THE ROUTLEDGE COMPANION
TO THE MAKERS OF GLOBAL BUSINESS

The Routledge Companion to the Makers of Global Business draws together a wide array of state-of-the-art research on multinational enterprises. The volume aims to deepen our historical understanding of how firms and entrepreneurs contributed to transformative processes of globalization.

This book explores how global business facilitated the mechanisms of cross-border interactions that affected individuals, organizations, industries, national economies and international relations. The 37 chapters span the Middle Ages to the present day, analyzing the emergence of institutions and actors alongside key contextual factors for global business development. Contributors examine business as a central actor in globalization, covering myriad entrepreneurs, organizational forms and key industrial sectors. Taking a historical view, the chapters highlight the intertwined and evolving nature of economic, political, social, technological and environmental patterns and relationships. They explore dynamic change as well as lasting continuities, both of which often only become visible – and can only be fully understood – when analyzed in the long run.

With dedicated chapters on challenges such as political risk, sustainability and economic growth, this prestigious collection provides a one-stop shop for a key business discipline.

Teresa da Silva Lopes is Professor of International Business and Business History and Director of the Centre for Evolution of Global Business and Institutions at the University of York, UK. She is also the President of the Business History Conference.

Christina Lubinski is Associate Professor at the Centre for Business History at Copenhagen Business School and Visiting Professor of Clinical Entrepreneurship at the Lloyd Greif Center for Entrepreneurial Studies, University of Southern California, USA.

Heidi J.S. Tworek is Assistant Professor of International History at the University of British Columbia, Canada. She received the Herman E. Krooss Prize for best dissertation in business history.

ROUTLEDGE COMPANIONS IN BUSINESS, MANAGEMENT AND ACCOUNTING

Routledge Companions in Business, Management and Accounting are prestige reference works providing an overview of a whole subject area or sub-discipline. These books survey the state of the discipline including emerging and cutting-edge areas. Providing a comprehensive, up to date, definitive work of reference, Routledge Companions can be cited as an authoritative source on the subject.

A key aspect of these Routledge Companions is their international scope and relevance. Edited by an array of highly regarded scholars, these volumes also benefit from teams of contributors which reflect an international range of perspectives.

Individually, Routledge Companions in Business, Management and Accounting provide an impactful one-stop-shop resource for each theme covered. Collectively, they represent a comprehensive learning and research resource for researchers, postgraduate students and practitioners.

Published titles in this series include:

The Routledge Companion to Critical Marketing
Edited by Mark Tadajewski, Matthew Higgins, Janice Denegri Knott and Rohit Varman

The Routledge Companion to the History of Retailing
Edited by Jon Stobart and Vicki Howard

The Routledge Companion to Innovation Management
Edited by Jin Chen, Alexander Brem, Eric Viardot and Poh Kam Wong

The Routledge Companion to the Makers of Global Business
Edited by Teresa da Silva Lopes, Christina Lubinski and Heidi J.S. Tworek

For more information about this series, please visit: www.routledge.com/Routledge-Companions-in-Business-Management-and-Accounting/book-series/RCBMA

THE ROUTLEDGE COMPANION TO THE MAKERS OF GLOBAL BUSINESS

Edited by Teresa da Silva Lopes,
Christina Lubinski and Heidi J.S. Tworek

LONDON AND NEW YORK

First published 2020
by Routledge
2 Park Square, Milton Park, Abingdon, Oxon OX14 4RN

and by Routledge
605 Third Avenue, New York, NY 10017

First issued in paperback 2021

Routledge is an imprint of the Taylor & Francis Group, an informa business

British Library Cataloguing-in-Publication Data
A catalogue record for this book is available from the British Library

Library of Congress Cataloging-in-Publication Data
Names: Lopes, Teresa da Silva, 1968- editor. | Lubinski, Christina, editor. | Tworek, Heidi, editor.
Title: The Routledge companion to the makers of global business /
[edited by] Teresa da Silva Lopes, Christina Lubinski and Heidi J.S. Tworek.
Description: Abingdon, Oxon ; New York, NY : Routledge, 2019. |
Series: Routledge companions in business, management and accounting |
Includes bibliographical references and index.
Identifiers: LCCN 2019007118 | ISBN 9781138242654 (hardback) |
ISBN 9781315277813 (ebook)
Subjects: LCSH: International business enterprises. | International trade. |
International economic relations.
Classification: LCC HD2755.5 .R686 2019 | DDC 338.8/8–dc23
LC record available at https://lccn.loc.gov/2019007118

ISBN 13: 978-1-03-209137-2 (pbk)
ISBN 13: 978-1-138-24265-4 (hbk)

Typeset in Bembo
by Wearset Ltd, Boldon, Tyne and Wear

CONTENTS

FIGURES

TABLES

CONTRIBUTORS

Michael Aldous, Queen's University Belfast

Rolv Petter Amdam, Norwegian Business School

Isabel Bartolomé Rodríguez, Universidad de Sevilla

Ann-Kristin Bergquist, Umeå University

Marten Boon, Norwegian University of Science and Technology

Marcelo Bucheli, University of Illinois at Urbana-Champaign

Youssef Cassis, European University Institute

Catherine Casson, University of Manchester

Mark Casson, University of Reading

Andrea Colli, Bocconi University

Asli M. Colpan, Kyoto University

Alvaro Cuervo-Cazurra, Northeastern University

Paula de la Cruz-Fernández, Florida International University

Teresa da Silva Lopes, University of York

Thomas David, University of Lausanne

Pierre-Yves Donzé, Osaka University

Paloma Fernández Pérez, University of Barcelona

Álvaro Ferreira da Silva, Universidade Nova de Lisboa

Robert Fitzgerald, Royal Holloway University of London

Neil Forbes, Coventry University

Robert Fredona, University of York

Patrick Fridenson, École des Hautes Études en Sciences Sociales

Valeria Giacomin, Copenhagen Business School

Gelina Harlaftis, Ionian University

Niels Viggo Haueter, Swiss Re

Jan-Otmar Hesse, University of Bayreuth

Kristoffer Jensen, Danmarks Industrimuseum

Richard R. John, Columbia University

Geoffrey G. Jones, Harvard Business School

Matthias Kipping, Schulich School of Business, York University

Takafumi Kurosawa, Kyoto University

Andrea Lluch, Universidad de la Pampa/CONICET, Argentina and Universidad de los Andes

Christina Lubinski, Copenhagen Business School and University of Southern California

Christopher W. Miller, Glasgow University

Ishva Minefee, Iowa State University

Peter Miskell, University of Reading

Mads Mordhorst, Copenhagen Business School

Pasi Nevalainen, University of Jyvaskyla

Patrick Neveling, University of Bergen

Gijsbert Oonk, Erasmus University Rotterdam

Gaspar Martins Pereira, University of Porto

Véronique Pouillard, University of Oslo

Sophus A. Reinert, Harvard Business School'

Neil Rollings, University of Glasgow

Raymond G. Stokes, University of Glasgow

Espen Storli, Norwegian University of Science and Technology

Heidi J.S. Tworek, University of British Columbia

Kazuo Wada, University of Tokyo

R. Daniel Wadhwani, University of the Pacific

Gerarda Westerhuis, Utrecht University

Ben Wubs, Erasmus University Rotterdam

Mary A. Yeager, University of California Los Angeles

FOREWORD

Mira Wilkins

This Handbook provides an up-to-date survey of research on various aspects of the history of multinational enterprise.[1]

There have been recently (and in earlier times), many histories of the world economy, western civilization, international finance, and capitalism. There have been conferences on law and the history of capitalism. Over the years, the reach of these studies has greatly expanded. They go back further in time (from Babylon to Bernanke, as one book's subtitle reads). They extend beyond the West and ask new questions on dating and understanding the "Great Divergence" between the West and East, between the West and "the Rest."

With some few exceptions, most of these histories neglect business as an actor in the transformation of the world economy. Individual entrepreneurs are mentioned, but the role of the firm seems shortchanged. It seems to me that our discipline, business history, and particularly students of the history of multinational enterprise, have a critical contribution to make.

What is a multinational enterprise? It is a business. It produces and sells goods and services, buys inputs and end products as well as services, and engages in numerous added business-related activities. It is a firm that extends over borders, so that it has representation, however small, outside the boundaries of its home jurisdiction. It does not necessarily take the corporate form. It typically involves a cluster of companies (subsidiaries and affiliates). It does more than trade. It invests abroad. Yet, it moves more than capital; as a firm, the multinational enterprise allocates other resources, for example personnel, technology, information, research and development, marketing knowhow, brands and trademarks, engineering expertise, general knowledge, and most of all management. The latter includes managerial design as well as the actual managing of the resource allocation within the firm. The multinational enterprise expects a return on the package it owns internationally, not simply on the investment of capital.

Multinational enterprises change over time. They grow; they retreat; they merge; they divest. They are in many different businesses, from mining and agriculture, to public utilities, manufacturing, marketing (wholesale and retail), banking, real estate, consulting services, and so forth. At any time, it becomes difficult defining "the firm" as the enterprise's managers change strategies and structures through the years, often through the decades, and sometimes with even greater longevity. Individual firms are not confined to a single business sector. A multinational enterprise may carry out many different activities, operating in a range of countries, industries, product lines, with both vertical (backward and forward) and horizontal integration. There is nothing static in the history of multinationals.

There is now a large and growing body of literature on the history of (and theory of) multinational enterprise. There appear to be five basic considerations that shape the historical course of multinational enterprises: (1) the search for *opportunity*. Managers of every multinational enterprise believe there is an opportunity of some kind when the firm makes a foreign investment. But, (2) there are *political and economic* constraints. For example, for many years, American multinationals saw opportunities in investment in Cuba, but politically (and economically) it was impossible to invest. All other things being equal (which they never are), (3) *familiarity* shapes the direction of initial investments. Firms tend to invest initially in geographically nearby countries, or in countries with historical connections (part or once part of empire, common language), or where corporate executives have personal knowledge. Then there are (4) *third country* rationales. Companies will make investments in countries to assist strategies. Thus, for example, for years companies with investment in oil production in Venezuela, refined in Aruba and Curaçao – the safe Dutch West Indies. And, finally, (5) the *existing investment configuration* of the firm. Firms over time shape their investment plans based on actual or management perceptions of the outcome of prior decisions.

Students of the history of multinational enterprises have pushed back their histories thousands of years. I do not want to summarize the expanding literature on early multinationals. The Handbook has a sampling, from the medieval period onward. Instead, I want to focus on the history of the *modern* multinational enterprise, which most scholars date from the late nineteenth century when steamships and railroads shortened distances; when the cable and the telegraph linked far flung areas; when sizeable migration (and travel) enhanced information flows, when connections around the world were spurred by the spread of empires (and the end to empire, in Latin America and elsewhere). The modern multinational enterprise emerged in the new economic and political milieu where technological change was accelerating and multinationals took part in that technological advance.

I want to argue that there is a serious gap in the literature, in our understanding of the role of multinationals in the transformation of the world economy from the mid- to late nineteenth century to the present. The Handbook is a start in filling that gap. When we think of major developments in the modern world, we need to factor in the activities of multinational enterprise. They transformed the contours of the modern world.

It has become increasingly evident as research has mounted on the history of the multinational enterprise that these firms made a major contribution to world economic development through their spread of information, technology, research and development, intangible assets, engineering talents, and also capital. That these were managed activities is important. Management of resource allocation made a difference. Multinationals moved individuals within the firm to participate in diverse activities. Multinational enterprises mattered in changing, in shaping, global history.

This was true, for example, in such different but transforming worldwide businesses, as sewing, harvesting, and automobiles, but also in such services as banking and insurance. Think about the application of the machine to sewing and its impact on the household and the workshop (the transformation in daily life that took place with ready-made clothing). Consider the role of harvesters in revolutionizing agriculture. Automobiles reshaped so many aspects of our existence. Research has shown that the international reach of some big banks and of insurance providers made a difference in the economies of nations. In all these cases multinationals were deeply engaged in the introduction and spread of innovations that altered global history.

Multinationals participated in numerous other services. The operations of consulting firms-as-multinationals provide a framework for helping us understand the spread of and application of managerial forms. Similarly, the internationalization of accounting firms spread new norms. Advertising firms became global and changed buyers' habits around the world.

So, too, the story of mining, processing, manufacturing, and distribution over time needs to be told through the lens of the history of multinational enterprise. The history of multinational enterprises in the emergence and dispersion of the global oil and gas industry was and continues to be crucial. Research on global electrification and on communication shows the vital and complex operations of multinational enterprises in providing the organizational impetus (and the directions) for the international spread of electrification and telecommunication. The timing of the contributions needs to be charted.

In numerous industries from food and beverages, to electrical and electronics manufacture, to chemicals and pharmaceuticals, to entertainment, through time, multinational enterprises had a fundamental (and positive) impact in developed as well as developing nations. It was the multinational enterprise that served an entrepreneurial function.

As we moved into the age of the computer and then into the digital age, once again, multinationals mattered (introduced, influenced, set the pattern) in the sharp and dramatic changes that have characterized the late twentieth and the early decades of the twenty-first century. Multinationals changed over the years, but were very much in evidence.

Often, we talk about US, UK, French, German, Japanese, Brazilian, and Chinese multinationals. We do *comparative* studies of homes and hosts to multinational enterprise. Yet, I am convinced that far more important to the study of the history of multinational enterprise and intimately associated with their place in world economic development is the *integrative* role of the multinational enterprise. As the firm moves over borders at different paces, it has the ability to make entrepreneurial choices, choices on where and how to introduce and to develop innovations. It selects opportunities. It is the entrepreneurial firm (far more, in the long run, than the inventor or individual-named managerial entrepreneur) that provides the organizational framework as well as the network for the allocation of global resources and that over an historical span sustains the process of resource allocation. New firms as well as evolving ones (that establish new operations and/or participate in mergers and acquisitions and also spin off segments of the business) have been and continue to be prominent in the history of the world economy. It is a highly complex story that varies sharply by industry but one on which there is now emerging substantial research with multiple studies and convincing evidence on the historical significance of multinational enterprises. Research on multinationals helps us understand why one country is able to adopt ideas, including technologies and productivity improvements, which are diffused through multinational enterprise, and another unable to do so. We learn about the spread and absorption of the offerings of the multinational – of the whole firm and not only the spread of and allocation of capital (which is only one facet of the storyline). The study of the history of multinational enterprises aids us in understanding the timing of global economic growth and development.

I have long realized that individual multinationals function in an ever changing economic, political, social and cultural environment. Over the years, however, I have become convinced that they should be viewed as actors in the changing world economy. Entrepreneurial firms have become crucial agents of change, not transcending individual nations (as an earlier literature once implied) but rather by taking on a critical role in the allocation of many different types of global resources and in prompting global change. The resources allocated include, to repeat, technology, research findings, information, capital, marketing methods, engineering, but most of all the diffusion of managerial methods. The multinational firm makes choices on where to explore for oil, where to look for minerals. It makes choices on where, as well as whether and when, to build manufacturing plants or when to shut them down. It makes choices on whether to make or buy goods and services from outsiders. It organizes complex supply chains. It makes choices on licensing and franchising and on framing contractual relationships. It is able to learn from one country (or one investment) and spread that learning to other locales. The spread is not simply bilateral, it is multilateral, taking advantage of the global scale and scope of the multinational enterprise. The multinational may begin small with mere representation; today, many multinationals operate through an immense collection of business entities and have business relationships in over 100 countries in a multiplicity of heterogeneous activities.

The place of the multinational enterprise (as it takes on different forms and changes through time), as it succeeds and also as it fails has now been documented in many individual studies. It is time to recognize *the overall pattern* and to include multinationals in histories of the world economy, capitalism, and western civilization. Their entrepreneurial role is central to the story of modern global change. It involves more than capital; it is the multinational's management and allocation of resources that should be incorporated in the story of the transformation of the modern global economy. Management of resources matters. Clearly, not only have multinational enterprises reshaped the world economy, but they have altered social and cultural norms. Imagine for a moment a world without electricity, automobiles, or advanced medicines. We have to think about where multinationals fit in the establishment of these basics that we take for granted. The presence of multinational enterprises exists in a political world and has generated state responses, from those in the fiscal sphere to those in regulatory regimes (to those related to expropriation and to subsidies and many other public choices). Governments have a kaleidoscope of associations with the firm. The activities of multinationals in political (and diplomatic) history require much more systematic exploration, based on archival sources. Multinationals are neither heroes nor villains. The research seems, however, to be very clear that they had a profound impact on the spread of economic, social, and cultural change. The entrepreneurial role of key firms and the impact of management by multinationals needs to be brought into the general historical literature. The Handbook offers valuable research that contributes to fulfilling the academic goals as discussed in this foreword.

Addendum: The above mentions no names of individuals, who have contributed to this literature.

I am including below a list of living and dead academics who have done useful work on the history of modern multinationals (the list is just a beginning, and very incomplete).

I should begin with Geoffrey Jones, who has done major work on the history of multinationals. In alphabetical order, the following selected individuals (and I apologize for the omissions of many others) have written on and most are still contributing on the history of multinational enterprise. Tetsuo Abo, Maria Ines Barbero, Martin Boon, Hubert Bonin, Peter Borscheid, Marcelo Bucheli, Peter Buckley, John Cantwell, Ann Carlos, Fred V. Carstensen, Youssef Cassis, Mark Casson, Roy Church, Sherman Cochran, Andrea Colli, Asli N. Colpan, James Cortada, Howard Cox, Paula de la Cruz-Fernández, Stephanie Decker, Pierre-Yves Donze, Larry Franko, Robert Fitzgerald, Patrick Fridenson, Louis Galambos, Ben Gales, Andrew Godley, Andrea Goldstein, Benjamin Gomes-Casseres, Leslie Hannah, Niels-Viggo Haueter, Will Hausman, Witold Henisz, Jean-François Hennart, Peter Hertner, Takashi Hikino, Takeo Kikkawa, Matthias Kipping, Takafumi Kurosawa, Stephen Kobrin, Bruce Kogut, Norma Lanciotti, Pierre Lanthier, Don Lessard, Andrea Lluch, Teresa da Silva Lopes, Christina Lubinski, Ragnhild Lundstrom, Joe Martin, Chris McKenna, David Merritt, Michael Miller, Rory Miller, Margrit Mueller, Aldo Musacchio, Viv Nelles, Stephen Nicholas, Robin Pearson, Joe Pratt, Jorge Ramos, Karl Sauvant, Luciano Segreto, Harm Schroeter, Keetie Sluyterman, Dick Sylla, Graham Taylor, Kevin Tennent, Stephen Tolliday, Stephen Topik, Heidi J.S. Tworek,

Pierre van der Eng, Alain Verbeke, Simon Ville, Kazuo Wada, Daniel Wadhwani, Lou Wells, Gerarda Westerhuis. Eleanor Westney, Ben Wubs, Shakila Yacob, Daniel Yergin, David B. Yoffie, Tsunehiko Yui, and Takeshi Yuzawa.

And, then there are the now deceased group that among their many contributions made pioneering ones in the study of the history of multinational enterprise: the late Alice Amsden, V.I. Bovykin, Rondo Cameron, Alfred Chandler, T.A.B. (Tony) Corley, John Dunning, Wilfried Feldenkirchen, Gerald Feldman, David Fieldhouse, Ralph Hidy, Charles Kindleberger, Christopher Kobrak, Henrietta Larson, Cleona Lewis, Douglass North, D.C.M. (Christopher) Platt, Edith Penrose, Richard Roberts, A.E. (Ed) Safarian, Robert Stobaugh, John Stopford, Alice Teichova, Clive Trebilcock, Ray Vernon, and Charles Wilson.

Note

1 This foreword is based on a presentation made on January 8, 2016, at a Business History Conference session at the American Historical Association meetings in Atlanta. I have updated that presentation, based on post-2016 research.

PART I

Introduction and context

1

INTRODUCTION TO THE MAKERS OF GLOBAL BUSINESS

Teresa da Silva Lopes, Christina Lubinski, and Heidi J.S. Tworek

Introduction to the makers of global business

This *Handbook* draws together a wide array of state-of-the-art research on the makers of global business. It aims to deepen our historical understanding of how firms and entrepreneurs contributed to transformative processes of globalization. We see the volume making two main contributions. First, the chapters cumulatively explore how the multinational enterprise (MNE) impacted not just economic interactions, but also political, social, technological, and environmental patterns and relationships. Second, the volume analyzes how global business facilitated the mechanisms of cross-border interactions that in turn affected individuals, organizations, industries, national economies, and international relations. The chapters span the Middle Ages to the present day. They explore dynamic change as well as continuities, both of which often only become visible when analyzed in the long run.

Cross-border economic activity is a phenomenon of great relevance today. World trade has increased from 24 percent of world GDP (gross domestic product) to more than 50 percent. A similar trend can be observed in foreign direct investment (FDI), which amounted to 4.4 percent of world GDP in 1960 and reached 37 percent in 2017 (World Bank 2018; UNCTAD 1994; OECD 2018). This accelerated growth of international trade and investment arguably originated in the late nineteenth century, during what became known as the "first global economy" (Jones 2005a).[1] The trend temporarily turned sluggish during World War I and the Great Depression of 1929 (although how much is a matter of debate), before a second wave of globalization after World War II. From the 1980s onwards, the ratio of world FDI to world GDP overtook the levels reached before World War I. Both waves of globalization are characterized by radical transformations: movements of people, transfers of knowledge and capital, shrinking distances between regions, changing lifestyles and consumer habits. Together they contributed to greater interdependencies between countries, regions, and cultures (Jones 2005a, 2008a).

This volume aims to expand current thinking on the evolution and the makers of global business by including long-term developments based on historical sources and methodologies. It provides new evidence about the multiplicity of entrepreneurs, institutions, and governance arrangements that "made" or created global business, while avoiding false labeling of some phenomena as "new." The volume also analyzes the origins and evolution of global industries, while highlighting the many challenges that entrepreneurs and institutions have encountered when entering foreign markets. Finally, it addresses the long-term impact of the makers of global business on the environment, and on social and economic development.

There are many historical studies of globalization by economists, economic historians, and historians, explaining how it developed and its impact on the world economy. Many studies focus on macroeconomic factors such as countries' policies and institutions (Williamson 1997; O'Rourke and Williamson 1999; James 2001), and the integration of national markets for capital, commodities, and labor (Bordo *et al.* 2003). Historians of capitalism, including global historians (Beckert and Sachsenmaier 2018), have focused on the movement of people, commodities, and ideas (e.g., Beckert 2014; Elmore 2014; Ogle 2017; Topik and Wells 2014; Beckert *et al.* 2014; Conrad 2016). Business historians, including Wilkins (2015, 2016) and Jones (1999, 2002, 2008a, 2013, 2014), point to the need to acknowledge the complexities arising when business enterprises are introduced as actors in cross-border economic activity.

Any attempt to define the MNE in a historical study is aiming at a moving target because, over time, MNEs go through different stages and invest in myriad assets. Moreover, contextual change requires adjustments in MNE strategy, often making one type of MNE particularly suited or unsuited for a specific historical time period. In this volume, we define the MNE broadly as an organization that "controls operations and income-generating assets in more than one country" (Dunning 1993a). More importantly, we look at these MNEs as essential for transferring (and sharing) physical and knowledge resources, developing innovations, creating new jobs, opening new markets, and leading to economic development. The field of international business history provides the detailed (often archive-based) evidence to capture the dynamics within firms as well as between firms and institutions. From this unique standpoint, business history can make valuable contributions to the history of globalization and the history of capitalism as well as the fields of international business, entrepreneurship, management, and strategy.

The field of international business history

International business history today has become a well-advanced field of inquiry. It might be traced back to the longitudinal work of Ray Vernon (1966), and his students John Stopford (1974) and Larry Franko (1974), but they were international business scholars with a somewhat ahistorical approach. The pioneer was Mira Wilkins (1969, 1970, 1974). Wilkins is the doyenne of historians of international business and deserves credit for opening up a previously neglected subject area in business history (Jones and Zeitlin 2008). As early as 1964, Wilkins (Wilkins and Hill 2011 [1st ed.: 1964]) published an archive-based analysis of the Ford Motor Company's early internationalization; this was around the same time as the term MNE was first coined (Hymer 1968; Jones 2008a: 142).

Wilkins shaped the field because many of her findings were later formalized in economic theory, particularly in international business. Wilkins' epilogue of *The Maturing of the Multinational Enterprise* (1974) developed an evolutionary model of the development of US MNEs that anticipates the original Uppsala School model (Johanson and Vahlne 1977). In the 1980s, Wilkins identified the "free-standing company" as a type of multinational enterprise, conceptually distinguishing it from what prior literature had conceived as portfolio investments (Wilkins 1988; Wilkins and Schröter 1998; see also, Hennart 1994). Wilkins' two-volume *The History of Foreign Investment in the United States* (1989, 2004) provided a detailed analysis of both foreign direct and foreign portfolio investments. Other influential topics included technological transfer and diffusion (Wilkins 1974) and neglected intangible assets such as trademarks (Wilkins 1992).

Wilkins' important body of work confirms the great relevance of historical research for understanding international business development both chronologically and conceptually.

Drawing on the work of renowned scholars, such as Alfred D. Chandler (1962, 1977, 1990), Ronald Coase (1937), John Dunning (1958, 1970), Stephen Hymer (1976), Charles Kindleberger (1969), Edith Penrose (1959), and Raymond Vernon (1966, 1971), Wilkins' subsequent career focused on and significantly advanced the study of the history of MNEs, including major contributions to their impact on the process of globalization (Wilkins 1986, 1970, 1974; Wilkins and Schröter 1998; Wilkins 1994, forthcoming). Wilkins' historical work pays close attention to the firm in its economic, social, and political environment, clarifying many of the complex issues of mutual interactions between firms, public policy makers, and societal stakeholders.

Following Wilkins' line of research, Geoffrey Jones' extensive work on the evolution of international business broadened the research agenda. Like Wilkins, he relies heavily on primary archival sources and connects their analysis, even more formally, with other disciplines, in particular with the economic theory of the multinational enterprise. Many of his contributions bring together the present and past by foregrounding patterns of the evolutionary and cumulative nature of international business, one important prerequisite for any interdisciplinary dialogue. Jones mapped the historical growth of businesses abroad and showed how and why business contributed to the integration of economies – for better or worse. His work pioneered many new areas of research, such as multinational banking (Jones 1993), business groups and multinational trading (Jones and Wale 1998; Jones 2000), and the consumer goods and beauty industries (Jones 2005b, 2008b, 2010). Many scholars have followed this tradition including Kipping (1999), da Silva Lopes (2007), and Fitzgerald (2015). This body of research has widened our understanding of multinational growth by exploring service providers such as management consultants and the role of brands.

Over the last decade, Jones has moved toward exploring critically the cultural, ecological, gender, and social impact of global capitalism over time (Jones 2010; Jones and Lubinski 2012; Jones, 2017; Jones and Spadafora, 2017). He has worked to shift the discipline of international business history from focusing on the history of the developed West toward much greater engagement with the historical experiences of Africa, Asia, and Latin America. Businesses in these regions faced widespread institutional voids and political and economic instability, to which they responded differently from in the West (Jones and Lluch 2015; Colpan and Jones 2016; Austin *et al.* 2017; Gao *et al.* 2017; Jones and Spadafora 2017, see also Jones, Origins, in this *Handbook*).

The field of international business history has thus matured and found its way into academic curricula, for example through the widely read and taught textbooks by Jones (2005a) and Robert Fitzgerald (2015). Increasingly, business historians also make important contributions to journals of international business (Jones and Khanna 2006; Bucheli and Kim 2012; da Silva Lopes *et al.* 2018) and international strategy (Bucheli and Kim 2015; Gao *et al.* 2017; Bucheli *et al.* 2018; Lubinski and Wadhwani 2019), where they use their historical approach to revisit big research debates, push new agendas forward, and contextualize ahistorical accounts.

This *Handbook* is part of these efforts. It aims to provide students, researchers, managers, and policy makers with an overview of current scholarship on how history has made modern global business. To do so, the editors have gathered an international team of authors from history and economics departments as well as business schools. The chapters discuss the emergence of institutions and actors as well as relevant contextual factors for global business development. They also suggest areas for future research and provide in-depth case studies to illustrate how the dynamics of global business have functioned in the past. While engaged first and foremost in historical analysis, many contributors also open their discussions to adjacent fields and audiences.

Some draw on economics and management literature, while others are inspired by and contribute to political science, gender studies, and sociology. The contributions reflect the methodological eclecticism of business history by relying on different, mostly qualitative approaches (Friedman and Jones 2017; Decker *et al.* 2015).

Temporal and spatial embeddedness

The chapters in this volume excel in tracking the embeddedness of actors and actions across both time and space. Jeffrey Fear (2014: 177) has argued that historical reasoning establishes the significance of a moment or period "by relating events, actions, and actors' reasons to past, present and future developments." One frequently used tool of the historian is therefore *periodization*, i.e., the division of larger timeframes into smaller units, marked by significant events or turning points, to organize coherent eras or epochs. Defining a period's beginning (possibly including antecedents), an endpoint, and important junctures is a genuinely historical act of interpretation (Rowlinson *et al.* 2014; Wadhwani and Decker 2017). Throughout the *Handbook*, the authors highlight that historians' guiding questions frequently include "when" questions and result in chronological interpretations with real analytical impact on broader fields of inquiry (Aldous; Fernández Pérez in this volume). To situate the makers of global business in their temporal and spatial context is thus one important contribution of this volume.

Because periodization necessarily changes with the subject of research, there is no pre-defined scheme for all chapters in this volume. A research question focused on climate change requires a different periodization from one that considers the global expansion of insurances or cars. Periodization does not easily translate from one context to another – a fact that several of the authors in this volume address by identifying heterogeneous chronologies for different sets of actors (see e.g., Colpan and Cuervo-Cazurra on the different development paths for business groups based on origin). However, in comparing the chapters, some repeating patterns or nested temporal frames emerge, as well as some equally important discrepancies between periodizations.

First, while the majority of the chapters support the argument that the first rise of global integration can be placed in the mid- to late nineteenth century, several chapters explore *antecedents* of this first global economy. These are important because they establish (some) path dependency and shed light on how organizations, actors, and practices emerged. Catherine Casson's discussion of guilds from 1200 to 1500 argues for rapid expansion of global trade around 1500, which reduced the attractiveness of guild membership. Reinert and Fredona focus on the role of merchants in Europe's prosperity during the early modern period as an antecedent and causal explanation for the "great divergence" between the West and the rest in the mid-eighteenth century. Identifying "the story before the story" helps them both to criticize earlier historiography and to explain an evolutionary development.

Second, several complementary periodization schemes emerge from the chapters. The most widely used is based on Jones (2005a) and distinguishes roughly between a First Global Economy (1840–1918/1929), a Deglobalization period (1918/1929–1979), and a Second Global Economy (1945/1979–2008), with significant overlaps and possible further turning points in particular during the post-World War II period. The First Global Economy can roughly be described as the process of global integration starting in the second half of the nineteenth century, enabled by international business networks (David and Westerhuis in this volume) and technological advances of the second industrial revolution (Jones, Origins; Lopes, Lluch, and Pereira; Cassis; de la Cruz-Fernández; Storli all in this *Handbook*). Depending on the specific theme or industry, some authors see its endpoint in World War I (de la Cruz-Fernández for manufacturing industries; Boon for oil; Cassis for financial institutions; Fitzgerald for decentralization; Rollings for business–government relations, Kurosawa, Forbes, and Wubs for business during the war). Others point to the Great Depression of 1929 as the event concluding this period (Jones, Origins, on the development of global business; da Silva and Bartolomé Rodríguez on electricity; Harlaftis on shipping).

The subsequent Deglobalization period, roughly from 1914/1929 to the late 1970s, presented a series of new challenges for global business – new government regulation, expropriations, war and nationalism, fragmentation of corporate structures, and many more – which are described in detail across the chapters (Jones, Origins; Jones, Divergence; Cassis all in this volume). Some authors stress turning points within this period for their specific topics, such as the beginning of the Cold War, which is of particular relevance to commodity traders (Storli), or the process of decolonization, which impacted decentralization and international management (Fitzgerald). Other authors question whether the term "deglobalization" adequately describes this period. They propose seeing the period instead as one when the relationship between governments and multinational companies was fundamentally reordered, particularly outside Europe, but not necessarily when global engagement declined (Rollings in this volume; Dejung and Petersson 2012; Fitzgerald 2015).

The Second Global Economy emerged slowly and first in the Western world in the decades after World War II. Several authors find that the makers of global business started engaging in their ventures in this period of postwar recovery, whether the internationalization of executive education (Amdam) or the global expansion of the automobile industry (Fridenson and Wada). By the late 1970s and early 1980s, this Second Global Economy became global, incorporating ever more areas of the world. This period was marked by deregulation and pro-market reforms leading to organizational responses, including the global expansion of emerging market business groups (Colpan and Cuervo-Cazurra), transformations of global value chains (Hesse and Neveling), and the gradual decline of state-owned national champions (Colli and Nevalainen). It was also the era of new practices, such as intensified cross-border production, off-shoring, and contracting-out (Fitzgerald) as well as new environmental strategies by corporate actors in response to increased pollution (Bergquist; Stokes and Miller).

This basic timeline serves as a temporal map for most authors in this volume. Some, however, find divergence from it for their particular topics. For the luxury industry, Pouillard and Donzé see the entire pre-1945 period as one unit, followed by an early globalization (1945–1980). Like other contributions, they confirm the change in character of the global luxury industry in the early 1980s. For the issues of sustainability, pollution, and climate change, the authors prefer to extend the first period up to the 1960s, labeling it "pre-global" (Bergquist) or the "first wave of environmentalism" (Stokes and Miller). Both chapters follow the perception of their actors and situate the newly emergent awareness of pollution and sustainability in the early 1960s. Both Jones' and Cassis' contributions indicate a newly emerging transition period after the financial crisis of 2007/2008 and the subsequent great recession, which might be characterized as a new form of deglobalization. It includes a surge in micro-protectionism, new export taxes, and trade distorting subsidies as well as discrimination against foreign firms.

Some chapters potentially fit neatly into a subset of these timelines, while accounting for the antecedents of the developments that they analyze. For example, Amdam pays close attention to the forerunners of the global spread of executive education back to the late 1920s even if his primary research interest lies in the post-World War II era; Bucheli and Minefee stress the importance of the Foreign Corrupt Practice Act (1977), but describe the period from the Progressive era to Watergate in the United States as a backstory to this development.

Finally, some authors make an explicit effort to provide *historical analogies* which can help to contextualize present concerns. Tworek and John, for example, use the communications industry to explain how the present is not the first historical epoch when enormous technical advances have reshaped the world economy and reordered assumptions about time, speed, and space. They explicitly discuss the lessons from history, most importantly the importance of institutional arrangements fostering and perpetuating political and market power.

Identifying new periodizations and challenging existing ones matters because different types of causal explanations emerge from different historical organizations of time. For example, selecting shorter research periods usually assigns greater agency to individuals, while longer timeframes tend to foreground structural factors (Wadhwani and Decker 2017). In this volume, the authors often switch between zooming in on events and individual actors and zooming out to show structural developments that illuminate complex causalities over time.

While periodization embedded historical actors in time, the authors of this volume also advance arguments about actors' embeddedness in space. Several authors highlight particular places of global business, such as large globally connected cities (Cassis; Kipping) or global networks of academic campuses (Amdam). Unsurprisingly, most of the chapters track transfers of goods, services, and ideas from one space to another, contributing among others to the large historical literature on colonialism (Aldous; Giacomin; Oonk) and Americanization (Amdam; Miskell; Kipping). Many find that over time, centers of gravity shift between different locations, as in the case of commodity trading, which was first based in Europe, then shifted to the United States after 1945, then back to Europe in the 1960s, and after 2000 to Southeast Asia (Storli).

The relationship between the global and the local permeates all chapters of this volume in different ways. First, several authors describe the efforts of globally active companies to localize their offerings, be that in response to anti-foreign sentiments or critical government policies, including taxation (Jones, Origins; Kurosawa, Forbes, and Wubs; Rollings) or to better serve customers (Amdam; Kipping). Strategies to accomplish localization include information gathering via agents or local partners (Jones; Storli; Lubinski and Wadhwani), cloaking strategies designed to hide country of origin or fraudulently display a false origin (Lopes, Lluch, and Pereira), and incorporating local companies or hiring local staff (Kipping). Authors also stress that localization efforts could be unsuccessful or have unintended consequences, for example in the consulting industry, where consultants instigated offshoring and outsourcing, which then stimulated the emergence of local service providers that became competitors (Kipping).

Many chapters trace the myriad frequent tensions between the global and the local. Some criticize past historical research, arguing that it unjustly overemphasized the local over the global, or vice versa. For example, Giacomin shows that the literature on clusters focuses strongly on the local elements as sources of competitiveness. It becomes "location-obsessed" and loses sight of how clusters entertained global linkages and fostered internationalization. Other authors highlight tensions that the historical actors themselves experienced, as for example in the cooperative movement that for a long time had celebrated its deep embeddedness in local communities and then found itself faced with a legitimacy crisis when it started to globalize (Mordhorst and Jensen). Tensions also emerged because legal frameworks remain a preserve of the nation-state and are seldom global or even transnational. They thus require forms of local implementation, creating challenges for globally active companies, for example with regards to heterogeneous corruption laws (Bucheli and Minefee) or protective laws against imitation (Lopes, Lluch, and Pereira).

Main themes

This book addresses several research desiderata recently identified by business historians (Friedman and Jones 2011; Scranton and Fridenson 2013) that can help to make historical research "matter" to other disciplines such as economics, political science, management, and law. The topic of this *Handbook* and the archival evidence on how firms and institutions responded, drove, and framed their activities within a global context, addresses these recent appeals. Many chapters individually provide evidence of spillover effects by foreign investors to local business. Other chapters address topics which only recently started to receive attention in business history, such as business and sustainability, pollution and climate change, the role of government and state-owned enterprises on economic growth and globalization, and the great divergence and great convergence.

Some topics appear throughout the volume, even if they are not addressed in a specific chapter. These include the impact of different types of non-profit-making institutions, such as religious groups on efforts to combat corruption (Bucheli and Minefee), environmental associations (Bergquist), and foundations' effects on global knowledge transfers (Amdam). Several chapters address colonialism and imperialism, a topic that has recently attracted significant attention from business historians and historians of capitalism (see the special issue in *Business History Review*, June 2012). While entrepreneurship, gender, and race have affected globalization, the reverse is also true, and empires played an important role in this process (Yeager in this volume). Several chapters deal with obstacles to trade, providing an important context for the origins and development of global business (Jones, Divergence; Fitzgerald; Kurozawa, Forbes, and Wubs; Lopes, Lluch, and Pereira). Many of the chapters address cases of less rational or irrational business behavior, including conflict, speculation, and non-rational decision-making processes. While the Western world plays a central role in many chapters, either as home country or host country, the authors committed themselves to exploring global flows of goods, people, and ideas.

The chapters in this *Handbook* address a key set of themes to understand why and how, over time, the makers of global business shaped and challenged the complex processes of globalization. These themes are briefly discussed below. They include: (i) entrepreneurship as a driver of change; (ii) international transfer of resources; (iii) organization and coordination of multi-market activities; (iv) political economy; and (v) long-term impact. While some of these themes are explicitly the topic of one part of the book, all of them also cut across the contributions.

Entrepreneurship as a driver of change

The concept of entrepreneurship is usually connected with the development of business activities which involve uncertainty and risk bearing, and lead to innovations which, over time, bring about historical change. Entrepreneurship is thus a creative process, by which actors imagine and pursue future forms of value. Chapters 3 to 5 of this *Handbook* address the topic of entrepreneurship explicitly. Mark Casson as well as Lubinski and Wadhwani review the key literature in business history and highlight how entrepreneurship shaped the process of business internationalization, how entrepreneurs identified and pursued opportunities across borders, and how they legitimized their international ventures. Yeager focuses on the contribution of female and non-white entrepreneurs to globalization, showing how race and gender intertwined to create unequal and exploitative hierarchies, with white men generally benefitting most from globalization. She also examines how globalization affected employability and working conditions of females and non-whites.

Many other chapters in the *Handbook* contribute to understanding the multiple drivers that led entrepreneurs to trade and invest abroad. Harlaftis' chapter on shipping discusses how Aristotle Onassis, a Greek shipper, pioneered the formation, development, and consolidation of the modern model of ownership and management of global bulk shipping companies after 1945.

Oonk discusses collective entrepreneurship and shows how diaspora communities formed networks coordinated essentially through family ties, where trust bonds substituted contracts, and which were decisive in the emergence of long-distance trade between pre- and post-colonial societies in the Indian Ocean.

Most chapters discuss productive opportunities (Baumol 1990, 2010), often based on product or service innovations, as illustrated in Fridenson and Wada's chapter on the automobile, de la Cruz-Fernández' chapter on Singer sewing machines, or Fernández Pérez' chapter on healthcare services. Some international business activities, however, take advantage of loopholes in the institutional environment. Lopes, Lluch, and Pereira show how, in the nineteenth century, wine producers in the New World developed a new wine industry by imitating brands, grape casts, and the types of wines produced. While in the short term these activities might have been considered unproductive, they led in the long term, to regional economic development, increased consumer choices, and contributed to the making of global business.

International transfer of resources

International business has contributed to globalization by transferring different types of resources between home and host countries. The process of knowledge transfer is usually associated with exports, FDI, licensing agreements, among other modes of entry in foreign markets. The resources transferred take the form of knowledge, people, physical goods, financial resources, or a combination. Much research has examined the types of knowledge transferred (or shared), ranging from patents and technologies, brands and trademarks, to organizational practices such as accounting and administrative practices, financial resources used for the financing of investments abroad, and people used to manage, provide training, and operate businesses abroad (Wilkins 1976).

In this *Handbook* several chapters review the literature on the topic and offer new evidence. Kipping examines the role of consultants in the making of global business, while Amdam analyzes the role of executive management programs set up by Harvard Business School and the transfer of management practices globally. Both authors argue that these agents shaped policies and practices of organizations and their stakeholders in multiple ways, and often crowded out other forms of less commercially driven knowledge sharing. Storli and Harlaftis show how shipping companies were essential in the transfer of goods across the globe. Their transportation of raw materials and other goods between different regions of the world was instrumental in creating global value chains. Cassis discusses how banks and capital markets transferred financial resources across the world. Banks were central in following investors in foreign markets, and financial centers were critical intermediaries in financing business investments.

Organization and coordination of multi-market activities

International business activity requires firms with operations in multiple markets to organize and coordinate their activities (Hymer 1968; Buckley and Casson 1976; Hennart 1982; Dunning 1993b). Research in international business history has also contributed to this topic, providing relevant evidence to help refine theory (Wilkins 1970, 1974, 1988, 1989, 2004, 2015; Jones 2000, 2005a; da Silva Lopes 2007; da Silva Lopes *et al.* 2018). Several chapters in this *Handbook* discuss the coordination of businesses with activities in multiple markets.

Part III on "Organizational Forms" provides detailed examples of the types of modes of coordination and integration of activities carried out by different businesses and institutions with international activity. Aldous shows how trading companies affected Anglo-Indian international trade in the nineteenth century. Over time, traders diversified their operations away from intermediation to include production and related activities such as financial services, and adopted diverse ownership and organizational forms. Catherine Casson shows how medieval guilds helped individual traders to create, strengthen, and coordinate networks and infrastructure and also provided them with the training and quality control which were essential in developing sustainable global supply chains. Kurosawa, Forbes, and Wubs focus on the case of Roche from Switzerland before World War I and highlight how this MNE implemented strategies and structures to survive in the high-risk political environment of the war.

Political economy

Several chapters explore the key importance of the macroeconomic environment in facilitating or constraining globalization, particularly the role of governments and politics. Part V on "Challenges and Impact" examines how changes in the business environment created obstacles for business success and survival. Bucheli and Minefee analyze the efforts by governments to combat corruption in business between the Cold War and the 2010s. Jones' chapter on the "Origins and Development of Global Business" highlights the role of government policies, major crises such as wars, the Great Depression, and communism in shaping global business from the late nineteenth century until the twenty-first century. Several chapters, including Rollings, Tworek and John, Lubinski and Wadhwani, trace the intertwined nature of business and politics. They suggest that "political economy" can be a useful lens for historians when thinking about global and international history. Richard John (2008: 488–9) has defined "political economy" as "the relationship of the state and the market." Indeed, one may criticize an international history that focuses too strongly on nation-states, diplomacy, and conflicts, while ignoring the important role of multinationals (Fitzgerald 2015: 1). While home governments supported their MNEs abroad, host nations used myriad political tools to gain from foreign investment. As a consequence, MNEs always interacted with politics in different forms and with wide-ranging consequences. Moreover, political decisions laid the groundwork for some of the most persistent path dependencies during the time period studied here. The complicated interactions between MNEs and political stakeholders certainly deserves more attention.

Long-term impact

This *Handbook* provides illustrations of how exactly business contributed to globalization in the long term, going beyond the usual macroeconomic indicators such as aggregated flows of trade, investment, capital, and people. Jones (Chapter 2) offers quantitative and qualitative macro-data on the origins and development of global business, but also shows how specific businesses affected and were affected by globalization since the late nineteenth century. Giacomin focuses on two clusters from emerging economies – the palm oil cluster in Southeast Asia and the eco-tourism cluster in Costa Rica – showing how these clusters facilitated investments into these countries, which became spaces of global integration. As such, they affected economic activity beyond their location and became building blocks of today's global economy.

Some of the effects of MNE activities are cultural rather than economic. Cruz-Fernández, for instance, shows how sewing machines allowed people to make clothing and ornaments at home, generating cultural experiences that became ingrained within households' economies and national cultures. Haueter's chapter on insurance argues that culture and local idiosyncrasies, and the legal environment, shaped the development of the global insurance industry.

Multinational investment also had a huge impact on environmental sustainability. Sustainability, climate change, and pollution are key challenges for humanity. Bergquist shows how polluting firms sought to reduce environmental impact, and in recent years created sustainability in for-profit businesses, developing new product categories such as organic foods as well as wind and solar energy. Stokes and Miller focus on the impact of globalized businesses on pollution and climate change from the earliest days of industrialization to the present and the strategies that firms have developed to deal with this.

Jones' chapter in the concluding part of this volume expands the discussion about impact to include social equality. He shows that global business created both wealth and inequality contributing to the great divergence between the West and the Rest, and the more recent great convergence. He appeals to the multiple obligations of business to pursue corporate strategies and executive compensation schemes to help legitimize capitalism again and reduce inequality, even if that comes at a cost for management and shareholders.

Organization of the volume

The volume comprises 37 chapters divided into five parts. The opening part introduces the volume, provides an overview of the development of global business, and engages with inter-national *entrepreneurship* as a major driver of international business. Part II discusses prominent *institutions* that the makers of global business interacted with, namely governments, capital markets, educational institutions, and consultants. Part III gives an overview of the myriad *organizational forms* found in past international business, from guilds, merchants, and trading companies, to business groups and clusters, to the creative organizations by diaspora and international networks, to cooperatives and state enterprises. The sheer diversity raises new questions for modern-day businesses and how they can be conceptualized. As many of the more interesting research questions can only be addressed on the micro- and industry-specific level, Part IV of the volume makes selected deep dives into a few major *industries* that became global or enabled the spread of business around the world, namely automobiles, insurances, healthcare, manufacturing, luxury goods, electricity, commodity trading, communication, film, shipping, and oil. While this provides only a selection of industries, we have endeavored to cover a range of goods and service industries to explore some ways that industries interacted with and shaped globalization. Finally, Part V engages with some of the big *challenges* to global business and its broader *impact*. Major challenges have constantly confronted global business in the past, and continue to create obstacles for global business: political risk, imitation, corruption, excessive decentralization, and the need for environmental sustainability. Two closing chapters examine the *impact* of global business, particularly the two primary and most heatedly debated consequences of globalizing business: the effects on pollution and climate change, and on the great divergence and social inequality.

All chapters first survey and assess the relative significance of changes, continuities, and discontinuities. Different regions are examined both as originators of global business and also as hosts of foreign investments; many chapters provide international comparative analysis. Others focus on in-depth original case studies, highlighting how particular agents contributed to globalization beyond their narrow scope of activity, when seen in a larger time frame. Internet submarine cables, for instance, are laid along the same lines as telegraph cables were in the nineteenth century – a path dependency that can only become visible in the long run (Tworek and John). The contributions reveal causal relationships and detect patterns in the past through the detailed analysis of businesses which provide learning opportunities and raise new questions.

Despite the very agentic title of the volume, business is neither the hero nor the villain of the chapters in this volume. In some cases, business constrained globalization; in others, it created or facilitated the process. We often think of booms and busts in business, and the chapters are certainly full of experiences of failure, setbacks, obstructions, and problems. Yet, the longer history of multinationals shows that many experienced surprising longevity and were well equipped (or learned) to deal with the challenges that they encountered. While individuals, organizations, and institutions emerged and disappeared, became successful, were challenged, failed, and dissolved, the relevance of global business today is greater than ever. The multinational nature of their ventures may have waxed and waned, but many of the makers of global business proved astonishingly resilient in the long run. However, global business today also faces serious opposition, which may require decision makers to explore new forms and new ethics of international business behavior – a formidable task, which can be facilitated by exploring the deep historical roots of the makers of global business.

Note

1 There is evidence of early forms of globalization as far back as 2000 BC when the Old Assyrian Kingdom expanded international trade and investment. During the following centuries, empires rose and fell, trade routes opened and closed, and international commerce expanded and contracted in response to shifting political, economic, social, and physical environments around the globe. The late fifteenth and sixteenth centuries, when explorers navigated the world, accelerated world integration (Wilkins 1970: 3; Carlos and Nicholas 1988; Moore and Lewis 2000, 2009).

References

Austin, Gareth, Dávila, Carlos, and Jones, Geoffrey (2017), "The Alternative Business History: Business in Emerging Markets," *Business History Review*, 91 (3), 537–69.

Baumol, William J. (1990), "Entrepreneurship: Productive, Unproductive, and Destructive," *Journal of Political Economy*, 98 (5), 893–921.

Baumol, William J. (2010), *The Microtheory of Innovative Entrepreneurship* (Princeton, NJ: Princeton University Press).

Beckert, Sven (2014), *Empire of Cotton: A Global History* (New York: Penguin).

Beckert, Sven and Sachsenmaier, Dominic (eds.) (2018), *Global History, Globally: Research and Practice around the World* (London: Bloomsbury).

Beckert, Sven, Burgin, Angus, Hudson, James, Hyman, Louis, Lamoreaux, Naomi, Marler, Scott, Mihm, Stephen, Ott, Julia, and Scranton, Philip (2014), "Interchange: The History of Capitalism," *Journal of American History*, 101 (2), 503–36.

Bordo, Michael D., Taylor, Alan M., and Williamson, Jeffrey G. (eds.) (2003), *Globalization in Historical Perspective* (Chicago, IL: University of Chicago Press).

Bucheli, Marcelo and Kim, Min-Young (2012), "Political Institutional Change, Obsolescing Legitimacy, and Multinational Corporations," *Management International Review*, 52 (6), 847–77.

Bucheli, Marcelo and Kim, Minyoung (2015), "Attacked from Both Sides: A Dynamic Model of Multinational Corporations' Strategies for Protection of Their Property Rights," *Global Strategy Journal*, 5 (1), 1–26.

Bucheli, Marcelo, Salvaj, Erica, and Kim, Minyoung (2018), "Better Together: How Multinationals Come Together with Business Groups in Times of Economic and Political Transitions," *Global Strategy Journal*, doi.org/10.1002/gsj.1326.

Buckley, Peter J. and Casson, Mark (1976), *The Future of the Multinational Enterprise* (London: Macmillan).

Carlos, Ann, and Stephen Nicholas (1988) "'Giants of an Earlier Capitalism': The Chartered Trading Companies as Modern Multinationals," *Business History Review*, 62 (3), 398–419.

Chandler, Alfred D. (1962), *Strategy and Structure: Chapters in the History of the Industrial Enterprise* (Cambridge, MA: MIT Press).

Chandler, Alfred D. (1977), *The Visible Hand: The Managerial Revolution in American Business* (Cambridge, MA: Belknap Press of Harvard University Press).

Chandler, Alfred D. (1990), *Scale and Scope: The Dynamics of Industrial Capitalism* (Cambridge, MA: Belknap Press of Harvard University Press).

Coase, Ronald H. (1937), "The Nature of the Firm," *Economica*, 4, 386–405.

Colpan, Asli M. and Jones, Geoffrey (2016), "Business Groups, Entrepreneurship and the Growth of the Koç Group in Turkey," *Business History*, 58 (1), 69–88.

Conrad, Sebastian (2016), *What is Global History?* (Cambridge: Cambridge University Press).

Da Silva Lopes, Teresa (2007), *Global Brands: The Growth of Multinationals in the Alcoholic Drinks Industry* (New York: Cambridge University Press).

Da Silva Lopes, Teresa, Casson, Mark, and Jones, Geoffrey (2018), "Organizational Innovation in the Multinational Enterprise: Internalization Theory and Business History," *Journal of International Business Studies* (pre-published online).

Decker, Stephanie, Kipping, Matthias, and Wadhwani, Daniel R. (2015), "New Business Histories! Plurality in Business History Research Methods," *Business History*, 57, 30–40.

Dejung, Christof and Petersson, Niels P. (eds.) (2012), *The Foundations of Worldwide Economic Integration: Power, Institutions, and Global Markets, 1850–1930* (Cambridge: Cambridge University Press).

Dunning, John H. (1958), *American Investment in British Manufacturing Industry* (London: Allen & Unwin).

Dunning, John H. (1970), *Studies in International Investment* (London: Allen & Unwin).

Dunning, John H. (1993a), *Multinational Enterprises and the Global Economy* (Wokingham, UK: Addison-Wesley).

Dunning, John H. (1993b), *The Globalization of Business: The Challenge of the 1990s* (London, New York: Routledge).

Elmore, Bart (2014), *Citizen Coke: The Making of Coca-Coca Capitalism* (New York: Norton).

Fear, Jeffrey (2014), "Mining the Past: Historicizing Organizational Learning and Change," in Marcelo Bucheli and R. Daniel Wadhwani (eds.), *Organizations in Time: History, Theory and Methods* (Oxford: Oxford University Press), 169–91.

Fitzgerald, Robert (2015), *The Rise of the Global Company: Multinationals and the Making of the Modern World* (Cambridge: Cambridge University Press).

Franko, Lawrence (1974), "The Origins of Multinational Manufacturing by Continental European Firms," *Business History Review*, 48, 277–302.

Friedman, Walter A. and Jones, Geoffrey (2011), "Business History: Time for Debate," *Business History Review*, 85 (1), 1–8.

Friedman, Walter A. and Jones, Geoffrey (2017), "Debating Methodology in Business History," *Business History Review*, 91 (3), 443–55.

Gao, Cheng, Zuzul, Tiona, Jones, Geoffrey, and Khanna, Tarun (2017), "Overcoming Institutional Voids: A Reputation-Based View of Long-Run Survival," *Strategic Management Journal*, 38 (11), 2147–67.

Hennart, Jean-François (1982), *A Theory of Multinational Enterprise* (Ann Arbor, MI: University of Michigan Press).

Hennart, Jean-François (1994), "Free-Standing Firms and the Internalisation of Markets for Financial Capital: A Response to Casson," *Business History*, 36 (4), 118–31.

Hymer, Stephen H. (1968), "The Large Multinational 'Corporation,'" in Mark Casson (ed.), *Multinational Corporations* (London: Edward Elgar), 6–31.

Hymer, Stephen H. (1976), *The International Operations of National Firms: A Study of Direct Foreign Investment* (Cambridge, MA: MIT Press).

James, Harold (2001), *The End of Globalization: Lessons from the Great Depression* (Cambridge, MA: Harvard University Press) vi, 260 p.

Johanson, Jan and Vahlne, Jan-Erik (1977), "The Internationalization Process of the Firm: A Model of Knowledge Development and Increasing Foreign Market Commitments," *Journal of International Business Studies*, 8 (1), 23–32.

John, Richard R. (2008), "Bringing Political Economy Back In," *Enterprise & Society*, 9 (3), 487–90.

Jones, Geoffrey (1993), *British Multinational Banking, 1830–1990* (Oxford: Clarendon Press).

Jones, Geoffrey (1999), "Company History and Business History in the 1990s," in Wilfred Feldenkirchen and Terry Gourvish (eds.), *European Yearbook of Business History* (Aldershot, UK: Ashgate Publishing), vol. 2, 1–20.

Jones, Geoffrey (2000), *Merchants to Multinationals: British Trading Companies in the Nineteenth and Twentieth Centuries* (Oxford: Oxford University Press).

Jones, Geoffrey (2002), "Business Enterprises and Global Worlds," *Enterprise & Society*, 3 (4), 581–605.

Jones, Geoffrey (2005a), *Multinationals and Global Capitalism: From the Nineteenth to the Twenty-First Century* (Oxford, New York: Oxford University Press).

Jones, Geoffrey (2005b), *Renewing Unilever: Transformation and Tradition* (Oxford: Oxford University Press).

Jones, Geoffrey (2008a), "Globalization," in Geoffrey Jones and Jonathan Zeitlin (eds.), *The Oxford Handbook of Business History* (Oxford: Oxford University Press), 141–68.

Jones, Geoffrey (2008b), "Blonde and Blue-Eyed? Globalizing Beauty, c.1945-c.1980," *Economic History Review*, 61 (1), 125–54.

Jones, Geoffrey (2010), *Beauty Imagined. A History of the Global Beauty Industry* (Oxford, New York: Oxford University Press).

Jones, Geoffrey (2013), *Entrepreneurship and Multinationals: Global Business and the Making of the Modern World* (Northampton, MA: Edward Elgar Publishing).

Jones, Geoffrey (2014), "Business History and the Impact of MNEs on Host Economies," in Jean J. Boddewyn (ed.), *Research in Global Management: Multidisciplinary Insights from New AIB Fellows* (Bingley, UK: Emerald Group Publishing), 177–98.

Jones, Geoffrey (2017), *Profits and Sustainability: A History of Green Entrepreneurship* (Oxford: Oxford University Press).

Jones, Geoffrey and Khanna, Tarun (2006), "Bringing History (Back) Into International Business," *Journal of International Business Studies*, 37, 453–68.

Jones, Geoffrey and Lluch, Andrea (eds.) (2015), *The Impact of Globalization on Argentina and Chile: Business Enterprises and Entrepreneurship* (Cheltenham, UK; Northampton, MA: Edward Elgar Publishing).

Jones, Geoffrey and Lubinski, Christina (2012), "Managing Political Risk in Global Business: Beiersdorf 1914–1990," *Enterprise & Society*, 13 (1), 85–119.

Jones, Geoffrey and Lubinski, Christina (2014), "Making 'Green Giants': Environment Sustainability in the German Chemical Industry, 1950s–1980s," *Business History*, 56 (4), 623–49.

Jones, Geoffrey and Spadafora, Andrew (2017), "Creating Ecotourism in Costa Rica, 1970–2000," *Enterprise & Society*, 18 (1), 146–83.

Jones, Geoffrey and Wale, Judith (1998), "Merchants as Business Groups: British Trading Companies in Asia before 1945," *Business History Review*, 72, 367–408.

Jones, Geoffrey and Zeitlin, Jonathan (eds.) (2008), *The Oxford Handbook of Business History* (Oxford: Oxford University Press).

Kindleberger, Charles P. (1969), *American Business Abroad: Six Lectures on Direct Investment* (New Haven, CT: Yale University Press).

Kipping, Matthias (1999), "American Management Consulting Companies in Western Europe, 1920–1990: Products, Reputation and Relationships," *Business History Review*, 73 (2), 190–220.

Lubinski, Christina and Wadhwani, R. Daniel (2019), "Geopolitical Jockeying: Economic Nationalism and Multinational Strategy in Historical Perspective," *Strategic Management Journal*, accepted author manuscript. doi:10.1002/smj.3022.

Moore, Karl and Lewis, David Charles (1999), *Birth of the Multinational: 2000 Years of Ancient Business History, From Ashur to Augustus* (Copenhagen: Copenhagen Business School Press).

Moore, Karl and Lewis, David Charles (2009), *The Origins of Globalization* (New York: Routledge).

O'Rourke, Kevin H. and Williamson, Jeffrey G. (1999), *Globalization and History: The Evolution of a Nineteenth-Century Atlantic Economy* (Cambridge, MA: MIT Press).

OECD (2018), *National Accounts Data Files* (Paris: OECD).

Ogle, Vanessa (2017), "Archipelago Capitalism: Tax Havens, Offshore Money, and the State, 1950s-1970s," *American Historical Review*, 122 (5), 1431–58.

Penrose, Edith Tilton (1959), *The Theory of the Growth of the Firm* (Oxford: Oxford University Press).

Rowlinson, Michael, Hassard, John, and Decker, Stephanie (2014), "Research Strategies for Organizational History: A Dialogue Between Historical Theory and Organization Theory," *Academy of Management Review*, 39 (3), 250–74.

Scranton, Philip and Fridenson, Patrick (2013), *Reimagining Business History* (Baltimore, MD: Johns Hopkins University Press) x, 260 p.

Stopford, John M. (1974), "The Origins of British-Based Multinational Manufacturing Enterprises," *Business History Review*, 48 (3), 303–35.

Topik, Steven, and Wells, Allen (2014), *Global Markets Transformed, 1870–1945* (Cambridge, MA: Belknap Press of Harvard University Press).

UNCTAD (1994), *World Investment Report* (Geneva: UNCTAD).

Vernon, Raymond (1966), "International Investment and International Trade in the Product Cycle," *Quarterly Journal of Economics*, 80 (2), 190–207.

Vernon, Raymond (1971), *Sovereignty at Bay: The Multinational Spread of U.S. Enterprises* (New York: Basic Books).

Wadhwani, R. Daniel and Decker, Stephanie (2017), "Clio's Toolkit: The Practice of Historical Methods in Organizational Research," in Raza Mir and Sanjay Jain (eds.), *Routledge Companion to Qualitative Research in Organization Studies* (New York and Abingdon: Routledge), 113–27.

Wilkins, Mira (1969), "An American Enterprise Abroad: American Radiator Company in Europe, 1895–1914," *Business History Review*, 43 (3), 326–46.

Wilkins, Mira (1970), *The Emergence of Multinational Enterprise: American Business Abroad from the Colonial Era to 1914* (Cambridge, MA: Harvard University Press).

Wilkins, Mira (1974), *The Maturing of Multinational Enterprise: American Business Abroad from 1914 to 1970* (Cambridge, MA: Harvard University Press).

Wilkins, Mira (1976), "Multinational Companies and the Diffusion of Technology in Africa: An Historical Perspective," in D. Babatunde (ed.), *Importing Technology into Africa* (New York: Praeger), 25–42.

Wilkins, Mira (1986), "Defining a Firm: History and Theory," in Peter Hertner and Geoffrey Jones (eds.), *Multinationals: Theory and History* (Aldershot: Gower), 80–95.

Wilkins, Mira (1988), "The Free-Standing Company, 1870–1914: An Important Type of British Foreign Direct Investment," *Economic History Review*, 41 (2), 259–82.

Wilkins, Mira (1989), *The History of Foreign Investment in the United States to 1914* (Cambridge, MA: Harvard University Press).

Wilkins, Mira (1992), "The Neglected Intangible Asset: The Influence of the Trade Mark on the Rise of Modern Corporation," *Business History*, 34, 66–95.

Wilkins, Mira (1994), "Comparative Hosts," *Business History*, 36 (1), 18–50.

Wilkins, Mira (2004), *The History of Foreign Investment in the United States, 1914–1945* (Cambridge, MA: Harvard University Press).

Wilkins, Mira (2015), "The History of Multinationals: A 2015 View," *Business History Review*, 89 (3), 405–14.

Wilkins, Mira (2016), "Business and Borders: Capitalism," Speech at the American Historical Association (8 January).

Wilkins, Mira (forthcoming), *History of Foreign Investment in the United States, 1945–2012* (Cambridge, MA: Harvard University Press).

Wilkins, Mira and Hill, Frank Ernest (2011 [1st ed.: 1964]), *American Business Abroad: Ford on Six Continents* (2nd edn.; Cambridge, New York: Cambridge University Press).

Wilkins, Mira and Schröter, Harm G. (eds.) (1998), *The Free-Standing Company in the World Economy, 1830–1996* (Oxford: Oxford University Press).

Williamson, Jeffrey G. (1997), "Globalization and Inequality, Past and Present," *World Bank Research Observer*, 12 (2), 117–35.

World Bank (2018), *World Bank Accounts Data* (Washington, DC: World Bank).

2

ORIGINS AND DEVELOPMENT OF GLOBAL BUSINESS

Geoffrey G. Jones

Introduction

This chapter surveys the current state of research on the origins and development of global business. Since the middle of the nineteenth century, firms have been the strongest institution to operate across national borders. Multinational firms, defined as firms owning and controlling assets in more than one country, have been major drivers of the trade and capital flows which have characterized the globalization waves since the middle decades of the nineteenth century (Jones, 2005a; Jones, 2014).

Figure 2.1 provides a visual representation of these globalization waves. The metric of cross-border integration aggregates capital, trade, and migration flows.

It should be emphasized that Figure 2.1 is a pictorial representation of the overall historical pattern. It makes no claim to be based on statistical estimates – it would be challenging to

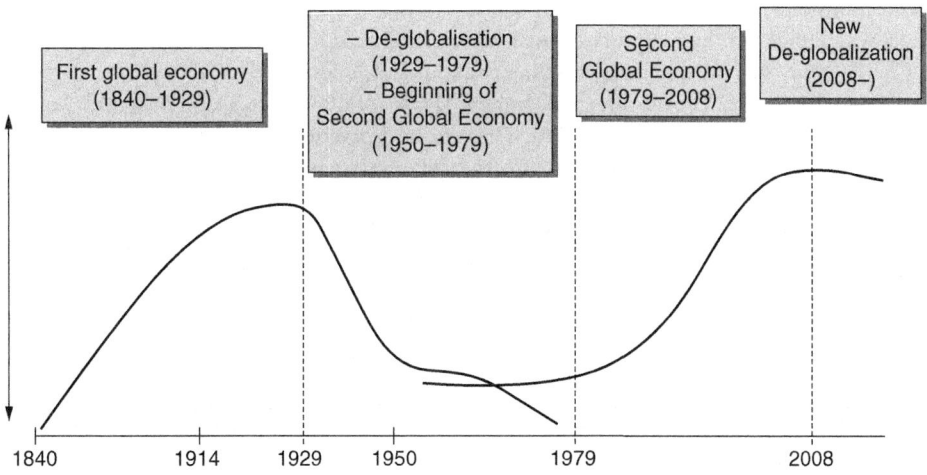

Figure 2.1   Globalization framework

Source: The author.

formulate a data series which combines trade, capital, and migration. It does not claim that there was zero international trade, capital flow or migration in 1840. Indeed, as argued elsewhere (Jones, 2013) globalization could be legitimately traced back to when homo sapiens migrated from Africa about 80,000 years ago. Rather the point is that from 1840s the scale of international trade, capability, and migration intensified, increasingly integrating different regions of the world (Bordo *et al.*, 2003).

The first wave of globalization stumbled during World War I. There were new controls on trade. The Gold Standard was suspended. A surge of racism resulted on ethnicity-based restrictions on migration flows in the United States, Australia, and elsewhere. The Wall Street Crash in 1929 resulted in the collapse of the first global economy as tariffs and exchange controls massively reduced capital and trade flows. While international trade increased again from the 1950s, migration and capital movements remained subdued until the end of the 1970s. Large parts of the world, including the Soviet Union and the People's Republic of China, excluded global firms and international trade. Subsequently capital flows and international trade rose very quickly, although migration flows were much less. This second global economy was ended by the global financial crisis in 2008. Enhanced regulations, a huge increase in non-tariff barriers, and other restrictions resulted in trade and capital flows becoming subdued. Within a decade anti-globalization populist movements had come to power in multiple countries entirely changing the policy context in which global firms worked.

The following five sections will consider the role of global firms in each of the chronological eras of globalization. A final section concludes.

Global business and the first globalization wave 1840–1929

From the mid-nineteenth century thousands of firms, largely based in Western countries which had experienced the Industrial Revolution, established operations in foreign countries. Merchant houses and banks were among the first businesses to become multinational. The search for raw materials and food led firms abroad too. The first instances of multinational manufacturing included small Swiss cotton textile firms in the 1830s (Jones and Schröter, 1993). The phenomenon intensified from mid-century. Multinational manufacturing was stimulated by the spread of protectionism from the late nineteenth century. Firms were able to "jump" over the tariff barriers which blocked their exports by establishing local production. This strategy was prominent in industries such as chemicals, machinery and branded consumer products.

As Table 2.1 shows, foreign direct investment (FDI) rose to a percentage of world output which it would not reach again until 1990. These firms drove the rapid increase in trade flows during this era. Latin America and Asia were especially important as host economies, attracting well over half of the total world stock of foreign direct investment. Possibly one half of world FDI was invested in natural resources, and a further one-third in services, especially financing, insuring, transporting commodities and foodstuffs (Wilkins, 1970; Jones, 2005a; Dunning and Lundan, 2008).

Table 2.1 World foreign direct investment as a percentage of world output, 1913–2010 (%)

1913	1960	1980	1990	2010
9.0	4.4	4.8	9.6	30.3

Source: Jones, 2014.

The firms of different countries varied in their propensity to invest abroad. Britain alone was the home of nearly one half of world FDI in 1914, and the United States and Germany accounted for a further 14 percent each. Firms from a number of small European countries, especially the Netherlands, Sweden and Switzerland, were very active internationally (Jones and Schröter, 1993). During the first global economy, the fact that the majority of foreign direct investment was in natural resources and related services, meant that the biggest host economies were countries of recent settlement and primary producers in the periphery. A listing of the ten largest host economies in 1929 included India, Cuba, Mexico, Argentina, Chile, Malaya, and Venezuela. FDI in these countries was overwhelmingly in resources and services. Manufacturing FDI went to three other countries – Canada and the United States in first and second place, and Britain in eighth place. Canada and the United States also attracted considerable FDI in resources (Wilkins, 1994).

The spread of global firms rested crucially on the overall political economy of the period. The expansion of Western Imperialism over much of Asia and Africa, the spread of an international legal system and legal norms which enforced contracts and private property rights, numerous trade treaties, and the international Gold Standard, reduced the risks of doing business abroad, primarily for firms from the West. After tariffs rose in the United States and Europe from the middle of the nineteenth century, business enterprises "jumped" over them to create multinational manufacturing operations (Magee and Thompson, 2010; Fitzgerald, 2015). Access to capital was facilitated by the growth of large globally oriented capital markets in London and elsewhere. Trading in commodities was facilitated by the rapid growth of futures markets in the second half of the century. Transport and communication innovation was vital too. The advent of steam driven railroads from the 1830s, and faster sailing ships and then steamships, shrank geographical distance. The discovery of the principles of electricity was vital too. It permitted the revolution in communication costs caused by the invention of the electric telegraph. Although the impact of the telegraph was not immediate, as submarine technology was so expensive it was mainly used by governments and large firms (Müller, 2016). Over an extended period of time it became fundamental in enabling the boundaries of firms to expand, inside countries and then over borders. It made formal managerial control over distant operations much easier (Jones, 2014).

The growth of global firms was enabled by innovation in organizational structures which reduced the risks of operating internationally. There was constant experimentation with organizational design, and the organizational forms employed were heterogeneous. As described by Chandler, the nineteenth century saw the creation of large firms with managerial hierarchies (1962, 1977, 1990). Many began as small entrepreneurial ventures, but a handful became global giants. Singer Sewing Machines was one example. By 1914 it accounted for 90 percent of the sewing machines built in the world. Singer's development of installment plans and direct selling enabled millions of relatively low income consumers from Russia to Japan to purchase the machine (Carstensen, 1984; Godley, 2006; Gordon, 2011).

Singer, and other large firms such as Standard Oil and Lever Brothers, co-existed with numerous small and family owned firms. European firms, especially from smaller economies such as Sweden, made foreign investments at early stages of their corporate lives (Olsson, 1993). Thousands of "free-standing" firms, which conducted little or no business in their home economies, were established in Britain and the Netherlands especially, exclusively to operate internationally (Wilkins and Schröter, 1998). These free-standing firms were once seen as inferior to US-style managerial hierarchies. In her path-breaking article on the subject, Wilkins observed their "high mortality rate" and the managerial challenges of a "tiny head office" (Wilkins, 1988: 271, 277). However, subsequent research found them to have often been robust, employing socialization methods of control in place of formal bureaucracy. In many cases free-standing firms were not genuinely free-standing at all, but formed parts of clusters of businesses, or business groups organized around trading companies (Jones, 1998, 2000).

Merchant networks established by *diaspora* communities were also important drivers of global business. The Greek *diaspora* spread over the Mediterranean, and Russia was active in wide-ranging international commercial and shipping business, creating a cosmopolitan business network based on kinship ties extending over central Europe and even reaching France and Britain (Minoglou and Louri, 1997). In Asia, Chinese and Indian commercial *diaspora* operated within and between European empires (Brown, 1994, 2000; Fitzgerald, 2015).

The minority of firms which survived the challenge of global operations long enough to build viable businesses drove globalization by creating trade flows, constructing marketing channels, building infrastructure, and creating markets. By 1914 the production or marketing of most of the world's mineral resources was controlled by US and European firms. Foreign firms also dominated the production and marketing of renewable resources including rubber, tropical fruits, and tea. A high proportion of world trade in primary commodities was intra-firm. The commodity chains created by these firms were fundamental actors in the process of world economic integration (Topik *et al.*, 2006).

Much of the infrastructure of the global economy – the telegraph, ports, railroads, and electricity and gas utilities – was also put in place by international business enterprises (Hausman *et al.*, 2008; Geyikdagi, 2011; Fitzgerald, 2015). International shipping companies carried the world's oceanic trade and moved millions of people (Harlaftis and Theotokas 2004; Munro 2003). Trading companies both facilitated and created trade flows between developed and developing countries, often investing in creating plantations and opening mines, and the processing of minerals and commodities (Jones, 1998, 2000; Jonker and Sluyterman, 2000). European overseas banks built extensive branch networks throughout the Southern Hemisphere and Asia, and financed the exchange of manufactured goods for commodities (Jones, 1993: 13–62).

World War I was a major economic and political shock for global firms. The expropriation of German-owned affiliates by US, British, and other Allied governments not only virtually reduced the stock of German FDI to zero, but also signaled the end of the era when foreign companies could operate in most countries on the same terms as domestic ones. The Russian Revolution in 1917 resulted in France and Belgium losing two-thirds of their total foreign investment (Jones, 2013; Fitzgerald, 2015).

Yet multinational investment resumed during the 1920s, even if short-term and speculative capital flows became much more prominent in the world economy. The giant American mining company, the Guggenheim Brothers, made very large investments in Mexico, Chile, and elsewhere. There were large foreign investments during that decade by US automobile manufacturers Ford and General Motors. The Swedish Match Company, led by Ivar Kreuger, consolidated the fragmented match industry and by 1930 controlled 40 percent of the world match market. By then the company also owned other Swedish multinationals, including the electrical company Ericsson, ball bearing manufacturer SKF, and the mining company Boliden. Yet the experience of Swedish Match also reflected the new fragility of the global economy. After the mid-1920s, the company raised capital on the American stock exchange and lent it to sovereign governments in Europe and elsewhere unable to finance their deficits in the capital markets. In 1932, after Ivar Kreuger's suicide, it was discovered that Swedish Match's growth had rested on systemic accounting fraud (Hildebrand, 1985).

The impact of these global firms was considerable. Multinational manufacturing companies transferred products and brands across borders during this era of fast globalization. Bayer introduced the aspirin to the United States. There were hundreds of other examples (Wilkins, 1989).

Firms which built factories in foreign countries transferred new techniques and work practices. Beginning with a factory in Glasgow, Scotland, in 1867, Singer took mechanized sewing machine manufacture around the world. In Tsarist Russia, it built the largest modern engineering factory in the country, employing German and British managers to supervise both the production process and new methods of labor management (Carstensen, 1984). Companies also transferred the values behind brands. For example, the international growth of the beauty industry drove a worldwide homogenization of beauty ideals and practices. The features and habits of White people became established as the benchmarks of global beauty (Jones, 2010).

Technology transfer was not limited to multinational manufacturing. The establishment and maintenance of mines, oil fields, plantations, shipping depots, and railroad systems involved the transfer of packages of organizational and technological knowledge to host economies. The Guggenheims moved mining technologies developed in the United States to their businesses in Mexico and Chile. They also collaborated with other mining companies, such as Sweden's Boliden, to exchange technology (Bergquist and Lindmark, 2016). Given the absence of appropriate infrastructure in many countries, foreign enterprises frequently not only introduced technologies specific to their activities, but also social technologies such as police, postal, and education systems (Jones, 2000). In some cases they created entire towns: an example was Ford Motor Company's ultimately unsuccessful Fordlandia started in Brazil in 1928 (Wilkins and Hill, 1964: 169–70, 176–8, 184). The building of transport and distribution infrastructure enabled entrepreneurs to access world markets for the first time. In so far as access to markets had been a constraint on capitalist enterprise in many parts of the world, this relieved it. However there were also huge costs. The movement of crops and plants around the world resulted in massive losses of biodiversity and other environmental damage beginning a process of environmental degradation which has yet to be reversed (Jones, 2017, 2018).

There was, therefore, considerable potential for global firms to facilitate the closing of the wealth gap which had opened up as Western Europe and North America underwent industrialization from the nineteenth century, whilst the rest of the world did not, and lost once large craft industries. In practice, this did not happen, except in isolated incidences. Knowledge spillovers from multinational investment to the non-Western world were limited. Technological diffusion worked best when foreign firms went to a country with the institutional arrangements, human capital, and entrepreneurial values to absorb transferred knowledge, much of which was tacit and not readily codified (Bruland and Mowery, 2014). Consequently, while the first global economy saw multinational firms become the conduits for significant technological and organizational transfers from the United States to Western Europe, and Western Europe to the United States, their role in transferring knowledge and capabilities from the West to the rest of the world was more modest. Global firms can be seen as part of the explanation for the convergence of technologies and incomes within the West, and the lack of convergence between the West and the rest (Harley, 2014).

Both the strategies of global firms and their management practices contributed to this situation. Most FDI in developing countries was in resources and related services. These natural resource investments were highly enclavist. Minerals and agricultural commodities were typically exported with only the minimum of processing. This meant that most value was added to the product in the developed economies. Foreign firms were large employers of labor at that time. However, expatriates were typically employed in the higher skill jobs (Piquet, 2004). As a result, the diffusion of organizing and technological skills to developing host economies was far less than to developed economies. Certainly some developing countries, such as Mexico, experienced significant economic growth before World War I, as foreign firms developed and exported minerals and commodities, and built the railroads and ports that allowed them access to foreign markets (Allen, 2014). However on the whole, and with exceptions, Western firms in Mexico were not significant agents of technological diffusion into the domestic economy, given the formidable institutional, social, and cultural roadblocks in face of the transfer of technologies from advanced economies (Beatty, 2003, 2009).

In the broadest sense, many of the gains from the first global economy had not been evenly shared. This was most clearly seen in the cases of the huge natural resource concessions which colonial regimes and assorted dictators had granted to Western firms. In order to entice firms to make investments in mines, railroads, and so on, foreign firms were often given large, long-term, and tax-free concessions by governments in Latin America and elsewhere. These concessions turned Western companies into supporters of repressive governments, and associated Western capitalism with dictatorships and colonial regimes (Jones, 2013). Global capitalism had flourished within the context of Western colonialism, and became associated with the political and racial injustice of such regimes. In interwar India, for example, Gandhi's campaign against British imperialism encompassed a wider criticism of global capitalism as a whole (Tripathi, 2004; Nanda, 2003).

During the last decades of the first global economy income gaps increased not only between the West and the Rest, but also within countries. Global firms were significant drivers of this story. As commodity exports surged in Latin America, income inequality soared as the owners of land became wealthy (Williamson, 2010). Meanwhile mining and other extractive Western companies employed thousands of local people typically paid low wages and offered few avenues for improvement. The creators and owners of large global corporations in the United States (and Europe) also became hugely wealthy. This contributed to the huge rise in income inequality seen evident by the early 1900s (Piketty, 2014). Inequality and unfairness prompted the growth of labor movements and socialist parties. In 1917 the Bolsheviks seized power in Russia, and proceeded to abolish capitalism. Global firms such as Singer Sewing Machines and Shell lost their large assets in the country.

Global business in the era of de-globalization 1929–1979

Global firms encountered numerous challenges after 1929 as liberal policy regimes gave way to numerous government restrictions on trade, capital flows, and migration. If the management of geographical distance had been a major managerial challenge before the 1920s, the management of governments and their policies rose sharply up corporate agendas subsequently (Jones and Lubinski, 2012). Between 1929 and 1938 the real value of world exports declined by 9.4 percent. By the end of the 1930s half of world trade was affected by tariffs. There was no recovery to 1929 levels until after World War II. The integration of world markets went into reverse (Fitzgerald, 2015).

This changed policy regime happened despite the fact that transport and communication innovations continued to reduce the costs of geographical distance. Telephones and automobiles became items of mass consumption, especially in the United States. Air travel became quite widespread, if costly. The advent of cinema and radio also provided unprecedented opportunities to see lifestyles real or imagined elsewhere, and facilitated the further diffusion of cultural influences (Grazia, 2005). Yet as technology facilitated human beings to travel and observe one another as never before, so they disliked what they saw. Nationalism and racism proliferated. Governments sought to block foreign companies, alongside foreign imports and capital flows, and immigrants.

The nationality of firms rose rapidly up political agendas after World War 1, and receptivity to foreign firms did not recover after the end of the war. Although the United States shifted from being the world's largest debtor nation to being a net creditor over the course of World War I, this was accompanied by a growing nationalism which resulted in major restrictions on foreign ownership in shipping, telecommunications, resources, and other industries (Wilkins, 2002, 2004). The world became, and remained, much riskier for firms crossing national borders.

After the end of World War II, the spread of Communism, decolonization and subsequent growth of restrictions on foreign firms, and widespread nationalization of foreign-owned natural resource investments in the developing world, combined to dramatically reduce foreign investments beyond the West. By 1980 the six largest hosts for FDI were the United States, Britain, Canada, Germany, France and the Netherlands. Brazil, the first developing economy, was in seventh place. Australia, Indonesia, and Italy followed (Dunning and Lundan, 2008; Jones, 2014).

Although capital flows, trade flows, and migration flows all fell sharply, global business did not disappear during these decades. A number of rabidly nationalistic regimes, such as Japan in the 1930s, blocked new foreign investment, and squeezed existing foreign-owned businesses. However, Nazi Germany, while it used exchange controls to block profit remittances, exercised few restrictions on foreign businesses beyond requiring that they excluded Jews and others considered undesirable from the management of affiliates in Germany. As a result, US and other foreign firms such as General Motors and IBM were able to sustain growing businesses, albeit ones whose profits they needed to plough back into their German operations, and as a result contribute to strengthening the Nazi state (Wilkins, 1974; Turner, 2005). Meanwhile consumers in Nazi Germany continued to watch the same Hollywood movies and purchase the same American cosmetic brands, as their counterparts in the United States (Grazia, 2005; Jones, 2010). More generally, the ability of multinationals to finance their subsidiaries by ploughing back profits, or lending from local banks, meant that their businesses were much less impacted by the interwar collapse of capital flows than might have been expected.

Business enterprises were more robust than an aggregate view of markets would suggest. From the perspective of firms, globalization was constrained rather than totally reversed. During the 1920s German firms rebuilt international businesses (Jones and Lubinski, 2012). In interwar Great Britain, as elsewhere, there were significant divestments as manufacturing multinationals closed down their affiliates, but there were at least as many new entrants (Bostock and Jones, 1994; Jones and Bostock, 1996). US and other firms in fast-growing consumer products such as automobiles – and component industries such as tires – invested heavily in manufacturing in foreign markets (Fitzgerald, 2015). There were strong continuities, rather than massive disruption, in the global maritime world of shipping, trading, and ports (Miller, 2011). Despite an era of falling commodity and mineral prices, multinational companies made vast investments developing new sources of supply, such as copper mines in east Africa and the Belgian Congo, and petroleum in Venezuela (Jones, 2005a).

Numerous international cartels strove to regulate prices and output on a global scale. By the 1930s a high percentage of world trade was controlled by such international cartels. In manufacturing, the world electric lamp cartel controlled three-fourths of world output of electric lamps between the mid-1920s and World War II (Reich, 1992). Commodities such as oil, tin, and tea saw wide-ranging and quite long-lasting international cartels. While they may be seen as part of the story of growth-retarding institutions during this era, it is evident that most cartels were rarely able to control them for too long before new competitors appeared, unless they were strongly supported by governments. More importantly, however, they were often not agents of de-globalization. They often represented competition by another means rather than the elimination of competition altogether. They were sometimes powerful actors in the transfer of knowledge and intellectual property across borders (Fear, 2008).

Global firms faced much greater restrictions after World War II. The Communist states of the Soviet Union, eastern Europe and China excluded capitalist firms from their borders. The Communist world resembled an "alternative" global economy, but one without capitalist firms, at least until the deterioration of political relations between China and the Soviet Union halted attempts at economic integration (Kirby, 2006). Yet, even here, global firms kept marginal presences. In consumer products such as hair care, Western firms sold ingredients to Soviet and other eastern European state-owned firms from at least the 1970s, and sometimes licensed their technology also (Jones, 2010).

Leaving aside the Communist countries, much of the world restricted or banned foreign companies in some or all industries. In European and many other developed countries, tight exchange controls enabled governments to vet or sometimes prohibit investments from other firms. In major European economies such as France, Britain, and Italy, large swathes of industry were nationalized and taken out of capitalist control, domestic or foreign. The United States was broadly more open to foreign firms, although they were blocked from sectors considered strategic, including defense, airlines, and broadcasting (Wilkins, 2002).

In the postcolonial world, the restrictions on global capitalism were much greater. In both Africa and Asia there was widespread restriction and expropriation of foreign firms. Entrepôts and colonial outposts which remained open to foreign multinationals, such as Singapore and Hong Kong, experienced rapid economic growth, although their equally successful "Newly Industrializing Countries" (NIC) counterparts South Korea and Taiwan adopted Japanese-style restrictions on wholly owned foreign companies. During the 1970s Western firms lost ownership of much of the world's natural resources, as Middle Eastern and other governments expropriated assets. Within the non-Western world, there was enormous concentration of FDI flows. In Asia, there was no FDI in China, and almost none in Japan and India (Jones, 2005a).

Global business and the origins of the second global economy 1945–1979

After World War II ended, global firms made significant contributions to the reconstruction of a global economy. Service firms such as management consultants, advertising agencies, hotels and film distributors served as significant conduits for the international diffusion of American management practices, values, and lifestyles (West, 1987; Quek, 2012). However their activities involved limited capital investment compared to manufacturing or mining. This meant that their growing importance was not captured by FDI figures. This was one reason why levels of FDI remained well below their pre-1914 peaks.

As US management consultancies, such as McKinsey, globalized from the late 1950s, they both created and served markets for consultancy services. They diffused managerial best practice from the United States, initially primarily to Western Europe where they opened branches (Kipping, 1999; McKenna, 2006). Trading companies developed global networks exploiting information asymmetries. Japan's general trading companies (*sogo shosha*) survived their dismantling by the Allied occupation after World War II to become the central drivers of Japan's foreign trade and FDI (Yonekawa, 1990).

Long-established European trading companies, many of whom had had their businesses devastated during the war, were also rebuilt and re-invented. Jardine Matheson and Swire, for example, lost their substantial assets in China after the 1949 Revolution. However they developed new businesses in the British colony of Hong Kong and elsewhere in the region, building and operating ports, wharves, and shipping companies, and creating airlines. Swire's development of Cathay Pacific created, by the 1960s, a major airline which facilitated regional economic integration (Jones, 2000).

Shipping firms were especially important actors in the postwar growth boom. They carried the bulk of international trade, including much of the energy, raw materials, and food that the Western world and Japan required. A new generation of Greek ship-owners, headed by Aristotle Onassis and Stavros Niarchos, built new bulk shipping companies, taking advantage of regulatory arbitrage opportunities by, for example, registering ships using flags of convenience, and basing themselves in tax havens such as Monaco (Harlaftis, 1993, 2014, 2019).

Multinational banking assumed a new importance. A number of European overseas banks, such as HSBC, diversified from their regional bases to become large global banks active in both developed and developing countries (Jones, 1993: 285–371; Roberts and Kynaston, 2015). As British and US banks took advantage of the Bank of England's liberal policies toward foreign exchange markets during the late 1950s, the development of the Eurodollar markets in London provided a dynamic new source of funding for global capitalism. In the interests of financial stability, governments had sought to tightly regulate their financial markets since the Great Depression, and had separated them from each another by exchange controls. The new unregulated Eurocurrency and Eurobond markets soon began to capture a rising share of financial intermediation from regulated domestic markets. The new financial markets were global in scope, but physically located in a small number of financial centers, of which London stood at the apex, and in offshore centers such as Bermuda, the British Virgin Islands, and the Cayman Islands, typically small British colonies, where the primary attraction was not the size of domestic markets, but a combination of regulations and fiscal conditions, and political stability (Jones, 1992; Roberts, 1994; Schenk, 2001, 2011; Young, 2013; Hauter and Jones, 2017; Ogle, 2017).

The commercial and investment banks in the new Euro markets innovated financial products on an accelerating scale with the tacit, and later explicit, support of the British and US governments (Helleiner, 1994). However the financiers who created these markets also subverted the strategies of governments to closely regulate their financial markets. In some instances, such as the British merchant bank Warburg, they were explicitly motivated by political and economic ambitions to erode national sovereignties and foster European integration (Ferguson, 2009).

The physical location of international financial markets in a few geographies formed part of a wider pattern of the concentration of business activity in certain cities and regions during the postwar decades. The advantages of proximity and agglomeration drove such patterns. While such clustering had always been a feature of the world economy, the growing importance of knowledge, and knowledge workers, intensified the trend. This was evident in the origins of the Silicon Valley technology cluster during the 1950s and 1960s, where an unusual convergence of technological skills, educational institutions, and venture capital led to the creation of multiple entrepreneurial firms which were to dominate innovation in many parts of the IT industry for the remainder of the century (Lécuyer, 2005).

During the 1950s, most of the international cartels of the interwar years were dismantled, while US manufacturing companies invested on a large scale in Western Europe, initially in response to the "dollar shortage," which encouraged US firms to establish factories to supply customers in countries that lacked the dollars to buy American products (Wilkins, 1974). There was initially little rationalized production, and intra-firm trade was low. However, from the 1960s, firms began to seek geographical and functional integration across borders. The process of building integrated production systems was difficult. While a European company such as Unilever was a prominent proponent of European economic integration from the 1950s, it struggled to achieve regional integration of its own production and marketing facilities (Jones and Miskell, 2005).

The postwar decades were the classic era of the Chandlerian large corporation managed by professional managers, which served as powerhouses of innovation in many manufacturing industries, especially in the United States. US-based firms were pre-eminent in new technologies, and they sought to maintain innovation and other value-added activities within firm boundaries. In the computer industry, for example, it proved impossible for western European firms, let alone those from developing countries, to build sustainable businesses. Advanced knowledge was locked within the boundaries of such large Western corporations, as well as geographical clusters such as Silicon Valley.

Global business also often changed its form, rather than disappearing, and resilience remained a prominent feature. Whilst foreign ownership of natural resources vastly declined, especially during the 1970s, foreign orchestration of commodity trade flows and dominance of higher value-added activities did not. World trade in commodities was increasingly handled by giant commodity trading firms such as Cargill, the grain trader and largest private company in the United States (Broehl, 1992, 1998). While large integrated oil companies lost control of their oil fields in many countries, they kept control of refineries, tankers, and distribution facilities. New forms of independent trading companies emerged as key players in the global economy. A number of the most important, including Andre and Philipp Brothers were either based in Switzerland or used Swiss-based affiliates to book most of their transactions. Switzerland offered a low tax environment and corporate secrecy, with the added benefit of not belonging to the United Nations (Guez, 1998). This enabled the companies to trade with governments, such as that of apartheid-era South Africa, subject to trade embargoes. The most noteworthy example was the trading house of Marc Rich, founded in 1974 by disgruntled former employees of Philipp Brothers, which had revenues of $15 billion by 1980. It flourished as the world's largest independent oil trader by clandestinely selling Iranian oil to Israel and South Africa (Ammann, 2009).

Firms proved adept at pursuing strategies to respond to anti-foreign sentiments or critical governmental policies. They assumed local identities. In 1947 Sears, the US department store chain, started a successful business in Mexico, a country which had only a decade earlier expelled foreign oil companies and was widely regarded as highly nationalistic. Sears carefully crafted its strategy to appeal to Mexicans, representing policies such as profit-sharing, pensions, and low priced meals as in the traditions of the Mexican Revolution (Moreno, 2003). Unilever retained its large consumer goods business in India, and other emerging markets such as Turkey, by means of employing local nationals in senior management positions, selling equity shares to local investors, and investing in industries deemed desirable by governments, such as chemicals in India (Jones, 2005b, 2013).

Multinationals also learned that interventionist government policies could work in their favor. In Latin America, postwar governments imposed high tariffs to achieve import substitution manufacturing, but they did not prohibit ownership of industries by foreign firms. The Brazilian and other Latin American governments offered incentives to attract foreign firms to build manufacturing facilities. Although such import substitution strategies have since been widely derided, in part as they became associated with the chronic macro-economic mismanagement which resulted in hyperinflation in Brazil and elsewhere during the 1970s and 1980s, they resulted in the building of much new industrial capacity.

A striking example was the creation of a large automobile industry in Brazil from the late 1950s. While the US automobile giants Ford and General Motors initially refused to respond to the government's desire to start local production, the upstart German car maker VW began local manufacturing, benefitting from exchange rate subsidies. It was able to rapidly overturn the large market share of the US firms which had relied upon importing knock-down kits for assembly. By 1980 Volkswagen, eventually joined by the leading US and other firms, had given Brazil an annual production of over one million vehicles a year, making the country the world's tenth largest automobile industry. The downside was excess capacity and low productivity, but

VW and the other firms had also laid the basis for the sub-continent's largest automobile industry (Shapiro, 1994).

Global business and the second global economy 1979–2008

As the world spectacularly re-globalized from the 1980s, among the most dramatic changes was the worldwide policy embrace of global capitalism. State planning, exchange controls, and other instruments of interventionist policies were abandoned. Instead, practically every government on the planet eventually came to offer incentives for global firms to invest. The most spectacular change came in China which, after 1978, opened its economy once more to global firms. In 2001 China joined the World Trade Organization (WTO), resulting in significant cuts in Chinese tariffs. Just over ten years later the fall of the Berlin Wall and the collapse of the Soviet Union re-opened eastern Europe to global business. In some federal systems, such as the United States, individual states competed with one another to attract foreign investors.

The role of global business in the growth and dynamics of the second global economy is considerable. The ratio of inward FDI stock to GDP (gross domestic product) rose in the world from 9.6 percent to 30.3 percent between 1990 and 2010. The same increase applied to the developed world as a whole, but there were outliers. In Britain, inward FDI stock rose from 20.1 percent of GDP to 48.4 percent between 1990 and 2010. In the developing world as a whole the ratio increased from 13.4 percent to 29.1 percent, but again there were outliers. In India the ratio of inward FDI stock rose from a very low 0.5 percent in 1990 to a much higher 12.0 percent in 2010. In China, it rose from 5.1 percent to 9.9 percent (UNCTAD, 2011).

As during the fast globalization during the late nineteenth century, global firms were drivers of economic integration. Multinational investment grew far faster than world exports or world output. International production systems developed within which firms located different parts of their value chain across the globe. In some industries such production systems became highly externalized through outsourcing.

There was a striking globalization of many services. These included insurance and re-insurance, where firms such as AIG, Allianz and Swiss Re expanded globally. In leisure and retailing, the coffee chain Starbucks, which made its first investment outside the United States in Japan in 1996, and retail companies such as Wal-Mart, Zara, and Uniqlo became symbolic of the new global era. In media, News Corporation built a newspaper, movie, television, and cable business with large market shares in Australia, Britain, India, and the United States (Fitzgerald, 2015; Hauter and Jones, 2017).

The global significance of firms based beyond North America, western Europe, and Japan also rose. During the 1960s and 1970s, some manufacturers from South Korea and Taiwan began to invest abroad, typically in other emerging markets. They were usually small scale and used labor-intensive technology. A second wave of firms, based in both Asia and Latin America, began to expand globally from the 1980s, often after they had built scale and corporate competences in their protected domestic markets. They were prominent in assembly-based and knowledge-based industries including electronics, automobiles, and telecommunications. These investments often originated from firms embedded in the business groups which characterized emerging markets, including the Korean *chaebol* and the *grupos economicos* in Latin America. (Amsden, 2003; Kosacoff, 2002; Khanna and Palepu, 2006; Barbero, 2014).

The ability of firms from emerging markets to become significant actors in global capitalism rested on several factors. They were sometimes able to piggyback on incumbent Western or Japanese firms as customers through subcontracting and other linkages (Mathews, 2002). The spread of management education, as well as the growing number of international students at leading US business schools, provided firms outside the developed core with well-trained and globally minded managers. Finally there was a new generation of state-owned, or partly owned firms, which could invest in building global businesses without the constraint of having to deliver private shareholder returns. The growth of state-owned firms was particularly evident in China, where state support enabled highly competitive local firms to emerge even in high-technology sectors. Examples included Huawei, the internet networking firm, and wind and solar energy firms such as Xinjiang Goldwind. The number of Chinese companies among the global top ten turbine manufacturers went from zero to four between 2006 and 2010 (Buckley *et al.*, 2011; Clifford, 2015; Jones, 2017).

The dynamic growth of global firms, drawn from a widening range of home countries, was apparent. There remained little or no aggregate evidence of spillovers from multinational firms to local firms in the same sector, especially in developing countries, although there was evidence of positive linkages between multinationals and suppliers. Foreign affiliates were often more demanding in their specifications and delivery targets, while more willing to provide assistance and advice to local firms. Multinationals continued to have no incentive to encourage know-ledge leakages to competitors. In many developing countries, local firms also still lacked the capabilities to compete with large multinationals, and the greater the technology gap, the more difficult this gap was to fill (Alfaro *et al.* , 2004). Governments sought to attract foreign firms and create whole industries by designating free trade areas or export processing zones. Most export processing zones, whether in Asia, Africa, or Latin America, have failed to attract more than the low value-added, low-skill segments of industry value chains (Steinfeld, 2004; Cling *et al.*, 2005).

As global firms moved resources across borders in pursuit of profitability opportunities, they also continued to reinforce trends more than counter them. Despite the availability of technologies which permit the dispersal of economic activities, global firms served as major actors in the clustering of higher value-added activities in "global cities" and regions such as Silicon Valley and Bangalore. A significant difference with earlier eras may have been that US firms started to "outsource" domestic jobs to foreign countries. Apple, for example, outsourced manufacturing of its iconic iPhone to the Taiwanese company Foxconn, which produced them in China. In 2016 half of the world's iPhones were made at a Foxconn plant in Zhengzhou, China, where the venture received massive subsidies from the local and provincial government (Barboza, 2016). The aggregate evidence on domestic employment loss and hollowing out in the United States was not straightforward. Longitudinal research has not generally been supportive of polit-ical rhetoric on the major threats to domestic employment (Harrison *et al.*, 2007). However there was little doubt that global firms played a significant role in the widening wealth gaps which became a feature of the second global economy. Enabled by the rise of theories of share-holder value and the rapid expansion of stock options, chief executives awarded themselves very large remuneration even as real incomes remained highly subdued, especially in the United States. The second global economy was also characterized by extensive gaming and outright corporate fraud among large global corporations, facilitated by the ability to transfer funds through offshore financial centers such as the Cayman Islands which had opaque reporting requirements (Salter, 2008; Balleisen, 2017).

Global business in the era of new de-globalization since 2008

As in the previous era of globalization, a financial crisis provided a massive shock to the global economy. The world financial crisis of 2008–2009 was itself the result in part of three decades of the financialization of capitalism, enabled by the deregulation of the financial services industry which had been tightly regulated by most governments between the 1930s and the 1970s.

The financial sector represented 8 percent of US corporate profits in 1950. By 1990 it was 20 percent. By 2003 it was 34 percent. Global financial assets rose from $56 trillion in 1990 to $206 trillion in 2007. Financialization was accompanied by a number of financial crises – including currency and stock market collapses in Asia in 1997 and the collapse of the US and other stock markets in 2000 – before the collapse of Lehman Brothers resulted in a full-scale global financial crisis.

The global financial crisis resulted in a severe economic downturn, but more fundamentally it provoked a change of sentiment about the benefits of liberal global capitalism. Policy regimes shifted in a more restrictive fashion toward global firms, especially initially in financial services. There were no more international agreements to reduce tariffs: the Doha round of multilateral trade negotiations stalled. Although tariff levels did not rise, governments took numerous other protectionist non-tariff measures. After 2008 there was a surge in micro-protectionism. There was a widespread adoption of local content rules, public procurement discrimination against foreign firms, export taxes, and quotas, and trade distorting subsidies. One study identified 3,500 new protectionist events between 2008 and 2016. This policy shift contributed to a significant stagnation in capital and trade flows. The ratio of world trade to output was basically flat between 2008 and 2016. FDI flows fell from a peak of $1.9 trillion in 2007 to $1.2 trillion in 2014 (Hufbauer and Jung, 2016; Ghemawat and Altman, 2016).

It was within the content of stagnation that a number of populist governments came to power which looked upon liberal and cosmopolitan capitalism with disfavor and pursued nationalistic agendas. This trend was first evident in emerging markets such as Turkey, Thailand, and the Philippines, as well as Russia, but subsequently spread to some Western economies characterized by extreme inequality and/or high levels of immigration. Britain's decision in 2016 to leave the European Union, motivated by popular desires to restrict migrant flows, had the potential – depending on how the decision was executed –to disrupt multinational supply chains in Europe and significantly diminish London's position as the world's leading global financial center. Donald Trump's assumption of the US Presidency in the following year was followed by a surge of trade protectionist and anti-immigrant rhetoric, as well as withdrawal from the Trans-Pacific Partnership (TPP) trade agreement and the Paris climate change agreement signed in 2015.

This political and economic environment rendered international corporate strategies more challenging. Some emerging markets firms which had gone global during the heady days of the second global economy experienced managerial and financial challenges. These included Indian companies such as the Tata business group and steel company Arcelor Mittal, which struggled to manage acquisitions in major Western and other markets. A number of globalized Brazilian firms were caught up in a massive corruption scandal which broke out in the country in 2014. However many emerging market businesses emerged as successful global competitors to Western incumbents (Jones, Chapter 39, this volume).

As in the previous era of deglobalization, global firms sought to accommodate nationalistic governments. In 2016 Cisco, which had once dominated internet networking in China, but whose business had shrunk as the government favored domestic competitors such as Huawei, merged its China business with the local company Inspur to create a joint venture. In January 2017, the public tweets of Donald Trump ahead of his assumption of the US Presidency, resulted in the Ford Motor Company cancelling plans to build a $1.6 billion automobile manufacturing plant in San Luis Potosi in Mexico. Companies with strong bargaining power sought to negotiate special deals with governments. In 2016, following the Brexit vote, the British government promised the Japanese automobile manufacturer Nissan special incentives should Brexit negotiations result in trade barriers which would hinder the company selling into the

European Union. As institutional structures weakened, global firms sought protection in special deals with governments.

Concluding remarks

Business enterprises have been powerful actors in the spread of global capitalism after 1840. Emerging out of the industrialized Western economies, global firms created and co-created markets and ecosystems through their ability to transfer a package of financial, organizational, and cultural assets, skills, and ideologies across national borders. They have been major drivers of trade growth, which they often organized within their own boundaries. They have been shapers of, as well as responders to, globalization waves over the last two centuries. There was a great deal of heterogeneity in the organizational forms employed in global business: indeed, mapping and accounting for such changes should form an important component of future research agendas.

Global firms were also actors in periodic de-globalization waves. This was because they functioned as reinforcers of gaps in wealth and income rather than disrupters of them. Business enterprises proved disappointing institutions for knowledge and technology transfer. During the first global economy, multinational resources and related investments were highly enclavist, and embedded in the institutional arrangements of Western imperialism and autocratic dictators. Western firms reinforced rather than disrupted institutional and societal norms which restricted growth in many countries outside the West. They often functioned, as a result, as part of the problem, rather than part of the solution. In the more recent globalization era, the strategies of Western corporations have moved far beyond the practices of the colonial past, but linkages and spillovers to local economies have often been disappointedly low. Their ability, and motivation, to locate value-added activities in the most attractive locations means that they strengthen clustering rather than encourage dispersion of knowledge. Business historians have concentrated far too much on the drivers of global business, and far too little on its impact. The next generation of research should focus far more on impact, including not only knowledge transfer, but also impact on inequality, gender, and ethnic relations, and environmental sustainability.

Evidently over the course of the second global economy the era when Western and Japanese business enterprises dominated global markets and innovation began to give way to one in which they competed as equals in a growing number of industries with firms whose homes were in China, India, the Arab Gulf, and elsewhere. Much more research needs to be undertaken on the historical origins of this shift. This will require business historians to shift their focus from the West and Japan. As wealth shifts East and with the consolidation of China as the world's largest economy, this trend can only accelerate, especially as the growing fragility of institutional structures in the United States and the European Union looks set to further weaken the competitiveness of firms based in those regions.

References

Alfaro, Laura, Rodríguez-Clare, Andrés, Hanson, Gordon H., and Bravo-Ortega, Claudio (2004), "Multinationals and Linkages: An Empirical Investigation," *Economía*, 4, (2), 113–69.
Allen, Robert. C. (2014), "The Spread of Manufacturing," in Larry Neal and Jeffrey G. Williamson (eds.) *The Cambridge History of Capitalism*, vol. 2. (Cambridge: Cambridge University Press), 22–46.
Ammann, Daniel (2009), *The Secret Lives of Marc Rich*. (New York: St. Martin's Press).
Amsden, Alice H. (2003), *The Rise of "the Rest": Challenges to the West from Late-Industrializing Countries*. (Oxford: Oxford University Press).
Balleisen, Edward J. (2017), *Fraud: An American History from Barnum to Madoff*. (Princeton, NJ: Princeton University Press).

Barbero, Maria I. (2014), "Multinacionales latinomericanas en perspectiva comparada, Teoría e historia," *Cátedra Corona, Universidad de los Andes*, 23.

Barboza, David (2016), "How China Built "iPhone City" with Billions in Perks for Apple's Partner," *New York Times*, December 29.

Beatty, Edward (2003), "Approaches to Technology Transfer in History and the Case of Nineteenth Century Mexico," *Comparative Technology Transfer and Society*, 1, (2), 167–200.

Beatty, Edward (2009), "Bottles for Beer: The Business of Technological Innovation in Mexico, 1890–1920," *Business History Review*, 83, 317–348.

Bergquist, Ann-Kristin and Lindmark, Marcus (2016), "Sustainability and Shared Value in the Interwar Swedish Copper Industry," *Business History Review*, 90, (2), 197–225.

Bordo, Michael D., Taylor, Alan M., and Williamson, Jeffrey G. (2003), *Globalization in Historical Perspective*. (Chicago, IL: University of Chicago Press).

Bostock, Frances and Jones, Geoffrey (1994), "Foreign Multinationals in British Manufacturing, 1850–1962," *Business History*, 36, (1), 89–126.

Broehl, Wayne G. (1992), *Cargill: Trading the World's Grain*. (Hanover, NH: University Press of New England).

Broehl, Wayne G. (1998), *Cargill: Going Global*. (Hanover, NH: University Press of New England).

Brown, Rajeswary A. (1994), *Capital and Entrepreneurship in South East Asia* (London: Macmillan).

Brown, Rajeswary (2000), *Chinese Big Business and the Wealth of Asian Nations*. (London: Palgrave).

Bruland, Kristine and Mowery, David C. (2014), "Technology and the Spread of Capitalism," in Larry Neal and Jeffrey G. Williamson (eds.) *The Cambridge History of Capitalism*, vol. 2. (Cambridge: Cambridge University Press), 82–126.

Buckley, Peter J., Voss, Hinrich, and Cross, Adam C. (2011), "The Emergence of Chinese Firms as Multinationals: The Influence of the Home Institutional Environment," in Robert Pearce (ed.) *China and the Multinationals: International Business and the Entry of China into the Global Economy*. (Northampton, MA: Edward Elgar), 125–57.

Carstensen, Fred V. (1984), *American Enterprise in Foreign Markets: Singer and International Harvester in Imperial Russia* (Chapel Hill, NC: University of North Carolina Press).

Chandler, Alfred D. (1962), *Strategy and Structure*. (Cambridge, MA: MIT Press).

Chandler, Alfred D. (1977), *The Visible Hand*. (Cambridge, MA: Harvard University Press).

Chandler, Alfred D. (1990), *Scale and Scope*. (Cambridge, MA: Harvard University Press).

Clifford, Mark L. (2015), *The Greening of Asia*. (New York: Columbia University Press).

Cling, Jean-Pierre, Razafindrakoto, Mireille, and Roubaud, François (2005), "Export Processing Zones in Madagascar: A Success Story under Threat?" *World Development*, 33, (5), 785–803.

Dunning, John H. and Lundan, Sarianna M. (2008), *Multinational Enterprises and the Global Economy*, 2nd ed. (Northampton MA: Edward Elgar).

Fear, Jeffrey (2008), "Cartels," in Geoffrey Jones and Jonathan Zeitlin (eds.) *The Oxford Handbook of Business History*. (Oxford: Oxford University Press), 268–92.

Ferguson, Niall (2009), "Siegmund Warburg, the City of London and the Financial Roots of European Integration," *Business History*, 51, (3), 364–82.

Fitzgerald, Robert (2015), *The Rise of the Global Company: Multinationals and the Making of the Modern World*. (Cambridge: Cambridge University Press, 2015).

Geyikdagi, V. Necla (2011), "French Direct Investments in the Ottoman Empire before World War 1," *Enterprise & Society*, 12, (1), 525–61.

Ghemawat, Pankaj and Altman, Steven A. (2016), *DHL Global Connectedness Index 2016: The State of Globalization in an Age of Ambiguity*. (Bonn: Deutsche Post DHL).

Godley, Andrew (2006), "Selling the Sewing Machine around the World: Singer's International Marketing Strategies, 1850–1920," *Enterprise & Society*, 7, (2), 266–314.

Gordon, Andrew (2011), *Fabricating Consumers: The Sewing Machine in Modern Japan* (Berkeley, CA: University of California Press).

Grazia, Victoria de (2005), *Irresistible Empire: America's Advance through 20th-Century Europe*. (Cambridge, MA: Harvard University Press).

Guez, Sébastien (1998), "The Development of Swiss Trading Companies in the Twentieth Century," in Geoffrey Jones (ed.) *The Multinational Traders*. (London: Routledge), 150–72.

Harlaftis, Gelina (1993), *A History of Greek-owned Shipping*. (London: Routledge).

Harlaftis, Gelina (2014), "The Onassis Global Shipping Business, 1920s–1950s," *Business History Review*, 88, (2), 241–71.

Harlaftis, Gelina (2019), *Creating Global Shipping: Aristotle Onassis, the Vagliano Brothers, and the Business of Shipping, c.1820–1970.* (Cambridge: Cambridge University Press).

Harlaftis, Gelina and Theotokas, John (2004), "European Family Firms in International Business: British and Greek Tramp-Shipping Firms," *Business History*, 46, (2), 219–55.

Harley, Kick (2014), "British and European Industrialization," in Larry Neal and Jeffrey G. Williamson (eds.) *The Cambridge History of Capitalism, Volume 1, The Rise of Capitalism: From Ancient Origins to 1848* (Cambridge: Cambridge University Press), 491–531.

Harrison, Anne E., McMillan, Margaret S., and Null, Clair (2007), "U.S. Multinational Activity Abroad and U.S. Jobs: Substitutes or Complements?" *Industrial Relations: A Journal of Economy and Society*, 46, (2), 347–65.

Hausman, William J., Hertner, Peter, and Wilkins, Mira (2008), *Global Electrification: Multinational Enterprise and International Finance in the History of Light and Power, 1878–2007.* (Cambridge: Cambridge University Press).

Hauter, Niels Viggo and Jones, Geoffrey (2017), "Risk and Reinsurance," in Niels Viggo Hauter and Geoffrey Jones (eds.) *Managing Risk in Reinsurance: From City Fires to Global Warning.* (Oxford: Oxford University Press), 1–46.

Helleiner, Eric C. (1994), *States and the Re-emergence of Global Finance* (Ithaca, NY: Cornell University Press).

Hildebrand, Karl-Gustaf (1985), *Expansion, Crisis, Reconstruction: Swedish Match 1917–1939.* (Stockholm: Liber Förlag).

Hufbauer, Gary C. and Jung, Euijin (2016), "Why Has Trade Stopped Growing? Not Much Liberalization and Lots of Micro-Protection," Peterson Institute for International Economics, March.

Jones, Geoffrey (1992), "International Financial Centres in Asia, the Middle East and Australia: A Historical Perspective," in Youssef Cassis (ed.) *Finance and Financiers in European History, 1880–1960.* (Cambridge: Cambridge University Press), 405–28.

Jones, Geoffrey (1993), *British Multinational Banking 1830–1990.* (Oxford: Clarendon Press).

Jones, Geoffrey (ed.) (1998), *The Multinational Traders.* (London: Routledge).

Jones, Geoffrey (2000), *Merchants to Multinationals.* (Oxford: Oxford University Press).

Jones, Geoffrey (2005a), *Multinationals and Global Capitalism: From the Nineteenth to the Twenty-First Century.* (Oxford: Oxford University Press).

Jones, Geoffrey (2005b), *Renewing Unilever: Transformation and Tradition.* (Oxford: Oxford University Press).

Jones, Geoffrey (2010), *Beauty Imagined: A History of the Global Beauty Industry.* (Oxford: Oxford University Press).

Jones, Geoffrey (2013), *Entrepreneurship and Multinationals: Global Business and the Making of the Modern World.* (Northampton, MA: Edward Elgar).

Jones, Geoffrey (2014), "Firms and Global Capitalism," in Larry Neal and Jeffrey G. Williamson (eds.) *The Cambridge History of Capitalism*, vol. 2. (Cambridge: Cambridge University Press), 169–200.

Jones, Geoffrey (2017), *Profits and Sustainability: A History of Green Entrepreneurship.* (Oxford: Oxford University Press).

Jones, Geoffrey (2018), *Varieties of Green Business: Industries, Nations and Time.* (Cheltenham, UK: Edward Elgar Publishing).

Jones, Geoffrey and Bostock, Frances (1996), "U.S. Multinationals in British Manufacturing before 1962," *Business History Review*, 70, (1), 207–56.

Jones, Geoffrey and Lubinski, Christina (2012), "Managing Political Risk in Global Business: Beiersdorf 1914–1990," *Enterprise & Society*, 13, (1), 85–119.

Jones, Geoffrey and Miskell, Peter (2005), "European Integration and Corporate Restructuring: The Strategy of Unilever c1957-c1990," *Economic History Review*, LVII, 113–39.

Jones, Geoffrey and Schröter, Harm G. (eds.) (1993), *The Rise of Multinationals in Continental Europe.* (Aldershot, UK: Edward Elgar).

Jonker, Joost and Sluyterman, Keetie (2000), *At Home on the World Markets.* (The Hague: Sdu Uitgevers).

Khanna, Tarun and Palepu, Krishna G. (2006), "Emerging Giants: Building World-Class Companies in Developing Countries," *Harvard Business Review*, 84, (10), 60–9.

Kipping, Matthias (1999), "American Management Consulting Companies in Western Europe, 1920–1990: Products, Reputation and Relationships," *Business History Review*, 73, (2), 190–220.

Kirby, William C. (2006), "China's Internationalization in the Early People's Republic: Dreams of a Socialist World," *China Quarterly*, 188, 870–90.

Kosacoff, Bernardo (2002), *Going Global from Latin America: The ARCOR Case*. (Buenos Aires: McGraw-Hill InterAmericana).

Lécuyer, Christophe (2005), *Making Silicon Valley: Innovation and the Growth of High Tech, 1930–1970*. (Cambridge, MA: MIT Press).

McKenna, Christopher D. (2006), *The World's Newest Profession: Management Consulting in the Twentieth Century*. (Cambridge: Cambridge University Press).

Magee, Gary B. and Thompson, Andrew S. (2010), *Empire and Globalization: Networks of People, Goods and Capital in the British World, c 1850–1914*. (Cambridge: Cambridge University Press).

Mathews, John A. (2002), *Dragon Multinational: A New Model for Global Growth*. (Oxford: Oxford University Press).

Miller, Michael (2011), *Europe and the Maritime World*. (Cambridge: Cambridge University Press).

Minoglou, Ioanna P. and Louri, Helen (1997), "Diaspora Entrepreneurial Networks in the Black sea and Greece, 1870–1917," *Journal of European Economic History*, 26, (1), 69–104.

Moreno, Julio (2003), *Yankee Don't Go Home* (Chapel Hill, NC: University of North Carolina Press).

Müller, Simone M. (2016), *Wiring the World: The Social and Cultural Creation of Global Telegraph Networks*. (New York: Columbia University Press).

Munro, J. Forbes (2003), *Maritime Enterprise and Empire*. (Woodbridge, UK: Boydell).

Nanda, B.R. (2003), *In Gandhi's Footsteps: The Life and Times of Jamnalal Bajaj*. (New Delhi: Oxford University Press).

Ogle, Vanessa (2017), "Archipelago Capitalism: Tax Havens, Offshore Money, and the State, 1940s–1970s," *American Historical Review*, 122, (5), 1431–1458.

Olsson, Ulf (1993), "Securing the Markets: Swedish Multinationals in a Historical Perspective," in Geoffrey Jones and Harm G. Schröter (eds.) *The Rise of Multinationals in Continental Europe*. (Aldershot, UK: Edward Elgar), 99–127.

Piketty, Thomas (2014), *Capital in the Twenty-First Century*. (Cambridge, MA: Belknap Press).

Piquet, Caroline (2004), "The Suez Company's Concession in Egypt, 1854–1956: Modern Infrastructure and Local Economic Development," *Enterprise & Society*, 5, (1), 107–27.

Quek, Mary (2012), "Globalizing the Hotel Industry 1946–1968: A Multinational Case Study of the Intercontinental Hotel Corporation," *Business History*, 54, (2), 201–26.

Reich, Leonard S. (1992), "General Electric and the World Cartelization of Electric Lamps," in Akiro Kudo and Terushi Hara (eds,) *International Cartels in Business History* (Tokyo: University of Tokyo Press), 213–31.

Roberts, Richard (ed.) (1994), *International Financial Centres*, Vol. 1. (Aldershot, UK: Edward Elgar).

Roberts, Richard and Kynaston, David (2015), *The Lion Wakes: A Modern History of HSBC*. (London: Profile Books).

Salter, Malcolm S. (2008), *Innovation Corrupted: The Origins and Legacy of Enron's Collapse*. (Boston, MA: Harvard Business School Press).

Schenk, Katherine (2001), *Hong Kong as an International Financial Centre: Emergence and Development 1945–65*. (London: Routledge).

Schenk, Katherine (2011), "The Re-emergence of Hong Kong as an International Financial Centre, 1960–1978," in Laure Quennouëlle-Corre and Youssef Cassis (eds.) *Financial Centres and International Capital Flows in the Nineteenth and Twentieth Centuries*. (Oxford: Oxford University Press), 199–253.

Shapiro, Helen (1994), *Engines of Growth: The State and Transnational Auto Companies in Brazil*. (Cambridge: Cambridge University Press).

Steinfeld, E. (2004) "China's Shallow Integration: Networked Production and New Challenges for Late Industrialization," *World Development*, 32, (11), 1971–1987.

Topik, Steven, Marichal, Carlos, and Frank, Zephyr (eds.) (2006), *From Silver to Cocaine: Latin American Commodity Chains and the Building of the World Economy, 1500–2000*. (Durham, NC: Duke University Press).

Tripathi, Dwijendra (2004), *The Oxford History of Indian Business*. (Oxford: Oxford University Press).

Turner, Henry A. (2005), *General Motors and the Nazis: The Struggle for Control of Opel, Europe's Biggest Carmaker* (New Haven, CT: Yale University Press).

UNCTAD, *World Investment Report*, various years.

West, Douglas C. (1987), "From T-Square to T-Plan: The London Office of the J. Walter Thompson Advertising Agency, 1919–1970," *Business History*, 29, 467–501.

Wilkins, Mira (1970), *The Emergence of Multinational Enterprise*. (Cambridge, MA: Harvard University Press).

Wilkins, Mira (1974), *The Maturing of Multinational Enterprise*. (Cambridge, MA: Harvard University Press).

Wilkins, Mira (1988), "The Free-Standing Company, 1870–1914: An Important Type of British Foreign Direct Investment," *Economic History Review*, XLI, (2), 259–85.

Wilkins, Mira (1989), *The History of Foreign Investment in the United States before 1914*. (Cambridge, MA: Harvard University Press).

Wilkins, Mira (1994), "Comparative Hosts," *Business History*, 36, (1), 18–50.

Wilkins, Mira (2002), "An Overview of Foreign Companies in the United States, 1945–2000", in Geoffrey Jones and Lina Gálvez-Muñoz (eds.) *Foreign Multinationals in the United States*. (London: Routledge), 18–49.

Wilkins, Mira (2004), *The History of Foreign Investment in the United States 1914–1945*. (Cambridge, MA: Harvard University Press).

Wilkins, Mira and Hill, Frank E. (1964), *American Business Abroad: Ford on Six Continents*. (Detroit, MI: Wayne State University Press).

Wilkins, Mira and Schröter, Harm (eds.) (1998), *The Free Standing Company in the World Economy, 1836–1996*. (Oxford: Oxford University Press).

Williamson, Jeffrey G. (2010), "Five Centuries of Latin American Income Inequality," *Revista de Historia Económica/Journal of Iberian and Latin American Economic History*, 28, (2), 227–52.

Yonekawa, Shinichi (1990), *General Trading Companies: A Comparative and Historical Study*. (Tokyo: United Nations University Press).

Young, Mary Alice (2013), *Banking Secrecy and Offshore Financial Centers: Money Laundering and Offshore Banking*. (New York: Routledge).

3

THE MAKING OF GLOBAL BUSINESS IN LONG-RUN PERSPECTIVE

Mark Casson

Introduction

This chapter highlights the role of entrepreneurship in the making of global business. It argues that global business needs to be seen as a self-contained system. The evolution of this system has been driven by many forces, one of which is human enterprise. Over the centuries human enterprise has generated new technologies and products, and financed major investments, which collectively have transformed the global business system.

Records of enterprise go back as far as Rome, Greece, and Babylon (Temin, 2002). But a continuous written record linking the past to the present only begins in Western Europe *c*.1200. From this date the role of enterprise can be clearly discerned from documents relating to commodity trade, taxes, tariffs and subsidies, licenses, property transactions, and the formation of business partnerships and merchant guilds. This evidence requires interpretation, and theories of entrepreneurship hold the key to this. This chapter applies entrepreneurship theory to interpret the history of global business since 1200 (Casson and Casson, 2013a).

Global business is an inter-dependent system. Every element in the system is connected, either directly or indirectly, to every other. A change in any part of the system sends ripples that spread to every corner, however remote (Samuelson, 1947). Innovations made at one location quickly spread to other locations. Disruption at one location stimulates adaptive responses, as other locations isolate the disrupted element and work around it.

The global system requires coordination, but is too complex to be coordinated by a single leader (Hayek, 1949; Klein, 2014). Where there are alternative ways of doing things, competitive market processes can select the most efficient solution; promoters of rival solutions compete and customers decide between them. Where there are no alternatives, management ensures that the correct solution is applied. Firms and markets work together. Firms manage plants which transform resources into products; markets distribute the products to consumers, supply raw materials to firms, and allocate workers to jobs.

Global business has emerged as the result of many inter-dependent and inter-related business decisions. Climate and natural resources frame business decision-making. Climate and resources vary considerably between locations, so that different locations favor different types of activity. Business location is a key decision in the global economy. Other key decisions relate to investment in transport and communications infrastructure. This connects different parts of the world and makes possible a spatial division of labor, in which different locations specialize in carrying out different activities. Each location exports large amounts of a few specialized products and imports for consumption small amounts of many products, generating significant international and inter-regional trade.

Other key decisions relate to the formation of institutions, such as multinational enterprises, which coordinate international operations through networks of foreign subsidiaries. These subsidiaries are linked to each other, and to their headquarters, by internal communications and by flows of semi-processed products, carried by the transport and communication infrastructure described above. International trade and investment are in turn regulated by international treaty organizations, such as the World Trade Organization and the United Nations.

Human beings play three main roles in this global system. First, they supply manual work by converting food into energy and then applying their skills to artisan production and factory work. Second, they act as entrepreneurs, developing new technologies and novel products. Each new technology adds to the stock of human knowledge and raises the base level from which the next generation of technology is developed. Each new product provides users with experience which suggests further improvements to design. And, third, they act as leaders in social, political, and religious life, presiding over a range of non-profit institutions, from small charities, through the nation state, to the treaty organizations mentioned above.

The focus in this chapter is on the entrepreneur. Entrepreneurs sit in the middle between managers and workers below them and political and religious leaders above them. Sometimes these roles can be combined; entrepreneurs may become political leaders, while self-employed entrepreneurs may work for themselves. These roles remain distinct, however, in terms of the functions they perform, as explained below.

The global business system evolves over time. The institutional environment has evolved through political initiatives; e.g., until recently the prevailing world order was very much a legacy of post-war reconstruction that created the United Nations, the World Bank, and so on. Business, too, drives the evolutionary process. Entrepreneurs are key drivers of change, and their investments, especially in infrastructure, create a legacy on which the future of the system is built.

The nature of entrepreneurship

Entrepreneurs as opportunity-seekers

In the business studies literature, entrepreneurs are typically portrayed as opportunity seekers, taking advantage of new technologies or emerging consumer trends to innovate new products or to move from small-scale craft production to mass production (Kirzner, 1973; Casson, 1982; Shane, 2003).

Identifying an opportunity requires imagination. It is necessary to visualize something that does not yet exist. It could be something revolutionary, such as a railway, or "iron road," as visualized in the 1820s, or the high-street chain store, which emerged in the 1850s once the railway network was in place (e.g., W.H. Smith in the United Kingdom, A&P in the United States). It could also be something quite mundane, such as an artisan gluten-free bakery in a provincial town today.

Success requires a combination of imagination, pragmatism, and good judgment. Judgment is about processing information effectively. A successful business venture needs to fulfill a demand, otherwise there will be no revenue stream. The entrepreneur must ask "What is the customer problem that my product solves?" "Do customers realize that they have this problem?" and "Are they aware that my product exists and that it solves their problem?" In other words, the entrepreneur must diagnose the customer's problem in order to create the demand (Godley and Casson, 2015).

Demand is not the only issue; there is also supply to consider. The cost of labor and materials can be high at start-up. Novel products often need to be introduced on a small scale and priced for a luxury market. Only when technology has matured can mass production be introduced, driving costs down through economies of scale and creating a global market. Airline travel, for example, was initially a luxury product; it was only in the 1990s that budget airlines used a cheaper generation of jet aircraft, no-frills service, and internet booking to create a low-price mass market.

Entrepreneurs as coordinators

Entrepreneurs are also coordinators. They devise mechanisms to bring supply and demand together. Coordination is usually effected through a firm; the firms acts as a nexus of contracts through which resources are procured and output sold (Casson, 2005; Foss and Klein, 2012). Workers are hired through a contract of employment in which the worker agrees to act under the direction of a manager (within limits set by law or custom) in return for a wage. The wage is fixed independently of the price for which the product sells; thus the commercial risk of weak demand and low price is borne by the entrepreneur rather than the worker. Managers too can be hired; this creates a hierarchy in which workers report to the managers and managers report to the entrepreneur.

A small firm may be wholly owned by the entrepreneur, but larger firms have independent shareholders too. If the independent shareholders between them hold a majority of shares then they effectively control the firm, provided they all agree; they can remove the entrepreneur from the management of the firm if they believe that his judgment is flawed.

Customers, suppliers, managers, workers, and shareholders all contract with the firm. In this context, the entrepreneur is simply a shareholder and possibly a top manager too. The firm is a legal institution set up to generate profit from the opportunity identified by the entrepreneur, and possesses certain legal privileges that facilitate the performance of this role (see below).

The customer does not deal directly with the worker who produced the product; they deal with the entrepreneur and his firm instead. The entrepreneur acts as a middleman, buying labor from the worker and selling the product on to the customer, thereby appropriating profit from the margin between selling price and production cost.

Advertisements, shop displays, websites, and credit-card payment all play an important role where consumer products are concerned. The entrepreneur decides the advertising medium and the message, they specify customer service (self-service, made-to-order, immediate delivery etc.), they hire the web designer, and they decide how much credit to offer.

The entrepreneur, therefore, takes responsibility of the choice of product, the pricing strategy, the hiring of workers, and the choice of marketing methods. If the entrepreneur's judgment is good, the product sells well and profits are high. High profit rewards the entrepreneur for quality of judgment, and for any risks taken. But the risk may not be so great as others perceive, because the entrepreneur's superior judgment may have been based on superior information. Lack of this information may have discouraged potential competitors from producing similar products. This strengthens the entrepreneur's monopoly power and increases profit. The more the entrepreneur's judgment diverges from popular opinion, therefore, the weaker the competition, the more profitable is the business, and the greater its opportunity for growth. Conversely, the weaker their judgment, the greater the risk of failure.

Entrepreneurship, as described above, is a *function*, and entrepreneurs are people who *specialize* in it. Where the function is relatively simple, e.g., marketing artisan products to a local market, the artisan can perform the role of the entrepreneur. This is the domain of small business. The self-employed artisan is incompletely specialized because entrepreneurship is only a part of their job. At the other extreme are highly complex functions, such as organizing the supply of an innovative mass-produced product to a global market. This is the domain of the multinational enterprise. In this context the entrepreneurial function may engage an entire team of people, each of whom has an entrepreneurial role.

In a large firm with a highly centralized (hierarchical) managerial structure the senior managers at head office operate as an entrepreneurial team. These managers instruct their subordinates, such as managers of foreign subsidiaries, how they are to play their roles. By contrast in a large decentralized firm (e.g., a "multi-divisional" or "network" firm) the entrepreneurial team is distributed across locations, with subsidiary managers having significant influence over global operations. With a decentralized structure the headquarters of the firm is a "hub" where information from different subsidiaries is pooled through discussion and global strategy is negotiated. Generally speaking, a centralized structure is most appropriate where generic technological or marketing knowledge in pre-eminent, and local conditions vary little, so that local knowledge can easily be obtained from local employees, while a decentralized structure is most appropriate where generic knowledge is of limited importance, and local variation is considerable, so that local knowledge is paramount. This point is explored further below.

Competition and cooperation

Competition can never be entirely eliminated, however. Innovation does not take place in a vacuum. There may be no close substitute for a new product, but there is usually some legacy product to contend with. Railways had no close substitutes for long distance travel until cars and planes arrived, but for short distances carts, wagons, and horseback all remained an option. Railways did not compete merely against other forms of transport. They also competed against other forms of leisure. Railway excursions proved popular with the working classes, diverting expenditure from local amusements such as the public house; indeed Thomas Cook's first railway excursion was to a temperance event (Brendon, 1991).

Innovation may also involve cooperation. Railways teamed up with hotels to accommodate passenger needs, and with local carriers to facilitate the collection and distribution of freight. Many contemporary innovations, such as the mobile phone, combine different technologies whose patents are held by different firms.

Firms can cooperate and compete at the same time. Where competitors cooperate, they may set up joint ventures for the purpose. A joint venture can operate as a firm within a firm. Each partner supplies the joint venture with only a subset of its knowledge and skills, reserving the remainder for competitive use. It reserves the right to buy its partner out should the venture begin to develop competitive products that could damage its overall position.

Entrepreneurs are interdependent therefore; they threaten each other as competitors but they can also support each other as collaborators and, in some cases, they can do both at the same time. It is, therefore, a mistake to analyze entrepreneurship in purely individualistic terms. Much of the entrepreneurship literature focuses on the individual entrepreneur, discussing their personality, social background, and the business they created, often using a case study method. This myopic focus often plays down the influence of other entrepreneurs. Most entrepreneurs have rivals; successful entrepreneurs have imitators whilst unsuccessful ones may be driven out of business by more efficient competitors. More to the point, entrepreneurs have collaborators; they may be business partners but, in many cases, they will be suppliers or distributors. Entrepreneurs not only compete with other entrepreneurs; they rely upon them too. This interdependence is evident in large multinationals with complex supply chains, that coordinate networks of contracts involving many independent subcontractors and franchises and licensees.

The role of infrastructure

It is easy to exaggerate the importance of entrepreneurs. Individual entrepreneurs rarely have the scientific skills needed to create inventions of their own; their innovations typically commercialize inventions made by others (Schumpeter, 1934). They rarely have sufficient wealth to fund major innovations by themselves. They often need to rely on family and friends, banks, and sometimes speculative investors too (Gompers and Lerner, 1999).

Entrepreneurs need support, not just from other people, but also supporting social and physical infrastructure. This section considers the various forms that this infrastructure takes. In global business, social interaction over distance relies on physical infrastructure. Several examples of investment in physical infrastructure are presented in later chapters; they provide a useful counterpoint to the investments in manufacturing industries which tend to dominate classic business history literature.

Physical infrastructure is typically large, complex, and durable. It ranges from docks and harbors to power stations and electricity grids (Hausman *et al.*, 2008). In the short run, endowments of infrastructure can be regarded as fixed. At any given time, much of the infrastructure inherited from the past will have been around for so long that it is simply taken for granted, both by business managers of the time and historians of the period. But taking a long-run view of business enterprise, as in this book, it is clear that infrastructure changes. In transport, roads give way to canals as the dominant mode of transport, canals to railways, and railways back to roads with the advent of the motor car.

Investment in canals, railways, and road improvements was complex and risky, and involved a mixture of private enterprise and state control. The making of global business is not, therefore, just the story of how global business responded to changes in infrastructure, but of how global businesses helped to change the infrastructure too. The evolution of global business involved the continuing interplay of agricultural, manufacturing, and service investments on the one hand and infrastructure investments on the other. Growing demand for manufacturing and services created demand for additional infrastructure, and investment in new infrastructure stimulated the supply of manufacturing and services. Enterprise in services and manufacturing depended on enterprise in infrastructure, and vice versa.

In many developed societies, much physical infrastructure is today owned and operated by nation states, city councils, or local public bodies. Private enterprise is rarely absent, however. State and local enterprise expanded considerably from 1870 to 1914 and again in the period 1945–70, but in many cases, this involved nationalizing existing private enterprises. Much of the equipment used in infrastructure systems was purchased by the operators from private producers, and construction was often in the hands of private building contractors and consulting engineers too. In some cases, an operator employed labor directly but in other cases labor was employed by franchisees or subcontractors who delivered customer service on behalf of the government or local community. Franchising was an important element of the "privatization" movement that gathered momentum in the 1990s.

Social infrastructure encompasses law, morals, social norms, and a collective sense of identity. It plays a crucial role in fostering or inhibiting entrepreneurship (Weber, 1947). Entrepreneurs can contribute to this invisible infrastructure by setting an example of social responsibility, personal achievement, and business success. But other players are important in building social infrastructure too like political and religious leaders, together with artists and intellectuals. Including these actors is important. "Everything depends on everything else" in business as elsewhere, and no more so than in global business. Business histories regularly allude to political and cultural influences on business behavior. Links between business leaders, artists, and intellectuals regularly feature in accounts of late Victorian enterprise, particularly in industries like textiles that are influenced by fashion and design. These linkages need to be viewed, however, in a wider and more strategic perspective.

Transport, communications, and utilities

Physical infrastructure comprises a set of facilities at different locations with linkages between them. Physical infrastructure enhances connectivity and increases interdependence within the global economy as a whole. Appendix Table 3.a.1 distinguishes four main types: transport, communications, broadcasting, and utilities. Each is examined in turn. A distinction is drawn between one-way and two-way communications, and between utilities that distribute things and those that collect unwanted things. This gives six categories altogether.

To create a mass market, transport infrastructure is required. Transport allows people to send consignments of goods to each other and to pay each other visits. Investment in transport infrastructure makes it possible to distribute product from a factory to villages, towns, and cities across a wide area; it also allows a factory to draw its resource inputs from a wide area (Chandler, 1965). If mass production is to be profitable then investment in transport infrastructure must be profitable too. If it cannot be made profitable then government may have to subsidize it, or even make the investment itself. Private provision of transport infrastructure therefore avoids having to raise taxes or increase public debt. On the other hand, private monopoly may restrict public access to infrastructure, while competition between private networks may lead to wasteful duplication (Bogart, 2009).

Communications infrastructure is also required. A product must be advertised in order to create a mass market. In the nineteenth century, popular print media provided the ideal instrument for mass-market advertising. This involved one-way communication from supplier to customer. Word-of-mouth recommendation by satisfied customers was an alternative, but was often too slow a mechanism to build up the level of demand required. Shops were important too; they facilitated two-way face-to-face communication. Telegraphy and telephone communication had a major impact on business generally and on the growth of organized commodity markets and financial markets in particular (John, 2000, 2010; Hoag, 2006; Müller and Tworek, 2015). The growth of retailing, especially in major centers of population, allowed potential customers to inspect samples of goods at first hand, and purchase them straightaway (Porter and Livesay, 1971). Since the interwar period, radio and TV broadcasting have transformed one-way communication, giving it a more immediate and visual aspect, while e-mail and interactive websites have expanded the range of options for two-way communication.

Utilities are also important. They distribute energy and power, and other essentials such as water. They also dispose of unwanted material, notably waste and sewage. The development of utilities was crucial in allowing industry to escape dependence on local supplies of fuel (notably coal) for power and heat, allowing it to move out of congested towns into new areas powered and lit by gas and electricity. Improvements in water management, meanwhile, led to better drainage, and brought many areas of the countryside into cultivation as marshland was turned into arable fields.

Both transport and two-way communications are often described as "network industries" (Shy, 2001). This is because the linkages they employ have a network structure. Linkages radiate from hubs and hubs are linked to other hubs, so that movement between any pair of terminals typically involves transit through several hubs. The hub and spoke structure is efficient because it minimizes the overall length of the connections in the network, subject to ensuring that every trip is reasonably short and more or less straight.

Utilities are broadly similar to network industries, but differ in detail. They typically involve one-way rather than two-way flows, e.g., from a gas works, a power station, or a reservoir to a large number of individual factories, offices, shops, and households. These systems often exhibit a more restricted type of network structure, such as a "root and branch structure" for water and a "grid" for electricity (see Chapter 21 on electricity).

It is debatable whether private enterprise is the best method for constructing complex infra-structure networks. Consider railways for example. Individual entrepreneurs may build individual linkages just to connect a specific pair of towns or cities and to cater for local traffic between them. Over time these individual linkages connect up to form a network. Through traffic then develops across the network. The value of each linkage then depends upon the amount of through traffic that it carries as well as the amount of local traffic. To operate the network efficiently it is therefore necessary for the private operators to agree charges for through traffic (Casson, 2009). The easiest to way to sort this out is to bring all the operators under common ownership and control. However, merger would create a monopoly (as happened in the United States). If mergers are prohibited in order to sustain competition, then companies may divert their traffic away from rival routes, leading to inefficient routing and high fares (as happened in the United Kingdom). Nationalization, on the other hand, can lead to slow and bureaucratic decision-making, leading to excessive costs (as happened in France). Further complications arise with continental systems that span different countries, where integration may be effected through unified ownership of trains rather than track (e.g., the Wagon-Lits company in Europe).The way these issues are resolved can impact significantly on the performance of national economies, and thereby affect the global economy too.

Markets as infrastructure

Markets can also be regarded as a form of infrastructure. Markets are centers of trade, where economic activities naturally tend to agglomerate. Markets can be regarded as a match-making device in which buyers are paired up with sellers (Gusfeld and Irving, 1989). In a perfectly competitive market, as described in classic economics texts, every buyer wants the same product and every supplier offers this same product. The only thing to negotiate is therefore the price. With perfect information no one can insist on buying at a lower price than anyone else because no one will sell to them, and conversely no one can sell at a higher price than anyone else because no one will buy from them; thus everyone must sell at the same price. The buying price and selling must be equal, for otherwise a seller could gain by cutting their price in order to profit from additional sales (Marshall, 1890). Thus a uniform equilibrium price prevails. In a global context, international transport costs, tariffs, and non-tariff barriers (e.g., different statutory quality standards) drive wedges between competitive prices for the same product in different countries. Equilibrium price divergence is sustained by the costs incurred by arbitrageurs in moving goods from low-price countries to high-price ones (Krugman, 1991).

Markets are not the only match-making device. Entrepreneurs may wish to match themselves to investors who are sympathetic to their product, or with wholesalers and retailers who are willing to distribute it. Introductions can be made at match-making business events, rather similar to the way that dates can be arranged between young people. Match-making is like a market in many ways: it involves making contact, and everyone wants to be paired up with someone else. But it is unlike a market in two important ways. In a perfectly competitive market any buyer can be paired with any seller and vice versa, but match-making requires a match with the perfect partner, or at least a compatible one. Second, match-making does not involve negotiations over price; that comes later. Match-making lets people decide who to negotiate with; negotiations are based on other characteristics as well as price, and deals are usually long term. Markets work best when setting prices for standardized products; match-making works best where requirements are specific and diverse, and compatibility is the major concern. Match-making complements markets, rather than substitutes for them. Appendix Table 3.a.2 illustrates some of the different forms that markets and match-making mechanisms can take.

Although markets and matching mechanisms may be classified as social infrastructure, they rely heavily on physical infrastructure too. Local markets and match-making institutions may have little need for transport and communications infrastructure, but national and international markets certainly do. Historically the expansion of markets has been key to economic and political integration. The combination of private and state investment in transport and communications played a vital role on the growth in the international entrepôt in the late middle ages, in the economic integration of the United States and more recently in the emergence of the European Union (Badenoch and Fickers, 2010; Lagendijk and Schot, 2007; Matterlart, 2000; Misa and Schot, 2005). Market integration through transport and communications has also played an important role in the development of empires too, as explained below.

Social infrastructure

Social infrastructure is intangible and largely invisible too. It can be given visible expression, however, e.g., in art and architecture. These provide symbolic expressions of the fundamental values and beliefs embedded in a culture. There is a substantial literature on this subject which is much cited in the chapters below. But there is little literature that integrates the discussion of social and physical infrastructure. This section examines the interaction of social and physical infrastructure from the perspective of entrepreneurship, as outlined above. Examples of these interactions can be found in reference works such as Jones and Wadhwani (2007), Casson and Casson (2013b) Jeremy (1984, 1990) Slaven and Checkland (1986–90), and Corley (2005).

From a business perspective, a shared culture aligns expectations and improves communications. It makes it easier for entrepreneurs to understand their customers, workers, investors, and suppliers and for the entrepreneur themselves to be understood well. A business culture may embody religious and moral principles shared by a business community, but it needs to be pragmatic too. A culture that promotes the idea that markets are evil, that profit stems from exploitation, and that wealth is a reward for corruption is unlikely to encourage entrepreneurial activity. On the other hand, a culture that demands that people be honest, that they negotiate in good faith, and that their profits are spent on good causes is likely to have a beneficial effect. Similarly, a culture that prescribes rigid rules and dogmatic beliefs will inhibit enterprise, while a culture that encourages flexibility and curiosity will encourage it instead (Casson, 1991).

Networks of trust

Trust reduces transaction costs. For the entrepreneur it reduces the risk of workers shirking and customers defaulting on payment or making false warranty claims. It also increases investors' confidence in the integrity of the entrepreneur. The family provides a convenient environment within which to build trust; it can be a powerful resource in funding business. Historically, marrying into a wealthy family has been an important way of raising business capital; introducing your brother or sister to a potential spouse in a wealthy family can prove successful too.

Friendship networks also build trust. These can be fostered by the local neighborhood, schooling, religion, political affiliation, and membership of special interest groups. Networks can also work negatively, though, as when people get drawn into criminal gangs. Building the right sort of network is therefore key for an entrepreneur. Breaking into exclusive social networks is particularly useful because that is where financial support and inside information can be obtained (Lane and Bachmann, 1998).

Reputation

Reputation is also important. Reputation makes it easier for an entrepreneur to raise finance from outside the family; reputation for product quality makes it easier to attract and retain customers, while reputation as a good employer makes it easier to attract and retain skilled workers. Reputation also works the other way around; by investigating other people's reputations the entrepreneur can avoid extending credit to heavily indebted customers, avoid seeking loans from banks that quickly foreclose, and avoid hiring lazy workers.

The personal aspect of reputation is very important where entrepreneurs are concerned; professional accreditation is mainly relevant to the people they employ. Personal reputation, however, dies with the individual. Historically, business reputation was often inherited, with an eldest son continuing the business under the father's name. Beginning in the nineteenth century, reputations became embodied in brands (see for example Chapter 32 on Imitation). The brand attached to the product rather than the individual; as a virtual entity it never died and could be bought and sold between businesses (Lopes and Casson, 2007).

The virtual nature of the brand made it easy to steal, however. It could be counterfeited, or simply imitated in such a way as to create confusion. The obvious solution was legal enforcement of trademarks. Once brands and trademarks could be registered under international agreements, the way was open for the development of global brands. Legal innovations backed by standardized protocols and enforced through international treaties were therefore a major step in strengthening product reputation in international business.

The brand is not the only kind of reputation possessed by a business, however. A diversified or "conglomerate" firm may produce several different products, each with its own brand name, but still enjoy a corporate reputation under a different name, e.g., the consumer products conglomerate Unilever or the drinks conglomerate Diageo. A good business reputation may enhance the share price, thereby making it easier for the business to raise capital; it may also enhance its ability to negotiate with governments over taxes or regulations.

Law

Reputation does not address every problem, as the Global Banking Crisis demonstrated when several highly reputable banks failed. Some industries need to be highly regulated; banks are entrusted with people's savings, pharmaceutical firms with people's health, and rail and bus operators with people's lives (see Chapter 7 by Cassis). Social norms and social sanctions alone cannot address the most critical issues: law and regulation are required. But over-regulation can discourage enterprise. The law itself requires a reputation for efficiency and impartiality. Some of the laws and regulations directly relevant to entrepreneurship are summarized in Appendix Table 3.a.3.

Self-governing associations

A self-governing association – often referred to simply as an "institution" – is a group of people who agree to conform to certain standards and to be disciplined by other members of the association if they fail to comply. A classic example is the democratic state. The firm is also an institution. It is a relatively late development. Early states were reluctant to authorize individuals to associate for fear of them plotting against them. Religious institutions were the earliest institutions authorized by Western European rulers *c.*600. These were largely self-governing institutions, having an elected senior officer and accountability to the Pope. Universities and colleges followed *c*.1200 (Catto, 1984). At that time association for businesses purposes was generally effected through partnerships, with training provided through apprenticeships. Guilds were developed for social and charitable purposes, but from 1300 onwards began to play an important role in organizing artisan production and trade. It was not until the 1850s, however, that the modern form of limited liability joint stock company (or corporation) emerged (other than those chartered specifically by the state) (see Chapter 13 by Aldous). The emergence of this type of firm was an important step in widening the scope of entrepreneurship as it allowed larger amounts of funding to be mobilized, it facilitated delegation of management, and it allowed a business to survive automatically beyond the founder's death.

Applications to global business

Global business is important because it produces useful products on a global scale. Popular fascination with multinational enterprises and their battles for global market share should not obscure the economic fundamentals: global business, like any business, transforms resources into products – it just does so on a larger scale and with wider reach. Resources are scarce, so they need to be used economically: to produce the right mix of products in the most efficient way. These products should be sold to those who value them most (although in practice this often means those who can most afford to pay).

Transforming resources into products requires technology. Until quite recently, however, economists used to assume that most technologies were free; if someone understood a technology then anyone could understand it, and no one could stop anyone else from using it. Although patents had existed for centuries, they were deemed expensive to obtain and difficult to enforce. Matters changed as a result of international patent agreements in the 1880s. By the 1930s international patent pools were quite common and often gave rise to international cartels (see Evenett *et al.*, 2001). Only with the postwar expansion of US multinationals did the importance of proprietary technology become widely understood. US firms producing in Europe were demonstrably more efficient that their local rivals because of their access to proprietary technology developed in the United States (and the use of superior management methods too) (Dunning, 1958).

The logic of the multinational enterprise is that it exploits proprietary technology by embodying that technology in global products which are produced and sold through subsidiary firms in different countries. The use of subsidiaries protects the firm from the competitive threat posed by imitations or improvements made by independent licensees, subcontractors, or franchisees (Buckley and Casson, 1976). The use of subsidiaries also affords more general advantages of vertical integration.

Social infrastructure has played an important role in encouraging the discovery of new knowledge and its commercial exploitation. Many of the earliest institutions in Western Europe were, in fact, knowledge-based institutions, and some of the earliest forms of international association were associations for purposes of research. For further details see the chronology in Appendix Table 3.a.4.

One of the major differences between global business and local business is in the type of knowledge used. It could be said, rather tritely, that global business utilizes global knowledge and local business utilizes local knowledge. This is partly true, but not entirely so. Global business certainly exploits global knowledge but it requires local knowledge too. This is because products have to be marketed in many different localities, and at each location local knowledge is required. Products also have to be produced somewhere, and wherever this is, some local knowledge is again required.

A similar point can be made about local businesses. Local businesses certainly exploit local knowledge, but they can play a role in exploiting global knowledge too. Many local businesses handle global products, e.g., as retailers, or as subcontractors undertaking local production.

A firm that controls a global technology but lacks local knowledge can, if desired, rely on local distributors to sell its products and on local subcontractors to produce them. Indeed, it could license its technology to a local firm that both produced and marketed the product.

The major difference between a global firm and a local firm, therefore, is that a global firm typically owns a proprietary technology which it chooses to exploit itself, with minimal reliance on local partners, whereas a typical local firm does not own global knowledge, but may assist a firm that does by acting as their retailer, subcontractor, or licensee.

This analysis applies to both manufacturing firms and to infrastructure suppliers, but the implications are rather different in the two cases. Knowledge of local conditions is crucial in infrastructure projects. Relevant conditions vary from location to location, and country to country, so that no two infrastructure projects are the same. They may depend on the same technology, but the technology always needs to be adapted to local conditions – possibly in an imaginative way.

Infrastructure investment is often undertaken as a one-off project, in contrast to continuous production which is common in manufacturing industry. The end of one project does not normally dove-tail with the start of another project in the same locality. Thus continuous flow mass production is not an option in infrastructure-building industries. The combination of one-off projects and intense demand for local knowledge encourages the use of local partners, who may be well-established local firms. It favors a consortium approach to project management whereby the owner of the proprietary technology acts as major shareholder, lead contractor, and overall coordinator but local partners also take an equity stake.

Invisible infrastructure and the generation of global knowledge

The history of the evolution of global business shows that at various times specific countries have dominated global business, in that many of the leading firms in the global economy were headquartered in that country. In the seventeenth century the Dutch were dominant, in the nineteenth the British, and in the twentieth the United States. Two millennia earlier it was the Romans. Dominance in global business is closely associated, it seems, with imperial power.

Although global business dominance is a contentious issue, a global systems view provides an additional perspective to some leading social and cultural historians (e.g., Colley, 2002). The global systems perspective often accords more closely with the view of global business leaders on the nature of their "achievements" (Platt, 1977). Still, historians have started to analyze the connections between global business and slavery (Beckert, 2014), the environment (Ellmore, 2015), or imperialism in Africa (Zimmerman, 2012), to give just a few examples.

From an economic perspective, there are two main ways of analyzing global business dominance. One is to say that military power, and especially naval power, leads to control of trade, and that control of trade then leads to global business dominance. The other is to say that access to advanced technology is the key, because it can underpin both military and commercial expansion (Casson *et al.*, 2009). The logic of empire, according to this view, is that knowledge is a public good (Mueller, 1979) and can therefore be shared between businesses in different countries, and that technology in particular is based on laws of nature that work across the globe. Knowledge exploitation by business therefore has potential global reach. Transport and communications infrastructure can help to exploit this global reach. But some sort of mechanism is required to exploit knowledge advantage in business. Empire is an example of such a mechanism because knowledge can also be used to exercise military power and subjugate colonized peoples.

It is one of the principles of global business, however, that those who gain access to proprietary technology must pay for it. Within an empire, indigenous businesses that cannot afford to pay will be excluded, and indigenous peoples who lack access to public education may be denied even a basic education that would allow them to understand and assimilate this knowledge. This protection of proprietary knowledge advantage is reflected today in the forms of contract used in developing countries, whereby foreign multinationals license, subcontract, or franchise local firms (whether expatriate or indigenous firms) on terms that protect the foreign firms from imitation, as noted earlier.

Knowledge advantages can arise in many ways. One answer is that they reflect the quality of social infrastructure, and the hierarchies of who can access knowledge through that social infrastructure. Within an empire such exclusion can be applied to people as well by restricting the access of certain groups to various forms of education. Property rights are also defended by exclusionary arrangements like patents. Exclusion is thus key to theories in international business about the relationship between empire and business.

One objection to this line of reasoning is that some countries appear to have achieved intellectual leadership without becoming an imperial power. China in the fifteenth century is often cited in this respect (Jones, 1981). The answer to this question may lie in the level of investment in physical infrastructure, and the type of infrastructure built. Imperial countries are noted for their commitment to building physical infrastructure, often as an expression of their confidence and status. But some imperialists have also built infrastructure for strictly economic purposes and others have not (Winseck and Pike, 2007).

For an imperial nation that has already developed a wide range of domestic commodity markets there is ample profit for entrepreneurs in developing commodity trade, e.g., the Dutch in spices. This expanding trade generates a demand for additional infrastructure, which can be paid for out of the profits of trade. Private demand encourages private enterprise in the provision of infrastructure. Private enterprise is particularly useful when government intervention would encounter obstacles to taxation, such as high administrative costs of tax collection or public ill-will.

Trading nations are therefore more likely to invest in transport and communications infrastructure than non-trading ones (Innis, 1950). The negative Chinese attitude to foreign trade, possibly stemming from Confucian values, may therefore have inhibited international expansion. Chinese politicians concentrated on the defense of land borders (the Great Wall) rather than exploitation of the seaboard with the South China Sea and the Indian and Pacific oceans; similar considerations may have applied in Japan before 1860 (Jones, 1981).

For a manufacturing nation access to foreign raw materials is a key consideration, e.g., cotton in the United Kingdom from the 1760s and oil in the United States from 1900. Britain followed the Dutch in becoming a long-distance trading nation, but its trade really took off with the Industrial Revolution. Early British railways were promoted with international trade and travel in mind. After 1830 trunk lines were quickly built from London to Liverpool, Bristol, Southampton, and Dover, and harbor improvements were also made. The Newcastle & Carlisle Railway was built as a "land bridge" between the North Sea and the Baltic to the east and Ireland and the Atlantic to the west. "Free standing companies" invested in port cities and harbors around the world, focusing not only on settler economies (e.g., Australia) but on anywhere where sources of raw materials could be found (e.g., Latin America, South Africa) (Wilkins and Schroter, 1998).

The other side of the coin concerns the type of product exported by the imperial power. The Dutch were mainly producers of artisan products, while the British exported factory products instead. Export demand not only encouraged British domestic expansion but also promoted "learning by doing" through which technological progress in manufacturing was sustained. This strategy of importing low-knowledge content products and exporting high knowledge-content products was further refined by the United States. From the 1890s the United States began to embody this not only in products produced for export in its own country but in products produced abroad for foreign markets too (Godley, 2006). This process gained momentum in the

1950s. The United States transferred its technology to foreign countries but retained control of it through foreign direct investment. This allowed it to combine its technology, not only with its own domestic resources, but with foreign resources too.

Conclusion

This chapter has attempted to synthesize some of the insights that can be gained from later chapters in this book. It has concentrated on general themes rather than specific points in individual chapters. These themes have been woven together using the concept of entrepreneurship.

Entrepreneurship has been examined in the context of the global business system, which has been viewed as an interdependent knowledge-based system in which infrastructure has a crucial role. This systems view has revealed that the making of global business represents more than just the sum of the separate contributions of individual entrepreneurs. Global business was made by the global business system which coordinated individual enterprise so that it became more than the sum of its parts.

While it is quite appropriate for global business history to focus on individual entrepreneurs – their lives, ambitions, successes, and failures – a full understanding of the subject can only be obtained by considering the contexts in which these people operated. Part of this context is provided by other entrepreneurs, and the infrastructure they created and used. More attention needs to be given to interactions between entrepreneurs, and their relations with infrastructure. These involve both competition and cooperation.

Competition between entrepreneurs has been of two main kinds. First, entrepreneurs competed to discover opportunities and to be the first to exploit them; in other words, they competed to identify and fill "gaps in the market" which others overlooked. Second, entrepreneurs entered markets already created by other entrepreneurs, to offer a new variety of an existing product or an identical product at a lower price; this was conventional market competition. Business history provides overwhelming evidence that this second "static" form of competition is by no means the most important form of competition, as conventional economics would suggest, and that the first more "dynamic" form of competition is key.

Entrepreneurs collaborated too. This collaboration was not necessarily the product of business partnerships between them; often it was collaboration coordinated impersonally by the market system. Many entrepreneurs invested, not in meeting the needs of consumers, but in meeting the needs of other entrepreneurs. For example, they responded to profit incentives by building infrastructure to meet the needs of expanding businesses in the manufacturing sector. These projects were undertaken both at home and abroad with the aim of improving international transport and communications.

These entrepreneurs undertook large risky knowledge-intensive projects, often in hostile environments; their achievements often remain today, in stone and iron, but they have left no household brand name by which they can be remembered. They are often more celebrated amongst engineers, or seamen, than they are amongst business historians, although fortunately many of them get a mention in this book.

More generally, this chapter has highlighted the crucial role of infrastructure investment in promoting long-term economic growth. Investments in infrastructure increased global connectivity and stimulated global trade. They also fostered knowledge transfer and thereby promoted foreign direct investment and multinational enterprise. The making of global business has lasted for more than 800 years (or even longer, if early empires are included). Many things have changed, but throughout this period entrepreneurship and investment in infrastructure have always played a crucial role.

Appendix

Table 3.a.1 Typology of physical infrastructure

Type	Terminal facility	Other facilities	Linkage	Vehicle/user
Two-way flows				
Transport with two-way traffic flows				
Foot	House	–	Footpath, track, road	Person
Road	Stables, garage, parking space	Road hub, inn, café	Road network	Horse, cycle, car, bus, coach, van, lorry
Sea	Dock and harbor	Transshipment port	"Sea route," "shipping channel"	Ship, boat
Canal/river navigation	Canal basin	Canal hub	Canal	Canal boat
Rail and tram	Station, depot	Rail-hub, tram interchange	Railway track	Train
Air	Airport	Air-hub	"Flight path"	Aircraft
Remote communications with two-way message flows				
Post (letter)	Postbox, post office	Sorting office	Transport system	Vehicles (e.g., mail-coach, mail-train, delivery van)
Telegraph (coded message)	Telegraph office	Exchange	Overhead wires	Message signal
Telephone (speech): landline	Home or office telephone, telephone box	Exchange	Landline	Message signal
Telephone (speech): mobile	Mobile phone	Exchange	Aerial, satellite, landline	Message signal
E-mail (message), Skype (see and speak)	Personal computer, mobile	Server	Aerial, satellite, landline	Message signal
One-way flows				
Remote communication with one-way message flows from center to periphery: publishing and broadcasting				
Print media (read)	Newsagent's shop	Print works and editorial office	Delivery of publication	Newspaper, journal, directory, or other publication
Radio broadcasting (listen)	Radio receiver in house, car, etc.	Studio, transmitter	Radio waves	Signal
Television broadcasting (watch and listen)	TV set	Studio, transmitter	Radio waves	Signal

Remote communication with one-way message flows from periphery to center: consultation systems that make use of infrastructure that is also used for other purposes

Voting system	Polling station	Election officer	Collection of ballot papers	Ballot paper
Telephone auction	Personal telephone	Auctioneer	Telephone system	Bid

One-way traffic flow from center to periphery: utilities involved in generation and distribution of essential services

Water	Tap, sink, wash basin, bath	Well, lake, reservoir, pumping station	Pipelines	Flow
Gas	Cooker, heater	Gas works, gasholder	Pipelines	Flow
Electricity	Household appliances, factory equipment, trains, etc.	Power station	Wires, cables, pylons	Flow

One-way traffic flow from periphery to center: utilities involved in the collection, aggregation, and disposal of surplus material

Drainage and flood control	–	Dams, embankments	Drains, rivers, pipelines,	Flow
Sewage	Toilets	Sewage processing works	Sewers	Flow
Rubbish	Bins	Landfill sites, recycling centers, authorized local tips	Refuse collection vehicles	Rubbish items

Note

The table is organized in the following way. First, a distinction is made between one-way and two-way traffic flow. Second, a distinction is made between the movement of physical traffic (e.g., transport of passengers or freight) and the transmission of messages (e.g., postal or telephone traffic). Third, where one-way traffic is involved a distinction is made between traffic flowing from center to periphery and traffic flowing in the opposite direction from periphery to center. This generates six types of infrastructure altogether. There are other dimensions along which infrastructure can be classified but they are not so relevant to this analysis.

For two-way traffic involving either transport or remote communications the "other facilities" listed in the third column are intermediating facilities (e.g., hubs, exchanges) because terminal facilities handle both incoming and outgoing traffic. For one-way traffic systems the "other facilities" are terminals; for broadcasting, publishing, and "generation and distribution' they are sources of flow, while for "consultation" and "collection and processing" they are destinations of flow. There are few complicating factors, however (e.g., where publications are purchased from booksellers or newsagents rather than by direct subscription the booksellers and newsagents also act as hubs).

Where transport and two-way communications are concerned, customers need to be connected to the specific destinations (the places to which they want to go and the people with whom they wish to communicate). Where utilities are involved, however, customers are usually indifferent about the location of the source from which their service is supplied. Punctuality is an important consideration in transport and communications, but continuity of supply is most important where utilities are concerned.

Table 3.a.2 Markets and other matching mechanisms

Matching mechanism	Terminal	Central facility	Traffic over linkages
Markets			
Markets for products	Household	Urban market place, shopping center, trade fair	Transport of shoppers to and from market; Transport of goods to and from shops and stalls
Markets for claims	Households and businesses	Organized exchange located in a city dealing in shares, bonds, insurance, commodity futures etc.	Transport of brokers to and from the exchange Telephoned instructions to buy or sell
Online markets for products and claims	Households and businesses	Internet server	Messages sent as signals
Matching mechanisms			
Vacancies and job-seekers (off-line)	Employers and employees	Publishers of newspapers and other media that carry job advertisements	Postage of application and transport to interview
Partner-seeking (off-line)	People seeking spouses, business partners, investors etc.	Organizers of "networking" events where introductions are made	Transport to event

Note
The table highlights types of markets and matching mechanisms that are specifically relevant to the theme of this chapter. There are many other variants too.

Table 3.a.3 Norms, standards, and their enforcement

Type	Examples	Enforcement agency
Product standards		
Full and accurate measure	Standard pint of beer, size of loaf	Legal system, trade, or professional association
Assured standard of quality	Heathy and safe to use	Legal system, trade, or professional association
	Performance under reasonable conditions conforms to specification/expectations	
	Interchangeable/compatible with other products as required	
Standards of behavior		
Towards other people	No violence or insults; show care and consideration	Law, morals, religion
Towards other people's property	No infringement of their rights, e.g., theft, fraud	Law, morals, religion
Towards society in general: anti-social behavior	Avoid vandalism/undermining collective effort e.g., through laziness/damaging collective reputation e.g., inappropriate behavior	Social norms supported through law, morals, and religion
Norms promoting low-cost transactions		
Negotiate quickly using agreed protocol	The only threat when negotiating a contract should be to switch to a competitor	Social norms within a trade or profession
Delivering products and services according to specification	No deception	Law, morals, religion
Pay punctually for products and services as agreed	No default or use of counterfeit currency	Law, morals, religion

Table 3.a.4 Institutions for knowledge discovery

Type	Dating for Western Europe	Role
Community of scholars: religious	600–1500	Monasteries and nunneries of various orders within the Catholic church
		Re-discovery and translation of classical texts in history and philosophy
Community of scholars: secular	1200–1950	Colleges and universities
		Development of law, medicine, philosophy, theology, history; natural sciences from 1800
Royal administration and civil service	1200–	Development of judicial systems, financial accounting, devolved regional administration
		Personal taxation from 1800
Modern university	1950–2000	Basic research funded by government
		Emphasis on natural science, technology, and social science
		Teaching of undergraduates by active researchers
Government research centers	1800–	Applied research in defense industries, agriculture, medicine, etc.
Corporate R&D laboratories	1900–	Applied research biased to patentable technologies, consumer durables, cosmetics, etc.
Political and social think-tanks and lobby groups	1930–	Identification of ideas that can be applied to government policy, political party manifestos, etc.
Post-modern university	2000–	Mass higher education
		Separation of teaching and research
		External sponsorship of research

References

Badenoch, Alec, and Andreas Fickers (eds.) (2010) *Materializing Europe: Transnational Infrastructures and the Project of Europe*, Basingstoke: Palgrave Macmillan.

Beckert, Sven (2014) *Empire of Cotton: A Global History*, New York: Knopf.

Bogart, Daniel (2009) Nationalisations and the development of transport systems: Cross-country evidence from railroad networks, 1869–1912, *Journal of Economic History*, 69 (1), 202–237.

Brendon, Piers (1991) *Thomas Cook: 150 Years of Popular Tourism*, London: Secker & Warburg.

Buckley, Peter J. and Mark Casson (1976) *The Future of the Multinational Enterprise*, London: Macmillan.

Casson, Catherine and Mark Casson (2013a) *The Entrepreneur in History: From Medieval Merchant to Modern Business Leader*, Basingstoke: Palgrave Macmillan.

Casson, Catherine and Mark Casson (2013b) *History of Entrepreneurship: Innovation and Risk-taking 1200–2000*, Cheltenham: Edward Elgar.

Casson, Mark (1982) *The Entrepreneur: An Economic Theory*, Oxford: Martin Robertson, New ed. 2003, Edward Elgar.

Casson, Mark (1991) *Economics of Business Culture*, Oxford: Oxford University Press.

Casson, Mark (2005) Entrepreneurship and the theory of the firm, *Journal of Economic Behaviour and Organization*, 58, 327–348.

Casson, Mark (2009) *The World's First Railway System*, Oxford: Oxford University Press.

Casson, Mark, Kenneth Dark, and Mohamded Azzim Gulamhussen (2009) Extending internalisation theory: From the multinational enterprise to the knowledge-based empire, *International Business Review*, 18, 236–256.

Catto, J.I. (1984) *History of the University of Oxford, Vol. I: The Early Schools*, Oxford: Oxford University Press.

Chandler, Alfred D., Jr. (1965) *The Railroads: The Nation's First Big Business*, New York: Harcourt Brace.

Colley, Linda (2002) *Captives: Britain, Empire and the World, 1600–1850*, London: Jonathan Cape.

Corley, T.A.B. (2005) *Oxford Dictionary of Business Biography*; over 100 biographies of entrepreneurs; search under "Author: Corley," www.oxforddnb.com (last accessed April 14, 2019).

Dunning, John H. (1958) *American Investment in British Manufacturing Industry*, London: Allen Unwin.

Ellmore, Bart (2015) *Citizen Coke: The Making of Coca Cola Capitalism*, New York: W. W. Norton.

Evenett, Simon J., Margaret Levenstein, and Valerie Y. Suslow (2001) *International Cartel Enforcement: Lessons from the 1990s*, Washington, DC: World Bank.

Foss, Nicolai J. and Peter G. Klein (2012) *Organizing Entrepreneurial Judgement: A New Approach to the Firm*, Cambridge: Cambridge University Press.

Godley, Andrew C. (2006) Selling the sewing machine around the world: Singer's international marketing strategies, 1850–1920, *Enterprise & Society*, 7 (2), 266–314.

Godley, Andrew C. and Mark C. Casson (2015) "Doctor, doctor…" Entrepreneurial diagnosis and market-making, *Journal of Institutional Economics*, 11(3), 601–621.

Gompers, Paul A. and Josh Lerner (1999) *The Venture Capital Cycle*, Cambridge, MA: MIT Press.

Gusfeld, Dan and Robert W. Irving (1989) *The Stable Marriage Problem: Structures and Algorithms*, Cambridge, MA: MIT Press.

Hausman, William J., Peter Hertner, and Mira Wilkins (2008) *Global Electrification: Multinational Enterprises and International Finance in the History of Light and Power*, Cambridge: Cambridge University Press.

Hayek, Friedrich A. von (1949) *Individualism and Economic Order*, London: Routledge & Kegan Paul.

Hoag, Christopher (2006) The Atlantic telegraph cable and capital market information flows, *Journal of Economic History*, 66 (2), 342–353.

Innis, Harold A. (1950) *Empire and Communication*, Oxford: Clarendon Press.

Jeremy, David (ed.) (1984) *Dictionary of Business Biography*, London: Butterworth.

Jeremy, David (1990) *Capitalists and Christians*, Oxford: Oxford University Press.

John, Richard R. (2000) Recasting the information infrastructure for the industrial age, in Alfred D. Chandler, Jr. and James Cortada (eds.), *A Nation Transformed by Information: How Information has Shaped the United States from Colonial Times to the Present*, New York: Oxford University Press, 55–105.

John, Richard R. (2010) *Network Nation: Inventing American Telecommunications*, Cambridge, MA: Belknap Press of Harvard University Press.

Jones, Eric L. (1981) *The European Miracle*, Cambridge: Cambridge University Press.

Jones, Geoffrey and R. Daniel Wadhwani (eds.) (2007) *Entrepreneurship and Global Capitalism*, Cheltenham: Edward Elgar.

Kirzner, Israel M. (1973) *Competition and Entrepreneurship*, Chicago, IL: University of Chicago Press.

Klein, Daniel B. (2014) *Knowledge and Coordination: A Liberal Interpretation*, New York: Oxford University Press.

Krugman, Paul R. (1991) *Geography and Trade*, Cambridge, MA: MIT Press.

Lagendijk, Vincent and Johan Schot (2007) Technocratic internationalism in the interwar years: Building Europe on motorways and electricity networks, *Journal of Modern European History*, 6, 196–216.

Lane, Christe and Reinhard Bachmann (eds.) (1998) *Trust Within and Between Organizations*, Oxford: Oxford University Press.

Lopes, Teresa da Silva and Mark Casson (2007) Entrepreneurship and the development of global brands, *Business History Review*, 81 (4), 651–680.

Marshall, Alfred (1890) *Principles of Economics, Volume I*, London: Macmillan.

Matterlart, Armand (2000) *Networking the World, 1794–2000*, Minneapolis, MN: University of Minnesota Press.

Misa, Thomas J. and Johan Schot (2005) Inventing Europe: Technology and the hidden integration of Europe, *History and Technology*, 21 (1), 1–22.

Mueller, Dennis C. (1979) *Public Choice*, Cambridge: Cambridge University Press.

Müller, Simone M. and Heidi Tworek (2015) The telegraph and the bank: On the interdependence of global communications and capitalism, 1866–1914, *Journal of Global History*, 10 (2), 259–283.

Platt, D.C.M. (ed.) (1977) *British Imperialism, 1840–1930*, Oxford: Clarendon Press.

Porter, Glenn and Harold C. Livesay (1971) *Merchants and Manufacturers: Studies in the Changing Structure of Nineteenth-century Marketing*, Baltimore, MD: Johns Hopkins University Press.

Samuelson, Paul A. (1947) *Foundations of Economic Analysis*, Cambridge, MA: Harvard University Press.

Schumpeter, Joseph A. (1934) *The Theory of Economic Development* (trans. Redvers Opie), Cambridge, MA: Harvard University Press.

Shane, Scott (2003) *A General Theory of Entrepreneurship: The Individual–Opportunity Nexus*, Cheltenham: Edward Elgar.

Shy, Oz (2001) *The Economics of Network Industries*, Cambridge: Cambridge University Press.

Slaven, Anthony and S.G. Checkland (1986–90) *Dictionary of Scottish Business Biography*, Aberdeen: Aberdeen University Press.

Temin, Peter (2002) Price behaviour in ancient Babylon, *Explorations in Economic History*, 39 (1), 46–60.

Weber, Max (1947) *The Theory of Social and Economic Organization* (Talcott Parsons, ed.) Glencoe, IL: Free Press.

Wilkins, Mira and Harm G. Schroter (eds.) (1998) *The Free-standing Company in the World Economy*, Oxford: Oxford University Press.

Winseck, Dwayne R. and Robert M. Pike (2007) *Communication and Empire: Media, Markets, and Globalization, 1860–1930*, Durham, NC: Duke University Press.

Zimmerman, Andrew (2012) *Alabama in Africa: Booker T. Washington, the German Empire, and the Globalization of the New South*, Princeton, NJ: Princeton University Press.

4

INTERNATIONAL ENTREPRENEURSHIP AND BUSINESS HISTORY

Christina Lubinski and R. Daniel Wadhwani

Introduction

There is a rich and diverse empirical tradition in business history that has implicitly examined international entrepreneurship within narratives that recount the makers of global business. In these studies, business historians have often used the term entrepreneurship loosely. They refer variously to enterprising individuals and business owners, to particular organizational forms, to innovation, and to new market exploitation, and sometimes have avoided the use of the term entrepreneurship altogether. This eclecticism has had its advantages, allowing for many different topics and approaches to emerge from the historical narratives that have been produced. However, it has also come at the cost of a lack of clarity about what is meant by entrepreneurship and why it has historically mattered to international business and the global economy. The lack of conceptual clarity inhibits dialogue on entrepreneurship in international business amongst historians and limits our ability to draw out the implications of historical research for broader debates on international entrepreneurship and globalization.

In this chapter, we aim to review existing literature and build on recent attempts to bring greater conceptual coherence to research in entrepreneurial history (Cassis and Pepelasis Minoglou 2005; Wadhwani and Jones 2014; Wadhwani and Lubinski 2017); and we use these concepts to re-interpret selected business history research in ways that draw out its implications for international entrepreneurship more broadly (see also, Jones and Wadhwani 2007, 2008). We define entrepreneurship not as a particular kind of individual, organization, or technology but rather as *the creative processes that propel economic change* (Wadhwani and Lubinski 2017). The emphasis on processes, rather than individuals, organizational forms, or technologies, focuses attention on historians' inherent interest in and ability to examine *how* change occurred, in this case between entrepreneurial actions and the evolution of global business. It allows us to re-read a selection of important historical studies with the goal of better examining how international entrepreneurial opportunities were identified and pursued.

The emphasis on entrepreneurial processes also presents historians with an opportunity to address one of the often lamented shortcomings of international business studies, namely the critique that the field has given greater attention to the organizational form that international entrepreneurship takes (e.g., born-global firms) than to the *processes* by which these entrepreneurial strategies are developed and implemented (Zahra and George 2002). Teece (2014), for example, argues that international business researchers have focused too narrowly on questions of corporate governance, such as internalization, and transaction cost optimization, but have failed to study truly entrepreneurial processes, such as market creation, learning processes, and the development of dynamic capabilities over time. Jones and Khanna (2006) make an explicit plea for bringing history (back) into international business because it can help scholars to (i) understand the impact of historical variation on international entrepreneurship, (ii) critique spurious labeling of phenomena as new, (iii) more carefully conceptualize the issue of path dependency, and (iv) open the field up to topics, which can only be addressed in the very long term. By focusing on such entrepreneurial processes, historians have an opportunity to use their empirical research to contribute both to debates about the role of entrepreneurship in international business and to the bigger question of how entrepreneurial actions drove historical change in international business and the global economy.

We begin by briefly summarizing what we mean by entrepreneurial history. Reviewing some classic conceptualizations of entrepreneurship, we articulate that entrepreneurial history differs by focusing on entrepreneurial processes as primary objects of study. In particular, we consider three entrepreneurial processes crucial for examining entrepreneurship from a historical perspective. We then review existing historical literature on international business using the lens and key constructs of entrepreneurial history and show how it contributes to a deeper and more complex understanding of each of these three processes. We conclude by identifying research opportunities at the intersection of international entrepreneurship and business history.

Entrepreneurial history as the study of processes

In a previous article (Wadhwani and Lubinski 2017), we argue that historians' interest in entrepreneurship has long stemmed from the understanding that entrepreneurial processes can help us grasp historical change. For this reason, definitions of entrepreneurship that focus on start-up activity or individual entrepreneurs (Brockhaus 1982; Miner 1996), in isolation from the question of how historical change happens, offer little promise in entrepreneurial history. Similarly, studies that de-emphasize the social context in which entrepreneurship takes place, such as universally applicable life cycle models (Kazanjian 1988), are of little use to historians (for a critique of decontextualized entrepreneurship research, see the contributions in Welter and Gartner 2016).

Many of the "classic" definitions of entrepreneurship focus primarily on the risk bearing function of entrepreneurship. Richard Cantillon and John Stuart Mill, for example, argue that entrepreneurial profits are the reward for the entrepreneur's risk taking. Cantillon (2001 [first published in French: 1755]) in his main work, published posthumously in 1755, defines discrepancies between supply and demand as opportunities for selling at a higher price than buying. Mill (1848: 218) highlights the great significance of entrepreneurship and distinguishes the wages of management or entrepreneurship, premiums for risk bearing, and interest as three conceptually different forms of profit. Frank Knight (1921) takes up this stream of research but differentiates between calculable risks and uncalculable and hence unpredictable uncertainties. He argues that entrepreneurs earn profits as a return for putting up with uncertainty.

A slightly different perspective was offered by the German Historical School (Campagnolo 2010; Nau and Schefold 2002; Shionoya 2005b, 2005a). Gustav von Schmoller (1904 [1897]), for example, defines entrepreneurship as the motor of economic development and sees the entrepreneur as a creative organizer and the initiator of new projects. Werner Sombart (1927) thinks in terms of historical consequences and assigns the entrepreneur an important role in the development of modern capitalism. He gives the entrepreneur an almost heroic persona when he describes him as inventor, explorer, organizer, and businessman. He also resembles Max Weber (1978 [German original: 1922]) in highlighting the inner motivations of entrepreneurs, which Weber explains with reference to the Protestant Ethic.

Joseph Schumpeter's (1947, 1989 [1951]) conceptualization of the entrepreneur as a creative and innovative agent propelling historical change builds on these predecessors of the Historical School (Ebner 2000; Jones and Wadhwani 2008; Shionoya 2005a). He highlights the importance of entrepreneurial innovation but distinguishes it from the act of invention. "The inventor produces ideas, the entrepreneur 'get things done,' which may but need not embody anything that is scientifically new" (Schumpeter 1947: 152). Entrepreneurs, in Schumpeter's thought, also do not have to bear the risk of entrepreneurial endeavors. Furnishing the capital or other resources does not define entrepreneurship, and entrepreneurs frequently convince others to invest in their ventures. (This thought echoes in more recent conceptualizations of entrepreneurship, such as Stevenson and Jarillo (1990) and Shane and Venkataraman (2010).) Instead, what distinguishes the entrepreneur is that her or his innovation changes "social and economic situations for good, or, to put it differently, it creates situations from which there is no bridge between those situations that might have emerged in its absence" (Schumpeter 1947: 150). With agency and creativity, entrepreneurs contribute to large-scale historical change. This is particularly the case if we look beyond the individual entrepreneur and include entrepreneurial teams and streams of opportunities. Arthur Cole (1959: 50, 76), who founded the "Harvard Research Center in Entrepreneurial History" in 1948, argued that entrepreneurship "is a social phenomenon" and that to understand large economic changes one has to focus on "the interaction of entrepreneurial units." (For a discussion of the Center in Entrepreneurial History, see Cuff 2002; Fredona and Reinert 2017.)

An alternative way of thinking about entrepreneurship shifts the attention to the role of the entrepreneur in identifying temporary disequilibria in the market. Friedrich Hayek and Israel Kirzner argue that entrepreneurs process information swiftly and thus discover windows of opportunity for arbitrage. Kirzner (1997: 72) highlights the entrepreneur's "alertness" which he defines as "an attitude of receptiveness to available (but hitherto overlooked) opportunities." In being alert, entrepreneurs discover market disequilibria, buy where prices are too low and sell at a profit, contributing, or continuously "nudging," toward the (ultimately unattainable) state of perfect market equilibrium. Hayek (1948) emphasizes that the battle for information is inherently rivalrous with entrepreneurs competing for higher levels of knowledge and thus better opportunities.

Building on these earlier positions, the most recent and most influential theory of the entrepreneur in business history is by Mark Casson. Casson (2003: 20) defines the entrepreneur as "someone who specializes in taking judgmental decisions about the coordination of scarce resources." According to Casson, the entrepreneur excels in judgment and processing of the unevenly distributed information in markets. Entrepreneurs thus fulfill an important function for society, synthesizing and exploiting economic information advantages using exceptional judgment. They coordinate resources based on this judgment, thus improving the overall allocation of societal resources. Casson's conceptualization of the entrepreneur is influential in business history and has been applied to a variety of different time periods and organizational settings (Alvarez *et al.* 2014; Casson and Casson 2013) and including application to employees if they act in an entrepreneurial way (Lopes and Casson 2007).

While all of these approaches to entrepreneurship have value and channel attention to different aspects of the entrepreneurial function, our approach is most closely related to, and inspired by, the German Historical School and in particular Joseph Schumpeter. We point out that the plurality of entrepreneurial motives, entrepreneurial creativity, and the temporality of entrepreneurial action had been key assumptions used by these earlier historical scholars, but became sidelined in mainstream entrepreneurship research and business history alike. We thus proposed in an earlier article to reinvent entrepreneurial history (Wadhwani and Lubinski 2017) because it may provide us with a systematic framework for analyzing the relationship between entrepreneurial action and historical change in business history.

We therefore chose our definition with a focus on the relationship between entrepreneurship and change. We define new entrepreneurial history as *the study of the creative processes that propel economic change* (Wadhwani and Lubinski 2017: 3), and emphasize that these creative processes involved the mechanisms by which actors imagined and pursued future forms of value beyond what was offered in their present. The focus on creative processes as primary objects of study, we contend, differentiates entrepreneurial history from other approaches to business history, including Chandlerian perspectives that focus on organizational form (Chandler 1962, 1977, 1990), institutional perspectives that focus on laws, rules, and norms governing behavior (North 1990), and transaction–cost approaches that focus on exchange (Guinnane 2002; Lamoreaux and Raff 1995).

It also differs in emphasis from some of the classic works of entrepreneurship discussed above. For example, entrepreneurial history recasts Frank Knight's binary conceptualization of the future as involving either insurable risks or unknowable uncertainties. Instead it moves the focus of the attention to the question of *how* entrepreneurs shaped the seemingly unpredictable future through entrepreneurial agency, for example in the form of rhetorical or narrative processes or product design. By highlighting temporality, entrepreneurial history draws attention to the question of how actors' imagined futures relate to their interpreted pasts. The recent literature on "uses of history" in entrepreneurship and organization studies (Foster *et al.* 2017; Suddaby *et al.* 2010) and Hargadon and Douglas's study (2001) on Thomas Edison's design of the light bulb are examples of these creative processes. Finally, while business history has traditionally emphasized the constraining effects of institutions on entrepreneurship, as exemplified in the work of William Baumol (1990) and David Landes (1949), entrepreneurial history following Schumpeter (1947: 153) highlights also the "bursting" influence of entrepreneurial processes on institutions.

None of our suggestions is entirely new and many historians have already contributed to this research agenda. However, we hope that entrepreneurial history provides a framework for synthesizing these earlier attempts and drawing out their implications more clearly. The promise of entrepreneurial history, we believe, is the opportunity to re-interpret well-examined subjects by analyzing the creative and agentic processes that drive economic change.

In particular, we identify three processes as the primary objects of study in entrepreneurial history: (i) how entrepreneurial opportunities are imagined and valued; (ii) how resources are allocated and reconfigured to serve such entrepreneurial endeavors; and (iii) how these entrepreneurial actions are legitimized given institutional contexts. A focus on these three processes allows us to re-examine the existing historical literature on international entrepreneurship in ways that bring out the mechanism underlying the pursuit of international business opportunities. In the next three sections, we re-examine selected empirical research in international business history, drawing out how historical research can deepen our understanding of these three processes and their historical role in international business.

Envisioning and valuing opportunities

International Entrepreneurship has been defined as "the discovery, enactment, evaluation, and exploitation of opportunities – across national borders – to create future goods and services"

(Oviatt and McDougall 2005: 540). This widely accepted definition reflects the increasingly common view that entrepreneurship research centers on processes of opportunity identification and exploitation (Shane and Venkataraman 2000). In the context of international entrepreneurship, this raises the question of *where* to locate and pursue such opportunities. However, the reasons for this choice may be more complex and contingent than traditional international business theory assumes. International business scholars have traditionally considered location choices to be based on transaction cost optimization, profitability, or asset seeking (Buckley and Casson 1976; Dunning 1981). Location choices can be motivated by minimizing transaction costs, as traditional internalization theory would argue, but could just as well be propelled by entrepreneurs interested in seeking new markets, guarding property rights, leveraging resources into new environments, or supporting learning processes. Although research on location choices is abundant, several international business scholars have lamented the fact that the *process* of making location choices is still underexplored (Buckley *et al.* 2007; Mudambi 1998). The sense-making processes of internationally active entrepreneurs therefore move to the center of a historical analysis of international entrepreneurship, rather than being reduced to one (ill-defined) component in a laundry list of ownership advantages that lead firms to invest across borders.

Historical research has a lot to offer for an analysis of context-sensitive enactment of opportunities as a counter to the assumption that international opportunities are objective and categorical. This has been most clearly articulated by Popp and Holt (2013) in the analysis of the merchant house T. E. Thomson & Co. and their business in nineteenth-century Calcutta. These authors show that the opportunity of establishing an international merchant house could in hindsight be seen as an obvious response to the vacuum left by the end of the East India Company's monopoly and the collapse of other merchant houses on the subcontinent. However, the historical analysis of ego-documents left by founder John Shaw demonstrates the importance of entrepreneurs "imagining forward" and projecting new but uncertain futures rather than discovering a disequilibrium left by the failure of existing firms (Popp and Holt 2013: 20–1). Popp and Holt emphasize in particular the emotional quality of such decision-making and how the protagonist based his decision on highly limited knowledge about the future.

The potential for such an emphasis on entrepreneurial imagination in international business is further elaborated on by Jones and Pitelis (2015: 313) who offer several definitions of imagination including "the faculty or function of forming ideas or mental images, the ability of the mind to be creative and resourceful." Jones and Pitelis use imagination in their conceptual article for understanding the processes by which multinational companies create and co-create the context for their opportunities rather than accepting it as given. Drawing on historical illustrations, these authors critique the ahistorical assumptions of economics and international business studies that treat the host country environment and socio-economic system as beyond or outside the realm of entrepreneurial action. They point out that multinationals have historically not only sought to shape the business context but also, when feasible, the wider institutional, regulatory, and even cultural contexts. In particular, they stress a study by Clegg (2017) that highlights how the East India Company created a business opportunity in the opium market by shaping the military and political environments in which it operated. Historically, international entrepreneurial opportunities were not simply identified by synthesizing information but were created by powerful actors able to shape the very context for their existence.

Entrepreneurial imagination is characterized not just by market and economic possibilities but also by political ones. This fact provides historians with a particularly fertile opportunity to contextualize the pursuit of international entrepreneurial opportunities within and in-between the history of nation states. Boon (2014, and in this volume) for instance shows that the pursuit of the opportunity to create a transnational European oil pipeline, integrating the continent's energy markets, was shaped by political calculations as well as economic ones. The leaders of major multinational oil companies saw and imagined opportunities for an economically optimal pipeline that ran across much of Europe; however, these visions were tempered by the perceived uncertainty in the political milieu of postwar Europe. Boon's account further unveils the frictions between how different actors, in this case the headquarters and regional offices, perceived and calculated these opportunities based on their position vis-à-vis the political environment. The findings emphasize that the imagining of cross-border business opportunities was shaped not only by understandings of political as well as economic conditions, but also by one's position and perspective within a multinational organization.

While Boon highlights the constraining impact of political environments, Fear's (2012, 2013) analysis shows that political contexts can also facilitate the pursuit of international entrepreneurial opportunities. The German "pocket multinationals," which Fear studies, were internationally successful in a variety of different sectors, including security products (safes, locks), chainsaws, laser cutting, and specialty ink. In the postwar period, they excelled at a deliberate micro-niche strategy that allowed them a global presence, despite the fact that they were relatively small, family-owned, and resource-constrained firms operating at an inconducive macroeconomic moment. Fear emphasizes the German institutional environment, such as an active network of chambers of commerce and other collaborative institutions, which facilitated and opened international opportunities for firms that would otherwise not have access to them.

While the previous cases show how entrepreneurial imagination was interwoven with political developments, de la Cruz-Fernández's (2014) study of Singer's international market development strategy focused on exploiting cultural cues. Whereas sewing machines in the nineteenth century were often associated with factory labor that was considered a threat to the domestic sphere and women's welfare, Singer actively recast the product identity in moving into markets such as Spain, where it positioned its sewing machines as a complement to domestic craft and home work (de la Cruz-Fernández in this volume). Taking advantage of the growing interest in embroidery and highly localized embellishment, Singer created a new market opportunity for its product by placing it in a cultural framework that was very different from the one it had initially defined in its domestic market.

Re-reading historical research from the lens of entrepreneurial history offers historians a way not only to compare the processes at work in imagining and valuing international opportunities but also a timely way to engage the literature on international business more broadly. Historical narratives implicitly already grapple with the nuances of how firms and entrepreneurs imagined and pursued global opportunities in highly uncertain economic, political, and cultural contexts. Moreover, they also stress the interactions and co-creation at work between business and other spheres of social life. The emphasis on the entrepreneurial mechanisms of imagining and valuing opportunities offers a fresh way of revisiting international business history that unveils the creative processes at work in the development of the global economy.

Allocating and reconfiguring resources

Entrepreneurial processes are not limited to opportunity identification, but inherently involve resource allocation and reconfiguration toward future opportunities as well. This second set of processes is much less well explored in international business research, and historical research – seen through the conceptual lens of entrepreneurial history – can provide new interesting insights in how international entrepreneurs managed to allocate resources toward cross-border business opportunities. In particular, history is unique in offering a variety of different and creative ways of understanding how entrepreneurs assembled resources to pursue such opportunities that are by no means limited to multinationals' foreign direct investments.

To pursue international opportunities, entrepreneurs have historically had to find ways to prioritize and organize the allocation of resources to uncertain future-oriented endeavors over present-oriented ones. Historical research is able to show how such allocations were based on complex judgments about future conditions, beyond purely rational calculations. Simone Müller and Heidi Tworek (2016) have emphasized the role of imagined future uses of technology as an important trigger for the allocation of new resources. For example, in a study of the telegraph before World War I, Tworek (2016) shows that the German government first created a colonial wireless network based on imagined fears of British uses of the technology (on the context of global communications see also, John and Tworek in this volume). In short, imagined futures may play a role not only in the opportunities entrepreneurs identified but also in the perceptions of competition and timing that prompted the allocation of resources to a particular entrepreneurial endeavor; either by the entrepreneurs themselves or by investors, including governments, in supporting entrepreneurs and subsidizing their research and development.

Historical research has also shown the wide variety of organized ways in which resources have been assembled to pursue future opportunities. The historical literature on free-standing companies, for instance, has made a significant contribution to our understanding of resource orchestration in international entrepreneurship. During the nineteenth century, thousands of (primarily British and Dutch) companies were formed exclusively to operate in foreign markets, with no prior domestic business and only a small head office in the home market. Mira Wilkins (1988; Wilkins and Schröter 1998) and Geoffrey Jones (2000) have both shown how these nominally independent free-standing companies were part of a wider business network or sometimes part of business groups. Valeria Giacomin (2017, 2018) in her research on the rubber and palm oil cluster shows the importance of the community of traders and free-standing companies for spreading information, negotiating and changing institutional settings, and responding to political risks. Free-standing companies were often linked to each other based on equity ties, debt and contracting relationships, and cross-directorates. Through the network, entrepreneurs had access to resources, monitoring, and advice as new opportunities were exploited.

Historians have also explored how international social networks have had similar resource orchestration effects (Baghdiantz McCabe *et al.* 2005; David and Westerhuis in this volume). Immigrant and diaspora entrepreneurs, for instance, often worked through ethnic networks to share information, allocate people, and pool capital to pursue entrepreneurial opportunities across borders. Andrew Godley (2001) shows in his comparative study of Eastern European Jews who emigrated to London and New York in the late nineteenth century that immigrants to New York were much more likely to move into entrepreneurship than those to London. He suggests that entrepreneurs in Britain were confronted with conservative craft values, which erected hurdles to introducing new technologies and working practices not found in New York.

Kilby (1971) is another author who connects resource assembly with institutional context. Based on his empirical work on entrepreneurship in West Africa, he found that entrepreneurial behavior in Africa is very different from its counterpart in more developed economies because the lack of organized markets for talent and political conditions required active entrepreneurial management – an argument that reverberates in the idea of "institutional voids" in emerging markets today (see Khanna *et al.* 2010). Kilby not only uses variations in the institutional context to critique the Western bias of the prevalent understanding of the entrepreneurial process but also argues that entrepreneurship in West Africa requires active context management to make resource assembly possible.

Historical research furthermore revealed how firms have cultivated new resources and capabilities in order to identify and pursue international opportunities. Teresa da Silva Lopes and Vitor C. Simões (2017) demonstrate that the continuous interactions between foreign investors and local players in Portugal over 300 years triggered the development of new firm-level capabilities, knowledge spillovers, and ultimately host-country economic development. The article provides one of the few examples of focusing very explicitly on the impact of entrepreneurial processes on historical change, using the case of Portugal. The importance of knowledge also is clear in Espen Storli's (2017) work on the metal trading firm founded by Ludwig Jesselson. The company developed a network of agents throughout the world whose information on local economic and political conditions were superior to even that of the CIA. This network of agents was vital to the information advantages that were crucial to competitive advantage in the metals trading industry. Likewise, research on the development of multinational oil companies in the early twentieth century shows how their ability to coordinate between new low-cost sources of crude and globally dispersed markets for petroleum played a major role in organizing the worldwide oil market. Companies like Standard Oil, Royal Dutch Shell, and British Petroleum created and reconfigured their capabilities in production, refining, and distribution of petroleum in order to stabilize the global market for gasoline (Yergin 2008).

Entrepreneurial processes of resource reconfiguration, however, extend even beyond the development of new firm-level routines and capabilities. They often also entail the creation of new relationships and combinations between firms, the emergence of whole new sets of firms, and changes in the relationships among firms, intermediaries, public authorities, and other actors. Indeed, reconfigurations in these inter-organizational relationships are often associated with broader historical changes in industries, sectors, and economies. Entrepreneurial history hence needs to tackle in more detail such topics as category, market, and industry emergence (and decline) as processes of resource reconfiguration between firms; and to that end can build on historians' previous work in this area (Forbes and Kirsch 2011; Khaire and Wadhwani 2010; Kirsch *et al.* 2014). The focus of such research would not be on studying form or structures – for example business groups (Colpan and Hikino 2010; Fruin 2007), associations (Lanzalaco 2007), or cartels (Fellman and Shanahan 2016) – but on the *processes* by which actors of various sorts recreate relationships, markets, and business ecosystems in order to collectively pursue a new form of value.

Legitimizing novelty

The third set of processes we focus on pertain to legitimacy. Legitimacy poses a problem in the entrepreneurial process because the new forms of value and new combinations of resources entrepreneurs propose often fail to conform to widely shared expectations. This is a particular challenge for entrepreneurs active in foreign markets because they easily find themselves confronted with conflicting expectations by home and host country stakeholders as well as global civil society.

Legitimacy can be defined as the "perception or assumption that the actions of an entity are desirable, proper, or appropriate within some socially constructed system of norms, values, beliefs and definitions" (Suchman 1995: 574). Legitimation processes thus pertain to the question of how entrepreneurial actors confront existing institutions. Institutions create pressures on actors to conform, and to some extent entrepreneurs who manage to conform confront more modest challenges when it comes to establishing their legitimacy. However, new entrepreneurial history does not focus on legitimate or illegitimate entrepreneurs but rather foregrounds the *process of legitimation*.

Within mainstream business and organizational research, the sources of legitimacy tend to be taken as static and given. This is particularly the case when researchers discuss cognitive legitimacy, which occurs when there is a strong congruence between the normative expectations of the firm and its environment (Hannan and Freeman 1986; for an overview of this literature see the review article by Suddaby *et al.* 2017). Often the state, law, and culture are seen as monolithic entities that confer legitimacy on entrepreneurs and organizations. But work by business historians has emphasized not only divisions and differences within these fields but also the contingent and contested processes by which entrepreneurs establish legitimacy for their endeavors (Bucheli and Kim 2014). Entrepreneurial legitimation is not a one way influence but a co-evolutionary process that changes states, societies, and markets (Favero 2017; Jones and Pitelis 2015). Empirical work by international business historians has already contributed extensively to how international entrepreneurship both depends on and shapes legitimizing mechanisms within the international arena.

One such set of contributions pertains to how entrepreneurship responds to the shock of rapid political and societal change (for an overview of different risk management strategies by foreign investors, see Casson and Lopes 2013). Bucheli and Salvaj (2013), for instance, draw on the case of the International Telephone and Telegraph Company (ITT) in Chile to examine the effects of a rapid regime change on the political legitimation strategies of a multinational. They point to the concept of "obsolescing political legitimacy" as a risk that international entrepreneurs face under swiftly changing conditions. In the case of ITT, successful efforts to incorporate domestic elites, a strategy well established to gain legitimacy in stable environments, backfired when political change undermined their authority and quickly changed the legitimizing context. Similarly, Andrew Smith (2016) considers the risks of war and nationalism to international business (see also the chapter by Kurosawa, Forbes and Wubs in this volume). Smith uses the historical case of the Hongkong and Shanghai Banking Corporation (HSBC) in World War I and finds that HSBC needed to distance itself from certain former markets and partnerships, for example with Germany, in response to German–British rivalry and heightened nationalism in the lead up to World War I. He illustrates the shifting focus of legitimizing efforts from the host country back to the home country in response to geopolitical concerns.

Business historians in that regard have been particularly attentive to the fact that the legitimacy of international entrepreneurial endeavors are not just dependent on host country political and social contexts but rather take place within the context of geopolitical interactions involving multiple nation states and organizations. Lubinski (2014) and Lubinski and Wadhwani (2019), for instance, explore the relative political advantages of German multinationals in late colonial India, where they found ways to take advantage of their national identity as "outsiders" to the conflicts of British imperialism. Focusing on entrepreneurs in the dyes industry (Lubinski 2015), she looks at the symbolic, rhetorical, and economic strategies these multinationals used to cultivate stronger relationships with Indian nationalists and in opposition to British rivals in the period leading up to Indian independence. The outsiderness opportunity allowed German firms leverage in entering emerging markets, not just in India but in several markets with strong nationalistic movements. Focusing on the flipside, Lopes and Simões (2017) find that British expatriate entrepreneurs, to avoid legitimacy challenges, downplayed their contribution to Brazil's economic development and rather disguised their activities as local. They had no established business in their home country but pursued an opportunity abroad relying on their international network for financing, trading, and other activities.

Grappling with the turbulences of international political relations over the nineteenth and twentieth centuries, historians have turned the traditional international business assumption that legitimizing environments tend to be stable on its head. They asked instead what successful multinationals have done over the long run to deal with the inherent instability of international political relations. Decker (2007, 2008), for instance, has considered how British multinationals in Nigeria and Ghana managed to survive through and beyond the period of decolonization, when their legitimacy was fundamentally questioned and African countries increasingly turned to an agenda of Africanization. She finds that British multinationals successfully engaged in marketing and advertising efforts to reinvent their image and recast their contribution to the development of the respective country. Decker emphasizes these strategic adjustments to corporate identity as crucial to long-term legitimation. In related work, Gao *et al.* (2017) consider the survival of multinationals over the very long run in the particularly volatile context of emerging markets. They find that reputation was crucial for multinationals' long-term survival in such situations and break down reputation as involving three components: prominence, perceived quality, and resilience.

The methodological strength of entrepreneurial history is that it incorporates historical and social context for action, while not reducing choice and agency to a function of contextual constraint. Thus, it addresses the complex interplay between entrepreneurship on the one hand and institutional and contextual change on the other hand. Legitimacy as a subjective assessment requires an inherently constitutive historical approach. Legitimation processes may seem more streamlined in hindsight than they are for the historical actors who experienced the uncertainty of an unknown future. Historical analysis may also enrich our understanding of legitimation processes through its focus on institutionally embedded (but not predetermined) perception, judgment, and imagination.

Conclusion: international entrepreneurship seen historically

In this chapter, we have used entrepreneurial history as a conceptual lens to re-read and re-interpret empirical research in international business history, highlighting the creative and imaginative role of entrepreneurial agency in the "making of global business." Such a lens foregrounds the creative processes at work in the identification and pursuit of cross-border business opportunities, in contrast to the organizational, institutional, and transactional lenses that have often been the focus of analysis and synthesis in business history scholarship. We have shown that historical research has much to offer in deepening our understanding of international entrepreneurship and its role in the global economy, but that unlocking this potential requires engaging key constructs from entrepreneurship theory.

Specifically, we found that historical research, when it engages with entrepreneurship theory, can help us more deeply analyze: (1) how exactly entrepreneurs imagined and enacted cross-border business opportunities, how this process interacted with broader political and social contexts, and how entrepreneurial actors' positioning may have shaped the futures they imagined; (2) how entrepreneurs allocated resources toward future value, including the role of imagined future uses and competition in this process and the role of social networks, novel organizational forms, and new capabilities as mechanisms through which resources were configured in new ways; and (3) how legitimation was pursued in a complex and changing multipolar world rather than the static, bi-polar world often assumed in international business theory.

This may be a particularly opportune time for historians to adopt such an entrepreneurial history lens. The growth of analytical interest in context and in processes within international entrepreneurship research, and in international business research more broadly, suggests that historians could play a pivotal role in these fields in the years to come. Such an opportunity, moreover, fits well with historians' inherent interest in incorporating contexts and analyzing processes in studies of business history. We therefore believe there are opportunities for historians to contribute to these theoretical debates as historians, with historical sources and methods as an important comparative advantage.

Finally, engaging with entrepreneurial history offers historians the opportunity to address one of the classical questions of historiography: how does historical change take place? Entrepreneurial history provides a specific approach to the question well suited to international business history in particular, in that it embraces the study of the sense-making processes by which actors identified and articulated plausible and attractive futures and pursued the resources and capabilities to make those futures present. Entrepreneurial history hence holds the promise of grappling with the processes driving change in global capitalism.

References

Alvarez, Sharon, Godley, Andrew, and Wright, Mike (2014), "Mark Casson: The Entrepreneur at 30: Continued Relevance?" *Strategic Entrepreneurship Journal*, 8 (2), 185–94.

Baghdiantz McCabe, Ina, Harlaftis, Gelina, and Pepelasē Minoglou, Iōanna (2005), *Diaspora Entrepreneurial Networks: Four Centuries of History* (Oxford; New York: Berg).

Baumol, William J. (1990), "Entrepreneurship: Productive, Unproductive, and Destructive," *Journal of Political Economy*, 98 (5), 893–921.

Boon, Marten (2014), *The Rotterdam Oil Port, Royal Dutch Shell and the German Hinterland, 1945–1975* (Rotterdam: Erasmus University Rotterdam).

Brockhaus, Robert H. (1982), "The Psychology of the Entrepreneur," in Donald L. Sexton and Karl H. Vesper (eds.), *Encyclopedia of Entrepreneurship* (Englewood Cliffs, NJ: Prentice-Hall), 39–57.

Bucheli, Marcelo and Salvaj, Erica (2013), "Reputation and Political Legitimacy ITT in Chile, 1927–1972," *Business History Review*, 87 (4), 729–56.

Bucheli, Marcelo and Kim, Jin Uk (2014), "The State as a Historical Construct in Organization Studies," in Marcelo Bucheli and R. Daniel Wadhwani (eds.), *Organizations in Time: History, Theory and Methods* (Oxford: Oxford University Press), 241–62.

Buckley, Peter J. and Casson, Mark (1976), *The Future of the Multinational Enterprise* (London: Macmillan).

Buckley, Peter J., Devinney, Timothy M., and Louviere, Jordan J. (2007), "Do Managers Behave the Way Theory Suggests? A Choice-Theoretic Examination of Foreign Direct Investment Location Decision-Making," *Journal of International Business Studies*, 38 (7), 1069–94.

Campagnolo, Gilles (2010), *Criticisms of Classical Political Economy: Menger, Austrian Economics and the German Historical School* (London; New York: Routledge).

Cantillon, Richard (2001 [first published in French: 1755]), *Essays on the Nature of Commerce in General* (Classics in economics series) (New Brunswick, NJ: Transaction Publishers).

Cassis, Youssef and Pepelasis Minoglou, Ioanna (eds.) (2005), *Entrepreneurship in Theory and History* (Basingstoke, UK: Palgrave Macmillan) XIII, 211 S.

Casson, Mark (2003), *The Entrepreneur: An Economic Theory* (2nd edn.; Cheltenham, UK; Northampton, MA: Edward Elgar) xii, 271 p.

Casson, Mark and Casson, Catherine (2013), *History of Entrepreneurship: Innovation and Risk-Taking, 1200–2000* (Cheltenham, UK: Edward Elgar Publishing).

Casson, Mark and Lopes, Teresa da Silva (2013), "Foreign Direct Investment in High-Risk Environments: An Historical Perspective," *Business History*, 55 (3), 375–404.

Chandler, Alfred D. (1962), *Strategy and Structure: Chapters in the History of the Industrial Enterprise* (Cambridge, MA: MIT Press).

Chandler, Alfred D. (1977), *The Visible Hand: The Managerial Revolution in American Business* (Cambridge, MA: Belknap Press of Harvard University Press) xvi, 608 p.

Chandler, Alfred D. (1990), *Scale and Scope: The Dynamics of Industrial Capitalism* (Cambridge, MA: Belknap Press of Harvard University Press) xviii, 760 p.

Clegg, Stewart R. (2017), "The East India Company: The First Modern Multinational?" in Christoph Dörrenbächer and Mike Geppert (eds.), *Multinational Corporations and Organization Theory: Post Millennium Perspectives* (Bingley, UK: Emerald), 43–67.

Cole, Arthur (1959), *Business Enterprise in its Social Setting* (Cambridge, MA: Harvard University Press).

Colpan, Asli M. and Hikino, Takashi (2010), "Foundations of Business Groups: Towards an Integrated Framework," in Asli M. Colpan, Takashi Hikino, and James R. Lincoln (eds.), *The Oxford Handbook of Business Groups* (Oxford; New York: Oxford University Press), 15–66.

Cuff, Robert D. (2002), "Notes for a Panel on Entrepreneurship in Business History," *Business History Review*, 76 (1), 123–32.

De La Cruz-Fernández, Paula (2014), "Marketing the Hearth: Ornamental Embroidery and the Building of the Multinational Singer Sewing Machine Company," *Enterprise & Society*, 15 (3), 442–71.

Decker, Stephanie (2007), "Corporate Legitimacy and Advertising: British Multinationals and the Rhetoric of Development from the 1950s to the 1970s," *Business History Review*, 81 (1), 59–86.

Decker, Stephanie (2008), "Building up Goodwill: British Business, Development and Economic Nationalism in Ghana and Nigeria, 1945–1977," *Enterprise & Society*, 9 (4), 602–13.

Dunning, John H. (1981), *International Production and the Multinational Enterprise* (London, Boston, MA: Allen & Unwin).

Ebner, Alexander (2000), "Schumpeter and the 'Schmollerprogramm': Integrating Theory and History in the Analysis of Economic Development," *Journal of Evolutionary Economics*, 10 (3), 355–72.

Favero, Giovanni (2017), "A Reciprocal Legitimation: Corrado Gini and Statistics in Fascist Italy," *Management and Organizational History*, 12 (3), 261–84.

Fear, Jeffrey (2012), "Straight Outta Oberberg: Transforming Mid-Sized Family Firms into Global Champions 1970–2010," *Jahrbuch für Wirtschaftsgeschichte/Economic History Yearbook*, 53 (1), 125–69.

Fear, Jeffrey (2013), "Globalization from a 17mm-Diameter Cylinder Perspective: Mittelstand Multinationals," in Christina Lubinski, Jeffrey R. Fear, and Paloma Fernández Pérez (eds.), *Family Multinationals: Entrepreneurship, Governance, and Pathways to Internationalization* (New York: Routledge), 73–95.

Fellman, Susanna and Shanahan, Martin (2016), *Regulating Competition: Cartel Registers in the Twentieth-century World* (New York; Abingdon: Routledge).

Forbes, Daniel and Kirsch, David (2011), "The Study of Emerging Industries: Recognizing and Responding to Some Central Problems," *Journal of Business Venturing*, 26, 589–602.

Foster, William M., Diego, M. Coraiola, Suddaby, Roy, Kroezen, Jochem, and Chandler, David (2017), "The Strategic Use of Historical Narratives: A Theoretical Framework," *Business History*, 59 (8), 1176–200.

Fredona, Robert and Reinert, Sophus A. (2017), "The Harvard Research Center in Entrepreneurial History and the Daimonic Entrepreneur," *History of Political Economy*, 49 (2), 267–314.

Fruin, W. Mark (2007), "Business Groups and Interfirm Networks," in Geoffrey G. Jones and Jonathan Zeitlin (eds.), *The Oxford Handbook of Business History* (Oxford: Oxford University Press), 244–67.

Gao, Cheng, Zuzul, Tiona, Jones, Geoffrey, and Khanna, Tarun (2017), "Overcoming Institutional Voids: A Reputation-Based View of Long-Run Survival," *Strategic Management Journal*, 38 (11), 2147–67.

Giacomin, Valeria (2017), "Negotiating Cluster Boundaries: Governance Shifts in the Palm Oil and Rubber Cluster in Malay(si)a (1945–1970 ca.)," *Management and Organizational History*, 12 (1), 76–98.

Giacomin, Valeria (2018), "The Emergence of an Export Cluster: Traders and Palm Oil in Early Twentieth Century Southeast Asia," *Enterprise & Society* 19 (2), 272–308.

Godley, Andrew (2001), *Jewish Immigrant Entrepreneurship in New York and London 1880–1914: Enterprise and Culture* (Basingstoke, UK; New York: Palgrave).

Guinnane, Timothy W. (2002), "Delegated Monitors, Large and Small: Germany's Banking System, 1800–1914," *Journal of Economic Literature*, 40 (1), 73–124.

Hannan, Michael T. and Freeman, John (1986), "Where Do Organizational Forms Come From?" *Sociological Forum*, 1 (1), 50–72.

Hargadon, Andrew B. and Douglas, Yellowlees (2001), "When Innovations Meet Institutions: Edison and the Design of the Electric Light," *Administrative Science Quarterly*, 46 (3), 476–501.

Hayek, Friedrich A. von (1948), *Individualism and Economic Order* (Chicago, IL: University of Chicago Press).

Jones, Geoffrey (2000), *Merchants to Multinationals: British Trading Companies in the Nineteenth and Twentieth Centuries* (Oxford: Oxford University Press).

Jones, Geoffrey and Khanna, Tarun (2006), "Bringing History (Back) Into International Business," *Journal of International Business Studies*, 37, 453–68.

Jones, Geoffrey and Pitelis, Christos (2015), "Entrepreneurial Imagination and a Demand and Supply-Side Perspective on MNE and Cross-Border Organisation," *Journal of International Management*, 21 (4), 309–21.

Jones, Geoffrey and Wadhwani, R. Daniel (2007), *Entrepreneurship and Global Capitalism*, 2 vols. (Cheltenham, UK: Edward Elgar Publishing).

Jones, Geoffrey and Wadhwani, R. Daniel (2008), "Entrepreneurship," in Geoffrey Jones and Jonathan Zeitlin (eds.), *The Oxford Handbook of Business History* (New York: Oxford University Press), 501–28.

Kazanjian, Robert K. (1988), "Relation of Dominant Problems to Stages of Growth in Technology-Based New Ventures," *Academy of Management Journal*, 31 (2), 257–79.

Khaire, Mukti and Wadhwani, R. Daniel (2010), "Changing Landscapes: The Construction of Meaning and Value in a New Market Category – Modern Indian Art," *Academy of Management Journal*, 53 (6), 1281–304.

Khanna, Tarun, Palepu, Krishna G., and Bullock, Richard J. (2010), *Winning in Emerging Markets: A Road Map for Strategy and Execution* (Boston, MA: Harvard Business Press) xii, 246 p.

Kilby, Peter (ed.) (1971), *Entrepreneurship and Economic Development* (New York: Free Press).

Kirsch, David, Moeen, Mahka, and Wadhwani, R. Daniel (2014), "Historicism and Industry Emergence: Industry Knowledge from Pre-emergence to Stylized Fact," in Marcelo Bucheli and R. Daniel Wadhwani (eds.), *Organizations in Time: History, Theory and Methods* (Oxford: Oxford University Press), 217–40.

Kirzner, Israel M. (1997), "Entrepreneurial Discovery and the Competitive Market Process: An Austrian Approach," *Journal of Economic Literature*, 60–85.

Knight, Frank H. (1921), *Risk, Uncertainty and Profit* (Boston, MA; New York: Hart, Schaffner & Marx).

Lamoreaux, Naomi R. and Raff, Daniel M. G. (eds.) (1995), *Coordination and Information: Historical Perspectives on the Organization of Enterprise* (Chicago, IL: University of Chicago Press).

Landes, David S. (1949), "French Entrepreneurship and Industrial Growth in the Nineteenth Century," *Journal of Economic History*, 9 (1), 45–61.

Lanzalaco, Luca (2007), "Business Interest Associations," in Geoffrey G. Jones and Jonathan Zeitlin (eds.), *The Oxford Handbook of Business History* (Oxford: Oxford University Press), 293–315.

Lopes, Teresa da Silva and Casson, Mark (2007), "Entrepreneurship and the Development of Global Brands," *Business History Review*, 81 (4), 651–80.

Lopes, Teresa da Silva and Simões, Vitor Corado (2017), "Foreign Investment in Portugal and Knowledge Spillovers: From the Methuen Treaty to the 21st Century," *Business History*, www.tandfonline.com/action/showCitFormats?doi=10.1080%2F00076791.2017.1386177.

Lubinski, Christina (2014), "Liability of Foreignness in Historical Context: German Business in Preindependence India (1880–1940)," *Enterprise & Society*, 15 (4), 722–58.

Lubinski, Christina (2015), "Global Trade and Indian Politics: The German Dye Business in India before 1947," *Business History Review*, 89 (3), 503–30.

Lubinski, Christina and Wadhwani, R. Daniel (2019), "Geopolitical Jockeying: Economic Nationalism and Multinational Strategy in Historical Perspective," *Strategic Management Journal*, accepted author manuscript. doi:10.1002/smj.3022.

Mill, John Stuart (1848), *Principles of Political Economy with Some of their Applications to Social Philosophy*, 2 vols. (Boston, MA: C.C. Little & J. Brown).

Miner, John B. (1996), *The 4 Routes to Entrepreneurial Success* (San Francisco, CA: Berrett-Koehler Publishers).

Mudambi, Ram (1998), "The Role of Duration in Multinational Investment Strategies," *Journal of International Business Studies*, 29 (2), 239–61.

Müller, Simone M. and Tworek, Heidi J. S. (2016), "Imagined Use as a Category of Analysis: New Approaches to the History of Technology," *History and Technology*, 32 (2), 105–19.

Nau, Heino Heinrich and Schefold, Bertram (2002), *The Historicity of Economics: Continuities and Discontinuities of Historical Thought in 19th and 20th Century Economics* (Berlin; New York: Springer).

North, Douglass C. (1990), *Institutions, Institutional Change, and Economic Performance* (Cambridge; New York: Cambridge University Press) viii, 152 p.

Oviatt, Benjamin M. and McDougall, Patricia P. (2005), "Defining International Entrepreneurship and Modeling the Speed of Internationalization," *Entrepreneurship Theory and Practice*, 29 (5), 537–54.

Popp, Andrew and Holt, Robin (2013), "The Presence of Entrepreneurial Opportunity," *Business History*, 55 (1), 9–28.

Schmoller, Gustav von (1904 [1897]), *Über einige Grundfragen der Sozialpolitik und der Volkswirtschaftslehre* (2nd edn.; Leipzig: Duncker & Humblot).

Schumpeter, Joseph A. (1947), "The Creative Response in Economic History," *Journal of Economic History*, 7 (2), 149–59.

Schumpeter, Joseph A. (1989 [1951]), "Economic Theory and Entrepreneurial History [Reprinted from Change and the Entrepreneur, Cambridge, MA 1949, 63–84]," in Richard V. Clemence (ed.), *Essays on Entrepreneurs, Innovations, Business Cycles and the Evolution of Capitalism* (New Brunswick, NJ; Oxford: Transaction Publishers), 253–71.

Shane, Scott and Venkataraman, Sankaran (2000), "The Promise of Entrepreneurship as a Field of Research," *Academy of Management Review*, 25 (1), 217–26.

Shionoya, Yūichi (2005a), *The Soul of the German Historical School: Methodological Essays on Schmoller, Weber, and Schumpeter* (New York: Springer) xv, 207 p.

Shionoya, Yūichi (2005b), "A Methodological Appraisal of Schmoller's Research Program," in Yūichi Shionoya (ed.), *The Soul of the German Historical School: Methodological Essays on Schmoller, Weber, and Schumpeter* (New York: Springer), 13–30.

Smith, Andrew David Allan (2016), "A LBV Perspective on Political Risk Management in a Multinational Bank during the First World War", *Multinational Business Review*, 24 (1).

Sombart, Werner (1927), *Die deutsche Volkswirtschaft im neunzehnten Jahrhundert und im Anfang des 20. Jahrhunderts: Eine Einführung in die Nationalökonomie* (7th edn.; Berlin: Bondi).

Stevenson, Howard H. and Jarillo, J. Carlos (1990), "A Paradigm of Entrepreneurship: Entrepreneurial Management," *Strategic Management Journal*, 11 (4), 17–27.

Storli, Espen (2017), "Ludwig Jesselson," in Daniel R. Wadhwani (ed.), *Immigrant Entrepreneurship: German-American Business Biographies, 1720 to the Present*, vol. 5 (German Historical Institute. Last modified March 24, 2014. www.immigrantentrepreneurship.org/entry.php?rec=167Aug).

Suchman, Mark C. (1995), "Managing Legitimacy: Strategic and Institutional Approaches," *Academy of Management Review*, 20 (3), 571–610.

Suddaby, Roy, Bitektine, Alex, and Haack, Patrick (2017), "Legitimacy," *Academy of Management Annals*, 11 (1), 451–78.

Suddaby, Roy, Foster, William M., and Quinn Trank, Chris (2010), "Rhetorical History as a Source of Competitive Advantage," *Advances in Strategic Management*, 27, 147–73.

Teece, David J (2014), "A Dynamic Capabilities-based Entrepreneurial Theory of the Multinational Enterprise," *Journal of International Business Studies*, 45 (1), 8–37.

Tworek, Heidi J. S. (2016), "How Not to Build a World Wireless Network: German–British Rivalry and Visions of Global Communications in the Early Twentieth Century", *History and Technology*, 32 (2), 178–200.

Wadhwani, R. Daniel and Jones, Geoffrey (2014), "Schumpeter's Plea: Historical Reasoning in Entrepreneurship Theory and Research", in Marcelo Bucheli and R. Daniel Wadhwani (eds.), *Organizations in Time: History, Theory and Methods* (Oxford: Oxford University Press), 192–216.

Wadhwani, R. Daniel and Lubinski, Christina (2017), "Reinventing Entrepreneurial History", *Business History Review*, 91 (4), 767–99.

Weber, Max (1978 [German original: 1922]), *Economy and Society: An Outline of Interpretive Sociology.* Translated by Ephraim Fischoff *et al.* (Berkeley, CA: University of California Press).

Welter, Friederike and Gartner, William B. (eds.) (2016), *A Research Agenda for Entrepreneurship and Context* (Cheltenham, UK: Edward Elgar Publishing).

Wilkins, Mira (1988), "The Free-Standing Company, 1870–1914: An Important Type of British Foreign Direct Investment," *Economic History Review*, 41 (2), 259–82.

Wilkins, Mira and Schröter, Harm G. (eds.) (1998), *The Free-Standing Company in the World Economy, 1830–1996* (Oxford: Oxford University Press).

Yergin, Daniel (2008), *The Prize: The Epic Quest for Oil, Money & Power* (New York: Free Press).

Zahra, Shaker A. and George, Gerard (2002), "Absorptive Capacity: A Review, Reconceptualization, and Extension," *Academy of Management Review*, 27 (2), 185–203.

5

GENDER, RACE, AND ENTREPRENEURSHIP

Mary A. Yeager

Business has always been associated with drama, some of it playing out in the melodramas of individual lives, much more of it associated with business institutions and the booms and busts of economies. No entry that explores the global connections between gender, race, and entrepreneurship can avoid the dramatic. Given business history's undeniable masculinism and a business world dominated by white male decision-makers and entrepreneurs, efforts to disrupt the taken-for-granted absence of others may be considered hopelessly naïve at best. At worst, such efforts can be perceived as a misguided strategy to disguise businesses' role in perpetuating some of the world's most intractable development problems. This chapter combines these three topics and examines their impact in creating economic shifts of wealth and power, which sometimes complicated and sometimes exacerbated inequality in the areas of entrepreneurship, gender, and race.

This entry mounts a global drama that unfolds in two "Acts," each scripted to highlight the connections between gender, race, and entrepreneurship as they play out in different historical contexts over time, and as they contribute to or hinder the making of global business (Laird 2008; Bayly 2018). The Acts will be preceded by a curtain raiser, laying out the three concepts as they have come to be embedded in their separate historiographies and understood by contemporary scholars inside and outside the discipline of business history. Act I, "Making the Invisible Visible," focuses on the second half of the twentieth century, when transformative social and political movements challenged glib assumptions about gender, sexuality, and race from centuries before. Act II, "Dangerous Crossings," ventures out into the world. It examines what happens when colonialism and imperialism are redefined as globalization. Let the drama begin.

Curtain raiser: three historically fluid concepts

Gender, race, and entrepreneurship are concepts constructed by societies to convey powerful realities about how people engage and interact with each other. As such, they are also powerful influences on the continuous process of creating and shaping global business. Each of these concepts has a long and contested historiography and history developed and used by scholars situated in separate academic silos. As developed within and across humanities and social science disciplines, gender and race occupy competing and overlapping positions as fluid and intertwined "meta-categories" of "social difference," always subject to change and fundamental to the structuring of all societies (Peterson and Runyan 2018; West and Zimmerman 2009). Entrepreneurship, by contrast, foregrounds the mutual influences of individual agency and societal change (Schumpeter 1934).

"Gender" is neither synonymous with woman nor a personal trait. It is rather an activity ("doing gender") of ongoing assessments, which constitutes belonging to a sex as based on the socially accepted dichotomy of "women" and "men." It is a process of doing, becoming, learning, and un-learning associated with living in the world. As a consequence, gender is always situational, rather than essentialist, and integral to self-making and social identities (Yeager 1999; Hofstede 1998; West and Zimmerman 2009; Kelan and Jones 2010; Søraa 2017).

Societies have created the gender puzzle about sexual differences that feminist theorists, gender scholars, and street fighters for women's equality have spent centuries trying to resolve. To separate the biological from the social was a radical political move, undertaken in the 1970s to empower women by exposing how ideas about sexual differences had historically and systematically disadvantaged women more than men (Rubin 1975; Taylor 2002). Since at least the European Enlightenment, when the idea of equality as a masculine universal became inextricably linked to female inequality, women have used both sexual differences and similarities to argue for equality with men. The assumption of a masculine universal made attention to sex and gender mostly a woman's affair. Universalizing the masculine enabled some men to take for granted what women have been compelled to explain and justify (Scott 1996; Stuurman 2017).

Inequality based on race is likewise associated with the powerful universalizing of a norm, in this case, whiteness. The meaning of the noun "race" is unstable, but by the nineteenth century the noun "racism" had acquired specific and negative connotations. The *Oxford English Dictionary* (Soanes and Stevenson 1975) records the first appearance of the word "whiteness" in the sixteenth century, when it meant "radiance" or "brilliance." Like the term "gender," "race" was a word constructed and used by societies to transform a physiological characteristic into a negotiable instrument of power (Bethencourt 2013; Jerkins 2018). The power and significance of ideas about race and gender stem from the conclusions that societies draw about biological/physiological differences and the way those differences are used to discriminate, divide, and subordinate (Baca Zinn and Thornton Dill 1996). All societies use sex/gender and race to structure and order human interactions.

"Entrepreneurship," a word borrowed from the French that first appeared in fifteenth-century Europe, was rarely used until the seventeenth and eighteenth centuries, when European observers of moral and political economy began to pay attention to the "Wealth of Nations" (Smith 1776; Murray 2017). The word threaded ideas about agency with actions and consequences. As it evolved across the centuries, it generated a stream of linguistic off-shoots – enterprise, enterprisers, entrepreneur, entrepreneurial – that have been used with greatest effect by scholars of economics and management studies, and in anthropology and sociology more than in history, where the study of "practice" takes second place to processes of change. It sweeps in all varieties of economic actors whose identities are presumed to be associated with a vector of actions that have historically encompassed risk-takers of all sorts, from capitalists to orchestra conductor (Foss and Klein 2012: 226). The entrepreneur, in short, has been incorporated into broader "social communities" of business enterprise (Kogut and Zander 2003: 516).

Not all societies have paid attention to entrepreneurship. Nor have they understood or assessed its significance in the same way (Hoselitz 1952; Leff 1979; Jones and Luch 2015; Bayly 2018). Entrepreneurship has been both productive and unproductive in terms of its effects on economic growth and development (Baumol 1990). At no point, however, has entrepreneurship been more popular or more integral to global and national policymaking efforts than in the decades before and immediately after the global financial crisis of 2008. Between the 1980s and 1990s, national efforts to deregulate domestic markets coincided with a revolution in global communications technologies that widened opportunities for some of the world's poorest populations. A large percentage of those people were women, many of whom assumed primary caretaking responsibilities for children and families, and 80 percent of whom still worked in agriculture. Governmental and nongovernmental institutions saw entrepreneurship as a new low-cost growth industry and poverty-reduction strategy. The World Bank and the International Monetary Fund (IMF) funded new data-gathering and educational efforts specially designed with women in mind. Microenterprises took off, using a new business model based on the capital-sharing and lending capabilities of women helping women (World Bank Enterprise Surveys (WBES) 2002–2011; World Bank Group 2015; World Development Report 2012; World Trade Organization 2016).

Entrepreneurship became a hot topic in academia as well. The increasing numbers of women receiving college and professional degrees meant that women were better positioned to undertake entrepreneurship and to educate themselves and others about it. Research on female entrepreneurs challenged the masculine assumptions embedded in the historiographies and histories of entrepreneurship. The result was to divide the study of the subject into two camps that seldom spoke the same language. On the one hand were women scholars whose interest in entrepreneurship derived mostly from an interest in women in business and management; on the other were entrepreneurship scholars for whom gender identities were irrelevant, except insofar as a masculine universal was assumed to be synonymous with gender neutrality.

Entrepreneurship spans the categories of poverty, self-employment, middle-class status, and big boot capitalist winners (Dexter 1924; Arum and Müller 2004). Its proponents and practitioners now use a discourse of creativity, empowerment, and ownership to stimulate and encourage business creation as a socio-economic escalator to a more prosperous future. Instead of class struggles and debates about power and exploitation, entrepreneurship studies now feature local enterprisers willing to take a chance on themselves in a global order, (allegedly) of their own making. It remains to be seen whether this "creative" turn in entrepreneurship will make global business more or less aware of gender and race (Wadhwani and Lubinski 2017; Csikszentmihalyi 2007; Redien-Collot 2009).

Act I: making the invisible visible

Contemporary scholars of business women and female entrepreneurs have weaponized gender and feminist theories to deconstruct the masculinism and patriarchy of national and global business worlds (Ahl 2002, 2004; Ahl and Marlow 2012; Besse 1996; Boulding 1992; Chamlee-Wright 1997; Chow 2003; Elam 2014; Enloe 1990, 2004; Eschle 2004; Mackinnon 1989; Pearson 2000; Gamber 1997, 1998). Before women could be valued as entrepreneurs, they first had to be seen and made visible in business.

Women paid attention to gender precisely because the history and historiography of business had rendered them invisible, a fate they shared with racial and ethnic minorities. The assumption that a masculine universal was synonymous with gender neutrality worked only as long as societal norms and institutional hierarchies held. Late in the twentieth century, these hierarchies began to crack unevenly in many national economies, under pressure from a convergence of forces. The second globalization wave in the last third of the twentieth century intensified rivalries among more mature and emerging economies, testing the ability of a mostly white corporate elite to innovate more effective managerial strategies (Livesay 1989: 6, 2017: 17). Cultural perceptions of womanhood and manhood began to change; demographic shifts brought more married women into the workplace; the number of women earning college and business degrees swelled, increasing the supply of managerial talent at the same time that demand for female talent intensified. Starting in the 1960s, a string of interconnected anti-war and liberation movements attacked established national and global institutions for their exclusionary practices and biased decision-making structures (Wajcman 1991; Freedman 2002; Snyder 2008).

The fall of the Berlin Wall in 1989 intensified distinct national efforts to deregulate and widen access to global markets. The rise and rapid spread of new knowledge-based creative industries based in communications, computers, and entertainment paved the way for a massive industrial restructuring that transformed economies into an increasingly complex global network of interlocking businesses. Business and national economic systems both shaped and reflected the neo-liberal currents that were intimately intertwined with new forms of multiculturalism, internationalism, and feminism (Meagher and Nelson 2004). In 1986, Joan Scott (1986) introduced gender as an analytical tool to give it purchase in those mainstream disciplines most impervious to concerns about women's issues and activities. She singled out military, diplomatic, and political history, but later cautioned that the tool might prove problematic in business history, especially if the analysis rested upon the emancipatory impulses underlying the study of women's and labor history (Scott 1998; Roper 2005).

Research revealed gender to be an important factor shaping access to and control over resources but also as a cause of women's powerlessness, marginality, and dispossession. It exposed the social construction of identities and institutions, including patriarchy and masculinism. While gender's effects were shown to vary across cultures, assumptions undergirding masculine and feminine behaviors were revealed to be uncannily similar. Stubbornly durable gender norms associated with family, school, and workplace rendered the economic survival strategies of women invisible (Scott 1998; Craig 2017; Melman 1993; UN DESA 2009).

Scholars of women's history used gender to dramatize "difference" by thrusting women's experiences onto a global stage where men remained in the shadows. A focus on women made differences with men more visible. The changeability and perspectival nature of gender were unmistakable (Jones 2008; Scott 1996; Als 2017). Difference corralled indifference, reviving age-old questions about Enlightenment ideas of equality and the justifications for women's subordination (Stuurman 2017).

Gender was in the 1980s a malleable but problematic concept. Legal scholar Catharine MacKinnon (1989) rewove the radical strands of Marx and his daughter Eleanor to expose gender as hierarchical and fundamental to sexualized power relations (Holmes 2014). Male dominance, she insisted, operates through rape, sexual harassment, prostitution, and pornography, all of which expressed "the distinctive power of men over women in society." (MacKinnon 1989: 162, 170, 127; Mikkola 2008/2017; Yeager 1999: 1–5). Philosopher Judith Butler (1990) insisted that gender is not what one is but something one does, a sequence of acts, a doing rather than being. Doing gender is like a theatrical performance for a social audience. Both script and audience change across generations, evolving with socially established meanings.

Business historians took their cues from business – they kept issues of sexism and harassment in the closet and rolled with capitalism's gender punches. Their cautious behavior reflected not only their precarious legitimacy in popular and scholarly communities; it also reflected a reluctance to tackle hot button social issues that might compromise standards of "scientific neutrality." They did not notice that management scholar Rosabeth Moss Kanter (1977) had already begun to deconstruct the "masculine mystique" of managerialism (Kanter, 1977; Ibarra, 1993, 2004; Ibarra *et al.* 2010). Scholars whose specialties rested on nationally oriented manufacturing industries engaged the global with renewed vigor, while others explored the neglected service sector, itself a growth-oriented Goliath (Walsh, 1996, 2000; Kwolek-Folland, 2007. Explorations of smaller, family-focused, specialty producers by Philip Scranton (1998), Mary Rose (2000), and Susan Ingalls Lewis (2009) generated new hypotheses about issues of gender and race at the intersections of small and big businesses at national and global levels.

Using the unique example of Japanese and American automobile cupholder design, Lipartito (1995, 2007) opened windows into managerial thinking just wide enough to reveal business history as a promising site of cultural analysis. For some, the cultural opening proved too wide. Attention to culture exposed both the left and right flanks of business systems previously bound by national ties of Cold War politics or beholden to economic leviathans. The cultural turn both unbalanced and enlivened the discipline. By the turn of the twenty-first century issues of racism, sexism, environmentalism, and after 2001, terrorism, took center stage (Galambos 2003; Amatori 2009; Kobrak and Schneider 2011; Rosen 2013, 2010, 2016; Rosen and Seller 1999; Jones 2017; Bergquist 2017).

Firms that enter international markets have strategized to transcend cultural boundaries, only to discover a new set of hazards. The introduction of gender and race not only challenged how knowledge about business came to be assembled, analyzed, and understood. It also demanded a re-valuation and re-consideration of authorial voices. Radical moments do not last forever, but effective gender and racial norm-busters often ride together on the collective power derived from a common history. Who professes to speak, and for whom? Who re-claims the history of excluded groups? And how is all this to be done? These questions matter deeply, particularly when the status quo is challenged. Alternative perspectives must be considered, but they do not resonate with the same weight at all times and places. Scholars take their cues from society too.

The scholars who first paid attention to what business historian Philip Scranton (1998: 185) has described as the "durable absence" of women from history were, with rare exceptions, mostly women scholars who were positioned in sub-streams of more mainstream fields. Before the late 1990s, many of these separate research streams developed along parallel lines, seldom intersecting, with each carrying the national markings of their own historical and historiographical traditions (Allen and Truman 1993; Yeager 2001).

A common thread connecting these traditions to processes of professionalization has been the exclusion of women (Smith, 2005). Inclusion did not get women to "equal," even in meritocratic-leaning academia. No sooner had national professional organizations appeared at the turn of the century than additional gatekeepers began to surveil the "appropriateness" of topics that challenged either the strong currents of public opinion or the gender order. In 1901, Vassar historian Lucy Maynard Salmon submitted a completed manuscript on "Imperialism" to prospective publishers. She linked domestic service to the history of colonization by showing how routine cleaning activities, like the cleaning of toilets and wiping of children's faces, paved the way for racial and class hierarchies. Publishers showed little interest. "Nobody cares a straw what a woman has to say on public questions," complained Salmon in a letter to a friend, "unless she writes to the newspapers on the horrors of war and signs the letter." "Imperialism" was never published. Salmon produced an alternative "History in a Back Yard," which used garden imagery to explore how "new trade routes are opened up in our lilies" and the "Dutch West India Company lives in our mulberry tree." Another rejection followed. Salmon's legacy was left for succeeding generations of women (Smith in Salmon 2001). They have kept the smaller backyards open (Kwolek-Folland 1998a; Lewis 2009; Buddle 2010).

Women had to become norm breakers to claim status as professionals and as individuals distinct from their relationships to men, children, and family. The legitimacy of women's professional claims have generally depended on the decisions of men, particularly in fields like economics, economic and business history, engineering and other STEM (Science, Technology, Engineering and Mathematics) fields (Eswaran 2014; Yeager 2015; Nelson 2006, 2016). Management scholar and sociologist Rosabeth Moss Kanter (1977) argued that "opportunity," "power," and "numbers" were more important than demographic factors in explaining women's career trajectories and experiences in (corporate) business (see also, Ibarra 1993, 2004; Ibarra *et al.* 2010). More recently, scholars have pointed to the negative impact of "gender norms" and "unconscious biases," a move which has fueled new debates about appropriate policy responses (Segal and Demos 2019; Sandberg 2013; Bohnet 2016; Bicchieri 2016).

In 1994, cultural and social historian Angel Kwolek-Folland framed her exploration of gender relations in America's financial and insurance industries around a managerial paradigm developed by an eminent business historian, Alfred D. Chandler, Jr. However, by dramatizing the transformation of the modern corporation from an efficient instrument of economic change to a problematic social institution, she upended Chandler's efficiency-based explanation of the modern corporation. Business historians paid attention. Four years later, she pioneered the first-ever synthesis of women and business in the United States, raising the curtain on a distinguished all-women multicultural and racially diverse cast of business characters, ranging from Spanish and Indian-Americans in female trade economies to media and movie moguls. Wendy Gamber (1997), who straddled the fields of business and social history, used Dun and Bradstreet's credit reports to document the creation of a distinctive "female economy" in the millinery and dressmaking trades, readying scholars for debates about the distinctiveness of female versus male economies.

By 1999, there was enough information about business women in developed areas of the world for this business history insider to assemble a three-volume edited collection of articles, *Women in Business* (Yeager 1999). The organizational structure of the volumes reflected a grounding in business rather than women's history. It divided women in business globally and by sectors, thereby urging business historians to give greater consideration to the interactions between women and men in the business world instead of positioning each alone on a single national stage. Included was an editor's essay with a teasing title, "Will There Ever Be a Feminist Business History?" More than two decades later, the question still hangs in the air, begging another question, "What about masculinities?" (Yeager 1999 [1]: 3–43; Guthey 2001; Bederman 1995; Connell 1995; Connell and Wood 2005; Kimmel 2002, 2005; Hinsch 2013).

In the United Kingdom and Europe, women scholars built upon different data bases and historiographical traditions. Early Medievalists Helen Maud Cam (1910) and Eileen Power (1975) dissected parliamentary institutions and medieval manors, respectively, without sacrificing either drama or women. Initially more attention was paid to class than to race and gender. Recent imperial histories are an exception. Nicola Phillips (2006) tracked women in business during the period 1700–1850, many of whom might well have carried on easy conversations with Gamber's American women in retail and millinery trades. Women invaded the manly turf of the Industrial Revolution. Jane Humphries (2011) spearheaded recent debates about women's wages, capabilities, and industriousness. Katrina Honeyman (2000), Hannah Barker (2017a, 2017b), and Kate Mullholland (2003) gave women agency as business owners, leaders, and strategists of family enterprises, toppling some popular stereotypes of family women as marginal helpmeets and casting doubt on separate sphere ideologies. With far longer history of banking and finance to examine than the United States, European scholars pursued the trail of women investors, stock and wealth holders, wealth creators, and entrepreneurial risk takers (Laurence *et al.* 2012; Aston 2016; Aston and di Martino 2014; Sanandaji 2018; Bishop 2015; Carlos and Neal 2004; Newton and Cottrell 2006; Rutterford and Maltby 2006, 2007; Green and Owens 2003). Most recently, Béatrice Craig (2016) has offered a compelling synthesis of women and business in Europe and North America since 1500 that bookends the earlier US-based synthesis by Kwolek-Folland (1994, 1998b). Craig (2017) has extended the imperial reach of female entrepreneurs by following the commodities they produce and sell in international markets.

Women were, and gender came to be, a fundamental category for analyzing the vast array of people-directed activities and institutions responsible for linking the local to the global, connecting big and small manufacturing, agricultural, transportation, and other services. The majority of businesses created by women still cluster in the traditional sectors of agriculture and services, but the latter sector has become a major growth engine in the twenty-first century (Schipani *et al.* 2006). If there is more constancy than change in the history of business women and entrepreneurship, the gender lens needs to be widened to encompass diverse narratives about how genders interact in cultures and economies to foster and constrain change.

Incorporating women into history as business owners raised questions about the terms of incorporation and their status as entrepreneurs. Are all enterprising women entrepreneurs by virtue of their efforts to create a business? Not everyone becomes an entrepreneur, so what differentiates female entrepreneurs from other women and from male entrepreneurs and other men? Ideas about gender frame assumptions about entrepreneurial activities, behaviors, and ambitions. Cultures may be slow to change, but entrepreneurs and entrepreneurial businesses have also precipitated change in economies and in gender norms.

Women management scholars first paid attention to female entrepreneurs in the mid-1970s and 1980s. Instead of assuming that there were no differences between male and female entrepreneurs, they carved out a subfield within a subfield by searching and accounting for "differences." They first corralled the men, and then proceeded to assemble data and information about the women who created businesses, their motives, the types and sizes of their enterprises, and the results of their efforts. This means-ends approach was practical and instrumental, designed to help women become entrepreneurs, to remove the obstacles to entrepreneurship, and to harness creativity and make difference pay (Ahl 2004, 2006; Ahl and Marlow 2012; Hisrich and Brush 1984; Brush *et al.* 2006; Brush and Cooper 2012).

The financial crisis of 2008 gave scholars of female entrepreneurship reason to exhale, and gender scholars and business historians new territories to explore. The crisis exposed new racial and global fault lines in mostly white, male-dominated banking institutions and tilted research on women and female entrepreneurs toward financialization processes and practices. Research documented the experiences of women in finance as bank CEOs, managers, traders, and analysts. A pioneering study of about thirty Wall Street women by anthropologist Melissa Fisher (2012) revealed the power of mostly white, female-centered networks in helping to overcome discrimination. She illuminated the emergence of a feminist consciousness among some women and the continued adherence to more conservative beliefs about women's essential differences and the merits of markets, among others. A strand of "market feminism" which had been criticized in the 1980s, had by 2010, regained its appeal for some women in finance and marketing (Maclaran 2012). In the hands of feminist business and social historian Susan Yohn (2006), the so-called "Witch of Wall Street" Hetty Green became a "crippled capitalist," handicapped by gender, children, and sexist media coverage. Not so crippled were scores of other women in finance who were revealed to be savvy investors, counterfeiters, speculators, fund managers, arbitragers, and CEOs (Walker 2017). Notable autobiographies of women in finance have also revealed that variation in behaviors and outcomes may well be more significant than either differences or similarities (Siebert 2002; Krawcheck 2017).

Crises of finance have often evolved alongside crises generated by wars. In 2001 a global war on terror erupted. Anthropologist Carla Freeman (2001) asked a troubling question: "Is Local: Global as Feminine: Masculine?" Freeman's gender frame invites reconsideration of ongoing debates about convergence or divergence and "the West and the Rest." Not only have micro-analyses of business firms gone missing (Jones, this volume); women and minorities have also disappeared. Manly states and militaries have regained the global stage (Hooper 2001; Mann 2013).

The literature on race is unusual in several respects, reflecting the deep complexities and contradictions of its subject. The gender and racial mix of its scholars is more varied; women and men interact on the same economic stage as both collaborators and competitors; entrepreneurship unfolds even under slavery and spans all sectors of economies (Perkins 1989). Where there is discrimination there is also uplift and empowerment. If studies demonstrate the significance of individual achievements, they also raise questions about personal costs within the black community and about the meaning of black enterprise in societies where whites do and do not dominate. Moreover, governments are ever-present institutions, alternately expanding and shrinking opportunities for enterprise (Walker 2004, 2017, 1998; Ingham 2002; Garrett-Scott 2011; Shaw 2015; Gill 2004; Smith 2005; Mutongi 2007; Spring 2002; Edoho 1997; Weems 1998, 2000, 2009; Butler 1991).

Context is everything and contradictions abound. In 2006, a mixed authorial team at Harvard Business School tracked the "*Paths to Power*" of American business leaders (Mayo *et al.* 2006: 1). They began with the "fearless" if self-evident disclosure "that yes, the vast majority of individuals in top leadership of U.S. businesses over the course of the past century were white men." Years earlier, in the Jim Crow era, W. E. B. DuBois stated this truth far more boldly, declaring that property is "white ownership of the earth." And yet Juliet Walker (2004: 259, 2017) has recently noted that "there were more black managers on plantations during the age of American slavery than there has been in the era of the New Economy." Change in business, like that in history, is never easy or automatic, but a matter of human effort and creativity.

Given these complexities, historians of race take nothing for granted. As both free and enslaved peoples, blacks and other racial minorities have long work histories and violent experiences with commercial, industrial, and post-colonial capitalisms, in both mature and underdeveloped regions in the world. As such, they have carved out businesses and claimed status as entrepreneurs in ways that dramatize both the dark and bright sides of capitalism, the ethical and unethical, the moral and uplifting, for good and ill.

But DuBois and Walker (2017) among others, dealt with the triangulated histories of entrepreneurship, race, and gender primarily if not exclusively within the borders of the United States. These histories broaden exponentially as one moves beyond national borders and beyond the horizon to consider the centuries-long transition from imperialism and colonialism to the contemporary globalized world.

Act II: dangerous crossings: what about imperialism and colonialism?

The sordid business of imperialism and colonialism is a drama unlikely to attract a time-starved business-friendly audience. Its scripts have proved problematic and changeable (Mann 2013: 2–8; Nagar *et al.* 2002; Eschle 2004). Yet, few topics are better able to expose what makes global business such a challenging and contested area of research. Historian Joyce Appleby (2010) has described the uneven historical development of capitalism as "relentless revolution," repeated in many different regions around the globe, and shaped by "coercion, culture, and contingency." Its wealth-generating capacities enable people to see a future different from the past. When and where capitalism expands is always important. But, she argues, there is nothing "inexorable, inevitable, or destined" about this history. Imperialism and colonialism are by-products of decisions made by "rulers as capitalists," whom Appleby (2010: 229) identifies as "kings and statesmen who become entrepreneurs in order to command subjects' labor and resources to make things for the market."

Appleby's understanding of capitalism gives globalization content but drains it of the distinct, multiple, overlapping sources of social power that Marx and contemporary fellow-travelers have associated with capitalist nation-states and empires. Neo-Marxist sociologist Michael Mann (2013: 3–5, Vol. IV) reminds us that globalization does not "do anything." Globalization involves political, economic, ideological, and military power and "results as human groups have sought to expand their collective and distributive powers to achieve their goals." Philosopher, historian, and social theorist Michel Foucault (1982) focuses on power as a "force," dispersed throughout society, that is exercised, although unequally, by people of all statuses (Foucault 1978/1991).

The entwined histories of imperialism and colonialism place power at the center of debates about globalization (Formes 1995). They reveal multiple levels and axes of power operating within macro- and micro-institutional structures, in the interstices of cultural economies, the spaces between private and public, intimate and institutional, business and government, local and global. They reveal gender power and racial dynamics to be constitutive of globalization, not only an effect but a shaping force (Bahramitash 2005).

As the curtain rises on Act II, global tensions have mounted. A diverse cast of international characters, each speaking different languages, struggles to converse. Andrew Thompson (1997: 147) has complained that "the terms 'empire' and 'imperialism' were like empty boxes that were continuously being filled up and emptied of their meanings." The same could be said about the term globalization. The larger point, of course, is that language has always been part of a political process allowing its users and interpreters some leeway in shaping discourse for different ends.

Globalization has a shorter and less distinguished historiography than imperialism. In 1960, Theodore Levitt (1960), a Harvard Business School Professor of Marketing, wrote a polemical article, "Marketing Myopia," which criticized business executives for too narrowly defining what their companies did at a time when changes in technology and social behaviors were allowing multinationals to sell the same products worldwide. Twenty-three years later, Levitt (1983) coined the word "globalization" in a now classic article, "The Globalization of Markets." Although David Harvey (2000) has confessed to feeling conned that "globalization" was simply a "promotional gimmick to make the best of a necessary adjustment in the system of inter-national finance," he carefully delineated globalization as "a process of production of uneven temporal and geographical development." His formulation better prepares us for the possibility of global backlash, or what Thomas Friedman has described as "a brakeless train wreaking havoc" (Harvey 2000: 61, quoting Friedman 1996).

Given that men have done most of the talking about globalization, and most of the talking is about disembodied forces, flows, and processes, exceptions are notable. Embedded within Patrick Wolfe's (1997: 416) synthesis of imperialism from Marx to postcolonialism is a rare acknowledgement:

> As in so many areas, feminist scholars of imperialism have been obliged to labor the most elementary of points before being able to move on to more demanding ques-tions. Thus they have had to remind us (or at least, too many of us) that women were there too and that women have colonized and been colonized in different ways to men. Much of this work has been recuperative, re-reading imperial archive to disclose its female dimension.

Contemporary scholars from different globalized fields compete for the attention of an internet-savvy audience more culturally sensitive to social, religious, and economic differences between and within nations. The costs and benefits of globalization continue to be spread unevenly, with notable differences between men, women, and ethnicities stubbornly persisting, despite slight improvements for women. In most countries, the rich have done better than the poor, men have done better than women, and racial majorities have fared better than minorities (Global Entrepreneurship Monitor, 2001–2016). Who is to frame the part of the debate that is likely to matter most to business scholars? What are the questions that are likely to shape debates? Who is to speak for whom, about what? (Chaudhuri *et al.* 2010).

At the intersection of gender and race, insightful contributions come from a group of male activist intellectuals, anti-colonial freedom fighters, and feminist scholars determined to explore the psychology and troubled legacies of colonialism (Mannoni 1950; Fanon 1952, 1961; Rodney 1972; Memmi 1965). Among the foremost Pan-Africanists to put "black power" and "third world" non-aligned Marxism at the center of anti-colonial movements was Walter Anthony Rodney, an activist historian and leader, born and assassinated in his native Guyana in 1980 (Benjamin and Kelley 2018). Rodney blasted imperialism as a "monstrous institution," blaming Europe for the underdevelopment of Africa. To underscore the white racist side of colonialism, he used a vivid metaphor: far from having two hands – one of oppression and the other of beneficence – Rodney called it "a one-armed bandit" (Agyeman 1973: 72–74; Dupuy 1996: 114). African-American scholar Robin Kelly has noted that Rodney's alignment of Western thought with the interests of bourgeois capitalism was not unlike the *Orientalism* analytic used by Edward Said (1978) to expose the occidental and imperial nexus of modern thinking. Rodney developed an explicitly global viewpoint from an African position, but both Rodney and Said emphasized the need for schools and education to challenge these dichotomies and the discourses behind them (Benjamin and Kelley, 2018: xxii).

By the 1990s, feminist activists and women scholars made their voices heard. They began to apply gender to reveal the limits of Said's model as well as older styles of imperial history that paid little attention to women or the experiences of the marginalized. They complicated what had been primarily patriarchal narratives revolving around political and economic developments. They reconceptualized imperialism as a highly gendered process, a powerful form of colonial discourse in and of itself (Midgley 1998; Desai 2008; Peterson and Runyan 2018).

Over time white patriarchal imperialism came under attack. Empires that were once defined by clear territorial borders were gendered masculine and feminine and rendered "intimate" (Rizzo and Gerontakis 2017). Exploring the intersections of gender, race, and class across various sites of imperial encounters, feminist and post-colonial scholars expanded the imperial "imaginary." Although business institutions and people played a minor role in their narratives, their attention to literary sources, to advertising, branding, and other visual and media technologies, has generated important insights about the sources of inspiration and impact of representations of gendered images and racialized bodies.

A single, illuminating example of this is Ann McClintock's *Imperial Leather* (1995), which maps the southern African and gendered connections between race, sexuality, and money in a way that vividly expresses "the governing themes of Western imperialism: the transmission of white, male power through control of colonized women; the emergence of a new global order of cultural knowledge; and the imperial command of commodity capital" (1995: 1). Since its publication, the number of enthusiastic reviews that appeared in a wide range of humanities-oriented journals and the flow of subsequent citations have assured the book's status as a classic (Karamcheti 1995: 16–17; Puri 1998: 532–535; Pickering 1997: 991–993; Nelson 1997: 383–386; Jolly 1997: 444–448; Lewis 1997: 148–149; Sinha 1998: 183–184; Ha 1997: 187–190; O'Donnell 1997: 310–312).

Business scholars disregarded McClintock's brand of "situated psychoanalysis" and other socio-psychological tools that post-colonial scholars have used to theorize gender in relation to other axes of power. They neglected the large issues of "desire," "sexuality," and "male power." They criticized discourse analysis as a limited and somewhat dangerous tool, especially if disconnected from an examination of how business actually works and decisions come to be made. They remained suspicious of profit-making and power dynamics that could not be measured or quantified (Blaszczyk 2009; McCloskey 2009; Davis and Huttenback 1983: 2; Powell 1991).

Scholars of economic development and management engaged more directly with data and policy-oriented analyses. By the 1990s, empirical data about the economic lives of women in various parts of the world had begun to be assembled. Danish economist Ester Boserup (1980), who worked for the United Nations and several other international organizations, made seminal contributions to the study of agrarian change and women in development. She theorized that population change drove the intensity of agricultural production. Although her empirically grounded work pointed to the disproportionate economic burdens carried by women, she retained an economist's optimism about opportunities. "The power of ingenuity," she once said, "would always outmatch that of demand." Amartra Sen's (2002) "capabilities" approach urged development economists and policy professionals to consider what women really needed in order to achieve the kind of life they valued, defined in terms of a set of valuable "beings and doings" (Sen 2002, 2005; Nussbaum 2003). Sen's work generated recurrent debates about which capabilities to prioritize in order to expand women's opportunities (Agarwal *et al.* 2006; Nussbaum 2003).

Entrepreneurship became a global policy priority when studies revealed that female entrepreneurs were far more likely than men to invest the income generated from business activities in the education of children and family well-being. Scholars began to focus on business creation to better understand why some economies and some women and men are more enterprising than others. In 1999, researchers in the United Kingdom and United States launched the Global Entrepreneurship Monitor (GEM) to better understand the relationship between entrepreneurial activity and economic growth, and to identify which policies boost entrepreneurship (Acs 2006; Acs *et al.* 2008a; Baker *et al.* 2005; Minniti and Arenius 2003; Minniti and Naude 2010).

Scholars of gender and female entrepreneurship, however, have remained wary. They have criticized some of the growth-oriented and gender assumptions on which these quantifiable datasets rest. They argue that a singular focus on economic growth minimizes the importance that some entrepreneurs have attached to other objectives, such as family survival, work–life balance, ecological, and health-related issues. Others have suggested that differentiating entrepreneurs on the basis of preconceived characteristics perpetuates gender stereotypes. As an example, they cite the distinctions between "necessity" and "opportunity" entrepreneurs, showing that more women than men place themselves in the "necessity" category. Data on informal businesses sweep in more women than men (Henry *et al.* 2016; Pines *et al.* 2010; Hamilton 2013). On the other hand, data on women, business, and the law from the IMF and World Bank shows why "getting to equal" has been so difficult. Women throughout the world experience greater difficulty in accessing institutions, using property, getting a job, building credit, going to court, and securing protection from violence (GEM 2015–2017; Acs *et al.* 2008a; Álvarez *et al.* 2014; Acs *et al.* 2008b;Johnson *et al.* 2006; Acs 2006; Amorós 2011; Amorós *et al.* 2013).

The turn toward global entrepreneurship and female entrepreneurs signaled changes in the identities and dynamics of imperial powers. Scholarship on imperialism shifted away from European industrializers scrambling for territories in Africa to the post-World War II invasion of European consumer markets by American multinationals. In *The Sex of Things*, social and intellectual historians De Grazia and Furlough (1996) placed gender at the heart of the analysis of

consumption. The edited volume showed how consumption has been associated with femininity across cultures, and how this association impacts masculinity and relationships of power. De
Grazia's (2005) subsequent study examined the "irresistible rise and inexorable decline" of
America's market empire. She connected the changing forms of Americanization and imperialism to the transmission, diffusion, and reception of particular marketing technologies and the
rhetoric of consumption. By demonstrating how European elites both cooperated with and
contested American influence, De Grazia joined other scholars who have forewarned of cultural
imperialism's waning power (de Grazia 2005; Blaszczyk and Spiekermann 2017; Van Elteren
2003, 2006; Stephan 2006; Danielsen 2008; Woodard 2012; Berger 1997). By ignoring the role
played by racial inequalities in projecting and contesting the American dream, she left the black
box of imperialism half-open.

The imperial strands that connect global businesses to diverse cultures involve gendered and
racialized assumptions about the sources, exercise, and impact of power (Chow 2003). These are
craftily revealed by scholars of global business who have focused attention on "agents of change
at work in business" (Blaszczyk 2009, 2015; Ibeh and Carter 2008). These scholars weave an
intricate net wide enough to capture the many gender and racial identities of an array of business
people and decision-makers, from global leaders responsible for strategy to critical intermediaries and workers embedded in global networks of exchange.

Of the numerous studies of imperial interconnections this entry singles out a few of the more
notable scholarly contributions in three areas: multinationals; cultural, creative, and service
industries; and commodities. Each of these areas has been selected because of distinct but uneven
contributions to ideas about gender, race, and entrepreneurship and the regional contexts that
differentiate the scholarship. For all its potholes, this road map points to possibilities for future
research incorporating and connecting gender, race, and entrepreneurship in historically specific
business contexts in different parts of the world.

By the turn of the twenty-first century, some multinational management scholars had begun
to warn of "the dangers of an imperial mind-set," which assumed "big emerging markets were
new markets for their old products, or a chance to squeeze profits out of sunset technologies"
(Prahalad and Lieberthal 2003). There were sightings of "business imperialism" in Africa whose
more fragile nation-states, smaller markets, and rich resources meant fewer foreign multinationals,
more opportunities for larger and smaller indigenous enterprises, and better outcomes. "Business imperialism in South Africa," Stuart Jones (1996: 20) concluded, "was made up of these
three ingredients, capital, skill, and entrepreneurial flair." Even the monopolistic diamond villain
De Beers was revealed to have paid out 70 percent of its profits to the South African government (Jones 1996: 18). However, few male management scholars paid attention to gender or
race in this narrative, not even Jones himself.

Business historian Paula de la Cruz-Fernández (2015, in this volume) has paid some attention. Her exploration of women's experiences with new sewing machines in Spain and Mexico
offered a different and more socially grounded view of the marketing strategies of Singer Sewing
Machine. Her interpretation of their histories gave women power and agency. Instead of passive
players or disempowered workers, women emerge as builders of multinationals who define the
idea of "modern" machine sewing on their own terms. On the other hand, de la Cruz-Fernández
left room for debate with those whose understanding of gender analysis involves a study of
power relationships, such as those between these women and their husbands or family members
and the largely male stratum of marketing executives.

The new realities of a global economy have been fueled by new technologies of communication and information. The widespread popular appeal of these cultural, creative, and service
industries created new opportunities for business scholars to explore transnational cultural

exchanges (Friedman and Jones 2011). In some ways, this shift in focus reflected and enabled an end-run around debates about power that had been associated with empires and different forms of imperialism. As long as entrepreneurship was linked more to creativity than to brute force, there was more to celebrate than to fear. An additional bonus was that the turn to creative industries pulled in people of all genders and racial minorities, as part of an intricate web of small and big, insider and outsider global makers (McRobbie 2002; Foss and Klein 2012; Thomas *et al.* 2010; Scranton and Fridenson 2013: 61–66).

The business of beauty is quicksilver and ill-defined. As such, the identities of its makers and users are all the more revealing of unstated assumptions about gender, race, and entrepreneurship. On the one hand, " '[m]aking up' is an integral component of the rituals of everyday life. Similar to fashion, cosmetics consumption is tightly tied with identity construction and expression of the self" (Jeacle 2006: 87). Globally, the beauty business is sprawling, fragmented, and changeable. It encompasses a mix of different sectors, a variety of skill sets, complex distribution networks, and is constantly on the defensive against charges of immorality and legality. Business scholars have offered accounts that connect shifting cultural ideals of beauty with advertising, aspirational brands, and fickle consumers whose choice-changes and brand-jumping keep destabilizing industry development patterns. They identify the sex and gender of the industry's global pioneers to underscore how a wide variety of actors influenced how beauty came to be imagined so differently by so many (Jones 2010; Peiss 1998, 2000; Gill 2004; Mazzeo 2008; McAndrew 2010; Scranton 2001/2014).

Like the beauty industry, the fashion industry presents many of the same historical challenges and opportunities for scholars of business, gender, race, and entrepreneurship (Abrahamson 1996; Boris 2017; Brasó-Broggi 2015; Gökariksel and Secor 2009; Hemphill and Suk 2009; Kawamura 2004). In both industries, every piece of the creative puzzle is likely to generate more questions than answers about the power of one nation to impose its cultural tastes on another. Business scholar Regina Blaszczyk's (2009: 6) popular history of America's consumer society explored "the evolution of the relationship between what Americans purchased and how they expressed their collective and individual identities." A subsequent edited collection, *Producing Fashion* (2015) drew global and gendered connections between commerce, culture, and consumers in a variety of national contexts. The charge of "color imperialism" that flew across the Atlantic in the 1930s is an example of the unusual power dynamics buried in these sources. *The Fashion Forecasters*, co-edited by Blaszczyk and Wubs (2018), reveals a hidden history of color and trend prediction. Contributors follow fashion forecasters around the globe as they struggle to choose the right color for the right season for different genders and races.

In the turn to commodities, scholars of racial, gender, and war capitalism discovered common ground with business and economic historians (Beckert, 2015 [2009]). A commodity-centered approach has the potential to integrate local and global, top-down and bottom-up perspectives to incorporate producers, distributors, and consumers as well as workers. Commodities provide an apt subject for histories of global capitalism that do not assume inevitability, greater equality, or homogeneity. As Erika Rappaport (2018) has so powerfully demonstrated in the case of tea, Appleby's three Cs ("culture, coercion, and contingency") are allowed full play. In addition to tea, the global businesses associated with feathers, cocoa, champagne, chocolate, rice, and shawls have been shown to construct the gender and race identities of producers and consumers (Stein 2008; Barrientos 2014; Craig 2016; Callaway 1987; Bray 1986; Robertson 2009; Mazzeo 2008; Ratten 2017).

Marx's understanding of commodity fetishism retains value. Globalization has not vanquished his ghost. Although capitalism has been gendered and racialized in ways that Marx did not anticipate, the legacies of imperialism and colonialism endure. Historians of capitalism and slavery have retraced the lives of those human beings forced to live their lives as commodities. They have described their interactions with business people in localities and regions where finance and racial capitalism rose together. Two recent examples stand out. Caitlin Rosenthal (2018) uses the account books of southern slaveholders in the United States to demonstrate the connections between profit and innovation, and violence and inequality. By linking a series of interconnected business histories and data practices to planters' control over their enslaved labor force, she establishes synergies between slavery and quantitative management. "[I]t is perilously easy," she concludes, "to render human figures as figures on paper and to imagine men, women and children as no more than hands" (Rosenthal 2018: xiv).

Peter Hudson (2017: 146) recovers a history of imperial bankers in the Caribbean, an area marginalized in business and economic history. Tracing the roots and precedents for racial capitalism to US continental expansion in the nineteenth century, he shows how particular banks "participated in the creation, replication, and reordering of Caribbean economies on racial lines while helping to reproduce the racist imaginaries and cultures in which finance capital was embedded and through which bankers functioned." Drawing from multinational sources, including the private papers of prominent bankers, Wall Street pamphlets, newspapers, and government reports, he demonstrates how bankers used social capital and government influence to counter regulatory constraints and gain advantages to compete on the international banking scene.

Curtain

Considerations of gender, race, and entrepreneurship complicate the displacement of notions of "imperialism" and "colonialism" even as they advance the global project. If these three intertwined themes were not on the radar of business historians in the mid-1990s, they have since become impossible to ignore. Communication and information technologies have galvanized global social movements. Environmentalism, racism, sexism, and empowerment issues have combined with global population shifts to push business firms closer to the center of global debates, where the dark shadows of imperial pasts hang over future generations. Yet if business scholars are to take the issues of race and gender seriously, they need to find ways to tackle common issues of enduring inequalities and accountability. Whether inequalities are due to colonialism, sexism, racism, or the legal and institutional structures of economies and cultures, business has become part of the global problem, and hopefully the solution as well. It is at this intersection of gender, race, and entrepreneurship that global business histories will have the greatest impact and that race and gender historians will be able to make a much needed contribution to our understanding of (all) makers of global business. There is no doubt that gender and racial dynamics are constitutive of globalization; they have been shaping and continue to shape global business and global order.

A major challenge for business history going forward is to re-assemble information, think creatively, and seek out the missing pieces in the drama of gender, race, and entrepreneurship. Two voices from the past articulated this challenge: in a provocative edited volume entitled *Imagining Britain's Economic Future*, the editors stress how Joseph Schumpeter and Benedict Anderson placed "the concept of imagination at the heart of the entrepreneurial process" (Thackeray *et al.* 2018). This concept marked an important interpretive shift from an emphasis on Schumpeter's heroic man of action to an interest in the softer, thinking side of his ungendered twin, endowed with "the capacity of seeing things in a way which proves afterwards to be true, even though it cannot be established [as such] at the time" (Thackeray *et al.* 2018: 2). The edited volume pivots on a provocative question: how are we to understand the economic imagination of people engaged in markets "making calculations about and placing faith in the future ... key qualities of investors and entrepreneurs?" (Thackeray *et al.* 2018). This large question begs others which pull at the gender and racial threads underlying each act of this entry's drama: how have women and racial minorities been imagined? By whom? And for what purposes?

Gender has been and continues to be a question central to historian Joan Scott's research. It is not a given. In her 2018 memorial lecture, presented when she was awarded the prestigious Edgar de Picciotto International Prize of the Graduate Institute of Geneva, Scott (2018: 5) explained: "this means asking of any society or culture *how* the difference of sex is being defined and regulated, as well as what ends it is seeking to secure." For Scott (2018: 3), the historical persistence of gender inequality is a result of the interdependency between gender and politics. "Gender, defined as the historically and culturally variable attempt to insist on the duality of sex difference – *becomes the basis for imagining social, political, and economic orders* [my emphasis]."

This entry's expansive, boundary-defying drama began with an imaginative leap. It has ended with more questions than answers. Global connections between gender, race, and entrepreneurship have been developed in ways that have confirmed and contested Joan Scott's understanding of the interdependencies between gender and politics. Gender and race did not always involve politics, although politics mattered most of the time in ways that disadvantaged women more than men. In accounting for gender inequality, Scott dismissed the usual suspects – capitalism, patriarchy, male self-interest, misogyny, and religion – although she considered them "useful categories to work with." Entrepreneurship eluded her categorical net.

This entry has revealed entrepreneurship to be a wild card, illuminating how creative processes and practices can disrupt economic orders, regardless of politics, gender, or race. Still, gender and racial inequalities persist, even in the domain of entrepreneurship. It did not come as a surprise to this historian at least, to learn that societies have always valued white male entrepreneurs and their creations far more highly than those developed by white women and minorities. Entrepreneurship may or may not fuel global business and economic growth; but it always reinforces inequalities. Entrepreneurship is, after all, about valuing difference differently (Mazzucato 2013, 2018).

Bibliography

Abrahamson, Eric (1996), "Management Fashion," *Academy of Management Review*, 21 (1), 254–285.

Acker, Joan (2006), *Class Questions: Feminist Answers* (Lanham, MD: Rowman & Littlefield).

Acs, Zoltan J. (2006), "How Is Entrepreneurship Good for Economic Growth?" *Innovations: Technology, Governance, Globalization*, 1 (1), 97–107.

Acs, Zoltan J., Desai, Sameeksha, and Hessels, Jolanda (2008a), "Entrepreneurship, Economic Development and Institutions," *Small Business Economics*, 31 (3), 219–234.

Acs, Zoltan J., Desai, Sameeksha, and Klapper, Leora F. (2008b), "What Does 'Entrepreneurship' Data Really Show?" *Small Business Economics*, 31 (3), 265–281; special issue: "Entrepreneurship, Economic Development and Institutions."

Agarwal, Bina, Humphries, Jane, and Robeyns, Ingrid (Eds.) (2006), *Capabilities, Freedom and Equality* (Oxford: Oxford University Press).

Agyeman, Opoku (1973), "Review of Walter Rodney: How Europe Underdeveloped Africa," *Africa Today*, 20 (3), 72–74.

Ahl, Helen J. (2002), "The Making of the Female Entrepreneur: A Discourse Analysis of Research Texts on Women's Entrepreneurship" (Jonkoping International Business School, JIBS Dissertation Series No. 015).

Ahl, Helen (2004), The Scientific Reproduction of Gender Inequality: A Discourse Analysis of Research Articles on Women's Entrepreneurship (Copenhagen: Copenhagen Business School Press).

Ahl, Helen (2006), "Why Research on Women Entrepreneurs needs New Directions," *Entrepreneurship Theory and Practice*, 30 (5), 595–621.

Ahl, Helen and Marlow, Susan (2012), "Exploring the Dynamics of Gender, Feminism and Entrepreneurship: Advancing Debate to Escape a Dead End?" *Organization*, 19 (5), 543–562.

Allen, Sheila, and Truman, Carole (1993), *Women in Business: Perspectives on Women Entrepreneurs* (New York: Routledge).

Als, Hilton (2017), "The Art of Difference," *New York Review of Books* (June 8), 30–32.

Álvarez, Claudia, Amorós, José Ernesto, and Urbano, David (2014), "GEM Research: Achievements and Challenges," *Small Business Economics*, 42 (3), 445–465.

Amatori, Franco (2009), "Business History as History," *Business History*, 51 (2), 143–156.

Amorós, José Ernesto (2011), "El Proyecto Global Entrepreneurship Monitor (Gem): Una Aproximación Desde El Contexto LatinoAmericano/The Global Entrepreneurship Monitor Project (Gem): A Latin-American Context Approach," *Academia, Revista LatinoAmericana de Administración*, 46, 1–15.

Amorós, Jose E., Bosma, Niels, and Levie, Jonathan (2011), "Ten Years of Global Entrepreneurship Monitor: Accomplishments and Prospects," *International Journal of Entrepreneurial Venturing*, 5 (2), 120–152.

Appleby, Joyce (2010), *The Relentless Revolution: A History of Capitalism* (New York: W. W. Norton).

Arum, Richard, and Müller, Walter (Eds.) (2004), *The Reemergence of Self-Employment: A Comparative Study of Self-Employment Dynamics and Social Inequality* (Princeton, NJ, and Oxford: Princeton University Press).

Aston, Jennifer (2016), *Female Entrepreneurship in Nineteenth-Century England: Engagement in the Urban Economy* (New York: Palgrave Macmillan).

Aston, Jennifer, and di Martino, Paolo (2014), "Risk and Success: Re-Assessing Female Entrepreneurship in Late Victorian and Edwardian England," *University of Oxford Discussion Papers in Economic and Social History*, no. 125.

Baca Zinn, Maxine, and Thornton Dill, Bonnie (1996), "Theorizing Difference from Multiracial Feminism," *Feminist Studies*, 22 (2), 321–331.

Bahramitash, Roksana (2005), *Liberation from Liberalization: Gender and Globalization in South East Asia* (London: Zed Books).

Baker, Ted, Gedajlovic, Eric, and Lubatkin, Michael (2005), "A Framework for Comparing Entrepreneurship Processes across Nations," *Journal of International Business Studies*, 36 (5), 492–504.

Barker, Hannah (2017a), "Gender and Business during the Industrial Revolution," in D. Simonton (Ed.) *Routledge History Handbook of Gender and the Urban Experience* (New York: Routledge), 45–57.

Barker, Hannah (2017b), *Family and Business During the Industrial Revolution* (Oxford: Oxford University Press).

Barrientos, Stephanie (2014), "Gendered Global Production Networks: Analysis of Cocoa-Chocolate Sourcing," *Regional Studies*, 48 (5), 791–803.

Baumol, William J. (1990), "Entrepreneurship: Productive, Unproductive, and Destructive," *Journal of Political Economy*, 98 (5), 893–921.

Bayly, C. A. (2018), *Remaking the Modern World 1900–2015: Global Connections and Comparisons*, Blackwell History of the World (Hoboken, NJ: WileyBlackwell).

Beckert, Sven (2015 [2009]), *Empire of Cotton: A Global History* (New York: Alfred Knopf: First Vintage Books edition).

Bederman, Gail (1995), *Manliness and Civilization: A Cultural History of Gender and Race in the United States, 1880–1917* (Chicago, IL: University of Chicago Press).

Benjamin, Jesse, and Kelley, Robin D. G. (Eds.) (2018), *The Russian Revolution: A View from the Third World*. By Walter Rodney (New York: Verso).

Berger, Peter L. (1997), "Four Faces of Global Culture," *National Interest*, 49 (Fall), 23–29.

Bergquist, Ann-Kristin (2017), "Business and Sustainability: New Business History Perspectives," Harvard Business School Working Paper 18-034.

Besse, Susan K. (1996), *Restructuring Patriarchy: The Modernization of Gender Inequality in Brazil, 1914–1940* (Chapel Hill, NC: University of North Carolina Press).

Bethencourt, Francisco (2013), *Racisms: From the Crusades to the Twentieth Century* (Princeton, NJ: Princeton University Press).

Bicchieri, Cristina (2017), *Norms in the Wild: How to Diagnose, Measure, and Change Social Norms* (New York: Oxford University Press).

Bishop, Catherine (2015), *Minding Her Own Business: Colonial Businesswomen in Sydney* (Sydney: NewSouth Publishing).

Blaszczyk, Regina Lee (2009), *American Consumer Society, 1865–2005: From Hearth to HDTV* (Wheeling, IL: Harlan Davidson).

Blaszczyk, Regina Lee (Ed.) (2015), *Producing Fashion: Commerce, Culture and Consumers* (Philadelphia, PA: University of Pennsylvania Press).

Blaszczyk, Regina Lee, and Spiekermann, Uwe (Eds.) (2017), *Bright Modernity: Color, Commerce, and Consumer Culture* (New York: Palgrave Macmillan).

Blaszczyk, Regina Lee, and Wubs, Ben (Eds.) (2018), *The Fashion Forecasters: A Hidden History of Color and Trend Prediction* (London: Bloomsbury Visual Arts).

Bohnet, Iris (2016), *What Works: Gender Equality by Design* (Boston, MA: Harvard University Press).

Boris, Eileen (2017), "Fashion Works," *Feminist Studies*, 43 (1), 169–192.

Boserup, Ester (1980), "Women in Development" Commission of the European Communities 38 (Brussels: Commission of the European Communities).

Boulding, Elise (1992), *The Underside of History: A View of Women Through Time*, Vol. 2, revised (Boulder, CO: Westview Press).

Brasó-Broggi, Carles (2015), "The Weft of Shanghai Fashion: Economic Networks in Shanghai's Modern Fashion Industry," *China Perspectives*, 3 (103), 5–11.

Bray, Francisca (1986), *The Rice Economies: Technology and Development in Asian Societies* (Berkeley and Los Angeles, CA: University of California Press).

Brush, Candida G. and Cooper, Sarah Y. (2012), "Female Entrepreneurship and Economic Development: An International Perspective," *Entrepreneurship and Regional Development*, 24 (1–2), 1–6.

Brush, Candida G., Carter, Nancy M., Gatewood, Elizabeth J., Greene, Patricia G., and Hart, Myra M. (2006), *Growth-Oriented Women Entrepreneurs and their Businesses: A Global Research Perspective* (Cheltenham, UK and Northampton, MA: Edward Elgar).

Buddle, Melanie (2010), *The Business of Women: Marriage, Family, and Entrepreneurship in British Columbia, 1901–1951* (Vancouver: University of British Columbia Press).

Butler, John Sibley (1991), *Entrepreneurship and Self-Help Among Black Americans: A Reconsideration of Race and Economics* (Albany, NY: State University of New York Press).

Butler, Judith (1990), *Gender Trouble: Feminism and the Subversion of Identity* (New York: Routledge).

Callaway, Helen (1987), *Gender, Culture and Empire: European Women in Colonial Nigeria* (New York: Palgrave Macmillan).

Cam, Helen Maud (1910), "The Education of Girls Before the Foundation of the Women's Colleges," Personal Papers of Helen Maud (Girton College Private Personal Correspondence – Archives, University of Cambridge) (GCPP CAM 3/1/25).

Carlos, Ann M., and Neal, Larry (2004), "Women Investors in Early Capital Markets, 1720–1725," *Financial History Review*, 11 (2), 197–224.

Chamlee-Wright, Emily (1997), *The Cultural Foundations of Economic Development: Urban Female Entrepreneurship in Ghana* (New York: Routledge).

Chaudhuri, Nupur, Katz, Sherry J., and Perry, Mary Elizabeth (Eds.) (2010), *Contesting Archives: Finding Women in the Sources* (Champaign, IL: University of Illinois Press).

Chow, Esther Ngan-Ling (2003), "Gender Matters: Studying Globalization and Social Change in the 21st Century," *International Sociology*, 18 (3), 443–460.

Connell, R.W. (1995), *Masculinities* (Berkeley and Los Angeles, CA: University of California Press).

Connell, R. W., and Wood, Julian (2005), "Globalization and Business Masculinities," *Men and Masculinities*, 7 (4), 347–364.

Cotton, Charlotte (2014), "State of Fashion," *Aperture* 216, "Fashion," 44–51.

Craig, Béatrice (2016), *Women and Business since 1500: Invisible Presences in Europe and North America?* (New York: Palgrave Macmillan).

Craig, Béatrice (2017), *Female Enterprise: Behind the Discursive Veil in Nineteenth-Century Northern France* (New York: Palgrave Macmillan).

Csikszentmihalyi, Mihaly (2007), *Creativity: Flow and the Psychology of Discovery and Innovation* (New York: Harpercollinsbooks.com).

Danielsen, Helge (2008), "The American Spirit in Europe Revisited?" *Contemporary European History*, 17 (1), 117–126.

Davis, Lance E., and Huttenback, Robert (1983), *Mammon and the Pursuit of Empire: The Political Economy of British Imperialism* (Cambridge: Cambridge University Press).

de Grazia, Victoria (2005), *Irresistible Empire: America's Advance through Twentieth-Century Europe* (Cambridge, MA: Harvard University Press).

de Grazia, Victoria, and Furlough, Ellen (Eds.) (1996), *The Sex of Things: Gender and Consumption in Historical Perspective* (Berkeley, CA: University of California Press).

de la Cruz-Fernández, Paula (2015), "Multinationals and Gender: Singer Sewing Machine and Marketing in Mexico, 1890–1930," *Business History Review*, 89 (3), 531–549.

Desai, Manisha (2008), *Gender and the Politics of Possibilities: Rethinking Globalization* (Lanham, MD: Rowman & Littlefield).

Dexter, Elizabeth Anthony (1924), *Women of Colonial Affairs: A Study of Women in Business and the Professions in America before 1776* (Boston and New York: Houghton Mifflin).

Dupuy, Alex (1996), "Race and Class in the Postcolonial Caribbean: The Views of Walter Rodney," *Latin American Perspectives*, 23 (2), 107–129.

Edoho, F. M. (1997), *Globalization and the New World Order: Promises, Problems and Prospects for Africa in the Twenty First Century* (London: Praeger).

Elam, Amanda Brickman (2014), *Gender and Entrepreneurship* (Cheltenham, UK: Edward Elgar).

Enloe, Cynthia (1990), *Bananas, Beaches, and Bases: Making Feminist Sense of International Politics* (Berkeley, CA: University of California Press).

Enloe, Cynthia (2004), *The Curious Feminist: Searching for Women in a New Age of Empire* (Berkeley, CA: University of California Press).

Eschle, Catherine (2004), "Feminist Studies of Globalisation: Beyond Gender, Beyond Economism?" *Global Society*, 18 (2), 97–125.

Eswaran, Mukesh (2014), *Why Gender Matters in Economics* (Princeton, NJ: Princeton University Press).

Fanon, Franz (1952 [1967]), *Black Skin, White Masks*, trans. Charles L. Markmann (New York: Grove Press; orig. pub. 1952 as *Peau noire, masques blancs* [Paris: Editions Seuil]).

Fanon, Franz (1961 [1963]), *The Wretched of the Earth*, trans. Constance Farrington (New York: Grove Press; orig. pub. as *Les Damnés de la Terre* [Paris]).

Fisher, Melissa S. (2012), *Wall Street Women* (Durham, NC: Duke University Press).

Formes, Malia B. (1995), "Beyond Complicity versus Resistance: Recent Work on Gender and European Imperialism," *Journal of Social History*, 28 (3), 629–641.

Foss, Nichola, and Klein, Peter G. (2012), *Organizing Entrepreneurial Judgment* (New York: Cambridge University Press).

Foucault, Michael (1978, 1991), *Discipline and Punish: The Birth of the Prison* (New York: Pantheon Books).

Foucault, Michel (1982), "The Subject and Power," *Critical Enquiry*, 8 (4), 777–795.

Freedman, Estelle B. (2002), *No Turning Back: The History of Feminism and the Future of Women* (New York: Ballantine).

Freeman, Carla (2001), "Is Local: Global as Feminine: Masculine? Rethinking the Gender of Globalization," *Signs*, 26 (4), 1007–1037; special issue: "Globalization and Gender."

Friedman, Thomas (1996), "Revolt of the Wannabes," *New York Times* (January 7), A19.

Friedman, Walter, and Jones, Geoffrey (2011), "Business History: Time for Debate," *Business History Review*, 85 (1), 1–8.

Galambos, Louis (2003), "Identity and the Boundaries of Business History: An Essay on Consensus and Creativity," in Franco Amatori and Geoffrey Jones (Eds.), *Business History Around the World* (New York: Cambridge University Press), 11–30.

Gamber, Wendy (1997), *The Female Economy: The Millinery and Dressmaking Trades, 1860–1930* (Champaign, IL: University of Illinois Press).

Gamber, Wendy (1998), "A Gendered Enterprise: Placing Nineteenth-Century Businesswomen in History," *Business History Review*, 72 (2), 188–218; special issue: "Gender and Business." doi: 10.2307/3116275.

Garrett-Scott, Shennette (2011), *Daughters of Ruth: Enterprising Black Women in Insurance in the New South, 1890s to 1930s*, PhD Dissertation (University of Texas at Austin: Mimeo).

Gill, Tiffany (2004), "Civic Beauty: Beauty Culturists and the Politics of African American Female Entrepreneurship, 1900–1965," *Enterprise & Society*, 5 (4), 583–593.

Global Entrepreneurship Monitor (GEM), various years.

Gökariksel, Banu, and Secor, Anna J. (2009), "New Transnational Geographies of Islamism, Capitalism and Subjectivity: The Veiling-Fashion Industry in Turkey," *Area*, 41 (1), 6–18.

Green, D. R., and Owens, A. (2003), "Gentlewomanly Capitalism? Spinsters, Widows, and Wealth Holding in England and Wales, c. 1800–1860," *Economic History Review*, 56 (3), 510–536.

Guthey, Eric (2001), "Ted Turner's Corporate Cross-Dressing and the Shifting Images of American Business Leadership," *Enterprise & Society*, 2 (1), 111–142.

Ha, Marie-Paule (1997), "Review of *Imperial Leather*," *Research in African Literatures*, 28 (2), 187–190.

Hamilton, Eleanor (2013), "The Discourse of Entrepreneurial Masculinities (and Femininities)," *Entrepreneurship and Regional Development*, 25 (1–2), 90–99.

Harvey, David (2000), *Spaces of Hope* (Berkeley, CA: University of California Press).

Hemphill, C. Scott, and Suk, Jeannie (2009), "The Law, Culture, and Economics of Fashion," *Stanford Law Review*, 61 (5), 1147–1199.

Henry, Colette, Foss, Lene, and Ahl, Helene (2016), "Gender and Entrepreneurship Research: A Review of Methodological Approaches," *International Small Business Journal*, 34 (3), 217–241.

Hinsch, Bret (2013), *Masculinities in Chinese History* (Lanham, MD: Rowman & Littlefield).

Hisrich, Robert, and Brush, Candida (1984), "The Woman Entrepreneur: Management Skills and Business Problems," *Journal of Small Business Management*, 22 (1), 30–37.

Hofstede, Geert (1998), *Masculinity and Femininity: The Taboo Dimension of National Cultures* (Thousand Oaks, CA, London, and New Delhi: Sage Publications).

Holmes, Rachel (2014), *Eleanor Marx: A Life* (New York: Bloomsbury Press).

Honeyman, Katrina (2000), *Women, Gender and Industrialisation, 1700–1870* (London: Macmillan).

Hooper, Charlotte (2001), *Manly States: Masculinities, International Relations, and Gender Politics* (New York: Columbia University Press).

Hoselitz, Bert F. (1952), "Entrepreneurship and Economic Growth," *American Journal of Economics and Sociology*, 12 (1), 97–110.

Hudson, Peter James (2017), *Bankers and Empire: How Wall Street Colonized the Caribbean* (Chicago, IL: University of Chicago Press).

Humphries, Jane (2011), *Gender, Work and Wages in Industrial Revolution Britain* (Cambridge: Cambridge University Press).

Ibarra, Herminia (1993), "Personal Networks of Women and Minorities in Management: A Conceptual Framework," *Academy of Management Review*, 18 (1), 56–87.

Ibarra, Herminia (2004), "Men and Women of the Corporation and the Change Masters: Practical Theories for Changing Times," *Academy of Management Executive*, 18 (2), 108–111.

Ibarra, Herminia, Carter, Nancy M., and Silva, Christine (2010), "Why Men Still Get More Promotions Than Women," *Harvard Business Review*, 88 (9), 80–85.

Ibeh, Kevin, and Carter, Sara (2008), "Editorial: Perspectives on Women, Globalisation, and Global Management," *Journal of Business Ethics*, 83 (1), 1–3; special issue on "Women, Globalisation and Global Management."

Ingham, John N. (2002), "Patterns of African American Female Self-Employment and Entrepreneurship in Ten Southern Cities, 1880–1930," in Alusine Jalloh and Toyin Falola (Eds.), *Black Business and Economic Power* (Rochester, NY: University of Rochester Press), 470–538.

Jeacle, Ingrid (2006), "Face Facts: Accounting, Feminism and the Business of Beauty," *Critical Perspectives on Accounting*, 17, 87–108.

Jerkins, Morgan (2018), *This Will Be My Undoing: Living at the Intersection of Black, Female, and Feminist in (White) America* (New York: HarperCollins).

Johnson, Peter, Parker, Simon, and Wijbenga, Frits (2006), "Nascent Entrepreneurship Research: Achievements and Opportunities," *Small Business Economics*, 27 (1), 1–4.

Jolly, Margaret (1997), "Review of *Imperial Leather*," *Journal of the History of Sexuality*, 7 (3), 444–448.

Jones, Geoffrey (2010), *Beauty Imagined: A History of the Global Beauty Industry* (New York: Oxford University Press).

Jones, Geoffrey (2017), *Profits and Sustainability: A History of Green Entrepreneurship* (New York: Oxford University Press).

Jones, Geoffrey, and Lluch, Andrea (2015), *The Impact of Globalization on Argentina and Chile: Business Enterprises and Entrepreneurship* (Cheltenham, UK; Northampton, MA: Edward Elgar Publishing).

Jones, Nikki (2008), "Working "the Code": On Girls, Gender and Inner-city Violence," *Australian and New Zealand Journal of Criminology*, 41, 63–83.

Jones, Stuart (1996), "Business Imperialism and Business History," *South African Journal of Economic History*, 11 (2), 1–20.

Kanter, Rosabeth Moss (1977), *Men and Women of the Corporation* (New York: Basic Books).

Kanter, Rosabeth Moss (1978), "Reflections on Women and the Legal Profession: A Sociological Perspective," *Harvard Women's Law Journal*, 1, 1–18.

Karamcheti, Indira (1995), "Dirty Secrets: Review of *Imperial Leather*," *Women's Review of Books*, 13 (2), 16–17.

Kawamura, Yuniya (2004), *The Japanese Revolution in Paris Fashion* (Oxford: Oxford University Press).

Kelan, Elisabeth K. and Jones, Rachel Dunkley (2010), "Gender and the MBA," *Academy of Management Learning and Education*, 9 (1), 26–43.

Kimmel, Michael (2002), "Global Masculinities: Restoration and Resistance," Paper presented at the XVth Congress of Sociology, International Sociological Association, Brisbane, Australia, July 7–13.

Kimmel, Michael S. (2005), *The History of Men: Essays on the History of American and British Masculinities* (Albany, NY: State University of New York Press).

Kobrak, Christopher, and Schneider, Andrea (2011), "Varieties of Business History: Subject and Methods for the Twenty-First Century," *Business History*, 53 (3), 401–424.

Kogut, Bruce, and Zander, Udo (2003), "Knowledge of the Firm and the Evolutionary Theory of the Multinational Corporation: 2003 Decade Award Winning Article," *Journal of International Business Studies*, 34 (6), Decade Award Issue Foreword from the Editor in Chief, 516–529.

Krawcheck, Sally (2017), *Own It: The Power of Women at Work* (New York: Crown).

Kwolek-Folland, Angel (1994), *Engendering Business: Men and Women in the Corporate Office, 1870–1930* (Baltimore, MD: Johns Hopkins University Press).

Kwolek-Folland, Angel (1998a), "Customers and Neighbors: Women in the Economy of Lawrence, Kansas, 1870–1995," *Business and Economic History*, 27 (1), 129–139.

Kwolek-Folland, Angel (1998b), *Incorporating Women: A History of Women and Business in the United States* (New York: Twayne).

Kwolek-Folland, Angel (2001), "Gender and Business History," *Enterprise & Society*, 2 (1), 1–10; special issue: "Gender and Business History."

Kwolek-Folland, A. (2007), "Gender, the Service Sector, and U.S. Business History," *Business History Review*, 81 (3), 429–450.

Laird, Pamela Walker (2008), "Looking Toward the Future: Expanding Connections for Business Historians," *Enterprise & Society*, 9 (4), 575–590.

Laurence, Anne, Maltby, Josephine, and Rutterford, Janette (Eds.) (2012), *Women and Their Money, 1700–1950: Essays on Women and Finance* (New York: Routledge).

Leff, Nathaniel H. (1979), "Entrepreneurship and Economic Development: The Problem Revisited," *Journal of Economic Literature*, 17 (1), 46–64.

Levitt, Theodore (1960), "Marketing Myopia," *Harvard Business Review*, 38 (4), 45–56.

Levitt, Theodore (1983), "The Globalization of Markets," *Harvard Business Review*, 61 (3), 92–102.

Lewis, Reina (1997), "Review of *Imperial Leather*," *Feminist Review*, 55 (1), 148–149.

Lewis, Susan Ingalls (2009), *Unexceptional Women: Female Proprietors in Mid-Nineteenth-Century Albany, New York, 1830–1885* (Columbus, OH: Ohio State University Press).

Lipartito, Kenneth (1995), "Culture and the Practice of Business History," *Business and Economic History*, 24 (2), 1–41.

Lipartito, Kenneth (2007), "Business Culture," in Geoffrey Jones and Jonathan Zeitlin (Eds.), *The Oxford Handbook of Business History* (Oxford and New York: Oxford University Press), 603–628.

Livesay, Harold C. (1989), "Entrepreneurial Dominance in Businesses Large and Small," *Business History Review*, 63 (1), 1–21.

Livesey, Finbarr (2017), *From Global to Local: The Making of Things and the End of Globalization* (New York: Pantheon).

McAndrew, Malia (2010), "A Twentieth-Century Triangle Trade: Selling Black Beauty at Home and Abroad, 1945–1965," *Enterprise & Society*, 11 (4), 784–810.

Maclaran, Pauline (2012), "Marketing and Feminism in Historic Perspective," *Journal of Historical Research in Marketing*, 4 (3), 462–469.

McClintock, Anne (1995), *Imperial Leather: Race, Gender, and Sexuality in the Colonial Contest* (New York: Routledge).

McCloskey, Deirdre Nansen (2009), "Slavery and Imperialism Did Not Enrich Europe," MPRA Paper 20696, University Library of Munich, Germany, RePEcArchive.

MacKinnon, Catherine (1989), *Toward a Feminist Theory of State* (Cambridge, MA: Harvard University Press).

McRobbie, Angela (2002), "Fashion Culture: Creative Work, Female Individualization," *Feminist Review*, 71, "Fashion and Beauty," 52–62.

Mann, Michael (2013), *The Sources of Social Power: Vol. 4, Globalizations, 1945–2011* (New York: Cambridge University Press).

Mannoni, Octave (1950), *Psychologie de la colonisation* (Paris: Seuil).

Mayo, Anthony J., Nohria, Nitin, and Singleton, Laura G. (2006), *Paths to Power: How Insiders and Outsiders Shaped American Business Leadership* (Boston, MA: Harvard Business School Press).

Mazzeo, Tilar J. (2008), *The Widow Clicquot: The Story of a Champagne Empire and the Woman who Ruled It* (New York: Harper Collins).

Mazzucato, Mariana (2013), *The Entrepreneurial State: Debunking Public vs. Private Sector Myths* (London and New York: Anthem Press).

Mazzucato, Mariana (2018), *The Value of Everything: Making and Taking in the Global Economy* (New York: Hachtte Book Group, Perseus Books).

Meagher, Gabrielle, and Nelson, Julie A. (2004), "Survey Article: Feminism in the Dismal Science," *Journal of Political Philosophy*, 12 (1), 102–126.

Melman, Billie (1993), "Gender, History and Memory: The Invention of Women's Past in the Nineteenth and Early Twentieth Centuries," *History and Memory*, 5 (1), 5–41.

Memmi, Albert (1965), *The Colonizer and the Colonized* (New York: Orion).

Midgley, Clare (1998), *Gender and Imperialism* (Manchester: Manchester University Press).

Mikkola, Mari (2008/2017), "Feminist Perspectives on Sex and Gender," *Stanford Encyclopedia of Philosophy*, Edward N. Zalta (Ed.), URL: https://plato.stanford.edu/archives/win2017/entries/feminism-gender/.

Minniti, Maria, and Arenius, Pia (2003), Women in Entrepreneurship: Report on "The Entrepreneurial Advantage of Nations: First Annual Global Entrepreneurship Symposium," United Nations Headquarters, New York, April 29.

Minniti, Maria, and Naude, Wim (2010), "What Do We Know About the Patterns and Determinants of Female Entrepreneurship across Countries?" *European Journal of Development Research*, 22 (3), 277–293.

Mullholland, Kate (2003), *Class, Gender and the Family Business* (London: Macmillan/Palgrave).

Murray, James M. (2017), "Entrepreneurs and Entrepreneurship in Medieval Europe," in David S. Landes, Joel Mokyr, and William Baumol (Eds.), *The Invention of Enterprise: Entrepreneurship from Ancient Mesopotamia to Modern Times* (Princeton, NJ; Oxford: Princeton University Press), 88–106.

Mutongi, Kenda (2007), *Worries of the Heart: Widows, Family and Community in Kenya* (Chicago, IL: University of Chicago Press).

Nagar, R., Lawson, V., McDowell, L., and Hanson, S. (2002), "Locating Globalization: Feminist (Re) readings of the Subjects and Spaces of Globalization," *Economic Geography*, 78 (3), 257–284.

Nelson, Diane M. (1997), "'The Horror': The Subject of Desire in Postcolonial Studies," *American Anthropologist*, 99 (2), 383–386.

Nelson, Julie (2006), "Can We Talk? Feminist Economists in Dialogue with Social Theorists," *Signs: Journal of Women in Culture and Society*, 31 (4), 1051–1074.

Nelson, Julie (2016), "Male Is a Gender, Too: A Review of 'Why Gender Matters in Economics' by Mukesh Eswaran," *Journal of Economic Literature*, 54 (4), 1362–1376.

Newton, Lucy, and Cottrell, Philip L. (2006), "Female Investors in the First English and Welsh Commercial Joint-Stock Banks," *Accounting, Business and Financial History*, 16 (2), 315–340.

Nussbaum, Martha (2003), "Capabilities as Fundamental Entitlements: Sen and Social Justice," *Feminist Economics*, 9 (2/3), 33–59.

O'Donnell, Lorraine (1997), "Review of *Race, Gender and Sexuality in the Colonial Context* by Anne McClintock," *Labour/Le Travail*, 40, 310–312.

Pearson, Ruth (2000), "Moving the Goalposts: Gender and Globalisation in the Twenty-First Century," *Gender and Development*, 8 (1), 10–19.

Peiss, Kathy (1998), *Hope in a Jar: The Making of America's Beauty Culture* (Philadelphia, PA: University of Pennsylvania Press).

Peiss, Kathy (2000), "On Beauty … and the History of Business," *Enterprise & Society*, 1 (3), 485–506.

Perkins, Edwin J. (1989), "The Entrepreneurial Spirit in Colonial America: The Foundations of Modern Business History," *Business History Review*, 63 (1), 160–186.

Peterson, V. Spike, and Runyan, Anne Sisson (2018), *Global Gender Issues in the New Millennium* (New York: Routledge).

Phillips, Nicola (2006), *Women in Business, 1700–1850* (Rochester, NY: Boydell Press).

Pickering, Michael (1997), "Review of *Imperial Leather: Race, Gender and Sexuality in the Colonial Contest* by Anne McClintock," *Journal of Social History*, 30 (4), 991–993.

Pines, Aya Malach, Lerner, Miri, and Schwartz, Defna (2010), "Gender Differences in Entrepreneurship: Equality, Diversity and Inclusion in Times of Global Crisis," *Equality, Diversity and Inclusion: An International Journal*, 29 (2), 186–198.

Powell, John (1991), "Review of *Mammon and the Pursuit of Empire: The Economics of British Imperialism*, by Lance E. Davis and Robert A. Huttenback," *Victorian Periodicals Review*, 24 (2), 91–92.

Power, Eileen (1975), *Medieval Women* (Cambridge: Cambridge University Press).

Prahalad, C. K., and Lieberthal, Kenneth (2003), "The End of Corporate Imperialism," *Harvard Business Review*, 76 (4), 109–117.

Puri, Shalini (1998), "Book Review of *Imperial Leather*, et al.," *Signs*, 23 (2), 532–535.

Rappaport, Erika (2018), *A Thirst for Empire: How Tea Shaped the Modern World* (Princeton, NJ: Princeton University Press).

Ratten, Vanessa (2017), "Gender Entrepreneurship and Global Marketing," *Journal of Global Marketing*, 30 (3), 114–121.

Redien-Collot, Renaud (2009), "Female Entrepreneurs' Authority: Is the Creative Aspect of Authority a Masculine Fiction in Managerial and Entrepreneurial Paradigms?" *Journal of Enterprising Culture*, 17 (4), 419–441.

Rizzo, Tracey, and Gerontakis, Steven (2017), *Intimate Empires: Body, Race, and Gender in the Modern World* (New York: Oxford University Press).

Robertson, Emma (2009), *Chocolate, Women and Empire: A Social and Cultural History* (Manchester, UK: Manchester University Press).

Rodney, Walter (1972 [2014]), *How Europe Underdeveloped Africa*, rev. ed. (n.p.: African Tree Press).

Roper, Michael (2005), "Slipping Out of View: Subjectivity and Emotion in Gender History," *History Workshop Journal*, 59 (1), 57–72.

Rose, Mary B. (2000), *Firms, Networks and Business Values: The British and American Cotton Industries since 1750* (Cambridge: Cambridge University Press).

Rosen, Christine Meisner (2009), "Business Leadership in the Movement to Regulate Industrial Air Pollution in Late Nineteenth and Early Twentieth Century America," *Jahrbuch für Wirtschaftsgeschichte/ Economic History Yearbook*, 50 (2), 23–44.

Rosen, Christine Meisner (2010), "The Role of Business Leaders in Community Sustainability Coalitions: An Historical Perspective," in Woodrow W. Clark II, (Ed.) *Sustainable Communities* (New York: Springer Science+business Media), 13–28.

Rosen, Christine Meisner (2013), "What is Business History?" *Enterprise & Society*, 14 (3), 475–485.

Rosen, Christine Meisner and Seller, Christopher C. (1999). "The Nature of the Firm: Towards an Eco-cultural History of Business: [Introduction]," *The Business History Review*, 73(4) , Business and The Environment, 577–600.

Rosenthal, Caitlin (2018), *Accounting for Slavery: Masters and Management* (Cambridge, MA: Harvard University Press).

Rubin, Gayle (1975), "The Traffic in Women," in Rayna A. Reiter (Ed.) *Toward An Anthropology of Women* (New York; London: Monthly Review Press), 157–210.

Rutterford, Janette, and Maltby, Josephine (2006), "The Widow, the Clergyman, and the Reckless: Women Investors in England, 1830–1914," *Feminist Economics*, 12 (1–2), 111–138.

Rutterford, Janette, and Maltby, Josephine (2007), "The Nesting Instinct: Women and Investment Risk in a Historical Context," *Accounting History*, 12 (3), 305–327.

Said, Edward W. (1978), *Orientalism* (New York: Pantheon Books).

Salmon, Lucy Maynard (2001), *History and the Texture of Modern Life: Selected Essays*, edited by Nicholas Adams and Bonnie G. Smith (Philadelphia, PA: University of Pennsylvania Press), 8–9.

Sanandaji, Nima (2018), "The Nordic Glass Ceiling," *Cato Institute Policy Analysis No. 835* (March 8), 1–16.

Sandberg, Sheryl (2013), *Lean In: Women, Work and the Will to Lead* (New York: Knopf).

Schipani, Cindy A., Dworkin, Terry M., Kwolek-Folland, Angel, and Maurer, Virginia (2006), "Women and the New Corporate Governance: Pathways for Obtaining Positions of Corporate Leadership," *Maryland Law Review*, 65 (2), 504–537.

Schumpeter, Joseph A. (1934), *The Theory of Economic Development*, trans. R. Opie (Cambridge, MA: Harvard University Press).

Scott, Joan W. (1986), "Gender: A Useful Category of Historical Analysis," *American Historical Review*, 91 (5), 1053–1075.

Scott, Joan W. (1988), *Gender and the Politics of History* (New York: Columbia University Press).

Scott, Joan W. (1996), *Only Paradoxes to Offer: French Feminists and the Rights of Man* (Cambridge, MA: Harvard University Press).

Scott, Joan W. (1998), "Comment: Conceptualizing Gender in American Business History," *Business History Review*, 72 (2), 242–249.

Scott, Joan W. (2018), "The Persistence of Gender Inequality: How Politics Constructs Gender, and Gender Constructs Politics," www.ias.edu/ideas/scott-gender-inequality (last accessed April 14, 2019).

Scranton, Philip (1998), "Introduction: Gender and Business History," *Business History Review*, 72 (2), 185–187.

Scranton, Philip (Ed.) (2001/2014), *Beauty and Business: Commerce, Gender and Culture in Modern America* (New York: Routledge).

Scranton, Philip, and Fridenson, Patrick (2013), *Re-Imagining Business History* (Baltimore, MD: Johns Hopkins University Press).

Segal, Marcia Texler and Demos, Vasilikie (Eds.) (2019), *Gender and the Media* (Bingley, UK: Emerald Publishing Limited).

Sen, Amartya (2002), "How to Judge Globalism," *American Prospect*, 13 (2), 1–14.

Sen, Amartya (2004), Capabilities, Lists and Public Reason: Continuing the Conversation," *Feminist Economics*, 10(3), 77–80.

Shaw, Stephanie J. (2015), *W. E. B. Du Bois and The Souls of Black Folk* (Chapel Hill, NC: University of North Carolina Press).

Siebert, Muriel (2002), *Changing the Rules: The Adventures of a Wall Street Maverick* (New York: Free Press).

Sinha, Mrinalini (1998), "Review of *Imperial Leather*," *American Historical Review*, 103 (1), 183–184.

Smith, Adam (1776), *An Enquiry into the Nature and Causes of the Wealth of Nations* (London: Strahan & Cadell).

Smith, Cheryl A. (2005), *Market Women: Black Women Entrepreneurs: Past, Present, and Future* (Westport, CT; London: Praeger Publishers).

Snyder, R. Claire (2008), "What is Third-Wave Feminism? A New Directions Essay," *Signs: Journal of Women in Culture and Society*, 34 (1), 176–196.

Soanes, Catherine, and Stevenson, Angus (Eds.) (1975), *Concise Oxford English Dictionary*, 11th ed. (Oxford: Oxford University Press).

Søraa, Roger Andre (2017), "Mechanical Genders: How Do Humans Gender Robots?" *Gender, Technology and Development*, 21 (1–2), 99–115.

Spring, Anita (2002), "Gender and the Range of Entrepreneurial Strategies: The Typical and the 'New' Women Entrepreneurs," in Alusine Jalloh and Toyin Falola (Eds.) *Black Business and Economic Power* (Rochester, NY: University of Rochester Press), 381–404.

Stein, Sarah Abrevaya (2008), *Plumes: Ostrich Feathers, Jews, and a Lost World of Global Commerce* (New Haven, CT: Yale University Press).

Stephan, Alexander (Ed.) (2006), *The Americanization of Europe: Culture, Diplomacy, and Anti-Americanism after 1945* (New York: Berghahn Books).

Stuurman, Siep (2017), *The Invention of Humanity: Equality and Cultural Difference in World History* (Cambridge, MA: Harvard University Press).

Taylor, Shelley E. (2002), *The Tending Instinct: Women, Men, and the Biology of Relationships* (New York: Henry Holt).

Thackeray, David, Thompson, Andrew, and Toye, Richard (Eds.) (2018), *Imagining Britain's Economic Future, c.1800–1975: Trade, Consumerism, and Global Markets* (New York: Palgrave Macmillan).

Thomas, Nicola J., Hawkins, Harriet, and Harvey, David C. (2010), "The Geographies of the Creative Industries: Scale, Clusters and Connectivity," *Geography*, 95 (1), 14–21.

Thompson, Andrew S. (1997), "The Language of Imperialism and the Meanings of Empire: Imperial Discourse in British Politics, 1895–1914," *Journal of British Studies*, 36 (2), 147–177.

United Nations Department of Economic and Social Affairs (UN DESA) (various years), *The World's Women* (New York: United Nations).

van Elteren, Mel (2003), "U.S. Cultural Imperialism: Today Only a Chimera," *SAIS Review*, 23 (2), 169–188.

van Elteren, Mel (2006), *Americanism and Americanization: A Critical History of Domestic and Global Influence* (Jefferson, NC: McFarland).

Wadhwani, R. Daniel, and Lubinski, Christina (2017), "Reinventing Entrepreneurial History," *Business History Review*, 91, 767–799.

Wajcman, Judy (1991), *Feminism Confronts Technology* (Cambridge, UK: Polity Press with Blackwell Publishers Ltd., reprinted 1993, 1996, 2000).

Walker, Juliet E. K. (1998), *History of Black Business in America: Capitalism, Race, Entrepreneurship* (New York: Twayne Publishers).

Walker, Juliet E. (2004), "White Corporate America: The New Arbiter of Race?" in Kenneth Lipartito and David Sicilia (Eds.) *Constructing Corporate America: History, Politics, Culture* (New York and Oxford: Oxford University Press), 246–293.

Walker, Juliet E. K. (2017), "Oprah Winfrey, the Tycoon," in Robert Weems, Jr. and Jason Chambers (Eds.), *Building the Black Metropolis: African American Entrepreneurship in Chicago* (Champaign, IL: University of Illinois Press), 212–233.

Walsh, Margaret (1996), "Not Rosie the Riveter: Women's Diverse Roles in the Making of the American Long-Distance Bus Industry," *Journal of Transport History*, 17 (1), 43-56.

Walsh, Margaret (2000), *Making Connections: The Long-Distance Bus Industry in the USA* (Burlington, VT: Ashgate Publishing Co.).

Weems, Robert E. (1998), *Desegregating the Dollar: African American Consumerism in the Twentieth Century* (New York: New York University Press).

Weems, Robert E. (2000), *Black Business in the Black Metropolis: The Chicago Metropolitan Assurance Company, 1925–1985* (Bloomington and Indianapolis, IN: Indiana University Press).

Weems, Robert E. (2009), *Business in Black and White: American Presidents and Black Entrepreneurs in the Twentieth Century* (New York and London: New York University Press).

West, Candace, and Zimmerman, Don H. (2009), "Accounting for Doing Gender," *Gender and Society*, 23 (1), 112–122.

Wolfe, Patrick (1997), "History and Imperialism: A Century of Theory, from Marx to Postcolonialism," *American Historical Review*, 102 (2), 388–420.

Woodard, James P. (2012), "Consumer Culture, Market Empire, and the Global South," *Journal of World History*, 23 (2), 375–398.

World Bank Enterprise Surveys (WBES) (2002–2011).

World Bank Group (2015), *Women, Business and the Law 2016: Getting to Equal* (Washington, DC: World Bank).

World Development Report (2012), "Gender Equality and Development," World Bank.

World Trade Organization (2016), *World Trade Report for 2016: Levelling the Trading Field for SMEs* (Geneva: World Trade Organization).

Yeager, Mary (2015), "Women Change Everything," *Enterprise & Society*, 16 (4), 744–769.

Yeager, Mary A. (Ed.) (1999), *Women in Business*, 3 vols. (Cheltenham, UK: Edward Elgar).

Yeager, M. A. (2001), "Mavericks and Mavens of Business History: Miriam Beard and Henrietta Larson," *Enterprise & Society*, 2 (4), 687–768.

Yohn, Susan M. (2006), "Crippled Capitalists: Gender Ideology, the Inscription of Economic Dependence and the Change of Female Entrepreneurship in Nineteenth-Century America," *Feminist Economics*, 12 (1–2), 85–109; special issue: "Women and Wealth."

PART II

Institutions

6

GOVERNMENT AND REGULATORS

Neil Rollings

In January 2017 *The Economist* published a leading article entitled 'In Retreat: The Multinational Company is in Trouble' (*The Economist* 2017). It noted: 'The retreat of global firms will give politicians a feeling of greater control as companies promise to do their bidding'. Talk of the end of an era for the global firm may be premature but it does capture the commonly perceived tension between national governments and multinational enterprises (MNEs). However, the standard account is of the rise of MNEs and the consequent decline of the nation-state and national governments. Certainly, the first time *The Economist* is believed to have referred to MNEs, that was the approach they took. 'Companies Outgrow Countries: A New Kind of Economic Animal – Mastodons of the Future? – Is Displacing Growing Weight Throughout the World Economy' was the title of a leading article which went on to highlight 'the inherent flexibility towards national sovereignty that internationally spread private companies possess' (*The Economist* 1964).[1] Since the 1960s multinational enterprise was increasingly viewed as the future and nation-states (and their governments) as 'just about through as an economic unit' (Kindleberger 1969: 207 and more recently Ohmae 1990 and Strange 1996). In the most extreme form of this zero-sum power game between multinationals and governments democracy is seen as being replaced by the quiet power of big business (for example Hertz 2001; Korten 2001; George 2015).

This strand of argument is extensive, reflecting popular concerns about the power of big business but has mainly taken the form of empirical studies, usually in the field of political economy, and dealing with the period since the Second World War. However, the starting point for this *oeuvre* was in international business studies. The landmark publication here was Raymond Vernon's *Sovereignty at Bay* (1971). In this seminal volume Vernon, 'the father of research on relations between nation states and MNEs' (Eden 2000: 335), set out that there would inevitably be conflicts between MNEs and both home and host countries. However, he did not see this as a simple zero-sum game in the way that many later writers have done. In *Sovereignty at Bay* and in subsequent works (1977 and 1998), Vernon did not foresee the demise of the nation-state. Rather he saw 'two systems, … each legitimated by popular consent, each potentially useful to the other, yet each containing features antagonistic to the other' (Vernon 1991: 191): it was not just nation-states whose sovereignty was at bay but also that of multinationals. What mattered, in Vernon's view, was the perception of a loss of sovereignty by nation-states, not that this was necessarily a reality (Boddewyn 2005: 37; Kobrin 2001: 183).

Despite such early engagement with this issue, most strands of the international business literature, in contrast to that in political economy, developed to say little directly about the relationship between MNEs and governments or their regulations (an exception is John Dunning (see Dunning and Lundan 2008)). Building on Stephen Hymer's (1976) work, the focus has been on internal explanations for the existence and growth of multinational enterprise (Fitzgerald 2015: 2–4). Government, its policies and regulations in this respect are exogenous variables to which MNEs respond and are therefore extraneous to many international business (IB) models of multinational enterprise.

There are issues with this separation. After all, at the heart of what distinguishes 'international business' from 'business' more generally is the issue of territoriality (Grosse 2005: 3). These enterprises are and have been multi-*national* or trans-*national* and it is this dimension which defines them. Given the centrality of governments to the very notion of the nation-state, what governments are like, how they act, how they change over time and how they perceive MNEs affects the very nature of MNEs. Indeed, the merging of two nation-states might well turn some MNEs into straightforward enterprises. Likewise, it is governments that establish the nature of property rights within their territorial domains, a key aspect of political risk (see the chapter by Wubs and Kurosawa in this volume).

However, in recent years there have been signs of a greater engagement with international business–government relations (IBGR) from management scholars, alongside a recognition of their importance (see Boddewyn 2016 for an overview). Building on the work of David Baron (1995), non-market strategy is now recognised as a key element of corporate strategy and of its study (Lawton and Rajwani 2015). The growth in studies of corporate social responsibility (CSR) (for example Barton *et al.* 2016) and corporate political activities (CPA) (for example Oliver and Holzinger 2008; and Henisz and Zelner 2010) is evidence of this development. Much of this literature examines the relationship between MNEs and emerging economies on the one hand in terms of dealing with the political risks faced by MNEs and, on the other, the potential for exploitation by MNEs (Lawton *et al.* 2012; Lawton *et al.* 2014). However, in many respects a focus on direct, quantitative effects of MNE activities has predominated, such as the impact of political donations on policy development (for example Bonica 2016). This may provide some minimum benchmark of the effectiveness of MNE corporate political activities but seems rather narrowly conceived.

As will be shown, business historians have explored many of these issues already, providing an excellent opportunity for a mutually beneficial conversation. In this respect, there are four relevant contributions that have emerged from the work by business historians. First, business historians, taking a more embedded view of the position of multinationals in society, highlight the pivotal role of governments, not just in implementing policies which impact directly on MNEs, but also in creating and developing the general framework in which MNEs operate. From this, and second, much business history research has highlighted the importance of context, complexity and contingency here. Third, and related to this, business historians have been able to provide rich and detailed accounts of the interaction of business and governments in the form of CPA, like lobbying, in a variety of political contexts. They are able to explore these in a more nuanced and sophisticated way than much of the current CPA literature. Finally, and most importantly, the IB literature has been heavily influenced by its roots in the experience of post-Second World War US manufacturing multinationals. The historical dimension provided by business historians has been important here in showing how widespread multinationals were before the Second World War. More relevant here, is the secondary finding that in the context of rising nationalism, interactions between MNEs and national governments were at least as visible before as after the Second World War. Likewise, the influence of empire and the consequences of empire have been highlighted, though again this influence was not insuperable.

The chapter begins by elaborating on the contribution of an historical perspective to the making of global business to our understanding of the relationship between multinationals and governments. Two areas of study are then explored in more depth to highlight the two-way and complex nature of the relationship. One examines the relationship between MNEs and government in the context of European integration, that is as a move away from national levels of governance; the other considers the highly topical and controversial subject of tax avoidance and tax evasion. Finally, there is space for some brief conclusions.

Business history literature

The early IB literature focused on US manufacturing multinationals and it was from studying their experiences that theories of multinational enterprise emerged. Business historians have taken a broader perspective. While they have contributed to our understanding of American multinationals at this time (for example Wilkins 1974; Rollings 2011), this has been only one of their fields of interest. One of the most obvious contributions by business historians was to show the existence of MNEs in other sectors of the economy, notably the service sector. This is relevant to IBGR because the service sector is often more regulated than manufacturing. Geoffrey Jones's (1990, 1993) work on banks as multinationals led the way here. Building on this, others have examined a range of service sectors. Thus Wilkins (2009) has shown the impact of regulation on the development of multinationals in the insurance industry. Similarly, Calvo (2008) and Clifton *et al.* (2011) have shown how differences in regulation impacted upon the internationalisation of telecommunications companies both before and after the Second World War. A different form of interaction with government has been found in the construction industry where government was often involved in purchasing (Linder 1994; Donzé 2015). In the case of the international hotel industry, government influence was felt through the encouragement of US governments to stimulate international travel and indirectly by international governance mechanisms, in this example the Convention in International Civil Aviation (Quek 2012).

Similarly, while the IB literature tended to concentrate on the internal dynamics of MNEs, business historians have readily acknowledged the importance of governments in determining the development of MNEs. Thus Colli (2016: 9) has recently written: 'Despite a very diffused perception of globalization as being incompatible with the role of national governments, the latter played and continue to play a pivotal role in the process of the internationalization of enterprises and entrepreneurs'. Such sentiments are readily found in other core business history texts (Jones 2005: 201; Jones 2008: 154). However, it is perhaps most thoroughly illustrated in Fitzgerald's recent contribution, *The Rise of the Global Company* (2015). Here, Fitzgerald (2015, 18) addresses many of the aspects of the relationship between MNEs and governments raised in the business history literature: 'Through law, taxation, subsidies, regulation, and policies, the state has been a strong influence on multinational business strategy, corporate organization, and employment'. That MNEs are embedded in a political and regulatory context has been viewed by business historians as crucial to understanding and explaining their development.

Much of the IB and political economy literature tends to focus on the nature of the relationship between MNEs and national governments in rather simple dichotomies – conflict or cooperation, or, who has more power? In contrast, business historians have highlighted that these relationships are more fluid and contingent, and, as they change, so this required MNEs to adapt as best they could to those changes, even if this meant accommodation with authoritarian political regimes (Kobrak and Hansen 2004; Wubs 2008). Donzé and Kurosawa (2013) suggest from the example of Nestlé in Japan that European multinationals tended to be more pragmatic and organisationally flexible than their American counterparts in dealing with difficult political environments. But this was not simply as part of some recalibration of the balance of power between the MNE and the home and/or host government: 'Business success is not only about power, it is also about navigating in politicized environments, in which economic considerations do not always come first' (Sandvik and Storli 2013: 130–1). Equally, this is not a simple two- or three-actor model of MNE, host government and (sometimes) home government as the IB literature often tends to assume. Just as the MNE is not a monolith so the same is the case for governments, as the political science literature has long understood (see for example Rhodes 1997). The cases presented by business historians of IBGR highlight, therefore, the complexity and contingency involved in assessing and managing political risk and that this is not simply a case of power relationships.

Managing political risk has also been a theme of another branch of the business historiography of IBGR, that is studies relating to MNEs and developing host economies. Business historians have, in particular, addressed the colonial and post-colonial dimension. Verma and Abdelrehim (2017) present a similar argument about the importance of context and contingency to those considered above, but in a post-colonial context: the relationships between Burmah Shell, the Burmah Oil Company and the Indian government fluctuated between cooperation and conflict in what was a complex relationship in which a legacy of imperial relationships continued to have influence. Sometimes this imperial legacy proved too much: Merrett (2007) has shown how the withdrawal of Australian MNEs from post-colonial Fiji and Papua New Guinea occurred, despite the host governments' desire for them to stay, because the companies were unable to adjust to this new context. In other cases, empire and the imperial legacy does not seem to have been that influential in determining market access (Decker 2011; Lubinski 2015).

The influence of empire on IBGR stretches back much further in time too. In the age of high imperialism at the end of the nineteenth century there were many examples of European governments turning informal empire into formal empire to protect the rights and assets of multinationals. MNEs exploited this to embark on their own scramble for Africa (Jones 2000: 75–80). Moreover, the British government revisited an old model of business by issuing charters to certain companies to create state-sanctioned monopolies for certain parts of Africa. Like the East India Company (Carlos and Nicholas 1988; Bowen 2005) and other chartered companies before them there was a direct relationship between home governments and the operation of these state monopolies. But this influence could also be less direct too: by spreading legal systems from the metropole to the rest of empire, investor risks were reduced by replicating property and other rights and by encouraging companies to operate outside their home country. Thus, Mira Wilkins (1998: 435) posed the question as to whether there was a link, perhaps related to reduced information asymmetries and colonial administration, between free-standing companies and empire because these companies were at their zenith in the age of high imperialism.

This strand of imperial and colonial business history is part of a third important contribution to our understanding of the development of IBGR by moving research beyond the era of the 'classic' US manufacturing multinational of the post-Second World War era. From an early date, business historians have shown that the history of multinationals is a long one (Wilkins 1970, 1974). Such work has included many insights relating to IBGR and from which some important findings have emerged. First, it has been conventional to view the First World War as marking a watershed in this IBGR (Jones 2005: 203). Prior to that date, unless there were strategic issues, governments did not seem that concerned by foreign ownership issues and MNEs had a relatively free hand. With the war restrictions and expropriation of assets without compensation by host governments became increasingly common. For example, Coats lost their mill in Russia following the Bolshevik revolution (Kim 1995). Thereafter, throughout the interwar period governments took far more interest in foreign multinationals with various restrictions and prohibitions imposed, notably in the United States (Wilkins 2004). This era is frequently associated with international cartelisation (Fear 2008; Kindleberger 1989: 233), and it became common to refer to the rise of MNEs after 1945 as, in part, the consequence of tighter regulation of cartels which made market access easier (Fitzgerald 2015: 258–331).

Yet, it is clear we should not take this too far (Dehne 2013). Indeed Tworek (2015) refers to the period from about 1850 to the Second World War as 'the age of multinationals'. And if one looks beyond Europe it has been suggested that 'the interwar years were not a period of deglobalization, but a period in which the relations between states and firms and between the West and the "rest" were reordered and renegotiated' (Déjung and Petersson 2013: 16). The first half of the twentieth century has received considerable attention from business historians interested in IBGR:

> What the period … between 1914 and 1929, and even more so from 1929 to 1948 … especially illustrated was the influence of home and host country governments on the activities of multinationals, and it revealed the power that nation states, even those in the developing economies of Latin America could impose on foreign-owned business. … [It also showed] how assertions of national sovereignty could strongly clash with the multinational's assertion of private property rights and preference for open cross-border trade.
>
> *(Fitzgerald 2015: 257)*

An example of how these policies developed even in countries traditionally with open trade policies and limited regulatory powers is provided by Scott and Rooth (1999). MNEs remained key actors at that time but they had to adjust their strategies in the light of the increased scrutiny that they faced. Frank (2009) has shown how Standard Oil tried to be flexible in its presentation of its Austrian subsidiary depending on the audience it was addressing. The same company (and its competitors) had mixed success with its legitimising strategies in South America (Bucheli 2010; Bucheli and Sommer 2014). Bucheli (2008) has also shown how in the case of the United Fruit Company in Central America that similar political interests (such as anti-unionism) were not sufficient to guarantee cooperation from a host government.

These cases illustrate not only the adjustment of market strategies by MNEs but also their non-market strategies. Corporate political activities, in the form of lobbying and relationship building with national governments were a core element of these MNEs' strategies, even if they were not always successful. These political activities took many forms (Nye 1974) – from outright illegal activities like bribery and corruption (Dosal 1993; Bucheli & Minefee in this volume) to behind-the-scenes lobbying (Culpepper 2011) and on to open involvement in standard-setting (Moguen-Toursel 2002; Ramírez Pérez 2007) and institution building (Ringe and Rollings 2000). Many of these activities occurred through the auspices of business interest associations but individual multinationals also acted directly. In addition, multinational firms were also at the heart of more general business lobbying (Rollings 2014; Phillips-Fein and Zelizer 2012; John and Phillips-Fein 2017; Waterhouse 2014). From this a more nuanced picture of political influence has emerged which has explored less direct and softer forms of influence but which, once more, illustrates the complexity and contingency of the relationship between MNEs and governments.

The final, if still emergent, contribution by business historians relates to the appropriate level of governance of MNEs. From the outset Raymond Vernon argued that conflict between MNEs and national governments was inevitable because of the ability of MNEs to exploit differences in national policies. Vernon became exercised over issues like transfer pricing and taxation (Eden 2000): governance and regulation needed to become more uniform, be it through bilateral treaties, or institutions of regional or global regulation. As many have argued, the danger without such action is a continued 'race to the bottom' in the desire to attract investment. The next two sections explore these issues in more depth by examining two particular areas of study. The first, business and European integration, is the more established but still developing, while the second, multinationals and taxation, remains nascent, despite Vernon's long-standing concerns.

European integration

European integration offers an interesting angle on IBGR because of its supranational dimension. What has been the effect of the existence of the European Union (EU) on the development of global business, as a market, as a regulator and as a new forum for MNE influence. Surprisingly few works in business history deal directly with the first issue. The most obvious exception to this is Jones and Miskell (2005) which examines Unilever's restructuring strategy in light of European integration. Ramírez Pérez (2007) has also published work on the automobile industry.

In terms of regulation, there is one area where MNEs have been directly and powerfully affected by European Economic Community (EEC)/EU institutions: competition policy. One needs only to think of the recent cases against Microsoft and Google over abuse of dominant position and the hefty fines imposed on numerous MNEs for cartel misbehaviour to be aware of the EU's profound influence here (Damro and Guay 2016; Cini and McGowan 2008). Historians have already developed an extensive historiography of the development of EEC competition policy and now business historians are also beginning to contribute to this field.[2] A forthcoming special issue of *Business History* (edited by Rollings and Warlouzet) presents cases of business responses to various aspects of EEC competition policy in the computer industry, aluminum industry, the paper and pulp industry, shipbuilding, car distribution and boiler makers.

The other side of the coin is the impact of MNEs on European integration. European integration is traditionally seen as something to the advantage of MNEs as they can exploit economies of scale associated with the larger market: the European Roundtable of Industrialists, for example, has been credited by some with relaunching European integration in the early 1980s (Green Cowles 1995). Politically there have also been possibilities for standardisation and harmonisation of regulatory regimes. On the other hand, the existence of supranational political institutions is likely to reduce the bargaining power of MNEs.

MNEs were closely linked with the process of integration. This was particularly the case of US multinationals which followed the lead of Marshall Aid to Western Europe by embarking on a massive expansion of foreign direct investment (Wilkins 1974). Such was the influx of US MNEs by the 1970s that not only was it common to refer to the notion of the Americanisation of Europe (McCreary 1964), but also that 'It has become a cliché that American companies have integrated the European economies' (Behrman 1972: 50; Wilkins 1996; Tolliday 2003). However, historians of European integration rejected this argument, proposing that European integration was a process internal to Europe. Initially, this historiography was dominated by diplomatic historians but even when economic historians analyzed European integration such arguments still held no sway (Milward 1992, 2006; Guirao *et al.* 2012). This was because the focus of European integration historians was on the emergence and development of the political institutions of the EEC and this placed national governments and the nation-state at the heart of European integration (for overviews see Dinan 2014: 345–75; Loth 2008; Kaiser and Varsori 2010).

Recently, historians of European integration have begun to reassess this position and to redefine the meaning of European integration and, with that, the key actors involved. The outcome has been an appreciation of a much broader notion of European integration. In the early years of European integration there were multiple competing and overlapping notions of European integration, not just the EEC. Limiting attention to the EEC is overly deterministic (Rollings and Kipping 2008). Linked to this has been a move to bring society back in (Kaiser and Starie 2005; Kaiser *et al.* 2009; Kaiser and Meyer 2013). One element here is the role of business actors and business lobbying in influencing the course of European integration. An increasingly extensive historiography has appeared looking at this from a national level and from a European level. Some of this relates to business representative bodies and trade associations (Morival 2014, 2015; Rollings 2007; Geven 2014; Badel and Michel 2011) where MNE influence on EEC political institutions can be seen but is indirect, but also to the direct actions of MNEs (Moguen-Toursel 2002, 2007; Ramírez Pérez 2007, 2008, 2009a, 2009b). This was particularly the case in areas of what might be termed low politics.

A separate, but related, development in the historiography of European integration has flowed from Misa and Schot's (2005) article on 'the hidden integration' of Europe. This was the starting point for a series of publications exploring the spread of technological innovations across Europe and the related network linkages. These provided the infrastructure for drawing Europe together, not necessarily on the basis of the six countries that went on to create the EEC but, nevertheless, providing a framework and linkages from which political integration might emerge (Kaiser and Schot 2014; Kohlrausch and Trischler 2014). Often these studies show how networks of experts, including businessmen, built links through the construction of transnational infrastructure projects (Van der Vleuten and Kaijser 2006; Lagendijk 2008; Badenoch and Fickers 2010; Högselius *et al.* 2015). Coming full circle in the historiography, Paju and Haigh (2016) draw inspiration from this approach to elaborate IBM's approach to Western Europe after the Second World War and show how IBM embraced European integration 'by engineering its own networks of interdependence among European nations' (268). We are beginning to see more clearly the ways in which MNEs contributed towards European integration both directly and indirectly and were affected by it too.

Multinationals and taxation

The second area of focus, multinationals and taxation, is clearly a current issue of popular concern with the publicity given to the low levels of corporate taxation paid by many multinationals. Historical analysis of the development of this trend is nascent but has moved forward significantly in the last couple of years. This offers two important ways to improve our understanding of the growth of multinationals. First, there are the organisational implications for multinationals. According to the *New York Times*, Enron at the time of its collapse had 881 subsidiaries in tax havens, including 692 in the Cayman Islands and 119 in the Turks and Caicos Islands (quoted in Palan 2003: 193 fn7). Related to this, a raft of literature exists on the phenomenon of transfer pricing, whereby multinationals move goods and services between subsidiaries to maximise tax efficiency (avoid taxation) (for an overview see Eden 1998), but most is from a narrowly economic or tax perspective. Little work, to date, has considered the organisational implications of the growing complexity of these structures, or the consequences in terms of the internal organisational dynamics of its operations, with the focus remaining on the production and delivery of goods and services. Business historians need to explore the historical development of these changing organisational forms.

Second, and developing this last point, the long-term development of this phenomenon requires exploration. Most work in this field assumes that this is a post-1945 phenomenon linked to the spread of US multinationals and the emergence of the Eurodollar markets. A literature is beginning to question this assumption but largely from the perspective of the establishment of tax havens (Palan *et al.* 2010; Zucman 2015; Sagar *et al.* 2013). Ogle (2017) and Palan (2003) have adopted a more historical approach. They both emphasise (a) the importance of a longer-term approach to the development of tax havens, often with their roots in empire and (b) that the tax havens often were of value to the very national governments who, as a result, lost tax revenue.

The period before the Second World War is also beginning to be studied on its own merits by a new generation of historians. Farquet (2013, 2016) has explored the interwar development of Switzerland as a tax haven. Similarly, Izawa in his PhD and various conference presentations has analysed the emergence of double taxation agreements after the First World War. Significantly, he also examines the role of multinational business in this process, including their development of subsidiaries to avoid double taxation (Izawa 2015) and their political activities (Izawa 2017). Here then is a nascent emergent field of study for business historians.[3]

Like the study of cartels, business records for the period before the Second World War can reveal the extent to which MNEs engaged with issues about taxation. For the period after 1945 business records may be less forthcoming given the lack of transparency around such issues, the sensitivity of companies to public disclosure of such activities and the complexity of the structures created. However, alternative sources do exist and are yet to be exploited systematically. First, there are the enormous collection of records of tobacco companies made available via the Truth Tobacco Industry Documents (previously known as the Legacy Tobacco Documents Library) (www.industrydocumentslibrary.ucsf.edu/tobacco/). The 15 million documents available online include some on tax avoidance and on the use of tax havens by tobacco companies. A second source is the collections of records released by the International Consortium of Investigative Journalists as the Panama Papers, the Paradise Papers and similar records, some of which date back to the 1970s (https://offshoreleaks.icij.org/). Finally, government records do sometimes deal with multinationals' tax affairs as well as tax havens, in addition to the studies carried out by international bodies like the Organisation for Economic Co-operation and Development (OECD). For example, in the 1970s the UK government carried out examinations of transfer pricing, concluding that fears about the practice were a good deal exaggerated and that there was no systematic and widespread abuse by multinationals. Nevertheless, what stood out was the diversity of practice: multinational structures provided scope for tax avoidance and in 1976 the Inland Revenue was examining 180 companies on this issue (TNA 1976). A year earlier a Customs and Excise 'Group of Four', established to examine these issues, noted that the cases which had been most financially productive for the UK included Fison (fertilisers), Beecham (pharmaceuticals) and the US multinational Halliburton in addition to the more famous case of Hoffmann La Roche (TNA 1975). Studying this topic may not be straightforward but is beginning to happen and seems timely given the significance attached to the topic.

Conclusions

If one accepts that markets and companies are embedded in a wider economic, social and political context then it is inevitable that governments will be a fundamental influence on business through their regulations, their laws, their taxes and their policies. As noted at the outset, territoriality distinguishes international business and MNEs from other forms of business. Without nation-states and national governments there would not be MNEs. European integration amends this picture but not in any fundamental way. In addition, while conflict between MNEs and governments may be widespread, there can also be cooperation. More importantly, this is only one element of a more complex relationship where context and contingency matter. Equally, this is a two-way relationship where multinationals also influence national governments via a range of corporate political activities. Yet, once more, this has not been a straightforward process of political influence. Historical study of the making of global business again shows the importance of contingency and context. As a result, it is only with further cases that we will begin to be able to discern patterns among those contingencies in any systematic way. In other words, there is plenty of need (and scope) for more of the same – for more case studies exploring MNE–home, and MNE–host-country government relations – to provide a fuller and more detailed understanding of the complexities of these relationships.

Raymond Vernon's solution to the potential conflicts between MNEs and national governments was to move towards forms of transnational governance. The history of European integration and studies around this issue of multinationals and taxation have shown that while this may offer some solutions these are, again, not straightforward. As illustrated in the case of tax havens, this is because it is false to depict the relationship between international business and governments as a zero-sum power game of political competitors. Rather, there is a symbiotic interdependent relationship but one which is fluid and dependent on context and circumstances.

Notes

1 According to Luyckx and Janssens (2016) this was the first article in *The Economist* to talk about MNEs directly.
2 For an overview see the introduction to the forthcoming *Business History* special issue.
3 There was a session on the topic at the 2018 World Economic History Congress in Boston.

References

Badel, Laurence and Hélène Michel (eds) (2011) *Patronats et Intégration Européenne: Pour un Dialogue Disciplinaire Raisonné* (Paris: L'Harmattan).
Badenoch, Alexander and Andreas Fickers (eds) (2010) *Materializing Europe: Transnational Infrastructures and the Project of Europe* (Basingstoke: Palgrave Macmillan).
Baron, David (1995) 'Integrated Strategy: Market and Nonmarket Components', *California Management Review* 37 (2), 47–65.
Barton, Dominic, Dezsö Horváth and Matthias Kipping (eds) (2016) *Re-Imagining Capitalism* (Oxford: Oxford University Press).
Behrman, Jack (1972) 'Industrial Integration and the Multinational Enterprise', *Annals of the American Academy of Politics and Social Science* 403, 46–57.
Boddewyn, Jean (2005) 'Early US Business-School Literature (1960–1975) on International Business–Government Relations: Its Twenty-First-Century Relevance', in Robert Grosse (ed.), *International Business and Government Relations in the 21st Century* (Cambridge: Cambridge University Press), 27–47.
Boddewyn, Jean (2016) 'International Business–Government Relations Research 1945–2015: Concepts, Typologies, Theories and Methodologies', *Journal of World Business* 51, 10–22.
Bonica, Adam (2016) 'Avenues of Influence: On the Political Expenditures of Corporations and their Directors and Executives', *Business and Politics* 18 (4), 367–94.
Bowen, Huw (2005) *The Business of Empire: The East India Company and Imperial Britain, 1756–1833* (Cambridge: Cambridge University Press).
Bucheli, Marcelo (2008) *Bananas and Business: The United Fruit Company in Columbia, 1899–2000* (New York: New York University Press).
Bucheli, Marcelo (2010) 'Multinational Corporations, Business Groups, and Economic Nationalism: Standard Oil (New Jersey), Royal Dutch-Shell, and Energy Politics in Chile 1913–2005', *Enterprise & Society* 11 (2), 350–99.

Bucheli, Marcelo and Gonzalo Romero Sommer (2014) 'Multinational Corporations, Property Rights and Legitimization Strategies: US Investors in the Argentine and Peruvian Oil Industries in the Twentieth Century', *Australian Economic History Review* 54 (2), 145–63.

Calvo, Angel (2008) 'State, Firms and Technology: The Rise of Multinational Telecommunications Companies: ITT and the *Compañía Telefónica Nacional de España*, 1924–1945', *Business History* 50 (4), 455–73.

Carlos, Ann and Stephen Nicholas (1988) '"Giants of an Earlier Capitalism": The Chartered Trading Companies as Modern Multinationals', *Business History Review* 62 (3), 398–419.

Cini, Michelle and Lee McGowan (2008) *Competition Policy in the European Union* (Basingstoke: Palgrave Macmillan).

Clifton, Judith, Francisco Comin and Daniel Díaz-Fuentes (2011) 'From National Monopoly to Multinational Corporation: How Regulation Shaped the Road towards Telecommunications Internationalisation', *Business History* 53 (5), 761–81.

Colli, Andrea (2016) *Dynamics of International Business: Comparative Perspectives of Firms, Markets and Entrepreneurship* (Abingdon: Routledge).

Culpepper, Pepper (2011) *Quiet Politics and Business Power: Corporate Control in Europe and Japan* (Cambridge: Cambridge University Press).

Damro, Chad and Terence Guay (2016) *European Competition Policy and Globalization* (Basingstoke: Palgrave Macmillan).

Decker, Stephanie (2011) 'Corporate Political Activity in Less Developed Countries: The Volta River Project in Ghana, 1958–66', *Business History* 53 (7), 993–1017.

Dehne, Phillip (2013) 'The Resilience of Globalisation during the First World War: The Case of Bunge and Born in Argentina', in Christof Dejung and Niels Petersson (eds), *The Foundations of Worldwide Economic Integration: Power, Institutions, and Global Markets, 1850–1930* (Cambridge: Cambridge University Press), 228–48.

Dejung, Christof and Niels Petersson (2013) 'Introduction: Power, Institutions, and Global Markets – Actors, Mechanisms, and Foundations of Worldwide Economic Integration, 1850–1930', in Christof Dejung and Niels Petersson (eds), *The Foundations of Worldwide Economic Integration: Power, Institutions, and Global Markets, 1850–1930* (Cambridge: Cambridge University Press), 1–17.

Dinan, Desmond (2014) *The Origins and Evolution of the European Union* (Oxford: Oxford University Press).

Donzé, Pierre-Yves (2015) 'Siemens and the Construction of Hospitals in Latin America, 1949–1964', *Business History Review* 89, 475–502.

Donzé, Pierre-Yves and Takafumi Kurosawa (2013) 'Nestlé Coping with Japanese Nationalism: Political Risk and the Strategy of a Foreign Multinational Enterprise in Japan, 1913–45', *Business History* 55 (8), 1318–38.

Dosal, Paul (1993) *Doing Business with the Dictators: A Political History of United Fruit in Guatemala 1899–1944* (Wilmington, DE: Scholarly Resources).

Dunning, John and Sarianna Lundan (2008) *Multinational Enterprises and the Global Economy* 2nd edn (Cheltenham: Edward Elgar).

Economist, The (1964) 'Companies Outgrow Countries: A New Kind of Economic Animal – Mastodons of the Future? – Is Displacing Growing Weight Throughout the World Economy', 17 October.

Economist, The (2017) 'In Retreat: The Multinational Company is in Trouble', 28 January.

Eden, Lorraine (1998) *Taxing Multinationals: Transfer Pricing and Corporate Income Taxation in North America* (Toronto: University of Toronto Press).

Eden, Lorraine (2000) 'The Realist Adjusts the Sails: Vernon and MNE–State Relations over Three Decades', *Journal of International Management* 6, 335–42.

Farquet, Christophe (2013) 'Tax Avoidance, Collective Resistance, and International Negotiations: Foreign Tax Refusal by Swiss Banks and Industries Between the Two World Wars', *Journal of Policy History* 25 (3), 334–53.

Farquet, Christophe (2016) *La Défense du Paradis Fiscal Suisse avant la Seconde Guerre Mondiale: Une Histoire Internationale* (Neuchâtel: Éditions Alphil).

Fear, Jeff (2008) 'Cartels', in Geoffrey Jones and Jonathan Zeitlin (eds), *The Oxford Handbook of Business History* (Oxford: Oxford University Press), 268–92.

Fitzgerald, Robert (2015) *The Rise of the Global Economy: Multinationals and the Making of the Modern World* (Cambridge: Cambridge University Press).

Frank, Alison (2009) 'The Petroleum War of 1910: Standard Oil, Austria, and the Limits of the Multinational Corporation', *American Historical Review* 114 (1), 16–41.

George, Susan (2015) *Shadow Sovereigns: How Global Corporations are Seizing Power* (Cambridge: Polity Press).

Geven, Ruud (2014) *Transnational Networks and the Common Market: Business Views on European Integration, 1950–1980* (Maastricht: Universitaire Pers Maastricht).

Green Cowles, Maria (1995) 'Setting the Agenda for a New Europe: The ERT and EC 1992', *Journal of Common Market Studies* 33 (4), 501–26.

Grosse, Robert (2005) 'Introduction', in Robert Grosse (ed.), *International Business and Government Relations in the 21st Century* (Cambridge: Cambridge University Press), 3–21.

Guirao, Fernando, Frances Lynch and Sigfrido Ramírez Pérez (eds) (2012) *Alan S. Milward and a Century of European Change* (Abingdon: Routledge).

Henisz, Witold and Bennet Zelner (2010) 'The Hidden Risks in Emerging Markets', *Harvard Business Review* 88 (4), 88–95.

Hertz, Noreena (2001) *The Silent Takeover: Global Capitalism and the Death of Democracy* (New York: Free Press).

Högselius, Per, Arne Kaijser and Erik van der Vleuten (2015) *Europe's Infrastructure Transition: Economy, War, Nature* (Basingstoke: Palgrave Macmillan).

Hymer, Stephen (1976) *The International Operation of National Firms: A Study of Direct Foreign Investment* (Cambridge, MA: MIT Press).

Izawa, Ryo (2015) 'The Formation of Companies for Tax Avoidance: The Relationship between UK Multinationals and International Double Taxation in the Interwar Period', *Business and Economic History On-Line* 13, 1–10.

Izawa, Ryo (2017) 'Dynamics of the British Multinational Enterprises and International Tax Regulation, 1914–1945', *Centre for Risk Research Shiga University Discussion Paper No. A-26*.

John, Richard and Kim Phillips-Fein (eds) (2017) *Capital Gains: Business and Politics in Twentieth-century America* (Philadelphia, PA: University of Pennsylvania Press).

Jones, Geoffrey (ed.) (1990) *Banks as Multinationals* (London: Routledge).

Jones, Geoffrey (1993) *British Multinational Banking 1830–1990* (Oxford: Clarendon Press).

Jones, Geoffrey (2000) *Merchants to Multinationals: British Trading Companies in the Nineteenth and Twentieth Centuries* (Oxford: Oxford University Press).

Jones, Geoffrey (2005) *Multinationals and Global Capitalism: From the Nineteenth to the Twenty-First Century* (Oxford: Oxford University Press).

Jones, Geoffrey (2008) 'Globalization', in Geoffrey Jones and Jonathan Zeitlin (eds), *The Oxford Handbook of Business History* (Oxford: Oxford University Press), 141–68.

Jones, Geoffrey and Peter Miskell (2005) 'European Integration and Corporate Restructuring: The Strategy of Unilever, c.1957–c.1990', *Economic History Review* 58 (1), 113–39.

Kaiser, Wolfram, Brigitte Leucht and Morten Rasmussen (eds) (2009) *The History of the European Union: Origins of a Trans- and Supranational Polity 1950–72* (Abingdon: Routledge).

Kaiser, Wolfram and Jan-Henrik Meyer (eds) (2013) *Societal Actors in European Integration: Polity-Building and Policy-Making 1958–1992* (Basingstoke: Palgrave Macmillan).

Kaiser, Wolfram and Johan Schot (2014) *Writing the Rules for Europe: Experts, Cartels, and International Organizations* (Basingstoke: Palgrave Macmillan).

Kaiser, Wolfram and Peter Starie (eds) (2005) *Transnational European Union: Towards a Common Political Space* (Abingdon: Routledge).

Kaiser, Wolfram and Antonio Varsori (eds) (2010) *European Union History: Themes and Debates* (Basingstoke: Palgrave Macmillan).

Kim, Dong-Woon (1995) 'J. & P. Coats in Tsarist Russia, 1889–1917', *Business History Review* 69, 465–93.

Kindleberger, Charles (1969) *American Business Abroad: Six Lectures on Direct Investment* (New Haven, CT: Yale University Press).

Kindleberger, Charles (1989) 'Summary: Reflections on the Papers and the Debate on Multinational Enterprise: International Finance, Markets and Governments in the Twentieth Century', in Alice Teichova, Maurice Lévy-Leboyer and Helga Nussbaum (eds), *Historical Studies in International Corporate Business* (Cambridge: Cambridge University Press), 229–39.

Kobrak, Christopher and Per Hansen (eds) (2004) *European Business, Dictatorship, and Political Risk, 1920–1945* (New York: Berghahn).

Kobrin, Stephen (2001) 'Sovereignty @ Bay: Globalization, Multinational Enterprise, and the International Political System', in Alan Rugman and Thomas Brewer (eds), *The Oxford Handbook of International Business* (Oxford: Oxford University Press), 181–205.

Kohlrausch, Martin and Helmuth Trischler (2014) *Building Europe on Expertise: Innovators, Organizers, Networkers* (Basingstoke: Palgrave Macmillan).

Korten, David C. (2001) *When Corporations Rule the World* 2nd edn (Bloomfield, CN: Kumarian Press).

Lagendijk, Vincent (2008) *Electrifying Europe: The Power of Europe in the Construction of Electricity Networks* (Amsterdam: Aksant).

Lawton, Thomas and Tazeeb Rajwani (eds) (2015) *The Routledge Companion to Non-Market Strategy* (Abingdon: Routledge).

Lawton, Thomas, Jonathan Doh and Tazeeb Rajwani (2014) *Aligning for Advantage: Competitive Strategies for the Political and Social Arenas* (Oxford: Oxford University Press).

Lawton, Thomas, Steven McGuire and Tazeeb Rajwani (2012) 'Corporate Political Activity: A Literature Review and Research Agenda', *International Journal of Management Reviews* 15 (1), 86–105.

Linder, Marc (1994) *Projecting Capitalism: A History of the Internationalization of the Construction Industry* (Westport, CT: Greenwood).

Loth, Wilfried (2008) 'Explaining European Integration: The Contribution from Historians', *Journal of European Integration History* 14 (1), 8–26.

Lubinski, Christina (2015) 'Global Trade and Indian Politics: The German Dye Business in India before 1947', *Business History Review* 89, 503–30.

Luyckx, Joost and Maddy Janssens (2016) 'Discursive Legitimation of a Contested Actor over Time: The Multinational Corporation as a Historical Case (1964–2012)', *Organization Studies* 37 (1), 1595–619.

McCreary, Edward (1964) *The Americanization of Europe: The Impact of Americans and American Business on the Uncommon Market* (Garden City, NY: Doubleday).

Merrett, David (2007) 'Sugar and Copper: Postcolonial Experiences of Australian Multinationals', *Business History Review* 81, 213–36.

Milward, Alan (1992) *The European Rescue of the Nation-State* (London: Routledge).

Milward, Alan (2006) 'History, Political Science and European Integration', in Knud Erik Jørgensen, Mark Pollack and Ben Rosamond (eds), *Handbook of European Union Politics* (London: Sage), 99–103.

Misa, Thomas and Johan Schot (2005) 'Inventing Europe: Technology and the Hidden Integration of Europe', *History and Technology*, 21 (1), 1–20.

Moguen-Toursel, Marine (2002) *L'Ouverture Des Frontieres Europeennes Dans Les Annees 50: Fruit D'Une Concertation Avec Les Industriels?* (Brussels: PIE – Peter Lang).

Moguen-Toursel, Marine (ed.) (2007) *Stratégies d'Éntreprise et Action Publique Dans l'Europe Intégrée (1950–1980): Affrontement et Apprentissage des Acteurs* (Brussels: PIE – Peter Lang).

Morival, Yann (2014) 'Passage à Bruxelles et Structuration Nationale de l'Intérêt Européen au sein du CNPF', *Relations Internationales* 157 (2), 97–109.

Morival, Yann (2015) 'Les Europes du Patronat: L'Enjeu "Europe" dans les Organisations Patronales Françaises depuis 1948' (PhD EHESS, Paris).

Nye, Joseph (1974) 'Multinational Corporations in World Politics', *Foreign Affairs* 53 (1), 153–75.

Ogle, Vanessa (2017) 'Archipelago Capitalism: Tax Havens, Offshore Money, and the State, 1950s–1970s' *American Historical Review* 122 (5), 1431–58.

Ohmae, Kenichi (1990) *The Borderless World: Power and Strategy in the Interlinked Economy* (New York: HarperCollins).

Oliver, Christine and Holzinger, Ingo (2008) 'The Effectiveness of Strategic Political Management: A Dynamic Capabilities Framework' *Academy of Management Review* 33 (2), 496–520.

Paju, Petri and Thomas Haigh (2016) 'IBM Rebuilds Europe: The Curious Case of the Transnational Typewriter', *Enterprise & Society* 17 (2), 265–300.

Palan, Ronen (2003) *The Offshore World: Sovereign Markets, Virtual Places, and Nomad Millionaires* (Ithaca, NY: Cornell University Press).

Palan, Ronen, Richard Murphy and Christian Chavagneux (2010) *Tax Havens: How Globalization Really Works* (Ithaca, NY: Cornell University Press).

Phillips-Fein, Kim and Julian Zelizer (eds) (2012) *What's Good for Business: Business and American Politics since World War II* (Oxford: Oxford University Press).

Quek, Mary (2012) 'Globalising the Hotel Industry 1946–68: A Multinational Case Study of the Intercontinental Hotel Corporation', *Business History* 54 (2), 201–26.

Ramírez Pérez, Sigfrido (2007) 'Public Policies, European Integration and Multinational Corporations in the Automobile Sector: The French and Italian Cases in a Comparative Perspective 1945–1973' (PhD, Florence: EUI).

Ramírez Pérez, Sigfrido (2008) 'La Politique de la Concurrence de la Communauté Économique Européenne et L'Industrie: L'Exemple des Accords sur la Distribution Automobile (1972–1985)', in *La Politique de la Concurrence Communautaire: Origins et Développement*, special issue of *Histoire, Économie & Société*, edited by Eric Bussière and Laurent Warlouzet (Paris: Armand Colin), 63–77.

Ramírez Pérez, Sigfrido (2009a) 'The Role of the Committee of Common Market Automobile Constructors', in Wolfram Kaiser, Brigitte Leucht and Morten Rasmussen (eds), *The History of the European Union: Origins of a Trans- and Supranational Polity 1950–1972* (Abingdon: Routledge), 74–93.

Ramírez Pérez, Sigfrido (2009b) 'The French Automobile Industry and the Treaty of Rome: Between Welfare State and Multinational Corporations 1955–1958', in Michael Gehler (ed.), *From Common Market to European Union Building: 50 Years of the Rome Treaties 1957–2007* (Vienna: Böhlau Verlag), 169–94.

Rhodes, R.A.W. (1997) *Understanding Governance: Policy Networks, Governance, Reflexivity and Accountability* (Buckingham: Open University Press).

Ringe, Astrid and Neil Rollings (2000) 'Responding to Relative Decline: The Creation of the National Economic Development Council', *Economic History Review* 53 (2), 331–53.

Rollings, Neil (2007) *British Business in the Formative Years of European Integration, 1945–1973* (Cambridge: Cambridge University Press).

Rollings, Neil (2011) 'Multinational Enterprise and Government Controls on Outward Foreign Direct Investment in the United States and the United Kingdom in the 1960s', *Enterprise & Society* 12 (2), 398–434.

Rollings, Neil (2014) 'The Twilight World of British Business Politics: The Spring Sunningdale Conferences since the 1960s', *Business History*, 56 (6), 915–35.

Rollings, Neil and Matthias Kipping (2008) 'Private Transnational Governance in the Hey-day of the Nation-state: The Council of European Industrial Federations (CEIF)', *Economic History Review* 61 (2), 409–31.

Sagar, Paul, John Christensen and Nick Shaxson (2013) 'British Government Attitudes to British Tax Havens: An Examination of Whitehall Responses to the Growth of Tax Havens in British Dependent Territories from 1967–75', in Jeremy Leaman and Attiya Waris (eds), *Tax Justice and the Political Economy of Global Capitalism, 1945 to the Present* (New York: Berghahn Books), 107–32.

Sandvik, Pål Thonstad and Espen Storli (2013) 'Big Business and Small States: Unilever and Norway in the Interwar Years', *Economic History Review* 66 (1), 109–31.

Scott, Peter and Tim Rooth (1999) 'Public Policy and Foreign-based Enterprises in Britain Prior to the Second World War', *Historical Journal* 42 (2), 495–515.

Strange, Susan (1996) *The Retreat of the State: The Diffusion of Power in the World Economy* (Cambridge: Cambridge University Press).

TNA (1975) The (UK) National Archives, IR 40/18828, FW Fawcett to Collins 'Manipulation of Transfer Pricing by Multinational Companies', 3 June.

TNA (1976) The (UK) National Archives, IR 40/18828, 'Report of an Interdepartmental Group on Multinationals and Artificial Transfer Pricing', July, 10.

Tolliday, Steven (2003) 'The Origins of Ford of Europe: From Multidomestic to Transnational Corporation, 1903–1976', in Hubert Bonin, Yannick Lang and Stephen Tolliday (eds), *Ford, 1903–2003: The European History Volume 1* (Paris: PLAGE), 177–241.

Tworek, Heidi (2015) 'Political and Economic News in the Age of Multinationals', *Business History Review* 89, 447–74.

Van der Vleuten, Erik and Arne Kaijser (eds) (2006) *Networking Europe: Transnational Infrastructures and the Shaping of Europe, 1850–2000* (Sagamore Beach, MA: Science History Publications).

Verma, Shraddha and Neveen Abdelrehim (2017) 'Oil Multinationals and Governments in Post-Colonial Transitions: Burmah Shell, the Burmah Oil Company and the Indian State 1947–70', *Business History* 59 (3), 342–61.

Vernon, Raymond (1971) *Sovereignty at Bay: The Multinational Spread of U.S. Enterprises* (New York: Basic Books).

Vernon, Raymond (1977) *Storm over the Multinationals: The Real Issues* (London: Macmillan).

Vernon, Raymond (1991) 'Sovereignty at Bay: Twenty Years After', *Millennium: Journal of International Studies* 20 (2), 191–6.

Vernon, Raymond (1998) *In the Hurricane's Eye: The Troubled Prospects of Multinational Enterprises* (Cambridge, MA: Harvard University Press).

Waterhouse, Benjamin (2014) *Lobbying America: The Politics of Business from Nixon to NAFTA* (Princeton, NJ: Princeton University Press).

Wilkins, Mira (1970) *The Emergence of Multinational Enterprise: American Business Abroad from the Colonial Era to 1914* (Cambridge, MA: Harvard University Press).

Wilkins, Mira (1974) *The Maturing of Multinational Enterprise: American Business Abroad from 1914 to 1970* (Cambridge, MA: Harvard University Press).

Wilkins, Mira (1996) 'US Multinationals and the Unification of Europe', in F. Heller and John Gillingham (eds), *The United States and the Integration of Europe: Legacies of the Postwar Era* (Basingstoke: Macmillan), 341–63.

Wilkins, Mira (1998) 'The Significance of the Concept and a Future Agenda', in Mira Wilkins and Harm Schröter (eds), *The Free-Standing Company in the World Economy 1830–1996* (Oxford: Oxford University Press), 421–39.

Wilkins, Mira (2004) *The History of Foreign Investment in the United States 1914–1945* (Cambridge, MA: Harvard University Press).

Wilkins, Mira (2009) 'Multinational Enterprise in Insurance: An Historical Overview', *Business History* 51 (3), 334–63.

Wubs, Ben (2008) *International Business and National War Interests: Unilever between Reich and Empire, 1939–45* (Abingdon: Routledge).

Zucman, Gabriel (2015) *The Hidden Wealth of Nations: The Scourge of Tax Havens* (Chicago, IL: University of Chicago Press).

7

BANKS AND CAPITAL MARKETS

Youssef Cassis

In the last analysis, global business comes down to international capital flows. And international capital flows require an intermediation process, which is provided by the financial institutions and markets gathered in the leading international financial centres. In the course of the last two centuries, financial institutions and markets have thus played a decisive role in the making of global business. In many ways, they could be seen as having *enabled* it. International financial centres provide a convenient vantage point from which to consider this role. They can be defined as the grouping together, in a given urban space, of a certain number of financial services; in a more functional way, they could be defined as a place where intermediaries coordinate financial transactions and arrange for payments to be made (Kindleberger, 1974; Roberts, 1994). A financial centre's influence can be limited to a single country, it can extend to a region of the world, or it can be truly global and provide financial facilities to the entire planet. The makers of global business are thus the financial institutions and markets – and those who run them – located in the handful of truly international, indeed global financial centres – though the global significance of lesser centres should not be entirely dismissed.

One of the particular features of international financial centres is the high concentration of global players that can be found on a fairly small geographical area – a square mile in arguably the most global of all, the City of London. Nowhere else has it ever been possible to find such a great number of multinational enterprises within a few hundred yards of one another. Banks have of course been the most significant – they include the head offices of domestic banks with a network of branches in other countries, as well as the branches, often of considerable dimension, of foreign banks. The same applies to other financial institutions, in the first place insurance companies. Moreover, leading multinational companies in other sectors (natural resources, manufacturing) have usually established their head office in an international financial centre – a trend that has increased in the course of the twentieth century. For their part, capital markets have been no less global, but in a different way, by issuing securities on behalf of borrowers from across the world, to investors from across the world, with the possibilities to trade them in a single exchange and arbitrate between exchanges.

The classic work on the history of international financial centre remains Youssef Cassis's *Capitals of Capital*, which provides an analysis of the rise and decline of the leading centres from the late eighteenth to the early twenty-first century (Cassis, 2006, 2010). The story has been further updated to take stock of the situation ten years after the crisis (Cassis and Wojcik, 2018).

Individual financial centres have been unevenly studied. While the history of the City of London is by now fairly well known (Michie, 1992; Kynaston, 1994, 1995, 2000, 2001), that of New York (Geisst, 1997; Fraser, 2005), Paris (Quennouëlle-Corre, 2015), or Berlin and Frankfurt (Pohl, 2002; Holtfrerich, 1999) offers scope for investigation on specific aspects of their development as well as broad syntheses; and there is no history of Tokyo as a financial centre available in English. Information and analysis on other centres, especially their very recent history, can be found in Richard Roberts's now slightly dated four volumes compendium (Roberts, 1994). Banks and capital markets have of course been extensively studied at both domestic and international levels. More specific works are available on multinational banking, with Geoffrey Jones's definitive study on Britain (1993), and more patchy works on other countries (Jones, 1990; Kobrak, 2008). On the international securities market, Ranald Michie's masterly study (2006) can be complemented by some of the essays gathered by Quennouëlle-Corre and Cassis (2011) on financial centres and international capital flows. A recent *Oxford Handbook* (Cassis *et al.*, 2016) presents the state of the art in banking and financial history, including on issues directly related to the making of global business, such as multinational and transnational banking, securities markets, international capital flows, or sovereign defaults.

This chapter will look at the makers of global business from the perspective of international financial centres, with particular attention to the multinational banks and global capital markets that have been at the heart of their activities. It will concentrate on the leading financial centres, which have been home to global business in the financial sector, and whose activities have enabled the emergence of global businesses in all sectors. It will follow a chronological order, with one globalisation of the world economy at each end – the first, starting in the 1870s, and the second a century later. The period in between, from the 1930s to the 1970s, was indeed a period of receding international capital movements and reduced activities of international financial centres, yet this did not herald the end of global businesses.

The first modern globalisation, 1870s–1914

Foreign investment began to grow substantially from the mid-1850s, the capital stock invested outside its country of origin going from just under $1 billion in 1855 (it was at the same level 30 years earlier) to $7.7 billion in 1870. It then rose to $23.8 billion in 1900 and to $38.7 billion in 1914 (Obstfeld and Taylor, 2004). Throughout these years, Britain was the largest exporter of capital (42 per cent in 1913), followed by France (20 per cent), and, later in the nineteenth century, Germany (13 per cent). The United States became a capital exporting country by the turn of the twentieth century; while small European countries (Belgium, the Netherlands, and Switzerland) exported substantial amounts of capital, especially when measured as a proportion of their GDP (gross domestic product). Global financial institutions and markets developed in the financial capital of these countries and enabled the development of global business across the world.

In the four decades preceding the First World War, the City of London was the world's leading financial centre (Michie, 1992; Kynaston, 1994, 1995; Cassis, 2006). Paris was a strong challenger in the 1850s and 1860s, but the defeat of France by Prussia in 1871 put an end to Parisian ambitions. London's position reflected Britain's dominant position in the world economy, even though it had been overtaken by the United States in terms of GDP by the early 1870s (Maddison, 2001). Britain's position rested on the leadership it retained in foreign trade, services and finance, and the role of the pound sterling as the cornerstone of the international monetary system, the gold standard, with the Bank of England, to use Keynes's words, as its 'conductor' and whose leadership the other central banks were prepared to follow in order to maintain monetary stability (Eichengreen, 1996).

The City of London offered an unrivalled range of financial services on a global scale. First, the bulk of world trade was financed through the medium of bills of exchange drawn on London. And, second, with nearly 50 per cent of foreign capital held by British investors, London was the main centre for the issue of foreign securities, on behalf of governments and large corporations, above all railway companies. These two essential functions were carried out by a group of private banking houses known as merchant banks – because of their former and in some cases persisting links with international trade (Chapman, 1984). The issuing business, the most prestigious activity in international business, was the preserve of the most select houses (Rothschilds, Barings, Morgan Grenfell, Hambros, Schroders, and a few others, including Kleinworts, the leading accepting house). The accepting business (in other words guaranteeing the payment of a bill of exchange when it came to maturity) was the bread and butter of a growing number of firms, possibly as many as 105 in 1914, several of them from abroad. Another group of merchant houses, described as 'investment groups' (Chapman, 1992) or 'trading companies' (Jones, 2000), moved towards a third line of global financial business and opted to organise and finance the often vast shipping, commercial, financial, and manufacturing operations carried out abroad and in the empire by their branches and correspondents – firms like Jardine Matheson, Mackinnon Mackenzie, Balfour Williamson, or Antony Gibbs, to quote but a few – and were also involved in accepting and issuing activities.

These merchant banks and investment groups were mostly long-established family-owned partnerships, operating at the very heart of the world's financial capital. The new joint stock banks, which had emerged in the mid-nineteenth century (Lloyds Bank, Midland Bank, London County and Westminster, National Provincial Bank, to name but the four largest in 1913), confined themselves to deposit banking activities within the domestic economy. But they provided the cash credit required by the City's international operations. However, another group of newly formed joint stock banks, known as overseas banks (London and River Plate Bank, Hong Kong and Shanghai Banking Corporation, Chartered Bank of India, Australia and China, Standard Bank of South Africa, and others) were directly involved in international finance. They usually had their head office in London (one exception was the Hong Kong and Shanghai Banking Corporation), but operated a network of branches in the formal and informal empire, providing facilities to merchants, especially foreign exchange, and banking services to the well-off members of the local community. While the number of overseas banks doubled (from 15 to about 30) between 1860 and 1913, the number of branches increased more than tenfold, from 132 to 1,387 (Jones, 1993).

As a result of its financial predominance, the City attracted large foreign banks that came there to seek profitable business opportunities. Crédit Lyonnais opened a branch in 1870, followed by Deutsche Bank in 1873, and during the ensuing decades most of the large foreign banks opened a branch in the City. They numbered 30 in 1913, belonging to 12 different countries, and included the major French and German banks. They were particularly strong in the field of discounting and acceptances, less so in the market for foreign loans, and participated in issue syndicates merely as members (Cassis, 2005).

Subscribers to the foreign issues floated by merchant bankers and other issuing houses were primarily individual investors. However, institutional investors started to make their mark. Insurance companies expanded considerably during this period and became more active investors with, in particular, foreign investment making up 40 per cent of their portfolio in 1914 – up from 7 per cent in 1870. And a new financial institution, investment trusts, emerged in the 1870s and matured in the 1890s and 1900s. Their assets reached £90 million by 1913 (as against £500 million for insurance companies), mainly invested in foreign stock, primarily American.

The City of London's other major activity as an international financial centre was the London Stock Exchange – a secondary market where the securities issued on the primary market could be negotiated. The nominal value of the securities listed there went from £2.3 billion in 1873 to £11.3 billion in 1913 – in other words, more than the New York Stock Exchange and the Paris Bourse combined (Michie, 1999). As evidence of its highly cosmopolitan character, foreign stocks, which represented between 35 and 40 per cent of the total in 1873, exceeded 50 per cent from 1893 onwards. By 1914 one-third of all securities in the world were quoted on the London Stock Exchange, with an increasing number of them quoted on at least one other centre, primarily New York. This gave rise to international arbitrage operations (Michie, 1987). In addition, the City hosted major commodity markets, such as the London Metal exchange (copper, tin, lead, zinc, and silver) and the Baltic Exchange (shipping).

The City also provided specialised professional services, especially legal and accounting, whose leading firms soon expanded abroad to follow their clientele or to build up a new one. Price Waterhouse, for example, opened a branch in New York in 1890 and another in Chicago in 1892, where its business took off very quickly (Jones, 1996). Finally, the City's contribution to the making of global business was partly reflected in the presence of the headquarters of a multitude of multinational enterprises for which it had been the main source of financing: shipping companies (see Harlaftis, in this volume); foreign and colonial railway companies; natural resources, including oil firms (see Boon, in this volume), like the Shell Transport and Trading Company; not to mention the London branches of companies established abroad but whose financing was largely provided by the City, such as the North American railways or the South African gold and diamond mines, like De Beers.

Such a concentration of global financial services and multinational financial companies could only be found in London. Paris has been accurately described by Alain Plessis as a "brilliant second" (2005). In the absence of any significant accepting business, its strength lay above all with its long-term capital market, especially for foreign securities, which was second only to London. However, while Britain's foreign investment was spread worldwide (with a distinct preference for the two Americas), French investors expressed a more marked preference for Europe, including Russia, as well as for the Middle East. Until the negotiations of the war indemnity loans in 1871–72, the issuing business, especially on behalf of foreign governments, had remained in the hands of the *Haute Banque* (Rothschild, Fould, Mallet, Hottinguer, Sellière, and a few others), a group of old-established banking houses akin to the London merchant banks. Thereafter, it was taken over by the new joint stock banks, in the first place the investment banks (Banque de Paris et des Pays-Bas). The *Haute Banque* remained influential and some of its members turned themselves into large investment groups. The Rothschilds, in particular, acquired major stakes in non-ferrous ores (especially in Spain) and in oil (Russia) – in addition to their banking business (Ferguson, 1998).

Unlike their British counterparts, the large French commercial banks (Crédit lyonnais, Société générale, Comptoir national d'escompte de Paris) were involved in international finance, though more in the placing than the issuing of foreign loans. They also established a network of foreign branches (Crédit lyonnais had 20 in 1913 and Comptoir d'escompte 28, not including those in the colonial empire). Overseas banks were less prominent than in the City of London, owing partly to competition from the commercial banks but mainly to France's weaker presence in the world. However, the most important among them (Banque Impériale Ottomane, Banque de l'Indochine) were forces to be reckoned with in international finance. Paris also attracted foreign banks, around 18 in 1913, more than any other centre bar London (Cassis, 2006). Finally, befitting its position as a world leading financial centre, Paris had a vibrant financial market. Though smaller and more regulated than the London Stock Exchange, the Paris Bourse was no less international, with a little over half of the stocks officially quoted having been issued by foreign governments or companies, and the proportion might well be higher if one includes the unofficial market, the *Coulisse* (Quennouëlle-Corre, 2015).

The bulk of global business took place in, or was financed through, London and Paris. Some of the international financial centres ranked behind them had a global outreach but were fairly small (Brussels, Amsterdam, Zurich); the others were fairly large but more domestically than internationally oriented (Berlin, New York).

Berlin's rise to financial prominence was a natural consequence of Germany's growing economic weight in the decades following its unification in 1871. More than anywhere else, business was dominated by the big banks (Deutsche Bank, Dresdner bank, Disconto-Gesellschaft, Darmstädter Bank). They were universal banks, engaged in both commercial and investment banking, and controlled most international financial transactions. They were also multinational banks, with a number of foreign branches, as well as subsidiaries established to conduct business in less developed countries. The Deutsche Bank, for example, created the Deutsche Überseeische Bank (active in Latin America) and the Deutsch-Asiatische Bank, the latter in conjunction with the Disconto-Gesellschaft and Bleichröder, a private bank (Hertner, 1990). German universal banks clearly supported German global businesses, especially in manufacturing industry. Interestingly, the electrical giants Siemens and AEG, which had close business and personal links with the big banks, also had their head office in Berlin. However, as a financial centre, Berlin was not in a position to rival seriously London or even Paris, if only because Germany invested far less capital abroad than Britain and France did. Significantly, only five foreign banks had a branch in Berlin in 1913 – though another nine could be found in Hamburg, a more dynamic trade centre (Cassis, 2016). Moreover, the Berlin Börse was strictly regulated in order to curb speculation and combat fraud – the law of 1896 considerably limited forward transactions, and actually prohibited them on the securities of mining and manufacturing companies. As a result, speculative transactions, which represented the bulk of stock-market business, moved out of Germany, towards Amsterdam and London in particular (Gömmel, 1992).

The financial capitals of small advanced economies could not compete on all fronts. They had to specialise in certain niches where they had a competitive advantage, and which could play a significant role in the development of global business. Brussels ranked first amongst these centres on account of the size of its largest bank, the Société Générale de Belgique, its Stock Exchange, and the presence of both multinational and foreign banks. More importantly, Brussels was the main centre for the financing of the tramways and then the power industry, mainly obtained through finance companies set up by the banks, and which usually took the form of holding companies (Société Générale Belge d'Entreprises Electriques, Sofina, Société Générale des Chemins de Fer Economiques). Brussels was ideally placed to host the headquarters of these firms, owing to the plentiful Belgian domestic savings that preferred this type of investment to foreign government funds, to the not very restrictive legislation on companies, especially in fiscal matters, and finally to the country's neutrality, enabling these companies to attract foreign – mainly German and French – capital (Hausman *et al.*, 2008). In the same way, finance companies such as Elektrobank in Zurich, Indelec in Basel, or the Société Franco-Suisse pour l'Industrie Electrique in Geneva contributed towards developing the power industry via their links with big German banks and electrical engineering companies (Paquier, 1998).

New York was in an altogether different position. It was the financial capital of the world's largest economy, yet its contribution to the making of global business was more as an entry point for foreign funds than as a point of departure for capital exports. The situation started to change in the early twentieth century: while remaining a net debtor until the War, the United States had also become a significant holder of foreign assets – mainly foreign direct investment, thus requiring a lesser involvement of the New York capital market. The leading Wall Street investment banks (JP Morgan, Kidder Peabody, Lee Higginson, Kuhn Loeb, Seligman, Speyer, and others), all family-owned partnerships, formed the cornerstone of New York's financial centre, though they faced competition from the largest national banks, with the National City Bank in the lead (Carosso, 1970; Cleveland and Huertas, 1985). They were primarily involved in the domestic securities business (railway companies and later large industrial concerns), but had close links to foreign financial centres, above all the City of London, as they were instrumental in attracting foreign capital. Likewise, the international character of the New York Stock Exchange came from its attraction to foreign investors rather than the securities traded there. Finally, regulation also played its part in limiting the development of a global banking business in New York, as national banks – but not trust companies – were forbidden to expand abroad until 1913; and the branches of foreign banks (15 in 1913) could not collect deposits and issue loans, though they could take part in financing foreign trade and operate on the foreign exchange market (Wilkins 1989).

Wars, depression, and regulation, 1914–1973

The First World War did not put an end to capital exports. Between 1914 and 1918, debts totalling nearly $20 billion – in other words an amount equivalent to the stock of British foreign assets on the eve of the war – were incurred among the Allies. However, these loans were essentially contracted between governments and did not activate the mechanisms usually associated with credit transfers between international financial centres. France, for example, borrowed $2.9 billion from the American government compared with only $336 million from banks, and $2.1 billion from the British government, compared with $625 million from banks, including the Bank of England. Only a few private intermediaries were involved in these operations, first and foremost the House of Morgan (Artaud, 1977).

Global financial transactions, both capital exports and trade finance, resumed after the War. Some $10 billion flowed from creditor to borrowing nations during the second half of the 1920s (Feinstein and Watson, 1995). One major difference with the pre-war years was the respective position of the financial powers. The great victor was the United States, which in a few years changed from a debtor country to a creditor country (having net private liabilities in excess of $3 billion in 1913 to net assets of $4.5 billion in 1919). Europe was no longer the world's banker. Germany lost nearly all its foreign assets; France most of them, probably three-quarters of its assets in Europe, mainly in Russia; and Britain some 20 per cent, essentially the $3 billion worth of American stock that it was obliged to sell. Nevertheless, Britain remained the largest holder of foreign investment in terms of stocks, but no longer the largest capital exporter in terms of annual flows, because of the constraints weighing down its balance of payments.

This role was now devolved to the United States: during the second half of the 1920s, foreign issues placed in New York generally exceeded those offered in London by 50 per cent (Burk, 1992). This foreign investment mainly flowed to Europe (41 per cent), ahead of Canada (25 per cent), Latin America (22 per cent), and Asia (12 per cent), with a very marked preference for public bonds that made up more than 95 per cent of issues between 1920 and 1929. Investment banks thus became more engaged in global finance, and J.P. Morgan, the undisputed leading international house in the 1920s, derived enormous prestige from its position at the hub of the world of business and politics, particularly in the field of financial diplomacy, not least as the lead manager of the Daws Loan. Another house, Dillon Read was particularly active in issues on behalf of large German companies (Carosso, 1970). The number of overseas branches of American banks increased significantly following the Edge Act of 1919 – from 26 in 1913 to

180 in 1920. But the number had fallen back to 107 by 1925, as American banks were quick to retreat to their national territory after making some heavy losses (Wilkins, 1999). Perhaps even more tellingly, all the major foreign banks now tried to establish a branch there (they numbered 26 in 1929) while others were represented by a subsidiary, usually set up jointly with another bank. And foreign capital continued to be invested in the United States, primarily through New York, spurred by the bullish trend of the New York Stock Exchange.

Did New York replace London as the world's leading financial centre? The point is debatable, but the answer is probably not. If London had to cede first place to New York in foreign issues, it soon regained its predominance in other activities, including acceptances, despite the success of acceptances drawn on New York thanks to the establishment of the Federal Reserve in 1913, which allowed national banks to accept bills of exchange. The pound remained the main trading currency, despite the difficulties in preserving this status and strong competition from the dollar (Eichengreen, 2012). And London was far ahead of New York in international banking, both as the home of British multinational banks and the host of branches of foreign banks. In spite of its new world role, New York remained as much an American as an international financial centre. Foreign issues, for example, played a secondary role to domestic issues and accounted for only 15 per cent of the total amount of new issues in the 1920s. This close interaction between domestic and international business was one of the main characteristics of New York when compared to London (Wilkins, 1999).

Paris fell behind London and New York. France was crippled by the weakness of the franc, capital flight, and reconstruction requirements. However, the stabilisation of the franc by Raymond Poincaré in December 1926 marked a turning point: Paris recovered part of its pre-war vitality, rekindling ambitions to compete with London and New York. Nevertheless, the French banks were weakened by the depreciation of the franc, the loss or closure of several foreign branches (in Russia, the Middle East, and Latin America) and the slow resumption of foreign investment – and didn't recover their pre-war dominant position. Berlin paid the price of defeat and hyperinflation in 1923. Germany became the world's largest capital-importing country in the 1920s, and it is mainly in this capacity that the German capital remained a significant international financial centre. Amsterdam, on the other hand, was commonly described in financial circles as Germany's effective financial centre during the years of inflation and hyperinflation (Houwink ten Cate, 1989). All the major banks set up there after the end of the War and were active on the foreign exchange market and later in the acceptance market, which enjoyed spectacular growth during the 1920s and established itself as the foremost in continental Europe. Zurich and the other Swiss centres (Geneva and Basel) played a lesser though not insignificant role in attracting foreign capital and redirecting it abroad – mainly to Germany (Cassis, 2006).

The Great Depression was a watershed in the history of global finance. Long-term capital investments almost completely stopped in the 1930s. New York saw its role as an international financial centre shrivel: foreign loans, which had been its speciality, fell to less than $300 million in 1931 – less than the issues offered in London – and to less than $100 million in 1932 and 1933. But the domestic capital market was also shaken. In London, foreign loans outside the empire ceased almost completely after September 1931, adding up to a mere £28.5 million between 1932 and 1938 – that is to say less than 3 per cent of the total amount of issues in London, as against 17 per cent for imperial issues (£186.7 million), which continued throughout the decade (Balogh, 1947). Britain's imperial retreat thus did not entirely end London's role in international business and finance. Overseas banks, for example, added another 1,000 branches to their worldwide, mainly imperial, network.

The crisis led to the introduction of regulatory measures, which in most countries – Britain was a notable exception – were to reshape the financial system. The most radical reforms were enacted in the United States, in particular the Glass-Steagall Act of 1933, which decreed the complete separation of commercial banking activities from investment banking activities; the Securities Exchange Act of 1934, which created the Securities and Exchange Commission (SEC). Universal banking, on the other hand, survived in Germany, where the banking law of December 1934 made do with strengthening bank supervision and introducing some restrictions on long-term deposits and on banks' representation on the supervisory boards of other companies(James, 1992).

The Second World War was different from the First if only because global financial activities had started to decline several years earlier. Moreover the state's hold over the economy was stronger than it had been during the Great War, leaving hardly any opportunity at all for bankers and financiers to take in charge the large financial transactions required by the war effort. Capital transfers mainly took place within each of the two camps and consisted of state-to-state transactions, or exactions – the American lend-lease programme on the Allied side, the extensive use of resources from the occupied territories made by the Reich on the Axis side (Milward, 1977).

The golden age of economic growth, between 1950 and 1973, when annual gross domestic product (GDP) growth averaged 5 per cent in Europe and 8 per cent in Japan, was not accompanied by intense international movements of private capital. The regulations inherited from the 1930s and those established in the immediate post-war years, including exchange controls, contributed to financial stability but limited the expansion of global business and its financing by banks and capital markets. The largest capital transfers were undertaken by governments, state bodies, and, to a lesser extent, multilateral agencies like the International Monetary Fund or the World Bank. Between 1955 and 1962, foreign issues floated in New York barely reached $4.2 billion – a feeble sum compared with the $126.5 billion for domestic issues, or the $98 billion in economic and military aid granted by the United States to foreign countries between 1945 and 1952 (Nadler *et al.*, 1955; Orsingher, 1964).

New York emerged as the world's financial capital and remained unchallenged until the 1960s. Its position relied first and foremost on the role of the dollar as the Bretton Woods System's reference currency. It also hinged on the influence of its financial institutions. New York's commercial banks (National City Bank, Chase National Bank, Manufacturers Trust, Central Hanover Bank, Chemical Trust, and J.P. Morgan) had, as a group, become the world's largest (Nadler *et al.*, 1955; Cleveland and Huertas, 1985). They all had well-organised departments for their international business and most of them had a presence overseas – in 1955 seven American banks, mainly from New York, had a total of 106 foreign branches. The investment banks, for their part, had fallen back into line following the crisis, competition from commercial banks and the New Deal regulations (Carosso, 1970). Twenty-one foreign banks (belonging to 12 different countries) had 'licensed agencies' in New York in 1954, on top of which there were numerous subsidiaries of foreign banks registered as banks or trust companies. And the Federal Reserve Bank of New York played a key role in international finance as the correspondent bank in the United States for the main foreign central banks and governments (Nadler *et al.*, 1955).

The New York Stock Exchange picked up again during the phase of economic expansion in the 1950s. It was still a market where mostly American stocks were traded, but in which traders from all over the world took part, giving it a truly international dimension (Geisst, 1997; Roberts, 2002). Foreign issues were expensive and remained relatively limited: on the one hand, American capital transfers abroad were mainly carried out through governmental and international agencies; and on the other hand, the bulk of private capital exported – $5.4 billion between 1950 and 1954 – was made up of direct investment, with a new wave of expansion in American multinationals, several of which, like General Electric, Standard Oil Co. of New Jersey (later EXXON), or IBM, were constituent parts of New York's financial centre where their registered offices were located. Foreign loans denominated in dollars were, nonetheless, issued on Wall Street on behalf of large enterprises, foreign governments, and multinational institutions, like the European Coal and Steel Community, or ECSC (Mensbrugghe, 1964).

London's position was considerably weakened after the war and its activities hampered by state intervention, in particular the restrictions on the movement of capital, controls over the distribution of credit, and bans on speculative stock market operations. Nevertheless, the City refocused on the Commonwealth and, particularly, on the sterling area, which enabled it to resume, in a more limited way, the role it had played on the world stage prior to 1914 (Michie, 1992; Kynaston, 2001). Paris's international position after 1945 was a mere shadow of what it had been only some 30 years earlier. Even more than in Britain, the state's grip ended up stifling the Parisian capital market, with foreign issues practically nil during this period (Quennouëlle-Corre, 2015). In Germany, Frankfurt took over from Berlin as the country's financial centre but remained a centre of national rather than international significance until the late 1970s (Holtfre-rich, 1999). Zurich was one of the rare financial markets, along with New York, to strengthen its international position, probably ranking third (together with Geneva, Basel, and to a lesser extent Lugano) behind New York and London, in the 1960s, as the Swiss markets quickly developed their role for accommodating and investing foreign capital, through international issues and wealth management (Iklé, 1970).

In a climate of state intervention and regulation, global business and finance resurfaced in the late 1950s with the advent of the Euromarkets. The Euromarkets are markets for transactions in dollars taking place outside the United States, free of American regulations. For various reasons, dollars started to accumulate in Europe, especially in London, in the 1950s – the cold war and the Soviet Union's fears of having its dollar deposits frozen in the United States; the US overseas investment and growing payment deficit; banking regulations, especially Regulation Q, which put a ceiling on the rate of interests which US banks paid on domestic bank deposits.

The Eurodollar market, a short-term money market, was the first to develop, when London banks began to use dollars rather than pounds to finance third party trade, after the British government had banned the use of sterling instruments for such purposes following the sterling crisis of 1957 (Schenk, 1998; Battilossi, 2002). With the European currencies' return to external convertibility in December 1958 and, from the early 1960s, the gradual relaxing of controls on capital flows, the Eurodollar market expanded rapidly. It was supplied mainly by American multinationals and by European central banks and provided credit on a worldwide scale and in hitherto unprecedented proportions, mainly to finance international trade and other short-term loans. From approximately $1.5 billion when it started in 1958, this market reached $25 billion ten years later and $130 billion in 1973 (OECD, 1996).

The Eurodollar market quickly gave birth to the Eurobond market, a long-term capital market using Eurodollars not only for bank loans but also for issuing dollar-denominated bonds, in London rather than in New York. The first Eurobond was issued in London in July 1963 by Siegmund Warburg, on behalf of Autostrada Italiana, a subsidiary of the state holding company IRI (Kerr, 1984; Ferguson, 2010). Eurobonds quickly proved very popular, especially as they were issued to bearer, which means that they were anonymous and exempt from withholding tax. The Eurobond market grew from about $250 million in 1963 to a yearly average of over $4 billion ten years later (OECD, 1996).

A third form of Euro credit – medium-term this time, lasting from three to ten years – developed in the mid-1960s, between short-term, mainly interbank, Eurodollar deposits, and long-term Eurobonds. These were international bank loans wholly financed by resources in Eurodollars and generally granted on the basis of floating interest rates. In view of the growing demand for these loans and the size of the amounts required, they took the form of syndicated loans bringing several banks together (Roberts, 2001). Despite the risks associated with interest rate fluctuations, the borrower found this a more flexible source of funding than a bond issue. From barely $2 billion dollars in 1968, Eurocredits quickly swelled to exceed $20 billion in 1973 − or more than four times the amount of Eurobonds (OECD, 1996).

The Euromarkets reshaped the world of international finance. They marked the start of the huge multinational expansion of American banks, which went from having 131 branches abroad in 1950 to having 899 in 1986, in addition to their 860 foreign subsidiaries. Europe was the preferred destination: by 1975 the eight largest American banks had set up 113 branches and 29 representative offices there, London alone having 58 of them (Huertas, 1990). European banks, especially British and French commercial banks, were also spurred into a new wave of internationalisation (Altamura, 2017). And the Euromarkets signalled the rebirth of the City of London, which quickly became their natural home. London was certainly well equipped for hosting these new financial activities − because of the age-old experience of its bankers, their expertise in international finance, and the diversity and complementarity of its institutions and markets. The positive attitude of the British monetary authorities, in contrast to that of their European counterparts, also made a difference. The first sign of the rebirth of the City was the attraction that it held for banks throughout the world: the number of foreign banks represented in London went from 59 in 1955 to 159 in 1970 and 243 in 1975 − nearly twice the corresponding number in New York (Baker and Collins, 2005).

Globalisation, deregulation, and innovations, 1973–2008

The end of the Bretton Woods system in 1971–73 opened a new era of international capital flows. According to recent estimates, in 2000, foreign assets ($28,984 billion) represented 92 per cent of world GDP, up from 25 per cent (with $2,800 billion) in 1980 and barely 6 per cent ($147.7 billion) in 1960 (Obstfeld and Taylor, 2004). At the turn of the twenty-first century, the United States was − as indeed it had been since the end of the Second World War − the largest holder of capital outside its territory, ahead of Britain, Japan, Germany, and France − the same countries, in a different order, as before 1914, with the addition of a newcomer, Japan. The destination of foreign investment, on the other hand, had changed. At the beginning of the twentieth century, it was the colonies and new countries that received the bulk of these transfers. A century later, it was the rich countries of Europe and North America that, with Japan, absorbed more than 80 per cent of foreign investment (Obstfeld and Taylor, 2004).

The upsurge in capital exports started with the demise of the Bretton Woods system in 1971–73. With the end of fixed exchange rates, free movements of capital became compatible with an independent monetary policy − in line with the Mundell-Fleming's trilemma, according to which only two of these three policy options can be pursued together. Their continued expansion took place within a new climate marked, in particular, by financial deregulations and innovations.

The deregulation movement started in the United States, with a liberalisation of the New York Stock Exchange (abolition of fixed commissions) in May 1975, making competition keener and leading to a consolidation in investment banking. The City of London followed in October 1986 with 'Big Bang', also a reform of the Stock Exchange (abolition of fixed commission and of the separation, unique to the London Stock Exchange, between the functions of brokers, who acted on behalf of clients, and jobbers, who were market-makers); it was also decided to open the London Stock Exchange, and by extension the City, to the outside world by permitting banks, both domestic and foreign, to buy member firms, hitherto banned. In Paris, the stockbrokers' monopoly was abolished in 1992. In Germany, the Bundesbank authorised floating-rate issues in

1984–85, despite its distrust of financial innovation, and allowed foreign banks to act as lead banks for foreign issues in Deutsche Marks. The wave of deregulation culminated in 1999 when the Glass-Steagall Act of 1933 was repealed by the Financial Modernisation Act. Commercial banking and investment banking could again be brought together on the grounds that new financial instruments justified greater concentration amongst the various intermediaries in the world of finance.

Financial innovation became, as never before, an integral part of global finance. Three main factors account for this development. One was the incredible progress made in computing, which enabled the new financial products to reach an otherwise impossible degree of sophistication. Another was the application to the market of theoretical advances made in the field of financial economics (Markowitz and Sharpe's modern portfolio theory, Fama's efficient market hypothesis, the Black Scholes options pricing model, and others), opening the way for the design of ever more complex financial products. And a third was the liberalisation of the financial markets, whose aim was to improve their efficiency by encouraging financial innovations – which remained very lightly if at all regulated.

The end of Bretton Woods offered an incentive. Modern derivatives, which have been at the heart of the financial revolution of the late twentieth century, came into being in Chicago in 1972 with the creation of the International Monetary Market, where currency contracts were traded – the initiative was taken to provide facilities for hedging against foreign exchange fluctuations. The Chicago Board Options Exchange, where options were traded on shares, was founded a year later. Europe followed with LIFFE (London International Financial Future Exchange) in 1982, MATIF (Marché à Terme des Instruments Financiers) in Paris in 1986, and DTB (Deutsche Termin Börse) in Frankfurt in the early 1990s (Cassis, 2006).

Derivatives were also combined with a new investment medium: alternative management funds, better known as hedge funds, which appeared in the 1980s (Mallaby, 2010). They were usually domiciled in an offshore centre, were highly leveraged, and took short positions, through derivatives or forward operations. Their managers, who often made the headlines in the financial press, earned high bonuses – generally reaching 20 per cent of profits above a certain threshold plus 1.5 to 2 per cent management fees – and, as a rule, invested their own funds alongside those of their clients. Their growth was phenomenal during the 1990s, from a few hundreds to nearly 3,000 by 2006, with nearly $1,000 billion of funds managed. And if they enjoyed spectacular successes (with George Soros allegedly making £1 billion in 1993) they also suffered severe setbacks, most spectacularly with the failure of LTCM (Long-Term Capital Management) in 1998, which had a debt-to-equity ratio of 25 to 1 and two economics Nobel prize winners (Robert Merton and Myron Scholes) on its board of directors.

Banking and financial practices have been deeply transformed by what has become known as securitisation – the conversion of various types of debt, especially loans, into marketable securities. Its novelty resided in the type of assets converted into securities and the type of financial products emerging from this conversion. Typically, they were derivatives. Mortgages were the first debts to be securitised, in the form of Mortgage-Backed Securities (MBS); other assets in particular consumer debt (insurance policies, car loans, credit card loans, student loans, and so on) were in turn securitized, bearing the generic name of Assets-Backed Securities (ABS); credit derivatives were also developed, in the first place Credit Default Swaps (CDS), which offered protection against the risk of default on a debt through a contract between two parties, the seller as it were insuring the buyer in return of the payment of a regular fee.

These developments were at once the cause and the consequence of the emergence of a new type of multinational banks, that some have called 'transnational banks', to underline both the quantitative and qualitative differences with their predecessors – in terms of size, internal organisation, geographical spread, and range of activities. The specialised British overseas banks, which had dominated multinational banking since the mid-nineteenth century, had lost their competitive advantage by the 1960s. By the turn of the twenty-first century, global finance was dominated by the world's leading universal banks (Citigroup, J.P. Morgan Chase, Bank of America, HSBC, RBS, Barclays, Deutsche Bank, BNP Paribas, UBS, Credit Suisse, and a few others). The largest, Citigroup, had offices in over 100 countries and employed nearly 370,000 people in 2007, before the crisis. It was engaged in all types of banking and financial activities, including retail banking, investment banking, trading, wealth management, and alternative investments such as hedge funds and private equity. Even more significantly, the bank had internalised its international activities, and was able to draw resources from one place and exploit them in another. All universal banks had more or less adopted this model (Kobrak, 2016).

New York and London played the leading role in the making of this new global financial business. By the turn of the twenty-first century, New York was still in first place, with by far the largest capital market, even if London had the edge in direct international financial activities, ranking first for international banking, asset management, and foreign exchange, and attracting the highest number of foreign banks – 481, as against 287 in New York (Roberts, 1998). New York clearly set the tone in international banking and financial business, if only because of the might of the American banks, mostly based in New York, and on which a great deal of London's international influence depended. In 2001, the two largest American banks, Citigroup and JPMorgan Chase had their head office in New York, as did the investment banks (Goldman Sachs, Merrill Lynch, and Morgan Stanley), which once again symbolised the United States' immense financial power. London's policy of opening up to the world had been kept up relentlessly and had borne fruit, at the cost, however, of a certain eclipse of British financial institutions (all merchant banks, with the exception of Rothschilds, were taken over by domestic and foreign financial institutions in the wake of the collapse of Baring Brothers in 1995) and the City's dependence on foreign banks – what has sometimes been called the 'Wimbledon effect'.

The major newcomer of the post-war era was Tokyo. As a result of Japan's rise to the rank of economic superpower, Tokyo established itself as a major international centre during the 1970s, going in 20 years from being a regional financial centre to a centre of world dimensions. And the possibility that Tokyo might overtake New York and become the world's leading financial centre did not seem entirely fanciful at the end of the 1980s, though such judgements proved too hasty. The American economy, far from declining, enjoyed spectacular growth in the 1990s whereas the Japanese economy went into a long slump after the burst of the stock exchange and property bubbles in 1990, which had severe repercussions for Tokyo's international position (Cassis, 2006).

Frankfurt only overtook Zurich and Paris to become Continental Europe's leading financial centre in the late 1980s. The decision in 1992 to establish the headquarters of the new European central bank in Frankfurt gave it a further boost, raising hopes that it might eventually overtake London, but this appeared highly unlikely a decade later. Paris regained some ground from the 1980s, without, however, really finding its role. Paris did not dominate any of the main fields of international financial activity, but held some aces, especially in asset management, as well as in the bond market and derivatives. Zurich and Geneva continued to figure amongst the leading centres, increasingly specialising in wealth management, with 35 per cent of the world's private offshore wealth in the early 2000s, as against 21 per cent for Britain and 12 per cent for the United States (Cassis, 2016).

The number of aspiring international financial centres increased significantly in the last two decades of the twentieth century. Several cities, especially in emerging economies, were actively promoted with the aim of gaining the status of regional or even global international financial centre. Two centres proved particularly successful: Singapore and Hong Kong (Roberts, 1994). Singapore's development was the result of a systematic effort made on the part of the authorities, immediately upon the country's independence in 1965, to turn it into an international financial centre, by hosting the nascent Asian dollar market (the counterpart of the Eurodollar market in London) and encouraging the emergence of a bond market. Singapore's financial markets really took off in the 1980s and the foreign exchange market grew in its wake to reach fourth position in 1998, behind London, New York, and Tokyo; derivatives started being traded in 1984 with the foundation of SIMEX; and as a result, an increasing number of foreign banks set up there, reaching 260 in 1995.

In Hong Kong, by contrast, the authorities adopted a non-interventionist stance, at the same time creating conditions conducive to developing financial activities, notably a favourable tax system and modern infrastructure, in addition to the absence of exchange control, a robust legal system, the existence of the rule of law, and its position as the door for a China that began to open up to the world at the end of the 1970s. Syndicated Euro-credits found a home here, with operations on behalf of enterprises and governments in the region's main economies – Japan, Taiwan, South Korea, Australia, and New Zealand, later joined by Thailand, the Philippines, and, above all, China. In the space of about ten years, Hong Kong established itself as the world's third centre for Euro-credits, behind London and New York. Its international status was mirrored in the presence of foreign banks, numbering 357 in 1995, that is to say more than any financial centre except for London (Roberts, 1994).

New York, London, Hong Kong, and Singapore stood at the apex of a hierarchy of financial centres. The *Global Financial Centres Index* listed 46 centres when it was first published in 2007, with London ranked first (in terms of competitiveness) and Athens 46th. The number had nearly doubled ten years later. Multinational banks considerably expanded in the second age of global finance, with a much stronger presence in the financial centres of both advanced and emerging economies – from about 20 per cent, in terms of number, in 1995, to 34 per cent in 2009, with some countries, especially in Eastern Europe having more than 50 per cent of assets controlled by foreign banks.

Epilogue: global finance after the crisis

The Global Financial Crisis of 2007–09 was the worst financial panic in modern history. Never before, even in the 1930s, did so many of the leading banks, in so many advanced economies, find themselves, at almost exactly the same moment, requiring state intervention to save them from failing. And yet its effects on the global financial business have been fairly limited – in sharp contrast with what happened during the Great Depression which, as an economic downturn, was of a far greater magnitude than the so-called Great Recession. The causes and consequences of this financial debacle cannot be discussed here, but two points can be briefly made in conclusion to this overview: one concerns the balance of power in global finance, the other the conduct of financial business. They reveal more continuity than change in the development of global finance.

Ten years after the debacle of 2008, only one new financial centre, Shanghai (together with Beijing) had been added to the top ten; and the ranking order had only been marginally altered, with Hong Kong and Singapore definitely overtaking Frankfurt and Paris and possibly also Tokyo. This should not come as a surprise: since the late nineteenth century, financial crises have never led to any real change in the hierarchy of international financial centres. In that respect, major changes have all been brought up by wars (Cassis, 2006). The French wars led to Amsterdam's final demise and its replacement by London as the world's leading financial centre at the turn of the nineteenth century. London was overtaken by New York a century-and-a-half later, as a result of the First and Second World Wars. At the same time, wars mainly accelerate long-term processes already under way: London had already overtaken Amsterdam as a trading centre in the late eighteenth century; and with the United States' GDP already twice as large as that of Britain by 1905 with about the same GDP per head, it was only a matter of *when* New York was going to supplant London. The Global Financial Crisis was thus unlikely to alter the balance of power in global finance in favour of Shanghai, the main contender amongst emerging markets: when it broke out in 2008, China's GDP was about one-third of that of the United States and its GDP per head less than a tenth. China has been catching up since then, but it will need time and will have to meet several conditions, not least in terms of wealth and openness, before claiming the mantle.

Within the leading financial centres, the financial crisis slowed down business activities. Most transnational banks suffered enormous losses and some were brought under state control. They eventually recovered, though unevenly, depending on countries but also on individual banks. New regulation was introduced in the wake of the crisis, with Basel III at international level, the Dodd-Frank Act in the United States, the Vickers Report in Britain, and the various steps towards the Banking Union in the Eurozone and several other countries of the EU. Less than ten years later, the question was whether regulation had gone too far in its burdensome and sometimes apparently unnecessary complexity, with people in the profession talking of regulatory tsunami (Sylla, 2018; Roberts, 2018). From the perspective of global finance, cross-border lending declined, especially on the part of European banks. On the other hand, foreign direct investment increased, though more often in search of lower taxes than actual investment. However, despite relying on local resources rather than capital transfers in their lending business, transnational banks continued to play a significant role in the making of global business.

References

Altamura, Edoardo (2017), *European Banks and the Rise of International Finance: The Post-Bretton Wood Era* (London: Routledge).

Artaud, Denise (1977), 'Les dettes de guerre de la France, 1919–1929', in M. Lévy-Leboyer (ed.), *La position internationale de la France. Aspects économique et financiers, XIXe–XXe siècles* (Paris: Editions de l'Ecole des Hautes Etudes en Sciences Sociales, 1977), 313–18.

Baker, Mae and Michael Collins (2005), 'London as an International Banking Centre, 1958–1980', in Youssef Cassis and Eric Bussière (eds), *London and Paris as International Financial Centres in the Twentieth Century* (Oxford: Oxford University Press), 247–64.

Balogh, Thomas (1947), *Studies in Financial Organization* (Cambridge: Cambridge University Press).

Battilossi, Stefano (2002), 'Introduction: International Banking and the American Challenge in Historical Perspective', in Stefano Battilossi and Youssef Cassis (eds), *European Banks and the American Challenge Competition and Cooperation in International Banking Under Bretton Woods* (Oxford: Oxford University Press), 1–35.

Burk, Kathleen (1992), 'Money and Power: The Shift from Great Britain to the United States', in Youssef Cassis (ed.), *Finance and Financiers in European History 1880–1960* (Cambridge: Cambridge University Press), 359–70.

Carosso, Vincent (1970), *Investment Banking in America* (Cambridge, MA: Harvard University Press).

Cassis, Youssef (2005), 'London Banks and International Finance', in Youssef Cassis and Eric Bussière (eds), *London and Paris as International Financial Centres in the Twentieth Century* (Oxford: Oxford University Press), 107–18.

Cassis, Youssef (2006), *Capitals of Capital: A History of International Financial Centres 1780–2005* (Cambridge: Cambridge University Press).

Cassis, Youssef (2010), *Capitals of Capital: The Rise and Fall of International Financial Centres 1780–2009* (Cambridge: Cambridge University Press).

Cassis, Youssef (2016), 'International Financial Centres', in Youssef Cassis, Richard S. Grossman, and Catherine R. Schenk (eds), *The Oxford Handbook of Banking and Financial History* (Oxford: Oxford University Press), 293–317.

Cassis, Youssef and Wojcik, Dariusz (eds) (2018), *International Financial Centres after the Global Financial Crisis and Brexit* (Oxford: Oxford University Press).

Cassis, Youssef, Grossman, Richard S., and Schenk, Catherine R. (eds) (2016), *The Oxford Handbook of Banking and Financial History* (Oxford: Oxford University Press).

Chapman, Stanley (1984), *The Rise of Merchant Banking* (London: Allen & Unwin).

Chapman, Stanley (1992), *Merchant Enterprise in Britain: From the Industrial Revolution to World War I* (Cambridge: Cambridge University Press).

Cleveland, Harold van B. and Huertas, Thomas (1985), *Citibank 1812–1970* (Cambridge, MA: Harvard University Press).

Eichengreen, Barry (1996), *Globalizing Capital: A History of the International Monetary System* (Princeton, NJ: Princeton University Press).

Eichengreen, Barry (2012), *Exorbitant Privilege: The Rise and Fall of the Dollar and the Future of the International Monetary System* (Oxford: Oxford University Press).

Feinstein, Charles H. and Katherine Watson (1995), 'Private International Investment Flows in Europe in the Inter-war Period', in Charles H. Feinstein (ed.), *Banking, Currency, and Finance in Europe Between the Wars* (Oxford: Oxford University Press), 94–130.

Ferguson, Niall (1998), *The World's Banker: The History of the House of Rothschild* (London: Weidenfeld & Nicolson).

Ferguson, Niall (2010), *High Financier: The Lives and Time of Siegmund Warburg* (London: Allen Lane).

Fraser, Steve (2005), *Wall Street: A Cultural History* (London: Faber & Faber).

Geisst, Charles R. (1997), *Wall Street: A History* (Oxford: Oxford University Press).

Global Financial Centres Index, since 2007.

Gömmel, Rainer (1992), 'Entstehung und Entwicklung der Effektenbörse im 19. Jahrhunderts bis 1914', in H. Pohl (ed.), *Deutsche Börsengeschichte* (Frankfurt: Knapp), 135–210.

Hausman, William J., Hertner, Peter, and Wilkins, Mira (2008), *Global Electrification: Multinational Enterprise and International Finance in the History of Light and Power, 1878–2007* (New York: Cambridge University Press).

Hertner, Peter (1990), 'German Banks Abroad before 1914', in Geoffrey Jones (ed.), *Banks as Multinationals* (London: Routledge), 99–119.

Holtfrerich, Carl-Ludwig (1999), *Frankfurt as a Financial Centre: From Medieval Trade Fair to European Banking Centre* (Munich: C.H. Beck).

Houwink ten Cate, Johannes, (1989), 'Amsterdam als Finanzplatz Deutschalnds (1919–1923)', in Gerald D. Feldman and J. Th. M. Houwink ten Cate (eds), *Konsequenzen der Inflation* (Berlin: De Gruyter), 152–89.

Huertas, Thomas F. (1990), 'U.S. Multinational Banking: History and Prospects', in G. Jones (ed.), *Banks as Multinationals* (London: Routledge), 248–67.

Iklé, Max (1970), *Die Schweiz als internationaler Bank- und Finanzplatz* (Zürich: Orell Füssli).

James, Harold (1992), 'Banks and Bankers in the German Interwar Depression', in Youssef Cassis (ed.), *Finance and Financiers in European History 1880–1969* (Cambridge: Cambridge University Press), 263–81.

Jones, Edgar (1996), *True and Fair: The History of Price Waterhouse* (London: Hamish Hamilton).

Jones, Geoffrey (1990) (ed.), *Banks as Multinationals* (London: Routledge).

Jones, Geoffrey (1993), *British Multinational Banking 1830–1990* (Oxford: Clarendon Press).

Jones, Geoffrey (2000), *Merchants to Multinationals: British Trading Companies in the Nineteenth and Twentieth Centuries* (Oxford: Oxford University Press).

Kerr, Ian M. (1984), *A History of the Eurobond Market: The First 21 Years* (London: Euromoney Publications).

Kindleberger, Charles (1974), 'The Formation of Financial Centers: A Study in Comparative Economic History', *Princeton Studies in International Finance*, 36, 1–78.

Kobrak, Christopher (2008), *Banking on Global Markets: Deutsche Bank and the United States, 1870 to the Present* (Cambridge: Cambridge University Press).

Kobrak, Christopher (2016), 'From Multinational to Transnational Banking', in Youssef Cassis, Richard S. Grossman and Catherine R. Schenk (eds), *The Oxford Handbook of Banking and Financial History* (Oxford: Oxford University Press) 163–90.

Kynaston, David (1994), *The City of London: volume I, A World of Its Own 1815–1890* (London: Chatto & Windus).

Kynaston, David (1995), *The City of London: volume II, Golden Years, 1890–1914* (London: Chatto & Windus).

Kynason, David (2000), *The City of London: volume III, Illusions of Gold 1914–1945* (London: Chatto & Windus).

Kynaston, David (2001), *The City of London: volume IV, A Club No More 1945–2000* (London: Chatto & Windus).

Maddison, Angus (2001), *The World Economy: A Millennial Perspective* (Paris: OECD).

Mallaby, Sebastian (2010), *More Money Than God: Hedge Funds and the Making of the New Elite* (London: Bloomsbury).

Mensbrugghe, Jean van der (1964), 'Foreign Issues in Europe', *International Monetary Fund Staff Papers*, 11, 327–35.

Michie, Ranald (1987), *The London and New York Stock Exchanges 1850–1914* (London: Allen & Unwin).

Michie, Ranald (1992), *The City of London: Continuity and Change, 1850–1990* (Basingstoke and London: Macmillan).

Michie, Ranald (1999), *The London Stock Exchange: A History* (Oxford: Oxford University Press).

Michie, Ranald (2006), *The Global Securities Market: A History* (Oxford: Oxford University Press).

Milward, Alan S. (1977), *War, Economy and Society, 1939–1945* (London: Allen & Unwin).

Nadler, M., Heller, S., and Shipman, S. (1955), 'New York as an International Financial Center', in *The Money Market and Its Institutions* (New York: Ronald Press), 283–302.

Obstfeld, Maurice and Taylor, Alan (2004), *Global Capital Markets: Integration, Crisis and Growth* (Cambridge: Cambridge University Press).

OECD (1996), *International Capital Markets Statistics, 1950–1995* (Paris: OECD).

Orsingher, R. (1964), *Les banques dans le monde* (Paris: Payot).

Paquier, Derge (1998), *Histoire de l'électricité en Suiss : La dynamique d'un petit pays européen 1875–1938*, 2 vols (Geneva: Editions Passé Présent).

Plessis, Alain (2005), 'When Paris Dreamt of Competing with the City ...', in Youssef Cassis and Eric Bussière (eds), *London and Paris as International Financial Centres in the Twentieth Century* (Oxford: Oxford University Press), 42–54.

Pohl, Hans (ed.) (2002), *Geschichte des Finanzplatzes Berlin* (Frankfurt: Knapp).

Quennouëlle-Corre, Laure (2015), *La place financière de Paris au XXe siècle: Des ambitions contrariées* (Paris: Comité pour l'Histoire Economique et Financière de la France).

Quennouëlle-Corre, Laure, and Cassis, Youssef (2011), *Financial Centres and International Capital Flows in the Nineteenth and Twentieth Centuries* (Oxford: Oxford University Press).

Roberts, Richard (ed.) (1994), *International Financial Centres*, 4 vols (Aldershot: Elgar).

Roberts, Richard (1998), *Inside International Finance* (London: Orion).

Roberts, Richard (2001), *Take Your Partners: Orion, the Consortium Banks and the Transformation of the Euromarkets* (Basingstoke: Palgrave).

Roberts, Richard (2002), *Wall Street* (London: The Economist).

Roberts, Richard (2018), 'London: Downturn, Recovery and New Challenges – But Still Pre-eminent', in Youssef Cassis and Dariusz Wojcik (eds), *International Financial Centres after the Global Financial Crisis and Brexit* (Oxford: Oxford University Press), 37–60.

Schenk, C. (1998), 'The Origins of the Eurodollar Market in London, 1955–1963', *Explorations in Economic History*, 35 (2), 221–38.

Sylla, Richard (2018), 'New York: Remains A, if not The, Pre-eminent International Financial Centre', in Youssef Cassis and Dariusz Wojcik (eds), *International Financial Centres after the Global Financial Crisis and Brexit* (Oxford: Oxford University Press), 16–36.

Wilkins, Mira (1989), *The History of Foreign Investment in the United States to 1914* (Cambridge, MA: Harvard University Press).

Wilkins, Mira (1999), 'Cosmopolitan Finance in the 1920s: New York's Emergence as an International Financial Centre', in Richard Sylla, Richard Tilly, and Gabriel Tortella (eds), *The State, the Financial System and Economic Modernization* (Cambridge: Cambridge University Press), 271–91.

8

THE INTERNATIONALIZATION OF EXECUTIVE EDUCATION

Rolv Petter Amdam

The emergence of the modern global economy gives rise to questions such as who has managed the firms during this process and how these managers have been prepared for their jobs. Most of the historical literature on the relationship between education and management positions and performance has focused on the role of formal degree programs, such as the MBA degree and engineering degrees, and on their different impact in different contexts (e.g., Locke 1989, 1984; Engwall *et al.* 2016). These comparative studies have highlighted the international aspects of business education. National systems of business education have received ideas from abroad and changed and, after World War II, especially the international impact of ideas and concepts from the United States had a strong impact globally. However, the studies also show that national variations are still strong despite international exchange of ideas on how to educate future managers.

This chapter narrows down the question of how to prepare for top executive positions to one type of education that aims to train them directly: non-degree executive education. Executive education as we have known it in recent decades is a typical post-World War II phenomenon, although the concept of executive education was not used before the 1960s (Amdam 2016). In the US, and in some other countries, selected business schools offered courses before World War II that predated the first executive programs. In the US, Harvard Business School offered a program called Special Sessions for Executives from 1928 and the course Business Executive Discussion Group from 1935, both approaching executives. However, both lasted for only a couple of years (Amdam 2016). In, for example, Paris, France, Centre de preparation aux affaires (CPA) was established in 1931 with the same purpose (Fridenson 2017). We date the birth of modern executive education to 1945, when Harvard Business School (HBS) began to offer a 13 week full-time on-campus non-degree program to men – and, from 1963, also to women – who were top management, or aspired to become top managers. At HBS, which was the first US business school to offer this kind of program, the program was called the Advanced Management Program (AMP). The idea was that the business schools should prepare people for top executive positions and improve top executives' performance. These programs represented an attempt to strengthen the involvement of business schools in the development of professional executives, and to do so more directly than the MBA programs (which attracted young people who might be top executives one day in the future). In the context of the history of higher education, executive education represented a powerful new logic that was different from the general academic trend in the business school programs after World War II. For the executive programs, recruitment was not based on previous grades, degrees or entry exams but on a person's hierarchical position within a corporation. The participants were often chosen by enterprises and not selected by universities, and no grades or degrees were awarded after graduation (Amdam 2016).

Executive education, defined as short full-time on-campus non-degree programs for top executives or potential top executives, was a major innovation within the field of executive development. From the 1950s to the early twenty-first century, this concept spread globally in a remarkably standardized form, which makes it a good example of a real global product. The executive education programs could have different names, such as the Management Development Program or the Executive Development Program. As early as 1968, there were around 50 programs of a similar format to the HBS's AMP at different US universities (West 1970). The aim of many of the programs was to train top executives for international assignments in a period when US corporations were internationalizing rapidly. Globally, there were similar programs modeled on those of US business schools – or organized by US business schools – in countries such as Japan, the Philippines, India, Morocco, South Africa, Switzerland, France, Italy, Costa Rica, and Chile. All of them had the purpose of training people who were in – or were about to be in – top executive positions.

The 1950s and 1960s were a formative period for executive education across the world. Among the top ten executive programs in the *Financial Times'* 2017 ranking of open executive programs, seven, including HBS's program of 1945, were created in this period. Six of the ten were run by European business schools. Faculty members from HBS were actively involved in establishing three of these in the 1950s: Institut européen d'administration des affaires (INSEAD), Instituto de Estudios Superiores de la Empresa (IESE) in Spain, and l'Institut pour l'étude des méthodes de direction de l'entreprise (IMEDE), later the International Institute for Management Development (IMD) in Switzerland. The Ford Foundation was actively involved in establishing the fourth of them, the London Business School, in 1965.[1]

The chapter argues that, globally, executive education is a relatively standardized US-influenced concept that has been neglected in the research literature on the development of business education. Based on this, it outlines some main patterns of development in the formative period 1945–1970 by defining the spread of the executive education "product" as an international process influenced by strong institutional factors. In the last part of the chapter these arguments are illustrated by exploring some prestigious business schools in Europe and India, based on secondary literature as well archival studies of the Harvard Business School and Ford Foundation archives.

The chapter offers two contributions to the existing literature. First, it shows that the development and functions of executive education should be studied as a unique phenomenon, but also as a phenomenon related to business education in general. According to HBS's Professor Kenneth R. Andrews, the new wave of executive programs was "an educational experiment unique in the history of education" (Andrews 1959: 593). Second, this chapter claims that, more so than for business education in general, the internationalization of "the American model" was a success in the way that it spread and developed in a surprisingly standardized form. This does not mean that there were no conflicts. Existing research on the international history of business education has highlighted the resistance in many countries to adopting American educational formats such as the MBA degree. This chapter also highlights the tension between competing US models for educating executives.

Literature and perspectives

Within the historical literature on business education, the non-degree top-executive activity of the business schools has, with a few exceptions, been neglected. It has been mentioned in short paragraphs or sub-chapters in some scholarly written anniversaries of business schools, and Matthias Kipping is one of a few who has addressed this sector as a separate research field (Cruikshank 1987; Epstein 2016; Kipping 1998; Sedlak and Williamson 1983; Wilson 1992). The question of the different logics of the degree and non-degree executive sectors of business schools has only recently been addressed. While the first sector recruits young students on the basis of their degrees, grades and/or enrolment tests, and awards grades, the second recruits on the basis of a position in a corporate hierarchy, has no exams, and awards no grades. Graduates of the first sector are young people who might end up in top executive positions after ten or 20 years; graduates of the second are people who are already in – or are close to – top executive positions (Amdam 2016).

Since Robert R. Locke's (1989, 1984) seminal books comparing the development of US, German, French, and British management education, there have been several comparative studies of the development of modern business education (e.g., Amdam 1996, 2008; Amdam *et al.* 2003; Engwall and Zamagni 1998; Gourvish and Tiratsoo 1998; Kipping *et al.* 2009). The recent study by Lars Engwall *et al.* (2016) explores the development of business education (and media and the consulting industry) from the perspective of organizational fields, where an organizational field is defined as "a set of interdependent populations of organizations participating in the same cultural and social sub-system" (Scott 2008: 434). Historically, business education as a field has developed within different national contexts. By drawing on DiMaggio and Powell (1983), the argument is that the actors within a field tend to become more similar or isomorphic with one another because of mimic, normative, and coercive processes. According to Engwall *et al.* (2016), business schools have in general become more similar and closer to a US-dominated global model. Another expression of the institutionalization process is that they have developed from surviving to gaining legitimacy and authority. The role of executive education in this perspective is, however, not researched.

Changes within organizational fields may be the result of endogenous processes of interaction between actors or of exogenous shocks such as Americanization. Americanization is here defined as a political–economic–cultural institution that reflected an attempt to diffuse American ideas on how to organize modern societies and economies, especially in the period from 1945 to 1973 when the US's international position was very strong (Berghahn 2010). The term was frequently used in business history studies around the millennium turn, and expressed a cultural turn in business and economic history (e.g., Berghahn 2010; Kipping and Bjarnar 1998; Djelic 1998; Zeitlin and Herrigel 2000).

This chapter will draw upon the organizational field perspective. However, it argues that we can talk about a specific field of top executive development that is related to – but is not identical with – the field of business education. Within this field of top executive development, business corporations and associations, in addition to business schools, other course providers, and institutions such as the Ford Foundation, played an active role. Further, I perceive the international diffusion of the AMP executive education model as a process of internationalization, and we draw upon the Uppsala model of international business (IB) to explore it. According to the Uppsala approach, organizations internationalize gradually in two ways: first, by moving from simple exporting to engaging in foreign direct investment (FDI) by establishing subsidiaries, and, second, by investing initially in countries that are close in terms of psychic distance and then expanding geographically after having accumulated international experiential knowledge

(Johanson and Vahlne 1977). In their revised model, however, Johanson and Vahlne (2009) suggest that networks may replace psychic distance, so that firms' patterns of FDI may be a result of networks that existed prior to their investments. In other words, being in networks that reduce the distance to foreign markets has a strong shaping effect on firms' behavior regarding internationalization. However, Forsgren (2016) has questioned this shaping effect, and argues that more research is needed to understand the relationship between the characteristics of these networks and firms' foreign investment behavior as it relates to pace, direction, and level of commitment.

The internationalization process perspective is relevant for several reasons. First, in this period, we can perceive the AMP as a product that was exported to foreign units, such as management development centers or business schools, where programs were organized and taught by or in close cooperation with US business schools, especially HBS. The AMP was copied or adjusted according to the local context, but the basic idea of a limited number of weeks of extensive management development training, focused on general management and aimed at preparing participants for top management positions, remained. Most of these new units later developed into full degree-awarding business schools, but organizing such short executive programs was a key objective during their first years. Second, the relationships between the US business schools and the foreign units were similar to the relationships we find within other international organizations. The various relationships between the US business school partner and the foreign unit can be understood by using concepts from IB and by defining the unit as a licensing partner, an export agent, a strategic ally, or even a greenfield subsidiary. Third, among US business schools there was an awakening understanding of this process as something that was partly aimed at supporting the creation and development of US multinational enterprises (MNEs).

The network perspective is strongly highlighted in the literature that studies the role of the Ford Foundation in the Americanization process in the 1950s and 1960s. The Ford Foundation financed many of the projects that contributed to the export of US executive programs, such as the establishment of the London Business School, INSEAD in Fontainebleau, France, Instituto Postuniversitario di Organizzazione Aziendale (IPSOA) in Turin, Italy, and the Indian Institute of Management Ahmedabad (IIMA). According to Gemelli (1998), who has studied the Ford Foundation and the growth of European business education in general (not just executive education), transatlantic political and intellectual networks were very important for the development of business education, especially in Italy and France. Parmar (2012), who has studied the global impact of the three largest US foundations, has approached the topic from a perspective inspired by the French sociologist Pierre Bourdieu and has shown how transatlantic elite networks emerged around the Ford Foundation's international operations.

Executive education and Americanization

In a broader sense, the internationalization of executive education was part of the Americanization process, which was aimed at transforming global capitalism and business practices on the basis of American models (Kipping and Bjarnar 1998; Djelic 1998). Seen from the US, this process was driven by a symbiosis of different forces, among which the most important were the foreign policy of the US state, expressed in the Marshall Plan and later the European Productivity Agency (EPA), the Ford Foundation, American enterprises that internationalized, and educational institutions (David and Schaufelbuehl 2015). All three of the US Technical and Productivity Program (USTAP) (McGlade 1998), the EPA (Boel 1998), and the Ford Foundation (Gemelli 1998) highlighted management education in a broader sense as a key element in what was later called Americanization.

From an internationalization process perspective, the Americanization process was an institutional framework, which, according to North (1990), represents both constraints and possibilities. The institutional possibilities that supported the internationalization of executive education were, most of all, financial grants. For example, the USTAP and the EPA financed visits from several hundred professors and potential professors from foreign business schools and training centers who stayed at HBS, MIT, and other US business schools in order to learn how to teach business in their home countries (McGlade 1998; Boel 1998). The Ford Foundation funded several projects, including those at US business schools (among which HBS was the largest recipient) and with foreign partners, in order to initiate new business education programs abroad. It also contributed to the establishment of some educational institutions that developed into prestigious business schools, such as INSEAD in France (Barsoux 2000), the London Business School (Barnes 1989), and the IIMA (Hill *et al.* 1973).

Among these actors, strong personal networks emerged through meetings, project cooperation, and mobility. For example, Paul G. Hoffman came from a position as director of the Economic Cooperation Administration, managing the Marshall aid program, to a position as president of the Ford Foundation (from 1950 to 1953). Among the Ford Foundation's most active trustees was Donald D. David, HBS's dean. Such networks illustrate the informal aspects of the institutional context. Seen from the perspective of the main exporter of executive education, HBS, the networks gave it access to information and a wider international reputation. As HBS's dean said in 1954, after a trip to Europe during which he had noticed that HBS was well known, "I think they give us too much credit. ... Since America has skills and the Harvard Business School teaches it, HBS must be mainly responsible. Naturally this is an overstatement – pleasing but embarrassing."[2]

The institutions also acted as constraints to internationalization, since the actors had different motives and roles within the bigger picture of Americanization. HBS and the Ford Foundation often cooperated in exporting executive education, but sometimes their interests clashed. HBS's model of short intensive executive programs was driven by a strong belief in training professional top executives to complete the managerial revolution (Amdam 2016). The Ford Foundation was in no way against this corporate transformation, but it had other concerns as well. One of these was the geopolitical perspective, since it was an institutional actor, albeit a soft one, in the Cold War. This motive explains its strong support for management education in Turkey in the 1950s and India in the 1960s (Parmar 2012).

Another of the Ford Foundation's concerns arose because it initiated a huge project to turn American business schools into academic institutions. This New Look, as the project has been named, was based on an analysis that US business education was too practical and too remote from the academic standards of the universities. As was demonstrated in the Pierson report of 1959 on US business education (Pierson 1959) and in several grants to leading American business schools, among which the Carnegie Mellon School of Administration was a role model, the Ford Foundation played a major role in this transformation (Augier and March 2011). The idea was that business education should be more scientific, which, in particular, meant a stronger focus on mathematics, statistics, organizational behavior, and, to some extent, economics. Interestingly enough, this process did not include executive education but related primarily to the degree logic of the business schools (Andrews 1959). Consequently, the Ford Foundation did not intervene in the internationalization process in the content of executive education. However, as we will see from some archival examples, in some cases the Ford Foundation introduced constraints by offering or supporting alternatives, and especially degree alternatives, to the HBS model of executive education.

The Ford Foundation's efforts were formed in the geopolitical context of the Cold War and were combined with a strong belief in science. The HBS model was, to a larger degree, formed in the context of completing the managerial revolution by offering the new group of professional top executives a program that trained and socialized them into their new positions (Amdam 2016). This perspective also formed the mantra of HBS's international activity. The school's external presentation of its international efforts in executive education said: "(T)he School has responded actively to global appeals to share what some have called the 'management' revolution deriving from the steady advances in administrative skills achieved in the United States over the past half century."[3]

The internationalization process of the AMP

The internationalization of executive education, which here is defined as short non-degree on-campus programs for top executives or potential top executives, developed largely according to the Uppsala model, but there were some important modifications. The original model holds that internationalization tends to happen in countries that are close in terms of psychic distance (having similar culture, language, and institutions), and the internationalization of AMP to Canada and Hawaii illustrates this (see Table 8.1). In both Canada and Hawaii, HBS professors, such as Ralph H. Hower and Kenneth Andrews, offered an AMP that was a shorter copy of the HBS AMP, and they did this on an individual basis with the informal approval of HBS.[4]

Table 8.1 Some examples of executive education programs that had various degrees of involvement from US business schools and/or the Ford Foundation, 1949–1968

Year of first entry	Country	Institution/place
1949	Canada	Huron College London, Ontario
1953	Hawaii	Honolulu
1953	Italy	IPSOA, Turin
1954	Turkey	University of Istanbul
1956	Philippines	AMP in the Far East, Baguio
	Chile	JEFT/ICARE, Valparaiso
1957	Japan	Kawanda, Keio University
	France	INSEAD
1958	Switzerland	IMEDE, Lausanne
1960	Nigeria	Nigeria Institute of Management and Administration
	Mexico	IMAN, Mexico City
1961	India	Indian Institute of Management Ahmedabad
	Egypt	Management Development Institute
1962	Pakistan	West Pakistan Institute of Management
1964	Central America	INCAE
	UK	British Institute of Management (HBS alumni organization)
1965	Israel	Tel Aviv
	South Africa	Witwatersrand University
1967	Tunisia	CAMSED
	Venezuela	IESA
1968	Argentina	IDEA
	Singapore	Singapore Institute of Management

Sources: Compiled from various documents in Harvard Business School Archives and the Ford Foundation Archives.

Some of the new programs were also the results of personal networks. One type of network was the MBA alumni networks. From 1955 to 1959, HBS received requests for cooperation from 76 countries.[5] Most of these were through visitors to Cambridge, MA, and many of them were MBA alumni who asked for cooperation in establishing an AMP in their home country; Mexico is an example here. In 1954, a group of Mexican alumni from the HBS MBA program contacted the HBS faculty, who agreed to teach for some years, and in 1958 the Ford Foundation awarded the Mexican institution a grant to write Mexican cases under the instruction of the HBS professors.[6]

Another type of personal network was the network of an individual's faculty or previous faculty. In the case of INSEAD, George Frederic Doriot, who had been professor at HBS before World War II, was very active in the process that led to the creation of INSEAD in France in 1957. As early as 1930, he, together with a small group of French entrepreneurs, had created CPA in Paris to offer programs for top managers. In the 1950s, he worked with the business community, and especially Olivier Giscard d'Estaing (later member of the French parliament 1968–1973), Roger Godino (later advisor to the Premier Minister 1988–1991), and Claude Janssen (a French businessman in international banking), who were all HBS alumni, to establish INSEAD (Barsoux 2000; Gemelli 1998).

Networks of the third type were political networks such as that of George Cabot Lodge. Prior to being appointed as a lecturer at HBS in 1962, Lodge had worked as Assistant Secretary of Labor for International Affairs, having been appointed by President John F. Kennedy. He used his political networks to get HBS actively involved in offering an AMP in the new Latin American Business School, INCAE, in 1964.[7]

This internationalization pattern resulting from distance and networks was modified by two factors: geopolitical concerns, and alternative educational models that represented the New Look alternative in business education. First, concerning the geopolitical concerns, the Americanization movement with all its features has to be regarded in the light of the Cold War. The efforts of the Marshall aid administration, the EPA, and the Ford Foundation to include top management training and development as core initiatives in programs to strengthen the geopolitical position of the US contributed to a greater international demand for programs such as the AMP as well as the pattern of geographical localization of these programs during their internationalization. HBS categorized their international partners into three groups. First, there were partners with whom HBS had made formal cooperation agreements lasting between five and ten years; second, there were informal partners; and third, there were foreign business schools and management development centers where HBS professors taught AMPs on an individual basis.

In the first group, there were only three formal academic partners: the University of Istanbul, Turkey, IIMA in India, and INCAE in Central America. The formal agreements were the result of geopolitical initiatives. In the case of Turkey and India, the initiatives came from the Ford Foundation.[8] In India, some regional management training centers were set up in the early 1950s; one of these was the Administrative Staff College, which was modeled on the Administrative Staff College in Henley in the UK and was set up in 1957. In the geopolitical post-war landscape in the 1950s, India was, due to her growing interests in the Soviet Union in the 1950s, given the Ford Foundation's highest priority among countries outside the US (Sackley 2012). In 1955, Dr. Douglas Ensminger, the head of the Ford Foundation's office in India, met with the Indian Minister of Science and Research. They agreed that the regional focus of the management training centers, and the middle-management focus of the Administrative Staff College, did not meet the requirements for training top executives in a post-colonial context. As a result, Ensminger organized a study tour to the US to allow representatives from the government and the business elite to meet US business schools that offered programs for top managers (Hill *et al.* 1973).

This process exemplifies how the US offered alternative models for executive programs even in the early phases of the New Look. In the US, the Indian group met four business schools with quite different focuses on training top executives: (1) HBS "stressed the training of practitioners, especially in general management"; (2) the Carnegie-Mellon School of Administration "defined its primary purpose as extensions of the frontier of knowledge, especially in the quantitative area"; (3) MIT "based its programs on a strong foundation of knowledge of quantitative methods and the behavioral sciences"; and (4) the University of Chicago "rests heavily on Chicago's strength in the social sciences, especially in economics" (Hill *et al.* 1973: 37). In the case of the Indian developments, the Ford Foundation pushed for a consortium of MIT and UCLA, representing a quantitative approach, to provide an MBA program instead of a short executive program.[9] However, as a result of strong and long-term pressure from the business community in Ahmedabad, which included several local HBS alumni, IIMA chose "the Harvard doctrine." In 1963/1964 it offered its first program, an AMP, for 120 participants, and it later became a full business school with degree programs. At the same time as IIMA was established in 1961, the India Institute of Management Calcutta (IMMC) as established in Calcutta with MIT as its main American partner. IIMA was formally recognized by HBS as an institutional partner, and, until 1969 when the agreement ended, HBS sent seven faculty members to Ahmedabad every year to teach. For five years IIMA sent eight faculty members to HBS to be trained in case method teaching for executives (Hill *et al.* 1973; Anubhai 2011).

Another example of a business school for which HBS and the Ford Foundation presented conflicting models, and for which HBS's model was chosen, was IMEDE, which was established in 1957 by the multinational company Nestlé in Lausanne, Switzerland. In 1990 IMEDE merged with Centre d'Etudes Industrielles (CEI) in Geneva to become IMD (David and Schaufelbuehl 2015). When planning IMEDE, two top managers from Nestlé contacted HBS for cooperation. They looked to HBS to gain legitimacy, and HBS responded by taking an active part in shaping and managing IMEDE, which started as a management training center offering executive programs. According to the *Boston Sunday Herald* newspaper, IMEDE was "the first attempt to blend American teaching with the business practice and production methods of Europe and other parts of the world."[10] Seven HBS professors went to the new school to teach on the basis of HBS case methods. Within this cooperative framework, HBS convinced the Nestlé directors to change the focus of IMEDE from an internal corporate focus to one that approached the European market for top managers. They even established a "Boston Committee" in 1957, with three of the HBS professors who taught at IMEDE acting on an advisory committee for IMEDE's management. The committee was frequently contacted regarding strategic questions on how to develop IMEDE.

The first program at IMEDE was a non-degree executive program, but it lasted for eight months rather than the 13 weeks offered at HBS. This reflected the fact that IMEDE was an independent institution that, from the beginning, focused on executives from a lower level of the corporate hierarchies than the HBS AMP. The length of the course was also affected by the fact that IMEDE had a strong international profile and primarily attracted European participants from outside Switzerland who needed time to adjust to a multicultural setting.[11]

From the first year of cooperation, HBS made several efforts to push IMEDE toward the shorter AMP model.[12] After an initiative from the "Boston Committee," the creation of a short AMP was on the IMEDE board's agenda in 1964.[13] The HBS faculty at IMEDE met resistance from two parties. The first of these contained the majority of the small number of permanent IMEDE faculty. Not all of the permanent faculty were enthusiastic about the case methods, and especially the AMP, which, they argued, was too short to go into any depth. There was also a question of who within IMEDE should make the decision or, as IMEDE's director Chaffee E. Hall, Jr. wrote,

Should this be a function of the Faculty, or should an Advanced management programme be planned by the Advisory Committee at Harvard in the same way that the
original IMEDE programme was planned? And what role do the Trustees play?[14]

HBS also met resistance from the Ford Foundation, which promoted a change from the
eight-month program toward a degree program in cooperation with the University of Lausanne.
The Ford Foundation was concerned that IMEDE was too dependent on HBS and its case
tradition, and at the beginning of the 1960s this led to negative responses from the Ford Foundation when IMEDE applied for funding (David and Schaufelbuehl 2015: 92). When, later in the
1960s, the IMEDE faculty began to articulate its lack of enthusiasm for the short AMP concept
and argued in favor of a longer program and more research, representatives from the Ford
Foundation had several meetings with the faculty and management at IMEDE. They were told
that, in the US, the Ford Foundation did not support MBA or short management development
programs, but preferred research-based activities, such as PhD programs.[15] They were also
encouraged to develop the relationship with the University of Lausanne and to prepare for the
introduction of a degree program.[16]

As a result of its strong position at IMEDE, and because of a demand from business for
shorter programs, HBS managed to continue its campaign for shorter executive programs. HBS
regarded the length of the program as an important success factor if a program should be able to
attract real top executives. In 1966, a new four-week AMP was offered, nine years before the
MBA degree was formalized in 1975. CEI, which was established in 1946 by Alcan and
cooperated closely with HBS in the 1950s, also started with a longer non-degree residential
program of 11 months and moved toward shorter programs by offering an AMP in 1963. The
MBA came in 1979. At INSEAD in France, the first program, from 1957 onwards, was a ten-
month program. The first AMP was offered in 1966. The MBA degree, however, was introduced as late as 1969 (David and Schaufelbuehl 2015; Barsoux 2000). All these highly ranked
European business schools, including IESE in Barcelona,[17] started as business schools offering
what today we call executive programs, and strengthened their profiles by introducing AMP
before later expanding to offer degree-awarding programs.

Conclusion

Globally, modern executive education is a viable and profitable division, particularly in the most
prestigious business schools, and it is presented in formats of different length and content. Within
this great variety of programs and courses, the short non-degree AMP model has achieved a
position as the preferred format for executive education. This format emerged at HBS as a contribution to the completion of the managerial revolution by preparing the new group of professional top executives who were detached from the knowledge and norms of the owners. In
some countries, there were national initiatives prior to this process, and in some countries the
process has been stronger than in others. The model spread globally, partly through the mechanisms of closeness and networks that are prescribed in internationalization process theories, but
it was also modified by the institutional context of Americanization, with the Ford Foundation
as a key actor. The emergence of a new non-degree logic directed toward managers in top or
close to top positions, with the AMP as the core, was anchored in a strong demand from business for short intensive programs. In many countries, the Ford Foundation tried to push the
process in a more academic direction into the degree format. However, this aim was of secondary order and subordinated to the general aim of developing business education. Therefore, the
foundation was basically a supporter, and if possible, a modifier to the process where the US

business schools were the providers of a new concept for executive education and local actors key partners to implement executive education in a new context.

Research on the development of executive education does not only contribute to our knowledge about the formation of top executives in a period of globalization. Since most of the non-American business schools that began to offer this program in the period 1945–1970 started with executive programs and then began to develop MBA, PhD and other degree programs, the emergence of this sector also leads to a more nuanced perception of the general development of business schools. First, by including the development of executive education within the business school we modify the impression of radical changes toward a rigorous academic logic linked to the New Look movement that attempted at making the schools more scientific and more detached from business practice. Second, this study shows that US concepts, such as executive education, had a strong impact when institutional constraints, such as national regulations, were of less importance than in the degree-part of business education.

This story is about the globalization of the business of executive education. It is basically the narrative of the internationalization of a concept for how to develop top executives. Although not explicitly discussed here, it also relates to the internationalization of students since some went abroad to attend such programs. The story also includes the question of education and training as tools to develop skills that are required for the creation and development of MNEs, which came in focus from the late 1960s. The impact these programs had on the development of MNEs has not yet been addressed as a question for historical studies.

Another topic for further studies is the role of local actors and institutions in adjusting the general idea of executive education to the local context. This chapter argues that the influence from the US was strong in this field, and that national institutions were different compared to the educational system in general since executive education did not challenge national degree-specific institutions. This does not mean that national institutions and actors were not important. Indeed, they were of great relevance and their influence should be explored further in future studies. A third interesting and so far underexplored research field is the content of these programs. Since they were short and intense in time, and emphasized on-campus location where participants lived together and worked in groups, we can hypothesize that the main aim of the programs was to socialize the participants into the world of executives and establish social networks. If so, this has potential implications for the future development of executive education. While business schools today are concerned with how to meet the new digitalized world by introducing new technology into the programs, the key to the future of top executive education could depend more on their ability to develop the social dimensions that require on-site activities.

Acknowledgement

I am thankful to the archivists at the Historical Collection, Baker Library, Harvard Business School, and at Rockefeller Archive Center, which stores the Ford Foundation archives, for all their help.

Notes

1 The two other European business schools on the top ten list of open programs in 2017 were the Saïd Business School, University of Oxford, established in 1993, and ESTM Berlin, founded in 2002. See www.rankings.ft.com, accessed 1 August 2017.
2 *Harvard Business School Bulletin*, vol. 30, no. 3 (1954): 6.
3 *Harvard Business School Bulletin*, vol. 44, no. 3 (1968): 22.
4 "Management Training Course 1953. General Information 1953," box 3, folder "Western Ontario Management Training, 1953," Ralph M. Hower's papers, Baker Library, Harvard Business School.

5 "Documents for consideration, 1963–1964," Memo to Dean George P. Baker, from Ad hoc Committee on the School's International Activities, December 13, 1962, box 1, Division International Activities papers, HBS Archives (hereafter HBS/DIA).
6 HBS/DIA, Policies and Program Committee, Minutes of Meeting, June 2, 1959. Report from the Task Force Committee on International Management Training, box 1, folder "Hansen report 1963," HSB/DIA.
7 "INCAE: The Early Years," note http://conocimiento.incae.edu/EN/biblioteca/recursos-servicios/historia-incae/pdf/INCAE-The-Early-Years.pdf, accessed 1 February 2017.
8 E.g., *Harvard Business School Bulletin*, vol. 30, no. 3 (1954): 3–19; vol. 40, no. 3 (1964): 5–6; vol. 44, no. 3 (1968): 22–25.
9 Request for Grant Action, 30 October 1964; Grant file 62-520; FA732D, reel 1921, Ford Foundation Record, Rockefeller Archive Center (hereafter FFR).
10 *Boston Sunday Herald*, 5 May 1957, box 28, folder "Teaching Control Course, 1957 (IMEDE)," Robert N. Anthony papers, HBS Archives.
11 E.g., Report – IMEDE visit – 1959, from C. Roland Christensen, box 74, folder "IMEDE, Memos, reports 1958–1959," Kenneth Andrew's paper, HBS Archives (hereafter HBS/Andrews).
12 E.g., Clark E. Meyer (Director), Comments of the director on the Smith–Christensen report, June 17, 1959, box 74, folder "IMEDE, Memos, reports 1958–1959," HBS/Andrews.
13 Chaffee E. Hall, Jr. Director IMEDE to Prof. Robert N. Anthony, 6 October 1964, box 8, folder "IMEDE, Advanced Management Program, Summer 1966," HBS Archives, George Albert Smith's paper.
14 Ibid.
15 Mariam K. Chamberlain, Discussion with Pierre Goetschin, note 12 June 1967, Log files 1957–1976, FA734, Reel L-220; FFR.
16 Mariam K. Chamberlain to Marshall A. Robinson, 22 September 1967, Log files 1957–1976, FA734, Reel L-220; FFR.
17 *Harvard Business School Bulletin*, vol. 40, no. 2 (1964): 11–12.

References

Amdam, Rolv Petter, ed. 1996. *Management education and competitiveness: Europe, Japan, and the United States.* London: Routledge.
Amdam, Rolv Petter. 2008. "Business education." In *The Oxford handbook in business history*, edited by Geoffrey Jones and Jonathan Zeitlin, 581–602. Oxford: Oxford University Press.
Amdam, Rolv Petter. 2016. "Executive education and the managerial revolution: The birth of executive education at Harvard Business School." *Business History Review* 90 (4): 671–690. doi: 10.1017/S0007680517000010.
Amdam, Rolv Petter, Ragnhild Kvålshaugen, and Eirinn Larsen, eds. 2003. *Inside the business school: The content of European business education.* Oslo: Abstrakt.
Andrews, Kenneth R. 1959. "University programs for practicing executives." In *The education of American business: A study of university-college programs in business administration*, edited by Frank C. Pierson, 577–608. New York: McGraw-Hill.
Anubhai, Prafull. 2011. *The MBA story: The DNA of an institution.* Noida and London: Random House India.
Augier, Mie, and James G. March. 2011. *The roots, rituals, and rhetoric of change: North American business schools after the Second World War.* Stanford, CA: Stanford University Press.
Barnes, William. 1989. *Managerial catalyst: The story of London Business School, 1964–1989.* London: Paul Chapman.
Barsoux, J.-L. 2000. *INSEAD: From intuition to institution.* Basingstoke: Macmillan.
Berghahn, Volker R. 2010. "The debate on 'Americanization' among economic and cultural historians." *Cold War History* 10 (1): 107–130. doi: 10.1080/14682740903388566.
Boel, Bent. 1998. "The European Productivity Agency and the development of management education in Western Europe in the 1950s." In *Missionaries and managers: American influence on European management education, 1945–60*, edited by Terry R. Gourvish and Nick Tiratsoo, 34–45. Manchester and New York: Manchester University Press.
Cruikshank, Jeffrey L. 1987. *A delicate experiment: The Harvard Business School 1908–1945.* Boston, MA: Harvard Business School Press.

David, Thomas, and Janick Marina Schaufelbuehl. 2015. "Transatlantic influence in the shaping of business education: The origins of IMD, 1946–1990." *Business History Review* 89 (1): 75–97. doi: 10.1017/S0007680515000069.

DiMaggio, Paul J., and Walter W. Powell. 1983. "The iron cage revisited: Institutional isomorphism and collective rationality in organizational fields." *American Sociological Review* 48 (2): 147–160.

Djelic, Marie-Laure. 1998. *Exporting the American model: The post-war transformation of European business.* Oxford: Oxford University Press.

Engwall, Lars, and Vera Zamagni, eds. 1998. *Management education in historical perspective.* Manchester: Manchester University Press.

Engwall, Lars, Matthias Kipping, and Behlül Üsdiken. 2016. *Defining management: Business schools, consultants, media.* New York and London: Routledge.

Epstein, Sandra. 2016. *Business at Berkeley: The history of the Haas School of Business.* Berkeley, CA: Berkeley Public Policy Press.

Forsgren, Mats. 2016. "A note on the revisited Uppsala internationalization process model: The implications of business networks and entrepreneurship." *Journal of International Business Studies* 47 (9): 1135–1144. doi: 10.1057/s41267-016-0014-3.

Fridenson, Patrick. 2017. "La formation continue des dirigeants d'entreprise en France depuis 1944." In *Les trames de l'histoire: entreprises, territoires, consommations, institutions. Mélanges en l'honneur de Jean-Claude Daumas*, edited by Jean-Paul Barrière, Régis Boulat, Alain Chatriot, Pierre Lamard, and Jean-Michel Minovez, 143–160. Besançon: Presses Universitaires de Franche-Comté.

Gemelli, Guiliana, ed. 1998. *The Ford Foundation and Europe (1950s – 1970s): Cross-fertilization of learning in social science and management.* Brussels: Europe Interuniversity Press.

Gourvish, Terry, and Nick Tiratsoo, eds. 1998. *Missionaries and managers: American influence on European management education, 1945–1960.* Manchester: Manchester University Press.

Hill, Thomas M., W. Warren Haynes, and Howard Baumgartel. 1973. *Institution building in India: A study of international collaboration in management education.* Boston, MA: Harvard University, Graduate School of Business Administration, Division or Research.

Johanson, Jan, and Jan-Erik Vahlne. 1977. "The internationalization process of the firm: A model of knowledge development and increasing foreign market commitments." *Journal of International Business Studies* 8 (1): 23–32.

Johanson, Jan, and Jan-Erik Vahlne. 2009. "The Uppsala internationalization process model revisited: From liability of foreignness to liability of outsidership." *Journal of International Business Studies* 40 (9): 1411–1431. doi: 10.1057/jibs.2009.24.

Kipping, Matthias. 1998. "The hidden business schools: Management training in Germany since 1945." In *Management education in historical perspective*, edited by Lars Engwall and Vera Zamagni, 95–110. Manchester and New York: Manchester University Press.

Kipping, Matthias, and Ove Bjarnar, eds. 1998. *The Americanisation of European business: The Marshall Plan and the transfer of US management models.* London and New York: Routledge.

Kipping, Matthias, Lars Engwall, and Behlül Üsdiken. 2009. "The transfer of management knowledge to peripheral countries." *International Studies of Management and Organization* 38 (4): 3–16.

Locke, Robert R. 1984. *The end of the practical man: Entrepreneurship and higher education in Germany, France, and Great Britain, 1880–1940.* Greenwich, CT and London: JAI Press.

Locke, Robert R. 1989. *Management and higher education since 1940.* Cambridge: Cambridge University Press.

McGlade, Jacqueline. 1998. "The US technical assistance and productivity program and the education of Western European managers, 1948–58." In *Missionaries and managers: American influences on European management education, 1945–60*, edited by Terry R. Gourvish and Nick Tiratsoo, 13–33. Manchester and New York: Manchester University Press.

North, Douglass C. 1990. *Institutions, institutional change and economic performance.* Cambridge: Cambridge University Press.

Parmar, Inderjeet. 2012. *Foundations of the American century: The Ford, Carnegie, and Rockefeller Foundations in the rise of American power.* New York: Columbia University Press.

Pierson, Frank C. 1959. *The education of American businessmen: A study of university–college programs in business administration.* New York: McGraw-Hill.

Sackley, Nicole. 2012. "Foundation in the field: The Ford Foundation's New Delhi office and the construction of development knowledge, 1951–1970." In *American Foundations and the Coproduction of World Order in the Twentieth Century*, edited by John Krige and Helke Rausch, 232–260. Göttingen: Vandenhoeck & Ruprecht.

Scott, W. Richard. 2008. *Institutions and organizations: Ideas and interests.* Thousand Oaks, CA: Sage Publications.

Sedlak, Michael W., and Harold F. Williamson. 1983. *The evolution of management education: A history of the Northwestern University J. L. Kellogg Graduate School of Management 1908–1983.* Urbana and Chicago, IL: University of Illinois Press.

West, Jude P. 1970. "A comparative analysis of university executive development programs conducted in 1958 and 1968." PhD dissertation, University of Iowa.

Wilson, John F. 1992. *The Manchester experiment: A history of Manchester Business School, 1965–1990.* London: Paul Chapman Publishing Ltd.

Zeitlin, Jonathan, and Gary Herrigel. 2000. *Americanization and its limits: Reworking US technology and management in post-war Europe and Japan.* Oxford: Oxford University Press.

9

CONSULTANTS AND INTERNATIONALIZATION

Matthias Kipping

Introduction

A recent book on economic policy-making characterizes the twenty-first century as the "century of consultants, advisors and experts" (Levy and Peart 2017: 3). It is no surprise that consultants are named first. They have indeed been shaping economic policy, as that book demonstrates in some detail. More consequentially, consultants have also come to define "best practices" and "excellence" for a wide range of public and private organizations around the globe, determining the strategic directions of these organizations and reshaping their operations as well as the work experiences and life worlds of millions of people (for details and additional references, see Kipping and Wright 2012; Engwall *et al.* 2016). In the process, consulting firms have grown significantly and are today larger than many of their clients (see Table 9.1).

These large consulting firms are also very global. First-ranked Deloitte for example claimed to employ more than 260,000 people in over 150 countries and territories in 2017 (Deloitte 2017)

Table 9.1 Estimates of the world's largest consulting firms by revenue in 2013 (billion USD)

	Gartner			Kennedy Consulting		
		Revenues (USD billion)	*Growth (%)*		*Revenues (USD billion)*	*Growth (%)*
1	Deloitte	14.7	6.0	Deloitte	18.3	7.0
2	PwC	12.7	10.0	PwC	16.1	10.5
3	EY	12.1	12.7	EY	13.7	10.1
4	KPMG	10.7	5.2	KPMG	11.3	6.5
5	Accenture	4.1	4.4	Accenture	7.3	−2.5
6	IBM	4.0	2.1	IBM	6.0	−0.4
7	McKinsey & Co.	2.3	5.5	McKinsey & Co.	5.9	4.5
8	Booz Allen Hamilton	2.1	−2.9	BCG	3.6	7.0
9	CGI	1.5	3.4	Booz Allen Hamilton	3.4	−5.5
10	CSC	1.4	-3.6	Mercer	3.3	1.6

Source: See Engwall et al. 2016: 241.

– even if probably not all these locations offered consulting services. Accenture boasts offices in more than 200 cities in 53 countries with over 435,000 employees (Accenture 2018) – though quite a large proportion in technology and outsourcing services. McKinsey & Co., still considered the "premier" management consulting firm by many, employed around 11,000 in more than 120 cities in over 60 countries (www.mckinsey.com/locations). Few other sectors have such an extensive international presence. However, this is only the case for the largest consulting firms, since the vast majority of management advice is provided by myriad individual and small-scale service providers that operate locally or nationally. These nevertheless contribute to globalization – albeit in a different way, to be discussed below.

Few publications have addressed the internationalization of larger consulting firms specifically (see, especially Jones 2003; Morgan *et al.* 2006; Roberts 2006). There has been more research on the internationalization of other service firms (e.g. Enderwick 1989; Aharoni and Nachum 2000; Roberts 2015), namely banks (see Youssef Cassis in this volume) and knowledge-based services (e.g. Harrington and Daniels 2006). There has also been work on the globalization of professional services more generally (see, e.g. Bäumer *et al.* 2012), such as accounting (e.g. Daniels *et al.* 1989; Cooper *et al.* 2000). This contrasts with the large number of scholarly studies devoted to the international expansion and global activities of manufacturing firms (see, e.g. Paula de la Cruz-Fernández and Patrick Fridenson in this volume). Moreover, much of this limited literature focuses on the recent period and links it with the overall globalization of the economy since the late twentieth century – even if Kipping (1999) shows that consultants were active outside their home countries since the beginning of that century (see also Engwall *et al.* 2016).

To provide a more comprehensive – and long-term – overview, this chapter assembles information from a wide range of historical and contemporary treatments of the management consulting industry and its various stakeholders. The extant research has come from scholars in multiple academic disciplines, namely business and management history, economic geography, international business, organization studies, and even law. Some additional information is derived from the business press and – cognizant of their potential biases – from commissioned or internal histories of consulting firms or their client companies. As noted, very few of these accounts were written with a specific focus on internationalization, which means the present overview will remain tentative as well as incomplete.

But despite these constraints in terms of the available evidence, it seems safe to suggest that consulting has been both an integral part and a driver of global business since the early twentieth century. This becomes evident by examining (i) when and how management consulting firms themselves expanded internationally; (ii) how far their ideas and practices were adopted – or adapted – globally; and (iii) whether and in what ways consultants influenced the international expansion of their client organizations. The following sections of the chapter will address each of these questions by (a) summarizing and critically reviewing the findings of the extant literature – rather than conducting new empirical work – and (b), whenever possible, considering how far these findings conform with the main theories and frameworks in international business or challenge them. The final section of the chapter will summarize the main overall insights and point out some promising avenues for future studies.

The global expansion of management consulting firms

The large consulting firms of today took one of two avenues toward their global presence: they either *internationalized* by establishing offices outside their home country – an ongoing process since the beginning of the twentieth century; or they expanded abroad based on different though adjacent activities such as accounting or IT services and then *diversified* into consulting – a process that also started early but accelerated significantly over recent decades. Both types of firms predominantly originated in the United States, with the United Kingdom and other Western European economies as secondary home countries. The first of these two processes has been studied mainly by historians – and often ignored by scholars in other disciplines; the second has found some interest among organizational scholars – though they have tended to focus on internal conflicts within these conglomerates and on what appears as their ultimate failure to establish truly global structures and policies. Both processes are detailed in the following sub-sections, with a third sub-section looking at how India became increasingly important since the end of the twentieth century both as a host and a home country for global consulting activities.

From local to global and back: consultants internationalizing

As historical research has shown, at the outset consulting was an activity dominated by engineers, in particular under the umbrella of "scientific management" or "Taylorism" due to the visible role played by Frederick W. Taylor (1853–1915) in its foundation (see, for a summary, Wright and Kipping 2012). These consultants focused, originally, on efficiency enhancements on the shop floor – soon extended to offices, public administration and even society as a whole. In terms of internationalization, at the beginning of the twentieth century most of these "consulting engineers" or "efficiency experts", as they were known at the time, worked as individuals, generally based in the United States (Nelson 1995). But these people travelled and did spread their "gospel" globally (see, e.g. Merkle 1980; the contributions in Nelson 1992; Spender and Kijne 1996; and, for a summary, Engwall *et al.* 2016: ch. 8). Three main ways can be distinguished: (i) Taylor and his many competitors spent short periods abroad proselytizing their systems among fellow engineers or carrying out projects; (ii) foreigners wanting to observe scientific management and its implementation in action visited the US – taking the ideas back to their home countries; (iii) events and other dissemination efforts were organized, since 1924, by the International Committee of Scientific Management, CIOS (*Comité Internationale de l'Organisation Scientifique du Travail*) and, between 1925 and 1934, the Geneva-based International Management Institute (IMI).

A first attempt to establish a wider presence in the US and a more permanent one outside came from the firm founded by Taylor's competitor Harrington Emerson in 1907 under the name Emerson Company Engineers, later changed to Emerson Efficiency Engineers (Quigel 1992). Emerson established multiple offices in the US and some of its engineers, led by the Italian A. M. Morinni, also moved to Paris, France in 1913 – though the outbreak of World War I cut their efforts short. At the same time, the war and its aftermath brought other efficiency engineers to Europe to help with production and reconstruction efforts. Some of them stayed and established a more permanent presence there, including, most prominently C. Bertrand Thomson and Wallace Clark, the former based in Paris (Wren *et al.* 2015) and the latter running his European offices from New York (Wren 2015). Most successful among them was Charles E. Bedaux, a French immigrant to the US, who familiarized himself with scientific management when working as an interpreter for the above mentioned Morinni, whom he also accompanied to Paris in 1913. Upon his return to the US, Bedaux developed his own system and his own firm in the Midwest in 1916. Following projects for well-known companies, such as GE and Kodak, the firm quickly expanded across the US, opening multiple offices. In 1926, Bedaux ventured abroad starting in London, followed by Paris, Milan and Berlin – with a somewhat more ephemeral presence in other parts of the globe, including Africa, Australia and Japan. By the mid-1930s, his firm employed several hundred consultants around the world (Kreis 1992; Kipping 1999; Weatherburn 2014).

Small in comparison with today's global consulting giants, Bedaux and his firm were never-theless significant and highly visible at the time. In comparison, the firm established by account-ing professor James O. McKinsey in Chicago in 1926, which is today among the leading global service providers, had less than 50 consultants based in Chicago, New York and Boston around the mid-1930s (McDonald 2013: 31). McKinsey belonged to a new "wave" of consulting firms that examined organizations more comprehensively and suggested changes to their overall struc-tures and operations rather than focusing on the optimization of (productive) efficiency (Kipping 2002; McKenna 2006; McDonald 2013). Most of these firms were established in in the US during the interwar period, generally under the label of "consulting management engineers". They saw a significant expansion during the Great Depression, when they assisted in the re-organization of troubled companies, and even more so during World War II, when they con-ducted projects for the US government or the military, and converted companies for wartime production – and then re-converted them after the war. Government-related work continued during the Cold War and also led to their first forays abroad to countries such as Egypt, Iran and Nigeria with projects sponsored by the US Agency for International Development (AID) (Engwall *et al.* 2016: 177, 182). Only during the 1960s did these firms establish a more perma-nent international presence in Europe (see Table 9.2).

In terms of internationalization, these were neither the first nor the last. An early mover was the firm founded by former bible salesman George S. May during the inter-war period, which expanded rapidly due to aggressive sales methods. May set up an office in Düsseldorf in 1955, apparently after playing in a golf tournament there, and claimed to have a total of nine European offices by the mid-1960s – but his firm seems to have faltered thereafter since it apparently promised more than it could deliver (Engwall *et al.* 2016: 182). The Boston Consulting Group (BCG) was a latecomer, established in 1963 by a Boston bank and gaining its independence only about a decade later. BCG nevertheless internationalized almost immediately, based on acquisi-tions in what appeared more marginal and probably less competitive markets, namely Italy and Japan in 1965 and 1966 respectively, followed by a joint venture in London in 1968 (see Higdon 1969; Engwall *et al.* 2016: 179–184).

With the possible exception of May and BCG, the international expansion of all these firms conforms at least partially to a "follow-thy-client" strategy, which is still widely seen as the main motivation for the internationalization of service businesses (e.g. Kundu and Merchant 2008). Bedaux's initial projects in Europe, for instance, were for the foreign subsidiaries of his US client Kodak. For similar reasons, Arthur D. Little and Booz Allen established their first European offices in Switzerland, where many US multinationals had moved their European headquarters during the war (see also Kurosawa and Wubs, in this volume). But local companies also "invited" these consultants, seeking their help in dealing with growing competition, namely from US

Table 9.2 The expansion of US management consultants in Europe in the 1960s

	No. of offices		No. of consultants		Revenues in 1969	
	1962	1969	1962	1969	USD million	% of total
McKinsey & Co.	1	6	15	160	8	35
Arthur D. Little	1	4	30	53	6	16
Booz Allen	1	2	70	111	5	9
A. T. Kearney	0	5	0	60	2	15

Source: See Kipping 1999: 210.

multinationals. This was the case with Italy's Fiat and Bedaux in the 1930s or, on a much larger scale, after World War II, when large European firms became concerned by the influx of American multinational enterprises (MNEs) following the creation of the European Economic Community (EEC) in 1957, which also disrupted their own market-sharing arrangements (Servan-Schreiber 1967; Kipping 1999; McKenna 2006). Some of these European companies gained initial experiences with US consultants in the Americas. The Anglo-Dutch oil company Shell for instance first hired McKinsey for a project in Venezuela (Kipping 1999: 212). Hence, for the internationalization of the US consulting firms, multinationals from both their home country and the host countries in Europe acted as "bridges" (Kipping 1999: 193, 199).

Once in Europe, the US consulting firms quickly localized their staff – increasingly hiring host country nationals – and their offices, establishing strong presences in the major financial and business centers such as London, Paris and Amsterdam. To quickly build relationships with local elites they relied on well-placed individuals as "connectors" (Kipping 1999; see also, in general, Glückler 2006). Bedaux for instance appointed leading industrialists, such as Fiat's Giovanni Agnelli, to the boards of his various subsidiaries and hired consultants from top engineering schools, like France's *grandes écoles*. McKinsey recruited a well-connected former civil servant as a director in the UK and supported the establishment of the London Business School and INSEAD (Institut européen d'administration des affaires) in France. And, in Germany, it established close relations with the long-time head of Deutsche Bank, Hermann-Josef Abs, and frequently attended the bi-annual meetings of the country's top managers and their potential successors in the Black Forest spa town of Baden-Baden (see Figure 9.1). Last not least, the US consulting firms also prompted the creation of local competitors through spin-offs and new

Figure 9.1   McKinsey connecting with German CEOs in Baden-Baden

Source: Industriekurier, 21 February 1970; reprinted with permission of the cartoonist, Klaus Pielert.

foundations. The Americans nevertheless remained dominant, also and especially in cultural, behavioral and even linguistic terms, with consultants across Europe imitating the "McKinsey look of successful young professionals" or letting "drop the odd Americanism" (quoted from contemporary publications by Kipping 1999: 215).

All of this suggests that from their early days, consulting firms followed an internationalization process akin to the recently "revisited" version of the so-called Uppsala model (Johanson and Vahlne 2009). In their original model, Johanson and Vahlne (1977) had focused on the liability of foreignness due to cultural or as they called it "psychic" distance between suppliers and customers. Now business is seen as a "web of relationships", where foreign firms are "outsiders" with trust-building as an important way to overcome this outsider status. Johanson and Vahlne (2009) have linked these revisions to recent changes in business practices as well as advances in international business (IB) theory. However, consultants seem to have already developed mechanisms to access networks within host countries since the inter-war period, namely by using MNEs as "bridges" and by hiring "connectors" – highlighting once again the need for the IB literature to become more sensitive to service activities, on the one hand, and to historical research, on the other.

International first: diversifying into consulting

Many of the large global consulting firms of today took a different pathway to their current position: diversification. This mainly concerns three types of organization that provided services in adjacent areas: accounting and auditing; information technology, including hardware, software and services; and communications, in particular advertising. Firms in all three areas internationalized *before* or while becoming involved, to varying degrees, in consulting activities, which in many cases now represent the largest share of their revenues. In line with the limited research on the internationalization of services, not much has been done to examine their global expansion – though there has been some recent research questioning how far their organizations and policies are truly global (Boussebaa 2009; Boussebaa *et al.* 2012). By contrast, scholars have paid some more attention to the antecedents and consequences of the diversification processes, namely with respect to the tensions within these firms regarding (a) the distribution of profits between the consultants and those on the traditional, less dynamic side of the business, whose relationships facilitated the diversification originally (e.g. McDougald and Greenwood 2012) and (b) regulatory concerns regarding possible conflicts of interests between the different parts of these conglomerates (e.g. Coffee 2006). The remainder of this sub-section quickly recounts the internationalization and diversification processes for each of the three types of firms.

In *audit and accounting* a first wave of internationalization occurred in the late nineteenth century as British accountants expanded into the US, partially following British investors. But UK and US operations soon separated and grew independently (see, for the case of Price Waterhouse, Jones 1995; Allen and McDermott 1993, respectively). With the exception of Peat Marwick, Mitchell, & Co., established through a merger between a UK and a US firm in 1925, the large service providers only internationalized again after World War II – at a time when many of them also started expanding their consulting activities and established internal units to provide these "management advisory services". This internationalization occurred in a variety of forms (Daniels *et al.* 1989). On one extreme were loose international alliances, where partner firms retained their own identity, structures, policies etc. under a common umbrella with Klynveld Main Goerdeler (KMG) as a prime example. KMG was formed in 1979 by firms from the Netherlands, the US, West Germany, Canada, the UK, Australia, Switzerland, France and Denmark (Daniels *et al.* 1989: 82); it merged in 1987 with Peat Marwick to form KPMG. On the other extreme was the firm established in Chicago by accounting professor Arthur Andersen in 1913, who limited expansion to a few other US offices and imposed tight control namely through a uniform culture. It was only after the founder's death in 1947 that his successor expanded internationally reaching 92 offices in 26 countries by the early 1970s – all fully owned and unified through corporate culture (Squires *et al.* 2003: 44–45).

Consolidation, internationalization and diversification accelerated since the 1970s. Mainly drawing on their early expertise in the application of information technologies, the so-called "Big Eight" accounting and audit firms expanded their consulting activities to such an extent that, by 1982, seven of them were listed among the top 20 consulting firms in the US by revenue, with Andersen ranked first overall (Engwall *et al.* 2016: 184–186). In terms of consolidation, after two more mergers, the number of the largest firms was reduced to six by the end of the decade and ultimately to five with the creation of PricewaterhouseCoopers (PwC) in 1998 – all of them highly international. But these developments also resulted in significant internal and external challenges. Internally, conflicts emerged between audit and consulting partners with the latter now bringing in most of the profits and the former insisting that "their" relationships had been making that success possible. At Arthur Andersen, the creation of a highly autonomous division, called Andersen Consulting (AC) in 1989 managed to delay full scission, which eventually occurred in 2001, when AC spun off under the name Accenture (Squires *et al.* 2003: chs 5 and 6; for an overview, McDougald and Greenwood 2012).

Pressure to split auditing and consulting also came from the regulators, concerned with the conflict of interest inherent in cross-selling these services (Stevens 1991). These concerns were proven justified with the Enron bankruptcy in 2001, where Andersen had provided both audit and consulting services, which it had re-developed internally following the creation of AC and then Accenture. Consequently, Andersen was prohibited from auditing publicly quoted companies and quickly disintegrated with most partners joining the remaining "Big Four". KPMG, PwC and Ernst & Young sold or spun off their consulting activities at the time, but also ended up redeveloping them – with the revenue growth and profits they keep providing apparently difficult to forgo. Only Deloitte pulled back from such a separation, which might explain its leading position today. Recently, these firms moved further into the "core" of management consulting, acquiring remnants of former strategy consultants: Deloitte buying Michael Porter's Monitor and PwC Booz & Co., renamed Strategy& (Engwall *et al.* 2016: 239–250).

The second type of organizations entering consulting from the outside were *IT services providers*. In terms of internationalization, many, but not all of them, internationalized before diversifying into consulting – and that diversification occurred largely through acquisitions, reflecting their latecomer status. Outcomes varied widely. Thus, Electronic Data Services (EDS), which was founded by Ross Perot in 1962, went public in 1968 and was owned by General Motors (GM) between 1984 and 1996, made a major push into consulting during the 1990s. Thus, in 1995 it acquired A. T. Kearney (ATK), which itself had separated from McKinsey in the early post-World War II period. The objective for the combined firm was to become "a new competitive force in the global management consulting arena" (EDS History Timeline 2008: 12). But it failed in that intent, spinning off ATK again in 2006 and selling itself to Hewlett-Packard (HP), which was also unable to revive its flagging fortunes, formally split its consumer and enterprise businesses in 2015 and merged HPE Enterprise Services with the Computer Sciences Corporation (CSC) into DXC Technology in 2017 operating in 70 countries. EDS, HPE, CSC and now DXC, like many others attempting to expand their consulting activities, ultimately remained "pure-play IT services" providers (Cornell 2017).

Most successful among these new entrants was IBM, which had been operating internationally for almost a century by the time it decided in 1992 to amalgamate a group of 1,500 employees "to provide management and information technology-related consulting services to companies and organizations in 30 countries" (IBM, 7 January 2016; for more details, see IBM Corporate Archives 2002). Under the leadership of a former Booz Allen Hamilton partner that group grew organically to 30,000 people over the next decade. It doubled in size in 2002 with the acquisition of the consulting activities from PwC, propelling it among the largest global consulting firms – though still with a focus on technology-based solutions.

The third and most recent development concerns the entry of the *large global advertising agencies* into consulting activities. Like the audit and accounting firms, after World War II these agencies also embarked on a process of consolidation and internationalization, largely through acquisitions, leading by the beginning of the twenty-first century to another "Big Four": Paris-based Publicis, WPP of London as well as Omnicom and Interpublic of New York (Elliott 2002; for the earlier internationalization, Weinstein 1977). Their diversification into consulting is more recent and very partial. It is probably related to the growing need for organizations to communicate with all their stakeholders and the public at large. Possibly the earliest indication for their push into the consulting space was the offer by Saatchi & Saatchi, now part of Publicis, to acquire Arthur Andersen's consulting division in the late 1980s – ultimately rejected by the latter (Squires *et al.* 2003: ch. 5). Publicis has been the most active in developing consulting activities, namely through the acquisition of Razorfish in 2009 and Sapient in 2015. Both companies had their origins in the 1990s and were among the first to see the potential of the internet and digital technologies for marketing as well as, in the case of Sapient, for broader business services. They suffered when the dot-com bubble burst in the early twenty-first century, but Sapient in particular moved most of its software operations to India (see also below) and continued to grow its service offerings and global footprint through a number of acquisitions. Publicis merged its digital advertising activities into SapientRazorfish and, more importantly, continues to offer technology-based consulting under the name Publicis.Sapient, which recently won a major global contract, jointly with Paris-based Capgemini, to (digitally) enhance the dining experience at McDonald's, beating out Accenture, among others (Stein 2017).

Targeted internationalization and its consequences: to and from India

Over the last three decades, the international expansion of all these consulting firms has taken a new direction: India. Today, Western consulting firms such as Accenture or Deloitte employ tens if not hundreds of thousands of consultants there – often outnumbering those in any other country. This rapid expansion is a surprising development, given that India only opened up to foreign investment since the early 1990s (Malik and Nilakant 2015). Moreover, the country has brought forth its own consulting firms, many of which are now operating globally (e.g. Shainesh *et al.* 2012). Thus, India nowadays serves both as a host and a home country for many of the largest consulting firms in the world – a significant, possibly seminal, break with the past for an industry that from its inception in the early twentieth century and during its subsequent global expansion has been dominated by firms with a Western, mainly US origin (see above). How and why India emerged as such a hub for the management consulting industry has not yet been the subject of specific research, though it has been touched upon by scholars pursuing research interests other than consulting per se and some more popular writing. The remainder of this sub-section briefly sketches the development of India as a consulting hub and summarizes the available insights from the extant literature.

When it comes to the origins of the move to India, and those pioneering it, the relevant literature generally tends to offer very brief and rather divergent accounts (e.g. Grimme and Kreutter 2012). For example, the former President of the country's National Association of

Software and Services Companies (Nasscom), founded in 1988, suggests that its starting point was a deal between General Electric (GE) CEO Jack Welch and the Indian government in 1989, with the former agreeing to outsource software work for US$10 million to India in exchange for the purchase of aircraft engines (Karnik 2012). Others point to the Harvard Business School graduate and former McKinsey consultant Kumar Madheva, who in 1994 convinced Dun & Bradstreet to form a joint venture with the Indian software firm Satyam, which itself had been founded in 1987. The company was renamed Cognizant Technology Solutions in 1996, separated from D & B as part of a restructuring, bought out Satyam in 1997, and became fully independent in the early 2000s (Dinger and Caudill 2013).

As to the broader motivations, the underlying drivers apparently included the widespread knowledge of English and excellent engineering education combined with low wages, even for those highly qualified, as well as a good dose of local entrepreneurship (e.g. Zahee *et al.* 2009; Malik and Nilakant 2015). These conditions seem to have prompted the Western consulting firms to move a large share of their IT-based activities to India. They also advised their clients to do the same and usually offered to take on these activities on their behalf – meaning that from a Western point of view India became a center for "offshored outsourcing", which has been examined by scholars from a variety of perspectives (e.g. Lee *et al.* 2003; Metters and Verma 2008), including international business (Doh *et al.* 2009). The firms of Indian origin, led by Infosys, Tata Consultancy Services (TCS) and Wipro, initially also provided outsourcing for Western clients. But they have since expanded their activities globally, offering services that go well beyond outsourcing (Schwarz and Hentrich 2012).

These Indian firms have attracted some attention, though largely in regard to their earlier activities in the outsourcing of software development and maintenance (e.g. Cusumano 2006; Ghemawat and Altman 2007). Among them, the unique trajectory of Wipro from a vegetable seller founded in Mumbai in 1945 to a major outsourcer has been chronicled in some detail (Hamm 2007). Other studies looking at these firms usually treat them as a case for broader questions such as corporate governance (e.g. Khanna and Palepu 2004) or, more frequently, knowledge management (e.g. Oshri *et al.* 2007). Recently, these Indian consulting firms have also been mentioned in the growing literature on multinationals from emerging economies (e.g. Kumar 2009) – though, with rare exceptions (e.g. Schwarz and Hentrich 2012), there has been little in-depth work on their expanding consulting activities. Neither has there been much interest in the particular organizational form adopted by most of these consulting operations in India, where consultants both work and live in the same place, generally referred to as a "campus" (cf. some of the contributions in Malik and Rowley 2015).

Spreading uniform business models around the globe

In probably one of the most widely cited management articles, DiMaggio and Powell (1983) identify consultants as one of the mechanisms driving what they refer to as "isomorphism", i.e. the tendency for organizations everywhere to become increasingly similar: "Large organizations choose from a relatively small set of major consulting firms which, like Johnny Appleseeds, spread a few organizational models throughout the land" (p. 152). This is part of what they refer to as mimetic processes, which, in addition to normative and coercive processes, promote isomorphism (see also Kipping and Wright 2012). Subsequent studies have picked up on this idea, though focusing increasingly on the legitimacy consultants provide for changes within organizations rather than the uniformity they might be causing (e.g. Jackall 1988). Others have highlighted the largely discursive nature of consulting work, arguing that even initially superficial linguistic changes might eventually lead to more profound transformations (e.g. Czarniawska and Joerges 1996). Relatedly, there is now a relatively widely held view that questions the "reality" of the increases in organizational efficiency invariably promised by consultants – in particular as new organizational models and management ideas seem to follow each other in a fashion-like manner (Abrahamson 1991; Ernst and Kieser 2002).

Empirically, historians have been the ones providing evidence of how new organizational models spread, albeit without necessarily acknowledging their discursive nature or questioning – and, on the contrary, often assuming – their efficiency effects. Studies of their dissemination were sometimes subsumed under the notion of "Americanization" since many of these models had their origins in the United States – with some discussion about whether these US models were suitable elsewhere (for a summary, Kipping and Wright 2012). However, research on the role(s) of consultants in these processes remains spotty. Thus, much of the earlier literature on the first of these major ideas, scientific management, has focused almost exclusively on the role of specific individuals in developing and spreading their gospel, with a particular emphasis on the role of Taylor and his system (see above). These individuals did indeed play an important part, especially early on, in proselytizing the ideas of how to organize work, organizations and even whole societies more efficiently and – more than they have been given credit for – harmoniously (cf. Nyland and Bruce 2012). Ultimately, not individuals but consulting firms applied these systems around the world for much of the twentieth century (see above). At present, many of the large global consulting firms carry out similar optimization work, in production and, increasingly, in the supply chain (for more details, see Wright and Kipping 2012; Engwall *et al.* 2016: ch. 8).

Consultants were also instrumental in spreading what has been called the most significant management innovation of the twentieth century, the decentralized multidivisional organization or M-form (Whittington *et al.* 1999). But their contribution is largely ignored in the quite extensive economics and management literature, which focuses almost exclusively on the question whether or not the M-form improved efficiency – without reaching a clear-cut conclusion (for a summary, Kipping and Westerhuis 2012). Here again empirical evidence on the role of consultants has come from historical studies. Chandler (1962), who was the first to systematically examine the origins and subsequent adoption of the M-form in the United States already mentioned "the very significant role that management consultants … have had in bringing about the introduction of the new structure" (pp. 381–382). Some of the subsequent studies covering other countries confirm this assertion, though with some differences in the degree of consulting input. Thus, for Great Britain, Channon (1973: 239) found that consultants participated in the decentralization processes at 32 of the largest 100 industrial companies – with McKinsey involved in 22 of them. Examining the largest 100 industrial companies in France and Germany, Dyas and Thanheiser (1976) mention their role "in some of the major French divisionalisations" (p. 247), while among the top German companies they identified 18 cases, 12 of which were advised by McKinsey, which "met with difficulties" in three of them (pp. 112, 120–121).

A number of historical case studies found similar "difficulties", i.e. latent or open conflicts between consultants and (middle) managers in a wide range of companies (for a summary, see Kipping and Armbrüster 2002). A recent study has looked at how consultants, and in particular McKinsey, spread the multidivisional structure in the banking sector in a number of countries since the late 1960s (Kipping and Westerhuis 2014). It shows how McKinsey had clear ideas what structure a "modern" banking organization *should* have, drawing extensively on the model of the M-form pioneer GM, which at the time was considered a highly successful global organization and whose President and CEO had just published his memoirs (Sloan 1964). The consultants used a report on "Developing Future Bank Management", originally prepared for the Trustees of the Banking Research Fund at the Association of Reserve City Bankers in the US, as a kind of "blueprint" for all their clients. Regardless of the country- or organization-specific context, they tried to convince the bankers that they should behave like "managers," namely in terms of being more aggressive when it came to increasing revenues and profits. Overall, this study confirms the important mimetic pressures exercised by consultants in order to disseminate a single model of management around the globe, and also highlights the importance of getting them to espouse a specific management terminology in the process. More tentatively, the research also suggests that the consequences of these changes introduced by the consultants might have been detrimental in the longer run, since the structures and incentives created to sell cars were not necessarily suited for selling mortgages and other loans.

Consultants seem to have played a similar role in the spread of more recent management ideas and practices around the globe. Most of the corresponding research has used citation analysis to demonstrate the flow and ebb of fashions and fads (see, for a summary and critique, Clark 2004), paying limited attention to whether or how consulting firms contributed to these processes (cf. Ernst and Kieser 2002). There are some indications, mainly from the more practitioner-centric literature that Western, and in particular US, consultants were heavily involved in spreading manufacturing and quality control models from Japan during the 1980s and early 1990s (e.g. Stalk and Hout 1990) – once again demonstrating their (cultural) hegemony. There has also been some work, based on the popularization of "business process re-engineering", suggesting that consultants were as much driven by the dissemination of fashionable ideas as they were driving it – "hitchhiking on a hype", as Benders *et al.* (1998) put it. Maybe best researched is the influence consultants had in developing and disseminating "new public management", the introduction of business principles and practices in all kinds of public sector entities (see, especially Saint-Martin 2000). By contrast, their more recent impact on changing the boundaries of organizations through "transformational" outsourcing (see above), has yet to be examined in more detail.

Last not least, there is also the important suggestion that their role in spreading uniform business models goes beyond large global consulting firms advising multinational clients – which is the scenario examined by most of the extant scholarship. Thus, based on an ethnographic study of a sole consulting practitioner in Italy, Crucini and Kipping (2001) pinpoint their role in translating – literally as well as figuratively – the ideas of the large global consultants into a local context dominated by small- and medium-sized enterprises – though, unsurprisingly, with a rather limited adaptation to that context (see also McKenna *et al.* 2003).

Promoting internationalization: push thy clients

Another aspect of how consultants have impacted the internationalization of business and globalization more generally concerns the international expansion of client organizations. Many consultants initially followed their clients abroad – as the international business literature would suggest (see above). At the same time, these consulting firms pushed clients from their home country, namely the US, to become more international. And as they expanded themselves to new markets, they not only disseminated new management ideas and practices there, which, as discussed in the previous section, usually originated in the US, they also prompted their local clients in these new host countries to expand abroad.

This sequence is quite clearly at display in the expansion of the US consulting firms to Europe after World War II. These firms initially came to Europe to serve their domestic multinational clients there, hence often setting up their first offices in neutral Switzerland, or to work with European multinationals, for which they had done projects in the Americas, as exemplified by the case of Shell and McKinsey (see above). But they appear to quickly have leveraged their new positions in Europe to entice other US companies to expand there. Thus, already in 1962, shortly after it had opened its first office in Europe, McKinsey published a booklet entitled *International Enterprise: A New Dimension of American Business* (see Kipping 1999: 210). It is difficult to assess the extent to which consultants contributed to the growth of US foreign direct investment in Continental Europe (visualized in Figure 9.2) – in addition to other factors such as the creation of the Common Market in 1957. But whatever the ultimate drivers, or combination thereof, these developments clearly benefitted the consulting firms, since it prompted European companies to hire them to learn more about the modus operandi of their US competitors (Servan-Schreiber 1967).

But the consultants did *not* stop with disseminating US management ideas and practices to their European clients. They apparently also encouraged the latter to expand abroad, namely to – not surprisingly – the United States. The M-form constituted an ideal vehicle in this respect, since the model introduced by McKinsey in the banks, for instance, invariably contained an international division in addition to the ones focusing on domestic banking and other financial products/services – even if most of their European banking clients did not have much of an international presence at the time (Kipping and Westerhuis 2014). The archival material available at the banks in this ongoing research shows that, after introducing the M-form, the consulting firm managed to convince most of them to fill in that international division, namely through acquisitions, often in the US – with McKinsey producing large numbers of reports identifying and evaluating possible targets.

These internationalization efforts and their results have yet to be examined more systematically. The evidence available from bank histories suggests that they often ended in failure and retreat (see, e.g. for the Dutch cases, Westerhuis 2008). Japan's Sumitomo Bank, for instance, suffered such a fate. After completing divisionalization in 1979, its CEO pushed an international expansion, turning Sumitomo into the "leading Japanese bank in foreign markets" (Salamie

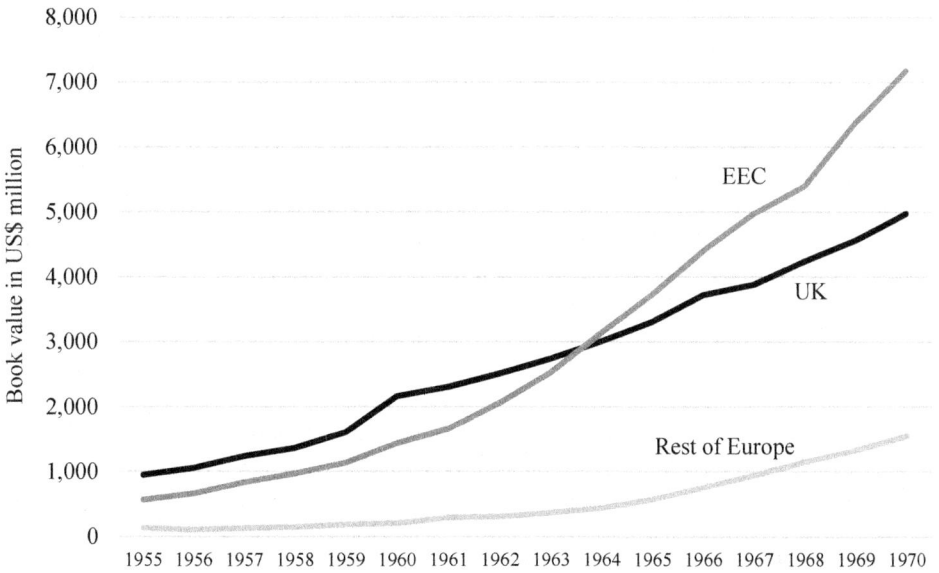

Figure 9.2 US manufacturing foreign direct investment in Europe (book value in US$ million)

Source: Based on Wilkins 1974: Table XIII.3.

1999: 456). Results were mixed though, and much of the expansion was later reversed – often at significant losses. The example of the British Midland Bank is particularly telling. McKinsey made its usual recommendations to create three separate divisions, including an international one, in 1971. Implementation took some time and a head of the international division was only named in 1974. Initial efforts consisted of increasing the bank's stake in South Africa's Standard Chartered, which was, however, liquidated – for political reasons – in 1978–79 (Holmes and Green 1986: 282–296). Subsequently, Midland acquired majority shares in smaller banks in Germany and Switzerland. And in 1981 it made the largest foreign takeover of a US bank at that time by acquiring 57 per cent of Crocker National Bank in California – propelling itself into the top ten global banks. But what was meant to be the "centerpiece" of Midland's internationalization strategy quickly turned into an unmitigated disaster due to Crocker's bad real estate loans and large share in Latin American debt (www.company-histories.com/Midland-Bank-plc-Company-History.html). Following massive losses, Midland terminated its "Californian adventure" by acquiring the remaining shares in 1985 and selling off the lot to Wells Fargo in 1986, reducing "the bank to a shadow of its former eminence". It was eventually acquired by HSBC in 1992 (Anon. 2004).

This pattern, where the entry of MNEs created more competition, which led local companies to call for help from (foreign) consultants, who in turn first introduced (foreign) business models to these companies and then pushed them to expand abroad, appears to have repeated itself a few more times since – though with some twists. Thus, similar mechanisms were probably at work when the former Eastern bloc countries opened their economies after 1989 (Kostera 1995). Western consultants assisted in privatization efforts and then encouraged their Western clients to enter these markets, often through acquisitions, resulting in pressure on local firms to quickly become more competitive – creating additional opportunities for the consultants. Foreign expansion of companies from Eastern Europe seems to have been more limited though. And, as seen above, in the Indian case consulting firms were definitely among the instigators of the IT offshoring rush to India over recent decades, making clients follow their example – though they preferred clients outsourcing these activities to them. As an unintended consequence, the massive growth in outsourcing activities also stimulated the expansion of local service providers, which are increasingly giving the Western consultants a run for their money, even in the latter's home markets.

China is yet another interesting case with a twist. Following the economic reforms since the late 1970s, consultants must have written countless reports for Western firms recommending they take advantage of low production costs and fast-growing markets in the country. Using the Western multinationals as "bridges" for their own entry, they did establish a presence in China – though with less success than in their earlier international expansions to Western and Eastern Europe. This, according to a veteran insider with experience in US and Chinese consulting firms, was mainly due to the fact that the Western consultants "just want to sell the same thing everywhere" (quoted by Edwards 2015) – an impression confirmed by an earlier academic study (Wang and Wright 2008). The large number of state-owned or -controlled enterprises and their apparent preference for local services providers might have also played a role here. To what extent the Western consulting firms have played an integral part in the global "buying spree" by Chinese companies has yet to be explored – though they have certainly written reports offering advice to Chinese companies about "what should they do differently going forward" *and* to Western targets "to ensure that the deals they strike with Chinese companies deliver the returns they are seeking" (McKinsey 2017: 1) – once again demonstrating how the consultants aim to benefit from internationalization efforts at both ends of the process.

Summary and outlook

There is no doubt that consulting firms are today among some of the most global organizations – at least when it comes to the largest among them. And they are also among the organizations with most impact on international business. Based on a critical summary of the extant research, this chapter has shown how these firms have established a global presence since the beginning of the twentieth century. A first set of individuals and firms expanded from their home country, the United States, during the interwar period focusing mainly on Western Europe. A second wave of different service providers followed the same path during the 1960s and 1970s, with a few also venturing into Asia, namely Japan. A third wave of firms, those dominating the industry today, were already present in many countries based on their original activities in accounting and auditing or IT services by the time they started providing consulting services at a larger scale. These firms were also instrumental in developing India as a major host for outsourcing and consulting activities since the 1990s, with Indian firms subsequently expanding outward. Much of this is quite well documented in the literature from various angles, though a more thorough academic investigation of the role of India as both a host and home country for IT-related consulting services seems warranted – as is an examination of the incursion of the large advertising agencies into consulting.

But, as the chapter has also shown, the importance of management consultants within the study of international business and globalization goes well beyond their own expansion and presence. From the outset, they have been instrumental in introducing uniform management discourses and practices in organizations around the globe. This includes locally based individual and small-size consulting providers "translating" global concepts for their clients. The consultants' impact in this respect is well understood theoretically, while its extent and consequences continue to be debated among scholars. Empirically, much of the research is based on single or – rarely – comparative case studies. A systematic compilation of all extant cases might be a way to provide more general insights – though is possibly too daunting a task given the secrecy that continues to surround consulting projects. We know even less about how consultants have contributed to business internationalization by pushing clients to expand beyond their home country. Doing so clearly benefits consultants in multiple ways but, as the few known cases suggest, might be premature if not detrimental for their clients.

In terms of future directions for research, there is still considerable scope for more empirical studies regarding all of these topics. There is also a need for theorizing the multiple roles of consultants in globalization. And there are a number of big questions that have yet to be addressed, which include, but are not limited to, (i) the possible co-evolution between consulting firms and "global cities" (Sassen 2005; see also Wood 2002), (ii) the constitution of a new global elite by former consultants, not only in business but also in government, politics and even academia, and (iii), relatedly, their contribution to not only spreading, but also reforming global capitalism (Engwall *et al.* 2016).

References

Abrahamson, E. (1991). "Managerial fads and fashions: The diffusion and rejection of innovations". *Academy of Management Review* 16/3: 586–612.

Accenture (2018). "Accenture fact sheet Q1 FY18", https://newsroom.accenture.com//content/1101/files/Accenture_Factsheet_Q1_FY18_FINAL%203Jan.pdf [accessed 7 March 2018].

Aharoni, Y. and Nachum, L. (eds) (2000). *The Globalization of Services: Some Implications for Theory and Practice*. London: Routledge.

Allen, D. G. and McDermott, K. (1993). *Accounting for Success: A History of Price Waterhouse in America 1890–1990*. Boston, MA: Harvard Business School Press.

Anon. (2004). "Obituaries: Geoffrey Taylor", *Telegraph*, 6 December; www.telegraph.co.uk/news/obituaries/1478299/Geoffrey-Taylor.html [accessed 29 April 2018].

Bäumer, U., Kreutter, P. and Messner, W. (eds) (2012). *Globalization of Professional Services: Innovative Strategies, Successful Processes, Inspired Talent Management, and First-hand Experiences*. Berlin: Springer.

Benders, J., van den Berg, R.-J. and van Bijsterveld, M. (1998). "Hitch-hiking on a hype: Dutch consultants engineering re-engineering". *Journal of Organizational Change Management* 11/3: 201–215.

Boussebaa, M. (2009). "Struggling to organize across national borders: The case of global resource management in professional service firms". *Human Relations* 62/6: 829–850.

Boussebaa, M., Morgan, G. and Sturdy, A. (2012). "Constructing global firms? National, transnational and neocolonial effects in international management consultancies". *Organization Studies* 33: 465–486.

Chandler, A. D., Jr. (1962). *Strategy and Structure: Chapters in the History of the Industrial Enterprise*. Cambridge, MA: MIT Press.

Channon, D. F. (1973). *The Strategy and Structure of British Enterprise*. London: Macmillan.

Clark, T. (2004). "The fashion of management fashion: A surge too far?" *Organization* 11/2: 297–306.

Coffee, J. C. (2006). *Gatekeepers: The Professions and Corporate Governance*. Oxford: Oxford University Press.

Cooper, D. J., Rose, T., Greenwood, R. and Hinings, B. (2000). "History and contingency in international accounting firms", in Y. Aharoni and L. Nachum (eds), *The Globalization of Services: Some Implications for Theory and Practice*. London: Routledge, pp. 93–124.

Cornell, J. (2017). "Hewlett Packard Enterprise completes spin-merger to form DXC Technology", forbes.com, 4 April [accessed 5 March 2018].

Crucini, C. and Kipping, M. (2001). "Management consultancies as global change agents? Evidence from Italy". *Journal of Organizational Change Management* 14/6: 570–589.

Cusumano, M. A. (2006). "Envisioning the future of India's software services business". *Communications of the ACM* 49/10: 15–17.

Czarniawska, B. and Joerges, B. (1996). "Travel of ideas", in B. Czarniawska and G. Sevón (eds), *Translating Organizational Change*. Berlin: de Gruyter, pp. 13–48.

Daniels, P. W., Thrift, N. J. and Leyshon, A. (1989). "Internationalization of professional producer services: Accountancy conglomerates", in P. Enderwick (ed.), *Multinational Service Firms*. London: Routledge, pp. 79–106.

Deloitte (2017). "Deloitte announces record revenue of US$38.8 billion", Press release, 14 September, www2.deloitte.com/global/en/pages/about-deloitte/articles/global-revenue-announcement.html [accessed 7 March 2018].

DiMaggio, P. J. and Powell, W. W. (1983). "The iron cage revisited: Institutional isomorphism and collective rationality in organizational fields". *American Sociological Review* 48/2: 147–160.

Dinger, E. and Caudill, C. (2013). "Cognizant technology solutions corporation", in K. Hill (ed.), *International Directory of Company Histories*, Vol. 139. Detroit, MI: St. James Press, pp. 122–128.

Doh, J. P., Bunyaratavej, K. and Hahn, E. D. (2009). "Separable but not equal: The location determinants of discrete services offshoring activities". *Journal of International Business Studies* 40: 926–943.

Dyas, G. P. and Thanheiser, H. T. (1976). *The Emerging European Enterprise: Strategy and Structure in French and German Industry*. London: Macmillan.

EDS History Timeline (2008). https://web.archive.org/web/20090331200616/http://www.eds.com/about/history/timeline.aspx [accessed 27 August 2015].

Edwards, S. (2015). "The dawn of Chinese consultancy companies?" *China Business Review*, March 10, www.chinabusinessreview.com/the-dawn-of-chinese-consultancy-companies/ [accessed 8 March 2018].

Elliott, S. (2002). "Advertising's big four: It's their world now". *New York Times*, 31 March.

Enderwick, P. (ed.) (1989). *Multinational Service Firms*. London: Routledge.

Engwall, L., Kipping, M. and Üsdiken, B. (2016). *Defining Management: Business Schools, Consultants, Media*. New York: Routledge.

Ernst, B. and Kieser, A. (2002). "In search of explanations for the consulting explosion", in K. Sahlin-Andersson and L. Engwall (eds), *The Expansion of Management Knowledge*. Stanford, CA: Stanford University Press, pp. 47–73.

Ghemawat, P. and Altman, S. P. (2007). "The Indian IT services industry in 2007", www.aacsb.edu/~/media/AACSB/Publications/CDs%20and%20DVDs/GLOBE/Cases/indian-it-industry.ashx [accessed 8 March 2018].

Glückler, J. (2006). "A relational assessment of international market entry in management consulting", *Journal of Economic Geography* 6: 369–393.

Grimme, K. and Kreutter, P. (2012). "Consolidation patterns in the IT outsourcing market: Past, present, and future", in U. Bäumer, P. Kreutter and W. Messner (eds), *Globalization of Professional Services: Innovative Strategies, Successful Processes, Inspired Talent Management, and First-hand Experiences*. Berlin: Springer, pp. 10–21.

Hamm, S. (2007). *Bangalore Tiger: How Indian Tech Upstart Wipro is Rewriting the Rules of Global Competition*. New York: McGraw-Hill.

Harrington, J. W. and Daniels, P. W. (eds) (2006). *Knowledge-Based Services: Internationalisation and Regional Development*. Farnham: Ashgate.

Higdon, H. (1969). *The Business Healers*. New York: Random House.

Holmes A. R. and Green, E. (1986). *Midland: 150 Years of Banking Business*. London: B. T. Batesford Ltd.

IBM (7 January 2016). "1992", www-03.ibm.com/ibm/history/history/year_1992.html [accessed 7 January 2016].

IBM Corporate Archives (2002). "IBM global services: A brief history", www-03.ibm.com/ibm/history/documents/pdf/gservices.pdf [accessed 20 August 2015].

Jackall, R. (1988). *Moral Mazes: The World of Corporate Managers*. New York: Oxford University Press.

Johanson, J. and Vahlne, J.-E. (1977). "The internationalization process of the firm: A model of knowledge development and increasing foreign market commitments". *Journal of International Business Studies* 8/1: 23–32.

Johanson, J. and Vahlne, J.-E. (2009). "The Uppsala internationalization process model revisited: From liability of foreignness to liability of outsidership". *Journal of International Business Studies* 40: 1411–1431.

Jones, A. (2003). *Management Consultancy and Banking in an Era of Globalization*. London: Palgrave Macmillan.

Jones, E. (1995). *True and Fair: A History of Price Waterhouse*. London: Hamish Hamilton.

Karnik, K. (2012). *The Coalition of Competitors: The Story of Nasscom and the IT Industry*. Noida, India: Collins Business.

Khanna, T. and Palepu, K. G. (2004). "Globalization and convergence in corporate governance: Evidence from Infosys and the Indian software industry". *Journal of International Business Studies* 35/6: 484–507.

Kipping, M. (1999). "American management consulting companies in Western Europe, 1920 to 1990: Products, reputation and relationships". *Business History Review* 73/2: 190–220.

Kipping, M. (2002). "Trapped in their wave: The evolution of management consultancies", in T. Clark and R. Fincham (eds), *Critical Consulting*. Oxford: Blackwell, pp. 28–49.

Kipping, M. and Armbrüster, T. (2002). "The burden of otherness: Limits of consultancy interventions in historical case studies", in M. Kipping and L. Engwall (eds), *Management Consulting*. Oxford: Oxford University Press, pp. 203–221.

Kipping, M. and Westerhuis, G. (2012). "Strategy, ideology and structure: The political processes of introducing the M-form in two Dutch banks", in S. J. Kahl, B. S. Silverman and M. A. Cusumano (eds), *History and Strategy*. Bingley: Emerald, pp. 187–237.

Kipping, M. and Westerhuis, G. (2014). "The managerialization of banking: From blueprint to reality". *Management and Organizational History* 9/4: 374–393.

Kipping, M. and Wright, C. (2012). "Consultants in context: Global dominance, societal effect and the capitalist system", in M. Kipping and T. Clark (eds), *The Oxford Handbook of Management Consulting*. Oxford: Oxford University Press, pp. 165–185.

Kostera, M. (1995). "The modern crusade: The missionaries of management come to eastern Europe". *Management Learning* 26/3: 331–352.

Kreis, S. (1992). "The diffusion of scientific management: The Bedaux Company in America and Britain, 1926–1945", in D. Nelson (ed.), *A Mental Revolution: Scientific Management since Taylor*. Columbus, OH: Ohio State University Press, pp. 156–174.

Kumar, N. (2009). *India's Global Powerhouses: How They are Taking on the World*. Boston, MA: Harvard Business Press.

Kundu, S. K. and Merchant, H. (2008). "Service multinationals: Their past, present, and future". *Management International Review* 48/4: 371–377.

Lee, J.-N., Huynh, M. Q., Kwok, R. C.-W. and Pi, S.-M. (2003). "IT outsourcing evolution: Past, present, and future". *Communications of the ACM* 46/5: 84–89.

Levy, D. M. and Peart, S. J. (2017). *Escape from Democracy: The Role of Experts and the Public in Economic Policy*. New York: Cambridge University Press.

McDonald, D. (2013). *The Firm: The Story of McKinsey and its Secret Influence on American Business*. New York: Simon & Schuster.

McDougald, M. S. and Greenwood, R. (2012). "Cuckoo in the nest? The rise of management consulting in large accounting firms", in M. Kipping and T. Clark (eds), *The Oxford Handbook of Management Consulting*. Oxford: Oxford University Press, pp. 93–116.

McKenna, C. D. (2006). *The World's Newest Profession: Management Consulting in the Twentieth Century*. New York: Cambridge University Press.

McKenna, C., Djelic, M.-L. and Ainamo, A. (2003). "Message and medium: The role of consulting firms in globalization and its local interpretation", in M.-L. Djelic and S. Quack (eds), *Globalization and Institutions*. Aldershot: Edward Elgar, pp. 83–107.

McKinsey (2017). "A pocket guide to Chinese cross-border M&A", April, http://mckinseychina.com/wp-content/uploads/2017/04/McKinsey_A-Pocket-Guide-to-Chinese-Cross-Border-MA-English.pdf [accessed 10 March 2018].

Malik, A. and Nilakant, V. (2015). "Context and evolution of the Indian IT industry", in A. Malik and C. Rowley (eds), *Business Models and People Management in the Indian IT Industry: From People to Profits*. London: Routledge, pp. 15–34.

Malik, A. and Rowley, C. (eds) (2015). *Business Models and People Management in the Indian IT Industry: From People to Profits*. London: Routledge.

Merkle, J. E. (1980). *Management and Ideology: The Legacy of the International Scientific Management Movement*. Berkeley, CA: University of California Press.

Metters, R. and Verma, R. (2008). "History of offshoring knowledge services". *Journal of Operations Management* 26: 141–147.

Morgan, G., Sturdy, A. and Quack, S. (2006). "The globalization of management consultancy firms: Constraints and limitations", Working Paper No. 168, University of Warwick, Centre for the Study of Globalisation and Regionalisation.

Nelson, D. (ed.) (1992). *A Mental Revolution: Scientific Management since Taylor*. Columbus, OH: Ohio State University Press.

Nelson, D. (1995). "Industrial engineering and the industrial enterprise", in N. R. Lamoreaux and D. M. G. Raff (eds), *Coordination and Information: Historical Perspectives on the Organization of Enterprise*. Chicago, IL: University of Chicago Press, pp. 35–50.

Nyland, C. and Bruce, K. (2012). "The demonization of scientific management and the deification of human relations", in N. Lichtenstein and E. Shermer (eds), *The American Right and Labor: Politics, Ideology, and Imagination*, Philadelphia, PA: University of Pennsylvania Press, pp. 50–84.

Oshri, I., Kotlarsky, J. and Willcocks, L. (2007). "Managing dispersed expertise in IT offshore outsourcing: Lessons from Tata Consultancy Services". *MIS Quarterly Executive* 6/2: 53–65.

Quigel, J. P. (1992). "The business of selling efficiency: Harrington Emerson and the Emerson efficiency engineers, 1900–1930", Doctoral dissertation, State College, PA: Pennsylvania State University.

Roberts, J. (2006). "Internationalisation of management consultancy services: Conceptual issues concerning the cross-border delivery of knowledge intensive services", in J. W. Harrington and P. W. Daniels (eds), *Knowledge-Based Services: Internationalisation and Regional Development*. Farnham: Ashgate, pp. 101–124.

Roberts, J. (2015). "Globalization of services", in J. R. Bryson and P. W. Daniels (eds), *Handbook of Service Business: Management, Marketing, Innovation and Internationalisation*. Cheltenham: Edward Elgar, pp. 257–277.

Saint-Martin, D. (2000). *Building the New Managerialist State: Consultants and the Politics of Public Sector Reform in Comparative Perspective*. New York: Oxford University Press.

Salamie, D. E. (1999). "The Sumitomo Bank, Limited", in J. P. Pederson (ed.), *International Directory of Company Histories*, Vol. 26. Detroit: St. James Press, pp. 454–457.

Sassen, S. (2005). "The Global City: Introducing a Concept". *Brown Journal of World Affairs* XI/2: 27–43.

Schwarz, S. and Hentrich, C. (2012). "Transformation journey from offshore service provider to global innovator", in U. Bäumer, P. Kreutter and W. Messner (eds), *Globalization of Professional Services: Innovative Strategies, Successful Processes, Inspired Talent Management, and First-hand Experiences*. Berlin: Springer, pp. 225–240.

Servan-Schreiber, J.-J. (1967). *Le défi américain*. Paris: Denoël.

Shainesh, G., Sultan, Z. and Weigand, J. (2012). "Market entry and expansion strategies of Indian IT firms into the European IT outsourcing industry", in U. Bäumer, P. Kreutter and W. Messner (eds), *Globalization of Professional Services: Innovative Strategies, Successful Processes, Inspired Talent Management, and First-hand Experiences*. Berlin: Springer, pp. 23–31.

Sloan, A. P. (1964). *My Years with General Motors*. New York: Doubleday.

Spender, J.-C. and Kijne, H. (eds) (1996). *Scientific Management: Frederick Winslow Taylor's Gift to the World?* Boston, MA: Kluwer.

Squires, S. E., Smith, C. J., McDougall, L. and Yeack, W. R. (2003). *Inside Arthur Andersen: Shifting Values, Unexpected Consequences*. London: FT Press.

Stalk, G. and Hout, T. M. (1990). *Competing against Time: How Time-Based Competition is Reshaping Global Markets*. New York: The Free Press.

Stein, L. (2017). "McDonald's taps Publicis.Sapient, Capgemini for global IT", http://adage.com/article/agency-news/mcdonald-s-taps-publicis-sapient-capgemini-global/310267/, August 28 [accessed 8 March 2018].

Stevens, M. (1991). *The Big Six: The Selling Out of America's Top Accounting Firms*. New York: Simon & Schuster.

Wang, Y. and Wright, C. (2008). "How management consultancies strategize knowledge in emerging markets: The case of China", 22nd ANZAM Annual Conference, Auckland, New Zealand, 5 December.

Weatherburn, M. R. (2014). "Scientific management at work: The Bedaux system, management consulting, and worker efficiency in British industry, 1914–48", Doctoral Dissertation. London: Imperial College.

Weinstein, A. K. (1977). "Foreign investments by service firms: The case of multinational advertising agencies". *Journal of International Business Studies* 8/1: 83–91.

Westerhuis, G. K. (2008). *Conquering the American Market: ABN AMRO, Rabobank and Nationale-Nederlanden Working in a Different Business Environment, 1965–2005*. Amsterdam: Boom.

Whittington, R., Mayer, M. and Curto, F. (1999). "Chandlerism in post-war Europe: Strategic and structural change in France, Germany and the United Kingdom, 1950–1993". *Industrial and Corporate Change* 8/3: 519–551.

Wilkins, M. (1974). *The Maturing of Multinational Enterprise: American Business Abroad from 1914 to 1970*. Cambridge, MA: Harvard University Press.

Wood, P. (2002). "Knowledge-intensive services and urban innovativeness". *Urban Studies* 39/5–6: 993–1002.

Wren, D. A. (2015). "Implementing the Gantt chart in Europe and Britain: The contributions of Wallace Clark". *Journal of Management History* 21/3: 309–327.

Wren, D. A., Greenwood, R. A., Teahen, J. and Bedeian, A. G. (2015). "C. Bertrand Thompson and management consulting in Europe, 1917–1934". *Journal of Management History* 21/1: 15–39.

Wright, C. and Kipping, M. (2012). "The engineering origins of management consulting and their long shadow", in M. Kipping and T. Clark (eds), *The Oxford Handbook of Management Consulting*. Oxford: Oxford University Press, pp. 29–49.

Zahee, S., Lamin, A. and Subramani, M. (2009). "Cluster capabilities or ethnic ties? Location choice by foreign and domestic entrants in the services offshoring industry in India". *Journal of International Business Studies* 40: 944–968.

PART III

Organizational forms

10

GUILDS

Catherine Casson

Introduction

The term "guild" requires careful definition because it has been used loosely in the literature. Guilds can be defined as associations of individuals formed for a common purpose, using a subscription model of membership (Hunt and Murray 1999: 34–5). Guilds may be differentiated by their primary function: religious observance, social interaction, or trade promotion. Many guilds had more than one function, for example combining social interaction with trade promotion. This chapter focuses on guilds whose primary function was trade promotion, but whose activities also encompassed social interaction and religious devotion. Trade promotion was split between merchants and artisans. Members of merchant guilds were usually involved in the sourcing, creation, or distribution of exports and the distribution of imports. Members of artisan guilds were generally focused on the creation of exports and of items for the domestic market.

Guilds were generally centered on a town or city, and possessed a clear urban identity. Religious and social guilds were primarily local (centered on a single town) in scope whereas merchant guilds could be local, regional, and international. The focus of this chapter is on the local and regional guilds and their members. Guilds were distinct from companies. This chapter covers individual members and partnerships between guild members. It does not cover federations of guilds, which are covered in the subsequent chapter. Guild members were usually from a specific town or city but sometimes there were also visiting and associate members from other locations. It was possible for guilds from different towns or cites to federate, as discussed in the subsequent chapter. Particularly detailed evidence survives on the operations of members of English guilds, and their activities will be the focus of the chapter. Evidence on the presence of guilds in other countries is discussed below.

Three main methods were available to co-ordinate trade in the Middle Ages. The first was that of a merchant operating alone but supported by a guild; the second was a partnership formed between members of a guild; the third was a corporate model in which the guild operated as a whole. This chapter focuses on the individual and partnership models (the corporate model is discussed in the next chapter.) The individual would pay a fee to join the guild, in return for which they would receive membership benefits. To provide the membership services, most guilds elected officials on an annual basis to take responsibility for tasks such as quality control inspections.

Guild members, operating as sole traders or partnerships, could engage in global trade by co-ordinating supply chains. Guild members would engage in part of a supply chain but rarely all of it. Some members might specialize in sourcing, others in production and others in distribution. This chapter focuses on the period *c.*1200 to *c.*1500 during which global trade operated through a series of supply chains. The Silk Road was an important overland route which provided a supply chain across central Asia, linking up with the distribution network of the Mediterranean. Venice served as a hub from which goods from Asia were distributed to the rest of Europe (Boulnois 2003; UNESCO 2017). Shorter supply chains around the English Channel, the North Sea, and the Baltic Sea fed into the longer global supply chain by providing export goods from England, Scandinavia, the Low Countries, France, and Germany and distributing imports (Barron 2004: 76–117; Miller and Hatcher 1995: 143). Most countries specialized in particular products or services which they exchanged for imports. England's key export was wool, which it sent to the Continent in exchange for wine from France and woad and alum (used in wool and cloth processing) and spices which arrived from Asia via Venice.

Internal trade routes, often organized by members of merchant guilds, supported the external supply chains. Manufactured items from London, for example, were distributed to the Continent through the ports of London and Southampton while those from York were distributed to Scandinavia via Hull (Hicks 2015). Wool from Norfolk and salted herring were distributed from Great Yarmouth while agricultural produce from the west of England was exported through Bristol and Exeter. Many of the raw materials traded by the merchant guilds and the manufactured products produced by craft guilds reached the global market through those internal routes. On some occasions goods were also purchased directly by visiting merchants. Members of the Italian super-companies, for example, frequently visited England to arrange the advance purchase of wool, as did other overseas merchants. Records from Leicester's merchant guild, among others, reveal that guild members traded directly with foreign merchants and were sometimes asked to arrange business trips for them (Bateson 1899: 187, 203–4).

The presence of guilds outside Western Europe is the subject of ongoing academic research. It has been suggested that formal guilds were absent from medieval Islamic cities such as Damascus, but that trades were informally organized into different groups, and that sometimes leaders of particular trades were asked to liaise with the sultan (Lapidus 1984: 95–107). It is possible that those informal groups were used by the central authorities as a convenient means through which to regulate certain trades, especially for taxation purposes. However, it seems unlikely that the informal groups performed the same range of functions as did some guilds in Europe, and especially England. In China, it has been suggested that kinship organizations, known as clans, were "an important conduit for economic exchange" in the Middle Ages (Greif and Tabellini 2010: 139). It has been proposed that merchant networks and organizations of craft and manufacturing producers existed in China from at least the mid fourteenth century, but there is debate amongst historians over whether they can be accurately referred to as "guilds" as not all of them had formal regulations or were recognized by other institutions (Moll-Murata 2008). Chinese organizations were probably utilized for the administration of tax collection, and it has been suggested that their members also engaged in religious and welfare activities and convened training and dispute resolution (Moll-Murata 2008).

Guilds and supply chains

The contribution made by guild members to international trade was described in an account of a Venetian official visiting England in 1496–7. He first described the raw materials available for export by guild members, noting that:

the riches of England are greater than those of any other country in Europe, as I have been told by the oldest and most experienced merchants, and also as I myself can vouch, from what I have seen. This is owing, in the first place, to the great fertility of the soil, which is such that, with the exception of wine, they import nothing from abroad for their subsidence. Next, the sale of their valuable tin brings in a large sum of money to the kingdom, but still more do they derive from their extraordinary abundance of wool, which bears such a high price and reputation throughout Europe.

(Amt 2001: 487–96)

The official continued his account by describing trading conditions in London, a city where many guilds were located. The city's transport links through the river Thames and the sea provided "all the advantages desired in a maritime town." As a trading center and place of residence

the city abounds with every article of luxury, as well as the necessaries of life … in one single street, named the Strand, leading to St Paul's, there are fifty-two goldsmith's shops, so rich and full of silver vessels, great and small, that in all the shops in Milan, Rome, Venice and Florence put together, I do not think there would be found so many of magnificence seen in London.

Members of London's goldsmiths craft guild were responsible for the creation of the beautiful items and guild officials fostered consumer confidence by policing the quality of goods made by members, as described later in this chapter.

The account illustrates how members of different guilds co-ordinated different parts of the global supply chain. Members of merchant guilds, individually or in partnership, could source wool from the countryside, organize its production into cloth or arrange its distribution to be turned into clothes by consumers. Members of artisan guilds could manufacture products to be sold directly to consumers in the domestic market, or to be sourced and distributed as exports by merchants.

Potential for supply chain conflict existed in such a situation. Conflicts could occur amongst merchant guilds if members of one guild decided to diversify their trading interests from their original specialty, thereby overlapping with the trading interests of another guild. In fourteenth-century London rivalries developed between the guilds of the grocers, the drapers, and the mercers, who all had interests in the wool and cloth trades (Barron 2004: 231). The grocers exported wool and imported spices, the drapers exported cloth and imported a wide range of goods, while the mercers imported "linens, silks and expensive textiles" but also exported a variety of items (Nightingale 1989: 12). The groups were in conflict over the location of the staple – the key port which was selected by the English king to administer and collect the revenues from overseas trade. The grocers favored a staple in Bruges or Calais, where they could easily obtain spices from Genoese traders, while the mercers and drapers favored staples in Antwerp or Middleburg, which were more convenient for the cloth trade.

Conflict could occur between merchant and artisan guilds if merchant guilds imported products that competed with those produced locally. In London in the 1310s and 1320s tensions occurred between the cappers guild on the one hand and the haberdashers and mercers guilds on the other. The cappers claimed that the haberdashers were selling imported caps of "inferior materials," imported by the mercers, rather than caps manufactured locally by the cappers. In defense, the haberdashers and mercers argued that the cappers "sold old caps for new, and that they dyed black caps made of white and grey wool" (Archer 1991: 8).

The Venetian's account, however, shows that guild members could also contribute to the overall prosperity of England's economy. Guild members allowed natural resources to reach international markets, and their craft skills added value to raw materials. Guild officials policed the quality of the goods distributed and manufactured by members, allowing customers to shop with confidence and contributing to the positive reputation of English products. Guild members also contributed to the economic performance of the town in which they were located. A large town or city, such as London, might have many specialist guilds producing a wide range of consumer products that attracted buyers for the domestic and global markets. An overview of crafts and companies in London in 1328–1518 demonstrates that, in the area of metal working alone, there were guilds of "armourers, bladesmiths, braziers, cardmakers [who made combs for carding wool], coppersmiths, cutlers, ferrours, founders, goldsmiths, ironmongers, latteners, lorimers, pewterers, pinners, plumbers, smiths, spurriers and wiresellers" (Barron 2004: 220).

Early discussion of guilds

Having considered the views of a medieval commentator, it is useful to examine the views of the earliest academics who studied the operation of guilds. Scholars have varied in their emphasis or marginalization of the functions of religious observance, social interaction, and trade promotion. They have also differed in their opinions on the benefits that guilds provided to individual members and to the overall economic performance of the town or city in which they were based (Richardson 2001).

Gross is credited with establishing guilds as a field of study. Focusing on the merchant guilds of medieval England, Gross emphasized their contribution to the regulation of trade at the local level (1890: 37). He was especially interested in the relationship between merchant guilds and local government and viewed the merchant guild as essentially "a department of town administration" whose members had the right to trade freely in the town, usually in return for a small entrance fee (Gross 1890: 44). Those who were not members of the guild, in contrast, faced more restrictions, including having to pay tolls, being barred from retail trade, and prohibited from buying certain items (Gross 1890: 45). Gross argued that an individual could be member of a guild without being a citizen of the town, or could be a citizen without being a member of the guild, or could live in the town without having the full rights of citizenship or being a member of the guild (1890: 66, 69, 71–2). He suggested that such distinctions were less rigid in locations where the merchant guild had taken more general responsibility for the regulation of trade in the town.

Other literature has been more critical of guilds, arguing that they created barriers to trade. This argument is prominent in the work of Ogilvie, who referred to guilds as "exclusive organizations for middle-class businessmen" (2011; 2014: 173). The monopoly possessed by guilds, Ogilvie (2014: 184) argued, created barriers to innovation by "blocking entry by venturesome upstarts." Ogilvie was critical of the quality control responsibilities of guilds, suggesting that guild inspectors would sometimes accept the use of poorer quality materials if that was the only way for a profit to be made while failing to recognize situations where consumers were willing to pay a cheaper price for a lower quality item (Ogilvie 2014: 179–81). That argument has recently been contested by Davids and de Munck and their colleagues (2014) who have proposed that guilds in Italy and the Low Countries updated their practices to respond to changing consumer preferences in the fifteenth century, for example for glass tableware or high-quality mid-range cloth (Ammannati 2014; Maitte 2014).

The relationship between the artisan or craft producers of manufactured items and the merchants who distributed manufactured goods and raw materials has been questioned by historians

(Brentano 1870). Some scholars, notably Brentano and Swanson, suggested that the earliest merchant guilds welcomed artisans as members, as many artisans also traded the raw materials that they used in manufacturing. They argue that a division of labor then occurred, in which the trade in raw materials became increasingly concentrated amongst merchants to the exclusion of artisans (Brentano 1870: lxiv–cxcix, cvii, cviii; Swanson 1989). At the same time, the financial burdens placed on the artisans increased, including the expectation of payments for special events and hospitality. Recent scholarship has taken a more positive view of the relationship. Examining merchant guilds involved in long distance trade Grafe and Gelderblom (2010: 478) proposed that there was "complementarity between different providers of services to merchants, for example ruler and guilds." Strong merchant guilds, they suggested, were able to help the wider community by using their influence to lobby central government for initiatives which benefitted not just themselves but other participants in the economy who were "outside the guild" (Grafe and Gelderblom 2010: 510). This view was echoed by Epstein and Prak (2008: 4), who suggested that guilds helped to reduce transaction costs by promoting investment in training, co-ordinating "complicated production processes," and communicating accurate information about product to consumers.

The networking potential of guilds and their welfare provision was the focus of research by Toulmin Smith *et al.* (1870) and Rosser (2015). They emphasized the role of guilds as providers of "mutual help," "charity," and religious activity for the lay community. Rather than seeing guilds as closed organizations, both scholars highlighted evidence of the diverse membership of guilds, including evidence of the admission of women. They argued that the social capital aspects of guild membership meant that great importance was attached to the general behavior and personal reputation of members and prospective members, and not just the quality of their products. The guild of St Anne, based in the Church of St Laurence, London, for example, expelled members if they were found to lie too long in bed in the morning and refused to work once they had risen! (Toulmin Smith 1870: xxx, xxxix, xl).

Membership services

Individual merchants and craftspeople were encouraged to join a guild because of the membership services provided, alluded to above, and outlined below. These services were obtained in return for the payment of a member's annual subscription.

Membership services: trade networks and infrastructure

Accurate and detailed information about markets and traders could limit some of the risks of global trade. Membership of a guild provided merchants operating the inland and overseas trade routes with access to social capital. Surviving registers reveal that some guilds drew their members from well beyond their immediate location, a situation which reflected the importance of networking along trade routes. Holy Trinity Guild in Luton in the south-east of England was founded in 1474 in order to pray for the souls of its founders after death. However, even with a strong religious focus, it appears that the guild served as a networking hub for traders on the long-distance inland trade routes which sourced wool and cloth for export. Members came from as far away as Canterbury in Kent, Coventry in the Midlands, Boston in Lincolnshire, Halifax in Yorkshire, and Kendal in Cumbria as well as the international trade center of London (Tearle 2012: xxii). Meanwhile the Guild of the Holy Cross in Stratford-upon-Avon, despite also having a religious focus, quickly attracted members from Bristol, Coventry, and London, including members from the London mercers' guild, after its foundation in 1269 (Macdonald

2007: 24–5). It is probably not surprising, therefore, that some guilds eventually changed their emphasis from primarily religious to primarily economic. The York mercers' guild was initially founded as a religious fraternity in 1357, before transforming into the mercers guild in the early fourteenth century and subsequently the York company of merchant adventurers in the sixteenth century (Wheatley 2008: 14–15).

Financial capital could also be an important outcome from guild membership and networking. Members of the York mercers' guild, who were usually engaged in overseas trade with the Low Countries and Scandinavia, sometimes went into partnership with one another to organize and share the costs of shipping (Wheatley 2008: 15–16). There is also evidence that guild members obtained credit from each other, which facilitated their ability to make bulk purchases.

The annual guild feast was a key networking event, which provided an opportunity for social interaction between members and between members and representatives of other local and national institutions (Rosser 1994). Some guilds had rules that governed behavior at the feasts, including that conversations should only be about "peace and love" and that any disputes between members had to be resolved at the event (Rosser 1994: 441). Feasts were often impressive affairs; the wax chandlers guild of London consumed

> a loin of beef, a leg of mutton, two loins of veil and two loins of mutton, a goose, a capon, a pig and a rabbit, a dozen of pigeons, a hundred of eggs, a gallon of wine and 16 gallons of ale.
>
> *(Dummelow 1973: 16–17)*

The surroundings could be equally attractive, as many guilds used membership payments and additional donations to construct a hall to provide a permanent base for hospitality, philanthropy, and business meetings. Between its foundation in 1269 to its dissolution in 1547 the guild of Holy Cross in Stratford-upon-Avon constructed an impressive range of buildings, comprising a guild hall, almshouses, and a chapel with wall paintings on subjects including the Last Judgement and the Dance of Death (Giles 2017). The York mercers' guild constructed their guild hall in the fourteenth century with an upper story for business functions, an undercroft which served as a hospital, and a chapel for religious devotion (Giles 2000; Merchant Adventurers Hall 2017). The "outsiders and gentry" invited to the feasts would have left with a positive impressive of the behavior of guild members in the spheres of trade, welfare, and religion (Rosser 1994) and may have helped to lobby on behalf of the guild for favorable economic policies.

Membership services: training and quality control

Membership of a guild provided an indication of the quality of manufactured goods and raw materials, information which was important to the merchants who sourced goods for export. Many merchant and craft guilds had rules that regulated the quality of the product, for example the cleanliness of the wool traded and the nature of the materials used in manufactured products. The rules were enforced in guild courts, for those guilds that had them, as well as in local courts. Domestic and foreign merchants could therefore purchase in confidence, knowing that they would receive a product of a certain standard and that, if anything went wrong, they could seek redress in a guild or local court.

Guilds provided access to specialist craft training which promoted certain production standards. In order to become a journeyman (a wage earner but not a member of a guild) or a master in a guild it was necessary to complete the apprenticeship, usually of seven years, and in London apprenticeship was an important step toward urban citizenship (Hovland 2006: 154–6; Minns and Wallis 2012; Wallis 2012; Wallis 2008). Masters were expected to provide bed and board, and education in business or manufacturing practices. Inadequate training or early termination of apprenticeships damaged the process of knowledge dissemination, however (Schalk *et al.* 2016). The goldsmiths records reveal that in 1386–7 some members caused problems by taking on apprentices who then left their training early having "learnt a little of the said craft and … its privities [trade secrets]" and then traveled to other towns where they did work that was "not proper and not up to the legal standard … to the great discredit of the people of the said mistery" (Jefferson 2003: 219). The threat that such practices posed to the reputation of all guild members meant that inadequate instruction of apprentices was an offense that could be prosecuted in both guild and town courts (Hovland 2006: 95).

Quality control was often delegated to guilds by local government, who recognized the benefits that trained expertise could provide. Control included ensuring that items were supplied in the correct quantity and quality and were safe to consume (Casson 2012). Wine was a key commodity in global trade but the health of consumers was threatened, and the reputation of the city diminished, by unscrupulous practices by members of the vintners' guild, who imported the wine, and coopers' guild, who made the barrels for it. The increased popularity of expensive sweet Romney wine in the fifteenth century resulted in some local and foreign merchants

> putting wine of Spain and Rochelle and other remnants of broken, sodden[or] reboiled … wine of other countries, which are enfeebled in colour and nothing in value, in various butts and other vessels that are scraped to make resin adhere, gummed with pitch, cobblers wax and other horrid and unwholesome things in order to reduce and bring again a pleasant colour and likely manner drinking of Romney to smell and taste, to the deceit of all.
>
> *(Crawford: 1977)*

As members of the vintners' guild had responsibility for policing taverns, the local authorities asked them to be vigilant for this offense, which was punishable by a spell in the stocks.

There was recognition that in a mutual association of guild members, poor quality goods produced by one member risked undermining the reputation of the products produced by others. The resolution of disputes with customers and the maintenance of quality are revealed in prosecutions in the goldsmiths' court, including that of Gerard van Sweck, prosecuted in 1369–70 for soldering nails with tin when altering a gold girdle for the Duke of Lancaster (Jefferson 2003: 125). Reflecting the links between the members, his offense was recorded as being "to the disgrace" of the whole guild and he was ordered to pay half mark into the alms funds in recompense. The money from the fine went toward the support of those members of the guild and their families who had fallen on hard times, a further demonstration of the varied functions of medieval guilds.

On some occasions, the civic authorities and guild collaborated to prosecute offenses by guild members. In 1355 the civic authorities and wardens of the goldsmiths of London jointly charged guild member Henry Lyrpol with using counterfeit metal to create a harness, a seal, and two small plates (Casson 2009: 290; Thomas 1926: 242–3). After returning a guilty verdict, the court barred Lyrpol from trading for six months and confiscated the false materials. Guilds were willing and able enforce rules relating to quality control, and to co-operate with civic authorities to prosecute members whose behavior threatened the reputation of the guild and city as a whole. Their efforts in this area contributed to consumer confidence in

England's export items, further enhancing the country's ability to participate in global trade networks.

Membership services: welfare

Welfare provision during sickness and devotion after death were further benefits of guild membership (Rosser 1994). In a period before state welfare institutions, many guilds collected money toward the provision of healthcare facilities and accommodation for members and their families. Court fines, membership fees, and bequests from members helped to fund such provision. In 1446, for example, the vintner Guy Shuldham left land to the vintners' guild of London for the construction of a guild hall and 13 almshouses for "poor and needy" members (Barron 2004: 225). Upon death, guild membership provided access to commemoration. Guild members were expected to provide prayers for the souls of deceased members and attend their funerals, and fines were levied on those who did not participate in those activities (Jefferson 2003: 101).

Performances of plays at religious festivals provided an opportunity to combine religious devotion with an element of trade advertising. In York the subject matter of the annual plays of the Corpus Christi religious festival reflected the expertise of the craft performing them, for example *Noah's Ark* was portrayed by the fishmongers and mariners and the *Three Kings* by the goldsmiths (Purvis 1969: 33). Indeed, the popularity of these plays often threatened to undermine the religious significance. In 1426 Friar William Melton complained that the audience "gave themselves over to feasting, boozing, carousing, sing-songs, and other improper behaviour" (Sellers 1914: 156–8).

The role of guild members in England's economic performance

As well as providing benefits for their members, and potentially also their urban location, the activities of guild members also contributed to the performance of the English economy as a whole. In medieval England, the crown had overall responsibility for the performance of each town, and of the realm. The crown held ultimate control over the operation of English towns, although in some locations it delegated this power to local authorities in return for an annual payment and the right to intervene if the town was poorly administered. Tax on international trade provided a key source of royal income and so the English crown took a close interest in the regulation of the wool and cloth trades, the tax on which was a key source of royal income. The crown provided and policed the currency and the standard system of weights and measures. This ensured continuity in transactions between different locations within the country, fostered the confidence of foreign traders in English products, and made England an attractive trading location for foreign traders.

The English crown, historians have argued, appreciated the benefits of formally organized groups of merchants or artisans as a source of specialist expertise and quality control. In London and Winchester there is evidence that the earliest guilds to be officially recognized by the crown involved export commodities (the weavers' and fullers' guilds), the currency (the goldsmiths' guild) and food necessities (the guilds of the bakers and fishmongers) (Barron 2004: 201–3; Keene 2005: 15). The crown also realized that the expertise of guild members could be applied to the affairs of central government, particularly in the maintenance of the strong currency (Keene 2005). From at least the thirteenth century, members of the London goldsmiths' guild held roles in the Royal Mint (Reddaway and Walker 1975: 304).

The crown recognized the potential to apply best-practice from one guild to others in order to strengthen an entire sector of the English export economy. The crown promoted the use of the London goldsmiths' guild as a model for the conduct of the provincial goldsmiths. By 1300 the standards of the London goldsmiths' guild were rolled-out to provincial goldsmiths and in the late 1320s the London goldsmiths appointed officials to supervise the goldsmiths of Oxford and York (Alsford 2017a). In London itself, the crown encouraged the clustering of the trade around Cheapside, as described by the Venetian visitor, to facilitate the supervision of the trade. The goldsmiths' royal charter of 1327 stressed that no goldsmiths' shops were to be opened in London outside that area (Alsford 2017a). Quality control was therefore an area in which the interests of guilds and of the crown overlapped (Keene 2005: 11, 14–15).

On some occasions, however, the interests of the crown and of the members of merchant and artisan guilds diverged. Competition from foreign merchants in areas of global trade covered by English merchants was a source of tension throughout the Middle Ages. The English crown saw foreign merchants as a source of both luxury goods and taxation income. On various occasions (especially in the reign of Edward I) overseas merchants were therefore encouraged to settle in England (Barron 2004: 94–101). In the 1280s, for example, merchants from the Hanseatic League established headquarters in the Steelyard in London (Alsford 2017b). In periods of prosperity, relations were fairly cordial, as the foreign merchants were customers for English manufactured products and their trade routes often complemented those used by the English merchants. Economic recession and warfare, however, intensified competition, particularly over the trade routes used for the distribution of raw materials. In the 1380s, war between England and France meant that many English merchants decided to focus their attentions on northern Europe, where trade was controlled by the Hanseatic League. Some English merchants wished to establish an English base in Gdansk to mirror that of the Hanse merchants in London. The new king Richard II supported this move, and imposed restrictions on Hanse merchants in England to put pressure on the Hanseatic League. In this tense situation, a number of disputes developed, including in 1385 when merchants from London, York, Beverley, Lynn, and Norwich collaborated to petition the Grand Master of the Hanseatic League to resolve offenses that they claimed had been committed against them by Hanse merchants, including the seizure of their goods, the failure to pay correct value for them, violence against some English merchants, and failure to settle debts (Alsford 2017c). The English merchants stated that they were "quite astonished" that, rather than providing a remedy, the Prussian authorities had encouraged Hanse members to bring "all kinds of trumped up counter-charges ... against the English." In an attempt to resolve the situation an exchange of ambassadors occurred between the English king and the Grand Master, and both sides were ordered to return to each other seized goods while other claims were to be properly heard and settled.

Change over time

The membership services outlined above made guild membership an attractive proposition for individuals engaged in the sourcing, production, and distribution of items in global supply chains. The quality control facilities and skills of members could be positive attributes to a town, while the crown also saw a potential alignment between its goals and the services provided by guild officials to guild members. However, the rapid expansion of global trade from *c.*1500 was coupled by a decline, rather than enhancement, in the attractiveness of guild membership. The reasons for this situation are unclear, but changes in the political and economic environment may have played a part. The royal enquiry of 1388–9 and the dissolution of the chantries in 1547 demonstrated that guilds, though useful to the crown, were not immune from challenge. The 1388–9 enquiry occurred in the aftermath of the Peasants' Revolt of 1381 and reflected a fear of the potential use of religious and craft guilds as organizations for social unrest, as well as a mounting concern with the amount of land that was under guild control. Guilds across England were asked to state their "aims, resources and activities," although there is little surviving evidence to reveal what purpose, if any, the information collected was used for (Jones 1974; Rosser 2015: 64–5; Toulmin Smith *et al*. 1870). The dissolution in 1547 was part of the English Reformation and primarily affected guilds with a religious focus. The English crown, it appears, became more suspicious of the activities of guilds as the Middle Ages progressed.

Competition between England and other countries intensified from *c.*1450 onwards, posing a particular challenge to the merchant guilds and raising questions about their usefulness to members engaged in the distribution networks for global trade. The control of the London vintners' guild over the Gascon wine trade, for example, became less significant as competition from other products, notably beer from the Low Countries and sweet wines from the Mediterranean, intensified. Guild members also suffered disruption in their supply chain due to the English crown's loss of Gascony in 1453 (Crawford 1977: 54, 61). The vintners' guild responded by successfully petitioning the crown, on behalf of its members, to extend their control to other types of wines. Members of the guild enjoyed a brief resurgence in their fortunes until royal legislation in 1553 placed significant restrictions on the volume of wine that could be stored for trade and on the number of taverns an individual vintner could operate. As guild membership began to be associated with limitations on trade, rather than opportunities, there was less incentive for merchants or artisans to pay a fee to join.

The relocation of manufacturing from towns to the countryside may have contributed to the decline of guilds whose members were engaged in production. From *c.*1450 onwards some industries, including cloth making, became more reliant on mechanized production rather than hand production. The countryside provided easier access to fuel and water power for such production (Britnell 2009: 174–5). Raw materials and manufactured products for the global trade routes could increasingly be sourced directly from the countryside or from the new factories, rather than needing to be obtained from guild members.

Mechanization encouraged the centralization of production in factories organized by a single entrepreneur, rather than in individual workshops. There was therefore less incentive to use a model of business organization that co-ordinated craft producers working in individual workshops. Furthermore, mechanization aided the standardization of production, potentially reducing the need to provide quality inspections through the guild system (Gross 1890: 52). There was therefore little need to establish guilds in the new rural locations, while established urban guilds saw membership diminish as manufacturers relocated.

Conclusion

This chapter has outlined the contribution that members of merchant and artisan guilds made to global supply chains during the Middle Ages. It has shown that guild members sourced, created, or distributed exports or distributed imports. By focusing on English guilds, it shows that merchant and artisan guilds provided trade promotion services for their members as well as opportunities for religious observance and social interaction. Some of the services provided helped members to reduce the risks of overseas trade, for example through the potential for partnerships and access to specialist knowledge. Other services, such as quality control and training, helped to boost consumer confidence in products. The importance of the services provided by guild officials to guild members was recognized by local and central government, with whom guild members shared the common goals of promoting a good reputation for the products of their town and a strong performance of their country in the global marketplace.

References

Alsford, Stephen (2017a), "Goldsmiths," in Stephen Alsford, *Medieval English Towns*, http://users.trytel. com/~tristan/towns/florilegium/popcom20.html (accessed 3 January 2017).

Alsford, Stephen (2017b), "Home Front of International Commerce," in Stephen Alsford, *Medieval English Towns*, http://users.trytel.com/~tristan/towns/florilegium/eccom_i6.html#pt7 (accessed 3 January 2017).

Alsford, Stephen (trans.) (2017c), "Perils of Engaging in International Trade," in Stephen Alsford, *Medieval English Towns*, http://users.trytel.com/~tristan/towns/florilegium/economy/eccom20.html (accessed 3 January 2017).

Ammannati, Francesco (2014), "Craft Guild Legislation and Woollen Production: The Florentine Arte della Lana in the Fifteenth and Sixteenth Centuries," in Karel Davids and Bert de Munck (eds.) *Innovation and Creativity in Late Medieval and Early Modern European Cities* (Farnham: Ashgate), 55–80.

Amt, Emilie (2001), *Medieval England 1000–1500: A Reader* (Peterborough, ON: Broadview Press).

Archer, Ian W. (1991), *The History of the Haberdashers' Company* (Chichester: Phillimore & Co Ltd).

Barron, Caroline M. (2004), *London in the Later Middle Ages: Government and People 1200–1500* (Oxford: Oxford University Press).

Bateson, Mary (ed.) (1899), *Records of the Borough of Leicester: Being a Series of Extracts from the Archives of the Corporation of Leicester, 1103–1327* (London: J. C. Clay & Sons).

Boulnois, Luce (trans. Loveday, Helen with additional material by Mayhew, Bradley and Sheng, Angela) (2003), *Silk Road: Monks, Warriors and Merchants of the Silk Road* (Hong Kong: Odyssey).

Brentano, Lujo (1870), "On the History and Development of Gilds, and the Origin of Trade-unions," in Lucy Toulmin Smith, Joshua Toulmin Smith, and Lujo Brentano (eds.) *English Gilds: The Original Ordinances of More than One Hundred Early English Gilds* (London: Early English Text Society), lxiv–cxcix.

Britnell, Richard (2009), *The Commercialisation of English Society 1000–1500* (Cambridge: Cambridge University Press).

Casson, Catherine (2009), "A Comparative Study of Prosecutions for Forgery in Trade and Manufacturing in Six English Towns, 1250 to 1400" (PhD thesis, University of York, 2 vols.).

Casson, Catherine (2012), "Reputation and Responsibility in Medieval English Towns: Civic Concerns with the Regulation of Trade," *Urban History*, 39 (3), 387–408.

Crawford, Anne (1977), *A History of the Vintners' Company* (London: Constable).

Davids, Karel and de Munck, Bert (eds.) (2014), *Innovation and Creativity in Late Medieval and Early Modern European Cities* (Farnham: Ashgate).

Dummelow, John (1973), *The Wax Chandlers of London: A Short History of the Worshipful Company* (London: Phillimore).

Epstein, S. R. and Prak, Maarten (eds.) (2008), *Guilds, Innovation and the European Economy, 1400–1800* (Cambridge: Cambridge University Press).

Giles, K. (2017), "Digital Creativity and the Wall Paintings of 'Shakespeare's Guildhall', Stratford-upon-Avon," *Internet Archaeology*, 44, doi.org/10.11141/ia.44.6.

Giles, Kate (2000), *An Archaeology of Social Identity: Guildhalls in York 1350–1630* (Oxford: Archaeopress).

Goldberg, Jessica (2012), *Trade and Institutions in the Medieval Mediterranean: The Geniza Merchants and Their Business World* (Cambridge: Cambridge University Press).

Grafe, Regina and Gelderblom, Oscar (2010), "The Rise and Fall of Merchant Guilds: Re-thinking the Comparative Study of Commercial Institutions in Pre-modern Europe," *Journal of Interdisciplinary History*, 40 (4), 477–511.

Greif, Avner and Tabellini, Guido (2010), "Cultural and Institutional Bifurcation: China and Europe Compared," *American Economic Review*, 100 (2), 135–40.

Gross, Charles (1890), *The Guild Merchant: A Contribution to British Municipal History Vol. 1* (Oxford: Clarendon Press).

Hicks, Michael (ed.) (2015), *English Inland Trade 1430–1540: Southampton and its Region* (Oxford: Oxbow Books).

Hovland, Stephanie R. (2006), "Apprenticeship in Later Medieval London, (*c.*1300–*c.*1530)" (PhD thesis, Royal Holloway University of London).

Hunt, Edwin and Murray, James (1999), *A History of Business in Medieval Europe: 1200–1550* (Cambridge: Cambridge University Press).

Jefferson, Lisa (ed.) (2003), *Wardens' Accounts and Court Minute Books of the Goldsmiths' Mistery of London 1334–1446* (Woodbridge, UK: Boydell & Brewer).

Jones, William R. (1974), "English Religious Brotherhoods and Medieval Lay Piety: The Inquiry of 1388–89," *Historian*, 36 (4), 646–59.

Keene, Derek (2005), "English Urban Guilds, *c*.900–1300: The Purposes and Politics of Association," in Ian A. Gadd and Patrick Wallis (eds.) *Guilds and Associations in Europe, 900–1900* (London: University of London), 3–27.

Lapidus, Ira M. (1984), *Muslim Cities in the Later Middle Ages* (Cambridge: Cambridge University Press).

Macdonald, Mairi (ed.) (2007), *The Register of the Guild of the Holy Cross, Stratford-upon-Avon* (Stratford-upon-Avon: Dugdale Society).

Maitte, Corine (2014), "The Cities of Glass: Privileges and Innovations in Early Modern Europe," in Karel Davids and Bert de Munck (eds.) *Innovation and Creativity in Late Medieval and Early Modern European Cities* (Farnham: Ashgate), 1–34.

Merchant Adventurers Hall (2017), Homepage, www.merchantshallyork.org/history-and-collections/ (accessed 20 September 2017).

Miller, E. and Hatcher, J. (1995), *Medieval England: Towns, Commerce and Crafts 1086–1348* (London: Longman).

Minns, Chris and Wallis, Patrick (2012), "Rules and Reality: Quantifying the Practice of Apprenticeship in Premodern England," *Economic History Review*, 65 (2), 556–79.

Moll-Murata, Christine (2008), "Chinese Guilds from the Seventeenth to the Twentieth Centuries: An Overview," *International Review of Social History*, 53, 213–47.

Nightingale, Pamela (1989), "Capitalists, Crafts and Constitutional Change in Late Fourteenth-century London," *Past and Present*, 124, 3–35.

Ogilvie, Sheilagh (2011), *Institutions and European Trade: Merchant Guilds, 1000–1800* (Cambridge: Cambridge University Press).

Ogilvie, Sheilagh (2014), "The Economics of Guilds," *Journal of Economic Perspectives*, 28 (4) 169–92.

Purvis, J. S. (1969), *From Minster to Market Place* (York: St Anthony's Press).

Reddaway, T. F. and Walker, Lorna E. M. (1975), *The Early History of the Goldsmiths' Company 1327–1509* (London: Edward Arnold).

Richardson, Gary (2001), "A Tale of Two Theories: Monopolies and Craft Guilds in Medieval England and Modern Imagination," *Journal of the History of Economic Thought*, 23 (2), 218–41.

Rosser, Gervase (2015), *The Art of Solidarity in the Middle Ages: Guilds in England 1250–1550* (Oxford: Oxford University Press).

Rosser, Gervase (1994), "Going to the Fraternity Feast: Commensality and Social Relations in Late Medieval England," *Journal of British Studies*, 33, 430–46.

Schalk, Ruben, Wallis, Patrick, Crowston, Clare, and Lemercier, Claire (2016), "Failure or Flexibility? Exits from Apprenticeship Training in Pre-modern Europe," Economic History Working Papers, 252/2016, London School of Economics and Political Science, Economic History Department.

Sellers, Maud Sellers (ed.) (1914), *York Memorandum Book, Part II (1388–1493)* (York: Surtees Society) available in Stephen Alsford, *Medieval English Towns*, http://users.trytel.com/tristan/towns/florilegium/community/cmreli21.html (accessed 3 January 2017).

Swanson, Heather (1989), *Medieval Artisans: An Urban Class in Late-Medieval England* (Oxford: Basil Blackwell).

Tearle, Barbara (ed.) (2012), *The Accounts of the Guild of Holy Trinity, Luton 1526/7–1546/7* (Woodbridge, UK: Boydell & Brewer).

Thomas, A. H. (ed.) (1926), *Calendar of the Plea and Memoranda Rolls of the City of London Vol. 1: 1323–1364* (London: Corporation of London).

Toulmin Smith, Lucy, Toulmin Smith, Joshua and Brentano, Lujo (1870), *English Gilds: The Original Ordinances of More than One Hundred Early English Gilds* (London: Early English Text Society).

UNESCO (2017), "The Silk Road," http://en.unesco.org/silkroad/about-silk-road (accessed 3 January 2017).

Wallis, Patrick (2008), "Apprenticeship and Training in Premodern England," *Journal of Economic History*, 68 (3), 832–61.

Wallis, Patrick (2012), "Labor, Law and Training in Early Modern London: Apprenticeship and the City's Institution," *Journal of British Studies*, 51 (4), 791–819.

Wheatley, Louise Russell (2008), "The Mercers in Medieval York 1272/3 to 1529: Social Aspirations and Commercial Enterprise" (PhD thesis, University of York).

11

MERCHANTS AND THE ORIGINS OF CAPITALISM

Sophus A. Reinert and Robert Fredona[1]

The emergence of business history as a distinct discipline, first in the United States in the late 1920s, and the development of the history of commerce in late medieval and Renaissance Europe were, from the very beginning, inextricably linked. N.S.B. Gras, the "father" of business history and holder of the first chair in the discipline at Harvard Business School (Boothman 2001; Fredona and Reinert 2017), fruitfully encouraged business historical work on premodern merchants and mercantile firms both in the United States and in Europe (Ferguson 1960: 13–17). Gras believed he had discovered, in the rise of what he called the "sedentary merchant" (understood in contrast to the earlier "traveling merchant" who accompanied his own goods to market or trade fairs), the crucial moment in the development of "mercantile capitalism" in Europe, the stage of economic development in which Europe first rose to undisputed economic prominence on the global stage (Gras 1939). The articles on medieval and Renaissance merchants published in the foundational *Cambridge Economic History of Europe*, written by Gras's MBA student Raymond De Roover (1963b) and by Robert S. Lopez (1952), whom Gras had helped bring to the United States from Italy, bore the clear marks of Gras's influence. Lopez's piece, for example, used the phrase "sedentary merchant" nine times. And the later impresario of economic history Frederic Lane's (1944) early study of the fifteenth-century Venetian merchant Andrea Barberigo was explicitly conceived of as a case study of one such "sedentary merchant". In Gras's view, the sedentary merchant, freed from the demands of travel to trade fairs because he conducted his business through agents and by means of commercial correspondence, was able to develop revolutionary managerial techniques for the administration of business. And these techniques ushered in, or, more properly, developed alongside a "commercial revolution" in the later Middle Ages, focused around a long thirteenth century, a fertile conceptual nexus first coined by De Roover (1942) in response to Gras and later associated with Lopez's (1976) widely read and debated book of that name, which presented the case for such a revolution (more broadly understood) even earlier.

The medieval "commercial revolution" – not to be confused with Early Modern commercial or financial "revolutions" in the Low Countries and England (involving the long-term development of the bourse, exchange banks, joint stock companies, and so on) that built upon it (e.g. Roseveare 1991) – saw the invention, diffusion, or earliest perfection of holding companies, of cashless transactions using bills of exchange, of contracts for marine insurance, and of advanced bookkeeping techniques including so-called "double-entry" accounting, practices

171

which together allowed for the radical facilitation and expansion of long-distance trade, inter-national banking, and commercial and industrial partnerships. Although Gras's schematic and stadial view, with the "sedentary merchant" as point of historical rupture, is doubtlessly an over-simplification of complex, contingent, and overlapping historical processes, there can be little doubt that the period of the "commercial revolution" saw a remarkable transformation of mer-cantile practices, practices by which merchants were able to create a global trade in both com-modities and luxury goods and to thereby enrich and empower urban Europe. Gras, along with Italian pioneers like Gino Luzzatto and Armando Sapori (Varanini 2014; Franceschi 2014, 2018), understood that business records (chiefly account books and commercial correspond-ence), mercantile manuals, and the personal memoranda of merchants (called, in Italy, *ricordi* or *ricordanze*) could give a clearer picture of the development of commerce and of business prac-tices than the normative sources (guild statutes, laws, and so on) that had largely informed earlier (especially nineteenth-century and German) work. This chapter will briefly sketch the develop-ment of medieval and Renaissance mercantile practices, focusing especially on Italian merchants in the Mediterranean, for it was in large part Italian merchants who invented or developed the techniques of modern business, not least of accounting and banking, and thereby created the world of pre-industrial global capitalism.

The commerce of the Mediterranean

The fall of Rome in the West, concomitant with the "invasion" of by then already Romanized "barbarians", witnessed the collapse of the movement of surplus wealth from North Africa and Egypt to the imperial center and to its politico-cultural aristocracy, which had long been enriched in this way, thereby shattering the unity of the Roman Mediterranean as a commercial space. Although it did not dissolve as a political unit or as a regional power (albeit a limited one) until the middle of the fifteenth century, Byzantium, the empire in the East centered at Con-stantinople, similarly survived as a major commercial power only until it lost its wealth-generating provinces in Egypt and the Levant to Islamic expansion, beginning in the seventh century (Lewit 1991; Wickham 2005). European Christians nonetheless maintained a presence, as pil-grims and traders, in North Africa and the Levant well beyond this period, and, although not necessarily predominant, commercial motivations inspired the Crusades, *c.*1095–1291, which saw the foundation and then loss of Christian states in the Levant, created new or larger Euro-pean markets for Eastern goods, and allowed merchants from the Italian city-states to take advantage of new opportunities for West–East trade and seaborne transport (Abulafia 1993; Phillips 1988). Before Europe's epochal geographic expansion in the fifteenth century – begin-ning perhaps as early as 1415 with the Portuguese capture of Ceuta near Gibraltar, but punctu-ated and defined most powerfully by the discovery of the Americas and the navigation of the Indian Ocean in the 1490s (Chaunu 1995) – the mastery of global trade, from a European per-spective, meant constructing anew a system of lucrative shipping lanes and proto-colonies in what had once been the Roman Mediterranean, a process fully underway already by the tenth century, when Lopez saw the first evidence of a "commercial revolution". And even up to and throughout the sixteenth century, as Europe began the process of creating maritime empires in the Indian Ocean and in the Americas, the Mediterranean remained an essential zone for Euro-pean merchant activity.

No scholarly approach to the Mediterranean has been more influential than that of Fernand Braudel (1972), who viewed the Mediterranean as a single unit of analysis, where interactions were defined more by long-term underlying ecological and geographic structures and by periodic cyclical changes in relation to these structures than by the profusion of "events" that preoccupied earlier political and economic historians. More recent approaches have stressed the Mediterranean's numerous tiny micro-regions and the connectivities, including economic ones, between them (Horden and Purcell 2000) or the resilience of the Mediterranean's environment in the face of millennia of human exploitation (Grove and Rackham 2003), but until the creation of the Atlantic economy, i.e. from antiquity to the sixteenth century, the Mediterranean was a (if not, indeed, the) chief locus of long-distance trade and dynamic wealth creation in the West. The industrial and mercantile cities of northern Italy, enriched by the Eastern trade, formed the bottom pole of an almost continuous geographic corridor of advanced, wealthy, and densely populated urban communities stretching across the continent to the Low Countries and ultimately southern England (Brunet 2002). This corridor was the historical axis of capitalism, trade, and civilization in the West.

Even before the revival of global trade in earnest, the desire of European elites (in cities and in monasteries as at royal courts) for luxuries from the East was met by small merchant communities of Jews, Greeks, and Arabs or by traveling middlemen (Vercauteren 1964). But, not surprisingly, it was the Italian cities with the closest ties to Byzantium and its trade in the eastern Mediterranean – places like Genoa and Venice, with commanding positions on the Tyrrhenian and Adriatic Seas, and cities along the Italian coast like Amalfi – that had the first major medieval breakthroughs in establishing effective and secure sea routes (McCormick 2001: 501–47). European merchants, chiefly Italian, without the control of territory within the Muslim and Byzantine polities of North Africa and the Eastern Mediterranean, regularly established diasporic trading colonies there, following a pattern established by earlier commercial diasporas, of Jews, of Egyptians, of Greeks. By the twelfth century, merchants from Venice, Genoa, and Pisa had already established extensive networks of such colonies – often small and often centered around a *fondaco* (from the Greek *pandocheion* by way of the Arabic *funduk*), a combination warehouse and inn, where Christian merchants were permitted to trade and to pray, and where they were supervised and regularly subject to local taxes and duties; but sometimes large enough to house thousands of expatriate merchants, extending to entire neighborhoods or city districts, as at Constantinople – all along the Mediterranean basin. Similarly, foreign trading colonies existed within the mercantile cities of premodern Italy: the most famous is surely the Fondaco dei Tedeschi, or German traders' colony, at Venice, which was established in the early thirteenth century and which housed several hundred northern traders (Constable 2003). The communal nature of diasporas certainly mitigated the dangers of international trade before it was facilitated by more permanent institutions (Greif 2006), but they could also remain competitive even into the eighteenth century, as in Francesca Trivellato's (2009) important case of the Sephardim of the Tuscan free port of Livorno.

The commerce of Europe

Gras's sedentary merchant must naturally be understood in contrast to the so-called "traveling merchant" who defined an earlier but, to a significant extent, contemporary period of long-distance overland trade in Europe, a trade facilitated by the existence of regular circuits of commercial fairs across Northwestern Europe in the Middle Ages. Originally local or regional in character, linking town and countryside or economic center and periphery, these fairs soon became hubs of inter-regional and international merchant activity, linking the premier commercial and industrial zones of Europe. The traveling merchant who attended these fairs accompanied his goods to market, bargained face-to-face with buyers and sellers there, and personally assumed the burdens, costs, and risks of overland travel, from bandits and wolves to unstable infrastructure and inclement weather. Commercial fairs are attested as early as the seventh century in France, but the ninth through thirteenth centuries witnessed an explosion of both long-distance overland trade and the establishment of fairs. The most important fairs were those of Flanders and of the Champagne-Brie region of northeastern France. A cycle of fairs spread over the course of the calendar year (eventually there were six six-week events) and across the region, the Champagne fairs gained particular prominence because of their geographical position – there Flemish cloth dealers, bearing wool and linen cloth from the advanced industrial centers of the Low Countries, could meet with Italian merchants, bearing the goods of Italy and the Mediterranean trade – and because of the protection provided them by the Counts of Champagne. The protection of the Counts, out of which ultimately developed reliable systems of policing, debt enforcement, and dispute resolution, inspired confidence in the Champagne fairs. A sign of the importance and assurance of these fairs: by the late twelfth century, the coins of Provins (one of the Champagne fair towns) were regularly used in Southern Europe and the system of weights associated with Troyes (another) was commonly used in the North. In addition to the direct buying and selling of goods, the Champagne fairs, as those of Flanders had earlier, became centers for financial transactions, money markets, and clearing centers facilitated by letters obligatory and by investment and association contracts, such that credit could reliably be extended at one fair and debt paid back at another (Bautier 1970; Epstein 1994; Cavaciocchi 2001). By the end of the thirteenth century, the largest European fairs were in decline. Although it is difficult to establish causation in one direction or the other, the foundation and increasing regularity and safety of direct sea routes connecting Italy (and thus the West–East trade) with Northwestern Europe was a parallel and related phenomenon. One possibility is that these direct routes, which passed by Gibraltar and linked the Mediterranean with other European sea spaces for trade, reduced the need for the fairs and for overland travel, for which increasingly endemic warfare and instability in Europe had radically increased transportation costs (Munro 2001).

Of course, the Mediterranean was not the only commercially important European sea space in the period. The Black Sea, fed by the Danube and directly open to Constantinople through the Bosporus (along with the connected Sea of Azov, fed by the Don), was an important source of foodstuffs and others goods for Byzantium, serving as a commercial crossroads that linked the Eastern Empire to Eastern Europe, Russia, and Central Asia. As early as the eleventh century, Byzantine concessions to Genoa allowed the Italian city-republic to trade and establish colonies there; and by the mid-thirteenth century, the Genoese controlled much of the direct seaborne trade of the Black Sea with the Mediterranean (Todorova 1987). More importantly, the East–West trade of Northern Europe, like that of the Mediterranean, was a lucrative source of both profit and power for premodern merchants. The German Hanse, a largely commercial but later loosely political organization of merchants in dozens of towns on and around the North and Baltic Seas – stretching from London and Bergen to Bruges and Lübeck and on to Novgorod in Russia – allowed merchants from northern Germany to successfully mediate (though never to monopolize) the trade between the Eastern Baltic and Germany, Flanders, England, and Scandinavia. Although there were Eastern markets for Western goods, like woolen textiles, the Hanse largely satisfied the continental demand for grain, foodstuffs like salted fish, raw materials like wood and metal, and even luxury goods like fur and amber from Scandinavia and especially from the Baltic and regions east (Hammel-Kiesow 2000). But as lucrative as this trade was, it has nonetheless recently been estimated, on the basis of available records from Lübeck and Genoa in the second half of the fourteenth century, that the total value of the Hanseatic trade then represented as little as one-fifteenth ($c.6.6$ percent) of that of the Mediterranean trade (Spufford 2002).

Commercial innovations

The desire for merchant credit and decreased transaction costs in long-distance trade led to the use of moneys-of-account and the creation of the earliest instruments of international finance; the most fundamental of the latter was the "bill of exchange", the *lettera di cambio* or *di pagamento*, a multi-party payment order executable in a foreign currency in a distant location, which was invented in northern Italy, widespread already in the fourteenth century, and in use – largely unchanged – until the eighteenth. Cashless exchanges had occurred at the fairs, on the basis of obligatory letters or so-called *lettres de foire*, but the bill of exchange was revolutionary because the issuer could thereby order a distant third party to pay the debt in another currency, which allowed the bills to circulate widely and function as instruments of both credit and transfer in international trade. The interest or profit from issuing such bills of exchange could be included (or perhaps better, given the usury prohibition, hidden) within the exchange rate, artificially raised in the lender's favor (De Roover 1953). By the 1320s, Florentine merchants were importing the highest quality raw English wool for local manufacturing directly from Southampton rather than through continental middlemen. Florentine merchant-bankers were also simultaneously dominating both international finance and the incredibly lucrative collection of papal taxes; as a result, the largest Florentine companies were able to make extensive loans to the English crown, secured by income from English duties on the export of wool. In this environment, for example, bills of exchange could be employed to great advantage, allowing Florentines resident in England to buy English wool with English papal taxes and to have their partners resident in Italy give the Pope profits from other transactions in lieu of those English taxes (Lloyd 1977: 60–140). The extension of credit, indeed of trust, through formal mechanisms like the bill of exchange, facilitated trade between merchants who no longer were meeting face-to-face, and brought together those with capital and those in need of it.

Primitive methods for spreading risk through indemnification, akin to so-called "bottomry" loans, high interest maritime loans nullified by the loss of the ship itself, may have been known to the ancient world (Andreau 1987), but insurance as we understand it today appears largely a development of the fourteenth century in the maritime cities of northern Italy, where the risks and rewards of business were stark enough and big enough to create regular entrepreneurial opportunities to offer premium insurance for profit. Although there were certainly earlier and undocumented developments, the earliest known insurance contracts that can properly bear that name (even though they hid their interest-bearing nature for legal or ethical reasons) are Genoese and cover a 1343 voyage from Pisa to Sicily and a 1347 voyage from Genoa to Mallorca (Melis 1972: 7; Bensa 1884: 192). A wide range of insurance contracts (Zeno 1936) rapidly developed side-by-side with advances in maritime transport, and the resulting parallel decrease in risk and in shipping rates fed an explosive growth of trade, such that by the late fourteenth century, according to Federigo Melis, a real insurance market had emerged and merchants, originally in Tuscany, had turned insurance into a matter of issuing private contracts (rather than public, notarized documents) and began to include insurance premiums as discrete debits in their bipartite (credit–debit) accounts (Melis 1975; 1984). The next great advance would have to await the mathematics of probability and the mathematization of risk (Daston 1987), and the related growth of large-scale insurance firms, but in the Renaissance the insurance market was highly fragmented and merchants had to rely on a large pool of small-time insurers, since these other merchants and merchant-bankers were willing to underwrite only relatively small policies to avoid catastrophic loss. Between 1390 and 1401, for example, the fabled Prato merchant Francesco Datini, whom we will discuss below, had to rely on some 490 insurers to underwrite 128 policies (Goldthwaite 2009a: 99).

175

The initial and profound expansion of the Mediterranean trade in the tenth and eleventh centuries was also symbiotically accompanied by the creation of new, legally recognized forms of commercial cooperation that appreciated the special characteristics of long-distance merchant ventures, which were high risk and required large initial capital investment. The best known of these is the so-called *commenda*, signified by numerous contemporary names, a contract for pooling capital and sharing the risks and rewards of overseas commerce, which likely evolved from earlier Islamic commercial agreements. A recent analysis of notarial records in medieval Genoa suggests that over 90 percent of all commercial partnerships there before the mid-fourteenth century were based on *commenda* contracts (van Doosselaere 2009). *Commenda* contracts varied in details, but one (sometimes called a "bilateral *commenda*") might look like this: a passive investor, resident in Genoa, puts up two-thirds of the necessary capital for the commercial sea voyage; an active investor – a traveling merchant who will accompany the goods in transit and provide commercial expertise – puts up one-third; profits are shared equally; losses shared are shared in proportion to the initial investment (based on Lopez and Raymond 1967, doc. 84). Contracts of this sort, abundantly available in medieval notarial cartularies, allow us to trace the activities of merchants first hand, but these activities must always be placed in the context of Genoa's contemporary trade wars with its Mediterranean rivals, like Venice and Pisa; its development of colonies as far away as Kaffa on the Black Sea and maintenance of Pera, the Christian trading quarter of Constantinople; and its early creation of a public debt to finance costly naval construction and maritime expansion (Epstein 1996; Miner 2018). The line between Genoese government action and commerce was often exceptionally indistinct: the Genoese colony at Chios, on the Aegean, for example, was administered by a consortium (called the *maona*) of Genoese investors who had funded its capture in 1346 and who exploited its resources to pay dividends to its members (Argenti 1958). Unlike agreements based on a single sea voyage, other forms of partnership agreements were created for firms engaged in longer-term commerce; in Italy such a firm was commonly called a *compagnia*, related to our own word "company", and its members *compagni*. Partnership agreements specified the duration of the partnership (often three years), the initial capital investment (*corpo*) and ultimate shares of the profits, how later investment of capital (*sopraccorpo*) would be handled, which partner(s) would actively run the business either in person or through agents and which would remain passive "investors", and they often depicted the partnership's *segno* or trademark and laid down guidelines for its portability to other firms. Firms could vary in size, but most had only a handful of partners, often blood relatives (even if only distantly related), and the size or scale of partnerships in Tuscany seems to have been under largely downward pressure after the mid-fourteenth century (Goldthwaite 2009a: 64–79). Although the strength of the Renaissance family has become something of a popular trope, dynastic family businesses, with ownership descending through a single patriline, remained relatively rare (though see the example in Caferro 1996) and most firms were, for lack of a better term, ad hoc, with merchants seeking to expand their business creating new partnerships as needed. Partnership agreements, largely unchanged throughout the period, also created – unlike the modern corporation – unlimited personal liability in the partners, even though legislation could (as in Florence after 1408) grant external, passive investors limited liability (Melis 1991).

The sedentary merchant, seen by Gras as defining the first (mercantile) stage of capitalism, achieved what Alberto Tenenti in a suggestive profile of the Renaissance merchant (1988) has called the "gradual and organized control of time, space, and risk" by becoming a manager instead of a trader, and this management required him to transform the world around him into information, into words and numbers. In the jargon of the Tuscan merchant of the late Middle Ages and Renaissance, the word for a firm and the word for its set of account books could, not coincidentally, be the same: *ragione*, from the Latin *ratio*, a count, an accounting, a calculation, a reckoning (Edler 1934: 236). In the firm's books, as in its articles of association, the theoretical body achieved something like a concrete existence. Although the limited-liability joint stock company was a much later innovation, business corporations of a significant size – with a home office, distant branches (*filiali*), directors, partners, agents, and employees – emerged, "constructed out of sedentary merchants", in the second half of the thirteenth century in Tuscany (Padgett 2012, quotation at 121), where and when we also find the earliest references, as in an incomplete 1281 cash book of the Sienese Salimbene company, to complex accounting procedures involving interrelated accounts books (De Roover 1974b). Tuscan account books came to be routinely written in the bilateral or *contrapposto* format, showing debits verso and credits recto, a century later (Padgett and McLean 2006: 1539–43), sometimes using the so-called "double entry" (*partita doppia*) technique, which is often associated with its first systematic exposition by Luca Pacioli near the end of the fifteenth century and which did not gain widespread European acceptance until the seventeenth century (De Roover 1974b; Yamey 2004). Jacob Soll (2014) has recently shown the clear relationship between these methods and the viability ever since of political communities, indeed of the modern state itself, which has historically flourished when accompanied by a culture of accountability.

Mercantile culture and artefacts

If the figures presented by the historian Giovanni Villani are to be believed, already in the 1330s Florence had a boyhood schooling rate as high as 83 percent (Grendler 1989: 72), and, nearly a century later, self-submitted property surveys confirm an overall urban male literacy rate of around 80 percent (a rate not reached in England, for example, until the late nineteenth century). In the Florentine context, before classicizing humanism transformed childhood education in the late fifteenth century, literacy meant the basics of reading and writing in the Tuscan vernacular followed by the arithmetic training necessary for a life in commerce (Black 2004). Literacy and numeracy together were, not surprisingly, the twin foundations of a thriving commercial culture, one evidenced by the abundance of literature left behind by early Renaissance merchants – men like Villani himself, who was a *factor* (business agent) of the Peruzzi bank in Bruges as a young man in the first decade of the fourteenth century (Luzzati 1969) – and by the super-abundance of business records left behind by their compatriots: approximately 2,500 account books from the thirteenth through the fifteenth centuries are extant in the archives of Florence and nearby Prato, more than for the rest of Italy and Europe combined (Tognetti 2012). And these extant books are, of course, but a fraction of the number of books produced: in the 1343 bankruptcy proceedings of the large Acciaiuoli family company, some 1,500 of the firm's account books were referenced (Hoshino 2001).

Merchants, again especially in Tuscany, and not surprisingly given the culture out of which they arose, seem to have been afflicted with a *furor scribendi*, a compulsion to write. In an important early study of these merchant-writers, Christian Bec (1967) showed how generically capacious pre-humanist merchant writing could be, with "*marchands moralistes*", "*marchands conteurs*", "*marchands mémorialistes*", and "*marchands historiographes*" producing advice books, short story (*novella*) collections, family chronicles, and histories. All of these genres, though, orbited around a central and vaster phenomenon, the keeping by merchants of run-of-the-mill *libri di ricordi* or *ricordanze*, personal memoranda books, usually recorded chronologically; quintessential records of "economics" in the pure, premodern sense of household or estate management (from the Greek *oikos*, home), these books laconically recorded chiefly personal business accounts, family data (births, marriages, deaths, etc.), and only occasionally events outside the family–household sphere (Ciappelli 2014). The proverbial or aphoristic wisdom of merchant advice books, like that of Paolo da Certaldo, provides us with a glimpse into the ethos (sometimes start-ling, often all too familiar) of the premodern merchant (Branca 1986: 1–99). More apropos of the long-distance trade, manuals (*pratiche*) of commercial practices were also produced and examples, largely Tuscan and Venetian, remain from the fourteenth and fifteenth centuries: books, covering the width and breadth of the geography of the long-distance merchant's world, in which information useful to merchants – trade routes; distances; local currencies, weights, and measures; lists of spices and other goods; duties and tariffs; carriage costs – was compiled directly or second-hand from correspondents (Dini 1980, especially 53). The most complete specimen, written between 1310 and 1340 by Francesco di Balducci Pegolotti, who worked for the Bardi company in London and Cyprus, is extraordinary in scope, covering thousands of exotic coins, commodities, and measures in hundreds of cities from Acre, as it were, to Zara (present-day Zadar in Croatia). The first route described by Pegolotti, for example, takes a mer-chant (or, more likely, his agents and goods) from the Italian colony of Tana (today Azov, Russia) to Canbalecco (Beijing), around 6,000 kilometers away (Evans 1936).

After 500–700 years, we possess, quite understandably, only a small sample of the business records produced in the late Middle Ages and Renaissance. And when we do possess such records they are often incomplete, even fragmentary. More complete collections are unique and uniquely valuable: as we will describe below, it is precisely and only because so many of the account books and other materials from the businesses of the famous Prato merchant Francesco Datini survive that scholars, from Enrico Bensa (b. 1848) to Federigo Melis (b. 1914) to the current generation of Italian economic historians, have been able to reconstruct the organization and management of his businesses. Harvard Business School's Baker Library possesses another uniquely complete collection (as per De Roover 1974c: 74), which, unlike the extraordinary Datini fonds, has barely been examined in the last 75 years (roughly since the important work of Edler 1934; and De Roover 1974a [1941 original]). The so-called "Selfridge Collection" of Medici family business records, donated to Harvard Business School by the Anglo-American retail magnate Harry Gordon Selfridge, contains about 150 manuscripts through which it is pos-sible to trace the businesses – predominantly wool manufacturing and export – of one branch of Florence's Medici family. The most important merchant covered in the Harvard Business School collection is Francesco de' Medici (1450–1528) whose books, along with those of his father Giuliano di Giovenco (d. 1499), his son Raffaello (d. 1555), and his grandson Giuliano (d. 1565), make up more than 80 percent of the collection. Francesco began his business career in local banking by making petty loans in and around Florence (Goldthwaite 1985) and by selling the wares of goldsmiths; in 1472 he personally journeyed to Pera (the Christian trading quarter of Constantinople) and to Bursa (at the end of the Silk Road); after 1500 he was one of Flor-ence's more prestigious entrepreneurs, regularly holding positions of honor in the city, and overseeing a sizable importing and exporting operation between Spain, Lyons, Florence, Ragusa (on the Italian Dalmatian coast), and the Ottoman cities of Constantinople and Adrianople, exporting finished woolens and importing raw wool from Spain, and silk, spices, and other luxuries from the East. Throughout his career, Francesco's business interests remained varied (lending small sums, dying wool, buying and selling leather, scrap cloth, silk, and jewels, etc.) and most often he had no partners (operating as "Francesco di Giuliano de' Medici and Company"); when he did have partners they were about half the time members of his close family (his father, brothers, and son) and half other Florentine merchants, especially one other local banker and several merchants with similar interests in the Levant trade.[2]

When Gras conceived of the sedentary merchant, he most certainly had in mind the even more exceptional figure of Francesco di Marco Datini (1335–1410), about whom he commis-sioned an article for publication in the early journal of business history that he co-edited with

Harvard Business School's first dean Edwin F. Gay (Brun 1930). Datini, who achieved something like lasting fame in modernity with the publication of Iris Origo's lively account *The Merchant of Prato* (1957), left behind a superabundance of records – over 600 account books, and over 140,000 pieces of commercial correspondence including hundreds of bills of exchange – that is unparalleled for any other premodern merchant. An orphan, Datini first made his fortune with a warehousing and export–import business in Avignon, where the presence of the papal court had created a thriving commercial and financial center, one linked to Tuscany with regular overland mercantile and diplomatic traffic. In the 1380s he returned to Prato, which had been annexed to the Florentine regional state in 1351, and from there operated a massive international enterprise, which has been called a system of businesses or of firms (*sistema di aziende*; Melis 1962) and which foreshadowed, albeit imperfectly, the multinational trading companies of the nineteenth century (Jones 2002) and the hierarchically administered multiunit firm of the twentieth century (Chandler 1977). With major branches in Avignon, Prato, Pisa, Florence, Genoa, Barcelona, Valencia, and Mallorca, Datini's commercial empire involved banking, industrial production (chiefly of woolen textiles), and hundreds of commercial partnerships with junior partners, agents, and employees. Of course Datini's system was far from representative of the usually much smaller and more abundant mercantile partnerships of the era, and these were equally far from the still more abundant shops of the petty merchants of Prato in the same period, who kept only rudimentary accounts, dealt with the long-distance trade through local small bankers (*tavolieri*), and occupied a circumscribed world dominated by personal trust and rampant consumption loans (Marshall 1999). Late in life, and strongly influenced by a friend, the notary Lapo Mazzei, Datini became increasingly devout and left his fortune to a charitable organization for the poor of Prato that he established called the *Ceppo dei poveri* (Guasti 1880; Nigro 2010).

Although Datini regularly opened his new accounts in the name of "God and profit", as many Italian merchants of the time did, he also, again like many of his contemporaries, increasingly grew anxious about his wealth and its possibly deleterious effect on his salvation. The relationship of religion to capitalism and its origins became a major question around the beginning of the twentieth century: Max Weber's (2010; original 1905) famous argument that the "spirit" of capitalism did not arise until Calvinist and Puritan doctrines gave work, as a secular vocation (*Beruf*), a dignified place within God's plan was formulated in reaction to those of Werner Sombart (1902; Lehmann 1993), who held that capitalism emerged from a mixture of acquisitiveness and the rational calculation of profit, and whose powerful synthetic vision of a "modern" (or post-sixteenth-century) economy formed by entrepreneurs, states, and technologies cast a long shadow in the twentieth century (especially in the heavily revised form of Sombart 1916). Although the larger question of "spirit" – a cultural rather than empirical one – remains moot, capitalism as it developed in the medieval West did so alongside an often hostile religious or ethical mindset, most commonly associated in the most widely known scholarly literature with the usury prohibition and the just price doctrine.

Usury, understood as *any* interest rather than excessive interest, was forbidden by the Biblical and Koranic traditions, but was allowed in Byzantium, where legal rates were set by imperial legislation. The increased trade of the twelfth century created a demand for commercial credit and prompted increasing condemnations from church councils, like the Third Lateran Council of 1179, as well as theologians and preachers. Pawnbrokers and moneylenders, often Jews because the Jewish usury prohibition was understood to extend only to loans to other Jews and not to gentiles, were understood to be preying on the Christian poor and were regularly subjected to rhetorical and physical violence (Le Goff 1988). Moneychangers and bankers provided their services and loans of capital at interest, but they often obscured the interest, as we have already noted, under the guise of otherwise licit transactions. And theologians and canon lawyers, already in the thirteenth century, had moreover created innovative doctrines to support commercial credit on the basis of risk, opportunity costs, and the legitimacy of remuneration for performing financial services. The Provençal theologian and Spiritual Franciscan Peter John Olivi even distinguished productive capital from money, a non-productive or "sterile" medium of exchange in the Aristotelian and Scholastic traditions (Spicciani 1990). There is some evidence that the usury prohibition retarded the growth of financial markets in medieval Italy, and surviving testaments show that merchants often experienced moral doubts about their commercial and credit activities, leading them to make general restitution to the church for ill-gotten gains and sometimes specific restitution to individuals and institutions from whom usury had been exacted (Edler De Roover 1957; Petti Balbi 2011). Nonetheless, the impact of the usury prohibition upon merchants and upon the development of commercial instruments remains an open question still debated in a vibrant historiography (Barile 2008; Todeschini 2009). It should also be noted here that the famous "just price", with which the scholastic economic ethic is commonly identified, was rarely understood by medieval theologians and canonists, in practice and under ordinary conditions, as anything other than the market price (De Roover 1958). That said, certain essential staple goods, like grain – subject to unpredictable crop failures, and thus life or death matters for rulers and their subjects – were highly regulated (De la Roncière 1982) and continued to be for centuries (Kaplan 2015: xxii–xxiv); and neither the trades nor trade were "free" in premodern urban Europe: guilds and governments alike erected barriers to trade protecting local merchants and industries including quality, price, and exchange controls; tariffs and levies; subsidies and privileges; and franchises and legal monopolies (Munro 1977; Mackenney 1987; Mauro 1990).

Venice: merchants and the state

In approaching the trade of the Mediterranean, the case of Venice, the preeminent commercial power of the later Middle Ages and Renaissance, is exemplary; foreshadowing the mercantilist and national powers of the seventeenth century, in Venice more purely commercial activity went hand-in-hand with industrial-technological advancement and state intervention, creating for the Serenissima a set of partially overlapping commercio-political empires on the Italian mainland (the so-called *Terraferma*, ultimately extending to the plains of Lombardy and including cities like Brescia, Cremona, Padua, and Verona), in Istria and on the Dalmatian coast, and all across the Eastern Mediterranean, controlling and fortifying possessions along the Strait of Otranto, the Gulf of Corinth, the Peloponnese (or *Morea*), and beyond, including Crete and Cyprus. Although undisputed Venetian mastery of the Eastern Mediterranean was brief, lasting between the end of a series of commercial wars with Genoa and the start of Ottoman encroachment, its commercial and industrial power writ large was extraordinarily long lived (Chambers 1970; Lane 1973). A symptom of Venice's stable and expansive mercantile power: although Florence and Genoa both minted gold coins before Venice did, with the former's famed Florin quickly displacing North African gold coins and gold dust as the foremost medium of exchange for high payments in Europe, the Venetian Ducat – first minted in 1285 – was rapidly used and copied throughout the Eastern Mediterranean and, in the fifteenth century, overtook the Florin as the premier gold coin of Europe (Lane and Mueller 1985; Stahl 2000). Venice had been a vassal state under the jurisdiction of Byzantium until the late ninth century, it established major trade routes in the eleventh century, and by the start of the thirteenth century – when, in 1204, Doge Enrico Dandolo diverted the Fourth Crusade to sack Constantinople – it conspicuously rivaled or equaled the Eastern Empire due to its maritime prowess (Nicol 1988; Laiou-Thomadakis 1980–81). Venice's slow loss of mercantile supremacy in (and colonial rents from) the Eastern Mediterranean, offset in part by increased expansion in the Terraferma, sped up only in the seventeenth century, when North-western European national powers, the Dutch and the English, began to capture significant parts of the Levantine trade as a result of their burgeoning naval and economic power. The English Levant Company, a politico-commercial entity, came to trade directly with the Ottomans, entirely sidestepping the Venetians and similarly, when necessary, small and mobile communities of English merchants would deal with Greek rather than Venetian traders in territories under Venetian domination (Fusaro 2015). Such reversals of fortune often follow successful politico-mercantile emulation (Reinert 2011).

In Venice, as elsewhere in northern and central Italy, industry and trade were intimately and harmoniously linked. To take one famous example: although the Venetian glass industry, centered on the island of Murano, began as early as the tenth century, it was the astonishing wealth of Venice's merchants in the late Middle Ages and Renaissance that supplied the large capital investment necessary for growth and technological development and it was these merchants' mastery of Mediterranean sea lanes that facilitated both the importation of raw materials and the export of luxury glasswork (McCray 1999). Similar arrangements also existed on a much larger scale. The massive industry of turning raw timber, culled locally or from Venetian forests in Istria and Dalmatia, and long one of Venice's chief commodities for sale, into ships for war and trade lay at the heart of the Venetian enterprise: the Arsenal, Venice's shipyard, built in stages from the thirteenth through the fifteenth centuries, employed as many as 16,000 shipbuilders in the 1420s and achieved remarkable productivity (Appuhn 2009; Concina 2006). The production of the Arsenal fed the system of public galley convoys that had long been central to Venice's maritime trading and war-making capacity, a system that collapsed only in the sixteenth century when the private interests of the Venetian patriciate could no longer be reconciled with the city's public interest (Judde de Larivière 2008).

The scale of mercantile enterprises

Throughout the Middle Ages and Renaissance, merchant partnerships and companies, even those with "global" reach, tended to remain both small in size and limited in duration, and are often best viewed as particularistic entities embedded in much larger and sometimes overwhelming mercantile networks, trade routes, and flows of goods and precious metals, but there were exceptions: late medieval Florence, for example, saw the creation of what Edwin S. Hunt (1994) has called "super-companies": the Bardi, Peruzzi, and Acciaiuoli family companies of the fourteenth century. The Peruzzi company, defined by a series of renewed short-term partnership agreements, lasted nearly 70 years and grew to a conspicuously large size: in addition to a main branch in Florence and others in some of the political and economic centers of Europe (Avignon, London, Paris, Bruges), the company, in 1335, had subsidiary branches all over the Mediterranean world – Pisa, Venice, Naples, Barletta, Sicily, Sardinia, Mallorca, Tunis, Cyprus, and Rhodes – and employed 90 salaried agents. By comparison, the papacy in Avignon, by far Europe's largest administrative operation, employed about 250 there. The Bardi company was even larger and its assets, again in 1335, were an astonishing 4.5 times larger than the net receipts of the English crown nearly a century later. The scale of these companies allowed them to obtain trading privileges with kings and other political rulers in exchange for the large cash loans required to wage war. The three companies went bankrupt in the 1340s. It was long believed, due to the historic centrality of the wool trade in Florence, that the Peruzzi company's failure resulted from Edward III, the English king, defaulting on the enormous loans that secured for the company control of the supply of high-quality raw English wool, but Hunt has shown that the Peruzzi instead fell victim to decreasing profit margins in the grain trade, which formed the real core of their business. Even if the "super-companies" did not collapse due to sovereign defaults, lending to kings, city-states, and other large institutions could be a very dangerous business for premodern merchants and merchant bankers. The case of Jacques Coeur is exemplary: the Bourges merchant, who amassed a fortune by importing tapestries and silk through Damascus, financed French military campaigns in the 1440s before ultimately running afoul of the court, having his property confiscated, and fleeing arrest to Rome (Mollat 1988).

Some Renaissance family companies also grew to extraordinary size and attained equally large geopolitical influence, most famously the Medici bank of fifteenth-century Florence and the Fugger bank of sixteenth-century Augsberg, both of which profited from the collection of papal taxes, from the sale of insurance, from the regular fluctuation of international exchange rates, and from loans to merchants and princes. And both the Medici and Fugger companies, with branches all over Europe, in addition to these more bank-like activities, acted as vast international holding companies (or perhaps multinational business groups), operating manufacturing and mining enterprises and export–import businesses. Using the abundant and meticulous extant records of the Medici bank, including some of its "secret books" (*libri segreti*) discovered by his wife Florence Edler, Raymond de Roover (1963a) showed that the bank's success relied not on innovative banking techniques but on managerial prowess – insulating the central company from losses, incentivizing branch managers to increase profits, requiring the regular presentation of financial statements – and that its failure, between 1464 and the ultimate collapse of 1494, likewise was the product of mismanagement by the younger generation. Jakob Fugger, the richest man in Europe, personally helped finance the 1516 royal election of Charles I of Spain (later the Emperor Charles V), and his family bank, its fortunes tied to Spain, reaped enormous profits and gained incredible holdings in land and mines (by which unpaid loans to the crown were redeemed) but, in the second half of the sixteenth century, was battered by a series of Spanish state bankruptcies (Kellenbenz 1990).

Conclusion

It has lately become fashionable to suggest that the West's clear economic advantage over the East is a relatively recent phenomenon, with Europe overtaking China only in the mid-eighteenth century (Pomeranz 2000), even though earlier periods, like the fourteenth century, have been more persuasively presented on the basis of economic data (Maddison 2006). But the most commercially advanced regions of Europe, like the urban centers of Flanders and north-central Italy, were extreme outliers much earlier, both globally and within Europe itself. Italy's was the leading world economy *c.*1300 and, even with a steady and long decline from then to the 1880s (Malanima 2011), England's did not overtake it (in terms of real wages) until the eighteenth century (Malanima 2013). Although the Industrial Revolution allowed for unprecedented prosperity and brought about modern economic growth (Hartwell 1971), Michael Mitterauer (2010) is right that Europe was set on its "special path (*Sonderweg*)" in the Middle Ages, but his search for causes – from the cultivation of rye to the centralization of the Papal church – largely overlooks the patent cause of Europe's distinct late medieval prosperity, which spurred revolutionary advancements in shipping, communications, and manufacturing: the long-distance trade of merchants. Indeed, to speak of the makers of global business must be, first of all, to speak of merchants.

In this chapter, with its focus on the Mediterranean trade of the Middle Ages and Renaissance, we have shown how the merchant – Gras's "sedentary merchant", freed from the harsh demands of travel by his mastery of information and by the seismic innovations of the medieval "commercial revolution" – emerged as a truly global figure. Then, as now, merchants pooled capital and shared risk to enrich themselves and their polities, utilizing the infrastructure and markets that they helped to make, and creating new legal and financial instruments to facilitate their ventures. Premodern merchants bequeathed to the businessmen of later centuries essential techniques of trade and bookkeeping, but also their commercial ethos, their institutions, and the very riches for which they competed and often risked their lives. It is not by chance that the politico-economic system that followed is called the mercantile system, as in Adam Smith's (1976: 396–417) pejorative usage, or simply mercantilism, for, broadly understood, it held that the competition for trade lay at the essential core of state power (Reinert 2013). The violent Genoese–Venetian struggle for the Mediterranean trade, the aggressive emulation of Italian banking practices in the Low Countries, and so on, are forerunners of the mercantilist age and, indeed, of the perpetual competition, diversity of forms (political and economic), and innovation that has marked the development of the West.

Let us conclude with an example, from the Low Countries instead of Italy, which encapsulates much of what had already been said. Bruges, the quintessential merchants' city, spatially positioned to benefit from the decline of the Champagne fairs and from regional advances in textile manufacturing, was by 1350 a center of trade, finance, and industry: politically responsive to mercantile interests, densely urbanized, concentrating and exploiting the resources of the surrounding countryside, attracting skilled craftsmen as immigrants, hosting large merchant colonies (of Italians and German Hanse traders, of course, but of many others as well), and importing and exporting commodities and luxury goods in a trade covering the known world and extending beyond it, the Flemish seaport was also a center for deposit banking and credit creation, and a clearing house for commercial information (De Roover 1948; van Houtte 1982). A search for the "origins" of capitalism in any essential sense is futile, and capitalist or proto-capitalist activities and ideas may be transhistorical phenomena, but to see one of the European merchant metropolises of the late Middle Ages or Renaissance – to see a city like Bruges or like Venice – was, we may say with crystalline hindsight, to glimpse the very future of global business.

Notes

1 The authors wish to thank William Caferro, Julius Kirshner, and Erik S. Reinert for their helpful criticisms, and Geoffrey Jones and Walter Friedman of Harvard Business School's Business History Initiative for their support and encouragement. Robert Fredona's research was funded in part by a grant from the European Union's Horizon 2020 research and innovation programme under the Marie Skłodowska-Curie grant agreement No. 793583.
2 The collection (briefly described in de Ricci 1935) was acquired by Selfridge at auction in London (see Tyler 1919). HBS Medici Family Collection, Baker Library Special Collections, Harvard Business School, ms. 495, fascio C, pp. 89–146 for Francesco's sojourn in Turkey; ms. 519 [not physically with the collection, on which see Goldthwaite 2009b] for some of his earliest businesses; Francesco's activities from 1471 to 1525 are represented by at least 11 partnership agreements [in ms. 495] and 27 manuscript books [mss. 514, 516, 518–21, 523–4, 526, 528–34, 536 (2–6), 537–9, 543(1), 545–6, 568(1)], many of them ledgers (*libro debitori e creditori*), with a sizable number of other types, including journal (*giornale*), memoranda (*ricordanze*), and letter copybook (*copialettere*), and a single *libro segreto*.

References

Abulafia, David (1993), *Commerce and Conquest in the Mediterranean, 1100–1500* (Aldershot: Variorum).
Andreau, Jean (1987), *La vie financière dans le monde romain: Les metiers de manieurs d'argent* (Rome: École Française de Rome).
Appuhn, Karl (2009), *A Forest on the Sea: Environmental Expertise in Renaissance Venice* (Baltimore, MD: Johns Hopkins University Press).

Argenti, Philip P. (1958), *The Occupation of Chios by the Genoese and their Administration of the Island, 1346–1566* (Cambridge: Cambridge University Press).

Barile, Nicola Lorenzo (2008), "Il dibattito sul prestito a interesse negli ultimi trent'anni tra probabilisti e rigoristi: Un bilancio storiografico", *Nuova rivista storica* 92, 835–74.

Bautier, Robert-Henri (1970), "The Fairs of Champagne", 42–63, in Rondo E. Cameron (ed.), *Essays in French Economic History* (Homewood, IL: R.D. Irwin).

Bec, Christian (1967), *Les marchands écrivains: Affaires et humanisme à Florence, 1375–1434* (Paris: La Haye).

Bensa, Enrico (1884), *Il contratto di assicurazione nel Medio Evo: Studi e ricerche* (Genoa: Tipografia marittima).

Black, Robert (2004), "Education and the Emergence of a Literate Society", 18–36, in John M. Najemy (ed.), *Italy in the Age of the Renaissance* (Oxford: Oxford University Press).

Boothman, Barry E.C. (2001), "A Theme Worthy of Epic Treatment: N.S.B. Gras and the Emergence of American Business History", *Journal of Macromarketing* 21, 61–73.

Branca, Vittore (1986), *Mercanti scrittori: Ricordi nella Firenze tra Medioevo e Rinascimento* (Milan: Rusconi).

Braudel, Fernand (1972), *The Mediterranean and the Mediterranean World in the Age of Philip II*, trans. Siân Reynolds (New York: Harper).

Brun, Robert (1930), "A Fourteenth-Century Merchant of Italy: Francesco Datini of Prato", *Journal of Economic and Business History* 2, 450–6.

Brunet, Roger (2002), "Lignes de force de l'espace Européen", *Mappemonde* 66, 14–19.

Caferro, William (1996), "The Silk Business of Tommaso Spinelli, Fifteenth-Century Florentine Merchant and Papal Banker", *Renaissance Studies* 10, 417–39.

Cavaciocchi, Simonetta (ed.) (2001), *Fiere e mercati nella integrazione delle economie europee secc. XIII–XVIII* (Florence: Le Monnier).

Chambers, David S. (1970), *The Imperial Age of Venice, 1380–1580* (London: Thames & Hudson).

Chandler, Jr., Alfred D. (1977), *The Visible Hand: The Managerial Revolution in American Business* (Cambridge, MA: Harvard University Press).

Chaunu, Pierre (1995), *L'expansion européenne du XIIIe au XVe siècle*, 3rd rev'd ed. (Paris: Presses universitaires de France).

Ciappelli, Giovanni (2014), *Memory, Family, and Self: Tuscan Family Books and Other European Egodocuments (14th–18th Century)* (Leiden: Brill).

Concina, Ennio (2006), *L'Arsenale della Repubblica di Venezia* (Venice: Electa).

Constable, Oliva Remie (2003), *Housing the Stranger in the Mediterranean World: Lodging, Trade, and Travel in Late Antiquity and the Middle Ages* (Cambridge: Cambridge University Press).

Daston, Lorraine J. (1987), "The Domestication of Risk: Mathematical Probability and Insurance, 1650–1830", vol. I: 237–60, in L. Krüger, L.J. Daston, and M. Heidelberger (eds.), *The Probabilistic Revolution*, two vols (Cambridge, MA: Harvard University Press).

De la Roncière, Charles Marie (1982), *Prix et salaires à Florence au XIVe siècle*, vol. 2 (Rome: Ecole Française de Rome).

De Ricci, Seymour (1935), *Census of Medieval and Renaissance Manuscripts in the United States and Canada*, vol. 1 (New York: Wilson,), 1052–3.

De Roover, Raymond (1942), "The Commercial Revolution of the Thirteenth Century", *Bulletin of the Business Historical Society* 16, 34–9.

De Roover, Raymond (1948), *Money, Banking, and Credit in Mediaeval Bruges: Italian Merchant Bankers, Lombards, and Money-Changers* (Cambridge, MA: Medieval Academy of America).

De Roover, Raymond (1953), *L'evolution de la lettre de change, XIVe–XVIIIe siècles* (Paris: A. Colin).

De Roover, Raymond (1958), "The Concept of the Just Price: Theory and Economic Policy", *Journal of Economic History* 18, 418–38.

De Roover, Raymond (1963a), *The Rise and Decline of the Medici Bank, 1397–1494* (Cambridge, MA: Harvard University Press).

De Roover, Raymond (1963b), "The Organization of Trade", 42–118, in M.M. Postan, E.E. Rich, and Edward Miller (eds), *Cambridge Economic History of Europe*, vol. 3 (Cambridge: Cambridge University Press).

De Roover, Raymond (1974a), "A Florentine Firm of Cloth Manufacturers: Management and Organization of a Sixteenth-Century Business" [1941], 85–118, in Julius Kirshner (ed.), *Business, Banking, and Economic Thought in Late Medieval and Early Modern Europe* (Chicago, IL: University of Chicago Press).

De Roover, Raymond (1974b), "The Development of Accounting Prior to Luca Pacioli According to the Account Books of Medieval Merchants" [1956], 119–80, in Julius Kirshner (ed.), *Business, Banking, and Economic Thought in Late Medieval and Early Modern Europe* (Chicago, IL: University of Chicago Press).

De Roover, Raymond (1974c), "The Story of the Alberti Company of Florence, 1302–1348, as Revealed in its Account Books" [1958], 39–84, in Julius Kirshner (ed.), *Business, Banking, and Economic Thought in Late Medieval and Early Modern Europe* (Chicago, IL: University of Chicago Press).

Dini, Bruno (ed.) (1980), *Una pratica di mercatura in formazione (1394–1395)* (Florence: Istituto Datini).

Edler, Florence (1934), *Glossary of Mediaeval Terms of Business, Italian Series, 1200-1600* (Cambridge, MA: Medieval Academy of America).

Edler De Roover, Florence (1957), "Restitution in Renaissance Florence", 773–90, in *Studi in onore di Armando Sapori*, vol. 1 (Milan: Istituto editoriale cisalpino).

Epstein, Stephen (1994), "Regional Fairs, Institutional Innovation, and Economic Growth in Late Medieval Europe", *Economic History Review* 47, 459–82.

Epstein, Stephen A. (1996), *Genoa and the Genoese, 958–1528* (Chapel Hill, NC: University of North Carolina Press).

Evans, Allan (1936), *Francesco Balducci Pegolotti: La Pratica della mercatura* (Cambridge, MA: Medieval Academy of America).

Ferguson, Wallace K. (1960), "Recent Trends in the Economic Historiography of the Renaissance", *Studies in the Renaissance* 7, 7–26.

Franceschi, Franco (2014), "Armando Sapori e la storia economica *à part entière*", *Storia economica* 17.2, 367–83.

Franceschi, Franco (2018), "Armando Sapori e la storiografia internazionale", 73–100, in Stefano Moscadelli and Achille Marzio Romani (eds), *Armando Sapori* (Milan: Egea).

Fredona, Robert and Reinert, Sophus A. (2017), "The Harvard Research Center in Entrepreneurial History and the Daimonic Entrepreneur", *History of Political Economy* 49, 267–314.

Fusaro, Maria (2015), *Political Economies of Empire in the Early Modern Mediterranean: The Decline of Venice and the Rise of England, 1450–1700* (Cambridge: Cambridge University Press).

Gras, N.S.B. (1939), *Business and Capitalism: An Introduction to Business History* (New York: Crofts).

Greif, Avner (2006), *Institutions and the Path to the Modern Economy: Lessons from Medieval Trade* (Cambridge: Cambridge University Press).

Grendler, Paul (1989), *Schooling in Renaissance Italy* (Baltimore, MD: Johns Hopkins University Press).

Goldthwaite, Richard A. (1985), "Local Banking in Renaissance Florence", *Journal of European Economic History* 14, 5–55.

Goldthwaite, Richard A. (2009a), *The Economy of Renaissance Florence* (Baltimore: Johns Hopkins University Press).

Goldthwaite, Richard A. (2009b), "The Return of a Lost Ledger to the Selfridge Collection of Medici Manuscripts at Baker Library", *Business History Review* 83, 165–71.

Guasti, Cesare (ed.) (1880), *Ser Lapo Mazzei: Lettere di un notaro a un mercante del secolo XIV, con altre lettere e documenti*, two vols (Florence: Le Monnier).

Grove, A.T. and Rackham, Oliver (2003), *The Nature of Mediterranean Europe: An Ecological History* (New Haven, CT: Yale University Press).

Hammel-Kiesow, Rolf (2000), *Die Hanse* (Munich: Beck).

Hartwell, R.M. (1971), *The Industrial Revolution and Economic Growth* (London: Methuen).

Horden, Peregrine and Purcell, Nicolas (2000), *The Corrupting Sea: A Study of Mediterranean History* (Oxford: Oxford University Press).

Hoshino, Hidetoshi (2001), "Nuovi documenti sulla compagnia degli Acciaiuoli nel Trecento", 83–100, in Franco Franceschi and Sergio Tognetti (eds), *Industria tessile e commercio internazionale nella Firenze del tardo medioevo* (Florence: Olschki).

Hunt, Edwin S. (1994), *The Medieval Super-Companies: A Study of the Peruzzi Company of Florence* (Cambridge: Cambridge University Press).

Jones, Geoffrey (2002), *Merchants to Multinationals: British Trading Companies in the Nineteenth and Twentieth Centuries* (Oxford: Oxford University Press).

Judde de Larivière, Claire (2008), *Naviguer, commercer, gouverner: Économie maritime et pouvoirs à Venise (XVe–XVIe siècles)* (Leiden: Brill).

Kaplan, Steven L. (2015), *The Stakes of Regulation: Perspectives on Bread, Politics and Political Economy Forty Years Later* (London: Anthem).

Kellenbenz, Hermann (1990), *Die Fugger in Spanien und Portugal bis 1560: Ein Grossunternehmen des 16. Jahrhunderts*, two vols (Munich: Vögel).

Laiou-Thomadakis, Angeliki E. (1980–81), "The Byzantine Economy in the Mediterranean Trade System: Thirteenth-Fifteenth Centuries", *Dumbarton Oaks Papers* 34–35, 177–222.

Lane, Frederic C. (1944), *Andrea Barbarigo, Merchant of Venice, 1418–1449* (Baltimore, MD: Johns Hopkins University Press).

Lane, Frederic C. (1973), *Venice: A Maritime Republic* (Baltimore, MD: Johns Hopkins University Press).

Lane, Frederic C. and Mueller, Reinhold (1985), *Money and Banking in Medieval and Renaissance Venice*, vol. 1, *Coins and Moneys of Account* (Baltimore, MD: Johns Hopkins University Press).

Le Goff, Jacques (1988), *Your Money or Your Life: Economy and Religion in the Middle Ages* (New York: Zone Books).

Lehmann, Hartmut (1993), "The Rise of Capitalism: Weber versus Sombart", 195–208, in Hartmut Lehmann and Günther Roth (eds), *Weber's Protestant Ethic: Origins, Evidence, Context* (Cambridge: Cambridge University Press).

Lewit, Tamara (1991), *Agricultural Production in the Roman Economy, A.D. 200–400* (Oxford: Oxford University Press).

Lloyd, Terence (1977), *The English Wool Trade in the Middle Ages* (Cambridge: Cambridge University Press).

Lopez, Robert S. (1952), "The Trade of Medieval Europe: The South", 306–401 in M.M. Postan and Edward Miller (eds), *Cambridge Economic History of Europe*, vol. 2 (Cambridge: Cambridge University Press).

Lopez, Robert S. (1976), *The Commercial Revolution of the Middle Ages, 950–1350* (Cambridge: Cambridge University Press).

Lopez, Robert S. and Raymond, Irving W. (1967), *Medieval Trade in the Mediterranean World: Illustrative Documents* (New York: Norton).

Luzzati, Michele (1969), "Ricerche sulle attività mercantili e sul fallimento di Giovanni Villani", *Bullettino dell'Istituto Storico Italiano per il Medio Evo e Archivio Muratoriano* 81, 173–235.

McCormick, Michael (2001), *Origins of the European Economy: Communications and Commerce A.D. 300–900* (Cambridge: Cambridge University Press).

McCray, Patrick (1999), *Glassmaking in Renaissance Venice: The Fragile Craft* (Aldershot: Ashgate).

Mackenney, Richard (1987), *Tradesmen and Traders: The World of the Guilds in Venice and Europe, c. 1250–1650* (Totowa, NJ: Barnes and Noble).

Maddison, Angus (2006), *The World Economy: A Millennial Perspective*, two vols (Paris: OECD).

Malanima, Paolo (2011), "The Long Decline of a Leading Economy: GDP in Central and Northern Italy, 1300–1913", *European Review of Economic History* 15, 169–219.

Malanima, Paolo (2013), "When Did England Overtake Italy? Medieval and Early Modern Divergence in Prices and Wages", *European Review of Economic History* 17, 45–70.

Marshall, Richard K. (1999), *The Local Merchants of Prato: Small Entrepreneurs in the Late Medieval Economy* (Baltimore, MD: Johns Hopkins University Press).

Mauro, Frédéric (1990), "Merchant Communities, 1350–1750", 255–87, in James D. Tracey (ed.), *The Rise of Merchant Empires: Long-Distance Trade in the Early Modern World, 1350–1750* (Cambridge: Cambridge University Press).

Melis, Federigo (1962), *Aspetti della vita economica medievale: Studi nell'Archivio Datini di Prato* (Siena: Monte dei Paschi).

Melis, Federigo (1972), *Documenti per la storia economica dei secoli XIII–XVI con nota di paleografia commerciale a cura di Elena Cecchi* (Florence: Olschki).

Melis, Federigo (1975), *Origini e sviluppi delle assicurazioni in Italia (secoli XIV–XVI)*, vol. 1, *Le Fonti*, Bruno Dini and Elena Cecchi (eds) (Roma: Istituto Nazionale delle Assicurazione).

Melis, Federigo (1984), *I trasporti e le comunicazioni nel medioevo*, Luciana Frangioni (ed.) (Florence: Le Monnier).

Melis, Federigo (1991), "Le società commerciali a Firenze dalla seconda metà del XIV al XVI secolo", 161–180, in Federigo Melis, *L'azienda nel Medioevo*, Marco Spallanzani (ed.) (Florence: Le Monnier).

Miner, Jeffrey (2018), "Genoa, Liguria, and the Regional Development of Medieval Public Debt", 1–28, in Robert Fredona and Sophus A. Reinert (eds), *New Perspectives on the History of Political Economy* (London: Palgrave).

Mitterauer, Michael (2010), *Why Europe? The Medieval Origins of its Special Path* (Chicago, IL: University of Chicago Press).

Mollat, Michel (1988), *Jacques Cœur, ou L'Esprit d'entreprise au XVe siècle* (Paris: Aubier).

Munro, John H. (1977), "Industrial Protectionism in Medieval Flanders", 229–68, in Harry Miskimin, David Herlihy, and A.L. Udovitch (eds), *The Medieval City* (New Haven, CT: Yale University Press).

Munro, John H. (2001), "The 'New Institutional Economics' and the Changing Fortunes of Fairs in Medieval and Early Modern Europe: The Textile Trades, Warfare, and Transaction Costs", *Vierteljahrschrift für Sozial- und Wirtschaftsgeschichte* 88, 1–47.

Nicol, Donald M. (1988), *Byzantium and Venice: A Study in Diplomatic and Cultural Relations* (Cambridge: Cambridge University Press).

Nigro, Giampiero (ed.) (2010), *Francesco di Marco Datini: L'Uomo, il mercante* (Florence: Firenze University Press).

Origo, Iris (1957), *The Merchant of Prato, Francesco di Marco Datini, 1335–1410* (New York: Knopf).

Padgett, John F. (2012), "The Emergence of Corporate Merchant-Banks in Dugento Tuscany", 121–67, in John F. Padgett and Walter W. Powell (eds), *The Emergence of Organizations and Markets* (Princeton, NJ: Princeton University Press).

Padgett, John F. and McLean, Paul D. (2006), "Organizational Invention and Elite Transformation: The Birth of Partnership Systems in Renaissance Florence", *American Journal of Sociology* 111, 1463–568.

Petti Balbi, Giovanna (2011), "Fenomeni usurari e restituzioni: La situazione ligure (secoli XII–XIV)", *Archivio storico italiano* 169, 199–220.

Phillips, J.R.S. (1988), *The Medieval Expansion of Europe* (Oxford: Oxford University Press).

Pomeranz, Kenneth (2000), *The Great Divergence: China, Europe, and the Making of the Modern World Economy* (Princeton, NJ: Princeton University Press).

Reinert, Sophus A. (2011), *Translating Empire: Emulation and the Origins of Political Economy* (Cambridge, MA: Harvard University Press).

Reinert, Sophus A. (2013), "Rivalry: Greatness in Early Modern Political Economy", 248–70, in Philip J. Stern and Carl Wennerlind (eds), *Mercantilism Reimagined: Political Economy in Early Modern Britain and its Empire* (Oxford: Oxford University Press).

Roseveare, Henry (1991), *The Financial Revolution, 1660–1760* (London: Longman).

Smith, Adam (1976), *An Inquiry into the Nature and Causes of the Wealth of Nations*, Edwin Cannan (ed.) (Chicago, IL: University of Chicago Press).

Soll, Jacob (2014), *The Reckoning: Financial Accountability and the Rise and Fall of Nations* (New York: Basic Books).

Sombart, Werner (1902), *Der moderne Kapitalismus*, two vols (Leipzig: Duncker & Humblot).

Sombart, Werner (1916), *Der moderne Kapitalismus* (Munich and Leipzig: Duncker & Humblot).

Spicciani, Amleto (1990), *Capitale e interesse tra mercatura e povertà nei teologi e canonisti dei secoli XIII–XV* (Rome: Jouvence).

Spufford, Peter (2002), "The Relative Scale of Medieval Hanseatic Trade", 125–33, in Rolf Hammel-Kiesow (ed.), *Vergleichende Ansätze in der hansischen Geschichtsforschung* (Trier: Porta Alba).

Stahl, Allan M. (2000), *Zecca: The Mint of Venice in the Middle Ages* (Baltimore, MD: Johns Hopkins University Press).

Tenenti, Alberto (1988), "Il mercante e il banchiere", 214–19, in Eugenio Garin (ed.), *L'uomo del Rinascimento* (Rome-Bari: Laterza).

Todeschini, Giacomo (2009), "Eccezioni e usura nel Duecento: Osservazioni sulla cultura economica medievale come realtà non dottrinaria", *Quaderni storici* 44, 443–60.

Todorova, Elisaveta (1987), "The Thirteenth Century Shift of the Black Sea Economy", *Études balkaniques* 23, 112–16.

Tognetti, Sergio (2012), "Mercanti e libri di conto nella Toscana del basso medioevo: Le edizioni di registri aziendali dagli anni '60 del novecento a oggi", *Anuario de estudios medievales* 42, 867–80.

Trivellato, Francesca (2009), *The Familiarity of Strangers: The Sephardic Diaspora, Livorno, and Cross-Cultural Trade in the Early Modern Period* (New Haven, CT: Yale University Press).

Tyler, Royall (1919), *Catalogue of the Medici Archives* (London: Clowes for Christie's).

Van Doosselaere, Quentin (2009), *Commercial Agreements and Social Dynamics in Medieval Genoa* (Cambridge: Cambridge University Press).

Van Houtte, J.A. (1982), *De Geschiedenis van Brugge* (Tielt: Lannoo).

Varanini, Gian Maria (2014), "Gino Luzzatto: Alle origini della storia economica italiana", in Luigi di Matteo, Alberto Guenzi, and Paolo Pecorari (eds), *Le radici della Storia economica in Italia: La costruzione di un metodo*, special issue of *Storia economica* 17.2, 413–26.

Vercauteren, Ferdinand (1964), "La circulation des marchands en Europe occidentale du vie au Xe siècle: aspects économiques et culturels," 393–411, in *Centri e vie di irradiazione della civiltà nell'alto Medioevo* (Spoleto: Centro Italiano di Studi sull'Alto Medioevo).

Weber, Max (2010), *Die protestantische Ethik und der Geist des Kapitalismus*, Dirk Käsler (ed.) (Munich: Beck).

Wickham, Chris (2005), *Framing the Early Middle Ages* (Oxford: Oxford University Press).

Yamey, Basil S. (2004), "Pacioli's *De scripturis* in the Context of the Spread of Double Entry", *De Computis: Revista Española de Historia de la Contabilidad* 1, 142–54.

Zeno, Riniero (ed.) (1936), *Documenti per la storia del diritto marittimo nel secoli XIII e XIV* (Turin: Lattes).

12

DIASPORA NETWORKS

Gijsbert Oonk

Introduction

Long-distance trade across cultural lines may be one of the most important issues in global expansion and history. It connects varying kingdoms and monarchs, cultures, religions, and areas with different languages, different forms of exchange (shells, ivory, gold, silver, coins), and various specializations or produce. The big questions are: how did long-distance traders overcome cultural differences? How did traders with different backgrounds develop trust and create lasting economic relationships? These cross-cultural traders were not only traders and businessmen, but also cross-cultural brokers: they were interpreters and translators and they were creative trust creators.

The Greek historian Herodotus wrote about the gold trade with Ghana and Carthage in the fifth century BCE. In his famous book *The Histories* he describes one of the earliest forms of cross-cultural trade:

> Another story is told by the Carthaginians. There is a place in Libya, they say, where men live beyond the Pillars of Heracles; they come here and unload their cargo; then, having laid it in order along the beach, they go aboard their ships and light a smoking fire. The people of the country see the smoke, and, coming to the sea, they lay down gold to pay for the cargo, and withdraw from the wares. Then the Carthaginians disembark and examine the gold; if it seems to them a fair price for their cargo, they take it and go away; but if not, they go back aboard and wait, and the people come back and add more gold until the sailors are satisfied. In this transaction, it is said, neither party defrauds the other: the Carthaginians do not touch the gold until it equals the value of their cargo, nor do the people touch the cargo until the sailors have taken the gold.
>
> *(Herodotus, Book IV Chapter 196; translated by A.D. Godley)*

In this so-called "silent trade," two parties could exchange valuable goods for gold without speaking to each other and without an interpreter or a mediator (Grierson 1903; de Moraes Farias 1974). Trade with limited communication and without contracts or contract enforcement lies at the heart of much global history, from ancient times to the modern era. Herodotus does not describe how this silent trade emerged. How did traders decide where to meet? What happened if one of the parties cheated the other and took away the gold *and* the cargo? What is interesting in this account, however, is that it highlights these important topics that feature in long-distance trade throughout history like intercultural communication, intercultural exchange, and intercultural trust. These topics are at the core of this chapter.

In this chapter I will focus on specific trading and entrepreneurial communities that were able to overcome the challenges of long-distance trade. That is, the emergence of trading diasporas and middlemen minorities as powers of global trade throughout global history, with a special emphasis on the nineteenth and twentieth centuries. Trading diasporas and middlemen minorities are often portrayed as having overcome the main issues of long-distance trade, including transcultural communication and trust. Well-known examples include Jewish Indian, Chinese, Armenian, and Lebanese diasporas (Cohen 1997). The role of middlemen is highlighted as the interlink between two or more geographical divided culturally diverse groups. These groups often provided the links between the European empires and local societies. Moreover, these diasporas developed their own trading networks beyond empires. In general, diaspora traders were able to overcome long distances over sea or land in a network of community, clan, and kinship based traders. In other cases, they were appointed as custom agents in port-cities from which they intermediated between the shipowners and local businessmen. Or they acted as colonial agents between local producers and European businesses. These "in-between" groups are neither "local" nor "distant." Understanding trade diasporas and the role of their merchants may help us to understand the emergence of the world economy and how they shaped globalization.

In 1971 Abner Cohen may have been the first to coin the term "trading diaspora." He refers to "a type of social grouping":

> Its members are culturally distinct from both their society of origin and from the societies among which they live. Its organisation combines stability of structure, but allows a high degree of mobility of personnel. It has an informal political organisation of its own which takes care of stability of order within the one community, and the coordination of activities of its various member communities in their perpetual struggle against external pressure. ... It also has its own institutions of general welfare and social security. In short a diaspora is a nation of socially interdependent, but spatially dispersed communities.
>
> *(Cohen 1971: 267)*

As Cohen stresses the importance of the political organization of the overseas community, the world historian Phillip Curtin emphasized the relationship of cross-cultural traders with their hosts, with each other, and the way they organized cross-cultural trade (Curtin 1984). Curtin emphasizes the importance of the "cultural broker" in global trade. He assumed that cross-cultural long-distance trade needed "cross-cultural brokers" who mediated between cultural differences. He argued that within trading settlements there were two types of traders: the typical ones who moved back and forth with their trades, and the outsider settlers who were strangers settling in a certain area. The collaboration and integration of the typical traders and the outsider settlers eventually became part of larger diaspora network. An important aspect of trading diasporas is the relationship between the trading community and the host society. Strikingly, the balance of power between traders and their host society was necessarily asymmetrical. The diaspora traders more often than not were specialists in a particular kind of trade or economic sector such as liquor, luxury goods like diamonds, or money lending.

Abner Cohen and Phillip Curtin, used the term "trading diaspora" long before the field of diaspora studies became popular in the late 1990s. They both argued that people of a trade diaspora were not only members of an urban society: they were also members of a plural society, where two or more cultures existed side by side (Curtin 1984; Cohen 1997). They were often part of larger – sometimes hostile – environments with many other occupations, class stratification, and political divisions between the rulers and the ruled. At times, they had close-knit relationships with the powerful elites who may have granted them certain privileges, but they were also vulnerable to discrimination and exclusion (Bonacich 1973).

This chapter has three sections. In the first section I describe the emergence of the "stranger" and the "middleman" in the sociological and economic literature on long-distance trade and economic development. The second section highlights the notion of trust within the diaspora networks, and how trust was gained and lost within these networks. In the third and final section I emphasize the role of intercultural communication and language(s). The subjects mentioned in these three sections should not be seen as separate entities: they are instead interrelated and reinforce one another. However, for the sake of clarity and organization of this text, and for analyzing the extensive literature on this subject, they are presented separately.

Long-distance trade: the role of middlemen minorities and diasporas

Herodotus and the case of "silent trade" does not provide us with insights on the how disputes were resolved. What was entirely absent in Herodotus' description of the silent trade was the middleman, the intermediary. How did these traders communicate over disagreements on the qualities of the products they delivered?

In the late nineteenth century, however, German sociologists like George Simmel and Werner Sombart emphasized the importance of "the stranger" in long-distance trade and economic development (Simmel 1950; Sombart 1982 [1911]). Simmel and Sombart were interested in the role of visible minorities in trade and economic development, most notably the role of Jewish minorities. Even if these minorities settled in their new societies, they argued, they would be seen as outsiders and would remain "strangers." But these settlers were different from wanderers, who would be "here today, gone tomorrow." The settled strangers would arrive today, and stay tomorrow. They would be known locally, while remaining outsiders. This might help them in developing their business. On the one hand strangers may fill economic niches that local business communities were not allowed to fill, like selling liquor. On the other, strangers developed a more detached attitude toward the local markets, which could help them to set prices at a more profitable rate. Last but not least, the stranger was aware of prices elsewhere and he was able to exploit this knowledge profitably. In other words, Simmel stressed the advantage the "stranger" had in commercial transactions in terms of exploiting knowledge of distant markets and the use of "objectivity" (Shack and Skinner 1979).

In the 1970s the sociologist Edna Bonacich referred to these "strangers," who were neither integrated nor foreign, as "sojourners" or middlemen minorities. She noticed that some of these "outsider communities" or "strangers" were very successful economically, in contrast to most migrant communities or ethnic minorities. Good examples are Jewish communities in various cities in Europe, Indian communities in East Africa, Chinese communities in Southeast Asia, and Lebanese communities in West Africa. Bonacich seeks to explain the success of these communities as the result of in-group solidarity and trust relations while being alienated by the majority groups. She emphasizes the importance of the process of settlement of these commercial groups in cities, with the transformation from sojourner to settler. What is important in this process is that a trader or sojourner often enough ends up understanding the local habits and

191

cultures, but he remains an outsider as he returns to his home elsewhere. The sojourner becomes part of a middlemen minority once he decides to settle in his new environment and invites his wife, family, and community members to his new home. However, despite the fact that they become settlers, they remain outsiders in the eyes of local communities as a result of their reluct-ance to intermarry locally (Oonk 2007, 2013). In the Indian Ocean trade between East Africa and northwest India, members of the Hindu Gujarati traders in Zanzibar, Mombasa and Dar es Salaam would try to find their brides in Gujarat even after two or three generations of settlement in East Africa between 1860–1920. This was not only important for the cultural orientation of the group, but it would also reinforce the trading relations between the continents (Oonk 2013). Others would add that the local minority status caused major social distress in all kinds of discrimination, like not being allowed to own land, not being allowed to do certain jobs etc. Thus they developed a strong motivation to show that they could become successful (Bonacich 1973; Dobbin 1996). At the same time, locally, they may have acted as a buffer for elites, bearing the brunt of mass hostility, because they directly dealt with the latter. This is especially true within colonial empires where middlemen minorities became the "in-between traders" between local producers and colonial rulers and businesses.

In the nineteenth century, European empires actively encouraged sojourners from trading groups to settle in the overseas trading hubs of the empires. The Dutch encouraged the Chinese to settle in Batavia and the British encouraged South Asians to settle in Zanzibar and Nairobi. They were seen as suitable middlemen to support the colonial empires abroad. More often than not, these groups were not only important as traders and suppliers of goods, but they also played an important role as translators, informants, and local bureaucrats. The Hindu Bhatia Jairam Sewji, for example, was appointed as the chief customs collector in Zanzibar, and with the exception of some brief periods, he served in this position for almost 70 years. Jairam Sewji used to travel from Zanzibar to Aden and west India every two or three years. He obviously talked to interested traders and financers about the economic potential of East Africa and the business opportunities in Zanzibar. As a result, some decided to send their sons to Zanzibar to explore the economic options for their families (Oonk 2013). This firm helped recruit hundreds of other Bhatias from India and set them up in business within the Zanzibar commercial empire. Besides acting frequently as customs collectors along the coast, Bhatias were also moneylenders and traders. The fact that these businessmen belonged to non-majority groups meant that many colonial governments supported these groups as their local suppliers, translators, informants etc. In this way these groups are often seen as collaborators in the Marxist as well as nationalist his-toriographies (Louis 1976).

Here the concept of middlemen minorities in this literature tends to be Eurocentric. The Asians are seen as literally the middle between the Europeans and the Africans. Yes, Asians depended on European rulers for their trading licenses, tax exemptions, and building educa-tional institutions. At the same time, however, the Europeans depended on the Asians to fill the civil services, pay tax, and explore trading opportunities that were difficult for the Europeans to exploit, like inland trade and agricultural products. For Europeans, the Asians were middlemen partners between the local producers and themselves. For the Asians, Europeans were the mid-dlemen between themselves and the European markets (Bishara 2017; Oonk 2013).

As noted earlier, Curtin (1984) describes the Chinese in Southeast Asia or the Indians in East Africa in the nineteenth and twentieth centuries as prototypes of early diasporas. In his view, these communities were often small trading settlements with strong ties to their homelands and the local traders and businessmen, as well as local rulers. As in Simmel's notion of the "stranger" as the prototype of the diaspora trader, Curtin combines his local and global familiarity of the world. He often translates the names and quality of products literally with his knowledge of local and foreign languages; he is able to exploit his understanding of local and global prices and markets and exchange rates. The success of these groups is usually seen as the result of two – sometimes intertwined – factors. One emphasizes cultural factors, like Chinese (Confucian values and the *guanxi* or networking capabilities) and Indian values within the Hindu and Parsee religions. However, the other focuses on favorable market conditions and relations with the (colonial) state. A more revisionist perspective portrays a more complex picture of intergroup competition, the relation with the homeland, and the centrality of the family-eldest and the role of business familism (Liu 2012).

Therefore, we acknowledge that most studies on the diaspora tend to focus on specific family businesses within larger diasporic networks. One such case is a study by Murray Weidebaum and Samuel Hughes of what they call the *Bamboo Network*. The subtitle of their book is even more telling: *How Expatriate Chinese Entrepreneurs are Creating a New Economic Superpower in Asia* (Weidebaum and Hughes 1996). The book focuses on the importance of transnational Chinese family relations in the twentieth century. Weidebaum and Hughes follow important business families like the Charoen Pokhand group, the Li Ka-shing family, the Salim group, and Ong Beng Seng. Most of them started in the agri-business (tea related) and then diversified into local (building) industries as well finance and electronics. These are Chinese family firms that have developed transnational relations within Southeast Asia. The authors' overall conclusion is that these Chinese family firms operate through a network of (family owned and managed) enterprises rather than a unitary company (like Ford, Phillips, or Heineken). They often rely on strict centralized control (the role of the family's eldest). In the Chinese diaspora, like the Indian, the family eldest – more often than not – lives outside the motherland. Murray and Weidebaum (1996) highlight the importance of informal transactions and trust to minimize the company bureaucracy.

There are, however, just a few studies in business history and diasporas that analyze the long-distance networks involved over a larger timeframe. One is Claude Markovits' *The Global World of Indian Merchants, 1750–1947: Traders of Sind from Bukhara to Panama* (2000). His study makes a strong case against the idea of permanent settlement. He argues that the majority of Indian migrants in the nineteenth century were not permanent migrants, but rather temporary migrants (Markovits 1999). Markovits argues that – in the case of the Sindhi traders – it is doubtful to use the term "diaspora." He shows that between 1830 and 1950 more than 90 percent of the departures from India do return to their home towns and villages, albeit to leave again. Hence, he follows the type of sojourning diaspora as proposed by Curtin ("the typical ones who went back and forth") and distances himself from the more mainstream definition that became prevalent in the late 1990s where long-term physical separation from the homeland (imagined or not) is key. The neglect of the importance of circulation is – according to Markovits – the consequence of the colonial sources that often counted arrivals and departures of migrants in absolute numbers and therefore missing the point that these were often the same traders and businessmen traveling back and forth. In this perspective, migration includes circular migration that re-enforces the ties with homeland. The major aim of a "network" is the cheap circulation of capital, credit, information, goods, and produce. Markovits' work transcends the family networks mentioned by Weidebaum and Hughes.

Some studies look carefully into the consequences of being a small – usually well-off – diasporic community in a larger hostile community. Bruce Whitehouse has formulated an interesting set of shared expectations, rights, and duties that local authorities and majorities might expect from middlemen minorities. In many cases, as with the South Asians in East Africa or the Chinese in Indonesia, they are full citizens of these countries, but they cannot claim the same citizenship rights. For his case on Muslim Congolese merchants in Ghana in the nineteenth and twentieth century, Whitehouse (2012) formulates a "Stranger's Code" that includes formal and informal rules and expectations like: "Do not get involved in host countries' politics"; "Do not flaunt your wealth; keep it modest"; "Do not protest violation of your rights." In all these cases local majorities use their local strength (in numbers as well as contacts with law enforcement institutions) to put these middlemen minorities "in place" informally. The Stranger's Code, or a local mechanism between majorities and minorities, may also apply to many other visible middlemen minorities in global history (Whitehouse 2012).

The examples above are based on empirical case-studies related to long distance trade. The examples come from Chinese in Southeast Asia, South Asians in East Africa, and Muslims Congolese in Ghana from the sixteenth until the twentieth century. If we look closely at the fascinating organizational structure of the family business in the diaspora, we may be surprised to see the striking similarities with family business structures in the Middle Ages in Europe as studied by Avner Greif (1989, 1993). The mother company, often directed by the family eldest, is the center of the family business. Each associate (often, but not always, the sons) has to produce their monthly or annual business reports to the mother company from their distant regions. The associates may open branches in different areas in the name of the mother company. However, they are often allowed to make their private business deals outside branch and the mother company. In addition, the mother company or its branches may develop partnerships or formal joint-ventures with other companies (families). It is fascinating to note that this pre-industrial family business structure was dominant in European as well as throughout global history. A part of the explanation may be because diaspora traders had to overcome the same type of institutional and cultural differences, like trust, language differences, and cultural adaptation (Prange 2006).

Long-distance trade and the importance of trust

The importance of the middleman is denied and is missing in Herodotus' example of the "silent trade." The notion of trust is acknowledged, however. Herodotus expresses surprise when he mentions that the traders do not touch the cargo until the sailors have taken the gold. But it is unclear why the traders are so honest and reliable. What is the mechanism behind this attitude? Are they honest because of their upbringing, their faith, and religion, or are other mechanisms at work?

Abner Cohen (1969, 1971) explains how members of a particular family, ethnic, or religious group cooperate in long-distance trade. They are able to overcome basic logistical challenges such as financial constraints, access to local information and network, and the coordination of transport. It is generally assumed that these basic challenges are much easier to overcome within ethnic networks, where kinship ties, language, and a similar legal system reinforce solidarity. To put it succinctly, within these networks a good name is easily lost. Thus, a merchant will think twice before cheating on his fellow member within these networks (Oonk 2013). Conflict regulation on trust relations between ethnic groups – in long-distance trade – usually requires the role of a charismatic trader or legal institution that can enforce contracts. But this is often a far more expensive solution.

James Coleman uses a classic example of the benefits of social capital and trust in a paper on the wholesale diamond market in the late twentieth century in New York. In this market, diamond dealers frequently hand over bags of diamonds, often worth thousands of dollars, to other merchants to examine at their leisure. There is no insurance; there are no contracts; and no witnesses. This may be regarded as an extremely risky venture, but it is in fact very successful, cheap, and efficient. It would actually become highly bureaucratic, time-consuming and expensive if exchange contracts were to be made, pictures of the trade were produced, and witnesses were arranged. There is an unwritten agreement that information flows freely and exchanges can be made without expensive contracts and legal formalities; in short, this reduces transaction costs considerably (Coleman 1998). The individual trader is expected to obey specific rules of conduct and to espouse a distinct business culture. More often than not, this culture is not open to others (Siegel 2009).

Similar notions of trust may be found in the diamond trade in Antwerp. But this network of Jewish diamond traders is complemented with a cross-cultural, cross-religious, and cross-gender diamond merchant network operated between the cities of Antwerp, London, Amsterdam, and Lisbon. This network is active beyond national boundaries, and connected with other religious and trading networks, most notably an English Catholic in Antwerp and French Huguenots in Lisbon in the eighteenth century (Vanneste 2011). Unfortunately, there is little evidence on how trust relations between diaspora groups are generated. This is an under-researched area that is worthwhile pursuing.

Another area of under-researched opportunities is the competition between different diaspora trading networks. Again, the Antwerp diamond industry may serve as an illustration. In the popular imagination diamonds, the Jewish community, and Antwerp are indistinctly connected with each other. The Jewish community was able to regain control over the diamond community after World War II, despite the fact that most of its population was exterminated. Nevertheless, recent observations in newspapers' travelogues have shown that the Indian diaspora has come to control more than three-quarters of the Antwerp diamond industry (Aiyar 2015). The explanation given by Indian informants may not be convincing: "We will work on the weekends. We will do whatever it takes to get a client. And we are willing to work this hard even for small margins." (Aiyar 2015: 134). A more profound explanation is probably determined by a shift of the global commodity chain. Diamonds and the finishing industry reached Europe in the fifteenth and sixteenth centuries. However, the industry faced a recent shift from finishing and polishing techniques and labor from Antwerp to India again (Hofmeester 2013). In the 1970s, the skilled diamond processing labor force amounted for more than 25,000 people. This number is down to less than 1,000. It is more likely than not than the familiarity with India, and the Indian business culture (including the knowledge of Gujarati) was a big advantage for the Indian diamond traders in Antwerp (Aiyar 2015).

This notion of trust is especially relevant in the literature that includes a strong emphasis on non-western minority groups. It attempts to explain the economic success of Chinese, Indian, or Jewish businessmen in terms of trust based on ethnic backgrounds and trading networks. The major aim of a network is the cheap circulation of capital, credit, information, goods, and produce, as in the case of Coleman's diamond traders (Coleman 1998; Markovits 2000). Long-distance trade and is scarcity of information fuel the importance of trust. Often a merchant did not travel to distant markets with his goods, but delegated this task to an agent (a family member? his neighbor? an ethnic community member?). The merchant had to trust the overseas far away agent. He could simply disappear with the trade. Or, more subtly, he could tell the merchant that the prices were low overseas and he could not sell at a better price, while pocketing the difference. It was almost impossible for the principal merchant to check the market and quality conditions overseas (Aslanian 2006). Nevertheless, cheating happened, but it was trust that kept the business going.

Why and how does trust function in day-to-day affairs among long-distance traders and intercultural communication? To answer this question and to understand some of the complexities behind it, economic historian Avner Greif refers to the concept of trust as a "reputation-based economic institution" (Greif 2006: 58). In this concept the importance of future rewards or penalties in economic and social transactions are made conditional in the transaction here and now, so as to guarantee future trust relations. To put it straightforwardly and simply, if in the Coleman diamond market one of the diamond dealers cheated on another dealer, he would become an outcast in that market. He would forego all future dealings (economic liability), he would not be allowed to marry within the families running the diamond trade (social liability), and most probably he would have to move to some other city or place. What makes the Greif study fascinating and original is the fact that he supports his historical finding from the Maghribi traders (in the eleventh century) with the findings of modern economic game theory (Greif 2006: Appendix C). However, Sebouh Aslanian shows that trust must be understood not solely as an outcome of informal institutions, such as reputation-regulating mechanisms discussed by Greif, but also as a result of the simultaneous combination of both informal and semi-formal legal institutions (Aslanian 2006). Overall, we assume that notions of the same religion, language, and regional background reinforce concepts of "trust," mutual aid, and shared values among migrant traders and businessmen. In migrant communities, this is often reinforced by the fact that they arrive in specific neighborhoods where they also reproduce the culture, through community centers, mosques, and temples. In most literature, the system itself is not questioned, but reservations are expressed about *how* the members of a business community derive advantage from it.

As a rule, this type of literature tends to emphasize the "success stories" in migrant business communities. More often than not, networks are seen as a rather static, informally organized system, which is used as a tool by its various members. Most of these explanations, one way or another, emphasize the socioeconomic advantages of outsider minorities as an explanation for their economic virtue. What these explanations have in common is that they don't include the point of departure of migrants, the class background, their educational background, former experiences, and – with some exceptions – the way they were received by the local rulers. These explanations only gain significance in a particular historical setting. They cannot explain why some members of the same group were not successful at all, and were not gifted with a "superior" business mind.

In my own work (Oonk 2013), I have tried to balance the success stories of South Asian traders with examples of bankruptcies and failures. In this book, I argue that, as mentioned by Markovits, the transformation of circular migration to settlement was rather slow. Many members who followed the lead of successful pioneers in the diaspora did not make it, returning to their homelands. In other words, those who remained active in the diaspora had proven the capacity to survive. Some had been supported by a family member or clan members, others were supported by local (colonial) rulers (as in the previous section). From here, through trial and error, they developed local trading and business acquaintances and business networks. What is important here is the use of trust and credit. I present many examples where fathers, uncles, and community members were the first to supply credit to their sons and relatives. Nevertheless, they were the first – if needed – to file a bankruptcy. So trust was not self-evident in these family and community networks. Trustworthiness could easily be gained and lost within the network. In other words, the networks' most effective function is to signal dishonesty and disloyalty. This adds to the earlier findings (Markovits 2000) where Markovits argues against the importance of "ethnic" notions of trust. In the case of migrant traders "the inside ethnic network" may be as important as local networks, whether ethnic or not. In other words, trading groups can never rely solely on "inside" sources, but are dependent on information, power, and knowledge from other groups as well. In fact, their ability to trade *outside* the ethnic group plays a crucial role in determining the success or failure of business communities/groups (Trivellato 2009).

Long-distance trade and the significance of communication

The "silent trade" of the Greek historian Herodotus simply ignores the problem of cross-cultural communication. The communication is not just silent – it is absent. It is difficult to imagine that conflicting interests on the quality and quantity of products could be resolved by just bringing more or less silver and gold in exchange without further communication. In every public market and bazaar, we see customers bargaining for the best prices in words and non-verbal languages. This is more than just a ritual – it is the essence of deal-making. The import-ance of communication and trust in global trade cannot be overestimated. Long-distance cross-cultural communication in pre-modern and early modern times would be in letters and through messengers. Particularly in the pre-modern era, long-distance written communication could take weeks, if not months. Once the letter arrived – if it arrived – the situation might have already changed. This could put pressure on trust relations between partners, especially when the stakes and interests were high.

Communication and trust interrelated key elements in explaining the emergence of long-distance trade. One the one hand we may argue that that societies with a strong written culture and tradition (like Jewish, Christian, Chinese, Muslim, and Hindu) may have had an advantage in cross-cultural long-distance trade. On the other hand, it could be argued that trade and commerce were driving forces in the spread of literacy (Lydon 2009: 353). In this sense, the ancient historical long-distance trading routes like the Silk Road (overland; see Frankopan 2017) or the Indian Ocean region (over-seas; see Alpers 2013) may be seen as the first transcontinental trading routes, as well as communica-tion and information highways. In addition, being able to read and write and understand local legal contracts was vitally important for handling cross-cultural trade. Access to local languages was neces-sary for the communication in local markets and bazaars, and to develop an understanding of local cultures. Carefully explaining the quality of products, delivery dates, and means of payment lies at the heart of every business, both then and now. Excellent language skills may provide access to local rules or to religious authorities. If you – often literally – speak the language of the rulers, you have access to their legal system and indeed to the people in power. Diasporic trading families were able to overcome cultural and language differences, because they were locally well embedded and at the same time had access to their larger family networks in different parts of the world.

Most research focuses on communication within diaspora – often co-religionist – groups. These studies argue that the perspective of the stranger or outsider enables these migrant traders to share a particular objective and neutral perspective on the market. They were aware of the prices and qualities of products "here and there." These minorities were often exempt from local professions and from opportunities like owing land and selling liquor. Despite this – or maybe because of it – they would develop their local niches in economic opportunity areas where there were local taboos. Within their ethnic enclaves they were able to circulate informa-tion, women, and knowledge. These intergroup trust relations, their shared culture and lan-guage as well knowledge of languages would eventually enable them to prosper in long-distance trade (Arsan 2014; Dobbin 1996; Markovits 2000).

One interesting exception to this bulk of work is the study by Francesca Trivellato. In her widely acclaimed book *The Familiarity of Strangers*, she argues that long-distance business cooperation among diasporic groups, as well as *between* strangers, relied on language, customary norms, and social networks. She argues that the success of the Sephardic Diaspora in the early modern period relied more on intra-group cooperation than on the progressive rise of the state and legal institutions. In other words, the formalization of institutions, some of which are dis-cussed in the previous section, is less important than previously thought. She emphasizes the importance of letter writing. In her words:

A "good correspondency" was the most rewarding compensation for the many hours every merchant spent at his desk reading, dictating and writing letters. It was more than a metaphor. It was part of the cost-benefit calculations of the price of trust. When was it advantageous to forgive the debt of a correspondent who might deliver in the future?

(Trivellato 2009: 190)

In her focus on "communication" rather than communities or ethnic groups, Trivellato is able to transcend the focus of long-distance trade from *communities* of mercantile trust to *networks* of mercantile trust. But "good correspondency" was probably not only important in the past. In the nineteenth century, the emergence of the global telegraph network changed the way businesspersons (and others) corresponded on trustworthy information, like prices, new technologies, quality of products, and reliability of fellow businessmen (Tworek 2015). Catherine Davies (2016), however, rightly emphasizes that while bankers successfully used telegraphic cables to communicate intelligence, written letters proved superior as a medium for establishing personal trust. During crises and disagreements, the new technology was blamed for the paucity of information.

In the late twentieth and early twenty-first centuries, we noted an unprecedented revolution in communication with the arrival of the internet. This enabled quick email exchanges and Skype interviews. And this may have changed the culture of writing business letters considerably. However, the ultimate test of building trust relations remained face-to-face exchange relations. In my own research, I once spent some time in London visiting the trading office of a South Asian family who had settled in London. One day a week I visited the trading office in the financial district. I usually sat next to the director, watching him making phone calls, write emails, and instruct his secretaries. He was born in East Africa, but joined the London office in the 1960s. His son was born and raised in London. In fact, I was sitting at the desk of his son, who had just opened an office in Dubai. The father would phone his son at least once a day to enquire about the daily affairs and to coach him in running the Dubai business. In their case they were shipping vegetables from various sources in the Indian Ocean region to destinies in East Asia, East Africa, and Western Europe. They never owned the cargo, but they financed its shipment. The bulk of the trade was agricultural products. One day they had a dispute on the quality of the cargo that had passed from Mombasa to the Seychelles. They agreed to a meeting in Delhi to solve the problem. The son flew from Dubai to Delhi. The father came from London, and the counterparts flew from the Seychelles to have a face-to-face meeting. What we see here is very interesting, because it shows the importance of face-to-face communication. Despite the modern technology of using email or making Skype conference calls, the importance of a face-to-face meeting was still relevant. Notwithstanding legal institutions and modern insurance, it still seemed to be relevant to "see each other in person." More often than not, after such "crisis" meetings it was decided whether the business partners would continue their relationship or not. In fact, this is the same type of judgment the merchants in Trivellato's work had to make, but then based on written letters (Oonk 2013: 19; Trivellato 2009).

Conclusion

Diasporic communities are unquestionably of decisive importance in the emergence of long-distance trade, and therefore in the growth of the global economy. Diasporas were successful in pre-modern and pre-colonial societies, colonial societies and post-colonial societies. They were an important mover of cross-cultural trade in the pre-modern era. Curtin (1984) describes examples from Mesopotamian trade, ancient trade in Egypt, early Chinese trade, and so on. Nevertheless, the bulk of the literature and the examples in this chapter relate to Africa and Asia from the sixteenth to the twentieth century. These areas shared a long period of foreign domination, strong state intervention in the economy, and institutional weaknesses. It is suggested (Austin *et al.* 2017) that these continents were on the wrong side of the Great Divergence, but they developed their own instruments and strategies in developing trade and business. Informal, rather than formal, business fueled the emergence of migrant entrepreneurs and diasporas. More often than not, the British, Dutch, and French colonial elites and administrators actively attracted overseas businessmen to act as middlemen between them and traders and businesses in the local interiors. These diasporic businessmen would then invite their family members and clan members to join them. The strength of diaspora networks, however, is that they also flourished in Europe (especially the Jewish networks) and the United States and Canada (the Jewish, the Indian, and Chinese diaspora). In their day-to-day practices, tasks, and dealings they had to overcome language differences, trust issues, and cultural dissimilarities. Unlike the so-called "silent trade" described in the introduction, these diasporic communities facilitated transnational business, intercultural communication, and trust.

Nowadays we may wonder whether this "silent trade" actually existed. But we do know that the history of the Silk Route and the trans-Sahara trade routes go back more than 2,000 years. These routes connected peoples of different origins, languages, and cultures. But it was not the routes themselves that made trading possible – rather it was the traders, merchants, and money-changers who enabled this trade. They aided the development of formal and informal institutions in which long-distance trade could flourish. The interplay between merchant communities of kin, tribe, and religion with incomplete economic institutions of partnerships and coalitions created long-distance trade. More often than not it was this incompleteness that created space for trade and profit, and it was the down-to-earth attitude of these diasporic traders that made cross-cultural interaction possible. To use the well-known metaphor of the Sahara caravan traders: "Trust in God, but tie up your camel."

References

Aiyar, Pallavi (2015), *New Old World: An Indian Journalist Discovers the Changing Face of Europe*, (New York: St. Martin's Press).

Alpers, Ned (2013), *The Indian Ocean in World History*, (Oxford: Oxford University Press).

Arsan, Andrew (2014), *Interlopers of Empire: The Lebanese Diaspora in Colonial French West Africa*, (Oxford: Oxford University Press).

Aslanian, Sebouh David (2006), "Social Capital, 'Trust' and the Role of Networks in Julfan Trade: Informal and Semi-formal Institutions at Work," *Journal of Global History* 1 (3), 383–402.

Austin, Gareth, Davilia, Carlos, and Jones, Geoffrey (2017), "The Alternative Business History: Business in Emerging Markets," *Business History Review* (91), 1–33.

Baghdiantz McCabe, Ina, Harlaftis, Gelina, and Pepelasis Minoglou, Ioanna (eds.) (2005), *Diaspora Entrepreneurial Networks: Four Centuries of History*, (Oxford; New York: Berg Publishers).

Bishara, Fahad (2017), *A Sea of Debt: Law and Economic Life in the Western Indian Ocean, 1780–1950* (Oxford: Oxford University Press).

Bonacich, E. (1973), "A Theory of Middleman Minorities," *American Sociological Review* 38, October, 583–594.

Cohen, Abner (1969), *Custom and Politics in Urban Africa: A Study of Hausa Migrants in Yoruba Towns*, (Berkeley, CA: University of California Press).

Cohen, Abner (1971), "Cultural Strategies in the Organisation of Trading Diasporas," in Claude Meillassoux (ed.), *The Development of Indigenous Trade Markets in West Africa*, (London: Oxford University Press), 266–284.

Cohen, Robin (1997), *Global Diasporas: An Introduction*, (Seattle, WA: University of Washington Press).

Coleman, J.S. (1998), "Social Capital in the Creation of Human Capital," *American Journal of Sociology* (94) Supplement, S95–S120.

Curtin, Philip D. (1984), *Cross Cultural Trade in World History*, (Cambridge: Cambridge University Press).

Davies, Hannah Catherine (2016), "Spreading Fear, Communicating Trust: Writing Letters and Telegrams during the Panic of 1873," *History and Technology* 32 (2), 159–177.

De Moraes Faria, P.F. (1974), "Silent Trade: Myth and Historical Evidence," *History in Africa* (1), 9–24.

Dobbin, Christine (1996), *Asian Entrepreneurial Minorities: Conjoint Communities in the Making of the World Economy, 1570–1940* (Richmond: Curzon).

Frankopan, Peter (2017), *The Silk Roads: A New History of the World*, (London: Vintage).

Greif, Avner (1989), "Reputation and Coalitions in Medieval Trade: Evidence on the Maghribi Traders," *Journal of Economic History*, 49 (4), 857–882.

Greif, Avner (1993), "Contract Enforceability and Economic Institutions in Early Trade: The Maghribi Traders' Coalition," *American Economic Review*, 83 (3), 525–548.

Greif, Avner (2006), *Institutions and the Path to the Modern Economy: Lessons from Medieval Trade*, (Cambridge: Cambridge University Press).

Grierson, Hamilton (1903), *The Silent Trade: A Contribution to the Early History of Human Intercourse*, (Edinburgh: W. Green).

Herodotus, book IV chapter 196: with an English translation by A. D. Godley. Cambridge, MA: Harvard University Press, 1920. See also: www.perseus.tufts.edu/hopper/text?doc=Perseus:abo:tlg,0016,001:4:196 (seen 29 May 2017).

Herodotus, *The Histories*, translated by David Grene. University of Chicago Press, 1987.

Hofmeester, Karin (2013), "Shifting Trajectories of Diamond Processing: From India to Europe and Back, from the Fifteenth Century to the Twentieth," *Journal of Global History* (8), 25–49.

Liu, Hong (2012), "Beyond a Revisionist Turn: Networks, State and the Changing Dynamics of Diasporic Chinese Entrepreneurship," *China: An International Journal* 10 (3), 20–41.

Louis, R.W. (1976), *Imperialism: The Robinson and Gallagher Controversy*, (New York: New Viewpoints).

Lydon, Ghislaine (2009), *On Trans-Saharan Trails: Islamic Law, Trade Networks, and Cross-Cultural Change in Nineteenth-Century Western Africa*, (Cambridge; New York; Melbourne: Cambridge University Press).

Markovits, C. (1999), "Indian Merchant Networks outside India in the Nineteenth and Twentieth Centuries: A Preliminary Survey," *Modern Asian Studies* 33 (4), 883–911.

Markovits, Claude (2000), *The Global World of Indian Merchants 1750–1949: Traders of Sind from Bukhara to Panama*, (Cambridge: Cambridge University Press).

Oonk, Gijsbert (ed.) (2007), *Global Indian Diasporas: Exploring Trajectories of Migration and Theory*, (Amsterdam: Amsterdam University Press).

Oonk, Gijsbert (2013), *Settled Strangers: Asian Business Elites in East Africa 1800–2000* (New Delhi; London; Singapore: Sage Publishers).

Prange, Sebastian (2006), "'Trust in God, but Tie your Camel First': The Economic Organization of the Trans-Saharan Slave Trade between the Fourteenth and Nineteenth Centuries," *Journal of Global History* (1), 219–239.

Shack, William A. and Skinner, Elliot P. (eds.) (1979), *Strangers in African Societies*, (Berkeley, CA and London: University of California Press).

Siegel, D. (2009), "Jews, Indians, and Arabs: On Diamond Markets and Traders," in Dina Siegel, *The Mazzel Ritual: Culture, Customs and Crime in the Diamond Trade*, (New York: Springer), 79–118.

Simmel, G. (1950), "The Stranger," in K.H. Wolff (ed.), *The Sociology of George Simmel* (New York and Glencoe, IL: Free Press), 402–408.

Sombart, W. (1982 [1911]), *The Jews and Modern Capitalism*, (London: Transaction Books).

Trivellato, F. (2009), *The Familiarity of Strangers: The Sephardic Diaspora, Livorno, and Cross-Cultural Trade in the Early Modern Period* (New Haven, CT: Yale University Press).

Tworek, Heidi J.S. (2015), "Protecting News Before the Internet," in Richard R. John and Jonathan Silberstein (eds.), *Political Economy of Journalism in Britain and America from the Glorious Revolution to the Internet*, (Oxford: Oxford University Press), 196–222.

Vanneste, Tijl (2011), *Global Trade and Commercial Networks: Eighteenth-Century Diamond Merchants* (London: Pickering & Chatto).

Weidebaum, Murray and Hughes, Samuel (1996), *Bamboo Network: How Expatriate Chinese Entrepreneurs are Creating a New Economic Superpower in Asia*, (New York: Simon & Schuster).

Whitehouse, Bruce (2012), *Migrants and Strangers in an African City: Exile, Dignity and Belonging* (Bloomington and Indianapolis, IN: Indiana University Press).

13

TRADING COMPANIES

Michael Aldous

Introduction

Long-distance trade has fascinated historians almost as long as history has been written. Herodotus described the "Silent trade" conducted on the north coast of Africa between Carthaginian and local merchants, exchanging goods for African gold (Herodotus 2003: Book 4). Merchants and trade have been motifs in historical accounts of nearly all world regions and across time periods with trade networks and interconnections used to explain the development of the Mediterranean, Indian Ocean, and the Atlantic worlds (Braudel, 1995; Riello and Roy, 2009; Williams, 1944).

Business and economic historians have extensively examined the evolution in the organization and scale of international trade. Their studies can be broadly categorized into two sets of questions. First, when, how, and why does the organization of trade change (Chapman, 2004; Jones, 2000)? Second, how do these changes affect the flows and value of trade (Daudi *et al.*, 2010; Findlay and O'Rourke, 2009)? Analysis has sought to identify factors which led to expansion and contraction, the subsequent effects on national and regional economies, and the processes of globalization (Jones, 2007; Pomeranz, 2000).

Business historians have focused on the first set of questions, particularly examining the role played by entrepreneurs and firms in shaping the patterns of global trade and investment. This has revealed a striking heterogeneity of actors, particularly prior to the twentieth century, involved in the coordination of global trade. Producers and manufacturers were linked to consumers by merchants, brokers, agents, and auctioneers who intermediated flows of goods, credit, and information needed to synchronize markets (Aldous, 2017; Van Driel, 2003). They were supported by an array of specialist service providers such as shipping companies, financiers, and insurers (see Chapters 23 and 28 on Insurance and Shipping; Harlaftis and Theotokas, 2004).

Historical analysis of the organization of international business has identified the evolution from individual merchants to the formation of trading companies as a critical development in driving the expansion in the scale and value of international trade. Trading companies developed functions and specializations that mitigated problems of long-distance trade and improved the efficiency of intermediation and coordination between markets (Chapman, 2004; Jonker and Sluyterman, 2000). They were key makers of global business between the seventeenth and nineteenth centuries, growing global commodity trades, and were the main vehicles for foreign direct investment (FDI) until the early twentieth century (Jones, 1998). Multinational enterprises (MNEs), which grew in scale and scope across the twentieth century (Wilkins, 1991), may have reduced their importance, yet to this day general trading companies such as Mitsubishi Co., Cargil Co., and Glencore Plc., remain globally significant entities (see Chapter 29 on Commodity Traders)

Over time, and across geographies, trading companies developed significant variations in terms of their role, ownership, and organization. Merchant houses organized as partnerships, were "intermediary service providers in the supply chain between producers and consumers, as a rule without either producing goods themselves, or selling directly to the final consumers" (Jonker and Sluyterman, 2000: 10). Conversely, chartered trading companies, were organized as joint-stock corporations. Whilst intermediating trade, these firms vertically integrated into host markets through ownership of production and manufacturing facilities (Carlos and Nicholas, 1988). Additional variation occurred through specialization by region and product, and diversification into areas such as banking, insurance, and related services.

Further organizational forms involved in facilitating international trade, have been identified as increasingly important in the nineteenth century. Business groups used networks of legally distinct firms to cooperate through hybrid forms of ownership and control, to coordinate trade and production activities across national borders (see Chapters 15 and 16 on Business Groups and Networks). Whilst free-standing companies, incorporated in major capital markets like London or Amsterdam, vertically integrated international operations in sectors such as mining and plantations (Wilkins, 1988b).

These variations, shown in Table 13.1, raise questions as to when and why did trading companies diversify and change their ownership form and organizational structure? Subsequently, how do such choices effect firm and economic performance? This chapter explores these debates, setting out the main explanations for these experiments with organizational forms, and considering the effects these innovations had on the scale of international trade.

In particular, the chapter highlights methodological issues associated with analysis of trading companies caused by identification and definitional problems. The significant variation in function and organization, make sharp definitions, and subsequent categorization of trading companies difficult (Jones, 2000). To mitigate these problems, and ensure "like-with-like" analysis and robust findings, research tends to focus analysis on discrete forms. This approach potentially limits analysis of change between different forms, and subsequent examination of effects on wider phenomena such as economic growth and divergence. How, then, should trading companies be defined and analyzed?

Rather than narrowly focus on specific forms, the chapter proposes that researchers utilize longitudinal studies of the organization of international trade focused on understanding why different organizational forms emerged and evolved. This level of analysis accounts for the wide

Table 13.1 Typology of European firms involved in international trade, seventeenth to nineteenth centuries

Firm type	Ownership form	Organizational structure
Merchant house	Partnership	Networks of trading firms
Chartered trading company	Joint-stock	Vertically integrated, diverse operations
Business group	Hybrid	Group of managed firms
Free standing company	Joint-stock	Vertically integrated, specialized operations

Sources: Adapted from Chapman (2004), Jones (2000), Jonker and Sluyterman (2000), Wilkins (1988).

ecology of firms involved in international trade. It specifically considers the conditions under which change of form occurs, and allows analysis of correlation with the economic development of regions and industries.

This approach is illustrated through current research into the nineteenth century Anglo-Indian trade (Aldous, 2015). It shows how merchants used a wide range of business forms in innovative combinations, to address various economic and managerial challenges. These developments are correlated with the dramatic expansion of the trade, which saw India become one of Britain's largest import and export markets by the 1850s (Chapman, 2004: 8), and can be more widely linked to the expansion of the value of Britain's international trade as a share of gross domestic product (GDP), which rose from 21 percent in 1820 to 44 percent by 1870 (Daudi *et al.*, 2010: 106).

The focus of this chapter is limited to analysis of European trading companies between the seventeenth and nineteenth centuries. The emergence of the joint-stock chartered trading companies, and subsequent heterogeneity of business types involved in the expansion of Europe's international trade, are crucial factors in explaining the growth of international trade and globalization. Yet, important new research into the operations of merchants indigenous to India, China, the Levant, and Africa is revealing that innovation in mercantile activity and growth of global trade activity was not solely a European phenomenon. The expansion of networks, innovation of organizational structures, and diversification of activities was undertaken, both alongside and distinct from European activities, and had significant impact on the patterns of international trade (Machado, 2014; Markovits, 2000; Mathew, 2016).

A historical narrative of European trading companies

Long-distance trade in Europe expanded during the medieval period as innovations, such as the *commenda* contract, enabled individual merchants to enter legally recognized and enforced partnerships and build international networks. These innovations supported the pooling of capital and diversification of risks, which increased the scale and scope of mercantile operations (Grief, 2006). In the late medieval period, these trading networks were formalized and strengthened by institutional arrangements such as the Hanseatic League, and partnerships between merchant families, like the Medici, and the governments of Italian city states, such as Venice and Genoa (see Chapter 11 on merchants and origins of capitalism). The early modern period, saw merchants develop proto-firm structures, often using partnerships, which extended their reach and capacity throughout Europe, and into wider trade routes in the Mediterranean, Levant, and Asia.

Yet, it was the response of entrepreneurs to the opportunities opened by European explorers in Africa, Asia, and the Americas in the fifteenth and sixteenth centuries that resulted in the most dramatic changes to the organization of long-distance trade. The size of the risks, in part exacerbated by the long distances between European mercantile centers and the new markets, and the scale of the opportunities offered by high value products such as spices, called for levels of investment beyond the scope of individual merchants or existing partnership networks. The need for deep capital reserves that could be retained and reinvested year after year encouraged entrepreneurs to utilize the joint-stock corporate form (Gelderblom *et al.*, 2013).

These early modern chartered trading companies, such as the English East India Company (EIC), Dutch East India Company, and Hudson's Bay Company used joint-stock ownership to enable investment in infrastructure, allowing the firms to extend their operations in Asia, Africa, and North America (Chaudhuri, 1965). This facilitated the establishment of permanent trading settlements and production facilities, increasing integration into the host economies, which, in time, supplanted local economic and political systems (Bowen *et al.*, 2002).

The chartered trading companies dominated many long-distance routes, in part because they were protected by government granted monopolies, locking out competition in return for significant contributions to state finances (Bowen, 2005). Yet, by the end of the eighteenth century, a growing free-trade movement saw monopolies rescinded and the chartered trading companies were swept away (Webster, 2009). International trade in the nineteenth century was dominated by private enterprise; predominantly organized as partnerships these firms acted as both intermediators and, depending on the structure of the host market, integrated into local industries (Chapman, 2004). Indigenous merchants also reasserted themselves, and new entrants, particularly from the United States, arrived (Downs, 2015; Oonk, 2013).

Increasing levels of competition, emergence of new industries, and development of new technologies in transport and communication, such as the telegraph, all encouraged extensive experimentation with the organization of trade across the nineteenth century (North, 1968; McCusker, 2005). Firms organized as partnerships still undertook import and export trade, but innovative business forms such as business groups and free-standing companies emerged, alongside increasingly specialized brokers and financiers.

These developments reduced the risks and improved the efficiency of the flows of goods and finance now circling the globe. The result was a dramatic increase in the level of international trade in the period between 1875 and 1913, described as the first wave of globalization (O'Rourke and Williamson, 1999).

The final twist in the historical story of the trading companies began in the late nineteenth century, as firms successful in their domestic markets expanded their operations internationally. The early MNEs were predominantly industrial firms that established overseas subsidiaries to secure supply chains and open new markets for their products (Wilkins, 1971). The vertical and horizontal integration of these activities into a single business entity reduced the scope for trading companies to provide intermediary services. The MNE model was rapidly entrenched in Europe, the US, and parts of Asia and dominated international trade in the second half of the twentieth century (Wilkins, 1991). Yet, trading companies, having evolved and diversified to find new opportunities, remain important in certain regions and industries to this day (Broehl, 1998).

Major themes of analysis

Central to this narrative, and one of the dominant questions for business historians is, how did merchants coordinate markets over thousands of kilometers with communication reduced to the speed of foot and sail (Aldous, 2015; Carlos, 1992; Jones, 2000)? The separation of market participants by time and space created difficulties in coordination and decision making. These challenges were exacerbated by volatility in political and economic conditions in home and host markets. Business historians seek to understand the nature of these challenges and how merchants mitigated these risks. This analysis can be broadly categorized into three themes: examining the organization of the firms, understanding the environment in which they operated, and assessing the outcomes of their activities.

The firm

The narrative of the European trading companies identified the emergence of proto-firms in the late medieval period, the proliferation of the chartered trading companies using the joint-stock form in the seventeenth century, and the innovation and experimentation with business forms in the nineteenth century, as developments that stimulated significant increases in the scale and scope of trade. These innovations, and their effects on scale, can be linked to changes in operations and ownership.

Their main operations were, initially, as intermediators for commodities and goods, acting as import–export agents, brokers, and resellers. However, the efficient functioning and coordination of markets required flows of information, credit, and capital, as well as the provision of services such as transportation and shipping. Trading companies created organizational structures, such as networks of agents, to facilitate the exchange of information and knowledge. They also diversified their activities into industries such as banking, to facilitate flows of credit and capital, particularly in regions with thin financial markets and lacking services and infrastructure (Casson, 1998; Jones, 1995).

In certain regions and industries, they also integrated upstream into manufacturing and production, particularly when transaction costs could be lowered, and local expertise and knowledge was crucial (Hennart, 1998). Over time, the firms developed wide-ranging capabilities, diversifying and innovating in areas such as marketing, merchant banking, infrastructure development, and manufacturing, as conditions demanded (Llorca-Jaña 2012; Webster, 2005)

The evolving nature of these activities encouraged innovation with ownership and organization. The chartered trading companies utilized the joint-stock form to deepen capital reserves and diversify risks for investors, allowing greater levels of investment to be channeled overseas. This allowed integration into more capital intensive activities such as manufacturing (Chaudhuri, 1965; Carlos and Nicholas, 1988).

Yet, the joint-stock chartered trading companies, due to the separation of owners and managers inherent in the ownership structure, were troubled by difficulties in controlling their agents at distance (Adams, 1996; Carlos and Nicholas, 1990). Partnership firms utilized their ownership structure, involving capital investment and profit share, to align the interests of networks of geographically dispersed partners, improving control and coordination (Dejung, 2013). This gave them agility and flexibility to respond to the volatile risks and opportunities in international markets (Jones, 2000).

Trading companies faced a trade-off between the joint-stock form's capacity to expand operational scope and achieve scale efficiencies, and the partnership's governance systems to successfully operate at distance. This encouraged innovation to address the weaknesses of the organizational forms. Trading companies were at the forefront of experiments with incentives, such as private trade, and control mechanisms like employment contracts, to better control agents at distance (Hejeebu, 2005; Yates *et al.*, 2002). Whilst innovation in ownership saw entrepreneurs experiment with business groups to achieve scale and resolve governance problems, and free-standing companies to more efficiently channel capital investments (Buchnea, 2014; Jones and Wale, 1998; Wilkins and Schroter, 1998).

The environment

The analysis of the relationship between organizational form and function show that diversification into more resource and capital intensive activities, like banking and manufacturing, were key factors driving change in the structure of trading companies. These processes can be closely related to developments in the economic and political environment, as institutions, industries, infrastructure, and financial systems evolved in home and host markets.

One of the widely identified drivers of change was technological innovations in transportation and communication. Improvements to ship design, coupled with infrastructure developments, dramatically improved the speed of communication, improving the coordination of activities, and reducing freight costs (Kaukiainen, 2001; Rönnbäck, 2016). Similar effects were delivered through technological changes in communication. In the nineteenth century, the telegraph revolutionized the capacity of firms to communicate between distant markets and agents (Hugill, 1999). The telegraph also enabled new financial transactions and markets based on futures contracts (Engel, 2015). Whilst these innovations lowered costs of international business, they also allowed coordination functions to be internally integrated, reducing the need for intermediation (Wilkins, 1988a).

The new technologies created investment opportunities, as did emerging and expanding industries such as rubber and jute (Resor, 1977; Sethia, 1996). They required increased levels of capital investment and managerial expertise, which were often in short supply outside Europe. Trading companies utilized their networks to act as conduits for factors of production and expertise between the developed European capital markets and developing markets. However, the increasing capital intensity of these operations incentivized direct ownership and management to reduce transaction costs and improve control, encouraging experimentation with the free-standing company model (Hennart, 1998; Hennart and Kryda, 1998). Change in the structure of markets and industries encouraged experimentation with organizational and ownership solutions.

Similarly, developments in financing also played a significant role in expanding and changing the nature of international trade. Systems of credit requiring transfers of bullion were gradually replaced by innovations like the "Bill of Exchange," and more nuanced accounting practices for advancing credit, enabling expansion of geographically dispersed credit networks (Gervais *et al.*, 2014; Llorca-Jaña, 2011). However, advances in merchant and correspondent banking saw specialization in the funding of international trade reduce the need for trading companies to undertake these activities (Chapman, 1984). Innovation and growth in capital markets, such as Amsterdam and London, allowed entrepreneurs and investors to increasingly utilize the joint-stock form to channel capital into foreign investments (Gelderblom and Jonker, 2004).

A key determinant of the opportunities and constraints facing trading companies was change in the institutional frameworks in both home and host markets. The proliferation of joint-stock companies and growth in capital markets were closely correlated, and enabled by innovation in legal and financial institutions (Steengard, 1982). These processes were shaped by interactions between merchants, financiers, and politicians defining policies toward trade (Bowen, 2005; Jones, 1987), which over time saw a gradual shift from mercantilist to free trade ideologies. Similarly, philosophies of imperialism reshaped access to colonial markets (Gallagher and Robinson, 1953). These developments determined how and where the trading companies could operate.

The outcomes

Interaction between trading companies and their home and host environments drove experimentation and innovation in firm organization. The effects were varied, but innovations in business form that leveraged networks structures to channel flows of credit, information, and managerial expertise, and vertically integrated structurers which enhanced control and efficiencies, improved the capacity and performance of the firms, growing the scale and flows of trade (Jones, 2000; Wilkins, 1988a). Take-offs in the eighteenth century and late nineteenth century have been identified through analysis of levels of market integration achieved through the quantification of the flows of goods, capital, and people (Bordo *et al.*, 2003).

Changes in these flows have been used to analyze economic development in the regions involved. The innovative capacity of British merchants generated flows of resources, profits, and expertise that drove the industrial revolution (Davies, 1979). However, the extent to which host countries, such as India and China, benefited from this trade is widely debated (Roy, 2000).

Increased levels of FDI sparked industrial development, but extractive colonial regimes saw the returns from trade and market integration unequally distributed between the core and periphery (Wallerstein, 2011). The asynchronous and unequal returns generated by international trade have been linked to the "Great divergence" as Western European economies rapidly outgrew those of Qing China, Japan, and Mughal India in the eighteenth and nineteenth centuries (Pomeranz, 2000).

The outcomes for the trading companies themselves are also widely debated. Chartered trading companies achieved great scale and importance in the seventeenth and eighteenth centuries. Yet, technological change, market integration, and innovations in the ownership and organization of firms reduced the scope for intermediation and enabled the proliferation of MNEs. Despite these changes, Jones (1998: 2) remarks that trading companies are, "highly entrepreneurial corporate forms, constantly alert to new opportunities and resourceful in setting up the systems and creating flexible organizations." Their adaptability, coupled with expertise in the creation and management of information and knowledge, continued to provide sources of competitive advantage throughout the twentieth century (Jones and Wale, 2006).

Current debates

Determining the causation and correlation between changes in business form, the economic and political environment, and effects on firm and economic performance is widely debated. There is no consensus on a historically optimal business form, instead entrepreneurs have selected from a "menu of organizational choice"; their choice shaped by variation in legal and economic institutions (Guinanne *et al.*, 2007). The different capabilities of the joint-stock, partnership and cooperative business forms in mitigating the effects of a range of economic problems, and the impact of these choices on firm performance and economic development, are widely debated (Lamoreaux *et al.*, 2003)

International trade has been less widely covered in these debates, yet offers interesting possibilities to advance them due to the use of diverse business forms. Growth in the eighteenth century was driven by joint-stock chartered companies, but the dramatic expansion in the late nineteenth century was correlated with a variety of business forms. The trade-off between the need for capital depth provided by the joint-stock form and strong governance inherent in the partnership, were particularly acute when doing business at distance (Hilt, 2006; Silverman and Ingram, 2017). Identifying an optimal form to address the challenges of international trade is an open question.

In the case of the trading companies these debates are further complicated by a definitional and identification problem. The diverse nature of ownership and broad scope of the trading companies' operations make precise definitions and identification of a firm type difficult. Chapman (2004: 3), defined merchants as, "taken to be entrepreneurs engaged in foreign (overseas) commerce as wholesale traders." Yet, it is hard to define trading companies as discrete entities, when many functioned as networks or groups with shared ownership but unrelated functions (Jones, 2000). Defining the boundaries, activities, and organization of the trading firms to obtain a neat unit of analysis is problematic.

This creates a methodological issue of selection. Analysis of a set, and subsequent comparisons between them, requires a definition so that the sets can be clearly distinguished (Lamoreaux, 2006). Although sharing common antecedents, should merchant houses and chartered trading companies be grouped in a single set? Should business groups or free-standing joint-stock firms, pursuing activities as varied as merchant banking and plantation management, be classified as trading companies? Indeed, can trading companies be analyzed as a homogeneous group?

To mitigate these problems, historians have tended to focus on discrete business types. For example, Jonker and Sluyterman (2000: 9–10) specifically identify, and limit their analysis to, merchant houses. There are clear methodological benefits of a narrowly defined unit of analysis, yet this approach potentially limits explanations. Narrow identification strategies limit analysis of the dynamics between and amongst types. It may also lead to potentially important forms being ignored and explanations overdetermined in favor of a neatly defined ideal type, and subsequently limits claims around performance and impact.

How, then, should researchers expand the scope of their explanations? Jones (1998: 3) notes that, "little can be done about such definitional problems beyond pointing them out." Indeed, the definitions allow diversification and hybridization to be identified, and subsequent analysis can focus on the factors shaping these changes.

This approach can be taken further through longitudinal studies of the organization of international trade, which rather than narrowly focus on specific forms, explicitly analyzes the transitions between different organizational forms. Research can focus on a region or product to understand the conditions under which trading companies adapt and innovate, and specifically consider decisions to diversify or integrate activities. This level of analysis accounts for the wide ecology of firms involved in international trade, and embraces the debates on the menu of organizational choice. The outcomes of these decisions can be assessed in terms of firm performance, and correlation with the economic development of regions and industries.

Trading companies in nineteenth century Anglo-Indian trade

New research into change in the organization of the Anglo-Indian trade across the nineteenth century can illustrate the opportunities of this approach in explaining the changing role and impact of trading companies. The longevity of British mercantile interests in India, stretching from the sixteenth century to the present day, saw significant changes in the organization of the trade over time. One of the most dramatic transitions occurred in 1813 when the EIC's monopoly on trade with India was rescinded, opening new opportunities to private merchants. Those entering the market had, however, to reorganize the EIC's established system of trade that encompassed complex flows of credit to fund the manufacturing, purchase, and marketing of goods (Furber, 1948).

The extant literature has identified three distinct business types involved in the organization of the trade after 1813. First, the agency houses bear greatest similarity to merchant houses. Organized as partnerships, they operated in conjunction with corresponding trading firms in Britain to facilitate a flow of goods, such as Indian indigo and British manufactured goods, and credit between Britain and India (Tripathi, 1980). Initially acting as commission agents, agency houses, such as John Palmer and Co., became increasingly engaged in local industries, particularly indigo, as direct investors and owners (Singh, 1966; Webster, 2007).

The second are managing agents, which can be defined as diversified business groups based around a central firm organized as a partnership (Jones and Wale, 1998). The managing agent promoted joint-stock firms and used contractual mechanisms such as cross-directorates to control them (Lokanathan, 1935). This diversified the risks of integration into local industries such as tea and jute. Managing agents, like Carr, Tagore and Co., coordinated the flow of capital, credit, managerial expertise, and products amongst the group and between Britain, India, and other international markets (Kling, 1966; Jones, 2000).

Third, joint-stock firms incorporated in both Calcutta and London, some of which can be classified as free-standing companies, fully integrated production and marketing functions between India and Britain. Firms such as the Assam Co., and Jorehaut Co., proliferated in industries such as tea and jute (Antrobus, 1957; Chapman, 1998; Rungta, 1970).

Table 13.2 Typology of firms operating in the nineteenth century Anglo-Indian trade

Firm	Ownership form	Organizational structure	Location	Main activities
Agency house	Partnership	Network of trading firms	HQ in Calcutta, linked to independent trading companies	Commission traders, investors in local industries
Free-standing company	Joint-stock	Vertically integrated	Incorporated in both London and Calcutta	Production and marketing fully owned and managed
Managing agent	Hybrid	Group of managed firms	HQ in Calcutta, linked to group by cross-holdings, cross-directorates, and contracts	Promotion and management of firms

Sources: Adapted from Chapman (1998, 2004), Jones (2000).

Questions remain as to when and why the different business forms proliferated or failed, and the subsequent effect of the organization of business on the level and value of trade. The dominant explanations describe how the agency houses diversified to become managing agents around the middle of the century (Chapman, 2004; Roy 2014). Through this process the managing agency system became the dominant method of business organization in India by the end of the nineteenth century. Yet, these explanations have tended to focus analysis either on the agency houses (Singh, 1966; Tripathi, 1980; Webster, 2005) or the managing agents (Lokanathan, 1935; Misra, 1999), whilst the importance of independent joint-stock firms have been marginalized (Chapman, 1998). Less attention has been placed on understanding the factors that shaped the transitions between the different forms. Indeed, a lack of basic quantification of the number, size, and scope of the different organizational forms has made it difficult to accurately assess trends in the changes of the organization of business, and subsequent correlation with the scale and value of trade.

To address these questions new data drawn from nineteenth century Bengal business registers is used to categorize firms involved in the trade typologically and chronologically, clarifying and quantifying how and when the organization of trade changed. This data is correlated with longitudinal analysis of the organization of key export products including indigo and tea, to examine factors determining the changes in ownership and organization.

Identifying changes in organization

The data from the registers, shown in Table 13.3, reveals three significant trends. The first was the growth in number of agency houses. Although the two decades after 1813 were dominated by a stable number of around 25 agency houses, there was a sharp increase in the number of trading partnerships after credit crises in the 1830s and 1840s saw large incumbents removed. The number stabilized at around 80 after 1848.

The second trend was the rapid proliferation of joint-stock firms after 1853. Prior to 1840 the use of the joint-stock form was virtually non-existent with only a handful of joint-stock banks established by government charter. Subsequently, a small number of firms in transport,

Table 13.3 Number of trading companies and value of the Anglo-Indian trade, 1813–1868

Year	Agency houses	Joint-stock firms	Managing agents	Managed joint-stock	Value of trade
1813	25	1	–	–	£11,408,510.00
1824	24	4	–	–	–
1834	25	2	–	–	–
1838	44	2	–	–	£22,831,943.00
1843	62	11	–	–	£22,046,714.00
1848	60	15	–	–	£22,565,996.00
1853	75	16	–	–	£30,902,006.00
1858	86	30	28	9	£41,408,784.00
1863	80	58	37	15	£84,398,889.00
1868	88	173	62	72	£96,173,711.00

Sources: Benchmark years of the merchant and company lists in Calcutta and Bengal commercial registers published between 1813 and 68 in the British Library (BL). Value of trade from Chaudhuri (1971), and DSAL statistics section, No. 27 and 31 (1841–1865) and No. 18 and 24 (1860–69). The values are real and have been deflated using the GDP deflator index in Broadberry and Van Leeuwen (2010) .

infrastructure, and manufacturing, incorporated. In India, the passing of a Companies Act in 1850, and a Limited Liability Act in 1857, simplified the administrative process of incorporation, and embedded the benefits of limited liability. In the decade after these changes the number of Calcutta registered joint-stock firms rose from 30 to 173. The form initially became dominant in the tea sector, which accounted for 40 percent of all joint stock firms in 1868.

The third trend shows that as the number of joint-stock firms increased in the late 1860s, both the number of managing agents and the number of joint-stock firms contracted to them rapidly increased. The number of firms acting as managing agents doubled between 1858 and 1868. By 1868 42 percent of joint-stock firms were contracted to agents. This trend was most notable in the tea sector. After its foundation in 1840, the industry dramatically expanded in the 1860s as demand grew in the UK. The number of joint-stock firms proliferated from a handful in the 1850s to 70 at the end of the 1860s (Griffiths, 1967). Yet, of these, 46 were listed as having a managing agent (Chapman, 1998).

The correlation between change in the role and organization of the trading companies and the growth in the value of the trade is striking. The gradual increase in the number of agency houses, in the years between 1813 and 1840, stimulated fitful growth. Yet, between 1848 and 1858, the decade in which the joint-stock form proliferated, saw the value of the trade almost double. Similarly, between 1858 and 1868 the value more than doubled again.

Analysis of the organization of the production, financing, and marketing of key export products, can shed light on the questions of change in organizational form. After 1813, the major Indian export products by value included raw cotton, indigo, sugar, and silk. In the first half of the nineteenth century indigo was the most valuable export crop in Bengal and it was the product which became synonymous with the agency houses (Chaudhuri, 1971). Initially the agency houses intermediated the trade, acting as commission agents for corresponding British trading houses.

However, the indigo industry was characterized by dramatic fluctuations in the level of production in Bengal, leading to volatility in supply and prices (Chowdhury, 1964). The trade was also affected by the limitations of the local financial system. Credit in Calcutta was relatively expensive and predominantly short term, whilst supply was also volatile, with the Bengal economy racked by credit crises in the 1830s and 1840s (Tripathi, 1980) This resulted in periods of underinvestment and overproduction as factory owners reacted to the availability and cost of credit.

These limitations encouraged the agency houses to explore different mechanisms to organize the market. Utilizing relationships with firms in Britain gave them access to London's financial markets, which placed them at the center of financing networks that funneled credit and capital into Bengal, particularly making loans to indigo factory owners. This saw the agency houses increasingly integrated into production, as they took ownership of factories as loans defaulted. (Webster, 2007).

The role played by the trading firms changed significantly, from intermediaries, to investors of capital, and ultimately managers of plantations and factories. The thin capital markets caused innovation with upstream integration, but this shifted risk onto the agency houses, who now owned not just the product, but also the means of production.

The challenges of capital and integration were intensified by the emergence of significant new opportunities and risk in the second half of the nineteenth century. The production of jute increased markedly, and its export value rose rapidly after the 1850s. Tea followed a similar trend, as the Indian tea industry went from supplying less than 5 percent of the UK's total tea imports to 34 percent between 1866 and 1883 (Griffiths, 1967: 125).

The new industries were significantly different from indigo. The cultivation of tea required extensive capital investments in new plantations and infrastructure in the distant tea regions of Assam. In the late 1860s, rising demand in the UK created favorable conditions to attract capital from both British and Indian investors. A tea mania saw an explosion in the number of firms entering the industry. The Bengal registry for 1868 listed 70 joint-stock tea firms incorporated in both London and Calcutta, a dramatic increase on the handful operating in the late 1850s (Griffiths, 1967).

Innovating the trading company

Resolving the challenges of capital and integration encouraged experimentation with models of ownership and organization. The joint-stock form allowed entrepreneurs to address the growing scale of infrastructure investment, and diversify the escalating risks, by raising capital from shareholders in London and Calcutta and channeling it into the new industries. These developments allowed the integration of production and marketing activities, with many tea companies directly exporting to Britain for sale at auction and to wholesalers (Griffiths, 1967).

Yet, the decisions to fully integrate operations had implications for the internal organization and management of the firms. Owners and shareholders in London and Calcutta faced significant difficulties in establishing control over their managers in the far-off tea regions, with malfeasant and opportunistic behaviors an endemic feature of the operations, leading to declining profitability. Efforts to innovate governance mechanisms proved ineffectual in resolving these problems (Aldous, 2015). These governance challenges encouraged further experimentation.

The managing agency system allowed the joint-stock form to be leveraged to address the need for capital investments and gain benefits from integration. Yet, overarching firm governance was determined by the partnership form. The use of profit share and capital investment meant each partner, had "skin in the game," with remuneration tied to firm performance, reducing the risks of opportunism. Many of the managing agent firms also drew on extensive experiences in controlling decentralized trade operations which equipped them with versatile managerial control systems, allowing them to successfully control and coordinate activities amongst the industrially diverse and geographically dispersed portfolio of managed firms (Jones, 2000).

211

Take-off in the Anglo-Indian trade

The expansion and take-off in the Anglo-Indian trade was facilitated by the experimentation with business forms. The thinness of the colonial financial markets encouraged diversification and subsequently the widespread use of the joint-stock form, enabled and incentivized by the institutional and economic developments of the 1850s. This significantly increased the flows of FDI allowing capital investment and the integration of operations in nascent industries, whilst the innovation of the managing agent system addressed the weakness of the joint-stock firms' internal management, allowing the scope of the firms to expand and efficiencies of operations to improve.

The expansion of new industries and improved efficiencies of the firms had wider effects on the Anglo-Indian trade, with India becoming an increasingly large proportion of Britain's total trade balance. Asia and the Near East's share of British exports increased from 7 to 20 percent between 1805 and 1845 and accounted for 20 percent of British imports in 1845 (Chapman, 2004: 8). By 1845, Asia had become Britain's second largest export market, with only Europe receiving a greater quantity of goods. The growth in the scale and scope of international trade saw the total value of Britain's international exports and imports as a share of GDP increase from 21.4 percent in 1820 to 27.8 percent in 1850 and 43.6 percent by 1870 (Daudi *et al.*, 2010: 106).

Trading companies in the long-run

Trading companies were the key makers of global trade from the seventeenth to the nineteenth centuries. As these findings show, merchants in the nineteenth century Anglo-Indian trade developed innovative organizational solutions to balance an evolving set of challenges resulting from changes in the economic and business environments. This experimentation improved market coordination, increased flows of FDI, and expanded industries and trade.

The explanation of the organization and expansion of the Anglo-Indian trade are improved through longitudinal analysis of these experimentations with business forms. Extending the analysis to investigate a wider ecology of firm types involved in the trade highlighted the important, but problematic, role of the joint-stock free-standing companies, mainly ignored in the literature. This improves understanding of the emergence and proliferation of the managing agent system.

Addressing the debates around the role of business forms enabled this research to show the importance of hybrid forms of ownership in solving the multifaceted challenges of international trade. It was notable that the take-off in the trade in the 1850s was strongly correlated with innovation in business forms, but occurred before major developments in transportation and communication, including the completion of the Suez Canal and London to Calcutta telegraph line in 1870.

This opens possibilities to rethink the evolution of trading companies beyond the nineteenth century. There was no ideal or optimal type, but an iterative and adaptive set of processes saw a broad typology of trading companies become active and successful. The experimentation and innovation in response to external and internal challenges led to wide-ranging diversification and hybridization of business forms to undertake international trade.

The problems with definition and categorization of what constitutes a trading company are clear. Yet, it is crucial to analyze the processes driving change between forms to understand their evolving role and importance. Whilst complicating analysis, and leading to modest findings that are bound by regional and industry contexts, research needs to systematically extend beyond the archetypal activities of intermediation, and explain the upstream integration into production and diversification into services such as banking. This approach will improve understanding of why trading companies became important makers of global business, and offer propositions to explain their further innovation and longevity.

Further comparative work on regions and industries would allow analysis to distinguish more clearly the effects of change in the institutional and economic environment on organizational innovations. This would deepen understanding of the contingent effects of the environment and path dependency in shaping decisions around firm organization. It would better explain the emergence and evolution of business forms active in international business and allow contemporary studies to consider how the long-run development of their antecedents shape modern MNEs; considering them as part of an evolutionary process of adaptation, rather than a monolithic optimal type. This can potentially improve understanding of the effects that innovation in business organization has had on the expansion of trade and FDI and the shape and velocity of globalization.

References

Adams, J. (1996). "Principals and Agents, Colonialists and Company Men: The Decay of Colonial Control in the Dutch East Indies." *American Sociological Review* 61/1: 12–28.

Aldous, M. (2015). "Avoiding Negligence and Profusion: The Failure of the Joint-Stock Form in the Anglo-Indian Tea Trade, 1840–1870." *Enterprise & Society* 16/3: 648–685.

Aldous, M. (2017). "Rehabilitating the Intermediary: Auctioneers and Brokers in the 19th Century Anglo-Indian Trade." *Business History* 59/4: 525–553.

Antrobus, H. (1957). *The History of the Assam Company 1839–1953*. Edinburgh: Constable Ltd.

Bordo, M., Taylor, A., and Williamson, J. (eds.) (2003). *Globalization in Historical Perspective*. Chicago, IL: University of Chicago Press.

Bowen, H. (2005). *The Business of Empire: The East India Company and Imperial Britain, 1756–1833*. Cambridge: Cambridge University Press.

Bowen, H., Lincoln, M., and Rigby, N. (eds.) (2002). *The Worlds of the East India Company*. Woodbridge, UK: Boydell & Brewer.

Braudel, F. (1995). *La Méditerranée et le Monde Méditerranéen a l'époque de Philippe II*, English translation. Berkeley, CA: University of California Press.

Broadberry, S., and Van Leeuwen, B. (2010). "British Economic Growth and Business Cycle, 1700–1870: Annual Estimates," CAGE Online Working Paper Series.

Broehl, W. G. (1998). *Cargill: Going Global*. Hanover, NH: University Press of New England.

Buchnea, E. (2014). "Transatlantic Transformations: Visualizing Change Over Time in the Liverpool–New York Trade Network, 1763–1833," *Enterprise & Society* 15/4: 687–721.

Calcutta and Bengal Commercial Registers. British Library (BL) Shelf mark OIR 954.14 ST 1216 CH.

Carlos, A. (1992). "Principal–Agent Problems in Early Trading Companies: A Tale of Two Firms," *American Economic Review* 82/2: 140–145.

Carlos, A., and Nicholas, S. (1988). "'Giants of an Earlier Capitalism': The Chartered Trading Companies as Modern Multinationals." *Business History Review* 62/3: 398–419.

Carlos, A., and Nicholas, S. (1990). "Agency Problems in the Early Chartered Companies: The Case of the Hudson's Bay Company." *Journal of Economic History* 50/4: 853–875.

Casson, M. (1998). "The Economic Analysis of Multinational Trading Companies," in Jones, G. (ed.). *The Multinational Traders*. London: Routledge.

Chapman, S. (1984). *The Rise of Merchant Banking*. London: George Allen & Unwin.

Chapman, S. (1998). "British Free-Standing Companies and Investment Groups in India and the Far East," in Wilkins, M., and Schröter, H. (eds.). *The Free-Standing Company in the World Economy, 1830 to 1996*. Oxford: Oxford University Press.

Chapman, S. (2004). *Merchant Enterprise in Britain: From the Industrial Revolution to World War I*. Cambridge: Cambridge University Press.

Chaudhuri, K. N. (1965). *The English East India Company: The Study of an Early Joint-Stock Company, 1600–1640*. London: Cass.

Chaudhuri, K. N. (1971). *The Economic Development of India under the East India Company 1814–58: A Selection of Contemporary Writings*. London: Cambridge University Press.

Chowdhury, B. (1964). *Growth of Commercial Agriculture in Bengal*. Calcutta: Quality Printers.

Daudi, G., O'Rourke, K., and Prados de la Escosura, L. (2010). "Trade and Empire," in Broadberry, S., and O'Rourke, K. (eds.). *The Cambridge Economic History of Modern Europe, Vol. 1, 1700–1870*. Cambridge: Cambridge University Press.

Davies, R. (1979). *The Industrial Revolution and British Overseas Trade*. Leicester: Leicester University Press.

Dejung, C. (2013). "Worldwide Ties: The Role of Family Business in Global Trade in the Nineteenth and Twentieth Centuries." *Business History* 55/6: 1001–1018.

Downs, J. (2015). *The Golden Ghetto: The American Commercial Community at Canton and the Shaping of American China Policy, 1784–1844*. Hong Kong: Hong Kong University Press.

Engel, A. (2015). "Buying Time: Futures Trading and Telegraphy in Nineteenth-Century Global Commodity Markets." *Journal of Global History* 10/2: 284–306.

Findlay, R., and O'Rourke, K. (2009). *Power and Plenty: Trade, War, and the World Economy in the Second Millennium*. Princeton, NJ: Princeton University Press.

Furber, H. (1948). *John Company at Work*. Cambridge, MA: Harvard University Press.

Gallagher, J., and Robinson, R. (1953). "The Imperialism of Free Trade." *Economic History Review* 6/1: 1–15.

Gelderblom, O., and Jonker, J. (2004). "Completing a Financial Revolution: The Finance of the Dutch East India Trade and the Rise of the Amsterdam Capital Market, 1595–1612." *Journal of Economic History* 64/3: 641–672.

Gelderblom, O., de Jong, A., and Jonker, J. (2013). "The Formative Years of the Modern Corporation: The Dutch East India Company VOC, 1602–1623." *Journal of Economic History* 73/4: 1050–1076.

Gervais, P., Lemarchand, Y., and Margairaz, D. (2014). *Merchants and Profit in the Age of Commerce, 1680–1830*. London: Pickering & Chatto.

Greif, A. (2006). *Institutions and the Path to the Modern Economy: Lessons from Medieval Trade*. New York: Cambridge University Press.

Griffiths, P. (1967). *The History of the Indian Tea Industry*. London: Cloves & Son.

Guinanne, T., Harris, R., Lamoreaux, N., and Rosenthal, J-L. (2007). "Putting the Corporation in Its Place." *Enterprise & Society* 8/3: 687–729.

Harlaftis, G., and Theotokas, J. (2004). "European Family Firms in International Business: British and Greek Tramp-shipping Firms." *Business History* 46/2: 219–255.

Hejeebu, S. (2005). "Contract Enforcement in the English East India Company." *Journal of Economic History* 65/2: 496–523.

Hennart, J-F. (1998). "Transaction–Cost Theory and the Free-Standing Company," in Wilkins, M., and Schröter, H. (eds.). *The Free-Standing Company in the World Economy, 1830 to 1996*. Oxford: Oxford University Press.

Hennart, J-F., and Kryda, G. (1998). "Why do Traders Invest in Manufacturing?" in Jones, G. (ed.). *The Multinational Traders*. London: Routledge.

Herodotus. (2003). *The Histories*. London: Penguin Classics.

Hilt, E. (2006). "Incentives in Corporations: Evidence from the American Whaling Industry." *Journal of Law and Economics* 49/1: 197–227.

Hugill, P. (1999). *Global Communications since 1844: Geopolitics and Technology*. Baltimore, MD: Johns Hopkins University Press.

Jones, C. (1987). *International Business in the Nineteenth Century: The Rise and Fall of a Cosmopolitan Bourgeoisie*. New York: Columbia University Press.

Jones, G. (1995). *British Multinational Banking 1830–1990*. Oxford: Oxford University Press.

Jones, G. (ed.) (1998). *The Multinational Traders*. London: Routledge.

Jones, G. (2000). *Merchants to Multinationals: British Trading Companies in the 19th and 20th Centuries*. New York: Oxford University Press.

Jones, G. (2007). "Globalization," in Jones, G., and Zeitlin, J. (eds.). *Oxford Handbook of Business History*. New York: Oxford University Press.

Jones, G., and Wale, J. (1998). "Merchants as Business Groups: British Trading Companies in Asia before 1945." *Business History Review* 72/3: 367–408.

Jones, G., and Wale, J. (2006). "Diversification Strategies of British Trading Companies: Harrisons & Crosfield, c.1900–c.1980." *Business History* 41/2: 69–101.

Jonker, J., and Sluyterman, K. (2000). *At Home on the World Markets: Dutch International Trading Companies from the 16th Century until the Present*. The Hague: Sdu Uitgevers.

Kaukiainen, Y. (2001). "Shrinking the World: Improvements in the Speed of Information Transmission, 1820–1870." *European Review of Economic History* 5/1: 1–28.

Kling, B. (1966). "The Origin of the Managing Agency System in India." *Journal of Asian Studies* 26/1: 37–47.

Lamoreaux, N. (2006). "Business Organization," in Carter, S., Gartner, S., Haines, M., Olmstead, A., Sutch, R., and Wright, G. (eds.). *Historical Statistics of the United States*, Millennial Edition On Line. Cambridge: Cambridge University Press.

Lamoreaux, N., Raff, D., and Temin, P. (2003). "Beyond Markets and Hierarchies: Towards a New Synthesis of American Business History." *American Historical Review* 108: 404–433.

Llorca-Jaña, M. (2011). "The Organization of British Textile Exports to the River Plate and Chile: Merchant Houses in Operation, c. 1810–59." *Business History* 53/6: 821–865.

Llorca-Jaña, M. (2012). *The British Textile Trade in South America in the Nineteenth Century*. New York: Cambridge University Press.

Lokanathan, P. (1935). *Industrial Organization in India*. London: George Allen & Unwin.

McCusker, J. (2005). "The Demise of Distance: The Business Press and the Origins of the Information Revolution in the Early Modern Atlantic World." *American Historical Review* 110/2: 295–321.

Machado, P. (2014). *Ocean of Trade: South Asian Merchants, Africa and the Indian Ocean, c.1750–1850*. Cambridge: Cambridge University Press.

Markovits, C. (2000). *The Global World of Indian Merchants, 1750–1947: Traders of Sind from Bukhara to Panama*. Cambridge: Cambridge University Press.

Mathew, J. (2016). *Margins of the Market: Trafficking and Capitalism across the Arabian Sea*. Berkeley, CA: University of California Press.

Misra, M. (1999). *Business, Race, and Politics in British India, c. 1850–1960*. New York: Oxford University Press.

North, D. (1968). "Sources of Productivity Change in Ocean Shipping, 1600–1850." *Journal of Political Economy* 76/5: 953–970.

O'Rourke, K., and Williamson, J. (1999). *Globalization and History: The Evolution of a Nineteenth-century Atlantic Economy*. Cambridge, MA: MIT Press.

Oonk, G. (2013). *Settled Strangers: Asian Business Elites in East Africa 1800–2000*. London: Sage.

Pomeranz, K. (2000). *The Great Divergence: China, Europe and the Making of the Modern World Economy*. Princeton, NJ: Princeton University Press.

Resor, R. (1977). "Rubber in Brazil: Dominance and Collapse, 1876–1945." *Business History Review* 51/3: 341–366.

Riello, G., and Roy, T. (eds.) (2009). *How India Clothed the World: The World of South Asian Textiles, 1500–1850*. Leiden: Brill.

Rönnbäck, K. (2016). "Transaction Costs of Early Modern Multinational Enterprise: Measuring the Transatlantic Information Lag of the British Royal African Company and its Successor, 1680–1818." *Business History* 58/8: 1147–1163.

Roy, T. (2000). "De-Industrialisation: Alternative View." *Economic and Political Weekly* 35/17: 1442–1447.

Roy, T. (2014). "Trading Firms in Colonial India." *Business History Review* 88/1: 9–42.

Rungta, R. (1970). *The Rise of the Business Corporation in India 1851–1900*. Cambridge: Cambridge University Press.

Sethia, T. (1996). "The Rise of the Jute Manufacturing Industry in Colonial India: A Global Perspective." *Journal of World History* 7/1: 71–99.

Silverman, B., and Ingram, P. (2017). "Asset Ownership and Incentives in Early Shareholder Capitalism: Liverpool Shipping in the Eighteenth Century." *Strategic Management Journal* 38: 854–875.

Singh, S. (1966). *European Agency Houses in Bengal 1783–1833*. Calcutta: Firma K.L Mukhopadhyay.

Steengaard, N. (1982). *The Dutch East India Company as an Institutional Innovation*. Cambridge: Cambridge University Press.

Tripathi, A. (1980). *Trade and Finance in the Bengal Presidency 1793–1833*. Calcutta: Oxford University Press.

Van Driel, H. (2003). "The Role of Middlemen in the International Coffee Trade since 1870: The Dutch Case." *Business History* 45/2: 77–101.

Wallerstein, I. (2011). *The Modern World-System I: Capitalist Agriculture and the Origins of the European World-Economy in the Sixteenth Century*. Berkeley, CA: University of California Press.

Webster, A. (2005). "An Early Global Business in a Colonial Context: The Strategies, Management and Failure of John Palmer and Co of Calcutta." *Enterprise & Society* 6/1: 98–133.

Webster, A. (2007). *The Richest East India Merchant: The Life and Business of John Palmer of Calcutta 1767–1836*. Woodbridge, UK: Boydell Press.

Webster, A. (2009). *The Twilight of the East India Company: The Evolution of Anglo-Asian Commerce and Politics 1790–1860*. Woodbridge, UK: Boydell Press.

Wilkins, M. (1971). *The Emergence of Multinational Enterprise: American Business Abroad from the Colonial Era to 1914*. Cambridge, MA: Harvard University Press.

Wilkins, M. (1988a). "European and North American Multinationals, 1870–1914: Comparisons and Contrasts." *Business History* 30/1: 8–45.

Wilkins, M. (1988b). "The Free-Standing Company, 1870–1914: An Important Type of British Foreign Direct Investment." *Economic History Review* 41/2: 259–282.

Wilkins, M. (1991). *The Growth of Multinationals*. Cheltenham: Edward Elgar.

Wilkins, M., and Schröter, H. (eds.) (1998). *The Free-Standing Company in the World Economy, 1830 to 1996*. Oxford: Oxford University Press.

Williams, E. (1944). *Capitalism and Slavery*. Chapel Hill, NC: University of North Carolina Press.

Yates, J., O'Leary, M., and Orlikowski, W. (2002). "Distributed Work over the Centuries: Trust and Control in the Hudson's Bay Company, 1670–1826," in Hinds, P., and Kiesler, S. (eds.). *Distributed Work*. Cambridge, MA: MIT Press.

14

CO-OPERATIVES

Mads Mordhorst and Kristoffer Jensen

Co-operatives between stable ideals and a fast changing context

The co-operative way of organizing economic activity has a history as long as business has existed itself. European guilds and trade associations of the Hanseatic League in the Middle Ages, for example, were organized in a co-operative way (Battilani and Schröter 2012: 4; Catherine Casson in this volume). Still, most of us when thinking of co-operatives relate to the "modern" form developed in the nineteenth century as a response to the downsides of industrialism. Saving banks, consumer-, producer-, and, later, workers' co-operatives were created to stimulate self-help for the less favored classes (Davis and Payne 1958; Wadhwani 2011; Robertson 2012; Bátiz-Lazo and Billings 2012; McLaughlin 2014; Fernández 2014; Hilson *et al.* 2017; Toms 2012; Henriksen *et al.* 2012; Perotin 2012).

An initiative in 1844 by the "Rochdale Pioneers" proved particularly influential for the co-operative way of organizing. The Pioneers were around thirty weavers and other artisans who opened a consumer co-operative in the town of Rochdale, England. The co-operative was a grocery shop selling basic foodstuffs like sugar, butter, and oatmeal at affordable prices to the local workers (Wilson *et al.* 2013: 34–42). What proved more important in a larger perspective, though, was the ability of the Pioneers to narrate about their initiative in a way that inspired others to follow suit. The Rochdale co-operators became highly influential for the evolution of the co-operative business form by setting the standard for how to organize and regulate co-operative societies. They soon came to be seen as the founding fathers of an entire co-operative movement. As it is stated today on the website of the International Co-operative Alliance (ICA):

> The principles that underpinned co-operatives' way of doing business are still accepted today as the foundations upon which all co-operatives operate. These principles have been revised and updated, but remain essentially the same as those practiced by the Pioneers in 1844.
>
> *(International Co-operative Alliance n.d.a)*

According to ICA, these principles included that: "a co-operative is an autonomous association of persons united voluntarily to meet their common economic, social, and cultural needs and aspirations through a jointly owned and democratically-controlled enterprise" (International Co-operative Alliance n.d.b).

The Pioneers in Rochdale inspired others across the world to embark on similar ventures. When ICA argues that a whole co-operative world today rests on "essentially the same" principles as the ones the weavers developed in the 1840s, they nevertheless stretch the term to its essential limits. The Rochdale Pioneers did not use the term "Principles," rather they talked about "Objects," and some of the principles set as defining by ICA, such as the "democratic" cornerstone, the "one man one vote," and the free and open membership, were not part of the original "Objects" (Rochdale Society 1844).

The historian Eric Hobsbawm (1983: 1–14) introduced the concept of "invented tradition" to grasp how the introduction or reshaping of traditions of supposedly long heritage were used to build nations and communities. Invented traditions could help craft identity and thereby stimulate unity. By narrating the actions of the Rochdale Pioneers of the 1840s as the timeless shared cradle of a co-operative world, ICA as an interest organization works to knit an otherwise diverse and fragmented co-operative movement together. As Zerubavel (2003: 8) stated, "exaggerating one's antiquity" is a common tool in that regard.

For historians, it is not surprising that even traditions change over time. The co-operative world has had to respond to a dramatically changing context since 1844. For identity purposes ICA has an interest in downplaying the changes made to the founding principles, but we will argue that ICA at the same time created a tension for the business activities of a co-operative sector and its need to respond to a globalizing world. The principles set the boundaries for what is regarded as legitimate behavior. Given that they are constructed as eternal, they put limits on the strategic maneuverability of co-operative firms which increasingly find themselves in need of adapting to new contexts. A line of ambiguities and tensions seems to exist in a global era: innovation vs. historical principles, social movement vs. profitable enterprise, and national vs. global. In this chapter we explore the strategic response of co-operative management toward globalization and the resulting outcome. The empirical foundation is two selected Danish co-operatives: the consumer co-operative Coop and the dairy producer co-operative Arla. Both tried to meet the challenges from the recent wave of globalization through mergers in the Nordic region.[1]

To explore the role of co-operatives as "makers of global business," we start by reviewing the existing literature on co-operatives. We then develop the tensions which large-scale co-operatives need to address in the context of global pressures. Next we discuss how the identified tensions impacted the co-operative sector in Denmark and how it has come to be seen as an important pillar of Danish society. Our two cases allow us to empirically analyze how co-operatives respond to these challenges in detail. We conclude by stressing what we believe can be learned from these cases on a larger scale and by identifying promising research topics for the future.

Literature review

When ICA talks about the co-operative as a means to meet "common economic, social, and cultural needs and aspirations" (International Co-operative Alliance n.d.b), it becomes clear that co-operatives are shaped by both a business-logic and a movement-logic. The success criterion of the first is the ability to generate growth and profits, while the second measures success on a broader scale. The successful co-operative is not only able to secure growth of sales and profits for itself, but will have to also demonstrate how it has benefited the common good. This can be done, for instance, by having provided honest products at a fair price for consumers, good conditions for suppliers, decent labor conditions for the workforce, or by more indirectly having been able to promote democratic principles and social justice.

As a business form, co-operatives can be defined as jointly owned enterprises engaging in the production or distribution of goods or the supply of services, and operated by their members for their mutual benefit (Dictionary.com n.d.). A consumer co-operative is thus owned by its members on the principle of "one member one vote" and with its dividends distributed according to how much turnover each member secures for the organization. In a producer co-operative, such as the dairy company Arla, the dairy farmers jointly own the production facilities and share the profits proportionally to the amount of milk delivered.

Robert Owen famously created New Harmony in the 1820s as a utopian town in the US state of Indiana based on co-operative principles, and in the mid-1800s John Stuart Mill came to see the co-operative form as holding great business potential because it could create a partnership between capital and labor (Wilson 1967). Nevertheless, the dominating view among economists came to be that the success of co-operatives would fade as societies modernized. Neo-classical economists paid little attention to co-operatives, which they considered less efficient than capitalist firms due to their democratically controlled governing bodies. Capitalist firms had the advantage of concentrating on a single goal – profit seeking – while co-operatives inherently had split personalities, constantly balancing profit seeking with some sort of benevolence (Whyman 2012). In modern-day societies of the developed world co-operatives might have a role in limited periods of economic contraction, but in periods of macro-economic growth they, in the eyes of influential economists, would not be able to compete (Medina-Albaladejo 2015). As a result they have also moved to the margins of economic thought.

In the field of business history, co-operative business has also lived on the margins of scholarly interest. When co-operative enterprises were in fact discussed in the leading journals of the field like the *Business History Review*, *Business History*, and *Enterprise & Society*, it nearly always concerned co-operative initiatives of the pre-World War II period (Bamfield 1998; Purvis 2006; Sørensen and Pedersen 2007). In Scandinavia, however, enterprises organized as co-operatives could not be so easily overlooked, and Mordhorst (2007, 2014) and Hansen (2001, 2007) made valuable contributions showing how co-operative dairies and Danish saving banks after World War II had their strategic choices limited by being culturally interwoven in greater narratives stipulating what it meant to be and act Danish. Martin Jes Iversen and Steen Andersen (2008) in the ambitious textbook *Creating Nordic Capitalism* even labeled the entire Danish business system "co-operative liberalism." Still, co-operatives at first were far from becoming a mainstream research topic in business history. The otherwise comprehensive *Oxford Handbook of Business History*, published in 2009, gave a "state-of-the-art survey of research in business history" (Jones and Zeitlin 2009) but did not devote a chapter or even a full section to co-operative business.

Researchers neglecting the co-operative form of business could partly find justification in the fact that many co-operatives throughout the world had been in decline since the 1960s. Consumer co-operatives had been on the forefront of modernizing retailing in many places in Europe from the interwar years and up until the early 1960s, but since then many of them lost the initiative to privately owned retail chains (Alexander 2008; Sandgren 2009; Gurney 2012; Jensen 2016; Brazda and Scediwy 2011).

Since the end of World War II, conditions within the retail sector have dramatically changed. Before World War II, consumer co-operatives in most countries competed only with small independent grocers. After the war – despite great differences between countries – the main competitors increasingly became chain store businesses, some of which were controlled by multinationals. This development happened as former legislative impediments were removed and new technologies became available, and at the same time significant economic growth changed consumer behavior. The co-operative societies were by nature local in their orientation and therefore devoted to the neighborhood shop, even though economic and demographic developments in many cases rendered them obsolete and called for supermarkets located in new suburbs (Ekberg 2012a, 2012b).

Despite the observations presented by Brazda and Scediwy (2011) and a competitive situation in the global north that since the late 1980s has only increased, the consumer co-operative sector has, to the surprise of many observers, been able to survive and even thrive in some countries. This fact has helped spur a new research interest. The year 2012 was appointed the International Year of Co-operatives by the United Nations, and that same year *Business History* published two special issues devoted to not-for-profit financial institutions and to co-operatives and Cambridge University Press produced an edited volume on co-operative business since the 1950s (Bátiz-Lazo and Billings 2012; Webster and Walton 2012; Battilani and Schröter 2012). Hilson *et al.* (2017) put out a comprehensive edited volume on consumer co-operatives since 1850 in an effort to include not only the histories of consumer co-operatives in the global north, but as inspired by global history to also include parts of the world that had previously tended to get marginalized in the historiography. These publications blended in with a stream of important monographs analyzing consumer cooperation in individual countries (Lange 2006; Wilson *et al.* 2013; Knupfer 2013; Jensen 2016).

The new wave of studies had a shared core as they discussed the role of co-operatives in previous times and also foregrounded their continued present-day importance in some countries and sectors, thereby stressing that co-operatives had competitive advantages overlooked by mainstream economists. In a history of Italian co-operative enterprises, Battilani and Zamagni (2012) discussed the managerial transformation that took place within the co-operative movement after World War II seeing it as one of the preconditions for the co-operative sector in Italy to have flourished. Also, in Denmark, the recruitment of well-educated managers had been key to the movement's ability to counter the challenges of a new era. However, Jensen (2016) discussed that newly hired managers educated at business schools contributed to the internal tensions within the co-operative firms. Electorates feared that the co-operative firms were in the process of losing their distinctiveness (Hilson *et al.* 2017; Jensen 2016).

The new interest in co-operatives was connected to the global financial crisis of the mid-2000s, which had reminded us of the weaknesses of the market economy and the insufficiency of public regulation. The stories that surfaced, as the financial crisis unfolded, illustrated that individual profit seeking did not necessarily benefit the majority. The new interest in co-operatives thus resembles the one that occurred during the 1930s recession. Then, in a highly influential book, the American journalist Marquis Childs (1936) presented Sweden as a model society which prompted President Roosevelt to initiate a 1936 inquiry about the "Nordic Middle Way" and the role of co-operatives (Hilson 2013).

Since the financial crisis, and stimulated by the international year of co-operatives in 2012, business historians have argued for the need to increase the focus on co-operatives. A large share of the resulting literature has been permeated by a clear political agenda, presenting the co-operative model as a solution for societal challenges. As Waterhouse (2014) rightfully points out this double ambition to analyze and agitate is somewhat problematic. Still, important new insights have been provided as the study on co-operative business has moved closer to the core of the field. As a sign indicating that the new interest in co-operatives is genuine, a whole chapter of *The Routledge Companion to Business History* (Webster 2017) is devoted to them.

The growing research interest devoted to co-operative business since 2012 has until now predominantly benefited our knowledge of consumer co-operatives. A void is left concerning the producer version of the species and especially their development during the second wave of globalization since the 1980s. Filling that void should be an important direction for future research: a growing attention toward producer co-operatives might tell us something highly relevant regarding co-operatives as partakers in the global economy. Wilson *et al.* (2013: 126–133) showed how the wholesale organization of the English consumer co-operative movement (CWS) became an early MNE in the 1880s and 1890s by setting up purchase offices abroad and by investing in plantations and foreign manufacturing facilities. In a later publication they called for further research into the international expansion of CWS before World War II with a specific focus on why it did not in the end prove more successful (Webster *et al.* 2017). Friberg (2017), with a focus on the interwar period, illustrates how the ICA worked to promote international co-operative trade as well as arguing for the need to establish an institutional framework to handle it. Such an institution was *Nordisk Andelsforbund* (NAF) set up by the consumer co-operative wholesalers in the Nordic countries in 1918. Throughout the 1920s the NAF started to develop multinational activities with a purchase office in London followed with offices in Valencia, Santos, San Francisco, Buenos Aires, Bologna, and Hamburg. The aim was to bypass the middlemen and secure goods for the Nordic co-ops that were not produced locally, such as coffee, dried fruits, and spices (Hummelin 1997).

The above examples illustrate that some members of the co-operative movement from an early stage were "makers of global business." We also know from existing research that producer co-operatives were important in helping farmers access global markets (Fernández 2014; Higgins and Mordhorst 2008, 2015). Which role producer co-operatives have played for local producers to access foreign markets during the recent wave of globalization and the organizational forms taken on to achieve such goals are open questions and we need further investigation to address them. The literature is full of evidence showing how co-operatives historically have been intertwined with different national political agendas and cultures, but it largely fails to answer which links emerged or were revived in the recent wave of globalization. Too little interest has been devoted to the internal tensions of the co-operative sector in a globalized economy: Did the allegedly "timeless" co-operative principles contribute to or hinder the continued success of co-operatives since the 1980s? And under which circumstances have the "eternal" principles in reality been modified in order to secure the continued success of a co-operative business?

Movement or business: tensions and ambiguities

We will argue that the modern-day co-operative sector is inherently threatened by the internal tensions, which we schematically lay out in Table 14.1. Not all individual co-operatives will face all the challenges all the time. Especially small-scale co-ops, part of a new wave of the "sharing economy," may for some time be able to escape some of these tensions. For co-operatives with a longer history, which have expanded beyond a local community and with ambitions for continued growth, the tensions nevertheless have to be taken into account.

Table 14.1 Tensions within the co-operative sector

Stable, long lived, path dependency ↔ Innovation
Social movement ↔ Economic entity
Local, national ↔ Global
Small scale ↔ Big business

Source: developed by the authors.

There might be other tensions but we focus on these because they are rooted in the long history of the co-operatives, and are tensions that under the present influence of globalization have grown and become issues for the co-operatives' internationalization strategies. The figure could thus be read the following way: the values on the left-hand side (stable, movement, local, and small scale) were historically legitimized by the narratives created by the co-operative sector itself, while the values on the right-hand side (innovation, economic entity, global, and big business) have become influential in the general business world today in which large-scale co-operatives engage.

Co-operatives have shown remarkable survival skills. However, one could argue that co-ops often had difficulties being innovative. Many of the larger co-ops of today have their origin in the nineteenth century, and there seems to be a strong tendency for stability and even path dependency. As the insights from the above reviewed literature on co-operatives suggest, co-ops today play a much larger role in mature, labor-intensive, and low-tech industries than in emerging industries based on new inventions and highly skilled labor. Information technology and robotics coupled with ongoing globalization nevertheless also call for innovation in dairies and in retailing, which we will argue makes it necessary for the co-ops to speed up the process of change.

Another inherent ambiguity is between co-operatives as economic enterprises on the one hand, and as part of a social and democratic movement on the other. Co-operatives came into being when a group of people agreed to economically cooperate by sharing investments, responsibilities, and profits. In isolation, this does not necessarily indicate an initiative with a social agenda or responsibility or a pronounced democratic profile. The democratic discourse that draws on historical rhetorical resources and narratives has however become a central part of the idea of the "co-operative movement." In this discourse, co-operatives are seen as social organizations in line with other movements (i.e., for social rights or the labor movement). The idea of co-ops as part of a social movement is built on the narrative that co-operatives constitute an alternative "third sector" in the economy, neither public nor private, neither capitalistic nor socialist. The need for such a sector is based on the argument that privately owned companies in their quest for profit often turn into "villains" acting against the interest of society as a whole by creating cartels, putting the environment at risk (cf. Bergquist; Stokes and Miller both in this volume), or by suppressing their workforce. The co-operatives on the other hand, according to the narrative, work for the collective good and for the less privileged classes. The duality between the economic activities of the co-operative and the social ambitions is often reflected in the way co-operatives are organized: a business side is run by professional managers, while an association side is meant to secure the relationship with the members and to administer "movement like" activities such as educational programs. The structural tension between being a business that has to be competitive on the market and at the same time being an association with moral responsibilities is not an easy one to balance.

Similarly, a tension seems today to exist between local commitment and big business. The Pioneers created a small-scale shop where all members were meant to play an active part (Wilson *et al.* 2013). Since then the co-operative idea has been clearly linked to the role of the local community. Co-operatives are to play an active part in people's everyday life, and the members are to take part in the co-operative through its democratic bodies. As opposed to that, multinational big business was traditionally framed as evil in the co-operative narratives: the need for co-operatives arose in the first place when neither the state nor big business could secure the interest of the middle and lower classes (Hilson 2017; Patmore 2017). But today many long-lived co-operatives have grown big themselves.

Taken together the tensions mentioned above create a challenge for co-operatives in a globalized economy. The processes of globalization create a push toward economies of scale reaching across borders, which historically have been challenging for co-operatives to embrace (Webster *et al.* 2017). This we will illustrate through the analysis of two Danish cases: FDB/Coop as a consumer co-operative, and Arla as a producer co-operative dairy company. Both of them are market leaders: Coop holds more than 35 percent of the Danish retail market for food-stuff and Arla controls more than 90 percent of Danish milk processing. Despite their success on the national market, both have faced the pressure of globalization but have reacted to it differently: Arla originated as a merger between the leading Danish and Swedish dairies in 2000, and has since then developed into a multinational dairy business. Coop tried to internationalize through a merger with the Swedish and Norwegian counterparts in 2002 to form Coop Norden. This merger, however, fell apart in 2007.

The co-operative movement in Denmark in a historical perspective

In Denmark the co-operative idea was first tried out in the 1850s based on English and German models (Mordhorst 2008, 2014). The first co-operatives were consumer based but experienced very limited success until 1866, when a co-operative in Thisted, in the northern part of Jutland, was opened and became the first sustainable co-operative in Denmark (Thestrup 1986). In Thisted, the vision was to create a grocery store as well as to educate the workers of the town to become enlightened consumers and good citizens. Hereafter the idea spread relatively fast to other villages and towns. It was, however, not the spread of consumer co-operatives alone that came to characterize the development in Denmark, rather it was the spread of the co-operative idea to other sectors. Co-operative business became a central element in Denmark's transformation from a nation in deep crisis in the middle of the nineteenth century to a modern and relative prosperous nation by the turn of the twentieth century. Still, exactly which role the co-operative sector played has recently triggered intense debate among historians (Lampe and Sharp 2015; Boje 2016).

In Denmark, co-operatives came to play a role not only as businesses but also in regard to the shaping of a grand narrative about the entire modernization of the country. The *Danish Encyclopedia* thus describes the cooperative movement as follows:

> An understanding of co-operation [in Denmark] cannot be based on its particular legal, financial or organizational characteristics alone, but must also include the historical and cultural community, which has its roots in the structure of the rural community in the late 19th century. In the minds of the public, the Co-operative Movement is viewed as a unique economic/democratic Danish tradition, which is important to the rise of modern Denmark.
>
> *(Lund 2004: 38)*

The co-operative sector was able to gain such a position in the Danish self-conception due to its rise in a period of crisis in Denmark. In 1864 – two years before the Thisted co-operative opened – Denmark was defeated in a war against Prussia and was forced to withdraw from the duchy of Schleswig-Holstein. As a result, Denmark was reduced to being a small state and heavily dependent on agricultural exports. When the grain prices dropped in the 1870s it threatened the entire Danish economy, but a way forward was found by rearranging the agricultural production to animal products – especially bacon and butter – valued in the new international economy. The co-operative organizational form came to play a decisive role in this transformation of Danish farming (Henriksen and Kærgård 2014).

The establishment of the first co-dairy plant in Hjedding in 1882 is usually mentioned as the beginning of an entire co-operative sector that reached beyond retailing (Bjørn 1998: 71). Ten years later, 1,100 co-dairy plants had been established (Bjørn 1988: 372). From here on the co-operative model spread rapidly to a wide range of other industries related to farming such as slaughterhouses, corn, feed businesses, manure, egg transport, and insurance. It is estimated that during World War I more than 4,000 co-operative businesses existed in Denmark (Drejer 1929: 45). Around 1900, co-operative umbrella organizations were formed and they became highly politically influential (Bukstil 1974).

The *Co-operative Magazine*, published by the Co-operative Commission from 1899, originally coined the term "co-operative movement." The concept was fleshed out in a range of books with the words "co-operative movement" in the title that were published after 1910 (Degerbøl 1931; Hertel 1917; Kruchow 1946; Nielsen 1910; Ravnholt 1943). In the bulk of this literature, co-operatives are seen as part of a moral and social movement with higher aims than just making money for its shareholders. Severin Jørgensen, one of the founders of FDB and one of the founding fathers of the Danish co-operative movement in 1903 wrote:

> The movement has a far higher, far more important goal than increasing the population's economic well being. The most important and most meaningful goal is to lift the population to a higher moral level, to make the members of the co-operative movement more competent and more independent, but most importantly, to make them better people.
>
> *(quoted in: Drejer 1929: 33)*

Jørgensen was part of a genre portraying the co-operative movement in a purely positive light. This stream of literature placed farming and the co-operative movement as the heroes of Denmark's more recent history by making the co-operative movement a social, cultural, and national movement representing the best aspects of the Danish national character. The co-operative movement in Denmark was thus established on a nationalistic ideological foundation. The paradox is, however, that the co-operative bacon and butter production not only lifted Denmark out of the economic and ideological crises after the defeat in 1864; it also integrated Denmark into the globalized and work-divided economy.

Globalization and competition changed the structure of the co-operatives in Denmark. While they spread with an impressive speed in the late nineteenth century, the structural development since the 1960s has been reversed. The co-operatives have merged into still larger units. In 1993, the Danish Dairy Company (Mejeriselskabet Danmark, MD) reached a market share of more than 90 percent seen in relation to the amount of milk being processed in Denmark. The co-operative slaughter house Danish Crown reached a similar share of the meat and bacon market in 2002 after a take-over of the last privately owned slaughter house (Strandskov 2011). FDB (renamed Coop in 2002) reached a marked share of more than 35 percent of the grocery retail market in the 1990s and had by then taken over two-thirds of the former independent co-operatives.

The structural development was a response to the evolution of a new global economy changing the Danish business system (Mordhorst 2008). The problem however was that this same concentration threatened the co-operative identity of being different. The co-operative sector narrated and branded itself as a movement focused on small-scale activities easy to influence by individuals and connected to democratic ideals and national identity. The fight against monopolies and cartels controlled by big business had been a cornerstone in these narratives.

From the Danish Dairy Company to Arla

After the acquisition of the second largest dairy in Denmark in 1999 and controlling more than 90 percent of the domestic market for milk, the management of MD realized that they had more or less reached the limit for growth in Denmark. Since around 1990 they had believed that international expansion would be necessary if the company were to survive on a still more globalized market for dairy products (Bigum and Kjelstrup 2007: 494). Thus, in 1990 MD had made their first acquisition outside Denmark by buying Associated Fresh Foods, the fifth largest dairy company in Britain. Another breakthrough came when MD – then the largest dairy in Scandinavia – joined in a strategic co-operation with the second largest dairy in Scandinavia, the Swedish co-operative dairy Arla in 1995. The strategic alliance led to a full-fledged merger in 2000 under the Arla brand. With this merger, a milestone was reached. The former Danish co-operative movement had become a leading multinational business and was ready to take up the challenges of a still more globalized market for foodstuffs. The "home market" was now Sweden, Britain, and Denmark making up nearly three-quarters of Arla's turnover. The ambition was to become the leading dairy on the European continent (Bigum and Kjelstrup 2007: 506).

A range of factors had made Arla's management consider international expansion attractive and even necessary. Most prominently, Danish membership of the European Union had made Brussels more important than Copenhagen in central areas of legislation, planning, subsidies, and trade. Second, the process of internationalization and globalization had contributed to instituting a much less regulated and more liberal business system in Denmark. A third motivation was the realization that agriculture and dairy production had gradually lost its importance for the Danish economy; dairy production had become just one among other export industries. And last, a general belief in the need for economies of scale and continued growth for all business had come to permeate the Danish business system.

Arla grew to become a large company, but the changes came not without failures and problems. In the decade from 2003 to 2013, Arla suffered from a more or less permanently bad reputation in Denmark. The reputation crises were closely connected to the idea of the co-operative movement as a special Danish and local way of doing business. Even though Arla was still structured as a co-operative, it had become everything the co-operative narrative traditionally had distanced itself from – an industrial multinational with monopolistic attitudes resembling the business practices of its capitalistic opponents.

The series of crises began in December 2003 when the small Hirtshals Dairy, located in northern Jutland, accused Arla Foods of exploiting its size to keep the Hirtshals Dairy's products off the shelves of the major supermarket chains. This started a media storm against Arla. The Danish Competition Authority took up the case and charges were filed against Arla based on Hirtshals' claims. On February 10, 2006, Arla was found guilty of engaging in unfair business practices on the national market and was penalized with the largest fine of its kind in Denmark. Hirtshals' accusation in December 2003 caused a snowball effect and, in the months that followed, Arla faced fresh accusations in the media on a weekly basis. In the media, Arla was presented as a near-monopoly that exploited the dairy farmers, bullied the smaller dairies, and made the consumers pay too much for their products. Danish consumers started to boycott Arla's products. Arla answered with apologies and promised to change. As Åke Modig, the CEO of Arla said in an interview in 2004:

> Arla is a fantastic company, and we have good prospects to win next year's battle for survival against the large dairy plants of Europe. But we also need to win the battle in Denmark. We have to teach the Danish population to love Arla.
>
> *(Arlas nye profil, Jyllands-Posten, January 18, 2004)*

However, Arla was not successful in that regard. The consumer boycott prevailed and Arla's market share in Denmark decreased by more than 10 percent. The problems at home came to influence Arla's possibilities abroad. In December 2004, Arla declared that it would initiate "the largest business fusion in Danish history, which would create the largest dairy enterprise in the world" by amalgamating with the Dutch dairy plant Campina. However, the idea never became reality and the project was abandoned by the spring of 2005 (e.g., see "Spildt mælk," *Jyllands-Posten*, April 22, 2005). One reason was national conflicts between the managements of Arla and Campina but another was that Arla's tarnished image at home had led to doubts within Campina's management (Bigum and Kjelstrup 2007: 541).

Also on the international stage, Arla had to deal with reputation problems. In 2006, through a series of misfortunes, Arla became a central part of what came to be known as the "Danish Cartoon Crisis." The conflict had started with the publication of twelve cartoons of the prophet Muhammad in the Danish newspaper *Jyllands-Posten* in September of 2005. This action was regarded as blasphemy and was denounced by Muslims in both Denmark and abroad. In January, religious and political leaders in Saudi Arabia called for a boycott of all Danish products. As Arla was by far the most important Danish business in the Middle East, the boycott became synonymous with boycotting Arla.

Though the crises of Hirtshals, Campina, and the Muhammad cartoons have different backgrounds, they were all placed in the tension between national and global concerns. The crises resulted in problems on the national market and had a negative effect on Arla's global strategy. The structural development and takeovers that lead to the Hirtshals' crisis was at least partly initiated by the pressure of international competition, the merger with Campina failed due to the national heritage of Arla, and the cartoon crisis had consequences for Arla both in the Middle Eastern market and in the Danish home market.

While Arla suffered from bad-will in Denmark, in Sweden it continued to be perceived as a high-quality brand. That was possible because Danes, despite the formal merger, still predominantly considered Arla to be Danish, whereas Swedes considered Arla to be Swedish. Both Danes and Swedes could at the time find support in empirical evidence: the Arla name came from the Swedish dairy which had been merged into the new Arla giving Swedes reason to consider Arla as Swedish, whereas Danes related to the fact that the company headquarters were located in Denmark. The logo and graphical design contained elements that could be traced back to the two national dairies, and Arla's communication on national webpages in the years after the merger told stories with national angles. If you opened the section entitled "History" at the Danish webpage (Arla.dk), you would get a narrative that told the story of Arla as a company with Danish origin. When you opened the same section at the Swedish webpage (Arla.se) you would get a narrative that claimed that Arla, throughout history, had been a Swedish company. While Arla as a business on international markets acted as a multinational, in Denmark and Sweden they still legitimized themselves as national co-operatives, addressing the different national cultures and historical narratives.

Starting in 2008 Arla began to change strategy and merge the two cultures. First, it replaced the individual history sites at the webpages with one common narrative told in a short video with the plot "it started in Scandinavia and now we are a global company" (Arla Danmark 2010). By focusing on a shared Scandinavian heritage, Arla tried to tell its history in a way that could bridge national cultures. Furthermore, the company downplayed the heritage all together by painstakingly reducing the amount of information about the time before the merger in 2000. Today there is nothing but a short statement saying that Arla has its origins in Denmark and Sweden but that the "cooperative idea also flourished in other countries and through recent mergers cooperative owners in the UK, the Netherlands, Germany, Belgium and Luxembourg have joined Arla Foods. And we will continue to grow stronger" (Arla n.d.). This new type of storytelling reflects that Arla during the last years has developed into a truly global company and has decoupled itself from national identities. Between 2008 and 2016 Arla experienced rapid growth and nearly doubled the amount of milk processed (Arla Danmark 2008).

From FDB to Coop Norden to Coop Denmark

Competitive positioning was also at the core of the second case of a co-operative going global presented in this chapter. In 1997, the management of the co-operative FDB sought advice from the consulting firm McKinsey and Company as they saw a desperate need to improve their competitive position. In the late 1990s FDB acted as a wholesale organization serving the entire consumer co-operative sector in Denmark, but also acted as a retailer through direct ownership of the Fakta discount chain stores, the Irma supermarkets, and the majority of the Brugsen and Kvickly stores located in the larger cities. In addition, individual co-operatives existed with a stronghold in smaller communities. Since 1970 the focus of the FDB management had been on the national competitive situation and the problems in dealing with the main competitor, Dansk Supermarked. In the late 1990s the FDB management nevertheless feared that multinational competitors like Royal Ahold, Tesco, or Carrefour would soon enter Denmark and make the competitive environment even fiercer.

The McKinsey consultants concluded that FDB lagged seriously behind its rivals in terms of efficiency and in the ability to engage in swift decision-making. Thus, the consultants only confirmed the beliefs held by FDB's professional management that the co-operative model had turned into an impediment for long-term survival: democratic governing bodies interfered in matters they had no professional understanding for, labor movement representatives hindered change, and individual co-operative societies served their own special interests rather than contributing to the competitive position of the entire consumer co-operative sector (Jensen 2016: 331–338).

To counter the challenge of globalization and solve the inherent organizational problems of FDB at the same time, the FDB management presented for its board of directors a merger with either Royal Ahold or Tesco as an attractive solution. The FDB board of directors should work to secure the competitive position of FDB, but at the same time they should represent the co-operative membership and the co-operative ideals. Therefore they were very skeptical toward a merger with a privately owned foreign multinational. They agreed with the management that drastic solutions were needed to keep the consumer co-operation competitive in the long run, but wanted to maintain co-operative distinctiveness. In that situation they favored a merger with the Norwegian and Swedish consumer co-operatives. It would create the economies of scale they believed globalization called for, set the stage for an organizational new-orientation, and at the same time make it possible to maintain a co-operative core (Jensen 2016: 339–356).

After long discussions, Coop Norden came into being in 2002 as a full-fledged merger of the business entities of the consumer co-operatives in Scandinavia. A new enterprise – according to turnover ranking tenth among Scandinavian firms – had been created, controlling 3,000 shops and employing 64,000 people. Coop Norden was organized as a joint stock company with FDB owning 38 percent, NKL in Norway 20 percent, and KF in Sweden 42 percent of the shares (Jensen 2016: 357). Coop Norden would handle the business activities, while co-operative member activities would still take place on a purely national basis. The movement would own a business but no longer run it. Coop Norden should be able to operate at a safe distance from co-operative members, who now solely could use their democratic right to appoint members to the Coop Norden general assembly which in turn elected the members of the Coop Norden board of directors (Ericson 2006). Still, it soon became apparent that Coop Norden as a business would not have an uncomplicated life.

Seen from the perspective of the FDB management, Coop Norden should solve the problems related to insufficient financial results and a threatening debt through the advantages of economy of scale, while at the same time securing a more stringent governance structure making it possible to respond to competitive pressure with more agility.

In addition to the Danes though, the Norwegians and Swedes also brought their own agendas into Coop Norden (Weiss 2009: 118). In Norway, NKL had remained a wholesale organization and was not running shops on its own. For them, Coop Norden should ideally work only to secure common purchases in order to reduce costs (Lange 2006: 572). Seen from a Swedish perspective, Coop Norden should similarly improve the competitive strength of the consumer co-operative movement, but it was also of pivotal importance that co-operative distinctiveness was kept alive in the process. In Sweden, co-operative heritage proved to have a slightly different meaning from its meaning in Denmark. The Danish consumer co-operative movement had from the outset navigated a tension between a rural co-operative tradition with producers' co-operatives like dairies and slaughterhouses and links to the liberal party on one side, and workers' co-operative movements with a stronghold in the larger cities and links to the social democratic party on the other. At least in the assessment of the Danish born Coop Norden chairman, Ebbe Lundgaard, that proved not to be the case for consumer cooperation in Sweden, which he came to see as too closely associated with the social democratic party (Weiss 2009: 123).

For the FDB management the primary vision for Coop Norden was to improve competitiveness and Coop Norden's first year did not prove convincing in that regard. Therefore Ebbe Lundgaard was glad in 2003 to present the Swede Svante Nilsson as the new Coop Norden CEO. It was assumed that Nilsson would speed up the integration process to position Coop Norden "clear-cut and strong in the market-place" (Gamelby, 2002). Svante Nilsson came with experience from ICA, which for long had been the main competitor for the Swedish consumer co-operative sector. Nilsson knew retailing, yet the Swedish members of the Coop Norden board came to believe that he sacrificed co-operative principles in the process of making Coop Norden a profitable business. Hence Svante Nilsson, to the frustration of chairman Lundgaard, was fired in 2005 by a majority vote of the board. As stated at the time by Börje Fors from KF, "what is right for a capitalist isn't always right for a co-operator" (*Berlinske Tidende* 2005).

Both the conflict concerning Nilsson and the different views on the political implications of the co-operative heritage illustrated that divergent understandings of the role of a "third sector" in the economy existed between the partners. In both Denmark and Sweden co-operative business had become entwined in broader national cultural understandings, which problematize the notion made by the ICA about the shared core of the co-operative sector. The ideological non-alignment made it difficult to create international co-operative business (Ekberg and Jensen 2018).

At the same time as discussions were taking place in the Coop Norden governing bodies concerning ideology, it became clear that globalization was not reshaping the Nordic market for grocery retailing the way co-operative managers had envisaged. Consumer taste remained highly differentiated across borders making it much more difficult to reap the scale advantages that Coop Norden's vision rested on. Privately owned retail chains to a large extent came to the same conclusion and still today national players dominate food retailing in the region (Ekberg and Jensen 2018).

A flawed understanding for the impact of globalization on retailing combined with ideological disagreements in 2005 made it clear that Ebbe Lundgaard's and the FDB management's vision for a strongly integrated Coop Norden had to be buried. Lundgaard stepped down to a position as vice-chairman, while Nilsson's successor reinstated individual management in each

Scandinavian country. In 2006 it became clear internally that Coop Norden did not have a future, and in 2007 Coop Norden was formally dissolved. The consumer co-operatives in Scandinavia went back to being solely national in their orientation (Jensen 2016: 357–373).

To explain the survival of an isolated consumer co-operative in Australia, Balnave and Patmore (2015) stress the ability of the co-operative to engage with the local community. Local engagement was not seen as a strength, however, for the consumer co-operative leaders in Denmark. They believed globalization called for economies of scale and clear-cut strategies laid out by well-informed managers with retail competences rather than strong feelings for a co-operative heritage. After the failure of Coop Norden the value of local ties has at least to some extent been rediscovered in the Danish consumer co-operation, which has been able to maintain its position as market leader despite the Coop Norden failure and the vanished ambition for becoming a maker of global business.

Conclusions

The co-operative business form is an interesting case of nineteenth-century globalization, and how globalization historically has emerged with unintended consequences. The cooperative societies were in their origin responses to local problems, but from its roots in Rochdale the movement swiftly spread geographically and beyond retail into other sectors. The co-operative movement also created global institutions such as the ICA and NAF, while the wholesale organization of the British consumer co-operative movement established its own network of offices throughout the world to secure supplies. And still in 2013 it was estimated that worldwide more than one billion individuals were members of a co-operative (Worldwatch Institute 2012).

Despite the failure of Coop Norden, both Arla and Coop today stand as strong examples of the continued importance of co-operatives in a global era. The two examples nevertheless also illustrate how co-operatives became embedded in national cultural contexts thereby problematizing the prominent view held by the ICA that the co-operative sector rests on common ground. The entwinement between national cultures and co-operative ideology became an impediment when co-operative leaders wished to become makers of global business. Further research is needed on whether this local embeddedness played a more crucial role in the Nordic setting than elsewhere because the co-operative sector here was seen as crucial for modernizing entire nations.

Both Arla and Coop rest on a long and influential heritage. The heritage proved not to be a total advantage around the turn of the new millennium. Both co-operatives tried to respond to a new competitive situation with mergers, fast growths, and economies of scale. Mergers were for both also seen as a shortcut to decouple the movement and democratic part from the business side, and to ultimately give more autonomy to the business side. More freedom to pursue strict business logic was seen as pivotal in an era of globalization. As such it can be argued that they became makers of global business more out of a defensive and adaptive strategy than an innovative one. When international partners were needed they were found among the co-operative's long established "friends." Yet in the merger process the new companies had a tendency to isomorph and become difficult to distinguish from their privately owned counterparts.

Arla and Coop do however differ in how they handled the ambiguity between national and global. Arla's strategy was in the long run successful, while Coop Norden's proved to be a strategic mistake. The starting point was in many aspects similar. The nationality and national roots of the co-operatives was a challenge in both mergers, even though the mergers took place between partners within Scandinavia that had a long established tradition for collaboration. Three elements might explain the different outcome. (1) They acted in different sectors with different commitments to global markets: more than 80 percent of Arla's products are exported to markets outside Denmark and Sweden. The purpose of the merger was to expand the market share on the international markets. Coop is much more embedded in the national market with many local suppliers, and its turnover is secured through indigenous shops. The main argument behind the creation of Coop Norden was thus to protect domestic markets. (2) Arla's merger was in a business sense developed step-by-step, starting in 1995. In contrast, Coop Norden was created at a time when the Danish and Swedish consumer co-operatives were in crisis and needed fast results. (3) The Arla merger was downplayed in terms of cultural consequences making it possible for both Swedes and Danes in a period of transition to consider the firm respectively both Swedish and Danish. On the structural side though, the Arla merger was done wholeheartedly from the outset with both the business and the association side merged into one organization. At Coop it was the opposite: only the business side was integrated, while national bodies continued to exist on the association side. As challenges were encountered, that made it difficult to agree on a clear-cut strategy. National interest continued to dominate between the owners.

Both Arla and Coop became makers of global business, but only Arla proved able to sustain its business as a multinational entity. We have in this chapter highlighted some of the possible reasons for that. A few of these are related to the co-operative ownership structure, but just as important is the historically created legitimacy. This requires a management that not only possesses a huge historical and contextual knowledge, but also has the skills to handle and use this past for present purposes.

Note

1 This chapter draws on previous research done by Mads Mordhorst and Kristoffer Jensen, most importantly: Mordhorst 2014; Jensen 2016; and Ekberg and Jensen 2018.

References

Alexander, A. (2008), "Format development and retail change: supermarket retailing and the London Co-operative Society," *Business History*, 50 (4), 489–508.

Arla (n.d.), "About us: History," http://mea.arla.com/company/history/ (accessed 11.14.17).

Arla Danmark, *Annual Reports 2008–2016*. Arla, Copenhagen.

Balnave, N. and Patmore, G. (2015), "The outsider consumer co-operative: lessons from the Community Co-operative Store (Nuriootpa), 1944–2010," *Business History*, 57 (8), 1133–1154. https://doi.org/10.10 80/00076791.2015.1015998.

Bamfield, J. (1998), "Consumer-owned community flour and bread societies in the eighteenth and early nineteenth centuries," *Business History*, 40 (4), 16–36.

Bátiz-Lazo, B. and Billings, M. (2012), "New perspectives on not-for-profit financial institutions: organizational form, performance and governance," *Business History*, 54 (3), 309–324.

Battilani, P. and Schröter, H.G. (eds.) (2012), *The cooperative business movement, 1950 to the present: comparative perspectives in business history* (New York: Cambridge University Press).

Battilani, P. and Zamagni, V. (2012), "The managerial transformation of Italian co-operative enterprises 1946–2010," *Business History*, 54 (6), 964–985. https://doi.org/10.1080/00076791.2012.706893.

Berlinske Tidende (2005), "Ebbe Lundgaards vision for Coop Norden lider skibbrud," Berlingske Bus. www.business.dk/content/item/200030 (accessed November 14, 2017).

Bigum, J. and Kjelstrup, P. (2007), *Mælkevejen: fra landsbymejerier til global koncern; Jens Bigums erindringer fortalt til Peter Kjelstrup* (Copenhagen: Hovedland).

Bjørn, C. (1988), *Det danske landbrugs historie*, vol. 3: 1810–1914 (Odense: Landbohistorisk Selskab).

Bjørn, C. (1998), *Dengang Danmark blev moderne: eller historien om de virkelige danske utopi* (Copenhagen: Fremad).

Boje, P. (2016), "Why Denmark became rich: on the history of the Danish Innovation System," in Sogner, K., Lie, E., and Aven, H.B. (eds.), *Entreprenørskap* (Oslo: Novus forlag), 29–56.

Brazda, J. and Scediwy, R. (2011), *A time of crises: consumer co-operatives and their problems around 1990* (Vienna: University of Geneva). https://genos.univie.ac.at/fileadmin/user_upload/genossenschafts wesen/Genos/consum.pdf (accessed April 4, 2019).

Bukstil, J. (1974), *Et enigt Landbrug* (Aarhus: Aarhus Universitetsforlag).

Childs, M.W. (1936), *Sweden: the middle way* (London: Pelican Books).

Davis, L.E. and Payne, P.L. (1958), "From benevolence to business: the story of two savings banks," *Business History Review*, 32 (4), 386–406.

Degerbøl, S. (1931), *Andelsbevægelsen* (Copenhagen: Gyldendalske Boghandel).

Dictionary.com (n.d.), "Cooperative," www.dictionary.com/browse/cooperative (accessed November 14, 2017).

Drejer, A.A. (1929), *Den Danske Andelsbevægelse* (Copenhagen: Martins Forlag).

Ekberg, E. (2012a), "Confronting three revolutions: Western European consumer co-operatives and their divergent development, 1950–2008," *Business History*, 54 (6), 1004–1021. https://doi.org/10.1080/00 076791.2012.706894.

Ekberg, E. (2012b), "Organization: top down or bottom up? The organizational development of consumer cooperatives, 1950–2000," in Battilani, P. and Schröter, H.G. (eds.), *The cooperative business movement, 1950 to the present* (Cambridge: Cambridge University Press), 222–242. https://doi.org/10.1017/CBO9781139237208.012.

Ekberg, E. and Jensen, K. (2018), "The non-globalisation of modern food retailing: the case of the failed Coop Norden merger," *Scandinavian Economic History Review*. https://doi.org/10.1080/03585522.2018.1454340.

Ericson, M. (2006), "Exploring the future exploiting the past," *Journal of Management History*, 12 (2), 121–136. https://doi.org/10.1108/13552520610654032.

Fernández, E. (2014), "Selling agricultural products: farmers' co-operatives in production and marketing, 1880–1930," *Business History*, 56 (4), 547–568. https://doi.org/10.1080/00076791.2013.809524.

Friberg, K. (2017), "A co-operative take on free trade: international ambitions and regional initiatives in international co-operative trade," in Hilson, M., Neunsinger, S., and Patmore, G. (eds.), *A global history of consumer co-operation since 1850: movements and businesses* (Leiden: Brill), 201–225.

Gamelby, P.F. (2002), "Ny koncernchef i COOP Norden," http://finans.dk/artikel/ECE4232326/Ny-koncernchef-i-COOP-Norden/ (accessed November 14, 2017).

Gurney, P.J. (2012), "Co-operation and the 'new consumerism' in interwar England," *Business History*, 54 (6), 905–924. https://doi.org/10.1080/00076791.2012.706896.

Hansen, P.H. (2001), *Da sparekasserne mistede deres uskyld: en historie om sparekasser og samfund i opbrud, 1960–90* (Odense: Odense Universitetsforlag).

Hansen, P.H. (2007), "Organizational culture and organizational change: the transformation of savings banks in Denmark, 1965–1990," *Enterprise & Society*, 8 (4), 920–953. https://doi.org/10.1017/S1467222700006492.

Henriksen, I. and Kærgård, N. (2014), "Dansk landbrugs største og mest succesrige omstilling," *Tidsskrift for landøkonomi*, August, 1–14.

Henriksen, I., Hviid, M., and Sharp, P. (2012), "Law and peace: contracts and the success of the Danish dairy cooperatives," *Journal of Economic History*, 72 (1), 197–224.

Hertel, H. (1917), *Andelsbevægelsen i Danmark* (Copenhagen: Gyldendal).

Higgins, D.M. and Mordhorst, M. (2008), "Reputation and export performance: Danish butter exports and the British market, c.1880–c.1914," *Business History*, 50 (2), 185–204. https://doi.org/10.1080/00076790701868601.

Higgins D.M. and Mordhorst, M. (2015), "Bringing home the 'Danish' bacon: food chains, national branding and Danish supremacy over the British bacon market, c. 1900–1938," *Enterprise & Society*, 16 (1), 141–185. https://doi.org/10.1017/eso.2014.14.

Hilson, M. (2013), "Consumer co-operation and economic crisis: the 1936 Roosevelt inquiry on co-operative enterprise and the emergence of the Nordic 'middle way,'" *Contemporary European History*, 22 (2), 181–198. https://doi.org/10.1017/S0960777313000040.

Hilson, M. (2017), "Consumer co-operation in the Nordic countries, c. 1860–1939," in Hilson, M., Neunsinger, S., and Patmore, G. (eds.), *A global history of consumer co-operation since 1850: movements and businesses* (Leiden: Brill), 121–144.

Hilson, M., Neunsinger, S., and Patmore, G. (eds.) (2017), *A global history of consumer co-operation since 1850: movements and businesses* (Leiden: Brill).

Hobsbawm, E.J. (1983), "Inventing traditions," in E.J. Hobsbawm and Ranger, T.O. (eds.), *The invention of tradition* (Cambridge, New York: Cambridge University Press), 1–14.

Hummelin, K. (1997), *Nordisk Andelsforbund NAF 1918–1993: Konsumentkooperativt samarbete i Norden* (København: Nordisk Andelsforbund).

International Co-operative Alliance (n.d.a), "History of the co-operative movement," https://ica.coop/en/whats-co-op/history-co-operative-movement (accessed July 5, 2017).

International Co-operative Alliance (n.d.b), "Our identity," https://ica.coop/en/what-co-operative (accessed November 14, 2017).

Jensen, K. (2016), *Brugsen: En anderledes forretning? Dansk brugsbevægelse for pastor Sonne til det moderne Coop* (Albertslund: Samvirke).

Jones, G. and Zeitlin, J. (2009), "Introduction," in Jones, G. and Zeitlin, J. (eds.), *The Oxford handbook of business history* (Oxford: Oxford University Press).

Knupfer, A.M. (2013), *Food co-ops in America: communities, consumption, and economic democracy* (Ithaca, NY: Cornell University Press).

Kruchow, E. (1946), *Dansk landbrugs andelsbevægelse* (Copenhagen: Ejnar Munksgaard).

Lampe, M. and Sharp, P. (2015), "How the Danes discovered Britain: the international integration of the Danish dairy industry before 1880," *European Review of Economic History*, 19 (4), 432–453. https://doi.org/10.1093/ereh/hev013.

Lange, E. (ed.) (2006), *Organisert kjøpekraft: forbrukersamvirkets historie i Norge* (Oslo: Pax forlag).

Lund, J. (ed.) (2004), *Den Store Danske Encyklopædi, vol. 1* (Copenhagen, Gyldendal).

McLaughlin, E. (2014), "Profligacy in the encouragement of thrift: savings banks in Ireland, 1817–1914," *Business History*, 56 (4), 569–591. https://doi.org/10.1080/00076791.2013.837887.

Martin, J.I. and Andersen, S. (2008), "Co-operative liberalism: Denmark from 1857 to 2007," in Fellman, S., Iversen, M., Hans, S., and Thue, L. (eds.), *Creating Nordic capitalism: the business history of a competitive periphery* (New York: Palgrave Macmillan), 265–334.

Medina-Albaladejo, F.J. (2015), "Co-operative wineries: temporal solution or efficient firms? The Spanish case during late Francoism, 1970–1981," *Business History*, 57 (4), 589–613. https://doi.org/10.1080/00076791.2014.982105.

Mordhorst, M. (2007), "Fire historier om smør og fortællingens magt," in Christiansen, N.F. (ed.), *Fra kætter til koryfæ: Festskrift til Ole Lange* (Copenhagen: Gyldendal), 102–116.

Mordhorst, M. (2008), "Arla: from decentralised industry to multinational enterprise," in Fellman, S., Iversen, M., Hans, S., and Thue, L. (eds.), *Creating Nordic capitalism: the business history of a competitive periphery* (New York: Palgrave Macmillan), 351–358.

Mordhorst, M. (2014), "Arla and Danish national identity: business history as cultural history," *Business History*, 56 (1), 116–133. https://doi.org/10.1080/00076791.2013.818422.

Nielsen, A. (1910), *Andelsbevægeslen* (Copenhagen: Gyldendal).

Patmore, G. (2017), "Fighting monopoly and enhancing democracy: a historical overview of US consumer co-operatives," in Hilson, M., Neunsinger, S., and Patmore, G. (eds.), *A global history of consumer co-operation since 1850: movements and businesses* (Leiden: Brill), 507–526.

Perotin, V. (2012), "The performance of workers' co-operatives," in Battilani, P. and Schröter, H.G. (eds.), *The cooperative business movement, 1950 to the present: comparative perspectives in business history* (New York: Cambridge University Press), 195–221.

Purvis, M. (2006), "Stocking the store: co-operative retailers in north-east England and systems of wholesale supply circa 1860-77," *Business History*, 40 (4), 55–78. https://doi.org/10.1080/00076799800000338.

Ravnholt, H. (1943), *Den danske andelsbevægelse* (Copenhagen: Det danske selskab).

Robertson, N. (2012), "Collective strength and mutual aid: financial provisions for members of co-operative societies in Britain," *Business History*, 54 (6), 925–944. https://doi.org/10.1080/00076791.2012.706895.

Rochdale Society (1844), *Laws and objects of the Rochdale Society of Equitable Pioneers* (Rochdale: Jesse Hall).

Sandgren, F. (2009), "From 'peculiar stores' to 'a new way of thinking': discussions in self-service in Swedish trade journals, 1935–1955," *Business History*, 51 (5), 734–753. https://doi.org/10.1080/00076790903125636.

Sørensen, P. and Pedersen, K. (2007), "Limits to scale and scope: the failure of a Danish slaughterhouse merger in 1890/91," *Business History*, 49 (5), 595–624. https://doi.org/10.1080/00076790701695566.

Strandskov, J. (2011), *Konkurrence og koncentration: svineslagteriernes fusionshistorie 1960–2010* (Odense: Syddansk universitetsforlag).

Thestrup, P. (1986), *Nærbutik og næringslovs-omgåelse: en undersøgelse af brugsforeningerne og deres placering i innovationsprocessen i Danmark mellem 1850 og 1919* (Odense: Odense universitetsforlag).

Toms, S. (2012), "Producer co-operatives and economic efficiency: evidence from the nineteenth century cotton textile industry," *Business Industry*, 54 (6), 855–882. https://doi.org/10.1080/00076791.2012.706900.

Wadhwani, R.D. (2011), "The institutional foundations of personal finance: innovation in U.S. savings banks, 1880s–1920s," *Business History Review*, 85 (3), 499–528. www.jstor.org/stable/41301432.

Waterhouse, B.C. (2014), "The cooperative business movement, 1950 to the present," *Business History Review*, 88 (1), 227–230. https://doi.org/10.1017/S0007680513001487.

Webster, A. (2017), "The 'third sector': co-operatives, mutual, charities and social enterprises," in Wilson, J.F., Toms, S., Jong, A.d., and Buchnea, E. (eds.), *The Routledge companion to business history* (London, New York: Routledge), 123–138.

Webster, A. and Walton, J.K. (2012), "Introduction," *Business History*, 54 (6), 825–832. https://doi.org/10.1080/00076791.2012.706897.

Webster, A., Wilson, J.F., and Vorberg-Rugh, R. (2017), "Going global: the rise of the CWS as an international commercial and political actor, 1863–1950: scoping an agenda for further research," in Hilson, M., Neunsinger, S., and Patmore, G. (eds.), *A global history of consumer co-operation since 1850: movements and businesses* (Leiden: Brill), 559–583.

Weiss, K. (2009), *Når vikinger slås: hvorfor skandinaviske virksomheder har det så svært med hinanden* (Copenhagen: Kirsten Weiss).

Whyman, P.B. (2012), "Co-operative principles and the evolution of the 'dismal science': the historical interaction between co-operative and mainstream economics," *Business History*, 54 (6), 833–854. https://doi.org/10.1080/00076791.2012.706903.

Wilson, J.F., Webster, A., and Vorberg-Rugh, R. (eds.) (2013), *Building co-operation: a business history of the co-operative group, 1863–2013* (Oxford: Oxford University Press).

Wilson, W.E. (1967), *The angel and the serpent: the story of new harmony* (Indiana, IN: Indiana University Press).

Worldwatch Institute (2012), "Membership in co-operative businesses reaches 1 billion," www.worldwatch.org/membership-co-operative-businesses-reaches-1-billion (accessed November 14, 2017).

Zerubavel, E. (2003). *Time maps: collective memory and the social shape of the past* (London: University of Chicago Press).

15

BUSINESS GROUPS

Asli M. Colpan and Alvaro Cuervo-Cazurra

Introduction

Business groups have risen to play essential roles in industrial development since the Second Industrial Revolution in the late nineteenth century. While business groups have been a crucial organizational form in many economies, they have been most resilient and remained dominant actors in contemporary emerging economies (Colpan *et al.*, 2010; Colpan and Hikino, 2018a; Khanna and Yafeh, 2007). Business groups have generated an extensive and increasing literature that has mostly focused on their diversification strategies and pyramidal structures, and the performance implications of group affiliation (e.g., Carney *et al.*, 2011; Cuervo-Cazurra, 2006, 2018a; Khanna and Rivkin, 2001; Morck and Yeung, 2003; see literature reviews in Colpan and Hikino, 2010; Colli and Colpan, 2016; Khanna and Yafeh, 2007). However, the literature has paid less attention to the internationalization of business groups as an organizational form, and to how companies affiliated with business groups are influenced by the parent organization in their internationalization (e.g., Guillen, 2000; Kumar *et al.*, 2012; Tan and Meyer, 2010; Yiu, 2011; see a review in Yaprak and Karademir, 2010).

Hence, in this chapter, we examine the internationalization strategies taken by business groups to understand how business groups act as "makers of global business." After providing a broad discussion of different varieties of business groups and their internationalization patterns in historical context since the nineteenth century, we concentrate on the cases of emerging market business groups for analytical focus and logical clarity. These emerging market business groups have shown active involvement in overseas markets, especially since the implementation of pro-market reforms after the 1980s induced them to improve the competitiveness of their component businesses (Cuervo-Cazurra *et al.*, 2019). Advanced economy business groups also expanded their international presence in this period, while at the same time several of them refocused their product portfolios (Colpan and Hikino, 2018a). We focus on emerging market business groups after the 1980s for two reasons. First, emerging market business groups, and consequently their internationalization, differ in their basic resource endowments and institutional settings from those in advanced economies. Firms in emerging economies often lack the support of superior national innovation, capital, and educational systems that have helped the internationalization of companies in industrialized economies. Second, research on emerging economy business groups and the internationalization of their firms has surged recently, providing new and rich material.

We examine the case of the Koç group, the largest and one of the most internationalized Turkish business groups, with operations in automotive, consumer electronics, energy and petrochemicals, banking and insurance, tourism, and information technology. This broad examination of the internationalization of business groups at the entire group-level in an evolutionary perspective differentiates the present chapter from previous research on the topic. As such, the case serves as the basis for understanding the internationalization of business groups in emerging economies and the identification of the following conclusions.

First, we propose and explain how the affiliation of a company with a business group provides it with not only benefits, but also constraints on its internationalization. On the one hand, business groups assist component firms with the financial, managerial, and knowledge support needed to undertake investments that are critically lacking in emerging markets and that form the basis for internationalization. On the other hand, membership in a business group may constrain internationalization because affiliated firms may have fewer incentives to internationalize given their advantageous and often dominant positions in domestic markets.

Second, we propose and explain how the internationalization of emerging market business groups has been driven by the adoption of pro-market reforms that have supported their global expansion since the 1980s. Such reforms had critical effects on the timing and momentum of internationalization of business groups as the component firms were forced to improve their competitiveness. This is illustrated in the Koç group's accelerated internationalization efforts as the country opened up its domestic markets to overseas competition after the 1980s.

The rest of this chapter is organized as follows. In the next section, we provide a brief overview of the literature on the internationalization of business groups in historical context to present a broad picture of the topic. We then introduce our arguments on the influence of business groups on internationalization in emerging markets. We illustrate these with a historical overview of the internationalization of the Turkish Koç group. We conclude with suggestions for future studies and the overall impact on the development of global business.

Business groups and internationalization: historical context

Business groups are a collection of legally independent firms operating in unrelated product markets and connected via equity and other formal and informal ties.[1] Business groups can be considered under the category of "multi-unit" enterprises, which consist of a headquarters unit and operating units that illustrate the division of labor between the task of administrative control and the actual production of goods and services (Colpan and Hikino, 2010). Business groups differ from other organizational models especially regarding their strategy and structure. First, they show technology- and market-unrelated product portfolios. Second, their operating units are structured in legally independent subsidiaries and affiliates that are connected via multiple ties; those units are often partially (rather than wholly) owned by the headquarters.

Table 15.1 illustrates the difference between business groups and other multi-unit enterprises. It shows that business groups differ from other multi-unit enterprises as they are composed of legally independent firms that operate in unrelated industries and have a degree of coordination, control, and ownership links. Thus, business groups differ from acquisitive conglomerates (no strategic coordination), multidivisional firms (no legally independent firms and no unrelated diversification), multinational firms (no unrelated diversification), or holding companies (no strategic coordination and no unrelated diversification).

There is a perception that business groups are an organizational form characteristic of emerging markets, known by various names such as *grupos económicos* in Latin America or *chaebol* in South Korea, since many of the largest companies in emerging economies are linked to business

Table 15.1 Business groups and other multi-unit enterprises

Characteristics					Type of enterprise
Legally independent firms	Ownership link[1]	Central control	Strategic coordination	Unrelated diversification	
Yes	Yes (often partial)	Yes	Yes[2]	Yes	(Diversified) business group
Yes	Yes	Yes	No	Yes	Acquisitive conglomerates, private equity
No	Yes	Yes	Yes	No	Chandlerian multidivisional enterprise
Yes	Yes	Yes	Yes	No	Multinational enterprise
Yes	Yes	Yes[3]	No	No	"Holding-company"[3]

Notes

The above classifications give the archetypal characteristics of some of the comparable organizational models.

1 Ownership link here denotes equity ties between the different units of the organization.

2 Conventionally, often limited and unsystematic.

3 The "holding company" model is based on Chandler-Williamson, which includes a pure holding company with limited and *lose* control of operating subsidiaries that are concentrated on focused or narrowly related product categories

groups. For example, among the largest publicly listed firms in Forbes (2017) one finds the South Korean Samsung Electronics, which is part of Samsung group's operations in construction and real estate, consumer electronics, medical services, shipbuilding, and financial services; the Chinese technology conglomerate Alibaba operating in e-commerce, finance, artificial intelligence, information technology services, distribution, and media; the Indian conglomerate Reliance Industries that has operations in telecommunications, oil and gas, refining and petrochemicals, retail, biotechnology, and transportation; and the Saudi holding Saudi Basic Industries Corporation that operates in chemicals, fertilizers, and metals.

Many of the billionaires from emerging markets derive their wealth from the ownership of business groups. For example, among the list of billionaires in Forbes (2018), one finds Carlos Slim Helu of Mexico whose wealth comes from telecommunication, construction, mining, real estate, and consumer goods firms; Wang Jianlin of China whose wealth is associated with commercial real estate, hotels, tourism, and entertainment; Gennady Timchenko of Russia, who has investments in gas, petrochemicals, railways, and construction; and Mukesh Ambani of India whose wealth is derived from oil and gas, telecommunications, petrochemicals, and retail.

However, business groups are not exclusively an emerging market phenomenon; they have also played critical roles in the world's most advanced economies especially in Europe since the late nineteenth century and they continue to be a prevalent form of large enterprise in many developed economies. For instance, the Wallenberg group in Sweden is presently active in engineering, finance, wood and paper, pharmaceuticals, and medical equipment industries and others; and the Exor group in Italy operates in insurance, motor vehicles, heavy machinery, media, and sports management (see Colpan and Hikino, 2018a; Jones and Khanna, 2006; Morck, 2005).

We argue that the internationalization of business groups can be understood in three broad categories depending on the historical context in which they were formed: trading, early industrializing, and late industrializing business groups. The contextual conditions can primarily be understood in terms of the period of industrialization of the national economy (early industrializing nations that underwent their initial phase of industrialization by the late nineteenth to early twentieth century, and late industrializing ones had their modern economic growth in the twentieth century and especially after the 1950s) and the economic nature of central institutions within the groups (overseas trading companies versus banks and financial institutions) (Colpan and Hikino, 2018b). The three types of traditional business groups, however, should not be viewed as a comprehensive set of business groups and patterns of internationalization that were prevalent at a particular time in history. Instead, they show how the prevailing types of business groups within a specific developmental context have followed various internationalization patterns.

The first type is the trading business groups. Firms in early industrializing economies used the abundant capital in those economies to invest abroad in the mid to late nineteenth century. In some economies, such as Britain, business groups were formed to exploit market imperfections in developing, and particularly colonial, economies (Jones, 2000). Their objective was to take advantage of investment opportunities in those developing countries that were at the initial stage of industrialization and lacked domestic capital. These groups often had contacts with colonial administrators and local businesses in the regions where they invested, and leveraged their regional knowledge competencies. These business groups were thus international from their beginning, operating in a variety of foreign nations (Jones and Khanna, 2006). Examples of these groups are overseas merchant business groups, such as the British-trading company centered groups Swire's and Jardine Matheson, and the US overseas groups Grace and United Fruit, which were established in the mid to late nineteenth century (Jones, 2000; Jones and Colpan, 2010; Hikino and Bucheli, 2018). The merchant houses were the core firm within each group, whereas their separately listed or incorporated affiliates operated plantations, mines, processing facilities, and others. For instance, Harrisons and Crosfield was founded as a Liverpool-based partnership in the 1840s and managed tea trading and rubber plantations, as well as import, shipping, and insurance agencies, mostly in South Asia and Southeast Asia. The overseas companies were placed in publicly quoted entities in which Harrisons and Crosfield held equity and board positions (Jones and Colpan, 2010).

The second type is the early industrializing business groups. These groups were bank-centered groups appearing in the late nineteenth to early twentieth centuries in countries like Belgium, Germany, and Sweden. In those groups, the commercial and investment banks functioned as reorganizing mechanisms by restructuring existing industrial firms and forming business groups around the banks (Colpan and Hikino, 2018b). In these instances, banks (or financial holdings linked to banks after the 1930s when banks experienced limitations on their control of industrial enterprises) reorganized large industrial firms with proprietary resources and capabilities in technology and brands. Business groups served as providers of capital when necessary, but the internationalization of the industrial companies often targeted additional revenues for those firms to exploit their capabilities. Swedish industrial firms belonging to the biggest business group in the country, Wallenberg group, fit this case (Larsson and Peterrson, 2018).[2] An example is Skega, founded in the 1920s by the Svensson family in Sweden to produce working shoes and rubber gloves, which experienced early internationalization attempts in the mid-1960s under agent agreements. However the real internationalization momentum of the company came when it was acquired by the Wallenberg group company, Incentive, in 1969. Skega by itself had failed to export capital from Sweden under the tight capital markets of the time, and could not find local financiers abroad either. Under the new ownership of the Wallenberg group and an introduction letter from Marcus Wallenberg, Skega was able to access financial funds for its overseas investment. As a result, by the end of the 1970s it had established overseas subsidiaries in Chile, Canada, Mexico, South Africa, Singapore, Finland, and Brazil. Being a part of the Wallenberg group with its financial expertise and international network brought critical advantages in this affiliated company's international endeavor (Andersson, 2010).

The third type is the late industrializing business groups. These groups were formed as local entrepreneurs established several legally independent firms based on licensed and imported technologies, which then grew in protected domestic markets, especially since the 1950s. In these economies, business groups emerged with an industry generating role, with entrepreneurs creating multiple enterprises and gathering them within diversified business groups (Colpan and Hikino, 2018b). Examples are current emerging market business groups such as the Indian Tata group, which was created in 1869 and by 2017 had 100 operating companies, 29 of which were publicly traded. The group has operations in metals, automobiles, information technology, consulting, energy, chemicals, food and beverages, and hotels, and obtained 64 percent of its total revenues from its international operations (Tata, 2018).[3] Firms in these economies actively went overseas, particularly since the 1980s after their home countries implemented pro-market reforms that forced component firms to improve their capabilities (Cuervo-Cazurra and Dau, 2009b), seeking to invest in more advanced economies to acquire superior resources and capabilities (Luo and Tung, 2007). They also invested in other emerging countries to exploit their firm-specific capabilities (Sarkar, 2010; Colpan, 2010), taking advantage of their knowledge on how to operate in the challenging conditions of emerging economies (Cuervo-Cazurra and Genc, 2008; del Sol and Kogan, 2007). Being part of a business group was more critical in the internationalization of these emerging economy firms relative to the advanced economy ones, because the group membership brought a range of resources and advantages that affiliated firms critically lacked in supporting their overseas expansion (Pedersen and Stucchi, 2014).

Given the differences in the apparent roles and functions of business groups across the historical developmental patterns of countries, in this chapter, we will focus on the third case for analytical focus and logical clarity. While business groups share similar organizational characteristics across countries, they have served different roles and functions depending on the historical context in which they were created. The first two types have been discussed elsewhere (for instance see Colpan and Hikino, 2018a; Jones 2000; Hausman *et al.*, 2008; Pedersen and Stucchi, 2014). They reflect not only the ability of business groups as an organizational form to provide component firms with necessary resources, but also the nature of advanced economies in comparison to emerging ones in terms of institutional endowments and their ability to facilitate the internationalization of companies. This facilitation in advanced economies was done in the early stages via colonial relationships, and in the latter stages via the provision of superior innovation systems.

The distinctive growth strategies pursued by emerging economy business groups relative to those pursued by large enterprises in mature industrial economies has attracted broad interest not only from scholars of international business, but also from scholars in other disciplines including economics, sociology, and business history, as well as in policy and practitioner circles (Colpan *et al.*, 2010). Interest on emerging market multinationals has also been growing (see, for example, Cuervo-Cazurra *et al.*, 2016; Goldstein, 2007; Guillen and Garcia-Canal, 2012; Ramamurti and Singh, 2009). Nevertheless, the two domains of research on business groups and the international growth of emerging market firms have tended to evolve separately.

Below we try to integrate those arguments to provide a broader framework to understand this phenomenon. Once we discuss the literature and our research questions, we will explore them in a specific case of the internationalization of the largest business group in Turkey, the Koç group, in the next section.

The internationalization of emerging market business groups

The conventional wisdom in international business research is that internationalization takes place around a set of core ownership advantages such as technology and brands, which usually is the formula for competitive success abroad (Dunning, 1977). Since emerging market firms tend to have such proprietary assets in a less sophisticated form, one critical resource to exploit is leveraging business group affiliation. This is a common argument underlining most of the literature that has studied the internationalization of business groups in emerging markets and that was attributed above (Chari, 2013; Pedersen and Stucchi, 2014; Yaprak *et al.*, 2018; Yiu *et al.*, 2013).

The affiliation with the business group helps individual operating companies internationalize in several ways. Affiliated firms can tap into intra-group capital markets and accumulated management skills that less developed economies critically lack (Khanna and Yafeh, 2007). Such resource endowments place the affiliated firms in an advantageous position in their internationalization attempts, either by supporting the development of firm-specific assets to be exploited overseas or by assisting in the acquisition of such assets in international markets. Accumulated international contacts and established overseas networks within the group can also be instrumental in affiliated companies' internationalization efforts. The group brand name by itself may function as a critical competitive asset insofar as it enjoys international recognition (Bonaglia *et al.*, 2007; Mukherjee *et al.*, 2018).[4] Exclusive rights and subsidies from governments given to the largest business groups may be another critical factor in certain groups' overseas endeavors as well (Yiu *et al.*, 2013). Kim (2013) argues that the Korean business groups have exploited their domestic advantages in accessing and mobilizing generic resources, mainly financial and human resources, to develop firm-specific advantages. Those firm-specific advantages including technological and marketing capabilities were then transferred to overseas markets. Such firm-specific advantages, therefore, provided the business group firms with adequate motivation as well as the capability to pursue entry into international markets.

However, firms affiliated with business groups, relative to their stand-alone counterparts, may also internationalize and profit less from internationalization as they may have fewer incentives to internationalize. Business groups often enjoy advantageous, dominant, and privileged positions in their domestic markets that guarantee high enough levels of profitability to prevent them from taking the unnecessary risks of venturing into unknown overseas markets (Pedersen and Stucchi, 2014). Carney *et al.* (2011) found a negative relationship between business group affiliation and the degree of internationalization. The primary resources and capabilities, such as contact capabilities or project execution capabilities, that business groups have used to grow in their domestic markets, may not be transferable to foreign markets (Kim, 2013). Gaur and Kumar (2009) found that in India, firms affiliated with business groups show lower performance from internationalization compared to non-group affiliated ones. The business group uses some of its most successful companies to help support other affiliated firms, thus establishing some constraints on their internationalization. These constraints can take the form of using financial resources from companies and their international operations to subsidize underperforming member companies in the business group, limiting the funds available for internationalization.

The internationalization of business groups changes with the transformation of the home country and particularly with its opening after pro-market reforms (Barbero, 2015; Guillen, 2000; Pedersen and Stucchi, 2014). In a closed economy, business group affiliated companies, relative to independent firms, enjoy advantages from their access to intra-group markets as well as from the relationship between the business group and the government, which provides them with the opportunity to expand and perform well within their home country (Ghemawat and

Khanna, 1998; Kock and Guillen, 2001). Thus, these companies are less likely to explore international markets given that most of the source of their advantage relies on their home country. The adoption of pro-market reforms in the home country, on the other hand, has helped many business groups to expand rather than reduce their businesses, and notably supported their internationalization. The result has been that pro-market reforms have forced business groups and their affiliated companies to improve their level of international competitiveness, although some of them may have disappeared as a result of their inability to compete in an open economy (Barbero, 2015; Cuervo-Cazurra and Dau, 2009a; Kumaraswamy *et al.*, 2012). The business group affiliated company is more likely to achieve a competitive advantage because it is better positioned to receive support from the business group for its transformation toward internationally competitive levels. In contrast, unaffiliated companies may not have the necessary resources to improve their competitiveness in the face of foreign competition.

Thus, in the following section, we take into account these influences on the internationalization of business groups and their affiliated companies in a specific case of the internationalization of the largest business group in Turkey, the Koç group.

The internationalization of the Koç group

The Koç group is one of the oldest and the top business group in Turkey, and one of the most internationalized. In 2016 it was the only Turkish firm in the Fortune Global 500 ranking with its revenues of US$15.6 billion, representing 6 percent of the gross domestic product (GDP) of Turkey and its total exports representing 9 percent of Turkey's exports (Koç, 2017) (see Table 15.2 for the Forbes Global 2000 ranking of Turkish firms in 2017 that ranks Koç Holding at the top of the list). The group is active in a diverse range of products and industries including automotive (automobiles, car retailing, and others), consumer durables (white goods and consumer electronics), energy (refinery, distribution, power generation, natural gas), finance (including banking, leasing, real estate investment), and other businesses. The Koç group is also one of the most internationalized groups in the country (Colpan, 2010). It was Turkey's largest exporter, and four of its component firms were among the top ten of Turkey's exporters in 2016 (Koç, 2017). The group thus well illustrates the internationalization of business groups from emerging markets.

Table 15.2 Ranking of the largest publicly traded Turkish firms that appear in the Forbes Global 2000 list, ranked by sales, 2017

Forbes Global 2000 rank	Company	Sales (US$ bn)	Profits (US$ bn)	Assets (US$ bn)	Market value (US$ bn)
567	Koç Holding	23.50	1.10	25.10	10.40
739	Sabanci Holding	11.90	0.88	87.90	5.40
527	Isbank	11.70	1.80	118.00	7.90
1,511	Turkish Airlines	9.70	−0.02	18.50	2.00
523	Garanti Bank	9.20	1.70	88.10	10.20
585	Akbank	7.90	1.50	91.60	9.20
932	Halkbank	7.00	0.73	71.00	3.50
951	VakifBank	7.00	0.69	69.00	3.70
1,744	Turkcell	4.70	0.51	9.00	7.10
1,870	Enka	3.50	0.59	7.60	6.80

Source: Forbes (2018).

Koç group's origins go back to the 1920s when Vehbi Koç, its founder, started his business as a retail merchant in the city of Ankara. Building on his initial contacts with international companies through his relationships especially with ethnic minorities (Greeks, Armenians, and Jews) in the country and the government, Koç grew in the Turkish market as it secured franchise deals and representative positions like for the US companies Standard Oil (New Jersey) and Ford Motor (Colpan and Jones, 2016). Koç partnered with foreign multinationals, such as General Electric, US Rubber, and Siemens, as it leveraged the establishment of contact capabilities with overseas, and especially, US companies (Colpan and Jones, 2013). When import substitution measures, such as import restrictions and tariff barriers, began to be implemented in Turkey from the early 1950s due to the shortage of foreign exchanges, Koç turned to domestic manufacturing via joint ventures and licensing agreements with international companies (Colpan, 2010; Colpan and Jones, 2016). At the same time, Koç also attempted to establish a group-wide Research and Development (R&D) center in 1975, which would become the first such center in the private sector in Turkey.

Nonetheless, serious efforts to accumulate skills in technology to develop indigenous products only materialized when Turkey turned from import substitution toward export-led growth and liberalization starting in the 1980s. With the opening of the domestic market to international companies, the increase in imports and inward investment by those international companies brought growing competition within the Turkish market. The 1996 customs agreement with the European Union reduced tariffs and created a free trade area in manufacturing goods. The following liberalization of the economy accelerated domestic competition.

The closed economy partly caused the delay in the internationalization of companies, including the Koç affiliated firms, as they could enjoy advantageous positions in the Turkish market. The new environment of pro-market reforms, in contrast, pushed them to compete with international companies not only in their home market but also in overseas markets leading to the advancement of the group's globalization efforts (Colpan, 2010).

The internationalization of the Koç affiliated company Arçelik illustrates these points, because it has been the principal company in the Koç group to lead a rapid internationalization process especially after the 1980s. Arçelik was founded in 1955 by Vehbi Koç and his partners to produce steel office furniture. The company quickly moved into home appliances such as washing machines and refrigerators in the late 1950s and early 1960s by establishing technical assistance and licensing agreements with firms from Belgium and Israel and purchasing key components such as motors and gearboxes from overseas. With these, they manufactured the first locally produced washing machines and refrigerators in the country. Restrictions and difficulties in importing prompted the company to begin domestic manufacturing of more parts, such as electric motors and compressors in partnership with General Electric. This was followed by technology licensing agreements with General Electric and Bosch-Siemens in the late 1960s (Colpan and Jones, 2013). Arçelik became a prime white-goods enterprise in the protected domestic market, but depended on licensed technology until the 1980s.

The company took a two-pronged strategy in its internationalization: exports and acquisitions.[5] The first was organic growth that started with exporting, opportunistically at the beginning, to neighboring countries in the Middle East and North Africa from the 1970s. The main motivation was to exploit the company's production surplus. The company did not have any separate exporting model in these initial attempts, e.g., the first machines sold to Saudi Arabia did not have any manuals in Arabic (Bonaglia *et al.*, 2007). The company also needed foreign exchange to pay for its imported parts due to the severe foreign exchange shortage in Turkey. Neighboring countries such as Iran, Pakistan, Iraq, Syria, and Tunisia, and their government institutions, in particular, were the major buyers (Colpan and Jones, 2015). These exports were originally conducted with the cooperation of the Koç group's foreign trade company RAM, after which Arçelik established its export division in 1983. The company then turned towards original equipment manufacturing (OEM), which was first secured with Sears Roebuck in the USA in 1988 to produce refrigerators. It did not rely on OEM only, however. The company also began investing heavily in its technology and brands to overcome the potential challenges of the gradual opening of the domestic market to international competition starting in 1980. By the late 1990s, the company had set up sales offices in France, Germany, and the UK (Bonaglia *et al.*, 2007; Colpan, 2010; Colpan and Jones, 2015) to sell its branded products.

The second part of the internationalization strategy was the targeted acquisition of international companies to obtain superior brands and technology and enter into new markets. In the early 2000s, Arçelik began its purchases with European companies that included Blomberg in Germany, Elektra Bregenz in Austria, Arctic in Romania, the Leisure (cookers) and Flavel (appliances and TV sets) brands in Britain, and Grundig in Germany (Bonaglia *et al.*, 2007). The aim was to enter these markets by building on these strong brands that the company lacked in international markets. As the company upgraded its capabilities, it established itself as one of the most significant players in the white-goods industry, expanding first into close geographical markets and later on to more distant ones such as China, especially since the late 2000s (Colpan and Jones, 2015). By the late 2010s, the company had manufacturing plants in China, Russia, Romania, and South Africa and operated sales and marketing companies in 19 countries (Bonaglia *et al.*, 2007; Colpan and Jones, 2015).

For its rapid and successful internationalization, leveraging the business group membership was instrumental for the company. A critical membership advantage was tapping into intra-group capital and managerial markets which independent firms lacked. Arçelik not only had access to intra-group resources in its development of technology and brands, but it also benefited from those resources available group-wide when necessary in its foreign expansion. For instance, some of the company's top executives came from other group companies, like Beko Ticaret which had been active for the marketing and sales of electronics products (Colpan, 2010; Bonaglia *et al.*, 2007). Some others also came from Koç Holding, giving a broad exposure to the business group headquarters and its knowledge resources. Further, Arçelik undoubtedly benefited from the group-wide technological know-how and especially overseas networks available within the group. When it integrated in 2001 with another Koç affiliated firm, Beko Elektronik, that integration brought benefits not only in terms of operational efficiency and cost-effectiveness, but also in overseas expansion as the usage of the Beko brand name in international markets was useful since that brand was already known in several markets in Europe. Finally, the reputation associated with the Koç brand name, which enjoyed international recognition especially among foreign manufacturers and distributors was also a significant asset when Arçelik, or any other group affiliated firm for that matter, ventured abroad (Bonaglia *et al.*, 2007; Colpan, 2010).

Apart from Arçelik, however, the international expansion of other Koç group companies was overall limited. The automobile companies, Ford Otosan and Tofaş contributed to exports through their international joint partners' networks; but at the same time, those joint ventures limited the pursuit of independent international expansion, because the vehicles produced were models from the international companies (Ford and Fiat) and Koç auto companies were only a manufacturing hub for the vehicles. In banking, the situation was similar with the joint venture partner Unicredit restricting an independent internationalization strategy for Koç affiliates. In energy, on the other hand, a newly acquired company in 2005 (Tupras in refining and petrochemicals) had a wide export presence, but the knowledge from these export markets has yet to be shared and utilized within the group (Koç Holding, 2012; Colpan and Jones, 2015).

Arçelik thus remained the only company with overseas production facilities, whereas other group companies have contributed to the group's increasing international sales via exports. As a result, Koç group's international sales overall increased from 7 percent in 1990 to more than 30 percent by the mid-2010s (Colpan and Jones, 2015).

The above narrative provides some support for our research questions. In a protected market environment before the 1980s, Koç companies were in a favorable position to access technology and establish alliances with foreign companies. International contacts were beneficial as such know-how for accessing overseas companies could be shared across different affiliated companies. Koç group affiliated companies, therefore, did not internationalize before pro-market reforms because their sources of advantages lay within their home country where the Koç group enjoyed a dominant position. However, some of those same companies, especially Arçelik, internationalized rapidly after pro-market reforms because the business group affiliation provided them with the ability and resources (especially capital, managerial talent, technology, and brands) to compete overseas initially in neighboring countries of the Middle East and Europe and later in more distant ones such as East Asia and Africa. Table 15.3 shows that while all large business groups in the country exploited the opportunities in international markets after the 1980s, by 2007 the Koç group had become the most international group with operations in 23 countries (Colpan, 2010). By 2016 it had gained about 30 percent of its total revenues from foreign sales and remained active in 23 overseas markets (Koç, 2017).

Our narrative about the Koç group also illustrates that Arçelik established its capabilities by investing in research and development and acquiring overseas brands; while other Koç companies like Ford Otosan and Tofaş relied on their foreign joint venture partners with sophisticated technology and international brands. Those international partners continued to work with Koç because it had controlled a vast dealership network in the country and had extensive knowledge of the local market. Affiliation to the Koç group brought some affiliated firms wider

Table 15.3 Internationalization of Turkish business groups, 2007

	Export commitment (export sales total sales)	International scope (number of countries shown below)				
		100%-owned manufacturing	*Joint-venture manufacturing*	*100%-owned non-manufacturing*	*Joint-venture non-manufacturing*	*Total number of countries*
Group A	25–50%	2–3	2–3	7–10	7–10	23
Group B	11–24%	7–10	2–3	10+	1	14
Group C	50%+	2–3	2–3	10+	10+	15
Group D	25–50%	7–10	7–10	6–10	0	10
Group E	50%+	2–3	2–3	10+	2–3	11
Group F	25–50%	4–6	0	7–10	0	13
Group G	11–24%	4–6	4–6	7–10	0	16
Group H	1–10%	2–3	0	4–6	2–3	6
Group I	25–50%	1	1	7–10	7–10	8
Group J	25–50%	1	0	7–10	0	8
Group K	11–24%	1	2–3	4–6	0	7

Source: Colpan (2010).

Note
Business groups are ranked based on their number of employees. Koç is the top-ranked group shown as Group A above.

Table 15.4 Ranking of Turkish multinationals, 2007

Rank	Name	Industry	Ownership type	Foreign assets (US$ mn)
1	Enka Construction	Diversified	Business group	3,877
2	Turkcell	Communication	Part of business group	2,331
3	Çalık Holding	Diversified	Business group	2,002
4	Koç Holding	Diversified	Business group	1,742
5	Anadolu Group	Diversified	Business group	1,629
6	Turkish Petroleum Corporation (TPAO)	Oil and gas	State owned enterprise	1,121
7	Şişecam A.Ş.	Glass	Part of business group	977
8	Tekfen Holding	Diversified	Business group	751
9	Sabancı Holding	Diversified	Business group	640
10	Eczacıbaşı Holding	Diversified	Business group	266
11	Borusan Holding	Diversified	Business group	223
12	Zorlu Enerji Group	Energy	Part of business group	152
Total				15,711

Source: Adapted with additions from Vale Columbia Center on Sustainable International Investment, Kadir Has University and DEIK survey of Turkish multinationals, 2009.

internationalization. However, this was not homogeneous across all affiliated firms. Arçelik undoubtedly benefited from being a group member as it received financial, managerial, and knowledge resources from the parent and affiliated companies (Colpan and Jones, 2015).

Table 15.4 shows the first-ever ranking of Turkish multinationals investing abroad in 2007; as of 2017 this ranking had not been updated. A close look at the largest Turkish multinationals shows that business groups and their affiliated firms dominate the top of the list by their foreign assets (Vale Columbia Center, 2009). The table also illustrates that all the firms in the list except for one are (or belong to) business groups. This supports our argument about the broader internationalization of business group firms relative to independent firms.

Conclusions

This chapter has analyzed the internationalization of business groups, concentrating on the cases of emerging market business groups and examining the case of the Turkish Koç group. Although the use of one case cannot be regarded as a defining test for the abovementioned ideas, some generalizations can be made from the historical development of our case. We argued that emerging market business groups assert a dual influence on the international expansion of the member companies that often originally lack the necessary resources for internationalization. On the one hand, business groups support affiliated companies' internationalization by providing them with intra-group financial, managerial, and knowledge resources. On the other hand, business group affiliation establishes constraints on internationalization by limiting the expansion of affiliated companies that enjoy dominant positions and privileges in their home markets. We also proposed that the conditions of the home country influence these international expansions, and that the pro-market reforms of the home country lead a company affiliated with a business group to expand faster.

There are several similarities with business groups in other emerging markets, such as the intra-group resource support to help internationalization (e.g., Pedersen and Stucchi, 2014) and the push for internationalization in business groups following pro-market reforms after the

1980s and 1990s (e.g., the Argentina groups in Barbero, 2015). There are also differences, however. Contrasting with some other cases where business groups achieve a significant presence in global markets (such as those in India, e.g., Khanna and Palepu, 2009), Turkish groups lack behind other emerging market multinationals regarding their level of foreign expansion (Vale Columbia Center, 2009). This might be related to the low competitiveness of Turkish products and businesses in international markets and the delayed internationalization of Turkish companies that benefited from the closed economy of the country that gradually opened from the 1980s (Colpan, 2010). These differences suggest that any generalizations need to take the country of origin and the timing of internationalization into consideration. With this caveat, we conclude that business groups acted as contributors to the internationalization of their component firms and the globalization of markets.

These ideas contribute to a better understanding of the literature on business groups by bringing a historical perspective. There have been limited analyses on the internationalization of business groups and many of these have tended to study the determinants or impact of internationalization within a short period. This has yielded new insights but a historical perspective helps expand, enrich, and in some cases challenge them by bringing a long-term view.

We proposed that there have been three broad categories of internationalization of business groups in historical context: trading, early industrialization, and later industrialization business groups. The first type was trading business groups in early industrializing economies with abundant capital that used this capital and colonial relationships to expand widely abroad, exemplified by the British nineteenth century overseas merchant groups. The second type of business groups appeared in early industrializing economies with advanced technologies. Business groups were centered around banks and financial holding companies, which often provided the capital, and their affiliated industrial firms used indigenous technological capabilities to expand abroad, exemplified by the Swedish groups. The third type is business groups from late industrializing countries with limited proprietary assets. These business groups grew in protected economies and later used their intra-group resources and domestic advantages to expand abroad as their economies opened; this type is illustrated by emerging market business groups.

In sum, the internationalization of business groups can only be understood in the context in which they emerged and expanded. Business groups have played a crucial role in the making of global business at different points in time and in different locations. They have promoted the integration of economies into the global arena, not only in their home countries by facilitating exports, but also in other countries by facilitating imports from host countries and the coordination of global value chains dispersed across a multitude of nations. Their diversified operations in the home country have reinforced the links across countries, with one business's foreign operations serving as a bridgehead for subsequent investments and trade connections for other businesses. This contextual and historical account has the critical implication of challenging the assumption that insights from studies of business groups in one economy can be automatically transferred to business groups in other economies; the contextual conditions that determined the creation and internationalization of the business groups play a role that cannot be assumed away. This same contextual and historical account helps explain the variation in the characteristics of globalization across time and the pre-eminence of particular business groups in it.

Notes

1 We adopt the definition of "diversified business groups." For detailed typology and other types of business groups, such as network types, see Colpan and Hikino (2010; 2018a) and for a discussion by their ownership see Cuervo-Cazurra (2006, 2018b).

2 For the earlier overseas investment of groups focused on public utilities from nations including Belgium and Germany, see Hausman *et al.* (2008). We do not explore such groups further here as they are typically operating in one industry rather than being unrelatedly diversified.

3 For the map of the historical development of the international business of the Tata group, see Regan (2015a).

4 Mukherjee *et al.* (2018) argue that a business group's reputation quality is heterogeneous and may serve as a positive or a negative factor as the groups expand internationally.

5 For the map of the historical development of the international business of Arçelik, see Regan (2015b).

References

Andersson, S. (2010). "Suppliers' international strategies," *European Journal of Marketing*, 36 (1/2): 86–110.

Barbero, M. I. (2015). "Business groups in nineteenth and twentieth century Argentina," in Jones, G. and Lluch, A. (eds.) *The Impact of Globalization on Argentina and Chile: Business Enterprises and Entrepreneurship*, Cheltenham: Edward Elgar.

Bonaglia, F., Goldstein, A., and Mathews, J. (2007). "Accelerated internationalization by emerging multinationals: the case of white goods sector," *Journal of World Business*, 42: 369–383.

Carney, M., Gedajlovic, E. R., Heugens, P., van Essen, M., and van Oosterhout, J. (2011). "Business group affiliation, performance, context and strategy: a meta-analysis," *Academy of Management Journal*, 54 (3): 437–460.

Chari, M. D. R. (2013). "Business groups and foreign direct investments by developing country firms: an empirical test in India," *Journal of World Business*, 48 (3): 349–359.

Colli, A. and Colpan, A. M. (2016). "Business groups and corporate governance: review, synthesis, and extension," *Corporate Governance: An International Review*, 24 (3): 274–302.

Colpan, A. M. (2010). "Business groups in Turkey," in Colpan, A. M., Hikino, T., and Lincoln J. (eds.) *Oxford Handbook of Business Groups*, Oxford: Oxford University Press.

Colpan, A. M. and Hikino, T. (2010). "Foundations of business groups: towards an integrated framework," in Colpan, A. M., Hikino, T., and Lincoln J. (eds.) *Oxford Handbook of Business Groups*, Oxford: Oxford University Press.

Colpan, A. M. and Hikino, T. (2018a). *Business Groups in the West: Origins, Evolution and Resilience*, Oxford: Oxford University Press.

Colpan, A. M. and Hikino, T. (2018b). "The evolutionary dynamics of business groups in the West: history and theory," in Colpan, A. M. and Hikino, T. (eds.) *Business Groups in the West: Origins, Evolution and Resilience*, Oxford: Oxford University Press.

Colpan, A. M. and Jones, G. (2013). "Vehbi Koc and the making of Turkey's largest business group," HBS case No: 9-811-081.

Colpan, A. M. and Jones, G. (2015). "Vehbi Koc and the making of Turkey's largest business group (B)," HBS case No: 9-815-078.

Colpan, A. M. and Jones, G. (2016). "Business groups, entrepreneurship and the growth of the Koc group in Turkey," *Business History*, 58 (1): 69–88.

Colpan, A. M., Hikino, T., and Lincoln J. (2010). *Oxford Handbook of Business Groups*, Oxford: Oxford University Press.

Cuervo-Cazurra, A. (2006). "Business groups and their types," *Asia Pacific Journal of Management*, 23 (4): 419–437.

Cuervo-Cazurra, A. (2018a). "The evolution of business groups' corporate social responsibility," *Journal of Business Ethics*, 153 (4): 997–1016.

Cuervo-Cazurra, A. (2018b). "Business groups in Spain: regulation and ideology drivers," in Colpan, A. M. and Hikino, T. (eds.) *Business Groups in the West: The Evolutionary Dynamics of Big Business*, Oxford: Oxford University Press.

Cuervo-Cazurra, A. and Dau, L. A. (2009a). "Pro-market reforms and firm profitability in developing countries," *Academy of Management Journal*, 52 (6): 1348–1368.

Cuervo-Cazurra, A. and Dau, L. A. (2009b). "Structural reform and firm exports," *Management International Review*, 49 (4): 479–507.

Cuervo-Cazurra, A. and Genc, M. (2008). "Transforming disadvantages into advantages: developing-country MNEs in the least developed countries," *Journal of International Business Studies*, 39 (6): 957–979.

Cuervo-Cazurra, A., Gaur, A., and Singh, D. (2019). "Pro-market institutions and global strategy: the pendulum of pro-market reforms and reversals," *Journal of International Business Studies*, https://doi.org/10.1057/s41267-019-00221-z.

Cuervo-Cazurra, A., Newburry, W., and Park, S. (2016). *Emerging Market Multinationals: Solving Operational Challenges in Internationalization*, Cambridge: Cambridge University Press.

del Sol, P. and Kogan, J. (2007). "Regional competitive advantage based on pioneering economic reforms: the case of Chilean FDI," *Journal of International Business Studies*, 38 (6), 901–927.

Dunning, J. H. (1977). "Trade, location of economic activity and the MNE: a search for an eclectic approach," in Ohlin, B., Hesselborn, P.-O., and Wijkman, P. M. (eds.) *The International Allocation of Economic Activity*, London: Macmillan.

Forbes (2016). "The world's billionaires." www.forbes.com/billionaires/ (Accessed February 13, 2017).

Forbes (2017). "The world's biggest public companies." www.forbes.com/global2000/ (Accessed February 13, 2017).

Forbes (2018). "The world's biggest public companies." www.forbes.com/global2000/list/#country:Turkey (Accessed February 13, 2018).

Gaur, A. S. and Kumar, V. (2009). "International diversification, business group affiliation and firm performance: empirical evidence from India," *British Journal of Management*, 20 (2): 172–186.

Ghemawat, P. and Khanna, T. (1998). "The nature of diversified business groups: a research design and two case studies," *Journal of Industrial Economics*, 46: 35–61.

Goldstein, A. (2007). *Multinational Companies from Emerging Economies: Composition, Conceptualization and Direction in the Global Economy*, New York: Palgrave-Macmillan.

Guillen, M. (2000). "Business groups in emerging economies: a resource-based view," *Academy of Management Journal*, 43(3): 362–380.

Guillen, M. and Garcia-Canal, E. (2012). *Emerging Markets Rule: Growth Strategies of the New Global Giants*, New York: McGraw Hill.

Hausman, W., Hertner, P., and Wilkins, M. (2008). *Global Electrification*, New York: Cambridge University Press.

Hikino, T. and Bucheli, M. (2018). "The United States before the mid-20th century: strange career of business groups in economic development," in Colpan, A. M. and Hikino, T. (eds.) *Business Groups in the West: Origins, Evolution and Resilience*, Oxford: Oxford University Press.

Jones, G. (2000). *Merchants to Multinationals: British Trading Companies in the Nineteenth and Twentieth Centuries*, Oxford: Oxford University Press.

Jones, G. and Colpan, A. M. (2010). "Business groups in historical perspectives," in Colpan, A. M., Hikino, T., and Lincoln J. (eds.) *Oxford Handbook of Business Groups*, Oxford: Oxford University Press.

Jones, G. and Khanna, T. (2006). "Bringing history (back) into international business," *Journal of International Business Studies*, 37 (4): 453–468.

Khanna, T. and Rivkin, J. W. (2001). "Estimating the performance effects of business groups in emerging markets," *Strategic Management Journal*, 22: 45–74.

Khanna, T. and Palepu, K. (2009). "House of Tata: acquiring a global footprint," HBS Case 708-446.

Khanna, T. and Yafeh, Y. (2007). "Business groups in emerging markets: paragons or parasites?" *Journal of Economic Literature*, 45: 331–372.

Kim, H. (2013). Panel presentation, "Internationalization and resilience of business groups in developing economies: a comparative and evolutionary perspective session," AIB Annual Meeting, Istanbul, Turkey.

Koç (2017). "The Koç Group at a glance." www.koc.com.tr/en-us/investor-relations/InvestorRelations/KO%C3%87%20GROUP%20AT%20A%20GLANCE.pdf (Accessed February 13, 2018).

Koç Holding (2012). "Investor presentation." www.koc.com.tr/en-us/investor-relations/presentations-and-bulletins/koc-holding-presentations (Accessed February 13, 2018).

Kock, C. and Guillen, M. (2001). "Strategy and structure in developing countries: business groups as an evolutionary response to opportunities for unrelated diversification," *Industrial and Corporate Change*, 10 (1): 77–113.

Kumar, V., Gaur, A. S., and Pattnaik, C. (2012). "Product diversification and international expansion of business groups," *Management International Review*, 52 (2): 175–192.

Kumaraswamy, A., Mudambi, R., Saranga, H., and Tripathy, A. (2012). "Catch-up strategies in the Indian auto components industry: domestic firms' responses to market liberalization," *Journal of International Business Studies*, 43: 368–395.

Larsson, M. and Peterrson, T. (2018). "Sweden: tradition and renewal," in Colpan, A. M. and Hikino, T. (eds.) *Business Groups in the West: Origins, Evolution and Resilience*, Oxford: Oxford University Press.

Luo, Y. and Tung, R. L. (2007). "International expansion of emerging market enterprises: a springboard perspective," *Journal of International Business Studies*, 38: 481–498.

Morck, R. K. (ed.) (2005). *A History of Corporate Governance around the World: Family Business Groups to Professional Managers*, Chicago, IL: University of Chicago Press.

Morck, R. and Yeung, B. (2003). "Agency problems in large family business groups," *Entrepreneurship Theory and Practice*, 27 (4): 367–382.

Mukherjee, D., Makarius, E., and Stevens, C. E. (2018). "Business group reputation and affiliates' internationalization strategies," *Journal of World Business*, 53 (2): 93–103.

Pedersen, T. and Stucchi, T. (2014). "Business groups, institutional transition and the internationalization of firms from emerging economies," in Cuervo-Cazurra, A. and Ramamurti, R. (eds.) *Understanding Multinationals from Emerging Markets*, Cambridge: Cambridge University Press.

Ramamurti, R. and Singh, J. V. (eds.) (2009). *Emerging Multinationals in Emerging Markets*, Cambridge: Cambridge University Press.

Regan, J. (2015a). Tata Group International Businesses 1903–2014. www.hbs.edu/businesshistory/courses/resources/historical-data-visualization/Pages/details.aspx?data_id=16 (Accessed February 13, 2018).

Regan, J. (2015b). Arçelik Corporation (Koç Group) 1955–2014. www.hbs.edu/businesshistory/courses/resources/historical-data-visualization/Pages/details.aspx?data_id=4 (Accessed February 13, 2018).

Sarkar, J. (2010). "Business groups in India," in Colpan, A. M., Hikino, T., and Lincoln J. (eds.) *Oxford Handbook of Business Groups*, Oxford: Oxford University Press.

Tan, D. and Meyer, K. E. (2010). "Business groups' outward FDI: a managerial resources perspective," *Journal of International Management*, 16 (2): 154–164.

Tata (2018). Tata group profile. www.tata.com/aboutus/sub_index/Leadership-with-trust (Accessed February 13, 2018).

Vale Columbia Center (2009). "Survey provides the first ever ranking of Turkish multinationals investing abroad," Istanbul and New York, December 3. http://ccsi.columbia.edu/files/2013/11/Turkey_2009.pdf (Accessed February 13, 2018).

Yaprak, A. and Karademir, B. (2010). "The internationalization of emerging market business groups: an integrated literature review," *International Marketing Review*, 27 (2): 245–262.

Yaprak, A., Yosun, T., and Cetindamar, D. (2018). "The influence of firm-specific and country specific advantages in the internationalization of emerging market firms: evidence from Turkey," *International Business Review*, 27 (1): 198–207.

Yiu, D. W. (2011). "Multinational advantages of Chinese business groups: a theoretical exploration," *Management and Organization Review*, 7 (2): 249–277.

Yiu, D., Ng, F., and Ma, X. (2013). "Business group attributes and internationalization strategy in China," *Asian Business and Management*, 12 (1): 15–38.

16

INTERNATIONAL BUSINESS NETWORKS

Thomas David and Gerarda Westerhuis

Introduction

Both markets and hierarchies are primary and complementary governance mechanisms, used to regulate the production and exchange of economic goods and services. Business historians, among others, identify networks as separate organising institutions, in between markets and hierarchies (Casson and Cox 1993). Networks often act as the negotiating interface between firms, workers, state, and society, in different constellations. Therefore, they are often associated with cooperation rather than competition.

A network consists of firms and persons, also known as a two-mode network in social network analysis. Granovetter (1985) shows that they are constrained by the structure of the network but are also important actors that change and influence this structure. Networks and individuals do not operate in isolation, but have to deal with the changing environment they operate in. We therefore follow Carnevali (2011: 910) by conceptualising "networks not as structures (that shape action in a linear fashion) but as 'processes of relations' in which actors define each other in interaction and on the basis of their context". When studying business networks, we should be aware of these external and internal dimensions of their activities. Internally, they have members to consider and, externally, an environment in which they operate. Thus internally networks articulate shared interests, values, and ethics to which members feel acquainted. An important aspect in doing so is the management of diversity in order to get internal cohesion. The external environment, consisting of the state, non-governmental organisations (NGOs), labour, and competitors, possess constraints on and opportunities for them (David and Westerhuis 2014).

Why do business networks, i.e. tightly knit networks of businessmen, exist alongside hierarchies and markets? In other words, why do rational self-interested individuals form business networks? Networks emerge when market institutions fail (when they are weak or don't exist at all) and individuals start relying on personal connections based on trust (on the notion of trust, see Guinnane 2005). The concept of network has proved to be a useful analytical tool in the context of risk-reducing strategies and the building of interpersonal and informal trust relations. A business network reduces information asymmetries and enhances information flows. In this way their power relies on "their ability to set the parameters of the corporate environment within which all large enterprises must act" (Scott 1991: 188).

International business networks facilitate the integration of foreign markets by building trust when contract enforcement is weak to nonexistent. It is a relatively secure way to expand economic activities across borders. We distinguish among three different obstacles to global market integration that international business networks might help overcome. First, individuals from different parts of the world have different tastes, values, and cultural backgrounds, which might complicate economic transactions. Second, international trade only works efficiently when there is enough information. In other words, individuals can make optimal economic decisions only when they have been adequately informed of all possible options. A third barrier has to do with policies and regulations limiting (international) economic activity.

Thus, globalisation, or the integration of markets, depends on the ongoing mitigation of these obstacles. Business networks can reduce these barriers. First, they can create cohesion among business elites by lessening tensions or taking on common competitors. Second, these networks operating across national borders can help to overcome problems of contract enforcement and provide information about trade opportunities (Rauch 2001). Third, because the state can facilitate these developments by removing obstructions, providing protection, and creating infrastructure, we often see close links between business networks and the state.

International business networks have attracted attention in various fields: business history, sociology, political science, economics, and management. Business history in particular has shown that international business networks are not a recent phenomenon, nor have they been replaced by more formal ways of economic coordination (e.g. by multinationals). In fact, long distance trade was important during the medieval and modern period (Braudel 1981–1984 [1967–1979]). At that time, networks based on kinship, family, or religious ties helped to reduce uncertainty linked to international trade and promote trust (Pearson and Richardson 2008; Gelderblom and Trivellato 2018; see also Chapter 12 on diaspora networks in this volume). With the second industrial revolution, two interconnected trends occurred. First, partly due to innovations in communication and transport, more institutionalised and formal-legal arrangements for doing business emerged (Pearson and Richardson 2008; Rauch 2001). Second, towards the end of the nineteenth century, large companies started becoming increasingly more important in many parts of the world. Economic activities began to be more and more coordinated within multidivisional firms, often having activities across borders, rather than by means of market exchange (Casson and Cox 1993; Chandler 1990). In theory, due to these trends there should have been less of a need for the existence of business networks. However, as we will see, the emergence of formal arrangements and the growing importance of multinationals did not replace international business networks (Rauch 2001).

In this chapter we will explore the role of international business networks in the process of globalisation. We will address the question of how these networks contributed to the making of global business. As it is a very broad topic, we decided to focus on two types of international business networks that connect business leaders at the global level: corporate networks and Business Interest Associations (BIAs) over the course of the last two centuries. Corporate networks are defined as ties between companies created by directors sitting on more than one board (Stokman *et al.* 1985; David and Westerhuis 2014). A BIA is a type of business network whose goal is to further the interests of businesses (Schmitter and Streeck 1999). One important characteristic of a BIA is that its members are firms that are autonomous entities that "voluntarily" take part in the network. This is in contrast to a business group, for example, which is a group of firms consisting of a parent and subsidiaries that function as one single economic entity (on business groups, see Chapter 15 in this volume).

Although there have been debates among historians and economists on the beginning of globalisation, going back to the sixteenth, eighteenth or nineteenth century (see O'Rourke and

Williamson 1999; Flynn and Giraldez 2004; De Vries 2010), we will focus on the period from the mid-nineteenth century to today. We will see that international business networks flourish during periods of globalisation such as the second half of the nineteenth century or the period after the Second World War, in particular after the 1980s. However, the creation and diffusion of international business networks were not interrupted during the other periods. For example, the First World War "did not serve as a pivot making a decisive retreat from transnational network building" (Rosenberg 2012a: 6; see also Sluga and Clavin 2017).

Another debate concerns the concept used to characterise the networks which favour the exchange of men, goods, and capital across borders, which make possible the economic relations, circulations, or connections between nations. Which term should we use? International, trans-national, global, or cosmopolitan business networks? We found all these expressions in the liter-ature. We decided to use international business networks even if, to avoid repetitions, we will sometimes use other expressions. In this sense, we agree with Saunier (2013: 3) when he writes about the debate concerning global/transnational/international histories: "The differences between these approaches are ... less important than their common emphasis on relations."

The chapter proceeds as follows. This section is followed by three consecutive sections on corporate networks, international elites, and BIAs, respectively. In each section we start with an overview of the literature followed by historical insights on the topic. The following section nuances the link between international business networks and the making of global business. In the conclusion we share some ideas on future research.

International corporate networks and transnational elite

Members of (international) corporate networks consist of financial members (banks, institutional investors, insurance companies) and non-financial members (often dominated by listed firms). These networks are used to channel information and communication, via which business can be spread (Mizruchi 1996 for national networks and Nollert 2005 for international ones). These networks are also used to create a kind of cohesion among a certain group of firms and contri-bute to the lessening of tensions. For example, they might help to reduce opportunistic beha-viour by imposing an ethical code of conduct on the members of the business elite (Windolf 2009). Networks might also give access to (financial) resources. Thus information and transac-tion costs are lowered, and privileged access to markets can be obtained. Externally corporate networks are confronted with the state, NGOs, labour, and so on.

The study of corporate networks has a long history, which goes back to the beginning of the twentieth century with the studies of Jeidels (1905) and Hilferding (1910) in Germany, and of Brandeis (1914) in the United States. Until the 1970s, these studies mostly focus on the national links between corporate networks via interlocking directorates. It is only since the 1970s that scholars begin to look at transnational board interlocks (see e.g. Fennema 1982), a trend that has accelerated since the beginning of the twenty-first century.

National corporate networks, which emerged in many countries with the second industrial revolution at the end of the nineteenth century, began to erode slightly after the 1980s, a decline which sped up during the 1990s (see David and Westerhuis 2014 for the development of cor-porate networks in various countries). One of the most important explanatory factors for this disintegration has been a conscious strategic choice of disengagement from industrial companies on the part of the banks due to the effects of globalisation and financial deregulation. Another explanation for the decline is the increasing focus of firms on shareholder value and on the pro-fessionalization of boards (on the notion of shareholder value, see Lazonick and O'Sullivan 2000). According to some scholars, the recent decline of national networks is also concomitant to the emergence of a growing transnational corporate network linking the largest multinational firms across the world. Heemskerk *et al.* (2016) show, in a comparison of the 176 largest firms in the world economy between 1976 and 2013, that transnational networks increased in relative importance during this period.

A way to study international corporate networks is to look at the nationality of the boards of the world's largest companies. According to Staples (2007), there is evidence that between 1993 and 2005, the board composition of the world's largest multinationals became more international at a rather rapid pace. However, he puts things into perspective by arguing that this transnationalisation has not yet reached very deep: "Only very few of the corporations studied had more than 50 per cent non-national directors" (Staples 2007: 317–318; see also Burris and Staples 2012).

Others investigate this postulate even more vigorously. For example, Hartmann highlights the persistence of national specificities in the profile of economic elites despite economic globalisation. In a study based on the boards of the 1,000 largest firms and the 1,000 wealthiest persons in the world, he concludes that there is no transnational or global economic elite: the number of foreigners on the boards of these firms is very low, and the business leaders of these companies generally haven't had vast experience in foreign countries before joining the boards of these firms. He claims that the traditional models and systems of national careers continue to prevail nowadays and constitute an obstacle to the transnational mobility of business elite. Hartmann concludes by saying that a global economic elite is a mythos, and the economic elite is recruited at the national level (2016).

These debates among sociologists and political scientists are interesting but fail to take into account the historical perspective. Most contributions to the transnationalisation of corporate networks and elites deal with recent years (Sklair 2001; Robinson 2004). Widespread evidence shows that this phenomenon already existed in the nineteenth century during the first wave of globalisation. Hannah (2007: 651) formulates this very well when describing London in 1900:

> At a time when it took sixty days to travel round the world and international communication was by cable, not the more natural telephone, the social cement of a relatively homogeneous, international elite of merchants and businessmen, with a common European cultural heritage, no doubt aided global business development.

Jones (1987) describes the existence of a cosmopolitan bourgeoisie during the nineteenth century that is linked by international partnerships, kinship ties, and a common liberal ideology. Commercial networks created by diaspora communities, such as Chinese, Indian, or Greek communities, were key players in international trade during this period (Jones 2008: 146–147; see also Chapter 12 on diaspora networks in this volume). Moreover, the place of registration and nationality of shareholders and managers of large firms were clearly not confined to national borders. It is only during the interwar period that this "cosmopolitan capitalism" was replaced by national identities, a process reinforced by the Second World War (Jones 2006; see also Wagner 2005 or Hannah 2007).

The Swiss case is very representative of this transnational dimension before the First World War and the process of nationalisation thereafter (see Mach *et al.* 2016). The proportion of foreigners among the largest Swiss firms was more significant in 1910 (11 per cent) than in later decades. Indeed, only 3 to 4 per cent of foreigners sat on the boards of the largest Swiss companies from the 1930s to the 1980s. It is only since the 1980s that the number of foreigners has been increasing to the point that Swiss boards are actually among the most internationalised among developed countries (Ruigrok and Greve 2008).

Other, more peripheral, countries, where foreign multinationals play an important role, are interesting cases because they show that international corporate networks are not only influenced by changes in the economic environment, but also by alterations in political regimes. For example, foreigners (French, German) and minorities members (mostly Jews) were very present in the Bulgarian big business scene during the interwar period. During the Great Depression their influence started to diminish but it was only with the communist regime that foreigners vanished almost entirely from Bulgarian firms (Ivanov and Ganev 2014). Hungary experienced the same evolution as Bulgaria during the communist period. However, after the fall of the Berlin Wall, foreign-owned firms became progressively more integrated into the broader corporate network (Stark and Vedres 2006). In Argentina, too, the process of nationalisation led by Peron after the Second World War saw the decline of the "cosmopolitan" corporate network where foreign and local capital forged coalitions and built collaborative strategies (Lluch and Salvaj 2014). After Taiwan (which was conquered by Japan in 1895) had its first taste of independence in 1947, all the Japanese companies' assets were transferred to the new government of Chiang Kai-Shek, which transformed them into publicly owned firms (Lee and Velema 2014).

We know international corporate networks exist, but it remains difficult to assess these networks' real influence across borders in order to lower transaction and information costs. This influence is often assumed; only some papers focusing on the national level deal explicitly with the question. Davis (1991) for example finds that firms that are centrally located in the network and are interlocked with firms that have already adopted the poison pill are more likely to adopt this takeover defence as well. Haunschild (1993) investigates inter-organisational imitation by analysing the relation between interlocks and the acquisition activities of firms. She finds that directors transfer information on the efficiency of certain policies by observing the consequences of management decisions. There is even less evidence of the transfer of information and ideas on an international level. For example, it would be very interesting to see how the idea of shareholder value became so dominant over the last four decades (Lazonick and O'Sullivan 2000). The ideas of agency theory, which form the basis of the shareholder value conception of the firm, are "derived not from inductive observation and practical experience but, instead, from the theoretical musings of a newly revitalised neoclassical economic theory" (Fourcade and Khurana, 2013: 151). Economists brought the deductive, theoretical approach to business schools. For example, William Meckling and Michael Jensen, both graduates from the University of Chicago, played an important role in the dissemination of these ideas, both within academia as well as in the press (for more details on the spread of these ideas, see Fourcade and Khurana 2013: 151–153). Heilbron *et al.* (2014) show the role of corporate raiders and pension funds in the diffusion of the shareholder value conception. According to them, corporate raiders used the economic crisis of the early 1980s to oppose management and acquire shares in undervalued firms, while threatening to restructure and partially sell shares in the name of shareholders' interests. The Council of Institutional Investors was founded in 1985 in tandem with the adoption of the shareholder value doctrine, introducing organised activism to pension funds with regard to the management of firms (Heilbron *et al.* 2014; see also David *et al.* 2015 for the Swiss case). However, more research needs to be done on how ideas spread and what role international corporate networks play. Business schools seem to play an important role, which brings us to the inner circle of transnational elites and the importance of education and social clubs.

Creating cohesion among the transnational elite

The inner circle forms an important component within corporate networks. This close group of well-connected elites with shared norms and values is expected to defend not only their own interests, but also those of the business elite as a whole. "It has the capacity to discipline corporations and corporate elite members whose individual behavior may be contrary to the interests of all; and it can legitimately represent itself as the general voice of big business" (Useem 1980: 62). The inner circle often has political ties and can influence state policies. At the international level, there are very few studies on the interactions between these business networks. However, it seems that an "inner circle of cosmopolitans" exists at the end of the twentieth century, composed of corporate directors sitting on the boards of companies in different countries and belonging at the same time to transnational policy groups (Nollert 2005; Caroll 2010: ch. 2).

For transnational class to be able to lower obstacles to globalisation, it is important to build trust and shared norms and values; in other words, to build a strong inner circle. One way to do so is by standardising education; yet another is by participating in social clubs. Useem (1984) emphasises the importance of inner circle educational networks for two reasons. First, people who study in the same institution create strong social bonds. Second, schools help to create common ideas and values among business elites. Some scholars argue that after the Second World War (in particular since the 1980s), managers have increasingly held MBAs from American or European business schools, which has helped to create a transnational community. For example, Brezis finds that more than 40 per cent of the business and political elites of the developed countries have attended one of the top 50 universities in the world, which she calls the international elite universities. "In consequence, we face today a scenario where the elites of the world become uniform. They obtain the same education, move in the same milieu, and imbibe the same culture" (see Brezis 2010: 16). Others disagree with this statement. Hartmann (2016) is sceptical about this trend. Interestingly, the transnationalisation of elites through education is not new. During the nineteenth century, the recruitment and education of elites was a family business: heirs of family firms were often sent abroad in a form of apprenticeship, either to foreign agents or to firms with which the family firm had close working relationships (Byrkjeflot 2001; Wagner 2005). It is since the end of the nineteenth century that we see progressively emerging national models of management education, which would dominate until the 1980s (see Chapter 8 in this volume).

Useem also emphasises the importance of social clubs for the cohesion of the inner circle: "Social cohesion implies that the inner circle is truly a circle: acquaintanceship networks are dense, mutual trust and obligation are widespread, and a common sense of identity and culture prevail" (1984: 63). Sociologists have underlined the importance of such clubs for the contemporary transnational elite (Cousin and Chauvin 2012; Beaverstock 2011). Historically, however, they have also played a role for the social cohesion of the transnational elite. For example, Rotary expanded during the twentieth century to become a "globe-spanning organisation" (Wikle 1999; see also De Grazia 2006). Even if these clubs show strong differences at the regional and national level, as a transnational network, Rotary International evolved during the interwar period "into a middle ground for U.S. and non-U.S. business and professional classes" (Goff 2008: 326). Other studies emphasise the importance of social clubs at the transnational levels, which strengthens interlocking directorates. For example, Brayshay *et al.* (2005) analyse the networks of the capitalist elite of 12 major multinationals active across British imperial territories between 1900 and 1930 and show that in the early twentieth century, there was an interconnected corporate elite running large companies whose interests were spread across the world. This elite was not only linked through boards of directors, but they also belonged to the same social clubs, such as the Carlton Club (Brayshay *et al.* 2005: 217–219). In yet another article, they investigate the social network of Patrick Ashley Cooper who was appointed governor of the Hudson's Bay Company in 1931. Cooper's diary shows how his strong transnational social life was embedded in his international corporate network:

As in London, the diaries show that meetings were held in company premises, the dining rooms of banks and hotels, embassies, government offices and the official residences of ministers and other political figures. Moreover, just as in London, Cooper was made a member, or he was admitted as a guest, to gentlemen's clubs in the major cities that he visited in Argentina, the United States, Canada and South Africa.

(Brayshay et al. 2006: 995)

International corporate networks are an important source of international contacts and information sharing. They help to lower information and transaction costs, and to get privileged access to foreign markets. The evolution of international corporate networks shows that these cross-border networks are not a recent phenomenon, but rather they already existed in the nineteenth century. However, this section also shows that the networks are not strictly global networks, because important parts of the world, where large (multinational) firms do not or hardly exist, are not included in the networks. Although the transnational elite shares membership in social clubs and, more recently, standardised education, it seems reasonable to conclude that they still have deep-rooted connections with their home countries.

Thus, international business networks' contribution to globalisation is due to the fact that the inner circle is formed by a group of international businessmen whose new ideas and opinions have been spread across borders and who have tried to influence politics. The latter often happens by means of BIAs. BIAs help to coordinate the actions of corporate networks and strengthen their political influence. At the same time, corporate networks help to reduce internal divisions within BIAs:

despite their greater complexity and variety there seems to be a markedly lower level of tension, discord and conflict among BIAs than among the associations of any other class or status group. ... coordination is achieved through an invisible network of interlocking directorates and financial connections.

(Schmitter and Streeck 1999: 23–24; see also Ginalski and Eichenberger 2017)

We will now turn to the BIAs.

International BIAs

Schmitter and Streeck (1999) define two logics that frame the actions of BIAs. On the one hand, they engage with their members in a logic of membership. On the other hand, BIAs interact with the state, NGOs, and labour organisations (logic of influence). Their actions are situated at the intersection of these two logics, which implies constraints on and opportunities for them. The management of diversity due to the heterogeneity of its members' interests is central to the functioning and efficiency of these associations.

Various scholars have tried to make typologies of BIAs. The most common one is the distinction between trade associations and employers' associations. Trade associations are organised around a certain sector or product and provide services for their members but also act as lobbying groups in the political spheres. Employers' associations, on the other hand, are active in industrial relations issues (Lanzalaco 2008). The former, it would appear, are more likely to develop in international associations than the latter, which are organised more on a local or regional basis reflecting the labour market. Carroll (2010) puts forward another typology more focused on international BIAs and on the recent period. He identifies three (neoliberal) groups among international BIAs for the recent period. The first one "calls for a complete global laissez-faire, drawing on fundamental neoliberal tenets of monetarism, state deregulation, 'spontaneous' order of market relations, and possessive individualism" (Carroll 2010: 39; based on Robinson and Harris 2000). The International Chamber of Commerce (ICC) can be considered as representative of this stream. BIAs defined in the second group try to promote neoliberalism with a managerial role for the state in order to bring some stability to world markets. According to Carroll, the Bilderberg meetings belong to this second faction. The third one calls for a "broader regulatory apparatus" and includes organisations such as the World Business Council for Sustainable Development (WBCSD) created in 1995. Carroll (2010: ch. 2) states that these transnational policy groups play a very important integrative function among transnational boards.

The literature on international BIAs, dominated by political scientists and sociologists, has been concentrated on organised business in relation to European integration, resulting in a focus on associations established after the Second World War. However, this transnationalisation dates back even further in time. Galambos traced the roots of BIAs almost back to the Middle Ages: "Fundamentally, however, the organisations [Trade Associations] which businessmen in the modern world have employed to stabilise conditions have performed the same functions as the guilds and have developed along similar lines" (Galambos 1966: 4; see also Chapter 10 on guilds in this volume). Without going so far back in time, we see that already since the mid-nineteenth century business transnational elites met at international congresses. An important condition for the importance of these meetings has been the increasing mobility of individuals due to technological innovations in water transport (steam power and canals), communications (telegraph, overseas cables), and rapidly expanding railroads. As a result, a wide range of international congresses was organised in the United States and Europe beginning in the 1850s, when transnational knowledge was exchanged (Leonards and Randeraad 2015). More specifically, business elites tried to organise themselves during the second half of the nineteenth century when chambers of commerce took advantage of the World Exhibitions in order to create international contacts (Robins 2015; Druelle-Korn 2017). As we will see, the First World War did not put an end to this transnational spirit with the creation of a small – in comparison with the other periods – number of transnational BIAs.

After the Second World War, BIAs experienced another period of "transnationalisation", as well as "Europeanisation", characterised by the rapid emergence of many associations and federations that became active in lobbying and regulatory activities. According to Lanzalaco, this wave of transnational BIAs "can be interpreted as the attempt to create peaceful cross-border relationships among national capitalists, in order to avoid further military conflicts" (2008: 308). Rollings and Kipping (2008) show the importance of the economic function alongside the political function of these business associations. These kinds of forums were often informal meetings where ideas and information were multilaterally exchanged in uncertain times. This included, in part, the exchange of economic knowledge so as to reduce uncertainty and risks for firms. Lanzalaco (2008) identifies a last wave of transnationalisation of BIAs beginning in the 1980s, which is linked to the increasing process of regionalisation and globalisation of the economy.

We will now describe the activities of some of these transnational BIAs which are representative of the three categories put forward by Carroll and which reflect the three periods we just described. Even though ICC was created in 1919, it originated in the period before the First World War with the Union Internationale des Chambres de Commerce, created in 1905 (Rosengarten 2001). It was founded in order to facilitate international trade, a goal that it is still pursuing to this day. Only five countries were members of this organisation at its creation. Nowadays, more than 90 countries are affiliated. In order to promote international trade, ICC follows two approaches (Kelly 2005). On the one hand, it operates via political advocacy and lobbying directed at national governments and international organisations. For example, ICC has collaborated with other international organisations, such as the League of Nations (Ridgeway 1959) and the United Nations Conference on Trade and Development (UNCTAD) (Sauvant 2015) throughout the twentieth century. On the other hand, ICC provides services to business in general by creating international norms or standards (Kelly 2005). For example, ICC defined the Incoterms rules, or International Commercial Terms, after the interwar period (Jolivet 2003). ICC has also offered services in the domain of international commercial arbitration, having founded the ICC International Court of Arbitration in 1923 (Lemercier and Sgard 2015). By alleviating problems in contract enforcement and providing information about trade in numerous countries, ICC has tried to promote international trade throughout the twentieth century.

As we have seen, the internationalisation of BIAs after the Second World War was in part related to European integration. Numerous BIAs were created such as the Union des Industries de pays de la Communauté Européenne (UNICE) in 1958. However, elite networks were also created that involved non-state actors and that were not only related to European integration. An example is the Bilderberg meeting. Next to European issues, it was meant for improving relations with the United States. Thus, when Joseph Retinger founded the Bilderberg Group in 1952 with the help of Prince Bernhard of the Netherlands, Belgian Foreign Minister Paul van Zeeland, and Chairman of Unilever Paul Rijkens, one of its aims was to improve the increasingly tense relations between Western Europe and the United States. By bringing together an important group of Europeans and Americans, it contributed to a sense of shared values and interests on the transatlantic level between Western Europe and the United States (Richardson *et al.* 2011; Schaufelbuehl 2016).

The WBCSD was created in 1995 during the third wave of transnationalisation of BIAs. It is a worldwide organisation that focuses on environmental issues. It reflects,

> a maturing elite awareness that transnational corporate enterprise must be coupled with consensus over environmental regulation. … The WBCSD promotes, as an alternative to state regulation of capital, a global self-regulatory framework, emphasising benchmarking and "best practices" as voluntary means towards green capitalism.
>
> *(Carroll 2010: 216–217)*

By creating common values and interests, sharing important knowledge among their members, and lobbying for fewer and/or more consistent regulations, international BIAs (and international corporate networks) play an important role in lowering the barriers to globalisation. However, we want to make a few remarks in the next section to nuance this conclusion.

International business networks and global trade

First, international business networks are not a recent phenomenon, nor do they emerge only in times or places where market institutions fail. International business networks are clearly related to periods of globalisation, e.g. the period between 1870 and 1914 and the period after the 1980s. However, during periods of more protectionism and/or political tensions (or even war), they also seem to be important players to keep or improve relations. ICC clearly plays such a role during the interwar period (Rosengarten 2001).

Second, the evolution of different types of international business networks reveal that it is hard to speak of strictly global networks, as important parts of the world are not included in the networks. A more accurate term would be international, or transnational, networks. The members of these networks mostly come from Europe and North America, whereas African countries are often not involved. For example, Carroll (2010), in a study of the 500 largest firms, shows that in 2006 a North Atlantic ruling class remains at the centre of the process of transnational capitalist class formation, although it finds a modest participation of corporate elites from the Global South. Historically, Asian countries are extensively connected through regional networks, but have relatively fewer connections to other parts of the world (Lee and Velema 2014).

Third, also interesting is the fact that despite the existence of international networks, in many cases the national home country remains very important. These international networks and actors are profoundly embedded in national or urban networks. These different geographical levels (local, regional, national, or international) should not be opposed but integrated into a "scalar conception that suggests human societies, polities, activities and non-human factors are organised into levels that go from the local to the global, through the national, with each one fitted into the other according to some pyramidal structure" (Saunier 2008: 171; on the inter-actions between these scales, see also Tyrrell 2009 or Middell and Naumann 2010). During the eighteenth century, some British business networks were thus profoundly embedded in polit-ical, social, and cultural networks at the city and regional levels, and were at the same time very active in transnational trade through global connections (Pearson and Richardson 2008: 766; see also Lüthy 2005). This is still the case; for example, the organisation of ICC relies on national committees that are often closely linked to regional or urban chambers of commerce.

Fourth, in certain circumstances, international business networks can hinder the globalisation process (see also Chapter 32 on imitation and global business in this volume). We will show this by focusing on international *cartels*, which can also be considered as business networks (Fear 2008). Internally, it is important to coordinate their actions and to avoid cheating members. Communication and diffusion of information therefore play a very important role within the cartel. Externally, cartels aim to create barriers of entry in order to fight against competitors. Moreover, cartels have close and conflicting interaction with governments.

We emphasise two points that are relevant not only for international cartels, but also more broadly for international business networks in general. First, their perception and impact have been influenced by the economic, social, and political environment. The evolution of cartel legislation during the twentieth century illustrates this phenomenon. Second, we focus on the debate about the impact of international cartels on economic development.

Since the end of the nineteenth century, private international cartels – which comprise firms from more than one country – have been flourishing across the world (Schröter 1996). They have emerged in very different industries and sectors. Although the functions of international cartels seem not to have changed fundamentally since the end of the nineteenth century, their external institutional environment has evolved considerably, which explains why international cartels were progressively banned after 1945. The interwar years are often described as the golden age of international cartels – they controlled an estimated 30–40 per cent of world trade during the 1930s (Levenstein and Suslow 2008: 1108). It is interesting to note that international cartels gained legitimacy during this period. The collaboration of some of the active firms in these cartels with international institutions such as the League of Nations and ICC helped to forge a public discourse that was able "to transform private and secret organisations into instru-ments of public utility" (Bertilorenzi 2015: 45). After the Second World War, anti-cartel legis-lation was introduced in Germany and Japan partly due to the pressure of the US government (Freyer 2006). In 1962, Regulation 17 of the Treaty of Rome banned cartels and gave a clear priority to the fight against cartels in Europe. However, the implementation of this regulation proved difficult (Warlouzet 2016). The prosecution of international cartels was generally avoided for political and economic reasons:

In some cases, international cartels had the active support or participation of sovereign states, making prosecution politically sensitive, if not impossible. In others, international cartels were the sole source of supply of critical raw materials (such as potash), making prosecution risky for the economy as a whole.

(Levenstein and Suslow 2008: 1111)

It is only in the 1990s that prosecutions of international cartels became very active due to the globalisation process and adoption of corporate amnesty programs. This movement began first in the United States, then spread to Europe and other regions around the world (Freyer 2006).

Economists argue that cartels led firms to raise prices and restrict output. In a review on the function and impact of cartels, Levenstein and Sulow (2006: 86) emphasise that cartels seem to increase prices and profits, even though more careful studies would be necessary to fully understand the economic effects of international cartels. One of the reasons why international cartels do not stimulate international trade is that they create and enhance entry barriers. Indeed, Rauch (2001: 1200) writes that the "organisation of international trade through networks may hinder its growth if transnational networks tend to be closed to new members". These restrictions can lead to the creation of rents captured by private business networks (see Pearson and Richardson 2008 for the eighteenth century). This is an important conclusion: in certain cases, international business networks, such as the Mafia, can create harmful forms of cooperation, in which "bad behaviour spreads". Thus, these harmful forms of cooperation point out that networks "do not always include everybody; at times social networks work for some (the powerful) and harm others (the weak)" (Carnevali 2011: 909).

Future research

In conclusion, we would like to put forward three research avenues. First, more attention should be paid to agency in order to explain the role and evolution of these international business networks as emphasised by Rosenberg (2012b: 819) in her study of social and cultural transnational networks during the second part of the nineteenth century:

An examination of global currents helps direct attention to particular people who shaped the emergent networks and affiliations and who served as conduits for exchanges connecting several planes of analysis. A focus on people and their connections can help make visible how the realms of the transnational, the national, and the local intersected.

Second, it remains extremely difficult to measure the real influence of international business networks. In his study of the World Economic Forum, an influential agent in the global political economy, Graz (2003: 322) argues that it is almost impossible to measure the power of such groups, because "the influence of an elite club on a particular issue of global politics hinges, by definition, on loose and informal channels of power". It is the reason why more research is needed to analyse how knowledge and ideas are being spread through these networks. Third, studies on international business networks should not focus only on their positive impact. Business networks, such as international cartels, are vehicles of inclusion and exclusion. Because these international networks are often not truly global, they risk increasing the great divergence between the West and the rest of the world. In other words, the European and American dominated business networks might decide upon important societal issues without having listened to voices in the rest of the world. In studying international business networks, "we cannot shy away from investigating issues such as hegemony, conflict, and exclusion" (Carnevali 2011: 909). At their core, international business networks are driven not only by trust, but also by power.

References

Beaverstock, J. V., "Servicing British Expatriate 'Talent' in Singapore: Exploring Ordinary Trans-nationalism and the Role of the 'Expatriate' Club", *Journal of Ethnic and Migration Studies* 37(5), 2011, 709–728.

Bertilorenzi, M., "Legitimating the International Cartels Movement: The League of Nations, the International Chamber of Commerce, and the Survey of International Cartels during the Interwar Period". In: S. Fellman and M. Shahannan (eds), *Regulating Competition: Cartel Registers in the Twentieth Century World*, New York and London: Routledge, 2015, 30–48.

Brandeis, L. D., *Other People's Money: And How the Bankers Use It*, New York: F.A. Stockes, 1914.

Braudel, F., *Civilization and Capitalism, 15th–18th Century"*, 3 vols, New York: Harper & Row, 1981–1984 [French original 1967–1979].

Brayshay, M., M. Cleary, and J. Selwood, "Interlocking Directorships and Trans-national Linkages within the British Empire, 1900–1930", *Area* 37(2), 2005, 209–222.

Brayshay, M., M. Cleary, and J. Selwood, "Power Geometries: Social Networks and the 1930s Multi-national Corporate Elite", *Geoforum* 37(1), 2006, 986–998.

Brezis, E. S., "Globalization and the Emergence of a Transnational Oligarchy", Working paper, *World Institute for Development Economics Research* 10(5), 2010.

Burris, V. and C. L. Staples, "In Search of a Transnational Capitalist Class: Alternative Methods for Comparing Director Interlocks within and between Nations and Regions", *International Journal of Comparative Sociology* 53(4), 2012, 323–342.

Byrkjeflot, H., "Management Education and Selection of Top Managers in Europe and the United States", Bergen: LOS-Senter, Rapport 103, 2001.

Carnevali, F., "Social Capital and Trade Associations in America, c. 1860–1914: A Microhistory Approach", *Economic History Review* 64(3), 2011, 905–928.

Carroll, W., *Corporate Power in a Globalizing World*, Revised Edition, Toronto: Oxford University Press, 2010.

Casson, M. and H. Cox, "International Business Networks: Theory and History", *Business and Economic History* 22(1), 1993, 42–54.

Chandler, A. D., *Scale and Scope: The Dynamics of Industrial Capitalism*, Cambridge, MA: Belknap, 1990.

Cousin, B. and S. Chauvin, "L'économie symbolique du capital social: Notes pour un programme de recherche", *Actes de la recherche en sciences sociales* 193(3), 2012, 96–103.

David, T. and G. Westerhuis (eds), *The Power of Corporate Networks: A Comparative and Historical Perspective*, London: Routledge, 2014.

David, T., M. Lupold, A. Mach, and G. Schnyder, *De la "Forteresse des Alpes" à la valeur actionnariale: Histoire de la gouvernance d'entreprise suisse au 20ème siècle*, Zürich: Seismo, 2015.

Davis, G. F., "Agents without Principles? The Spread of the Poison Pill through the Intercorporate Network", *Administrative Science Quarterly* 36(4), 1991, 583–613.

De Grazia, V., *Irresistible Empire: America's Advance through Twentieth-Century Europe*, Cambridge, MA: Belknap Press of Harvard University, 2006.

De Vries, J., "The Limits of Globalization in the Early Modern World", *Economic History Review* 63(3), 2010, 710–733.

Druelle-Korn, C., "The Great War: Matrix of the International Chamber of Commerce, a Fortunate Business League of Nations". In: A. Smith, S. Mollan, and K. D. Tennent (eds), *The Impact of the First World War on International Business*, New York and London: Routledge, 2017, 103–120.

Fear, J., "Cartels". In: G. Jones and J. Zeitlin (eds), *The Oxford Handbook of Business History*, Oxford: Oxford University Press, 2008, 268–292.

Fennema, M., *International Networks of Banks and Industry*, The Hague/Boston, MA: Martinus Nijhoff Publishers, 1982.

Flynn, D. O. and A. Giraldez, "Path Dependence, Time Lags and the Birth of Globalization: A Critique of O'Rourke and Williamson", *European Review of Economic History* 8(1), 2004, 81–108.

Fourcade, M. and R. Khurana, "The Social Trajectory of a Finance Professor and the Common Sense of Capital", *History of Political Economy* 49(2), 2013, 347–381.

Freyer, A. T., *Antitrust and Global Capitalism, 1930–2004*, Cambridge: Cambridge University Press, 2006.

Galambos, L., *Competition and Cooperation: The Emergence of a National Trade Association*, Baltimore, MD: Johns Hopkins University Press, 1966.

Gelderblom, O. and F. Trivellato, "The Business History of the Preindustrial World: Towards a Comparative Historical Analysis", *Business History*, 12 February 2018, 1–35.

Ginalski, S. and P. Eichenberger, " 'Si vis pacem, para bellum': The Construction of Business Cooperation in the Swiss Machinery Industry", *Socio-Economic Review* 15(3), 2017, 615–635.

Goff, B. M., "The Heartland Abroad: The Rotary Club's Mission of Civic Internationalism", PhD dissertation in History, University of Michigan, 2008.

Granovetter, M., "Economic Action and Social Structure: The Problem of Embeddedness", *American Journal of Sociology* 91(3), 1985, 481–510.

Graz, J.-C., "How Powerful are Transnational Elite Clubs? The Social Myth of the World Economic Forum", *New Political Economy* 8(3), 2003, 321–340.

Guinnane, T. W., "Trust: A Concept too Many", *Jahrbuch für Wirtschaftsgeschichte/Economic History Yearbook* 46(1), 2005, 77–92.

Hannah, L., "Pioneering Modern Corporate Governance: A View from London in 1900", *Enterprise & Society* 8(1), 2007, 642–686.

Hartmann, M., *Die globale Wirtschaftselite: Eine Legende*, Frankfurt am Main: Campus, 2016.

Haunschild, P. R. "Interorganizational Imitation: The Impact of Interlocks on Corporate Acquisition Activity", *Administrative Science Quarterly* 38(4), 1993, 564–613.

Heemskerk, E. M., F. W. Takes, J. Garcia-Bernardo, and M. J. Huijzer, "Where is the Global Corporate Elite? A Large-scale Network Study of Local and Nonlocal Interlocking Directorates", *Sociologica* (2), 2016, 1–18.

Heilbron, J., J. Verheul, and S. Quack, "The Origins and Early Diffusion of 'Shareholder Value' in the United States", *Theory and Society* 43(1), 2014, 1–22.

Hilferding, R., *Das Finanzkapital: Eine Studie über die jüngste Entwicklung des Kapitalismus*, Frankfurt am Main: Europäische Verlagsanstalt, 1910 (1968).

Ivanov, M. and G. Ganev, "Bulgarian Business Elite, 1900s–2000s". In: T. David and G. Westerhuis (eds), *The Power of Corporate Networks: A Comparative and Historical Perspective*, London: Routledge, 2014, 213–233.

Jeidels, O., *Das Verhältnis der Deutschen Grossbanken zur Industrie mit Besonderer Berücksichtigung der Eisenindustrie*, Leipzig: Duncker & Humblot, 1905.

Jolivet, E., *Les Incoterms: Etude d'une norme du commerce international*, Paris: Litec, 2003.

Jones, C. A., *International Business in the Nineteenth Century: The Rise and Fall of a Cosmopolitan Bourgeoisie*, Brighton: Wheatsheaf Books, 1987.

Jones, G. "Globalization". In: G. Jones and J. Zeitlin (eds), *The Oxford Handbook of Business History*, Oxford: Oxford University Press, 2008, 141–171.

Jones, G., "The End of Nationality? Global Firms and Borderless Worlds", *Zeitschrift für Unternehmensgeschichte* 51(2), 2006, 149–166.

Kelly, D., "The International Chamber of Commerce", *New Political Economy*, 10(2), 2005, 259–261.

Lanzalaco, L., "Business Interest Associations". In: G. Jones and J. Zeitlin (eds), *The Oxford Handbook of Business History*, New York: Oxford University Press, 2008, 293–315.

Lazonick, W. and M. O'Sullivan, "Maximizing Shareholder Value: A New Ideology for Corporate Governance", *Economy and Society* 29(1), 2000, 13–35.

Lee., Z.-R. and T. A. Velema, "The Directorate Interlock Network in Taiwan Throughout the Twentieth Century". In: T. David and G. Westerhuis (eds), *The Power of Corporate Networks: A Comparative and Historical Perspective*, London: Routledge, 2014, 276–296.

Lemercier, C. and J. Sgard, "Arbitrage privé international et globalization(s)", [Rapport de recherche 11.11), Mission de Recherche Droit et Justice, CNRS Sciences Po, 2015.

Leonards, C. and N. Randeraad, "Building a Transnational Network of Social Reform in the 19th Century". In: D. Rodogno, B. Struck, and J. Vogel (eds), *Shaping the Transnational Sphere: Experts, Networks and Issues from the 1840s to the 1930s*, Contemporary European History, No. 14, New York: Berghahn Books, 2015, pp. 111–131.

Levenstein, M. C. and V. Y. Suslow, "What Determines Cartels Success?" *Journal of Economic Literature* XLIV, 2006, 43–95.

Levenstein, M. C. and V. Y. Suslow, "International Cartels". In: W. D. Collins (ed.), *Issues in Competition Law and Policy*, Chicago, IL: American Bar Association, Antitrust Section, 2008, 1107–1126.

Lluc, A. and E. Salvaj, "Longitudinal Study of Interlocking Directorates in Argentina and Foreign Firms' Integration into Local Capitalism (1923–2000)". In: T. David and G. Westerhuis (eds), *The Power of Corporate Networks: A Comparative and Historical Perspective*, London: Routledge, 2014, 257–276.

Lüthy, H., *La Banque protestante en France: De la Révocation de l'Edit de Nantes à la Révolution*, Zürich: Neue Zürcher Zeitung, 2005.

Mach, A., T. David, S. Ginalski, and F. Bühlmann, *Les élites économiques suisses au XXe siècle*, Neuchâtel: Alphil, 2016.

Middell, M. and M. Naumann, "Global History and the Spatial Turn: From the Impact of Area Studies to the Study of Critical Junctures of Globalization", *Journal of Global History* 5(1), 2010, 149–170.

Mizruchi, M., "What Do Interlocks Do? An Analysis, Critique, and Assessment of Research on Interlocking Directorates", *Annual Review of Sociology* 22, 1996, 271–298.

Nollert, M., "Transnational Corporate Ties: A Synopsis of Theories and Empirical Findings", *Journal of World-Systems Research* 11(2), 2005, 289–314.

O'Rourke, K. H. and J. G. Williamson, *Globalization and History. The Evolution of a Nineteenth-Century Atlantic Economy*, Cambridge, MA: MIT Press, 1999.

Pearson, R. and D. Richardson, "Social Capital, Institutional Innovation and Atlantic Trade Before 1800", *Business History* 50(6), 2008, 765–780.

Rauch, J. E., "Business and Social Networks in International Trade", *Journal of Economic Literature* 39(4), 2001, 1177–1203.

Richardson, I., A. Kakabadse, and N. Kakabadse, *Bilderberg People: Elite Power and Consensus in World Affairs*, London: Routledge, 2011.

Ridgeway, G. L., *Merchants of Peace: Twenty Years of Business Diplomacy through the International Chamber of Commerce 1919–1938*, New York: Columbia University Press, 1959.

Robins, J. E., "A Common Brotherhood for Their Mutual Benefit: Sir Charles Macara and Internationalism in the Cotton Industry, 1904–1914", *Enterprise & Society* 16(4), 2015, 847–888.

Robinson, W., *A Theory of Global Capitalism: Production, Class and State in a Transnational World*, Baltimore, MD: Johns Hopkins University Press, 2004.

Robinson, W. and J. Harris, "Towards a Global Ruling Class? Globalization and the Transnational Capitalist Class", *Science and Society* 64(1), 2000, 11–54.

Rollings, N. and M. Kipping, "Private Transnational Governance in the Heyday of the Nation-State: The Council of European Industrial Federations (CEIF)", *Economic History Review* 61(2), 2008, 409–431.

Rosenberg, E. S., "Introduction". In: E. S. Rosenberg, *A World Connecting, 1870–1945*, Cambridge, MA: Belknap Press of Harvard University Press, 2012a, 29–40.

Rosenberg, E. S., "Transnational Currents in a Shrinking World". In: E. S. Rosenberg, *A World Connecting, 1870–1945*, Cambridge, MA: Belknap Press of Harvard University Press, 2012b, 815–999.

Rosengarten, M., *Die Internationale Handelskammer: wirtschaftspolitische Empfehlungen in der Zeit der Weltwirtschaftskrise 1929–1939*, Berlin: Duncker und Humblot, 2001.

Ruigrok, W. and P. Greve, "The Rise of an International Market for Executive Labour". In: L. Oxelheim and C. Wihlborg (eds), *Markets and Compensation for Executives in Europe*, Bingley, UK: Emerald Group Publishing, 2008, 53–78.

Saunier, P.-Y., "Learning by Doing: Notes about the Making of the Palgrave Dictionary of Transnational History", *Journal of Modern European History* 6(2), 2008, 159–180.

Saunier, P.-Y., *Transnational History*, Basingstoke: Palgrave Macmillan, 2013.

Sauvant, K. P., "The Negotiations of the United Nations Code of Conduct on Transnational Corporations: Experience and Lessons Learned", *Journal of World Investment and Trade* 16(1), 2015, 11–87.

Schaufelbuehl, J. M., "The Transatlantic Business Community Faced with US Direct Investment in Western Europe, 1958–1968", *Business History* 58(6), 2016, 880–902.

Schmitter, P. C. and W. Streeck, "The Organization of Business Interests: Studying the Associative Action of Business in Advanced Industrial Societies", Working paper, *Max Planck Institut für Gesellschaftsforschung*, 1999, 1–95.

Schröter, H. G., "Cartelization and Decartelization in Europe, 1870–1995: Rise and Decline of an Economic Institution", *Journal of European Economic History* 25(1), 1996, 129–153.

Scott, J., "Networks of Corporate Power: A Comparative Assessment", *Annual Review of Sociology* 17(1), 1991, 181–203.

Sklair, L., *The Transnational Capitalist Class*, Oxford: Blackwell, 2001.

Sluga, G. and P. Clavin (eds), *Internationalisms: A Twentieth-Century History*, Cambridge: Cambridge University Press, 2017.

Staples, C. L., "Board Globalisation in the World's Largest TNCs 1993–2005", *Corporate Governance: An International Review* 15(2), 2007, 311–321.

Stark, D. and B. Vedres, "Social Times of Network Spaces: Network Sequences and Foreign Investment in Hungary", *American Journal of Sociology* 111(5), 2006, 1367–1411.

Stokman, F. N., R. Ziegler, and J. Scott (eds), *Networks of Corporate Power. A Comparative Analysis of Ten Countries*, Cambridge: Polity Press, 1985.

Tyrrell, I., "Reflections on the Transnational Turn in United States History: Theory and Practice", *Journal of Global History* 4(3), 2009, 453–474.

Useem, M., "Corporations and the Corporate Elite", *Annual Review of Sociology* 6, 1980, 41–77.

Useem, M., *The Inner Circle: Large Corporations and the Rise of Business Political Activity in the US and the UK*, New York: Oxford University Press, 1984.

Wagner, A.-C., "Les élites managériales de la mondialisation: angles d'approche et catégories d'analyse", *Entreprises et histoire* 41(4), 2005, 15–23.

Warlouzet, L., "The Centralization of EU Competition Policy: Historical Institutionalist Dynamics from Cartel Monitoring to Merger Control (1956–91)", *Journal of Common Market Studies* 54(3), 2016, 725–741.

Wikle, T. A., "International Expansion of the American-Style Service Club", *Journal of American Culture* 22(2), 1999, 45–52.

Windolf, P., "Coordination and Control in Corporate Networks: United States and Germany in Comparison, 1896–1938", *European Sociological Review* 25(4), 2009, 443–457.

17

CLUSTERS AS SPACES FOR GLOBAL INTEGRATION

Valeria Giacomin

Introduction

Clusters are geographically concentrated and interlinked agglomerations of specialized firms in a particular domain. Historically, clusters represented a primary form of organization for the spread of global capitalism. Multinationals operating in new markets channeled their investment in circumscribed geographies, to maximize the efficiency of their extractive activities in frontier locations (Fitzgerald 2016).

Social sciences research extensively examined the topic of localized industrial agglomeration: business and strategy scholars scrutinized how economic concentration impacted national competitiveness and firm strategies (Porter 1998b); economic geographers investigated how agglomeration forwards innovation and regional development (Storper and Walker 1989). Finally, sociologists and historians analyzed knowledge generation and exchange across cluster companies as well as the relationship between clustering and the institutional environment (Becattini 2004; Piore and Sabel 1984). However, these contributions over-empathized the impact of local dynamics over external influences. When considering non-local elements of cluster development, such as imported knowledge and technology, the literature studied how they were absorbed and repackaged to yield local competitiveness. Consequently, critics accused cluster scholarship of suffering from "self-containment" and a "local obsession" (Declercq 2019), while ignoring the role of transnational linkages. Despite several attempts to solve this theoretical puzzle, this research did not explicitly address clusters' impact on international business and globalization (Bathelt and Glückler 2014). By contrast, this chapter reviews the – so far partially under-researched – topic of longstanding clusters in developing countries, to explain how multinationals organized their activities at the global level. Given the limited infrastructure in emerging markets, multinational enterprises (MNEs) clustered their activities around service and port locations. This fostered knowledge dissemination and increased specialization, but also eased local exploitation and fast asset mobilization in times of political instability (Giacomin 2018).

This chapter first examines the major contributions at the core of cluster theory and argues for a new understanding of clusters as enabling the expansion of global capitalism. The next section reviews the multidisciplinary literature on industrial agglomeration and pinpoints the major contentions raised in the theoretical debate on clusters. The third section discusses clusters' contribution to globalization through global value chains (GVCs) and historical approaches. The fourth section includes two historical cases showing how MNEs' activities and investment in the form of, or within existing, clusters facilitated the internationalization of developing economies. The final section concludes by stressing clusters' role in the making of global business.

Industrial concentration as a foundation of cluster scholarship

Alfred Marshall's *Principles of Economics* (1920) is the standard reference for the study of industrial concentration. As the first to discuss the advantages of economic concentration, Marshall coined the expression "industrial districts" after observing the high density of specialized productions by small and medium-sized enterprises (SMEs) in selected UK regions, such as Lancashire cotton, Staffordshire pottery, and Sheffield cutlery. The companies co-locating in these industrial areas benefited from cost savings (i.e., lower input prices) and higher specialization. These advantages, later named "agglomeration economies," were understood as exogenous to each individual firm in the area, but endogenous to the group of companies there. Marshall identified a triad of sources for these positive externalities: a skilled labor pool; local non-traded inputs; and information spillovers due to proximity (McCann 2009).

In the post-war period, Marshall's theory re-emerged to explain the performance of new organizational forms surfacing in Europe as alternatives to the declining Fordist model (Piore and Sabel 1984; Trigilia 2002: 197–210). The concept of industrial district was adopted to define regionally concentrated systems of production based on highly specialized family-owned SMEs.

New industrial districts, learning regions, and self-containment

Since the 1980s, Marshall's ideas have inspired important contributions in several fields of the social sciences, defining the phenomenon in different ways: (neo-Marshallian) "industrial districts" (Bellandi *et al.* 2009), "learning regions," *milieux innovateurs* (Aydalot 1986; Scott 1985), and "clusters" (Porter 1998a; Karlsson 2008).

Economic historians and sociologists developed the neo-Marshallian district tradition, seeking to explain the growth of sectorial groups of SMEs in northeastern and central Italy – the so-called "Third Italy" – after the 1970s (Becattini 2004; Brusco 1990; Piore and Sabel 1984). In these neo-Marshallian districts, production occurs in dense industrial networks via an "extended division of labor between small and medium-sized firms specialized in distinct phases or complementary activities within a common industrial sector" (Zeitlin 2008: 223). Following Granovetter's (1985) concept of "social embeddedness," firms within these districts become more flexible by cooperating via trust and shared culture. This favors the rapid circulation of knowledge in non-codified (tacit) forms through informal, often face-to-face, exchange. Business historians joined this discussion by examining the long-term relationships between firms and districts' institutions (Zeitlin 2008: 222–224). Major influences included North's neo-institutionalism, examining how institutions drive economic change (North 1999); and the Varieties of Capitalism approach (Hall and Soskice 2001), studying systematic institutional differences (i.e., corporate governance, labor relations, financing, and innovation) across the industrialized world. Among them, Wilson and Popp (2003; Popp 2003) studied the business structures and culture in the pottery district of North Staffordshire. Carnevali (2004) researched how industrial associations impacted the cohesiveness of the Birmingham jewelry district. Parsons and Rose (2005) scrutinized the evolution of skills and technology in the Lancashire cotton district as outdoor trade expanded after the 1960s. Scranton (1997) investigated the US manufacturing districts, challenging the Chandlerian paradigm based on large corporations. Colli (1999) reinterpreted the Italian district tradition through archival material to describe the entrepreneurial elements underpinning the district; while Spadavecchia (2005a, 2005b) analyzed the sources of financing, innovation, and knowledge transfer among Italian SMEs. Lescure (2002) examined the development of financial institutions in French districts. Similarly, Hashino and Kurosawa (2013) worked on the linkages between firms, government, and trade associations for the promotion of districts in Japan.

Meanwhile, geographers developed their own interpretation, overcoming the district to introduce more malleable concepts such as "new industrial spaces" (Scott 1985; Storper and Walker 1989), *milieux innovateurs* (Crevoisier 2004; Maillat 1998), and "learning regions" (Lundvall 1995). This scholarship, also named "New Economic Geography," shared the district literature's focus on path dependency and social embeddedness, but differed in scope, questions, and methods. In terms of level of analysis, it shifted the focus to larger territories and interpreted Marshall's "information spillovers" as regional learning dynamics and technological trajectories (Mackinnon *et al.* 2002). As for methods, while the empirically rich district studies threatened the analytical power of the underlying agglomeration theory (Zeitlin 2008), economic geographers' theory-driven analyses often lacked empirical depth (Mackinnon *et al.* 2002). As a common weakness, both scholarships overstate the local economic outcomes and only indirectly recognize the advantages of industrial concentration for international business. As partial exceptions, some studies engaged in comparative analyses, though within the same country. Saxenian's (1996) ethnography of firms in the two tech-regions of Silicon Valley and Boston Route 128 identified local institutions as the major discriminant in their divergent performance. Historians Amdam and Bjarnar (2015) explained the opposite outcomes of two Norwegian clusters since the 1990s as resulting from differing strategic actions and attitudes toward internationalization. Perez-Aleman (2005) studied the emergence of two Chilean agricultural clusters emanating from the collaboration between the state, local actors, and multinationals. Overall, the reviewed literature showed that economic concentration generated specialization, local growth, and increased trade flows. However it seldom considered external sources of cluster development, and, if so, it did only to explain local competitiveness, rather than global connectivity. Thus, while indirectly suggesting that clustering enables internationalization, this scholarship did not explicitly acknowledge its role in the expansion of global capitalism.

From districts to clusters: the problem of the cluster in context

Michael Porter (1998b) famously revisited the Marshallian idea of economic concentration in the domain of business strategy to understand its impact on countries' competitiveness. Porter overcame the industrial district model based on systems of SMEs and coined the "cluster" concept. In Porter's most recent definition, clusters "are geographic concentrations of industries related by knowledge, skills, inputs, demand and/or other linkages" (Delgado *et al.* 2016: 1). As clusters include organizations of different sizes and types (Porter and Ketels 2009), industrial districts qualified as a type of cluster, comprising SMEs in light manufacturing industries (Declercq 2019: 15; Porter and Ketels 2009: 181). Further, drawing from the theory of comparative advantage, Porter interpreted the existence of specialized industrial locations as competitive tools for nations to succeed in the international markets. Thus, Porter conceived clusters the result of the interplay among different local elements: firm strategy and industry structure, supporting industries, demand conditions, environmental conditions, and government regulation – the so-called "diamond" (Porter 1998b; Rugman 2005). Although Porter popularized the debate on industrial concentration and introduced it into the fields of international business and strategy, his framework was criticized for being a "fuzzy" branding exercise, lacking analytical depth (Markusen 1999; Martin and Sunley 2003).

However, following the "cluster vogue," geographers outlined a "knowledge-based" cluster theory (Maskell 2001; Maskell and Kebir 2005) and an "evolutionary approach" to clusters (Bresnahan *et al.* 2001; Trippl and Todtling 2008). This work applies a bottom-up perspective and focus on the exchange of knowledge across cluster institutions (Wolfe and Gertler 2004: 1077). Clusters advance through a balanced interplay of tacit and codified knowledge, which members access via an integrated system of "local buzz" and "global pipelines" (Bathelt *et al.* 2004). The "buzz" identifies the Marshallian externalities resulting from proximity, constant comparison, and monitoring among firms. "Pipelines" are institutional arrangements channeling knowledge available elsewhere into the cluster (Maskell *et al.* 2007), requiring "a shared institutional context [for] joint problem solving, learning and knowledge creation" (Bathelt *et al.* 2004: 43).

This diverse scholarship synthetized the findings of previous studies on agglomeration and explicitly connected them with the concept of international competitiveness. However, it did not as yet offer a comprehensive solution to the problem of location specificity – or "tunnel vision" (Declercq 2019). By presenting clusters as the result of comparative advantage, Porter's theory over-empathized local dynamics relative to external linkages. Neither did the knowledge-based approach explicitly consider contextual contingencies, or external shocks, impacting the cluster's working, its evolution, or its role within the broader global economy. Conversely, both theories considered clusters as unique entities that can absorb external input, but are hardly reproducible away from their location of origin, thus underplaying the value of comparative analyses of clusters across distant locations. While Martin and Sunley argued that Porter's clusters are "self-contained entities abstract from the rest of the economic landscape" (2003: 17), Zeitlin observed that "the self-contained character of the districts has been overstated," calling for more research on the "relationship between districts and the wider world" (2008: 219). Finally, MacKinnon and colleagues (2002: 293) stated that economic geographers "underemphasize the importance of wider extra-local networks and structures."

Paul Krugman (1998) partially solved this problem by analyzing the endogenous effects of industrial concentration, applying mainstream economics to understand how geography impacts growth dynamics (Fujita *et al.* 1999). Krugman interpreted Marshall's agglomeration economies as the result of increasing returns to scale generated by proximity. This perspective enhanced the role of trade in industrial development, stressing that (several) inputs used in clusters' specialized production can be imported into a specific location from elsewhere. Indeed, while boosting national competitiveness via comparative advantage, clusters also reinforce international business. Recent economic geography work attempted to overcome location specificity and local–global duality by pinpointing the relational aspect of spatial interaction. Some promising studies investigated non-durable trans-local institutions, such as trade fairs, conventions, and conferences as "temporary clusters," where actors working in different locations exchange specialized knowledge (Maskell 2014; Henn and Bathelt 2015).

Clusters beyond location: MNEs, developing economies, and global integration

The previous section concluded that much of the available scholarship on industrial agglomeration suffered from "tunnel vision" (Declercq 2019: 11). Cluster studies overlooked the sources of cluster connectivity and the influence of non-local sources of growth, such as: foreign investment; imported inputs; dispersed sources of knowledge; market-driven standards and requirements; and other organizational forms, e.g. business groups (Colpan and Cuervo-Cazurra in this volume), similar distant clusters, GVCs, and global cities. The reason is twofold. First, most studies on economic agglomeration analyze industrialized countries, characterized by homogeneous availability of inputs, solid institutions, low trade barriers, and political stability. Second, cluster theory traditionally studied clusters to fathom relationships among localized (or local) firms, instead of examining their relevance for MNEs' strategies and transnational operations. Conversely, in the case of clusters in less-developed economies, sources of growth were rarely only location-specific, and more frequently depended on factors imported from other locations or even located elsewhere (Barton 2014). As these locations often lacked efficient institutional apparatus and extended infrastructure, non-local resources, such as foreign capital, specialized knowledge, and inputs, clustered around selected locations, in order to facilitate local extraction directed to international trade. Thus, examining the activities of MNEs and transnational entrepreneurs across different clusters in emerging economies illustrates how clustering traditionally supported the making of global business.

The GVC approach and clustering in less-developed countries

"Poor countries lack well-developed clusters" (Porter 1998a: 86), mostly because of structural deficiencies in their business environment. These are also defined "institutional voids," or missing intermediaries and poor institutions, impairing the smooth functioning of capitalist systems (Khanna and Palepu 2010). Because of the lack of widespread infrastructure in peripheral areas in developing economies, industrial activity tends to concentrate in selected locations, especially around capital and port cities (Fujita and Mori 1996; Jacobs *et al.* 2010). A rich literature in globalization and development studies recognized the importance of clustering for export-led development strategies and for the first stage of growth of local SMEs (Giuliani *et al.* 2005; Schmitz and Nadvi 1999; Dijk and Rabellotti 1997). Weijland (1999) showed that clusters of microenterprises sparked early development in Indonesia. Cramer (1999), studied the Mozambican cashew-nuts industry to understand whether sub-Saharan Africa can industrialize through primary commodities clusters.

Export-oriented clusters undergo (technological or sectorial) upgrading through insertion into broader production structures connecting specialized supplier locations across the globe, also theorized as global commodity chains or GVCs (Humphrey and Schmitz 2000; Bair 2016; Sturgeon *et al.* 2008). In the GVC view, "lead firms" – core actors (often multinationals) in cross-border business networks – control these chains and are crucial drivers behind successfully globalized clusters. They enforce control through coordination mechanisms that do not involve direct ownership of cluster firms or assets (Gereffi and Korzeniewicz 1994; Ponte and Sturgeon 2014), but rather consist of governance dynamics, i.e., the "coordination of economic activities through [inter-firm] non-market relationships" (Humphrey and Schmitz 2002: 4). The GVC approach overcame the problem of location specificity in two ways. First, it showed that cluster emergence and development could result from factors independent from the cluster location. Second, it conceptualized clusters as part of the broader global economic system. Since its inception in the late 1990s, the GVC framework sought to provide comprehensive theorization of chain governance, while documenting the diversity of mechanisms linking different nodes in the value chain (Ponte and Sturgeon 2014). However, the approach was accused of structuralism, as it argued that firms' choices are determined by type of chain where they operate. Only recently the scholarship acknowledged the downsides of export-led development strategies in the developing world (Gereffi and Lee 2016; Lund-Thomsen *et al.* 2014). Industrial concentration often polarized resources at the social and geographical level, reducing host economies as mere suppliers of low-value added products to the developed world (Pyke and Lund-Thomsen 2016). This resulted from MNEs outcompeting local players, but also from institutional stickiness at the local level. For example, Thomsen (2007) documented that in Vietnam, government authorities impacted the process of supplier selection for global buyers of garment and apparel.

Clusters in global perspective: MNEs' activity and cluster competition

Despite presenting clusters as elements of global capitalism, the chain approach struggled to connect different levels of analysis and to acknowledge the agency of multinationals and trans-national entrepreneurs. Conversely, the historical analysis of MNEs' long-term strategies in developing countries helped solving the structuralism in existing accounts on clusters and GVCs. Business history (Jones 2000, 2005, 2013: 190–207) and international business (Wilkins 1970; Kindleberger 1969) research documented the role of MNEs in the formation of the global economy since the nineteenth century.

Geographically, global capitalism expanded following international trade between indus-trialized economies of the "core" (Western Europe, USA, and later Japan in the North) and a system of clustered activities in the "periphery" (developing economies in the South), supplying natural resources and agricultural commodities. Charles Jones (1987) introduced the notion of *cosmopolitan bourgeoisie* – thick networks of families and dense ethnically heterogeneous trading communities concentrating in port locations and hubs for global trade – to retrace the social structures behind the genesis and the expansion of the British Empire (Barton 2014) and the development of the First Global Economy (Fitzgerald 2016; Jones 2005; Bayly 2004). Geoffrey Jones analyzed in depth the activities of trading firms, their subsequent transformation into busi-ness groups, and their role in international commerce and in the financing of (clustered) infra-structure for primary production in less-developed countries (van Helten and Jones 1989; Jones and Wale 1999). In his *Capitals of Capital* (2010), Youssef Cassis studied the tentacular develop-ment of global finance, through a net of global cities, i.e., clusters of interconnected financial services supporting the activities of MNEs and local companies in regional economies (Jones and Gallagher-Kernstine 2014). McCann and Acs (2011) adopted an historical perspective to illustrate how MNEs (including financial institutions) directly impacted locations' connectivity, being "the primary conduits via which global knowledge flows operate and the natural channels via which domestic firms can distribute their goods" (Aitken *et al.* 1997) during intense globali-zation. Goerzen *et al.* (2013) showed that MNEs are likelier to invest within existing clusters and global cities than in other locations due to their global interconnectedness, and proximity to advanced services and cosmopolitan networks. In some instances, MNEs contributed to the formation of clusters: several flower clusters emerged in Colombia, Ecuador, and Kenya out of Dutch investment (Porter *et al.* 2013). In other cases, MNEs invested into existing industrial poles to tap into specialized knowledge (Zeitlin 2008: 226). MNEs' acquisitions supported the regeneration and internationalization of north Italy's shoe district in Montebelluna, Veneto (Belussi 2003) and the biomedical equipment industry of Mirandola, Emilia (Biggiero and Sam-marra 2003). Conversely, MNEs' entry disrupted the collaborative and innovative dynamics in the mechanical engineering cluster of Jæren, Norway (Asheim and Herstad 2003).

Recent business history works emphasized the advantages of cross-fertilization, using theor-etical models developed in geography to direct their historical analysis. In his study of the fur district in Saxony during the nineteenth century, Declercq (2019, 2015) scrutinized the rela-tionship between GVCs and industrial districts, by retracing the long-term trans-border inter-action among fur entrepreneurs. His study explored how lead firms responded to external competition by leveraging local collaboration and collective action. Similarly, Sebastian Henn (2012, 2013; Henn and Laureys, 2010) studied the global diamond-cutting industry between Antwerp and Gujarat, stressing how transnational entrepreneurs functioned as "human global pipelines" across different cluster locations. After World War II, entrepreneurs from the Jainist community of Palanpuris in India managed to revive the declining Gujarat cluster by transferring knowledge, technology, and cutting-skills from the Antwerp cluster. Consequently, the Indian cluster directly competed with Antwerp, eroding Belgian diamond dominance in the United States. Finally, Cirer-Costa (2014) analyzed how Majorca's tourism sector outcompeted similar Mediterranean holiday destinations, as major luxury hotels and shipping companies actively promoted internationalization and sought for broad social consensus among islanders.

These examples show that an historical approach to MNEs' activities conceptualizes clusters as entities that are only partially entrenched at the local level, and can rather be moved and reproduced according to MNEs' strategies. Long-term comparisons of similar clusters in different geographies therefore overcome location specificity and document cluster competition. Different cluster locations indeed specialized on the same or homogeneous product and compete at a global scale; thus, in the context of emerging markets, MNEs have the option to operate across multiple locations, while diversifying their political risk (Giacomin 2018).

In summary, business history showed that MNEs long preferred to structure their investment across different locations through clustering. In aggregate, global capitalism spread from the developed to the developing world, as MNEs shaped an institutional architecture based on clustered production activities and connected across value chains and global cities (McCann and Acs 2011). A closer look at MNEs' operations in the developing world helps us examine the impact of clusters beyond their location and as organizational forms for the making of global business.

Clusters and global business: two cases from the developing world

The following subsections present two historical analyses of clusters in developing economies. The plantation (rubber and palm oil) cluster in Malaysia and Indonesia and the eco-tourism cluster in Costa Rica represent relevant examples of how MNEs fostered local growth via increased international exposure, by clustering their investment in foreign markets.

Despite differences in terms of region (Southeast Asia vs. Central America); industry (agriculture vs. services); size of cluster companies (big corporations vs. SMEs); historical period (colonial vs. postcolonial); and type of empirical material (archival sources and oral history), both cases show that clustered foreign direct investment (FDI) provided access to global markets and laid the foundations for long-term growth. Initially, a limited group of foreign companies recognized elements of exceptionality in the local environment, which appealed to global demand. Successively, these multinationals organized the import of locally unavailable inputs such as human resources, knowledge, and capital, while mobilizing native actors and existing resources to set up (or improve) the physical infrastructure and expand the scope of their activity *in loco*. Initially, these MNEs were also the ones to reap most benefits from clustering. Indeed, these clusters primarily emerged to serve the export markets, and eventually generated – positive and negative – spillovers for the local economy. Through the co-creation of new institutions, the resulting cluster organizations filled some of the existing institutional voids, and increased the competitiveness of these locations vis-à-vis potential competitors.

Rubber and palm oil plantation cluster in Southeast Asia (1900–1970)

The rubber cluster emerged in the colonial territories of British Malaya and Netherlands Indies in the early twentieth century. The need for tires in the bourgeoning automotive industry drove increasing demand for natural rubber. In the late nineteenth century the British businessman and adventurer Henry Wickham smuggled the rubber tree (*Hevea Brasiliensis*) from the Amazon, its native home, to colonial South Asia, a climatically similar but politically more stable environment (Wycherley 1968). In the same period, the colonial governments of both British Malaya and Netherlands Indies granted entrepreneurs and planters land concessions to launch estate ventures (Tate 1996). Public institutions such as the Botanic Gardens and Agricultural Departments attracted researchers (agronomists, botanists, biologists, and engineers) to support the development of plantations and the domestication of wild crops. In less than two decades, a dynamic community of European and ethnic Chinese planters transformed the pioneering rubber ventures in large-scale enterprises, leveraging the existing planting tradition (mostly on coffee and tobacco) and their contacts with trading houses and financiers in Singapore, the regional trading center. Simultaneously, a *cosmopolitan bourgeoisie* comprising Chinese, Indian, and Hadhrami Arab traders orchestrated the inflow of "coolies," migrant labor from overpopulated areas of China, India, and eventually Java, to employ as low-skilled workers in the plantations (Irick 1982). From Singapore, European traders channeled foreign capital via London, to strengthen the transport and production infrastructure, and to connect local supply with global commodity markets.

A cluster organization based on estate companies, industrial associations, public and private research institutions, and specialized supporting services, quickly emerged around Singapore, establishing itself as the major global rubber supplier (Huff, 1993). Rubber became the core commodity for several major trading houses and plantation companies – Guthrie, H&C, Barlows, Boustead, Socfin, Harper&Gilfillan, among the most influential – formally represented by the London-based Rubber Growers' Association (RGA). They vertically integrated by listing estate companies to fund acreage expansion, and by retaining shares of these ventures (Drabble 1973; Drabble and Drake 1981). When the price of rubber stabilized in the 1910s, a few of the largest companies came to control the bulk of the estates, acquiring smaller struggling ventures. Alongside industry associations, specialized institutions were created, such as the Rubber Research Institute and the Incorporated Planter Society along with outlets for knowledge dissemination such as the scientific magazine *Planter* (Giacomin 2018). In the 1920s, the spread of rubber estates in the region translated in lower entry barriers – access to seeds; technology; specialized knowledge on breeding, harvesting, and refining techniques; transport and service infrastructure. This enabled local smallholders to grow rubber as a family business in small plots adjacent to the large estates (Bauer 1948). Due to this rising Asian competition and increasingly volatile rubber prices, plantation companies such as Socfin and Guthrie introduced another imported crop in their estates, the West African oil palm (*Elæis Guineensis*), as an alternative to rubber (Tate 1996; Martin 2003). The oil palm was sufficiently similar to the rubber tree to leverage the synergies of the existing rubber organizational structure, but, being a more capital-intensive crop, it shielded large estates from smallholders' competition. Similarly to rubber, during the 1920s to 1930s, and after Japanese occupation, in the 1950s, the Southeast Asian cluster quickly established itself as the leading palm oil producer over the incumbent cluster in West Africa, where farmers still tapped wild palm grooves (Giacomin 2017). In the politically uncertain context of decolonization, MNEs looked to diversify their international exposure with regard to strategic raw materials. Unilever, the largest private palm oil buyer, holding extensive palm oil interest in West Africa since the 1910s, joined the Malaysian palm oil cluster through the acquisition of confiscated German estates in the Peninsula in the late 1940s (Giacomin 2018). In the 1950s and 1960s, the African and Asian clusters collaborated on R&D, but also competed for the supremacy as global palm oil exporters. While attempting to introduce plantations in West Africa following the Malaysian model, Unilever channeled specialized knowledge from its African facilities and promoted its circulation across Southeast Asia. Whereas, in order to counter the rising political risk due to communist guerrilla attacks, so-called

"Emergency," in Malaya (1948–1960), some estate companies considered investing in Africa despite its poorer institutions and lack of plantations. Since the mid-1960s, the major (foreign) plantation companies cooperated with the newly formed Malaysian and Indonesian governments to develop palm oil smallholdings, which represented a powerful engine of rural growth for the region in the next two decades (Sutton 1989). The political turmoil in West Africa reversed this trend by driving skilled human resources and investment toward Southeast Asia, now increasingly stable. This led to the definitive decline of West Africa as palm oil exporter in the 1970s.

First, the plantation example shows that although Malaysia and Indonesia provided climatically and politically conducive environments, non-local resources were major drivers of cluster emergence and success. Indeed, the cluster organization surfaced as a result of the strategies and investment of foreign companies, making use of imported inputs such as financial capital, specialized knowledge, migrant labor, and non-native crops. Knowledge circulated freely within the cluster thanks to the tight business networks residing in Singapore, several specialized public institutions, and extensive collaboration among private actors. While both the rubber boom and the diversification toward palm oil created lavish fortunes for foreign and local entrepreneurs, the plantation cluster ensured steady provision of natural rubber and vegetable oils to the industrialized world. At the local level, the cluster organization contributed to the rise of smallholders, supporting rural development enduring until today (Henderson and Osborne 2000).

Second, the comparative analysis of the African and Asian clusters showed that MNEs used clusters to diversify their investment across emerging markets to counter political risk. During the Malayan Emergency, prominent MNEs like Barlows considered moving to Africa, whereas when political turbulence hit West Africa, Unilever diverted resources to Asia and started exiting Africa (Giacomin 2018: 36). So clusters may facilitate the making of global business, as concentrated resources can be replicated or easily mobilized. Studies on clusters have traditionally eschewed the topic of cluster competition, as the very definition of cluster assumes product specialization and specificity in terms of actors and institutions. However, the palm oil case illustrates that clusters can move and compete according to the strategies of MNEs operating within them. By competing to attract MNEs and to join GVC, cluster locations supported the spread of global capitalism. However, this process depended heavily on political stability in the recipient locations, and often translated in lopsided development. In fact, cluster competition between West Africa and Southeast Asia initially informed institutional convergence, but eventually reinforced geographical concentration. Today, Malaysia and Indonesia together account for over 80 percent of global palm oil production (FAO 2016).

Costa Rica eco-tourism cluster (1940–2000)

Jones and Spadafora's (2017) analysis of the ecotourism cluster in Costa Rica also illustrates how clusters became preferred vehicles for international business in emerging economies. The authors use oral history to describe the creation and evolution of this cluster since the 1940s, which eventually made eco-tourism one of the largest revenue sources for the country. The cluster emerged as a successful case of making nature preservation commercially viable as a niche segment for global tourism. In the long run, the cluster transitioned into a mainstream tourism service provider and Costa Rica a major travel destination.

The basis story is one of co-creation by NGOs, the government, and private enterprise, sometimes acting together but mostly acting separately. A group of local and foreign (primarily American) institutions operating in the country since the 1940s, promoted the dissemination of scientific knowledge about Costa Rica's biodiversity and educational programs on wildlife conservation. Among them, the National School of Agriculture in the University of Costa Rica; the Inter-American Institute of Agricultural Sciences (later known as CATIE); the US-funded NGOs Caribbean Conservation Corporation and Tropic Science Center; and the (mostly US-led) university consortium Organization for Tropical Studies. These institutions included several highly committed scientists and researchers, who attracted significant funding and organizational infrastructure for protecting the country's biodiversity. These experts formed a transnational "epistemic community" (Cohendet *et al.* 2014), applying established research on environmental preservation into the country. Costa Rica became a sort of natural experiment as these "green" perspectives were popularized locally, propagating scientific knowledge, and boosting media coverage to raise global awareness.

These efforts produced positive spillovers in terms of both supply and demand for eco-tourism. In the 1980s, the government introduced a formal definition of biodiversity and created several national reserves and parks. This "environmental buzz" marketed the country's rainforests and untouched wildlife as attractive travelling spots for Western tourists. Several "rainforest enthusiasts" from overseas relocated to Costa Rica, invested in properties within or nearby the national parks, and devoted themselves to nature preservation. Some of them launched small-scale ventures offering lodging and guided tours in protected areas – often employing biodiversity researchers as guides or part of their staff. The success of these pioneers and their focus on conservation attracted additional transnational entrepreneurs, quickly leading to the emergence of the eco-tourism cluster, a system of companies and institutions profiting from "sustainable tourism," an appealing concept for environmentally minded international travelers. Thus, by concentrating their investment in the vicinity of natural reserves, foreign tour operators branded Costa Rica to global eco-tourists. Between the 1940s and the 1990s, the local government consciously supported the expansion of the tourism cluster. It invested in transport infrastructure, such as rail-lines, highways, and international airports. It also established the Costa Rica Tourism Institute and the national airline LACSA. As for regulation, it issued tax incentives for large-scale tourist ventures and legislation for environmental protection.

In terms of competition, as in Southeast Asia during decolonization, the political stability of Costa Rica relative to its neighboring locations like Guatemala or Nicaragua secured steady inflows of capital and visitors, strengthening the country's reputation as a "natural paradise," intact, and absolutely safe tourism destination.

Successively, the cluster institutional environment, originally serving the very specialized eco-tourism business, worked as the basis for the commercialization of mainstream tourism services. Both local and foreign entrepreneurs piggybacked on the successful image of Costa Rica as an untouched and exclusive travel destination, and built conventional tourism facilities across the country. While this increased the scale of Costa Rica's tourism infrastructure, the strategy of branding the country as a "conservation temple" revealed a double-edged sword. It successfully created longstanding international demand for tourism, but mainstream tourism ventures ended up watering down the very concept of sustainability at the core of the cluster, by free-riding on the "green" national image (Jones and Spadafora 2017: 176).

In sum, the case of Costa Rica offers a further example of how clustering supported international business. Like in the plantation case, Costa Rica's tourism flourished not only due to the country's resource endowment, but, primarily following a concerted effort by the government, transnational and local entrepreneurs, natural conservation NGOs, and scientific institutions, to co-create the eco-tourism cluster. As an unintended outcome, local companies established mainstream tourism ventures by "free-riding" on the cluster organization and on the country's "green" image.

Concluding remarks

Starting with Marshall, industrial concentration has been a recurring theme in the social sciences. Several meta-studies applied bibliometric techniques to categorize cluster scholarship in different fields (Cruz and Teixeira 2010; Lazzeretti *et al.* 2014; Hervas-Oliver *et al.* 2015). While recognizing some degree of "contamination" across disciplines, these studies show that cluster research remained largely segregated, with similar lines of inquiry developing in parallel within different disciplines. However most literature studying clusters was accused of "self-containment." By contrast, this chapter argued that clustering historically supported the expansion of global capitalism. MNEs traditionally structured their investment in colonial territories through clusters. During colonialism, emerging economies of the South became suppliers of raw materials for the industrialized North. Production clustered in specific locations due to geographical concentration of natural resources, limited infrastructure, and/or proximity to major service hubs, such as port cities. By concentrating FDIs in selected locations, MNEs maximized local exploitation and ensured easier mobilization in case of political turmoil. On the upside, the high degree of specialization and externalities due to proximity equipped these economies with the scale and capabilities to access the international markets. The long-term analysis of MNEs' location strategies in the developing world shows clusters' role as constitutive elements of the broader global economic system. In some cases, (colonial) MNEs propelled the emergence and expansion of these clusters, like in Costa Rica. In others, they tapped into existing clusters and integrated them into global value chains – i.e., MNEs leveraged local planting expertise to introduce foreign crops in Southeast Asia. Thus, MNEs provided these locations with linkages to access international demand and knowledge to increase specialization and competitiveness. In the long run, this allowed local companies to become MNEs in their own right. In both the Southeast Asia and Costa Rica cases, the cluster institutional framework responded to changes in demand and was repurposed for different products: palm oil in the former, and broader tourist packages in the latter. Further, both cases stress that knowledge circulation and political stability in the recipient locations are crucial for the making of global business. Government policy and public institutions supporting the production of specialized knowledge, FDI inflow, and MNEs' activities supported cluster advancement.

Finally, the two cases illustrate the local impact of globalization. Clustering was a disruptive development force. The plantation activity in Southeast Asia enriched foreign companies at the expense of indentured coolies for a long time. Only after independence, the palm oil industry expanded to include local firms and smallholders, but then started damaging biodiversity through deforestation. Similarly, in Costa Rica, the cluster organization born to promote natural conservation, indirectly supported the introduction of commercial tourism in the country. While this ensured higher income for the local population, it also affected the environment and delegitimized eco-tourism. In sum, by reproducing global capitalism, clustering entailed both negative and positive outcomes for the recipient locations. Economic concentration translated in increased export competitiveness and lower prices for global consumers, but skewed geographical and social development at the local level.

References

Aitken, B., Hanson, G. H., and Harrison, A. E. 1997. Spillovers, foreign investment, and export behavior. *Journal of International Economics*, 43, 103–132.
Amdam, R. P. and Bjarnar, O. 2015. Globalization and the development of industrial clusters: comparing two Norwegian clusters, 1900–2010. *Business History Review*, 89, 693–716.

Asheim, B. T. and Herstad, S. J. 2003. Regional clusters under international duress: between local learning and global corporations. *In:* Asheim, B. T. and Mariussen, Å. (eds.) *Innovations, Regions and Projects: Studies in New Forms of Knowledge Governance.* Stockholm: Nordregio.

Aydalot, P. 1986. *Milieux innovateurs en Europe,* Paris, GREMI.

Bair, J. 2016. Global capitalism and commodity chains: looking back, going forward. *Competition and Change,* 9, 153–180.

Barton, G. A. 2014. *Informal Empire and the Rise of One World Culture,* Basingstoke, Palgrave Macmillan.

Bathelt, H. and Glückler, J. 2014. Institutional change in economic geography. *Journal of Economic Geography,* 38, 340–363.

Bathelt, H., Malmberg, A., and Maskell, P. 2004. Clusters and knowledge: local buzz, global pipelines and the process of knowledge creation. *Progress in Human Geography,* 28, 31–56.

Bauer, P. T. 1948. *The Rubber Industry: A Study in Competition and Monopoly,* London: Longmans, Green.

Bayly, C. A. 2004. *The Birth of the Modern World, 1780–1914: Global Connections and Comparisons,* Oxford, Blackwell.

Becattini, G. 2004. *Industrial Districts,* Cheltenham: Elgar.

Bellandi, M., Becattini, G., and De Propis, L. 2009. *A Handbook of Industrial Districts,* Cheltenham: Edward Elgar Publishing.

Belussi, F. 2003. The changing governance of IDs: the entry of multinationals in local nets. *In:* Asheim, B. T. and Mariussen, Å. (eds.) *Innovations, Regions and Projects: Studies in New Forms of Knowledge Governance,* Stockholm: Nordregio.

Biggiero, L. and Sammarra, A. 2003. The biomedical valley: structural, relational, and cognitive aspects. *In:* Belussi, F., Gottardi, G., and Enzo, R. (eds.) *The Technological Evolution of Industrial Districts,* Boston, MA: Kluwer.

Bresnahan, T. F., Gambardella, A., and Saxenian, A. 2001. "Old economy" inputs for "new economy" outcomes: cluster formation in the new silicon valleys. *Industrial and Corporate Change,* 10, 835–860.

Brusco, S. 1990. The idea of the industrial district: its genesis. *In:* Pyke, F., Becattini, G., and Sengenberger, W. (eds.) *Industrial Districts and Inter-firm Co-operation in Italy,* Geneva: International Institute for Labour Studies.

Carnevali, F. 2004. "Crooks, thieves, and receivers": transaction costs in nineteenth-century industrial Birmingham. *Economic History Review,* 57, 533–550.

Cassis, Y. 2010. *Capitals of Capital: The Rise and Fall of International Financial Centres, 1780–2009,* Cambridge: Cambridge University Press.

Cirer-Costa, J. C. 2014. Majorca's tourism cluster: the creation of an industrial district, 1919–36. *Business History,* 56, 1243–1261.

Cohendet, P., Grandadam, D., Simon, L., and Capdevila, I. 2014. Epistemic communities, localization and the dynamics of knowledge creation. *Journal of Economic Geography,* 14, 929–954.

Colli, A. 1999. *Legami di ferro: storia del distretto metallurgico e meccanico lecchese tra Otto e Novecento,* Molfetta: Edizioni Meridiana.

Cramer, C. 1999. Can Africa industrialize by processing primary commodities? The case of Mozambican cashew nuts. *World Development,* 27, 1247–1266.

Crevoisier, O. 2004. The innovative milieus approach: toward a territorialized understanding of the economy? *Economic Geography,* 80, 367–379.

Cruz, S. C. S. and Teixeira, A. A. C. 2010. The evolution of the cluster literature: shedding light on the regional studies–regional science debate. *Regional Studies,* 44, 1263–1288.

Declercq, R. 2015. Transnational entrepreneurs? German entrepreneurs in the Belgian fur industry (1880 to 1913). *Zeitschrift für Unternehmensgeschichte,* 60, 52–74.

Declercq, R. 2019. *World Market Transformation: Inside the German Fur Capital Leipzig 1870 and 1939.* London: Routledge.

Delgado, M., Porter, M. E., and Stern, S. 2016. Defining clusters of related industries. *Journal of Economic Geography,* 16, 1–38.

Dijk, M. P. V. and Rabellotti, R. 1997. *Enterprise Clusters and Networks in Developing Countries,* London: Frank Cass.

Drabble, J. H. 1973. *Rubber in Malaya 1876–1922: The Genesis of the Industry,* Oxford: Oxford University Press.

Drabble, J. H. and Drake, P. J. 1981. The British agency houses in Malaysia: survival in a changing world. *Journal of Southeast Asian Studies,* 12, 297–328.

FAO (Food and Agriculture Organization of the United Nations) 2016. Statistics. www.fao.org/statistics/en/ (last accessed April 16, 2019).

Fitzgerald, R. 2016. *The Rise of the Global Company: Multinationals and the Making of the Modern World*, Cambridge: Cambridge University Press.

Fujita, M., Krugman, P., and Venables, A. J. 1999. *The Spatial Economy: Cities, Regions and International Trade*, Cambridge, MA: MIT Press.

Fujita, M. and Mori, T. 1996. The role of ports in the making of major cities: self-agglomeration and hub-effect. *Journal of Development Economics*, 49, 93–120.

Gereffi, G. and Korzeniewicz, M. 1994. *Commodity Chains and Global Capitalism*, Westport, CT: Praeger.

Gereffi, G. and Lee, J. 2016. Economic and social upgrading in global value chains and industrial clusters: why governance matters. *Journal of Business Ethics*, 133, 25–38.

Giacomin, V. 2017. The emergence of an export cluster: traders and palm oil in early-20th-century Southeast Asia. *Enterprise & Society*, 1–29.

Giacomin, V. 2018. The transformation of the global palm oil cluster: Dynamics of cluster competition between Africa and Southeast Asia (c. 1900–1970). *Journal of Global History*, 13, 3, 374–398.

Giuliani, E., Pietrobelli, C., and Rabellotti, R. 2005. Lessons from South-American clusters. *World Development*, 33, 549–573.

Goerzen, A., Asmussen, C. G., and Nielsen, B. B. 2013. Global cities and multinational enterprise location strategy. *Journal of International Business Studies*, 44, 427–450.

Granovetter, M. 1985. Economic action and social structure: the problem of embeddedness. *American Journal of Sociology*, 91, 481–510.

Hall, P. A. and Soskice, D. 2001. *Varieties of Capitalism: The Institutional Foundations of Comparative Advantage*, Oxford: Oxford University Press.

Hashino, T. and Kurosawa, T. 2013. Beyond Marshallian agglomeration economies: the roles of trade associations in Meji Japan. *Business History Review*, 87, 489–513.

Henderson, J. and Osborne, D. J. 2000. The oil palm in all our lives: how this came about. *Endeavour*, 24, 63–68.

Henn, S. 2012. Transnational entrepreneurs, global pipelines and shifting production patterns: the example of the Palanpuris in the diamond sector. *Geoforum*, 43, 497–506.

Henn, S. 2013. Transnational entrepreneurs and the emergence of clusters in peripheral regions: the case of the diamond cutting cluster in Gujarat (India). *European Planning Studies*, 21, 1779–1795.

Henn, S. and Bathelt, H. 2015. Knowledge generation and field reproduction in temporary clusters and the role of business conferences. *Geoforum*, 58, 104–113.

Henn, S. and Laureys, E. 2010. Bridging ruptures: the re-emergence of the Antwerp diamond district after World War II and the role of strategic action. *In:* Fornahl, D., Henn, S., and Menzel, M.-P. (eds.) *Emerging Clusters: Theoretical, Empirical and Political Perspectives in the Initial Stage of Cluster Evolution*, Cheltenham: Edward Elgar Publishing.

Hervas-Oliver, J.-L., Gonzalez, G., Caja, P., and Sempere-Ripoll, F. 2015. Clusters and industrial districts: where is the literature going? Identifying emerging sub-fields of research. *European Planning Studies*, 23, 1827–1872.

Huff, W. G. 1993. The development of the rubber market in pre-World War II Singapore. *Journal of Southeast Asian Studies*, 24, 285–306.

Humphrey, J. and Schmitz, H. 2000. *Governance and Upgrading: Liking Industrial Cluster and Global Value Chain Research*, Brighton: Institute of Development Studies.

Humphrey, J. and Schmitz, H. 2002. How does insertion in global value chains affect upgrading in industrial clusters? *Regional Studies*, 36, 1017–1027.

Irick, R. L. 1982. *Ch'ing Policy Toward the Coolie Trade, 1847–1878*, Taipei: Chinese Materials Center.

Jacobs, W., Ducruet, C., and De Langen, P. W. P. 2010. Integrating world cities into production networks: the case of port cities. *Global Networks*, 10, 92–113.

Jones, C. A. 1987. *International Business in the Nineteenth Century: The Rise and Fall of a Cosmopolitan Bourgeoisie*, London: Prentice Hall/Harvester Wheatsheaf.

Jones, G. 2000. *Merchants to Multinationals*, Oxford: Oxford University Press.

Jones, G. 2005. *Multinationals and Global Capitalism*, Oxford: Oxford University Press.

Jones, G. 2013. *Entrepreneurship and Multinationals: Global Business and the Making of the Modern World*, Cheltenham: Edward Elgar Publishing.

Jones, G. and Gallagher-Kernstine, M. 2014. "Walking on a tightrope": maintaining London as a financial center *Harvard Business School Case Study*, 804-081.

Jones, G. and Spadafora, A. 2017. Creating ecotourism in Costa Rica, 1970–2000. *Enterprise & Society*, 18, 146–183.

Jones, G. and Wale, J. 1999. Diversification strategies of British trading companies: Harrisons & Crosfield, c.1900–c.1980. *Business History*, 41, 69–101.

Karlsson, C. 2008. *Handbook of Research on Cluster Theory*, Cheltenham: Elgar.

Khanna, T. and Palepu, K. 2010. *Winning in Emerging Markets: A Road Map for Strategy and Execution*, Boston, MA: Harvard Business Review Press.

Kindleberger, C. P. 1969. American business abroad. *Thunderbird International Business Review*, 11, 11–12.

Lazzeretti, L., Sedita, S. R., and Caloffi, A. 2014. Founders and disseminators of cluster research. *Journal of Economic Geography*, 14, 21–43.

Lescure, M. 2002. *Entre ville et campagne: l'organisation bancaire des districts industriels. L'exemple du Choletais*, Tours: Presses universitaires François-Rabelais.

Lund-Thomsen, P., Lindgreen, A., and Vanhamme, J. 2014. Industrial clusters and corporate social responsibility in developing countries: what we know, what we do not know, and what we need to know. *Journal of Business Ethics*, 133, 9–24.

Lundvall, B.-Å. 1995. *National Systems of Innovation*, London: Pinter.

McCann, P. 2009. Regional development: clusters and districts. *In:* Basu, A., Casson, M., Wadeson, N., and Yeung, B. (eds.) *Oxford Handbook of Entrepreneurship*, New York: Oxford University Press.

McCann, P. and Acs, Z. J. 2011. Globalization: countries, cities and multinationals. *Regional Studies*, 45, 17–32.

Mackinnon, D., Cumbers, A., and Chapman, K. 2002. Learning, innovation and regional development: a critical appraisal of recent debates. *Progress in Human Geography*, 26, 293–311.

Maillat, D. 1998. From the industrial district to the innovative milieu: contribution to an analysis of territorialised productive organisations. *Recherches Économiques de Louvain/Louvain Economic Review*, 64, 111–129.

Markusen, A. 1999. Fuzzy concepts, scanty evidence, policy distance: the case for rigour and policy relevance in critical regional studies. *Regional Studies*, 33, 869–884.

Marshall, A. 1920. *Principles of Economics*, Basingstoke: Palgrave Macmillan.

Martin, R. and Sunley, P. 2003. Deconstructing clusters: chaotic concept or policy panacea? *Journal of Economic Geography*, 3, 5–35.

Martin, S. M. 2003. *The UP Saga*, Copenhagen: Nordic Institute of Asian Studies.

Maskell, P. 2001. Towards a knowledge-based theory of the geographical cluster. *Industrial and Corporate Change*, 10, 921–943.

Maskell, P. 2014. Accessing remote knowledge: the roles of trade fairs, pipelines, crowdsourcing and listening posts. *Journal of Economic Geography*, 14, 883–902.

Maskell, P. and Kebir, L. 2005. What qualifies as a cluster theory? *In:* Asheim, B., Cooke, P., and Martin, R. (eds.) *Clusters and Regional Development: Critical Reflections and Explorations*, Abingdon: Routledge.

Maskell, P., Bathelt, H., and Malmberg, A. 2007. Building global knowledge pipelines: the role of temporary clusters. *European Planning Studies*, 14, 997–1013.

North, D. C. 1999. *Understanding the Process of Economic Change*, London: Institute of Economic Affairs.

Parsons, M. and Rose, M. 2005. The neglected legacy of Lancashire cotton: industrial clusters and the U.K. outdoor trade, 1960–1990. *Enterprise & Society*, 6, 682–709.

Perez-Aleman, P. 2005. Cluster formation, institutions and learning: the emergence of clusters and development in Chile. *Industrial and Corporate Change*, 14, 651–677.

Piore, M. J. and Sabel, C. F. 1984. *The Second Industrial Divide: Possibilities for Prosperity*, New York: Basic Books.

Ponte, S. and Sturgeon, T. 2014. Explaining governance in global value chains: a modular theory-building effort. *Review of International Political Economy*, 21, 195–223.

Popp, A. 2003. "The true potter": identity and entrepreneurship in the north Staffordshire potteries in the later nineteenth century. *Journal of Historical Geography*, 29, 317–335.

Porter, M. and Ketels, C. 2009. Clusters and industrial districts: common roots, different perspectives. *In:* Becattini, G., Bellandi, M., and De Propris, L. (eds.) *A Handbook of Industrial Districts*, Cheltenham: Edward Elgar Publishing.

Porter, M. E. 1998a. Clusters and the new economics of competition. *Harvard Business Review*, 76, 77–90.

Porter, M. E. 1998b. *The Competitive Advantage of Nations*, London: Macmillan.

Porter, M. E., Ramirez-Vallejo, J., and Van Eenennaam, F. 2013. The Dutch flower cluster. *Harvard Business School Case Study*, 711–507.

Pyke, F. and Lund-Thomsen, P. 2016. Social upgrading in developing country industrial clusters: a reflection on the literature. *Competition and Change*, 20, 53–68.

Rugman, A. M. 2005. *The Regional Multinationals: MNEs and "Global" Strategic Management*, Cambridge: Cambridge University Press.

Saxenian, A. 1996. *Regional Advantage: Culture and Competition in Silicon Valley and Route 128*, Cambridge, MA: Harvard University Press.

Schmitz, H. and Nadvi, K. 1999. Clustering and industrialization: introduction. *World Development*, 27, 1503–1514.

Scott, A. J. 1985. Location processes, urbanization, and territorial development: an exploratory essay. *Environment and Planning A*, 17, 479–501.

Scranton, P. 1997. *Endless Novelty: Specialty Production and American Industrialization, 1865–1925*, Princeton, NJ: Princeton University Press.

Spadavecchia, A. 2005a. Financing industrial districts in Italy, 1971–91: a private venture? *Business History*, 47, 569–593.

Spadavecchia, A. 2005b. State subsidies and the sources of company finance in Italian industrial districts, 1951–1991. *Enterprise & Society*, 6, 571–580.

Storper, M. and Walker, R. 1989. *The Capitalist Imperative*, Oxford: Blackwell.

Sturgeon, T., Van Biesebroeck, J., and Gereffi, G. 2008. Value chains, networks and clusters: reframing the global automotive industry. *Journal of Economic Geography*, 8, 297–321.

Sutton, K. 1989. Malaysia's FELDA land settlement model in time and space. *Geoforum*, 20, 339–354.

Tate, D. J. 1996. *The RGA History of the Plantation Industry in the Malay Peninsula*, Kuala Lumpur: Oxford University Press.

Thomsen, L. 2007. Accessing global value chains? The role of business state relations in the private clothing industry in Vietnam. *Journal of Economic Geography*, 7, 753–776.

Trigilia, C. 2002. *Economic Sociology*, Oxford: Blackwell.

Trippl, M. and Todtling, F. 2008. Cluster renewal in old industrial regions: continuity or radical change? *In:* Karlsson, C. (ed.) *Handbook of Research on Cluster Theory (Vol. 1)*, Cheltenham: Edward Elgar Publishing.

Van Helten, J.-J. and Jones, G. 1989. British business in Malaysia and Singapore since the 1870s. *In:* Davenport-Hines, R. P. T. and Jones, G. (eds.) *British Business in Asia since 1860*, Cambridge: Cambridge University Press.

Weijland, H. 1999. Microenterprise clusters in rural Indonesia: industrial seedbed and policy target. *World Development*, 27, 1515–1530.

Wilkins, M. 1970. *The Emergence of Multinational Enterprise: American Business Abroad from the Colonial Era to 1914*, Cambridge, MA: Harvard University Press.

Wilson, J. F. and Popp, A. 2003. *Industrial Clusters and Regional Business Networks in England, 1750–1970*, London: Routledge.

Wolfe, D. A. and Gertler, M. S. 2004. Clusters from the inside and out: local dynamics and global linkages. *Urban Studies*, 41, 1071–1093.

Wycherley, P. R. 1968. Introduction of the Hevea to the Orient. *Planter*, 4, 1–11.

Zeitlin, J. 2008. Industrial districts and regional clusters. *In:* Jones, G. G. and Zeitlin, J. (eds.) *Oxford Handbook of Business History*, Oxford: Oxford University Press.

18

GLOBAL VALUE CHAINS

Jan-Otmar Hesse and Patrick Neveling

Introduction

In 2013, the United Nations for the first time dedicated its "World Investment Report" to Global Value Chains (GVCs). As recent fast growth of global trade had been driven increasingly by trade in semi-finished goods, the report illustrated that an incremental share of global trade resulted from a global disintegration of production processes organized by large transnational corporations, which operated as managers of GVCs. A total of 80 percent of global trade – so the spectacular figure of the report claims – were transfers of intermediates within GVCs. Since these goods moved back and forth between the different national affiliations of one and the same multinational enterprise (MNE) or its subcontractors, GVC-related trade also led to substantial double-counting in trade statistics, which was estimated as 28 percent of the total (UNCTAD 2013: X). Thus, as the trade specialist Robert Feenstra (1998) suggested in a seminal article, the significant integration of world markets by trade, globalization, is in part an effect and mirror-image of the "disintegration of production."

International economists have discussed this development intensively in recent years. Richard Baldwin and Javier Lopez-Gonzalez have generated input–output tables from a newly released database with trade statistics to account for the many production networks behind the trade flows and discovered that these are regional production clusters rather than the long-distance international production chains often featured in the media. They named three regional production networks with Germany being the "headquarters economy" in the European cluster, Japan in Asia, and the US in the Americas (Baldwin/Lopez-Gonzalez 2015). This trend started in the "second unbundling" of the 1970s, when transportation and information costs declined significantly and thereby enabled the global disintegration of production (Baldwin 2014: 212–219). Much more provocatively, the German economist Hans-Werner Sinn already in 2005 attacked the German "bazaar economy" for trading in goods rather than manufacturing them and thereby abandoning the German economy's traditional strength (Sinn 2005).

Yet, these are preliminary findings and provocations, curbed by the fact that national accounting is poorly equipped to make GVCs visible. Therefore, research has foremost focused on analyzing the value chains of particular multinationals or industries and has left a gap in our knowledge of their impact on global trade (Timmer *et al.* 2014: 99–118). This is where business history comes into play.

It is hard to imagine, from that discipline's perspective, that transnational production processes and transnational collaboration along the transformation of raw materials into finished goods are novel in the history of capitalism. Instead, business historians have long provided evidence that sourcing strategies and international cooperation have been common practice for centuries. However, the field has not thus far contributed rich empirical material to the most recent international debate. We therefore know little about the long-term transformation of value-chain production and especially so about the driving forces behind that trajectory. Is the disintegration of production a novel development, triggered by a sharp decline of transportation and communication costs in the 1970s, as Baldwin states? Or do trade politics interfere in this analysis? Can we find similar disintegration processes in other historical periods, in the "first globalization wave," for instance? This contribution elaborates whether long-term transformations of GVCs can explain changes and evolutions of global business. We start with a summary of chain-approaches over the last 40 years – from Terence Hopkins and Immanuel Wallerstein's notion of "commodity chains" (Hopkins/Wallerstein 1986) to recent GVC approaches and their relevance for business history. The second section shows how the changing nature of trade statistics and actual trade policies shaped the evolution of GVCs. The third section offers selected historical examples and the fourth section offers ideas for further research.

From "commodity chains" to "value chains" and "production networks"

There is a long tradition of thinking about (global) connections of production processes going back to Karl Marx' second volume of capital and Eugen Böhm-Bawerk's notion of "roundabout production" (Böhm-Bawerk 1902: 87–121). For modern historical research, Immanuel Wallerstein's world systems approach was fundamental. Wallerstein was interested in the economic exploitation of the world by expansive European capitalism and therefore aimed at reconstructing ties between historically changing economic "centers," "semiperipheries," and "peripheries" from the fourteenth century onward (Wallerstein 1974; Wallerstein/Hopkins 1982). In a seminal article, co-authored in 1986 with Terence Hopkins (1986: 159–160), Wallerstein developed the idea of "commodity chains," which the two authors identified as "a network of labor and production processes whose end result is a finished commodity," to "show the totality of the flows or movements that reveal the real division, and thus the integration, of labor in complex production processes." The pair explored in particular the flow of goods linked to "plantation economies" across the Atlantic that fueled the triangular trade in slave labor, tobacco, sugar, and cotton. The strong global connection of farmers, merchants, retailers, and consumers in different parts of the world at the same time served as the underlying story for Sidney Mintz' (1986) path-breaking book on *Sweetness and Power*, which, similarly to the work of another anthropologist, Eric Wolf (1982), emphasized that the industrial revolution was fueled by the inflow of cheap calories from Caribbean sugar into Britain's new urban industrial centers.

Yet, such discussions of "commodity chains" emphasized connections between historical centers and peripheries without attention to systematically describe particular patterns of business relations, trade, or types of production. A paramount interest in the evolution of capitalism also prevented research on when and why commodity chains emerged and in which sectors. Via the works of Stephen Topik, William Gervase Clarence-Smith, and others (Topik *et al.* 2006), the approach entered the more recent field of "global history." The focus on commodity chains as markers of "global entanglements" and "transregional connectedness" continues, however, with Sven Beckert's *Empire of Cotton* (2014) as the most recent example. Thus, important empirical issues remain unsolved in research on early and contemporary capitalist chains. Who actually governed and organized historical commodity chains? And what factors induced change over time?

While "world systems theory" became a stronghold of sociology rather than historical research, business historians focused on the evolution of big business and multinational corporations. Following Alfred D. Chandler, these new organizational forms of global capitalism were often seen as the result of mergers and "vertical integration" that culminated in national "big businesses" or dominant MNEs (Wilkins 2008: 251–266). This perspective was challenged in the 1980s when Charles Sabel and Jonathan Zeitlin's article on "historical alternatives to mass production" (1985: 133–176) pointed to the many examples of successful small and specialized corporations that did not use economies of scale. While mass-production could be the proper solution for the production of some goods, disintegrated and specialized production might be more fitting for others. However, this brilliant contribution did not trigger research on the transnational disintegration of production. Rather, it drew attention to national production clusters in which different specialized small firms collaborated often on a regional basis. Gerry Herrigel's book (1996) on the south-west German machine industry cluster was eye-opening because it explained why so many small and medium, often family-based firms, survived in a technology-driven, internationalized economy. Possibly because of the difficulty to reconstruct and measure the collaboration of companies beyond national boundaries, business history has only recently begun to study the global extension and organization of the regional networks studied in the footsteps of Herrigel. Yet, a paradigmatic approach for business history research is missing until today.

This is, in our view, because the commodity-chain approach of the 1980s and its recent application by "global historians" maintain three disadvantages that prevent them from gaining a strong analytical position in economic and business history. First, there is the above-discussed analytical focus on the emergence of capitalism and global exploitation. As this is mirrored in an empirical focus on the commodity chains of luxury goods, the stories published so far highlight the role of global production for European consumers and end in the late nineteenth century. This, second, means that a crucial turning point in many chain histories is missing, namely the changes in global trade and production that took place once raw-material scarce (Western) economies succeeded in replacing imported luxury goods with new mass consumer products: cane sugar with sugar beets, and later the invention of chemical dyestuff and fertilizer, and of synthetic fibers, oil, and rubber. Such histories of major commodities of the twentieth century and their chains are not only absent in research on the *Trentes Glorieuses*, but also for the interwar period, which therefore too often is perceived as a time of "de-globalization." Thus, in a long-term perspective, "chain stories" and the analysis of GVCs disappear from the agenda once economic and global historians turn from the nineteenth to the twentieth century. This, third, has an effect in research on the "second globalization wave" of the 1970s and 1980s also, for which sociologists and also contemporary historians treat the emergence of commodity chains, GVCs, and also the rise of global production networks as novel historical phenomena. Yet, a long-term historical analysis of chains and GVCs should point us in the opposite direction. Not least from the perspective of business history research on the interwar period we know that many corporations, and not the least the early MNEs of that period, found ways to continue global business (Chandler/Mazlish 2005). The challenge for research would seem to help us better understand their strategies and what these meant for the post-1945 period.

Instead, economic geographer Peter Dicken (1986) prominently diagnosed a "global shift" of manufacturing from advanced capitalist nations to the developing world since the 1970s and other scholars criticized the offshoring and outsourcing strategies of large firms in Europe for their economic impact on both deindustrializing regions in Europe and newly industrializing regions in the Third World (Fröbel *et al.* 1981). However, as for the case of MNE operations in the interwar period and other business practices discussed above, also the shifting of manufacturing to foreign countries (i.e., offshoring) or the subcontracting of production processes to partners (i.e., outsourcing) have a long history as business practices – though as historical business practices they were named differently (e.g., "third party contracting").

Business historians thus could make an important contribution to research that so far centers on contemporary sourcing strategies of global multinationals. Of special relevance here is the advanced GVC paradigm proposed by the contributors in an edited volume by Gary Gereffi, John Humphrey, and Tim Sturgeon (2005), which calls for systematic research on the redistribution of value-added along global production "chains." Via a comparison of various industries – textiles, apparel, consumer electronics, and automobiles – they discovered that in some cases GVCs are "governed" by the producers while in other cases the buyers are the more powerful actors. More recent research identified production processes that are more like "snakes" while others are like "spiders" (Baldwin/Venables 2013).

Economic geographers have added to this the concept of global production networks (GPNs), which identify the global organization of subcontracting, part-processing, and assembly of complex products under the auspices of MNEs, ranging from laptops to Barbie dolls. The core feature of both, GPNs as well as GVCs, is that their global chains lack formal integration and organization of the different units; the central organizing feature in the transfer of commodities within global "networks" or "chains," from raw materials until the consumption of the finished good, is mostly the dependency of nodes in those networks on other nodes and not the legal structure of the units as such. Such dependencies are not easily detected and connecting all nodes to identify the GPN or GVC may be a major challenge. The power differentials among the actors and business units involved in commodity chains, GVCs, and also GPNs are therefore essential aspects of research, especially for identifying how the value-added is distributed among the actors along the (global) value chain (Bair 2009: 1–35; 2016: 326–335).

Still, certain aspects of the GVCs concept must remain metaphorical because the notion of "chains" suggests that research could clearly identify a transformation process from a raw material to a finished consumer good across all the different global production steps. However, within a given subcontracting business unit any given production step in one such chain might take place in connection with other production processes entangled in entirely different chains. Therefore, it is difficult in practice to identify that subcontractor's contribution to one particular chain, even if company audits and accounts were available to the researcher. The cargo of a ship, for example, often includes different goods and thus such a vessel operates within more than only one value chain at a time. For similar reasons, the fraction of value-added that is attributed to one production activity along the value-chain of one good is difficult to detect in practice.

However, the very notion of GVCs pushes scholars to think about the individual production steps as much as of the pre- and the post-production steps without which the production of a finished manufacturing good would simply not happen. Taking this back to our earlier remarks about the long (business) history of commodity chains and GVCs it is important to consider that already in a very early stage of the industrial revolution many corporations actively researched the different global supply options for a particular raw material and that the same and other companies produced entirely for very distant markets. Information about sourcing possibilities or export markets was often available via diplomatic channels or through family relations. When no such flow of information existed, specialized agents could be contracted to obtain it. Such practices occurred even in very small businesses, which underlines that merchant activities and manufacturing were much less separated than most of the literature in business history suggests. Very small chinaware companies in a poor region in northern Bavaria sold their complete production to the United States in the late nineteenth century via a network of specialized sales agents (Kluge 2018). As Kluge shows, even though these companies were local businesses without formal relationships to world markets initially, they could insert themselves successfully in a GVC and thus become "global businesses." Likewise, early nineteenth century cane-sugar planters in small island colonies such as Mauritius associated in Chambers of Commerce and Chambers of Agriculture and actively sourced information about their British export market and their buyers via British–Mauritian joint venture companies, the local colonial administration, and also by inviting agents from the UK to advise them on the kind of packaging and presentation that would make London buyers most happy with Mauritian cane-sugar supplies (Neveling 2012). On the other side of that spectrum there were, of course, large multinationals with significant power in global markets that set up GVCs for their own input or output, e.g., when direct integration of foreign pre- or post-production units was not possible for political or economic reasons.

If archival and statistical material is available, the GVC approach gives business historians a standard procedure to explore the nature and transformation of manufacturing, trade, marketing, and many more aspects in a long historical perspective via the following steps: isolate a single production process starting from a finished good; follow the stream of materials and services that are used for the composition of the good backwards to the raw material or source; analyze to which extent the different production steps are in the hands of a single economic actor (individuals or organizations); try to estimate the value-added in every single production step; analyze how all these aspects have changed over time; find the driving forces behind particular transformations. In this, the driving forces are of particular relevance to identify how local or national industries transformed into global businesses. Research so far has detected technology, market power received by branding or specialized knowledge, and state intervention, especially trade policy, as the driving forces for this transformation. The following illustrates that the last aspect in particular connects research on GVCs to business history research on the evolution of global trade.

GVCs and international trade

In principle, value-chains and the disintegration of production also exist in national economies – we mentioned the cases explored by Gary Herrigel above. Yet, here our interest is with global sourcing and supply. The most simple such transaction is ordinary foreign trade, i.e., the purchase of finished or semi-finished goods on international competitive markets, which is also what trade statistics account for and trade theory elaborates on. Yet, the only possibility to discover whether a global production process is behind trade integration is to observe the relative share of raw material as opposed to semi-finished and finished goods in a given country's overall trade statistics. When a country imports all raw materials and only exports finished goods, we may assume that the national economy processes a significant share of the raw materials imported into the consumer product and exploits the value-added from the production. When raw material imports decline and semi-finished products are increasingly imported, we assume that a country "moved up the value chain," i.e., it specialized in the more valuable manufacturing processes.

Therefore foreign trade statistics can, to some extent, reveal structural adjustment processes in a national economy. For good reason, no systematic, global overview over the evolution of the composition of trade in this respect exists so far, as the required input–output tables are not available for most of the twentieth century in most national statistics. In fact, even an advanced industrial nation such as the Federal Republic of Germany (FRG) only began to release input–output tables on a regular basis in the 1960s and without such tables it is difficult to distinguish, for example, whether a decline in raw material imports was the effect of a decline in domestic manufacturing or the effect of manufacturing "moving up the value chain" – possibly extended backward along the chain by the fact that initial processing of raw materials now occurred in the same country that previously supplied the raw materials. Without input–output tables it is thus impossible to gain reliable information from trade statistics on the actual changes in the structure of production in a given national economy.

This gap could be closed in part by combining trade statistics with information on foreign direct investment (FDI). Yet, similar to input–output tables, most countries began reporting FDI flows comparatively late. FDI in most cases results from an increase in the frequency of trade flows between two ends of a GVC. If these flows become more regular and costlier, it might pay for the company on one end of the chain to buy the manufacturing facility on the other end. John Dunning (1982) systematized the three main advantages of such purchases in his eclectic paradigm; these are ownership, location, and internalization. There exist several other historical examples of cross-border integration of production processes, such as the "free stand-ing company" detailed by Mira Wilkins (1988). Yet, there are also numerous historical instances when, for political, legal, or also economic reasons, it did not make sense for global businesses to integrate across borders. This leaves us with historical GVC connections that do not show up either in trade statistics or in FDI statistics or in foreign portfolio statistics. GVCs therefore rest on relations of dependency between formally independent organizations across borders and their importance today is marked by the fact that European and American corporations invest significant sums to gain full control over their "global supply chains" and by the fact that global supply chain management is now a genuine field of training in management and business schools (Alfalla-Luque/Medina-López 2009).

The scholars who published the 2013 UN report mentioned in the introduction above identify a "correlation" between trade volume and GVCs, i.e., an increase in trade usually is driven, at least in part, by a disintegration of production. Yet, this again refers to the most recent evolution of world trade and we doubt if this correlation is valid in a long-term historical per-spective. Instead, on the one hand, we can assume that during the "first globalization wave" of the late nineteenth century and again during the "second wave" since the 1970s not only trade-to-GDP ratio increased worldwide but also new GVCs emerged in each period (Findlay/O'Rourke 2007). On the other hand, and as mentioned above, we further need to account for the interwar period: this is counter-intuitive to the many studies in business history. Though trade in many regions decreased, we observe still high FDI activity, but more so new forms of the organization of GVCs. Zurich and Amsterdam appeared as new financial centers in those decades, partly as a result of the transfer of assets from Germany during that nation's increasing hyperinflation years (Cassis 2006).

"Cloaking" played a large role during the war and the interwar period. Former direct links between foreign and domestic subsidiaries had to be disconnected, mainly for political reasons. The result was in many cases the replacement of trade with foreign production that was not legally attached to the former multinational (Aalders/Wiebes 1985; Jones/Lubinski 2012). There was thus a collapse of global trade especially during the Great Depression, but does this indicate a parallel collapse of the global economy and global business? Or did global business simply apply different and new forms of transactions that led to an increase of more subtle connections? And, if so, could we study the latter by using the concept of GVCs? The bilateral trade agree-ments and also international cartels that emerged in the times of crises might appear as aspects of the transformations of GVCs rather than a sign of "de-globalization."

The period after World War II was driven by the return to trade liberalization. The General Agreement on Tariffs and Trade (GATT) of 1947 reduced tariffs and other trade barriers and thereby successfully promoted a rapid increase in global trade. At the same time, however, the GATT also had many exemption clauses and "emergency" paragraphs that have been used in the years since 1947 to effectively protect national industries from global competition (Irwin 1995: 127–150; Bown/Irwin 2015). These Janus-headed provisions of the GATT have led trade scholars to use contradictory labels like "liberal protectionism" or "selective protectionism" to refer to the inconsistent trade policies of many nations (Aggarwal 1985; Wiemann 1983).

When, for example, the textile and clothing industries of the United States and Western Europe came under pressure in the 1950s, the GATT framework was used to delay rather than promote trade liberalization in these sectors. Using article XIX about "emergency action" in cases when increased imports would "threaten serious injury on domestic producers," Western countries restricted textile imports, especially from Japan. The GATT article XIX allows for the introduction of import quotas and other protectionist measures for a limited time period when consultations with export nations have failed and a national economy is threatened. This article was invoked 132 times between 1950 and 1986 and foremost by the United States, Canada, Australia, and European Economic Community (EEC) member-states (Sykes 1991). With reference to that article the US government pushed Japan into a "voluntary self restraint" arrangement in 1957, which meant limiting Japan's textile exports to the United States (Sugihara 2004: 527; Rivoli 2009: 193). European countries negotiated bilateral trade agreements in a similar spirit since the late 1950s. Though Japan became a member of the GATT in 1957, West Germany kept its import restrictions toward Japan with special permission by the GATT secretariat in 1959 and only later, under the aegis of the EEC in 1970, joined the prolongation of the "Long-term Arrangement in Cotton Textiles" (LTA) that was originally signed in 1962 (Minister of Economics, 1969; see also: Rivoli 2009: 193–196) and that, by the early 1970s, had already grown into a multilateral system of "self-restraint" arrangements encompassing more than 20 countries. Finally, the LTA was transformed into the well-known, often criticized "Multi-Fibre Arrangement" (MFA) of 1974 (Wiemann 1983: 122–127), which, under the surface of the GATT, consolidated a system of national and regional protectionist policies that ultimately sought to shield textiles and apparel manufacturing as well as other sensitive industries of the Western world from the exports of developing nations.

The example of textile and apparel industry

In textile and apparel manufacturing, protectionism triggered an astonishing "global hopping" of production, as described in Pietra Rivoli's seminal contribution. As soon as the textile industry discovered a country without restrictive export quotas to the United States and the EEC, it shifted its production facilities. Once the MFA quota system was extended to the new country, the industry moved on. Thus, the textile and apparel industry that made Hong Kong one of the leading textile producers worldwide in the 1960s was not a "new" industry, but to a large extent Japanese industries that relocated or subcontracted to Hong Kong partners in order to circumvent quota ceilings for Japan. In the 1970s, the dynamic reached its peak with the MFA signed among 50 countries, which extended the system of "voluntary self restraints" to synthetic fibers. From then on, 75 percent of US textile imports were "voluntarily" restricted by the export nations (Rivoli 2009: 193–207). The MFA, as well as its successor arrangements in the following decades, was preceded by a series of consultations and arrangements that provisioned for a step-by-step phasing out of the MFA toward a free world market without quotas. Only because of such promises the GATT tolerated protective arrangements, but, in fact, the successor arrangements to the MFA in particular included ever lower import quotas and therefore effectively increased protectionism in a time when Western nations struggled with high unemployment and economic crises after the oil-price shock (Rivoli 2009: 193–207; Wiemann 1983: 125–126). Since then, the liberalization of global trade in textiles has been consistently moderated in the negotiations of new fiber arrangements that often saw tiny increases in export quotas to Western markets for developing nations, among which the PR China took the most powerful position during the 1990s. With the establishment of the World Trade Organization in 1995, quotas did not fall, but the MFA system was replaced with another regulatory framework, the Agreement on Textiles and Clothing, that maintained the MFA's institutional structure for roughly another decade. Only as of 2005, did China and other rapidly expanding developing nations such as Bangladesh, Vietnam, and Cambodia obtain more or less free access to European and American markets.

Similar dynamics have existed in other industries for decades, especially so in electronics where investment in fixed capital is low and labor costs account for the lion's share in production costs, similar to the textile and garment sector, and where the level of political regulation is equally significant. In these sectors, the global spread of export processing zones (EPZ) and special economic zones has been most proliferated as the zones offer attractive conditions for global businesses and their permanent need for relocation. Puerto Rico offered the first EPZ-style investment incentives package with turnkey factories, tax and customs waivers, and quota-free access to the mainland US market in the late 1940s. Initial relocations from US mainland firms further moved to the Philippines and Mexico in search of cheaper labor in the late 1950s and many other EPZs, such as Hong Kong in the 1960s, later Taiwan, and from the late 1970s onward coastal cities with zones in the PR China, also attracted corporations from the United States, Asia, and Europe to shift or subcontract their production in search of cheaper labor and increasingly in search for quotas to Western markets (Neveling 2017: 23–40). While trade unions in the developed and developing countries fought against the rise of "runaway shops" and a downward spiral in global wages since the 1970s, tax waivers and state subsidies lured corporations into the industrial estates of ever new zones or countries without necessarily shifting capital or integrating production processes. While textile and apparel as well as consumer electronics might remain the most prominent case in this respect, similar changes in GVCs took place in car manufacturing, and more recently also in steel industries, pharmaceuticals, IT and call centers, and in agriculture.

Another strategy was discovered by the industry in the extensive use of "outward processing" (OP) starting in the mid-1960s. Again the textile and apparel industry serves as an example for a practice that myriad businesses widely used. OP refers to a particular practice of saving duties for businesses that need to process a certain product abroad, e.g., for reasons of quality improvement or refinement. If tariffs apply between the two countries, the businesses would have been charged twice: when exporting a good to the foreign country and again when importing the processed good back to the home country. Governments have therefore often waived the additional duty and agreed only to claim a duty for the value-added that was "re-imported" from the foreign country. Since businesses had to report this value-added to governments, we have figures on the volume of OP trade in statistics, though companies might exceed the volume of tax-reduced trade (Fröbel *et al.* 1981: 116–120). We find the same procedure, that was here exemplified for Germany, under different names in other countries. In the United States the practice was named "international subcontracting" in contemporary language (Sharpston 1976: 333–337).

Industry used OP especially when FDI was insecure or impossible, but quality control and information flow could be achieved. In the German textile and apparel industry, for example, OP was an option for economic relations with Eastern Europe, in particular. When the political tensions of the Cold War relaxed in the 1960s, the West German government increasingly promoted economic relations with the East (Rudolph 2004). The government actively supported

OP in the textile and apparel industry to improve the productivity of the domestic industry with its high labor costs. At least since 1965, the changing ministers of economics used OP as a strategy to improve the productivity of the German textile and apparel industry (Minister of Economics, 1965; see also: Gertschen 2013: 192). For political reasons, the FRG government treated the German Democratic Republic (GDR) as part of the FRG territory in customs so OP regulation did not apply there (Fäßler 2006: 263–268). OP was, however, extensively applied to all other Eastern European countries, because FDI was restricted or prohibited and political circumstances meant that FDI would have been insecure.

Eight percent of the value of all fabrics exported from West Germany in 1974 went to Eastern Europe (Soviet Union, Poland, Czechoslovakia, Hungary, Romania, Bulgaria) and 8.2 percent of import in cloths derived from there. The most important country in that year was Yugoslavia, which alone received 7.1 percent of West German export fabrics and accounted for 7.9 percent of all German imports of cloths (Fröbel *et al.* 1981: 252). The country became a manufacturing center of the German textile and apparel industry. In the years after 1945, Yugoslavia had switched back and forth between the Eastern and the Western economic and political systems, which caused difficult economic relations with the FRG in the 1950s. When Yugoslavia turned to "market socialism" in 1965, private business activity, FDI, and trade with the Western World followed (Kukić 2018: 8). West Germany ranked as Yugoslavia's second-largest trading partner behind Italy. A total of 92 percent of apparel imports to West Germany were conducted as OP (Fröbel *et al.* 1981: 116–122). German economic policy used OP both to enable Eastern European countries to earn foreign currency to buy expensive German manufactures as well to incentivize productive manufacturers in textiles and apparel to further improve their competitiveness. Therefore, when Karl Schiller negotiated an extension of import quotas for textiles from Eastern Europe in March 1969, he suggested increasing both the quota for regular imports by 20 percent and the tax-free proportion of OP traffic by 33 percent (Federal Chancellery 1969b). For trade with Yugoslavia, unrestricted imports from outward processing was considered. But the plan was cancelled after protests from those in the West-German textile and apparel industry that did not profit from this activity (Federal Chancellery 1969a). Unfortunately more detailed research on the East European side of the chain is rare if not absent and usually focuses on the post-1989 period (Smith 2003).

On the European level too, there was constant debate about the share of revenue that OP was allowed to generate. Apparently, German textile and apparel companies could engage in OP more easily than French, Italian, and British firms. The member countries of the EEC therefore restricted OP activities at the Eastern border. Only 30 percent of total revenue was allowed in the 1970s, increasing to 50 percent in the 1990s. While French revenue in outward processing reached 200 million euro, and British 41 million euro, West German revenue reached 1.2 billion euro in 1988 (European Commission 2006: 260; Lane/Probert 2005). The German textile and apparel industry apparently relied on OP to confront market pressures much more than their European competitors.

Increased international sourcing was of course paralleled by a domestic decline of textile and apparel manufacturing. A total of 23,000 employees of the German textile and apparel industry worked abroad in 1966, while domestic employment declined from 1.2 million in 1958 to only 950,000 in the mid-1960s. By 1970, domestic employment had dropped further and sank below half a million in 1990; international employment had doubled between 1966 and 1970 (Gertschen 2013: 190). While the international workforce equaled 6 percent of the total domestic employees in textiles and apparel in 1970, that proportion reached 19 percent in 1983. The number of foreign subsidiaries reached 174 in textiles and 139 in clothing in 1983, mainly located in the EEC and European Free Trade Association (EFTA) countries or Asia, while OP dominated the Eastern bloc countries (Mühleck 1992: 222; Lindner 2001: 168). According to the official figures from the German apparel industry, in 1976, 25 percent of the total import of clothes resulted from OP (Beese/Schneider 2001: 116). As early as 1964, the Ministry of Economics had estimated that 30 percent of imports from Hong Kong, which had been highly criticized by the textile and clothing industry as "unfair competition," actually was re-imported from the industry's OP (Gertschen 2013: 192). In 1978, 9 percent of the total revenue in the textiles sector and 18 percent in the clothing sector resulted from outward processing, as well as 17 percent from the import value in textiles and 28 percent in apparel. This only reflects the public figures (Mühleck 1992: 224; Fröbel *et al.* 1981: 116). Most authors however suggest that the actual volume of OP was higher as the corporations might have exceeded the tariff-free volume in some categories.

So far, we can only identify few corporations that have engaged in OP and that could thus serve as case studies of global businesses that followed the GVC organization. This is partly due to restricted access to company archives and partly because historical research has yet to engage in detail the historical transformation of GVCs. A more generic reading of reports on textile company activities in newspapers provides first examples, however. The brand "Triumph," a lingerie manufacturer from south-western Germany, built its first factory outside Europe in Hong Kong as early as 1962 (Beese/Schneider 2001: 75). The company had opened its first foreign sales office in Switzerland in 1933. By the late 1970s, domestic employment decreased from 18,000 to 3,000, while manufacturing abroad grew. The company sold directly from Hong Kong to Japan and overseas markets so that foreign revenues increased while domestic revenues declined in overall company earnings (Schnaus 2017). Though the corporation relocated its headquarters to Switzerland in 1977 for tax reasons, it kept facilities in Germany, where its market share peaked at around 50 percent and where it has remained until today (Triumph 2018).

Sportswear became another successful field for German apparel manufacturers. Brands like Trigema and Gerry Weber, which was founded in 1973, profited from the tennis boom in Germany and specialized in clothes and equipment. Even more successful was the sports shoe manufacturer Adidas, which also expanded into apparel manufacturing in the 1970s. As GVCs for its shoe business were already established, setting up global production structures for tricot and sportswear manufacturing was easy for Adidas. One of the best-known brands of the surviving German apparel industry, by 2000 Adidas controlled a network of 1,082 contract partners in 65 different countries that supplied 97 percent of the textile and 76 percent of the apparel input for the company's exports from Germany (Ferenschild 2007: 46).

Among the successful brands from the apparel sector are also German producers of menswear, like the shirt manufacturer Seidensticker or the suit manufacturer Hugo Boss (Köster 2011; 2016). Less well known, though much larger, was the Steilmann-Group, which became one of the largest apparel producers in West Germany in the 1980s. It employed almost 8,000 workers domestically and another 18,000 in 43 foreign companies with 82 production facilities (Beese/Schneider 2001: 127–136, 189–194). The company was one of the most important contract partners for large fashion labels like Karl Lagerfeld but also sold to large department stores such as the German Karstadt AG and to fashion retailers like C&A. Retailers like Karstadt, Kaufhof, and Hertie had revenues of more than four billion dollars and ranked as the largest retailers for textiles and cloth in Europe in 1979 (Clairmonte/Cavanagh 1982: 212). Yet, the Steilmann Group and others were the actual drivers of this powerful position. In the UK, Marks & Spencer became an important organizer of GVCs in textiles and apparel (Clairmonte/Cavanagh 1982: 212; Toms/Zhang 2016: 9). C&A chain stores gained a similarly powerful position in European markets. Since the company archive does not hold any material for the time period after 1961 (Spoerer 2016: 12), an analysis of C&A's business practices is difficult. In contrast to M&S, the Brenninkmeijer family that founded and ran C&A used the suppliers of the Steilmann Group rather than individual manufacturers.

Though most examples of successful adjustment to global markets derive from the West German apparel industry, examples in the textiles industry exist too. Even capital-intensive parts of the production process like spinning or weaving were off-shored by companies like Kümper, a cotton spinner near Münster that bought a company in Greece in 1976. Some of the cotton manufacturers completely gave up their domestic business and became specialized traders in yarn or fabrics, e.g., the Beyerlein company in Bayreuth (Lindner 2001: 166–171). A shift to specialized fabrics that were patented in Germany but produced globally helped many of the textile manufacturers keep their company on track. Some of the producers reached agreements with the auto industry, others found niches, e.g., the production of fireproof textiles by Webatex AG. The leading company among the textile manufacturers became the Freudenberg company in Weinheim, which specialized in synthetic fibers that were used for everything from cleaning ("vileda") to industrial use, and later diversified into other branches, including floor-covering and gasket production. The company expanded abroad with production plants in the USA and Japan in the 1950s (Lindner 2001: 171). While most of German textile manufacturing disappeared or transformed into chemical industry we can find examples of businesses moving up the value chain even in this sector.

GVCs as organizational form

GVCs are not an institution or an organizational form as economic sociology would define the latter. The chains neither have a uniform hierarchy nor do they manifest as a coherent legal relationship. In fact, GVCs are not necessarily markers of capital connections. However, their existence reflects historical and contemporary patterns of dependencies that connect business units and institutions in different countries and possibly across different sectors and such dependencies enable one unit or institution to govern an entire GVC. It is because of the conjunction of these features that we suggest treating GVCs as a particular form of global business – a form that has, however, traveled below the radar of trade economics and history during most of its existence.

However, such dependencies have effects that not only create new global connections and reflect changing international trade regulations, they can also create significant poverty and misery, as is evidenced by the most recent political outrage over the killings of thousands of Bangladeshi garment workers in the Rana-Plaza building in 2013. That accident drew public and also academic attention to the many hidden dependencies and linkages in GVCs, where seemingly governing Western high street retailers have long lost sight of subcontracting networks, unwittingly and possibly also wittingly, and thus were not even able to say whether their garments were sewn by Rana Plaza workers and anxiously waited whether one of their labels would appear among the rubble and the dead bodies of exploited workers. This questions how we can guarantee the responsibility for death and damages caused by global profit-maximizing in the absence of legal connections (Donaghey/Reinecke 2018). And, yet, from a business history perspective we should also consider the long-term historical implications of the alleged novelty of Rana Plaza and other manifestations of GVC dependencies and governance: What are the similarities and what are the differences between the similarly devastating and globally debated Triangle Shirt Waist Factory Fire on New York's Lower East Side in 1911? Are we observing an entirely novel organizational form of global business in GVCs or can we find forerunners? How did these structures evolve over time? Where did they originate and what are the driving forces for their evolution? Who are the governors of GVCs and why did they come to govern? How did they gain the "power" to force distant organizations into a structure of global dependence?

This chapter has focused on the historical example of the German textile and apparel industry to highlight the explanatory power of the GVC approach. However, the approach is not restricted to that sector alone. High-end consumer electronics such as TV sets have been assembled in Western Europe and in the United States using parts supplied by global chains starting since the 1960s already (Teupe 2016). Thus, we see GVCs in many other branches, from consumer electronics and IT to the automobile industry and further into agriculture (Gereffi *et al.* 2005: 78–104). Historical research on the twentieth-century transformations of GVCs is still rare, but there are pioneering studies like Andrew Godley and Bridget Williams' (2009: 47–61) exploration of the supply chain of "industrial chicken" in the UK, Teresa da Silva Lopes (2003: 592–598) has examined the "branding" strategies of alcoholic beverages that also encompassed GVCs, and Pierre-Yves Donzé (2015: 295–310) wrote on the GVC for watches, to name just a few.

If we discovered that GVCs are not only mechanisms for the exploitation of wage differences but a more general organizational form of global production, it may be feasible to apply the concept to other branches, such as the service sector and to banking in particular. Finance always plays a role in GVCs as raising capital for FDI, for insuring risks to property, and for securing the risks of currency volatility in payments for imports and exports or simply of unreliable buyers. In fact, financial services may have taken on the organizational form of a GVC in their own right: the complexities and specifics of the Eurodollar-Market might be more accurately captured, for example, once we addressed its value-chain-like structure. Such money, accumulated in predominantly British accounts during the 1950s, was subsequently transformed into sovereign debt as it was "sold" to states in Latin America mainly by US banks initially and then extended by the inflow of Petro-Dollars during the 1970s (Rischbieter 2015: 465–493; Devlin 1993; Underhill 1997: 101–123).

However, in order to expand the GVC research agenda into services and banking, business history first needs to research and analyze the transitions and transformations of the well-researched colonial and imperial commodity chains of the nineteenth century during the twentieth century, and especially so with a view to the globalization patterns of the interwar period. Likewise, the subsequent emergence of a seemingly bipolar global economy during the Cold War decades and the second globalization wave since the 1970s could appear in new light once business historians scrutinize the emergence and transformation of GVCs during those decades. Thus, the concept of GVCs is – from our perspective – perfectly fitting to support a wide range of novel research.

References

Aalders, Gerard and Wiebes, Cees (1985), "Stockholm's Enskilda Bank, German Bosch and IG Farben: A Short History of Cloaking," *Scandinavian Economic History Review*, 33 (1), 25–50.
Aggarwal, Vinod K. (1985), *Liberal Protectionism: The International Politics of Organized Textile Trade* (Berkeley, CA: University of California Press).
Alfalla-Luque, Rafaela and Medina-López, Carmen (2009), "Supply Chain Management: Unheard of in the 1970s, Core to Today's Company," *Business History*, 51 (2), 202–221.
Bair, Jennifer (2009), "Global Commodity Chains: Genealogy and Review," in Jennifer Bair (ed.), *Frontiers of Commodity Chain Research* (Stanford, CA: Stanford University Press), 1–35.
Bair, Jennifer (2016), "The Corporation and the Global Value Chain," in Grietje Baars and Andre Spicer (eds.), *The Corporation: A Critical, Multidisciplinary Handbook* (Cambridge: Cambridge University Press), 326–335.

Baldwin, Richard (2014), "Misthinking Globalization: Twentieth-Century Paradigms and Twenty First-Century Challenges," *Australian Economic History Review*, 54 (3), 212–219.

Baldwin, Richard and Lopez-Gonzalez, Javier (2015), "Supply-chain Trade: A Portrait of Global Patterns and Several Testable Hypotheses," *World Economy*, 38 (11), 1682–1721.

Baldwin, Richard and Venables, Anthony J. (2013), "Spiders and Snakes: Offshoring and Agglomeration in the Global Economy," *Journal of International Economics*, 90 (2), 245–254.

Beckert, Sven (2014), *Empire of Cotton: A Global History* (New York: Alfred A. Knopf).

Beese, Birgit and Schneider, Brigitte (2001), *Arbeit an der Mode: Zur Geschichte der Bekleidungsindustrie im Ruhrgebiet* (Essen: Klartext).

Böhm-Bawerk, Eugen (1902), *Capital und Capitalzins, Zweite Abtheilung: Positive Theorie des Capitals* (Second Edition, Innsbruck: Verlag der Wagner'schen Universitäts-Buchhandlung).

Bown, Chad and Irwin, Douglas (2015), "The GATT's Starting Point: Tariff Levels Circa 1947," *NBER Working Paper 21782*.

Cassis, Youssef (2006), *Capitals of Capital: A History of Financial Centres, 1780–2005* (Cambridge: Cambridge University Press).

Chandler, Alfred D. and Mazlish, Bruce (eds.) (2005), *Leviathans: Multinational Corporations and the New Global History* (Cambridge: Cambridge University Press).

Clairmonte, Frederick and Cavanagh, John (1982), *The World in their Web: Dynamics of Textile Multinationals* (London: Zed).

Da Silva Lopes, Teresa (2003), "The Growth and Survival of Multinationals in the Global Alcoholic Beverages Industry," *Enterprise & Society*, 4 (4), 592–598.

Devlin, Robert (1993), *Debt and Crisis in Latin America: The Supply Side of the Story* (Princeton, NJ: Princeton University Press).

Dicken, Peter (1986), *Global Shift: Industrial Change in a Turbulent World* (London: Harper & Row).

Donaghey, Jimmy and Reinecke, Juliane (2018). "When Industrial Democracy Meets Corporate Social Responsibility: A Comparison of the Bangladesh Accord and Alliance as Responses to the Rana Plaza Disaster," *British Journal of Industrial Relations*, 56 (1), 14–42.

Donzé, Pierre-Yves (2015), "Global Value Chains and the Lost Competitiveness of the Japanese Watch Industry: An Applied Business History of Seiko since 1990," *Asia Pacific Business Review*, 21 (3), 295–310.

Dunning, John H. (1982), "Changes in the Level and Structure of International Production: The Last One-Hundred Years," in Mark Casson (ed.), *The Growth of International Business* (London: Allen & Unwin), 84–139.

European Commission (ed.) (2006), *The Moving Frontier: Changing the Geography of Production in Labour Intensive Industries* (Luxemburg: European Commission).

Fäßler, Peter (2006), *Durch den „Eisernen Vorhang": Die Deutsch-Deutschen Wirtschaftsbeziehungen 1949–1969* (Cologne: Böhlau).

Federal Chancellery (1969a), Note for the Secretary of State on the Protests of the Textile Industry, 12 August, Bundesarchiv (i.e., Federal Archiv of the FRG in Koblenz) B136, No. 7742.

Federal Chancellery (1969b), Activities of the German Government for Increases of Imports in Textile and Apparel Markets, 30 April, Bundesarchiv (i.e., Federal Archiv of the FRG in Koblenz) B136, No. 7742.

Feenstra, Robert C. (1998), "Integration of Trade and Disintegration of Production in the Global Economy," *Journal of Economic Perspectives*, 12 (4), 31–50.

Ferenschild, Sabine (2007), "Verliererinnen und Gewinner: Soziale Konsequenzen der Liberalisierung im Textil- und Bekleidungshandel," *Kurswechsel*, 4, 37–49.

Findlay, Ronald and O'Rourke, Kevin H. (2007), *Power and Plenty: Trade, War and the World Economy in the Second Millennium* (Princeton, NJ: Princeton University Press).

Fröbel, Folker, Heinchrichs, Jürgen, and Kreye, Otto (1981), *The New International Division of Labour: Structural Unemployment in Industrialized Countries and Industrialization in Developing Countries* (Cambridge: Cambridge University Press).

General Agreement on Tariffs and Trade (GATT) (1986), Text of the General Agreement (Geneva: GATT).

Gereffi, Gary, Humphrey, John, and Sturgeon, Timothy (2005), "The Governance of Global Value Chains," *Review of International Political Economy*, 12 (1), 78–104.

Gertschen, Alex (2013), *Klassenfeinde – Branchenpartner? Unternehmer und Gewerkschaft der Westdeutschen Textilindustrie vor der Herausforderung der Internationalisierung. 1949–1979* (Baden-Baden: Nomos).

Godley, Andrew C. and Williams, Bridget (2009), "The Chicken, the Factory Farm and the Supermarket: The Emergence of the Modern Poultry Industry in Britain," in Warren Belasco and Roger Horrowitz (eds.), *Food Chains* (Philadelphia, PA: University of Philadelphia Press), 47–61.

Herrigel, Gary (2010), *Manufacturing Possibilities: Creative Action and Industrial Recomposition in the United States, Germany and Japan* (Oxford: Oxford University Press).

Hopkins, Terence K. and Wallerstein, Immanuel (1986), "Commodity Chains in the World-Economy Prior to 1800," *Review (Fernand Braudel Center)*, 10 (1), 157–170.

Irwin, Douglas (1995), "The GATT's Contribution to Economic Recovery in Post-War Western Europe," in Barry Eichengreen (ed.), *Europe's Postwar Recovery* (Cambridge: Cambridge University Press), 127–150.

Jones, Geoffrey and Lubinski, Christina (2012), "Managing Political Risk in Global Business: Beiersdorf 1914–1990," *Enterprise & Society*, 13 (1), 85–119.

Kluge, Arndt (2018), *Die Deutsche Porzellanindustrie bis 1914* (Regensburg: Habilitationsschrift).

Köster, Roman (2011), *Hugo Boss, 1924–1945: Eine Kleiderfabrik zwischen Weimarer Republik und „Drittem Reich"* (Munich: Beck).

Köster, Roman (2016), "Geschichte von Seidensticker." Unpublished Manuscript.

Kukić, Leonhard (2018), "Socialist Growth Revisited: Insights from Yugoslavia," *European Review of Economic History*, 22 (4), 403–429.

Lane, Christel and Probert, Jocelyn (2005), "Domestic Capabilities and Global Production Networks in the Clothing Industry: A Comparison of German and UK Firms' Strategies," *Centre for Business Research Working Paper No. 318.*

Lindner, Stephan H. (2001), *Den Faden verloren: Die westdeutsche und die französische Textilindustrie auf dem Rückzug. (1930/45–1990)* (München: C.H. Beck).

Minister of Economics (1965), "Minutes of the talks with the trade union textiles and apparel on December 20, 1965," 21 December, Bundesarchiv (i.e., Federal Archive of the FRG in Koblenz), B102.

Minister of Economics 1969), "Trade Policy Towards Japan," 3 June, Bundesarchiv (i.e., Federal Archive of the FRG in Koblenz), B102/153900.

Mintz, Sidney Wilfred (1986), *Sweetness and Power: The Place of Sugar in Modern History* (New York: Penguin Books).

Mühleck, Peter (1992), *Krise und Anpassung der Deutschen Textil- und Bekleidungsindustrie im Lichte der Fordismus-Diskussion* (Frankfurt am Main: Lang).

Neveling, Patrick (2012), *Manifestationen der Globalisierung: Kapital, Staat und Arbeit in Mauritius, 1825–2005* (DPhil Thesis, Halle-Wittenberg: Martin-Luther-University).

Neveling, Patrick (2017), "The Global Spread of Export Processing Zones and the 1970s as a Decade of Consolidation," in Knud Andersen and Stefan Müller (eds.), *Social Regulation: State, Economy, and Social Protagonists since the 1970s* (Oxford: Berghahn Books), 23–40.

Rischbieter, Laura (2015), "Risiken und Nebenwirkungen: Internationale Finanzstrategien in der Verschuldungskrise der 1980er Jahre," *Geschichte und Gesellschaft*, 41 (3), 465–493.

Rivoli, Pietra (2009), *The Travels of a T-Shirt in the Global Economy: An Economist Examines the Markets, Power, and Politics of World Trade* (Hoboken, NJ: Wiley).

Rudolph, Karsten (2004), *Wirtschaftsdiplomatie im Kalten Krieg: Die Ostpolitik der Westdeutschen Großindustrie 1945–1991* (Frankfurt am Main: Campus-Verlag).

Sabel, Charles and Zeitlin, Jonathan (1985), "Historical Alternatives to Mass Production: Politics, Markets and Technology in the Nineteenth Century Industrialization," *Past and Present*, 108, 133–176.

Schnaus, Julia (2017), "Das leise Sterben einer Branche. Der Niedergang der deutschen Bekleidungsindustrie in den 1960er und 1970er Jahren," *Zeitschrift für Unternehmensgeschichte*, 62 (1), 9–34.

Seabrooke, Leonard and Wigan, Duncan (2017), "The Governance of Global Wealth Chains," *Review of International Political Economy*, 24 (1), 1–29.

Sharpston, Michael (1976), "International Subcontracting," *World Development*, 4 (4), 333–337.

Sinn, Hans-Werner (2005), *Die Basar-Ökonomie: Exportweltmeister oder Schlusslicht?* (Berlin: Econ).

Smith, Adrian (2003), "Power Relations, Industrial Cluster and Regional Transformations: Pan-European Integration and Outward Processing in the Slovak Clothing Industry," *Economic Geography*, 79 (1), 17–40.

Spoerer, Mark (2016), *C&A: A Family Business in Germany, the Netherlands and the United Kingdom 1911–1961* (Munich: Beck).

Sugihara, Kaoru (2004), "International Circumstances Surrounding the Post-War Japanese Cotton Textile Industry," in Douglas A. Farnie and David J. Jeremy (eds.), *The Fibre that Changed the World: The Cotton Industry in International Perspective, 1600–1990s* (Oxford: Oxford University Press), 521–551.

Sykes, Alan O. (1991), "Protectionism as a 'Safeguard': A Positive Analysis of the GATT 'Escape Clause' with Normative Speculations," *University of Chicago Law Review*, 58 (1), 255–305.

Teupe, Sebastian (2016), *Die Schaffung eines Marktes: Preispolitik, Wettbewerb und Fernsehgerätehandel in der BRD und den USA, 1945–1985* (Berlin: De Gruyter Oldenbourg).

Timmer, Marcel P., Erumban, Abdul Azeez, Los, Bart, Stehrer, Robert, and de Vries, Gaaitzen J. (2014), "Slicing Up Global Value Chains," *Journal of Economic Perspectives*, 28 (2), 99–118.

Toms, Steven and Zhang, Qi (2016), "Marks & Spencer and the Decline of the British Textile Industry, 1950–2000," *Business History Review*, 90 (1), 3–30.

Topik, Steven, Marichal, Carlos, and Frank, Zephyr L. (2006), *From Silver to Cocaine: Latin American Commodity Chains and the Building of the World Economy, 1500–2000* (Durham, NC: Duke University Press).

Triumph (2018), *Geschichte*, [online] Available at: www.triumph.com/de/de/7487.html [Accessed 7 September 2018].

UNCTAD (Ed.) (2013), *Global Value Chains: Investment and Trade for Development* (Geneva: UNCTAD).

Underhill, Geoffrey R. D. (1997), "The Making of the European Financial Area: Global Market Integration and the Single Market for Financial Services," in Geoffrey R. D. Underhill (ed.), *The New World Order in International Finance* (New York: Macmillan), 101–123.

Wallerstein, Immanuel (1974), *The Modern World System I: Capitalist Agriculture and the Origins of the European World-Economy in the Sixteenth Century* (New York: Academic Press).

Wallerstein, Immanuel and Hopkins, Terence K. (1982), *World System Analysis: Theory and Methodology* (Beverly Hills, CA: Sage).

Wiemann, Jürgen (1983), "Selektiver Protektionismus und aktive Strukturanpassung: Handels- und Industriepolitische Reaktionen Europas auf die zunehmende Wettbewerbsfähigkeit der Entwicklungsländer am Beispiel der Textilpolitik der EG," Dissertation, Berlin.

Wilkins, Mira (1988), "The Free-Standing Company, 1870–1914: An Important Type of British Foreign Direct Investment," *Economic History Review*, 41 (2), 259–282.

Wilkins, Mira (2008), "Chandler and Global Business History," *Business History Review*, 82 (2), 251–266.

Wolf, Eric R. (1982), *Europe and the People without History* (Berkeley, CA: University of California Press).

19

STATE-OWNED ENTERPRISES

Andrea Colli and Pasi Nevalainen

Introduction

State-owned enterprises (SOEs) are often considered to be relics of twentieth century history. They are understood as vanishing entities, soon rendered obsolete by the privatization policies of the 1980s and 1990s (cf. Toninelli 2000). Nonetheless, SOEs continue to exist in the most advanced countries (Christiansen 2011), and represent a growing factor in the international market (OECD 2015). Their relevance among the world's largest multinational enterprises (MNEs) is significant. Today, 15 percent of the world's largest multinational enterprises (MNEs), or 40 percent in emerging economies, are under the legal ownership of their home countries' governments (UNCTAD 2017). Our claim is that this development emerged from a fundamental change in the basic concept of the SOE.

The transformation in the basic concept of SOE is closely linked to two major recent developments in Western capitalism. The first was a worldwide process of dismantling the SOE system, which had historically characterized Western industrial capitalism after World War II (Toninelli 2000; Amatori *et al.* 2011) and a number of other countries in Asia and Latin America (Musacchio and Lazzarini 2014). The second was the simultaneous acceleration of globalization after the fall of the Berlin Wall in 1989, and its impact on the internationalization of business enterprises (Colli 2016; Fitzgerald 2016). Research so far has tended to see these two as largely separate phenomena. Our key point is instead that there is a firm relationship between the privatization and the internationalization of the former SOEs.

The literature has long stressed the connection between privatization and liberalization as well as the internationalization of privatized incumbents. Privatizations put the former state-owned assets in the "right" hands of private investors, largely motivated by the logic of economic efficiency, with a positive impact on the companies' internationalization. Recent research has challenged this perspective, finding a much more complex relationship between the ownership dimension of former "national champions" and their internationalization.

Even today, the attitude toward direct state involvement is mixed. "Traditional" SOEs (that is, those active as natural monopolies), are generally considered to be bureaucratic and inefficient organizations. Although common sense tends to emphasize the problems of state entrepreneurship in terms of efficiency, in some cases companies under the control of national governments have internationalized more successfully than those fully privatized – thanks mainly to the state's guiding role in the process (Colli *et al.* 2014; Kalasin *et al.* 2019). In the meantime, SOEs have become increasingly relevant in the international economy. The UNCTAD World Investment Report (2017) identified 1,500 state-owned multinational enterprises (SOMNEs) with more than 86,000 affiliates. Recent decades have seen the internationalization of traditional SOEs, but also the growth of emerging economies, where SOEs very often play a major role.

There were two major drivers of the revival of SOEs. The first was the transformation of the basic concept of SOE. Both in developed and developing countries, states have largely abandoned the idea of total control over "domestic monopolists" in charge of pursuing social and redistributive goals instead of economic ones. This perspective has progressively evolved into a concept of SOE built around the idea of partial state ownership coupled with economic efficiency. The pursuit of economic efficiency implied, of course, access to other markets than the domestic one.

A second driver was the liberalization of domestic markets. When liberalization forced SOEs to face competition in the home market, they were forced to seek new business from the international market. In these contexts, we must not forget the changes that have taken place in SOEs themselves. As a result of external factors, SOEs renewed their own practices, developed internationalization strategies and became part of globalization. Sometimes they became change factors themselves.

In the following sections we examine the process of change in the concept of SOEs and their impact in the making of global business. As we are looking at a global phenomenon, we define SOE and SOMNE according to the three most basic features. The changes in this model are examined at three different levels: international, corporate governance and firm perspectives. The different levels of change had different characteristics. From our empirical standpoint, we look at two advanced European countries, Italy and Finland, where state operations played a major role in the modernization process of the twentieth century and where the role of the state as an owner has changed dramatically. However, as we will see in recent debate, state ownership still has many faces. Even if we finally draw our conclusions into a simplified model, we want to emphasize that the variety of SOEs is still manifold.

The three defining elements of state-owned multinationals

The traditional SOE was established and developed in a variety of circumstances. This is why the definition and corporate structures differ from country to country (e.g., Millward 2011; Christiansen 2011). In general, the definition of SOE relies on state ownership and control, elements that are related but not the same. This very basic attribute has a major impact on SOEs' other basic characteristics as depicted in Figure 19.1.

These interconnected determining factors, as illustrated in Figure 19.1, are (1) the degree of state ownership, (2) the type of SOE organization and (3) the degree of SOE internationalization strategy. The first two, ownership and type of organization, are, above all, associated with the general modernization of the SOE. The degree of an SOE's internationalization, in turn, is linked to the emergence of SOMNE.

Although our definition for SOE/SOMNE remains broad (within the transparent box in Figure 19.1), it allows us to conceptualize the transformation from "old-school" SOEs to SOMNEs. In practice this has often meant moving from the bottom left (government agency) to the upper right corner (MNE). Generally, development from traditional SOE to modern SOMNE has taken place between these two extremes. The historical trajectory has mostly occurred gradually and usually on one dimension at a time – or at least the development can be analytically distinguished in this way.

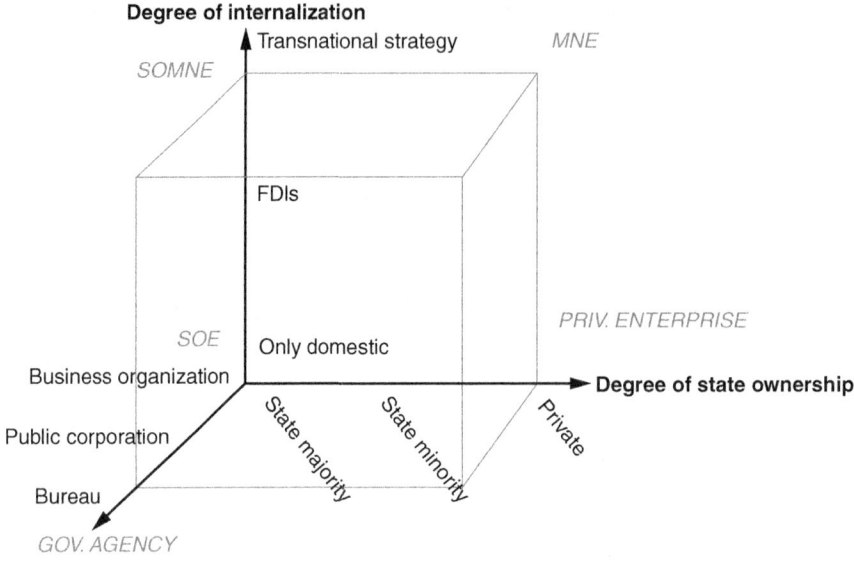

Figure 19.1   The determinants of SOMNE in three dimensions

Source: The authors.

The general, though debatable, view of the passage has gone so that SOEs are first incorporated and only then privatized, after which they have become internationalized.

State ownership varies between complete, majority and minority holding. How much of the holding would suffice for the company to be defined as "state-owned" varies. Typically, an SOE is a company in which the government holds a simple majority of the ownership rights. Seldom, however, does even a minority fraction suffice to give the state significant influence. For this reason, international comparative databases tend to define companies as SOEs also when the state's holding is very small. Ownership is closely related to control, and, for traditional SOEs in particular, this means a close interconnection with the national government.

SOEs have assumed various organizational forms: government agencies, intermediaries between the agency and the business enterprise, and state-owned limited liability companies (Millward 2005: 188). Especially those in a monopoly situation may also have had official duties, which is why separating them from other state organizations is not always straightforward. Because of this contradiction, they have sometimes been called "hybrid organizations" (Bruton *et al.* 2015; Aharoni 2018). In recent decades many SOEs have been corporatized and corporations have been directed toward "normal" business organizations whose official duties have most often been discontinued. In the same context, the sole purpose of the companies is to produce a profit. Business historians often associate this development with the emergence of the competitive market; but scholars of administration associate this development with the change in governance thinking. Either way, this shift often represents the generalization of market-oriented thinking, separating SOEs from the state's administrative functions, and has often proved an intermediate stage toward privatizations (e.g., Christensen and Pallesen 2001).

An important concept of MNE is often defined on the basis of company's foreign investment activity (FDIs) (Dunning and Lundan 2008). In the case of SOEs, a relatively small amount has been enough to meet the criteria of a SOMNE. For example, for Anastassopoulos *et al.*

(1987: 25), a mere 10 percent of turnover from abroad and operations in at least three countries was sufficient. This definition is particularly well suited for traditional SOEs whose internationalization was related to the acquisition of resources and the establishment of sales offices. In our view, however, internationalization should be understood as a strategic choice.

As Wilkins (2001: 6) recalls, an MNE provides "a tissue that unifies on a regular basis; it is not merely a channel for one time transactions but a basis for different sorts of external organizational relationships." Ghoshal and Bartlett (1998) divide the multinationals according to how internationalism is reflected in the company's strategy: does internationalization mean "only" the acquisition of resources and sales offices, or whether production or even strategic functions are decentralized across the globe, allowing the MNE to utilize various resources across borders and to specialize in managing value chains (also Aharoni and Ramamurti 2008). As we will see, such a change from national to multinational, especially when internationalization means a far-reaching transnational strategy, challenges the original idea of SOEs as tools for national purposes (Cuervo-Cazurra 2018). To understand the profundity of this change, we begin our historical analysis from the state owner's original interests.

How a faithful servant became a burden

The traditional SOE was a national creation. Although some of them were established centuries ago (e.g., royal armories, mines, posts and railways), their significance peaked during the twentieth century, when Europe went through the Second Industrial Revolution. According to Millward (2011; 2013), SOEs were instruments for promoting social and political unification, ensuring national defense and achieving economic growth. Basically, traditional SOEs can be divided into infrastructure and industrial facilities with differing purposes. Manufacturing-related SOEs were linked to nations' industrial strength (like machine shops, shipyards), while infrastructural enterprises (like energy and telecommunications) were chosen over other means (regulation, subsidies to private operators) to speed up construction processes or to avoid excessively high subsidy levels and to ensure necessary safety (Millward 2013; Toninelli 2000).

The behavior of SOEs reflected the quality and nature of governments, and their geopolitical situation. "Resource nationalism" is represented among other things by the national oil companies, whose task has been to ensure that the natural resource benefits remain in the home country (Stevens 2008). The defense aspects were particularly visible in network industries, which were partly designed for strategic considerations and security of supply, for which reason nature-based synergies between neighboring regimes (especially between the East and West) remained largely unexploited (Högselius et al. 2016).

In addition, in their country, SOEs had often a special political role as significant employers. Sometimes these were accompanied by significant national feelings. Such examples illustrate the fact that in the original concept of SOE, the economic efficiency could easily be overridden by political, military and ideological objectives. On the other hand, when looking at the behavior of these companies in the longer term, it should be remembered that they also developed their own business from their own perspectives. After they were established, their activities developed, expanded and extended to new areas which in many cases had little to do with the state's original purposes (e.g., Aharoni 2018; Vernon 1979).

The typical state-owned company had a certain built-in inconsistency. Since they were also at least partly business enterprises, they often had to balance between contradictory goals: to be profitable businesses and to accomplish political tasks. Partly because of this, they seemed inefficient in both respects (Heath and Norman 2004). Although the importance of financial targets grew markedly, the general public drew attention to the often impaired service level. Even though the typical public critique associated with them has sometimes been one-sided or exaggerated, it has had a major impact on their public image and hence the attitudes of the politicians responsible for the corporate governance of these companies (e.g., Aharoni 2000; Millward 2011).

The "Golden Age" of state-owned companies had begun in some European countries even before World War II. They generally reached their greatest significance during the decades immediately after the war, and public criticism of them increased as the post-war economic growth dissipated. The turn, which is usually in the late 1970s, was clear (e.g., Toninelli 2000; Millward 2005). In Europe, Margaret Thatcher's reforms in the UK represented the first systematic agenda for shrinking the public sector, providing relevant benchmarks for other countries (Parker 1999; Musacchio and Lazzarini 2014: 41–3). In fact, privatizing and opening up competition in its different forms progressed in Europe at different speeds, depending, *inter alia*, on country-specific political institutions (e.g., Thatcher 2004). In Finland, to take an example, the multi-party system, together with a strictly regulated legislative framework, practically prevented such dire turn of economic policy as that seen in the UK (see Nevalainen 2014: 155). Instead, reforms progressed gradually.

Earlier research has identified different levels of external factors that have been used to explain the change. We divide these into the following categories:

1 Supranational phenomena such as evolving technology (which weakened the foundations of old natural monopolies) and the increased popularity of neoliberal economics (perceiving state intervention as a major disturbance to the market).[1]
2 The impact of international cooperation within organizations like the Organisation for Economic Co-operation and Development (OECD), World Bank and the European Community (EC) (agreements on the dismantling of barriers to trade).
3 National level policies, involving a number of decision-making levels, such as politics, government administration and the influence of private companies (that finally led to deregulation efforts and changes in corporate governance policies at the national level, most prominently corporatization and privatization).

On the other hand, we must not forget the other side of the change. State-owned companies themselves wanted to cope with the change and thus become competitive business ventures.

SOEs as an issue for the free trade movement

International organizations began to be more negative about SOEs as of the late 1980s. This in turn had a great impact as the organizations, with their recommendations and norms, guided the world's states to adhere to the same basic principles, the most important of which was to remove barriers to trade. An important context was of course the Uruguay Round, the 123-nation negotiations that began in 1986 and led to the establishment of the World Trade Organization (WTO) in 1995. The elimination of barriers to trade highlighted the need to improve the efficiency of domestic markets. The term "Washington consensus" was introduced in 1989 to refer to the Washington-based institutions' commonly shared advice to developing countries, especially Latin America, for recovering from the economic crises of the 1980s (Williamson 2004). These usually ineffective SOEs were advised to privatize. This was repeated in the World Bank's (1995) publications as, according to "Bureaucrats in Business," inefficient SOEs slowed down the eradication of poverty.

The most interesting change from the standpoint of traditional SOEs occurred on the "old continent," the traditional core area of state capitalism. The European Commission, which had

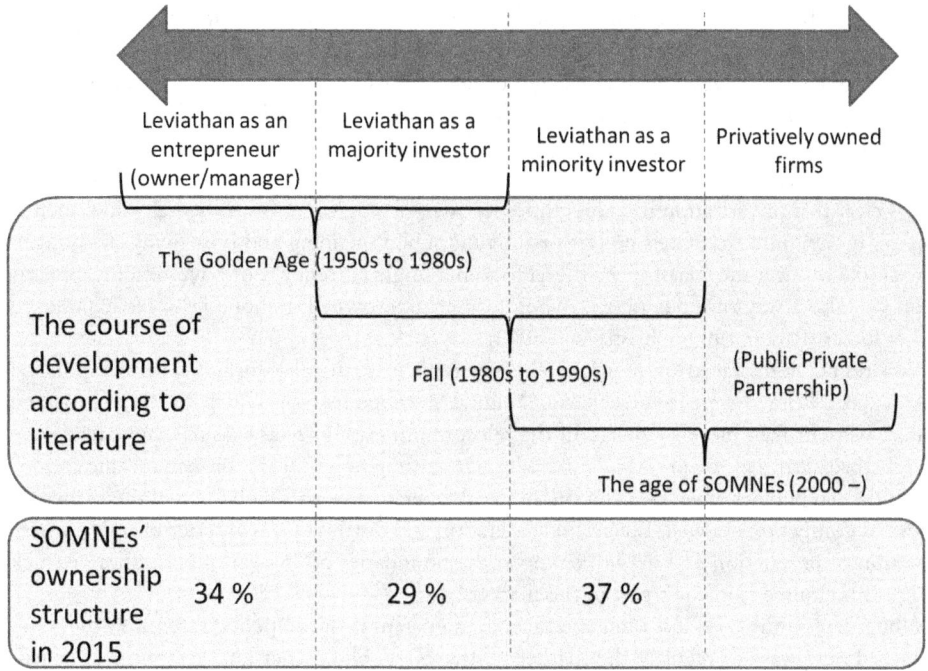

Figure 19.2   General trends in state capitalism and ownership of state-owned multinationals in 2015

Source: Elaborated on Musacchio and Lazzarini (2014: 8); UNCTAD (2017: 37).

Note
In the overview of international and international companies, it should be remembered that a large number of SOEs is domestic service establishments.

previously tolerated national solutions, changed its point of view. According to Parker (1999: 23) a particularly important turn was the Single European Act in 1986, which aimed at dismantling barriers to free trade within the EC by the end of 1992. As previously public goods were protected from competition, the EC applied pressure to Member States to open up competition in utility markets. In various industries, these developments progressed typically in stages, for example, Thatcher (2001) divided the EC's telecommunications policy change into three main phases: entry into regulation (1979–87), substantial but limited liberalization and re-regulation (1987–92), and the extension of the regulatory framework across the entire sector (1993–2000). The EC considered the single market a means to compete in a globalizing market.

   Although the trend in recent years has been a decline in state ownership, especially in Western countries, in a global review more than half of multinational state-owned companies are still majority state-owned (Figure 19.2).

Internationalization and corporate governance

Governments changed their attitude to natural monopolies and state ownership and control. At the same time as politicians adopted more market-liberal thoughts, the state administrations gradually adopted the ideas of *New Public Management* (NPM), according to which market-based models borrowed from the private sector were means to solve the public sector's contemporary efficiency problems. Unlike previous models aimed at improving administrative efficiency, NPM, despite its alleged neutrality, relied heavily on certain neoliberal perspectives (e.g., Pollitt and Bouckaert 2011). Deregulation was, according to this thinking, a means of exposing formerly protected industries to market mechanisms, which was believed to increase the efficiency of both the market and of SOEs. In this respect, privatization and deregulation actually served the same purpose.

It is clear that privatization had sometimes its own ideological or instrumental value, such as bringing money into the state's coffers or moving public spending and borrowing off-budget, for example to meet the Maastricht criteria to join a single currency. For governments, privatization was also a way of reducing risk when former state-owned monopolies were exposed to market forces (Parker 1999; Christiansen 2013).

As a result, SOEs faced momentous changes both in their relationships with the political system and in the competitive scenario. Natural monopolies, for which SOEs were often created, were broken piece by piece. In the telecommunications sector (as in many areas, such as public broadcasting), technology, especially wireless digital solutions, dismantled the monopoly of the old public networks. Later on, network operators were forced to open their lanes for the use of competitors as well. Electricity generation and distribution is another example where separation of production and network moved the boundaries of "natural monopolies" (Chick 2007: 113). Competitors took part in the markets.

While state institutions lost their special role as guarantor of the public interest as the states developed new ways to regulate the markets, "strategic public ownership" lost most of its past importance (Clifton *et al.*, 2011a, 2011b). In some cases, the state opted for funding or becoming an affiliate. In the United States, the practice of setting up privately owned, but government-funded organizational structures has been widely used since World War II. Such solutions were originally used in the development programs of the armaments industry, from which they quickly spread to other sectors as well (Radford 2013: 136).

The general discussion has been dominated by privatization, which was most pronounced in the mid-1990s, when up to 600 SOEs were privatized per year all over the world. In the 2000s, the development leveled off; roughly 200 reported cases per year (Musacchio and Lazzarini 2014: 44; Clifton *et al.* 2006) even though state functions previously carried out by authorities have been further incorporated into new SOEs. In the OECD area, the share of SOEs declined in comparison to emerging economies. The privatization was most marked in manufacturing, construction, finance, oil, coal, airlines and the non-grid parts of network utilities, such as electricity, train operations, telecommunications, road transport, shipping and ports (Kowalski *et al.* 2013; Christiansen 2011).

Starting from the beginning of the 2000s, the most common legal form of SOE has been the private limited liability company, followed by the joint stock company. According to the OECD (2004), SOEs in the majority of the OECD countries were considered to be the same as any other private company and were subject to the same legislation. With regard to direct ownership, states are often minority shareholders and tend to manage their equity portfolios professionally (Musacchio *et al.* 2015).

Table 19.1 summarizes the main differences between the "old" and the "new" models. Of course, the distinction between old and new models is both chronological ("old" was prevalent up to the 1990s) and conceptual/strategic ("old" is a model still diffused in many developing economies). Basically, the distinguishing characteristics of a state-owned company have changed significantly in all areas. While this depicts the principle, development is not always so unambiguous.

Existing state-owned companies are structurally different from the old ones: we look at this distinction from the viewpoint of corporate governance and the strategies chosen by SOEs.

Table 19.1 Differences between the old and new models of SOE

	Ownership	Legal form	Market	Rationale	Main corporate governance issues	Main assets of top management	Political economy goals	Instrument for international relations
Old model	Full	Agency; Joint Stock Company; Listed (few cases)	Domestic	Natural monopolies; redistribution; employment; regional development; consolidation of strategic industries; national championship	Relationship with political parties	Political connections	Yes, limited to internal consensus	No
New model	Partial; relative majority; always enough to exert control	Joint Stock Company; Listed Company	International	Profitability; international vertical integration; international championship	Relationship with minority shareholders	Professional skills and international connections	Yes, both for internal consensus but for international standing, supporting international relations	Yes

Source: The authors.

Both these areas have been greatly transforming under the pressure of globalization, and in many cases the result has been the present form of state ownership, no longer based on full ownership of domestic natural monopolies or national champions in strategic industries, but on the partial ownership of global players active at the international level. The internationalization of SOEs is, moreover, raising a number of issues both in the realm of political economy and international relations.

Empirical perspectives on corporate governance change

In the following, we examine the emergence of the "new" model in light of two national cases emphasizing different aspects of the change. Finland and Italy are examples of countries that were rapidly industrialized in the twentieth century with a high level of governmental involvement in the modernization. In both cases the governments changed their ownership policies strongly in response to the requirements of the globalizing economy. In addition to what we have already pointed out, these changes have been prompted by companies' own needs: to maintain market efficiency and profitability, basically enlarging their market strategy embracing internationalization. Although the political needs have been separated from everyday action, it is clear that the political and ideological trends have influenced policies and indeed continue to do so.

The Italian experience: from a highly centralized holding structure to an extensive privatization program

In Italy, the formation of an SOE system was particularly affected by the lack of private capital (Amatori 1997). In 1933, the Italian state ownership was concentrated in a holding company "Instituto di Riconstruzione Industriale" (IRI) to grant long-term loans to companies affected by the depression and to take over the industrial securities held by the country's major banks. In the absence of economic forces, IRI became a permanent owner. It was forced to provide a unified management of a consistent segment of the national economy. As a result, the Italian system became highly centralized.

The government policy was to create large business groups. For instance, in energy, the state supported the creation of a vertically integrated energy group, the Ente Nazionale Idrocarburi (ENI), a national agency producing and distributing electric energy under monopoly conditions (Amatori and Colli 2011: 190). At the peak of its expansion in the late 1960s, the Italian system of SOEs included the most important capital intensive and mass production industries, ranging from steel to chemicals; infrastructures (ranging from motorways and air transport to telecoms), energy and several other industries, including food and beverages, mass distribution and, last but not least, banking. The SOEs complex was basically the basis of the Italian postwar economic expansion and modernization, and was increasingly also used to reduce economic inequality between different regions of the country (Colli 2016).

This developmental role, however, was also the basis of a steady decline in one of the pillars of SOEs management, as SOEs tended to prioritize political objectives over economic efficiency and profitability. In the early 1990s, the losses turned public opinion against the SOEs. This, in turn, led to one of the most ambitious and intense European privatization programs, which resulted in the total or partial privatization of entire industries. The goal of the privatization process was not only the improvement of state finances but also the enhancement of the economic efficiency of the companies, the introduction of more industrial competition, the enlargement of the stock market and the internationalization of the Italian industrial system. The privatization process also created pressures for the revision of corporate law to give more serious consideration to the protection of rights of minority shareholders than had been the case in the past (Amatori and Colli 2000).

In addition to these, privatization had an important political goal. Italy wanted to be a major player in the European economic and political unification, starting with the Maastricht Treaty, which meant a need on the one hand to speed up the process of restoring the state's finances and on the other to follow the prescriptions emanating from the European Parliament, especially those concerning the participation of the state in the economic system and the elimination of monopolies in public utilities. However, at the same time as the Italian state retreated from specific sectors, the state's direct intervention in the economy through public enterprises has remained a stable feature (Cló *et al.* 2015).

The Finnish experience: fragmented ownership and the repetitive development of corporate governance

In Finland, the formation of SOEs was related, even more clearly than in Italy, to the building of a nation-state and promoting industrialization. In the early twentieth century, SOEs were acquired or set up for very practical reasons, such as to produce fertilizers for inefficient agriculture, to set up domestic armaments production and to build network industries. After World War II, Finland consolidated its position as a mixed market economy, joining the OECD in 1969. Strong economic growth, however, seemed to regress in the mid-1970s, which also marked a significant turn toward market-liberal economic policy. According to Junka (2010), the state's role as an industrialist was understood to have reached its endpoint.

SOEs themselves have faced increasing pressure from globalizing markets since the 1980s and many SOEs expanded abroad. Among companies it was commonly thought that only large players would survive in the globalizing business environment. Whereas in the early 1970s the eight largest SOEs had zero foreign affiliates, in 1987 there were already 80, mainly located in Western Europe and North America.[2] As SOEs needed more capital for investments, the pressure to list SOEs on the stock exchange grew (Ranki 2012). In 1988, the Prime Minister still underlined that listing some SOEs was not privatizing, but giving them an opportunity to gain risk financing from the private capital market (Junka 2010).

Another major line of development was the renewal of the corporate governance system, whose biggest problem was its "facelessness": it was not clear who represented "the state," and who was responsible for what part of the steering.[3] During the following years, the issue was investigated with a particular emphasis on internationalization. SOEs' corporate structures were to be adjusted to be consistent with "international practices and standards." As noted by the working group (1995): "Instead of a specific knowledge of social interests, it is becoming increasingly important to have a coherent understanding of international business and related risks"[4] (also Table 19.2).

The turning points of the ownership policy were characterized by failed projects. In the late 1970s the failure of the state-owned television CRT tube factory "Valco" had a dire impact on the general perception of the state's ability to handle business. The policy of the 2000s was affected by the telecommunications incumbent "Sonera," which was rapidly internationalized in the 1990s and transformed into a SOMNE. The partial privatization of the company in 1998 led to a heated public debate and the creation of the general privatization guidelines.[5] Interestingly enough, the development of recent decades also started in part from Sonera, which in 2002 was on the verge of bankruptcy after winning the licensing auctions (as a part of a consortium) for third-generation UMTS mobile licenses in Germany and Italy. As is well known, their

Table 19.2 The objectives and principles of the state's ownership policies in the 1990s and 2000s, Finland

Objectives (1990s):	Principles (1990s):
1 To secure companies' access to capital	1 The state requires the best possible return on capital
2 To strengthen capacities and international competitiveness	2 The state has long-term objectives, which are carried out taking into account the market conditions
3 To develop company structures in such a way that the companies develop steadily and are able to create jobs	3 The state defines and also takes into account the national interests (like defense)
4 Use the revenue from privatizations to strengthen the economy and the state's finances	*Principles (2004):*
5 Increase the value of state property by incorporating and rationalizing state institutions	1 Regulation and ownership should be strictly separated
6 To enhance corporate governance by developing management, pursuing active policy in dividends, improving incentive systems for management and employees	2 All the owners are equal 3 There should be a unambiguous division of power between parliament and government
7 To develop capital markets by activating investors and strengthening domestic ownership	4 Ownership policy belongs to the state, operative decisions to the company

Sources: Published memos: "Valtionyhtiöiden omistajapolitiikkaa selvittänyt työryhmä (1999)"; "Valtion yhtiöomistus (2004)."

value collapsed rapidly. The public debate asked whether the state – as the largest shareholder – should have prevented such ventures. The State Shareholding and Ownership Act (1368/2007) further defined the division of labor between government and parliament. It was also seen as an instrument in the final separation of the ownership function from regulatory and policy responsibilities.[6] According to OECD (2011), the reform created a comparatively centralized ownership structure.

Internationalization strategies: the pros and cons of state ownership

With the corporatization process, SOEs became more independent than before and they were relieved of their previous administrative and social obligations. Thus the old problem due to the contradictory objectives was, at least to some extent, removed. In these dynamics, stories of success go alongside blunders. Some companies have successfully become international leaders maintaining their character as state-owned entities, while others have failed. State ownership has both a useful (e.g., through privileged access to state resources) and a harmful side for the company (e.g., agency problems like excessively politicized and bureaucratic ownership steering) (e.g., Kalasin *et al.* 2019; Mariotti and Marzano 2019). In general, internationalization has been associated with an improved level of management; and vice versa, internationalization may be a means for corporate management to reduce the strict control of the state owner (e.g., Cuervo-Cazurra *et al.* 2014).

Anastassopoulos *et al.* (1987) summarized the key factors that influence SOEs' success in internationalization in two main points: (1) How does the top management organize its relationship with the state – in other words – how much freedom can it get to act as it sees fit; and (2) How well does the management learn to master international business – taking into account that, in addition to the strategy, the organization's business culture needs to be changed.

The existence of SOMNEs generates a series of legitimacy problems. SOEs are often seen as a mechanisms set up in order to achieve ideological and political goals, or, worse, to interfere in sovereign countries. For example, they can be used as instruments of foreign policy, or to achieve technological know-how. Sometimes their political goals and non-business motivations do clash with the interests of minority shareholders (Cuervo-Cazurra *et al.* 2014). Meyer *et al.* (2014) found that the Chinese SOEs expanding overseas faced different expectations and pressures than private-owned companies. This was attributed to the fact that an SOE is supposed to promote the (often non-financial) benefit of its owner. State ownership may also influence the geography itself of an internationalization strategy so that SOEs operate in their own industries (often in some way strategic) or exploit their own strengths. According to some studies (e.g., Knutsen *et al.* 2011; Amighini *et al.* 2013) SOEs are more inclined to invest in politically unstable countries than private companies.

From the private business point of view, SOMNEs are often accused of unfair competition, because their owners prefer them, provide them with financially secured positions or otherwise a loose framework for action. Problematic forms of support include for example direct subsidies, concessionary financing, state-backed guarantees, preferential regulatory treatment, exemptions from the antitrust enforcement of bankruptcy rules. For such reasons, privatization was seen as a prerequisite for inward investments, as with the lifting of competition, SOEs could use unfair means to block new entrants (Alonso *et al.* 2013).

It may not be surprising that privatization has often been considered by scholars to be an outright prerequisite for SOEs' internationalization. According to this line of thinking, privatization and market liberalization were supposed to encourage firms to expand abroad, as companies subject to competition in their domestic markets would look for new potential markets. In this competition, the first movers were supposed to gain an advantage. However, as Clifton *et al.* (2011a) have shown, early privatization was not enough to ensure the success of British Telecom.

The relationship between ownership, privatization and internationalization has been examined particularly in connection with telecommunications, which was one of the fastest growing industries in recent decades. While the new technologies enabled new kinds of business, the past monopolies were opened to competition, most commonly during the 1980s and 1990s. As a result of the combined effect of many factors, the industry's standards and practices were internationalized in exceptionally fast order (e.g., Thatcher 2004). Telecoms were often the first major privatizations, leading the way to further privatization programs, and turning themselves into international corporations.

Several studies have found that the SOEs' own process of change was gradual and that top management was often active (e.g. Erakovic and Wilson 2005). For telecom incumbents, it has been repeatedly stated that the long process allowed companies to change their ways of doing business (e.g., Karlsson 1998; Palcic and Reeves 2010). Many began internationalizing before privatizing. For example, the Finnish telecom incumbent Sonera became international in the early 1990s when it built its own networks in Estonia and Russia. These businesses were seen, above all, as proactive moves to safeguard the company's own domestic interests. However, the privatization in 1998 was clearly related to the fact that international business was seen as increasingly important. At this point Sonera itself found state ownership unpleasant, not only because of various administrative constraints, but also because of the company's reputation (e.g., Nevalainen 2017). After the listing in 1998, Finnish state ownership declined gradually to a minority, until the last shares were sold in winter 2018.

Then there are state-owned multinationals with unequivocal political dimensions. Energy companies, despite the internationalized business environment, have retained significant state

Table 19.3 SOMNEs in 2017: geographic distributions

European Union	420
Sweden	49
France	45
Italy	44
Germany	43
Belgium	32
Norway★	32
Portugal	26
Slovenia	24
Austria	23
Finland	23
Poland	21
Switzerland	20
Spain	19
Netherlands	11
Croatia	10
China	257
Malaysia	79
India	61
South Africa	55
Russian Federation	51
United Arab Emirates	50
Republic of Korea	33
Singapore	29
Qatar	27
New Zealand	24
Canada	18
Egypt	14
Brazil	12
Zimbabwe	9
Japan	6
Colombia	5
TOTAL	**1,150**

Source: UNCTAD (2017: 31).

Note
The most important sectors were finance, insurance and real estate (18 percent), electrics, gas and sanitary (10 percent), transportation (10 percent), holdings (7 percent) and mining (6 percent).
★   Not an EU member state.

ownership. In such cases, state control often takes place in different ways; for example, most of the national oil company governance systems are hybrids of corporate governance, public administration and regulation (Hults 2012). This has not always prevented them from succeeding. For instance, the case of ENI, the Italian oil company, transformed itself into an international player with significant investments around the world, and even in activities (such as the production of nuclear energy), outlawed in the country of origin.

A reappraisal? State-owned multinationals in the 2010s

Despite large-scale privatizations in the 1980s and 1990s and the clearly declining trend in Western countries, SOEs remained as significant actors in particular in network industries and the banking sector. As has already been shown their expansion to the international market is seen both as a threat and an opportunity. Being owned by the state, they can still be used as tools, for example, for the protection of domestic markets (Kowalski *et al.* 2013). Therefore the OECD considers it important that business and regulation are clearly distinguished. It underlines the importance of good corporate governance practices. In this regard, the World Bank (2006) also sees potential. Well-managed SOEs can serve as examples of good governance in emerging economies.

Especially during the financial crisis (2007–08), it was suspected that SOEs might be making a comeback. Governments rescued some companies that were considered particularly important or "too big to fall" (e.g., banks) (e.g., Stevens 2008; Florio 2013). Sometimes SOEs are still used to overcome obstacles to growth. Sometimes governments retain their holdings in order to avoid the risk of foreign ownership. However, structural changes in Europe have continued in recent years. Efficiency enhancing measures have ranged from modification of the legal framework and corporate governance (including corporatization and separation of activities) to selling assets to private parties or full privatizations. Other reforms have aimed at improving transparency and accountability. A recent wave of privatizations or preparatory steps has occurred mainly in the network industries, for example in power grids. According to the European Commission (2016), these efforts have been motivated by public finance constraints and the structural disadvantages that are still associated with state ownership.

While traditional research has focused on European SOEs, their significance has increased significantly with the growing importance of emerging economies, where the range is often also wider than in Europe (Table 19.3). Of particular importance is China, which in 2010 had the highest share of SOEs among its largest enterprises (Christiansen 2011; Kowalski *et al.* 2013). This is also reflected in the focus of the current discussion (Bruton *et al.* 2015). In recent years, public debate has focused on loss-making, state-owned "zombie companies" that cannot survive without substantial support. Chinese SOEs are often deemed less efficient and innovative than their private counterparts (e.g., Girma and Gong 2008; Girma *et al.* 2009). The reasons found resemble the content of the European debate: non-commercial objectives and loose budget constraints combined with inefficient management practices are seen to be characteristic in principle.

Conclusion

SOEs played a paramount role in the process of catching up and modernization starting from the mid-twentieth century, in Europe, Latin America, India and East Asia. Their pervasiveness reached a peak in the early 1980s. Everywhere governments acted as entrepreneurs in a huge variety of industries, both in manufacturing, and services. Globalization and above all the liberalization climate of the 1990s has dramatically transformed the nature of SOEs and their significance in the "making of global business."

In this chapter, we have looked at this change from the point of view of the three determinant factors (Figure 19.1): ownership, corporate governance and internationalization strategy. These factors we have examined at three levels: international cooperation, national decision-making and SOEs themselves. In Table 19.4 we summarize how these were related to each other. In the top line, we present features defining SOEs, while on the vertical axis we show how these characteristics were seen at the international, national and corporate levels. The table can be read in both directions. Although the phenomenon as a whole is still much more diverse, certain main tendencies are apparent.

Table 19.4 How the factors determining SOEs were seen at different levels

	State ownership (SO)	Corporate governance (CG)	SOEs' internationalization strategies
International layer: international organizations	SO was increasingly seen as a cause of market disturbance	Since SO was found to be a permanent phenomenon, good CG was a way to counteract abuses	SOEs were feared to be unfair competitors
National layer: governments	New regulation overrode SO's original significance	Regulatory and business functions were separated	Mixed attitude: suspicion changed to encouragement
SOE	Neutral or positive stance often changed to desire to become privatized	The general problem was contradictory objectives; SOEs' intention was to increase their freedom to do business	Was sometimes considered as an outright necessity with the internationalization of the markets

Source: The authors.

We want to continue to emphasize the importance of the gradual process whose starting point and background lie in economic globalization. Governments opened up markets because competition was seen to boost the economy. SOEs were subject to pressure not only from government but also from the market. When SOEs adapted to the international market, they themselves became multinational enterprises. Companies in which state ownership remained high became state-owned multinationals. If we look at the basic elements in Figure 19.1, it is noteworthy that although mainstream developments have gone from corner to corner (from a state institution to an MNE), different paths and outcomes are possible. Exceptional combinations are, however, most often seen as anomalies.

This development means a fundamental change in the basic concept of SOEs. Where SOEs originally acted as national safeguards against the unpredictable outside world, an international company is a living part of globalization. Although it appears at first sight that little remains of the traditional SOE except a thin slice of state ownership, many of the basic elements are still present. Most prominently, suspicions regarding SOMNEs. State ownership and control will be particularly contradictory if it is in the company's interest to adopt a transnational strategy, which means spreading its operations, including strategic functions over several countries. For these reasons, the general expectation is that when SOEs take an international turn, they should abandon their original obligations and eliminate their state owner's political influence. In part this problem is solved especially in Western countries, such as Italy and Finland, by separating ownership and steering, and reducing state ownership to a minority. This, of course, solves some of the contradictions, but the real significance of a state's strong minority ownership remains to be seen.

Notes

1 On public choice theory, agency theory, new economics of regulation and monetarism see Parker (2009: 12–22).

2 Thirty-seven were "only" marketing companies, 18 were associated with industrial production, nine were R&D facilities, but some were classified as "holding companies." Ministry of Trade and Industry's reports, Finnish National Archives: KTM teollisuusos. Hc:4.
3 Valtionyhtiölainsäädäntötyöryhmä 1989.
4 Valtionyhtiötyötyhmä 1995: 16–17, 24.
5 Valtionyhtiöiden omistajapolitiikkaa selvittänyt työryhmä 1999.
6 VNK omistajaohjausos. annual reports 2007–08.

References

Aharoni, Yair (2000), "The performance of state-owned enterprises," in: Pier Angelo Toninelli (ed.), *The Rise and Fall of State-owned Enterprise in Western World* (Cambridge: Cambridge University Press), 49–72.

Aharoni, Yair (2018), "The evolution of state-owned multinational enterprise theory," in: Alvaro Cuervo-Cazurra (ed.), *State-Owned Multinationals: Governments in Global Business* (Cham, Switzerland: Palgrave Macmillan), 9–44.

Aharoni, Yair and Ramamurti, Ravi (2008), "The internationalization of multinationals," in: Jean J. Boddewyn (ed.), *International Business Scholarship: AIB Fellows on the First 50 Years and Beyond* (Bingley, UK: Emerald Group Publishing), 177–201.

Alonso, José M., Clifton, Judith, Díaz-Fuentes, Daniel, Fernández-Gutiérrez, Marcos and Revuelta, Julio (2013), "The race for international markets: were privatized telecommunications incumbents more successful than their public counterparts?" *International Review of Applied Economics*, 27 (2), 215–36.

Amatori, Franco (1997), "Italy: The tormented rise of organizational capabilities between government and families," in Alfred Chandler Jr., Franco Amatori and Takashi Hikino (eds.), *Big Business and the Wealth of Nations* (Cambridge: Cambridge University Press), 246–76.

Amatori, Franco and Colli, Andrea (2000), "Corporate governance: The Italian story" (CGEP Working Paper).

Amatori, Franco and Colli, Andrea (2011), *Business History: Complexities and Comparison* (London: Routledge).

Amatori, Franco, Millward, Robert and Toninelli, Pier A. (2011), "Introduction," in: Franco Amatori, Robert Millward and Pier Angelo Toninelli (eds.), *Reappraising State-Owned Enterprise: A Comparison of the UK and Italy* (London: Routledge), 3–10.

Amighini, Alessia A., Rabellotti, Roberta and Sanfilippo, Marco (2013), "Do Chinese state-owned and private enterprises differ in their internationalization strategies?" *Chinese Economic Review*, 27, 312–25.

Anastassopoulos, Jean-Pierre, Blanc, Georges and Dussage, Pierre (1987), *State-owned Multinationals* (Chichester: John Wiley & Sons).

Bruton, Garry D., Peng, Mike W., Ahlstrom, David, Stan, Ciprian, and Xu, Kehan (2015), "State-owned enterprises around the world as hybrid organizations," *Academy of Management Perspectives*, 29 (1), 92–114.

Chick, Martin (2007), *Electricity and Energy Policy in Britain, France and the United States since 1945* (Cheltenham: Edgar Elgar).

Christensen, Jørgen and Pallesen, Thomas (2001), "The political benefits of corporatization and privatization," *Journal of Public Policy*, 21 (3), 283–309.

Christiansen, Hans (2011), "The size and composition of the SOE sector in OECD countries" (OECD Corporate Governance Working Papers No. 5). Retrieved from: http://dx.doi.org/10.1787/5kg54cwps0s3-en (January 12, 2017).

Christiansen, Hans (2013), "Balancing commercial and non-commercial priorities of state-owned enterprises" (OECD Corporate Governance Working Papers No. 6). Retrieved from: http://dx.doi.org/10.1787/5k4dkhztkp9r-en (January 10, 2017).

Clifton, Judith, Comín, Francisco and Díaz Fuentes, Daniel (2006), "Privatizing public enterprises in the European Union 1960–2002: Ideological, pragmatic, inevitable?" *Journal of European Public Policy*, 13 (5), 736–56.

Clifton, Judith, Comín, Francisco and Díaz-Fuentes, Daniel (2011a), "From national monopoly to multinational corporation: How regulation shaped the road towards telecommunications internationalization," *Business History*, 53 (5), 761–81.

Clifton, Judith, Lanthier, Pierre and Schröter, Harm (2011b), "Regulating and deregulating the public utilities 1830–2010," *Business History*, 53 (5), 659–72.

Clò, Stefano, DiGiulio, Marco, Galanti, Maria Tullia and Sorrentino, Maddalena (2015), "Italian state-owned enterprises after decades of reforms: Still public?" (Ciriec Working Paper 2015/19).

Colli, Andrea (2016), *Dynamics of International Business: Comparative Perspectives of Firms, Markets and Entrepreneurship* (New York: Routledge).

Colli, Andrea, Mariotti, Sergio and Piscitello, Lucia (2014), "Governments as strategists in designing global players: The case of European utilities," *Journal of European Public Policy*, 21 (4), 487–508.

Cuervo-Cazurra, Alvaro (2018), "State-owned multinationals: Introduction," in Alvaro Cuervo-Cazurra (ed.), *State-Owned Multinationals: Governments in Global Business* (Cham, Switzerland: Palgrave Macmillan), 1–6.

Cuervo-Cazurra, Alvaro, Inkpen, Andrew, Musacchio, Aldo and Ramaswamy, Kannan (2014), "Governments as owners: State-owned multinational companies," *Journal of International Business Studies*, 45 (8), 919–42.

Dunning, John and Lundan, Sarianna (2008), *Multinational Enterprises and the Global Economy* (2nd ed.) (Cheltenham: Edward Elgar).

Erakovic, Ljiljana and Wilson, Marie (2005), "Conditions of radical transformation in state-owned enterprises," *British Journal of Management*, 16 (4), 293–313.

European Commission (2016), *State-Owned Enterprises in the EU: Lessons Learnt and Ways Forward in a Post-Crisis Context* (Luxembourg: European Union). Retrieved from: http://ec.europa.eu/economy_finance/publications/ (January 12, 2017).

Fitzgerald, Robert (2016), *The Rise of the Global Company: Multinationals and the Making of the Modern World* (Cambridge: Cambridge University Press).

Florio, Massimo (2013), "Rethinking on public enterprise: Editorial introduction and some personal remarks on the research agenda," *International Review of Applied Economics*, 27 (2), 135–49.

Ghoshal, Sumantra and Bartlett, Christopher (1998), *Managing Across Borders: The Transnational Solution* (London: Random House).

Girma, Sourefel and Yundan, Gong (2008), "FDI, linkages and the efficiency of state-owned enterprises in China," *Journal of Development Studies*, 44 (5), 728–49.

Girma, Sourefel, Yundan, Gong and Holger, Görg (2009), "What determines innovation activity in Chinese state-owned enterprises? The role of foreign direct investment," *World Development*, 37 (4), 866–73.

Heath, Joseph and Norman, Wayne (2004), "Stakeholder theory, corporate governance and public management: What can the history of state-run enterprises teach us in the post-Enron era?" *Journal of Business Ethics*, 53, 247–65.

Högselius, Per, Kaijser, Arne and van der Vleuten, Erik (2016), *Europe's Infrastructure Transition: Economy, War, Nature* (New York: Palgrave Macmillan).

Hults, David (2012), "Hybrid governance: State management of national oil companies," in David G. Victor, David R. Hults and Mark Thurber (eds.), *Oil and Governance: State Owned Enterprises and the World Energy Supply* (Cambridge: Cambridge University Press), 62–120.

Junka, Teuvo (2010), *Valtionyhtiöt 1975–2008* [State-owned enterprises 1975–2008] (Helsinki: Valtion taloudellinen tutkimuskeskus).

Kalasin, Kiattichai, Cuervo-Cazurra, Alvaro, and Ramamurti, Ravi (2019), "State ownership and international expansion: The s-curve relationship," *Global Strategy Journal*, 2019, 1–33.

Karlsson, Magnus (1998), *The Liberalisation of Telecommunications in Sweden: Technology and Regime Change from the 1960s to 1993* (Doctoral dissertation) (Linköping: University of Linköping).

Knutsen, Carl, Rygh Asmund and Hveem, Helge (2011), "Does state ownership matter? Institutions' effect on foreign direct investment revisited," *Business and Politics*, 13 (1), 1–31.

Kowalski, Przemyslaw, Büge, Max, Sztajerowska, Monika and Egeland, Matias (2013), "State-owned enterprises: Trade effects and policy implications" OECD Trade Policy Papers No. 147 (Paris: OECD Publishing).

Mariotti, Sergio and Marzano, Riccardo (2019), "Varieties of capitalism and the internationalization of state-owned enterprises," *Journal of International Business Studies*, 2019, 1–23.

Meyer, Klaus, Ding, Yuan, Li, Jing and Zhang, Hua (2014), "Overcoming distrust: How state-owned enterprises adapt their foreign entries to institutional pressures abroad," *Journal of International Business Studies*, 45 (8), 1005–28.

Millward, Robert (2005), *Private and Public Enterprise in Europe: Energy, Telecommunications and Transport, 1830–1990* (Cambridge: Cambridge University Press).

Millward, Robert (2011), "Public enterprise in the modern western world: An historical analysis," *Annals of Public and Cooperative Economics*, 82 (4), 375–98.

Millward, Robert (2013), *The State and Business in the Major Powers: An Economic History, 1815–1939* (London: Routledge).

Moon, Myung Jae (1999), "The pursuit of managerial entrepreneurship: Does organization matter?" *Public Administration Review*, 59 (1), 31–43.

Musacchio, Aldo and Lazzarini, Sergio G. (2014), *Reinventing State Capitalism: Leviathans in Business, Brazil and Beyond* (Cambridge, MA: Harvard University Press).

Musacchio, Aldo, Lazzarini, Sergio G. and Aguileira, Ruth V. (2015), "New varieties of state capitalism: Strategic and governance implications," *Academy of Management Perspectives*, 29 (1), 115–31.

Nevalainen, Pasi (2014), *Virastosta liikeyritys: Posti- ja telelaitoksen muutosprosessi 1930–1994* [From State Department to Business Enterprise: The Finnish Post and Tele-communications Department and the process of change 1930–1994], Doctoral dissertation (Jyväskylä: University of Jyväskylä).

Nevalainen, Pasi (2017), "Facing the inevitable? The public telecom monopoly's way of coping with deregulation," *Business History*, 59 (3), 362–81.

OECD (2004), *Corporate Governance of State-Owned Enterprises: A Survey of OECD Countries* (Paris: OECD Publishing).

OECD (2011), *State-Owned Enterprise Governance Reform: An Inventory of Recent Change* (Paris: OECD Publishing).

OECD (2015), *OECD Guidelines on Corporate Governance of State-Owned Enterprises* (Paris: OECD Publishing).

Palcic, Do´nal and Reeve, Eoin (2010), "Organisational status change and performance: The case of Ireland's national telecommunications operator," *Telecommunications Policy*, 34, 299–308.

Parker, David (1999), "Privatization in the European Union: A critical assessment of its development, rationale and consequences," *Economic and Industrial Democracy*, 20 (1), 9–38.

Parker, David (2009), *The Official History of Privatisation: The Formative Years 1970–1987* (London: Routledge).

Pollitt, Christopher and Bouckaert, Geer (2011), *Public Management Reform: A Comparative Analysis: New Public Management, Governance, and the Neo-Weberian State* (3rd ed.) (Oxford: Oxford University Press).

Radford, Gail (2013), *The Rise of the Public Authority: Statebuilding and Economic Development in Twentieth-Century America* (Chicago, IL: University of Chicago Press).

Ranki, Risto (2012), *Niin Siinä Käy Kun Omistaa: Tarinaa Valtionyhtiöistä* [So it Happens When You Own: Story about State-Owned Enterprises], (Helsinki: Ministry of Economic Affairs and Employment, Edita).

Stevens, Paul (2008), "National oil companies and international oil companies in the Middle East: Under the shadow of governments and the resource nationalism cycle," *Journal of World Energy and Law Business*, 1 (1), 5–30.

Thatcher, Mark (2001), "The Commission and national governments as partners: EC regulatory expansion in telecommunications 1979–2000," *Journal of European Public Policy*, 8 (4), 558–84.

Thatcher, Mark (2004), "Varieties of capitalism in an internationalized world: Domestic institutional change in European telecommunications," *Comparative Political Studies*, 37 (4), 751–80.

Toninelli, Pier A. (2000), "The rise and fall of public enterprise: The framework," in: Pier Angelo Toninelli (ed.), *The Rise and Fall of State-Owned Enterprise in the Western World* (Cambridge: Cambridge University Press), 3–24.

UNCTAD (2017), *World Investment Report 2017: Investment and Digital Economy* (Geneva: United Nations). Retrieved from http://unctad.org/en/PublicationsLibrary/wir2017_en.pdf (January 12, 2017).

Vernon, Raymond (1979), "The international aspects of state-owned enterprises," *Journal of International Business Studies*, 10 (3), 7–15.

Wilkins, Mira (2001), "The history of multinational enterprise," in: Alan M. Rugman and Thomas L. Brewer (eds.), *The Oxford Handbook of International Business* (Oxford: Oxford University Press), 3–35.

Williamson, John (2004), "The strange history of the Washington consensus," *Journal of Post Keynesian Economics*, 27 (2), 195–206.

World Bank (1995), *Bureaucrats in Business: The Economics and Politics of Government Ownership* (New York: Oxford University Press).

World Bank (2006), *Held by the Visible Hand: The Challenge of State-Owned Enterprise Corporate Governance for Emerging Markets*. Retrieved from http://documents.worldbank.org/curated/en/3960714681 58997475/Held-by-the-visible-hand-the-challenge-of-state-owned-enterprise-corporate-governance-for-emerging-markets (August 1, 2017).

PART IV

Industries

20

GLOBAL COMMUNICATIONS

Heidi J.S. Tworek and Richard R. John

The harnessing of steam and electricity in the mid-nineteenth century created a new world of possibilities in business, politics, and public life. In no realm was this transformation more momentous than in communications, an activity commonly understood at this time to embrace not only the trans-local circulation of information, but also the long-distance transportation of people and goods (Matterlart 1996, 2000). For the first time in world history, merchants could convey overseas large quantities of goods on a regular schedule and exchange information at a speed greater than a ship could sail. New organizations sprang up to take advantage of this "communications revolution," as this transformation has come to be known (John 1994). Some were public agencies; others were private firms. Each was shaped not only by the harnessing of new energy sources, but also by the institutional rules of the game. These rules defined the relationship of the state and the market, or what economic historians call the political economy.

This chapter surveys this transformation, which we have come to view with fresh eyes following the commercialization of the Internet in the 1990s. It features case studies of two well-documented global communications organizations that originated in the nineteenth century – undersea cable companies and news agencies – which we have supplemented by a brief discussion of other important global communications organizations: radio, telephony, and the mail. We have not surveyed film, a topic addressed by Peter Miskell's chapter in this *Handbook*.

Four premises shape our chapter. First, the makers of global communications are best characterized as *organizations* rather than *private firms* or *public agencies*. They have sometimes been government owned and government operated and, especially recently, are often coordinated by ostensibly nonprofit and non-governmental technical bodies such as the Internet Corporation for Assigned Names and Numbers (ICANN) (Mackinnon 2012; DeNardis 2014). Many are multinational enterprises (MNEs), making this topic particularly pertinent for historians interested in the relationship between international business, technology, and the state.

Second, the organizations that the makers of global communications established are most aptly characterized as *networks* that consisted of links, nodes, and spaces-in-between, rather than as more-or-less seamless *systems*. All metaphors raise interpretative issues, and network is no exception (Marx 1994: 21–25). Yet *networks* are explicitly spatial, in contrast to *systems*, and, for this reason, better describe organizations that are entwined with sovereign states, technical standard-setting bodies, and multinational enterprises. In rejecting the system metaphor, we

315

break with much innovative recent scholarship on long-distance communications, which has posited that the leading organizations are best understood as components of a "large technical system," a concept popularized by historian of technology Thomas P. Hughes (1998, 2005). While this construct has the advantage of shifting attention away from the internal dynamics of particular firms, it presupposes a spatial uniformity that is hard to square with the historical record.

Our third premise is that the most influential makers of global communications were not confined to the ranks of visionary entrepreneurs or venture capitalists. Rather, they also included the political economy that facilitated – or in the case of the Soviet Union, stymied (Peters 2016) – the innovative process. Every political economy has a distinctive structure. And in global communications, as in so many other realms, *structure* shaped *strategy*: that is, the *political structure that incubated global communications organizations shaped the management strategies of private firms, the administrative mandates of public agencies, and the technical directives of standard-setting bodies.*

Our final premise is that the present is not the first historical epoch in which enormous technical advances in communications technology have reshaped the world economy, recalibrated perceptual horizons, and reordered conventional assumptions about time, space, and speed. On the contrary, the foundations of the present digital age were laid in a mid-nineteenth-century communications revolution that transformed the informational environment long before the laying of the first fiber optical cable (John 2000; Rosenberg 2012, Osterhammel 2014; Balbi and John 2015). The dominant organizations that this revolution spawned were not only or even primarily the byproducts of technical imperatives and economic incentives. On the contrary, they benefitted from institutional arrangements designed to promote political goals. In communications, probably more than in any other realm but national defense, governments have played favorites – hence why a small number of huge organizations with close ties to the state dominated the informational environment of modernity.

In the opening years of the twentieth century, German publications buzzed with excited reflections on a new concept: "the world economy" (*Weltwirtschaft*). New concepts are often devised to describe innovations in material life and this coinage was no exception. *Weltwirtschaft* received much of its plausibility from its association with "world traffic" (*Weltverkehr*), a related concept that described the circulation of information, people, and goods in commerce, communications, and transportation (Tworek 2015a). References to *Weltverkehr* became increasingly common in Germany in the decades following national unification in 1871, when the country emerged for the first time as a global economic powerhouse. This new way of thinking about business and technology would become so common by 1912 that a group of German academics established a journal entitled *Weltverkehr und Weltwirtschaft*.

But just how large was the world that these Germans imagined? To answer this question, postal administrator Max Roscher distinguished in 1914 between traffic that was merely national or international and traffic that was truly worldwide. Traffic linking neighboring countries such as Germany and France was international, but not global. *Weltverkehr*, by contrast, referred to "trade relationships encircling the whole world between areas ... that lie far apart" (Roscher 1914: 305, translated by the authors).

This chapter follows Roscher's lead by surveying historical scholarship on organizations that coordinated the movement of information, people, and goods between distant regions that were often separated by sea. These organizations relied upon two new energy sources: electricity, the circulating medium for the world's cable and telegraph networks; and steam, a motive power indispensable for overseas shipping. The first regularly scheduled steamship service between Great Britain and the United States went into operation in 1840. Before long, steamships would link most of the world's major ports (the subject of Harlaftis's chapter in this *Handbook*). The influence of steam and electricity upon commerce, politics, and the economy in the nineteenth century was "astounding," reflected a New York City-based wholesale merchant in 1875:

> Now, the whole world has become producers or traders, and in the event of scarcity at a given place, the news is flashed to the point of supply – under the ocean and around the earth even – and the giant power of steam hurries the products of the world to our doors.
>
> *(Thurber 1875: 623)*

The symbiotic relationship between innovations in communications and ocean-borne transportation has persisted to the present. In the early twentieth century, for example, private firms such as the U.S.-based United Fruit Company joined public agencies such as the British admiralty and U.S. Navy as early adopters of wireless telegraphy, or what we today call point-to-point radio (Hugill 1999; Winkler 2008). Following World War II, further innovations in information technology would transform supply-chain logistics in overseas trade (Levinson 2006; Miller 2012).

The transformations set in motion by steam and electricity hastened a new sensibility that can be properly called global, in the sense that they encouraged new and often highly expansive ways of thinking about knowledge, territoriality, and power. French scientists devised a new cosmology to describe a world in which steam power and the electric telegraph supplanted the clock as a metaphor for the natural order (Tresch 2012); American liberals linked technological innovation in transportation and communications with a more spatially expansive conception of moral progress (Ninkovich 2009); while British and American commentators invoked organic metaphors such as "nerves" and the global "body" to link the telegraph and cable with imperial projects and territorial expansion (Bell 2007; Otis 2011).

For the vast majority of the world's inhabitants, the most important long-distance communications network until quite recently was not the telegraph or the telephone, but the mail. The world's postal network expanded enormously in the nineteenth century, partly because of the widespread adoption of the steamship as a mode of transportation, and partly because of the establishment of an international organization – the Universal Postal Union – to coordinate the transnational movement of the mail (Hyde 1975; Laborie 2010; John 2015; Shulman 2015). Merchants relied on the mail to conduct routine business. Migrants used it to remain in touch with friends and family members back home (Gerber 2006; Laako 2007; Maischak 2013). The mail – and not the telegraph, as a journalist erroneously contended in a popular history written shortly after the commercialization of the Internet in 1995 (Standage 1998) – was the true "Victorian internet" (John 2010, 2013).

Until quite recently, all of the world's major postal systems were owned and operated by national governments and operated as monopolies, an uncomfortable fact for neoliberal champions of economic development, since the mail has long been an indispensable agent of globalization. Steamships remained the primary mode of long-distance postal conveyance until the mid-twentieth century, when they would be supplemented, and eventually largely replaced, by airplanes, the primary mode of long-distance postal conveyance today. Most of the organizations that conveyed the mail – from the Cunard Company in the mid-nineteenth century to Pan American Airlines in the 1930s – were not public agencies, but private firms. Even so, these companies relied on substantial government subsidies, particularly early on. Predictably, they quickly became oligopolies, which they largely remain today (Robinson 1964; Linden 2001).

By almost any measure, the mail remained the primary long-distance communications medium for almost everyone from the nineteenth century until the commercialization of the Internet in the 1990s. This included not only migrants eager to remain in touch with friends and family members back home, but also MNEs such as the Ford Motor Company, whose far-flung managers routinely relied on the mail to conduct routine business (Wilkins and Hill 1964). For certain groups of highly specialized users, however, the mail was supplemented – and partly supplanted – by a constellation of electrically mediated long-distance communications media: first the cable (or undersea telegraph), then wireless telegraphy (or what would come to be known as point-to-point radio), and eventually the telephone and the fax (Coopersmith 2015).

The electric telegraph was not the first long-distance communications medium to transmit information faster than a horse could gallop (Headrick 2000). That distinction goes to the optical telegraph, which, along with the guillotine and the metric system, deserves pride of place as one of the most fundamental of the technical advances to have emerged from the French Revolution. It was this innovation that gave the world the term "telegraph," a French neologism meaning, literally, writing at a distance. The French government owned and operated the most important optical telegraph. In its heyday in the early 1850s, it linked 556 towers in a network that extended over 2,900 miles. Except briefly during the Napoleonic era, this network did not operate outside France's borders (John 2010).

The first medium to transmit electrically mediated information over long distances between countries that lacked a common border was the undersea (or "submarine") cable. Undersea cables were almost always owned and operated as private firms, though they depended on the governments of the countries they linked for various privileges, particularly landing rights (Müller 2016).

Cable companies operated closely with country-specific land-line (or "inland") telegraph networks that were often government owned and government operated. Important exceptions (and there are others) included the British inland telegraph network before 1870 and the U.S. land-line telegraph network during its entire history. The cable network expanded rapidly: the English Channel was spanned in 1851; the Atlantic in 1866; and the Pacific in 1902. By 1879, around 100,000 miles of undersea cables had been laid. This total nearly doubled to 190,000 miles by 1900, when a wire network linked every continent other than Antarctica (Müller 2016: 227).

Historical writing on undersea cables is highly developed and falls into three main traditions. The first tradition highlights the close relationship between the cable network and the imperial designs of the European Great Powers, particularly Great Britain (Innis 1950; Headrick 1991; Hugill 1999; Headrick and Griset 2001; Wenzlhuemer 2013). The cable network, Daniel R. Headrick famously posited in 1991, was an "invisible weapon" that the British government deployed to maintain control over its sprawling imperial domain. The second tradition contends that the focus on imperial designs is often exaggerated (especially before 1890) and emphasizes the business strategy of individual cable companies and the economic benefits of oligopolistic collusion (Winseck and Pike 2007). The third tradition, and the one most aligned with this chapter's perspective (Müller and Tworek 2015; Müller 2016), shifts the focus to political economy, and, in particular, to the institutional rules of the game in which the global cable network evolved. This tradition has been shaped by the recent emergence of global history as a discrete field of inquiry. By decentering both the nation-state and the firm, it has shifted our attention to the network as the primary unit of analysis (Grewal 2008; Conrad 2016).

Though cable companies barely figure in standard accounts of large-scale enterprise, they share many features that historians associate with the rise of managerial capitalism (Chandler

1977). Capital-intensive and technically advanced, they were operated by an elite cadre of engineers who did much to invent the modern field of electrical engineering (Hunt 1997). The most important cable companies were headquartered in London, where a cohort of like-minded Anglo-American promoters, investors, and engineers – the "class of 1866" (Müller 2016) – oversaw the construction and operation of the global cable network during its heyday, which stretched from 1866 until World War I. Prominent among them was Cyrus Field, an American paper manufacturer who helped fund an unsuccessful 1858 Atlantic cable, and John Pender, a British textile manufacturer who invested heavily in the 1866 successful Atlantic cable, as well as the various telegraph companies linking the United Kingdom with its colonial possessions in South Asia. Though U.S.-based companies would contest the dominance of British firms in the North Atlantic market, only the British had the know-how, the natural resources, and the equipment to operate and maintain a global network (Winkler 2008). And since the fastest and most widely used North Atlantic cables all touched on British or Canadian soil, the British government retained the ability to monitor cable traffic to and from the United States, an affordance that would prove useful during World War I.

One of the most vital natural resources upon which cable promoters relied was gutta percha, a tree-based resin from Malaya that, beginning in the 1850s, cable manufacturers relied on to insulate undersea cables. British imperial control over much of Southeast Asia helped to guarantee British cable manufacturers cheap and reliable access to this indispensable raw material. By the early twentieth century, so much gutta percha had been extracted from the rain forests of the region that they had been stripped bare, creating a "Victorian ecological disaster" (Tully 2009).

The cable network was dominated by a small number of capital-intensive organizations that nineteenth-century economists dubbed "natural" monopolies (Mosca 2008; Wagner 2014). The huge sunk (literally!) costs of laying telegraph cables created formidable barriers to entry, as did the restrictions governments imposed on the granting of landing rights. The New York, Newfoundland and London Telegraph Company, for example, obtained from the Newfoundland government a fifty-year exclusive monopoly on cable landings in 1854, an enormously valuable asset, given the strategic location of Newfoundland in the North Atlantic market (Müller 2016).

Three business groups dominated the global cable network in its heyday: the Atlantic pool, the Eastern and Associated Companies, and a constellation of firms whose interests were often aligned with the Great Northern Telegraph Company. The Atlantic pool was dominant in the lucrative North Atlantic market. Led by the British-owned and British-operated Atlantic Telegraph Company – the firm that had laid the first successful Atlantic cable in 1866 – this pool was challenged in the 1880s by a number of rivals, including two based in the United States. Following a brief price war, the main players agreed to divide the market. By 1900, the thirteen cables that spanned the North Atlantic were owned and operated by a mere four companies, with a capitalization that was estimated to top £17 million, making them among the world's largest multinationals. Together, they sent around 10,000 messages each day between Europe and North America, in what was and would remain the single largest cable market in the world (Müller and Tworek 2015: 265).

The second group was the Eastern and Associated Telegraph Companies, a federation of British-owned and British-operated firms that controlled the cable network between Great Britain, its vast colonial empire, and much of the rest of the world. The most important cables in this group linked Great Britain, India, China, and Australasia; additional cables linked Great Britain to Central and South America (Brown 1927: 11–19). In 1898, this group owned and operated one-third of the world's total global cable mileage and transmitted two million messages

(Bright 1902: 167). By 1914, it had become, in the words of Daniel R. Headrick, "one of the world's most powerful multi-national conglomerates" (1988: 105).

The third group linked Europe with Asia and the United States with Latin America. While harder to characterize than the first two groups, it was dominated after 1869 by the Danish-based Great Northern Telegraph Company, which combined the assets of Danish, Norwegian, Russian, and English investors to link Europe with East Asia via the Baltic Sea by undersea cable and the vast Russian interior by land-line telegraph. Between 1871 and 1943, Great Northern partnered with a Japanese-based cable firm to boost East–West trade and reduce the cost of diplomatic dispatches (Yang 2010). Other cable companies linked the United States with Brazil and other South American countries by way of the West India and Panama Telegraph Company, the Brazilian Submarine Telegraph Company, and the Western and Brazilian Telegraph Company (Ahvenainen 2004; Britton 2013).

The cable network shaped global business in various ways. Though it did not annihilate time and space, as some contemporaries claimed, it helped to standardize time zones (Ogle 2015) and expand the futures market, a new economic institution that was based on the buying and selling of agricultural commodities in time rather than space. The new medium, or so Karl Marx predicted in 1855, was rapidly "transforming" the "whole of Europe" into "one single stock exchange" (Marx 1855: 167). Marx was wrong. Regional markets persisted and, in some places, the creation of a futures markets predated the laying of the first undersea cable: in Japan, for example, a futures market dated back to the Dojima rice market in Osaka in the early seventeenth century (Schaede 1989). Yet it was only after the Atlantic cable had linked the United States and Europe that a large-scale futures market emerged in Chicago (Engel 2015). Cable telegraphy also enabled steamship lines to buy, sell, and move goods around the world, while reducing the time that fleets had to remain in port (Lew and Cater 2006).

Undersea cables were most emphatically not the Victorian Internet (*contra* Standage 1998). Rates remained extremely high, and facilities limited. In the first several decades of the Atlantic cable, fewer than 100 businesses used it with any regularity. In fact, the cost of sending a cable was *so* exorbitant that one British MP, Henniker Heaton, complained in 1912 that the new medium was "beyond the means of 99 percent of the population" (Müller 2015). Until the 1890s, most cable investments strengthened pre-existing ties between major urban trading centers (Hoag 2006). Many parts of the world remained outside the network, an outcome based partly on prevailing assumptions about race, gender, and class. The vast majority of investors were men, though women would come to hold substantial shares in certain cable companies, just as they did in sailing vessels (Doe 2010; Müller 2016).

The cable network changed significantly in the 1890s, partly as a result of Great Power competition between Great Britain, France, and Germany, and partly because of the heightened U.S. presence in the Pacific that followed the U.S. acquisition of the Philippines and Guam during the Spanish–American War. No longer could it plausibly be contended that cable companies operated more-or-less independently of political fiat, a contention that had been at least partly true before this time for certain markets outside South Asia and Africa (Headrick 1988: 100, 107). The German government subsidized German cable companies because officials feared that Anglo-American cable companies put German firms at a disadvantage in international markets. The British government worked with its Canadian counterparts to lay a trans-Pacific cable that, when it went into operation in 1902, completed a global "All-Red Route" that linked British imperial possessions by landing only on British-controlled territory. And in 1903, the U.S. government provided technical assistance to a U.S. Pacific cable project that provided a direct cable link to Hawaii, the Philippines, and Guam. Neither Pacific cable was an economic success. Then and now, politics has its limits:

though geopolitical rivalry hastened their completion, it could not conjure new markets into existence. Built ahead of demand, the Pacific cables never generated enough traffic to cover their huge sunk costs (Müller and Tworek 2015).

An even more fundamental challenge to the cable network would emerge in 1901, when the British-Italian inventor-turned-promoter Guglielmo Marconi successfully demonstrated that he could transmit a point-to-point radio message across the Atlantic. The military and commercial significance of wireless telegraphy (as point-to-point radio transmission was then known) was self-evident to government officials in Great Britain, Germany, and the United States, setting in motion a global communications arms race that would ultimately have major implications not only for commerce, but also for geopolitics. To cement Marconi's dominant position in the wireless market, his company – Marconi Wireless – refused before 1912 to interconnect with rival wireless network providers, a business strategy that put Marconi at odds with government officials and rival network providers in the United States and Germany (Raboy 2016). The stakes were high: for the first time in world history, it was now possible for naval officers to maintain ship-to-shore contact with their fleets anywhere on the high seas, a logistical advantage that no great power could ignore. The geopolitical significance of technical advances such as wireless varied widely from nation to nation. For the British, as one historian has explained, technical advances helped "stabilize an international status quo" that was already "favorable to their nation"; for the Germans, in contrast, they could help "transform the international environment that stifled their political ambitions" by improving the position of German business and the German government in the global economy (Rieger 2005: 18).

The German government fostered innovation in wireless by restructuring private enterprise. In 1903, for example, it convinced two competing electrical manufacturing companies – Siemens & Halske and AEG – to form a jointly owned subsidiary known as Telefunken to undertake research and development in the mysterious new medium and manufacture wireless receivers. During the first eight years of its existence, Telefunken obtained between 70 percent and 80 percent of its revenue from government contracts. German officials were also active on the diplomatic front. Following an almost decade-long diplomatic standoff, German officials joined with British and U.S. officials in a 1912 international standard-setting meeting in London to force Marconi Wireless to make its receivers compatible with those of its rivals.

Within two years, Telefunken and Marconi established a cartel in wireless equipment. To gain control of market for ship-to-shore communications, the two companies agreed to pool patents. Of the 1,554 ship-to-ship stations then in existence, only 294 remained outside their control (Evans 2010: 213). Taking to the offensive, German officials underwrote the establishment of a global "All-Wireless Route" to link Germany and its colonies. Germany's defeat in World War I hastened the surrender of its wireless patents to the U.S. government, which transferred them to incumbent telephone network provider American Telephone & Telegraph (AT&T) and newly established radio equipment manufacturer Radio Corporation of America (RCA). These companies, in turn, would become major players in the U.S. radio broadcasting industry following its beginnings in 1920 (Aitken 1985). While Germany never regained its prewar position in wireless, it would remain a major player in the interwar period in broadcast radio (Tworek 2016).

The slow yet steady ascendency of the United States in global communications during the interwar period created path dependencies that have lasted until today. Rising American influence was on display in 1927 when an international radio conference agreed to allocate the spectrum by function rather than nation, a victory for U.S. companies and a defeat for Great Britain, France, and the other European Great Powers (Schwoch 1987). International standard-setting has a political dimension, as political theorist David Grewal has observed, since a successful standard can exert "network power" by fostering cooperation among network members, excluding non-members, and convincing would-be members to join the network even though membership might in certain respects be disadvantageous (Grewal 2008: 10). Since 1927, this kind of power increasingly bene-fitted the United States in its contest for global communications dominance first with Great Britain and, after 1945, the Soviet Union (Hills 2002, 2007). U.S. global communications policy has consistently favored private management over government administration. Since 1970, this pref-erence has become increasingly influential in global communications with the deregulation of many of the world's largest state-owned telecommunications network providers (Fitzgerald 2015).

For a brief period following World War II, it seemed conceivable that satellites might replace cables as the primary carrier of the world's global communications. Funded primarily by the United States and the Soviet Union, the first satellites – Sputnik for the Soviets; Comsat for the Americans – were players in a global Cold War (Schwoch 2009; Slotten 2013). Following the discovery of fiber optics, however, the balance has shifted back to undersea cables. As a con-sequence, today's Internet network resembles the global cable network in 1902 far more than the satellite network in 1970 (Finn and Yang 2009; Starosielski 2015). Little wonder, then, that one leader of a developing country, Tanzanian president Jakaya Kikwete, characterized the laying in 2009 by a pan-African business consortium of the first fiber optic cable between East Asia and the Arabian Peninsula as "the ultimate embodiment of modernity" (cited in Müller and Tworek 2015: 282).

While the cable network has long been hailed as a technological icon, the news agencies report-ing international news for the world's newspapers, radio programs, and television broadcasts are largely unknown even to specialists in the field. This is unfortunate, since their history reveals much about the evolution of global communications following the harnessing of steam and electricity.

Historical writing on international news agencies falls into two main categories: monographs on specific organizations and interpretative surveys. Organization-specific monographs are typically fact-laden and narrowly focused (Read 1992); interpretative surveys are more wide-ranging and often emphasize the interconnected influence of politics, new media, and business competition (Rantanen 2013; Silberstein-Loeb 2014; John and Silberstein-Loeb 2015; Stamm 2015; Shu 2016).

News agencies can be thought of as brokers or wholesalers that relied on a network of cor-respondents to generate news items in a specific territory that they repackaged as time-specific fillips of information for their "'retail' clients," which, in the late nineteenth century, were mostly newspapers (Boyd-Barrett and Rantanen 1998: 6). Of these newspapers, only the largest and best capitalized – e.g., the London *Times* and the *New York Herald* – could afford to hire their own international correspondents. As an alternative, many contracted with news agencies to send them up-to-date information via the mail, the telegraph, cable, and also, and in due time, the telegraph ticker, the telephone, and wireless.

The most important nineteenth-century European news agencies were the "Big Three": Agence Havas, founded in the early 1830s; Wolff's Telegraphisches Bureau, or Wolff, founded in 1849; and Reuters, founded in 1851. Each was named after an eponymous founder: Charles-Louis Havas, Bernhard Wolff, and Paul Reuter. Each relied on a far-flung staff of correspond-ents to gather news for newspapers, which were at the time the primary distributor of time-specific information on commerce and public affairs.

Their principal U.S. counterpart was the New York Associated Press (NYAP), which was founded in the mid-1840s, and the Western Associated Press (WAP), which was founded in 1862. The WAP succeeded the NYAP as the dominant U.S. newsbroker in 1892, when it renamed itself the Associated Press (AP) (Blondheim 1994). The news agency model proved highly successful. In the words of British journalist John Hobson, its ability to transmit real-time news to far-flung locations created an "immediate and simultaneous sympathy" that brought a "new element of sociality" into the world. "In this sense," Hobson elaborated, "we may say that the world has been recently discovered for the mass of civilized mankind" (1906: 17).

International news-gathering was, and is, expensive. To cover its cost, nineteenth-century news agencies relied on a far-flung network of overseas correspondents to report the news, and a global telegraph, telephone, and radio network to transmit it. On the eve of World War I, Wolff spent over $160,000 in news-gathering, while Reuters spent four to five times that much (Hansen 1914: 80). These were large sums for a time in which the capitalization of the then struggling London *Times* was a mere $2 million, the working capital of the entire Northcliffe newspaper empire no more than $8 million, and the financial value of news reporting an open question: then, as now, it was relatively easy to steal the news, or even to fake it.

Given the limited size of the newspaper market and the impunity with which news could be copied, it should come as no surprise that news agencies devoted much attention to protecting their reporting. Some tried to exclude rivals altogether; others to cut deals with government administrators to obtain exclusive access to official dispatches. To gain control over the market, Reuters, Havas, and Wolff formed a global cartel in 1870 that the Associated Press would eventually join. Henceforth, each was responsible for reporting on and circulating to each other whatever news they might have discovered on their particular "beat" (Silberstein-Loeb 2014).

Not everyone found this arrangement to its liking. Troubled by the global news cartel, and eager to tell its own story, the Japanese government in the 1930s entered into an agreement with cable network provider Great Northern (Akami 2012). The Japanese government's desire for autonomy in news provisioning hastened the departure from the global news cartel of the AP. Not until after World War II would the Japanese government give up its dream of a "Greater East Asian Co-Prosperity Sphere" that was independent of First World control (Yang 2010; Akami 2014).

Even more radical in his critique of the global news cartel was the Indian journalist and political activist Mahatma Gandhi. What was the ethical value, Gandhi asked during his years in South Africa, of the rapid transmission of up-to-date news? To answer this question, Gandhi founded a newspaper that championed an alternative ethic of slow reading (Hofmeyr 2013). After returning to India, Gandhi helped to transform the telegraph into "a double-edged sword" (Headrick 2010). Although the British had assumed the new media would consolidate British imperial control, Gandhi and his fellow Indian nationalists deployed it to counterbalance English-language reporting, challenge First World-style economic development, and coordinate pan-Indian resistance to British imperialism (Bonea 2016).

News agencies adapted to the advent of radio broadcasting in the 1920s in various ways. In Great Britain and Germany, the government regulated broadcasting tightly and radio stations were funded primarily by licensing fees. In both countries, news agencies at first provided the limited news sent over the airwaves. Only in the 1930s would the British government-licensed radio broadcaster, the British Broadcasting Corporation (BBC), begin to invest in an independent news-gathering apparatus (Tworek 2015b). The Soviet news agency, TASS, provided news for radio too, but radio in the Soviet Union was broadcast publicly through loudspeakers (Lovell 2015), rather than in private homes – the norm in Great Britain, Germany, and the United States.

In countries such as Argentina, news agencies sold news to advertising-based stations for producers intent on creating "authentically" Argentine programs for the working class (Karush 2012). Radio broadcasting in the United States was even more emphatically commercial. From the beginning, news agencies provided domestic radio stations with news, which they broadcast in the hopes of catching advertising dollars.

International broadcasting, by contrast, operated under different rules. Each of the principal U.S. overseas broadcast networks – Voice of America, Radio Free Europe, and Radio Liberty – were government owned and government operated (Puddington 2015). To prevent overseas news broadcasts from competing with domestic news broadcasts, lawmakers in 1948 prohibited the overseas networks from broadcasting inside the United States. The U.S. overseas networks confronted a different kind of obstacle from the government of the Soviet Union and its satellites. To prevent their broadcasts from penetrating the Iron Curtain, the Soviet government grew adept at blocking, or "jamming," their transmission (Siefert 2003).

The rapid dismantling of the European colonial empires following World War II confronted news agencies with additional challenges. Troubled by the continuing dominance in the global news market of news agencies headquartered in First World countries such as the United States and Great Britain, a coalition of Third World countries joined a group of left-leaning First World academics to establish a New World Information and Communication Order (NWICO) under the auspices of the United Nations Economic, Scientific, and Cultural Organization (UNESCO) (Brendebach 2018). In protest, both the United States and Great Britain briefly boycotted the UN organization.

In hindsight, it would seem indisputable that NWICO failed. Though the commercialization of the Internet has substantially transformed the global informational environment, the global influence of First World news agencies remains substantial. Ironically, several African nations received *more* news from Reuters after decolonization than they had during the colonial era, since Reuters squeezed out its Francophone rivals and pan-African cooperation stalled (Brennan 2015). Decolonization did not foster a new generation of post-colonial news agencies; instead, it consolidated a legacy news agency that was closely linked to the British Empire.

Newcomers such as Qatar-based Al Jazeera, China Central TV (CCTV), and Russia-based RT and Sputnik have tried to push back against what they regard as Anglo-American dominance of global news, thus far with limited success. Even so, the insurgents persist. "The ratings are almost beside the point" noted a *New York Times* reporter, in commenting on a Russian state-funded media project intended for viewers in the United States. What matters, declared Russian president Vladimir Putin, in a remarkably frank statement of his government's media policy, is to "break the monopoly of Anglo-Saxon global information streams," a policy goal that raises troubling moral questions in an age when the "weaponizing" of social media by foreign governments and multinational organizations is shaping popular culture and influencing electoral outcomes (Rutenberg 2017).

The dominant global communications organizations today are different in many ways from those that thrived in the nineteenth century. Yet they too have benefitted from path-dependent processes that owe as much to politics and culture as to technology and economics. For this reason, the organizations featured in this chapter – the cable companies that circulated information between the world's major commercial centers; the news agencies that created the content for the world's newspapers and broadcasters; and the postal and telecommunications networks that connected the world's peoples – created path-dependent institutional structures that have proved remarkably resistant to change.

How global communications will evolve in the future is an open question. Much will depend on the future configuration of the Internet, and, in particular, on the changing structure of the market for long-distance point-to-point communications (Balbi 2013). For much of the twentieth century, most of the world's telephone service was operated either as a government monopoly (which often combined the post, the telegraph, and the telephone in a single organization, and for this reason were known as PTTs) or, as in the United States, by a tightly regulated private firm, AT&T. The Bell System, as AT&T was known until its 1984 Supreme Court ordered break-up, operated primarily in the United States. Yet it also operated as an equipment manufacturer, Western Electric, that in the early years of telephony moved rapidly into global markets, as well as a research and development laboratory – Bell Labs – that developed a raft of innovations that would shape global communications, including the transistor, fiber optics, and cellular telephony.

Since 1970, the provisioning of telephone service has been unbundled, leading to a veritable explosion in foreign investment in networks that had formerly been government monopolies. This was true not only in Europe, but also in the Global South. Forty percent of all private investment in telecommunications in developing countries in 2000 came from overseas, mostly from incumbent providers in search of new markets. In fact, of the 100 largest nonfinancial transnational corporations in 2002, no fewer than eight were in telecommunications. Interestingly, each of these companies had formerly been a nationally based monopoly telecommunications service provider: six in Europe, one in Asia, and one in the United States (United Nations Conference on Trade and Development 2004: 117, 276–278).

Foreign investment by telecommunications corporations is nothing new. The U.S. telephone equipment manufacturer Western Electric opened a factory in Antwerp in 1882; the German cable manufacturer Siemens & Halske operated ten factories in five foreign countries in 1914, including China (Fitzgerald 2015: 128–132); the Swedish telephone equipment manufacturer Ericsson built one-third of its equipment outside Sweden in the 1930s (Jones 2005: 105). Direct foreign investment in telephone operating companies became increasingly precarious following World War II, as several governments took control of networks that had previously been operated by multinationals (Wilkins 1998: 117; Bucheli and Salvaj 2014). Even so, multinationals continued to supply much of the world's telephone equipment. The post-1970 period is distinguished, instead, by an increased reliance on outsourcing as an alternative to in-house manufacturing. In the period since 2000, for example, Ericsson, which in that year was the largest telecommunications corporations in the world, has reduced its foreign direct investments in manufacturing from seventy plants to fewer than ten (Fitzgerald 2015: 489).

Variegated and rapidly evolving – hastened, in particular, by the collapse of the once formidable technical barrier between digital computing and analog communications – these organizations are better characterized as network service providers than as large-scale technical systems. Privatization has fostered rapid innovation: of the ten largest mobile telephone operators in Africa in 2006, five were headquartered in Europe (United Nations Conference on Trade and Development 2008: 111). The results of this unbundling are evident to anyone who has visited Kenya, India, or China: mobile telephony has boomed.

Today's global communications network providers are among the leading beneficiaries of this post-1970 restructuring of the world's information infrastructure. This restructuring is often termed "deregulation," "liberalization," or even "neoliberalism," implying that governments no longer play a critical role in the informational environment of the digital age.

Nothing could be further from the truth. Government support has been instrumental not only in the promulgation of the technical standards that undergird the Internet (Russell 2014), but also in the scientific advances that made possible the Apple iPhone (Mazzucato 2013). Tax policy has shaped the location of brick-and-mortar facilities. The European Union has saddled Apple with huge fines for anti-competitive practices. A 1996 U.S. federal law immunized digital platforms from prosecution for the circulation of false, malicious, or libelous information; this hastened the weaponizing of these platforms by hostile powers. Governments in many countries work closely with network providers to surveil network users and to block subversive, obscene, or fake information (Tworek 2017).

What *has* changed is the scale on which these organizations operate. The markets in which Apple, Google, Facebook, Tencent, Nokia, and their rivals compete today are global rather than nationwide, making them in certain ways the heir to the undersea cable companies and news agencies of the past. New institutional arrangements abound. Facebook and Google, for example, are investing in fiber optic cables, a development reminiscent of the funding of a new Atlantic cable by the late-nineteenth-century newspaper baron James Gordon Bennett, Jr. More than any other factor, global competition between mobile telephone providers has hastened the quantitatively unprecedented expansion in connectivity on every continent, enabling billions of people to communicate at a remarkably low cost by email, voice, or even video with friends and relatives anywhere in the world.

This restructuring of the informational environment, in turn, opens up new possibilities for historical research. While we know a great deal about nineteenth-century undersea cables and pre-World War II news agencies, we know relatively little about the origins of today's fiber optic network and even less about the long history of global broadcasting, global censorship, and global surveillance. The significance of these phenomena is self-evident now that the relationship between global communications networks and the nation-state has become a topic of considerable contemporary concern. The recent spectacular rise of Google, Facebook, and Tencent also raises a spate of public-policy questions about the relationship between MNEs and the public good. If, for example, a digital platform can obtain a dominant market share in a media market by capitalizing on what economists call "network effects" – that is, the propensity of a network to become *more* valuable to its users as it expands – might not its very success become a rationale for its regulation?

The dizzying recent changes in global communications underscore the relevance of political economy as an analytical lens. Communications infrastructure is enormously expensive, giving the organizations that own and operate the world's communications networks and Internet service providers a vested interest in political stability. Conversely, the absence of political stability – as, for example, during World Wars I and II, or the early years of decolonization – has been enormously disruptive, with unpredictable consequences that have often proved irreversible.

Nothing is permanent. It is for this reason salutary to remember that influential elites have previously predicted that rapid, high-speed, global communications would bring economic prosperity and world peace. Writing in 1912, German economics professor Bernhard Harms hailed the "electrical transmission of news" as a more important factor in hastening overseas trade than even the steamship or the railway (Harms 1912: 141). Influential progressives in Great Britain, Austria-Hungary, France, and the United States went even further, contending that the world had become so interconnected that a global conflagration had become inconceivable.

The visionaries were mistaken. In 1914 – and once again in 1939 – the war came. Even so, the seductive allure of the profoundly mistaken assumption that technical advance will inexorably hasten moral progress endures – as anyone can attest who lived through the Internet boom of the 1990s. Paradoxes abound. International stability has never been more essential, yet diplomacy is disparaged. Information is ubiquitous, yet disinformation is endemic. Maintenance has never been more indispensable, yet disruptive innovation is all the rage. Never has the power of political economy to shape the institutional rules of the game been more palpable, yet rarely has the effects of these institutional arrangements been more emphatically denied. For if the history recounted in this chapter holds any lessons for the future, it is that the huge organizations that dominate today's global communications networks are driven less by technological imperatives than their champions proclaim, and are more dependent on political fiat than all but their most inveterate critics concede (Price 2002).

References

Ahvenainen, Jorma (2004), *The European Cable Companies in South America before the First World War* (Helsinki: Academia Scientiarum Fennica).

Aitken, Hugh G.J. (1985), *The Continuous Wave: Technology and American Radio, 1900–1932* (Princeton, NJ: Princeton University Press).

Akami, Tomoko (2012), *Japan's News Propaganda and Reuters' News Empire in Northeast Asia, 1870–1934* (Dordrecht: Republic of Letters).

Akami, Tomoko (2014), *Soft Power of Japan's Total War State: The Board of Information and D mei News Agency in Foreign Policy, 1934–45* (Dordrecht: Republic of Letters).

Balbi, Gabriele (2013), "Telecommunications," in Peter Simonson, Janice Peck, Robert Craig, and John Jackson, Jr. (eds.), *The Handbook of Communication History* (New York: Routledge), 209–222.

Balbi, Gabriele, and John, Richard R. (2015), "Point-to-Point: Telecommunications Networks from the Optical Telegraph to the Mobile Telephone," in Lorenzo Cantoni and James A. Danowski (eds.), *Handbook of Communications Science*, vol. 5: *Communication and Technology* (Berlin: De Gruyter Mouton), 35–55.

Bell, Duncan (2007), *The Idea of a Greater Britain: Empire and the Future of World Order, 1860–1900* (Princeton, NJ: Princeton University Press).

Blondheim, Menachem (1994), *News over the Wires: The Telegraph and the Flow of Public Information in America, 1844–1897* (Cambridge, MA: Harvard University Press).

Bonea, Amelia (2016), *The News of Empire: Telegraphy, Journalism, and the Politics of Reporting in Colonial India, c. 1830–1900* (Oxford: Oxford University Press).

Boyd-Barrett, Oliver and Rantanen, Terhi (1998), "The Globalization of News," in Oliver Boyd-Barrett and Terhi Rantanen (eds.), *The Globalization of News* (London: SAGE), 19–34.

Brendebach, Jonas (2018), "Towards a New International Communication Order? UNESCO, Development and 'National Communication Policies' in the 1960s and 1970s," in Jonas Brendebach, Martin Herzer, and Heidi Tworek (eds.), *International Organizations and the Media in the Nineteenth and Twentieth Centuries: Exorbitant Expectations* (Abingdon and New York: Routledge), 158–181.

Bright, Charles (1902), *Imperial Telegraphic Communication and the "All-British" Pacific Cable* (London: London Chamber of Commerce).

Brennan, James R. (2015), "The Cold War Battle over Global News in East Africa: Decolonization, the Free Flow of Information, and the Media Business, 1960–1980," *Journal of Global History*, 10 (2), 333–356.

Britton, John A. (2013), *Cables, Crises, and the Press: The Geopolitics of the New International Information System in the Americas, 1866–1903* (Albuquerque, NM: University of New Mexico Press).

Brown, J. (1927), *The Cable and Wireless Communications of the World: A Survey of Present Day Means of International Communication by Cable and Wireless* (London: Sir Isaac Pitman & Sons).

Bucheli, Marcelo, and Salvaj, Erica (2014), "Adaptation Strategies of Multinational Corporations, State-Owned Enterprises, and Domestic Business Groups to Economic and Political Transitions: A Network Analysis of the Chilean Telecommunications Sector, 1958–2002," *Enterprise & Society*, 15 (3), 534–576.

Chandler, Alfred D., Jr. (1977), *The Visible Hand: The Managerial Revolution in American Business* (Cambridge, MA: Belknap Press of Harvard University Press).

Conrad, Sebastian (2016), *What is Global History?* (Princeton, NJ: Princeton University Press).

Coopersmith, Jonathan (2015), *Faxed: The Rise and Fall of the Fax Machine* (Baltimore, MD: Johns Hopkins University Press).

DeNardis, Laura (2014), *The Global War for Internet Governance* (New Haven, CT: Yale University Press).

Doe, Helen (2010), "Waiting for Her Ship to Come In? The Female Investor in Nineteenth-Century Sailing Vessels," *Economic History Review*, 63 (1), 85–106.

Engel, Alexander (2015), "Buying Time: Futures Trading and Telegraphy in Nineteenth-Century Global Commodity Markets," *Journal of Global History* 10 (2), 284–306.

Evans, Heidi (2010), "'The Path to Freedom'? Transocean and German Wireless Telegraphy, 1914–1922," *Historical Social Research*, 35 (1), 209–33.

Finn, Bernard, and Yang, Daqing (eds.) (2009), *Communications under the Seas: The Evolving Cable Network and its Implications* (Cambridge, MA: MIT Press).

Fitzgerald, Robert (2015), *The Rise of the Global Company: Multinationals and the Making of the Modern World* (Cambridge: Cambridge University Press).

Gerber, David A. (2006), *Authors of Their Own Lives: The Personal Correspondence of Nineteenth Century British Immigrants to North America* (New York: New York University Press).

Grewal, David Singh (2008), *Network Power: The Social Dynamics of Globalization* (New Haven, CT: Yale University Press).

Hansen, N. (1914), "Depeschenbureaus und Internationales Nachrichtenwesen," *Weltwirtschaftliches Archiv*, 3 (1), 78–96.

Harms, Bernhard (1912), *Volkswirtschaft und Weltwirtschaft: Versuch der Begründung einer Weltwirtschaftslehre* (Jena: Gustav Fischer).

Headrick, Daniel R. (1988), *The Tentacles of Progress: Technology Transfer in the Age of Imperialism, 1850–1940* (New York: Oxford University Press).

Headrick, Daniel R. (1991), *The Invisible Weapon: Telecommunications and International Politics, 1851–1945* (New York: Oxford University Press).

Headrick, Daniel R. (2000), *When Information Came of Age: Technologies of Knowledge in the Age of Reason and Revolution, 1700–1850* (New York: Oxford University Press).

Headrick, Daniel R. (2010), "A Double-Edged Sword: Communications and Imperial Control in British India," *Historical Social Research*, 35 (1), 51–65.

Headrick, Daniel R., and Griset, Pascal (2001), "Submarine Telegraph Cables: Business and Politics, 1838–1939," *Business History Review*, 75 (3), 543–578.

Hills, Jill (2002), *The Struggle for Global Communication: The Formative Century* (Urbana, IL: University of Illinois Press).

Hills, Jill (2007), *Telecommunications and Empire* (Urbana, IL: University of Illinois Press).

Hoag, Christopher (2006), "The Atlantic Telegraph Cable and Capital Market Information Flows," *Journal of Economic History*, 66 (2), 342–353.

Hobson, John (1906), "The Ethics of Internationalism," *International Journal of Ethics*, 17 (1), 16–28.

Hofmeyr, Isabel (2013), *Gandhi's Printing Press: Experiments in Slow Reading* (Cambridge, MA: Harvard University Press).

Hughes, Thomas P. (1998), *Rescuing Prometheus: Four Monumental Projects that Changed Our World* (New York: Random House).

Hughes, Thomas P. (2005), "From Firm to Networked System," *Business History Review*, 79 (3), 587–593.

Hugill, Peter J. (1999), *Global Communications since 1844: Geopolitics and Technology* (Baltimore, MD: Johns Hopkins University Press).

Hunt, Bruce J. (1997), "Doing Science in a Global Empire: Cable Telegraphy and Victorian Physics," in Bernard Lightman (ed.), *Victorian Science in Context* (Chicago, IL: University of Chicago Press), 312–333.

Hyde, Francis E. (1975), *Cunard and the North Atlantic 1840–1973: A History of Shipping and Financial Management* (London: Macmillan).

Innis, Harold A. (1950), *Empire and Communication* (Oxford: Clarendon Press).

John, Richard R. (1994), "American Historians and the Concept of the Communications Revolution," in Lisa Bud-Frierman (ed.), *Information Acumen: The Understanding and Use of Knowledge in Modern Business* (London: Routledge), 98–110.

John, Richard R. (2000), "Recasting the Information Infrastructure for the Industrial Age," in Alfred D. Chandler, Jr. and James Cortada (eds.), *A Nation Transformed by Information: How Information Has Shaped the United States from Colonial Times to the Present* (New York: Oxford University Press), 55–105.

John, Richard R. (2010), *Network Nation: Inventing American Telecommunications* (Cambridge, MA: Belknap Press of Harvard University Press).

John, Richard R. (2013), "Communications Networks in the United States from Chappe to Marconi," in John Nerone (ed.), *The International Encyclopedia of Media Studies*, vol. 1: *Media History and the Foundations of Media Studies* (Malden, MA: John Wiley & Sons), 310–332.

John, Richard R. (2015), "Projecting Power Overseas: U.S. Postal Policy and International Standard-Setting at the 1863 Paris Postal Conference," *Journal of Policy History*, 27 (3), 416–438.

John, Richard R., and Silberstein-Loeb, Jonathan (2015), "Making News," in Richard R. John and Jonathan Silberstein-Loeb (eds.), *Making News: The Political Economy of Journalism in Britain and America from the Glorious Revolution to the Internet* (Oxford: Oxford University Press), 1–18.

Jones, Geoffrey (2005), *Multinationals and Global Competition from the Nineteenth to the Twenty-First Century* (New York: Oxford University Press).

Karush, Matthew (2012), *Culture of Class: Radio and Cinema in the Making of a Divided Argentina, 1920–1946* (Durham, NC: Duke University Press).

Laako, Seija-Riita (2007), *Across the Oceans: Development of Overseas Business Information Transmission, 1815–1875* (Helsinki: Finnish Literature Society).

Laborie, Léonard (2010), *L'Europe mise en réseaux: La France et la coopération internationale dans les postes et les télécommunications (années 1850-années 1950)* (Brussels: Peter Lang).

Levinson, Marc (2006), *The Box: How the Shipping Container Made the World Smaller and the World Economy Bigger* (Princeton, NJ: Princeton University Press).

Lew, Byron, and Cater, Bruce (2006), "The Telegraph, Co-ordination of Tramp Shipping, and Growth in World Trade, 1870–1910," *European Review of Economic History*, 10 (2), 147–173.

Linden, F. Robert van der (2001), *Airlines and Air Mail: The Post Office and the Birth of the Commercial Aviation Industry* (Lexington, KY: University Press of Kentucky).

Lovell, Stephen (2015), *Russia in the Microphone Age: A History of Soviet Radio, 1919–1970* (Oxford: Oxford University Press).

Mackinnon, Rebecca (2012), *Consent of the Networked: The Worldwide Struggle for Internet Freedom* (New York: Basic Books).

Maischak, Lars (2013), *German Merchants in the Nineteenth-Century Atlantic* (Cambridge: Cambridge University Press).

Marx, Karl (1855), "The Commercial Crisis in Britain," in James Ledbetter (ed.), *Dispatches for the* New York Tribune: *Selected Journalism of Karl Marx* (New York: Penguin, 2005), 166–171.

Marx, Leo (1994), "The Idea of 'Technology' and Postmodern Pessimism," in Yaron Ezrahi, Everett Mendelsohn, and Howard Segal (eds.), *Technology, Pessimism, and Postmodernism* (Dordrecht: Springer), 11–28.

Matterlart, Armand (1996), *The Invention of Communication* (Minneapolis, MN: University of Minnesota Press).

Matterlart, Armand (2000), *Networking the World, 1794–2000* (Minneapolis, MN: University of Minnesota Press).

Mazzucato, Mariana (2013), *The Entrepreneurial State: Debunking Public vs. Private Sector Myths* (London: Anthem Press).

Miller, Michael B. (2012), *Europe and the Maritime World: A Twentieth-Century History* (New York: Cambridge University Press).

Mosca, Manuela (2008), "On the Origins of the Concept of Natural Monopoly," *European Journal for the History of Economic Thought*, 45 (2), 317–353.

Müller, Simone M. (2015), "Beyond the Means of 99 Percent of the Population: Business Interests, State Intervention, and Submarine Telegraphy," *Journal of Policy History*, 27 (3), 439–464.

Müller, Simone M. (2016), *Wiring the World: The Social and Cultural Creation of Global Telegraph Networks* (New York: Columbia University Press).

Müller, Simone M., and Tworek, Heidi (2015), "The Telegraph and the Bank: On the Interdependence of Global Communications and Capitalism, 1866–1914," *Journal of Global History*, 10 (2), 259–283.

Ninkovich, Frank (2009), *Global Dawn: The Cultural Foundation of American Internationalism, 1865–1890* (Cambridge, MA: Harvard University Press).

Ogle, Vanessa (2015), *The Global Transformation of Time, 1870–1950* (Cambridge, MA: Harvard University Press).

Osterhammel, Jürgen (2014), *The Transformation of the World: A Global History of the Nineteenth Century* (Princeton, NJ: Princeton University Press).

Otis, Laura (2011), *Networking: Communicating with Bodies and Machines in the Nineteenth Century* (Ann Arbor, MI: University of Michigan Press).

Peters, Benjamin (2016), *How Not to Network a Nation: The Uneasy History of the Soviet Internet* (Cambridge, MA: MIT Press).

Price, Monroe E. (2002), *Media and Sovereignty: The Global Information Revolution and its Challenge to State Power* (Cambridge, MA: MIT Press).

Puddington, Arch (2015), *Broadcasting Freedom: The Cold War Triumph of Radio Free Europe and Radio Liberty* (Lexington, KY: Kentucky University Press).

Raboy, Marc (2016), *Marconi: The Man Who Networked the World* (New York: Oxford).

Rantanen, Terhi (2013), "'Quickening Urgency': The Telegraph and Wire Services in 1846–1893," in John Nerone (ed.), *The International Encyclopedia of Media Studies*, vol. 1: *Media History and the Foundations of Media Studies* (Malden, MA: John Wiley & Sons), 333–349.

Read, Donald (1992), *Power of News: The History of Reuters, 1849–1989* (Oxford: Oxford University Press).

Rieger, Bernhard (2005), *Technology and the Culture of Modernity in Britain and Germany, 1890–1945* (Cambridge: Cambridge University Press).

Robinson, Harold (1964), *Carrying British Mail Overseas* (London: G. Allen & Unwin).

Roscher, Max (1914), "Über das Wesen und die Bedingungen des Internationalen Nachrichtenverkehrs," *Weltwirtschaftliches Archiv*, 3 (1), 37–59.

Rosenberg, Emily S. (ed.) (2012), *A World Connecting, 1870–1945* (Cambridge, MA: Harvard University Press).

Russell, Andrew L. (2014), *Open Standards and the Digital Age: History, Ideology, and Networks* (Cambridge: Cambridge University Press).

Rutenberg, Jim (2017). "RT, Sputnik, and Russia's New Theory of War," *New York Times* (13 September).

Schaede, Ulrike (1989), "Forwards and Futures in Tokugawa-Period Japan: A New Perspective on the Dojima Rice Market," *Journal of Banking and Finance*, 13, 487–513.

Schwoch, James (1987), "The American Radio Industry and International Communications Conferences, 1919–1927," *Historical Journal of Film, Radio and Television*, 7 (3), 289–309.

Schwoch, James (2009), *Global TV: New Media and the Cold War, 1946–69* (Urbana, IL: University of Illinois Press).

Shu, Sheng-Chi (2016), "News as Internationally-Transacted Strategic Commodity: Reuters and the Party-State News Agencies of Twentieth-Century China, 1931–1957," (Ph.D. dissertation, University of Cambridge).

Shulman, Peter A. (2015), *Coal and Empire: The Birth of Energy Security in Industrial America* (Baltimore, MD: Johns Hopkins University Press).

Siefert, Martha (2003), "Radio Diplomacy and the Cold War," *Journal of Communications*, 53 (2), 363–373.

Silberstein-Loeb, Jonathan (2014), *The International Distribution of News: The Associated Press, Press Association, and Reuters, 1848–1947* (Cambridge: Cambridge University Press).

Slotten, Hugh (2013), "The International Telecommunications Union, Space Radio Communications, and U.S. Cold War Diplomacy, 1957–1963," *Diplomatic History*, 7 (2), 317–371.

Stamm, Michael (2015), "Broadcast Journalism in the Interwar Period," in Richard R. John and Jonathan Silberstein-Loeb (eds.), *Making News: The Political Economy of Journalism in Britain and America from the Glorious Revolution to the Internet* (Oxford: Oxford University Press), 133–163.

Standage, Tom (1998), *The Victorian Internet: The Remarkable Story of the Telegraph and the Nineteenth Century's On-Line Pioneers* (New York: Walker & Co.).

Starosielski, Nicole (2015), *The Undersea Network* (Durham, NC: Duke University Press).

Thurber, Francis B., "The Influence of Steam and Electricity," *International Review*, 2 (1875), 623.

Tresch, John (2012), *The Romantic Machine: Utopian Science and Technology after Napoleon* (Chicago, IL: University of Chicago Press).

Tully, John (2009), "A Victorian Ecological Disaster: Imperialism, the Telegraph, and Gutta-Percha," *Journal of World History*, 20 (4), 559–579.

Tworek, Heidi (2015a), "Der Weltverkehr und die Ausbreitung des Kapitalismus um 1900," *Themenportal Europäische Geschichte*, www.europa.clio-online.de/essay/id/artikel-3795 (accessed January 5, 2018).

Tworek, Heidi (2015b), "The Savior of the Nation? Regulating Radio in the Interwar Period," *Journal of Policy History*, 27 (3), 465–491.

Tworek, Heidi (2016), "How Not to Build a World Wireless Network: German–British Rivalry and Visions of Global Communications in the Early Twentieth Century," *History and Technology*, 32 (2), 178–200.

Tworek, Heidi (2017), "How Germany is Tackling Hate Speech: New Legislation Targets U.S. Social Media Companies," *Foreign Affairs*, www.foreignaffairs.com/articles/germany/2017-05-16/how-germany-tackling-hate-speech (accessed December 28, 2017).

United Nations Conference on Trade and Development (2004), *World Investment Report 2004: The Shift Toward Services* (New York: United Nations).

United Nations Conference on Trade and Development (2008), *World Investment Report 2008: Transnational Corporations and the Infrastructural Challenge* (New York: United Nations).

Wagner, Markus (2014), "Legal Perspectives and Regulatory Philosophies on Natural Monopolies in the United States and Germany," in Gunther Schulz, Mathias Schmoeckel, and William Hausman (eds.), *Regulation between Legal Norms and Economic Reality: Intentions, Effects, and Adaptation: The German and American Experiences* (Tübingen: Mohr Siebeck), 53–74.

Wenzlhuemer, Roland (2013), *Connecting the Nineteenth-Century World: The Telegraph and Globalization* (Cambridge: Cambridge University Press).

Wilkins, Mira, and Hill, Frank Ernest (1964), *American Business Abroad: Ford on Six Continents* (Detroit, MI: Wayne State University Press).

Wilkins, Mira (1998), "Multinational Enterprise and Economic Change," *Australian Economic History Review*, 38 (2), 103–134.

Winkler, Jonathan Reed (2008), *Nexus: Strategic Communications and American Security in World War I* (Cambridge, MA: Harvard University Press).

Winseck, Dwayne R., and Pike, Robert M. (2007), *Communication and Empire: Media, Markets, and Globalization, 1860–1930* (Durham, NC: Duke University Press).

Yang, Daqing (2010), *Technology of Empire: Telecommunications and Japanese Expansion in Asia, 1883–1945* (Cambridge, MA: Harvard University Press).

21

ELECTRIC POWER INDUSTRY

Álvaro Ferreira da Silva and Isabel Bartolomé Rodríguez

Introduction

This chapter focuses on the role of foreign investment and multinationals in the electric power industry. The industry went global from the first commercial ventures in electric lighting and power for industry and transport. Inventors and entrepreneurs – among them some larger-than-life characters like Edison and Tesla – aimed at a global public audience. International exhibitions provided stages to display spectacular commercial uses of the new technology (Schivelbusch 1995; Nye 2018).

The period from 1880 to 1930 was critical for developing the electric utility industry (Hughes 1983: 1). By 1900, the technological bases had emerged: the invention and commercial use of the dynamo, the central power station, the alternator, the use of long-distance transmission, and the polyphase system. This "dominant design" (Utterback and Abernathy 1975) created a de facto technological standard. In the 1920s the industry attained its maturity and was well established in developed countries and the urban centers of the peripheries (Hausman *et al.* 2008: 27). It settled the technological, managerial, and institutional components, which combined are the definition of any "large technological system" (Hughes 1983: 5–17; Hughes 1994): a standardized technology, electrical engineering experts and consultants, sources of venture capital, financiers and managers, government agencies, and educational institutions.

We argue that the electric power industry was global between 1880 to 1930. The electric utility holding integrated into a business form the technological, managerial, and financial components of the system. It represents the culmination of decades of experimentation in international business forms. As we show, the electricity industry tried almost every business model available to internationalizing firms during the first global economy: free-standing companies, multinational investment by manufacturing firms of electricity equipment, investment trusts, or consortia of investors, joining together manufacturing firms, financial and engineering interests (see the second and fourth sections below). This chapter studies the evolution of the organizational conduits for doing business abroad to understand why the electric holding company epitomized the multinational firm in the industry. This study builds upon the synthesis provided by Hausman and his co-authors (2008) and the insights from research on free-standing companies and other unconventional organizational forms in multinational activity, which "pushed forward thinking about different forms of multinational enterprise behavior over time" (Wilkins 2009: 18; see also Lopes *et al.* 2018).

The evolution of the electric utilities' foreign ownership (Hausman *et al.* 2008, table 1.4) outlines the dominance of global firms in the early 1930s. After that, foreign capital and multinationals ceased to define the industry. The Great Depression, and to a lesser extent World War I (see the fifth section below), triggered changes in the industry extrinsic to its economic and technological dynamics. The electric power industry deglobalized after the 1930s because of a combination of factors: the economic and political impact of the Great Depression; decreasing returns on investment; the financial excesses of the electric holding firms in the 1920s; the belief that the state should foster national integration of electricity networks. Nationalization policies were instrumental in ending the global electric holding.

Technological and economic issues in the development of the electric utility

The electric power industry had a similar network design to other infrastructures and utilities (see Tworek and John's chapter on communications in this volume), which influenced the industry's entrepreneurial form. The industry's commercial development crucially relied upon the early adoption of the central power station and networked transmission and distribution of energy, although the earlier innovations in electro-processing – Aluminium (Hall, 1888, Kensington, Pittsburgh, PA); Calcium Cyanamid (Frank-Caro 1898, Germany) – seemed to lead to a scattered geography. The dynamo created by the Belgian Zénobe Gramme in Paris around 1873 rapidly spread the networked design and was further reinforced by Edison's incandescent light bulb of 1878, the Pearl Street electrical station in 1882 in the USA, and the electric tram created in Germany in 1883 by Werner von Siemens. The first long-distance transmission of electricity was in the Electro-Technical Exhibition of Frankfurt in 1891, but its three-phase power was only recognized as a better method than Edison's DC and Tesla's biphasic system 20 years later (Dunsheat 1962; Devine 1990; Rosenberg 1994). Around 1900, the more effective generation and distribution design was based on powerful and efficient generators and the use of long-distance transmission grids, which permitted access to sources of hydroelectricity (Hirsh 2003: 36; Neufeld 2016: 33).

Larger electric utility networks shared with other networked industries the advantages of economies of scale but had one unique characteristic. The combination of different timing and sort of demands, and the total capacity of the larger electric network will always be lower than the summation of many smaller grids used for lighting, transport, and industrial power in a particular city or region. This is important to solving the "peak-load problem" in the efficient design of an electric network. Therefore, the peak of a larger network is always well below the sum of the peaks of the smaller ones (Hausman *et al.* 2008: 13).

In the early twentieth century, engineers and entrepreneurs acknowledged the advantages of larger, integrated networks in electric utilities. Private initiative dominated, and local or regional monopolies would turn out to be the most efficient solution to provide power for lighting, industrial uses, and transportation. Yet, the combination of private undertakings and monopolist operations raised important regulatory issues (Millward 2005: 76–87).

When commercial use of electricity began, invention and innovation were international, spanning across Germany, the USA, England, France, Austro-Hungary, Belgium, or Italy (Dunsheat 1962; Hughes 1983, chs. 4 and 5). In the early twentieth century, the industry concentrated in a few countries: Germany, the USA, and Switzerland. Electricity became a relatively complex technology, as the power and efficiency of generators, power stations, and transmission technology rapidly evolved.

The diffusion turned out to be increasingly complex. Extending networks, integrating different sources of energy (thermal and hydraulic), and designing the optimal power for efficiently overcoming the peak-load problem demanded specialized knowledge. The site-specificity of the network, power generation and transmission, and peak-load forecasts limited the degree of standardization. The design of the particular solution for a specific place demanded highly skilled engineering services. When hydroelectricity was an option, the engineering design was even more site-specific (Armstrong and Nelles 1988).

The development of electric utility demanded, thus, a much more site-specific technology transfer than in manufacturing (Rosenberg 1972, 1976). Water or sewerage networks raised similar challenges, as did the earlier installation of railways. The creation of free-standing companies provided the solution for spreading these new technologies to locations far from centers of technological knowledge. Free-standing companies synthesized the necessary capital, the engineering, and the management.

The electric utility industry shared another characteristic with networked utilities and infrastructures: these technological innovations demanded costly and highly transaction-specific capital investments in generation equipment, transmission and distribution lines, dams, and reservoirs. What was peculiar to the electric power industry was the much higher intensity of these initial capital costs. This prevented the use of retained earnings for financing a gradual investment or even for paying back the capital interest during the first years of operation. Hausman and his co-authors (2008: 19–23, particularly figure 1.4) emphasize the extraordinary capital intensity of the electric power industry during the late nineteenth and early twentieth centuries. Until World War I, the industry invested more in capital equipment than its total revenue, which was an abnormal situation, accumulating a high volume of capital without a remuneration out of the operational revenue (Neufeld 2016: 5). Moreover, capital costs did not end after the system launched. The electrical firms had to continually absorb not only intensive consumers – like chemical industries – but also competitors, namely urban gas and electricity distributors, in order to build a regional monopoly.

Managers perfectly understood the economics of the electric utility firm by the 1920s. Management practices accounted for the utility cost structure, its unusual balance between fixed and operating costs, the need to deal in the most efficient way with the peak-load factor, and the importance of price discrimination to entice customers to spread use evenly and thus decrease the maximum amount of energy generators should produce (Giannetti 1988; Hirsh 2003: 26; Neufeld 2016: 22).

These economic characteristics and the technological breakthroughs that favored larger electrical networks affected how the industry internationalized. The development of international business in electricity utilities became, thus, a rapid succession of experiments with several business models to find the most efficient solution for different issues: exceptional and transaction-specific capital costs; rapidly rising costs of the initial investment due to technological innovation and increasing scale; operating revenues hardly matching operating costs; much less remuneration of capital. This created a tension in the industry around the two poles of the Modigliani–Miller theorem (equity vs. corporate debt). On the one hand, debt was advisable for reducing financial risk in such a capital-intensive industry. On the other hand, long-term, foreign direct investment (FDI) was appealing to enforce control over the electric utilities' management, securing serial equipment orders, engineering services, and efficient management for protecting the capital tied up to the investment. Equity or debt, direct or portfolio investment remained thus a difficult choice for the firms driving early foreign investment in the industry.

The next section explains how manufacturers of electrical equipment had a strong interest in rapidly enlarging the market for the new technology both to sell capital equipment and appliances as well as to enforce their proprietary standards in the generation and transmission of technology. Investing in electric utilities at home or abroad was a way to attain these twinned objectives.

International business at the dawn of the first electricity ventures

Electricity became an international business at the same time as the industry became a commercial venture and the investment requirements were relatively modest (Segreto 1994: 162). In the late 1870s and 1880s, there was intense competition between different solutions for electric lighting and power. In France the Société Générale d'Électricité aimed to introduce electric lighting in the French main cities, but also in London and New York. At the beginning of the 1880s, Siemens created a subsidiary in London to promote the illumination of the British Museum (Hausman *et al.* 2008: 75). The American Edison Company expanded abroad, even before installing the Pearl Street electrical station in 1882, which created a new model for power management and distribution in the industry. A rush to secure the diffusion and the ownership rights of Edison's inventions abroad drove its international expansion: in Britain, an agreement with the banking house Drexel and Morgan to license Edison's inventions (1878); in Continental Europe, the creation of Edison Electric Light Company of Europe Ltd. (1880). The success of the New York power station launched many other initiatives across Europe and the Americas (Hughes 1983: ch. 3; list of Edison's companies at http://edison.rutgers.edu/list. htm#Lightfor).

This first phase of international expansion in the electricity industry depended upon inventors and manufacturers of electrical equipment. The Edison Company epitomizes this trend. Edison and his partners intended to diffuse abroad the new model of centralized power stations. The surge in Edison-affiliated companies around the world – from UK to Germany, France to Italy, Argentina to Cuba – was meant to secure concessions for urban lighting and enlarge the market. Contracts between the Edison Company in the USA and affiliates supported licensing agreements, striving to push a de facto standard for electricity production and transmission, at a time when a dominant design was still absent. These initiatives were short-lived as affiliates of the US company. Some of the firms were liquidated shortly after. Many others severed the initial ties with Edison and transformed into independent firms, as Società Edison in Italy, Deutsche Edison Gesellschaft (DEG) in Germany, or the Compagnie Continental Edison in France.

Thomson-Houston Electric Company, the rival of Edison in the USA (apart from Westinghouse with no experiences abroad) before both firms merged into International General Electric in 1892, moved into Europe differently during this first phase. Instead of creating affiliates and subsidiaries, it recycled Thomson-Houston's investments into marketable securities in operating utilities stock or bonds. The new securities were then sold to Thomson-Houston stockholders or on the market (Hausman *et al.* 2008: 81). Thomson-Houston International Electric Company (1885) was the vehicle used to export the firm's proprietary technology without a network of subsidiaries (Carlson 1991: 212–18). The American company also engaged in FDI through British and French Thomson-Houston, founded respectively in 1886 and 1893, but this was minimal compared to Edison.

At this time, different European manufacturing firms created competing solutions for lighting and power. The competition was technological *and* commercial, domestic *and* international. Germany witnessed a period of cooperation with the agreement between Siemens and Edison (1883). The German Edison subsidiary agreed to purchase generators and other equipment from Siemens, which would not litigate Edison incandescent lamps and would produce them for the

German domestic market. Besides Siemens & Halske, this agreement also included Thomas Edison, the Edison Electric Light Company of Europe Ltd., the DEG, the Continental Edison (which commercialized Edison patents in Europe), and three German banking houses, which supported the creation of Deutsche Edison (Hughes 1983: 68). Around 1900, when Allgemeine Elektricitäts-Gesellschaft (AEG) replaced DEG, the competition with Siemens became more intense. In 1903, AEG signed an agreement with the American General Electric splitting up the world into two main areas of influence. Europe was left to AEG, which had taken over UEG (founded in 1892), with close links with International General Electric.

Electrical manufacturers had strong incentives to establish electric utilities abroad through FDI, as the Spanish case exemplifies. AEG invested in electric utilities in Madrid (1889), Seville (1894), and Bilbao (1895) and acquired the British tram companies to create the Compañía General de Tranvías de Barcelona a Sans. In 1896, Schuckert started operating in Bilbao with Ahlemeyer Cía Anónima, and Siemens purchased a plant in Malaga (Lanciotti and Bartolomé 2014). They were crucial to expand the market for the new technological ensemble, selling generators, transmission equipment, or lamps, and channeling royalties from licensing the use of technological solutions. This occurred while there was still no set electro-technical solution for generating and transmitting electricity. The initial utility design could create path-dependency constraints preventing the use of other kinds of machinery. Thus, manufacturers established technological reliance on their own equipment in the initial phase by controlling the design of the electricity systems. This was essential to support a permanent flow of sales in electrical equipment and appliances. Manufacturers acted either as initiators, providing not only equipment but also engineering solutions, or in association with a foreign electrical manufacturer as an affiliate. However, downward vertical integration of light and power operating companies by manufacturers of electricity equipment was full of hazards and tied up capital for a long time. Manufacturing firms wanted to enlarge the market and sell their products but disregarded the direct involvement in running electrical utilities. In several instances and once the plant/system was running, manufacturers frequently sold to other investors (Hertner 1986; Segreto 1992a, 1992b).

Launching downward vertical integration of foreign electric utilities via electrical equipment manufacturers was the closest the electricity business came to the classic model of multinational firm, in which investment abroad starts after developing a consistent presence in the home country (Nelles 2003: 4). The German companies, AEG, Siemens-Halske, UEG, Schuckert, and the Swiss Brown-Bovery (specialized in hydro power) had their enormous technological potential stuck in limited domestic markets, in contrast with their American counterparts. This explains why they rapidly started to develop other options for enlarging the market for equipment and services abroad. In the very late nineteenth century they became the main experimenters in alternative business solutions to FDI in electric utilities.

Emulating railways and public works: the rise of consortia and holdings

A new business model for investments took shape in the late nineteenth century, as the industry's technology converged to more centralized solutions, exemplified by the central power station and the outcome of the "battle of currents" (David 1992). The demonstration of long-distance transmission at the Frankfurt exhibition (1891) showed the commercial viability of hydroelectricity, capable of supplying distant urban or industrial consumers and the use of polyphase systems (Hughes 1983: 127–39; Segreto 1994: 163). Investing in larger power stations and transmission infrastructure increased capital requirements.

The business model of international expansion during the 1880s owes much to American or German firms' experiences of internationalization in manufacturing. After 1890, the industry used previous practices for financing and constructing railways, ports, channels, water, and gas utilities, and trams (Schisani and Caiazzo 2016). The common characteristics of these industries and electricity explain the expansion of the new business model. The operating companies in railways, ports, water, and gas utilities were also highly capital-intensive and did not expand over borders. Business solutions for expanding abroad had relied on free-standing companies and consortia of investors for mobilizing capital and technology for investments in foreign locations.

The rising capital-intensity in electricity after the early 1890s favored the creation of consortia of investors in foreign ventures. The German, Swiss, and Belgium investment trusts or holdings after 1894 presented the first formalization of this process (Segreto 1994). One of the earliest was the Gesellschaft für Elektrische Unternehmungen (Gesfürel) created in 1894 in Berlin and joining German banks (Darmstädter Bank für Handel und Industrie, Dresden Bank, Disconto-Gesellschaft, Bankhaus S. Bleichröder, Privatbanken Born & Busse) and electrical manufacturers (AEG and Isidor Loewe). It was followed by similar initiatives centered on another manufacturer, Schuckert & Co.: Rheinische Schuckert-Gesellschaft für elektrische Industrie AG (1894) and the Continentale Gesellschaft für elektrische Unternehmungen (1895). Investment firms in Belgium and Switzerland made foreign operations a priority. In Switzerland, Elektrobank was promoted by AEG in 1895, Indelec by Siemens & Halske, and Motor established in 1895 by Brown-Boveri of Baden. In Belgium, UEG created the Société Générale Belge d'Enterprises Eléctriques in 1895, in partnership with Gesfürel, two Belgian railway holding companies (Société Générale des Chemins de Fer Économiques and Compagnie Générale des Chemins de Fer Secondaires), three Belgian banks (Cassel et Cie, la Banque de Bruxelles, Josse Allard) and the French bank Comptoir National d'Escompte (Bitsch 1994). In 1898, the same partnership between UEG and Gesfürel, Belgian banks (Cassel et Cie, Josse Allard, Mathieu et fils), German banks (Disconto-Gesellschaft and Dresden Bank), and other minor participations created the Société Financière de Transports et Enterprises Industrielles (Sofina).

The Belgian and Swiss initiatives had similar promoters to their German counterparts: equipment manufacturers and banks, which created these firms as a financial basis for channeling investments to operating companies in electrical power and urban transport. Banks had helped to establish public utility systems from the 1880s, when the initiative was led by equipment manufacturers. For instance, J. P. Morgan partnered with Edison in the first steps of internationalizing the American company. The banking house also participated in setting up the electricity project of Niagara Falls in the early 1890s. Banks provided access to capital markets and supported the issuing of equity and corporate debt, underwriting the securities. The association of manufacturers and financial firms in an investment trust or consortium constituted in itself a means for organizing a constellation of other investors for specific projects.

The Consortium of the Barcelona Tramways (1905) represents a clear example of the pivotal role played by these investment holdings in organizing a consortium of investors. Sofina led the consortium with 23 other partners. The German firm Gesfürel singled out with 30 percent of the capital, followed by the pivot firm (Sofina) with 23 percent and Belgian banking houses (Josse Allard and Cassel with a total of 18 percent). Many other examples of similar consortia in Constantinople or Lisbon could be added (see Thobie 1991 on Constantinople). Sofina's initial function was to spot opportunities: a city that wanted to franchise the modernization of lighting or transport using electrical power; a gas company or a tramway operator in difficulties for moving on to the new technology; a set of existing power and transport companies in a single city which could be combined in a more efficient one; an individual or society who got the franchise for electric lighting or transportation, but did not have the capital or the expertise to lead the process. If necessary, Sofina negotiated the franchise with the municipal or state authorities, created the consortium (or syndicate, as it was mentioned in contemporary documents), contracting the engineering solution, promoting the company, ensuring the securities issuing and underwriting by financial partners in the consortium, and finally launching the actual construction of electrical facilities. The members of these business alliances were meant to support the initial funding of the project, retain their shares for a period of time (usually one year), which might be extended through yearly agreements. This would create a convergent block of shareholders during the project management and construction phase, even if any single participation by an investor in the consortium was in clear minority.

The economic and political context facilitated the transnational business alliances underpinning these consortia. The international capital market and operators had extensive experience of similar investments in the railway sector, major public works, or other utilities. There was a perception of minimal political risks associated with these investments. Finally, the electricity sector experienced a very rapid innovation rhythm, typical of technological bubbles, and the rapid diffusion and adoption of innovations.

This model could be easily replicated in different geographies, in Lisbon or Constantinople, in Barcelona or Buenos Aires, explaining the proliferation of initiatives with the same agents in different countries and cities over the late nineteenth and early twentieth centuries. These early holdings and consortia were a conduit for foreign investment, but they rarely created stable multinational enterprises running utilities in foreign countries. Their participants were more interested in the engineering, manufacturing orders, financial revenues from the project phase, coupled with revenues from a portfolio investment.

Electric holdings: the face of the multinational enterprise in electric utilities

These consortia and investment firms in electricity had evident fragilities. They seemed much more devoted to serial projects, without entering into the actual process of management. They shared the characteristics of similar ventures for railway construction, mostly targeting the earnings obtained during the construction phase (Silva 2014: 727). Investment firms and consortia were more interested in getting the concession and constructing the power station, infrastructure of transmission, lighting, and traction, with the inherent equipment orders and engineering fees, as well as the underwriting fees and other earnings associated with the financial side of the business. The operation of the firm was beyond their strategic aims. They remained inherently unstable as a management block for long-term investments, as contemporaneous businessmen acknowledged (Heineman, 1931; Horn 1936).

The transformation of former electrical holdings into actual multinational firms addressed the fragility and short-termism of the entrepreneurial initiatives based on investment trusts. Holding is a catch-all term and with vague conceptual foundations, as economists like Bonbright and Means (1932), and businessmen, like Heineman, head of Sofina, recognized at the time. It could mean an organizational form similar to an investment trust, mostly dedicated to portfolio investments (Nelles 2003: 14). In other instances, the same designation was typical of multinational enterprises, taking over and controlling direct investments (Paquier 2001). Heinemann signals well this conceptual looseness ("a certain investment trust is named holding, and a holding is called trust," 1931: 9; also Hausman *et al.* 2008: 55). For Heinemann, the distinctive element of the holding is the control over the management of the firm, distinct from the portfolio investment typical of investment trusts ("the holding's purpose is to manage firms, not a portfolio," 1931: 10). The leader of Sofina emphasizes the role of the holding in managing the utility, keeping its autonomy but creating a pool of engineering and consulting services provided by the holding and coordinating different utilities. In some cases, the organizational form had a low, flatter, hierarchy. In other cases, it created a pyramid structure to maximize control over the affiliates (Morck 2005; Bonbright and Means 1932: 18–20, 147–8).

Manufacturing and financial interests led the initial establishment of electric holdings in the mid-1890s, but they acquired a life of their own. For instance, Sofina was a Belgian holding created by an electric manufacturer, the German UEG. Spotting investment opportunities continued to be the basis for its entrepreneurial activity. After signaling a favorable opportunity, Sofina organized a block of external investors, including financial intermediaries for the underwriting of securities in capital markets and the manufacturing firm(s) for supplying the equipment. The engineering talent for project design and management resources for supporting the operation were in-house capabilities.

These functions remained similar to consortia or investment firms. The novelty came from the investment's longer time horizon, as well as the internal capabilities in management and engineering. These holding firms were interested in garnering the revenues from the project management phase. But they also wanted to gain the profits from operations, as well as secure long-term fees for providing technical and management services. Sometimes – as in the case of Sofina – they started with a logic closer to a portfolio investment. Rapidly they evolved to a stable multinational endeavor to launch and control the operation of electric utilities.

The creation of electrical holdings provided a long-term orientation to foreign investments. They protected the manufacturers from the hazards of operating the utilities abroad, without renouncing the privileged access to foreign markets for supplying electrical equipment. They merged the entrepreneurial and venture creation ability of the first investment trusts with long-term multinational operation.

Countries like Belgium or Switzerland shared similar advantages for hosting firms with this double entrepreneurial and multinational function: neutral, with advantageous fiscal and company legislation as well as sophisticated financial institutions and integrated into the multinational networks of finance (Segreto 1994: 163; Hertner 1987: 343).

Besides Germany, the other major pole of technological innovation and entrepreneurial activity was the United States, where electric holdings developed later (Bonbright and Means 1932: 91).[1] The creation of holdings in the USA followed a similar pattern but a different chronology from continental Europe: they combined the interests of manufacturing firms (General Electric or Westinghouse, for instance), banks (Morgan House, Drexel, Bonbright), engineering firms, and electric utilities into financial devices to drive investment in utilities (Hausman and Neufeld 1990, 2004). The holding structure had showed its adaptive potential to the specificities of the electricity industry in the American domestic market before expanding overseas. Electric Bond & Share Co. created in 1905 by General Electric, is an earlier example of an electric holding. At the beginning it was mostly a financial vehicle to transform General Electric's portfolio of equity and bonds in different utility companies into marketable securities, evolving first to create holdings in domestic market and only expanding abroad later (Hughes 1983: 396; Hausman and Neufeld 1997; Schröter 2006).

Electric utility holdings in the American energy domestic market developed rapidly during the 1920s; by the early 1930s they controlled about 80 percent of total electric power generation in the USA (Bonbright and Means 1932: 94–5; Neufeld 2016: 97). The American holdings were less internationally oriented than their European counterparts, as the American domestic market was so large. The data collected by Bonbright and Means (1932: 103) indicate that only American & Foreign Power Company (led by General Electric) was involved in major international expansion into South America and Asia. Others had some investments across the border with Canada. The other American holding encompassing major foreign investment was Utilities Power and Light Corporation, a Chicago-based firm not even mentioned by Bonbright and Means but with interests in Britain (Hausman *et al.* 2008: 187).

Canada was another major pole for the creation of multinational holdings, once again later than in Continental Europe. The same fiscal and legal advantages enjoyed by Belgium and Switzerland explain the role played by Canada in clustering multinational activity in the electric industry, first through free standing companies in South America and later hosting holding companies in the 1920s (Hausman *et al.* 2008: 167–8). The Canadian holdings were in fact conduits for European and American entrepreneurs' multinational investment (Nelles 2003).

It is difficult to provide a quantitative and diachronic perspective on the role of these holdings in the international electricity business. The situation prior to World War I might be different from the late 1920s and 1930s, when one may rely on data collected by Schröter (2006). Two holdings stand out in terms of assets (see Table 21.1): Sofina and American & Foreign Power Company. The case of Sofina is the most impressive. It presided over several other holdings on Table 21.1, as Brazilian Traction, Light & Power Co., Chade, Barcelona Traction, Light & Power Co., Mexican Light & Power Co., and Sidro, controlling almost 50 percent of total assets in the table. Moreover, those 22 holdings clustered in a bimodal distribution, corroborating the different chronologies in the creation of international holdings on the two sides of the Atlantic. The oldest were set up around 1900, representing the forerunners of the electric holding in the first-moving European countries, as well as some prior free-standing companies which later evolved into international holdings (the Canadian firms created before World War I). The second peak is in the 1920s, when the American holdings emerged.

The holding firm prevailed as the most important business model for multinational activity in electric utilities until the mid-twentieth century, when the industry started to favor national networks and public ownership (Hausman *et al.* 2008: ch. 6; Millward 2005). It adapted to deal with two inherent characteristics of the electrical industry: the large sunk costs and the intrinsically stand-alone operation of electrical utilities. The second characteristic is shared by other activities (mining, public works, railways, and other utilities) where the attributes of on-site operation do not lead to the emergence of multinationals out of operating companies, as was the case of the classical multinationals in manufacturing activity (Casson 1998: 100).

The holding firms created across Europe and North America could maintain the inherent domestic and stand-alone characteristics of the electric utilities and, simultaneously, devise an adaptable business form to blend financing with engineering and management knowledge. The previously cited text on holdings by the head of Sofina, D. Heineman (1931: 10–11), clearly identified two fundamental functions: the use of financial capabilities and knowledge transfer (also Bonbright and Means 1932: 103ff.). Other functions are also mentioned, such as the procurement of equipment and raw materials over time, accounting, financial and technical consulting, but the financial and knowledge transfers are fundamental to understand the peculiar role assumed by these multinational firms. Kogut and Zander (1993) discussed multinationals as firms specializing in difficult to codify knowledge transfers. The emphasis on technical knowledge and site-specific engineering as major characteristics of electric holdings as multinationals goes well with this definition.

Investment trusts, consortia, and early holdings shared with the clusters of promoters of free-standing companies the same hands-off management perspective. In contrast, in the electric holdings the fee-based engineering, financial, and procurement services provided to utilities abroad coupled with hands-on management. This element of strategic and operational control is, in fact, another characteristic defining a multinational, besides knowledge and capital transfers to foreign locations.

Table 21.1 Foreign assets of electric utilities holdings, 1929 and 1937, in current US dollars

Name	Country of registration	Year	Assets 1929	Assets 1937
American & Foreign Power Co.	USA	1924	756	535
Société Financière de Transports et des Entreprises Industrielles SA (Sofina)	Belgium	1898	420	399
Brazilian Traction, Light & Power Co.	Canada	1912	369	426
Comp. Générale d'Entreprises Electriques et Industrielles SA (Electrobel)	Belgium	1929	194	218
Compania Hispano-Americana de Electricidad SA (CHADE)	Spain	1920	139	38
Barcelona Traction, Light & Power Co.	Canada	1911	116	190
The Mexican Light & Power Co.	Canada	1902	101	110
Electrotrust	Belgium	1928	50	98
Motor	Switzerland	1895	46	45
Soc. Internationale d'Energie Hydro-Electrique SA (Sidro)	Belgium	1923	44	91
Gesellschaft für Elektrische Unternehmungen (Gesfürel)	Germany	1894	43	63
Compagnie Financière d'Exploitations Hydro-Electriques SA (Hydrofina)	Belgium	1928	–	53
Italian Superpower Corp.	USA	1928	39	32
European Electric Corp.	Canada	1930	–	28
Schweizerisch-Amerikanische Elekrizitäts-Gesellschaft AG	Switzerland	1928	27	21
Bank für elektrische Unternehmungen AG (Elektrobank)	Switzerland	1895	23	30
International Power Co.	Canada	1926	15	21
Schweizerische Gesellschaft für elektrische Industrie AG (Indelec)	Switzerland	1896	11	11
Elektrische Licht und Kraftanlagen AG	Germany	1897	10	19
Société Financière Italo-Suisse	Switzerland	1902	9	14
Société Générale pour l'Industrie Electrique	Switzerland	1927	7	12
Société Centrale pour l'Industrie Electrique	France	1909	4	5

Source: Adapted from Schröter (2006: table 1).

Turning points and de-globalization: World War I and the Great Depression

Before the outbreak of World War I, foreign investment had turned electrification into a global business through multinational firms and international finance on a huge, but very uneven, scale. During the conflict, government intervention increased and ensured that energy supply became a priority, accelerating the development of hydroelectricity in European peripheries, where coal shortages had raised the energy prices (Hausman *et al.* 2008: ch. 4). In Britain, the USA, and Germany, governments also rationalized the production of electricity, expanding power capacity and transmission lines at a regional level. Furthermore, government involvement, stemming from growing nationalism, led to antiforeigner legislation. The authorities of belligerent countries subjected to monitoring overseas companies and imposed restrictions on capital exports. German authorities put under their control Belgian firms and intended to confiscate the assets belonging to French and English corporations. In turn, the UK and USA took over German investment in electric utilities, although it was small. In the USA, licenses, financial incentives, and support to build waterpower utilities were restricted to its own citizens. The Russian revolutionary government became the first state to nationalize all foreign properties, including electric utilities.

The war had deep consequences for global electrification. On the one hand, some of the key actors of foreign electrification were replaced. Electricity businesses abroad had ceased to be profitable during the war. In the European theater of hostilities but also in neutral countries, utility companies suffered from important imbalances between declining revenues and increasing operating costs, aggravated by currency depreciations during the early post-war. In the aftermath, getting supplies to the subsidiaries continued straggling the businesses for some years. Moreover, the Treaty of Versailles ratified the takeovers of German possessions abroad, as Keynes warned (1920: 37), using precisely the example of DUEG, the German electricity holding. Siemens and AEG lost a large part of their investment in Europe, Latin America, and Africa. German interests in the Swiss Electrobank and Indelec decreased and the former had to be redesigned while Motor coped with financial difficulties and had to merge with Columbus in 1923. Thus, an opportunity of entering sizable markets to other investors arose. US holdings' interests grew in Italy first and Latin American in the late 1920s, through American & Foreign Power Co. (Hausman *et al.* 2008: 145).

On the other hand, there were continuities. As early as 1919, German manufacturers decided to intensify their investments through Swiss or Belgian holding companies – e.g., Elektrobank, Sofina – and registered new distribution companies abroad. As the examples of the Iberian companies – Barcelona Traction Light and Power and CRGE of Lisbon – showed, German control was disguised by means of the openness to Iberian capital and the leading role of third countries. Shortages of capital due to Mark depreciation and the fear of confiscation of German shareholdings abroad as compensation for war reparations led to AEG selling DUEG-CATE, the Argentinian electric company. A Spanish banking consortium purchased it and the CHADE was registered as a Spanish company with interests in Argentina, Chile, and Uruguay. It soon became clear, however, that Sofina was backstage and German manufacturers were still involved in all contracts for the company's projects (Lanciotti and Bartolomé 2014).

After the war, governments were reluctant to abandon their commitment to rationalizing energy markets in general and electricity networks in particular. The takeover of German interests during the conflict enabled some governments to nationalize electric utilities and grids after the war. Particularly in Eastern Europe, takeovers eliminated the German presence, while in South America, Belgian, French, and British investment substituted for German interests. However, Britain had serious difficulties in restoring its position as the world's greatest electrical financial center and one of the most important registration places of foreign utility companies. Even the former almighty Canadian group started to withdraw from some markets while both US foreign investments in electric utilities and US finance acquired prominence in the 1920s. Monetary risk summed up political risk after the World War I (Coppersmith 2003). As Nelles (2003) has pointed out, foreign investment in electric companies was particularly hazardous in the aftermath of the war, due to currency exchange instability and the difficulty in restoring anything close to the fixed exchange rates of the pre-war gold standard. The companies attempted to keep the rates of foreign exchange of capital flowing under control in both senses and private electric holdings prevailed as the most suitable means to lead the process to rationalize electricity business operations during the interwar period. Sofina, the British Whitehall and the Canadian Securities (derived from the Toronto group), and Electric Bond and Share were still on the spot, but at the end of the 1920s new US companies and capital went abroad in a very tangled web of corporate structures, particularly through the American & Foreign Power Company. Nothing was ever the same again in overseas electrification after the war and US holdings featured the formidable expansion of electricity during these years.

The aftermath of the Great Depression revealed a divergence from other industries (Schröter 2006). Compared to the rest of the economy, the demand for electricity decreased very little in the United States and Europe while no significant effect is observed in most parts of the world. During the late 1920s, electricity had become a necessity for manufacturing, public lighting, and households. In spite of the differences in consumption per capita in 1932 and household electrification, the percentage of users of electricity in industrialized countries was above 90 percent (Table 21.2). The electricity market was broadened thanks to the increasing demand of new home appliances, advertised by the utility companies. Furthermore, the electricity industry had concentrated and rationalized, whilst internationalization was pursued. Thus, after the stock market crash, the electricity business was perceived as mature and the electricity companies as sound. Although the most ambitious projects, such as the Egyptian dam in Aswan, were promptly cancelled, the flow of overseas investment continued, and new actors emerged.

In 1930, foreign investments even intensified. As the prices of electricity securities fell, the American market opened to foreign investors on the cheap, while US holdings (Insull, Electric Bond & Share, and United Corporation), the British Whitehall, and some banks sought business abroad, most of them through loans guaranteed by governments like Italy and Spain. New actors also joined the venture, the Americans (American Foreign Power Corp., Amforp, subsidiary of Bond & Share) and the European Electric Corp. (EEIC), registered in Canada. Their funds were addressed to the peripheral countries, in Latin America and the south of Europe, where they all made sizable investments.

In the spring of 1931, the sector was perceived as vulnerable when US banks withdrew large amounts of money from Italian companies and the former Berlin City Elec. Co., which heavily relied on American loans. Furthermore, the crisis struck Latin America where sharp declines in exchange rates were experienced.

Political risks matched financial threat in 1932. Governments of FDI host countries discouraged foreign investment, primarily hampering the overseas transfer of dividends in a new era of capital controls. After 1933, foreigners with holdings in German securities lost not only their interest payments but also any chance of withdrawing their investments. Second, the new political setting favored the regulation of electricity prices and new taxations, like the Laval government in France. The diminishing profits perspective did not suit the new governmental requirements of electricity companies: huge amounts of additional investments in the form of both enlargement and densification of networks to cover rural areas and enhancing the security of supply of the whole electricity system. Foreign companies were seen with mistrust and the peril of expropriation against the will of the owners was embodied in some legislation. Accordingly, Gesfürel transferred its stake-holdings in CHADE to a Swiss subsidiary to avoid German nationalistic controls. At the same time, Electrobank diminished its holdings in the German electricity sector, whereas in Italy foreign investment was mostly rescued by IRI, the Italian state holding, in 1933.

When the Insull empire collapsed in 1932 (Neufeld 2016: 105–8), it became clear how the largely pyramid structures of holdings were at risk, exacerbated according to their degree of international exposure. As Hausman *et al.* (2008) put it, the electricity companies were caught up in these problems. Both American and British financiers increased domestic investments at the expense of overseas ones. However, as Schröter (2006) emphasized, electrification continued being a basic demand and most international holding companies were tied up by long-run investments. Thus,

Table 21.2 Some data on world electrification in 1932

	Canada	USA	Sweden	UK	Germany	France	Italy	Argentina	Spain	Portugal
Output per inhabitant	1,516	919	792	369	365	325	245	142	136	41
Percentage of users of electricity	n.a.	n.a.	91.7	97.4	87.7	97.6	93.4	n. a.	88	90
Percentage of electrification of households	n.a.	n.a.	84.5	43.7	75.3	93.6	73.5	n.a.	n.a.	n.a.

Sources: *Annuaire statistique de la Société des Nations* (1932–1933, 1933) Geneva: Bruno Seeger; El Consumo de Electricidad para alumbrado en Europa (1933) Madrid: Gráfica Administrativa.

they adopted a new set of survival strategies. First, the investments were diversified and the utility companies favored the reinvesting of profits; second, the concentration processes of large firms were reinforced; third, the collaboration with host country's entrepreneurs became a usual practice in order to avoid any kind of discrimination in concessions. Thus, Elektrobank diversified its portfolio of holdings in Europe and in the USA, where all the stakes were portfolio investments. Indelec expanded in Eastern Europe as did Siemens, but some residual investments in France remained in the 1930s whereas Motor-Columbus concentrated its interests in Switzerland and the Empain group in France. The difficulties of Sidro and Electrobel increased once the autarchic policies discouraged foreign investment in the south of Europe. The survivors focused on peripheral markets, particularly those in Eastern Europe and South American cities, like Motor-Columbus and particularly Sofina. This company remained a global business notwithstanding the most difficult environment. It transferred CHADE to a new Luxembourg company, SODEC, and reduced its holdings in both France and Turkey whereas obtained sizable ones in the USA.

The major change was the progressive trend to reverse the balance between foreign direct and portfolio investment in multinational holdings. Although Heineman maintained the hope of this crisis as transitory and opted for an increase of direct investments, most holding companies followed the opposite path. They maintained sizable stakes as international investors (Hausman *et al.* 2008: 219, Table 5.1) but more as portfolio investments than direct investments. Investors reduced their foreign exposure focused on a bunch of peripheral markets and reduced the number of their employees, in a clear sign that they were singling portfolio investment out of the Modigliani–Miller two poles. At the end of the 1930s the ties within and outside the electric multinationals had loosened.

Conclusion

This study on the Protean faces of international business in electric utilities privileged substantive and nuanced approaches to the taxonomies of foreign investment in the industry offered by Hausman *et al.* (2008: ch. 2) or Nelles (2003: 4). Behind many of the vehicles for investing abroad were very often the same manufacturing firms and entrepreneurs, banking houses and engineering firms, lawyers and politicians as brokers. The emphasis attributed to clusters of entrepreneurs and investors in the literature is consistent with the porosity revealed by the organizational forms and the human agency behind these investment vehicles. Hausman and his co-authors argued forcefully for the similarity between holdings and serial free-standing companies emerging frequently from the same clusters of investors (2008: 63). In fact, investment trusts and the early holdings consolidated in the multinational electric holding the informal alliances of manufacturers and banks formerly promoting foreign stand-alone investments through free-standing companies. The informal alliances did not disappear with the emergence of holdings and investment trusts in the mid-1890s. The consortia created for stand-alone investments in electric utilities (see the aforementioned examples of Barcelona or Constantinople) replicated those informal clusters of investors.

This chapter did not follow the presentation of divergent styles of foreign investment, separating German from American, Canadian from Belgian initiatives (Hertner and Nelles 2007; Nelles 2003). Indeed, the Canadian financial syndicates, so active in Latin America or in the second technological wave in electrifying Barcelona, replicated the consortia created in Europe by Swiss or Belgian investment trusts, German or Swiss manufacturers and banks from different nationalities since the 1890s. Once more: these large consortia of investors were not a novelty. The electric industry followed similar solutions for investing abroad in other capital-intensive and stand-alone foreign operations. Even the contractual agreement among the members of the Canadian syndicates to pool the common stock in a syndicate manager for a specified period of time appeared as a common solution in other national contexts and industries. To sum up, the entire range of organizational solutions was used irrespective of national affiliations or styles.

Jones and Khanna (2006: 459) warn against the fallacy of the new in international business studies. The variety of institutional conduits for promoting business ventures abroad in the electric industry belies the idea that late twentieth-century globalization created most of the brand-new and variegated forms of international business. In the short period of time covered by this chapter, different organizational models materialized, intertwined, coalesced, and evolved to foster new forms, sometimes reminiscent of current born-global firms or the flexible arrangements in joint ventures and business alliances.

The fallacy of the new should also not haunt the cross-industry comparison of institutional models in international business. Firm structures often seen as innovations instead emerged from adapting and invigorating business forms already tried in other industries (railways, other utilities, or public works). The organizational solutions experimented in the electric utilities addressed management tensions in the operation of the industry. These tensions heighten when running electric utilities as a result of the peculiar economic and technological conditions emphasized in the first section of the chapter. However, other industries faced comparable strains: stand-alone operations, site-specificity, capital intensity with high sunk costs, or the need to experiment on pricing to enlarge the consumer basis. A portfolio of organizational solutions to deal with these tensions was already available in the late nineteenth-century global economy. Therefore, the institutional conduits for foreign investment in electricity moved along an array of existing solutions: free-standing companies, formal and informal consortia of investors for capital intensive projects, investment trusts formalizing these alliances, manufacturing firms conveying abroad the goods or services provided in the home country.

Note

1 For a different perspective, emphasizing the pioneering role of Electric Bond & Share Co. and its manager, S. Z. Mitchell, in the creation of the electric holding company, see Hirsh (2003: 23).

Bibliography

Armstrong, Christopher and Nelles, Henry V. (1988): *Southern Exposure: Canadian Promoters in Latin America and the Caribbean, 1896–1930*. Toronto: University of Toronto Press.
Bitsch, Marie-Thérèse (1994): *La Belgique entre la France et l'Allemagne: 1905–1914*. Paris: Publications de la Sorbonne.
Bonbright, James C. and Means, Gardiner C. (1932): *The Holding Company, Its Public Significance and Its Regulation*. New York: McGraw-Hill.
Carlson, W. Bernard (1991): *Innovation as a Social Process: Elihu Thomson and the Rise of General Electric, 1870–1900*. New York: Cambridge University Press.
Casson, Mark (1998): "An Economic Theory of the Free-Standing Company," in Mira Wilkins and Harm Schröter (eds.), *The Free-Standing Company in the World Economy, 1830–1996*. Oxford: Oxford University Press, pp. 99–128.
Chick, Martin (2007): *Electricity and Energy Policy in Britain, France and the United States since 1945*. Cheltenham: Edward Elgar.
Coppersmith Jonathan C. (2003): "When Worlds Collide: Government and Electrification, 1892–1939," *Business and Economic History On-Line*, 2003/1, https://thebhc.org/sites/default/files/Coopersmith_0.pdf (accessed on April 9, 2019).
David, Paul A. (1992): "Heroes, Herds and Hysteresis in Technological History: Thomas Edison and the 'Battle of the Systems' Reconsidered," *Industrial and Corporate Change*, vol. 1, issue 1, pp. 129–80.
Devine, Warren D. (1990): "Early Developments in Electroprocessing: New Products, New Industries," in Sam Schurr, Calvin C. Burwell, Warren D. Devine, Jr., and Sidney Sonenblum (eds.), *Electricity in the American Economy: Agent of Technological Progress*. New York: Greenwood, pp. 77–98.

Dunsheat, Percy (1962): *A History of Electrical Engineering*. London: Faber & Faber.

Giannetti, Renato (1988): "Tecnologie di rete e intervento pubblico nel sistema elettrico italiano (1883–1996)," *Rivista di Storia Economica*, vol. 14, issue 2, pp. 127–160.

Hausman, William J. and Neufeld, John L. (1990): "The Efficiency of the US Electric Power Industry and the Rise of the Holding Company in the Early 20th Century," in Monique Trédé (ed.), *Électricité et électrification dans le monde*. Paris: Droz, pp. 307–22.

Hausman, William J. and Neufeld, John L. (1997): "The Rise and Fall of the American & Foreign Power Company: A Lesson from the Past?" *Electricity Journal*, vol. 10, issue 1, January–February, pp. 46–53.

Hausman, William J. and Neufeld, John L. (2004): "The Economics of Electricity Networks and the Evolution of the U.S. Electric Utility Industry, 1882–1935," *Business and Economic History On-Line*, vol. 2, issue 26, www.thebhc.org/sites/default/files/HausmanNeufeld_0.pdf (accessed on April 9, 2019).

Hausman, William J., Hertner, Peter, and Wilkins, Mira (2008): *Global Electrification: Multinational Enterprise and International Finance in the History of Light and Power, 1878–2007*. Cambridge: Cambridge University Press.

Heineman, Dannie (1931): "Rapport du Conseil d'Administration," *Société Financière de Transports et d'Entreprises Industrielles (SOFINA). Deuxième Exercice 1930*. Brussels: Imprimerie Industrielle et Financière.

Hertner, Peter (1986): "Financial Strategies and Adaptation to Foreign Markets: The German Electro-Technical Industry and Its Multinational Activities, 1890s to 1939," in Alice Teichova, Maurice Lévy-Leboyer, and Helga Nussbaum (eds.), *Multinational Enterprise in Historical Perspective*. Cambridge: Cambridge University Press, pp. 145–58.

Hertner, Peter (1987): "Les sociétés financières suisses et le développement de l'industrie électrique jusqu'à la Première Guerre mondiale," in Fabienne Cardot (ed.), *Un siècle d'électricité dans le monde, 1880–1980*. Paris: AHEF-PUF, pp. 341–53.

Hertner, Peter and Nelles Henry V. (2007): "Contrasting Styles of Foreign Investment: A Comparison of the Entrepreneurship, Technology and Finance of German and Canadian Enterprise in Barcelona Electrification," *Revue Économique*, vol. 58, pp. 191–214.

Hirsh, Richard F. (2003): *Technology and Transformation in the American Electric Utility Industry*. Cambridge: Cambridge University Press.

Horn, Max (1936): "Comments," in *Transactions of the Third World Power Conference*, vol. 5. Washington, DC: USGPO.

Hughes, Thomas P. (1983): *Networks of Power Electrification in Western Society, 1880–1930*. Baltimore, MD: Johns Hopkins University Press.

Hughes, Thomas P. (1987): "The Evolution of Large Technological Systems," in Wiebe E. Bijker, Thomas P. Hughes, and Trevor J. Pinch (eds.), *The Social Construction of Technological Systems: New Directions in the Sociology and History of Technology*. Cambridge, MA: MIT Press, pp. 51–82.

Hughes, Thomas P. (1994): "Technological Momentum," in, Leo Marx and Merritt Roe Smith (eds.), *Does Technology Drive History? The Dilemma of Technological Determinism*. Cambridge, MA: MIT Press, pp. 101–14.

Jones, Geoffrey and Khanna, Tarun (2006): "Bringing History (Back) into International Business," *Journal of International Business Studies*, vol. 37, issue 4, pp. 453–68.

Keynes, John M. (1920): *The Economic Consequences of the Peace*. London: Macmillan.

Kogut, Bruce and Zander, Udo (1993): "Knowledge of the Firm and the Evolutionary Theory of the Multinational Corporation," *Journal of International Business Studies*, vol. 24, issue 4, pp. 625–45.

Lanciotti, Norma S. and Bartolomé, I. (2014): "Global Strategies, Differing Experiences: Electricity Companies in Two Late-Industrialising Countries: Spain and Argentina, 1890–1950," *Business History*, vol. 56, pp. 724–45.

Lopes, Teresa Silva, Casson, M., and Jones, G. (2018): "Organizational Innovation in Multinational Enterprise: Internationalization Theory and Business History," *Journal of International Business Studies*. https://doi.org/10.1057/s41267-018-0156-6.

Millward, Robert (2005): *Private and Public Enterprise in Europe: Energy, Telecommunications and Transport, 1830–1990*. Cambridge: Cambridge University Press.

Morck, Randall (ed.) (2005): *A History of Corporate Governance Around the World: Family Business Groups to Professional Managers*. Chicago, IL: University of Chicago Press.

Nelles, Henry V. (2003): "Financing the Development of Foreign-Owned Electrical Systems in the Americas, 1890–1929: First Steps in Comparing European and North American Techniques", *Business and Economic History On-Line*, vol. 1. www.thebhc.org/sites/default/files/Nelles_0.pdf (accessed on April 9, 2019).

Neufeld, John (2016): *Selling Power: Economics, Policy, and Electric Utilities Before 1940*. Chicago, IL and London: University of Chicago Press.

Nye, David E. (2018): *American Illuminations: Urban Lighting, 1800–1920*. Cambridge, MA: MIT Press.

Paquier, Serge (2001): "Swiss Holding Companies from the Mid-Nineteenth Century to the Early 1930s: The Forerunners and Subsequent Waves of Creation," *Financial History Review*, vol. 8, issue 2, pp. 163–82.

Rainieri, Liane (2014): *Dannie Heineman: An Extraordinary Life (1872–1962)*. CreateSpace Independent Publishing Platform, 544 p.

Rosenberg, Nathan (1972): "Factors Affecting the Diffusion of Technology," *Explorations in Economic History*, (Fall), pp. 3–33.

Rosenberg, Nathan (1976): *Perspectives on Technology*. Cambridge, MA: Cambridge University Press.

Rosenberg, Nathan (1994): "Energy-Efficient Technologies: Past and Future Perspectives," in Nathan Rosenberg (ed.), *Exploring the Black Box: Technology, Economics and History*. Cambridge: Cambridge University Press, pp. 161–89.

Schisani, Maria Carmela and Caiazzo, Francesca (2016): "Networks of Power and Networks of Capital: Evidence from a Peripheral Area of the First Globalisation. The Energy Sector in Naples: From Gas to Electricity (1862–1919)," *Business History*, vol. 58, issue 2, pp. 207–43.

Schivelbusch, Wolfgang (1995): *Disenchanted Night: The Industrialization of Light in the Nineteenth Century*. Los Angeles, CA: University of California Press.

Schröter, Harm G. 2006. "Globalization and Reliability: The Fate of Foreign Direct Investment in Electric Power-Supply During the World Economic Crisis, 1929–1939," *Annales historiques de l'électricité*, vol. 1, issue 4, pp. 101–24.

Segreto, Luciano (1987): "Le nuove strategie delle societá finanziarie svizzere perl'industria electtrica (1918–1939)," *Studi Storici*, vol. 4, pp. 861–907.

Segreto, Luciano (1990): "Du 'Made in Germany' au 'Made in Switzerland': Les sociétés financiers suisses pour l'industrie électrique dans l'entre-deux-guerres" in M. Trédé (ed.), *Électricité et électrification dans le monde*. Paris: Droz, pp. 347–68.

Segreto, Luciano (1992a): "Imprenditori e finanzieri," in Giorigio Mori, *Storia dell'industria elettrice in Italia. I. Le origini. 1882–1914*. Roma: Laterza, Vol. II, pp. 249–331.

Segreto, Luciano (1992b): "Elettricità ed economia in Europa," in Giorgio Mori, *Storia dell'industria elettrice in Italia. I. Le origini. 1882–1914*. Roma: Laterza, Vol. II, pp. 696–750.

Segreto, Luciano (1994): "Financing the Electric Industry Worldwide: Strategy and Structure of the Swiss Electric Holding Companies, 1895–1945," *Business and Economic History*, vol. 23, issue 1, pp. 162–75.

Silva, Álvaro Ferreira da (2014): "Organizational Innovation in Nineteenth-Century Railway Investment: Peripheral Countries in a Global Economy," *Business History Review*, vol. 88, issue 4, pp. 709–36.

Thobie, Jacques (1991): "European Banks in the Middle East," in Rondo Cameron and V. I. Bovykin (eds.), *International Banking*. Oxford: Oxford University Press, pp. 406–40.

Utterback, James M. and Abernathy, William J. (1975): "A Dynamic Model of Process and Product Innovation," *Omega*, vol. 3, issue 6, pp. 639–56.

Wilkins, Mira (1970): *The Emergence of Multinational Enterprise: American Business Abroad from the Colonial Era to 1914*. Cambridge, MA: Harvard University Press.

Wilkins, Mira (2009): "The History of Multinational Enterprise," in Alan M. Rugman (ed.), *The Oxford Handbook of International Business*. 2nd ed. Oxford: Oxford University Press, pp. 3–35.

22

HEALTHCARE INDUSTRIES AND SERVICES

Paloma Fernández Pérez

Introduction

According to the Organisation for Economic Co-operation and Development (OECD), "health is determined by a number of factors, one of which is healthcare. Healthcare ... is defined as the combined functioning of public health and personal medical services" (Kelley and Hurst 2006). Healthcare corporations are defined in this chapter, accordingly, as those corporations that manufacture and sell products and services that are used by the public health system and by personal medical services.

Global healthcare corporations are not a homogeneous type of business. They are in fact extremely diverse and include public and private hospitals and clinics, pharmaceutical multinationals, health insurance groups, manufacturers and distributors of hospital equipment and medical supplies, vertically integrated business groups, clinical laboratories, networked consortiums of hospitals and laboratories, medium or large family-controlled firms and groups in highly specialized healthcare niches, and small start-ups with or without the participation of big healthcare groups. This diversity emerged from the combination of a path-dependent co-existence of business typologies and regulatory frameworks. Forbes 2000, Bloomberg, and Nasdaq include as healthcare corporations firms and groups that work in: the pharmaceutical industry; the biotechnology and life sciences; and instruments and medical equipment and services. In some countries, such as Japan or Spain, a single healthcare corporation has branches in some or all of these different industries. In other countries, such as Germany or the United States, healthcare corporations tend to specialize in a single branch, and in the United States vertically integrated businesses dominate.

From the late 1880s to today, global healthcare corporations have been praised as much as they have been condemned. Healthcare companies have contributed to reducing first deadly epidemic infectious diseases, and later chronic diseases, improving life expectancy and our quality of life (Billings 1901: 638). Since the late nineteenth and early twentieth centuries in the most developed economies, and from the 1950s elsewhere (except much of Africa), global public and private healthcare corporations have greatly helped to eradicate or at least control some of the deadliest diseases in human history: the bubonic plague; venereal diseases like syphilis; cholera and infectious diseases of the digestive system; smallpox (before 1900, smallpox killed around 500 million people); yellow fever; tuberculosis; influenza or flu; perinatal complications;

tetanus; malaria; leprosis; measles; pertussis; ebola; avian influenza; meningitis; heart diseases; autoimmune diseases; neuronal diseases; and mental illness.[1]

Despite the positive contributions of life sciences and healthcare corporations, newspapers have often published about their darker side: their mistakes, abuses, and scandals, particularly regarding their methods and their prices. Sometimes it was the uncertainty about new methods and drugs, and sometimes it was criminal behavior, that caused the poisoning and death of thousands of persons through drug or medicine experiments and trials. Such scandals started when large healthcare corporations began to globalize in the early 1900s. Thus, since the early twentieth century, health authorities in the United States, and in Europe, and (a bit later) in Asia and Latin America, slowly regulated quality control processes and, in some countries, set maximum prices for healthcare products.

Whether life-saving champions, speculators, or criminals, healthcare companies and business groups are business organizations, and therefore have diverse and changing structures and strategies. These structures and strategies both function for individual companies and for the industry as a whole through powerful oligopolies, interest groups, and lobbies. As such, healthcare corporations can be studied by business historians.

The following text is organized in four sections. The first identifies the leading internationalized healthcare companies headquartered in developed economies; I conclude that most of them were founded a century ago, and are enduring examples of the resilience and strength of the pioneering first-movers and their control of today's global markets in pharmaceutical products, biomedical products, and medical equipment. A second section explains this endurance and some of its consequences using an analytical model that combines four driving explanatory forces from the supply and demand side of the industries as well as broader social and entrepreneurial forces. A third section outlines three of business history's most relevant contributions to the heterogeneous scientific disciplines that have studied the creation of world healthcare systems and industries. Business history scholarship has, first, created a chronology of the industry's evolution since the mid-nineteenth century. Second, business historians have traced the complexity and variety of connections of industries, companies, and entrepreneurs within a broader social, economic, and institutional environment. Third, business historians have provided in-depth case studies that explore the dynamic path-dependent construction of the myriad healthcare systems that exist today. A fourth section presents very briefly some examples of this variety of healthcare systems and the diverse interplay between public and private initiatives that have shaped and shape the business of healthcare. The conclusion summarizes some of the key topics and debates about the dynamic evolution and origins of the diversity of the global healthcare systems and players.

Global corporations in the businesses of healthcare

Table 22.1 of leading healthcare listed corporations in stock market indexes for the year 2016 shows that most of them were founded before 1930.

Only a few companies were created after World War II during the golden age of capitalism or after 1980. This chronology confirms many of Chandler's (2005) observations about how the largest chemical and pharmaceutical corporations that pioneered the industry have endured, and created powerful barriers to entry for new entrants. Most of these resilient corporations have their headquarters in countries whose economies pioneered advanced knowledge and businesses in the chemical, pharmaceutical, electromechanical, and insurance industries around the turn of the twentieth century, when two revolutions took place in those countries: the therapeutic and the managerial.

Table 22.1 Internationalization of large healthcare companies in selected countries, 2017 (market capitalization of leading national stock market indexes, in billion US dollars 2017)

Nationality	Company	Sales (USD bn)	Employees	Market cap (USD bn)	Founded/year started	Subsidiaries (number of countries)	Internationalization started
USA	Johnson & Johnson	71.94	126,400	335.67	1886	60	1924
Switzerland	Roche Holding AG	50.40	94,052	222.35	1896	100	1897–1910
USA	Pfizer Inc.	52.82	96,500	204.45	1849	14	1950
Switzerland	Novartis AG	48.52	118,393	198.22	1996	155	
USA	Merck & Co. Inc.	39.81	68,000	182.50	1891	140	1912
USA	UnitedHealth Group Inc.	184.84	230,000	160.46	1977	125	–
France	Sanofi	36.36	115,631	112.90	2004	100	–
UK	GlaxoSmithKline Plc	42.15	101,255	101.51	2001	100	1891[1]
Germany	Bayer AG	50.29	115,200	98.66	1863	78	1881–1914
UK	AstraZeneca Plc	23.00	59,700	73.85	1999	100	
Germany	Merck KGaA	15.84	50,414	47.81	1668	66	1887
Germany	Fresenius SE & Co. KGaA	31.27	232,873	45.07	1912[2]	100	1955
Japan	Takeda Pharmaceutical Co. Ltd.	14.67	31,168	36.36	1781	40	1914
Japan	Astellas Pharma Inc.	11.14	17,217	28.99	1923[3]	50	1986
Italy	Luxottica Group SpA	9.77	78,933	25.20	1961	150	1981
Spain	Grifols SA	4.35	14,890	14.23	1940	26	1960
Italy	Recordati Industria Chimica e Farmaceutica S.P.A.	1.24	4,116	6.69	1926	31	1961
Sweden	Getinge AB	3.43	15,500	4.05	1904	40	1960

Source: Own elaboration. For market capitalization, leading stock market index in each country (Dow Jones for the US; SMI for Switzerland; CAC40 for France; FTSE100 for the UK; DAX30 for Germany; NIKKEI225 for Japan; MIB40 for Italy; IBEX35 for Spain; OMXS30 for Sweden).

Notes

1 Plough Court pharmacy established (1715).
2 Opening the Hirsch Pharmacy: 1462.
3 Yamanouchi Yakuhin Shokai(1923); Fujisawa Shoten (1894); Astellas Pharma (2005).

Table 22.1 uses leading stock market indexes of the United States, Switzerland, France, the United Kingdom, Germany, Japan, Sweden, and Spain to show that the top 11 companies in the healthcare businesses born before 1930 had their headquarters in the United States and Germany (three in each), in Japan (two), and in three small economies of North and Southern Europe (Italy, Sweden, Switzerland, one each). Three companies that started business between 1930 and 1980 were created in the United States, Italy, and Spain. The four largest healthcare companies created after 1980 are headquartered in Sweden, France, and two in the United Kingdom.

Seven of the 12 large healthcare corporations in Table 22.1 started operations abroad before World War II. These corporations were headquartered in the USA, Germany, UK, and Japan. The other five first internationalized after 1945 and have headquarters in the USA, Germany, Japan, Italy, and Spain.

The table confirms findings from available business history (Chandler 2005; Galambos and Sturchio 1998) suggesting that the leading economies of the second technological revolution pioneered the creation of global healthcare giants and global healthcare markets, and established powerful economic and scientific barriers to entry that very few healthcare corporations could surmount after 1945. Also, the inclusion in this table of other countries not often considered by North American scholars shows that, next to the pioneering giants in the pioneering industrial powers, there have been understudied or relatively ignored small or medium firms in late industrialized countries like Spain and Italy, in some specialized market niches in which they were able to grow and become competitive global champions.

Driving forces in the evolution of global healthcare players

The sample of corporations analyzed in the previous section are only the tip of the iceberg. The evolution of global healthcare markets and corporations over the last 200 years saw a complex long-term interplay between four driving forces: (1) healthcare demand; (2) healthcare supply; (3) the actions of social forces and public institutions to reduce inequalities in healthcare access; (4) entrepreneurship.

The first most important driving force has probably been the expansion of *healthcare demand*, first in the most developed economies, due to the increase in the purchasing power of the world population and the increase of life expectancy at birth. The expansion of healthcare demand fostered the slow transition from the old tradition of receiving informal non-regulated medical attention at home, to the increasing concentration of medical attention in regulated and controlled centers and institutions. This transition was a major revolution that occurred parallel to processes of demographic transition and urban growth. It started in the interwar period in large industrial cities such as Paris, Berlin, London, New York, and Tokyo, that experienced fast population growth (usually linked to an accelerated influx of migrants). This slowly expanded after the 1950s into rural areas with low density populations and into regions of the world with a weak and less regulated healthcare system.

Connected to increased demand was the second driving force of an evolving *healthcare supply* of products and services. Increased supply was intertwined with two parallel events: the accumulation of technological and scientific human capital in the life sciences; and the growth in scale and scope of companies able to manufacture and commercialize such innovations in domestic and foreign markets. From the nineteenth century until the 1980s, healthcare supply centers, scientists, and corporations have concentrated physically often in local or regional healthcare districts around Paris, London, Berlin, Harvard, New York, San Francisco, Buenos Aires, Mexico DF, Tokyo, Osaka, Geneva, Buenos Aires, or Barcelona. After the 1980s, the forces of globalization disseminated and reduced the territorial basis of those districts, favoring the global connections of distant healthcare supply forces in the world, and creating global clusters of healthcare between headquarters and subsidiaries as today is the case in the Siemens Group in medical equipment, and the Grifols Group in biomedicine and diagnostic equipment. In these leading global groups, cross-border globalized consolidation strategies are developed in close connection with strategies of national coordination with providers and clients by local management teams. Global value chains are essential for global healthcare clusters, connecting: (a) subsidiaries in regions of the world supplying good quality raw material; (b) subsidiaries in regions of the world with highly qualified human capital; (c) regions of the world with expanding markets; and (d) old metropolitan hubs of the world that concentrate abundant and varied supply of financial resources, and dynamic markets of intangible resources (patents, licenses, brands). One well-known example of the construction of global value chains is the case of the Grifols corporation, or the Almirall and Ferrer groups (Fernández Pérez *et al.* 2017; Fernández Pérez 2017).

A third major driving force has been the actions *of social groups, associations*, and *public institutions*. In some countries like the United States, United Kingdom, Switzerland, France, and Germany, locally or regionally embedded philanthropic individuals and associations pushed for better healthcare until World War I. A transnational approach started from the late 1880s and the interwar years with global initiatives aimed at disseminating and transferring innovation in healthcare knowledge: the International Health Commission of the Rockefeller Foundation founded in 1913 with programs in 80 countries; the Red Cross founded in 1863; the League of Nations Health Committee in 1922, and the International Hospital Association created in 1929. After World War II, these non-profit networks expanded with globalized institutions like the World Health Organization in 1948, UNICEF, and private foundations focused on healthcare initiatives as in the Bill and Melinda Gates Foundation from the United States, the Li Foundation in China, or the Center Esther Koplowitz for Biomedical Research in Spain.

Finally, *entrepreneurship* has shaped the form of the healthcare corporations, with great diversity in ownership and management. Bad practices may kill people, so owners, managers, and all employees in a firm must pay special attention to reducing health risks. Entrepreneurship, as startup entrepreneurs in healthcare with innovative ideas, was the driving force behind the first modern private clinics and hospitals in the United States, Japan, Germany, France, Spain, Argentina, or Mexico, during the last two decades of the nineteenth century and first decades of the twentieth century (Fernández and Sabaté 2016; Fernández 2017). Entrepreneurship, as entrepreneurial initiatives for funding, has been very important to sponsor and organize modern large public hospitals in the first half of the twentieth century in those countries like the Memorial Sloan Kettering Cancer Center in New York, or the Sant Pau Hospital in Barcelona. The biographies of founders and managers of innovative healthcare companies have stories of sacrifices and personal losses or suffering, when a new treatment or a new method of diagnosis was tried by an enthusiast healthcare entrepreneur in his/her own body or in the bodies of relatives, sometimes with fatal effects. César Comas Llabería, the pioneer of x-rays in Spain in 1896, died from the effects of radiation, for example (Portolés 2010; Sinca 2009).

The evolution of each of these four driving forces has varied dramatically around the world, creating path-dependent forces that explain the strengths and weaknesses of national healthcare systems, the rise and decline of healthcare corporations, and the inequalities in social access to healthcare products and services. There have been diverse typologies of national health systems, characterized by a dynamic and varied, often changing, relationship between the private and the public initiative (and power) in the provision of sanitary services and products to the population, a relationship often determined by the changing capacity of the state to encourage and use taxes for health spending with or without criteria of social equal access to healthcare. Depending on the equilibrium of such powers, there exists in the world different typologies of healthcare provision with more or less private initiatives. Where more private initiative has been allowed in the provision of national healthcare in the last two centuries, as in the United States or Japan, scholars usually find more large private corporations in the life insurance industry, the pharmaceutical and drug industries, the distribution of drugs, the construction of hospitals, and the provision of healthcare services, with subsidiaries abroad. Where less private initiative has been allowed, as in China, France, Australia, or Cuba, or Sweden, researchers usually find large national organizations manufacturing or distributing products and services, and fewer global makers of the healthcare industries. The most abundant typologies are mixed, with a combination of private (national, foreign) and public (governmental and non-governmental) initiatives fluctuating in the last century–and-a-half, as in Southern Europe, Latin America, Africa, and Asia.

Business history of healthcare corporations: an approach to major research directions

There is a vast bibliography about hospitals, and biographies about medical or pharmaceutical entrepreneurs, but a more limited number of monographs and studies about the history of healthcare corporations and their internationalization in the last century-and-a-half. There are a few overviews of recent published research on hospitals from a business history approach (Donzé 2005). Most research has focused on the financing of healthcare, the history of scientific and medical discoveries and technologies, and the history of the chemical and pharmaceutical corporations.[2] On financing healthcare and hospitals (Rosner 1982; Stevens 1999; Labish and Spree 2001; Gorsky and Sheard 2006; Domin 2008–2013); about medical technology in the hospitals (Löwy 1993; Howell 1995; Stanton 2002; Schlich 2002; Boersma 2003); and about the pharmaceutical industry from a business history perspective (Vagelos and Galambos 2004; Chandler 2005; Cramer 2015; Malerba and Orsenigo 2015). As the industry is so heterogeneous, scholars' sources, methodologies, and objectives have been similarly diverse. As specialists in the field have noted, the work of different disciplines overlaps in the study of large-scale firms that have tried to adapt to the external technological and market opportunities created in the last two centuries in healthcare (Galambos and Sturchio 1998; Donzé 2015).

The most significant research directions from a business history perspective include the context and chronology of technological waves of innovation in the pharmaceutical industries (Liebenau 1984, 1987a; Galambos and Sewell 1995; Galambos and Sturchio 1998; Malerba and Orsenigo 2002, 2015; Chandler 2005; Cramer 2015). Archival work and corporate case studies have provided a wealth of empirical evidence about the largest players and pioneers in the pharmaceutical and biomedical industries such as Merck, Sharp and Dohme, Mulford, Bayer, Cutter, Baxter, CSL, Green Cross, and Grifols (Galambos and Sewell 1995; Galambos and Sturchio 1998; Kobrak 2002; Chandler 2005; Malerba and Orsenigo 2002, 2015; Fernández Pérez 2016; Umemura 2014, 2016; Henderson *et al.* 1999; Hughes 2011; De Chadarevian 2011; Fernández Pérez *et al.* 2017). Business history has also analyzed the opportunities for growth for healthcare insurance corporations with the rise in demand for healthcare products and services, and how this led to the creation of a diversity of public and private health insurance corporations and systems (Ford Chapin 2010, 2015, 2016; Murray 2007; Pons and Vilar Rodríguez 2011, 2014). The urbanization and the increase in life expectancy that led to the transformation of charity-based hospitals to modern patient-based hospitals and clinics are processes studied by scholars focusing on the industry of hospital construction and hospital equipment, who have revealed the complex interactions between private and public interests, and between competition and cooperation in the private industry in very different countries like the United States (Sturdivant 1970; Howell 1995), Switzerland and Japan (Donzé 2005, 2007, 2015), and Spain (Fernández Pérez and Sabaté 2017). The same complex relationship between private and public interests in various periods and countries has been found in research about political regulations in manufacturing and commercialization of healthcare services and products (Jasso-Aguilar *et al.* 2005; Gandillière and Hess 2013); marketing (Gandillière and Thoms 2015), and the financing of healthcare (Gorsky and Sheard 2006; Rosner 1982; Domin 2008–2013), and the emergence of healthcare companies in late industrialized developing markets (Kale and Little 2007; Conroy 2006; Santesmases 1999; Fernández Pérez 2016; Fernández Pérez and Sabaté 2017). In all of these studies a recurrent issue of analysis and debate has been the existence of asymmetric information in national healthcare markets between producers and consumers that has resulted in myriad healthcare systems in the world. Also, second, these studies have revealed the existence of private firms and business groups that have lobbied in the last century-and-a-half, in very diverse institutional national settings, in Europe, North and South America, and Asia. The goals of many lobbies and healthcare insurance and pharmaceutical associations have usually been, first, to obtain protection with which to invest in healthcare innovation while reducing the market share of foreign competitors. And, second, and more often in corporations headquartered in late industrialized countries, grow by consolidation and acquisition, and the quick imitation or adoption of foreign technical and organizational healthcare knowledge. The diversity of interests and financial or political muscle to impose those interests by policymakers, consumers, startups, and global healthcare players, have been studied as determinant forces in the evolution of national and global healthcare industries.

Business historians of healthcare industries and services have demonstrated that these firms and groups have experienced three, or four, big waves of technological and economic revolutions in the last century-and-a-half. The first saw the gradual acceptance of the germ theory of disease at the end of the nineteenth century and first decades of the twentieth century; the second occurred during the chemical and therapeutic revolution from the 1930s to the 1960s. The third wave, based on recombinant (artificially produced) DNA technology and molecular genetics, called the biotechnological revolution, started in the 1970s and 1980s. A fourth is unfolding in the 2010s and focuses on personalized nanotechnological treatments for autoimmune and chronic neuronal diseases. These revolutions have shifted the focus of the industry from germs, to antibiotics, tissue biochemistry, cell biochemistry, molecular structure, and nano science. Each revolution has increased scientific and technological complexity of knowledge, manufacturing, and commercialization. Also, each revolution has increased the complexity of ethical and institutional regulations. Each revolution has produced industries and firms where high productivity, profits, and ROAs (return on assets) emerged from the firm's (own or acquired) dynamic capabilities to adapt to more challenging and expensive industry and regulatory requirements.

In the pharmaceutical and chemical industries, the pioneering firms first established scientific and technological new knowledge and learning bases between the 1870s and the 1930s. After World War II until the 1990s, the pioneers established solid barriers to entry to avoid competitors at home and particularly abroad in the markets they were creating with disruptive new products and services. Only from the end of the 1990s onwards did global competition from challengers erode the competitive basis of some first movers (Chandler 2005; Malerba and Orsenigo 2015). This chronology explains the establishment of leaders like Bayer, Ciba Geigy, and Sandoz, in the United States, Germany, France, the United Kingdom, Switzerland, and Japan. In late industrialized countries like Sweden, Japan, Italy, Spain, Cuba, Argentina, or

Mexico, many of these innovative products and services arrived due to early nineteenth-century contacts of scientists with the leading pioneering centers and corporations, and the efficient networks established among them by Faculties of Medicine and Pharmacy in Europe, America, and Asia to communicate quickly and efficiently knowledge about innovations.

In the manufacture and distribution of hospital equipment, in Europe, North America, Latin America, and Asia, small and medium companies with scientists–entrepreneurs soon started to register their commercial activity in order to take advantage of the expanding market opportunities opened with the concentration of millions of sick patients in the large industrialized cities that started to grow with industrialization and globalization after the mid-nineteenth century (Sturdivant 1970; Donzé 2015; Fernández Pérez and Sabaté 2017). Studies about trademarks and monographies of companies have revealed the coexistence of multiple pathways of development of this multiplication of small entrepreneurship in the production of chemical drugs and medicines that appeared in the mid- and late nineteenth century. Some grew serving the military needs of their armies (Nobel in Russia, Behring in Germany, Abbott and Baxter in the United States); some were transformed into large multinationals in the food industry in the twentieth century (like Nestlé, Danone, or Coca Cola); some developed due to government support to cover large population needs due to the isolation of key drug providers during war times (CSL in Australia); some changed headquarters due to war pressures and became large multinationals in other countries or continents (Danone moved from Spain to France; Andrómaco from Spain to the United States and then to Central and Latin America). But from the long lists of small laboratories that existed before the 1920s, very few remained after the 1950s: many did not survive the two world wars and the collapse of global trade in the interwar period.

After World War II, there was a decline in the number of small- and medium-sized family-owned companies in the healthcare industries in Western Europe, particularly in the United Kingdom, and a concentration of the chemical, pharmaceutical, and medical drugs business into larger corporations. North American corporations were particularly well placed to assume leadership, also in the healthcare industries of manufacturing and distribution of hospital equipment and drugs. As the need for complex technologies and medical drugs expanded with population growth in the post-war period, and as hospitals grew in numbers to serve this increased number of potential sick people, hospitals needed to purchase diagnostic instruments, pharmaceuticals, and laboratory equipment, such as sterilizers, masks, gloves, and microscopes. During the late nineteenth century in the United States, as in Europe, there were many small manufacturers of such items like the Gendron Wheel Chair Company (1872), Davol Rubger Company (1874), American Sterilizer Company (1894), Beckton, Dickinson and Company (1897), Bard-Parker Company Inc (1915). In the pharmaceutical industry, Merck and Company, Abbott Laboratories, Cutter Laboratories, and Mead Johnson and Company were founded between 1883 and 1900 (Sturdivant 1970: 7). However, most manufacturers had to sell their products directly to thousands of hospitals spread through the country, and the transaction costs were high. The American Surgical Trade Association founded in 1902 had tried to organize the industry, but unsuccessfully. By contrast, a talented medical supplies salesman named Foster McGaw founded the American Hospital Supply Corporation in 1921, By 1985, it became one of the world's largest wholesale distributors of hospital supplies (Sturdivant 1970). New hospital supply companies succeeded because they connected distant manufacturers, established price convergence across distant hospitals in the country and abroad, and organized a professional salesforce specially trained in the products they had to sell. This "Chandlerian" corporation would be difficult to imitate in other countries until the late 1980s. In Western Europe, particularly in Germany and German-speaking countries, the concentration took place, though for different reasons. Around 20 local manufacturers and distributors were taken over during World

War I by the X-ray equipment producer Reiniger, Gebbert & Schall, a company based in Erlangen and founded in 1887. In 1921, a holding company, Industrie-Unternehmungen AG (INAG) took control of this group to provide all the technical equipment needed by hospitals and independent doctors. In 1924, Siemens & Halske purchased INAG and established itself as a leader in hospital equipment business.

Business historians have also studied how organizational forms of large corporations have adapted with more or less success to the challenges of technoeconomic revolutions and diverse regulatory frameworks after World War II. On the one hand, healthcare corporations adapted to the changes in the scientific advances by combining hierarchical integrated forms of business organization (often for products and services belonging to past technoeconomic healthcare revolutions where greater scale and scope is needed), with alliances and joint ventures with smaller very innovative companies and start-ups (for new technoscientific challenges where risks are high and long-term patient investments needed). On the other hand, healthcare corporations have adapted to the historical waves of globalization and de-globalization, and to changing national healthcare regulations, that had for instance opened a period of fast foreign direct investment (FDI) in the healthcare businesses for the pioneering US, German, Swiss, and Japanese healthcare corporations in the rest of the world between the 1930s and the 1980s (Galambos and Sewell 1995; Galambos and Sturchio 1998; Chandler 2005); and a period of relative decline in growth rates of FDI of these pioneers with a parallel increase in shares of world FDI of the healthcare industries led by corporations from emerging markets (Fernández Pérez 2016; Fernández Pérez *et al.* 2017).

The diversity of world healthcare systems: between public and private initiative and pressures

Changes in public healthcare systems strongly influenced the expansion of commercial healthcare markets (Lethbridge 2005; Jasso Aguilar *et al.* 2005). In countries with a public healthcare sector, or the influence of public institutions in shaping rules of the game, healthcare companies tried to access their clients with strategies that prioritized the expansion into public sector markets. This applies to the diverse European national healthcare systems created since the mid-nineteenth century, despite the European Union's efforts to standardize practices and rules. A good example of this is Sweden. In a context of economic underdevelopment, an agricultural economy, and sparsely populated territory, Sweden brought together in the early eighteenth century local governments and religious sanitary centers in cities, and established provincial doctors for the rural areas financed with state funds from 1773. Between 1946 and the early 1990s the government controlled healthcare. Over 80 percent of doctors worked in government-run hospitals, and private healthcare almost disappeared. Healthcare corporations had to adapt to Sweden's strict regulations, including a state monopoly over the distribution of pharmaceutical drugs with price controls. Problems appeared in the 1990s and first years of the twenty-first century, with long waiting lists and complaints, which led to reform and some privatization of primary health services (Hogberg 2007).

In China, economic underdevelopment, a largely agricultural economy, and a very dispersed population in rural regions meant high mortality rates during waves of famines, until at least the 1950s. The lack of resources made Chinese local, regional, and national authorities use provincial rural doctors to heal the sick in the rural districts, as happened in Sweden. From the mid-twentieth century, there was a sharp rise in the construction of publicly funded and regulated public hospitals in larger cities. Thus medical services and products were controlled by rural practitioners with little formal educational; large corporations only appeared after 1950. In

1951, for instance, the Department of Health of the Guangdong Province established China Pharmaceutical Company Guangdong Branch (the predecessor of Guangzhou Pharmaceuticals Corporation) in Shamian, Guangzhou, which in 1955 established a first attempt of joint public–private business, and a joint venture with foreign interests in 2007 to distribute pharmaceuticals (Guangzhou Pharmaceuticals Corporation undated).

By contrast, in countries where the public sector was weak, companies prioritized strategies of introducing diverse healthcare systems of health insurance, which favor high and middle income groups' access to private healthcare and establish tough penalties for low income and poor people, like in the United States (Ford Chapin 2015).

In Australia, a public-led healthcare system of innovation unfolded during the twentieth century, and some of the most outstanding healthcare corporations in 2016 were created during the two revolutionary healthcare periods: the therapeutic revolution of vaccines during the first third of the twentieth century, and the biomedical cellular and molecular revolutions after the 1980s. During the first revolution, the following corporations were created: Australian Pharmaceutical Industries (1910), Sigma Pharmaceuticals (1912), CSL Limited (1916). After the 1980s some of the new outstanding healthcare companies in Australia were Biopharm Australia (1980), Cochlear Limited (1981), Healthscope (1985), Florigene (1986), Ausmed (1987), Chemeq (1989), IQNovate (2011). The geographical distance with Western centers of healthcare supply, and several wars in Europe during the twentieth century made the Australian policymakers well aware of the need to be self-sufficient, and, second, about the driving role of the state in long-term investment in research and development of healthcare products and services for Australians. Excellent scientific networks with leading Western centers and state support explain the strength in Australia of public healthcare corporations, until the 1990s when major private groups and funds started becoming major players first in partnership with state firms and then alone in the Australian healthcare markets, like in the case of the plasma derivatives industries and the vaccines industries.

Conclusions

Healthcare is a basic human need. Protectionist healthcare regulations sometimes ignore that disease is a global problem requiring cooperative approaches. Political ignorance about the complexities of the economics of healthcare, protectionist regulations, and economic de-globalization have made the role of global healthcare corporations of outstanding relevance today to help us face the challenges of an aging population in the developed world, and the resurgence of old infectious deadly diseases everywhere in the world, as classic drugs and vaccines become less effective. Germs do not know borders and do not respect immigration controls.

More research is needed to analyze and understand how the business of healthcare products and services changed from a preindustrial system of production and distribution, controlled by individuals educated in the power of natural remedies, to our current world controlled by the interests of distant drug and technology manufacturers, health insurance companies, and the changing regulations of political parties.

Also, more research is needed in the archives of governments about the role of imperial powers and military interests to finance new scientific centers and new scientists to support their imperial conquest, reduce the risks of deadly diseases in their armies and employees, and their contribution to subsidize some of the first pioneering global corporations in the pharmaceutical and healthcare industries. Behrinwerke in Germany, Cutter and Armour in the United States, CSL in Australia, or Siemens, for instance, first grew to serve the public needs of their armies in war times, and grew in scale and scope, thus establishing the enduring basis of global corporations in the biomedical or hospital equipment industries. In other cases, global private non-governmental institutions subsidized scientific research in close connection with economic imperial projects, like in the case of the International Health Division of the Rockefeller Foundation Commission.

There is also much research to do on the evolution of the markets and how conditions of the external environment created business opportunities, first used by scientists–entrepreneurs in the pioneering countries where conditions were more favorable to generate investments in research: Germany, Switzerland, France, the United Kingdom, the United States, Japan. Scientists–entrepreneurs received public and private resources to advance discoveries, and also increase the scale and scope of the manufacturing and distribution of new medical and pharmaceutical products.

New archival research could also uncover the diversity of healthcare policies. Healthcare corporations very early established for technological and economic reasons tough entry barriers to their knowledge, and their markets. They also had the extraordinary positive opportunity to meet the growing and stable demands of an expanding market, due to the increase in life expectancy in the world after the 1880s, first in the Western world, and after the 1950s to 1960s in the rest of the world. In this context, lobbies emerged very early close to the centers of political power, to influence laws regarding barriers to local and foreign competitors, though we have little research to date on the consequences of this development.

There are many debates in the media today about the degree of coverage and efficiency of privately based and public supported healthcare systems, but we know very little about their origins in every country, and above all we must try to establish new methodologies that allow international comparisons and a historically based narrative about the global construction of healthcare systems.

Finally, more research is needed on the management of the global players of the healthcare industries, such as their efficiency, their lobbies, and connections with interest groups and regulators. We also need to know more from national public agencies about safety and in helping to guarantee a fair price, about the abuses and frauds they commit, and the transparency and efficiency of and access to these corporations' healthcare products and services.

Acknowledgments

The author acknowledges the support for research and writing of this chapter of one of the first Ayudas a la Investigación en Socioeconomía of Fundación BBVA. Generous suggestions and continuous intellectual dialogue with co-editors of this book Heidi Tworek and Christina Lubinski have greatly contributed to improve the organization, the details, and the coherence of the arguments. Usual disclaimer of responsibility applies.

Notes

1 http://list25.com/25-deadliest-diseases-in-human-history/ (accessed March 2017)
2 See, forthcoming, in *Business History*, the Special Issue Health Industries guest edited and with an Introduction by Pierre-Yves Donzé and Paloma Fernández Pérez, with an Introduction that provides an overview to some of the most outstanding authors and contributions.

References

American Red Cross (undated), "A Brief History of the American Red Cross", http://embed.widencdn.net/pdf/plus/Americanredcross/uua0vkekh3/history-full-history.pdf?u=0aormr, accessed 25 January 2019.
Billings, John S. (1901), "Progress of medicine in the nineteenth century", by New York Evening Post Company, reprinted with permission of G.P. Putnams Sons in Smithsonian Institution (1901), *Annual*

Report of the Board of the Regents of the Smithsonian Institution showing the Operations, Expenditures and Condition of the Institution for the Year Ending June 30 1900. Washington, Government Printing Office, 637–644.

Boersma, F.K. (2003), "Structural Ways to Embed a Research Laboratory into the Company: A Comparison between Phillips and General Electric 1900–1940". *History and Technology*, vol. 19, no. 2, pp. 109–126.

Conroy, Mary Schaeffer (2006), *The Soviet Pharmaceutical Business during its First Two Decades*. Bern, Peter Lang.

Cramer, Tobias (2015), "'Building the "World's Pharmacy': The Rise of the German Pharmaceutical Industry, 1871–1914". *Business History Review*, vol. 89, no. 1, pp. 43–73.

Chandler, Alfred D. Jr. (2005), *Shaping the Industrial Century: The Remarkable Story of the Evolution of the Modern Chemical and Pharmaceutical Industries*. Cambridge MA, Harvard University Press.

De Chadarevian, Soraya (2011), "The Making of an Entrepreneurial Science: Biotechnology in Britain, 1975–1995". *Isis*, vol.102, pp. 601–633.

Domin, J.P. (2008–2013), *Une histoire économique de l'hôpital, XIXe-XXème siècles*, 2 vols. Paris, CHSS.

Donzé, Pierre-Yves (2005), "Les systèmes hospitaliers contemporains, entre histoire sociale des techniques et business history". *Gesnerus*, vol. 62, pp. 273–287.

Donzé, Pierre-Yves (2007), "L'ombre de César". *Les chirurgiens et la construction du système hospitalier vaudois (1840–1960)*. Lausanne, Editions BHMS.

Donzé, Pierre-Yves (2015), "Siemens and the Construction of Hospitals in Latin America, 1949–1964", *Business History Review*, vol. 89, no. 3, pp. 475–502.

Fernández Pérez, P. (2016), "Laboratorios Andrómaco: Origins of the First Subsidiary of a Spanish Pharmaceutical Multinational in the United States (1928–1946)".*Journal of Evolutionary Studies in Business*, vol. 2, no. 1, pp. 266–275.

Fernández Pérez, Paloma (2017), "Partners in a Journey to the Centre of the World: Spanish and Japanese Knowledge Transfer and Alliances in the Spanish Healthcare Industries (1960s–1980s)". *Business History*, pre-published online 2017, https://doi.org/10.1080/00076791.2017.1348498.

Fernández Pérez, Paloma and Ferran Sabaté (2017), "Entrepreneurship and Management in the Therapeutical Revolution: The Modernization of Labs and Hospitals in Barcelona, 1880s–1960s". Unpublished paper presented at the Workshop on Health Industries organized at the Faculty of Economics and Business, University of Barcelona, 25 November 2016 (forthcoming in *Investigaciones de Historia Económica*). https//doi.org/10.1016/j.ihe.2017.09.001.

Fernández Pérez, Paloma, Nuria Puig, Esteban García-Canal, and Mauro F. Guillén (2017), "Learning from Giants: Early Exposure to Advance Markets in the Growth and Internationalisation of Spanish health care corporations in the twentieth century", *Business History*, pre-published online 2017, https://doi.org/10.1080/00076791.2017.1369528.

Ford Chapin, C. F. (2010), "The American Medical Association, Health Insurance Association of America, and Creation of the Corporate Healthcare System". *Studies in American Political Development*, vol. 24, October, pp. 143–167.

Ford Chapin, Christy (2015), *Ensuring America's Health: The Public Creation of the Corporate Healthcare System*. New York, Cambridge University Press.

Ford Chapin, Christy (2016), "The Politics of Corporate Social Responsibility in American Healthcare and Home Loans". *Business History Review*, vol. 90, no. 4, pp. 647–670.

Galambos, Louis and Jeffrey Sturchio (1998), "Pharmaceutical Firms and the Transition to Biotechnology: A Study in Strategic Innovation". *Business History Review*, vol. 72, pp. 250–278.

Galambos, Louis and Jane Eliot Sewell (1995), *Networks of Innovation: Vaccine Development at Merck, Sharp&Dohme and Mulford, 1895–1995*. Cambridge, Cambridge University Press.

Gandillière, Jean Paul and V. Hess (2013), *Ways of Regulating Drugs in the Nineteenth and Twentieth Centuries*. Basingstoke: Palgrave Macmillan.

Gandillière, Jean-Paul and Ulrike Thoms, eds. (2015), *The Development of Scientific Marketing in the Twentieth Century: Research for Sales in the Pharmaceutical Industry*. Abingdon, Routledge.

Global Health Work Alliance (undated), "International Hospital Federation", www.who.int/workforce alliance/members_partners/member_list/ihf/en/ accessed 25 January 2019.

Gorsky, Martin and Sally Sheard (2006), *Financing Medicine: The British Experience since 1750*. Abingdon: Routledge.

Guangzhou Pharmaceuticals Corporation (undated), "Milestones", www.gzmpc.com/index_en.php/About/index/cid/7 accessed online 19 April 2017.

Henderson, Rebecca, Luigi Orsenigo, and Gary Pisano (1999), "The Pharmaceutical Industry and the Revolution in Molecular Biology: Interactions among Scientific, Institutional, and Organizational Change". In *Sources of Industrial Leadership: Studies of Seven Industries*, edited by David Mowery and Richard Nelson. Cambridge, Cambridge University Press.

Hogberg, David (2007), "Sweden's Single-Payer Health System", National Policy Analysis, www.nationalcenter.org/NPA555_Sweden_Health_Care.html accessed 25 January 2019.

Howell, Joel D. (1995), *Technology in the Hospital: Transforming Patient Care in the Early Twentieth Century*. Baltimore, MD: Johns Hopkins University Press.

Hughes, Sally (2011), *Genentech: The Beginnings of Biotech*, Synthesis. Chicago, IL, University of Chicago Press.

Jasso-Aguilar, R., H. Waitzkin, and A. Landwehr(2005), "Multinational Companies and Healthcare in the United States and Latin America: Strategies, Actions and Effects". In *Commercialization of Healthcare: Global and Local Dynamics and Policy Responses*, edited by M. Mackintosh and M. Koivusalo. Basingstoke, Palgrave Macmillan.

Kale, Dinar and Steve Little (2007), "From Imitation to Innovation: The Evolution of R&D Capabilities and Learning Processes in the Indian Pharmaceutical Industry". *Technology Analysis and Strategic Management*, vol. 19, no. 5, pp. 589–609.

Kelley, E. and J. Hurst (2006), "Healthcare Quality Indicators Project: Conceptual Framework Paper", OECD Health Working Papers, No. 23, OECD Publishing, Paris. DOI: http://dx.doi.org/10.1787/440134737301.

Kobrak, Christopher (2002), *National Cultures and International Competition: The Experience of Schering AG, 1851–1950*. Cambridge, Cambridge University Press.

Labish, A. and R. Spree, eds. (2001), *Krankenhaus-Report 19. Jahrhundert*. Frankfurt, Campus Verlag.

Lethbridge, Jane (2005), "Strategies of Multinational Healthcare Companies in Europe and Asia". In *Commercialization of Healthcare: Global and Local Dynamics and Policy Responses*, edited by M. Mackintosh and M. Koivusalo. Basingstoke, Palgrave Macmillan.

Liebenau. Jonathan (1984), "Industrial R & D in Pharmaceutical Firms in the Early Twentieth Century". *Business History*, vol. 26, no. 3, pp. 329–346.

Liebenau, Jonathan (1987a), "The British Success with Penicillin". *Social Studies of Science*, vol. 17, no. 1, pp. 69–86.

Liebenau, Jonathan (1987b), *Medical Science and Medical Industry: The Formation of the American Pharmaceutical Industry*. Baltimore, MD, Johns Hopkins University Press.

Löwy, I., ed. (1993), *Medicine and Change: Historical and Sociological Studies of Medical Innovation*. Paris and London, INSRM and John Libbey Ltd.

Malerba, Franco and Luigi Orsenigo (2002), "Innovation and Market Structure in the Dynamics of the Pharmaceutical Industry and Biotechnology: Towards a History Friendly Model". *Industrial and Corporate Change*, vol. 11, pp. 667–703.

Malerba, Franco and Luigi Orsenigo (2015), "The Evolution of the Pharmaceutical Industry". *Business History*, vol. 57, no. 5, pp. 664–687.

Murray, J. E. (2007), *Origins of American Health Insurance: A History of Industrial Sickness Funds*. New Haven, CT, London, Yale University Press.

Pons Pons, J. and M. Vilar Rodríguez (2011), "Friendly Societies, Commercial Insurance, and the State in Sickness Risk Coverage: The Case of Spain (1880–1944)". *International Review of Social History*, vol. 56, pp. 71–101.

Pons Pons, J. and M. Vilar Rodríguez (2014), *El seguro de salud privado y público en España: Su análisis en perspectiva histórica*. Zaragoza, Prensas Universitarias de Zaragoza.

Portolés, Francesca (2010), "César Comas, the Man who Introduced X-Rays in Spain", *Imagen Diagnóstica*, vol. 1, no. 1, pp. 28–35.

Rockefeller Archive Center (undated), "International Health Division", https://rockfound.rockarch.org/es_ES/international-health-division accessed 25 January 2019.

Rosner, D. (1982), *A Once Charitable Enterprise: Hospitals and Healthcare in Brooklyn and New York 1885–1915*. Cambridge, Cambridge University Press.

Santesmases, María Jesús (1999), "Antibióticos en la autarquia: Banca privada, industria farmacéutica, investigación científica y cultura liberal en España 1940–1960". *Documento de Trabajo 9906 Fundación Empresa Pública*, www.funep.es/phe/hdf9906.pdf accessed 10 August 2018.

Schlich, T. (2002), *Surgery, Science and Industry: A Revolution in Fracture Care 1950s–1990s*. Basingstoke, Palgrave Macmillan.

Sinca, Genís (2009), *Vida secreta dels nostres metges: Retrat de quinze gegants de la medicina catalana*. Barcelona, Angel Editorial.

Stanton, J., ed. (2002), *Innovations in Health and Medicine: Diffusion and Resistance in the Twentieth Century*. London and New York, Routledge.

Stevens, R. (1999), *In Sickness and in Wealth: American Hospitals in the Twentieth Century*. New York, Basic Books

Sturdivant, Frederick D. (1970), *Growth Through Service: The Story of American Hospital Supply Corporation*. Evanston, IL, Northwestern University Press.

Umemura, Maki (2016), "Divergent Responses in the Troughs of Disillusionment: Building the Monoclonal Antibody and Regenerative Medicine Industries". Unpublished paper presented at the Workshop on Health Industries organized at the Faculty of Economics and Business, University of Barcelona, 25 November 2016.

Vagelos, P.R. and L. Galambos (2004), *Medicine, Science and Merck*. Cambridge, Cambridge University Press.

World Health Organization (undated), "Archives of the League of Nations, Health Section Files", www.who.int/archives/fonds_collections/bytitle/fonds_3/en/ accessed 25 January 2019.

23

INSURANCE

Niels Viggo Haueter

Introduction

An old adage says that insurance is sold, not bought. Nevertheless, this European invention of turning risk into a marketable product has conquered the world. In 2016, insurance premiums accounted for 6.3 percent of world gross domestic product (GDP) or a staggering US$4,732,188 million (*sigma* 3 2017). Still, insurance has not yet reached the entire world. Many countries remain heavily underinsured. In 2015, for example, the life insurance market of South Africa was still about two-and-a-half times the size of the entire rest of the continent (*sigma* 3 2016: Table III).

The main reason is that insurance needs a certain level of economic development and consumers with disposable income to do any business at all. Insurance thrives with sound economies and reciprocally helps them thrive. Conversely, struggling economies and people with low incomes shun expenses on insurance and accordingly increase their risks and potential setbacks. Cultural and religious factors also play a role. Life insurance in Muslim countries, including economically powerful areas such as Saudi Arabia, is almost non-existent.

Being dependent on somewhat developed markets implies that insurance was never a first mover in globalization. Its supporting function for other business, however, is most likely significant, yet difficult to measure. The historian H.M. Robertson once stated that the "crux of capitalism lies in the function of risk-bearing" which prompted Swiss historian Jean Halpérin to declare insurance the very foundation of capitalist development (Halpérin 1946; Robertson quoted in Halpérin 1946: 24). Others implied that the support of insurance was limited. Frank Knight (1921), the American economist, pointed out that insurance was only suitable for calculable risks while it could not deal with uncertainties, and uncertainties provided the main opportunity for making profits. Others again, especially proponents from the non-governmental organization (NGO) sector, have argued that insurance creates risks rather than making the world safer because it entices people and companies to take on risks that they would otherwise not assume.[1]

The extent of such support further varied according to the different risks insured. Three main lines of business – marine, fire, and life – developed almost independently and along different paths for much of their histories. Marine insurance directly benefitted the shipping community while life insurance only started entering corporate strategies with industrial life insurance in the late nineteenth century. Fire insurance, as Pearson (2004) finds, mainly insured private risks but had a limited function in insuring corporations during the Industrial Revolution. Even the same lines of business developed in different ways in separate markets as insurance depends heavily on local regulation, risk landscapes, and differing cultures that lead to different risk awareness and consumer behavior. Risk profiles differed enormously for marine, fire, and life and naturally led to different insurance products and business models. Reinsurance, finally, the insurance of insurance, also developed along an individual path. An overarching history of insurance is difficult if not virtually impossible to write.

This chapter will therefore restrict itself to looking at the main forces that allowed insurance to internationalize in its initial stages. It will also consider some of the hindrances. The first three sections will explore how the three lines differed in the way they spread internationally. The focus is on the early periods of internationalization for each: marine insurance from the fourteenth to the mid-eighteenth century, fire insurance from the early eighteenth to the early nineteenth century, and life insurance from the late eighteenth to the late nineteenth century. This periodization sheds more light on the internationalization processes specific to these forms of insurance. Later globalization, especially from the 1970s and 1980s onwards, reveals fewer differences to other industries as larger composite companies dominated. Corporate reinsurance, which came about in the mid-nineteenth century, will not be a main focus of this chapter.

The international spread of the different lines of business was in those early stages supported by different actors. The fourth section of this chapter will therefore discuss what importance can be attributed to companies in the process of globalization, particularly focusing on the role of joint stock companies. I will argue that the advantages of joint stock companies should be re-evaluated. Also, the importance of companies in globalizing insurance should be revisited and compared to the equally important impacts of imitation and migration.

Marine insurance

The emergence of contractual practices, so-called *respondentia, commenda*, and later bottomry contracts, to protect against transport risks is assumed to have started with Babylonian overland trade.[2] These products offered credit where repayment was contingent on the safe arrival of the freight. The nature of long distance trade made such predecessors to insurance inherently international. This helped them spread to other regions, including India before 600 BC (Trenerry 1926: 61ff.). In the early seventeenth century, they reached Japan via Portuguese traders (Yoneyama 2012: 493). These systems evolved alongside other concepts of creditor protection, limiting liability, or otherwise shielding entities and owners and in essence hedged against financial liabilities. They do not necessarily classify as insurance business as they consisted mainly of clauses in credit agreements. However, they share some important attributes with insurance in that risk is transferred and, in these cases, interest rates functioned in lieu of premium payment as they were set at a level high enough to compensate the financer for the risk (Kingston 2013: 3).

It is challenging to define when risk protection started qualifying as insurance. Schug (2011) attempts a meticulously detailed analysis of the notion of insurance (*Versicherungsgedanke*) in the wide variety of risk-hedging activities from the Code of Hammurabi to the present day. Most scholars now agree that modern insurance appeared in the wake of Italian sea trade in the mid-fourteenth century. This view is based on two assumptions: (1) insurance needs to be premium based as opposed to communal arrangements financing losses *ex post*; (2) insurance qualifies as an independent business when its function is separated by individual contracts from the credit function (e.g., Raynes 1948). Much research on the origins of insurance therefore emerged out of legal historians' interest in detecting contracts that were drawn up separately from trading agreements (e.g. Bensa 1884; Salvioli 1884; Chaufton 1886). La Torre (1993) argues that the Commercial Revolution of the thirteenth and fourteenth centuries set the stage for premium-based insurance to appear, implying that insurance emerged as a consequence of trade. Bonß (1995) identifies a cultural shift as risk acquired positive connotations with the spread of entrepreneurship. This gradually replaced religious morale that interpreted risk taking in order to make profits as sinful. He sees this changing attitude toward risk as a prerequisite for both modern business and insurance to emerge. Bonß, however, also points out that even after modern insurance contracts started appearing, they remained isolated, albeit frequent, instruments and rarely led to the creation of insurance companies. Bogatyreva (2016) identifies the late seventeenth century as the time when the idea of corporate marine insurance became more popular with proponents stressing the increased financial security of corporate insurers.

For much of its history, marine insurance was carried out by traders, ship-builders, and owners who would often offer insurance alongside other services (Wright and Fayle 1928: 35; Supple 1970: 6). Coffeehouses associated with the shipping industry came to serve as trading places. They offered the opportunity to be in touch with the latest news. Eventually, though, groups specializing on insurance morphed into clubs, associations, broker offices, and, in the seventeenth century, the Lloyd's marketplace. The first significant joint-stock companies only appeared in the 1720s in London with the support of royal charters.

This implies that the first international expansion of insurance was not driven by companies. It spread, at least initially, with the help of individuals through an already existing network of the marine community. It was an informal and largely unregulated market based on a relatively simple instrument, the insurance contract, which survived in its basic form for many centuries. Offering insurance among themselves allowed the shipping community to profit from their unusually intimate knowledge about the risks insured. With this, somewhat idiosyncratic organizational forms, such as clubs and associations, have survived (Pearson and Doe 2015). From the start, marine insurance expanded in almost identical forms across Mediterranean and European Atlantic trade regions imitating Italian practices. Italian templates for insurance contracts were used universally and it was not uncommon to see them used in Italian language even outside Italy (Kingston 2013: 9).

This standardization of legal documents across differing jurisdictions led to marine merchants establishing committees responsible for out of court settlements of disputes, often bypassing local legislation, to form part of the supranational *Lex Mercatoria*. If we distinguish between "international" as referring more to cross-border activities (i.e., *inter nationes*) and "global" as implying a certain degree of unification across countries, we can say that marine insurance in this early stage shows many hallmarks of a globalized, rather than just an international, industry. It was applied across nations and used a congruous business and legal network across borders. This global network appears to have functioned rather well until different players entered the market and governing institutions started appearing.

Some current research therefore focuses on the institutional change in marine insurance (Kingston 2007, 2013; Leonard 2016). For Kingston (2013), it was an information asymmetry inherent to marine insurance as well as moral hazard which required an increased role of regulatory institutions to intervene and deal with a "lemons problem" in which the insured possessed more information about the risk than the insurer. Leonard (2016) further argues that the growth of the business led to a large number of market entries that were impossible to absorb in a small, informal community of merchant insurers. In the case of intruding corporate insurers without any vested interest in the safety of the marine business, this could lead to disruptions between the market economy and purely financial capitalism as well as to increasing disputes. Legal institutions gradually adapted the *Lex Mercatoria* into local law and the business was subject to increasing regulation. Kingston (2013), however, argues that the success of governing institutions overall was rather limited. Institutional interventions also led Kingston (2007) and Leonard (2016) to analyze marine market developments against Institutional Economics theories to account for different developments of international markets. According to Kingston, institutional change helps explain the different paths along which British and US marine insurance developed. In North America and the later United States, the joint stock form thrived while in Britain the 1720 Bubble Act prohibited the foundation of new joint stock companies without a royal charter.

In 1720, the first significant British joint stock marine insurance company, the Royal Exchange Assurance (REA), was founded. A second chartered company, London Assurance, soon joined it. For over 100 years, the two companies enjoyed a monopoly in marine insurance. Private underwriting, however, was still permitted. Underwriting of both the London and the REA remained comparatively modest throughout the eighteenth century while the Lloyd's market and private underwriting flourished. Marine business was difficult to embed in departmental workflows. As Supple (1970: 200) points out, "even within a Corporation, marine underwriting was very much an individual and personal activity." Corporate insurance thus failed to compete effectively with the informal market where crucial information was much more readily available, especially at Lloyd's. Kingston (2007) therefore sees one of the main reasons for the relatively poor performance of corporate marine insurance in the agency problem inherent to insurance.

By having a monopoly, the marine corporate companies oddly protected the idiosyncratic landscape in marine insurance by preventing more corporate competition, which led to Lloyd's consolidating its leading position. It to some extent also prevented the London market from growing fast enough during the eighteenth century to absorb increasing business from booming trade and a surge in prices with the Napoleonic wars. This helped other English markets grow but also several other European and US–American markets. Britain, however, dominated. Countries such as Chile, for example, had nearly all their risks insured in Britain, including "cross-risks" where ships did not call on British ports (Llorca Jaña 2011: 19).

Marine insurance thus spread internationally in conjunction with trade and can hardly be seen as a main driver of globalization. It was confined, for obvious reasons, to economically developed areas with according shipping infrastructure. Dedicated companies were a relatively late phenomenon with, initially, limited success. Both the informal market and the corporations had to adapt gradually to local institutional circumstances. In some ways, this inherently international and even global business de-globalized as local markets and local regulation developed, which led to different marine markets internationally. In Genoa, Copenhagen, and Naples, for example, this even resulted in state monopolies in the mid eighteenth century (Pearson 2015: 3).

Fire insurance

Fire risks were stationary, so, while marine insurance lent itself to becoming international or even global from the start, protecting against fire remained a local and mutually organized concern at least up to the late seventeenth century. Clubs and associations offered protection through fire brigades and sometimes included some form of mutual financial help. After the 1666 Great London Fire, joint stock fire insurers appeared along with several mutual foundations. Joint stock companies, especially, were to thrive with the Industrial Revolution and with growing trade in the Empire.

Pearson (2004) discusses how the changing economic balance affected the development of fire insurance as well as the impacts of insurance on the Industrial Revolution. Fire insurance grew enormously and profited from the growth of population and the associated boom in housing and other property but much less from manufacturing. However, according to Pearson's findings, it did not directly insure the Industrial Revolution.

Fire insurance spread to other British cities via an agency system that the Sun Fire Office had developed in the early eighteenth century (Pearson 2004: 107ff.; Dickson 1960). But growing trade in the British Empire was the driving force for fire insurance to diffuse internationally. It was, though, also thanks to one pioneering company, the Phoenix Assurance. No "other company entered the foreign market with such incisive rapidity or precocious application" (Trebilcock 1985: 162). A group of sugar refinery owners who found it difficult to obtain cover on the market had founded the joint stock company in 1782. Only three years later, their "Committee on Foreign Insurances" discussed a detailed business plan "to further consider the Extension of Business in Foreign Parts" (Trebilcock 1985: 181). Why did the Phoenix lead this expansion? The sugar business was colonial and the sugar refiners were intimately familiar with the international risks. Trebilcock also points to the industrial origins of the company and the composition of the management board which, unlike at other fire insurers, consisted exclusively of businessmen. One of the founders called the Phoenix "the First Commercial Insurance Company" (Trebilcock 1985: 172). Choosing the joint stock form appears to have been obvious in order to raise the capital necessary for expansion. As we will see later, the role of the corporate form was, though, limited. The success was largely due to the first international agency system, which allowed expanding without heavy infrastructure. During the first two decades, over 90 percent of foreign business came from Hamburg. The Hamburg agency consequently developed into a considerably sized bureau which expanded locally by appointing agents as far away as later Poland–Lithuania. Operating through agents rather than establishing subsidiaries or branches brought several advantages as costs mainly occurred in the form of commissions. Agents were also familiar with local conditions and better equipped to assess the risks.

The Phoenix' endeavors were later copied with companies demonstrating their global ambition in names such as the Globe, the Atlas, or the Imperial.[3] On the continent, company founders showed even less inhibition to imitate and the French, German, and Spanish markets subsequently had their national versions of *Phénix*, *Phönix*, and *Fénix*. Also, companies all over the world later started calling themselves Lloyd's without in any way being related to the their London namesake. The insurance model that internationalized was strongly influenced by the British models for fire insurance. Imitation may have played an equally important role in this spread as the expansion of British companies' business in European Atlantic seaports and the Baltics. Several German fire insurers, for example, copied "every aspect except [the Phoenix'] legal form, from operational structure to its technical accounting and risk classification system" (Liebig 1911: 23–24, quoted from Borscheid and Haueter 2012: 99).

Fire insurance depended on developed markets in order to expand. It thus followed traders and their risks wherever they went and used their networks to do business. As such, traders became not only clients of insurance companies but insurers often entrusted them to represent their business abroad. Agency houses' contacts with local traders eventually led to the first foundations of local insurance companies for example with the involvement of Parsee traders in India and so-called *compradores* in Hong Kong (Borscheid and Haueter 2012: 416–17; for the role of local merchants see Leonard 2012; see also Aldous' chapter in this volume). However, despite the involvement of local traders in India and Hong Kong, fire insurance remained very much a business done by Europeans with other Europeans.

Fire insurance thus spread globally in a different way from marine insurance. It appears that joint stock companies with innovative business ideas were the main driver. Yet, the fire insurers were heavily dependent on an infrastructure set up by trade. Similar to marine, an intimate knowledge of the risks insured was crucial at least in the case of the leading fire insurance company, the Phoenix. Imitation also appears to have played an important role but there is no systematic research available on this subject.

Life insurance

The first expansion of life insurance was driven much less by agents or companies. It also differed from the expansion of early marine markets through networks. Agents in some cases sold life insurance but usually only to fellow Europeans. Borscheid and Haueter (2012) identify other forces for the expansion of life insurance. Migration to the New World was possibly just as important as internationalizing companies were. Several waves of mass exodus of Europeans brought the idea of life protection to all white settler colonies, often in the form of mutual insurance. Company names such as Franco-Argentina, or Germano-Argentina referred to the origins of the mutuals and addressed specific client segments. European offspring also founded local subsidiaries of fraternal organizations. Freemasonry modeled on British lodges appeared in the USA from the early eighteenth century on (Beito 2000: 5). Friendly societies, the Manchester Unity, or Oddfellows, especially, founded hundreds of subsidiaries in white settler colonies. It was only toward the end of the nineteenth century, that mainly North American life insurance companies conquered international markets with modern advertising methods.

The other significant factor was imitation of prototype life insurers. British companies sold life insurance for example in Hamburg, but at inflated prices made possible by the absence of local competition (Braun 1925: 212). Business was also hampered by some failures of British companies to pay out claims. This, Braun, concludes, led to the foundation of the first significant German life insurance company, Gothaer in 1827. The company served as a model for later Japanese life insurance but was itself a copy of British life insurance. The model imitated goes back to the British Equitable. In the 1770s, it had been the first to adopt an actuarial approach to calculating premiums. Mortality tables allowed calculating different premiums for different ages and helped managing reserves in a more efficient way. Alborn (2009), however, shows how life insurance in Britain throughout the nineteenth century and beyond relied surprisingly little on actuarial insight. Still, such actuarial practices became a kind of a blueprint for starting life insurance companies in other markets. Actuarial books traveled more easily to new potential markets than companies did. Actuarial sciences developed somewhat independently of insurance companies through academic and professional associations. Even throughout the de-globalizing period that started with World War I, actuarial networks continued to function internationally. Hence, actuarial history has a long tradition with Braun (1925) still providing the most comprehensive and reliable study. Hacking's *Emergence of Probability* (1975) brought the development of probability theories during the Enlightenment back as a research subject and Daston (1988) examined probability and its influence on views on rationality while Porter (1986) examined the rise of statistical thinking. While none of the latter focuses on the expansion of the insurance industry, they are important for our understanding of the business rationale that allowed especially life insurance to spread.

These contributions to the literature also help understand why insurance was, at least initially, a product more easily sold in Western cultures. The concept of life insurance is strongly tied to cultural parameters and societal organization.[4] Early forms of, for example, burial clubs or widow funds had emerged around somewhat homogeneous groups of participants where an underlying solidarity principle was evident. Mutuals, to some degree, maintained this group feeling as they evolved around certain professions as well as cultural and sometimes religious identities. The shift from solidarity organizations to actuarially based business was difficult for a variety of reasons and met with considerable opposition. Turning life insurance into a business meant putting a price on someone's life. This in itself was difficult before the advent of sound actuarial methods but it also provoked criticism, notably from religious quarters. Probabilistic calculation had moral implications, as the Church interpreted the forecasting of death as tampering with Divine providence. Ceccarelli (2001), however, gives some more detailed insights into the subject and shows how clerics differed and partly disagreed in their view on insurance. Borscheid (2013: 31) further points to the fact that mortality statistics later used by insurance companies were the work of clerics who attempted to prove a divine order. The magistrates, however, also eyed insurance practices with suspicion, especially as early life insurance companies soon expanded into speculation and some turned the business into gambling-like practices in the late seventeenth and eighteenth centuries (Clark 1999). Much life insurance was banned in European countries and England curbed speculative life business in 1774 with the Gambling Act (Alborn 2008). Zelizer (1979) describes how moral opposition to life insurance persisted in the United States well into the nineteenth century. This moral objection extended to the managers of life insurance companies as Braun (1925: 302) illustrates. He quotes Elizur Wright, the "father of insurance regulation" in the United States as saying that life insurance was "the most available, convenient, and permanent nidus for rogues that civilization had ever presented."

Skepticism about European life insurance according to Borscheid and Haueter (2012) was one of the main hindrances for it to spread to different non-European characterized societies. Muslim societies up until today share early European doubts about how religiously or morally acceptable insurance can be. This may account for the scarcity of life and other insurance in Muslim countries. Skepticism was often mutual. One hindrance to the expansion of life insurance companies was therefore self-imposed. Many companies abroad only targeted white people as they did not believe that the indigenous could be trusted (Borscheid and Haueter 2012: 10–15). Reciprocally, many locals did not trust Western insurance companies and perceived some threat to their traditional solidarity networks. As insurance companies started globalizing in the late nineteenth century, clients of foreign cultures were only slowly targeted and often with difficulties. Some companies later had to go to some lengths in order to convince locals. The Shanghai Life Insurance Company for example, in the early twentieth century is reported to have provided its Chinese policy-holders with free accommodation on their travels and founding English schools for children of Chinese clients (Wright 1908: 827).[5] In the USA, African-Americans were often denied insurance well into the twentieth century and fraternal organizations provided attractive alternatives to those without ready access to life insurance. Even masonic lodges, despite being associated with the elite appeared to have been accessible. As early as 1775, Prince Hall started African-American freemasonry (Beito 2000: 7; on Prince Hall and the insurance activities of lodges see Muraskin 1975).

Makers of global business: institutional forms

So, who were the makers of the global insurance business? Companies played a crucial role and it is tempting to assume that joint stock insurers were at an advantage with easier access to capital and more freedom in management decisions. Yet, mutuals later globalized after reaching the necessary size to do so. The respective roles of mutuals and joint stocks have provoked several debates. Some older authors (e.g., Halpérin 1946, 1952; Raynes 1948) assumed a single evolutionary line along which insurance developed from charity and mutual help into a superior modern business carried out by joint stock companies. But views on organizational forms of insurance often show hallmarks of political preferences. Both capitalist and left-wing quarters claimed insurance for their purposes (Puskar 2006: 50–51). The left saw mutual insurance based on solidarity as an alternative to purely capitalist business. Insurance served as a model for a more social enterprise within capitalism as it builds on solidarity among the insured and, in essence, practices a redistribution of means. Fraternal, especially friendly societies, fit this view even more as they were even further removed from profit making. Consequently, in the late nineteenth century they were considered hotbeds of communist ideas (Wallace 2000). State intervention, more than competition from corporate insurance, came to spell the gradual decline of fraternal organizations. Bismarck designed his wide-ranging social security and pension system primarily as a means to "bribe" (in Bismarck's own words) the working classes into having something to look forward to and take their minds off revolutionary thoughts (Andreas 1926: 195–196).

Conservative quarters, on the other hand, stressed the benefit of corporate insurance to the economy and through this to society overall. Halpérin (1946) places insurance at the heart of capitalist development and argues that older forms of communal security had to be replaced by calculable capitalist methods with money assuming the role of bridging the present with the future. Family ties and guilds, according to Halpérin (1946: 20), prevented insurance from turning into a business end of its own (for guilds see Catherine Casson's chapter in this volume). This, he argued, was because mutual help "paralyzed" the development of modern insurance and, with it, business per se.[6] Clark (1999: 7) dismantles Halpérin's claims that such capitalist insurance business was based on sound calculations by showing how little systematic risk management such early modern companies applied. Febvre (1956), in direct response to Halpérin, argues that insurance was a side effect of developing capitalism which led to a split of the notion of security into material security, on the one hand, and safety in the hereafter on the other. He dismisses Halpérin's distinction of security provided by insurance versus solidarity and that the latter was gradually superseded by the former.

The difference between mutually organized insurance and joint stock players was described later by La Torre (1993). La Torre still stresses the business end as a main identifier of modern insurance. The disconnection of the insured's interest (i.e., the risk) from the financial interest of the insurer lessens the potential for conflict, he argues. Thus, insurers mainly interested in financial gain were optimally suited to insure marine risks as they did not have any directly vested interests and as such were more disposed to provide risk capital. Mutuality, though, still had its place in that it is better suited to cover regular and statistically more predictable risks, for example in agriculture or life. Marine insurance, however, with its short term and less predictable risks, La Torre continues, was better suited for modern, capitalist insurance. The evolution of mutual and modern insurance (in La Torre's sense) was thus parallel rather than linear with each of them suited to specific purposes. Yet, as La Torre notes, mutuality also reached certain limits with increasing size and number of the risks. The gradual change from mechanical to organic societies, to use Durkheim's (1893) terminology, thus meant that voluntary mutuality had to become compulsory, eventually paving the way for state-backed social insurance.

La Torre's view that mutual and joint stock insurance are, respectively, better suited for certain lines of business is commonly accepted today. This view may explain the frequency of mutuals in life insurance and the fact that this branch spread mainly via emigration and imitation. Recent research, however, suggests that other factors were influential as well. Some suggest that life insurance across continents is economically not viable (Biener *et al.* 2015). Conditions for life insurance vary enormously in respect of regulation, product design, sales channels, consumer behavior, income distribution, competition from pension systems, tax incentives, differing life styles, dietary habits, climates, and many more factors. While these factors may have had less importance historically, it might still be interesting to research whether cross-border life insurance was a profitable business in the past.

Pearson (2004: 235) remarks that unincorporated joint stock partnership was the most common form found among British fire insurers founded before 1850. Due to the Bubble Act of 1720 which limited the foundation of further joint stocks without a royal charter, the joint stock principle was somewhat corrupted. Insurers without a charter had to find legal loopholes to operate. Pearson (2004) finds that fire insurers significantly developed the relatively new corporate form of the joint stock company. This eventually paved the way to the repeal of the Bubble Act in 1825. James (2013a: 8) sees the need to raise larger amounts of risk capital as a main reason for the rise of joint stock insurance companies from the eighteenth century on. He also points to the connection of the two composite companies, the REA and the London, with a "revolution in corporate form," during what Supple (1970: 5) called a "context of economic growth and financial experiment." Some early joint stock fire insures had enjoyed reasonable success after the Great Fire of London but many suffered from immature business logic and the turbulences of the early eighteenth century bubble. In some ways, also the foundations of the REA and the London may have been premature. At least initially, they did not offer the financial stability James (2013a: 8) attributes to the "more stable" business form of the joint stock company. As Supple (1970: 35) points out, the REA, shortly before the South Sea Bubble, had "implicitly committed itself to a dependence on the booming stock market."

Naturally, a certain size was required for insurance companies to engage in global business. According to James, the joint-stock principle was decisive in the development of large-scale insurance (2013a: 8–9). The two monied companies, the REA and the London Assurance, enjoyed the monopoly privileges of their charters because the government perceived the security of shipping and trading to be of public interest. Soon after their foundation, they received additional charters for fire and life business despite the fact that with the Sun an already powerful fire insurance company existed. Yet, the fire companies grew business mainly in their home markets and internationalized only toward the later nineteenth century. The London Assurance only started opening foreign agencies in the 1850s (Drew 1949: 89). The REA only seriously increased foreign business from the late nineteenth century on with an increase between 1885 and 1910 from a mere 2 percent to 64 percent (Supple 1970: 241–242; percentage calculation by Jones 1977: 54). Supple attributes this lack of internationalization to management failure. The scarce expansion of many insurers up until the second half of the nineteenth century can partly be explained by the Napoleonic wars, which on the one hand increased prices but also made international business riskier. Another factor may be attributed to exceptional growth opportunities in home markets. A further reason for extended international growth may have been the appearance of professional reinsurance in the mid-nineteenth century as an additional safeguard to conduct international business.

It was, though, a joint-stock company that drove the first significant and relatively early internationalization of fire insurance. This may seem self-evident but a closer look at the outset of the Phoenix reveals that the company was prevented from fully profiting from this organizational form. Trebilcock dwells in detail on the delicate legal implications that the foundation of a joint stock company involved (1985: 67ff.). There is no evidence that the choice of institutional form was made with a view to expand business internationally. Rather, it was based on the wish to be granted a royal charter and its benefits of limited liability and a monopoly. A few years before the foundation of the Phoenix, Adam Smith, who, as James (2013a: 8) points out, was rather skeptical of joint stock companies, noted in his *Wealth of Nations* that the joint stock principle was best suited for insurance companies but that they did not need a charter (Smith 1776: 416). Charters, in Smith's view, were justified mainly for companies dealing with "remote and barbarous nations" (1776: 415).

The Phoenix did not obtain the charter, which meant that it could not operate with limited liability. This constituted a risk to investors and policyholders. Furthermore, the practice of issuing shares with a high proportion of uncalled capital proved difficult to implement. Uncalled capital functioned as a kind of risk reserve in that a call on capital could cover unexpected expenses and claims. It, however, also meant that shareholders faced potentially large liabilities for which they expected to be compensated by high dividends (Acheson *et al.* 2012). The Board of the Phoenix feared that the high proportion of uncalled capital (£250 versus only £50 paid up) might deter sugar refiners who were already suffering from a difficult market. The overall capital was then lowered from an originally envisaged £97,500 to £16,500. Such relatively low capitalization, unlimited liability, not being chartered, and operating without a monopoly suggest that the Phoenix' success was not exactly based on a strong capital structure. Rather, it was due to a legal trick. The Phoenix' operations were based on a Deed of Settlement that had been drafted in order to secure utmost liberty in management decisions and to limit the influence of shareholders. Furthermore, the fact that no charter had been granted proved to be beneficial as it allowed the company to decide independently of the government and spared them from paying substantial amounts to the government.[7] It is safe to assume that the liberty to decide on their business strategy (the international agency system) proved the decisive factor for the Phoenix Board to enable international expansion. Asking for shares to be fully paid up also proved advantageous as dividends could be issued rather restrictively.

More research is needed into the importance of organizational form for companies to internationalize. The case of the Phoenix may not be exemplary, yet the imperfection of the joint stock principle at the time and the successful ways in which other corporate elements were applied suggest that question of mutuals versus joint stocks in globalization is not that easy to answer. Recent research indicates that the distinction between mutual and joint stock was not always clear (Pearson and Yoneyama 2015). Many hybrid forms existed and continue to exist. Organizational choice was often based on necessity and exogenous factors because "the law dictated the institutional forms available to insurance entrepreneurs, and the interpretation of law entirely controlled which fields remained open for daring exploitation and which became merely the source of later frustration" (Trebilcock 1985: 69). The main factors influencing decisions were regulatory environments with some governments favoring mutuals, the ease of access to capital, cultural views, and also entrepreneurial ideologies (Pearson and Yoneyama 2015). The founder of Japan's first mutual insurer based his organizational choice on Confucian principles despite being an ardent supporter of a free market economy (Yoneyama 2015). Some joint stock companies during the Industrial Revolution resorted to applying methods borrowed from mutuals and attempted to increase business by asking shareholders to take out policies (Pearson 2004: 246) while some mutuals in twentieth century Japan introduced with-profit policies (Jiang 2015). The Canadian Sun Life, one of the most global life insurers, started as "The Sun Mutual Life Insurance Company" in 1871, despite being a joint stock company. The "mutual" in its name was purely for marketing purposes (Darroch and Kipping 2012: 258). The fake mutuality was abandoned ten years later when the failures of several real mutual societies were felt to taint the mutual principle but the company mutualized in the 1950s to fend off foreign takeover attempts (Darroch and Kipping 2012: 264). International expansion of mutuals appears to be a phenomenon of the later nineteenth century. The idea of mutuality was easy to export but the mutual institutions, initially, were less fit for cross-border or multinational business. In the seventeenth and eighteenth centuries, they were the "classic associations of small traders and shopkeepers clubbing together for defense" (Trebilcock 1985: 6). The mutual principle matured from communal organizations into mutual companies with longer lasting success. From the later eighteenth century to the early nineteenth, Britain witnessed mainly joint-stock foundations in life business, most of which, however, rapidly disappeared while the fewer mutual foundations proved more resistant (Braun 1925: 206). Mutual organizations reached impressive sizes during the nineteenth century especially in white settler colonies. In Japan, mutual insurance organizations produced some of the world's largest insurers in the twentieth century, albeit all of them active almost exclusively in their home market.

Yet, the role of transnational and multinational companies, mutual or joint stock, is easy to overestimate in the early modern era. Insurance, initially, spread very much as a concept. Copying business models, as we have seen, was frequent in fire and in life insurance. In some ways, also marine insurance thrived on imitation as insurance contracts and business practices were copied throughout European ports. Imitation was not limited to certain organizational forms. Emigrants, however, the possibly most important force to export life insurance in the nineteenth century, appear to have preferred mutual organizations. They also brought fraternal forms of insurance to the new world such as freemasonry and friendly societies (see e.g., Carlyon 2001 for foundations in New Zealand). These organizations covered an important share of life and health insurance (see van Leeuwen 2016 for the insurance function of friendly societies). Toward the end of the nineteenth century, Germany started offering social insurance, a concept imitated by other states subsequently. Insurance spread as a cultural good as much as a business concept and thrived mostly in European-influenced cultures.

Conclusion and suggestions for further research

Research into the globalization of insurance is relatively scarce. Borscheid and Haueter (2012) provide the main overview of the spread of insurance to twenty different markets. Different actors supported the diffusion of insurance. Companies played an important role but may not have been the dominant force during these early stages. Migration and imitation were possibly equally important. The basic concept of insurance was easy to reproduce and led to a rapid expansion of marine insurance from the fourteenth century without producing any notable companies before the 1720s. In all lines of business described here, marine, fire, and life, imitation proved successful. As insurance depends on local idiosyncrasies in terms of the risk landscape, legal environments, cultural parameters, and many more factors, imitation and adaptation to local conditions may have been a more effective way of spreading insurance. There is a large field open here for further research.

Migration as a promoter of insurance proved powerful as well and, through the large number of emigrants, produced important mutual insurance institutions, indeed some of the world's largest insurance companies. The role of mutuals in engaging in cross-border business and internationalization endeavors is, though, not well researched. Although friendly societies and other fraternal organizations globalized from the eighteenth century on and covered a large part of the insurance sector, their role has so far been neglected in academic writing. Joint stock companies, finally, may have been the main drivers for companies' diffusion. Past research concentrated more on mutual than on joint stock insurance. Some insight into possible advantages of the joint stock form in globalizing is also necessary. If, as some imply, joint-stock insurers are more supportive of other business, an account of how companies used insurance in order to expand is necessary. A more detailed analysis of the relationship and links between risks, institutional forms, market environments, and exogenous factors that created different insurance markets would be welcome. Finally, a comparative account of the spread of insurance and other financial services or the service sector altogether might provide some interesting insight into the aptness of insurance as a cross-border or international business.

Notes

1 See for example the recent campaign of several NGOs urging insurance companies to stop underwriting coal exploration and mining. https://unfriendcoal.com/coal-insurance/ (accessed 9 April 2019).
2 See Trenerry (1926) for the history of pre-modern forms of insurance. For the origin of *commenda* contracts see Hillman (1997: 621–624), and La Torre (1993: 181ff.). Udovitch (1962) traces the *commenda* back to Islamic *Qirad* financial instruments. See Schug (2011) for a classification of insurance and insurance similar activities from antiquity on.
3 Mutuals, on the other hand, expressed the solidarity of their members in names such as *Hand in Hand* or their professions such as in *Jeweller's Mutual*.
4 See Ewald (1986) for the societal function of insurance; Lobo-Guerrero (2011, 2012, 2016) for the notion of security that insurance produces.
5 This has continued into the present for example in China, where products linked to death touched on taboos (Chan 2012). When the PRC opened up to insurance in the 1980s, life insurance was to lead the way. It was praised as something in between insurance and stock speculation. Life insurance, it was argued, promised a guaranteed return unlike, for example, motor insurance. At the same time, it carried little risk as opposed to many financial instruments. (Interview with Qixiang Sun, C.V. Starr Professor, Associate Dean of School of Economics and Director of the China Center for Insurance and Social Security Research (CCISSR) at Peking University, 6 June 2007.)
6 "[C']est précisément l'assistance mutuelle familiale, sociale ou professionelle qui a paralysé le développement de l'esprit d'entreprise" (Halpérin 1946: 20).
7 The REA and the London together had offered the government the sum of £300,000 in order to obtain charters.

References

Acheson, Graeme A., Turner, John D., and Ye, Qing (2012), "The Character and Denomination of Shares in the Victorian Equity Market," *Economic History Review*, 65 (3), 862–886.
Alborn, Timothy (2008), "A License to Bet: Life Insurance and the Gambling Act in the British Courts," *Connecticut Insurance Law Journal*, 14 (1), 1–20.
Alborn, Timothy (2009), *Regulated Lives: Life Insurance and British Society, 1880–1914* (Toronto: University of Toronto Press).
Andreas, Willy (ed.) (1926), *Bismarck: Die gesammelten Werke* (Stollberg).
Beito, David T. (2000), *From Mutual Aid to the Welfare State: Fraternal Societies and Social Service, 1890–1967* (Chapel Hill, NC: University of North Carolina Press).
Bensa, Enrico (1884), *Il contratto di assicurazione nel medio evo: studi e ricerche* (Genova: Tipografia Marittima).
Biener, Christian, Eling, Martin, and Jia, Ruo (2015), "Globalization of the Life Insurance Industry: Blessing or Curse?" Working paper. www.wriec.net/wp-content/uploads/2015/07/8E1_Biener.pdf (accessed 6 September 2016).
Bogatyreva, Anastasia (2016), "England 1660–1720: Corporate or Private?" in Adrian Leonard (ed.), *Marine Insurance. Origins and Institutions, 1300–1850* (Basingstoke: Palgrave Macmillan), 179–204.
Bonß, Wolfgang (1995), *Vom Risiko: Unsicherheit und Ungewissheit in der Moderne* (Hamburg: Hamburger Edition).
Borscheid, Peter (2013), "Global Insurance Networks," in Harold James (ed.), *The Value of Risk: Swiss Re and the History of Reinsurance* (Oxford: Oxford University Press), 23–144.
Borscheid, Peter and Haueter, Niels Viggo (eds.) (2012), *World Insurance: The Evolution of a Global Risk Network* (Oxford: Oxford University Press).
Braun, Heinrich (1925), *Geschichte der Lebensversicherung und der Lebensversicherungstechnik* (Nürnberg: C. Koch).
Carlyon, Jenny (2001), "New Zealand Friendly Societies, 1842–1941." Thesis submitted to Auckland University. https://researchspace.auckland.ac.nz/handle/2292/1033 (accessed 29 June 2016).

Ceccarelli, Giovanni (2001), "Risky Business: Theological and Canonical thought on Insurance from the Thirteenth to the Seventeenth Century," *Journal of Medieval and Early Modern Studies*, 31 (3), 602–652.

Chan, Cheris Shun-Ching (2012), *Marketing Death: Culture and the Making of Life Insurance in China* (Oxford: Oxford University Press).

Chaufton, Albert (1886), *Les Assurances, leur passé, leur présent, leur avenir en France et à l'étranger, études théoriques et pratiques* (Paris: Librairie A. Maresq).

Clark, Geoffrey (1999), *Betting on Lives: The Culture of Life Insurance 1695–1775* (Manchester: Manchester University Press).

Darroch, James and Kipping, Matthias (2012), "Canada: Taking Life Insurance Abroad," in Peter Borscheid and Niels Viggo Haueter (eds.), *World Insurance: The Evolution of a Global Risk Network* (Oxford: Oxford University Press), 251–273.

Daston, Lorraine (1988), *Classical Probability in the Enlightenment* (Princeton, NJ: Princeton University).

Dickson, Peter G.M. (1960), *The Sun Insurance Office, 1710–1960: Two and a Half Centuries of British Insurance* (London: Oxford University Press).

Drew, Bernard (1949), *The London Assurance: A Second Chronicle* (Plaistow: Curwen Press).

Durkheim, Emile (1893), *De la division du travail social: étude sur l'organisation des sociétés supérieures* (Paris: F. Alcan).

Ewald, François (1986), *L'Etat Providence* (Paris: Grasset).

Febvre, Lucien (1956), "Pour l'histoire d'un sentiment: le besoin de sécurité," *Annales. Économies, Sociétés, Civilisations*. 11e année, N. 2, 244–247.

Hacking, Ian (1975), *The Emergence of Probability* (Cambridge: Cambridge University Press).

Halpérin, Jean (1946), *Les Assurances en Suisse et dans le monde: Leur rôle dans l'évolution économique et sociale* (Neuchâtel: Éditions de la Baconnière).

Halpérin, Jean (1952), "La Notion de sécurité dans l'histoire économique et sociale," *Revue d'Histoire Économique et Sociale*, XXX, 1.

Hillman, Robert W. (1997), "Limited Liability in Historical Perspective," *Washington and Lee Law Review*, 54 (2), 613–627.

James, Harold (2013a), "The Insuring Instinct," in Harold James (ed.), *The Value of Risk: Swiss Re and the History of Reinsurance* (Oxford: Oxford University Press), 1–22.

James, Harold (ed.) (2013b), *The Value of Risk: Swiss Re and the History of Reinsurance* (Oxford: Oxford University Press).

Jiang, Ying Ying (2015), "The Development of the Mutual Form and Its Influence on the Life Insurance Industry," in Robin Pearson and Takau Yoneyama (eds.), *Corporate Forms and Organizational Choice in International Insurance* (Oxford: Oxford University Press), 217–242.

Jones, Charles (1977), "Insurance Companies," in D.C.M. Platt (ed.), *Business Imperialism, 1840–1930: An Inquiry Based on British Experience in Latin America* (Oxford: Oxford University Press), 53–74.

Kingston, Christopher (2007), "Marine Insurance in Britain and America, 1720–1844: A Comparative Institutional Analysis," *Journal of Economic History*, 67 (2), 379–409.

Kingston, Christopher (2013), "Governance and Institutional Change in Marine Insurance, 1350–1850." www.amherst.edu/system/files/media/governance.pdf (accessed 31 October 2016).

Knight, Frank H. (1921), *Risk, Uncertainty and Profit* (Boston, MA: Hart, Schaffner & Marx; Houghton Mifflin Co.).

La Torre, Antonio (1993), "L'assicurazione nella storia delle idee. I-IV," *Assicurazioni*, 3–42; 170–204; 283–300; 510–538.

Leonard, Adrian B. (2012), "Underwriting British Trade to India and China 1780–1835," *Historical Journal*, 55 (4), 983–1006.

Leonard, Adrian B. (ed.) (2016), *Marine Insurance: Origins and Institutions, 1300–1850* (Basingstoke: Palgrave Macmillan).

Llorca Jaña, Manuel (2011), *La historia del seguro en Chile, 1810–2010* (Madrid: Fundación MAPFRE).

Lobo-Guerrero, Luis (2011), *Insuring Security. Biopolitics, Security and Risk* (Abingdon: Routledge).

Lobo-Guerrero, Luis (2012), *Insuring War: Sovereignty, Security and Risk* (Abingdon: Routledge).

Lobo-Guerrero, Luis (2016), *Insuring Life: Value, Security and Risk* (Abingdon: Routledge).

Muraskin, William A. (1975), *Middle-class Blacks in a White Society: Prince Hall Freemasonry in America* (Berkeley, CA: University of California Press).

Pearson, Robin (2004), *Insuring the Industrial Revolution: Fire Insurance in Great Britain 1700–1850* (Aldershot: Ashgate).

Pearson, Robin (2015), "Escaping from the State? Historical Paths to Public and Private Insurance between the Eighteenth and Twentieth Centuries," Paper for session S2258, XVIIth World Economic History Congress, Kyoto, August 2015.

Pearson, Robin and Doe, Helen (2015), "Organizational Choice in UK Marine Insurance," in Robin Pearson and Takau Yoneyama (eds.), *Corporate Forms and Organizational Choice in International Insurance* (Oxford: Oxford University Press), 47–67.

Pearson, Robin and Yoneyama, Takau (eds.) (2015), *Corporate Forms and Organizational Choice in International Insurance* (Oxford: Oxford University Press).

Porter, Theodore M. (1986), *The Rise of Statistical Thinking 1820–1900* (Princeton, NJ: Princeton University Press).

Puskar, Jason (2006), "William Dean Howells and the Insurance of the Real," *American Literary History*, 18 (1), 29–58.

Raynes, Harold E. (1948), *A History of British Insurance* (London: Sir Isaac Pitman & Sons).

Salvioli, Giuseppe (1884), *L'assicurazione e il cambio marittimo nella storia del diritto italiano* (Bologna: N. Zanichelli).

Schug, Albert (2011), *Der Versicherungsgedanke und seine historischen Grundlagen* (Göttingen: V&R unipress).

sigma (various issues), Zurich: Swiss Re. www.swissre.com/institute/research/sigma-research.html (last accessed 17 April 2019).

Smith, Adam (1776), *An Inquiry into the Nature and Causes of the Wealth of Nations*. http://en.wikisource.org (accessed 15 May 2016).

Supple, Barry (1970), *The Royal Exchange Insurance: A History of British Insurance, 1720–1970* (Cambridge: Cambridge University Press).

Trebilcock, Clive (1985), *Phoenix Assurance & The Development of British Insurance, 1782–1870* (Cambridge: Cambridge University Press).

Trenerry, Charles Farley (1926), *The Origin and Early History of Insurance* (London: P.S. King & Sons).

Udovitch, Abraham L. (1962), "At the Origins of the Western Commenda: Islam, Israel, Byzantium?" *Speculum*, 37 (2), 198–207.

van Leeuwen, Marco H.D. (2016), *Mutual Insurance: From Guild Welfare and Friendly Societies to Contemporary Micro-Insurers* (London: Macmillan).

von Liebig, Eugen Friedrich Wolfgang (1911), *Das deutsche Feuerversicherungswesen* (Berlin: J. Guttentag Verlagsbuchhandlung).

Wallace, Elizabeth K. (2000), "The Needs of Strangers: Friendly Societies and Insurance Societies in Late Eighteenth-Century England," *Eighteenth-Century Life*, 24 (3), 53–72.

Wright, A. (ed.) (1908), *Twentieth Century Impressions of Hongkong, Shanghai, and other Treaty Ports of China: Their History, People, Commerce, Industries, and Resources* (London: Lloyd's Greater Britain Publishing Company).

Wright, Charles and Fayle, C. Ernest (1928), *A History of Lloyd's: From the Founding of Lloyd's Coffee House to the Present Day* (London: Macmillan).

Yoneyama, Takau (2012), "Japan: The Role of Insurance in the Rapid Modernization of Japan," in Peter Borscheid and Niels Viggo Haueter (eds.), *World Insurance: The Evolution of a Global Risk Network* (Oxford: Oxford University Press), 495–521.

Yoneyama, Takau (2015), "Tsunetana Yano, Founder of the First Mutual Company in Japan," in Robin Pearson and Takau Yoneyama (eds.), *Corporate Forms and Organizational Choice in International Insurance* (Oxford: Oxford University Press), 29–46.

Zelizer, Viviana (1979), *Morals and Markets: The Development of Life Insurance in the United States* (New York: Columbia University Press).

24

ENTERTAINMENT AND THE FILM INDUSTRY

Peter Miskell

Any attempt to analyze the internationalization of the film industry over the last century must inevitably focus on firms based in the United States. This is not because the United States is home to the only important center of film production in the world. Nor is it the only country to have produced film companies with the ambition to become multinational enterprises. However, only the oligopoly of firms that emerged in the United States in the 1910s and 1920s (and which has remained broadly intact since then) has consistently produced feature-length content that was widely distributed and consumed on an international basis (Thompson, 1985; Jarvie, 1992; Vasey, 1997; Segrave, 1997; Trumpbour, 2002; Guback, 1969). These firms were remarkable not for their size, but for their reach and cultural influence. Even in 1946, the peak year for cinema attendance in the United States, the industry accounted for just 0.5 percent of national income and employment (Gomery, 1986). Yet by the mid-1920s American films accounted for around 75 percent of those screened around the world (North, 1926). In seeking to explain the remarkable success of these multinational firms, this chapter will focus not just on their film-making activities, but more specifically on their role as distributors. The creation of durable global distribution networks provided these firms with the vital organizational infrastructure to sustain their global reach and cultural influence.

The emphasis on distribution derives from two broader assumptions that inform the chapter. The first is that there is an important distinction between American-based film companies and "Hollywood." It is certainly the case that since the 1910s Hollywood has formed the epicenter of feature film *production* within the United States (Bordwell *et al.*, 1985; Maltby, 2003; Scott, 2005). But while the major US film companies may have based their main production activities in southern California, these firms were typically headquartered in New York, where their *distribution* networks were centered (Gomery, 1986). Hollywood, therefore, was an important production hub that supplied the major film distributors with the content they needed. As we will see, however, it was not the only source of content to which these distributors could turn.

This is not to downplay the creativity and efficiency of the Hollywood production system in itself. Hollywood has undoubtedly proved a powerful attraction for creative artists, performers, and technicians from around the world (Phillips and Vincendeau, 2006; Petrie, 2002). The pull of this creative cluster has simultaneously enabled Hollywood to draw on a wide range of talents and cultural influences, while also depleting other film production centers of key creative personnel. Economic geographers have identified Hollywood as a classic industrial district,

377

exhibiting enduring agglomeration effects that ensured film-making would continue to be concentrated in southern California long after the demise of the studio system and the collapse of vertical integration (Storper and Christopherson, 1987; Storper, 1989; Scott, 2005). This begs the question why Hollywood has been more attractive than other production centers – to which the most obvious answer is that it offers film-makers and performers the opportunity to reach an international audience. A circular argument can easily start to develop here, whereby Hollywood's international reach is explained by its status as the leading global creative cluster, while its attractiveness as a cluster hinges on its success in producing films for international markets. While these trends are no doubt self-reinforcing, and agglomeration effects have played an important role in the industry's development, we should not assume that there was anything inevitable about Hollywood's pre-eminence. "The iron law of American dominance" as Bakker (2008: 192) reminds us, "is not iron and is not a law."

To understand the functioning of a global "hits-based" industry such as film, we need to broaden our focus beyond film production and examine the wider structures of distribution, to which Hollywood studios were just one supplier of content. Organizations in the business of producing hits require not just the capacity to create content, but also to ensure that it is widely circulated and promoted (Thompson, 2017). The multinational firms that came to dominate this industry were distributors as much as they were producers, and their construction of international distribution networks constituted a critical form of foreign direct investment. A distribution network on its own, of course, was of little use without a regular supply of suitable content. But equally, large-scale production was not viable without a reliable mechanism by which films could be brought to mass audiences. Successful film multinationals were those that proved capable not just of producing content that audiences around the world wanted to see, but also of building the distribution infrastructure that enabled them to see it.

The second assumption informing the chapter is that a study of the makers of globalization in this industry requires a firm-level focus, rather than a product-level one. While an emphasis on firms is quite natural for business historians, studies of the film industry do not typically adopt this approach. There are certainly scholars (such as Douglas Gomery, Janet Wasko, Tino Balio, and Richard Jewell) who examine the industry through the lens of business organizations, but their work is outweighed by studies focused on the work of particular directors, producers, actors, or the development of specific genres or national cinemas. In the context of globalization, studies tend to focus less on the business strategies of individual firms than on the activities of the industry-wide trade body, the Motion Picture Export Association (MPEA) or its predecessor the Motion Picture Producers and Distributors of America (MPPDA). This is understandable in that the trade body (with the backing of the US State Department) did play an important role in pressuring foreign governments to open up their markets to American film imports. In pressing for a more favorable international trading environment US firms did act collectively, but the international growth of these firms was not a matter of trade policy alone. The literature on international film policy, rather like that on the economic geography of Hollywood, is important and insightful, but it can run the risk of treating the industry as a homogeneous entity in which individual firms are assigned little meaningful identity or agency. There are surprisingly few studies of film companies as multinational enterprises, considering their development in the context of international business (IB) theory (Walsh, 1999; Bakker, 2004; Miskell, 2009a; Miskell and Nicoli, 2016).

This chapter is concerned with the role of firms in the long-run process of internationalization within the film industry. IB theory offers different perspectives on this process. Traditional IB theory emphasizes the "ownership" advantages that firms must possess (and exploit) in order to survive as multinationals. These "firm specific advantages" provide multinationals with the means to overcome "liabilities of foreignness" when competing against domestic rivals in foreign markets. Such advantages can originate either with the corporate parent or a foreign subsidiary, but the conception of multinationals as vehicles for disseminating innovative business practices or strategies throughout international markets remains an important feature of much IB research. Balancing this is an equally important strand of IB theory which sees multinationals not just in terms of the competitive advantages they introduce to foreign markets, but as organizations that learn from their experience of operating abroad. This line of thinking, sometimes referred to as the Uppsala model, envisages the process of internationalization as incremental, with firms gradually extending their commitment to foreign markets as they acquire more knowledge and experience of operating outside their home market. It is a view of international business quite at odds with the notion of "born global" firms, which are established from the outset as fully functioning multinational organizations. A survey of the global film industry over the last century provides a useful opportunity to reflect on these theoretical perspectives. Were American film multinationals "born global" in the 1910s and 1920s, or did their internationalization evolve over time as they accumulated more knowledge and experience?

The enterprises built by the likes of Adolph Zukor, William Fox, Louis B. Mayer, and Carl Laemmle in the 1910s and 1920s formed the basis of organizations that have endured for a century. Over the course of that century, we can identify important developments in the functioning of, and the nature of competition within, the global film industry. Here I examine three distinct, if overlapping, phases of internationalization, with a section of the chapter devoted to each phase. I should stress that though broadly chronological, these should not be considered as strictly sequential "stages" of development, with one leading inevitably to the next. Rather, they represent approaches to internationalization, which could (and did) function simultaneously. Examples of all

Table 24.1 The global evolution of American film distributors – an explanatory framework

Phase of development	Strategic objective	Source of content	Nature of competitive environment	Source of competitive advantage
American expansion: 1910s to 1940s	Provide international outlet for films of parent company.	In-house studios, Hollywood	US firms compete for status as global producer-distributors. Race for quality and quantity.	Generic quality and quantity of content.
American adaptation: 1930s to present	Provide international outlet for Hollywood's global content.	In-house + outside producers, Hollywood.	US firms exert political pressure to reduce restrictions on access to foreign markets.	Quality of content: international orientation.
Global integration: 1960s to present	Provide international outlet for global film content from multiple sources.	Outside producers, international.	International producers compete for access to the international distribution networks of US firms.	Quality of content: international and national orientation.

three approaches can be found throughout the period. The dates provided here represent the periods in which these approaches were most prevalent, with the "start point" of each phase being triggered by a moment of particular upheaval (or disruption) within the industry.

The first approach, at its peak from the 1910s to the 1940s, I describe as a process of American expansion. This involved the international distribution of films that were produced primarily for a domestic American market. The critical development here was the emergence in the 1910s of the feature film as the industry standard, and the inability of European (or other) film-makers to match American levels of investment in this new form of production. The second approach I call American adaptation, in which US firms consciously sought to develop content with a strong international orientation in order to appeal to audiences in major markets outside the United States. This became most apparent following the transition to sound, which heightened the cultural specificity of films, and is still in evidence today. The third approach, dating from around 1960 to the present, I call global integration. It involves US distribution networks acting not just as conduits for the spread of content produced by their parent corporations, but as something more like global media platforms, seeking out content from leading producers around the world. The breakdown of vertical structures within the industry is a complex and multifaceted story, but shifting patterns of consumption brought about by the emergence of television and other media forms was a key driver of change. The concluding section asks whether the recent emergence of digital media platforms is likely to disrupt (or to reinforce) these patterns of development.

The rise and fall of the first film multinationals

The internationalization of the film industry pre-dates the emergence of the feature film as the dominant mode of motion picture entertainment. The first movie multinational was probably the American Mutoscope Company, which established a foreign subsidiary (the British Mutoscope and Biograph Company) in 1897. This quickly became the leading film company in Britain, building its own indoor film studio in London in 1900. Its business model, however, was based on individual film consumption via coin-operated machines at fairgrounds. Once this mode of consumption was rendered obsolete, the firm's demise was as rapid as its ascent (Brown and Anthony, 1999). As motion pictures progressed from fairgrounds to more permanent sites of exhibition, European firms were at the forefront of internationalization, and moved quickly to establish international distribution exchanges. Nordisk Film was an important pioneer, with a particularly strong position in Germany prior to the reorganization of that country's film industry and the formation of Universum Film-Aktien Gesellschaft (UFA) in 1917. Nordisk also created an American affiliate, the Great Northern Film Company in 1908, though this proved less successful (Mottram, 1988). By 1907 European (predominantly French) films constituted around half of the screen entertainment shown in the United States. This generated some adverse sentiment in the United States, to which firms such as Pathé, Gaumont, and George Méliès' Star Films responded by establishing their own American production subsidiaries (Bakker, 2008). The Motion Picture Patents Company (MPPC), formed by Thomas Edison in 1908, included two French firms: Pathé and Star Films. Like the other members of the MPPC, however, neither of these firms formed part of the new oligopoly of film companies that emerged in the 1910s and 1920s. Star Films was partially sold to another MPPC member (Vitagraph) in 1911. Pathé, a larger and more ambitious organization, essentially cut its ties with the MPPC in 1912, established its own distribution subsidiary in the United States, and embarked on a program of feature film production.

At this point Pathé was almost certainly the world's pre-eminent film multinational with production facilities on both sides of the Atlantic and extensive international distribution activities. In common with other European firms, however, World War I severely curtailed its production activities at home, while in the United States, Pathé found its newsreels and serials to be a much more reliable source of profit than its feature length productions. Just as the US film industry was coming to be dominated by producers of big-budget feature films – the winners of the so-called "quality race" (see below) – Pathé's American subsidiary became increasingly focused on short films. By the early 1920s the company had been forced to sell off its film business operations in most countries. Its American subsidiary, the Pathé Exchange, was sold to Merrill Lynch and continued to function largely as a distributor of shorts and serials made by independent producers (Ward, 2016). A similar fate befell other French companies with international ambitions prior to World War I, such as Gaumont and Éclair (Bakker, 2008).

The US firms that emerged to become successful multinationals in the 1910s and 1920s did not invent the feature film. Nor were they the first to establish the production of such films on an industrial scale, or to organize their distribution and marketing on an international basis. In his insightful account of how entertainment became industrialized in the early twentieth century, Gerben Bakker (2008) astutely focused attention on the "quality race" in film production, and the emergence of the Hollywood production system as the undisputed "winner" of that race. He convincingly shows that the emergence of the feature film as the standard product format within the industry triggered a rapid escalation in film production budgets. Production of these high budget pictures was risky, but with a relatively small number of hit films generating a substantial proportion of industry revenues, entrepreneurs that were able to consistently produce "hits" quickly came to dominate the industry. These producers reinforced their position by hiring and retaining the most prominent film stars, and by outbidding rivals in their acquisition of rights to popular stories (Bakker, 2001, 2008).

Firms such as Pathé and Gaumont, which had established a strong position in film production and distribution by 1914, were effectively excluded from this "quality race" as it entered its crucial phase during World War I. Unable to keep pace with American levels of investment in feature film production, their films became uncompetitive in international markets, and their distribution offices were left without a source of advantage. The European firms which might have been best equipped to compete with the Americans in feature film production were the Italians, who had pioneered this form of film-making before 1914. As well as being hampered by World War I, however, these firms had not invested in foreign distribution, and so were ill-equipped to mount any substantive challenge to American dominance after the war (Bakker, 2008).

US film-makers may not have been the only ones with the incentive, ambition, or talent to reach international markets. But having established a clear advantage in feature film production, and with distribution offices and sales teams in 50 or more countries around the world, US companies were the only ones with the capacity to ensure that their content was widely marketed and screened to international audiences. Indeed, the possession of an international distribution network, rather than ownership of a Hollywood film studio (or a chain of movie theaters), was the defining characteristic of the firms that constituted the US film oligopoly: often referred to collectively as "the majors." By the 1930s eight major firms had emerged to dominate the industry. These included the "big five" (Fox, Loew's-MGM, Paramount, Warner Bros., and RKO) which were vertically integrated organizations covering film production, distribution, and exhibition. Alongside these were the so-called "little three" (Universal, Columbia, and United Artists), which did not control cinema chains, operated much more limited production activities, and in the case of United Artists produced no films at all (Gomery, 1986; Balio, 1976). The common feature of all these firms was their investment in extensive networks of distribution offices around the world. This provided the essential mechanism by which they ensured that filmed entertainment became internationalized. These networks remained critical long after the demise of the so-called "studio system" when most of the major firms scaled back their film production activities. The emergence of Disney as a major film company in the post-war decades coincided with its development of its Buena Vista distribution arm (Wasko, 2001; Gomery, 1994).

American firms expand to international markets

The emergence of an infrastructure to export, market, and monitor the spread of American films in international markets served to bolster Hollywood's position as the world's leading production center. Having won the "quality race" in feature film production, the creation of these distribution networks ensured that Hollywood entertainment would be actively promoted to global audiences. Not only did US firms benefit from privileged access to the world's largest domestic film market, they were the only firms able to set production budgets on the basis of reliable returns from international markets as well (Thompson, 1985; Vasey, 1997).

The mutually reinforcing advantages bestowed by rapidly escalating production budgets and equally fast proliferating distribution networks provide a powerful explanation for the global dominance of US firms in the 1920s. However, the story does not end there. The influx of US films into international markets was not universally welcomed, with many critics in those markets voicing concerns about the cultural and economic impact of "Americanization." Political reactions included a movement to boycott American films in Japan (Itatsu, 2008) as well as a raft of legislation in Europe and Latin America to limit the volume of foreign film imports in the 1920s (Lewis, 1933; Jarvie, 1992; Dickinson and Street, 1985, Ulff-Möller, 1998). Further,

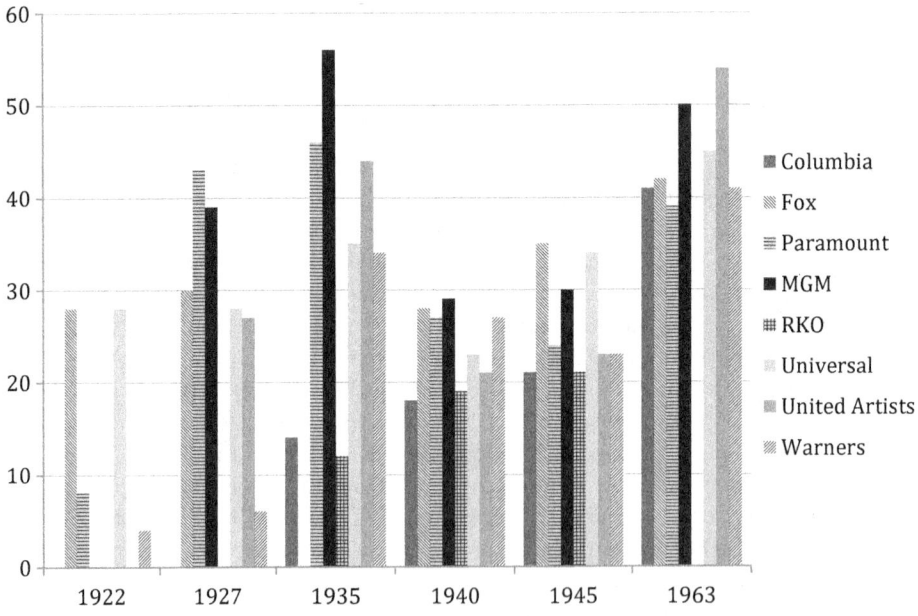

Figure 24.1 Number of international markets in which US distributors had offices, 1922–63
Source: Film Daily Yearbooks.

the introduction of sound technology at the end of the 1920s also served to heighten the cultural specificity of film, making it more difficult for movies to cross national borders without incurring "non-tariff barriers" associated with language, dialogue, or spoken accents (Maltby and Vasey, 1994). While such developments proved fatal to European efforts to counter American dominance, effectively killing off the "Film Europe" movement of the 1920s (Higson and Maltby, 1999), they also presented challenges to US multinationals. It became more difficult for US distributors to rely on a perceived "quality" advantage, when the foreignness of their content was becoming increasingly apparent.

"Quality," however, was not the only advantage on which these distributors traded. Equally important, though less discussed, was the sheer quantity of content at their disposal. The rapid escalation in spending on film production in the 1910s was driven as much by an increase in the quantity feature films made by the leading firms as by their quality. Fox Film Corp., for example, expanded production from just four films in 1914, to 71 in 1920, before stabilizing at just over 50 films per year by the end of the 1920s. Average production costs per film rose from $13,000 in 1914 to $60,000 in 1920, and to $300,000 by 1929 (Fox, 1930). To understand why quantity mattered as well as quality requires an appreciation of the processes of film exhibition and consumption in an era when cinema was the predominant form of public entertainment in most developed economies.

Just as contemporary media content is often released through a series of distinct distribution "windows," in the era before television films entered markets via a carefully managed process involving a strict hierarchy of cinema venues. Atop this hierarchy were first run cinemas, typically large city center venues, which screened the latest film releases and charged the highest prices. After a first-run release, films would be withdrawn from the market for a period before commencing a second run in the next tier of slightly less prominent and less expensive cinemas. The process would be repeated through a third, fourth, or fifth run until films had played the full range of cinema venues from the most palatial dream palaces to the cheapest local fleapits. The process took up to a year, and enabled films to be consumed by diverse audiences, in contrasting environments whose willingness to pay varied very widely (Maltby, 2003).

Accounts of the domestic growth of the major American film companies usually emphasize their control over first run film exhibition (Gomery, 1986). By ensuring a first-run release for their films, the "big five" could generate interest and publicity that would help to secure bookings throughout the release hierarchy – as well as capturing an important share of exhibition revenues (Sedgwick and Pokorny, 2005). This pattern of achieving market dominance through exclusive access to the highest profile films and direct control of first-run exhibition was evident in the domestic American market, but it provides a less powerful explanation of how the leading US firms operated internationally.

Closer scrutiny of the international activities of US film distributors reveals a more complex picture than one of major productions simply being pushed out to leading first-run cinemas and subsequently filtering down through the rest of the market (Sedgwick *et al.*, 2014; Miskell and Nicoli, 2016). There certainly were Hollywood movies that followed this pattern, but they were by no means the norm. Starting at the top of the release hierarchy, the most exclusive first-run cinemas in major metropolitan centers booked films for extended runs (often four weeks or more). American films often struggled to compete against leading domestic productions for access to such venues, which led some US firms to build or acquire their own showcase cinemas in key cities. In most towns and cities the largest cinemas changed programs weekly, and if part of a chain (which they often were) bookings were managed centrally. US firms did not typically own or control cinema chains in foreign markets, and they had to compete for access to these screens. In the UK, Warner Bros. did acquire a stake in the ABC cinema chain

(Porter, 2001), while Paramount and United Artists also made some investments in cinema exhibition (Miskell, 2006, 2009b). In most international markets, however, ownership of leading cinema chains by US firms was rare and bookings with these circuits could not be guaranteed. As we move lower down the release hierarchy, however, we come to venues that changed their changed their programs twice or three times weekly, relying as they did on the patronage of relatively small but loyal audiences of regular local cinemagoers. These types of venues did not screen the most recent major releases, but they did require access to a high volume of content that would be of a reliably consistent quality and which would appeal to an audience of habitual moviegoers. Here, US distributors held a distinct advantage over local competitors, in that they could offer a large quantity of low or medium budget pictures that held a popular appeal. Studies of cinema consumption in the 1930s from Bolton in the north of England to Sydney in Australia, have found that smaller suburban second- or third-run cinemas showed a higher proportion of American content than larger first-run venues in city centers (Richards and Sheridan, 1987; Sedgewick *et al.*, 2014). Trumpbour (2002: 285) similarly observes many European working-class provincial audiences rejected the films of the "European metropolis" which they regarded as "more alien than the products of Hollywood." The business model adopted by US distribution subsidiaries in many foreign markets from the 1920s through the 1940s, therefore, involved establishing a strong market share among lower tier cinemas through the regular and reliable supply of a large volume of content. To this relatively secure base could be added a smaller number of films that were able to achieve a more widespread popular appeal in specific markets.

American firms adapt to international markets

But what were these "hit" films that managed to attract extensive international audiences? Were they the same films that topped the box-office charts in the United States?

We know that the major American producer-distributors were adept at constructing balanced film portfolios during the studio era. Such portfolios enabled firms to convert the inherent uncertainty associated with film production, into a form of risk that could be managed (Sedgwick and Pokorny, 1998). Film executives were well aware that that the distribution of revenues within the industry was highly skewed, with a few hit films generating a large proportion of earnings. They were also aware that predicting each season's hit movies was not possible with any degree of certainty. Richard Caves (2000) refers to this as the "nobody knows" principle, in reference to William Goldman's oft-cited quip that "nobody knows anything" in Hollywood. Within a wider film portfolio, however, the potential losses from big budget productions could be offset by the much more reliable (if modest) profits from a large body of low or medium budget pictures (Pokorny and Sedgwick, 2010). In constructing their film portfolios, however, firms needed to be mindful of international audiences as well as domestic ones.

The film portfolios of the major distributors certainly contained a mix of big budget pictures with larger volumes of more modestly financed ones. If we measure films on the basis of their "international orientation," however, we find a similar pattern. The majority of films handled by the major US distributors during the studio era was based on American characters and settings, and employed mainly American creative talent. Yet each season's slate of pictures also contained a minority with a much more international flavor. Based on foreign stories or historical events familiar to audiences in many parts of the world, such films typically employed foreign-born actors, directors, or scriptwriters. A recent study that measured the international orientation of more than 1,000 films released by US distributors from the 1920s to the early 1950s found a strong positive correlation between the international content of these pictures and the proportion of revenue they generated in foreign markets. This relationship was particularly pronounced in the period following the transition to sound film (Miskell, 2016). During the 1930s and 1940s the "hit" films released by American distributors in foreign markets were very often those with strong international themes – which ranged from Errol Flynn as Robin Hood, through Greta Garbo as *Mata Hari*, to Michèle Morgan in *Joan of Paris*. These were the sorts of films for which US distributors were most likely to secure an extended first-run release in the most prestigious cinemas in the largest international markets (Glancy, 1999; Garncarz, 1994). The wider body of more obviously "American" content also received national distribution in these markets, but often found its most receptive audiences in smaller neighborhood cinemas in the suburbs or provinces.

The demise of the local neighborhood cinema in the 1950s and 1960s, however, rendered the high volume of modestly budgeted American-themed films unsustainable. Shifting consumption patterns, with television replacing the habitual twice-weekly attendance at local cinemas, caused Hollywood studios to scale back production quite dramatically in the late 1950s and early 1960s (Sedgwick, 2002). The films that continued to get made and internationally released, however, were typically big budget productions that scored highly on the international orientation measure, such as *Roman Holiday*, *Cleopatra*, or *Mary Poppins*. Such staples of studio production in the 1930s as the *Lassie*, *Thin Man* or *Andy Hardy* films, meanwhile, either ceased or switched to television. What had, in the 1930s and 1940s, been an important but relatively small component of the distribution portfolios of the American majors had, by the 1960s, become a core feature of their product offering (Miskell and Li, 2014).

The pattern of Hollywood studios routinely developing content based on international stories, settings, and characters to appeal to as broad a global audience as possible remains very much in evidence today. The film franchises based on the fictional creations of Ian Fleming,

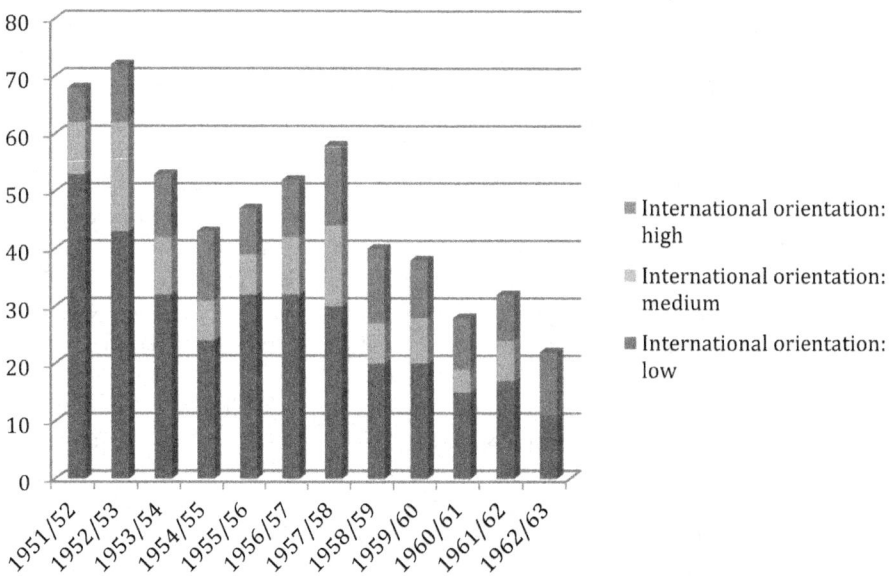

Figure 24.2 International orientation of film distributed by MGM and Warner Bros., 1951–63

Source: Miskell and Li (2014).

J. R. R. Tolkien, or J. K. Rowling are rooted very firmly in this tradition. The same can be said for many of the casting decisions and settings of the films created by Disney's Marvel Studios (or indeed LucasFilm). None of this is to deny that American film-makers can and do make pictures reflecting social and cultural circumstances within the United States itself. Yet it is striking just how many of Hollywood's most prominent big-budget film franchises continue to involve characters, settings, and actors that cannot be readily identified as American. Whereas the vast majority of such films in the 1930s and 1940s were based on European (often British) themes or settings, in recent years US studios have increasingly sought out Chinese content or characters, reflecting the growing importance of this market.

The model of global enterprise envisaged thus far has essentially been one in which American film companies constructed extensive multinational distribution networks for the purpose of promoting and marketing their own content on an international scale. Even during the height of the so-called studio era, however, the major US film distributors were known to source content from outside producers. Indeed, one of the major US distributors, United Artists, was formed in 1919 for the very purpose of providing a distribution outlet for Hollywood producers operating outside the studio system (Balio, 1976). Another of the major vertically integrated firms (RKO) regularly handled pictures by independent producers such as Sam Goldwyn and Walt Disney in the 1930s and 1940s (Jewell, 2012). As the major Hollywood studios started to scale back production in the 1950s, however, US distributors became increasingly reliant on outside producers for content. Moreover, in seeking content that would be suitable for international markets, US distributors did not restrict themselves to American producers.

American firms integrate international markets

The final approach to internationalization outlined here is described as global integration, which involved an important evolution in the function performed by the international distribution networks of US firms. Until the 1950s, these networks served mainly to disseminate Hollywood produced content *to* the wider world. By the 1960s, however, they increasingly provided a mechanism for the circulation of films *from* other parts of the world to international audiences. The practice of US distributors handling the release of foreign-produced films was not unheard of in the inter-war decades. United Artists, for example, had been quite reliant on the output of British producer Alexander Korda in the 1930s (Miskell, 2006). MGM handled the release of Abel Gance's *Napoleon* in the 1920s (Ulf-Möller, 1998). Such examples had been exceptions in the 1920s and 1930s. By the 1960s they were becoming more like the norm. We see in Figures 24.2 and 24.3 the dramatic reduction in the number of films for which MGM and Warner Bros. held worldwide distribution rights in the 1950s. By the early 1960s, not only were such films more likely to be internationally oriented, they were also much more likely to have been internationally produced.

Leading centers of film production outside the United States in the 1960s included the UK and Italy. American distributors were keen to strike deals with leading producers from these markets to supplement their dwindling supply of internally produced content. They often provided financial backing to these projects, and in some cases the films were jointly produced with American companies. Such deals enabled the US distributors to maintain a supply of content with a strong international orientation that could be expected to play well internationally. US firms found themselves in competition with each other (and with national distributors in domestic markets) to reach agreements with the most prominent international producers or directors. For film-makers in the UK, Italy, or elsewhere, these deals provided a valuable opportunity to ensure that their work reached a truly international audience. For such film-makers the

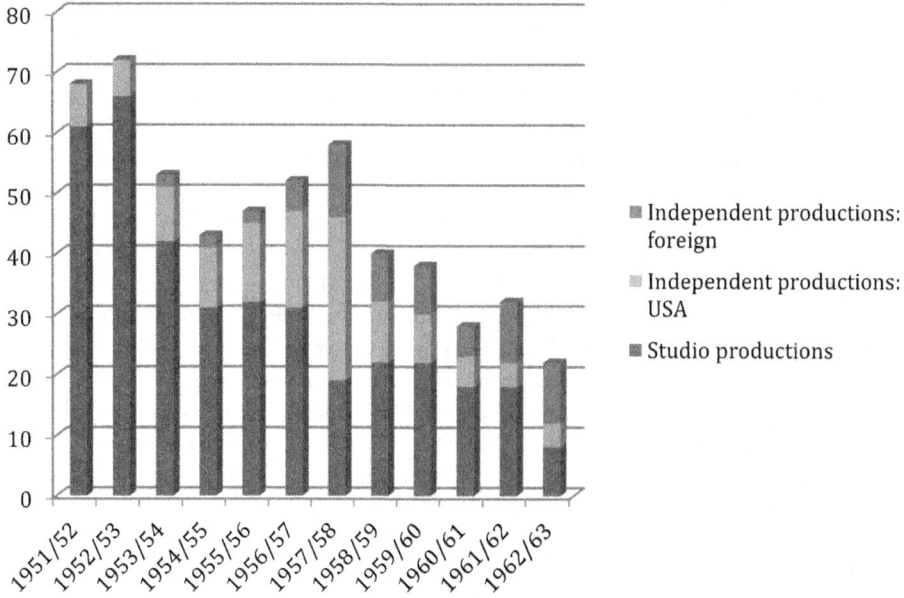

Figure 24.3 Production origin of films released by MGM and Warner Bros., 1951–63

Sources: For MGM, the Eddie Mannix ledger, held at the Margaret Herrick Library of the Academy of Motion Picture Arts and Sciences; for Warner Bros., the William Schaefer ledger, held at the University of Southern California Film and Television Archives, Los Angeles.

key competitive challenge became less about fending off the threat of American competition, and more about securing access to the American-controlled global distribution networks. In some cases, independent American producers established companies overseas, such as Sam Spiegel's Horizon Pictures, which made *Bridge Over the River Kwai* and *Laurence of Arabia* – both released through MGM. Woodfall Productions (set up by Tony Richardson, John Osborne, and Harry Saltzman) released a series of films through United Artists, including *Tom Jones*, *The Charge of the Light Brigade* and *Kes*. Saltzman, with Cubby Broccoli, was also behind Eon Productions which produced the *James Bond* films – also distributed through United Artists (Walker, 1974). In Italy, MGM worked with the producer Carlo Ponti to develop *Doctor Zhivago*, while Dino De Laurentis produced epics such as *Barabbas* for Columbia and *The Bible* for Twentieth Century Fox.

Another way of interpreting this development is to see it as a continuation of the longstanding process by which leading film-making talent from around the world succumbed to the gravitational pull of the major American firms. What changed in the post-war decades was that US firms were increasingly attracted by the prospect of organizing production activities away from southern California. Disintegrating vertical structures, combined with the trend toward "runaway production" (Bernstein, 1957), meant that instead of hiring talented producers or directors to work under contract in Hollywood, it became increasingly attractive to support their film-making activities in their home markets.

Hollywood has, of course, remained an important site of film production to this day, and it continues to be a key location in which deals are struck and decisions are made about which films get to be made and widely distributed. Hollywood producers continue to develop content that is designed to appeal to as wide a global audience as possible (as they have since at least the 1930s). But for US film distributors the practice of sourcing content from international providers has also endured. The year 1992 saw Universal establish a distribution joint venture called Gramercy Pictures with PolyGram – an ambitious UK-based film company which distributed well over 50 films in the 1990s including *Four Weddings and a Funeral* and *Priscilla, Queen of the Dessert*. In 1998 Universal acquired PolyGram, and continued to handle content from its "stable" of producers (Kuhn, 2002). More recently we have seen US distributors turn their attention from Europe to Asia, in search of producers able to develop content that appeals to audiences in China as well as western markets. Ang Lee's *Crouching Tiger, Hidden Dragon* (2000) was a notable success in this regard, and the director has subsequently worked on a number of high-profile Hollywood productions. Recent years have seen a number of deals struck between American and Chinese companies. Dalian Wanda has been at the forefront of such developments, acquiring an American production studio (Legendary Entertainment) and the AMC cinema chain (Clover and Ju, 2017). The firm has also formed a strategic alliance with Sony Pictures to co-finance film production (Hornby and Inagaki, 2016). The China Media Capital investment fund has built strong equity stakes in IMAX and Oriental DreamWorks (Sender, 2016), while Jack Ma's Alibaba has acquired a stake in Steven Spielberg's Amblin Partners (Mitchell, 2016). The growth of the Chinese cinema market in recent years has made it increasingly attractive to US producers and distributors, while Chinese firms are keen to expand their international reach. At the time of writing the most high profile Chinese-American film co-productions have yet to achieve widespread international appeal, though Hollywood blockbusters do appear to be popular with Chinese audiences. It remains to be seen whether the Chinese market will gradually become more open to internationally themed Hollywood productions, or whether Chinese-owned firms will succeed in securing a stronger hold over film production and distribution in international markets (Kokas, 2017).

Concluding reflections

The trends sketched out here might be construed as the Americanization of the film industry, but the process could more usefully be described as the internationalization of US firms. Did this process of internationalization involve gradually increasing levels of commitment to international markets, as per the Uppsala model (Johanson and Vahlne, 1977, 2009)? The speed with which US firms created global distribution networks in the 1920s does not, on the face of it, seem to be consistent with the type of incremental expansion predicted by the Uppsala theory. Indeed, a plausible case could be made that some of these firms were virtually "born global." The story of what happened to these companies after they became multinational enterprises, however, is much more consistent with Uppsala theory. The narrative outlined here is one of US firms becoming increasingly committed to international markets and, as they did so, refining and developing their approach to internationalization. The rapid construction of international distribution networks in the 1920s provided US firms with a mechanism for exporting their content on a global scale. The knowledge acquired from these markets enabled US multinationals to increase their commitment by adapting (some of) their content specifically for international audiences from the 1930s. Finally the longstanding ties that US distributors had established in many international markets by the 1960s put them in a strong position to form agreements or alliances with leading film producers in these locations. The impetus behind the shifting approaches may have come from exogenous shocks (such as sound technology and television), but the knowledge and connections that US firms had acquired over time helped them to mount an effective response to such events.

What types of upheaval has the industry faced since the 1960s? The emergence of video technology in the 1970s and 1980s threatened at one stage to endanger the industry, but the distinctive appeal of watching films in a communal space and on a large screen endured. Rather than eroding box office revenues in the 1970s and 1980s, video, along with pay TV and cable channels, instead added to them, creating secondary distribution "windows" through which films passed after their initial cinema release. This helped to re-create something similar to the second- and third-run cinema distribution tiers that existed in the era before television. Waterman (2005: 291) estimates that the addition of these new revenue streams saw total industry revenues grow from $3.5 billion in 1981 to $39.8 billion in 2003. However, just as secondary markets for film were eroded by the spread of television in the post-war decades, digital technologies are now replacing DVD sales. While it seems unlikely that viewing films online will replace the experience of going to the cinema, the shifting control over this extremely valuable secondary market does mark a potentially important moment in the evolution of international film distribution. Over the last century, the global networks through which filmed entertainment has been disseminated to international audiences have been controlled by a relatively stable oligopoly of US distributers (albeit ones that have undergone several changes of ownership since the 1960s). The emergence of new digital distribution platforms, such as Netflix, Amazon, or Apple, has provided an alternative means by which consumers can access entertainment. In some ways, these platforms offer a service analogous to that of cable TV providers, bundling together large packages of film or TV content into a subscription service. Such pay TV packages provided a reliable source of income to US distributors from the 1980s to the early 2000s but, crucially, not a growing one. The real growth in US distributor revenues during this period came from video or DVD releases (Waterman, 2005: 67). The prospect of the secondary film market becoming largely controlled by online subscription services would likely mark a significant shift in the balance of power between the copyright owners of individual films (the "traditional" distributors) and the so-called "aggregators" of online content. Indeed, the likes of Amazon, Netflix, and Apple have recently begun to invest in film production themselves, to ensure that they are able to offer exclusive access to some content (Garrahan, 2017). The competitive rivalry between these two groups, traditional distributors and aggregators, seems set to become a key battleground in the next phase of global competition within this industry.

References

Bakker, Gerben (2001), "Stars and stories: how films became branded products," *Enterprise & Society*, 2 (3), 461–502.

Bakker, Gerben (2004), "Selling French films on foreign markets: the international strategy of a medium-sized film company," *Enterprise & Society*, 5 (1), 45–76.

Bakker, Gerben (2008), *Entertainment Industrialised: The Emergence of the International Film Industry, 1890–1940* (Cambridge: Cambridge University Press).

Balio, Tino (1976), *United Artists: The Company Built by the Stars* (Madison, MI: University of Wisconsin Press).

Bernstein, Irving (1957), *Hollywood at the Crossroads* (Hollywood, CA: Hollywood AFL Film Council).

Bordwell, David, Staiger, Janet, and Thompson, Kristin (1985), *The Classical Hollywood Cinema* (London: Routledge).

Brown, Richard and Anthony, Barry (1999), *A Victorian Film Enterprise* (Trowbridge: Flick Books).

Caves, Richard (2000), *Creative Industries: Contracts Between Art and Commerce* (Cambridge, MA: Harvard University Press).

Clover, Charles and Ju, Sherry Fei (2017), "Wanda replaces US founder of Legendary studios with one of its own," *Financial Times*, 20 January.

Dickinson, Margaret and Street, Sarah (1985), *Cinema and State: The Film Industry and the British Government, 1927–1984* (London: BFI).

Fox Film Corp. (1930), "Annual Report."

Garncarz, Joseph (1994), "Hollywood in Germany: the role of American films in Germany, 1925–1990," in David Ellwood and Rob Kroes (eds.), *Hollywood in Europe* (Amsterdam: VU University Press), 94–135.

Garrahan, Matthew (2017), "Disrupting Hollywood: Amazon goes to the Oscars," *Financial Times*, 17 February.

Glancy, Mark (1999), *When Hollywood Loved Britain* (Manchester: Manchester University Press).

Gomery, Douglas (1986), *The Hollywood Studio System* (London: BFI).

Gomery, Douglas (1994), "Disney's business history: a reinterpretation," in Eric Smoodin (ed.), *Disney Discourse* (London: Routledge), 71–86.

Guback, Thomas (1969), *The International Film Industry: Western Europe and America since 1945* (Bloomington, IN: Indiana University Press).

Higson, Andrew and Maltby, Richard (1999), *"Film Europe" and "Film America": Cinema, Commerce and Cultural Exchange, 1920–1939* (Exeter: Exeter University Press).

Hornby, Lucy and Inagaki, Kana (2016), "Sony Pictures and Wanda in tie-up to market films in China," *Financial Times*, 23 September.

Itatsu, Yuko (2008), "Japan's Hollywood boycott movement of 1924," *Historical Journal of Film, Radio and Television*, 14 (1), 353–69.

Jarvie, Ian (1992), *Hollywood's Overseas Campaign: The North Atlantic Movie Trade, 1920–1950* (Cambridge: Cambridge University Press).

Jewell, Richard B. (2012), *RKO Radio Pictures: A Titan is Born* (Berkeley, CA: University of California Press).

Johanson, Jan and Vahlne, Jan-Erik (1977), "The internationalisation process of the firm: a model of knowledge development and increasing foreign market commitments," *Journal of International Business Studies*, 8 (1), 23–32.

Johanson, Jan and Vahlne, Jan-Erik (2009), "The Uppsala internationalisation process model revisited: from liability of foreignness to liability of outsidership," *Journal of International Business Studies*, 40 (9), 1411–31.

Kokas, Aynne (2017), *Hollywood Made in China* (Oakland, CA: University of California Press).

Kuhn, Michael (2002), *One Hundred Films and a Funeral: The Life and Death of Polygram Films* (London: Thorogood).

Lewis, Howard (1933), *The Motion Picture Industry* (New York: D. Van Nostrand).

Maltby, Richard (2003), *Hollywood Cinema* (Oxford: Blackwell, 2nd edition).

Maltby, Richard and Vasey, Ruth (1994), "The international language problem: European reactions to Hollywood's conversion to sound," in David Ellwood and Rob Kroes (eds.), *Hollywood in Europe* (Amsterdam: VU University Press), 68–93.

Miskell, Peter (2006), "'Selling America to the world'? The rise and fall of an international film distributor in its largest foreign market: United Artists in Britain, 1927–1947," *Enterprise & Society*, 7 (4), 740–76.

Miskell, Peter (2009a), "Resolving the global efficiency versus local adaptability dilemma: US film multinationals in the largest foreign market in the 1930s and 1940s," *Business History*, 56 (5), 689–723.

Miskell, Peter (2009b), "The film industry in twentieth century Britain," in Richard Coopey and Peter Lyth (eds.), *Business in Britain in the Twentieth Century* (Oxford: Oxford University Press), 306–29.

Miskell, Peter (2016), "International films and international markets: the globalisation of Hollywood entertainment, 1921–1951," *Media History*, 22 (2), 174–200.

Miskell, Peter and Li, Yunge (2014), "Hollywood studios, independent producers and international markets: globalisation and the US film industry c. 1950–1965," Henley Business School Working Paper, IBH-2014-07.

Miskell, Peter and Nicoli, Marina (2016), "From outsiders to insiders? Strategies and practices of American film distributors in post-war Italy," *Enterprise & Society*, 17 (3), 546–90.

Mitchell, Tom (2016), "Alibaba's Jack Ma joins up with Spielberg's film group Amblin," *Financial Times*, 9 October.

Mottram, Ron (1988), "The Great Northern Film Company: Nordisk film in the American motion picture market," *Film History*, 2 (1), 71–86.

North, C. J. (1926), "Our foreign trade in motion pictures," *Annals of the American Academy of Political and Social Science*, 128, 100–8.

Petrie, Graham (2002), *Hollywood Destinies: European Directors in America, 1922–1931* (Detroit, MI: Wayne State University Press).

Phillips, Alastair and Vincendeau, Ginette (eds.) (2006), *Journeys of Desire: European Actors in Hollywood* (London: BFI).

Pokorny, Michael and Sedgwick, John (2010), "Profitability trends in Hollywood, 1929–1999: somebody must know something," *Economic History Review*, 63 (1), 56–84.

Porter, Vincent (2001), "All change at Elstree: Warner Bros., ABPC and British film policy, 1945–1961," *Historical Journal of Film, Radio and Television*, 21 (1), 5–35.

Richards, Jeffrey and Sheridan, Dorothy (1987), *Mass-Observation at the Movies* (London: Routledge).

Scott, Allen J. (2005), *On Hollywood: The Place, the Industry* (Princeton, NJ: Princeton University Press).

Sedgwick, John (2002), "Product differentiation at the movies: Hollywood, 1946–1965," *Journal of Economic History*, 62 (3), 676–705.

Sedgwick, John and Pokorny, Michael (1998), "The risk environment of film-making: Warner Bros. in the inter-war years," *Explorations in Economic History*, 35, 196–220.

Sedgwick, John and Pokorny, Michael (2005), "The film business in the United States and Britain during the 1930s," *Economic History Review*, 58 (1), 79–112.

Sedgwick, John, Pokorny, Michael, and Miskell, Peter (2014), "Hollywood in the world market: evidence from Australia in the mid-1930s," *Business History*, 56 (5) 689–723.

Segrave, Kerry (1997), *American Films Abroad: Hollywood's Domination of the World's Movie Screens* (Jefferson, NC: McFarland).

Sender, Henny (2016), "Chinese business: Beijing's mogul," *Financial Times*, 19 October.

Storper, Michael (1989), "The transition to flexible specialisation in the US film industry: external economies, the division of labour and the crossing of industrial divides," *Cambridge Journal of Economics*, 13 (2), 273–305.

Storper, Michael and Christopherson, Susan (1987), "Flexible specialization and regional industrial agglomerations: the case of the US picture industry," *Annals of the Association of American Geographers*, 77 (1), 104–17.

Thompson, Derek (2017), *Hit Makers: How Things Become Popular* (London: Allen Lane).

Thompson, Kristin (1985), *Exporting Entertainment: America in the World Film Market* (London: BFI).

Trumpbour, John (2002), *Selling Hollywood to the World: US and European Struggles for Mastery of the Global Film Industry, 1920–1950* (Cambridge: Cambridge University Press).

Ulff-Möller, Jens (1998), "The origin of French film quota policy controlling the import of American films," *Historical Journal of Film, Radio and Television*, 18 (2), 167–82.

Vasey, Ruth (1997), *The World According to Hollywood, 1918–1939* (Madison, WI: University of Wisconsin Press).

Walker, Alexander (1974), *Hollywood England: The British Film Industry in the Sixties* (London: Michael Joseph).

Walsh, Mike (1999), "Options for American foreign distribution: United Artists in Europe, 1919–1930," in Andrew Higson and Richard Maltby (eds.), *Film Europe and Film America* (Exeter: University of Exeter Press), 132–56.

Ward, Richard Lewis (2016), *When the Cock Crows: A History of the Pathé Exchange* (Carbondale, IL: Southern Illinois University Press).

Wasko, Janet (2001), *Understanding Disney* (Cambridge: Polity).

Waterman, David (2005), *Hollywood's Road to Riches* (Cambridge, MA: Harvard University Press).

25

AUTOMOBILES

Patrick Fridenson and Kazuo Wada

Among multinationals, the automobile industry most strongly facilitates the movement of persons and goods. It can either improve or hinder mobility infrastructures like power, rail, and road transport. It is to a large extent an assembly industry: the parts have diverse origins and are combined in branched networks alongside supply chains. The main actors in these complex value chains are the final assemblers. The automobile industry depends upon "an industrial infrastructure for parts and components, skilled labor, and a sizable domestic market" (Shapiro, 1996: 28). Unlike other industries, however, it is both labor intensive and capital intensive. This makes large economies of scale essential. The barriers to entry for newcomers are high, because the industry requires large fixed investments, distribution and service networks (including importation, homologation, research, sales and marketing, warranty, after sales service, finance), and brand-name recognition (Volpato, 1989). Car markets themselves in each country have two peculiarities: the strength of the second-hand market, which influences strategies for car models; and the availability of financing for installment plans for both customers and dealers. These features have created an industry dominated by a small number of multinational corporations whose strategies are interdependent.

Auto multinationals are also political or semi-political organizations: they may create jobs, boost consumption, generate substantial income and financial flows, or potentially increase road accidents and damage natural resources (with hevea culture or oil extraction) and the environment at the national and global levels. They deal directly with governments before they enter, work in, or leave a country. Their executives exert political influence to obtain subsidies, reduce firms' tax burdens, and shape public policy. Their political power is also evident in international trade agreements. Yet car manufacturers are forced to adjust to certain conditions regarding national production systems with specific rules for local investment and distribution. For instance, during the import-substitution industrialization regime in Mexico from the 1970s up to the 1980s, and after the economic opening of China in the 1980s, producers were obliged to comply with local production quotas (Gandlgruber *et al.*, 2014). Automobile executives thus develop political capabilities akin to other multinational industries like oil.

Mainstream economics explain the birth and development of automobile multinationals through the advantages created by economies of scale and scope. They partly account for the differences in firms' trajectories through political factors and see the main impact of their history as the flow of capital that each firm carries for the purpose of foreign direct investment (FDI). One early exception was the British economist George Maxcy (1981). On the other hand, radical economics present multinational firms as tools to uniformize technology and consumption, exploit low wage populations, send profits outside the nations of production, and pollute massively (Hymer, 1979). Similarly, industrial sociology emphasizes the spread of an all-powerful Fordism that was replaced by an all-powerful Toyotism, from 1988 onward renamed lean production or often simply "lean."

Business history's narrative is different in many ways. Building on Mira Wilkins and Frank Hill's pioneering work of 1964, it focuses on actors, networks, chains, on practices and representations, and on how change emerges: after crises, Fordism transformed, so did Toyotism. It is often counter-intuitive: because cars and trucks are heavy, producing abroad would have seemed logical once financial resources were available, but history shows why some managers were reluctant. Moreover, business history has other priorities. First, it is interested in how the products of these multinationals fostered mobility. Second, it wonders whether hegemonic methods or learning processes develop both among multinationals and host countries. Third, it takes multinationals seriously, as creating webs of links between different countries. Fourth, it considers auto multinationals not as eternal powers but as fragile entities; their size does not protect them from decline or death. Fifth, it does not explain the trajectory and strategy of a leading multinational according to the primacy of the domestic market or simply economies of scale. On the one hand, it analyzes the conditions and demands of "each nation (and region)" and "all kinds of ongoing multilateral interrelationships" (Wilkins and Hill, 2011 (1964): XV). On the other hand, it outlines the structuring presence of the state on business strategy both at home (Tolliday, 2000, 1995) and in host countries, be they as different as Britain or Iran (Pardi, 2017; Mehri, 2017).

Finally, business history takes into account the varying cultural meaning of the same model in different countries, such as the Volkswagen Beetle. In West Germany, it symbolized an economic miracle; in the United States, suburbia and then hippie counterculture; in Latin America "sturdy" toughness necessary to thrive amid "economic instability" (Rieger, 2013: 331). At the other end of the market, a Mercedes is an upper-middle-class car in Europe and the US; in Russia it is often a car for the mafia; in Japan it long was the favorite car for yakuza, whereas today a number of them choose high-class Japanese models. The same multinational models have a second life as used cars in emerging countries where they may cripple domestic makers. In Africa, the state of Benin is the cornerstone of the continent's second-hand market of cars coming from Europe and the US (Beuving, 2004). Japanese used cars, auctioned mostly by Pakistani companies, finish their career in northern Russia and in Pacific islands (Shioji, 2018).

The business history approach also benefits from the development of global economic geography (Bloomfield, 1978; Dicken, 1986 [2015], whose relevant chapter is called "Wheels of change"). It also converges with research in international business (IB) emphasizing internationalization as a process where learning, experiential knowledge, and networks matter and stressing the importance of subsidiaries in decision-making (Forsgren *et al.* , 2015).

In this chapter, we first present an overview of how the auto industry became multinational, including two related sectors beyond cars: trucks and buses, and parts makers. Then we move outside production, illuminating several dimensions of the process still neglected in the literature and illustrate considerable change over the years. Finally, we focus on challenges for both companies and societies when auto manufacturers go global.

History

Our historical overview differentiates the trajectories to globalization of the industry's three branches: cars, trucks, and components makers. The volumes produced, the customers, and the business cycles are not the same (Tilly and Triebel, 2013).

In cars, after built-up vehicles were exported, European auto companies were the first to develop distribution organizations. Then an American firm (Ford) created manufacturing facilities abroad. To expand the competitive advantage of the mass-produced Model T, Ford opened its first foreign factory in Canada (1909), and a second one in Britain (1911). On a much smaller scale, Europeans chose three different patterns: a free standing company, which English venture capitalists founded in 1902 to acquire one of the French leaders, Darracq; a joint venture, which the French firm Peugeot operated in Turin, Italy, from 1905 to 1914; an assembly subsidiary, as another French maker, Renault, after creating a distribution subsidiary in Russia in 1914, opened a factory in Petrograd the same year and another one in Rybinsk in 1916 (Bardou *et al.*, 1982).

Crossing national boundaries thus began before World War I. After 1918, Ford's assembly plants spread far and wide: before World War II it had assembly plants in Canada, Mexico, Argentina, Chile, Brazil, Uruguay, England, Ireland, France, Belgium, Holland, Germany, Denmark, Spain, Italy, Romania, Turkey, Japan, India, Malaya, Australia, New Zealand, and South Africa. Ford spread its assembly plants over all continents, as the subtitle of Mira Wilkins and Frank Hill's book, *Ford on Six Continents*, suggests (2011). GM also began its overseas operations by exporting complete cars and by shipping abroad completely knock-down kits. It was initially less pervasive and more inclined to acquire shares of a company abroad: in Britain, Australia, Germany. The latter type of entry is quicker but has a higher risk and low flexibility.

In his best-selling memoirs from 1963, Alfred P. Sloan, GM's long-time president, chairman, and CEO, shows that going multinational was not a replica of home production and distribution. Producing outside home country constantly concerned management:

> For the overseas market is no mere extension of the United States market. In building up our Overseas Operations Division, we were obliged, almost at the outset, to confront some large, basic questions: We had to decide whether, and to what extent, there was a market abroad for the American car – and if so, which American car offered the best growth prospects. We had to determine whether we wanted to be exporters or overseas producers. When it became clear that we had to engage in some production abroad, the next question was whether to build up our own companies or to buy and develop existing ones. We had to devise some means of living with restrictive regulations and duties. We had to work out a special form of organization that would be suitable overseas. All of these problems were considered fully within the corporation for a period of several years in the 1920s when the basic policies were established.
>
> *(Sloan, 1963: 313–314)*

Even after World War II, the proportion of overseas production was relatively small.

> In 1955, the world looked like a very different place. Four out of every five cars in the world were made in the US, half of them by GM. No other car companies had the capital or the know-how to enter the global car business. GM's main US rival, Ford, was half its size. The largest foreign carmaker, VW, was little bigger than GM's own German subsidiary, Opel and only had one model – the VW Beetle. And Toyota was not even on the horizon. It made 23,000 cars in 1955 in Japan, compared to 4 million manufactured by GM in the US.
>
> *(Schifferes, 2007)*

Still in 1962, just 12 percent of total production at GM – then the largest auto company in the world – occurred overseas. Sloan hoped to vastly expand overseas, because he found even

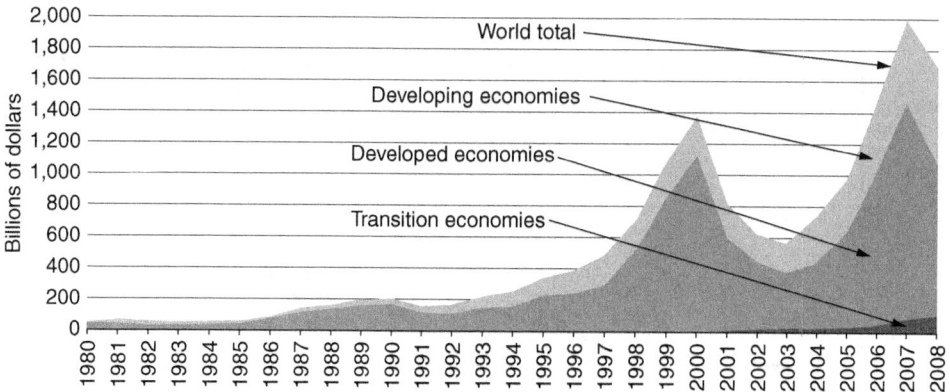

Figure 25.1   FDI inflows, global and by groups of economies, 1980–2006

Source: UNCTAD (2007: 3).

the European Common Market underdeveloped. There was only one car for every nine people, compared to one for every three in the US (Sloan, 1963: 313–314). This suggested that both European makes and latecomers such as the Japanese, and later the Koreans, could acquire large markets if the company could offer vehicles and services satisfying customers there.

Alongside the desire to become multinational, the emergence of many regional free trade associations was key. First the European Common Market (1957) and the European Free Trade Association (1960) were created, then after 1990: Mercosur 1991, ASEAN 1992, European Union 1992, North American Free Trade Agreement 1994. FDI surged, with automobile companies playing a significant role. Many of them became multinationals in those years, some beginning outside their region (like the Swedish Volvo in Canada in 1963, the German BMW in South Africa in 1973, or the Korean Hyundai in 1985, also in Canada) (Wilkins, 1981; Laux, 1992; Lansbury *et al.*, 2007; Biss, 2017).

These free trade associations also influenced car companies' behavior: they did not just cross borders, but also sought to handle each region as a whole (Carrillo *et al.*, 2004). The two leading American firms created Ford of Europe in 1967 and GM Europe in 1979. These reorganizations were traumatic, yet the European operations were able to bail out their parent companies between 1967 and 1989. Especially, it became important for them to build efficient supply chains among countries in the region, or between the region and the home country because cars' heft and bulk made rationalizing production vitally important. For instance, a GM US model, "modified with a better engine," was introduced in Europe in 1981 as both the Opel Ascona and the Vauxhall Cavalier. "Its engines came from Australia, transmissions from Japan and the United States, stampings from Germany, and carburetors from France." Its sales were quite successful (Laux, 1992: 223). Alongside the proliferation of regional trade associations (RTAs), auto companies faced the establishment of the World Trade Organization (WTO), in 1995. Like other RTAs, the WTO lowered customs and import duties.

Top managements were faced with a series of dilemmas which were not just "make or carry," as both the Honda and Toyota cases in the US make clear. In 1980, in a climate of trade frictions on imports of Japanese cars, Honda announced it would be the first Japanese auto manufacturer to open a plant in the US. But it had to change the organization of its operations and create a specific engineering division for the US. In November, 1982, its first car rolled off its Ohio assembly line (Demizu, 2003). Toyota had received proposals from numerous states.

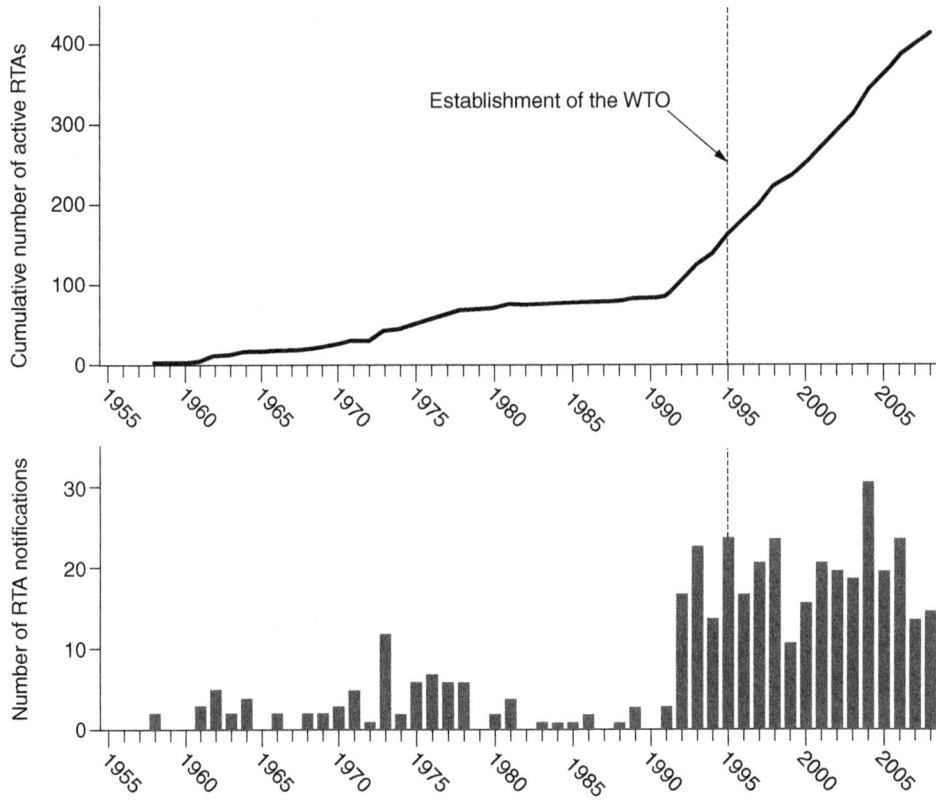

Figure 25.2   The acceleration in regional trade agreements, 1955–2008

Source: Dicken (2011: 203).

Yet it was more cautious and chose a joint venture with Ford as partner. But their long negoti-ations failed. Shortly after, in 1981, GM offered a proposal for a joint venture in California. Although a joint venture "required relatively little investment," Toyota's

> Production Related divisions felt uneasy about publicly disclosing production exper-tise in a joint venture plant, and the Sales and Marketing Division was worried about supplying a leading model to a competitor. In addition, cooperation with the United Auto Workers Union (UAW) was also a major issue.
>
> *(Toyota, 2012)*

Despite these concerns, the joint venture, called NUMMI, opened in 1984 on a shuttered GM site; the joint venture lasted until 2010.

Already in 1985, however, Toyota began to consider establishing its own plant as the volun-tary export restraints imposed on Japan by the US in 1981 "were causing supply shortages, and as a result, expanding supply by setting up independent operations" (Toyota, 2012) became the preferred option. Some executives opposed the idea because it would be much less expensive to ship finished cars to the US. But the CEO Eiji Toyoda thought that the company had to estab-lish a plant in the US because of the political situation. After selecting and building the plant in

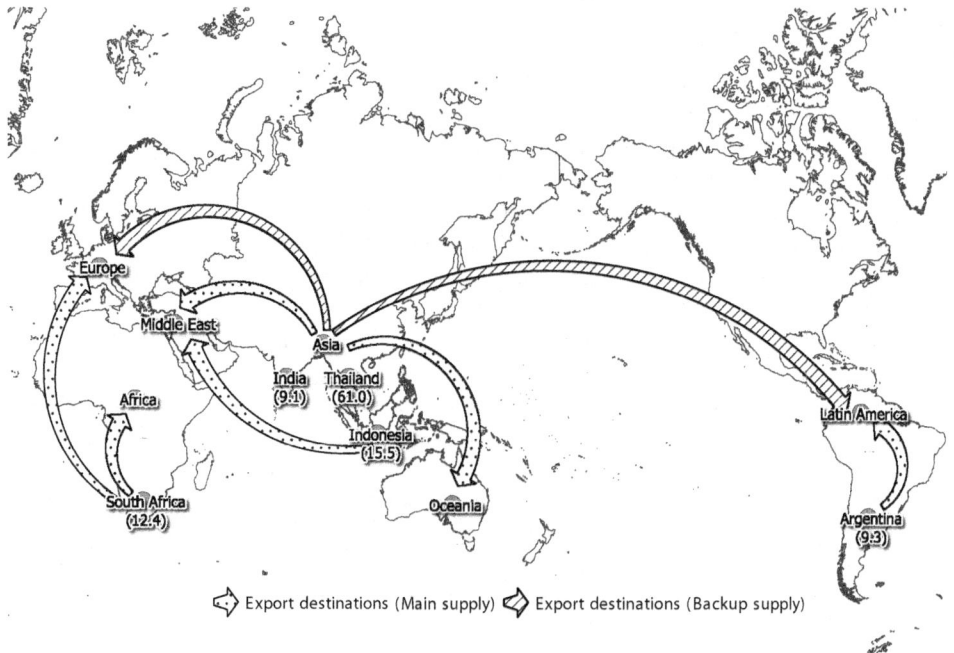

Figure 25.3   The distribution system of the finished IMV project cars

Source: Nikkan Kogyou Shinbun (The Daily Industry Newspaper), December 26, 2013. This map was reproduced by C. Brando (CRH, EHESS) with Quantum GIS.

Note
In parentheses, the number of units produced in 2012 (10,000 units). Besides this, Toyota is producing knockdown in eight countries.

Kentucky, which opened in 1989, Toyota faced difficulties getting good parts because most Japanese component makers had not built their own plants. Toyota also had not experienced American supplies yet. In such situations, the extensive use of container ships in the late 1980s (Levinson, 2006) helped Toyota and its suppliers to reduce costs. Toyota set up a collection center for parts, where parts suppliers brought their own parts and then Toyota would handle bringing them by container ships. Such measures reduced costs.

This focus on regional trade associations was quite fruitful in emerging countries, as the Toyota case illustrates again. The plants located there often had excess production capacities to supply their own home markets. From now on, each plant specialized its products and several countries jointly produced finished cars, bringing their parts together. Maybe it would increase costs but otherwise the plants in the emerging markets could not survive. In fact, during the Asian currency crisis in 1997, the plants in Thailand faced a crisis of survival. From the early 2000s onward, the pace of globalization quickened and many car makers made themselves able to use regional trade associations as a springboard to the whole world. Toyota launched a platform, the Innovative International Multi-purpose Vehicle (IMV) project in ASEAN (Association of Southeast Asian Nations) countries, and then the project widened to include countries such as South Africa and others in the Southern Hemisphere.

Pattern dot black arrows show shipments from main assembly plants to the market. Hashed black arrows show "backup supplies" from assembly plants. Because of the increasing demand or any other reasons, main assembly plants could not supply enough cars to the market, and some assembly plants, originally aimed at supplying a particular market, were mobilized to serve other markets. In 2014, South Africa plants produced 124,000 cars; Thailand 610,000; India 91,000; Indonesia 155,000; Argentina 93,000. In addition to the above plants, knock-down production was carried out in eight other countries.

In the early years of the IMV project, Japan's plants assisted the operations of plants in ASEAN. Also, plants were located to take advantage of lower customs and import duties while parts, engines, or bodies were moving around among the ASEAN countries. The IMV project enabled an easier globalization, a greater solidarity within the multinational, and the design of multilocal cars.

The relationship to markets and consumers was not the same in the trucks industry, as it is an equipment industry. This makes it very cyclical once customers are equipped. Multinationalization thus occurred differently. Unlike cars, truck making is a business-to-business industry. Truck makers produce vehicles for specific companies, fleets, road haulers, and for government or the army. Therefore, they must have common possible designs and be able to design highly specialized vehicles. This fostered an organization of research and development (R & D), which is closer to engineering or aircraft than autos. Here the role of production methods is less important than R & D. The series are smaller and the dealers' network is different. In recent years, for large road trains, a division has appeared between the driving platform which is made by truck makers and the trailers which are quite different companies and often very specialized. By 1955, the US share of world car manufacturing was 71.6 percent on cars, but only 43.3 percent on trucks and buses (Automobile Manufacturers Association, 1956: 28). Multinationalization of both distribution and production came later, on a smaller scale, and more often through multiple takeovers and resales of truck companies in search of profitability. Over the last 40 years, this increasing concentration has led to the dominance of two regions: the state of Michigan and the southern half of the major island of Japan, Honshu.

The multinationalization of components makers has been even more diversified. Here, we only discuss component makers specializing in the auto industry, who are both business-to-business and business-to-consumer. This also means that the international distribution of parts for the aftersales market is part of the product lifecycle. The internationalization of manufacturing began early, for Bosch in Paris in 1905 or Michelin in Turin, Italy, the city of Fiat, in 1906, then the US in 1907 (Bähr and Erker, 2015). However, there were alternative options. This was due to both the economic advantages of exports and to the protection offered in some of these sectors by international cross-licensing (which in the interwar years gave a comfortable monopoly to the British firm Lucas Industries over the British auto makers) (Nockolds, 1976–1978).

Moreover, different patterns emerged. For some components, the suppliers were subsidiaries of the car makers (see Peugeot and Faurecia, or Toyota and Nippondenso, later Denso). In other cases, auto firms twisted the arm of suppliers who did not want to invest in manufacturing countries (Scranton and Fridenson, 2013). Three trends are important. First, sometimes component makers went multinational to take advantage of their specific competitiveness, without following car makers (see in the US the Budd Company, a major supplier of body components to the auto industry, or in Germany Bosch for electrical parts) (Bähr and Erker, 2015). Second, the sensitivity to economies of scale led to the concentration of the domestic industry and to the internationalization of the domestic leaders' distribution and production by the multiplication of subsidiaries abroad. This is certainly true of the tire industry, whose leaders today are Michelin (French) and Bridgestone (Japanese), followed by Goodyear (US), and, far behind, Continental (German) (Erker, 2005). Third, the same suppliers became partners of different multinational companies, specializing in certain areas and combining their own knowledge base and adaptation to each consumer. But a major change appeared when some car makers, instead of embarking on production abroad with their usual components makers, decided in the mid-2010s to rely on local suppliers, in a move to reduce costs and benefit from local capabilities, as for Renault-Nissan in India for up to 98 percent of parts on the low-cost model developed for the subcontinent (Midler *et al.* , 2017).

Throughout this long history, four main sets of dynamics occurred.

Long term dynamics

On the whole, multinationalization is a process which changes the multinationals themselves and tends to bring them closer to their customers. First, design and development moved from centralization to partial localization. The initial logic of international production was centralization. Doing R & D and design/style at headquarters and producing identical models abroad was meant to exemplify economies of scale. After World War I, Henry Ford imposed British Model T to have left-hand drive. Sales dropped, and in 1922 Ford had to return to right-hand control (Wilkins and Hill, 2011). British consumers taught the leading multinational that local conditions might warrant modifications to its product. Furthermore, in the 1930s European consumers showed that they could not be satisfied by American models exceeding their wishes and needs. Therefore the two main US multinationals, Ford and GM, moved from indifference to local needs to partial adaptation and designed Ford or GM models for European markets (Tolliday, 2000) or for Australia (from where in turn GM models were exported to Asia) (Conlon and Perkins, 2001).

After World War II, European car makers producing abroad stuck to economies of scale for a long time. The best example is the Volkswagen Beetle that was successful abroad far longer than at home (Rieger, 2013). From the 1960s, a number of European makers produced models in Latin America, Africa, or Iran which were obsolete on the domestic European market. Only since the 1990s have most multinational car makers shifted to the idea that partially or totally adapting the product was both suitable and economical. The only exception remains the German premium brands, who however have built many plants abroad (Biss, 2017). This trend has extended to designing specific models for national or regional markets. A new key ingredient has been localizing parts of design centers in Spain, Germany, California, etc. For instance, the Korean Hyundai Ceed which appeared in 2018 was designed in Frankfurt, Germany, and produced in Slovakia. A further development happened when a car designed for a region other than its metropolis was sold in other regions at the price of significant adaptations, and produced elsewhere, which therefore can be called multilocal. Since 2003 the Renault company has made this strategy a specialty for its low-cost cars. This has also become the practice of Toyota in Asia, and of Hyundai.

A second dynamic is the management of cadres and of the labor force. Initially, auto multinationals appointed expatriates to run their foreign subsidiaries for homogeneity and control. But history soon showed the difficulty of top management from a distance. These expats enjoyed de facto great autonomy which created regular conflicts with headquarters over more investment or calls for local adaptation. Local employees or managers came to resent the glass ceiling for their promotion. Since the 1980s, auto multinationals worldwide have ended the existence of local kings, and have organized international careers with both regular mobility and consideration of local performance (Reiche *et al.* , 2012). Expats are in small numbers because they are a rare and expensive resource and because headquarters aim to train local managers. Yet, as a thorough comparison of German and Mexican car companies reveals, problems remain in terms of "constant participation in decision making, knowledge flow and control procedures" as well as "assigning adequate jobs to the returning expatriates." Also different mobility patterns have appeared despite similar tendencies, because of differences in terms of size and production volume, in positions within the global value chain of the car industry, and in localization of factories and research centres (Gandlgruber *et al.* , 2014: 81–83).

A much broader issue is that of blue collars. Attempting to transfer the knowledge, organization, and pace of work of the home country at lower wages has been the credo of multinationals. This implied more and more detailed rules or training periods sticking to the original routines, with the Japanese doing their best to transfer their wage and overtime system. From the start, workers demanded unionization, and Ford rejected it, sticking to the open shop, thus setting a pattern for other companies (Wilkins and Hill, 2011). Only in a minority of transplants has unionization prevailed. Moreover, the ability of national unions to coordinate internationally within one multinational has proved either weak or fragile (Bonin *et al.* , 2003; Fetzer, 2012). A local labor force might prove more productive than domestic labor, which in some cases was a lesson to a nation-centric management but in other cases, combined with wage levels, was an incentive to deindustrialize the home countries. The growth of information technologies contributed to these changes in human resource management.

The growing impact of information systems is the third, more recent, dynamic. It is obviously essential for internationalizing components makers, their multiple partnerships, and growing use of local suppliers. It is key for project management and styling and design. It is the base for the leading innovation which was the creation of modularization and platforms from the 1990s onward. It matters for the economy of variety which characterized most makers from the 1970s onward. What is not often underlined, however, is the connection between the spread of company activity beyond national boundaries and efficient use of communication systems. The spread of activities came to require the formation of supply chains. Speedy communication became necessary to manage the resulting international supply system efficiently. Furthermore, an efficient production of assembly products such as automobiles required a thorough list of all the parts needed (and eventually reducing their number). Toyota pioneered such a list, called the bill of materials (BoM). It used to be paper-based but moving toward a digital list happened in the domestic market in the 1970s. This specifications management system (SMS) ensured more efficient domestic production. But, until the mid-1990s, data transmission across borders was limited. This was one reason for Toyota's smaller globalization. The spread of the Internet facilitated new solutions; in the 2000s, Toyota strove to build a new SMS, attuned to more advanced information and communication technology, which could cover the entire planet. *Inter alia*, it allowed Toyota to cope better with variety while shortening the lead time to the final product (Wada, 2015). Other manufacturers faced similar problems. Making information systems more fluid, flexible, and resource-oriented became a cornerstone of globalization.

The fourth dynamic was building finance capabilities integral to the international activities of the auto companies themselves. The car makers which crossed borders had generally created their own installment plan financial subsidiary for both consumers and dealers; this competed with traditional retail banks. Once again moving abroad did not replicate domestic situations. Holdings and financial subsidiaries had to be built (Biss, 2017). Installment plans would not necessarily be the same. A variety of new risks had to be faced (exchange rates, interest rates, political crises, changes in tariff barriers, international conflicts, etc.). The lack of foreign currency among emerging countries or communist nations had to be overcome. The spaces for learning were quite limited: London, New York, Switzerland, with Switzerland also providing low taxes.

Car makers and components manufacturers made progress thanks to a series of new opportunities: first the development of the Eurodollar market and of the early regional trade associations, later the opening of foreign capital markets and a trend toward securitization and disintermediation in financial markets. Gradually companies created new organizational forms and conducted new types of financial activities in response. They turned the new risks into sources of profits, shortened payment periods, and offered consumer loans and leases to car buyers abroad, as well as business loans and lines of credit to dealerships, while being able to issue bonds. In Europe since 2010 the growth of lease with purchase option increased the sales of new cars and customer loyalty: it sold more than one out of two new cars in 2017, at the expense of traditional time payments and the share of banks. These financial arms also issued commercial paper and other debt instruments. GM and Ford, then Chrysler, who had pioneered domestic specialized financial entities, moved ahead with foreign subsidiaries. But today only one of these financial arms survives as such: Ford Credit. The other two have been either spun off or sold in the aftermath of the financial and automotive industry crisis of 2008–2010.

In Europe, Michelin and Renault were the pioneers and founded their main financial arms in Switzerland from 1960 onward (Fridenson and Fixari, 2009). The Japanese auto multinationals created their international finance subsidiaries much later. Toyota's managers learnt the tricks of the trade in London. After the establishment of financial subsidiaries both in Australia and the US in 1982, Toyota Finance Corporation emerged in 1988. Today it covers the company's operations on global financial markets and in 35 countries. The Koreans followed suit. Hyundai Capital Services since 1993 has grown steadily, later developing a strategic partnership with the US conglomerate General Electric, which increased its know-how in treasury, risk management, finance product design, IT, and corporate culture. After China, it is establishing footprints in emerging markets. These international financial activities have generally been quite profitable because of the size of the flows involved. However, their ultimate refinancing depends on banks. Hence auto companies may suffer when banks are in crisis internationally. So, these financial activities are the product of industry, but their volatility may result from financialization itself. Like in other multinationals, transfer pricing methods came into use to determine costs when divisions transact with each other, to get funding across the group, and to assess the taxable income (Financier Worldwide, 2010).

While internationalizing the auto industry brought achievements, it is also fraught with problems linked to the growing diversity of their markets and their products.

Challenges

Like all multinationals, auto multinationals face a high uncertainty due to the variety of their markets, but also to consumer choices on each national market. Let us take the example of the year 2016. Large pick-ups (Dodge and Ford) are very popular in the US. Latin Americans prefer heavy-duty vehicles. Indians privilege micro-cars. In Europe the market is dominated by French urban and German compact autos. In Iran, a sedan: the Peugeot 405 reigns. These differences reflect geopolitical effects, cultural specificities, purchasing power, installment plan regulation, condition of the road network, oil and fuel prices, and taxes. The leading multinational on each market in that year does not dominate more than ten nations; even then, a different model dominates in each nation (auto-moto.com, 2016). Such variety calls for enormous resources in terms of information, coordination, knowledge and skills, finance, and logistics. It is compounded by floating exchange rates since the Nixon shock of 1971 and by political instability in many emerging countries.

Auto multinationals face three main challenges: the relation to each host country's state, the necessary amount of interfirm co-operation, and the rate of exits and failure. None of these challenges is peculiar to auto multinationals, but their intensity is characteristic.

In this industry, politics matter. It goes far beyond the traditional issues of tariff barriers or taxes. Because the auto creates jobs and wealth, national governments may want to create their own firm and bar private foreign multinationals from their land: see the Soviet Union (1929–1989) or capitalist Malaysia with Proton (1983–2017), then half-sold to a Chinese firm. Similarly, the Indian government supported the birth of a national champion, Maruti in 1981, but it became a Japanese-owned subsidiary (Hansen and Nielsen, 2017). Even in officially open markets, domestic firms may lobby government to limit foreign competition. In Fascist Italy, Mussolini backed Fiat's request to prevent Ford's expansion in 1926, though this after Ford missed the chance to reach an agreement with Fiat (Toninelli, 2009). In India, most domestic car makers were subtler when they proposed and in 2013 obtained the creation of a tax on cars longer than four meters to forbid the entry of multinationals planning to produce a low-cost car.

In emerging countries, governments want to attract one or several foreign auto companies. Latin American governments in the 1970s followed three distinctive approaches: export promotion in Brazil and Mexico; market liberalization in Chile and Argentina; (unsuccessful) import substitution in the Andean Pact. By the 1980s, however, common trends prevailed: progressive internationalization of capital, heightened competition, and the homogenization of market products and demand (Jenkins, 1987). Iran is a nice case in two different and successive ways. After the Islamic revolution of 1979, the new government nationalized two private producers that had made foreign models under licensing agreements with a minority of their capital held by the foreign makes. From 2002 onward, soliciting Western and Asian companies, industrial nationalists "constructed a network of politically effective relationships to open up space for successful local industrial development, and then tapped into a set of important global linkages to create an industry with high local manufacturing content." It is the nation's largest source of employment, producing more than one million vehicles per year with 60 percent local content (Mehri, 2017: 4). Similarly, in 2014 the Russian government sold the state-owned company Avtovaz to Renault-Nissan provided it kept 49 percent of the capital.

Such relations occur in developed economies too. Local US states have funded multinationals to build greenfield plants since the 1980s. Paradoxically, during the late 1970s and early 1980s, the British government bargained for many months with the Japanese company Nissan and subsidized its establishment despite the fact it was injecting substantial amounts of capital into the recently nationalized firm British Leyland. This was not because of the Tory government's neoliberalism, but rather a strategy to keep alive the main British suppliers. In the 1990s Nissan was followed into the UK by Honda and Toyota (Demizu, 2003; Pardi, 2017). Continental European governments did the same later with Japanese then Chinese firms.

In both emerging and mature economies, local and national governments exert a continuous pressure to increase the local contents of the parts and vehicles produced and sold by multinationals. In the long run, these pressures have been successful and increased the industrializing power of these auto companies. On the other side, since the late 1960s safety, energy, and environment issues have been added to the panoply of government's relations or deals with auto multinationals, often at the request of consumers or citizens' movements. Here governments have deeply altered the technology and cost perspectives of the international auto industry.

All in all, these multiple developments show that corporate business has had to develop political capabilities. They include cutting a deal, long term strategy, adaptations to unexpected ups and downs (such as political shakeups or state managers' sudden fall from grace). There is a thin line to avoid the perils of corruption or, as with car emissions tests, of deceiving drivers and regulators (which may also happen with domestic firms). Simultaneously, car companies must balance between making concessions to enter new territories and maintaining quality and technological standards to preserve the make's global reputation. Market and production scale may be large locally but international competitiveness weak for a while. There is, however, no single pattern of response by auto multinationals to national considerations. Let us consider Russia since the late 2000s. As for modes of entry, "Hyundai-Kia, VW, and GM make ample use of outsourced production. Renault-Nissan is strengthening its commitment via M&A. Toyota uses the least foreign capital of all." For models, "all of the manufacturers other than Toyota have a multi-brand strategy, selling models in all segments. Toyota has the lowest rate of local production and the lowest rate of outsourced production." And for local strategic cars, three manufacturers "have developed local strategic cars and launched vehicles adapted to the Russian market: Hyundai-Kia, Renault-Nissan-Avtovaz, and the VW Group. Moreover, these three groups have a high rate of local production that they undertake themselves" (Tomiyama, 2016: 63–66).

Politics matter on a much broader scale. Like oil or armament multinationals, auto companies may also be confronted with the risk of international economic sanctions against the local government, as South Africa, Iran, and Russia have experienced. War too changes calculations. Even before war the military may interrupt a major agreement between auto multinationals and national firms in the name of national security. In December 1939, the Japanese military killed a joint venture between Ford, Nissan, and Toyota to manufacture civilian cars in which Ford would have had the majority. This short term decision may have changed the future of both the Japanese and US car industries (Wada and Yui, 2002). Governments also press multinationals to get involved in arms production. Subsidiaries of the same multinational may be situated in enemy nations (Turner, 2005; Wilkins and Hill, 2011; Bähr and Erker, 2015; Imlay and Horn, 2014). A resulting peace may lead either to the loss of markets or plants because of their own nation's role in the war or to new borders, which may reshape the commitments of auto multinationals.

The second set of challenges is interfirm co-operation, as in many other industries. Co-operation has increased over time, whether as contractual tie ups or formal joint ventures. They all are an alternative to straight competition; in the auto industry, the same two companies can be both partners and competitors. Co-operation reduces the flow of direct investment and in theory reduces the risks attached, though it is not straightforward.

Co-operation may result from political constraints or incentives. This definitely applies to Communist countries. The Soviet Union in the 1930s with Ford and in the 1960s with Fiat (or Renault for trucks) used Western multinationals as contractors to build or update a national automobile industry. Similarly, Communist Poland from 1965 onward renewed Poland's prewar connections with Fiat and in 1968 started production of models under license. After the Eastern bloc's return to the market economy, in 1992 Fiat purchased one of the Polish factories (Castronovo, 2005). China opened its doors in Shanghai in 1985 to Volkswagen as a 50–50 joint venture. It still benefits from a first mover advantage. However, during the same period China invited two smaller Western companies: American Motors (for the Jeep) and Peugeot. As has frequently occurred elsewhere since the 1960s, Peugeot sent outdated, complete knockdown kits that could neither compete with imported cars nor foster technology transfer. Therefore in 1994 when China generalized joint ventures as a mode of entry on the domestic market for multinationals, it imposed regulations on the use of domestic content and majority shares for state-owned Chinese companies as partners (Chin, 2010). Today, a company like GM says on its Chinese website that it "has ten joint ventures and two wholly owned foreign enterprises as well as more than 58,000 employees," offering "the broadest lineup of vehicles and brands" (GM China, 2018). The Party–state's strategic use of foreign investment and technology increased the Chinese individual's mobility, made China the world's largest auto market, transferred technologies and methods, as well as trained a labor force and a dedicated population of employees. It soon became profitable to foreign multinationals but it also enabled some Chinese firms to invest in Western firms like Volvo (totally) or (in minority) later PSA Peugeot Citroën, in order to prepare themselves to become multinationals.

In capitalist countries, local or national governments may encourage co-operation with multinationals to boost employment or innovation. Toyota tried independently in 1950, but was stymied by the Korean War. Thereafter, the Japanese government insisted on co-operation with Western makers in the early 1950s. This saved other Japanese first movers time in order to update and increase their capabilities (Cusumano, 1985). In the late 2000s, the state of California created an experimental station in Sacramento, where rival multinationals tested electric vehicles and exchanged information about their practices among themselves and with state representatives. On the other hand, in the same capitalist countries co-operation may develop for purely economic motives, mostly to share the costs of adding competences for a new vehicle or a new technology. One typical example is the joint venture between Ford and Volkswagen in Brazil: Autolatina (1987–1995) (Wellhöner, 1996). Another is the joint venture in the Czech Republic between Toyota and PSA Peugeot-Citroën, decided in 2001 and underway since 2005 for entry vehicles. It was later extended to commercial vehicles made by Peugeot in France.

Components makers have championed international co-operation since the 1960s as they often serve competing car makers and have increased the technological level of their R&D. The German Bosch and Continental, the French Valeo and Faurecia, the Canadian Magna, the Japanese Denso *et al.* are successful in such a position as they specialize on high value segments. They develop huge staffs of R & D and deep partnerships with each of their clients. Co-operation may be combined with capital controls (Hiraoka, 2000). If this does not guarantee either success or resilience, control may also take advantage of partners' complementary strengths. The Renault–Nissan alliance, which started in 1999, reduced costs, increased the attractiveness and variety of their products, and enabled entry into new countries. The alliance also led Japanese employees to pay greater attention to shareholders as one category of stakeholders. Since 2009, it added elements of integration in the following way. The visible parts of the car belong to each brand (design, product, marketing, strategy, selling); the invisible may be handed to the Alliance. The latter has built gradually common entities: first purchase, logistics, human resources, engines, production, engineering; then (2018) aftersales, quality, and business development. These entities serve as a toolbox. Analysts debate the pros and cons of alliance vs. full integration. Meanwhile, the Alliance has grown production and opened to other partners such as Daimler and Mitsubishi. This has made the Alliance one of the world's top producers alongside Volkswagen and Toyota. No American firm belongs any more to that circle.

The third and final set of challenges is frequent failure and exit on foreign markets. This applies to pocket multinationals, such as the Italian Lancia, only produced in France from 1934 to 1937 (Amatori, 1996). More broadly, economies of scale and scope are no permanent protection abroad. Some exits are linked to political risks: the few foreign auto companies present in Russia before 1917 lost their factories in the post-revolutionary nationalizations, or after the revolution in Iran in 1979, followed by the Iran–Iraq war (1980–1988) and US sanctions against the regime. Other exits are due to a combination of poor knowledge of the foreign market, insufficient organization there, and product quality problems. Renault left the US in 1960 after five years of boom; Nissan and Toyota initially failed in California in 1960 (Rae, 1982); the Korean company Hyundai's first foreign venture into Canada opened in 1989 and failed in 1993

(Lansbury *et al.* , 2007). Local management and shareholders may revolt, as with the merger of Volvo in Sweden with Renault, planned since 1989 but rejected in 1993 (Fridenson, 2015).

Other exits show the decline of competitiveness on a foreign market: Ford and GM left France in the 1950s, Chrysler left Europe in the 1970s (Hyde, 2003), BMW failed to make Leyland profitable, Peugeot left Nigeria in 2005, in 2007 Ford sold the British Jaguar and Rover to the Indian Tata and the Swedish Volvo to the Chinese Geely, and in the 2010s Ford abandoned Japan and GM left not only India and South Africa (Fourie, 2016) but also Germany and Britain. The same is true for suppliers. By 1996, two of Lucas Industries' strategic sites for diesel fuel injection, Japan and California, closed (Cheeseright, 2005). This last type of exit shows the intensified competition with greater globalization. GM's Opel was in the red from 2000 to 2017. It had an 80 percent use rate of its factories in 2017. The ratio of the payroll to the turnover was 16 percent instead of 10.3 at its European competitors. The dealers' network was too dense and disparate (PSA, 2017). GM's Vauxhall experienced similar decline and losses. Both subsidiaries were sold by GM to the French PSA in 2017. Multinationalization needs investment and a sense of local changes. Otherwise multinationals may destroy value. By 2017, all Japanese and American makes had pulled out of Australia. Unlike other fields, American firms have withdrawn from numerous countries and shown a diminishing ability to be global.

Yet comeback is possible. On a small scale, GM and Ford returned to France in the mid-1960s as producers of specialized parts for their global empire. On a big scale, Japanese first movers returned to the US in the 1960s. After increasing the quality and style of their models while cutting costs, they became immensely successful. In 1999 Nissan helped Renault back to Mexico. Both Renault and Peugeot have recently returned profitably to Iran, at least until the US economic sanctions of 2018. Renault's second entry to the US from 1979 shows that returns do not always work; by 1986 it had failed again. Return is possible; but it has a high intellectual, organizational, human, and financial price.

International competition can be brutal. For instance, during the 1980s, the ten Japanese auto companies established themselves to some extent in the world market. But during the 1990s they faced tough competition. By the end of the twentieth century, most of them had to associate with foreign companies, and only two companies (Honda and Toyota) remained independent.

Three effects are clear. First, auto multinationals have increased the technical and commercial base, the skills, and productivity of host countries. This includes the supply of top managers. Heinz Nordhoff, VW's first CEO, came from GM's Opel, Shotaro Kamiya, Toyota Motor Sales's first president, from GM Japan, Jose Lopez, VW's recent cost-killer, also from GM. Conversely, wages as well as industrial and commercial employment increased in host countries. Second, multinationals have increased auto pollution worldwide, with extreme levels in countries like Nigeria, South Korea, China, and India. Third, most car firms have repatriated most of the profits, making home country firms and elites richer. However, each of these three features may be qualified. The spread of dealerships and factories never quite ensured the convergence of products (and consumption). Hybridization became the rule in host countries. Although the number of parts in a model diminished and commonalization of parts between models increased, the variety of products and technologies became wider. In a major revision, Bosch, a leading proponent of diesel engines, began to go green after 2003, making losses in the solar business (Bähr and Erker, 2015). In a number of countries, local state elites have brought their own savings to nascent foreign manufacturing subsidiaries: see FASA in Spain for Renault in 1950, Oyak in Turkey in 1969 also for Renault, and Peugeot in Nigeria in 1970 (Laux, 1992) and thus got a share of the profits yielded by the multinationals. Contemporary China may emulate this pattern.

Conclusion

This chapter has stressed not only the underlying trends in the automobile industry's globalization, but also how the industry itself has changed over time: from multidomestic to multilocal as firms better adjusted to market variety and developed more fluid information systems. Many promising avenues for research remain. One is the place of auto multinationals in postcolonial nations, particularly Africa. Did the state see them as too independent (which may explain for instance why Indian governments in 1960, 1970, and 1977 abandoned projects to attract multinationals in order to develop mass mobility) (Maxcy, 1981)? How do former colonial makers lose a factory and a thriving market (Loubet, 2016)? How are foreign cars "used differently outside the centers of global capitalism" and stand in for both "patriarchal power and capitalist achievement," as in West Africa (Green-Simms, 2017: 5)?

On the other hand, we still know too little about how far host countries can influence the strategy and workings of auto multinationals: by expressing distinctive consumers' preferences and uses of vehicles, by building institutional incentives or barriers in areas such as energy and environment, safety, mobility, infrastructures, but also fiscal policy, labor relations, government relations with industry, national involvement in regional trade associations, by "understanding that learning is a two-way process, that the local operation almost certainly will have something to teach the rest of the global organisation" (Olcott, 2009: 55). Finally, coordination within auto multinationals may attract new interest: how do they assess at each period the potential of different countries? How are performance management systems developed to increase managers' results? Do common rules and tools plus multicultural management really weaken national differences within auto multinationals or alliances (Chiapello and Godelier, 2015)? Or do they touch preferably "people who are really open to other cultures, very globally minded, with a lot of understanding of different points of view," as a French manager at Nissan explained in 2007 (Olcott 2009: 248)? How do headquarters combine competition and co-operation with similar firms, suppliers, and inventors of today's start-ups? How do they comply with national regulations, lobby governments to have them modified, or simply cheat when they are threats to their profitability as we have seen in various scandals implicating diesel engine producers (like VW)?

There was "nothing at all inevitable" about how car companies became multinational, GM's Alfred Sloan remarked (1963: 313–314). At that point, auto multinationals still conducted relatively little economic activity abroad, compared to their cultural influence in labor and leisure. There was nothing inevitable about their dramatic expansion in the five following decades. International sales and production became strikingly important to the auto multinationals. An array of new players from emerging countries appeared, whereas a number of preexisting multinationals had to withdraw from countries where they were no longer profitable. In two countries, Britain and Sweden, local multinationals ceased to be independent or were dismantled. Pure players in the truck industry disappeared, and specialized component makers became major sources of innovation. Meanwhile buying new cars in the old industrial countries became the privilege of either companies (with fleets) or of the better-paid and older segments of the population, while such purchases attracted a growing part of the population of emerging countries.

The core of these multinationals is currently changing. Multinationalization has often led to competition with home countries, causing smaller pension allowances and a smaller labor force. This trend also affects the engineering and design centers in headquarters. Since around 2000, employment there has generally declined in favor of new technical centers and design studios located in the BRICS (Brazil, Russia, India, China, and South Africa) or Europe which host large numbers of engineers (some 10,000 people for a typical auto multinational). The continuous growth of onboard electronics and the industrial requirements to meet more demanding clean energy standards necessitate new knowledge and new organizations; they also open up new forms of value. With the help of suppliers and start-ups, these multinationals have kept up with challenges like searching for alternative energies, developing connected or autonomous vehicles, and creating efficient information systems. They also open the field to new entrants and innovative models produced by other industries such as software giants and aircraft makers. Global alliances flourish, with first-tier suppliers as cornerstones, although their success will not be easy. One massive alliance for autonomous vehicles includes Bosch, Tesla, Apple, Google, Intel, Baidu, and Lyft. Ridesharing platforms like Uber and Lyft have made "car ownership less aspirational" and Toyota has invested in Uber, VW and GM in Uber's rivals Gett and Lyft (Goyal, 2017). Automobile multinationals face fierce new and old competition; national and international regulation prompted by emissions and accidents also remains challenging. Alongside the unceasing pressure of global shareholders and financial markets, politics continue to matter.

References

Amatori, Franco (1996), *Impresa e mercato. Lancia 1906–1969* (Bologna: Il Mulino).

auto-moto.com (2016), "Découvrez le modèle leader sur chaque marché, dans plusieurs pays." www.auto-moto.com/lesderapages-auto-moto-com/decouvrez-le-modele-leader-sur-chaque-marche-dans-plusieurs-pays-85776.html#item=1 (accessed July 5, 2018).

Automobile Manufacturers Association (1956), *Automobile Facts and Figures* (36th ed., New York).

Bähr, Johannes and Erker, Paul (2015), *Bosch: History of a Global Enterprise* (Munich: C. H. Beck).

Bardou, Jean-Pierre, Chanaron, Jean-Jacques, Fridenson, Patrick, and Laux, James M. (1982), *The Automobile Revolution: The Impact of an Industry* (Chapel Hill, NC: University of North Carolina Press).

Beuving, Joost (2004), "Cotonou's Klondike: African Traders and Second-hand Car Markets in Benin," *Journal of Modern African Studies*, 42(4) 511–537.

Biss, Annika (2017), *Die Internationalisierung der Bayerischen Motoren Werke AG: Vom reinen Exportgeschäft zur Gründung eigener Tochtergesellschaften im Ausland 1945–1981* (Berlin: De Gruyter).

Bloomfield, Gerald T. (1978), *The World Automotive Industry* (Newton Abbot, UK: David & Charles).

Bonin, Hubert, Lung, Yannick, and Tolliday, Steven W. (eds.) (2003), *Ford, 1903–2003: The European History*. (Paris: Editions P.L.A.G.E.), 2 vols.

Carrillo, Jorge, Lung, Yannick, and van Tulder, Rob (eds.) (2004), *Cars, Carriers of Regionalism?* (Basingstoke: Palgrave Macmillan).

Castronovo, Valerio (2005), *Fiat: Una storia del capitalismo italiano* (Milan: Rizzoli).

Cheeseright, Paul (2005), *Lucas: The Sunset Years* (London: James & James).

Chiapello, Eve and Godelier, Eric (eds.) (2015), *Management interculturel* (Palaiseau: Editions de l'Ecole Polytechnique), 2 vols.

Chin, Gregory T. (2010), *China's Automotive Modernization: The Party-State and Multinational Corporations* (Basingstoke: Palgrave Macmillan).

Conlon, Robert and Perkins, John (2001), *Wheels and Deals: The Automotive Industry in Twentieth-Century Australia* (Aldershot: Ashgate).

Cusumano, Michael A. (1985), *The Japanese Automobile Industry: Technology and Management at Nissan and Toyota* (Cambridge, MA: Harvard University, Council on East Asian Studies).

Demizu Tsutomu (2003), *Honda: Its Technology and Management* (Osaka: Union Press).

Dicken, Peter (2011), *Global Shift*, 6th ed. (New York: Guilford).

Dicken, Peter (1986 [2015]), *Global Shift: Mapping the Changing Contours of the World Economy* (New York: Guilford Press, 7th edition).

Erker, Paul (2005), *Vom nationalen zum globalen Wettbewerb: die deutsche und amerikanische Reifenindustrie im 19. und 20. Jahrhundert* (Paderborn: Schöningh).

Fetzer, Thomas (2012), *Paradoxes of Internationalisation: British and German Trade Union Politics at Ford and General Motors* (Manchester: Manchester University Press).

Financier Worldwide (2010), "Transfer Pricing for the Automotive Sector." www.financierworldwide.com/transfer-pricing-for-the-automotive-sector/#.WwZvLdTRB9M (accessed July 5, 2018).

Forsgren, Mats, Holm, Ulf, and Johanson, Jan (eds.) (2015), *Knowledge, Networks and Power: The Uppsala School of International Business* (Basingstoke: Palgrave Macmillan).

Fourie, Louis F. (2016), *On a Global Mission: The Automobiles of General Motors International* (Victoria, BC: Friesen Press), 3 vols.

Fridenson, Patrick (2015), "Renault et l'ouverture au monde," in Françoise Berger, Michel Rapoport, Pierre Tilly, and Béatrice Touchelay (eds.), *Industries, territoires et cultures en Europe du Nord-Ouest XIXe-XXe siècles: Mélanges en l'honneur de Jean-François Eck* (Roubaix: Archives nationales du monde du travail), 35–47.

Fridenson, Patrick and Fixari, Daniel (2009), "Financement et organisation: les transformations de Renault de 1981 à 1999," in Laure Quennouëlle-Corre and André Straus (eds.), *Financer les entreprises face aux mutations économiques du XXe siècle* (Paris: Comité pour l'histoire économique et financière de la France), 329–352.

Gandlgruber, Bruno, Heske, Stephanie, Maletzky, Martina, Mark, Tino, Mercado, Alejandro, and Pries, Ludger, (2014), "Staff Mobility in German and Mexican Car Companies," in Christel Adick, Bruno Gandlgruber, and Martina Maletzky (eds.), *Cross-Border Staff Mobility: A Comparative Study of Profit and Non-Profit Organisations* (Basingstoke: Palgrave Macmillan), 43–83.

GM China (2018), "About GM China." www.gmchina.com/company/cn/en/gm/company/about-gm-china.html (accessed July 5, 2018).

Goyal, Malini (2017), "How Carmakers are Striking Strategic Alliances to Tackle Threats of Various Hues," *Economic Times*, 2 April.

Green-Simms, Lindsey B. (2017), *Postcolonial Automobility: Car Culture in West Africa* (Minneapolis, MN: University of Minnesota Press).

Hansen, Arve and Nielsen, Kenneth Bo (eds.) (2017), *Cars, Automobility and Development in Asia: Wheels of Change* (Abingdon: Routledge).

Hiraoka, Leslie S. (2000), *Global Alliances in the Motor Vehicle Industry* (Westport, CT: Quorum).

Hyde, Charles K. (2003), *Riding the Roller Coaster: A History of the Chrysler Corporation* (Detroit, MI: Wayne State University Press).

Hymer, Stephen H. (1979), *The Multinational Corporation: A Radical Approach* (New York: Cambridge University Press).

Imlay, Talbot and Horn, Martin (2014), *The Politics of Industrial Collaboration during World War II: Ford France, Vichy and Nazi Germany* (Cambridge: Cambridge University Press).

Jenkins, Rhys (1987), *Transnational Corporations and the Latin American Automobile Industry* (Basingstoke: Palgrave Macmillan).

Lansbury, Russell D., Suh, Chung-Sok, and Kwon, Seung-Ho (2007), *The Global Korean Motor Industry: The Hyundai Motor Company's Strategy* (London: Routledge).

Laux, James M. (1992), *The European Automobile Industry* (New York: Twayne).

Levinson, Mark (2006), *The Box: How the Shipping Container Made the World Smaller and the World Economy Bigger* (Princeton, NJ: Princeton University Press).

Loubet, Jean-Louis (2016), "Renault en Algérie: Automobile, pétrole et politique dans les Vingt Glorieuses," *Histoire, économie et société*, 35 (3), 114–124.

Maxcy, George (1981), *The Multinational Motor Industry* (London: Croom Helm).

Mehri, Darius (2017), *Iran Auto: Building a Global Industry in an Islamic State* (Cambridge: Cambridge University Press).

Midler, Christophe, Bernard, Jullien, and Lung, Yannick (2017), *Rethinking Innovation and Design for Emerging Markets: Inside the Renault Kwid Project* (Boca Raton, FL: CRC Press).

Nockolds, Harold (1976–1978), *Lucas: The First Hundred Years* (Newton Abbot, UK: David & Charles), 2 vols.

Olcott, George (2009), *Conflict and Change: Foreign Ownership and the Japanese Firm* (Cambridge: Cambridge University Press).

Pardi, Tommaso (2017), "Industrial Policy and the British Automotive Industry under Margaret Thatcher," *Business History*, 59(1), 75–100.

PSA (2017), "Avec le Plan PACE! Opel/Vauxhall est en route vers un avenir rentable, électrique et mondial." http://media.groupe-psa.com/fr/avec-le-plan-pace-opelvauxhall-est-en-route-vers-un-avenir-rentable-%C3%A9lectrique-et-mondial (accessed July 5, 2018).

Rae, John B. (1982), *Nissan-Datsun: A History of Nissan Motor Corporation in the U. S. A. 1960–1980* (New York: McGraw-Hill).

Reiche, B. Sebastian, Stahl, Günter K., Mendenhall, Mark E., and Oddou, Gary R. (2012), *Readings and Cases in International Human Resource Management and Organizational Behavior* (New York-London: Routledge, 5th edition).

Rieger, Bernhard (2013), *The People's Car: A Global History of the Volkswagen Beetle* (Cambridge, MA: Harvard University Press).

Schifferes, Steve (2007), "The Decline of Detroit," *BBC News*. http://news.bbc.co.uk/g o/pr/fr/-/2/hi/ business/6346299 (accessed July 5, 2018).

Scranton, Philip and Fridenson, Patrick (2013), *Reimagining Business History* (Baltimore, MD: Johns Hopkins University Press).

Shapiro, Helen (1996), "The Mechanics of Brazil's Auto Industry," *NACLA Report on the Americas*, 29(4), 28–33.

Shioji, Hiromi (2018), "Abandoned Vehicles Problem in Pacific Ocean Islands Countries," Conference Paper at the Gerpisa international colloquium, São Paulo, 11–14 June 2018.

Sloan, Alfred P. (1963), *My Years with General Motors* (Garden City, NY: Doubleday).

Tilly, Stephanie and Triebel, Florian (eds.) (2013), *Automobilindustrie 1945–2000: Eine Schlüsselindustrie zwischen Boom und Krise* (Munich: Oldenbourg Verlag).

Tolliday, Steven W. (1995), "Enterprise and State in the West German Wirtschaftswunder: Volkswagen and the Automobile Industry, 1939–1962," *Business History Review*, 69(3), 273–350.

Tolliday, Steven W. (2000), "Transplanting the American Model? US Automobile Companies and the Transfer of Technology and Management to Britain, France and Germany, 1928–1962," in Jonathan Zeitlin and Gary Herrigel (eds.), *Americanization and its Limits: Reworking US Technology and Management in Postwar Europe and Japan* (Oxford: Oxford University Press), 76–119.

Tomiyama, Eiko (2016), "How do the Marketing Strategies of Major Foreign Automobile Manufacturers in the Russian Market Differ?," *Northeast Asian Economic Review*, 4(1), 47–66.

Toninelli, Pier Angelo (2009), "Between Agnelli and Mussolini: Ford's Unsuccessful Attempt to Penetrate the Italian Automobile Market in the Interwar Period," *Enterprise & Society*, 10(2), 335–375.

Toyota (2012), "75 Years of Toyota." www.toyota-global.com/company/history_of_toyota/75years/ (accessed July 5, 2018).

Turner, Henry A. (2005), *General Motors and the Nazis: The Struggle for Control of Opel, Europe's Biggest Carmaker* (New Haven, CT: Yale University Press).

UNCTAD (United Nations Conference on Trade and Development) (2007), *World Investment Report* (New York, Geneva: United Nations).

Volpato, Giuseppe (ed.) (1989), *Commercializzare l'automobile* (Padua: Cedam).

Wada, Kazuo, (2015), "Why did Toyota Respond Less Quickly to Globalisation?," *Entreprises et Histoire*, no. 80, 134–154.

Wada, Kazuo and Yui, Tsunehiko (2002), *Courage and Change: The Life of Kiichiro Toyoda* (Nagoya: Toyota Motor Corporation).

Wellhöner, Volker (1996), *"Wirtschaftswunder," Weltmarkt, westdeutscher Fordismus: Der Fall Volkswagen* (Münster: Westfälisches Dampfboot).

Wilkins, Mira (1981), "Automobiles and International Markets," in Akio Okochi and Koichi Shimokawa (eds.), *Development of Mass Marketing: The Automobile and Retailing Industries* (Tokyo: University of Tokyo Press), 193–209.

Wilkins, Mira and Hill, Frank Ernest (2011), *American Business Abroad: Ford on Six Continents* (Cambridge: Cambridge University Press, 2nd edition).

26

MANUFACTURING AND THE IMPORTANCE OF GLOBAL MARKETING

Paula de la Cruz-Fernández

Introduction

Shortly after winning the sewing machine patent war in the United States in 1863 and establishing itself as a major US manufacturing company, Singer plants opened around the world to meet increasing global demand. This was an epoch-making event in the history of global manufacturing and illustrates the determinants behind why and how manufacturing companies expanded to global markets. As with the makers of radiators, reapers, bicycles, and automobiles, mass manufacturing and patenting were pivotal for Singer to win domestic and global markets for sewing machines. During the first five decades of activity, the US-headquartered company exceeded the production and international sales of any other manufacturer of sewing machines (Wilkins 1970; Hounshell 1984: 94–96).

The Singer case is known for its manufacturing, yet the company's adamant goal of controlling the demand side was also important (Davies 1976; Hounshell 1984: 84). While other small technology makers also invested in sales branches, Singer was particularly innovative because it built up its own global selling organization (Wilkins 1970: 35–64). "By 1905 Singer employed twice as many workers in marketing compared with its production operations," Andrew Godley calculates, mostly in canvassing: taking domestic sewing machines to virtually every interested home was a marketing pillar of the corporation. A system of installment payments was also offered to individual purchasers and a network of Singer (only) shops and warehouses greatly advanced Singer over its competitors at home and abroad (Godley 2006: 267, 280).

At the turn of the twentieth century, Singer was not the only US-headquartered company producing and selling its goods abroad. Other companies such as Kodak, the American Radiator Company, and International Harvester also produced and sold outside the United States (Wilkins 1970). The American Radiator Company had manufacturing and selling subsidiaries in France and Germany by the end of the nineteenth century, where consumers had demonstrated interest in the American technology over local manufacturers (Wilkins 1969). International Harvester's agricultural machinery was also distributed across Europe. In Russia, the company realized the importance of providing credit to farmers and having a sales organization that could better understand the consumers' economy (Carstensen 1984: 225–229). What made Singer unique, and successful for so long, however, was the building of globally connected markets based on cultures of private consumption.

When Singer sewing machines were introduced in households, they generated new markets for clothing. Their availability also attracted new female consumers in countries like Japan, and India, where sewing was primarily done by men (Gordon 2008; Arnold 2011). High demand for sewing machines worldwide was met by hundreds of canvassers who traveled across countries and cities knocking on doors and selling sewing machines to individual households. Although millions of sewing machines were used in workshops, whether large or family based, such a system worked because most sewing and embroidered products were done inside the home. Even in advanced industrialized nations such as the United States and the United Kingdom, where family or home-based workshops also remained important alongside factory establishments, wide availability of ready-to-wear clothing was not generalized in urban centers until the early twentieth century (Burman 1999; Green 1997; Zakim 2003). The same household-focused marketing system was gradually introduced, and generally successfully, throughout the world (Davies 1976).

Along with traveling agents and salesmen, Singer was made up of a robust and extended salesforce that focused on the products of machine sewing, namely embroidery and plain sewing, to make sewing machines more marketable. Although often outside official employees' records, women within the organization created marketing strategies that connected with the practices of everyday life, such as the making of house linens or embroidering for infant clothes. "Singer women," i.e., sales people making products for the home and representing the company by using only Singer sewing machines, created a strong connection between private, customary household practices, and the global organization. Because it extends to the realm of culture, historians of international business have largely overlooked the role of sewing and embroidery household practices in building the multinational corporation. This chapter looks at window fronts, sewing and embroidery exhibitions, and home sewing and embroidery lessons that were part of Singer's organization in every country where it operated by the 1920s. These visually attractive scenes demonstrate that marketing reached within the limits of the private home and thus explains the importance of maintaining a global, centrally managed organization for more than a century. While historians of multinationals focus primarily on manufacturing operations, a market analysis of how the products reach the consumer captures the role of culture and social practices in global business. This chapter builds upon the current scholarship on Singer and US multinational corporations (Bucheli 2005; Bonin and de Goey 2009; Wilkins and Hill 2011; Arnold 2013; Gordon 2012), by bringing women, culture, and the consumer side into the analysis of global corporate organization. By exploring why women sewed and embroidered, the products they made, and how these became symbols and marketing strategies of the Singer Sewing Machine Corporation globally, this study brings the company–customer relations element to the front of the analysis of multinational corporations.

First, this chapter examines the organization of international exhibitions, where manufacturers met to showcase their progress in the late nineteenth century and first decades of the twentieth century. These exhibitions became Singer's initial marketing strategy to address global markets. Second, the chapter explores Singer's system of shops and window fronts, well established by the 1920s, to situate Singer's marketing efforts both locally and globally. The sources of this research, mostly visual culture materials or marketing tools elaborated with the aim of selling, are unconventional in the study of multinationals' history. These were made at different Singer departments such as the Embroidery Department, a unit created in the 1890s to support the company's marketing efforts, and the Education Department, created in the mid-1920s. Andrew Gordon (2012) points to their development and clear influence in creating new consumers for sewing machines in Japan in the twentieth century. These efforts, this study demonstrates, were global and constituent of the multinational corporate organization. Departments that focused on marketing were key both for the success of the company and for its corporate global organization that only continued to grow after 1900.

Going global, going domestic: international exhibitions and the global marketing of traditional home sewing and ornamental embroidery

Beginning in the 1870s, Singer developed a unique strategy that combined marketing with family and traditional sewing and embroidery practices and focused on international consumers. At international exhibitions in the United States, manufacturers celebrated modernity through their exhibits of machines, large and small, linking industrialization prowess with civilization and economic advancement. Singer, unlike its sewing machine competitors, placed special emphasis on these events, organizing large displays at the Philadelphia World's Fair in 1876, the Chicago World's Fair in 1893, and at the Louisiana Purchase Exhibition of 1904. The 1851 British Great Exhibition of the Works of Industry of All Nations had set up a precedent for international meetings concentrated on manufacturing progress around the globe. International exhibits, celebrated regularly in the United States after the 1870s to show the country's recovery from war and its world leadership in machine manufacturing, were exemplary encounters of manufacturers and consumers embracing the novelties of a new era of industrialization (Rydell 1993). At the Machinery Hall in Philadelphia, for example, thousands of newly invented machines, from stoves and typewriters to foundries and engines, were exhibited.

At its first large exhibit in 1876, Singer began hiring women to oversee these events (or at least to decide what and how to display). Rather than highlighting mass manufacturing of clothing, Singer maintained its preference to display how and what women sewed and embroidered for private purposes. In doing so, the company elevated the consumer (as a producer) to an important element of its organization. Sewing machines were sold to make products, becoming a household tool continuously running and thus making home manufacturers dependent on both the company's maintenance service and its creative experts who came up with ideas of what to make with the sewing machine.

Singer's attention to women and their sewing appeared even earlier on in the company's history. In 1850, the Singer Co. was created. By 1865, Singer's Family model became the company's most popular machine (Hounshell 1984: 87–91). From then on, Singer's technology varied slightly. Decorations in the machine or attachments for sewing styles were added, though changes to the basic model were limited. Before the American Civil War (1861–1865), in fliers and in store demonstrations in the United States, it was women who demonstrated for other customers what to do with a sewing machine. And it was women who the company was trying to attract when it began decorating its showrooms and hiring salesmen to take the sewing machine to households (Burman 1999; Bacon 1946; Daly Goggin and Fowkes Tobin 2009).

Singer was not alone in targeting women, yet the company's investment in marketing with women was larger than other companies' efforts. Other US manufacturers such as Domestic, New Home, Household, or Wheeler and Wilson issued trade cards that sought to attract women and housewives as consumers. In 1882, for example, Domestic published a trade card featuring a couple getting married. A sewing machine, the card explained, was the perfect present for the newly married woman. To show its manufacturing counterparts and competitors that the company was on the rise after the war, Singer hosted the largest display the company would ever organize at a national convention. Internationalizing enterprises such as McCormick or International Harvester also organized displays within exhibits manufacturing halls (Carstensen 1984).

Yet Singer went bigger than others. It put up an entire building to show what the family sewing machine, a sewing machine manufactured for individual and domestic use, could achieve.

At the Centennial Building, the products on display ranged from cushions to bibs, all items that were considered to make a comfortable home. Women across Singer stores in the United States, and some from the newly opened shops in Germany and England, sent samples of their work, such as embroidered table covers, curtains, and embroidered scarfs. Robes, pillow shams, children's clothes, and embroidered aprons filled up the rooms of Singer's building in Philadelphia's most important industrial exhibit of the nineteenth century (Centennial Singer Manufacturing Co.'s Catalog of Exhibits, 1876: 4–9).

Philadelphia's exhibit meant an important shift in corporate organization. Although a specific department was not created until the company prepared to participate in Chicago's World Exhibition in 1893, significant employee and branding efforts were directed toward making Singer look like a company that cared for households, or at least for their ornamentation and for keeping sewing and embroidery traditions alive. As Elizabeth Bacon (1946: 90) put it, Singer "blaz[ed] the trail" in marketing and advertising sewing machines. The world's largest manufacturer of sewing machines, the Singer Sewing Machine Company, had already taken the lead in marketing by 1900 (Bacon 1946; Godley 2006). By displaying the insides of an ideal household and the products that women could put in it, Singer penetrated the environments of private life more effectively than issuing trade cards with images of aristocratic looking women and families. At exhibitions, women were talking to women and showing them that sewing machines were there to ease their labor and to enhance their role in the home. The company recognized that sample making of household items, such as tablecloths or curtains, something that was generally taught to girls along with reading or cooking, was an effective, low cost marketing strategy. Although women did not become Singer canvassers, because traveling and selling were not considered appropriate activities for respectable women to engage in, they became a pillar of Singer's permanent marketing strategies (Friedman 2004: 53, 60).

For the Chicago exhibit, Singer had already created a department to make samples to be displayed in stores and in international showrooms. Women working at stores in the United States and in Singer's foreign markets in the early 1890s, such as Germany, England, and Spain, sent samples to demonstrate the products of their labor. By 1893 the Embroidery Department, filled with women both skilled and in training, took care of sample making. They also oversaw the preparation of showrooms for domestic sewing machines at exhibitions. At the Chicago's World Exhibition, Singer announced its exhibit of "Fine Sewing and Art Needlework" to be hosted in the Manufacturers Liberal Arts building. Here, the official catalogue for the exhibit explained, "a half core of young ladies, [demonstrated] all the different kinds of sewing and Art Needle Work that can be accomplished on the Sewing Machines." Embroidered curtains, bed covers, and tablecloths, all made on Singer domestic sewing machines, transformed household rooms into modern homes, they explained (The Singer Manufacturing Co.'s Exhibit of Family Sewing Machines and Art Embroidery 1893; A New Era in Family Sewing Machines for Fine Sewing and Art Needlework 1893).

Machines made a home modern because domestic tasks were done more efficiently and economically. Such was a common association among advertisers of new technology in the nineteenth and twentieth centuries. Advertisers of washing machines focused on time saving before the twentieth century, and on washing efficiency in the 1940s (Woersdorfer 2017). Also, common among manufacturers, though not specifically US sewing machines companies, was Singer's extension of its product's association with modernity to its international consumers. Singer sewing machines were manufactured at three locations, the United States, England, and Germany in the 1880s, and in at least four factories in four different countries by 1900. By 1905, machines were delivered by thousands of canvassers and sold throughout the world. For Chicago's grand exhibit in 1893, Singer prepared a collection of postcards portraying either families or women by themselves from around the world using the sewing machine in a domestic looking setting and making traditional embroidery items. Only in the case of India's postcard were men the ones using the sewing machine because they were mostly in charge of tailoring. The *darzi* or tailor was commonly seen with a sewing machine, but the idea of sewing as a domestic and proper activity for women in the home gained acceptance over the nineteenth and twentieth century (Arnold 2011: 411–416, 426). The same type of advertising was used at the Pan-American Exhibit in 1901 (Buffalo, New York) and the Louisiana Purchase Exposition of 1904 (St. Louis, Missouri). In St. Louis, as had happened almost thirty years earlier, Singer had its own pavilion where "examples of beautiful needlework done on Singer machines for family use," were on display while trade cards were given as a handout (*Sewing Machine Times* 14(312) 1904). Following nineteenth-century cultural attitudes that highlighted the United States' superior role in terms of development and industry over indigenous peoples and overseas competitors, Singer cards described the sewing machine as a modernizing tool (Adas 2009; Domosh 2006).

Cultural constructions of race and gender traveled alongside commodities such as sewing machines and reapers as their advertisers built up an image of civilization and modernity around their consumption (Domosh 2006). The gender component was key as well within Singer's descriptions and images, showing the sewing machine as woman's most important technology to satisfy and achieve a western-based definition of domesticity around the world. Singer's homogenizing assumptions of what it meant to be a woman in the 1900s, and the race-based characterization of a civilized world versus the yet-to-be civilized indigenous peoples, was part of most of its advertising for exhibits in the United States. Women in Cuba, a territory under US jurisdiction after 1898, commonly used Singer sewing machines to make their "light, loose dress[es], befitting the climate and her surroundings." The Philippines card, which like the Cuban one showed a woman alone wearing traditional attire, praised the US role in liberating and developing this part of the world after centuries of formal colonialism. "Ladies of Manila" now used Singer sewing machines, which, "like in every other part of the world, [are] one of the foremost factors of civilization." In most cases, Singer trade cards celebrated women's beauty and their devotion to the home or the family. The descriptions averaged both a condescending and a celebratory tone, placing the responsibility of social progress, modernity, and the protection of culture, tradition, and even racial superiority upon women and their prescribed domestic role in the home. "The Spanish woman," a 1904 Singer card for Spain described, "has none of the creole languor of the Spanish-descended woman of Cuba, Mexico and tropical America." By "industrious[ly]" making traditional embroidered items and sewing on modern Singer sewing machines, she, "better than the man of her race," would light Spain's future (Singer National Costume Cards, Wolfsonian Museum, 1904).

Exhibit visitors who read and kept Singer's cards were possibly affirmed in their conviction of the international attraction and wonders of modern, and American, industrial innovation. The 1901 and 1904 cards included more locations in Latin America where Singer sewing machines and other US-made manufacturers were being delivered beginning in the twentieth century, and where the United States had more and more geopolitical interests (O'Brien 1996). By publishing the cards depicting people from 36 nations, from every location in the world where the company had a manufacturing plant (five in Europe and the United States by 1905) or a retail organization, however, Singer also showed the extension of its marketing system. At the turn of the twentieth century, Singer had a distribution system in place capable of moving hundreds of thousands of machines across borders and oceans, and on a wide variety of transportation systems including canoes and donkeys, whatever it took to connect with consumers all around the world (*Red S Review* 1920–1950).

Singer's investment in marketing in the United States and overseas was high. There is no data to compare with other sewing machine manufacturers in the nineteenth century mostly because Singer's overseas marketing operations were larger than any of its American competitors. Singer spent half of its earnings in retail stores, employee salaries, and travel all around the world (Godley 2006). Singer's marketing developed quickly as a response to high competition in the United States in the 1860s and 1870s, yet global marketing took its own path as the company did not have plants everywhere its machines were sold. Merchants and wholesalers were selling goods made in plants in the United States and Great Britain all around the world, but Singer's exclusive selling system already in place in 23 countries by 1905 was incomparable to any other global manufacturer at the time (Jones 2005: 195; Godley 2006: 285; Singer Sewing Machine Co. *Directory of Shops* 1905).

Contracting canvassing men to transport sewing machines, and staging elaborate displays at international exhibitions, were the company's main interests around 1900. Singer shops, however, became Singer's best way to market in a more permanent way in the United States and abroad. Unlike temporary international exhibitions, shops could act as showrooms. While other sewing machine manufacturers chose to sell their machines at new and expanding department stores opening in large urban centers throughout the world in the last third of the nineteenth century, Singer refused to do so, maintaining exclusivity through a unique system of selling, demonstrating, and technology maintenance all within one location. Within stores, all sorts of activities to sell machines were organized. Singer shops hosted permanent demonstrations, group lessons, manuals, contests, and schools. At the stores and in the manuals, what mattered was household sewing and ornamental embroidery. The Embroidery Department, initially created to make samples for exhibits and schools, was now composed of women and men from all around the world applying and adjusting the sewing machine to household and family purposes. The strategy was so successful in increasing sales of the family machine that Singer created another department for marketing purposes in the mid-1920s, the Education Department. While the Manufacturing Trade Department had grown in the first four decades of expansion by opening plants across Europe, both the Embroidery and the Education Departments were on the rise. Globally, during the first half of the twentieth century, they would become Singer's most important and successful part of the corporate organization.

Global marketing for global domesticity

Salesmen knocking on doors and retail establishments were a common scene of early twentieth-century urban centers. This was a time of automobile manufacturing expansion, for example, and yet the Singer Sewing Machine Company, after opening its Russian factory in 1902, almost exclusively expanded through its marketing organization (Carstensen 1984; Wilkins 1970). While Singer shops and buildings were opening in large cities and small towns throughout the world, the number of company manufacturing plants stayed static (except for Italy's 1934, Australia's and Istanbul's in 1960) and were capable of supplying Singer retail locations in every continent. Trade limitations of Singer's first global expansion, namely counterfeiting and competition, had been tackled through marketing as well; and this strategy continued to be effective against other global manufacturers such as the German Pfaff at least until the mid-twentieth century (Gordon 2012: 151–185; Arnold 2013). Since the 1870s, Singer sewing machines were only sold at Singer locations and by Singer agents, and such strategy was applied overseas as well. Singer built up its name by making it visible not only in its sewing machines, but also in stores in the most crowded locations of towns and cities, at schools, at exhibitions, and through their hundreds of salesmen and saleswomen that traveled all throughout each country where the company operated. Sewing machine companies worldwide were using stores and canvassers as well, but well below the level of Singer (Berghahn 2014: 58–62; Hausen 1985; Iza-Goñola de Miguel 2005; Gordon 2012). Although by the 1920s, canvassers were still an essential part of Singer's (retail) organization, Singer's marketing focus was turning to two departments – the Embroidery Department and the Education Department. Both remained concerned about reaching remote locations and offering credit options to consumers, but the idea that the Singer sales person had to be more in alliance with the customer's sewing and embroidery preferences and practices gained more relevance.

The Embroidery Department had been created to organize displays at international exhibits and stores, and it concentrated on ornamentation and artistic sewing. Prescriptive literature on domesticity in the nineteenth century included sewing as an activity that girls would ideally learn as they became young women, and eventually wives and mothers. Embroidery was fundamental for legitimizing the use of an industrial technology in the house because it allegedly uplifted the practice of home sewing from a house chore to an artistic, female identity enrichment practice. Embroidered or decorated family and household objects carried the maker's unique touch, the embroiderer's original sense and appreciation of beauty, and an understanding of decoration (Boris 1986; Burman 1999). An additional element that embroidery brought to marketing was its culturally specific attribution. Decorative motifs were distinct depending on location. Whether geometric, floral, or figurative, many embroidery designs were exclusive to certain regions, cultures, and nations and such diversity of patterns and styles added even more value to the work that women around the world were doing by making samples of embroidered objects with a Singer sewing machine. Because it could be used in decorating the home, or in adding a personal touch to the family's clothes, embroidery brought the private sphere to Singer.

Embroidery schools were a widespread practice in every region where Singer had a branch or a retail organization by the beginning of the 1930s. These schools became the company's central method of marketing traditional and household-related sewing and embroidery. The official establishment of these courses began in the early 1910s (*Red S Review* 2(3 and 4) 1930). They were a result of the success of sewing and embroidery one-to-one demonstrations. Since the company opened its first stores, sales people had been encouraged to show potential clients the range of objects that they could make with a sewing machine. Canvassing agents, mostly with the help of instructresses, also found that demonstrations would attract more customers. It was extra time that the sales agent could spend with a client. Either inside homes, at markets, or in the streets of small towns, sample making was an extended Singer practice throughout the world. In a market in Kajang, British Indies, a location controlled by the Singapore Agency, two men demonstrated sewing to a crowd in a street market. Similar reports arrived at Singer's British Central Office from agents in Spain and Portugal. In the early 1900s, women accompanied Mexican Singer agents to advertise sewing machines in rural areas. Later in 1931, Singer's Mexico City Office reported that "travelling instructresses" that went with male sales agents in their automobiles, "[were] helping the business along and creating enthusiasm in embroidery." (*Red S Review* 9(1) August 1928, 14(3) March 1931, 15(11) July 1934, 12(7) March 1932; González 1974: 99).

Courses generally enrolled about fifteen students but fluctuated significantly. For example, when the Mexico Academy of Instruction opened in Mexico City in 1928, 300 students enrolled over the course of two months. Classes took place within Singer shops unless there was a specific room or even an entire floor of a Singer building that could be dedicated to instruction and sampling. Such was the case of Teheran's School of Embroidery, for example, which had "attracted much attention, [embroidery] being a traditional art in Persia." The items made within Singer embroidery lessons were often used for window decoration and for occasional exhibits. At times, local exhibits also served as an extraordinary event to connect not only with the regular customer but also with government officials that were implementing needle-work and sewing within public education systems. Peru's president Augusto B. Leguía, along with other Catholic Church and government officials, visited the inauguration of Lima's central office exhibit in January of 1927. They greeted exhibitors, admired their work on Singer sewing machines, and they contracted with the company to supply machines for man-datory sewing instruction at girls' schools (*Red S Review* 7(2) October 1925, 9(9) May 1928, 8(11) August 1927).

Singer students and Singer instructors around the world all made products related to home activities and family traditions. The patterns and motifs, however, varied across borders. Images from Singer schools in Central Europe and the Middle East showed rows of students using sewing machines to make cushion covers, tablecloths, bed sheets, monochrome pillow covers and napkins, and children's clothes such as "pinafores, frocks, [and] jumper suits." They made these using Singer's updated domestic sewing machines attachments such as the binder, the under braider, the ruffle, or the quilter (*Red S Review* 1(1), 2(2–5, 7) 1920). Eventually, the company's marketing organization gathered these designs and products and created sewing machines manuals, which would then be used in schools and stores to provide the client with a quick look of what the sewing machine could do. In the early twentieth century, household appliances like vacuum cleaners were accompanied by general user manuals. Kitchen appliances, such as blenders, might have been sold along with cook books or recipes for usage with the technology. Singer published both of these manuals, in different languages, explaining the mechanics and how to use different parts of the machine. Singer's sewing departments published the applied sewing manuals, a more instructional, personal manual that explained how to make products for the home and clothing for the family. These were also translated, yet their content was the same for all markets, thus assuming homogeneity of embroidery making (Singer *Manual of Modern Embroidery* 1893; *Libro Singer de bordados* 1922). Women in each location, however, adjusted the manuals' instructions to their own needs and loves. In a photograph from the Hard-enger office in Norway sent in 1927, for example, women wore the "traditional head-dresses and aprons of countrywomen." Here, the Singer editor reminded, the sewing machine was "assisting the preservation and use of these traditional costumes" (*Red S Review* 9(1) 1927: 16–18). Singer encouraged this as locally tailored advertising. The company praised instructors who taught how to make local designs in each school. The appeal to local traditions continued to be present throughout the twentieth century in Singer's marketing efforts, as it had been at international exhibitions in 1893 and 1904 showing images of women and men in regional attire using the sewing machine.

Items taught at Singer's exclusive embroidery schools were then displayed in the company's store windows. Besides "cleanliness, neatness, activity, colour, [and] simplicity," windows would be sources of "magnetism" when properly decorated with embroidery and sewed objects made with a Singer sewing machine (*Red S Review* 10(9) 1929: 6). "Appealing to the Spanish taste," saleswomen in Spain decorated store windows with embroidery hoops that were used to make "elaborate arrangements" for individual store displays. Singer allowed and supported locally made advertising, knowing that the ultimate focus of it was the company's sewing machine. The company granted independence in the way exhibits and products followed local and traditional calendars and motifs, which also appeared to solve the idea that sewing machines were all about making women work more hours. In addition, it gave the name of the company a local flavor that made local consumers not necessarily know where the machine was made. To encourage employees from each of the retail locations to commit to marketing, in Spain and

Uruguay, for example, managers organized window display competitions. Onsite and window demonstration were also popular. Saleswomen could make "little articles, simple in construction, [and] neat in appearance," so that viewers could easily see how to use the sewing machine at home (*Red S Review* 2(5) 1920, 3(12) 1922, 6(6) 1923, 9(4, 5) 1928).

Embroidery became so crucial for Singer marketing strategies that by 1927 all staff members at every store were urged to learn to make small items or ornaments on the sewing machine. "Study groups," as staff courses were called, were at first all taken by women. Offices in Aradippou (Cyprus), Khartoum (Sudan), and Ebiar (Syria), sent photographs of their establishments offering such classes and making goods that would be shown to potential clients at their homes, in street markets, or inside the stores. Over the years, managers and employees realized that "giving demonstrations" would get sales people "into more homes." As they put it, "something simple and something original" would have a "dramatic effect," as customers would see both the speed and beauty that using a sewing machine would deliver. Male employees, especially the canvassers who worked on commission, would benefit from knowing some basics of home sewing and embroidery making. In England, instructional courses to staff began in 1924. The company began issuing employee certificates in the early 1930s to encourage this group of employees to come aboard on the demonstration marketing strategy (*Red S Review* 9(2) 1927, 7(9) 1926, 9(5) 1928, 12(8) 1931). Whether this specific practice was fully applied around the world is difficult to track due to the independence that regional offices had in terms of marketing. There was, however, a global, an all-encompassing level of commitment to institutionalize embroidery as a marketing strategy.

Plain sewing and home dressmaking were also marketing allures along with ornamental embroidery throughout the late nineteenth and early twentieth centuries, yet these gained more relevance later in the 1920s and 1930s. Such ascendancy coincided with the institutionalization and normalization of home economics within national education systems. Also called domestic science, women across the world were involved in the rationalization of housework, including cooking, cleaning, and sewing. Schools and leagues were created to train women in household management and the publication of home economics manuals and prescriptive literature boomed in the 1920s and 1930s following nineteenth-century educators like Catherine Beecher in the United States (1845) or Pilar Pascual de San Juan in Spain (1878). Companies were fully integrated in this movement in the United States, where salesmen and research departments from corporations such as General Electric collaborated hand in hand with government home economists introducing technology into the classroom. Singer was also able to work with government officials and private organizations around the world. In the United Kingdom and in Spain, for example, Women's Institutes and schools welcomed Singer instructors to their sewing courses, and Singer women were major players in Japan and India as home-dressmaking and dressmaking professionalization systems developed in the first third of the twentieth century (Goldstein 2012; Gordon 2012; Arnold 2013; *Red S Review* 10(9) 1928).

Home-dressmaking lessons were easily added to Singer courses that took place at Singer locations because instructors were generally acquainted with the practice of family and home-based clothing. Home-dressmaking classes at Singer stores resembled those taking place at government-led education institutions (like the Bureau of Home Economics in the United States) and at companies' research programs, such as Procter & Gamble that hired home economists to lead research and advertising of food oil, or Sears that incorporated a home economics graduate to test and demonstrate consumer appliances in the United States in the 1920s. Singer offered sewing and cutting courses directly to schools and vocational institutes and also supplied the sewing machines. The company's Educational Department was created in 1925 to coordinate these courses and the supply of sewing machines to schools. Manuals were also published to supplement the lessons of public teachers, allowing total independence of lessons in the class-room (*Red S Review* 7(1) 1925). At Singer dressmaking courses, students would first learn how to draw patterns. Manuals taught them how to cut them too, and to alter already-made patterns to fit specific measurements. As the Singer's manual, *How to Make a Dress* (1932) described, assembling the cloth parts was not the last step, however, because fitting and decorating a dress by tucking, ruffling, making buttonholes, or plaiting would also be possible on the sewing machine and it would assure that piece of clothing "to have a distinctive value."

Like most of the students who took Singer-led courses, instructors of both the Embroidery Department and the Educational Department were women. The social composition of this group of employees is unclear. Mostly, they were lower- to middle-class young women who could apply their sewing abilities to the world of sales. At times, saleswomen left their positions when they married, yet because sewing was an activity accepted to be part of women's domestic role, many of Singer's saleswomen remained in the company throughout their lives. Women occupied other positions as well such as cashiers, clerks, and testing machines in the manufacturing plant. Regularly, Singer recognized "long periods of faithful and effective service" by issuing certificates or featuring the story of an employee in the company's marketing magazine *Red S Review*. In 1923, the company praised the work of New York's office art embroidery operator, Miss Elizabeth Boehm. A saleswoman as well, Miss Boehm was "an expert in hand embroidery" before becoming part of Singer where she stayed for more than thirty years (*Red S Review* 4(10) 1923, 8(2) 1926: 10–12).

To become part of Singer's Embroidery and Educational Departments, knowledge and expertise on sewing and embroidery were a must. In England, both departments were clearly defined within the company's corporate organization. Women instructresses attended company events as employees and both departments followed the structure of other parts of the business, having managers, employees, and apprentices. In some parts of the world, however, both departments existed because women had been participating in the business accompanying canvassers, organizing exhibits, and teaching embroidery courses, but there was not a clear separation between sewing experts and the rest of the selling organization. Ever since the company began having stores and traveling agents, the figure of the instructress has existed and throughout the twentieth century her presence and role continued to be shaped. "Moving instructions," for example, which were Singer vans that carried sewing machines and samples in the back, were widely introduced by the 1930s in the United States, Mexico, and in Europe. In 1931, Mexico's Singer central office reported that their automobiles, which were "equipped with samples of all kinds of sewing and embroidery work, machines, and accessories," had an essential role in creating new customers. In all of them, "Travelling instructresses," accompanied the district's canvasser, and they "[were] creating enthusiasm in embroidery" and thus propelling sales, the manager assured (*Red S Review* 12(7) 1931: 18–19).

Singer's marketing system varied little from country to country, yet it was a culturally flexible system. It was composed of local personnel that generally catered to local traditions and times which is evidence of both the flexibility of Singer's marketing system and the openness of nineteenth and twentieth centuries culture to industrial consumer goods that forged the modern world. Scholars often search for organizations' capacity to adapt, while undermining the demand's side to adjust and rebuild itself to integrate novelty. Singer's Embroidery and Education Departments were composed of local personnel in every country where the multinational operated. These units went from somewhat unplanned sewing and embroidery demonstrations in the 1870s to acquiring an official space in the organization worldwide by the 1930s. In each country, both departments adapted a versatile machine to local uses by creating samples and new manuals, decorating Singer stores, and staffing "moving instructions" vans. Women assembled exhibits addressing local taste and traditions, and sewing experts connected with local officials, making Singer sewing machines part of schools. Marketing personnel made Singer local.

By 1914, Singer was one of several multinationals with factories overseas. However, its integrated selling organization continued to be unique in the sewing machine industry and even in the distribution of other branded goods. Manufacturers of branded goods and chemicals owned and managed factory locations across borders like Singer did by the beginning of World War I. French Saint-Gobain glass production was produced in eight countries, while the British Lever Brothers managed the production of soap in thirty-three locations. During the interwar years, Singer continued its multinational organization, controlling from production to customer relations. It did so like other multinationals such as Ford, Nestlé, or Coca-Cola that developed international operations, generally using a franchise system to sell products (Jones 2005). For Singer, canvassing continued to be the company's key for selling beyond large urban centers and controlling accounts, and women were a fundamental part of this marketing strategy (Gordon 2008, 2012).

World War II disturbed global production and even though the company returned its factories to produce sewing machines, and revitalized its selling organizations throughout the world by opening new buildings and continuing investment in marketing activities, Singer never recovered its 1920s global market dominance. In locations like Japan or Spain, for example, local competition was already strong by the 1940s. After the war, product diversification also intensified, and Singer also sold vacuum cleaners, irons, and sewing accessories such as trimmers or electrical scissors. During this time, other manufacturers of washing machines, refrigerators, and vacuum cleaners such as General Electric or Hoover expanded and modernized their technologies rather fast. Household electrification intensified these developments, and the manufacturing and selling of small household appliances, especially for the kitchen, expanded greatly worldwide. Singer locations in 1951 were celebrating the company's centenary, praising their canvassers and the potential of home dressmaking, but Singer had already lost its exclusivity as a manufacturer of consumer goods. Singer's largest manufacturing plant, the Clydebank factory, closed its doors in 1980.

Conclusions

Through marketing, global manufacturer Singer connected industry to culture worldwide for almost a century. The scholarship on global manufacturing has mostly centered on manufacturing capabilities (Wilkins 1969, 1970; Wilkins and Hill 2011; Hounshell, 1984; Jones 2005), but marketing was equally important for creating and maintaining global sales. Mass marketing secured the Singer Sewing Machine Company's corporate success around the world by making the company's name and its sewing machines part of the private sphere, of family, personal, and local life. Targeting some of the most private practices of the home, the making of clothing and ornaments, became one of the pillars of one of the first US multinational enterprises. Paying attention to consumers as experts on sewing machines and making them part of the company's selling organization beginning in the 1860s was central to Singer's national and global expansion.

Manufacturers of chemicals, machinery, and branded consumer goods led multinational manufacturing at the turn of the twentieth century (Jones 2005). For Singer, manufacturing and marketing grew hand in hand between the 1860s and World War I, but marketing continued to advance throughout the twentieth century, opening markets in countries where manufacturing might have been non-viable. While expensive at first, building up an exclusive marketing organization in different locations – with most of its agents being native – across the globe paid off by averting competitors and creating long-term relationships with consumers. Shops, international exhibits, sewing courses, embroidery contests, and the canvassers gave the company's name and its sewing machine the opportunity to be part of everyday life, both in the home and in the public sphere, connecting these spaces in ways that not only promoted new forms of economic activity, but also generated cultural experiences that became ingrained within households' economies and national cultures.

Though consumer goods were some of the first industries to expand multinational operations, and the distribution channels and relations with consumers prove essential to understanding global expansion, studies of consumers and producers are often done separately in the case of international business. This study demonstrates that women were key to building up Singer's global marketing and rethinks the role of consumption and gender as elements that are central to understand global manufacturing and marketing. Experts on sewing, generally women, were not passive consumers of sewing machines. Women and others who sew were technically knowledgeable and experts in threads, patterns, designs, and traditions. Thus, consumers were producers as well, of clothes and house linens, of objects that often carried meanings important to local cultures and lives. Whether to create new consumers, as Singer women did in Japan (Gordon 2012), or to maintain local cultural practices that had embroidery and sewing at the center, the integration and understanding of consumption practices within the organization's strategies opened new and exclusive markets for Singer throughout more than a century.

Bibliography

Adas, Michael. (1989), *Machines as the Measure of Men: Science, Technology, and Ideologies of Western Dominance* (Ithaca, NY: Cornell University Press).

Adas, Michael. (2009), Dominance by Design: Technological Imperatives and America's Civilizing Mission (Cambridge, MA: Harvard University Press.

Arnold, David. (2011), "Global Goods and Local usages: The Small World of the Indian Sewing Machine, 1875–1952," *Journal of Global History*, 6(3), 407–429.

Arnold, David. (2013), *Everyday Technology: Machines and the Making of India's Modernity* (Chicago, IL: University of Chicago Press).

Bacon, Elizabeth. (1946), "Marketing Sewing Machines in the Post-Civil War Years," *Bulletin of the Business Historical Society*, 20(3), 90–94.

Berghahn, Volker R. (2014), *American Big Business in Britain and Germany: A Comparative History of Two "Special Relationships" in the 20th Century* (Princeton, NJ: Princeton University Press).

Besse, Susan K. (1996), *Restructuring Patriarchy: The Modernization of Gender Inequality in Brazil, 1914–1940* (Chapel Hill, NC: University of North Carolina Press).

Bonin, Hubert and de Goey, Ferry. (2009), *American Firms in Europe: Strategy, Identity, Perception and Performance (1880–1980)* (Genève: Libraire Droz).

Boris, Eileen. (1986), *Art and Labor: Ruskin, Morris, and the Craftsman Ideal in America* (Philadelphia, PA: Temple University Press).

Boris, Eileen. (1994), *Home to Work: Motherhood and the Politics of Industrial Homework in the United States* (Cambridge, New York: Cambridge University Press).

Boris, Eileen and Daniels, Cynthia R. (1989), *Homework: Historical and Contemporary Perspectives on Paid Labor at Home* (Urbana, IL: University of Illinois Press).

Bucheli, Marcelo (2005), *Bananas and Business: The United Fruit Company in Colombia, 1899–2000* (New York: New York University Press).

Burman, Barbara. (ed.), (1999), *The Culture of Sewing: Gender, Consumption and Home Dressmaking* (Oxford: Berg).

Carstensen, Fred V. (1984), *American Enterprise in Foreign Markets: Studies of Singer and International Harvester in Imperial Russia* (Chapel Hill, NC: University of North Carolina Press).

Daly Goggin, Maureen and Fowkes Tobin, Beth. (2009), *Women and the Material Culture of Needlework and Textiles, 1750–1950* (Abingdon: Routledge).

Davies, Robert B. (1976), *Peacefully Working to Conquer the World: Singer Sewing Machines in Foreign Markets, 1854–1920* (New York: Arno Press).

de la Cruz-Fernández, Paula. (2014), "Marketing the Hearth: Ornamental Embroidery and the Building of the Multinational Singer Sewing Machine Company," *Enterprise & Society*, 15(3), 442–471.

de la Cruz-Fernández, Paula. (2015), "Multinationals and Gender: Singer Sewing Machine and Marketing in Mexico, 1890–1930," *Business History Review*, 89(3), 531–549.

Domosh, Mona. (2006), *American Commodities in an Age of Empire* (New York: Routledge).

Friedman, Walter A. (2004), *Birth of a Salesman: the Transformation of Selling in America* (Cambridge, MA: Harvard University Press).

Godley, Andrew. (2006), "Selling the Sewing Machine Around the World: Singer's International Marketing Strategies, 1850–1920," *Enterprise & Society*, 7(2), 266–314.

Goldstein, Carolyn M. (2012), *Creating Consumers: Home Economists in Twentieth-century America* (Chapel Hill, NC: University of North Carolina Press).

González, Luis. (1974), *San José de Gracia: Mexican Village in Transition*. Translated from English by John Upton (Austin, TX: University of Texas Press).

Gordon, Andrew. (2008), "Selling the American Way: The Singer Sales System in Japan, 1900–1938," *Business History Review*, 82(4), 671–699.

Gordon, Andrew. (2012), *Fabricating Consumers: The Sewing Machine in Modern Japan* (Berkeley, CA: University of California Press).

Green, Nancy L. (1997), *Ready-To-Wear and Ready-To-Work: A Century of Industry and Immigrants in Paris and New York* (Durham, NC: Duke University Press).

Hausen, Karin. (1985), "Technical Progress and Women's Labor in the Nineteenth Century: The Social History of the Sewing Machine," in Georg G. Iggers (ed.), *The Social History of Politics: Critical Perspectives in West German Historical Writing since 1945* (Leamington Spa: Berg), 259–281.

Hounshell, David A. (1984), *From the American System to Mass Production, 1800–1932: The Development of Manufacturing Technology in The United States* (Baltimore, MD: Johns Hopkins University Press).

Iza-Goñola de Miguel, Francisco Javier. (2005), *Alfa, S.A. Motor social y económico de la vida eibarresa* (Eibar: Ayuntamiento de Eibar & Comisión Ego Ibarra).

Jones, Geoffrey. (2005), *Multinationals and Global Capitalism: From the Nineteenth to the Twenty-First Century* (Oxford, New York: Oxford University Press).

Moura, Shawn. (2015), "Try it at Home: Avon and Gender in Brazil, 1958–1975," *Business History*, 57(6), 800–821.

O'Brien, Thomas. (1996), *The Revolutionary Mission: American Enterprise in Latin America, 1900–1945* (Cambridge: Cambridge University Press).

Reagin, Nancy R. (2007), *Sweeping the German Nation: Domesticity and National Identity in Germany, 1870–1945* (Cambridge: Cambridge University Press).

Rydell, Robert. (1984), *All the World's a Fair: Visions of Empire at American International Expositions, 1876–1916* (Chicago, IL: Chicago University Press).

Rydell, Robert. (1993), *World of Fairs: The Century-of-Progress Expositions* (Chicago, IL: Chicago University Press).

Scott, Peter. (2017), *The Market Makers: Creating Mass Markets for Consumer Durables in Inter-War Britain* (Oxford: Oxford University Press).

Smith, Stephanie J. (2009), *Gender and the Mexican Revolution: Yucatán Women and the Realities of Patriarchy* (Chapel Hill, NC: University of North Carolina Press).

Wilkins, Mira. (1969), "An American Enterprise Abroad: American Radiator Company in Europe, 1895–1914," *Business History Review*, 43(3), 326–346.

Wilkins, Mira. (1970), *The Emergence of Multinational Enterprise: American Business Abroad from the Colonial Era to 1914* (Cambridge, MA: Harvard University Press).

Wilkins, Mira. (1974), *The Maturing of Multinational Enterprise: American Business Abroad from 1914 to 1970* (Cambridge, MA: Harvard University Press).

Wilkins, Mira and Hill, Frank Ernest. (2011), *American Business Abroad: Ford in Six Continents* (Cambridge: Cambridge University Press).

Woersdorfer, Julia S. (2017), *The Evolution of Household Technology and Consumer Behavior, 1800–2000* (Abingdon: Routledge).

Zakim, Michael. (2003), *Ready-Made Democracy: A History of Men's Dress in the American Republic, 1760–1860* (Chicago, IL: University of Chicago Press).

Archival sources

"19th century American Trade Cards," Boston Public Library.

A New Era in Family Sewing Machines for Fine Swing and Art Needlework. Catalog. World's Columbian Exposition, (1893); Hagley Museum and Library, Imprints collection.

Centennial Singer Manufacturing Co's Catalog of Exhibits (1876), Hagley Museum and Library, Pictorials Collection.

Gilbert, Keith R. (1897), *The Story of the Sewing Machine* (1897) (New York: Press of F.V. Strauss).

"National Costume cards," from exhibitions in 1893, 1901, and 1904. Smithsonian's National Museum of American History, Archives; Warsaw Collection. Box 3; Hagley Museum and Library, Pictorials Collection, and the Wolfsonian Museum, Library (Florida International University).

Red S Review (various years), West Dunbarton-shire Libraries and Cultural Services, Dunbarton, U.K.

Sewing Machines: Science Museum Illustrated Booklet (Great Britain: H.M.S.O, 1970).

Singer Sewing Machine Co. (1905), *Directory of Shops, 1905*; Singer Sewing Machine Company Records, Wisconsin Historical Society.

The Singer Manufacturing Co.'s Exhibit of Family Sewing Machines and Art Embroidery (1893), Smithsonian's National Museum of American History, Archives; Warsaw Collection.

The Singer Manufacturing Co.'s Exhibit of Family Sewing Machines and Art Embroidery (1893), Catalog. (Singer Manufacturing Co.). Smithsonian's National Museum of American History, Archives Center; Warsaw Collection of Business Americana.

27

LUXURY

Pierre-Yves Donzé and Véronique Pouillard

Introduction

Luxury is one of the most globalized businesses in the consumer goods industries. A handful of multinational enterprises dominate the sector and control global sales networks. In 2013, the ten largest luxury goods companies had an aggregated 48.9 percent share of global sales of luxury goods (Deloitte 2015). The largest, the French conglomerate LVMH Moët Hennessy-Louis Vuitton SA (hereafter, LVMH), had a share of more than 10 percent. Although 84 of the top 100 luxury companies are based in Western Europe and the United States, sales are global. The largest market remains the United States (78.6 billion USD of sales in 2015), with Japan in second place (20.1 billion USD), China in third (17.9 billion USD), South Korea in eighth (10.8 billion USD), the Middle East in ninth (8.1 billion USD), and Hong Kong in tenth (6.8 billion USD) (D'Arpizio *et al.* 2015). A second indicator of the globalization of the luxury industry is the high degree of standardization of goods and the existence of global brands (Jackson 2004; Jain 2007).

Together with alcoholic beverage, luxuries were one of the first consumer goods for which companies adopted global brands (Lopes 2007). Yet, discussing the "luxury business" leads to the methodological problem of defining the object (Donzé and Fujioka 2017a). There is no common, shared concept of "luxury." The nature of the products does not define the luxury industry, as it does in the case of cars, electronics, or insurance. Rather luxury is a particular segment of the market, and can include almost any type of good or service. Some scholars in management introduced the idea of several levels between luxury and common goods. Allérès (1991) used the concepts of "intermediary luxury" and "accessible luxury," while Silverstein and Fiske (2008) proposed the concept of "new luxury." Kapferer and Bastien (2009) offer the most useful definition: luxury brands are defined by their marketing strategy, which differs from, and is the opposite of, common marketing strategy. Elements commonly stressed by companies in their definition of luxury (craft, heritage, know-how, quality, etc.) are less relevant. As luxury products form a segment of the market, the strategy that makes it possible to position and keep them positioned in this high-end segment is the most important determining factor.

Since the end of the nineteenth century, luxury companies have pursued differentiation from the manufacturers of common goods in the same industry and positioning in niche markets as key strategies to ensure their success. The current highly globalized luxury business however is not the outcome merely of expanding on these strategies. As we show here, today's global luxury industry is not the result of a linear expansion, but is rather mostly the outcome of a major industrial transformation that occurred during the 1980s, characterized by the foundation of large conglomerates through the merger of small family firms and the use of capital from financial markets, which happens to closely follow the rise of neoliberalism (Donzé and Fujioka 2017b). In our research, we have observed that the development of luxury as a global business does not follow the general model in three stages of first global economy, deglobalization, and second global economy proposed by Jones (2005). Rather, there were three periods of internationalization and globalization in the luxury business – internationalization (before 1945), early globalization (1945–1980), and mature globalization (since 1980) – and deglobalization during the interwar period. In this chapter, we focus on these three periods of internationalization and globalization that, we contend, are specific to the luxury business.

To discuss these various issues, we have selected two major sectors of the luxury consumer goods business – fashion and accessories (including leather goods), and watches and jewelry. Sales for fashion and accessories and for jewelry and watches amounted to, respectively, 25.7 percent and 26.3 percent of the gross sales of the top 100 luxury companies in 2013 (Deloitte 2015). Although these two sectors differ in terms of their products, consumers, and industrial organization, they both embody common trends that illustrate the dynamics of the luxury business in the global market. Service and marketing matter in all luxury industries. Luxury services, transportation, and housing are examples of other sectors, which sometimes interconnect. For example, the Armani Hotels & Resorts is a luxury chain that carries the signature of fashion magnate Giorgio Armani. The analysis below focuses on four large themes that are characteristic of the dynamics in the luxury business and of its evolution: (i) firms and entrepreneurs; (ii) markets; (iii) craftsmanship, know-how, and production; and (iv) marketing.

First stage: internationalization (before 1945)

International trade drove the first stage of globalization in the luxury industry. However, the flow of goods, as well as the range of luxury products, experienced a major shift after the Industrial Revolution. During the seventeenth and eighteenth centuries, Europe imported food, spices, porcelains, precious woods, and textiles from Asia, Africa, and the Americas, buying and consuming them as luxury goods (Anderson 2012). Pre-industrial trading firms, such as the British East India Company, the Dutch East India Company, the Royal African Company, and the Hudson's Bay Company, brought these goods to the West (Chaudhury 1978; Subramanyam 1990). Although the Industrial Revolution modified the status of many goods and brought a wide range of products to the masses, historians of the Ancien Régime underscore that a relative democratization of "luxury" – products other than necessity goods – was already underway before the Industrial Revolution. The same historians point to the second-hand trade and barter of luxury goods, and the increasing demand for "demi-luxe" or "populuxe" items (Palmer and Clark 2004; Fairchild 1993; Berg 2005). These various levels of "luxury" denote the emergence of a society in which consumption had become a widely available means for expressing social distinction.

During the Ancien Régime, the system of guilds (see Catherine Casson in this volume), which regulated professions and commerce, resulted in a specialization in handcrafts and retail structure that restricted the modernization of the distribution and sale of luxe and demi-luxe products (Coquery 2011). The Industrial Revolution, and the revolution in retail which started in the mid-nineteenth century, marked by the development of the department store, played decisive roles in expanding the sales of goods that had previously been reserved to the elites

(Chandler 1990, 255; Miller 1981). Western Europe and the United States were still the major markets of luxury goods, but had become also the producers of these goods. Instead of purchasing products imported from overseas, mostly from Asia, Westerners began consuming luxuries made in their own cultural environment, and the links to Asian countries weakened. Hence, the scope of globalization of this industry between 1815 and 1914 is open to debate. It can be argued that consumption actually de-globalized, in comparison with the Ancien Régime, in these years. Thus, we emphasize the *internationalization*, rather than the *globalization*, of the luxury business. Although Western countries shared intense commercial and cultural exchanges with regard to luxury goods, this new industry did not really extend to Asia, Latin America, and Africa.

Before 1914, fashion was aspirational, according to sociologists Thorstein Veblen and Georg Simmel (Veblen 1899; Simmel 1904). Simmel notably defined it as "change for the sake of change," first and foremost in textiles, clothes, and accessories, and also in the domains of interior decor, food, and cosmetics, to cite a few (Simmel 1904). New designs trickled down from the high classes to be imitated by lower strata, indicating that luxury and fashion had a symbiotic relationship during this era. The entry of women in the workforce, exemplified by the turn-of-the-century *Gibson Girl*, an active woman portrayed by advertising designer Charles Dana Gibson in the United States, and by the working women during the Great War in Europe, profoundly affected the fashion system. From the nineteenth century onwards, the generalization of ready-to-wear democratized fashion. Since the 1970s and 1980s, the rise of fast fashion has resulted in the quick adaptation of trends at any price point. Luxury gradually became associated with classic, iconic, and even static items, such as the Chanel tweed suit or the Hermès Kelly handbag. Although garments and accessories remain central to the luxury industry, the relationship between fashion and luxury and, hence, between novelty and luxury, has changed. Fashions democratized, and novelty stopped being essential to the definition of personal luxury goods.

With the opening in 1858 of the House of Worth in Paris by Englishman Charles-Frederick Worth and his Swedish business partner Otto Bobergh, a cluster of firms describing their activity as "Haute Couture," high-end, creative fashion designs made-to-measure for the clients, came to dominate fashion design in the West and, to some extent, in colonial empires until recent decades (Bayly 2004, Kuldova 2016). Haute couture marked a shift from pre-Revolutionary dressmaking when the most famous entrepreneur was Rose Bertin, and where the client directed the design of her dress starting from the textile. Worth presented himself as a creator, even a "dictator," of styles who directed clients to the styles he found most appropriate for them. Paris was the epicenter of haute couture for women, and London for high-end clothing for men and for sportswear (a category of dress that then included tailoring) for both sexes. Creation, fitting, and retail all took place within the walls of the haute couture house, which was, from the outset, cosmopolitan. Clients converged on Paris and London from all over the Western world. In the late nineteenth century, a cluster of early multinationals, with main locations in Paris, London, Vienna, and retail branches overseas, catered to the elites (Troy 2003). These firms, such as Boué Sœurs, Paquin, and Redfern, were overall very profitable, and some of them, notably Paquin, were listed on the stock exchange. Paquin showed a nearly continual increase in profits until World War I. In 1900, the firm's net profits were £88,868, an important sum at the time (Pouillard 2016, 200). The fashion industry, like the beauty industry, was characterized by a greater number of opportunities for women entrepreneurs, including in early international commerce (Jones 2010).

Haute couture developed an unparalleled marketing of exclusivity. Materials were costly. They included silks and brocades, woven in Lyons and sometimes directly made to order for haute couture firms, as well as precious laces and furs. Fittings make haute couture expensive as well. The trade adapted made-to-measure to serialization. For example, Worth conceived a series of bodices that could be fitted interchangeably to a series of skirts. He also ordered designs reproduced in a variety of fabrics, with variations in ornamentation. Selling haute couture to foreign buyers for reproduction abroad was the most profitable part of the industry, since it meant no fitting costs. It also transferred innovation to the foreign entrepreneurs, who copied Parisian know-how. Yet couturiers realized that the extent of the copying of haute couture was beyond their control and deprived them from a part of the profit they expected to make. From the nineteenth century onwards, they retaliated by suing copyists on domestic and international markets. They also lobbied governments in order to receive better legal protection for design (Troy 2003). Protecting original design from appropriation in the manufacturing of substitute goods remained very difficult, but the protective actions taken by the couturiers had the effect of marketing their brand names in a durable manner (Pouillard 2011, 319–344).

The growth of luxury fashion was supported by a handful of institutions that engaged in controlling production and in promotion. First, most of the Paris haute couture entrepreneurs organized in a prestigious professional syndicate, the Chambre Syndicale de la Couture Parisienne, founded in Paris in 1868. The Chambre safeguarded good practices and know-how, and lobbied public authorities in the pursuit of professional interests (Pouillard 2015). In 1927, the Chambre opened its own school to educate a specialized workforce for Paris haute couture firms. Second, the international spread of fashion media, including unauthorized fashion journals produced in Berlin, Brussels, Vienna, and in the biggest cities of North and South America, played a role in the promotion of haute couture. Although these luxury products were out of reach for the masses, the fashion media created powerful consumer imaginaries, making couturiers' names familiar to larger audiences, and fostering aspirational consumption and the imitation of styles designed for elites (Leach 1993).

Third, some fashion entrepreneurs launched accessories, such as perfume and leather goods. Perfume would become the most popular tie-in product for couture. Over the nineteenth century, the perfume industry became internationalized. French entrepreneur Alphonse Rallet founded a firm in Russia in 1843, and Brocard, another one in 1861. Technology transfers between the French perfumery center of Grasse, and the German chemistry industry, notably, created conditions for the take-off of this industry (Briot 2015). In 1911, couturier Paul Poiret created a perfume line, the Parfums de Rosine, and other tie-in product lines, notably accessories and home decor. Although Poiret did not give his own name to his perfumes (he used his daughter's), he started a future business model for haute couture (Troy 2003). This diversification into accessories was fostered by the Great Depression, which resulted in economic hardship for haute couture and a necessity to sell cheaper products and lines.

The leather goods industry was still distinct from the fashion business at this point. The oldest high-end leather goods firm to exist without interruption is the Belgian firm Delvaux, based in Brussels. Delvaux was founded by Charles Delvaux in 1829, and made trunks and other travel accessories. The business was fueled by Brussels' central position in continental Europe, and the 1935 opening of the first railway line on the continent, the Malines–Brussels line. Travel, and the expertise of horse saddlery and trunk making, form the basis of the oldest firms in the leather goods sector that are still active today – notably Hermès (1837), Moynat (1849), Goyard (1853), and Louis Vuitton (1854). Today a part of Bernard Arnault's LVMH group, the Louis Vuitton firm pioneered the development of the luxury leather goods industry. To this day, Louis Vuitton and the other brands put craftsmanship traditions – often reinvented – at the core of their marketing strategies.

In the watch and jewelry business, the forces driving internationalization were similar to those in fashion. Individual entrepreneurs organized the sales of their products to wealthy customers throughout the world, focusing on Western countries. This was a niche market but it was not limited to aristocracy like in the late eighteenth and early nineteenth centuries. Burgeoning urban bourgeoisie was a major target and a key determinant for the expansion of the markets. Luxury watch and jewel makers essentially opened offices and subsidiaries in large Western cities. For example, Tiffany established branches in Paris (1850) and London (1868) (Phillips 2006), whereas Omega had offices in Paris (1888), Moscow (1905), and Berlin (1905) (Richon 1998). However, most jewel and watch makers had no direct access to markets. They worked with independent agents, who sold their goods to wealthy customers on local markets. In this way, the Swiss watch company Omega could enter Japan (1896), the United States (1898), United Kingdom (1902), Italy (1909), Spain (1914), and other countries.

Nevertheless, production was realized not only by artisans but also by industrialists who adopted new manufacturing technology. For example, Tiffany & Co. opened a workshop in New Jersey in the 1870s, and then a modern factory in New Jersey in 1894 (Phillips 2006). Yet, although it employed 1,700 factory workers in 1901, Tiffany did not mass-produce jewels and silverware. It focused, rather, on custom and batch production, that is, on a specialty production system that enabled it to manufacture a high variety of goods for expanding markets (Scranton 1997). In the watch industry, the situation was slightly different due to the technical specificities of the product. The quality and reputation of watches were based on their precision and durability, so that process innovation for the movement was decisive. There was a division of labor between the industrial production of movements and the decoration of the complete watch. The latter was done by small companies in the context of industrial districts, enabling a high variety of designs (Donzé 2011). The growth of this specialty production relied not only on manufacturing technology, but also on retaining traditional know-how and training a new generation of skilled workers. Hence, Tiffany opened in 1878 an apprenticeship program to train designers and craftsmen. In Switzerland, a total of nine watch-making schools were founded between 1865 and 1914.

Second stage: early globalization (1945–1980)

Like other industries, the luxury business suffered from recessions, protectionism, and wars between 1914 and 1945. The higher cost of the franc in the 1920s and then the Great Depression hit French haute couture and other luxury trades hard (Jones and Pouillard 2009/2017). Haute couture exports fell consistently each year, from 2.4 billion French francs in 1925 to 49.2 million at the lowest point in 1936 (Rouzaud 1946). The import of French luxury products, such as haute couture and champagne, was subjected to high tariffs and sometimes prohibited entirely. For example, in spring 1932, French champagne was forbidden in Denmark for a few weeks, before a policy of quotas was introduced, and, in 1929, Romania temporarily forbade imports of French haute couture (Rouzaud 1946, 135).

Couturiers seeking to cope with the loss of international clients and raising tariffs increasingly turned to tie-in products, especially perfume and cosmetics, and the strategy of expanding boutiques selling couture-branded ready-to-wear. The French interwar luxury industries were pioneers in marketing techniques. Advertising techniques developed more slowly in France than in the United States, yet the French luxury firms Cartier, Lucien Lelong, and Worth hired American PR guru, Edward L. Bernays, to organize events and monitor press coverage of their brands (Martin 1992). Couturiers complained that the difficulties encountered on the global markets resulted in an increase of counterfeits. In reaction, they tried to build intellectual property rights portfolios to protect their designs and brands. This had limited impact on counterfeiters, but developed into an efficient way of marketing exclusivity (Pouillard 2011). During the postwar reconstruction of France, luxury expert Claude Rouzaud made the case that haute couture, as an industry, created large value from small quantities of raw materials. Economic and political experts thus saw French couture and luxury goods as leaders in renewing the export of French goods (Rouzaud 1946).

After nearly three decades of stagnation and decline, the Western luxury business entered a new phase of growth and internationalization. During the postwar high-growth years, the structure and organization of luxury companies (mostly small family firms), as well as the luxury industry's customers (wealthy people) basically did not change. However, one new non-Western market did emerge in the late 1960s: Japan. Its share of the total export of French leather goods between 1965 and 1980 rose from 0.8 percent to 18.1 percent, and for Swiss watches in the same years, from 1.9 percent to 3.6 percent. This first extension beyond Western markets was a period of early globalization. Companies had to learn how to organize their expansion in culturally different environments, making adaptations, for example, in market-entry strategy, distribution, and brand management.

In haute couture, the beginning of this second internationalization was marked by the foundation of the house of Christian Dior in 1946. The Paris-based firm became a multinational in 1948, with the opening of Christian Dior-New York. Other branches followed suit. C.D. Models was the British brand, founded in 1952; Christian Dior Venezuela, Inc. was founded in Caracas in 1953; and Christian Dior Del Sur, also founded in 1953, was the financial arm of the company in South America. During the oil boom in Venezuela, other French luxury businesses simultaneously opened branches there, notably jeweler Cartier and couturier Pierre Balmain. During the same years, the house of Dior signed exclusivity deals with high-end retailers in order to cover the markets of Mexico (1950), Cuba (1951), Chile (1952), and Australia (1952) (Okawa 2007; Palmer 2009; Jones and Pouillard 2009/2017). Dior was one the first French haute couture brands to enter Japan. It signed a licensing agreement with Daimaru department store in 1953, a strategy followed by numerous Western fashion companies up until the 1970s (e.g., Pierre Cardin in 1959, Lacoste in 1963, Burberry in 1970) (Donzé and Fujioka 2015).

Dior's new business model globalized the haute couture brand on the basis of a series of licenses for perfumes, cosmetics, accessories, and ready-to-wear for women, and, later, for men and children. This model depended on the financial support of Marcel Boussac, France's "king of cotton" who was also known as a breeder of racehorses. Boussac's industrial group focused on mass-manufactured textiles, but included household appliances and French media. Dior was, thus, the luxury outpost of Boussac's group. In 1957, the Dior firm accounted for 5 percent of total French exports. A major challenge was to avoid spreading the field of licenses too wide. Christian Dior put even his name on car interiors, and considered expanding into flower retail and food, but the latter initiatives were never pursued concretely.

Yet, the postwar growth of the French luxury business resulted not only from the action of individual firms such as Christian Dior, but also that of collective institutions, in continuity with the previous period. Most of the firms were small and medium-sized enterprises (SMEs), and thus they could not engage alone in lobbying and promotion. Hence, in 1954, the perfumer Jean-Jacques Guerlain founded the Comité Colbert. This trade association federates most of the French luxury firms and lobbies the French government for favorable tax conditions, protection from substitute products, and to promote the image of the French luxury industries on domestic and international markets (Okawa 2007; Palmer 2009).

The postwar period was also characterized by the development of new fashion centers besides Paris, notably London and a group of Italian cities. These new fashion cities were often nurtured by older industrial or creative clusters. Florence, Milan, and Rome competed for the title of fashion capital until the 1960s, when Milan came to the fore. Milan now hosts one of the four big global fashion weeks, along with London, New York, and Paris. Paris weeks of haute couture shows had been organized consistently since 1911, and the New York fashion week was institutionalized by the city authority in 1957 (Merlo and Polese 2006). Gucci had been founded by Guccio Gucci in Florence in 1921 and specialized first and foremost in leather goods. It became a symbol of Italian luxury, along with Prada (1913), Fendi (1925), Salvatore Ferragamo (1928), and Bottega Veneta (1966). Italian leather goods had their fashion ups and downs. In the 1970s and 1980s, firms such as Bottega Veneta and Gucci became characterized by the overuse of logos, one of the markers of a loss of prestige and consumer saturation. Such cases therefore nuance the idea that personal goods are static designs, and show that luxury brands remain sensitive to trends (Merlo and Polese 2006).

After World War II, the watch- and jewel-making industries were characterized by the coexistence of small traditional companies, which followed the model of the previous period, and other enterprises that moved to a new model of large companies. New investors outside founding families supported this second group of firms, and transformed their management. In jewelry, most firms, such as Bulgari, Harry Winston, and Cartier, were still small family businesses that developed luxury goods for wealthy customers, mostly in Western countries. As for Tiffany, it embodies the example of a small business gradually transformed into a large enterprise. After its takeover by an investing company, Hover Corporation, Tiffany adopted a new product development strategy, based on cooperation with star designers, and the launch of cheap jewelry to expand its customers base (Phillips 2006). Moreover, at the same time, Tiffany started to open other branches outside New York in the United States, particularly in California (1963–1966). In 1972, it inaugurated a salon in Mitsukoshi department store in Tokyo, Japan. The consequence of this development was a growth in annual sales from seven million USD in 1955 to 23 million USD in 1970 (International Directory 1996).

The Swiss luxury watch industry presents the same divide. Several small family firms, such as Patek, Philippe & Co., and Vacheron & Constantin, pursued their business model based on manufacturing of a broad range of models for niche markets. A few newcomers established in the luxury watch business following this model, the best example being Piaget. This company was originally a supplier of watch movements and complete watches for other firms, among them Cartier and Tiffany. In 1959, it opened its own shop in Geneva, followed by a plant the next year, and then launched its own brand of jewel watches. During these early postwar years, other companies chose to adopt a new work organization, characterized by the standardization of models and mass production, in order to expand sales and their customer base. Using machines rather than artisans to make watches did not harm the luxury branding of these watches, since high precision and durability are key elements in determining the marketplace competitiveness of watches. Among the companies following this pathway to modernization were Longines, Omega, and, especially, Rolex. The latter was not particularly famous as a luxury brand before the 1950s. It became a worldwide symbol of luxury and individual success through a two-fold strategy. First, it rationalized the number of models and engaged in the mass production of high-quality goods to ensure the best level of accuracy. Production rose from about 40,000 watches in 1960 to nearly 200,000 in 1970. These figures show that Rolex watches were not aimed at niche markets and a small international wealthy elite, but rather at the new urban upper-middle classes. This marketing target was the second part of Rolex's strategy. It focused mainly on the United States, where the company opened a sales subsidiary in 1948 (Donzé 2011). This early globalization, or second phase in the global development of luxury, creates a slightly different chronology than for other industries. New investments in capital, the rise of new elites, and the democratization of luxury are characteristics of the development of luxury during the Thirty Glorious Years.

Third stage: mature globalization (since 1980)

The luxury industry experienced a major change during the 1980s, characterized by three features (Donzé & Fujioka 2017b). First, multinational enterprises and public joint stock companies became the major actors in this business. Mergers and acquisitions (M&As) gave birth to diversified large groups, such as LVMH (1987) and Compagnie Financière Richemont (1988), which dominate the luxury industry today (Deloitte 2015). Smaller and less diversified companies followed the same strategy to take over other firms and build a portfolio of brands. For example, during the 1980s, L'Oréal Luxe acquired Helena Rubinstein and purchased licenses to produce cosmetics for the brands Ralph Lauren, Paloma Picasso, and Giorgio Armani (Marseille 2009). This industrial reorganization necessitated a large amount of capital, and thus most of the luxury companies entered stock exchanges to finance their expansion. In 2015, among the top 25 luxury companies ranked by Deloitte, only three were not listed (Giorgio Armani, Rolex, and Swarovski) (Deloitte 2015). Despite this entry into financial markets, most of the luxury companies are controlled, usually through special voting rights, by a new generation of entrepreneurs, such as Bernard Arnault (LVMH), François Pinault (Kering), and Nicolas Hayek (Swatch Group), who built these groups and implemented new strategies for the last phase of globalization.

The second change was the globalization of brands, which was fostered by the emergence of Asia as the fastest growing market for luxury goods (Donzé & Fujioka 2017b). Until the 1970s, the international expansion of luxury goods essentially relied on cooperation with local partners, through licensing or sales agreements, so that the brand identity and design differed, depending on the country and region. However, building global brands, that is, brands with highly standardized identities that were strongly controlled by headquarters, became a new challenge for global expansion in the 1990s (Lopes 2007). This strategy of brands globalization went hand in hand with the development of vertical distribution, particularly through the development of mono-brand stores (Moore *et al.* 2010), in which Louis Vuitton was a pioneer. The company opened its first independent store in the United States in 1980 and steadily developed its sales network (owning 345 mono-brand stores, worldwide, in 2005). The total number of stores owned by LVMH amounted to 1,286 in 2000 and 3,860 in 2015 (LVMH 2000, 2015). This expansion of retail was made possible by the capital provided by the access to stock exchanges. It made it possible to internalize profits from sales and to better control the image of the brand, particularly in emerging countries such as China.

Finally, the third characteristic feature of this period was the democratization of consumption, which was linked to the industrial reorganization and the globalization of brands. The newly transformed luxury companies aimed at improving their financial profitability, through the extension of their customer base. The democratization of luxury consumption has been shown to be a driving force for the growth of this business (Danziger 2005). For example, Fernie *et al.* (1997) showed that the development of mono-brand stores in big cities such as London enabled producers of luxury goods to reach directly a growing number of new customers. Using celebrities as ambassadors also facilitated communication between brands and mass consumers (McCracken, 1989) as did the hiring of celebrity designers to create or style a collection for the mass market. Some marketing scholars have coined the term "masstige" (combining "mass" and "prestige") to refer to this new strategy of promoting the mass consumption and democratization of luxury goods (Truong *et al.* 2009).

Fashion and accessories remain at the heart of the large luxury industry groups. From the 1960s onwards, the haute couture model became obsolete. The rising price of labor costs in Europe directly affected the cost of haute couture garments, and the clientele able to afford them shrank. Haute couture has become a creative laboratory for other fashion and luxury industries, and sells to only a few hundred clients across the world.

Over the last decade, luxury firms, notably Chanel and Prada, have bought workshops and small firms specializing in rare handcrafts. Chanel, a private luxury group owned by Alain and Gérard Wertheimer, whose grandfather acquired a controlling share in Gabrielle Chanel's perfumes in 1924, has been steadily gathering such workshops into a special branch called "Paraffection," which includes embroidery house Lesage (formerly Michonet, founded in 1858), flower maker Guillet (1869), feather artisan Lemarié (1880), bootmaker Massaro (1884), glove maker Causse (1892), hatmaker Maison Michel (1936), Montext embroidery (1939), costume jeweler Robert Goossens (1953), and the Scottish knitwear firm Barrie (1903) (Deloitte 2015). Managers of luxury groups state that the purpose of such a strategy is not to acquire full control over their suppliers, but, rather, to preserve craftsmanship heritage from creative destruction.

Many luxury fashion firms have switched from haute couture to luxury or designer ready-to-wear, that is best suited to the evolution of the luxury business in the twenty-first century. Haute couture remains a creative reference on which luxury groups have built global brands that sell perfumes, accessories, and leather goods globally. Today, just over a dozen haute couture firms satisfy the stringent membership criteria originally designed to define and protect the know-how and prestige of the industry in the Chambre Syndicale de la Couture Parisienne. Before World War II, there were over 100 (Grumbach 2008).

Handbags in particular have become central to the strategies of luxury firms. During the last globalization of the luxury industries, luggage entrepreneurs started producing haute couture or luxury ready-to-wear lines as a way to market their products. In a symmetrical movement, most haute couture firms now retail their own leather goods, in addition to selling branded ready-to-wear, perfumes, and cosmetics. As we have seen, in some instances, leather goods are at the core of the know-how of luxury groups. But, for the most part, they are no longer produced to satisfy the whims of regular customers. Rather luggage makers' core business depends on product lines that offer a relatively limited number of sizes and options. Because luxury brand handbags sold worldwide do not require fitting, they yield important margins. The margins become particularly significant when brands known for leather goods launch lines in other materials, as in the case of Prada's nylon bags, which are status-enhancing goods yet at the same time quite cheap to produce (Thomas 2007). Luxury groups have also relocated parts of production outside Europe, as did Burberry and Delvaux in the 2000s, when they outsourced some production to China and Vietnam. The acquisition of know-how by non-Western countries has changed traditional views about the places of production, including for high luxury (Tokatli 2008).

Firms, such as Gucci and Bottega Veneta, that lost prestige during the 1980s were next reinvigorated by new management that either re-focused the brand or the core craftsmanship expertise (Bottega Veneta) and/or hired new creative designers to revive their brands (Gucci). Today, some firms seem to prefer to remain more exclusive, such as Goyard and Moynat, yet these businesses are growing, notably in Asia, and their relative discretion therefore appears to be a part of a marketing strategy that uses relevant channels of communications, such as influencers, and digital media.

The Belgian brand Delvaux has adopted similar strategies of exclusivity, but has grown globally, especially since 2011, when 80 percent of the shares were bought by Hong Kong based Fung Group and stores were opened in Asia. Such developments created new challenges, yet these concern marketing rather than product quality. Louis Vuitton, for example, states that its products continue to be made, using traditional methods, in the workshops of Asnières, in the *banlieue* of Paris, although some manufacturing for the brand has been relocated abroad.

Hermès remains a powerful and remarkably stable brand in the leather goods business. In contrast to Vuitton, it is still controlled by descendants of the founder's family. Starting in 2001 however, LVMH group acquired shares of Hermès through derivatives, and, by 2010, it controlled over 14 percent of the private group. At that point, the French authority on financial markets (AMF) investigated Hermès's ownership, and litigation between Hermès and LVMH ensued. In 2011, the LVMH's ownership in Hermès rose to 22 percent. Eventually, the AMF found that LVMH had secretly bought shares of Hermès with the intent of building a minority stake, and possibly realizing an equity swap without Hermès group knowing it. In 2014, LVMH agreed to release its Hermès shares to minority shareholders who had no intention of buying more shares in the private-owned group. The Hermès family was thus able to maintain control over the group (Roberts 2014).

Counterfeits are both a challenge to the luxury trade, and an indicator of a brand's success (Nueno and Quelch 1998, 63). Historically, France has had the strictest policies against counterfeiters. The European Union has largely followed suit, its policies fostered by Germany and France, both of which feature among the most protective intellectual property rights systems, and also by Belgium and Italy. To this day, there is no streamlined international counterfeiting law, and experts disagree about the harmfulness of counterfeits (Nia and Lynne Zaichkowsky 2000).

A more tangible challenge for luxury brands is the dilution of brand identity and value that can result from the overuse of licenses. A textbook case is French couturier Pierre Cardin, whose image was permanently altered by allowing licenses for too wide an array of products, including small consumer goods such as tablecloths and ashtrays. Other brands, such as Gucci and Dior, have also based their global growth on licenses. These two brands experienced important erosions of their images in the 1980s but, unlike Cardin, they were able to recover. Restoring the image of luxury brands is often a decades-long process. The strategies of decentralization pursued by groups such as LVMH under the helm of Bernard Arnault have actively recruited designers and given them conditions to nurture their creativity, thereby adding the luster of art to the visibility of the brand.

Another – and to some extent related – challenge for luxury global firms occurs when a brand is attracting clients whom the brand management does not consider to be desirable. In the 1980s and 1990s, Vuitton and Gucci experienced saturation. The British firm Burberry, at some point favored by the British subculture of the Chavs, was a case of a firm confronted with the need to regain the trust of a more traditional clientele, and to restore its image that had been altered by the specific subculture exposed by its new clients through their use of the brand codes (Hayward and Yar 2006).

In the jewel and watch industries, most of the individual companies were merged into large groups or entered stock exchanges, and followed the new strategy described above. Cartier is a case in point. The French jeweler faced financial problems in the early 1970s and was taken over by Alain-Dominique Perrin, backed by a few investors, among which the South-African businessman Anton Ruppert. In 1973, he launched a new collection of accessories named "Must de Cartier," re-positioning the brand as an accessible luxury and accelerating worldwide sales. The need for capital to pursue expansion, notably by purchasing other companies, led Ruppert to invest more actively in Cartier. He founded Richemont in 1988, which controls Cartier, and the same year, he took over the Swiss watch companies Piaget and Baume & Mercier. This launched the basis of a multinational enterprise which is today number two in the luxury business (Donzé 2017).

Although most jewel and watch brands belong today to luxury groups, their acquisition occurred for two different reasons. In the case of jewelry, independent companies were acquired by investors interested in adding a jewelry brand to their portfolios, as in the cases of Cartier and

Van Cleef & Arpels (acquired by Richemont in 1999), Boucheron (Kering in 2000), Bulgari (LVMH in 2012), and Harry Winston (Swatch Group in 2013). Tiffany remains the only independent jewel maker today. It was purchased by the cosmetic group Avon Products (1978), and became public in 1987. As for watch brands, even if they are also acquired by large groups in order to diversify their portfolio, they have a second function different from jewels: internalizing manufacturing capabilities made it possible to launch watches for other brands, particularly in fashion. LVMH provides a good, but not unique, example. In 1999, it took over two Swiss watch companies, Tag Heuer and Zénith, and, two years later, opened a workshop to assemble watches for Christian Dior and Louis Vuitton. This process of creating synergies between brands is what Moore and Birtwistle (2005) call the "parenting advantage."

Conclusion

The areas covered and the products sold by the luxury business have changed over time.

Luxury became more profitable when it became accessible. In this chapter, we focused on personal luxury goods. Other classical areas of luxury that are mainstays include gastronomic restaurants and luxury automobiles. The notion of service, which is a part of the specific marketing of luxury, is essential to the development of the luxury industry as a lifestyle industry, and the rise of concepts such as the luxury apartment.

New transformations occurred in recent decades when luxury industries encountered the digital age, which both challenged the notion of personal service to the client, but also offered new possibilities, notably in terms of the information available about clients and their preferences (Nueno and Quelch 1998, 66). Luxury brands increasingly have their own webshops. Specialized websites, such as MyTheresa and Net-à-Porter, have flourished, bringing the digital retailing of luxury through a period of a fast, steep growth.

The globalization of the luxury business occurred in four stages. First, internationalization occurred before 1914, and saw, in addition to the ancient global commerce of luxury products, the development of early luxury multinationals. This network was largely dismantled in the next period, which included the economic upheavals of the Great Depression as well as the economic impact of the two world wars. The third stage was marked by a second and incomplete globalization during the economic boom following World War II. Luxury brands developed licensing strategies, allowing them to capitalize on luxury-brand image at the global level. This model suffered from the first oil shock in the early 1970s, and the image of many firms was eroded by the over-use of licenses. The fourth stage, and the third period of globalization, began in the 1980s and is characterized by the construction of global luxury groups through M&As.

The entrepreneurs and companies of the luxury industry also contributed to making the world more global through the diffusion of a highly unified culture of consumption. Since the early modern period, the expansion of this industry geographically (from Western countries to the whole world) and socially (the so-called democratization of luxury) has been closely related to the desire of a fast-growing number of people throughout the world to express their sense of belonging to a developed, wealthy, and global elite through the consumption of luxury goods.

Bibliography

Allérès, D. (1991), "Spécificités et stratégies marketing des différents univers du luxe," *Revue française du marketing*, 132, 71–96.
Anderson, J. L. (2012), *Mahogany: The Costs of Luxury in Early America*, Cambridge, MA: Harvard University Press.

Bayly, C. (2004), *The Birth of the Global World 1780–1914: Global Connections and Comparisons*, London: Blackwell.

Berg, M. (2005), *Luxury and Pleasure in Eighteenth-Century Britain*, Oxford: Oxford University Press.

Bergeron, L. (1998), *Les industries du luxe en France*, Paris: Odile Jacob.

Briot, E. (2015), *La fabrique des parfums: Naissance d'une industrie de luxe*, Paris: Vendémiaire.

Chandler, A. D. (1990), *Scale and Scope: The Dynamics of Industrial Capitalism*, Cambridge, MA: Belknap Press.

Chaudhury, K. N. (1978), *The Trading World of Asia and the English East Asia Company, 1660–1760*, Cambridge: Cambridge University Press.

Coquery, N. (2011), *Tenir boutique à Paris au XVIIIe siècle: Luxe et demi-luxe*, Paris, CTHS Histoire.

D'Arpizio, C., Levato, F., Zito, D., and Montgolfier, J. de (2015), "Luxury goods worldwide market study: Fall–Winter 2015 – A time to act: How luxury brands can rebuild to win," Bain & Company. Retrieved from: www.bain.com/Images/BAIN_REPORT_Global_Luxury_2015.pdf (accessed 14 November 2016).

Danziger, P. (2005), *Let Them Eat Cake: Marketing Luxury to the Masses – As Well As the Classes*. Chicago, IL: Kaplan.

Daumas, J.-C., (2010), "Bernard Arnault," in: J.-C. Daumas ed. *Dictionnaire historique des patrons français*, Paris: Flammarion, 32–34.

Deloitte (2015), "Global powers of luxury goods 2015: Engaging the future luxury consumer," Deloitte Touche Tohmatsu Ltd. Retrieved from: www2.deloitte.com/content/dam/Deloitte/ch/Documents/consumer-business/ch-en-cb-global-powers-of-luxury-goods-2015.pdf (accessed 14 November 2016).

Donzé, P.-Y. (2011), *History of the Swiss Watch Industry from Jacques David to Nicolas Hayek*, Berne: Peter Lang.

Donzé, P.-Y. (2017), *L'invention du luxe: histoire de l'horlogerie à Genève de 1815 à nos jours*, Neuchâtel: Alphil-Presses universitaires suisses.

Donzé, P.-Y. and Fujioka, R. (2015), "European luxury big business and emerging Asian markets, 1960–2010," *Business History*, 57 (6), 822–840.

Donzé, P.-Y. and Fujioka, R. (2017a), "Luxury business," *Oxford Research Encyclopedia of Business and Management*. Retrieved from: http://oxfordre.com/business/view/10.1093/acrefore/9780190224851.001.0001/acrefore-9780190224851-e-96?rskey=R0ScHi&result=1 (accessed 17 April 2019).

Donzé, P.-Y. and Fujioka, R. (eds.) (2017b), *Global Luxury: Organizational Change and Emerging Markets in the Luxury Industry since the 1970s*, Basingstoke: Macmillan.

Fairchild, C. (1993), "The production and marketing of populuxe goods in eighteen-century Paris," in: J. Brewer and R. Porter eds. *Consumption and the World of Goods*, London: Routledge, 228–248.

Fernie, J., Moore, C., Lawrie, A., and Hallsworth, A. (1997), "The internationalization of the high fashion brand: The case of central London," *Journal of Product and Brand Management*, 6 (3), 151–162.

Grumbach, D. (2008 [Seuil, 1993]), *Histoires de la mode*, Paris: Editions du Regard.

Guy, K. M. (2003), *When Champagne Became French: Wine and the Making of a National Identity*, Baltimore, MD: Johns Hopkins University Press.

Hayward, K. and Yar, M. (2006), "The *chav* phenomenon: Consumption, media, and the construction of a new underclass," *Crime, Media, Culture: An International Journal*, 2 (1), 9–28.

International Directory (1996), "Tiffany & Co. history," *International Directory of Company Histories*, Vol. 14, London: St. James Press.

Jackson, T. (2004), "A contemporary analysis of global luxury brands," in: M. Bruce, C. Moore, and G. Birtwistle eds. *International Retail Marketing: A Case Study Approach*, London: Routledge, 155–169.

Jain, S. C. (2007), "State of the art of international marketing research: Directions for the future," *Journal of Global Business Advancement*, 1, 1, 4–19.

Jones, G. (2005), *Multinationals and Global Capitalism: From the Nineteenth to the Twenty-First Century*, Oxford: Oxford University Press.

Jones, G. (2010), *Beauty Imagined: A History of the Global Beauty Business*, Oxford: Oxford University Press.

Jones, G. and Pouillard, V. (2009/2017), "Christian Dior: A New Look for Haute Couture", Boston, MA: Harvard Business School case no. 809–159.

Judah, H. and Pouillard, V. (2009), *Delvaux: 180 Years of Belgian Luxury*, Brussels: Lannoo Publishers.

Kapferer, J.-N. and Bastien, V. (2009), *The Luxury Strategy: Break the Rules of Marketing to Build Luxury Brands*, London and Philadelphia, PA: Kogan Page.

Kuldova, T. (2016), *Luxury Indian Fashion: A Social Critique*, London: Bloomsbury.

Leach, W. (1993), *Land of Desire: Merchants, Power, and the Rise of a New American Culture*, New York: Vintage.

Lopes, T. da Silva (2007), *Global Brands: The Evolution of Multinationals in Alcoholic Beverages*, New York: Cambridge University Press.

LVMH (2000, 2015), *Annual report*.

McCracken, G. (1989), "Who is the celebrity endorser? Cultural foundations of the endorsement process," *Journal of Consumer Research*, 16 (3), 310–321.

Marseille, J. (2009), *L'Oréal, 1909–2009*, Paris: Perrin.

Martin, M. (1992), *Trois siècles de publicité en France*, Paris: Odile Jacob.

Merlo, E. and Polese, F. (2006), "Turning fashion into business: The emergence of Milan as an international fashion hub," *Business History Review*, 80 (3), 415–447.

Miller, M. B. (1981), *The Bon Marché: Bourgeois Culture and the Department Store, 1869–1920*, Princeton, NJ: Princeton University Press.

Moore, C. M. and Birtwistle, G. (2005), "The nature of parenting advantage in luxury fashion retailing: The case of Gucci group NV," *International Journal of Retail and Distribution Management*, 33 (4), 256–270.

Moore, C. M., Doherty, A. M., and Doyle, S. A. (2010), "Flagship stores as a market entry method: The perspective of luxury fashion retailing," *European Journal of Marketing*, 44 (1/2), 139–161.

Nia, A. and Lynne Zaichkowsky, J. (2000), "Do counterfeits devalue the ownership of luxury brands?" *Journal of Product and Brand Management*, 9 (7), 485–497.

Nueno, J. L. and Quelch, J. S. (1998), "The mass marketing of luxury," *Business Horizons*, 41 (6), 61–68.

Okawa, T. (2007), "Licensing practices at Maison Christian Dior," in: R. Blaszczyk ed. *Producing Fashion: Culture, Commerce, and Consumers*, Philadelphia, PA: Pennsylvania University Press, 82–107.

Palmer, A. (2009), *Dior: A New Look, A New Enterprise (1947–57)*, London: Victoria and Albert Museum Publishing.

Palmer, A. and Clarke, H. (2004), *Old Clothes New Looks: Second Hand Fashion*, London: Berg.

Phillips, C. (2006), *Bejewelled by Tiffany 1837–1987*, Chicago, IL: Art Institute of Chicago.

Pouillard, V. (2011), "Design piracy in the fashion industries of Paris and New York in the interwar years," *Business History Review*, 85 (2), 319–344.

Pouillard, V. (2013a), "Keeping designs and brands authentic: The resurgence of the post-war French fashion business under the challenge of US mass production," *European Review of History*, 20 (5), 815–835.

Pouillard, V. (2013b), "The rise of fashion forecasting and fashion public relations, 1920–1940: The history of Tobé and Bernays," in: T. Kuehne and H. Berghoff eds. *Globalizing Beauty: Body Aesthetics in the Twentieth Century*, New York: Palgrave, 151–169.

Pouillard, V. (2015), "Managing fashion creativity: The history of the Chambre Syndicale de la Couture Parisienne during the interwar period," *Investigaciones de Historia Economica/Economic History Research*, 12 (2), 76–89.

Pouillard, V. (2016), "A woman in international entrepreneurship: The case of Jeanne Paquin," in: K. Sogner, E. Lie, and H. B. Aven eds. *Entreprenørskap i næringsliv og politikk: Festskrift til Even Lange*, Oslo: Novus Forlag, 189–210.

Richon, Marco (1998), *Omega Saga*, Bienne: Omega SA.

Roberts, A. (2014), "Arnault's LVMH to relinquish $7,5 billion Hermes stake," *Bloomberg*, 3 September. Retrieved from: www.bloomberg.com/news/articles/2014-09-03/lvmh-plans-to-distribute-hermes-shares-to-investors-this-year (accessed 5 January 2017).

Rouzaud, C. A. (1946), *Un problème d'intérêt national: Les industries du luxe*, Thèse pour le doctorat d'Etat, Strasbourg: Librairie du recueil Sirey.

Scranton, Philip (1997), *Endless Novelty: Specialty Production and American Industrialization, 1865–1925*, Princeton, NJ: Princeton University Press.

Silverstein, M. J. and Fiske, N. (2008), *Trading Up: Why Consumers want New Luxury Goods – And How Companies Create Them*, New York: Portfolio.

Simmel, G. (1904/1957), "Fashion," *American Journal of Sociology*, 62 (6), 541–558.

Simpson, J. (2011), *Creating Wine: The Emergence of a World Industry, 1840–1914*, Princeton, NJ: Princeton University Press.

Subramanyam, S. (1990), *Merchants, Markets, and the State in Early Modern India*, Oxford: Oxford University Press.

Thomas, D. (2007), *Deluxe: How Luxury Lost its Luster*, London: Penguin.

Tokatli, N. (2008), "Global sourcing: Insights from the global clothing industry – the case of Zara, a fast fashion retailer," *Journal of Economic Geography*, 8 (1), 21–38.

Troy, N. J. (2003), *Couture Culture: A Study in Modern Art and Fashion*, Cambridge, MA: MIT Press.

Truong, Y., McColl, R., and Kitchen, P. J. (2009), "New luxury brand positioning and the emergence of masstige brands," *Journal of Brand Management*, 16 (5), 375–382.

Veblen, T. (1899), *The Theory of the Leisure Class: An Economic Study of Institutions*, New York: Macmillan.

28

SHIPPING

Gelina Harlaftis

On November 2016, the tanker *Olympic Leopard* was anchored in China loaded with two billion barrels of crude oil from Brazil waiting to discharge. It was built in South Korea and owned by a Liberian company which in turn was owned by a Panamanian company, which in turn was owned by a Lichtenstein company. The vessel sailed under the Liberian flag, it carried Greek and Philippino crew, and was owned by Greek shipowners. The shipping business was one of the first to use global institutions extensively after World War II: offshore companies and "flags of convenience," or open registries as they are called today (Metaxas 1985; Harlaftis 1989). Deep-sea going shipping is an international industry par excellence; its business has been to work beyond political borders. The shipping industry was one of the first global makers in the last centuries and one of those that has led the way to globalization. After all, shipping was a leading sector in the early modern European economic growth that connected the local with the global (Lucassen and Unger 2011).

In 2015, the largest number of ships in the world sailed under the Panama flag followed by Liberia, Marshall Islands, Hong Kong, Singapore, and Malta (see Table 28.1). But these ships were not owned by Panamanians or Liberians. The "beneficial owners" of the world fleet were Greeks, followed by Chinese, Germans, and Singaporeans. Gone were the days of a century before. In 1914, the leading maritime nation was Great Britain: a vessel would be built in Britain, hoist a British flag, be owned by a British shipowner, and carry British crews from the British Empire. Despite the globalization of shipping, however, until the last third of the twentieth century, European shipping firms ran world shipping. Despite major transformations, even today one-third of the world fleet is still run by traditional European nations of southern and northern Europe: Greece, Norway, UK and Germany (Table 28.1) (Ojala and Tenold 2017).

Shipping has been a main driver of trade growth and hence has contributed to the emergence and expansion of a global economy. The importance of shipping in the integration of world economy and globalization has been recognized in many recent studies (Unger 2011; Miller 2012; Harlaftis *et al.* 2012). Globalization is about global connections; as the sea covers three-quarters of the Earth's surface, these are mainly maritime connections. Shipping is international by nature and global by coverage; it can hardly occur without crossing borders and seas, without dealing constantly with maritime links between different countries, economies, and cultures. The shipping enterprise was one of the main institutions that facilitated international trade; by

Table 28.1 The top shipping fleets of the world according to registry and beneficial ownership, 2015 (in thousand deadweight tonnage, above 1,000 dwt)

Registry	Dwt	% of the world fleet	Beneficial ownership	Dwt	% of the world fleet
1 Panama	352,192	20.1	1 Greece	279,430	16
2 Liberia	203,832	11.6	2 Japan	230,675	15.7
3 Marshall Islands	175,345	10.0	3 China	157,557	9
4 Hong Kong (China)	150,801	8.6	4 Germany	122,036	8.9
5 Singapore	115,022	6.6	5 Singapore	84,022	3.9
6 Malta	82,002	4.7	6 South Korea	80,182	3.5
7 Greece	78,728	4.5	7 Hong Kong (China)	75,321	3.5
8 Bahamas	75,779	4.3	8 United States	60,263	3
9 China	75,676	4.3	9 United Kingdom	48,382	2.9
10 Cyprus	33,664	1.9	10 Norway	46,370	2.8

Source: UNCTAD (2015).

coordinating resources and designing and implementing business strategies, it connected distant markets and promoted market integration.

Despite its global dimension and international nature, shipping sprang from small places, islands, and port towns first engaged within particular maritime regions. The evolution of the shipping firm, the transformation of the institution from the regional to the national and international level and its globalizing effect has been largely a European matter. European colonial expansion in the early modern and modern period meant that by 1900, European nations owned more than three-quarters of world shipping. This primacy continued to the twenty-first century. European shipping firms have thrived in specific maritime regions from the north to the south, in which small, medium, and big maritime centres developed.[1]

A shipping firm is the economic unit that uses the factors of production to produce and provide sea transport services (Theotokas 2018: 10–12). It consists of a person or group of persons that make the decisions for the employment (or not) of the factors of production (Metaxas 1981: 13–14). In this context, shipowners have to judge which markets they will pursue, the types of ships needed for these markets, the timing of ship investments, the sources to be mobilized to draw finance and human labor, and the kind of administration they are going to follow. The function of the shipping firm is ship administration and operation and its product the sea transport services – the movement of a cargo from point A to point B. The price of this movement is the freight rate. Shipping is a derived demand, it is dependent on trade, and hence fluctuations in trade result in violent fluctuations in freight rates, thus confirming that shipping can be a risky business (Stopford 1997; Haueter's chapter in this volume). As it is a business that takes place beyond national borders and beyond the land base of the shipping firm where trust and communication was of prime importance, it grew and flourished in particular maritime regions, small places that developed maritime tradition, international networks, and a know-how to run ships. Later, the entrepreneurship of the small regions furnished the formation of large maritime centers within- and inter-regions.

This chapter analyzes the evolution of the European shipping company in the two main markets that were consolidated in the nineteenth century and are relevant to the present day: liner and tramp shipping of deep-sea/ocean going vessels. It does not include coastal, short-sea, lake, or river shipping businesses. The shipping markets were divided according to the type of cargo and ship. Liner ships carried general cargoes (finished or semi-finished manufactured goods) and tramp ships carried bulk cargoes (like coal, ore, grain, fertilizers, oil). Furthermore, liner shipping carried cargoes on regular routes, and tramp shipping on demand. Maritime economists like to call liner ships the "buses" and tramp ships the "taxis" of the oceans (Stopford 1997).

The analysis follows the path from local to global within the developments in world shipping and formation of the shipping markets in the nineteenth and twentieth centuries. It distinguishes five stages of development of the European shipping firm (Harlaftis 2019): (1) up to the 1820s; (2) from the 1830s to 1870s; (3) from the 1880s to 1930s; (4) from the 1940s to 1970s; and (5) after the 1980s. Its aim is, first, to indicate the landmarks in the structural transformations and changes in the European shipping firm since the nineteenth century. Second, it brings out their importance as global makers by using global shipping institutions like open registries and offshore companies. And, third, it emphasizes the importance for globalization of the maritime tradition and know-how of small European maritime regions.

First stage: up to the 1820s

From the fifteenth to the eighteenth centuries, European commercial and shipping business developed along the lines of their colonial empires, and the inter-imperial and national external trade was operated by close-knit business networks. Deep-sea shipping developed in certain maritime regions around Europe as indicated in Figure 28.1. There are five seas – the Baltic Sea, the North Sea, the European Atlantic, the Mediterranean, and the Black Sea – and twelve maritime regions with shared common characteristics and transactions. During this first stage, it was mainly the shipping fleets of small port towns and islands of the Baltic Sea, the North Sea, and

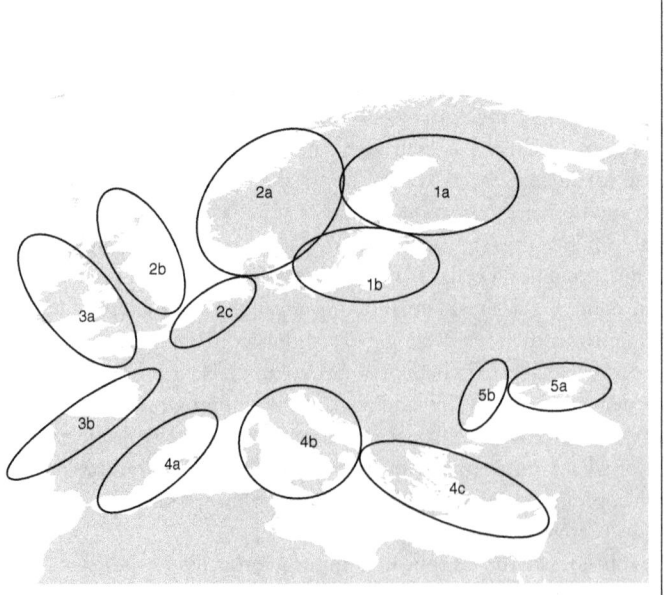

1. Baltic
    1a Northern Baltic
    1b Southern Baltic

2. North Sea
    2a Eastern North Sea
    2b Western North Sea
    2c Southern North Sea

3. Atlantic Europe
    3a Northern European Atlantic
    3b Southern European Atlantic

4. Mediterranean
    4a Western Mediterranean
    4b Central Mediterranean
    4c Eastern Mediterranean

5. Black Sea
    5a Northern Black Sea
    5b Western Black Sea

Figure 28.1   European maritime regions

the European Atlantic that developed deep-sea going sailing ship fleets to serve the colonial empires. In each maritime region, one or more big ports were formed to link hinterland and foreland and were served by the shipping fleets of the smaller places of the area. Whereas the fleets of the northern seas were engaged in deep-sea going trade, the eastern Mediterranean and Black Sea fleets started traveling beyond the inner sea from the last third of the eighteenth century onwards.

Two types of enterprise in European shipping emerged: the chartered companies and the free traders (see Figure 28.2). The big chartered merchant companies, British, Dutch, French, or

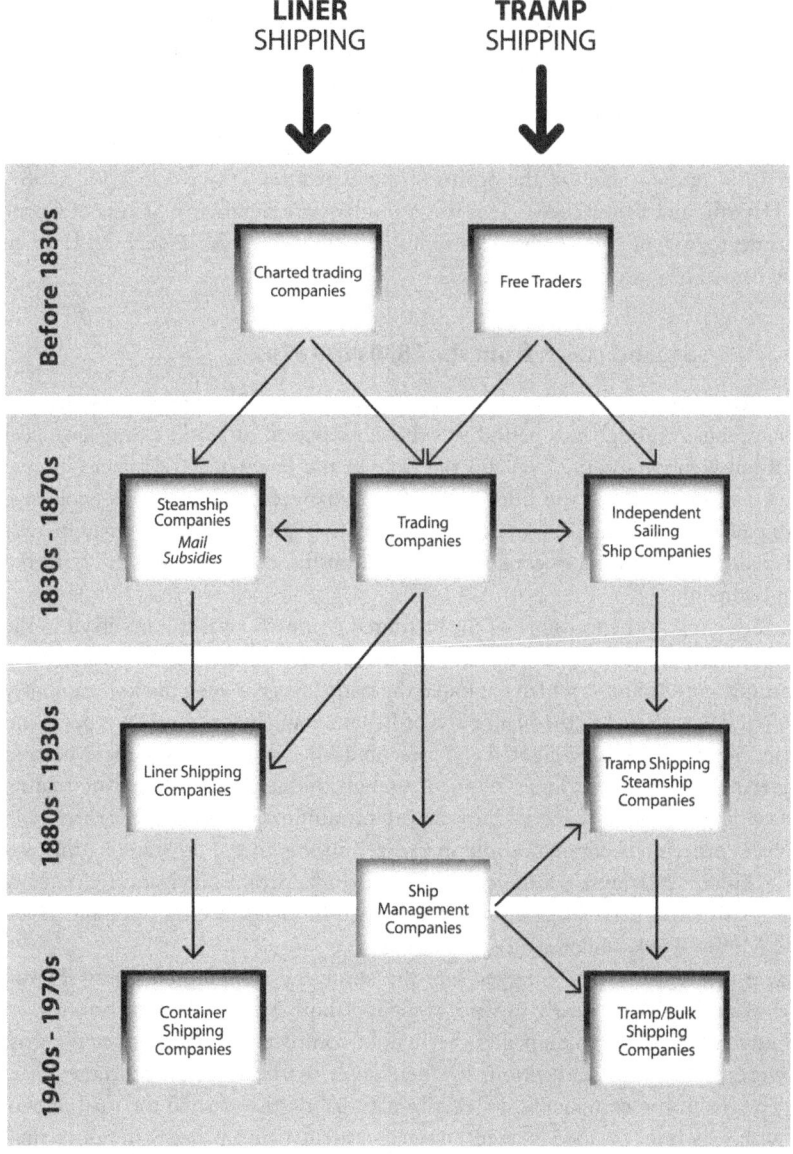

Figure 28.2   The evolution of the European shipping firm

Nordic, had special monopolistic trading privileges to trade in certain countries and overseas maritime regions. They carried out sea trade, owned fleets, and raised finance. As their trade was regularized, we can treat them as the predecessors of the liner shipping companies that followed. The growth of the international trade in the new modern industrial era revealed their limits and brought the need for structural changes and the demolition of most of the chartered companies by the end of the 1820s.

The free traders were the independent shipowners, who developed tramp shipping based on small port towns and islands in Europe's maritime regions. Free traders were ships outside the control of the chartered companies and were initiated by shipmasters or merchants who attracted investors in partnerships (Kirkaldy 1914; Davies 1962). At that stage, the tramp sailing ship was involved in a dual activity; sailing ships apart from providing sea transport services were simultaneously traders. The sailing vessel was then also a merchant trader and it comprised two functions: commercial and maritime. The beginning of a commercial voyage started with raising capital to purchase a cargo. This capital was usually raised from a small or large group of investors, and it enabled the master to have a cargo to sell on the voyage. The investor/creditor did not receive interest but rather a share in the profits of the expedition (Davis 1962; Ville 1987; Scheltjens 2015; Harlaftis and Laiou 2008). This was a similar system either in St Ives of Cornwall in the maritime region of the northern European Atlantic (area 3a, Figure 28.1) or in Cephalonia in the Ionian Sea (area 4c, Figure 28.1).

Second stage: from the 1830s to 1870s

During this stage, the effects of industrialization and the unprecedented size of cargoes changed the structure of shipping. Although this period was the culmination of world sailing ship fleet and the apogee of sail technology, this was also the time of the emergence of steamships and coexistence of sail and steam. After the institution of the chartered company was abolished, three types of companies were formed that carried world trade (Figure 28.2). The first type was the international trading company, the second the liner steamship company, and the third the tramp sailing ship company.

The first type, following in the footsteps of the chartered company, was still involved in the triple activity of trade, shipping, and finance. They were transformed into the overseas trading companies of the nineteenth century, which exploited the trade links between the home country and the colonies. They were based in the main ports of Britain, namely London, Liverpool, and Glasgow. Historian Geoffrey Jones highlighted and presented a detailed analysis of the evolution of the British big trading companies (Jones 2000). Although the majority of these big trading companies in the twentieth century evolved into important multinationals with diversified and multifaceted activities other than shipping, some specialized in shipping. For example, this was the case when Mackinnon Mackenzie founded the British India Steam Navigation Company known as BI, one of Britain's giant shipping concerns, based in Glasgow (Marriner and Hyde 1967; Jones 2000; Munro 2003; Miller 2012).

The second type of company that emerged was the steamship shipping company (Figure 28.2). As the new steamships were clearly superior to sailing ships, most European nations used state subsidies to establish steamship companies that would compete for control over the seas. These subsidies were mostly mail subventions by their states (Kirkaldy 1914; Sturmey 1962; Shulman 2015). The steamship companies of a certain nationality, that carried the mail of particular countries with which they traded for free, enjoyed particular advantages with tax exemptions within these countries. Their obligation was to serve a particular route a certain number of times per week or month. Britain, France, Belgium, Germany, Italy, Austria-Hungary,

Holland, Denmark, Sweden, Russia, Greece, and the Ottoman Empire, to name a few, established steamship companies which competed in cargo and passenger transportation in the European waters and the world's oceans.

Like the chartered companies, the liner shipping companies targeted maritime regions in particular distant seas. They became the most famous part of the shipping industry as they, at the time, carried "human cargoes," i.e., people with specialized passenger vessels (Williams 1990). As a general rule, liner companies were based in the big central home ports, whereas tramp shipping companies were based in the maritime regions of small port towns and islands. Liner shipping in Britain, the largest in Europe and in the world, was based in London, Liverpool, Glasgow, and Hull, where strong shipping business elites were formed. For example the Peninsular and Oriental (P&O) was based in London, established by the shipbroker Brodie McGhie Willcox, the seaman Arthur Anderson, and Captain Richard Bourne in 1837, which specialized in carrying the trade of the Indian Ocean. In Liverpool was the Ocean Steam Ship Company known as the Blue Funnel Line, established by the engineer and shipowner Alfred Holt in 1865, which specialized in trade with south-eastern Asia. Hull was the home port of the Wilson Line, established by the Wilson family that traded in all oceans and seas (Hyde 1957; Davies 1973; Starkey 1996; Harlaftis and Theotokas 2004; Boyce 2012a).

France's main liner shipping companies were based in the country's main ports. For example, Messageries Maritimes, established in 1851, and the Compagnie Fraissinet, established in 1836, were based in Marseille. The Compagnie Générale Transatlantique established in 1861 was based in Paris-Havre (Caty and Richard 1986). In the Austro-Hungarian Empire, the Austrian Österreichischer Lloyd, also known as Lloyd Austriaco, based in Trieste was formed in 1833. The Hamburg-American Line was formed in Hamburg in 1847 (HAPAG, Hamburg-Amerikanische Packetfahrt-Actien-Gesellschaft) and in Bremen, Norddeutscher Lloyd (NDL) in 1857. In Italy, the Navigazione Generale Italiana was established in Genoa in 1881 (after the unification of shipping lines formed in the 1840s), and was the largest shipping company of Italy. In Greece, the Hellenic Steamship Navigation was formed in 1856 based in Syros. In the Ottoman Empire, the Idarei Massousieh (Ottoman Steam Navigation Co.) in the early 1840s and Sirket-i Hayriye (Bosphorus Steam Navigation Company) in 1851 were formed and established in Constantinople (Harlaftis and Kardasis 2000). In Russia, the Russian Steam Navigation and Trading Company (known as ROPIT) was formed in 1856 and based in Odessa. Equally, in Scandinavia a number of liner companies developed toward the end of the century to serve the large transmigration trade from Central and Eastern Europe (Sebak 2013). All the above companies, apart from liner cargo vessels, operated large transoceanic passenger vessels to serve the massive immigration wave of the nineteenth to mid-twentieth century to the Americas and Australia (Feys 2013).

The third type of shipping company that served tramp shipping was the independent sailing shipowners, usually captains from Europe's maritime regions. What characterizes this period and differentiates it from the previous one is the separation of trade and shipping and specialization into shipping services. Indicative is that the term "shipowner" appeared in the London directories only in 1815 (Davis 1962: 81–109). Previously, the term was "merchant" or "trader" and by this term was usually meant a triple activity: trade, shipping, and finance. It was in the last third of the nineteenth century that specialization into the profession of shipowner and the shipping firm took place. The sailing ship was no longer a merchant trader, but only a carrier providing shipping services. The sailing shipowners drew capital from their home towns through co-ownerships and specialized in sea transport by forming large sailing ship fleets. Joint ownership practices were usual in the sailing ship era all over Europe.

The most dynamic deep-sea going sailing ship fleets of the Atlantic that developed during this period were by the British and the Scandinavians that were serving world trade, in fact their own and the northern European colonial trade. The northern European maritime communities lay in the eastern and northern coasts of the North Sea (areas 2a, 2b and 2c, Figure 28.1), in the northern European Atlantic (area 3a, Figure 28.1) (Nordvik 1985; Kaukiainen 1993; Craig 2003; Harlaftis and Theotokas 2004; Iversen and Thue 2008; Sheltjens 2015; Tenold *et al.* 2012; Tenold 2018). In southern Europe, deep-sea going tramp shipping thrived in Spain, on the Basque coastline (area 3b, Figure 28.1), on the north-western coast of the Italian peninsula in Liguria, and on the south-western coast, most particularly along the Sorrento coastline (area 4b, Figure 28.1). The Adriatic Dalmatian coastline developed an important maritime culture, while the Ionian and the Aegean islands, nourished the most important tramp operators of the Eastern Mediterranean and the Black Sea (areas 4b, 4c, 5a and 5b, Figure 28.1) (Frascani 2001; Valdaliso 1993; Harlaftis 1996; Pagratis 2009; Papadopoulou 2010; Delis 2012, 2016).

Southern Europeans served the Mediterranean and Black Sea trade whereas the northern Europeans served the north European ocean trade. Greeks, British, Norwegians, Dutch, French, Italians, Spanish continued practicing co-ownerships with strong local island or kinship ties and merchant family networks. The system of co-ownership was followed in all the maritime regions of Europe where a strong maritime culture had been nurtured (Palmer 1973; Nordvik 1985; Valdaliso 1993; Harlaftis 1996; Craig 2003; Papadopoulou 2010; Delis 2016).

Third stage: from the 1880s–1930s

The period from the 1880s to the 1930s was a watershed in the evolution of the shipping firm. It is characterized by the consolidation of the steamships that overtook sailing ships, the destruction of many traditional sailing ship areas, and the formation of new maritime centers in big ports. From 1880 to the eve of World War II, despite its declining share, Great Britain was the undisputable world maritime power, owning from 43 to 31 percent of the world fleet. The United States and Germany along with France and Italy tried to compete in vain in liner shipping (Cafruny 1987; Broeze 1991). Norway, Japan, and Greece competed in tramp shipping; they managed to surpass Britain only after World War II (Harlaftis 1996: Fig. 6.6). Over 95 percent of the world fleet belonged to fifteen countries that formed the so-called "Atlantic economy" (Fischer and Nordvik 1986).

There were at the time six maritime regions that nourished the most dynamic European fleets (areas 2a, 2b, 2c, 3a, 3b, and 4c, Figure 28.1), namely at the North Sea, the European Atlantic and the north-east Mediterranean), where British, German, Norwegian, and Greek shipowners developed the main liner and tramp shipping companies of the time. The French, Dutch, Spanish, and Italians concentrated mainly in the state subsidized liner companies. Europe remained at the core of the world sea-trade system. Until the eve of World War I, three-quarters of world exports in value and almost two-thirds of world imports featured the old continent (Fischer and Nordvik 1986). It does not come as a surprise then, that European countries owned the largest part of the world fleet. The interwar period was characterized by the attempt of the United States to keep a large national fleet with costly subsidies. However, most of the increase of the world fleet in the interwar period was due to the Japanese, the Norwegians, and the Greeks, who were involved in tramp shipping, and the Italians and the Dutch, involved in liner shipping. It was the first three that proved the most dynamic fleets of the second half of the twentieth century.

This period was characterized by the effect of new technology: the industrial revolution entered the shipping business in the form of steamships. Although steamships were operating since the 1820s, the world was still mainly run by sailing ships up to the 1870s. The transition from sail to steam took place between the 1880s and 1910s (Kaukiainen 1992; Armstrong and Williams 2008, 2010; Jackson and Williams 1996). The number of ships and tonnage of ships had shot up to serve the continuously increasing demand of raw materials, particularly grain, cotton, and coal which were the main bulk cargoes that filled the holds of the world fleet. Apart from increasing the availability of cargo space at sea, the advent of steamships caused a revolutionary decline in freight rates (North 1958; Harley 1988; Saif and Williamson 2004; Kaukiainen 2006). Steamships required much larger investments. Connection with the large home ports and international centers like London, on the one hand, and strong ties from the regional network, on the other, provided sources for drawing investment funds and control over business (Milne 2009; Starkey 1996). London provided the key maritime institutions that facilitated not only British but also European and world shipping. The Baltic Mercantile and Shipping Exchange was the global charter market where freight rates were fixed. Lloyd's Register of Shipping became the most important classification society for ships worldwide (followed by other European and American ones). Lloyd's of London became the main maritime insurance market, along with other commodity and financial markets, which facilitated international shipping (Boyce 2012b).

The development of the telegraph further facilitated business and communication. In 1914, Britain practically controlled the global telegraphic network (281,828 km versus 100,831 for the United States and over 43,000 each for Germany and France) (Scholl 1998; Müller and Tworek 2015).

Prior to this period, the shipping market was unified, meaning that cargoes neither determine the type of ship nor the organization of the trade. By the latter decades of the nineteenth century, the shipping market gradually formed two categories: liner and tramp shipping (Harlaftis

Table 28.2 World's largest fleets, 1880–2000

Country	1880 % of world tonnage	1937 % of world tonnage	1960 % of world tonnage	2000* % of world tonnage
Great Britain	43	31	15	3
Germany	8	6	3	3
USA	8	18	16	6
Norway	10	6	9	7
France	6	4	–	–
Japan	3	7	–	13
Italy	4	5	4	–
Holland	3	4	4	–
Sweden	3	2	3	–
Austria-Hungary	2	–	–	–
Russia-USSR	4	2	4	–
Spain	4	1	1	–
Greece	3	3	10	16
Hong Kong	0	–	–	4
China	0	–	–	5
South Korea	–	–	–	3
Taiwan	–	–	–	2

Sources: For 1880 from Kirkaldy (1914: Appendix XVII); Lloyd's Register of Shipping (1914, 1937, 1963); Lloyd's Statistical Tables (1990, 1992); UNCTAD (2015); Harlaftis (1996).

Note
* Beneficial ownership.

and Theotokas 2002). Although there was substitution between the two distinct markets, the main structures of each one were diametrically different: oligopoly and protectionism for the liner market with the formation of the shipping cartels, the conferences, from the 1880s, and almost perfect competition for the tramp ships (Sturmey 1962; Davies 1973; Palmer 1985; Cafruny 1987; Davies 1996; Greenhill 1982).

Consequently, two types of shipping companies were consolidated to serve the two different markets: the liner steamship companies and the independent steamship companies (Figure 28.2). Trading companies either specialized in shipping, like the Mackinnon group, or diversified in industry, mining, or other trading activities worldwide. Liner shipping companies carried packaged and/or industrialized goods and developed special ships, the passenger ships, to serve the ever-growing migrant trade of millions of people that crossed the oceans. Continuous development and harsh competition worldwide brought a wave of mergers and consolidation that took place from the beginning of the twentieth century. By the interwar period, particularly in Britain, most of the liner shipping firms had merged into large conglomerates. The economic crisis of the 1930s, however, hit British shipping and its companies hard. The colossus, the Royal Mail group, a public company that owned 11 percent of the whole British fleet, collapsed. The liner companies that retained their family character, and belonged to shipping families such as the Holts or Furnesses, were better able to withstand the financial turbulence. British banks intervened heavily to save British shipping (Green and Moss 1982).

Moreover, ship administration changed too with specialized ship management companies and the emergence of shipbroking and ship agencies to handle the exponential growth in international trade. Tramp shipping grew in Europe's maritime regions, areas that developed fleets in small port towns, islands, or regional maritime centers. In Britain, for example, until the nineteenth century the traditional areas of free traders were, apart from the London area, the south-west ports and the West Country (Craig 2003). With the industrial revolution, the main tramp shipping areas of Britain in the nineteenth century developed along with deep-sea export coal trade: the north-east English ports and Wales became the main hubs of British tramp operators in combination with those of the Clyde in Scotland which were traditionally connected with the worldwide trading networks of the Scottish merchants. By 1910, tramp shipping formed the largest part of the British merchant fleet up to the Great War with 462 companies owning 55 percent of the fleet (Boyce 1995; Argyros 2012; Craig 2003; Harlaftis and Theotokas 2004).

Most European tramp shipping companies were family owned companies that kept ownership and management of the companies and used intermarriages to expand and keep the business within closed circles. Maritime communities developed with strong regional ties. Shipping companies from Europe's maritime regions thrived within the framework of European colonial empires and their own private network foundations, according to the origin or links of their owners (Starkey 1996; Munro and Slaven 2001; Craig 2003; Argyros 2012). The local population of each port provided the financial and human capital for the shipping ventures. It was more usual than not for a shipmaster from a particular port to recruit seamen from the same port and have a partnership with investors from there.

In the modern steamship era, the usual practice of co-ownerships of the sailing ship era was further developed and re-invented by the British in their regional maritime areas. By the late 1870s, the single ship companies of unlimited liability were introduced, and this change produced a real boom in the market in the main tramp shipping areas of Britain (Boyce 1995; Craig 1980, 2003). In this way, the British invented the modern form of a tramp shipping company, which appeared to be the managing agent of a number of joint-stock single ship companies nominally distinct from each other but having the shipowner in firm control of all. Shrewd captains and other businessmen could satisfy their ambition to become shipowners at very little cost to themselves, by tapping sources of investment from a wider public (Craig 2003: 187–210). The other characteristic of the tramp shipping business sector was that it comprised a large number of single-ship companies. These were usually family-based shipping companies drawing sources from the maritime region where they came from. They formed, in reality, the reproduction hotbed of European shipping.

The choices and exploitation of technological advances by shipping entrepreneurs determined the path of world shipping. The first half of the twentieth century was characterized, on the one hand, by the use of steam engines and their gradual replacement by diesel engines, and, on the other, by the massive standard shipbuilding projects during the two world wars. From 1914 to 1918, 5,861 ships or 50 percent of the allied merchant fleet was sunk. Replacement of the sunken fleet took place between 1918 and 1921 in US and British shipyards. The "standard" ships became the main type of cargo ship during the interwar period; they were steamships of a standard type of 5,500 grt built on a large scale. It was these "standard" ships that Greeks, Japanese, and Norwegian tramp operators purchased en masse from the British secondhand market and expanded their fleets amongst the world economic crises.

For similar reasons during World War II, the United States and Canada launched the most massive shipbuilding programs the world had known, using a new and much quicker method of building ships: welding. During four years, the United States Maritime Commission managed to build about 4,700 vessels of all kinds, both commercial and military; out of these about 2,700 were the well-known Liberty ships that formed the standard dry-bulk cargo vessel for the next twenty-five years, and about 500 tankers of the so-called T2 type (Achee-Thornton and Thomson 2001). The Liberty ships and tankers of T2 type formed the basis for the world shipping fleet in the immediate post-World War II era.

Fourth stage: the 1940s–1970s

The period from 1945 to 1975 experienced almost uninterrupted economic and commercial growth. The volume of seaborne trade between the end of World War II and 1973 expanded more than six-fold, from 490 million metric tons in 1948 to 3,210 million metric tons in 1973. About 60 percent of the large increase between 1948 and 1973 was caused by an almost nine-fold increase in oil shipments (Harlaftis 1996: 246–251). Impressive also was the growth of the five main bulk cargoes: ore, bauxite, coal, phosphates, and grain. To carry the enormous volumes required to feed the industries of the West and East Asia, the size of ships carrying liquid and dry cargoes had to be increased. This period was characterized by the gigantic sizes of ships and their specialization according to the type of cargoes. Flags of convenience or open registries, as they were later called, and offshore companies were among the prime manifestations of the globalized shipping businesses. Flags of convenience were cheap flags with low taxes, which provided cheap sea transport and were supported by large American corporations like the oil companies. In the immediate post-war years, they were used more extensively by Greek and American shipowners mainly in the carriage of oil (Metaxas 1985; Cafruny 1987; Harlaftis 1989, 1996; Theotokas and Harlaftis 2009).

Today the use of offshore companies is a common practice by most businesses and businessmen. Back in the 1940s and 1950s, in the nation-centered post-World War II era, the practice of using offshore companies was a novelty, considered even an anomaly by state administrators. Offshore companies that sprang up during World War I started to be used on a small scale during the interwar period, and grew on a larger scale on the eve of World War II to reach unprecedented development since that time (Wilkins 2009: 823–824). What the offshore companies and the flags of convenience introduced was the abolition of the "genuine link" between ownership and operation, and the creation of global shipping in a globalizing world.

Michael Miller has emphasized Europe's maritime tradition and continuation of its supremacy in world shipping in the twentieth century. He examined globalization through maritime business connections, demonstrating the dramatic changes in the organization and mechanisms of European and world shipping during the second half of the twentieth century. Miller emphasizes the importance of the new shipping men who became the agents of change, the "world connectors" and "architects of transport" of the new oil transportation era. The new men in the new global tanker shipping era were involved in oil; he mentions that the "movers and shakers in tankers" were the Greeks, and among the pacesetters Aristotle Onassis (Miller 2012: 309).

Onassis pioneered in forming, developing, and consolidating the modern model of ownership and management of the global tramp/bulk shipping company after 1945 (Harlaftis 2019). This model had three components. The first one was the extensive use of the institution of the offshore company, mainly Panamanian and Liberian companies. The key became the multiple-holding offshore companies that rendered the owner of a ship practically invisible. The second one was the choice of flags of convenience or open registries. The third was the management of the shipping business group from many locations, which means that there was not an abode in only one particular country, but businesses run by "agencies" in different locations. These practices, which were very much frowned upon at the time, have been consolidated and are now considered the proper and common way of organizing and running shipping companies around the world to the present day. Although Onassis did not invent these practices, he was among the first worldwide, along with the Norwegian Erling Dekke Naess, the American Daniel Ludwig, and the Greek Stavros Niarchos, to put them altogether and consolidate them, thus creating the model of the global shipping enterprise of the twentieth and twenty-first century.

The 1970s were the landmark decade for the liner industry: unitization of the cargoes, also called containerization, brought a revolution in the transport of liner cargoes. Containerization included radically new designs for vessels and cargo-handling facilities, global door-to-door traffic, early use of information technology, and structural change of the industry through the formation of consortia, alliances, and international mega-mergers (Broeze 2003; Levinson 2009). This led to a total transformation of the liner shipping company that became the archetype of a globalized multinational shipping company (Figure 28.2).

Despite the importance of liner shipping companies, it is worth mentioning here that, to the present day, more than two-thirds of the volume of world trade is carried by tramp/bulk shipping and less than one-third by liners/container ships (Harlaftis and Theotokas 2002). The general pattern of trading has not changed over the last 130 years and the tramp/bulk shipping companies have remained, to a large extent, family businesses (Harlaftis 1996; on family business Colli and Rose 2003; Colli 1993; Jones and Rose 1993). However, what was lost during this period was the connection of the regional and human dimension.

Tramp shipping had developed with a path dependency in particular areas of Europe. For example, in Britain the hundreds of small operators in British maritime regions had traditionally been the nursery of British shipping. When this was lost, British shipping lost its strength and the ability to reproduce itself (Harlaftis and Theotokas 2004). On the contrary the Greeks continued along the lines of their path dependence and held partly the ties with the maritime islands of the Ionian and the Aegean islands that continued to be a major source of maritime entrepreneurship and labor during this period (Harlaftis 1996; Theotokas and Harlaftis 2009). The trend, however, was irreversible. During this time, many tramp operators lost their national culture and became international companies.

Fifth stage: after 1980s

The rise of the price of oil and the concomitant decline of economic activities led to a prolonged period of shipping crises with multiple recessions in the shipping markets from 1973 to 1986. By the end of the crises, world shipping had changed. The 1970s thus marked a new era characterized by a gradual loss of the predominance of European maritime nations. Still, the Greeks continued to keep their first position, while Norway, Germany, and the United Kingdom have kept a share of the market (Table 28.1).[2] The rise of maritime nations from Asia is evident. Apart from Japan in the second position, China occupied third place, followed by Singapore and South Korea. The division of labor in the world shipping had changed dramatically (Thanopoulou 1995).

In liner shipping, containerization rose abruptly. While in 1970 the world container fleet was of 500,000 teu, in 1980 it increased by more than six times to reach the 3,150,000 teu (Stopford 1997: 341). The new organization of liner shipping that demanded excessive investments in infrastructure (terminals, cargo handling facilities, ships, equipment, and agencies), led to an increase of ship and port productivity, increase of ship size, economies of scale, and decrease of transportation costs (Haralambides 2008). The above led to a total transformation of the liner shipping companies that became the archetype of a globalized multinational shipping company. Liner companies were forced to establish global networks in order to meet their customers' needs. The Danish Maersk became the biggest liner shipping company in the world, with a market share of 15 percent, operating more than 500 containerships (two million teu), more than fifty terminals, and more than 150 local offices worldwide at the beginning of the twentieth century. In 1999, Maersk acquired Sealand, the biggest American liner shipping company and the first company in the world that introduced the innovative technology of containers. In 2005 it bought the P&O Nedlloyd, then the third biggest liner company in the world.

On the contrary, the development of tramp shipping did not involve such innovative technological developments and no dramatic changes in the organization and structure of markets took place (Figure 28.2). Since the 1970s we are not talking of tramp shipping anymore but of bulk shipping moving from a label that emphasized the type of the ship to one focusing on cargoes. Four main categories of bulk cargo are distinguished (Stopford 1997: 16–17): liquid bulk (crude oil, oil products, and liquid chemicals), the five major bulk cargoes (iron ore, grain, coal, phosphates, and bauxite), minor bulk cargoes (steel products, cement, sugar, forest products etc.), and specialist bulk cargoes with specific handling or storage requirements (motor vehicles, refrigerated cargo, special cargoes).

Despite its global character, European shipping retains its national and local dimension and its closely knit business groups. Bulk shipping consists of companies of various sizes, which vary from large companies of more than fifty large ships to single-ship companies that directly compete with each other. For example, the Greek-owned shipping companies and the Norwegian shipping companies operating more than sixty ships co-existed and competed with the various Bergen-based and Piraeus-based small companies that operated ships of similar characteristics. No matter what the size of these enterprises was, their organization and structure and their strategies had very much in common (Harlaftis and Theotokas 2002; Tenold 2018). Big, medium, and small European bulk shipping companies shared four characteristics. The first important aspect of these shipping companies was their connection with a specific home port. The second one was the ownership and management of the company by distinct families for multiple generations. The third was the use of a regional network for drawing investment funds, and the fourth was the existence of an international network of overseas agencies.

Conclusions

European shipping firms have been the makers of the global shipping business, carrying cargoes in the world's oceans from European expansion in the fifteenth century to the present day. In the nineteenth and twentieth centuries, two types of shipping firms developed: the liner and tramp shipping companies. They mainly sprang from small regional maritime communities and acted as the main providers of capital, labor, and entrepreneurship for the large maritime centers. Maritime communities formed Europe's maritime regions, i.e., geographic entities with specific historical maritime traditions. These functioned as regional markets but also contributed to making the big port cities and eventually the European shipping markets.

From the nineteenth century to the mid-twentieth century, northern European shipping companies reigned in world shipping, particularly the British gigantic shipping companies followed by the Germans and the Scandinavians. The second half of the twentieth century brought changes; the shipping industry of southern Europe replaced the northern European leadership. The British gigantic companies had been replaced by the Greeks in the 1970s followed by the Scandinavians. And in the twenty-first century, Asian companies proved the most dynamic players in global shipping, still sharing it, however, with the Europeans led by the Greeks to the present day.

The analysis of shipping firms and the main markets has revealed the structural transformations and changes that occurred during the twentieth century. The hierarchy of maritime powers changed, as new maritime nations emerged and many of Europe's traditional maritime countries lost their competitiveness and decreased their market share. Shipping markets have followed the path to globalization and specialization has become the drive for their development. The maritime tradition of Europe's maritime regions in Greece, Scandinavia, and Britain, however, has meant that Europe has continued its primacy by using on the one hand the global shipping institutions like open registries and offshore companies and on the other hand the local dimension of its maritime regions. There is great scope for potential future comparative research on maritime businesses and maritime regions in Europe and beyond. The importance of the maritime tradition of small port towns and islands in the making of global shipping remains under investigated. Maritime businesses are still examined from a national/local point of view and almost never from a comparative point of view. Moreover, for the case of Scandinavian, continental, and Mediterranean shipping businesses research is "hidden" in publications in national languages. The evolution of the organizational forms of shipping businesses during the twentieth century is still under researched. Similarly, the institutions of shipping, like the insurance companies, the classification societies, or the Baltic Exchange have not received proper attention from the academic community. Breach of international maritime law, modern piracy, and maritime fraud, and how shipping businesses deal with these issues is a subject usually left to the reporters. Academic research is yet to be done. The impact on the environment of carrying oil at sea, a post-World War II phenomenon, is usually left to economists or environmental scientists.

Maritime businesses connect the world's oceans and seas. They are part of the history of the seas and oceans, of global history, an integral part of the globalization process. The history of navigation and shipping routes, of the entrepreneurship of ports and islands, of maritime transport logistics – connections of hinterland with foreland – of seamen, of maritime communities around the world that have produced particular maritime cultures need more and comparative research. Shipping companies are global makers that always remember home. Hence they are the quintessence of "local to global" that still remains to be fully explored.

Notes

1 This chapter is based on research on archival material in Greek and other European archives and inter-national bibliography on maritime business over the last thirty years. I encountered research for the international shipping business for the first time at the end of my first PhD year in Oxford, in 1984, in the Maritime History Conference at Greenwich Maritime Museum with the theme "The Shipowner in History." The leading role in the research of British shipping companies (and in fact for the creation of the academic journal *Business History*) was played by the so-called "Liverpool School" mostly developed during the 1950s to 1960s founded by Professor Francis Hyde and continued by Professor Peter N. Davies who was my PhD thesis co-supervisor. Since 1989 that the International Maritime Economic History Association (IMEHA) was formed. Either as a member or an officer of IMEHA (today IMHA) I have profited from discussions, exchange of archives and ideas with Lewis R. Fischer, Helge Nordvik, Frank Broeze, Robin Craig, David Williams, Lars Scholl, Sarah Palmer, Malcolm Tull, David J. Starkey, Jesus Valdaliso, and Stig Tenold. The Greek team of maritime historians that has taken off in the last decade has also contributed substantially in providing research, ideas, archival material, papers, books: Ioannis Theotokas, Gerassimos Pagratis, Apostolos Delis, Katerina Galani, Alexandra Papadopoulou, and Panayotis Kapetanakis.
2 Fierce world competition led Scandinavian and German shipping, despite its year-long resistance to open registries, to introduce a new invention the "international registry." Norwegians, followed by Danes and Germans established a "double" national registry.

References

Achee-Thornton, Rebecca and Thomson, Peter (2001), "Learning from Experience and Learning from Others: An Exploration of Learning and Spillovers in Wartime Shipbuilding," *American Economic Review* 91 (5), 1350–1368.

Armstrong, John and Williams, David M. (2008), "The Steamship as an Agent of Modernisation, 1812–1840," *International Journal of Maritime History* 19 (1), 145–160.

Armstrong, John and Williams, David M. (2010), "Technological Advances in the Maritime Sector: Some Implications for Trade, Modernization and the Process of Globalization in the Nineteenth Century," in Maria Fusaro and Amelia Polonia, (eds.), *Maritime History as Global History* (St. John's, Newfound-land: International Association of Maritime Economic History), 177–202.

Argyros, Leonidas (2012), "Burrel and son of Glasgow: A Tramp Shipping Firm, 1861–1930," Unpub-lished PhD thesis (Newfoundland: Memorial University of Newfoundland).

Boyce, Gordon (1995), *Information, Mediation and Institutional Development: The Rise of Large-Scale Enterprise in British Shipping, 1870–1919* (Manchester: Manchester University Press).

Boyce, Gordon (2012a), *The Growth and Dissolution of a Large-Scale Business Enterprise: The Furness Interest 1892–1919* (St. John's, Newfoundland: International Maritime History Association).

Boyce, Gordon (2012b), "The Development of Commercial Infrastructure for World Shipping," in Gelina Harlaftis, Stig Tenold, and Jésus M. Valdaliso (eds.), *World's Key Industry: History and Economics of Inter-national Shipping* (London: Palgrave Macmillan), 106–123.

Broeze, Frank (1991), "Albert Ballin, the Hamburg–Bremen Rivalry and the Dynamics of the Conference System," *International Journal of Maritime History* III (1), 1–32.

Broeze, Frank (2003), *The Globalisation of the Oceans: Containerisation from the 1950s to the Present* (St. John's, Newfoundland: International Maritime Economic History Association).

Cafruny, Alan (1987), *Ruling the Waves: The Political Economy of International Shipping* (Berkeley, CA: University of California Press).

Caty, R. and Richard, E. (1986), *Armateurs Marseillais au XIXe siecle* (Marseilles: Chambre de Commerce et d'Industrie de Marseilles).

Colli, Andrea (1993), *The History of Family Business 1850–2000* (Cambridge: Cambridge University Press).

Colli, Andrea and Rose, Mary (2003), "Family Firms in Comparative Perspective," in Franco Amatori and Geoffrey Jones (eds.), *Business History Around the World at the End of the 20th Century* (Cambridge: Cam-bridge University Press), 339–352.

Craig, Robin (1980), *The Ship: Steam Tramps and Cargo Liners, 1850–1950* (London: HMSO).

Craig, Robin (ed.) (2003), *British Tramp Shipping, 1750–1914* (St. John's, Newfoundland: International Economic History Association).

Davies, Peter N. (1973), *The Trade Makers: Elder Dempster in West Africa 1852–1972* (London: George Allen & Unwin).

Davies, Peter N. (1996), "Nineteenth Century Ocean Trade and Transport," in Peter Mathias and John A. Davis (eds.), *International Trade and British Economic Growth from Eighteenth Century to the Present Day* (Oxford: Blackwell).

Davis, Ralph (1962), *The Rise of the English Shipping Industry in the Seventeenth and Eighteenth Centuries* (London: Macmillan).

Delis, Apostolos (2012), "Shipping Finance and Risks in Sea Trade during the French Wars: Maritime Loan Operations in the Republic of Ragusa," *International Journal of Maritime History* 24 (1), 229–242.

Delis, Apostolos (2016), *Mediterranean Wooden Shipbuilding. Economy, Technology and Institutions in Syros in the Nineteenth Century* (Leiden: Brill).

Feys, Torsten (2013), *The Battle for the Migrants: The Introduction of Steam Shipping on the North Atlantic and its Impact on the European Exodus* (St. John's, Newfoundland: International Maritime Economic History Association).

Fischer, Lewis R. and Nordvik, Helge W. (1986), "Maritime Transport and the Integration of the North Atlantic Economy, 1850–1914," in Wolfram Fischer, R. Marvin McInnis, and Jurgen Schneider (eds.), *The Emergence of a World Economy, 1500–1914* (Wiesbaden: Franz Steiner Verlag), 519–544.

Frascani, Paolo (ed.) (2001), *A Vela e a Vapore. Economie, culture e istituzioni del mare nell' Italia dell' Ottocento* (Rome: Donzelli Editore).

Greenhill, Robert G. (1982), "Competition or Co-operation in the Global Shipping Industry: The Origins and Impact of the Conference System for British Shipowners before 1914," in D. J. Starkey and G. Harlaftis (eds.), *Global Markets: The Internationalization of the Sea Transport Industries since 1850* (St. John's, Newfoundland: International Maritime Economic History Association), 53–80.

Green, Edwin and Moss, Michael (1982), *A Business of National Importance: The Royal Mail Shipping Group, 1902–1937* (London: Methuen).

Haralambides, Hercules (2008), "Structure and Operations in the Liner Shipping Industry," in D. A. Hensher and K. J. Button (eds.), *Handbook of Transport Modelling*, 2nd ed. (Amsterdam, London: Elsevier), 607–621.

Harlaftis, Gelina (1989), "Greek Shipowners and State Intervention in the 1940s: A Formal Justification for the Resort to Flags-of-Convenience?" *International Journal of Maritime History* 1 (2), 37–63.

Harlaftis, Gelina (1996), *A History of Greek-Owned Shipping: The Making of an International Tramp Fleet, 1830 to the Present Day* (London: Routledge).

Harlaftis, Gelina (2019), *Creating Global Shipping: Aristotle Onassis, the Vagliano Brothers and the Business of Shipping, c.1820–1970* (Cambridge: Cambridge University Press).

Harlaftis, Gelina and Kardasis, Vassilis (2000), "International Bulk Trade and Shipping in the Eastern Mediterranean and the Black Sea," in Jeffrey Williamson and Sevket Pamuk (eds.), *The Mediterranean Response to Globalization* (London: Routledge), 233–265.

Harlaftis, Gelina and Laiou, Sophia (2008), "Ottoman State Policy in Mediterranean Trade and Shipping, c.1780–c.1820: The Rise of the Greek-Owned Ottoman Merchant Fleet," in Mark Mazower (ed.), *Networks of Power in Modern Greece* (London: Hurst), 1–44.

Harlaftis, Gelina and Theotokas, Ioannis (2002), "Maritime Business during the 20th Century: Continuity and Change," in C. Th. Grammenos (ed.), *Handbook of Maritime Economics and Business* (London: Lloyd's of London Press), 9–34.

Harlaftis, Gelina and Theotokas, Ioannis (2004), "European Family Firms in International Business: British and Greek Tramp-Shipping firms," *Business History* 46 (2), 219–255.

Harlaftis, Gelina, Tenold, Stig, and Valdaliso, Jésus M. (eds.) (2012), *The World's Key Industry: History and Economics of International Shipping* (London: Palgrave Macmillan).

Harley, C. Knick (1988), "Ocean Freight Rates and Productivity, 1740–1913: The Primacy of Mechanical Invention Reaffirmed," *Journal of Economic History* 48, 851–875.

Hyde, Francis E. (1957), *Blue Funnel: A History of Alfred Holt and Company of Liverpool, 1865–1914* (Liverpool: Liverpool University Press).

Iversen, Martin Jes and Thue, Lars (2008), "Creating Nordic Capitalism: The Business History of Competitive Periphery," in Susanna Fellman, Martin Jes Iversen, Hans Sjögren, and Lars Thue (eds.), *Creating Nordic Capitalism: The Business History of a Competitive Periphery* (Basingstoke/New York: Palgrave Macmillan), 1–19.

Jackson, Gordon and Williams, David M. (1996), *Shipping, Technology and Imperialism* (Hans: Scolar Press).

Jones, Geoffrey (2000), *Merchants to Multinationals: British Trading Companies in the Nineteenth and Twentieth Centuries* (Oxford: Oxford University Press).

Jones, Geoffrey and Rose, Mary (eds.) (1993), *Family Capitalism* (London: Frank Cass).

Kaukiainen, Yrjö (1992), "Coal and Canvas: Aspects of the Competition between Steam and Sail, c. 1870–1914," *International Journal of Maritime History* 4 (2), 175–191.

Kaukiainen, Yrjo (1993), *A History of Finnish Shipping* (New York: Routledge).

Kaukiainen, Yrjö (2006), "Journey Costs, Terminal Costs and Ocean Tramp Freights: How the Price of Distance Declined from the 1870s to 2000," *International Journal of Maritime History* XVIII (2), 17–64.

Kirkaldy, Adam Willis (1914), *British Shipping: Its History, Organisation and Importance* (London: K. Paul, Trench, Tübner & Co. Ltd.; New York: E.P. Dutton & Company).

Levinson, Marc (2006), *The Box: How the Shipping Container Made the World Smaller and the World Economy Bigger* (Princeton: Princeton University Press).

Lucassen, J. and Unger, R. W. (2011), "Shipping, Productivity and Economic Growth," in R. W. Unger (ed.), *Shipping and Economic Growth, 1350–1850* (Leiden: Brill), 4–44.

Marriner, Sheila and Hyde, Francis E. (1967), *The Senior: John Samuel Swire 1825–98. Management in Far Eastern Shipping Trades* (Liverpool: Liverpool University Press).

Metaxas, Basil N. (1981), *The Economics of Tramp Shipping* (2nd ed.) (London: Athlone Press).

Metaxas, Basil N. (1985), *Flags of Convenience* (London: Gower Press).

Miller, Michael B. (2012), *Europe and the Maritime World: A Twentieth-Century History* (Cambridge: Cambridge University Press).

Milne, Graeme J. (2009), "North East England Shipping in the 1890s: Investment and Entrepreneurship," *International Journal of Maritime History* 21 (1), 1–26.

Müller, S. M. and Tworek, H. J. S. (2015), "Telegraph and the Bank: On the Interdependence of Global Communications and Capitalism, 1866–1914," *Journal of Global History* 10 (2), 259–283.

Munro, Forbes J. (2003), *Maritime Enterprise and Empire: Sir William Mackinnon and his Business Network, 1823–1893* (Woodbridge, UK: Boydell).

Munro, Forbes J. and Slaven, Tony (2001), "Networks and Markets in Clyde Shipping: The Donaldsons and the Hogarths, 1870–1939," *Business History* 43 (2), 19–50.

Nordvik, Helge (1985), "The Shipping Industries of the Scandinavian Countries," in Lewis R. Fischer and Gerald E. Panting (eds.), *Change and Adaptation in Maritime History: The North Atlantic Fleets in the Nineteenth Century* (St. John's, Newfoundland: International Maritime History Association), 117–148.

North, Douglass C. (1958), "Ocean Freight Rates and Economic Development, 1750–1913," *Journal of Economic History* XVIII (4), 537–555.

Ojala, Jari and Tenold, Stig (2017), "Maritime Trade and Merchant Shipping: The Shipping/Trade Ratio since the 1870s," *International Journal of Maritime History* 29 (4), 1–17.

Pagratis, Gerassimos (2009), "Οργάνωση και διαχείριση της ναυτιλιακής επιχείρησης στην Κέρκυρα στο πρώτο ήμισυ του 16ου αιώνα" ["Organisation and administration of the shipping firm in Corfu in the first half of the 16th century"], *Mnemon* 30, 9–35.

Palmer, Sarah (1973), "Investors in London Shipping, 1820–1850," *Maritime History* 2, 46–68.

Palmer, Sarah (1985), "The British Shipping Industry 1850–1914," in Lewis R. Fischer and Gerald Panting (eds.), *Change and Adaptation in Maritime History: The North Atlantic Fleets in the Nineteenth Century* (St. John's, Newfoundland: International Maritime Economic History Association), 87–114.

Papadopoulou, Alexandra (2010), "Ναυτιλιακές επιχειρήσεις, διεθνή δίκτυα και θεσμοί στη σπετσιώτικη εμπορική ναυτιλία, 1830–1870. Οργάνωση, διοίκηση και στρατηγική" ["Maritime businesses, international networks and institutions in the merchant shipping of the island of Spetses. Organisation, Management and Strategy"], Unpublished Ph.D. thesis (Corfu: Ionian University).

Saif, Mohammed I. and Williamson, Jeffrey G. (2004), "Freight Rates and Productivity Gains in British Tramp Shipping 1869–1950," *Explorations in Economic History* 41 (2), 172–203.

Scheltjens, Werner (2015), *Dutch Deltas: Emergence, Functions and Structure of the Low Countries' Maritime Transport System, ca. 1300–1850* (Leiden: Brill).

Scholl, Lars U. (1998), "The Global Communication Industry and Its Impact on International Shipping before 1914," in David J. Starkey and Gelina Harlaftis (eds), *Global Markets: The Internationalization of the Sea Transport Industries Since 1850* (St. John's, Newfoundland: International Association of Maritime Economic History), 201–212.

Sebak, Per Kristian (2013), "Russian-Jewish Transmigration and Scandinavian Shipping Companies: The Case of DFDS and the Atlantic Rate War of 1904–1905," in Tobias Brinkmann (ed.), *Points of Passage: Jewish Transmigrants from Eastern Europe in Scandinavia, Germany, and Britain 1880–1914* (New York: Berghahn Books).

Shulman, P. (2015), "Ben Franklin's Ghost: World Peace, American Slavery, and the Global Politics of Information before the Universal Postal Union," *Journal of Global History* 10 (2), 212–234.

Starkey, David J. (1996), "Ownership Structures in the British Shipping Industry: The Case of Hull, 1820–1916," *International Journal of Maritime History* VIII (2), 71–95.

Stopford, Martin (1997), *Maritime Economics* (London: Routledge).

Sturmey, Stanley G. (1962), *British Shipping and World Competition* (London: Athlone Press).

Tenold, Stig (2018), *Norwegian Shipping in the 20th Century. Norway's Successful Navigation of the World's Most Global Industry* (Cham, Switzerland: Palgrave).

Tenold, Stig, Martin Jes Iversen, and Even Lange (2012), *Global Shipping in Small Nations: Nordic Experiences after 1960* (Basingstoke: Palgrave)

Thanopoulou, Helen (1995), "The Growth of Fleets Registered in the Newly-Emerging Maritime Countries and Maritime Crises," *Maritime Policy and Management* 22 (1), 51–62.

Theotokas Ioannis (2018), Management of Shipping Companies (London: Routledge).

Theotokas, Ioannis and Harlaftis, Gelina (2009), *Leadership in World Shipping: Greek Family Firms in International Business* (Basingstoke: Palgrave Macmillan).

UNCTAD (2015), *Review of Maritime Transport* (New York and Geneva: UN).

Unger, R. W. (ed.) (2011), *Shipping and Economic Growth, 1350–1850* (Leiden: Brill)

Valdaliso, Jesus (1993), "Spanish Shipowners in the British Mirror: Patterns of Investment, Ownership and Finance in the Bilbao Shipping Industry, 1879–1913," *International Journal of Maritime History* 5 (2), 1–30.

Ville, Simon P. (1987), *English Shipowning during the Industrial Revolution* (Manchester: Manchester University Press).

Wilkins, Mira (2009), *The History of Foreign Investment in the United States, 1914–1945* (Cambridge, MA: Harvard Studies in Business History).

Williams, David (1990), "Bulk Passenger Shipping, 1750–1870," in Lewis R. Fischer and Helge W. Nordvik (eds.), *Shipping and Trade, 1750–1950: Essays in International Maritime Economic History* (Pontefract, UK: Lofthouse Publications), 43–61.

29

GLOBAL COMMODITY TRADERS

Espen Storli

Introduction

Access to natural resources has always been the bedrock of economic life; no society, however advanced, can survive without it. Yet, natural resources are spread unevenly across the globe and they are rarely found in the same place where they are consumed. Throughout human history, the need for natural resources has therefore been a basic driver of trade. The spread of industrialization during the nineteenth century magnified the demand for natural resources. This development picked up pace with the second industrial revolution from the 1870s onwards, as new technologies created demand for new resources. In addition, the fast-growing urban societies that grew up around new factories craved enormous amounts of foodstuffs to survive. This insatiable demand could only be met by moving huge volumes of basic materials from where they were found or grown to where they were needed to fuel industrial production and to feed the workers manning the machines. As a result, natural resources from all over the world were physically transformed into global value chains.

Companies, particularly multinational businesses, created global value chains in which a vertically integrated firm would control the different stages of the production process, for example from mine to smelter to end product. Global value chains could also be established through arm's length market transactions with producers specializing in one step of the production process and then selling on the commodity to a company involved in the next stage of production for further refining. The latter way of creating value chains opened up ample opportunities for middlemen to become involved. Specialized commodity-trading companies were one such type of middlemen. These companies did not usually mine, grow, refine, or smelt the commodities needed in production processes; they concentrated on physically linking the different stages of production together by buying the output from one stage, transporting it to another place, and selling the commodity to a producer involved in the next stage of production.

Specialized commodity-trading companies became increasingly important in the international economy toward the end of the nineteenth century. Some of the commodity traders grew to have a truly global presence, that is they were doing business on at least three different continents. For several important commodities, trading companies acquired a dominant role, combining their knowledge of markets with logistical and financial capabilities to transport, transform, and market commodities globally. It is notable that several of the trading companies

455

that grew large during the first global economy before 1914, such as Cargill and the Louis Dreyfus Company, have displayed a remarkable stability and still control important commodity markets today. While other big players have disappeared, new entities with links back to the initial movers often took over their position.

A commodity is most commonly defined as a basic good used in commerce that is interchangeable with other goods of the same type, or as bulk undifferentiated and unbranded goods (for a good discussion of the definition of commodities, see Topik and Wells 2012: 7–8). In a narrow sense, commodities might also be understood only as raw materials, but although ultimately all commodities come out of the ground, they might also have undergone one or several refining steps, and still be considered as a commodity. Commodities are usually grouped into two main types: hard and soft commodities. Hard commodities are typically natural resources that must be mined or extracted (such as gold, coal, and oil), whereas soft commodities are agricultural products or livestock (such as corn, wheat, coffee, sugar, soybeans, and pork).

A commodity is generally understood as a type of product of uniform quality. When a commodity is traded on a commodity exchange, it must fulfill specific quality requirements. The quality of the commodity on an exchange is thus essentially uniform across producers. However, as products that ultimately come from nature, the chemical form of a commodity depends on its origins, and thus there is really no such thing as a standard physical commodity (Buchan and Errington 2017). The distinctive physical properties of commodities are one of the basic foundations for the commodity traders' business model. Not only do they link producers and consumers by physically moving a commodity from one geographic location to another; they also change the properties of the commodity by blending commodities of different qualities to match the demands of the customer, and by storing them to time the delivery to maximize profits and suit the production timetable of the customer. The global commodity traders buy, transport, and sell the basic stuff that the world needs to function and on which modern life hinges – metals and minerals, oil and foodstuffs.

Global commodity traders continue to play an important role in the global economy; today a handful of companies control the flow of hundreds of billions of dollars of the world's commodities. Despite their importance, traders have traditionally not maintained a high public profile. Recent media articles on the traders have all played with different versions of the same chorus: they talk about "secretive giants," (*Daily Telegraph* 2011) "a cluster of publicity-shy companies," (Blas 2011) about "the hidden companies of the global economy," or "the biggest companies you never heard of" (Onstad *et al.* 2011).

This chapter argues that although there has always been widespread trade in commodities, global commodity trade only arose with the second industrial revolution in the latter decades of the nineteenth century. The revolution in information and transportation for the first time enabled companies to trade commodities actively on several continents. Over the last 150 years, the centers of commodity trading have shifted between different locations, but despite these shifts, there has been a remarkable stability in the industry. Overall, large commodity trading companies have played an important role in creating global value chains by physically transporting natural resources between different parts of the world and by transforming raw materials to make them into commodities.

Literature overview

In scholarship as well as the media, commodity trading companies have generally flown under the radar and we lack any broad studies of the role and impact of global commodity traders. Unlike the situation for general trading companies, where there is a wealth of studies, the existing literature on specialized commodity traders is limited and scattered (on general trading companies, see Michael Aldous' chapter in this collection). It can be divided into three broad categories: works on the economics of commodity trading, studies of the business history of specific companies, and, finally, popular journalistic investigations of aspects of commodity trading.

The most comprehensive work on the economics of commodity trading is Philippe Chalmin's (1989) book on *Traders and Merchants: Panorama of International Commodity Trading*. Chalmin analyzes the economic rationale for global trading firms and explains the different functions that the companies fulfill in the international economy. In addition, he gives a historical overview of the development of the major sectors of the commodity trade, with short histories of the dominant global traders in the 1980s, when the book was written. In addition to Chalmin's work, the economist Craig Pirrong (2014) has written a white paper commissioned by Trafigura, a global commodity trader, which discusses the fundamental economics of commodity trading. Pirrong's main argument is that commodity trading firms add value by identifying and optimizing transformations in commodities by reconciling mismatches between supply and demand.

Despite the size and historical importance of big commodity trading companies, there are only a limited number of works on their business history (for a short and concise overview of the history of commodity trading companies, see Jones 2005). Generally speaking, researchers have not had access to the companies' archives. Many of the existing works are therefore based on an outside-in perspective of the firms gained from published information or government archives. There are some notable exceptions, such as Wayne Broehl's (1992, 1998, 2008) monumental three-volume study of the giant grain trader Cargill, today the largest privately held corporation in the United States in terms of revenue. There are also a couple of other monographs on different aspects of Cargill (Morgan 1979; Kneen 2002). Cargill's historical competitors are not as well served, although there are some works on Bunge & Born (Green 1985; Dehne 2013) and Archer Daniels Midlands (Lieber 2000).

The role of commodity trading companies in other soft commodities has been less studied, but Philippe Chalmin's (1990) monograph on the history of the sugar company Tate & Lyle is important. Based on access to company archives, Chalmin analyzes how this global sugar giant developed from its origins as essentially a sugar refiner to focus increasingly on trading. There is also a growing literature on the history of Swiss commodity traders and their involvement in agricultural commodities, for instance Christof Dejung's (2013a, 2013b) work on the Volkart company and its involvement in the cotton and coffee trade.

The situation in hard commodities, especially metals, is similar. There are some important works on the most important specialized metal traders, such as Susan Becker's (2002) monograph on the pre-World War I history of the German company Metallgesellschaft, the biggest metal trader in the world before 1914, and Helmut Waszkis' (1992) book on Philipp Brothers, the American company that dominated international metal trading from 1945 until the 1980s. Becker based her works on the Metallgesellschaft archives, while Waszkis, who worked as a metal trader for Philipp Brothers, had access to internal correspondence and conducted a large number of interviews with company employees. Waszkis, together with his son (2003), has also written a very informative history of metal trading, tracing traders through history from antiquity to today, while Becker (1998) in a book chapter compares the pre-World War I development of Metallgesellschaft with that of its two biggest domestic competitors, Beer, Sondheimer & Co. and Aron Hirsch & Sohn.

The more recent history of trading in hard commodities is still a rather blank spot. There are no academic studies of the dominant global commodity traders of the last couple of decades, such as Glencore, Trafigura, Noble Group, or Vitol. Consequently, the move by metal traders into the oil markets has been virtually unexplored, although some journalists have written about this in books aimed at a more general market (Kelly 2014), and especially with a focus on the infamous Marc Rich (Ammann 2009; Copetas 1985).

The existing literature on the history of commodity trading companies is not extensive and there is still much to discover, but the historiography does show the importance of commodity traders in creating global markets for commodities by linking sites of primary production with manufacturing plants and consumer markets through physically moving and transforming natural resources. Some of the works also illustrate the key point that the definition of a commodity trading company can be a slippery affair, as for instance Tate & Lyle developed from a producer to become more and more of a trader, while a company like Glencore, which started out as essentially a non-ferrous metal trader, through its merger with the mining company Xstrata has become perhaps as much a miner and producer as a trading company. Helmut Waszkis' (2001) work on one of the Bolivian tin barons, Moritz Hochschild, illustrates this point well. Hochschild started out trading Bolivian tin ores with European producers, but then gradually took control also over mining operations, which eventually became the key focus for his operations. The existing body of work essentially focuses either on the economics of the industry or the business development of different companies. Only to a very limited extent do existing studies consider the national and international political economy in which global commodity traders have operated.

The development of global commodity traders

Large, specialized commodity trading companies with extensive international operations only came into existence in the second half of the nineteenth century, enabled by the technological advances of the second industrial revolution, and especially the advent of mass production and mass marketing, and the impact of the transport and information revolutions of this period (Dejung 2013b: 1005). The traditional small and middle-scale merchant houses, which for centuries had made a living through trading a wide range of products, often on a small scale, could not satisfy modern industrial manufacturers' gluttonous appetite for raw materials. That demand could be better met by traders that could build up extensive buying capacity in the areas where the commodities were first produced and also had the capital to invest in warehouses. In addition, these traders also built up effective selling organizations in the industrial districts where the commodities were transformed into consumer goods. By specializing on trading large volumes of one or a few commodities, some traders gradually grew into having a global presence.

The new demands for scale in commodity trading was not the only reason why larger specialized commodity traders became dominant in many commodities. Traditionally, the operations of many traders had relied on access to advances granted by purchasers. However, the introduction of the telegraph shifted the relations between the end-users and the middlemen and gave potential customers the ability to compare offers from different merchants, which meant that the traders increasingly had to start trading on their own account. The new business practices put a strain on liquidity, which could only be handled by securing short-term credit from merchant banks. Credit was generally more accessible to larger trading companies, and smaller entities were often pushed to the side by bigger competitors (Dejung 2013b: 1005).

As commodity traders increasingly traded on their own behalf, the time-lag between purchase and delivery made heavy demands on finance. It also carried the risks of price and currency fluctuations. To insure against risks, the traders embraced the growth of new commodity exchanges, where they could hedge their operations. Futures markets for globally traded articles such as cotton, coffee, and sugar emerged in the late 1860s and early 1870s, while the London

Metal Exchange was established in 1877. In the words of Alexander Engel (2015: 289), futures trading provided intermediaries with an important instrument to bridge the fast circulation of information and the slow circulation of goods.

The first trading companies which achieved a global presence could be found within the world of minerals and metals. A necessary condition for this development was the shift in energy used to fuel the smelters where pure metals were extracted from their ores (Evans and Saunders 2015). Since antiquity, metals, with their high value relative to weight, had always been traded over great distances, but this was not the case with metallic ores. Because of their bulky nature, ores were instead smelted in close proximity to the mines where they were extracted, using local timber for fuel. However, from the 1830s onwards, coal-fired smelters in coal-rich areas started to become dominant. The combination of advances in smelting technology and the reduction of transport costs, made it viable to break the traditional geological determinism of metal reduction and bring ores from faraway places to new giant smelters fed by coal. For instance, by the 1850s, the coal-fired smelters of Swansea extracted copper from ores that came from the Caribbean, Chile, Namaqualand in southern Africa, Algeria, Australia, from the Iberian peninsula, from the United States, and from Newfoundland (Evans and Saunders 2015: 4).

With metal smelting free from the constraints of geology, a brisk trade in metallic ores opened up, and especially in the second part of the nineteenth century, a host of new metal trading companies entered the business. Many of the new companies operated from London, but the German cities of Hamburg, Berlin, and, especially Frankfurt am Main, soon grew in importance as the steel- and non-ferrous industries took off in the German states. By the turn of the twentieth century, three big German companies dominated the international trade in non-ferrous metals and in metallic ores. The biggest of them, Metallgesellschaft, had roots both in London and in Frankfurt. The Cohen family of Frankfurt had traded in metals since the eighteenth century. In the late 1830s they established close links with the Merton family of London through marriage (Mosse 1987: 188). New generations of the families developed their trade both in Frankfurt and London, with the Frankfurt offices retaining a leading role. The company started out trading the traditional "old" metals – copper, lead, and zinc – but eventually it also tried to enter newer products like aluminum, nickel, and pyrites on a large scale. At the start, the company mostly traded the output of domestic mines to German-speaking customers, but after the family incorporated its German business as "Metallgesellschaft" in 1881, it started to look beyond central Europe. The company rapidly built up a network of representatives in the industrial centers of Europe and the United States, and in 1887 it set up a subsidiary company in New York. This signaled the start of a new strategy, and during the next decade, Metallgesellschaft set up new subsidiaries in places like Mexico, Australia, and Belgium. In this period, the company also started to make equity investments in mines and smelters, and it used its ownership interests to secure long-term contracts to sell the output of the producers it now partially owned (Becker 2002).

Metallgesellschaft's two biggest competitors were also based in Germany. Aron Hirsch & Co. was founded in 1805 in Göttingen, near the important mining district of Harz. Like Metallgesellschaft it started out doing local business, but it gradually expanded its reach by opening up offices in the principal industrial centers in Europe. Although not on the same scale as Metallgesellschaft, Aron Hirsch & Co. during the final decades of the nineteenth century bought ownership interests in metal works in France, Belgium, and Britain, as well as making investments into mines in Australia, the Americas, and the Far East (Becker 1998: 66–85). The last of the big three, Beer, Sondheimer & Co. was a more recent enterprise, and it was established when two senior salesmen from the Cohen/Merton company left to start on their own. Like the other two companies, Beer, Sondheimer grew quickly, and opened offices all over the world, especially focusing on the trade of lead, zinc, and copper, but also iron and manganese ore (Waszkis and Waszkis 2003: 130–131). By 1900, all three companies had representatives in all countries where metals were mined, processed, or consumed.

While the biggest commodity trading companies in metals and minerals had become global companies by the turn of the twentieth century, the same was not the case with traders dealing with other key commodities. Both in grain and cotton, two of the main globally traded commodities, there were large and important trading companies with a dominant market presence, but these companies would have more of a regional, rather than a global focus. Grain traders like Cargill, Bunge and Born, and Louis Dreyfus, or cotton traders such as Volkart or Ralli, sourced their commodities in specific regions of the world (Cargill in the US Midwest, Bunge and Born in Argentina, Louis Dreyfus in Russia and Romania, Volkart and Ralli on the Indian subcontinent) and sold in specific markets (Cargill mainly in the United States, Bunge and Born in Western Europe, Louis Dreyfus in Western Europe and Britain, Ralli in Britain and Western Europe, Volkart in Western Europe and Japan). Developing global organizations that could effectively penetrate what was in reality a number of regionally oriented markets was challenging.

While large trading companies became important in some commodities, this was not the case for all of them. Petroleum is one example. From the 1860s and onwards petroleum rapidly gained a market all over the world (see Boon's chapter on oil in this volume). Initially, trading companies were instrumental in bringing the product from the sites of production to where the petroleum was consumed, but as larger companies gradually took control over the production chain, traders were more and more pushed to the side. In the United States, Standard Oil, which by the 1880s had managed to take control over most of the oil refineries in the country and thus had a stranglehold on the whole US oil industry, at first exported petroleum through trading companies. However, by around 1890, the company started to develop its own marketing operations, both in Europe and the rest of the world. The company entered into alliances with European entrepreneurs and set up jointly owned companies to sell directly to the end users in the different markets. Independent traders were increasingly squeezed out from the business (Hidy and Hidy 1955: 147–151, 535–537). Standard Oil's strategies for taking control over the whole downstream production chain and its marketing operations were followed by the other large international oil companies in the period (see for instance Jonker and van Zanden 2007: 73–79).

The same development can also be seen in another "new" commodity: aluminum. Modern industrial production of aluminum only really started around 1890, and soon the three large German metal trading companies took an interest in the metal. Metallgesellschaft developed links with the pioneer producers, and in the first international cartel which the producers set up, Metallgesellschaft handled the cartel's sales on the German market. Aron Hirsch & Co. and Beer, Sondheimer on their side, entered into long-term contracts with several of the aluminum producers which were set up immediately after the original patent protection period of the Hall-Héroult process for producing aluminum expired. The metal traders supplied the smelters with metallic ores, and in return got privileged access to market the metal produced. However, as the large international aluminum producers integrated backwards in the production chain and took control over the bauxite mines which supplied the input factor, and also managed to take control over the smaller independent producers, the trading companies were gradually pushed out of the industry. After World War I, trading companies no longer played any important role in the aluminum industry (Storli 2010: 52–53; Becker 1998: 79).

As these examples illustrate, commodity traders played a significant part in the markets for some commodities, while for others they did not. This depended on the specific set-up of the industry. In commodities where there were bottlenecks in the production chain (either through limited deposits of a natural resource, or through technological or financial demands, such as the capital-intensive nature of oil refining and aluminum smelting), this often led to one group of producers taking control over the whole industry. Through vertical integration, the middlemen could be eliminated, and the producers would develop their own marketing organizations. However, in commodities with a large number of independent producers, which was generally the case with soft commodities such as coffee, cotton, and grain, middlemen tended to maintain an important role.

It was not only the set-up of an industry which affected commodity traders' room for maneuver. The political situation was also important. While the second half of the nineteenth century was characterized by few barriers to international trade and thus made it easier for trading companies to grow, the period from the outbreak of World War I and until the end of World War II proved disruptive for international trade and some of the old traders lost much of their importance. The large German metal traders were especially hard hit. During World War I, the Allied governments expropriated their international assets and destroyed their vertical integration strategies; during the 1920s, the German traders struggled to rebuild old global networks. Both Beer, Sondheimer and Aron Hirsch & Co. went bankrupt in 1930, while Metallgesellschaft continued as a shadow of its former self. The ascent of Hitler was also difficult for the company. Even though the Merton family, who ran the company, had converted to Christianity, they were still considered Jews by the Nazis and most of the directors had to leave the company (Auerbach 1965: 200–201). Also for traders in other commodities, the interwar years were challenging.

However, neither political currents nor the specificities of an industry were necessarily set in stone. After the end of World War II, political changes like the Cold War and decolonization enabled a handful of commodity trading companies to become truly global. The Cold War was especially beneficial for US traders, while decolonization tended to favor trading companies domiciled in small and tax-friendly European countries.

While trading companies based in Europe had dominated international trade in many commodities up to the outbreak of World War II, after the war had ended, US companies would soon take over the mantle in key commodities. Partially, this had to do with the experience of the war in itself, when the United States cemented its position as the center of the world economy, but just as important was what happened after the war. When an uneasy peace turned toward a Cold War, US authorities started to worry about their supplies of strategic raw materials. The US government built up massive stockpiles of strategic materials in preparation for a five-year future war. By December 1956, the different stockpiles in total contained 24.5 million tons of 75 different materials valued at $6.2 billion (Bidwell 1958: 46 fn. 22). These materials had been assembled partially through purchases from domestic producers, but increasingly they came from abroad. After 1954, with the installation of the Agricultural Trade Development and Assistance Act (popularly known as Public Law (PL) 480, US companies could barter surplus agricultural commodities for foreign raw materials. Between 1954 and 1961, US farm products worth a total of $1,354 billion were bartered through the PL480 program (*Fifteenth semiannual report on activities carried on under Public Law 480, 83 D Congress*, 1962).

These barter deals were important to the development of commodity traders. First of all, they were generally very lucrative for the companies, since the government provided generous credit arrangements as an incentive. More importantly, they allowed the companies participating in the operations to develop knowledge and contacts in foreign markets, and enabled them to grow their organizations in new parts of the world. For instance, the US grain trader Cargill, which up until then had concentrated on the US market, through the barter deals for the first time gained a foothold in Asia, particularly in India and Pakistan, but also in Europe (Broehl

1992: 791–792). The barter deals were even more important for the main New York-based metal traders, especially companies like Philipp Brothers, Associated Metals and Minerals, and Continental Ore Corporation. Not the least on the back of the barter deals, these three companies now emerged as the most important metal trading companies in the world with offices on all continents. Since all these three companies had been established by émigré German Jews who had left the country in the 1930s as a result of the Nazi regime, there was also a link back to the old dominant metal traders of the pre-1914 world (Waszkis and Waszkis 2003: 191–198).

After 1960, the same commodity trading companies increasingly became involved in trading the commodities of the Soviet Union and its satellites. To purchase industrial goods, the Soviet Union sold significant amounts of raw materials to the western world. These sales would often occur with the assistance of commodity traders. Either the traders would buy the commodities outright from the Soviet Union, or they would sell them on commission. For grains, the situation was the reverse. From 1963 and onwards, the Soviet Union would regularly need to buy grain from the West, and these operations were very lucrative for grain traders such as Cargill (Broehl 1998: 36–45). Up until the collapse of the Soviet Union in 1991, trade in commodities to and from the Soviet Union was an important factor in explaining the growth of large commodity traders.

The second important trend was decolonization which accelerated after 1960. This is important because after having gained political independence, the leaders in the new states also sought economic independence, especially through taking control over their own natural resources. Consequently, during the 1960s and the 1970s a nationalization wave swept over the non-western world. By the end of the 1970s, virtually all mines and oil wells outside the western world had been nationalized (Kobrin 1984: 338). This broke up the existing vertically integrated chains of production in a number of commodities. Commodity traders were adept at profiting from this development by contracting with the nationalized companies to market their output. For instance, when the newly independent state of Guyana in 1971 nationalized the biggest bauxite operation in the country, Philipp Brothers immediately sent representatives to Georgetown, the capital of Guyana. Two months after nationalization, Philipp Brothers were appointed as exclusive worldwide marketing agents for the new Guyanese state bauxite company (Storli 2015: 215).

The nationalization wave that followed decolonization also enabled commodity traders to break into the lucrative oil trade. Philipp Brothers was at the forefront of this development, and from a slow start in the late 1960s, the company already by the early 1970s was making huge profits on the oil trade. By 1978, oil contributed 50 percent of Philipp Brothers' total turnover (Chalmin 1989: 249). By the end of the 1950s, Philipp Brothers was already the biggest metal trader in the world; 20 years later it was an international giant, dealing in over 150 different industrial raw materials with representatives in virtually every country in the world (Storli 2014).

From the 1960s, Europe gradually again became a center for global commodity traders, with much of the trade being directed especially from Switzerland, but also from other small states such as the Netherlands and Luxembourg. Some of the big American traders had set up subsidiaries in Switzerland in the 1950s, and the number of commodity trading companies in the country only increased in the decades thereafter (Guex 1998: 166). There were three main attractions to Switzerland. First, the country had very benevolent tax policies, especially for companies engaged in international trade. Second, Switzerland was one of the banking centers of the world with strong banking secrecy regulations, which was important for commodity traders with their dependence on large short-term credit lines. Finally, Switzerland was politically neutral, which meant that Swiss-based companies would not be stopped by many of the political considerations that companies from other countries had to adhere to (Ammann 2009: 77).

Generally, the large commodity traders proved adept at profiting from instability and political risk. Unlike regular production companies, they did not run the risk of losing their assets through nationalization. It is, after all, difficult to nationalize a business which first and foremost is based on the ability to match a buyer and a seller, and not on bricks and mortar. Second, in many instances they were also able to secure loans to states which normal banks would not have done, because they could take the output from, for instance a state-owned mine, as collateral. Finally, because of their low profile and since they generally were private companies, and not publicly listed, they were less susceptible to popular pressure and were therefore able to operate in states which could be no-go zones for other international companies. The rapid growth of Marc Rich and Co., which in the 1980s became the dominant metals and minerals trading company in the world, is a good example of how the willingness to operate in zones where other companies were loath to go, could pay off handsomely. Between 1977 and 1988, for example, the company violated the United Nations' embargo against South Africa by exporting petroleum to the country. Allegedly, the company made a profit of over $2 billion dollars in South Africa in this period (Ammann 2009: 189–193).

One of the reasons why commodity traders were able and willing to operate in controversial areas was that they mostly were able to carry out business unnoticed by the general public. However, around 2000, traders increasingly came under scrutiny. Several large commodity trading companies were investigated for their role in the scandal surrounding the United Nations' Oil-for-Food Programme, the relief operation implemented after 1996 to avert a humanitarian crisis caused by the international sanctions imposed on Iraq. The Programme permitted Iraq to sell oil on the international market in return for purchasing food, medicine, and other civilian goods. Despite its noble intent, it suffered from allegations of massive fraud and corruption. The Independent Inquiry Committee which was set up to investigate the claims, in its final report detailed how several companies, including commodity traders like Vitol, Glencore, and Trafigura, had taken advantage of the Programme (Goldstone *et al.* 2005). Soft commodity traders, especially those involved in trading palm oil, have also come under criticism for their business practices. For instance, in *Newsweek*'s environmental ranking of the 500 largest publicly traded companies in the world, the Singapore-based commodity trader Wilmar came out on the bottom. As a result, Wilmar was named as the "worst company in the world" in headlines all over the world (*Newsweek* 2012).

Another key development in recent decades has been the rise of South East Asia, and especially China, as global centers for the use and consumption of commodities. In tandem with this development, some commodity trading companies based in the region have become globally active. This is especially the case in soft commodities, where companies such as Wilmar and Olam, both headquartered in Singapore, were established around 1990 and within a couple of decades had become among the top commodity trading houses by revenue (Buchan and Errington 2017). Starting out just a few years earlier with metals and minerals as its original focus, another newcomer, Noble Group based in Hong Kong, had a similar trajectory. All of these companies have gone public to strengthen their capital base, but, at the same time, this also means that they have to be more open to the public about their operations.

Concluding remarks

Over time, the centers of global commodity traders have changed. Before World War I, and to some extent before 1940, the big traders were generally European. They had started out with proximity to the end-users of commodities in the key European markets, be they German non-ferrous metal traders, British or Swiss cotton traders, French or Belgian grain traders. After 1945, the geographical center of commodity trading tended to shift to the United States, where a number of US-based traders became a dominant force. From the 1960s onwards, the center gradually gravitated back to Europe again, and especially to small, tax-friendly European countries such as the Netherlands, Luxembourg, or Switzerland. Especially Switzerland, which combined low taxes, political neutrality, and a well-developed finance sector with a well-developed sense of discretion, became an attractive place for trading companies. After 2000, there has been a new trend, where global trading companies based in South East Asia have become increasingly more important.

However, while the centers of commodity trading have shifted over time, there has been a remarkable continuity in the ranks of the dominant trading companies. This is especially evident in soft commodities, where the four largest traders today all can trace their history at least back to the nineteenth century (Archer Daniels Midland established in 1902, Cargill in 1865, Louis Dreyfus Company in 1851, and Bunge in 1818). In hard commodities, this trend is not as evident: all of today's top six trading companies were established well after World War II, and some even after 2000. Still, the founders of these companies were often trained in one of the older companies, which themselves had links back to the dominant German metal trading companies of the first global economy.

Although commodity traders have been among the key actors in the creation of global markets for commodities, the existing literature is remarkably scant. The main reason is the dearth of easily accessible company archives. However, by combining material from different sources, it will be possible to better assess the role and impact of global commodity traders. Future research would do well to investigate how commodity trading companies organized their businesses across borders and continents. Potential key questions include why some localities and industries have been more resilient to the penetration of traders than others, and how these actors worked to overcome barriers to trade. Another central issue is the question of how traders interacted with other important actors, such as local entrepreneurs and middlemen, multinational companies, and political players to set up global value chains. To understand economic globalization, it is important to understand how the different geographies were linked together in practice by investigating how the interactions of traders with other economic actors shaped global commodity markets and value chains, and how this changed over time. In short, it is important to embed the study of the companies in the international political economy in which they have operated. Finally, future research should help us understand the societal impact of global commodity traders. How have the operations of these companies affected the commodity producing states?

References

Ammann, Daniel (2009), *The King of Oil: The Secret Lives of Marc Rich* (New York: St. Martin Griffins).

Auerbach S. M. (1965), "Jews in the German Metal Trade," *Leo Baeck Institute Yearbook* 10 (1), 188–203.

Becker, Susan (1998), "The German Metal Traders Before 1914," in Geoffrey Jones, *The Multinational Traders* (Abingdon: Routledge), 66–85.

Becker, Susan (2002), "Multinationalität hat verschiedene Gesichter," *Formen internationaler Unternehmenstätigkeit der Vieille Montagne und der Metallgesellschaft vor 1914* (Stuttgart: Franz Steiner).

Bidwell, Percy (1958), *Raw Materials: A Study of American Policy* (New York: Harper & Brothers).

Blas, Javier (2011), "Trading Houses: Veil Slowly Lifts on a Secretive Profession," *Financial Times* 23 May.

Broehl, Wayne G. Jr. (1992), *Cargill: Trading the World's Grain* (Hanover, NH: University Press of New England).

Broehl, Wayne G. Jr. (1998), *Cargill: Going Global* (Hanover, NH: University Press of New England).

Broehl, Wayne G. Jr. (2008), *Cargill: From Commodities to Customers* (Hanover, NH: University Press of New England).

Buchan, David and Errington, Charlie (2017), "Commodities Demystified: A Guide to Trading and the Global Supply Chain," Guide commissioned by Trafigura Group, www.trafigura.com/media/3663/commoditiesdemystified-guide-en.pdf (accessed 22 January 2018).

Chalmin, Philippe (1989), *Traders and Merchants: Panorama of International Commodity Trading* (Chur: Harwood Academic Publishers).

Chalmin, Philippe (1990), *The Making of a Sugar Giant: Tate and Lyle, 1859–1989* (Chur: Harwood Academic Publishers).

Copetas, A. Craig (1985), *Metal Men: How Marc Rich Defrauded the Country, Evaded the Law, and Became the World's Most Sought-After Corporate Criminal* (New York: Harper Perennial).

Daily Telegraph (2011), "Top Ten Global Oil and Commodities Traders," 15 April.

Dehne, Philipp (2013), "The Resilience of Globalisation during the First World War: The Case of Bunge & Born in Argentina," in Christof Dejung and Niels R. Petersson, *The Foundations of Worldwide Economic Integration: Power, Institutions and Global Markets, 1850–1930* (Cambridge: Cambridge University Press), 228–248.

Dejung, Christof (2013a), *Die Fäden des globalen Marktes: Eine Sozial- und Kulturgeschichte des Welthandels am Beispiel der Handelsfirma Gebrüder Volkart* (Köln/Wien: Böhlau).

Dejung, Christof (2013b), "Worldwide Ties: The Role of Family Business in Global Trade in the Nineteenth and Twentieth Centuries," *Business History* 55 (6), 1001–1018.

Engel, Alexander (2015), "Buying Time: Futures Trading and Telegraphy in Nineteenth-Century Global Commodity Markets," *Journal of Global History* 10 (2), 284–306.

Evans, Chris and Saunders, Olivia (2015), "A World of Copper: Globalizing the Industrial Revolution, 1830–70," *Journal of Global History* 10 (1), 3–26.

Fifteenth semiannual report on activities carried on under Public Law 480, 83 D Congress, 87th Congress, 2d session, House Document no. 385, April 9, 1962, US Government Printing Office, Washington DC.

Goldstone, Richard J., Volcker, Paul, and Pieth, Mark (2005), "The Management of the United Nations Oil-for-Food Programme: Volume IV – Report of the Investigation: United Nations Administration, Part 2," in UN Documents and Publications (New York: United Nations).

Green, Raul H. (1985), *Bunge & Born: Puissance et secret dans l'agro-alimentaire* (Paris: Edition Publisud).

Guex, Sébastian (1998), "The Development of Swiss Trading Companies in the Twentieth Century," in Geoffrey Jones, *The Multinational Traders* (Abingdon: Routledge), 150–172.

Hidy, Ralph W. and Hidy, Muriel E. (1955), *Pioneering in Big Business: History of Standard Oil Company (New Jersey), 1882–1911* (New York: Harper).

Jones, Geoffrey (2005), *Multinationals and Global Capitalism: From the Nineteenth to the Twenty-First Century* (Oxford: Oxford University Press).

Jonker, Joost and van Zanden, Jan Luiten (2007), *A History of Royal Dutch Shell: From Challenger to Joint Industry Leader, 1890–1939, vol. 1* (Oxford: Oxford University Press).

Kelly, Kate (2014), *The Secret Club that Runs the World: Inside the Fraternity of Commodity Traders* (New York: Penguin).

Kneen, Brewster (2002), *Invisible Giant: Cargill and its Transnational Strategies* (London: Pluto Press).

Kobrin, Stephen J. (1984), "Expropriations as an Attempt to Control Foreign Firms in LDCs: Trends from 1960 to 1979," *International Studies Quarterly* 28 (3), 329–348.

Lieber, James B. (2000), *Rats in the Grain: The Dirty Tricks and Trials of Archer Daniels Midland* (New York: Basic Books).

Morgan, Dan (1979*), Merchants of Grain* (New York: Viking).

Mosse, Werner (1987), *Jews in the German Economy: The German-Jewish Economic Élite, 1820–1935* (Oxford: Clarendon Press).

Newsweek (2012), "Green Rankings 2012: Global Companies," 22 October, www.newsweek.com/2012/10/22/newsweek-green-rankings-2012-global-500-list.html (accessed 22 January 2018).

Onstad, Eric, MacInnis, Laura, and Webb, Quentin (2011), "The Biggest Company you Never Heard Of," Reuters Special report, 25 February.

Pirrong, Craig (2014), "The Economics of Commodity Trading Firms," White Paper commissioned by Trafigura, www.trafigura.com/media/1364/economics-commodity-trading-firms.pdf (accessed 22 March 2017).

Storli, Espen (2010), "Out of Norway Falls Aluminium: The Norwegian Aluminium Industry in the International Economy, 1908–1940," Doctoral thesis at NTNU, Trondheim, 117.

Storli, Espen (2014), "Ludwig Jesselson," in R. Daniel Wadhwani, *Immigrant Entrepreneurship: German-American Business Biographies, 1720 to the Present, vol. 5, German Historical Institute*. Last modified March 24, 2014. www.immigrantentrepreneurship.org/entry.php?rec=167 (accessed 12 April 2019).

Storli, Espen (2015), "The Birth of the World's Largest Tin Merchant: Philipp Brothers, Bolivian Tin and American Stockpiles," in Mats Ingulstad, Andrew Perchard, and Espen Storli, *Tin and Global Capitalism: A History of the Devil's Metal, 1850–2000* (London: Routledge), 202–220.

Topik, Steven C. and Wells, Allen (2012), *Global Markets Transformed 1870–1945* (Cambridge, MA: Belknap Press of Harvard University Press).

Waszkis, Helmut (1992), *Philipp Brothers 1901–1990* (Worcester Park, UK: Metal Bulletin Books, 2nd Edition).

Waszkis, Helmut (2001), *Dr. Moritz (Don Mauricio) Hochschild 1881–1965: The Man and His Companies. A German Jewish Mining Entrepreneur in South America* (Frankfurt am Main/Madrid: Vervuert/Ibero Americana).

Waszkis, Helmut and Waszkis, Peter (2003), *The Story of Metal Trading* (Worcester Park, UK: Metal Bulletin Books).

30

THE GLOBAL OIL INDUSTRY

Marten Boon

Introduction

The first big multinational companies of the modern era emerged from Europe's growing need for raw materials in the late nineteenth century (Jones 2005: 20, 45). One of those raw materials was oil. The modern oil industry started simultaneously around the mid-nineteenth century in Eastern Europe, the US, and Russia. Demand for lighting oil drove the industry's initial growth. As electricity substituted oil for lighting, the internal combustion engine sustained the industry's growth into the twentieth century. By 1914, the oil industry had given birth to multinational companies that roamed the globe searching for oil and markets. Military demands for fuels, lubricants, additives, and explosives during World War I, however, truly propelled the oil industry onto the global stage (Winegard 2016: 4; Yergin 1993: 167–8). Oil's strategic importance fostered technological innovations in exploration and production, transportation and refining in the 1920s and 1930s despite protectionism, economic nationalism, and depressed oil prices (Jonker and Zanden 2007: 334; Homburg 2006b, 2006a; Williamson 1963: 508–10). After World War II, oil displaced coal in most developed economies and became the vital resource it remains today.

The oil industry is uniquely global. It is the biggest of the internationally traded primary commodities (UN 2015: 221–8, 235). Oil companies, publicly traded, private, or state-owned, rank among the biggest companies in the world. Oil is above all an indispensable resource for modern economic life. But oil also has a dark side. Its strategic importance and value has fueled interstate conflicts as well as civil wars and insurgencies (Winegard 2016: 15; Adunbi 2015: 2). The global struggle over oil resources has concentrated wealth in the hands of national and global elites, creating massive global financial flows as well as horrendous inequality (Gray 2016; Devlin 2014: 43–4). Oil is also linked to authoritarian regimes and slower development in oil producing countries (Patey 2014: 6–7; Ross 2012: 553–4; Karl 1997: 16). The most pressing issue today, however, is the industry's future given climate change and the transition to low carbon energy sources (Berghoff 2017: 25–6; Haug 2011; Yergin 2011: 1369–71).

How did oil develop into the world's most controversial and prized resource and who were the actors shaping this giant global industry? By and large, the industry has been shaped by entrepreneurs and enterprises and the competitive forces and cooperative relations between them. However, the state has been highly influential too: as owner of subsoil resources, regulator

467

of domestic industries and markets, or as entrepreneur. The interplay between business and the state was a recurrent source of change, particularly since 1914. These relations were interdependent (Penrose 1968: 252–3). Oil companies controlled the technologies to explore and exploit oil, but oil producing countries controlled the access to oil. Government–business relations typically pivoted around control over oil reserves, rates of production, markets, and prices. There were no equilibrium outcomes in these disputes. Countries that nationalized their oil reserves and industries faced declining investments, falling production rates, and outdated technology. Oil-consuming countries that intervened in the domestic market often burdened consumers with higher prices or inflexible supply systems during oil crises.

Many of the disputes between states and companies hinged on prices being either too low for producers or too high for consumers. Whether the oil market was monopolistic, cartelized, oligopolistic, or competitive, the price of oil has been a persistent bone of contention. Without some kind of coordination of production levels, oil is prone to boom–bust cycles (McNally 2016: 57–8). Because price levels also determine the discovery of new oil reserves and long term supply (Radetzki 2008: 111–25; Sorrell *et al.* 2010: 5290–5; Adelman 1995: 11–17), the industry's central issue was and remains the problem of striking a price level that allowed for steady new investment while securing a reasonable profit to producers without imposing harmful costs on consumers.

Energy consultant Robert McNally (2016), argues that pricing regimes have alternated between competitive and coordinated market systems, creating three periods of boom–bust cycles and three periods of relative price stability since the 1860s (Figure 30.1).

Boom–bust cycles were prevalent between the 1860s and 1890s, between 1911 (after the break-up of the Standard Oil Trust) and the mid-1930s, and after 2004 when the Organization of Petroleum Exporting Countries (OPEC) was unable to ward off the run-up in prices in the

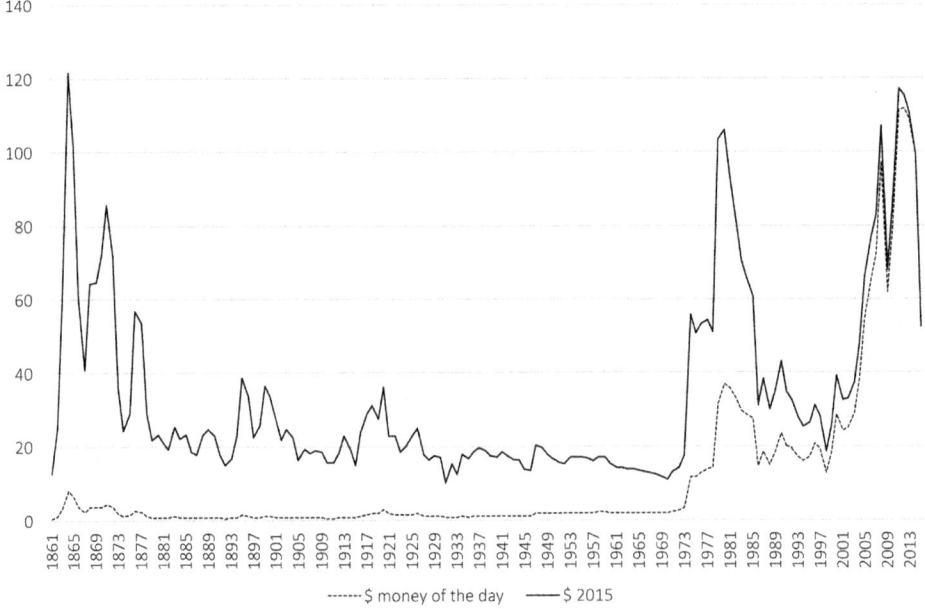

Figure 30.1 Crude oil price, 1861–2015

Source: BP Statistical Review of World Energy 2016.

2000s. Prices were relatively stable from the 1890s to 1911 during Standard Oil's monopoly in the US, between the mid-1930s and 1972 when the Texas Railroad Commission effectively regulated US, and indirectly world, oil prices and between 1973 and the early 2000s when OPEC attempted to manage the price of oil. McNally's periodization of alternating periods of coordination and competition encompasses the business and state forces that have jointly shaped the industry.

The chapter is organized in three sections. The first section gives a short overview of the main strands in the historiography. The second section chronologically examines the history of the industry from the 1860s to the present and highlights the relevant actors and historiographical debates connected to the industry's development. The third section concludes with a reflection on the role of the state in the industry and opportunities for future research.

Historiographical themes

Oil's central role in global affairs is reflected in its historiography; it touches virtually every subject imaginable. Here I examine the literature on the industry's globalization. The oil industry has been a core sector for studies on business organization (Chandler and Hikino 1994) as well as foreign direct investment, internationalization, and the formation of multinational enterprises (Jones 2005; Wilkins 1974a, 1970; Wilkins and Schröter 1998). Although the history of oil is littered with collusive business behavior, it was not very different from most other industries, especially before 1939. As such it doesn't figure particularly prominently in the historical cartel literature beyond the OPEC cartel (Fear 2008: 280).

The historiography of the industry itself has few comprehensive overviews (with the notable exception of Yergin 1993) and is spread across a broad range of literatures. A first, well-established genre is the company history – commissioned or not – starting with the critical study of the Standard Oil Trust by Ida Tarbell (1904). The major companies have by and large opened their archives for commissioned or condoned company histories (Pratt and Hale 2013; Jonker and Zanden 2007; Howarth and Jonker 2007; Sluyterman 2007; Bamberg 2000a, 1994; Ferrier 1982; Hidy and Hidy 1955; Larson *et al.* 1971; Gib and Knowlton 1956; Gerretson 1953). There are fewer histories of the state-owned oil companies of the producing countries that became prominent after the 1970s. A trailblazer could be the commissioned history of the Norwegian state-owned oil enterprise Statoil.[1] The state-owned enterprises of France (Total) and Italy (Ente Nazionale Idrocarburi, ENI) have exceptionally well-developed archives and an established body of work on their history (Labbate 2016; Bini 2016; Cricco 2014; Beltran 2010; Pozzi 2010).

Government–business relations and the role of the state are core themes in the industry's history. One subset studies the oil industry as an expression of British and US informal empire and geopolitics (Kuiken 2014; Dietrich 2014; Jones 2012; Painter 2012; Priest 2012; Galpern 2009). A critical strand questioned whether the oil companies were in fact more powerful than nation-states. This question started appearing when the government–business relations in the producing countries became increasingly strained in the 1960s (Penrose 1968; Hartshorn 1962), gained global attention in the wake of the 1973 oil embargo (Turner 1978; Engler 1977; Sampson 1975), and continues to inspire new scholarship today (Musso 2017; Bini *et al.* 2016; Glässer 2016; Petrini 2016; Graf 2018; Parra 2004).

A third major theme is the strategic and military use of oil. From World War I onwards, oil was an indispensable resource for waging war. Poor in domestic oil reserves, Nazi Germany pursued various strategies to achieve oil independence, including fuels from coal (Boon and Wubs 2016; Scherner 2008: 103–38; Stokes 1985), establishing a state-owned oil industry

(Toprani 2014; Overy 1994: 68), and capturing foreign oil fields (Klemann and Kudryashov 2012: 348; Karlsch and Stokes 2003, 213–23). Japan's dependence on foreign oil supplies also fueled its Southeast Asian campaigns (Yergin 1993: 325–6). Moreover, denying the Axis powers access to oil was vital to the Allied victory in 1945. During the Cold War, Soviet energy interference in the Middle East and Western Europe was a constant concern to Britain and the US (Perovic 2017; Cantoni 2017b, 2017a, 2015; Högselius 2012; Lippert 2011; Jensen-Eriksen 2007).

The globalization of oil

As in other extractive industries, oil started out as a domestic industry exploiting domestic deposits in the mid-nineteenth century. In the early nineteenth century, growing demand for lighting oil – known as petroleum or kerosene – spurred geologists, chemists, entrepreneurs, and adventurers to exploit oil deposits on a growing scale. Advances in drilling and refining started almost simultaneously in the US, Canada, Galicia, and Russia around the mid-nineteenth century but grew nowhere as rapidly as in the US and Russia (Frank 2009: 48; May 1998: 28–9; Tolf 1976: 44; Williamson 1959: 101–4).

From competition to monopoly

In the decade after Edwin Drake struck oil in the Pennsylvanian hills in 1858, the US oil industry boomed and busted repeatedly. The US regime of private natural resource ownership was based on the *rule of capture*, stipulating that whatever quantities of oil could be extracted from a patch of land belonged to the landowner, irrespective of the actual boundaries of the reservoir being drilled (Mommer 2002: 105; Skeet 1988: 35; Tugendhat and Hamilton 1975: 16–17). This incentivized drillers to produce as fast as possible because the neighbors were drilling in the same reservoir, resulting in a highly fragmented industry, incapable of stabilizing prices and production. More advanced techniques would much later rationalize the exploitation of wells, but it was John D. Rockefeller's Standard Oil that brought this initial period of volatile prices to an end by rationalizing, integrating, and concentrating the industry (Chandler 1977: 321–2). First establishing control over transportation (midstream) and refining (downstream), Rockefeller used his control over outlets to force production discipline on the drillers, before finally integrating backwards into crude production (upstream) in the 1880s (Hidy and Hidy 1955: 15–23).

From monopoly to oligopoly

Between 1860 and 1900, oil had grown into an internationally traded commodity centering on European markets. Standard Oil was the dominant player, but met with increasing competition from Russia, Galicia, Mexico, Romania, and the Asian colonies of the Dutch and the British empires (Brown 1987; Bud-Frierman et al. 2010; Yergin 1993: 132). Foreign capital and entrepreneurs opened these new oil areas. The Swedish Nobel brothers and the French Rothschilds invested heavily in Russian oil, establishing companies – Branobel and Bnito – in the Caspian town of Baku, in present-day Azerbaijan, in 1879 and 1884 respectively. In Galicia, French and Belgian capital, Canadian drillers, and laborers from across Central and Eastern Europe fueled the oil industry. In the British empire, Scottish merchants, London capital, and Canadian drillers explored the Indian subcontinent, establishing the Burmah Oil Company in 1886, which developed into a major British oil company by the early 1900s (Jones 2000: 281; Corley 1983b). Canadian drillers also traveled the Dutch East Indies, where Dutch entrepreneurs and mining engineers struck oil on the island of Sumatra in the 1880s (Poley 2000: 103) and established the Royal Dutch Petroleum Company in 1890. The British engineer Weetman Pearson obtained a concession in Mexico in 1889 while constructing a railroad (Brown 1987), establishing the Mexican Eagle Petroleum Company, although major oil finds would not materialize until 1909.

Standard Oil began to feel the sting of Russian competition when the Nobel brothers used economies of scale from their innovations in the bulk shipping of oil to challenge Standard's position in European markets (Tolf 1976: 50–60). Standard Oil responded by establishing foreign subsidiaries for distribution and marketing across Europe (de Goey 2002: 57). The British merchant Marcus Samuel picked up the Nobels' bulk innovation and subsequently managed to join together a number of British trading companies that marketed US and later Russian oil in Asia, to form the Tanker Syndicate in 1892 (Henriques 1960: 164). The syndicate, in 1897 incorporated into Shell Transport and Trading, established a major tanker fleet that shipped Russian kerosene to Asia and took Asian oil on the return trip to Europe. Although strong in transportation, the Shell company was weakly organized and lacked its own sources of supply. These were found in the Dutch East Indies, where Royal Dutch quickly grew during the 1890s. Royal Dutch's need for international marketing and Shell's lack of proprietary sources led to increasing cooperation between the two companies, culminating in the merger in 1907 (Jones 2000: 281).

The formation of Royal Dutch Shell as the principal international competitor of Standard Oil marked the industry's 'coming-of-age'. The lighting oil market declined with the ascent of electricity and town gas, but a new market for gasoline grew strongly with the introduction of the internal combustion engine. Royal Dutch was quick to recognize the opportunity, which strengthened its competitive position vis-à-vis Standard Oil (de Goey 2002: 60–4). The merger also illustrated the industry's early tendency for vertical integration to defend markets and stabilize production and prices. Moreover, the merger showed the superior organizational talents of the Group's skillful and mercurial CEO, Henri Deterding, who strengthened Royal Dutch's position considerably vis-à-vis the weaker organized Shell Company leading up to the merger in 1907 (Jonker and Zanden 2007: 63–5). Although later controversial because of his Nazi sympathies, Deterding was the mastermind behind Royal Dutch's rapid growth as Standard Oil's only global challenger by 1914 (Jonker and Zanden 2007: 475–86). The company rapidly expanded through the acquisition and establishment of companies in Egypt, Venezuela, and the US (Jones 1981: 77).

On the eve of the Great War, oil had grown into a vital fuel for propulsion, leading the British Navy to switch the fleet from steam coal to fuel oil. Subsequently, the British government sought to strengthen British control over foreign oil supplies (Jones 1981: 249–50), harnessing British capital and entrepreneurs in global oil ventures. The British *coup de grâce* came in Persia, where the Shah had invited British gold magnate William Knox D'Arcy to bankroll oil exploration in 1901. Persia's inhospitable interior was uninviting of foreign investment, but its pivotal role in the Great Game and the lure of profits stimulated private British investors to finance the venture. Additional funding came when Burmah Oil, desperately in need of new oilfields, decided to buy D'Arcy's concession in 1905 and floating a new company, Anglo-Persian Oil Company (APOC) on the Glasgow stock exchange in 1909 (Yergin 1993: 148; Corley 1983a: 98–103). The company's managing director Charles Greenway sought the favor of the British government to secure government contracts and funding to build the company's downstream business and reduce its reliance on competitors. But Greenaway did not solely rely on the British state and set out to build "an absolutely, self-contained organization": a vertically integrated oil company in the image of Royal Dutch Shell and Standard Oil (Ferrier 1982: 160).

In 1914, the British government took a 51 percent stake in APOC to secure oil supplies for the Navy but also to strengthen Britain's position in the development of oil reserves in the Ottoman Empire through the Turkish Petroleum Company (TPC), a joint venture between APOC, Royal Dutch Shell, Deutsche Bank, and the British National Bank of Turkey. Deutsche Bank's share in TPC reflected imperial Germany's designs to control foreign oil (Nowell 1994: 59). Established in 1911, TPC was financed with British and German capital and designed to coordinate the two rivals' interests in the region (Scazzieri 2015; Ferrier 1982: 197). After World War I, Deutsche Bank's foreign oil holdings were divided between the French state-owned Compagnie française des pétroles (1928) and APOC (Toprani 2017: 62). TPC illustrates well the interdependence between European empires and the oil companies.

British capital and entrepreneurs drove the internationalization of the oil industry until the 1920s. The examples of Burmah Oil, Shell Transport and Trading, and later APOC illustrate just how important British merchants and entrepreneurs were and how backward integration into oil production served to protect their positions in marketing (Jones 2000: 251). Strategies for establishing strong integrated companies differed, with Shell Transport and Trading choosing to merge with Royal Dutch, while Burmah Oil/APOC opted to shelter under the protective wing of the state. In both cases, however, consolidating, expanding, and diversifying a successful international oil business proved a task not for nimble traders but for capable administrators and technically skilled managers in the tradition of John D. Rockefeller, such as Standard Oil's Walter C. Teagle, Royal Dutch's Henri Deterding, or Anglo-Persian's John Cadman (Jonker and Zanden 2007: 491; Jones 2000: 252; Jones 1981: 170, 225; Wall 1974).

As Standard Oil was challenged by new competitors, its position further deteriorated with the breakup of the Trust in 1911 by the US Supreme Court – an event that still is one of the most powerful examples of how national legislation and jurisprudence can affect multinational enterprise. Nevertheless, by the 1920s, Standard Oil of New Jersey – the largest of the successor companies – had regained its dominant position. It expanded particularly abroad, such as in Venezuela (Wilkins 1974b: 414, 445–6) and Iraq, where it joined the Iraq (previously Turkish) Petroleum Company (IPC) in the Red Line Agreement of 1928 (Toprani 2017; Yergin 1993: 204). The agreement coincided with the famous As-Is or Achnacarry agreement of the same year, in which Royal Dutch Shell, Jersey Standard, and APOC formed a global oil cartel to defend their markets against competition from other Standard Oil successor companies and the rise of technologies to produce synthetic fuels from coal pioneered by the German chemical conglomerate IG Farben (Yergin 1993: 227–8; Nowell 1994: 236–51). Achnacarry marked the high point of a process of concentration and integration that had taken the industry from the Standard Oil Trust monopoly, to a fiercely competitive, and finally an oligopolistic market.

The Seven Sisters

The Great War had alerted states that it was imperative to control access to oil. During the post-war settlement of Middle Eastern oil interests, the US feared a British–French monopoly of the region's oil reserves and the US government supported US oil companies to gain a foothold in the Middle East (Painter 2010: 496–7). The ascent of US companies to the IPC signaled that the US too had joined the global race for oil. US companies went abroad driven by post-war fears over declining domestic oil production. Their attention focused on the vast unexplored deserts of the Arabian Peninsula. New prospecting techniques developed by geologists such as Everett DeGolyer aided their search for new oil reserves both at home and in the Middle East (Doel 2013: 401; Yergin 1993: 391–3).

Up to the 1920s, the Arabian Peninsula had failed to attract attention because the prospects of finding oil were deemed bleak. Initially, the British government blocked US companies in the region but Standard Oil of California (Socal), Gulf Oil, and Texaco were eventually allowed to acquire oil concessions from the rulers of Bahrain, Kuwait, and Saudi Arabia after 1929 (Yergin 1993: 282–3). Their international expansion into the largely untested Arabian Peninsula was a huge gamble and it illustrates how crucial crude oil supplies were to the survival and growth of oil companies.

Major oil finds were made in Kuwait and Saudi Arabia in the late 1930s, establishing the Middle East as the new epicenter of global oil. The new oil wealth was shared among the two Anglo-Dutch and five US companies, i.e., the so-called Seven Sisters that controlled the global oil market between the 1930s and the early 1970s. Although APOC, by then known as the Anglo-Iranian Oil Company (AIOC), exclusively controlled production in Iran, the Arabian concessions were run by joint ventures between these Seven Sisters. The IPC, jointly owned by CFP, AIOC, Royal Dutch Shell, and the American companies, controlled production in Iraq. In Saudi Arabia, Socal and Texaco jointly owned the concession through the California (later American) Arabian Oil Company, to which Jersey Standard and Socony were added in 1948. The Kuwait Oil Company, jointly owned by AIOC and Gulf Oil, was established in 1934 to develop the Kuwait concession.

Through the cross-ownership of the concessions, the majors informally coordinated prices and production rates, which, short of a formal cartel, allowed the companies a remarkably large degree of control over the world oil market (Adelman 1995: 48; Linde 1991: 60). This made for a new period of exceptionally stable prices lasting until the 1970s. The international price stability was considerably aided by the Railroad Commission of Texas (RTC), which from 1933 onwards regulated the output of the gigantic Texas oil fields that had been developed in the 1920s (Yergin 1993: 258–9).

The companies did not operate like a formal cartel; the US anti-trust laws cast a global shadow over the foreign operations of the US oil companies (Adelman 1995: 49). Rather, they attempted to maintain a price that allowed for stable downstream margins and a stable return on investment in new oil reserves, while being careful not to allow too much room for competitors. In retrospect, the oil price between 1945 and 1973 (Figure 30.1) appears low compared to the price hikes in the 1970s but because the development costs in the Middle East were (and still are) the world's lowest, even the prevailing "low" prices allowed for returns on investment that in some cases exceeded 400 percent (Adelman 1995: 19). Such rates of return allowed for the price of oil to decline in real terms over the course of the 1960s in response to increasing competition (Howarth and Jonker 2007: 180). The returns also allowed for a seemingly effortless expansion of production to keep up with the unprecedented growth in demand for oil during the post-war golden age of growth in Western Europe, the US, and Japan (Smil 2010: 31; Chapman 1991: 211).

The OPEC era

Despite stable prices and rapidly growing production, oil producing countries became increasingly displeased with the concession system. The Persian D'Arcy concession of 1901 was the first and it became the global standard in the following decades, giving oil companies near complete control over production rates and prices and reducing sovereigns to mere tax collectors with very little means to influence production policies or revenues.

Latin American states were the first to challenge the concession system. Oil became a rallying cause for democratic movements as well as national economic development projects (Mitchell

2013). Whereas earlier dictatorships in the region had invariably chosen the side of foreign investors (Bucheli 2008: 438–43), Mexico and Venezuela, among others, increasingly challenged the foreign companies (Wilkins 1974b: 445–6; Bucheli 2010: 341; Maurer 2011). The most radical expressions of resource nationalism were the nationalizations of foreign oil assets in Bolivia and Mexico in 1937–8. In Iran, the state disputed AIOC's concession since the 1920s (Ferrier 1982: 588, 628–31), culminating in the nationalization of AIOC assets in 1951. These nationalizations invariably provoked boycotts by the expropriated companies and their home governments – in the Iranian case even leading to an Anglo-American engineered *coup d'état* (Marsh 2007; Abdelrehim and Toms 2017; Heiss 1994) – highlighting the problems of asserting state ownership and control over industries that depended on foreign technology, capital, and markets.

The efforts of Latin American countries in the interwar period were a crucial step toward more state control over the oil industry. When Mexico chose to nationalize the assets of the foreign companies in 1938, it scared the Anglo-American companies and their home governments stiff. When Venezuela subsequently wanted better terms on its concessions, the companies granted a fifty–fifty split of profits in 1948 to stave off nationalization (Yergin 1993: 432–7). Fifty–fifty was a major improvement in the concession terms and quickly became the new standard for oil concessions across the globe.

Latin American state activism spilled over to the Middle East and fostered cooperation among oil producing countries, resulting in the founding of OPEC in 1960. OPEC developed into a powerful cartel that took control over oil reserves and domestic oil industries in the 1970s (Rubino 2008: 198; Yergin 1993: 583–8). Increasing Arab nationalism in the 1950s (Bamberg 2000b: 83; Stevens 2000) had prepared the minds in the Arabian Gulf to cooperate with the unknown Venezuelans and the deeply distrusted Persians to form OPEC.

The history of OPEC exemplifies how hard it was for oil producing states to regain control over the international oil regime and the infrastructures – pipelines, tankers, refineries – that the oil companies had managed to build in protection of their interests.[2] The British political economy scholar Timothy Mitchell recently argued that this transnational regime had thwarted nation building and democratization processes in oil producing countries (2013: 9, 108, 237). Indeed, reasserting sovereignty over oil resources in many oil producing countries since the interwar period was essentially a drive for nationhood, development, and, in some cases, democratization. As such, OPEC was an expression of the wider processes of decolonization and resource nationalism in the non-Western world, which fostered a movement for a fairer distribution of the gains from trade under the auspices of the UN Conference on Trade and Development in the early 1970s (Schenk 2011: 63–7).

Initially OPEC was ignored by the companies and the West, but when Libya and then Iran managed to extract higher taxes, royalties, and prices from the companies, OPEC gained strength and eventually forced the oil companies to negotiate with the organization itself in 1971 (Yergin 1993: 577–85). OPEC's ultimate goal was not higher revenues but control through participation in, or outright ownership of, production, refining, and marketing by state-owned oil companies (Parra 2004: 146). Some states opted to participate in the existing concession companies, such as in Saudi Arabia, Kuwait, and the other Arabian Gulf states (Al-Chalabi 1980: 22–7). Other countries chose to nationalize foreign assets, such as Algeria (1971), Iraq (1972), Libya (1973), and Venezuela (1975) (Parra 2004: 150–4).

By the early 1980s, the oil companies had lost their concessions and most of their assets in the OPEC member countries, with national oil companies taking over ownership and operations. OPEC's position was greatly enhanced by the evaporation of spare capacity in the US in 1972 (McNally 2016: 105). Surging demand in the late 1960s had left spare capacity only in the

Middle East. The OPEC revolution thus shifted pricing power to the OPEC countries, which used the Yom Kippur War of 1973 as a political excuse for an oil embargo against the Western allies of Israel to drive up the price of oil. Official OPEC prices more than quadrupled between 1972 and 1974 (Figure 30.1). The OPEC revolution ushered in an era of state control over the oil industry after four decades of disputing the powerful oligopoly of the Seven Sisters. The majors lost their powerful position and were forced to adjust their organizations and strategies, and to look for new sources of supply, pushing the frontier of oil exploration.

After OPEC

To contemporary observers of the oil industry, OPEC had stepped into the all-powerful position once occupied by the major oil companies (Tétreault 1985: 38). However, the OPEC revolution did not simply reverse the roles of company and state. It separated the majors from their most profitable oil fields, and forced them to adjust their tightly integrated businesses to acquire the majority of their crude supplies through the market, in most cases from the National Oil Companies (NOCs) of the producing countries. The disintegration also established the NOCs as emerging global companies. Not all NOCs succeeded in their integration and internationalization strategies, but Kuwait Petroleum International, Saudi Aramco, and PdVSA (Venezuela) were relatively successful integrating forwards into refining, transportation, and marketing in the 1980s (Tétreault 1995; Victor *et al.* 2011: part III).

The major oil companies had already started oil exploration in non-OPEC regions in the 1960s, especially in Alaska and the North Sea, where oil was struck in 1967 and 1969 respectively (Kemp 2012: 236; Ryggvik 2015). Production costs were high in these new oil frontiers but OPEC's price hikes accelerated activity in the 1970s as oil companies reinvested inflated profits into increased exploration activity (Petrie 2014: 49). Other non-OPEC countries saw an opportunity to give their oil industries a shot in the arm (Adelman 1995: 195–200; Yergin 1993: 569–74, 667–70; Linde 1991: 105–15). As a result, exploration and production in non-OPEC countries rose rapidly in the 1980s.

Increasing production and a dramatic reduction of demand after the second oil crisis of 1979 (Adelman 1995: 190) led to an oil price crash in 1986. As the biggest producer with most spare capacity, Saudi Arabia was the swing producer and attempted to maintain OPEC's high cartel price by continuously lowering its production between 1981 and 1986. In 1986, however, the kingdom ramped up production again to regain its lost market share, precipitating the price crash of 1986–7. This countershock brought many oil producing countries into financial distress, resulting in the partial retreat of the state. Privatization, balanced budgets, and foreign direct investment were the new recipes to revitalize domestic oil industries (Hartshorn 1993: 138–40). Especially where new oil reserves depended on high-cost and high-risk exploration, the state tended to retreat in favor of private enterprise and foreign investment (Nolan and Thurber 2012: 161–7; Stevens 2008: 27–8). However, this process was not linear because the rapidly rising oil prices of the 2000s enticed some of the states that had privatized their industries in the 1990s to reassert state control, particularly in Russia under Vladimir Putin and Venezuela under Hugo Chavez (Gustafson 2012: 187, 272ff.).

The multinational oil companies responded to the supply shocks of the 1970s and the countershock of 1986 with reorganizations, divestments, and mergers and acquisitions (M&As) to foster cost efficiencies and growth (Sluyterman 2007: 380–6). Two M&A waves, one in the early 1980s and another in the late 1990s, created supermajors from mergers between already exceedingly large oil companies, such as Exxon-Mobil and BP-Amoco (Petrie 2014: 52–3, 103–6).[3] In addition, most major companies shed their diversification investments in chemicals and non-hydrocarbon energy sources, focusing instead on natural gas as a cleaner burning altern-ative to oil, a strategy that was only strengthened by the challenges of climate change in the 2000s (Sluyterman 2010: 223). The restructuring also created room for smaller mini-majors as well as aggressively focused oil companies – petropreneurs – that took advantage of the divest-ments of the majors. Using advanced financing – increased private equity financing among others – and risk management methods, these companies developed focused businesses that specialized in a particular activity ranging from exploration and production, refining, trading, and transportation and storage (Bleakley *et al.* 1997).

The OPEC revolution had inadvertently helped to create a spot market for crude oil in the 1980s, which went on to develop into a global, financialized market, with myriad financial derivatives traded on futures and options exchanges in London, New York, Dubai, and Singa-pore as well as boutique derivatives sold in over-the-counter markets by a host of financial institutions (Gkanoutas-Leventis 2013: 77ff.; Razavi 1989). The rise of the petropreneurs and the internal decentralization of the supermajors were in many ways facilitated by this commodi-fication of oil, not least because of its expanding range of instruments to trade oil and manage price risks. Because the majors could no longer rely on abundant proprietary supplies of crude oil, trading and supply gained a larger role in managing supply and offtake between the up-, mid-, and downstream activities of the companies. This in effect externalized the market that these majors had organized internally before the 1970s. Shell and BP, for instance, were leading the development of the North Sea spot and forward markets, used today to price over half the world's trade in crude oil (Sluyterman 2007: 57–60; Horsnell and Mabro 1993; Mabro *et al.* 1986).

By the 2000s, global oil had developed into a thoroughly hybrid industry. States had taken a huge role by controlling the majority of oil reserves, but the major oil companies had not dis-appeared. Rather, the industry became much more varied than before the 1970s, with petro-preneurs, mini-majors, supermajors, and NOCs all competing in a global market. In the 2000s, moreover, China's giant state-owned petroleum enterprises rapidly internationalized in search of oil to fuel China's growth (Jiang 2012: 379ff.). Today, all these different types of players cooperate and compete across the up-, mid-, and downstream stages of the value chain. None of them fully controls the world market. OPEC intermittently sets a price range by regulating production levels, while the global market facilitates price discovery within the OPEC range. Recently, the oil shale and shale gas revolution in the US – a revolution driven by specialized and nimble exploration and production companies (Hinton 2012: 234) – has indeed caused a major reversal of long-standing global production and supply patterns (Sernovitz 2016: 6; Yetiv 2015: 15–34) as well as vindicating an increased focus on natural gas as an intermediate hydro-carbon on the road to the low carbon energy transition (Petrie 2014: 181, 191). The shale revolution exemplifies how the oil industry has developed into a global industry that is neither dominated by big multinationals nor powerful states, but a hybrid industry where domestic small, focused, and private companies have as much a role to play as publicly listed integrated supermajors or giant state-owned enterprises.

Conclusion

The makers of the global oil industry were the entrepreneurs, bankers, merchants, managers, and geologists who organized the industry's rapid expansion between 1860 and 1960. In the 1880s, the industry was still predominantly a fragmented industry consisting of mostly local or free-standing companies conducting exploration, production, and refining, while family-owned trading companies conducted international trade and marketing. The economies of scale and rationalization of production and prices realized by the professional and financially prudent management of John D. Rockefeller provided the organizational blue print for the industry's globalization in the decades after 1890. Standard Oil's virtual global monopoly, moreover, drew out the many foreign competitors that aspired to its business model. However, the process of developing an integrated, professionally managed business was arduous and, on many occasions, determined by sheer luck (Jones 1981: 247). The British trading companies and entrepreneurs that were among the first movers in oil merchanting excelled at organizing the financial, commercial, and logistical aspects of the business but their family-ownership often limited their ability to build and manage vertically integrated empires in the image of Standard Oil. Between 1900 and the 1920s, a new generation of technically skilled and financially astute professional managers emerged that focused on building the managerial and organizational processes and capabilities required to organize integrated, multinational enterprises.

The British empire provided the umbrella for the industry to develop. British companies emerged in the Asian colonies shielded from foreign competition while gaining access to the most promising oil reserves through British mandates and diplomatic pressure in the Ottoman Empire and Persia. Before World War II, the formation of the major oil companies was therefore significantly facilitated by empire. The concession system that was established in Persia in 1901, moreover, gave the companies virtually full control over the world's known oil reserves. First challenged in Latin America in the interwar period, however, the post-World War II era of decolonization rapidly diminished the role of empires and established the oil producing countries as the new powerful states in the oil industry. OPEC's successful challenge of the powerful oligopoly in the 1970s, however, did not completely reverse the roles of companies and states, while the rise of China and other emerging markets established non-OPEC state-owned enterprises as multinational oil companies in their own right. The oil industry today is a thoroughly hybrid industry in which big and small companies, state-owned, and private enterprises compete and cooperate.

In terms of historiography, much of the existing research focuses on the government–business relations connected to questions of ownership, control, access, and security of supply. However, in the past three decades, the need for low carbon energy sources to ward off the effects of global warming has become increasingly apparent. The question for the oil industry is no longer how much control producing states exert over access to oil reserves but how far consuming states, if not the global community, will restrict access to markets, i.e., the opportunities and threats posed by demands for clean energy. This future has been some time in the making, particularly considering oil companies' – often failed – investments in alternative energy sources over the past four decades. With recent pledges by, among others, Royal Dutch Shell and Exxon to invest in clean energy and improve their companies' carbon footprint, the impact of the environmental and sustainability movements on the oil industry have been more relevant than ever. This is still largely unexplored, providing major opportunities to reassess the role of states and companies in shaping the energy transition that will fundamentally change the global oil industry.

Notes

1 See for public announcement www.statoil.com/en/news/kick-start-for-statoils-50th-anniversary-history-project.html (accessed 14 December 2017).
2 Compare with Jones (2014). Jones argues that the historical development of power transport and transmission infrastructures, including oil pipelines, are a material expression of the political and entrepreneurial forces that shape energy transitions.
3 The merger was the biggest industrial merger ever at the time ("British Petroleum to Buy Amoco In Biggest Industrial Merger Ever," *Wall Street Journal*, 12 August 1998).

References

Abdelrehim, N. and Toms, S. (2017), "The obsolescing bargain model and oil: the Anglo-Iranian Oil Company 1933–1951," *Business History*, 59 (4), 554–71.

Adelman, M. A. (1995), *The genie out of the bottle: world oil since 1970* (Cambridge, MA: MIT Press).

Adunbi, O. (2015), *Oil wealth and insurgency in Nigeria* (Bloomington, IN: Indiana University Press).

Al-Chalabi, F. J. (1980), *OPEC and the international oil industry: a changing structure* (Oxford: Oxford University Press on behalf of the Organization of Arab Petroleum Exporting Countries).

Bamberg, J. H. (1994), *The Anglo-Iranian years, 1928–1954* (Cambridge: Cambridge University Press).

Bamberg, J. H. (2000a), *British petroleum and global oil 1950–1975: the challenge of nationalism* (Cambridge: Cambridge University Press).

Bamberg, J. H. (2000b), *British Petroleum and Global Oil, 1950–1975: the challenge of nationalism* (Cambridge: Cambridge University Press).

Beltran, A. (ed.) (2010), *A comparative history of national oil companies* (Bruxelles; New York: P.I.E. Peter Lang).

Berghoff, H. (2017), "Shades of green: a business-history perspective on eco-capitalism," in H. Berghoff (ed.), *Green capitalism? Business and the environment in the twentieth century* (Philadelphia, PA: University of Pennsylvania Press).

Bini, E. (2016), "Fueling modernization from the Atlantic to the Third World: oil and economic development in ENI's international policies, 1950s-1960s," in A. Beltran, E. Bussière, and G. Garavini (eds.), *L'Europe et la question énergétique: Les années 1960/1980* (Brussels: Peter Lang).

Bini, E., Garavini, G., and Romero, F. (eds.) (2016), *Oil shock: the 1973 crisis and its economic legacy* (London: I.B. Tauris).

Bleakley, T., Gee, D., and Hulme, R. (1997), "The atomization of big oil," *McKinsey Quarterly*, (2), 122–42.

Boon, M. and Wubs, B. (2016), "Property, control and room for manoeuvre: Royal Dutch Shell and Nazi Germany, 1933–1945," *Business History* [Online], 8 July. Available: https://doi.org/10.1080/0007679 1.2016.1205034 (accessed 8 January 2018).

Brown, J. C. (1987), "Domestic politics and foreign investment: British development of Mexican petroleum, 1889–1911," *Business History Review*, 61 (3), 387–416.

Bucheli, M. (2008), "Multinational corporations, totalitarian regimes and economic nationalism: United Fruit Company in Central America, 1899–1975," *Business History*, 50 (4), 433–54.

Bucheli, M. (2010), "Major trends in the historiography of the Latin American oil industry," *Business History Review*, 84 (2), 339–62.

Bud-Frierman, L., Godley, A., and Wale, J. (2010), "Weetman Pearson in Mexico and the emergence of a British oil major, 1901–1919," *Business History Review*, 84 (2), 275–300.

Cantoni, R. (2015), "Breach of faith? Italian-Soviet Cold War trading and ENI's international 'oil scandal,'" *Quaestio Rossica*, 132 (4), 180–98.

Cantoni, R. (2017a), *Oil exploration, diplomacy, and security in the early Cold War: the enemy underground* (New York: Routledge).

Cantoni, R. (2017b), "What's in a pipe? NATO's confrontation on the 1962 large-diameter pipe embargo," *Technology and Culture*, 58 (1), 67–96.

Chandler, A. D. (1977), *The visible hand: the managerial revolution in American business* (Cambridge, MA: Belknap Press).

Chandler, A. D. and Hikino, T. (1994), *Scale and scope: the dynamics of industrial capitalism* (Cambridge, MA: Belknap Press).

Chapman, K. (1991), *The international petrochemical industry: evolution and location* (Oxford: Blackwell).

Corley, T. A. B. (1983a), *A history of the Burmah Oil Company, 1886–1924* (London: Heinemann).

Corley, T. A. B. (1983b), "Strategic factors in the growth of a multinational enterprise: the Burmah Oil Company, 1886–1928," in M. C. Casson (ed.), *The growth of international business* (London: George Allen & Unwin).

Cricco, M. (2014), "ENI in Libya: from the Italian-Libyan treaty of 1956 to the negotiations of the seventies," *Nuova Rivista Storica*, 98 (2), 555–66.

de Goey, F. (2002), "Henri Deterding, Royal Dutch/Shell and the Dutch market for petrol, 1902–46," *Business History*, 44 (4), 55–84.

Devlin, R. (2014), *Debt and crisis in Latin America: the supply side of the story* (Princeton, NJ: Princeton University Press).

Dietrich, C. R. W. (2014), "'More a gun at our heads than theirs': the 1967 Arab oil embargo, Third World raw material sovereignty, and American diplomacy," in F. J. Gavin and M. A. Lawrence (eds.), *Beyond the Cold War: Lyndon Johnson and the new global challenges of the 1960s* (Oxford: Oxford University Press).

Doel, R. E. (2013), "The earth sciences and geophysics," in J. Krige and D. Pestre (eds.), *Companion encyclopedia of science in the twentieth century* (Florence: Taylor & Francis).

Engler, R. (1977), *The brotherhood of oil: energy policy and the public interest* (Chicago, IL: University of Chicago Press).

Fear, J. (2008), "Cartels," in G. Jones and J. Zeitlin (eds.), *The Oxford handbook of business history* (Oxford: Oxford University Press).

Ferrier, R. W. (1982), *The history of the British Petroleum Company: 1: the developing years 1901–1932* (Cambridge: Cambridge University Press).

Frank, A. (2009), "The petroleum war of 1910: Standard Oil, Austria, and the limits of the multinational corporation," *American Historical Review*, 114 (1), 16–41.

Galpern, S. G. (2009), *Money, oil, and empire in the Middle East: sterling and postwar imperialism, 1944–1971* (Cambridge: Cambridge University Press).

Gerretson, F. C. (1953), *History of the Royal Dutch: 4 volumes* (Leiden: Brill).

Gib, G. S. and Knowlton, E. H. (1956), *History of Standard Oil Company (New Jersey): the resurgent years 1911–1927* (New York: Harper).

Gkanoutas-Leventis, A. (2013), "The transformation of the oil market: A study of financialisation through crises" (Doctoral thesis, City University London).

Glässer, W. (2016), "Shifting power? The oil market between multinationals and petrostates 1960–1975," World Business History Congress/20th Annual Congress European Business History Association, Bergen, Norway, 26 August. Available: http://ebha.org/public/C3:paper_file:231 (accessed 8 January 2018).

Graf, R. (2018), *Oil and sovereignty : petro-knowledge and energy policy in the United States and Western* (New York: Berghahn Books).Gray, W. G. (2016), "Learning to 'recycle': petrodollars and the west, 1973–75," in E. Bini, G. Garavini, and F. Romero (eds.), *Oil shock: the 1973 crisis and its economic legacy* (London: I.B. Tauris).

Gustafson, T. (2012), *Wheel of fortune: the battle for oil and power in Russia* (Cambridge, MA: Belknap Press of Harvard University Press).

Hartshorn, J. E. (1962), *Oil companies and governments: an account of the international oil industry in its political environment* (London: Faber & Faber).

Hartshorn, J. E. (1993), *Oil trade politics and prospects* (Cambridge; New York: Cambridge University Press).

Haug, M. (2011), "Clean energy and international oil," *Oxford Review of Economic Policy*, 27 (1), 92–116.

Heiss, M. A. (1994), "The United States, Great Britain, and the creation of the Iranian Oil Consortium, 1953–1954," *International History Review*, 16 (3), 511–35.

Henriques, R. D. Q. (1960), *Marcus Samuel: first Viscount Bearsted and founder of the "Shell" Transport and Trading Company, 1853–1927* (London: Barrie & Rockliff).

Hidy, R. W. and Hidy, M. E. (1955), *History of Standard Oil Company (New Jersey): pioneering in big business 1882-1911* (New York: Harper).

Hinton, D. D. (2012), "The seventeen-year overnight wonder: George Mitchell and unlocking the Barnett shale," *Journal of American History*, 99 (1), 229–35.

Högselius, P. (2012), *Red gas: Russia and the origins of European energy dependence* (New York: Palgrave Macmillan).

Homburg, E. (2006a), "Explosives from oil: the transformation of Royal Dutch/Shell during World War I from oil to petrochemical company," in B. J. Buchanan (ed.), *Gunpowder, explosives and the state: a technological history* (Aldershot: Ashgate).

Homburg, E. (2006b), "Operating on several fronts: the trans-national activities of Royal Dutch/Shell, 1914–1918," in R. MacLeod and J. A. Johnson (eds.), *Frontline and factory: comparative perspectives on the chemical industry at war, 1914–1924* (Dordrecht: Springer).

Horsnell, P. and Mabro, R. (1993), *Oil markets and prices: the Brent market and the formation of world oil prices* (Oxford: Oxford University Press).

Howarth, S. and Jonker, J. (2007), *A history of Royal Dutch Shell: vol. 2: powering the hydrocarbon revolution, 1939–1973* (Oxford: Oxford University Press).

Jensen-Eriksen, N. (2007), "The first wave of the Soviet oil offensive: the Anglo-American Alliance and the flow of 'red oil' to Finland during the 1950s," *Business History*, 49 (3), 348–66.

Jiang, B. (2012), "China National Petroleum Corporation (CNPC): a balancing act between enterprise and government," in D. G. Victor, D. R. Hults, and M. C. Thurber (eds.), *Oil and governance: state-owned enterprises and the world energy supply* (Cambridge: Cambridge University Press).

Jones, C. F. (2014), *Routes of power: energy and modern America* (Cambridge, MA: Harvard University Press).

Jones, G. (1981), *The state and the emergence of the British oil industry* (London: Macmillan).

Jones, G. (2000), *Merchants to multinationals: British trading companies in the nineteenth and twentieth centuries* (Oxford: Oxford University Press).

Jones, G. (2005), *Multinationals and global capitalism: from the nineteenth to the twenty-first century* (Oxford: Oxford University Press).

Jones, T. C. (2012), "America, oil, and war in the Middle East," *Journal of American History*, 99 (1), 208–18.

Jonker, J. and Zanden, J. L. v. (2007), *A history of Royal Dutch Shell: vol. 1: from challenger to joint industry leader, 1890–1939* (Oxford: Oxford University Press).

Karl, T. L. (1997), *The paradox of plenty: oil booms and petro-states* (Berkeley, CA: University of California Press).

Karlsch, R. and Stokes, R. G. (2003), *Faktor Öl: die Mineralölwirtschaft in Deutschland, 1859–1974* (München: Beck).

Kemp, A. G. (2012), *The official history of North Sea oil and gas. vol. I: the growing dominance of the state* (London: Routledge).

Klemann, H. and Kudryashov, S. (2012), *Occupied economies: an economic history of Nazi-occupied Europe, 1939–1945* (London: Berg).

Kuiken, J. (2014), "Caught in transition: Britain's oil policy in the face of impending crisis, 1967–1973," *Historical Social Research*, 39 (4), 272–91.

Labbate, S. (2016), "ENI and North African oil producing countries during the 1970s: Egypt, Algeria and Tunisia," in A. Beltran, E. Bussière, and G. Garavini (eds.), *L'Europe et la question énergétique: Les années 1960/1980* (Brussels: Peter Lang).

Larson, H. M., Knowlton, E. H., and Popple, C. S. (1971). *History of Standard Oil Company (New Jersey): new horizons 1927–1950* (New York: Harper & Row).

Linde, C. v. d. (1991), *Dynamic international oil markets: oil market developments and structure, 1860–1990* (Dordrecht; Boston, MA: Kluwer Academic Publishers).

Lippert, W. D. (2011), *The economic diplomacy of ostpolitik: origins of Nato's energy dilemma* (New York: Berghahn Books).

Mabro, R., Bacon, R., Chadwick, M., Halliwell, M., and Long, D. (1986), *The market for North Sea crude oil* (Oxford; New York: Oxford University Press).

McNally, R. (2016), *Crude volatility: the history and the future of boom-bust oil prices* (New York: Columbia University Press).

Marsh, S. (2007), "Anglo-American crude diplomacy: multinational oil and the Iranian oil crisis, 1951–53," *Contemporary British History*, 21 (1), 25–53.

Maurer, N. (2011), "The empire struck back: sanctions and compensation in the Mexican oil expropriation of 1938," *Journal of Economic History*, 71 (3), 590–615.

May, G. (1998), *Hard oiler! the story of Canadians' quest for oil at home and abroad* (Toronto: Dundurn Press).

Mitchell, T. (2013), *Carbon democracy: political power in the age of oil* (London: Verso).

Mommer, B. (2002), *Global oil and the nation state* (New York: Oxford University Press).

Musso, M. (2017), "'Oil will set us free': the hydrocarbon industry and the Algerian decolonization process," in A. W. M. Smith and C. Jeppesen (eds.), *Britain, France and the decolonization of Africa* (London: UCL Press).

Nolan, P. A. and Thurber, M. C. (2012), "On the state's choice of oil company: risk management and the frontier of the petroleum industry," in D. G. Victor, D. R. Hults, and M. C. Thurber (eds.), *Oil and governance: state-owned enterprises and the world energy supply* (Cambridge: Cambridge University Press).

Nowell, G. P. (1994), *Mercantile states and the world oil cartel, 1900–1939* (Ithaca, NY: Cornell University Press).

Overy, R. J. (1994), *War and economy in the Third Reich* (Oxford: Clarendon Press).

Painter, D. (2010), "Oil, resources, and the Cold War, 1945–1962," in M. P. Leffler and O. A. Westad (eds.), *The Cambridge history of the Cold War: volume 1 origins* (Cambridge: Cambridge University Press).

Painter, D. S. (2012), "Oil and the American century," *Journal of American History*, 99 (1), 24–39.

Parra, F. R. (2004), *Oil politics: a modern history of petroleum* (London; New York: I.B. Tauris).

Patey, L. (2014), *The new kings of crude: China, India, and the global struggle for oil in Sudan and South Sudan* (London: Hurst & Company).

Penrose, E. (1968), *The large international firm in developing countries: the international petroleum industry* (London: Allen & Unwin).

Perovic, J. (2017), *Cold War energy: a transnational history of Soviet oil and gas* (Cham: Springer International Publishing).

Petrie, T. A. (2014), *Following oil: four decades of cycle-testing experiences and what they foretell about U.S. energy independence* (Norman OK: University of Oklahoma Press).

Petrini, F. (2016), "Eight squeezed sisters: the oil majors and the coming of the 1973 oil crisis," in E. Bini, G. Garavini, and F. Romero (eds.), *Oil shock: the crisis of 1973 and its economic legacy* (London: I.B. Tauris).

Poley, J. P. (2000), *Eroïca: the quest for oil in Indonesia (1850–1898)* (Dordrecht: Springer).

Pozzi, D. (2010), "Entrepreneurship and capabilities in a 'beginner' oil multinational: the case of ENI," *Business History Review*, 84 (2), 253–74.

Pratt, J. A. and Hale, W. E. (2013), *Exxon: transforming energy, 1973–2005* (Austin, TX: University of Texas).

Priest, T. (2012), "The dilemmas of oil empire," *Journal of American History*, 99 (1), 236–51.

Radetzki, M. (2008), *A handbook of primary commodities in the global economy* (Cambridge: Cambridge University Press).

Razavi, H. (1989), *The new era of petroleum trading: spot oil, spot-related contracts, and futures markets* (Washington, DC: World Bank).

Ross, M. L. (2012), *The oil curse: how petroleum wealth shapes the development of nations* (Princeton, NJ: Princeton University Press).

Rubino, A. (2008), *Queen of the oil club: the intrepid Wanda Jablonski and the power of information* (Boston, MA: Beacon Press).

Ryggvik, H. (2015), "A short history of the Norwegian oil industry: from protected national champions to internationally competitive multinationals," *Business History Review*, 89 (1), 3–41.

Sampson, A. (1975), *The seven sisters: the great oil companies and the world they made* (New York: Viking Press).

Scazzieri, L. (2015), "Britain, France, and Mesopotamian oil, 1916–1920," *Diplomacy and Statecraft*, 26 (1), 25–45.

Schenk, C. R. (2011), *International economic relations since 1945* (London: Routledge).

Scherner, J. (2008), *Die Logik der Industriepolitik im Dritten Reich: die Investitionen in die Autarkie- und Rüstungsindustrie und ihre staatliche Förderung* (Stuttgart: Steiner).

Sernovitz, G. (2016), *The green and the black: the complete story of the shale revolution, the fight over fracking, and the future of energy* (New York: St. Martin's Press).

Skeet, I. (1988), *OPEC: twenty-five years of prices and politics* (Cambridge: Cambridge University Press).

Sluyterman, K. (2007), *A history of Royal Dutch Shell: vol. 3: keeping competitive in turbulent markets, 1973–2007* (Oxford: Oxford University Press).

Sluyterman, K. (2010), "Royal Dutch Shell: company strategies for dealing with environmental issues," *Business History Review*, 84 (2), 203–26.

Smil, V. (2010), *Energy transitions: history, requirements, prospects* (Santa Barbara, CA: ABC-CLIO).

Sorrell, S., Speirs, J., Bentley, R., Brandt, A., and Miller, R. (2010), "Global oil depletion: a review of the evidence," *Energy Policy*, 38 (9), 5290–5.

Stevens, P. (2000), "Pipelines or pipe dreams? Lessons from the history of Arab transit pipelines," *Middle East Journal*, 54 (2), 224–39.

Stevens, P. (2008), "National oil companies and international oil companies in the Middle East: under the shadow of government and the resource nationalism cycle," *Journal of World Energy Law and Business*, 1 (1), 5–30.

Stokes, R. G. (1985), "The oil industry in Nazi Germany, 1936–1945," *Business History Review*, 59 (2), 254.

Tarbell, I. M. (1904), *The history of the Standard Oil Company* (New York: McClure, Phillips).

Tétreault, M. A. (1985), *Revolution in the world petroleum market* (Westport, CT: Quorum).

Tétreault, M. A. (1995), *The Kuwait Petroleum Corporation and the economics of the new world order* (Santa Barbara, CA: ABC-CLIO).

Tolf, R. W. (1976), *The Russian Rockefellers: the saga of the Nobel family and the Russian oil industry* (Stanford, CA: Hoover Institution Press).

Toprani, A. (2014), "Germany's answer to standard oil: the Continental Oil Company and Nazi grand strategy, 1940–1942," *Journal of Strategic Studies*, 37 (6–7), 949–73.

Toprani, A. (2017), "An Anglo-American 'petroleum entente'? The first attempt to reach an Anglo-American oil agreement, 1921," *Historian*, 79 (1), 56–79.

Tugendhat, C. and Hamilton, A. (1975), *Oil, the biggest business* (London: Eyre Methuen).

Turner, L. (1978), *Oil companies in the international system* (London: George Allen & Unwin).

UN (2015), *International trade statistics yearbook: vol. II trade by product* (New York: United Nations).

Victor, D. G., Hults, D. R., and Thurber, M. C. (2011), "Introduction and overview," in D. G. Victor, D. R. Hults, and M. C. Thurber (eds.), *Oil and governance: state-owned enterprises and the world energy supply* (Cambridge: Cambridge University Press).

Wall, B. H. (1974), *Teagle of Jersey standard* (New Orleans, LA: Tulane University).

Wilkins, M. (1970), *The emergence of multinational enterprise: American business abroad from the colonial era to 1914* (Cambridge, MA: Harvard University Press).

Wilkins, M. (1974a), *The maturing of multinational enterprise: American business abroad from 1914 to 1970* (Cambridge, MA: Harvard University Press).

Wilkins, M. (1974b), "Multinational oil companies in South America in the 1920s: Argentina, Bolivia, Brazil, Chile, Colombia, Ecuador, and Peru," *Business History Review*, 48 (3), 414–46.

Wilkins, M. and Schröter, H. G. (1998), *The free-standing company in the world economy 1830–1996* (Oxford: Oxford University Press).

Williamson, H. F. (1959), *The American petroleum industry: the age of illumination 1859–1899* (Evanston, IL: Northwestern University Press).

Williamson, H. F. (1963), *The American petroleum industry: the age of energy 1899–1959* (Evanston, IL: Northwestern University Press).

Winegard, T. (2016), *The first world oil war* (Toronto: University of Toronto Press).

Yergin, D. (1993), *The prize: the epic quest for oil, money and power* (London: Pocket Books).

Yergin, D. (2011), *The quest: energy, security and the remaking of the modern world* (New York: Penguin Press).

Yetiv, S. A. (2015), *Myths of the oil boom: American national security in a global energy market* (Oxford: Oxford University Press).

PART V

Challenges and impact

31

POLITICAL RISKS AND NATIONALISM

Takafumi Kurosawa, Neil Forbes, and Ben Wubs

Introduction

What impact did political risk and nationalism have on global business? Have wars and other conflicts caused by national interests and identities retarded or even reversed the trend towards globalization? When faced with political and geopolitical threats such as war, occupation, expropriation, economic blockade and sanctions, requisition, persecution, or boycott, how did multinational enterprises (MNEs) and other international economic actors manage (or fail) to overcome the situation they found themselves in? Also, how did the response of economic entities like MNEs transform global business, or change political risks and the sovereign state system? Furthermore, what insight does the examination of such phenomena present to business history and international business research?

In this chapter, risks arising from political phenomena including nationalism, are regarded as a part of various 'non-market risks'. Non-market risks include political as well as natural disasters and other risks (Casson and Lopes 2013, 377–379). One cannot always draw a clear line between political and other non-market risks, on the one hand, and market and economic risks on the other. In many cases, political risks influence MNEs and international economic activities indirectly, rather than directly, for example through changes in economic conditions (such as price, volume of transactions, and transaction conditions) in the market. Nonetheless, there are good reasons to regard political risk as a subject in its own right.

First, political and geopolitical phenomena may directly inhibit or promote business activities without waiting for market mediation, and therefore specific analysis is required. Second, political risk not only affects the profitability and competitiveness of the firm, but may also become an existential threat to the corporate assets, life, and property of managers, employees, and shareholders. Third, the dominant theoretical frameworks in business history and international business base themselves on economic logic, and the problem of political risk tends to be treated as an accidental, exogenous variable and as such has not been considered sufficiently (Bremmer and Keat 2009, 1–9).

Although risks will not hurt companies unless they materialize, once an awareness of such risks is developed, it triggers a response by economic entities. Risk is also an economic opportunity. If one entity can avoid risks more skilfully than others, it puts this entity in a relatively advantageous position in market competition. In this chapter, therefore, we focus on actual threats, the risks of those threats, and the actors' perceptions and expectations of those risks, threats, and opportunities.

Nationalism is a polysemous concept, but this chapter uses it in its broadest sense (Pickel 2005). In addition to perceptions and acts based on patriotism, nationalism also more widely encompasses action, including war, taken by a state to advance its own interests. It is not enough to discuss the relationship between 'business and state' and 'business and government' by focusing on a single state. Rather, the main focus of analysis should be on the fact that the international state-system comprises sovereign states which compete with each and whose relationships at times fluctuate between amicable and hostile. MNEs act within the realm of this international state-system and have to adapt to the various national legal conditions. Based on this perspective, this chapter considers the risks caused by conflict, especially between sovereign states, and between sovereign states and MNEs, while keeping in mind general political risk.

The first global economy

In the era of the first global economy preceding the First World War, political risk and nationalism were far from being the major obstacles facing modern businesses in crossing borders. During the century from the end of the Napoleonic War in 1815 to the First World War in 1914, there was no major or long-lasting conflict in Europe. Meanwhile, on a global scale, the colonial wars, regional conflicts, and political disturbances that occurred did not involve expropriation of foreign assets (Lipson 1985, 19), and in several cases such conflicts provided business opportunities for merchants based outside the region concerned. Military power was concentrated in a limited number of the world powers, and this was enough to protect foreign assets, at the time still largely confined to the vicinity of seaport cities.

Colonization and the wars it produced were part of the process of globalizing property rights and the modern state-system that protected them. Colonization extended the legal systems and governance structures of the home countries to various parts of the world, reducing the risks involved in foreign direct investment (FDI). For example, this process happened in Asia through the system of foreign concession and the acquisition of extraterritorial rights (Jones 1996, 27; Lipson 1985, 14). Global business was a promoter as well as a product of colonialism, imperialism, and 'gunboat diplomacy'.

For much of the nineteenth century, the UK-centred free trade system, the gold standard, and liberal economic thought made stable business possible. State intervention in economic society was miniscule, and the global economy was not organized around the logic of the national economy as its principal unit (Banken and Wubs 2017, 17–20). The major constraints for global business were the physical and cultural distances, not rivalry among the major powers and their policies. Few restrictions were imposed by the state on the movement of people, goods, and capital. Foreign firms were generally treated in the same way as local firms (Jones 2005, 201–202, 209–210). Though protective tariffs were introduced in the US in the 1860s and in many European nations after the 1880s, their rates were still not prohibitive. Even with the emergence of nationalistic discourse in Europe and the Americas regulation of foreign-owned enterprises was still limited, with some exceptions such as restrictions in the US banking business in the latter half of the nineteenth century (Wilkins 1989, 455; Jones 1996, 38–40).

Such openness was also effective in less developed regions. Merchants from diverse home countries, including small European nations and Canada, could enter the colonies of major powers freely. Swiss merchants in India provide a good example: their property rights were upheld and protected by the colonial government and German and American consulates (Dejung and Zangger 2010, 188). Before the First World War, ideas of race or civilization dominated the perceptions of people; cosmopolitanism based on imperialism, rather than nationalism, prevailed. In the Ottoman Empire, the policies from the end of the nineteenth century to the early twentieth century welcomed foreign capital, and as such political risk was small (Geyikdagi and Geyikdagi 2011, 395–397). In Japan in the latter half of the nineteenth century, the activities of foreign traders were confined within certain 'foreign settlements', but after resolving the unequal treaties at the end of the nineteenth century, this restriction was removed and foreign investment was introduced (Yuzawa and Udagawa 1990, 1–50; Jones 2005, 207).

How did the aforementioned situation influence international business? First, the nationality of the company was not explicit and made little difference in policy terms, despite all the nationalistic discourse (Jones 2006, 153–157). With the freedom of movement of capital as a precondition, multinational networks of entrepreneurs, owners, investors, and intermediaries were established. Second, 'born-global' firms – that is, firms founded with cross-border operations from their inception – were created in the nineteenth century (Jones and Khanna 2006, 459). The freestanding company was a representative example. Even if the actual business activities of such firms were performed in remote areas such as in colonies, the corporate headquarters were located in Europe, especially in London, with its abundant resources of capital and superior institutional and legal infrastructures (Wilkins, 1988). Third, a series of 'multi-regional' firms emerged along with cross-border regions, partially due to newly introduced tariffs and the differences in national legal systems. As there was an incentive to invest on the other side of the border, it prompted many multinational enterprises to be formed in the border areas of Germany and Switzerland, and also on the US–Canada border for example (Jones 2005, 22).

However, it is noteworthy that even in this age of relative stability and integration, political risks and apprehension towards nationalism also facilitated the emergence of unique corporate and investment forms. One such example is the case of holding companies, based in politically neutral states, emerging in the 1880s. In the infrastructure and utilities business, such as in railways and gas, and especially in electrification, a small number of engineering companies from a specific country (for example, Siemens, AEG, ABB in the case of the electrical sector) founded financing companies to establish firms in several parts of the world, and solicited investment funds from different countries all over the world. However, when investing in businesses in different regions through holding companies, investors considered public opinion and were wary of potential local opposition should domestic infrastructures and utilities be brought under the control of international bankers or the capital of a hostile country. In light of this, arrangements were made to locate headquarters in medium-sized or small countries such as Switzerland, Belgium, the Netherlands, and Canada, which had flexible corporate legislation (Hausman *et al.* 2008, 52–72).

The First World War and the 1920s

The First World War was a major turning point for global business. On the one hand, it ended the long-lasting era of relative peace, and signalled the start of an era of political instability and ideological conflict, revolution, dictatorship, and rampant (economic) nationalism. On the other hand, its impact on international business was ambiguous. While international business was hit hard by the war, it also showed amazing resilience. Many business historians who have written on this issue concur with Adam Tooze, the war historian, who has placed emphasis on the US-led postwar reconstruction of the global order (Tooze 2014). They claim that the First World War changed the course of globalization but did not reverse it (Smith *et al.* 2017, 26, 69, 142, 185, 211). Jones claims that the impediment for international business was not that large in the 1920s: fully fledged de-globalization is identified as taking place only from the 1930s (Jones 2005, 20, 28).

The disconnection and blows to the international order caused by the First World War are clear. The movement of people, goods, and finance, and the exchange of information across borders had become more difficult (Smith *et al.* 2017). Such problems also occurred between the belligerent and neutral states, destructing the business of the above-mentioned 'born international' enterprises. Difficulties hindering international business included military and economic blockades, the confiscation and freezing of enemy assets, the implementation of blacklisting and sanctions, currency control, rationing, the shift to military production and other economic controls, and boycotts against enemy or foreign companies. These outcomes favoured companies from neutral states, but dealt a blow to international business in general (Rossfeld and Straumann 2008; Fitzgerald 2015, 162–178).

During the First World War, nationality became a decisive factor for the first time. Companies dealing with enemy assets were sanctioned. Germany, UK, and later also the US launched for the first time ever a systematic survey on company ownership. There were more than 50,000 Germans in the UK, but after the war broke out, they were effectively excluded from economic life and many were interned, a trend which escalated during the course of the war (Panayi 1990). Internment was also undertaken in colonies (Lubinski *et al.* 2018). In order to confirm their neutrality, some multinational corporations domiciled in neutral countries, such as Switzerland, made the executives from belligerent countries resign and replaced them with neutral country personnel. Manufacturing enterprises established in Switzerland by German capital, such as AIAG, became a Swiss company in this way (Ruch *et al.* 2001, 125).

Foreign-affiliated companies in various countries continued with business even during the war by officially breaking ties with their parent company, leading to a fragmentation of multinational companies. Companies under the control of the enemy were condemned, but the business was maintained by trustees (custodian), and in the case of companies domiciled in the victorious nations, many were revived after the war. Even businesses domiciled in neutral nations but located in belligerent countries were continued – by increasing their independence and localizing their management (Kurosawa and Wubs 2019). The geographical composition of business and product strategy also shifted in line with the war situation. Neutral countries served as supply bases to the belligerent countries. Until then, Nestlé, for example, which had had its major production bases in Switzerland and the UK, made huge investments in the Americas and Australia during the war to convert them into supply bases for Europe (Fenner 2008). Not only the war itself, but also its sudden end dealt a blow to some companies that exploited or catered to wartime demand (Rossfeld and Straumann 2008, 78–87, 194–199, 330–337; Klemann 2007, 298–302).

The geopolitical consequences of the First World War were immense. Four empires collapsed, and, in Russia, the foreign capital-owned assets, including those in oil and electric businesses, were lost during the Bolshevik revolution and its aftermath. Many small sovereign states sprang up in Central Europe, where companies faced fragmented markets and nationalism after the break-up of the Austrian-Hungarian Empire. However, in some other regions, new international relations emerged that to some extent made up for the effects of division; Hungary's political split from Austria and subsequent strengthening link with the London market provides one such example (Forbes 2017).

On a global scale, the implications and consequences of what contemporaries called the 'Great War' were more ambiguous. For the war in Europe, human and material resources were mobilized globally, and global linkages intensified. The US emerged as the bearer of a Global Order, even if this was still a role it played only partially. The US retreated from the world stage politically with the failure of Congress to ratify membership of the League of Nations; but US companies began to expand internationally, particularly in Europe (de Goey 2009, 547).

US banks expanded their business in the issuing of foreign securities and set up new branches in Asia and Latin America (Stratton 2017). In Japan, import substitution and the formation of new industries during the First World War created the foundation for outward FDI to Korea and Taiwan in the following era. In South America, exports to Europe were also maintained, and companies with European roots became more localized in Latin America and integrated Latin American markets internationally (Dehne 2017).

Victory and defeat and the subsequent reparations and rearmament prohibition directly changed the competitive landscapes of countries and companies. German firms also faced the risk of reparation claims in addition to their losses of property conducted by the Allies. Confiscated properties, including patent and trademark rights, became the basis for the British chemical industry, including the establishment of ICI (Reader 1970). Firms from neutral states, such as Sweden, Switzerland, and the Netherlands, had improved their position after successfully continuing their business in and with both camps during the war, and by hosting German firms fleeing confiscation and postwar rearmament prohibition. Sweden's SKF (Golson and Lennard 2017) and Swiss companies in the chemical, electrical machinery, and metal sectors (Rossfeld and Straumann 2008) and Dutch incandescent lamp manufacturer, Philips (Sluyterman and Wubs 2009, 119–125) are good examples of this.

The First World War changed the strategy and organization of MNEs. Germany lost its overseas assets which were only partially recovered during the interwar period. It was only 50 years later, in the 1960s, that Germany's overseas assets finally returned to their pre-First World War level (Schröter 1993, 34). The low German level of FDI in mining and petroleum production was an outcome of Germany's defeat in the First World War (Jones 1996, 78). In the former German territory of Upper Silesia, special political measures had to be adopted to try to sustain German economic interests (Reckendrees 2013). The Netherlands in particular was a favourite destination for German banks and industrial companies during the 1920s (Sluyterman and Wubs 2009, 119–125). This was a response to the risk of confiscation (from reparation claims in the 1920s, and in expectation of another world war after the 1930s). IG Farben's investment in the US was Germany's largest FDI in that country, but its holding company was located not in Germany, but in Basle (König 2001, 31–38). German companies frequently secured their international business by joining international cartels, thereby avoiding the exclusive ownership of FDI, with its attendant risks of requisition (Schröter 1988; Jones 1996, 43).

Both during and after the World War, decentralization and localization were musts in dealing with market divisions and the complicated political situation. In the case of MNEs with multinational ownership and management prior to the war, head offices themselves tended to be pluralistic organizations. The relationship between the home country organization and affiliate of the host country also became looser and decentralized. The branches were transformed into local subsidiaries by incorporating local holding-companies (Wubs 2008, 23; Lüpold 2003, 216). American companies expanded in Europe after the War. In 1919, GE established International General Electric as a subsidiary for its overseas operations (Wilkins 1974, 138–151). Though this was a unitary organization, it invested in subsidiaries in each country according to their specific, national circumstances.

During the 1920s the use of holding companies became quite common. This was due to the rapid increase of the tax burden since the First World War that made double taxation of the parent company and foreign subsidiaries of multinationals an acute issue (Mollan and Tennent 2015; Izawa 2019). In the 1920s, complex corporate organizational architectures appeared. Multiple holding companies utilizing nominal 'shell companies' were established and tied up with complex ownership, borrower–lender relationships and differentiated voting rights. The aims were to obscure the owner's nationality, ownership, and controlling relations, to avert political risks and to avoid double taxation. For this purpose, Roche and Nestlé established a special, double corporate structure (Kurosawa and Wubs 2019), and IGC, a British gas utility firm that operated in multiple countries, did this through owning subsidiaries on the continent and providing loans to them (Izawa 2019). While Belgium had lost its position as a safe, neutral country after the German invasion, new tax havens such as Liechtenstein and Panama emerged in the 1920s. They offered flexible corporate legislation and tax laws favourable to holding companies (Kurosawa 2015, 238–239). But also the Netherlands, which remained neutral during the war and non-aligned after it, functioned as a tax haven, particularly for Dutch and German multinational companies. The Netherlands, which did not sign the Treaty of Versailles, kept taxes very low (corporate tax did not exist), had a law against double taxation, and was a relative small jurisdiction with political stability, and, moreover, had banking secrecy (Sluyterman and Wubs 2009, 116; Euwe 2010, 227). Behind the emergence of tax havens, such as Liechtenstein, Switzerland, Panama, and the Netherlands stood the activities of multinational companies, international bankers, lawyers, accounting firms, and the governments of the home countries of MNEs. It can be said that the international business elite developed the informal infrastructure or informal, international public goods by lobbying for changes in the legal and tax systems in several countries.

De-globalization, dictatorship, and the Second World War

The era spanning from the 1930s to 1940s was one in which international business was exposed to the most serious political and geopolitical risks so far (with the exception of the Russian Revolution). The Great Depression was followed by an era of protectionism, economic blocs, and autarchic economic policies, which fragmented the global economy *in extremis*. The threat of persecution by brutal political regimes seriously challenged international business and created several dilemmas related to ethics and legitimacy. The Second World War and foreign occupations brought about a threat to multinationals of a different magnitude compared to the First World War.

Changes in the political environment that triggered de-globalization in the 1930s were Janus-faced. On the one hand, tariffs were drastically raised, trade blocs formed, import substitution policies adopted, and currency controls and bilateral clearing system emerged; on the other hand, major Western countries still had a receptive attitude towards inward FDI (Jones 2005, 203–204). No serious cases of sequestration were observed until the war broke out (Lipson 1985, 65–84; Wubs 2008, 57), with the tragic exception of 'Aryanization' of Jewish companies in Nazi Germany (Bajohr 2002; Forbes 2007; Kohler 2016). To cope with these changes, MNEs shifted from trade to FDI and pursued decentralization, localization, and neutralization of their corporate organizations. Strict currency controls made it difficult for MNEs to remit their profits to their home country, forcing them to reinvest locally (Kobrak 2003; Wilkins 2004a, 28; Wubs 2007; Wubs 2008, 47–49). The number of foreign owned manufacturing subsidiaries grew fourfold from 1914 to 1938 (Teichova 1986, 364). The global business of the pre-war era, comprising a cosmopolitan, multinational network, had been reorganized into an agglomeration of decentralized MNEs, which were loosely integrated, highly self-sufficient domestic businesses, based on the premise of division by borders.

Economic nationalism and state intervention had become a global phenomenon in the inter-war period. In Latin America, government intervention and restrictions on foreign capital were strengthened, mainly for utilities and infrastructural projects, affecting ITT and other companies (Bucheli and Salvaj 2013). In Mexico, businesses in the agricultural sector based on foreign investment were nationalized (Lipson 1985, 77). In Japan, MNEs faced heavy competition with emerging local firms and their anti-foreign capital campaigns. Nestle's local subsidiary in Japan overcame this problem by replacing its manager and owner with a nominally Japanese one (Donzé and Kurosawa 2013). Oil, and the refining of oil products such as petroleum, which had become strategic goods, were a particular target for nationalization across the world. In Iran, Anglo Persian Oil Company's concession was temporarily suspended in 1932 (Andersen 2008, 642). The Bolivian government took over the assets of Jersey Standard in 1937, and in the following year Mexico nationalized the assets of Shell, and Standard Oil Company of California (Jonker and van Zanden 2007, 453–456). This was the first large-scale nationalization since the Russian Revolution. Government intervention also occurred in oil-consuming countries. In countries like Chile aiming at price control, and Japan targeting oil refining from a strategic viewpoint, local companies attempted to enter into the refining and distribution of oil backed by the government (Bucheli 2010; Kikkawa 2019).

The Second World War was not at all a replay of the First World War. With the surprisingly swift defeat of France, a much wider area was occupied than had been the case during the First World War, and a great part of the European continent came under the New Order of Nazi Germany. The occupied area included the important headquarters of several MNEs, such as those in the Netherlands, Belgium, France, and Czechoslovakia, which threatened not only overseas assets, but also entire companies and the life and property of their managers and shareholders. Except for what had happened in Belgium, such experiences were unprecedented: they were of an entirely different dimension from the risk of economic nationalism experienced during the 1920s and 1930s. The continental blockade mounted by the Allies and the counter-blockade set up by the Axis, divided the world market in two: a continental area under the control of the Axis and the rest of the world controlled by the Allies. This situation, together with the acute ethical challenges caused first by the persecution of the Jews, Gypsies, and political opponents followed by policies of racial genocide, made the decisions of economic actors in and outside the occupied territories extremely difficult and morally burdened (Lund 2006).

For MNEs headquartered in, respectively, allied, neutral, and occupied countries, most of the business was largely maintained given the lack of an alternative strategy. The German or continental subsidiaries of British or American MNEs continued their business by severing ties with their headquarters after the war broke out or upon the entry of the US into the War (for example, Dehomag, IBM's German subsidiary; Opel under GM). Anglo-Dutch multinationals Unilever and Royal Dutch Shell officially discontinued the relationship between the two headquarters – narrowly avoiding confiscation and direct control by the occupation authorities on the Dutch side – and managed to continue their businesses (Howarth and Jonker 2007, 86–97; Wubs 2008, 179–180). In the case of companies in neutral countries such as SKF (Sweden) and Georg Fisher AG (Switzerland), the property rights of the subsidiaries under German control were respected and it was relatively easy to maintain relations with them (Wipf 2001; Independent Commission of Experts Switzerland – Second World War 2002, 293–310). On the other hand, in the occupied countries, the situation was quite diverse (Lund 2006; Klemann and Kudryashow 2012). In Norway, a large-scale confiscation took place, and both the burden of the German occupation and German investments for strategic purposes were massive. In the case of firms from Denmark, it was possible to catch business opportunities in the *Grosswirtschaftsraum*, including in Norway (Lund 2006, 115–128; Andersen 2009). The ownerships of the local firms in occupied Eastern Europe were transferred to German, state-owned holding companies (Overy 2002). The assets of German companies under the control of Allied Powers had been much smaller by comparison as a result of the First World War and ensuing German strategies during the 1920s. The assets of the US subsidiary of IG Farben were frozen (König 2001,143–152).

Many studies have focused on the ethical aspects of corporate behaviour in this era. In works aimed at general readers, MNEs are often severely condemned for their cooperation with the Nazi dictatorship, including in relation to the war and the Holocaust. Most business historians nonetheless maintain a critical distance from moral condemnation. Instead, the constraints, dilemmas, and historical backgrounds of corporate behaviour are analysed as well as the impact of this on strategies and organizational structure, hypothesizing that most actions were based on economic rationality and survival strategies, rather than political ideology (Forbes 2000; Heide 2004; Kobrak and Hansen, 2004). According to these studies, the response of the companies varied greatly, depending on their size, resources, and capabilities, their dependency on business in the two camps and the countries they were operating in, the possibility of shifting their business to a safe area, the strategic importance of their products, the form of entry, the attitude and features of their home country government, and their room for manoeuvre (Boon and Wubs 2016).

Companies such as Nestlé, and Roche were relatively less dependent on the German market, thus they could manage to control risks and to maintain a certain distance from the oppressive government. In contrast, companies that relied heavily on the German market like Maggi were weak in the face of pressure from the regime (Ruch *et al.* 2001, 172–177). Insurance or financial companies such as Allianz, and producers with sizeable foreign market sales such as Schering, were especially vulnerable to the Nazi government's exchange controls, and that limited their freedom of action (Feldman 2001; Kobrak 2003). A company like Unilever, one of the largest multinationals in the world at the time, was simply too large, and its products were indispensable for the population and army. This gave the company enormous leverage over the Nazi regime. Companies were positioned in a competitive environment, thus they tended to be more keenly aware of the risk of withdrawal rather than that of cooperation with the regime (Forbes 2004). In Germany, the impact of political risks transformed more than corporate behaviour, it also greatly affected corporate organization (Kobrak 2002).

Although the above-mentioned financial and legal structures of companies using complex architecture were not necessarily all for the purpose of hiding their activities, they had also turned into a crucial means of cloaking (camouflage), especially when currency controls and war risk increased its importance. This was not just limited to German companies (Aalders and Wiebes 1996; Uhlig *et al.* 2001; Wilkins 2004a, 29; Kobrak and Wüstenhagen 2006; Jones and Lubinski 2012). MNEs from Allied and neutral countries also resorted to it. Not only Sweden and Switzerland, but also Latin America, South Africa, and other locations became bases for such activities, involving American, Dutch, Swiss, Swedish, and Danish 'nominees' (Wüstenhagen 2004; Wilkins 2004a). The Allies were aware of asset concealment by the Nazis and by German companies, and conducted an operation 'Safe haven' to contain it (Lorenz-Meyer 2007).

The reasons for cloaking were diverse. Dutch companies that had their home country occupied by the Nazis faced the risk of confiscation not only by Germany but also by the Allied authority (Van der Eng, 2017). They divided their parent companies into two, legally independent companies, and further evacuated their corporate overseas assets to safe areas in the Dutch Antilles or South Africa (Blanken 2002, 120–121; Wubs 2008, 63–65). Various organizational and legal structures were invented as seen in the 'Ring' structure established by Beiersdorf in Germany for their brand ownership (Jones and Lubinski 2012). While such financial and legal structures tended to be regarded as nominal ones, they sometimes threatened the control over the subsidiary by the parent company and thus the unity of the company, as in the cases of Nestlé and Roche (Lüpold 2003; Kurosawa 2015; Ruch *et al.* 2001, 86–211). On the other hand, Japanese companies, which experienced no serious damage during the Second World War, took no precaution against defeat or occupation of Japan.

The Second World War changed the competitive landscape significantly. For companies in the Axis nations, the effect of cloaking was limited, and they lost most of their assets (including trademarks and patents) outside the reduced territory. As a result, both German and Japanese companies focused more on exports than FDI for a few decades after the war. The position of firms of the victorious, occupied, and neutral countries varied, but Roche, Philips, and Unilever, for example, shifted their operations to the Western Hemisphere, transforming themselves from European-based MNEs to global ones (Blanken 2002, 312–314; Howarth and Jonker 2007, 103; Wubs 2008, 185; Kurosawa and Wubs 2019).

There was also a great impact on how MNEs organized themselves. Particularly in Europe, a decentralized and multi-domestic organizational structure had emerged during the interwar period. What had been established as an organizational architecture to survive war and occupation became a tool that could be used for political risk management during the Cold War and to avoid high taxation in the postwar period. In Japan, the wartime regime and occupation after the war fundamentally changed the corporate structure, and brought about bank-centred, horizontal business groups that were no longer based on the family ownership of Zaibatsu (Ohata and Kurosawa 2016, 170, 175–178).

Cold War, decolonization, and economic nationalism

The period from 1945 to the 1970s was marked by two elements: a bipolar world of the Cold War and proliferated economic nationalism. Although international business was eliminated from the Communist bloc and the risk that the Cold War could turn into a hot war was not unlikely (regional proxy wars were actually waged), serious threats to the home of Western MNEs did not disappear. The postwar period until the end of the 1970s was the era of mixed economies, state dirigism, and national industrial policies. It is true that the postwar General Agreement on Tariffs and Trade (GATT) and the International Monetary Fund (IMF) regime under American hegemony guaranteed financial stability and increasing free trade – international trade actually expanded dramatically – but the segmentation of global markets into national economies still stands out in comparison with the pre-First World War era (Jones 2006). Property rights, which were self-evident during the first globalization wave, were rendered vulnerable, and most nationalizations by governments in states that had formerly been colonies took place in this period (Lipson 1985, 85–139).

As a consequence of Sovietization in Central and Eastern Europe, and the Communist revolution in China, the international economic network both in Warsaw Pact countries and East Asia was dismantled. Private firms, including international businesses, were nationalized without compensation in Eastern Europe (Wubs 2008, 166–169). In East Asia, investments from Japan in Korea, Taiwan, and China (railways, electricity, cotton spinning in Shanghai, sugar industry in Taiwan) were taken over and domesticized by local governments. Intra East Asian FDI declined sharply. As a consequence of the Chinese Civil War, businesses, including foreign firms, had escaped to Hong Kong, or had been nationalized when physical transfer of assets was difficult (Jones 1996, 170). North Vietnam also followed this path of nationalization. In the 1960s, FDI from Japan to Asian countries, including Taiwan and South Korea, was resumed, but the full-scale economic reintegration of East Asia took place only after the 1980s. In Japan, the postwar re-establishing of American and European MNEs showed little progress due to restrictive regulations (Jones 2005, 220).

Up to the 1970s, interventionist-style economic policies and 'national' industrial policies were maintained in many West European nations and in Japan, despite the incremental (and eventual) abolition of exchange controls and regulations on capital. During the two decades after the War, for most German and Japanese manufacturers, exporting was much more important than FDI (Jones 1996, 47). MNEs from the UK, the Netherlands, Belgium, and France, however, soon revived their foreign activities and increased investments in Europe and the US (Sluyterman and Wubs 2009, 160–164; Wubs 2012). Most European MNEs maintained a 'parent–daughter' type of organization. The subsidiaries abroad often had a high level of autonomy, and control over them was often informal and personal. European companies often chose a multi-domestic model rather than an international or global model, even in the context of an increasing level of European integration; the degree of integration among their national subsidiaries lagged behind what was occurring with American companies (Jones 2005, 177). This, of course, corresponds to the actual division and fragmentation of markets and variations of national economies, but it was partially also a legacy of war and other political risk, or, at the very least, the influence of memory in helping to determine the decisions of business leaders.

Nationalization resulting from policies of economic nationalism in developing countries is symbolized by the nationalization of the Suez canal by Egypt in 1956: in fact, nationalizations increased in the 1960s, and peaked in 1975 (Lipson 1985, 97–123). Unlike the all-encompassing nationalization under Communist regimes, nationalization in developing countries usually focused on specific industries (typically oil, minerals, and utilities). With the exception of Cuba, Egypt, Iraq, and Syria, economic compensation was paid more or less at a reasonable rate. By 1976, virtually all oil-producing countries had nationalized crude oil production (Williams 1975; Jones 1996, 93). In the 1970s, many foreign-affiliated plantations in Asia were subject to nationalization or forced localization. In the mid-1980s, half of the extraction capacity of mining resources in developing countries had become state owned. As a result, direct ownership by multinationals in mineral resources and commodities decreased, thereby reducing the risk of expropriations (Kobrin 1984).

Besides nationalization, other forms of policies brought about political risk. In Chile and Japan, both lacking petroleum resources, the government preferred joint ventures between domestic firms and foreign multinational corporations, and ensured that this was realized (Bucheli 2010; Kikkawa 2019). Many developing countries such as Brazil adopted industrial policies, aiming at import substitution, and urged MNEs to set up factories in the host country (Jones 1996, 259–262). In Africa, a strategy of indigenization rather than nationalization was chosen (Decker 2008). In Indonesia after independence, a policy of so-called Indonesianization of human resources was adopted to achieve a higher level of economic independence (Sluyterman 2018). In some countries, economic nationalism took a form of ethnic policy. Policies in Indonesia and Malaysia constrained international business owned by migrant entrepreneurs and business groups with Chinese ethnicity. In Indonesia, political instability plagued foreign investment in general (White 2012).

MNEs were far from passive actors as regards these various policies and risks, and their proactive countermeasures transformed global business and political risk itself. The most extreme example was the political mobilization of home-country governments. In the *coup d'état* in Iran (against Mosaddegg in 1953) and in Chile (against Allende in 1973), MNEs resorted to motivate the US government to overthrow the host regime, which it did, and to maintain their favourable business position. Shocking though such blatant behaviour may be, these interventions carried their own risks, and the interests of the home country may not necessarily match the interest of the MNEs; so, in fact, it was not a commonly or preferred strategy of international business. However, in general, the relationship with the home country and its government remained important (Blaszczyk 2008; Bucheli 2008, 2013; Decker 2011).

Conversely, MNEs pursued exit strategies from foreign markets, or did so partially, with withdrawal from the ownership of assets in the host countries. MNEs that had lost their advantage in natural resource extraction often integrated the downstream part of the value chain and achieved vertical integration. Some withdrawals led to bold business transformation or diversification by tapping into unrelated sectors. In the mining industry and primary goods sectors, several MNEs adopted a strategy to avoid the risk of asset ownership. For example, United Fruit Company had a vertical integration strategy in Colombia up until the Second World War. However, it divested from that country, no longer owning plantations, but maintaining its influence in procurement (Bucheli 2008).

Localization by joint ventures and other means were also common. An 'absorption' strategy was used to internalize the source of political risk within the firm (Ring *et al.* 1990; Andersen 2009). In this case, typically, a joint venture with local business groups or the government-owned enterprises was formed, often by inviting government bureaucrats, politicians, and the local economic elite to be added as owners or managers. The investment by Japanese paper producers and steelmakers in Brazil were such examples. Whilst in Africa, they cooperated with the indigenization policy and secured their legitimacy by maintaining a favourable relationship with developing countries' elites (Decker 2008).

The effects of such actions, however, were sometimes seriously limited. The case of United Fruit Company in Central America shows that these beneficial relationships with the local elites depended on economic stability, and that democratization did not necessarily bring an open liberal policy to MNEs (Bucheli 2008). The examples of ITT in Chile and of Du Pont in Iran show that once the local elite had lost their legitimacy and fundamental social upheaval took place, great consequential blows can be brought about (Bucheli and Salvaj 2013; Blaszczyk 2008). Alternatively, the case of Sears Ruebuck and other firms that succeeded in Mexico where nationalization of oil companies was taking place, shows that political risks could be overcome, if the symbolic meaning of business (in this case, material prosperity, upward mobility, and consumer democracy) corresponded to the values of local society (Moreno 2003). A localization strategy was also important for the Philips, a technology company headquartered in Amsterdam. The survival of its subsidiary in Australia, for example, had to deal with a kind of 'post-colonial' context (van der Eng 2018).

After the Second World War, the existential threat to MNEs from their home countries reduced remarkably, and therefore the necessity for cloaking decreased. However, political and geopolitical risks in host countries as well as international taxation risks continued, and so MNEs often maintained complex legal structures for foreign subsidiaries and overseas projects. This coincided with the new emergence of host countries that provided safe infrastructures. 'Safe havens' emerged in the ocean of political instability; examples include Hong Kong during China's Communist revolution and Singapore amid Southeast Asia's heightened nationalism. Offering also a flexible corporate law and low tax rates, these locations also served as tax havens and centres for tax evasion or avoidance. Also, in the Western Hemisphere, Offshore Financial Centres (OFCs) were created in small jurisdictions in the Caribbean, for example in the Dutch Antilles (Curaçao) and British Cayman Islands (Van Beurden 2018, passim; Zucman 2015, 35). The rise of these tax paradises, however, did not happen in isolation; the geographical shifts of MNE operations during the 1950s and 1960s was closely linked to international developments and to regulatory and financial institutional changes in home countries.

Second global economy

After the 1980s, political and geopolitical risks for international businesses reached the lowest level since the outbreak of the First World War. Both the Cold War and ideological conflicts over the economic systems appeared to have ended. The Soviet state collapsed and collective property was rapidly 'privatized' and taken-over by 'oligarchs'. The former socialist countries in Eastern Europe entered the capitalist camp, privatized state-owned companies welcomed investments of foreign MNEs (King and Szelenyi 2005, 42). China had adopted an open door policy in 1978, and returned to the global market incrementally. In developed countries, privatization, financial liberalization, and market-oriented reforms created new opportunities (utility, transportation, insurance) for direct investments from abroad. In developing countries, nationalization policies became rare, and measures to attract foreign capital became paramount. As regional economic integration was promoted, trade expanded globally, and FDI increased even more.

Nevertheless, even under such conditions, political risks for international business did not disappear. In this period, potential trade conflicts between developed nations were an ever-present threat. For example, between Japan and the US a conflict began with fibres and extended to steel, automobiles, and semiconductors (Bergsten and Noland 1993). Under US diplomatic pressure, the Japanese manufacturers were forced to accept 'voluntary export restraints'. In the automobile industry, Japanese companies addressed concerns over American protectionism by means of FDI in the US. Political risk thus promoted multinationalization of Japanese car manufacturers (Anastakis 2017, 62–63). In the textile and steel industries, the protectionist measures taken by developed countries, such as the US and European nations, caused production shifts and outsourcing from the country targeted for such measures to third countries. In other words, political risk and MNEs' active response to it have given rise to today's global value chain (Gereffi 1999).

In former communist economies, market institutions and the rule of law were not sufficiently established; this caused significant uncertainty and posed risks for MNEs. China is an extreme example of such risk. During its open-door policy since the 1980s, access to the market was conditional on the transfer of technology. In the case of the car industry, foreign manufacturers could not enter the market without setting up joint ventures with local state-owned enterprises. Even after joining the World Trade Organization (WTO) in 2001, state intervention did not disappear. The Chinese government also used attacks on private enterprises as a means of putting diplomatic pressure on foreign governments. In the territorial dispute between Japan and China in 2012, Japanese companies in China faced state-approved attacks by mobs and boycotts by the public. In 2017, the Chinese government condemned the installation of a missile defence system by South Korea and openly boycotted South Korean MNEs.

As a result of the perpetual search by global enterprises for tax avoidance schemes and the competition among sovereign states to attract investments, the number of tax havens increased. The liberalization of international capital flows and financialization of entire economies also facilitated this phenomena (Ogle 2017, 1454). As in the case of attempted and failed 'corporate inversion' by Pfizer/Allagan in 2016 and Ireland's special position, these phenomena are becoming some of the decisive factors helping to shape the form and activities of MNEs.

It is still hard to assess the impact of the recent rise of right-wing populism in the advanced countries, the Brexit campaign in the UK, and the disruption of the postwar economic order by the President of the US. However, these developments have contributed to the realization by MNEs that political and geopolitical risks, and the threat of uncertainty, were not just problems of the past.

In what way did the international business change the international politics and international order? Needless to say, the political clout of multinational corporations and multinational banks has been one of the main drivers of globalization since the 1980s (Sluyterman and Wubs 2010, 822). Banks, law firms, accounting firms, consultants, among others, were practically involved in the design of taxation and corporate laws of the countries that are prominent in the financial offshore industry, including Dubai, the Netherlands, UK, and Ireland (Garcia-Bernardo *et al.* 2017, 1).

Likewise, these actors were active promoters of market-led economies and are evermore involved in government policy-making. In this sense, MNEs and other international business entities had a proactive and decisive role to play in the management of political risks as well as the creation of institutional and organizational loopholes designed to avoid the regulatory power of sovereign nations.

Conclusions

Political risk and nationalism have had major impacts on the development and retardation of global business. Two World Wars, the protectionism of the 1930s, and subsequent waves of economic nationalism damaged the global economy severely and threw it into reverse, though temporarily and partially, and changed the trajectory of globalization during the twentieth century. Wartime blockades, interwar trade barriers, and policies of sovereign nations protecting or serving national interests dealt a blow to the global integration of the market. The two World Wars also brought about technological innovation, and partly contributed to the rise of regions that had been traditionally on the periphery, and laid the basis for today's multipolar global economy.

Under these pressures, global business looked to transform itself from being based on a unitary structure to a multi-centred one: today's multinational corporations were created to operate beyond the constraints imposed by the sovereign states. In addition, the economic entities involved in global business created international public goods on their own, such as special safe havens, rather than remaining passive to the actions of sovereign states. Ironically, however, this seems to be creating a new kind of political risk and widespread anti-globalism.

The effects of political risks, due to their nature, showed significant geographical differences; they varied widely between European and US companies. In Europe, where serious risks such as war and occupation became a reality, the capability to address political risks had a great impact on the rise, fall, and survival of firms. A significant number of European MNEs survived, however, by adopting an organizational structure to control and resist political risk, or by strategically changing the allocation of geographical and business portfolios. Although business history has focused more on these issues recently, the situation after the Second World War and cases outside Europe are still under-researched. In addition, research on the history of corporate law and taxation and the effects on MNEs is only just emerging in the discipline, and interdisciplinary dialogues have not yet taken place. Herein lies an important opportunity for an exciting re-interpretation of international business history.

References

Aalders, G. and C. Wiebes, *The Art of Cloaking Ownership: The Secret Collaboration and Protection of the German War Industry by the Neutrals. The Case of Sweden.* Amsterdam: Amsterdam University Press, 1996.

Anastakis, D. 'Access to markets, investment, continentalization and competitiveness: The evolution of the Canadian auto sector'. In B. Bouwens, P. Y. Donzé, and T. Kurosawa, eds, *Industries and Global Competition: A History of Business Beyond Borders*, New York/Abingdon: Routledge, 2017, 47–67.

Andersen, S. 'Building for the Shah: Market entry, political reality and risks on the Iranian market, 1933–1939'. *Enterprise & Society*, 9 (4), 2008, 637–669.

Andersen, S. 'Escape from "safehaven": The case of Christiani & Nielsen's blacklisting in 1944'. *Business History*, 51 (5), 2009, 691–711.

Bajohr, F. *'Aryanisation' in Hamburg: The Economic Exclusion of Jews and the Confiscation of their Property in Nazi Germany.* New York/Oxford: Berghahn, 2002.

Banken, R. and B. Wubs, *The Rhine: A Transnational Economic History.* Baden Baden: Nomos, 2017.

Bergsten, C. F. and M. Noland, *Reconcilable Differences? United States–Japan Economic Conflict.* Washington, DC: Institute for International Economics, 1993.

Blanken, I. J. *De Geschiedenis van Koninklijke Philips Electronics N.V. Een industriële wereldfederatie: Deel 5.* Zaltbommel: Europese Bibliotheek, 2002.

Blaszczyk, R. L. 'Synthetics for the Shah: DuPont and the challenges to multinationals in 1970s Iran'. *Enterprise & Society,* 9 (4), 2008, 670–723.

Boon, M. and B. Wubs, 'Property, control and room for manoeuvre: Royal Dutch Shell and Nazi Germany, 1933–1945'. *Business History,* 2016, DOI: 10.1080/00076791.2016.1205034.

Bremmer, I. and P. Keat, *The Fat Tail: The Power of Political Knowledge in an Uncertain World.* New York, Oxford University Press, 2009.

Bucheli, M. 'Multinational corporations, totalitarian regimes and economic nationalism: United Fruit Company in Central America, 1899–1975'. *Business History,* 50 (4), 2008, 433–454.

Bucheli, M. 'Multinational corporations, business groups, and economic nationalism: Standard Oil (New Jersey), Royal Dutch-Shell, and energy politics in Chile 1913–2005'. *Enterprise & Society,* 11 (2), 2010, 350–399.

Bucheli, M. and E. Salvaj, 'Reputation and political legitimacy: ITT in Chile, 1927–1972'. *Business History Review,* 87 (4), 2013, 729–756.

Casson, M. and T. da Silva Lopes, 'Foreign direct investment in high-risk environments: An historical perspective'. *Business History,* 55 (3), 2013, 375–404.

de Goey, F. 'Dutch companies in the United States and American companies in the Netherlands'. In H. Krabbendam, C. A. van Minnen, and G. Scott-Smith, eds, *Four Centuries of Dutch-American Relations.* Amsterdam: Boom, 2009, 542–553.

Decker, S. 'Building up goodwill: British business, development and economic nationalism in Ghana and Nigeria, 1945–1977'. *Enterprise & Society,* 9 (4), 2008, 602–613.

Decker, S. 'Corporate political activity in less developed countries: The Volta River Project in Ghana, 1958–66'. *Business History,* 53 (7), 2011, 993–1017.

Dehne, P. 'Profiting despite the Great War: Argentina's grain multinationals'. In A. Smith, S. Mollan, and K. D. Tennent, eds, *The Impact of the First World War on International Business.* Oxford: Routledge, 2017, 67–86.

Dejung, C. and A. Zangger, 'British wartime protectionism and Swiss trading firms in Asia during the First World War'. *Past and Present,* 207 (1), 2010, 181–213.

Donzé, P.-Y. and T. Kurosawa, 'Nestlé coping with Japanese nationalism: Political risk and the strategy of a foreign multinational enterprise in Japan, 1913–45'. *Business History,* 55 (8), 2013, 1318–1338.

Euwe, J. 'Financing Germany: Amsterdam's role as an international financial centre, 1914–1931'. In P. Baubeau and A. Ögren, eds, *Convergence and Divergence of National Financial Systems: Evidence from the Gold Standards, 1871–1971.* London: Pickering & Chatto, 2010, 219–240.

Feldman, G. *Allianz and the German Insurance Business, 1933–1945.* Cambridge: Cambridge University Press, 2001.

Fenner, T. 'Nestlé & Anglo-Swiss: Vom Schweizer Milchimperium zum Multinationalen Nahrungsmittelkonzern'. In R. Rossfeld and T. Straumann, eds, *Der Vergessene Wirtscahftskrieg: Schweizer Unternehmen im ersten Weltkrieg.* Zurich: Chronos, 2008, 317–343.

Fitzgerald, R. *The Rise of the Global Company: Multinationals and the Making of the Modern World.* Cambridge: Cambridge University Press, 2015.

Forbes, N. *Doing Business with the Nazis: Britain's Economic and Financial Relations with Germany, 1931–1939.* London/Portland, OR: Frank Cass, 2000.

Forbes, N. 'Managing risk in the Third Reich: British business with Germany in the 1930s'. In C. Kobrak and P. H. Hansen, eds, *European Business, Dictatorship, and Political Risk, 1920–1945.* New York: Berghahn Books, 2004, 194–205.

Forbes, N. 'Multinational enterprise, "corporate responsibility" and the Nazi dictatorship: The case of Unilever and Germany in the 1930s'. *Contemporary European History,* 16 (2), 2007, 149–167.

Forbes, N. 'The flows of international finance after the First World War: The bank of England and Hungary, 1920–1939s'. In A. Smith, S. Mollan, and K. D. Tennent, eds, *The Impact of the First World War on International Business.* New York/Abingdon: Routledge, 2017, 211–224.

Forbes, N., T. Kurosawa, and B. Wubs, eds, *Multinational Enterprise, Political Risk and Organizational Change: From Total War to Cold War.* New York: Routledge, 2019.

Garcia-Bernard, J., J. Fichtner, F. W. Takes, and E. M. Heemskerk, 'Uncovering offshore financial centers: Conduits and sinks in the global corporate ownership network'. *Scientific Reports,* 2017, www.nature.com/articles/s41598-017-06322-9.pdf (accessed 25 April 2019).

Gereffi, G. 'International trade and industrial upgrading in the apparel commodity chain'. *Journal of International Economics*, 48 (1), 1999, 37–70.

Geyikdagi, V. N. and M. Y. Geyikdagi, 'Foreign direct investment in the Ottoman Empire: Attitudes and political risk'. *Business History*, 53 (3), 2011, 375–400.

Golson, E. and J. Lennard, 'Swedish business in the First World War: A case study of ball bearings manufacturer SKF'. In A. Smith, S. Mollan, and K. D. Tennent, eds, *The Impact of the First World War on International Business*. New York/Abingdon: Routledge, 2017, 89–102.

Hausman, W. J., P. Hertner, and M. Wilkins, *Global Electrification: Multinational Enterprise and International Finance in the History of Light and Power, 1878–2007*. New York: Cambridge University Press, 2008.

Heide, L. 'Between parent and "child": IBM and its German subsidiary, 1910–1945'. In C. Kobrak and P. Hansen, eds, *European Business Dictatorship and Political Risk*. New York: Berghahn Books, 2004, 149–173.

Howarth, S. and J. Jonker, *Stuwmotor van de koolwaterstofrevolutie, 1939–1973: Geschiedenis van Koninklijke Shell*, deel 2, Amsterdam: Boom, 2007.

Independent Commission of Experts Switzerland – Second World War, *Switzerland, National Socialism and the Second World War: Final Report*. Zurich: Pendo Verlag, 2002.

Izawa, R. 'Municipalisation, war, tax and nationalisation: Imperial Continental Gas Association in an era of turmoil, 1824–1987'. In N. Forbes, T. Kurosawa, and B. Wubs, eds, *Multinational Enterprise, Political Risk and Organizational Change: From Total War to Cold War*. New York: Routledge, 2019, 55–68.

James, H. and J. Tanner, *Enterprise in the Period of Fascism in Europe*. Aldershot/Burlington, NJ: Ashgate, 2002.

Jones, G. *The Evolution of International Business: An Introduction*. London: Routledge, 1996.

Jones, G. *The Multinationals and Global Capitalism: From the Nineteenth to the Twenty-first Century*. New York: Oxford University Press, 2005.

Jones, G. 'The end of nationality? Global firms and "borderless worlds"'. *Zeitschrift für Unternehmensgeschichte*, 51 (2), 2006, 149–165.

Jones, G. and T. Khanna, 'Bringing history (back) into international business'. *Journal of International Business Studies*, 37 (4), 2006, 453–468.

Jones, G. and C. Lubinski, 'Managing political risk in global business: Beiersdorf, 1914–1990'. *Enterprise & Society*, 13 (19), 2012, 85–119.

Jonker, J. and J. L. van Zanden, *From Challenger to Joint Industry Leader. Vol. 1, A History of Royal Dutch Shell*. Oxford: Oxford University Press, 2007.

Kikkawa, T. 'Foreign oil majors in Japan and the Second World War'. In N. Forbes, T. Kurosawa, and B. Wubs, eds, *Multinational Enterprise, Political Risk and Organizational Change: From Total War to Cold War*, New York: Routledge, 2019, 87–105.

King, L. P. and I. Szelenyi. 'The new capitalism in Eastern Europe: Towards a comparative political economy of post-communism'. In N. Smelser and R. Swedberg, eds, *Handbook of Economic Sociology*. Princeton, NJ: Princeton University Press, 2005.

Klemann, H. 'Ontwikkleing door Isolement'. In M. Kraaijestein and P. Schulten, eds, *Wankel evenwicht: Neutraal Nederland en de Eerste Wereldoorlog*. Soesterberg: Aspect, 2007, 271–309.

Klemann, H. and S. Kudryashow, *Occupied Economies: An Economic History of Nazi-Occupied Europe, 1939–1945*. New York: Berg, 2012.

Kobrak, C. 'Politics, corporate governance, and the dynamics of German managerial innovation: Schering AG between the wars'. *Enterprise & Society*, 3 (3), 2002, 429–461.

Kobrak, C. 'The foreign-exchange dimension of corporate control in the Third Reich: The case of Schering AG'. *Contemporary European History*, 12 (1), 2003, 33–46.

Kobrak, C. and P. Hansen, eds, *European Business, Dictatorship, and Political Risk 1920–1945*. New York: Berghahn Books, 2004.

Kobrak, C. and J. Wüstenhagen, 'International investment and Nazi politics: The cloaking of German assets abroad, 1936–1945'. *Business History*, 48 (3), 2006, 399–427.

Kobrin, S. J. 'Expropriation as an attempt to control foreign firms in LDCs: Trends from 1960 to 1979'. *International Studies Quarterly*, 28 (3), 1984, 329–348.

Kohler, I. *The Aryanization of Private Banks in the Third Reich*. Cambridge: Cambridge University Press, 2016.

König, M. *Interhandel Die schweizerische Holding der IG Farben und Ihre Metamorphosen: eine Affare um Eigentum und Interessen (1910–1999)*. Zürich: Chronos, 2001.

Kurosawa, T. 'Breaking through the double blockade: Inter-Atlantic wartime communications at Roche'. *Jahrbuch für Wirtschaftsgeschichte*, 56 (1), 2015, 227–256.

Kurosawa, T. and B. Wubs, 'Swiss and (Anglo)-Dutch multinationals and organizational change in the era of total war'. In N. Forbes, T. Kurosawa, and B. Wubs, eds, *Multinational Enterprise, Political Risk and Organizational Change: From Total War to Cold War*, New York: Routledge, 2019, 23–54.

Lipson, C. *Standing Guard: Protecting Foreign Capital in the Nineteenth and Twentieth Centuries*. Berkeley, CA: University of California Press, 1985.

Lorenz-Meyer, M. *Safehaven: The Allied Pursuit of Nazi Assets Abroad*. Columbia, MO: University of Missouri Press, 2007.

Lubinski, C., V. Giacomin, and K. Schnitzer, 'Internment as a business challenge: Political risk management and German multinationals in Colonial India (1914–1947)'. *Business History*, 2018, DOI: 10.1080/00076791.2018.1448383.

Lund, J. ed., *Working for the New Order: European Business under German Domination, 1939–1945*. Copenhagen: University Press of Southern Denmark/Copenhagen Business School Press, 2006.

Lüpold, M. 'Globalisierung als Krisenreaktionsstrategie: Dezentralisierung und Renationalisierung bei Nestlé 1920–1950'. In H.-J. Gilomen, M. Müller, and B. Veyrassat, eds, *Globalisierung-Chancen und Risiken: Die Schweiz in der Weltwirtschaft 18.-20. Jahrhundert/La globalisation-chances et risques. La Suisse dans l'economie mondiale 18e-20e siècles*. Zürich: Chronos, 2003, 211–234.

Mollan, S. and K. D. Tennent, 'International taxation and corporate strategy: Evidence from British overseas business, circa 1900–1965'. *Business History*, 57 (7), 2015, 1054–1081.

Moreno, J. *Yankee Don't go Home: Mexican Nationalism, American Business Culture and the Shaping of Modern Mexico, 1920–1950*. Chapel Hill, NC: University of North Carolina Press, 2003.

Ogle, V. 'Archipelago capitalism: Tax havens, offshore money, and the state, 1950s–1970s'. *AHR*, December 2017, 1431–1458.

Ohata, T. and T. Kurosawa, 'Policy transfer and its limits: Authorised cartels in twentieth-century Japan'. In S. Fellman and M. Shanahan, eds, *Regulating Competition: Cartel Registers in the Twentieth-century World*. Abingdon/New York: Routledge, 2016, 169–190.

Overy, R. J. 'Business in the Grossraumwirtschaft: Eastern Europe, 1938–1945'. In H. James and J. Tanner, eds, *Enterprise in the Period of Fascism in Europe*. Aldershot/Burlington, NJ: Ashgate, 2002, 151–177.

Panayi, P. 'German business interest in Britain during the First World War'. *Business History*, 32 (2), 1990, 244–258.

Pickel, A. 'Introduction: False oppositions: Recontextualizing economic nationalism in a globalizing world'. In E. Helleiner and A. Pickel, eds, *Economic Nationalism in a Globalizing World*. Ithaca, NY: Cornell University Press, 2005, 1–17.

Reader, W. J. *Imperial Chemical Industries: A History*. London: Oxford University Press, 1970.

Reckendrees, A. 'Business as a means of foreign policy or politics as a means of production? The German government and the creation of Friedrich Flick's Upper Silesian industrial empire (1921–1935)'. *Enterprise & Society*, 14 (1), 2013, 99–143.

Ring, P. S., S. A. Lenway and M. Govekar, 'Management of the political imperative in international business'. *Strategic Management Journal*, 11 (2), 1990, 141–151.

Rossfeld, R. and T. Straumann (eds), *Der Vergessene Wirtschaftskrieg. Schweizer Unternehmen in ersten Weltkrieg*. Zürich: Chronos, 2008.

Ruch, C., M. Rais-Liechti, and R. Peter, *Geschäfte und Zwangsarbeit: Schweizer Industrieunternehmen im 'Dritten Reich'*. Zurich: Chronos, 2001.

Schröter, H. 'Risk and control in multinational enterprise: German businesses in Scandinavia, 1918–1939'. *Business History Review*, 62 (3), 1988, 420–443.

Schröter, H. 'Continuity and change: German multinationals since 1850'. In G. Jones and H. Schröter, eds, *The Rise of Multinationals in Continental Europe*. Aldershot/Brookfield, VT: Edward Elgar, 1993, 28–48.

Sluyterman, K. 'Decolonisation and the organisation of the international workforce: Dutch multinationals in Indonesia, 1945–1967'. *Business History*, 2018, doi:10.1080/00076791.2017.1350170.

Sluyterman, K. and B. Wubs, *Over Grenzen: Multinationals en de Nederlandse Markteconomie*. Amsterdam: Boom, 2009.

Sluyterman, K. and B. Wubs, 'Multinationals and the Dutch business system: The cases of Royal Dutch Shell and Sara Lee'. *Business History Review*, 84 (4), Winter 2010, 799–822.

Smith, A., S. Mollan, and K. D. Tennent, *The Impact of the First World War on International Business*. New York/Abingdon: Routledge, 2017.

Stratton, T. 'Mammon unbound: The international financial architecture of Wall Street banks, 1915–1925'. In A. Smith, S. Mollan, and K. D. Tennent, eds, *The Impact of the First World War on International Business*. New York/Abingdon: Routledge, 2017, 185–210.

Teichova, A. 'Multinationals in perspective'. In A. Teichova, M. Lévy-Leboyer, and H. Nussbaum, eds, *Multinational Enterprise in Historical Perspective*. London: Cambridge University Press, 1986, 362–373.

Tooze, A. *The Deluge: The Great War and the Remaking of Global Order 1916–1931*. New York: Penguin, 2014.

Uhlig, C., P. Barthelmess, M. König, P. Pfaffenroth, and B. Zeugin, *Tarnung, Transfer, Transit Die Schweiz als Drehscheibe verdeckter deutscher Operationen (1939–1952): Hereausgegeben von der Unabhängigen Expertenkommission Schweiz – Zwiter Weltkrieg*. Zürich: Chronos, 2001.

van Beurden, T. 'De Curaçaose offshore: Ontstaan, groei en neergang van een belastingparadijs, 1951–2013'. PhD Amsterdam University, 2018.

van der Eng, P. 'Managing political imperatives in war time: Strategic responses of Philips in Australia, 1939–1945'. *Business History*, 59 (5), 2017, 645–666.

van der Eng, P. 'Turning adversity into opportunity: Philips in Australia, 1945–1980'. *Enterprise & Society*, 19, March 2018, 179–207.

White, N. 'Surviving Sukarno: British business in post-colonial Indonesia, 1950–1967'. *Modern Asian Studies*, 46 (5), 2012, 1277–1315.

Wilkins, M. *The Maturing of Multinational Enterprise: American Business Abroad from 1914 to 1970*. Cambridge, MA: Harvard University Press, 1974.

Wilkins, M. 'The free-standing company, 1870–1914: An important type of British foreign direct investment'. *Economic History Review*, 41 (2), 1988, 259–282.

Wilkins, M. *The History of Foreign Investment in the United States to 1914*. Cambridge, MA: Harvard University Press, 1989.

Wilkins, M. 'Multinationals and dictatorship: Europe in the 1930s and early 1940s'. In C. Kobrak and P. H. Hansen, eds, *European Business, Dictatorship, and Political Risk, 1920–1945*. New York: Berghahn Books, 2004a, 22–38.

Wilkins, M. *The History of Foreign Investment in the United States, 1914–1945*. Cambridge, MA: Harvard University Press, 2004b.

Williams, M. L. 'The extent and significance of the nationalization of foreign-owned assets in developing countries, 1956–1972'. *Oxford Economic Papers*, New Series, 27 (2), 1975, 260–273.

Wipf, H. U. *Georg Fischer AG 1930–1945: Ein Schweizer Industrieunternehmen im Spannungsfeld Europas*. Zürich: Chronos, 2001.

Wubs, B. 'Unilever's struggle for control: An Anglo-Dutch multinational under German occupation'. *Zeitschrift für Unternehmensgeschichte*, 52 (1), 2007, 57–84.

Wubs, B. *International Business and National War Interests: Unilever between Reich and Empire, 1939–45*. Abingdon/New York: Routledge, 2008.

Wubs, B. 'A Dutch multinational's miracle in post-war Germany'. *Jahrbuch für Wirtschaftsgeschichte*, 2012, 15–41.

Wüstenhagen, J. 'German pharmaceutical companies in South America: The case of Schering AG in Argentina'. In C. Kobrak and P. H. Hansen, eds, *European Business, Dictatorship and Political Risk, 1920–1945*. New York: Berghahn, 2004, 81–102.

Yuzawa, T. and M. Udagawa, *Foreign Business in Japan before World War II*. Tokyo: University of Tokyo Press, 1990.

Zucman, G. *The Hidden Wealth of Nations: The Scourge of Tax Havens*. Chicago, IL/London: University of Chicago Press, 2015.

32

IMITATION AND GLOBAL BUSINESS

Teresa da Silva Lopes, Andrea Lluch, and Gaspar Martins Pereira

Introduction

Imitation of goods is a growing and widespread phenomenon which has historically had great significance in the making of global business and also on the economic development of countries (Berg 2002; Béaur *et al.* 2007; Mihm 2007; Barry and Thrift 2007; among others). The concept of "imitation" never had a universal meaning. It changed over time and across cultures, but has always been associated with issues of appropriation of reputation and legitimacy that belong to an innovator. In the present day, a common way for innovators to prevent imitation in most markets is through protection of intellectual property, such as the registration of trademarks, patents, or copyrights (North 1981; Landes and Posner 2003; Maskus 2000; Horii and Iwaisako 2007). However, that has not always been the case, in particular before intellectual property laws were in place and enforced in different countries (Lopes and Casson 2012).

Imitation has affected virtually all industries, ranging from agricultural and manufactured goods to services. Imitation can be an unproductive activity when it has a few or more of the attributes of a truly innovative activity (Baumol 1990, 2010). But it can also be considered a productive activity. Entrepreneurs who imitate through, for example, reverse engineering or by creating substitute products, can be critical for technological progress. History is replete with examples of substantial improvements created by imitators, who adapted technologies to local conditions in new markets (e.g. of different size, with different consumer preferences, climatic conditions, or with different available complementary inputs). These are often called "new" innovations, when in fact they are "innovative imitations" (Levitt 1966). Imitation tends to proliferate in growing industries with low barriers to entry. It affects, in particular, successful products and services, relying on the exploitation of intangible assets such as successful brands and trademarks, or superior technologies and patents (Green and Smith 2002). Although it is difficult to provide precise estimates about imitation, studies indicate that in 2013 imitated goods corresponded to about 2.5 percent of total world trade, having increased from an estimated 1.9 percent in 2008 (US Chamber of Commerce 2016; OECD/EUIPO 2016).

This chapter provides an overview of the multiple dimensions and impacts of imitation on the making of global business. It will focus on the wine industry, which historically developed as one of the first global industries, and which was particularly affected by imitation and adulteration during late nineteenth and early twentieth centuries (Unwin 1991; Pan-Montojo 1994;

Pereira 2009; Stanziani 2003, 2009; Lopes *et al.* 2017a). This is also the period of the first global economy (1875–1914), discussed in Chapter 2 by Geoffrey Jones. During this period, the Western world was characterized by a revolution in transportation and communications (essentially in more developed economies), an expansion of urban consumption, and the development of mass distribution and marketing, in particular mass advertising, and mass packaging of branded goods (Chandler 1994; Jones 2005). These changes increased the choice of consumers in terms of selection of goods, their quality, and price (Wilkins 1989). This chapter compares and contrasts producer countries and consumers from two continents: the Old World, focusing on major producers such as Portugal, Spain, and France, and also major traders and consumers such as Great Britain; and the New World, including major producers of wines such as Argentina, and also major traders and consumers such as Brazil. The chapter adopts a supply side perspective, investigating the relations and the multiple dimensions of imitation strategies in the wines industry.

The second and third sections of the chapter provide a multidisciplinary review of the existing literature, particularly in business history, on how imitation affected the making of global business and economic development. The fourth section analyses the regulatory environment around the creation of geographical denominations of origin. Sections five and six provide evidence of imitation in wines in the Old and New World, and also of the strategies followed by innovators and imitators to compete internationally, in particular in weak institutional and regulatory environments. In the late nineteenth century and early twentieth centuries, world trade in alcoholic beverages comprised essentially wines (Lopes *et al.* 2017b). Finally, the seventh section provides some conclusions highlighting the significance of imitation and imitators in the making of the global business.

Different perspectives on imitation in business

The real impact of imitation on the making of global business and economic development remains an open debate. The prevailing view in legal studies is that imitation, and in particular counterfeiting, may harm society at large (Wilke and Zaichkowsky 1999; Naylor 2014). The legal literature discusses differences in intellectual property regimes between countries and how, over time, these dissimilarities have complicated the making of global business (Bently *et al.* 2008; Bently 2009). In the Western world, issues of imitation led to the development of strong intellectual property rights regimes, but a broad spectrum of legal traditions has developed against intellectual property rights infringement (Callman 1969; Ladas 1975; Takenaka 2013). Intellectual property regimes developed quite differently elsewhere. Several Latin American countries such as Argentina developed legal systems based on the so-called attributive system.[1] This principle provided privileged rights to the first registrant, who might not be the innovator. This created barriers to foreign exporters and manufacturers who often complained about the different trademark regimes in Latin America, claiming that valuable trademarks were being registered for purpose of piracy or to be given up to the rightful owner for a consideration.[2]

Several economic studies analyze the recent impact of imitations on the growth of global trade, on the profitability of businesses, and on consumers' wellbeing. Some economists consider innovation necessary for societal welfare, and believe that imitation may inhibit that process and make consumers worse off (Schumpeter 1949). Imitation and counterfeiting deprive brand owners from obtaining a return on the large investment, which are required to develop innovations (Grossman and Shapiro 1988). Therefore, and according to this strand of thinking, innovators, in order to avoid imitation, should improve overall market efficiency, match consumers' preferences with their own innovations, and register the trademarks of their products (Landes and Posner 1987: 269). The government has a role in protecting innovators against imitators, by facilitating organized intellectual property systems (North 1981). Retaliation measures such as protectionism are considered to be costly (Globerman 1988). Other economists have an opposite view and consider imitation and counterfeiting to be natural market reactions to situations in which easily reproduced goods are selling at exorbitant prices (Bagwell and Bernheim 1986). Without denying the ethics dimension of imitation and counterfeiting, they question the extent to which these practices actually damage brands or reduce their sales (Staake *et al.* 2009).

From the consumer's point of view, imitation can also be a form of competition, which helps to develop healthy and efficient markets (Schnaars 1994). Imitation can act as a strategic tool by increasing the distribution of products, technologies, and also ways of doing business when entering new markets. New product features and lower prices may benefit consumers by making goods and services more practical, useful, affordable, or accessible. Imitation also impacts on the welfare of consumers, by using the language of brands, as brand names represent information about a variety of attributes linked to a product, making it easy for consumers to talk or take decisions about products (McDonald and Roberts 1994). When imitators make use of existing brands that is called counterfeiting. Counterfeit is defined here as any good bearing, without authorization, a trademark which cannot be distinguished in its essential aspects from the trademark registered by the innovator for such goods (OECD/EUIPO 2016). Counterfeit is therefore a "direct" copy.[3] But imitations are also considered to misguide consumers and leave them worse off (Wilke and Zaichkowsky 1999). The argument is that it all depends on the ease of imitation, the type of imitation, and the information that consumers have about the quality of the imitators' goods (Teece 1988).

There are also psychological and cultural-ethical discussions about imitation and its impact (Zaichkowsky 2006). The ethical debate is not so obvious in nations which are importers of intellectual property (Chaudhry and Walsh 1996; McDonald and Roberts 1994). Many of the countries where imitation and counterfeiting flourishes are also highly collectivist in nature (Green and Smith 2002). Intellectual property rights seem to be better protected in individualistic countries (Ronkainen and Guerrero-Cusumano 2001).

Historical research agrees with other disciplines, confirming that imitation is a complex phenomenon and it is not possible to provide generalizations. It also shows that no single country has ever been free from imitation, piracy, and counterfeiting. It is possible to find evidence of such practices going back 2000 years, to civilizations such as Babylonian and Egyptian (Hopkins 2002). In *Fraud, Counterfeiting, and Contraband from Antiquity to Today* (Béaur *et al.* 2007), which compiles an impressive collection of historical essays, imitations and fraudulent and illegal practices are shown to have always been an important part of the market economy, and a persistent force behind the globalization of markets. State repression was always unable to stop those practices completely. Imitation, counterfeiting, piracy, forgery, and smuggling "underline" the inability of the market alone to regulate the mechanism of confrontation among producers, between producers and consumers, and between producers and public authorities.

Industries that developed in the nineteenth century, as diverse as publishing and banking in the United States, flourished as a result of imitation-driven practices by entrepreneurs who took advantage of loopholes in the law and also the slowness of regulatory institutions to protect consumers and investors (Khan 2005; Mihm 2007; Balleisen 2017, among others). In some cases, imitation of the same product had negative impacts, leading firms to withdraw their investments; while in others it led them to invest further in foreign markets by using modes of entry involving higher risk and control. An example is Pears soap, a very successful translucent British soap, which, at the time it was acquired by Lever Brothers in 1915, was a highly internationalized brand. Soon after the acquisition Lever's management had to deal with the huge number of imitators across different countries, which resulted from the success of the brand due to its innovative character and also marketing strategy. While in markets not considered strategic and where legal protection for intellectual property was weak the firm decided to withdraw; in other markets, considered to be more strategic, Lever Brothers increased their presence through the creation of wholly owned distribution channels, in substitution of agents working on commission (Lopes and Casson 2012).

Imitation in wines

Wines are one of the goods most affected by imitation and adulteration historically. The period starting in the last decades of the nineteenth century is, however, a particularly interesting one to study these phenomena (Gautier 1995; Stanziani 2003; Castro Coello 2004; Simpson 2011; Lopes and Casson 2012). A significant number of changes took place in the geography of production and international trade in wines, which was the main type of beverage traded globally. A series of diseases – oidium, phylloxera and mildew – affected all the vineyards in Europe from the 1850s, and that led to an abrupt drop in production across Europe. The countries affected by the diseases, the main wine producers, started to import wines to substitute the lack of local production, while simultaneously trying to replant the regions affected. All these joint initiatives led to a crisis of overproduction and a sharp drop in prices at the turn of the century (Simpson 2005). This transitional and unstable period created opportunities for the expansion of production and commercialization of imitations and adulterated wines worldwide (Lopes *et al.* 2017b). Some imitations resulted from wines which were produced artificially in Europe, in both traditionally producing and also in consuming countries. Wines were mixed with other chemical additives, dry grapes, water, industrial alcohol, and sugar, among other substances, which were added to fortify, provide color, or change the characteristics of the wines. These practices became frequent by different types of imitators in the global value chain, in particular by "wine manufacturers" (as imitators of wines were known), and wholesalers (Loubère 1978; Lachiver 1988; Pan-Montojo 1994). Imitation wines tended to be sold at cheaper prices; and often used fake denominations of origin with high and established reputation (Ramos 2010; Cardoso 2002).

A second type of imitation wines resulted from the production of imitations in new wine regions in the New World, in particular, Argentina, Algeria, Australia, and California in the United States (Lachiver 1988; Simpson 2011; Pinilla and Ayuda 2007). Indeed, they imitated production technologies and denominations of origin such as Jerez, Porto, and Marsala, names of regions which very quickly became known as generic beverages: they were written in lower case, in the same way as generic names of beverages like wine, water, or beer (Lachiver 1988; Morilla-Critz 1997; Lacoste 2003; Simpson 2011).

The attractiveness of foreign "styles" of wines in the New World is also associated with a large number of immigrants who arrived during the nineteenth and early twentieth centuries, in particular from Spain and Italy. They preferred to drink wines with certain characteristics associated with reputed regions in the Old World, in particular their own countries of origin. These countries were considered to have "identity poisoning" as foreign and local entrepreneurs, associated with the lack of action by the state, took advantage of these opportunities associated with nostalgia and acquired habits of consumption, by creating local wines which used reputed regions of origin (Lacoste *et al.* 2014). These contributed to explain the growing accusations of copycats and imitations in these regions of the world. Other alcoholic beverages sectors also affected by imitations were spirits and beer, but these sectors were mainly controlled by foreign companies or importers, most of whom were European immigrants.

Countries producers of imitation wines resisted international laws aimed at recognizing denominations of origin, as they considered theirs to be legitimate business given that they had adopted technologies used in the production of wines from reputed regions to the production of some "styles" of wines. They argued that they were not misleading the final consumer, given that they associated the product and the technology used to its real traditions but also informed them about the origin of the product (for example, Hamburg Port, Spanish Madeira, British Sherry, and Portuguese Champagne). They often mentioned that it was a wine produced using the "style" of wines from a particular region, and not that it was from that region. In many of these cases, these imitations of wines from reputed geographical regions also worked as substitutes to imports, stimulated both by technological and scientific innovations, by the expansion of the consumption of special wines, and also by the volatility in the international wine trade.

There are no clear historical estimates of the volumes of imitation and adulteration in wines. But it is possible to have an idea about its significance by looking at a series of proxies. For example, these include the number of protests by wine growers from highly reputed wine regions; the articles and advertisements published in newspapers about this phenomena; the treaties and regulations created by governments to protect geographical denominations of origin; and the number of conferences and conventions to protect intellectual property rights associated with both collective and commercial trademarks initiated by wine producers and traders (Simões 1932; Lopes and Duguid 2010: ch. 1).

There are, however, some partial estimates of the volume of imitation in wines, at country, regional, and product type level. For instance, in 1872, Great Britain was considered to be the country where most adulterated wines were sold, with imitations corresponding to approximately 20 percent of wine imports into the country (Simpson 2011: 95). In 1907 discussions in the Portuguese parliament mentioned that, out of 60,000 barrels of port wine exported, only one-third related to wines produced with grapes from the Douro region (from where port wine comes from) (Sousa 1907: 38). In that same year, more than 50,000 barrels of counterfeiting "port" were produced in California (Morilla-Critz 1997). Lopes *et al.* (2017b) compare the evolution of global wine trade with the total evolution of world trade, and argue that the dissemination of imitations in alcoholic beverages impacted on the sharp decline of the global wine trade. That contrasted with the fast growth of world trade in goods and foreign direct investment during this period, which as previously mentioned, is known as the first globalization wave of the world economy (Wilkins 1989; Jones 2005).

The regulatory environment: geographical denominations of origin

In the late nineteenth century, even after trademark laws for commercial marks were passed in many countries, there was no international legal system of protection of regions and geographical denominations of origin. That meant that imitators could easily appropriate the long-established reputation of certain categories of beverages, with reputations strongly linked to specific climates, soils in which the grapes used to produce certain wines developed, and casts of grapes (Lopes 1999).

Several wine-producing regions tried, as early as the eighteenth century, to deal with this risk of appropriation of collective reputation, by creating geographical demarcated regions for growing grapes used in the production of wines.[4] The widespread use of fake regional brands or fictitious geographical designations of origin at the end of the nineteenth century turned this into one of the most complex questions in international trademark law. It proved very hard to create harmonization among the countries, as they had different interests, and agricultural heritages. For instance, from the mid-1860s, the lack of regulation of the Douro region, which had been regulated from 1756 until 1865, facilitated the appropriation of a very reputed regional designation even by wine producers from other regions of Portugal. The same problem occurred in other reputed wine producing regions. As a result of this widespread practice of imitation of geographical denominations of origin, international law started to develop mechanisms for the protection of collective intellectual property and in favor of harmonization of laws, with the organization of international conventions, from the early 1880s. Although this principle was considered in the Convention of Paris in 1883, it did not have any practical applicability (Almeida 1999: 144). This led countries, producers of more reputed wines such as France, Spain, and Portugal, to fight for clarification with regards to denominations of origin. After the Convention of Rome 1886, the Madrid Convention in 1891 which aimed to repress the false denominations of origin was an important step in that direction (Holtmann 1992). Nonetheless, only eight countries signed the agreement – Brazil, Spain, France, Guatemala, Portugal, Great Britain, Switzerland, and Tunisia. Among these signatory countries there were some of the world's largest producers and exporters of wines (France, Spain, and Portugal), and also two of the most important importers (Great Britain and Brazil). The restricted number of countries limited the immediate legal effectiveness of the convention. The first stipulation concerning unfair competition was only adopted at the Brussels Conference of Revision in 1900, but no obligation was imposed on any country to afford remedies against acts such as imitation or counterfeiting (Ladas 1975: 1778). It was only at the Conference of The Hague in 1925 that the problem of international unfair competition was fully recognized.

The process through which some geographical denominations of origin, such as Bordeaux, the Douro (port wine region), and the Champagne region, were protected before international legislation came into place involved differentiated strategies. In some countries, such as in Spain in 1892, producers established enologic laboratories as a way to assure the quality and consistency of the characteristics of their wines. In other regions, such as in Champagne, firms invested collectively in the publicity of regional brands, through the creation and organization of associations. In the Champagne region, in 1882 the Syndicat du Commerce des Vins de Champagne was established, gathering more than 50 of the most well-known champagne brand owners, leading to the creation of the principles of denomination of origin. This was the result of the concerted actions of several producers, who advertised "pure champagne", produced in the region of Champagne using traditional techniques, against the use of the designation "champagne" as a generic name to sparkling wines produced in other regions of France and abroad (Guy 2003: 24–26).

In the beginning of the twentieth century, some of the wine producing countries created legally protected geographic denominations of origin. From 1905, the French government launched a series of laws, which culminated between 1908 and 1912, in the demarcation and regulation of production of various regions, which became controlled denominations of origin: Champagne, Cognac, Armagnac, Banyuls, and Bordeaux (Unwin 1991: 314). Also in Portugal, the law from 10 May 1907 re-established the demarcation of the Douro region and regulated the production and trade of port wine, creating also other denominations of origin in Portugal (fortified wines of Madeira, Carcavelos, and Moscatel from Setúbal; and also table wines from Colares, Bucelas, Dão, Bairrada, Borba, Torres, Cartaxo, Alcobaça, Douro, Vinhos Verdes – Minho, Amarante, Basto, Fuzeta, and Monção).

The principles used in the creation of geographical denominations of origin were accepted and disseminated throughout the twentieth century in Europe. But there continued to exist a great difficulty in harmonization with new producing countries, in particular in the New World, where wine was considered to be a manufactured good, with no connection or acknowledgment of the concept of denomination of origin. In Argentina it is from 1923 that the concern behind the excessive use of European denominations of origin for consumer products – including wines – lead to the passing of the Merchandise Identification Law (Breuer-Moreno 1946: 591–593). In fact, the official purpose of this law was to make obligatory that all articles manufactured in Argentina bore the label *Industria Argentina* (Argentine industry) a step taken by other countries as well. In Chile, Pisco brandies gained legal protection for denomination of origin in 1931 (Lacoste *et al.* 2014).

At the level of commercial or individual trademarks it was easier to reach some international harmonization since the last quarter of the nineteenth century. In fact, modern trademarks began with the creation of national registration systems during the second half of the nineteenth century (Wilkins 1992; Lopes and Duguid 2010). Most European countries (France 1857, Great Britain 1876, Portugal 1883), the United States, and many Latin American countries, set up national registration systems. Except for some Central American countries, most Latin American countries enacted their trademark laws before 1900, with Chile (1874) and Brazil (1875) pioneering this process. Argentina passed its first law on trademarks in 1876 (Act #787).

Strategies for imitation in wines

In the wine industry, it is possible to identify different types of strategies of imitation of commercial (or individual trademarks) and collective trademarks (with geographical origin). The meaning and the ethics associated with each type of strategy vary over time. They result from multiple factors, such as the level of regulation and the scope of activities, being the most significant ones. A trademark is a name, symbol, or other device that acts as a distinguishing feature of a product or of an entire range of products. It is part of the branding process.[5] And it is a crucial means for the conveyance and building of reputation, especially when extended distribution networks undermine the traditional familiarity between buyer and seller (Wilkins 1992: 68; Ramello 2006; Higgins 2010). The reputation effects conveyed by trademarks can assist new entries into markets where high search costs would otherwise represent a significant barrier to entry (Griffiths 2011). Collective trademarks are distinctive from commercial trademarks, in the sense that they are used by a group of entities (not just one) to identify themselves with a certain geographical region, and a certain level of quality.

Imitator entrepreneurs may follow different alternative imitation strategies in wines. Some imitate the product only but not the trademark. Others imitate the commercial (or individual) trademark; a third group may imitate the collective trademark (e.g. region); and a fourth group may imitate both – the commercial and collective trademark. When a product is imitated but not the trademark, the imitation is associated with the production of look-alikes (also known as copycats) (Horen 2010), but there is no trademark infringement. This is considered to be legitimate business, associated with processes of competition, or even with the first steps toward incremental innovation. In nineteenth century Spain, the modernization of "Rioja" wines is an example of imitation of a product – "Bordeaux" type of wines – with no imitation of the trademark. The expansion and modernization of the Rioja region, in the second half of the nineteenth century was the result, to a large extent, of techniques used for the production of wines in the Bordeaux region, where expressions such as "médoc alavês" or "médoc riojano" were being used. Sometimes, the actual technicians hired for the production of the Rioja wines were former employees in the Bordeaux wine region. The name of some firms and estates created during this period, such as "Bodegas Franco-Españolas" (1890) or "Chateau Ygay" (1893), also illustrate the French influence in the establishment of the Rioja region. The commercial flow of wines between Rioja and the Bordeaux region developed in the 1880s, as a result of phylloxera which had affected the Bordeaux wine production, and the fact that Rioja wines were attractive to former consumers of Bordeaux wines because of the taste and techniques used in its production.

In the beginning of the following decade, in the 1890s, with the reconstruction of many vineyards in France, the increase in imports of wines from Algeria, and the protectionist measures imposed by the French government, the imports of wines from Rioja and other foreign regions to France almost stopped (Gómez Urdáñez 2000: 62–66). As a result, the wine producers from Rioja, which had made large investments in the previous decade, had to change their strategies, trying to sell their wines in the domestic market and in other foreign markets, marketing those wines with French designations. For example, Bodegas Bilbainas traded, in the beginning of the twentieth century, among other beverages, "Cognac Faro", "Rioja Clarete", "Cepa Borgoña", and "Cepa Sauternes" (Gómez Urdáñez 2000: 78). Another illustration of a strategy of imitation without trademark infringement is the case of the Spanish sparkling wine "Cava", which developed around the same time, mainly in the region Catalunha. This type of sparkling wine developed as an imitation to "champagne", but with a different name (Pan-Montojo 1994: 352).

Another type of imitation strategy refers to cases where there is no imitation of the product type but there is imitation of the commercial or individual trademark. An illustration is Hiram Walker & Son the trademark known for Scottish whisky and owned in the late nineteenth century by the company with the same name. However, in Argentina, while Hiram Walker & Son registered the code of arms of the family a trademark for whisky in 1889 (trademarks 1686 and 1687), in 1893, Fernando Rossi, an Argentinian company, registered the same trademark for selling locally made "cognac" (trademark number 3639).

Imitation can also refer to cases where the product is not imitated but the collective trademark is. The imitator applies the collective trademark to one of his own products, rather than to a copy of the innovative good or service. It basically refers to cases of trademark infringement, or unauthorized brand extension. Here trademark infringement relates to the misuse of the geographical denomination of origin. Apart from the "cava" example provided above, in Brazil, in the last quarter of the nineteenth century firms registered trademarks which combined multiple reputed denominations of origin such as "cognac muscatel", "cognac fine champagne". These were artificial wines mostly manufactured in Rio de Janeiro and São Paulo.[6] Foreign imitators of reputed wines followed a similar practice. There is evidence of port wines originally from Hamburg, Tarragona, California, and other origins, and registered in different countries as genuine trademarks. There are also multiple examples of trademarks registered by foreign merchants such as "Cognac Gayarre" and "Cognac Tamarez" from Spain, and "Ginebra Llave" from Argentina.[7] In Portugal, at the end of the nineteenth century, there was a fashion among the urban middle classes, of drinking foreign beverages, in particular cognacs and champagnes. The adverts and trademark registrations from that period, apart from the original wines and spirits imported, also include a large number of imitation trademarks of such "styles" of foreign beverages produced in Portugal.

The most damaging scenario for the innovator relates, however, to those cases which involve the imitation of the product or service and also the trademark. Counterfeit goods are very likely to confuse the consumer and thereby take trade away from the innovator (Lopes and Casson 2012). In such cases the imitation of the trademark can relate to the commercial or individual trademark, or the collective trademark. For genuine nineteenth and early twentieth century wine producers, the fact that in most cases they were exported in barrels, that made imitation and adulteration easier at various points in the value chain. The press in different countries mentioned many cases of barrels which had the label of famous wines and spirits traders, and also bottles with famous brands which, once emptied, were refilled by producers of fraudulent wines, spirits, and beers, trying to take advantage of the reputation of established alcoholic beverages brands (Breuer-Moreno 1946: 400).[8] For example, a leading British wine merchant Gilbey's sued a grocer and wine and spirits merchant Wilkinson and Co. for using returned Gilbey's bottles and filling them with other spirits, without removing the original labels.[9]

Imitation through the misuse of the collective denomination of origin was the most common form of imitation of wines in the late nineteenth and early twentieth centuries. In many cases there was double counterfeit: imitation of the product and of both the commercial and collective trademarks. There are multiple cases of trademark registrations of imitations of "champagne", "madeira", "port", "sauternes", "Malaga", and French chateaux.[10] Registrations of imitations and adulterated beverages sometimes included more sophisticated names such as "Champagne Portugais Extra Dry", "Porto style", and "Champagne style". For example, many wines were circulated in the market with the label "port", and were produced in Lisbon, Tarragona, Sète, Hamburg, Cape Town, California, among other places (Simões 1932). The producers of such mixtures advertised themselves as "manufacturers of port wine" (Loubère 1978; Lachiver 1988; Pan Montojo 1994). Department stores, such as Armazéns Grandella, a market leader in Lisbon at the turn of the century, also registered trademarks such as "Château-Bordeaux", a wine produced in Benfica, a district of Lisbon. They were blamed by farmers and wine producers for creating a commercial crisis, and also for generating a lack of trust among consumers (Burnett 1999; Loubère 1978).

Innovators' strategies for dealing with imitation

In many countries such as Brazil and Portugal, the first years after trademark laws were passed, the process of registration was not effective as imitations were also registered as trademarks, and enforcement was very ineffective or nonexistent. Firms both with national and international activity had to find alternative ways to deal with such business risks associated with imitation (Lopes and Casson 2012; Lopes *et al.*, 2017a). Apart from conventional advertising strategies, firms sometimes used letters of apology sent by imitators which resulted from the brand owners' threats of ligation, as a way to show to the public how committed they were to sell genuine beverages. These pieces of news also alerted consumers that their products were genuine and of trusted quality, and informed indirectly potential imitators of the risks they faced of prosecution. For example, in Argentina Fratelli Branca, a producer of Italian liqueur published a note in eight newspapers to inform the public that they had no relation with an Argentinian producer of imitations who was trying to associate himself with the firm, through the widower of Luigi Branca.[11] This campaign appeared in national, regional, and local newspapers.

As a result, some firms developed marketing and technological innovations. An illustration is Gilbey's, which by the 1930s had its labels so widely copied that the company had to set up a special service to identify them. Often, only the printer could tell by the watermark if they were genuine. One ingenious racketeer bottled imitation Gilbey's gin in elaborately decorated cans, stating that no others were genuine (Waugh 1957: 91–92). To protect the consumer from spurious products, a square gin bottle was also produced. It was sand-blasted on three sides, with the label printed on both sides and visible through the one clear side. This was very difficult and costly to imitate.

Another way firms had of dealing with imitation was through the formation of horizontal alliances between competitors, or by creating vertical alliances with agents in the value chain (forward into retailing, or backward into production). An illustration is the alliance created by four companies Otard Dupoy y Cía. (France), Fratelli Branca (Italy), Cinzano (Italy), José Deu y Cía. (Spain and Argentina) between 1913 and 1917, to jointly take legal action against all imitators in the value chain (producers, wholesalers, and retailers of imitations of their own beverages). These allied companies not only sought litigation against imitators, manufacturers of fake liqueurs and vermouth, but also against the small traders in rural villages in Argentina who they accused of being accomplices by selling the imitated and counterfeited goods.[12]

Forward and backward integration was another strategy used by firms to prevent and mitigate imitation of their beverages. From the mid-1870s, the crisis in the global wine industry made it very difficult for large wine retailers such as the British firm Gilbey's to control the quality of the wines they were selling. Gilbey's depended traditionally on leading shippers in Jerez and Porto to select the wines they sold using the "Gilbey's" brand. This uncertainty led the company to integrate backward and purchase Château Loudenne in the Médoc in 1875. This investment reduced information costs associated with the firm's searches to buy suitable wines from local growers, and also cut operating costs (Faith 1983; Simpson 2011: 100). Other wine merchants followed this trend, and that eventually led to a change in the relations between the different agents in the global value chain.

In some cases, vertical integration meant investing forward in distribution in foreign markets through the establishment of commercial branches and/or the appointment of exclusive agents, or even the setting up of industrial facilities. In Argentina, firms such as Cinzano, Martini & Rossi, and Florio followed their consumers who had immigrated to foreign markets around the turn of the century.[13] Vertical integration allowed firms to overcome transaction costs. Exports through third parties were threatening their reputation, as imitators often acted opportunistically by trying to sell their beverages as if they were genuine.

Conclusion

This chapter provides a brief overview of the literature on imitation and the contribution of imitators as makers of global business. By focusing on the case of wines, historically one of the most internationally trade goods and also one of the most imitated, it offers an overview of the multiple dimensions and impacts of imitation on the making of global business, and on the strategies followed by both imitations and innovators in different institutional environments.

The wine industry was one of the earliest and most globalized in the world. It suffered a major backlash during the first wave of globalization, countering the growth trend in other industries during this period. Vineyards in the main European wine producing regions were devastated by various diseases since the 1850s. As a result, imitation and adulteration of wines spread, involving different agents within the global value chain. In the short-term this led to a lack of trust by consumers, and a decrease in international wine trade and wine consumption, in particular in traditional wine drinking markets.

In the medium and long run, imitation led to the development of global business. A new wine industry developed in most New World countries out of the production of wines, which were imitations of European wines, and used reputed denominations of origin. In these countries, consumption of wines increased very fast, in part because of the increase of supply of wines at cheaper prices, but mainly because of the large number of European immigrants and expatriates from Southern European countries. Governments in New World countries also created tariffs and other protective barriers for imports, and provided subsidies to help local entrepreneurs to develop new wine industries.

Imitation and adulteration had other consequences which impacted on the long-term making of the global wine business. It led to the creation of national and international trademark law;

the development of marketing and technological innovations; to processes of concentration in the industry; and to shifts in the power relations by agents involved in global value chains. Some firms formed alliances with competitors; others integrated forward into distribution, backward into production, or both. Imitation also had also a social and cultural impact. It disseminated habits of alcohol consumption around the world, in particular of certain categories of wines drunk by consumers with distinct social and economic income levels, and which would not have had purchasing power to drink the original wines. Because imitation and adulteration wines were cheaper, they could be consumed by people who would not have been able to drink the genuine beverages.

As with imitations of consumer goods in other industries, during the late nineteenth century and early twentieth century, imitations of wines were not originating from countries such as China, but rather from more developed countries, many of which throughout the twentieth century became leading economies such as the United States. While imitators, in the short term, might have impacted negatively on globalization by leading to sharp decrease in wine trade, the long-term implications in the making of global business were positive, as they helped disseminating production and consumption around the world.

Notes

1 Bolivia, Chile, Costa Rica, Ecuador, Nicaragua, Peru, Uruguay, and Venezuela. First usage was decisive in El Salvador, Honduras, Colombia, Mexico, and Panama. Brazil, opted for a mixed system.

2 *The Americas*, National City Bank of New York, 1915, May, 1(8), 15. However, Argentina and the South American countries were not the worst cases of trademark piracy according to information provided by the American Manufacturers' Export Association in 1922.

3 Illicit trading includes a wide variety of illegal or non-contractual activities, such as traffic in controlled substances, stolen and smuggled goods, trade of all kinds with products infringing intellectual property rights, and even parallel imports (Staake *et al.* 2009).

4 The first geographic boundaries were created for Chianti and Carmignano wines from Italy as early 1716, and for Tokay wines from the region of Tokaj-Hegyalja, Hungary, in 1737. Portugal follows in 1756 for the Alto Douro, the port wine production region (Unwin 1991).

5 A brand may be defined as an identity that differentiates a product from substitutes by associating it with specific characteristics. These characteristics may be objective, such as performance and reliability, or subjective, such as an association with particular celebrities or lifestyles. Brands are often used to signal quality and to enhance the perceived status of the consumer. They are particularly useful in signaling the value of nondurable goods in order to encourage repeat buys, as a memorable brand makes it easy for the consumer to recognize the product subsequently (Lopes 2002).

6 As illustrations for the case of Brazil, A. Cardoso Gouvêa & Comp. America do Sul registered trademark number 4697 "A. C. G. & Co. – Fino Champagne – Cognac" in 1906. He was a producer of beer liqueurs, syrups alcohol, and brandy in Rio de Janeiro. Alfredo F. Gomes Savedra, a producer and merchant of vinagre, syrup, and other beverages based in Rio de Janeiro, registered the trademark number 3957 "Ginebra Superior Savedra" in 1904.

7 See for example in Brazil trademark number 1467.

8 Argentina, Federal Court, *Emilio Gabay v. Juan Teic*, 1930, Patentes y Marcas, 1930: 363.

9 "Wine Merchants' Trade Mark Case", 23.

10 For example in Portugal there were registrations of "champagnes" from Bombarral (a town located in the middle west of Portugal), "Champagne de água-pé" (champagne from the alcoholic beverage made by pouring water on the husks of the grapes), "champagne de piquette", "champagne de mistura" (mixed champagne), as well as "champagnes" from Bairrada (a region south of Porto). Similar cases in Brazil include "cognac the Adrião", "cognac the carvão" (cognac made of coal), "superior ginebra", "champagne fino – produzido no Brazil" (fine champagne produced in Brazil), "Malaga from Brazil", "Porto Brazileiro", "Vinho de collares produce in Rio", "Château Rauzan" from Rio de Janeiro, "Alto Minho – Vinho Verde" produced in Rio de Janeiro, among others.

11 "Al Comercio y al Público", *Las Novedades* (1 October 1892).

12 Box 19, Reg. 312, 1917, File, A-1169, No. 321. "SA Importadora de Productos Cinzano y otros versus Pedro Aguirre", Falsificación. Usurpación de marca (Archivo Histórico Provincial Santa Rosa, La Pampa, Argentina).
13 In 1923, Cinzano opened its first industrial facility abroad, interested in maintaining its market share and the quality of its Vermouth (*Dinámica Social*, 74, November to December (1956): 69).

References

Almeida, Alberto Francisco Ribeiro de (1999), "Denominação de Origem e Marca", *Studia Luridica, 39* (Coimbra: Universidade de Coimbra Editora).
Bagwell, Laurie Simon, and B. Douglas Bernheim (1986), "Veblen Effects in a Theory of Conspicuous Consumption", *American Economic Review*, 86(3), 349–373.
Balleisen, Edward (2017), *Fraud: An American History from Barnum to Madoff, United States* (Princeton, NJ: Princeton University Press).
Barry, Gabriel, and N. Thrift (2007), "Gabriel Tarde: Imitation, Invention and Economy", *Economy and Society*, 36(4), 509–525.
Baumol, William J. (1990), "Entrepreneurship: Productive, Unproductive, and Destructive", *Journal of Political Economy*, 98 (5), Part 1 (October), 893–921.
Baumol, William J. (2010), *The Microtheory of Innovative Entrepreneurship* (Princeton, NJ: Princeton University Press).
Béaur, Gerard, Hubert Bonin, and Claire Lemercier (eds) (2007), *Fraude, Contrefaçon et Contrebande de l'Antiquité à nos Jours* [Fraud, Counterfeiting, and Contraband from Antiquity to Today] (Geneva: Droz).
Bently, Lionel (2009), "From Communication to Thing: Historical Aspects of the Conceptualisation of Trade Marks as Property", in G. Dinwoodie and M. Janis (eds), *Trade Mark Law and Theory: A Handbook of Contemporary Research* (Cheltenham: Edward Elgar), 3–41.
Bently, Lionel, Jane C. Ginsburg, and Jennifer Davis (2008), "The Making of Modern Trade Marks Law: The Construction of the Legal Concept of Trade Mark (1860–80)", in L. Bently, Jane C. Ginsburg, and J. Davis (eds), *Trade Marks and Brands: An Interdisciplinary Critique* (Cambridge: Cambridge University Press), 3–40.
Berg, Maxine (2002), "From Imitation to Invention: Creating Commodities in Eighteenth-Century Britain", *Economic History Review*, 55, 1–30.
Breuer-Moreno, Pedro C. (1946), *Tratado de Marcas de Fábrica y de Comercio*, 2nd edition (Buenos Aires: Editorial Robis).
Burnett, John (1999), *Liquid Pleasure: A Social History of Drinks in Modern Britain* (London: Routledge).
Callman, Rudolf (1969), *The Law of Unfair Competition, Trademarks and Monopolies.* (Mundelein, IL: Callaghan).
Cardoso, António Barros (2002), "Vinhos do Porto e Vinhos Portugueses Fabricados no Rio de Janeiro (1885)", in Javier Maldonado Rosso (ed.), *Actas del I Simposio de la Asociación Internacional de Historia y Civilización de la Vid y el Vino*. Vol. 2. (El Puerto de Santa María: Asociación Internacional de Historia y Civilización de la Vid y el Vino), 793–859.
Castro Coello (2004), "De la Identificación de los Vinos: Clases, Typos y Orígenes. De los Vinos Típicos, Artificiales y Facticios. Una Exposición Previa", in Alberto Vieira (ed.), *Actas do III Simpósio da Associação Internacional de História e Civilização da Vinha e do Vinho* (Funchal: Centro de Estudos de História do Atlântico), 793–859.
Chandler, Alfred (1994), *Scale and Scope: The Dynamics of Industrial Capitalism.* (Cambridge, MA: Belknap Press).
Chaudhry, Peggy E., and Michael G. Walsh (1996), "An Assessment of the Impact of Counterfeiting in International Markets: The Piracy Paradox Persists", *Columbia Journal of World Business*, 31(3), 34–48.
Faith, N. (1983), *Victorian Vineyard: Château Loudenne and the Gilbeys* (London: Constable).
Gautier, Jean-François (1995), *Le Vin et ses Fraudes* (Paris: Presses Universitaires de France).
Globerman, Steven (1988), "Addressing International Product Piracy", *Journal of International Business Studies*, 19(3), 497–504.
Gómez Urdáñez, José Luis (ed.) (2000), *El Rioja histórico: La Denominación de Origen y su Consejo Regulador* (Logroño: Consejo Regulador de la Denominación de Origen Calificada Rioja).
Green, Robert, and Tasman Smith (2002), "Executive Insights: Countering Brand Counterfeiters", *Journal of International Marketing*, 10(4), 89–106.

Griffiths, Andrew (2011), *An Economic Perspective on Trade Mark Law* (Cheltenham: Edward Elgar).

Grossman, Gene M. and Carl Shapiro (1988), "Foreign Counterfeiting of Status Goods", *Quarterly Journal of Economics*, 103(1), 79–100.

Guy, Kolleen (2003), *When Champagne Became French: Wine and the Making of French Identity, 1820–1920* (Baltimore, MD: Johns Hopkins University Press).

Higgins, David (2010), "Trademarks and Infringement in Britain, c1875–1900", in Teresa da Silva Lopes and Paul Duguid (eds), *Trademarks, Brands and Competitiveness* (Abingdon: Routledge), 102–118.

Holtmann, Monika (ed.) (1992), *Arreglo de Madrid: Cien Años de Marcas Internacionales, 1891–1991* (Madrid: Ministerio de Industria, Comercio y Turismo/Oficina Española de Patentes y Marcas).

Hopkins, A. G. (2002), *Globalization in World History* (New York: Norton).

Horen, Femke van (2010), *Breaking the Mould on Copycats: What Makes Product Imitating Strategies Successful?* (Ridderkerk: Ridderprint Offsetdrukkerij BV).

Horii, Ryo, and Tatsuro Iwaisako (2007), "Economic Growth and Imperfect Protection of Intellectual Property Rights", *Journal of Economics*, 90(1), 45–85.

Jones, Geoffrey (2005), *Multinationals and Global Capitalism: From the Nineteenth to the Twenty-First Century* (Oxford: Oxford University Press).

Khan, B. Zorina (2005), *The Democratization of Invention: Patents and Copyrights in American Economic Development, 1790–1920* (Cambridge: Cambridge University Press).

Lachiver, Marcel (1988), *Vins, Vignes et Vignerons: Histoire du Vignoble Français* (Paris: Fayard).

Lacoste, Pablo (2003), *El Vino del Inmigrante: Los Inmigrantes Europeos y la Industria Vitivinícola Argentina: Su Incidencia en la Incorporación, Difusión y Estandarización del uso de Topónimos Europeos 1852–1980* (Mendoza: Consejo Empresario Mendocino).

Lacoste, Pablo Alberto, Jiménez Cabrera, Diego Ingacio, Briones Quiroz, Félix Maximiano, Castro San Carlos, Amalia, Rendón Zapata, Bibiana Marcela, Jeffs Munizaga, and José Gabriel (2014), "Burdeos de Talca y Champagne de Mendoza: Denominaciones de Origen y contaminación identitaria de vinos en Argentina y Chile", *Mundo Agrario*, 15(29), 1–25.

Ladas, Stephen (1975), *Patents, Trademarks, and Related Rights: National and International Protection* (Cambridge, MA: Harvard University Press.).

Landes, William M. and Richard A. Posner (1987), "Trademark Law: An Economic Perspective", *Journal of Law and Economics*, 30(2), 265–309.

Landes, William M. and Richard A. Posner (2003), *The Economic Structure of Intellectual Property Law* (Cambridge, MA: Belknap Press).

Levitt, Theodore (1966), "Innovative Imitation", *Harvard Business Review* (September–October), 63–70.

Lopes, Teresa da Silva (1999), *Internacionalização e Concentração no Vinho do Porto, 1945–1995* (Porto: ICEP/GEHVID).

Lopes, Teresa da Silva (2002), "Brands and the Evolution of Multinationals in Alcoholic Beverages", *Business History*, 44(3), 1–30.

Lopes, Teresa da Silva, and Mark Casson (2012), "Brand Protection and Globalization of British Business", *Business History Review*, 86(2), 287–310.

Lopes, Teresa da Silva, and Paul Duguid (2010), *Brands, Trademarks and Competitiveness* (London: Routledge).

Lopes, Teresa da Silva, Carlos Gabriel Guimarães, Alexandre Saes, and Luiz Fernando Saraiva (2017a), "The 'Disguised' Foreign Investor: Brands, Trademarks and the British Expatriate Entrepreneur in Brazil", *Business History*, 59(2017), 1–25.

Lopes, Teresa da Silva, Andrea Lluch, and Gaspar Martins Pereira (2017b), "Imitation in Global Business: The Case of Alcoholic Beverages". Paper presented at the Annual BHC Conference Denver (30 March – 1 April 2017).

Loubère, Leo (1978), *The Red and the White: A History of Wine in France and Italy in the Nineteenth Century* (Albany, NY: State University of New York Press).

McDonald, Gael, and Christopher Roberts (1994), "Product Piracy: The Problem that Will not Go Away", *Journal of Product and Brand Management*, 3(4), 55–65.

Maskus, Keith E. (2000), *Intellectual Property Rights in the Global Economy*. (Washington, DC: Peterson Institute of International Economics).

Mihm, Stephen (2007), *A Nation of Counterfeiters: Capitalists, Con Men and the Making of the United States* (Cambridge, MA: Harvard University Press).

Morilla-Critz, José (1997), "A Califórnia e o Vinho do Porto entre Dois Séculos", *Douro. Estudos & Documentos*, 3, 123–141.

Naylor, R. T. (2014), *Counterfeit Crime: Criminal Profits, Terror Dollars, and Nonsense* (Montreal: McGill-Queen's University Press).

North, Douglass C. (1981), *Structure and Change in Economic History* (New York: Norton).

OECD/EUIPO (2016), *Trade in Counterfeit and Pirated Goods: Mapping the Economic Impact* (Paris: OECD).

Pan-Montojo, Juan (1994), *La Bodega Del Mundo: La Vid y el Vino en España (1800–1936)* (Madrid: Alianza Editorial).

Pereira, Gaspar Martins (2009), *O Nome do Vinho: Marcas e Denominações dos Vinhos Generosos do Douro, Séculos XVIII-XX* (Porto: FLUP) [mimeo].

Pinilla, V., and M. I. Ayuda (2007), "The International Wine Market, 1850–1938: An Opportunity for Export Growth in Southern Europe?", in G. Campbell and N. Gibert (eds), *Wine Society and Globalization: Multidisciplinary Perspectives on the Wine Industry* (New York: Palgrave Macmillan), 179–199.

Ramello, Giovanni B. (2006), "What's in a Sign? Trademark Law and Economic Theory", *Journal of Economic Surveys*, 20(4), 547–565.

Ramos, Luís A. de Oliveira (2010), "Contrafacções e Defesa da Marca 'Porto' em Finais do Século XIX", in Gaspar Martins Pereira (ed.), *Crise e Reconstrução: O Douro e o Vinho do Porto no século XIX* (Porto: Afrontamento), 335–353.

Ronkainen, Ilkka, and José-Luis Guerrero-Cusumano (2001), "Correlates of Intellectual Property Violation", *Multinational Business Review*, 9(1), 59–65.

Schnaars, Steven P. (1994), *Managing Imitation Strategies: How Later Entrants Seize Markets from Pioneers* (Don, Ontario: Free Press).

Schumpeter, Joseph A. (1949), "Economic Theory and Entrepreneurial History", in R. R. Wohl Can (ed.), *Change and the Entrepreneur: Postulates and the Patterns for Entrepreneurial History*, Research Center in Entrepreneurial History (Cambridge, MA: Harvard University Press).

Simões, J. de Oliveira (1896), "Marcas do País de Origem ou Contra- Marcas Nacionais", *Boletim da Propriedade Industrial*, 13 (19) 25.11.1896. (Lisboa: Ministério das Obras Públicas, Comércio e Indústria/ Imprensa Nacional), 200–201.

Simões, Nuno (1932), *Os Vinhos do Porto e a Defesa Internacional da sua Marca* (Coimbra: Imprensa da Universidade de Coimbra).

Simpson, James (2005), "Cooperation and Conflicts: Institutional Innovation in France's Wine Markets, 1870–1911", *Business History Review*, Autumn, 527–558.

Simpson, James (2011), *Creating Wine: The Emergence of a World Industry, 1840–1914* (Princeton, NJ: Princeton University Press).

Sousa, Teixeira de (1907), *A Questão do Douro* (Porto: Empresa Guedes).

Staake, Thorsten, Frédéric Thiesse, and Elgar Fleisch (2009), "The Emergence of Counterfeit Trade: A Literature Review", *European Journal of Marketing*, 43(3/4), 320–349.

Stanziani, Alessandro (2003), "La Falsification du Vin en France, 1880–1905: Un Cas de Fraude Agro-Alimentaire", *Revue D'Histoire Moderne et Contemporaine*, 50(2), 154–186.

Stanziani, Alessandro (2009), "Information, Quality and Legal Rules: Wine Adulteration in Nineteenth Century France", *Business History*, 51(2), 268–291.

Takenaka, Toshiko (ed.) (2013), *Intellectual Property in Common law and Civil Law* (Cheltenham: Edward Elgar).

Teece, David (1988), "Capturing Value from Technological Innovation: Integration, Strategic Planning, and Licensing Decisions", *Interfaces*, 18(3) (May–June), 46–61.

Unwin, Tim (1991), *Wine and the Vine* (London: Routledge).

US Chamber of Commerce (2016), "Creation of a Contemporary Global Measure of Physical Counterfeiting". Available at: www.uschamber.com/sites/default/files/documents/files/measuringthemagnitude ofglobalcounterfeiting.pdf (accessed 15 April 2019).

Waugh, Alex (1957), *Merchants of Wine: Being a Centenary Account of the House of Gilbey* (London: Cassell).

Wilke, Ricky, and Judith Lynne Zaichkowsky (1999), "Brand Imitation and its Effects on Innovation, Competition, and Brand Equity", *Business Horizons*, 42(6), 9–18.

Wilkins, Mira (1989), *The History of Foreign Direct Investment in the US to 1914.* (Cambridge, MA: Harvard University Press).

Wilkins, Mira (1992), "The Neglected Intangible Asset: The Influence of the Trade Mark on the Rise of the Modern", *Business History*, 34, 66–99.

Zaichkowsky, Judith Lynne (2006), *The Psychology behind Trademark Infringement and Counterfeiting* (Mahwah, NJ: Lawrence Erlbaum).

33

COMBATING CORRUPTION

Ishva Minefee and Marcelo Bucheli[1]

Introduction

This chapter studies efforts by governments to combat corruption between the Cold War and the 2010s. We show how Western powers shifted their stance toward corrupt activities of "their" multinational corporations (MNCs) abroad from turning a blind eye during the Cold War to gradually developing collective efforts to fight against corruption. The efforts to punish MNCs engaging in bribery abroad started in the United States of America with the adoption of the Foreign Corrupt Practices Act of 1977. For almost two decades, the United States was alone in this effort and the other Western powers did very little to fight against their MNCs' corrupt activities abroad. In the 1990s, however, other Western powers (mainly members of the Organisation for Economic Co-operation and Development [OECD]) joined the United States in developing a common front and practices to deal with this problem. We argue that efforts to fight corruption of domestic firms operating abroad are closely related to (a) big scandals that created social pressures for the government to fight against corruption; (b) external and political shocks that brought up to the surface existing corruption previously overlooked or ignored; and (c) pressures from the private sector to make the field of global business more competitive. Our chapter uses secondary sources in addition to the Public Papers of the Presidents of the United States for the Jimmy Carter administration, the United States Senate Church Committee Hearings on corruption, the United States General Accountability Office reports on global corruption, and reports on corruption published by the OECD.

Corruption and global business

At the time of this writing, corruption remains one of the most pressing challenges in global business. In a 1996 survey of high-ranking public officials and key members of civil society from more than 60 countries, respondents cited public sector corruption as "the most severe impediment to development and growth in their countries" (Gray and Kaufmann 1998: 7). Today, bribery alone is estimated to cost $1.5 to $2 trillion annually (International Monetary Fund 2016). Corruption – defined here as the abuse of public power for personal or private gain – permeates every society and represents an economic, legal, and ethical problem for national governments, international institutions, and MNCs.[2] It is a multifaceted phenomenon that affects the public and private sectors in both developed and developing countries. In tandem with the prevalence of corruption, however, there have been a multitude of institutional initiatives to reduce corruption. Although these initiatives have not eradicated corruption, they have shaped the landscape of global business practices and transactions.

There are various types of corruption in global business. The most common type of corruption is bribery, in which money and/or gifts are provided to foreign public officials in exchange for the procurement of business contracts or the facilitation of business transactions. In addition to bribery, MNCs may confront extortion, illicit taxes, and pressures for favors when they operate abroad (e.g., Doh *et al.* 2003).

Economic, political, legal, and cultural factors influence the prevalence of corruption across countries. Economic factors are often considered the primary contributors to corruption. For instance, Leite and Weidmann (1999) find that an abundance of natural resources in a country is positively correlated with corruption given that windfall gains present greater opportunities for corruption. Gutterman (2015) and Berghoff (2017) add that most cases of bribery from MNCs to government officials take place in the infrastructure and natural resources sectors, where there are large quantities of money involved, contracts require government approval, the sector is highly regulated by the government, and contracts are usually signed with just one firm (a "winner takes all" situation). High levels of economic inequality in countries also increase corruption as large numbers of the poor are more likely to be the targets of bureaucratic extortion in order to secure basic needs and services (e.g., You and Khagram 2005). Not all industrial sectors are equally affected by corruption. Politically, corruption is more prevalent in countries where authoritarian governments maintain power. Furthermore, corruption increases in countries where public officials have high levels of discretionary power (LaPorta *et al.* 1999; Rose-Ackerman 1997). Legally weak institutions also breed corruption as private property is not adequately protected (e.g., Rubin 1998). Culturally, corruption remains prevalent in high power-distance countries, in which less powerful members accept that power is distributed unequally, as subordinates often cover up scandals of their superiors due to an acceptance of questionable behavior (e.g., Husted 1999).

Corruption varies across countries on two general dimensions – pervasiveness (or level) and arbitrariness (uncertainty). According to Doh *et al.* (2003: 118), "the pervasiveness of corruption reflects the number and frequency of transactions (and individuals) with which (whom) the firm deals over the course of a fixed time period that involves illicit activities." The second dimension of corruption is arbitrariness, which refers to the predictability or uncertainty "of whom to pay, what to pay, and whether the payments will result in the promised goods or services" (Doh *et al.* 2003: 118). These dimensions intersect. If the pervasiveness of corruption is high but predictable, MNCs may perceive bribes as a tax or business expense. Conversely, when pervasiveness is low but arbitrariness is high, MNCs may not be able to estimate or budget for the costs of corruption.

All countries can be categorized along these dimensions. Attitudes toward corrupt activities of firms overseas have changed throughout time as well as efforts to fight against them. The following sections provide an overview of these changes focusing on the processes that sparked global efforts existing in the early twenty-first century.

So far away, so corrupt: denouncing corrupt activities overseas from the dawn of capitalism to the British Empire

The lack of control over the activities of firms or entrepreneurs abroad was considered for a long time a source of potential corrupt activities. This was apparent from when the newly created

European nation-states started their expansion beyond their continent. One example is that of the Spanish conquerors who defeated the indigenous communities in what is now known as Latin America. The Spanish conquest was not the result of a systematic military strategy led by the Spanish crown, but rather the result of a large number of uncoordinated private enterprises that armed themselves, crossed the Atlantic Ocean in their quest for gold, and legitimized their land grabbing by claiming the Spanish crown sovereignty over those lands. The process was chaotic and had no direct control from the Spanish authorities, who saw those conquerors as a potential destabilizing force composed of gold-thirsty thugs who abused the indigenous populations and did not follow the Spanish laws. Both the Catholic Church and members of the Spanish *Cortes* (parliament) wrote documents that harshly criticized the conquerors and legitimized the crown's efforts to control or punish them for their behavior. For the Spanish crown, the solution was more government presence in the Americas to stop the process of conquest from being one driven by private profits (Coatsworth *et al.* 2015; Velázquez 1991).

Corporations involved in the creation of the seventeenth and eighteenth centuries European empires were not free of criticism at home. Both the British and Dutch East India Companies were the focus of attention by many considering that the independence they had abroad allowed these organizations to follow corrupt behaviors that included the personal enrichment of some of their officials or government officials ruling areas of operation of both companies. In the eighteenth century, critics in Holland argued that officials of the Dutch East India Company made fortunes resulting from fraudulent businesses with the local societies (Nierstrasz 2012). An attempt led by Edmund Burke to impeach in the British Parliament the first governor general of India, Warren Hastings, in 1788–1795 led to a national debate on whether the activities of the East India Company were corrupt or not. In the end, Hastings was not impeached because those arguing that the benefits for the empire compensated the costs of corruption justified the firm's behavior (Dirks 2006). O'Neill (2017) adds that while Burke's criticisms of corrupt activities focused on individuals, Thomas Paine went further and focused on the East India Company as a corrupt organization.

Given their peculiar characteristics, organizations such as the East India companies are not considered MNCs, but proto-multinationals (Jones 2005). In fact, lots of the debates described here pointed to corrupt activities in territories formally acquired or "protected" by the imperial powers. The next section explores the first criticisms to corrupt activities by modern MNCs after the 1860s.

Modern multinationals and corruption in the first global economy

The first operations of modern MNCs started in the 1860s (Wilkins 1970), with growth patterns that differed depending on their home country characteristics. For the British case, for instance, many large multinationals started as such, partially because of the relatively small home market, lack of natural resources in Britain, or the advantages offered by the British empire (Wilkins 1988). For the case of US-based multinationals, on the other hand, most of these firms became large at home before moving abroad (Chandler 1980; Wilkins 1970, 1974). This section shows how attitudes and policies toward corruption abroad by American multinationals mirrored the ones toward big firms at home, especially when the multinational was accused of corrupt activities in the United States as well as abroad. When no accusations existed of corruption at home, corrupt activities abroad were largely ignored. We focus on the case of American firms because the United States eventually became the first country establishing clear rules punishing corrupt activities of "their" firms abroad.

1890–1972: from the progressive era to Watergate – journalism, Cold War, and domestic corruption in the United States

The creation of the large American corporations in the nineteenth century happened without serious political challenges. The men who came to be known as the "robber barons" built their fortunes in a political environment in which they could openly intervene in politics in order to protect their businesses, payments to politicians were part of the normal way of conducting business, and investigative journalism did not exist (Gentzkow *et al.* 2007). This meant that between the 1890s and 1910s corruption was rampant, particularly when it came to obtaining contracts for public works (Wallis 2007). Some actions were taken only in extreme cases when fraudulent operations harmed average citizens (Balleisen 2017). However, it was only after the 1920s, when major actions came from the government to control corruption. Wallis *et al.* (2007) posit that the expansion of the federal government, particularly after the Great Depression weakened local politicians' power to ask for bribes. The new role of the US government in the economy also translated into major pieces of legislation against bribery and fraud (Balleisen 2017). Additionally, in the 1920s the media became increasingly independent from politicians (corrupt or otherwise) and newspaper editors discovered that denouncing corrupt activities helped them to sell more newspapers (Gentzkow *et al.* 2007). As a result, being corrupt became too costly for politicians, leading to a general decrease of bribery in the United States (Glaeser and Goldin 2007).

A rise in the fight against corrupt activities of major corporations in the United States did not immediately translate into criticisms to their activities abroad. One example illustrates this divergence. During the first decades of the twentieth century, the US-based banana producing and marketing multinational United Fruit Company expanded its operations in Central America and the Caribbean. The high-handed way by which the firm conducted its businesses as well as its meddling in the host countries' domestic politics led United Fruit to gain a notorious reputation in the producing countries, where it became a symbol of American imperialism in the region (Bucheli 2005). In the United States, however, the firm had a different reputation. Aside from the classic *Banana Empire* by Kepner and Soothill (1935) in which the authors apply Vladimir Lenin's framework on imperialism to denounce the firm's operations in Latin America, some consumer protection activist groups (including those advocating for anti-fraud policies) as well as the newspapers criticizing corruption and power of big corporations in the United States portrayed the firm as a virtuous organization, a civilizing force in "the tropics," that provided the American working class with cheap food with high nutritional value and therefore deserved special treatment from the government (including no import tariffs) (Bucheli and Read 2006). Another illustrative example is the one related to the collusion of interests of some US senators with those of the Standard Oil Company of New Jersey in the 1920s, when the latter lobbied on Colombia's behalf to have the United States pay reparations to that country for the support Washington gave to a separatist movement that succeeded at seceding Panama from Colombia in 1903, a move that gave the United States sovereignty over the area where the Panama Canal was eventually built. Criticisms focused on the fact that reparations were going to allow Standard Oil of New Jersey to increase oil production in Colombia pressuring oil prices to fall without this fall translating into lower prices for consumers (Duran and Bucheli 2017). The fact that Standard Oil had obtained those oil concessions through a series of dirty maneuvers against British investors was not part of the public debate (Bucheli 2008a).

The Cold War did not create a favorable environment in the West to fight against corruption abroad. The payment of bribes to high-ranking officials by MNCs was even justified as a necessary evil in the war against Communism during the Cold War. Notorious examples include

Indonesian head of state Sukarno (who ruled between 1945 and 1967). Sukarno was a strong ally of the West and followed a friendly policy toward foreign MNCs. During his regime, he created a scheme to enrich himself and his family from contracts with MNCs, loans from multilateral institutions, or by simply consistently looting the national coffers. Even though the West was aware of the corrupt nature of his regime, he continued receiving political and economic support due to the geopolitical importance of his country.[3] Mobutu Sese Seko, president of Congo between 1965 and 1997 is another example. After taking over following the bloody defeat of the Belgian colonial forces, Mobutu quickly dismantled any resemblance of democracy and began a notorious authoritarian regime. After nationalizing the copper industry in 1967, Mobutu used the newly created firm as a source of personal income, which reached a level of $250 million a year. Mobutu remained as one of the darlings of the Western powers in Africa due to his strong anti-Communism commitment. The Western support only ended with the collapse of the Soviet Union (Cockcroft 2012). A similar case can be found with the United States turning a blind eye toward corrupt activities of the United Fruit Company in Central America due to the firm's close relationship with authoritarian anti-Communist regimes (Bucheli 2008b).

1972–1977: laying the foundation for global anti-corruption efforts

In the early 1970s, corruption in global business was still a widely accepted practice. Some economic analysts asserted that "multinational enterprises are among the foremost practitioners of corruption, particularly in the less-developed nations where they operate" (Waldman 1973: 93). In order to win business contracts, ensure a smooth process in business transactions, and maintain an economic foothold in various countries, managers of MNCs routinely paid bribes to foreign public officials. In essence, engaging in a form of corruption was business as usual.

The seemingly stable reality of global business was shaken following the Watergate scandal in the United States beginning in 1972 – a series of judicial investigations into illegal activities of President Richard Nixon's administration. These investigations revealed that several US corporations and executives used corporate funds for illegal domestic and foreign payments. In the United States, several corporations concealed the sources of political contributions and failed to report such payments to investors, both of which were in violation of federal securities laws (Koehler 2012). Outside the United States, the Securities and Exchange Commission (SEC) discovered that secret "slush funds" existed outside normal corporate financial accountability systems. These secret funds were partially used for questionable or illegal foreign payments (SEC 1976). Investigations by the Church Committee, headed by Senator Frank Church (Democrat – Idaho), also revealed that major corporations such as Gulf Oil, Mobil Oil, Lockheed, and Northrup made questionable payments to foreign government officials and political parties for business purposes (United States Senate, Church Committee 1975). Another scandal revealing collusion of interests between the International Telephone and Telegraph Company (ITT) with the Central Intelligence Agency (CIA) to overthrow Chile's elected president and a bribery scandal involving this same firm and high ranking members of the Republican Party only added fuel to the fire (Bucheli and Salvaj 2013). The February 3, 1975 suicide of Eli M. Black, CEO of the United Brands Company (known as United Fruit Company between 1899 and 1974 and re-named Chiquita Brands in 1989), following the discovery of a $2.5 million bribe that he offered to Honduran president Oswaldo López Arellano in exchange for a reduction of taxes on banana exports, symbolized the extent to which bribery was a problem for US corporations (Kim and Barone 1981). Further investigations by the SEC showed that the bribery scheme went all the way to European consuming countries, where it was discovered that the firm had bribed European officials to gain favorable terms of import (Bucheli 2005). In all these cases the role of investigative journalists was crucial. Consistent with the development studied by Gentzkow *et al.* (2007), the rise of investigative journalism helped to bring to light corruption cases. Watergate and the ITT scandal in particular emboldened investigative journalists who were seen by many as crusaders uncovering dirty operations at the highest levels of policy making and business (Feldstein 2010).

In 1975, the SEC announced a program whereby US corporations could voluntarily disclose questionable payments and activities without facing criminal prosecution or financial penalties (Kochan and Goodyear 2011) The SEC reported that "under this program more than 450 corporations admitted making questionable or illegal payments exceeding $300 million" (U.S. GAO 1981: 1). This stark reality, coupled with the previous investigations into corporations' activities, prompted reform efforts in Congress.

In 1977, Congress passed the Foreign Corrupt Practices Act (FCPA). Although domestic anti-corruption initiatives existed in nearly every society, the FCPA was the first initiative to criminalize corruption in foreign contexts. It amended the 1934 Securities and Exchange Act and made it unlawful for registered issuers of securities to make payments to foreign government officials or political parties for the purpose of obtaining or retaining business. The FCPA also required that corporations have adequate internal accounting control (i.e., monitoring) systems. These systems entailed good bookkeeping and transparent disclosure of all payments. Both individuals and corporations could be criminally charged if these requirements were violated. Anti-bribery violations could result in fines of up to $1 million for corporations. Individuals could incur a maximum of $10,000 fine and be sentenced to prison (Darrough 2010). The passage of the FCPA signaled a shift in the attitude toward corruption – in the United States at least, corruption among corporations was no longer seen as business as usual.

1978–1988: the limited global response

Although the FCPA represented a victory for US policymakers, challenges remained in persuading other countries to follow suit. Although representatives from 18 member countries of the United Nations drafted an international treaty on illicit payments in 1979, they failed to adopt the agreement (Kim and Barone 1981). Similarly, following a summit of executive politicians from seven countries, US President Jimmy Carter noted

> At the Venice Economic Summit meeting in June 1980 I urged that these seven industrial democracies renew efforts to work in the United Nations toward an agreement to prohibit illicit payments by their citizens to foreign government officials; and, if that effort falters, to seek an agreement among themselves, open to other nations, with the same objective.[4]

Despite President Carter's insistence on a collective effort, the attendees stated that they would engage in independent actions (Kim and Barone 1981). A major issue for several countries, such as Germany, France, and Japan, was that their legal systems allowed for the tax deductibility of bribes. Other countries, such as Switzerland, maintained bank secrecy laws, which allowed for MNCs to hide money off the books (Rubin 1998). Legalized corruption in several countries resulted in resistance to international efforts at combatting corruption. With the exception of Sweden's passage of a law criminalizing foreign bribery in 1978 (International Monetary Fund 2001), the United States was relatively alone in its efforts to combat corruption on a global scale.

The general lack of response by other countries resulted in negative consequences for US MNCs. For example, in a survey of 185 US corporations, more than 30 percent of respondents engaged in foreign business reported that they lost foreign business opportunities due to the FCPA (U.S. GAO 1981). Furthermore, 60 percent of respondents reported that they could not compete successfully against other foreign firms that engaged in bribery. Additionally, the Export Disincentive Task Force estimated that US MNCs could lose up to $1 billion as a result of the FCPA (Kim and Barone 1981). Many corporate executives believed that the FCPA reduced the competitiveness of US MNCs given that they did not operate on a level playing field.

Congress eventually made amendments to the FCPA following criticism by executives and foreign policy experts. In 1988, Congress shifted the definition of "corrupt payments" to focus on the purpose of the payment rather than to whom the payment was made (Kaikati *et al.* 2000). Congress allowed for "grease" (i.e., facilitating) payments to secure the performance of a routine government action. These actions included issuing business permits and licenses as well as processing visas. To determine the legality of a "grease" payment, the Department of Justice considered the size of the payment and the seniority of governmental officials involved in the transaction, among other factors. This amendment put US multinationals on a more even playing field with respect to multinationals from other countries (Gutterman 2015). In her study on the evolution of anti-corruption policies in the United States, Gutterman (2015) posits that after initially lobbying against the FCPA, American corporations realized the political and social environment was not on their side and that defending corruption was too costly for politicians. As a result, she maintains, firms opted for a different strategy consisting of lobbying for actions from the US government to make other countries develop a similar type of legislation. The next section studies that change.

1989–1999: toward a reversal of fortune

The late 1980s witnessed democratic transitions in Latin America and reform following the collapse of the Soviet Union. However, the adoption of market-friendly regimes in different parts of the world did not eliminate corruption, but in fact in some cases created new incentives for more corruption. A very telling case is the privatization of state property in Russia after the collapse of the Soviet Union. This process created a looting mentality among those with important government positions and opened the door for organized crime to influence politics at the highest levels (Cockcroft 2012). The chaotic nature of the transition facilitated the rise of corruption (Levin and Satarov 2000).

As Hall (1999) shows, privatization and liberalization of markets created opportunities for government officials to gain bribes from foreign multinationals bidding for the large amount of government property that was for sale. He demonstrates how this not only happened for the case of poor or emerging countries, but also for advanced countries such as France, the United Kingdom, or the United States. Similarly, the radical pro-market reforms adopted in Latin America during the 1980s and 1990s, hailed as policies that would clean those countries of corruption in fact created new opportunities for those benefitting from corrupt activities (Manzetti and Blake 2008). Some of the most pro-market presidents in that continent were eventually charged with corruption, including Carlos Menem (Argentina), Alberto Fujimori (Peru), and relatives of Chilean dictator Augusto Pinochet (Pop-Eleches 2009; Agnic 2006).

Despite opportunistic behavior among a few actors during this time, the global attitude toward corruption began to shift. In particular, the OECD formed an ad-hoc working group in 1989 to comparatively review national legislations regarding corruption. The review revealed that although several countries had laws that, in principle, applied to the bribery of foreign public officials, more effort was needed for effective action (International Monetary Fund 2001). Continued work by this group led to the 1994 Recommendation on Bribery in International Transactions, which encouraged OECD member countries to deter, prevent, and combat the bribery of foreign officials.

The OECD initiatives eventually resulted in the 1997 OECD Anti-Bribery Convention. This binding convention, signed by 29 OECD member countries and five non-members, criminalized the payment of bribes to foreign public officials. It was the first international convention to criminalize the bribery of foreign public officials. The convention came into effect on February 15, 1999 and has since been signed by all member countries of the OECD. The convention subjects its member countries to monitoring by the OECD Working Group on Bribery. Phase 1 of this monitoring entails an evaluation of the extent to which member countries change their legislation to reflect provisions of the convention (Cockcroft 2012).

In parallel to the OECD's actions, several other initiatives took place during this time period. Prior to the OECD Anti-Bribery Convention, 23 members of the Organization of American States (OAS) signed the Inter-American Convention Against Corruption in 1996. This convention was the first international convention to address corruption, as it called for member countries to strengthen legal mechanisms to deter and detect corruption. However, this convention did not require member countries to criminalize bribery. Similarly, the United Nations passed a resolution in 1996 that, although not legally binding, focused on the need to criminalize corruption and eliminate the tax deductibility of bribes to foreign officials (Rubin 1998). Beyond multilateral agreements, Transparency International was founded in 1993 with the goal of reducing corruption globally. This global nongovernmental organization (NGO) produces the annual Corruption Perceptions Index, which ranks countries in terms of perceived levels of corruption that occur in the public sector. This index helps to publicize corruption across countries and has triggered public opposition to corruption (Rubin 1998).

These international efforts were representative of the shift in the attitude toward corruption. Many of the major industrial nations adopted an anti-corruption stance under the assumption that multilateral efforts were more beneficial to combatting this issue relative to unilateral efforts. Multilateral efforts, in principle, leveled the playing field for all MNCs and increased the transparency in governmental actions in countries that adopted the aforementioned conventions.

2000 and beyond: bearing the fruits of hard labor

The beginning of the twenty-first century has witnessed continued progress in the global anti-corruption agenda. Beyond improving their internal monitoring systems, some MNCs have become more involved in the anti-corruption agenda by becoming signatories to the UN Global Compact – an initiative to encourage MNCs to engage in sustainable and socially responsible practices, with participating multinationals that include some firms often criticized for corrupt activities such as Shell or Siemens.[5] The 10th Principle of the Global Compact is "Businesses should work against corruption in all its forms, including extortion and bribery" (United Nations 2004). The principle stemmed from the 2003 United Nations Convention against Corruption. This convention required member countries to engage in preventative measures, criminalize various types of corruption such as money-laundering, cooperate with one another to combat corruption, and support the recovery of confiscated property or assets (United Nations 2017).

Besides the UN Global Compact, other organizations focused on particular industries emerged, such as the Extractive Industries Transparency Initiative (EITI), which not only focused on corruption, but also issues around environment destruction and human rights (EITI,

2017). During the 2000s, several multinationals directly participated along with different NGOs in the creation of the general principles defining guidelines for internal anti-corruption policies (Berkowitz *et al.* 2017). The presence of multinationals in the forums defining and evaluating actions against corruption is seen as problematic by some authors (Aaronson 2011; Van Altisne 2014; Smith *et al.* 2012), while others maintain that this leads to better and more efficient results (Baumann-Pauly and Scherer 2013; Haufler 2010; Rasche 2012).

The work of the United Nations complements the work of the OECD. Following Phase 1 of the OECD Anti-Bribery Convention, Phase 2 of the monitoring entails assessment of whether or not the anti-corruption legislation of a member country was applied effectively (OECD 2016b). Phase 3 focuses on the enforcement of the provisions of the 1997 convention. Furthermore, in 2009 the OECD adopted a recommendation regarding the tax deductibility of bribes of foreign officials, as the 1997 convention failed to eliminate this issue (OECD 2016c). Phase 4 of the monitoring began in 2016. It focuses on determining the progress made by member countries with regard to weaknesses in legislation efficacy and enforcement identified in previous phases.

Both the United States and the OECD have increasingly prosecuted individuals and MNCs engaged in corruption since 2000. Between 1977 and 1999, the Department of Justice (DOJ) and SEC in the United States made a total of 49 prosecutions in relation to the FCPA. Between 2000 and 2016, 448 prosecutions were made (Stanford Law School 2017) – the rise of prosecutions is partially the result of the opening of an FCPA division at the US Federal Bureau of Investigation (FBI) and the enlargement of the FCPA divisions in the SEC and the DOJ (Berghoff 2017). To date, the largest fine paid by a multinational under the FCPA has been the $1.6 billion Siemens paid both to the European and American authorities after being found guilty of creating a global bribery scheme to secure government contracts, followed by France's Alstom with a fine of $772 million in 2014 (Berghoff 2017). Similarly, as of 2016, nearly 400 individuals and more than 130 entities (e.g., MNCs) have been sanctioned in criminal proceedings since the implementation of the OECD Anti-Bribery Convention (OECD 2016a). As these trends suggest, there has been more emphasis on the enforcement of anti-bribery legislation since 2000.

Terrorism and fraud: twenty-first century challenges

Two major events forced society to re-evaluate how to fight against corruption at the global level. The first one was the terrorist attack from the Islamic radical group Al-Qaeda against several targets on US soil on September 11, 2001. Besides the American invasions of Afghanistan and Iraq and the creation of an internal security apparatus around the Department of Homeland Security, the September 11 attacks also had an effect on anti-corruption efforts. Shortly after the attacks, US Secretary of State Colin Powell showed the public a global list of illegal armed groups Washington classified as terrorists and enemies of the United States. Giving payments to these groups was equivalent to trading with the enemy, which generated problems for some American multinationals that could serve as precedent for future cases. One important example is the one involving the US banana marketing multinational Chiquita. Two of the groups Powell classified as terrorists included the right-wing militias United Self-Defense Forces of Colombia and the left-wing Colombian Revolutionary Armed Forces (AUC and FARC respectively in their Spanish acronym) (United States Department of State 2001). By the time of this designation Chiquita had been paying bribes to those two groups, so in order to avoid legal problems the firm came forward in 2004 and disclosed that for years they had paid money to both the AUC and the FARC, something they justified as a result of extortion or means to protect the lives of its employees (Baquero 2014). The disclosure of this information led to lawsuits by victims of the AUC and FARC against Chiquita (Frundt 2009), opening a new legal field in terms of how to fight against corruption. Legal scholars have debated whether payments to criminal groups threatening the lives of a multinational's employees should be treated in the same way as payments to a government official in exchange for a contract (Gaskins 2008). No other company came forward the way Chiquita did and to the date of this writing the legal challenges had not concluded. Some analysts even suggested that Chiquita did not benefit from being open about its activities (*Economist* 2012). However, the precedent of this case will surely guide future evaluations of corrupt activities.

The second event was the spectacular collapse of Enron, a major US-based energy firm in 2001. The scandal surfaced when the firm was not able to keep falsifying the information it provided to regulators and shareholders. Post-mortem analyses pointed to an existing general corporate-wide corrupt culture that led to an unmanageable downward spiral of corruption (Arbogast 2008; McLean and Elkind 2003). The gigantic losses generated by Enron's fall led to calls for further and tighter regulations, which translated into the 2002 Sarbanes-Oxley Act. This piece of legislation made top executives responsible for the functioning of internal control systems, which made it difficult for those executives to turn a blind eye or claim ignorance of corrupt actions. This new legal environment led several multinationals to plead guilty to bribery schemes abroad including Monsanto in Indonesia, Titan Corporation in Benin, and Switzerland's ABB in Angola, Nigeria, and Kazakhstan, while making others develop better internal control mechanisms (White 2009).

The road ahead

This chapter has reviewed the major institutional initiatives to combat corruption in global business. Beyond these unilateral and multilateral efforts, other initiatives on a smaller scale contribute to the global anti-corruption agenda. Although corruption remains a pressing problem, there has been rapid improvement in anti-corruption efforts, particularly over the past 20 years. Legislation continues to expand and monitoring of both governments and MNCs has been more transparent. This does not mean that these initiatives are free of challenges. Before being elected president of the United States, Donald J. Trump showed disdain toward the FCPA by describing it as a "horrible law [that] should be changed … the whole world is laughing at us" (Lynch 2016). Dismantling this piece of legislation, however, would not be an easy task. Other issues exacerbating corruption include the global growth of illegal drug trafficking that has shown its power to permeate all instances of government and the private sector from Colombia, Mexico, Brazil, and Italy to Guinea-Bissau, and the Balkans (Cockcroft 2012). This and the fact that new scandals keep emerging (such as the 2016–2017 global bribery scheme by the Brazilian multinational Odebrecht) shows the problem has not gone away (Tegel 2017). Whereas anti-corruption initiatives largely affect the demand side of corruption, more multilateral and unilateral efforts are needed to reduce the supply side of corruption. By the time of this writing, it was still uncertain how protectionist and isolationist policies adopted by several Western powers and the reaction toward those changes by emerging economies will affect global efforts to fight corruption.[6] Anti-corruption initiatives rapidly developed for a relatively short period of time with tangible positive results. How a collective action is maintained in the twilight of globalization constitutes an interesting research agenda for scholars and something to be watched closely by policy makers, activists, and private firms. The retreat from or resistance to cooperate with multilateral or international organizations by some countries (e.g., United Kingdom or the United States after the Brexit vote or the election of president Donald Trump) can make global coordinated efforts harder to achieve. Policies that put the interests of a country's firms first and the dismissiveness of ethical concerns might create new temptations by firms to return to unethical behaviors. Some of the "global" efforts have been done at the OECD level. This made sense in times in which the countries belonging to this exclusive group controlled most of the world's economy. However, the rise of emerging market multinationals that are not constrained by the OECD principles might generate new calls by OECD-based firms to either relax existing regulations or to pressure other governments to follow their initiatives. Moreover, some of the new large multinationals operating in the global scene do not come from democratic countries, but also from authoritarian regimes or countries notoriously corrupt (e.g., China or Russia). How to create global anti-corruption frameworks with those new actors can be a challenge.

Conclusion

The perception that many firms engage in what can be defined as "corrupt" activities when operating globally (or domestically) is not new. This chapter surveys governments' efforts to fight against corruption in the context of a changing global political landscape. As the chapter shows, serious efforts started relatively late (the 1970s) when considering how aware the world was about the existence of corruption and became a matter of global concern even later. We hope this chapter provides the readers with a general framework and chronology that explains why at certain points in history firms operating globally did not seem to see corruption as a matter of concern and when, how, and why this changed. We show how big political or economic shocks often generate the right environment to create new anti-corruption measures. The emergence of new multinationals from non-Western powers in the post-1990s period provides an interesting area of research to understand how firms originating from countries not participating in previous anti-corruption efforts adapt to the existing anti-corruption legal framework.

Notes

1 We thank comments to a previous version by R. Daniel Wadhwani, Hartmut Berghoff, other participants at the Business History Conference (Denver, 2017), Teresa da Silva Lopes, and Christina Lubinski. We also thank Thomas DeBerge for his research assistantship.
2 Cockcroft (2012: 2) provides another useful definition of corruption, which is consistent with our study as the "acquisition of money, assets, or power in a way which escapes the public view; is usually illegal; and is at the expense of society as a whole either at a 'grand' or everyday level."
3 Sukarno's protection of foreign property rights was selective. British business were expropriated during the confrontation Indonesia had against British-backed Malaysia (White 2012),
4 Public Papers of the Presidents of the United States – Jimmy Carter, 1980–1981, Book 2. Ann Arbor, MI: University of Michigan Library, 2005, pp. 1693–1694. https://quod.lib.umich.edu/p/ppotpus?ke y=title;page=browse;value=j (accessed April 14, 2019).
5 The long list of signatories of the UN Global Compact can be accessed in www.unglobalcompact.org/ what-is-gc/participants (accessed September 29, 2017).
6 The rise of nativist movements in the Western world, the election of an anti-globalization president in the United States in 2016, and the British decision to abandon the European Union have been pointed out as evidence that the second global economy that started in the 1970s as studied by Jones (2005) had come to an end (Agarwal and Raje, 2017).

References

Aaronson, Susan A. (2011), "Limited Partnership: Business, Government, Civil Society, and the Public in the Extractive Industries Transparency Initiative (EITI)," *Public Administration and Development*, 31 (1), 50–63.
Agarwal, Sapna and Raje, Aparna P. (2017), "We Are in a Deglobalization Period: Business Historian Geoffrey G. Jones," *LiveMint* (February 18) [online]. Available at: www.livemint.com/Companies/

tKamdGDvvyCt8Smn39TQMK/We-are-in-a-deglobalization-period-Business-historian-Geoff.html (accessed March 1, 2017).

Agnic, Ozren (2006), *Pinochet SA: La base de la fortuna* (Santiago: RIL).

Arbogast, Stephen (2008), *Resisting Corporate Corruption: Lessons in Practical Ethics from the Enron Wreckage* (Salem, MA: Scrivener).

Balleisen, Edward (2017), *Fraud: An American History from Barnum to Madoff, United States* (Princeton, NJ: Princeton University Press).

Baquero, Jairo (2014), *Layered Inequalities: Land Grabbing, Collective Land Rights, and Afro-Descendant Resistance in Colombia* (Berlin: LIT).

Baumann-Pauly, Dorothée and Scherer, Andreas (2013), "The Organizational Implementation of Corporate Citizenship: An Assessment Tool and its Application at UN Global Compact Participants," *Journal of Business Ethics*, 52 (1), 6–30.

Berghoff, Hartmut (2017), "'Organised Irresponsibility'? The Siemens Corruption Scandal of the 1990s and 2000s," *Business History*. http://dx.doi.org/10.1080/00076791.2017.1330332.

Berkowitz, Heloïse, Bucheli, Marcelo, and Dumez, Hervé (2017), "Collectively Designing CSR Through Meta-Organizations: A Case Study of the Oil and Gas Industry," *Journal of Business Ethics*, 143 (4), 753–769.

Bucheli, Marcelo (2005), *Bananas and Business: The United Fruit Company in Colombia, 1899–2000* (New York: New York University Press).

Bucheli, Marcelo (2008a), "Negotiating Under the Monroe Doctrine: Weetman Pearson and the Origins of US Control of Colombian Oil," *Business History Review*, 82 (3), 529–553.

Bucheli, Marcelo (2008b), "Multinational Corporations, Totalitarian Regimes, and Economic Nationalism: United Fruit Company in Central America, 1899–1975," *Business History*, 50 (4), 433–454.

Bucheli, Marcelo and Read, Ian (2006), "Banana Boats and Baby Food: The Banana in US History," in Marichal, C., Frank, Z., and Topik, S. (eds.), *From Silver to Cocaine: Latin America Commodity Chains and the Building of the World Economy* (Durham, NC: Duke University Press), 204–227.

Bucheli, Marcelo and Salvaj, Erica (2013), "Reputation and Political Legitimacy: ITT in Chile, 1927–1972," *Business History Review*, 87 (4), 729–756.

Chandler, Alfred (1980), "The Growth of the Transnational Industrial Firm in the United States and the United Kingdom: A Comparative Analysis," *Economic History Review*, 33 (3), 396–410.

Coatsworth, John, Cole, Juan, Hanagan, Michael, Perdue, Peter, Tilly, Charles, and Tilly, Louise (2015), *Global Connections: Politics, Exchange and Social Life in World History* (vol. 2) (Cambridge: Cambridge University Press).

Cockcroft, Laurence (2012), *Global Corruption: Money, Power, and Ethics in the Modern World* (Philadelphia, PA: University of Pennsylvania Press).

Darrough, Masako (2010), "The FCPA and OECD Convention: Some Lessons from the U.S. Experience," *Journal of Business Ethics*, 93 (2), 255–276.

Dirks, Nicholas (2006), *The Scandal of Empire: India and the Creation of Imperial Britain* (Cambridge, MA: Harvard University Press).

Doh, Jonathan, Rodriguez, Peter, Uhlenbruck, Klaus, Collins, Jamie, and Eden, Lorraine (2003), "Coping with Corruption in Foreign Markets," *Academy of Management Executive*, 17 (3), 114–129.

Duran, Xavier and Bucheli, Marcelo (2017), "Holding Up the Empire: Colombia, American Oil Interests, and the 1921 Urrutia-Thomson Treaty," *Journal of Economic History*, 143 (4), 753–769.

Economist (The) (2012), "Going Bananas," *The Economist* (May 31) [online]. Available at: www.economist.com/node/21551500 (accessed October 25, 2017).

Extractive Industries Transparency Initiative (EITI) (2017), *EITI* [online]. Available at: www.eiti.org (accessed September 29, 2017).

Feldstein, Mark (2010), *Poisoning the Press: Richard Nixon, Jack Anderson, and the Rise of Washington's Scandal Culture* (New York: Farrar, Strauss, & Giroux).

Frundt, Henry (2009), *Fair Bananas! Farmers, Workers, and Consumers Strive to Change an Industry* (Tucson, AZ: University of Arizona Press).

Gaskins, K. Curry (2008), "Chiquita Goes Bananas: Counter-Terrorism Legislation Threatens US Multinationals," *North Carolina Journal of International Law and Commercial Regulation*, 34 (1), 263–280.

Gentzkow, Matthew, Glaeser, Edward, and Goldin, Claudia (2007), "The Rise of the Fourth Estate: How Newspapers Became Informative and Why It Mattered," in Glaeser, E. and Goldin, C. (eds.), *Corruption and Reform: Lessons from America's Economic History* (Chicago, IL: University of Chicago Press), 217–229.

Glaeser, Edward and Goldin, Claudia (2007), "Corruption and Reform: Introduction," in Glaeser, E. and Goldin, C. (eds.), *Corruption and Reform: Lessons from America's Economic History* (Chicago, IL: University of Chicago Press), 3–21.

Gray, Cheryl and Kaufmann, Daniel (1998), "Corruption and Development," *Finance and Development*, 35 (1), 7–10.

Gutterman, Ellen (2015), "Banning Bribes Abroad: Enforcement of the Corrupt Practices Act," *Osgoode Hall Law Journal*, 53 (1), 31–66.

Hall, David (1999), "Privatisation, Multinationals, and Corruption," *Development in Practice*, 9 (5), 539–556.

Haufler, Virginia (2010), "Disclosure as Governance: The Extractive Industries Transparency Initiative and Resource Management in the Developing World," *Global Environment Politics*, 10 (3), 53–73.

Husted, Bryan (1999), "Wealth, Culture, and Corruption," *Journal of International Business Studies*, 30 (2), 339–360.

International Monetary Fund (2001), "OECD Convention on Combating Bribery of Foreign Public Officials in International Business Transactions" [online]. Available at: www.imf.org/external/np/gov/2001/eng/091801.pdf (accessed February 25, 2017).

International Monetary Fund (2016), "Corruption: Costs and mitigating strategies" [online]. Available at: www.imf.org/external/pubs/ft/sdn/2016/sdn1605.pdf (accessed February 24, 2017).

Jones, Geoffrey (2005), *Multinationals and Global Capitalism: From the Nineteenth to the Twenty-first Century* (Oxford: Oxford University Press).

Kaikati, Jack, Sullivan, George, Virgo, John, Carr, T. R., and Virgo, Katherine (2000), "The Price of International Business Morality: Twenty Years Under the Foreign Corrupt Practices Act," *Journal of Business Ethics*, 26 (3), 213–222.

Kepner, Charles David and Soothill, Henry (1935), *The Banana Empire: A Case Study of Economic Imperialism* (New York: Russell & Russell).

Kim, Suk H. and Barone, Sam (1981), "Is the Foreign Corrupt Practices Act of 1977 a Success or Failure? A Survey of Members of the Academy of International Business," *Journal of International Business Studies*, 12 (3), 123–126.

Kochan, Nick and Goodyear, Robin (2011), *Corruption: The New Corporate Challenge* (London: Palgrave Macmillan).

Koehler, Mike (2012), "The Story of the Foreign Corrupt Practices Act," *Ohio State Law Journal*, 73 (5), 929–1013.

LaPorta, Rafael, Florencio Lopez-de-Silanes, Andrei Shleifer, and Robert Vishny (1999), "The Quality of Government," *Journal of Law, Economics and Organization*, 15 (1), 222–279.

Leite, Carlos and Weidmann, Jens (1999), "Does Mother Nature Corrupt? Natural Resources, Corruption, and Economic Growth," *IMF Working Paper 99/85*, [online]. Available at: www.imf.org/external/pubs/ft/wp/1999/wp9985.pdf (accessed February 25, 2017).

Levin, Mark and Satarov, Georgy (2000), "Corruption and Institutions in Russia," *European Journal of Political Economy*, 16 (1), 113–132.

Lynch, David J. (2016), "US Anti-Bribery Law Set to Remain in Place under Trump," *Financial Times*, December 29 [online]. Available at: www.ft.com/content/a5b6d5e8-c951-11e6-8f29-9445cac8966f (accessed March 1, 2017).

McLean, Bethany and Elkind, Peter (2003), *The Smartest Guys in the Room: The Amazing Rise and Scandalous Fall of Enron* (New York: Penguin).

Manzetti, Luigi and Blake, Charles H. (2008), "Market Reforms and Corruption in Latin America: New Means for Old Ways," *Review of International Political Economy*, 3 (4), 662–697.

Nierstrasz, Chris (2012), *Remuneration and Corruption in the Shadow of the Company: The Dutch East India Company and its Servants in the Period of its Decline (1740–1796)* (Leiden: Brill).

O'Neill, Daniel (2017), "Burke and Paine on the Origins of British Imperialism in India," in Kapust, D. and Kinsella, H. (eds.), *Comparative Political Theory in Time and Place: Theory's Landscapes* (New York: Palgrave), 105–130.

OECD (2016a), "2015 Enforcement of the Anti-Bribery Convention" [online]. Available at: www.oecd.org/daf/anti-bribery/WGB-Enforcement-Data-2015.pdf (accessed February 28, 2017).

OECD (2016b), "Country Monitoring of the OECD Anti-Bribery Convention" [online]. Available at: www.oecd.org/daf/anti-bribery/countrymonitoringoftheoecdanti-briberyconvention.htm (accessed February 27, 2017).

OECD (2016c), "OECD Recommendation on Tax Measures for Further Combating Bribery" [online]. Available at: www.oecd.org/ctp/crime/2009-recommendation.pdf (accessed February 28, 2017).

Pop-Eleches, Grigore (2009), *From Economic Crisis to Reform: IMF Programs in Latin America and Eastern Europe* (Princeton, NJ: Princeton University Press).

Rasche, Andreas (2012), "Global Policies and Local Practice: Loose and Tight Couplings in Multi-Stakeholder Initiatives," *Business Ethics Quarterly*, 22 (4), 679–708.

Rose-Ackerman, Susan (1997), "The Political Economy of Corruption," in Kimberly Ann Elliott (ed.), *Corruption and the Global Economy* (Washington, DC: Institute for International Economics), 31–60.

Rubin, Nora M. (1998), "Global Efforts to Curb Corruption and Bribery in International Business Transactions," *American University International Law Review*, 14 (1), 259–325.

Smith, Shirley, Shepherd, Derek, and Dorward, Peter (2012), "Perspectives on Community Representation within the Extractive Industries Transparency Initiative: Experiences from South-East Madagascar," *Resources Policy*, 37 (2), 241–250.

Stanford Law School (2017), "Key Statistics from 1977 to Present" [online]. Available at: http://fcpa.stanford.edu/statistics-keys.html (accessed February 28, 2017).

Tegel, Simeon (2017), "Brazil's Huge Corruption Scandal is Spreading to the Rest of Latin America," *Washington Post*, February 12 [online]. Available at: www.washingtonpost.com/news/worldviews/wp/2017/02/12/brazils-huge-corruption-scandal-begins-to-affect-the-rest-of-latin-america/?utm_term=.4716dba85312 (accessed March 1, 2017).

United Nations (2004), "Principle Ten: Anti-corruption" [online]. Available at: www.unglobalcompact.org/what-is-gc/mission/principles/principle-10 (accessed February 27, 2017).

United Nations (2017), "United Nations Convention against Corruption" [online]. Available at: www.unodc.org/unodc/en/treaties/CAC/convention-highlights.html#Criminalization (accessed February 27, 2017).

United States Department of State (2001), "Designation of the AUC as a Foreign Terrorist Organization," *US Department of State Archive* [online]. Available at: https://2001-2009.state.gov/secretary/former/powell/remarks/2001/4852.htm (accessed September 30, 2017).

United States Senate, Church Committee (1975), "Multinational Corporations and United States Foreign Policy: Hearings Before the Subcommittee on Multinational Corporations of the Subcommittee on Foreign Relations," *94th Congress* (Washington, DC: US Government Printing Office).

U.S. General Accountability Office (GAO) (1981) "Impact of Foreign Corrupt Practices Act on U.S. Business," *Report AFMD-81–34* (Washington, DC: U.S. General Accountability Office).

U.S. Securities and Exchange Commission (SEC) (1976), "Report of the Securities and Exchange Commission on Questionable and Illegal Corporate Payments and Practices."

Van Altisne, James (2014), "Transparency in Resource Governance: The Pitfalls and Potential of 'New Oil' in Sub-Saharan Africa," *Global Environment Politics*, 14 (1), 20–39.

Velázquez, Nelly (1991), "Los resguardos de indios en la provincia de Mérida en el Nuevo Reino de Granada (siglo XVII) y la integración socio cultural," in García Jordán, P. and Izard, M. (eds.), *Conquista y Resistencia en la Historia de América* (Barcelona: Universitat de Barcelona), 111–122.

Waldman, Joseph M. (1973), "Corruption and the Multinational Enterprise," *Journal of International Business Studies*, 4 (1), 93–96.

Wallis, John J. (2007), "The Concept of Systematic Corruption in American History," in Glaeser, E. and Goldin, C. (eds.), *Corruption and Reform: Lessons from America's Economic History* (Chicago, IL: University of Chicago Press), 23–62.

Wallis, John Joseph, Fishback, Price, and Kantor, Shawn (2007), "Politics, Relief, and Reform: Roosevelt's Efforts to Control Corruption and Political Manipulation During the New Deal," in Glaeser, E. and Goldin, C. (eds.), *Corruption and Reform: Lessons from America's Economic History* (Chicago, IL: University of Chicago Press), 343–372.

White, Nicholas (2012), "Surviving Sukarto: British Business in Post-Colonial Indonesia, 1950–1967," *Modern Asian Studies*, 46 (5), 1277–1315.

White, William B. (2009), "The Influence of Sarbarnes-Oxley on the Foreign Corrupt Practices Act," *International Journal of Global Management Studies Quarterly*, 1 (2), 18–30.

Wilkins, Mira (1970), *The Emergence of Multinational Enterprise: American Business Abroad from the Colonial Era to 1914* (Cambridge, MA: Harvard University Press).

Wilkins, Mira (1974), *The Maturing of Multinational Enterprise: American Business Abroad from 1914 to 1970* (Cambridge, MA: Harvard University Press).

Wilkins, Mira (1988), "The Free-Standing Company, 1870–1914: An Important Type of British Foreign Direct Investment," *Economic History Review*, 41 (2), 259–282.

You, Jong-Sun and Khagram, Sanjeev (2005), "A Comparative Study of Inequality and Corruption," *American Sociological Review*, 70 (1), 136–157.

34

MULTINATIONAL MANAGEMENT

Robert Fitzgerald

Multinational management and business history

The organization and management of multinational firms have reflected phases in the development of the international economy. Evolving global and national contexts, economic and political, influenced internal company structures, and the external links multinationals formed with governments and other firms. Through historical analysis, we can also show how multinationals contributed dynamically to the expansion and impact of global business. Theories in business strategy and organization imply certainty about global best practice, or they offer a suite of distinct organizational options. Actual choices have been replete with difficulties, implemented tentatively, or constantly adjusted. Furthermore, firms have had to respond to dramatic events, such as expropriations, occupations, policy changes, and economic crashes, while adapting by design or piecemeal to more slowly moving shifts in the global economy. In real time, multinationals have encountered unknowns rather than certainties. The activities and investments of multinationals have been formative influences on national economies and the international balance of power: in the creation of infrastructure, commodity production, and transcontinental trading and finance links in the period before 1914; the growing transfer of technology and management know-how from parent firm to foreign subsidiaries from the 1950s; or in the increasing exploitation of locational advantages since the 1990s through the combination of integrated cross-border production chains and contracting-out.

The first section of this chapter will look at mainstream ideas in business and multinational organization, namely the role of managerial hierarchies in utilizing the core capabilities of large firms, and the role of a parent multinational in utilizing its "ownership" advantages or core capabilities in foreign markets through a cross-border managerial hierarchy. In doing so, this chapter brings in insights from business history. The second section will consider some of the debates around international business theory, specifically multinational subsidiaries, cross-border networks, emerging economy multinationals, and governments, and suggests ways in which business historians might contribute to these issues. The third section looks at trends in multinational business organization since the nineteenth century, indicating similarities and differences between periods, the variety of strategies and outcomes, and their contribution to the development of the global economy.

Foreign direct investment (FDI) theory and business organization

Business history has contributed significantly to theories of internal management, most obviously through Alfred Chandler's writings (1962, 1977). In this well-known canon, technological and market trends favoured strategies of internalizing commercial activities within large-scale manufacturing firms. Business structures enabled strategies to be fulfilled, and managerial hierarchies and divisional structures made policies of mass production and mass marketing effective. Arguing that the success or failure of a national economy depended on the internal management of its large firms, Chandler's *Scale and Scope* (1990) underplayed the importance of government, institutions, finance systems, labour, and skills as alternative or more plausible causes. It ignored, in turn, how these factors shaped the industrial structures of economies, the size of firms, and ultimately internal business organization; they explain, furthermore, variations in the organization of multinational business operating across borders. Chandler extended his model into international enterprise, and described how firms founded international and regional divisions with their own management teams. Through such a division, a parent multinational assumed the major responsibility for controlling, coordinating, and monitoring key resources and capabilities located in different economies (Chandler and Mazlish, 1997). The practice of parental multinational control could be more problematic than the theory. General Electric offers, as early as 1919, an example of a US firm forming an international division, as does Du Pont, in 1958, after which began the historically significant post-war surge in transatlantic investment into Western Europe (Fitzgerald, 2015, 2017). Long-distance management proved partial or just inappropriate for varying market contexts, and so space was created for local decision-making (Jones, 2005a; Fitzgerald, 2015). Cross-border internalization and a tiered management pyramid were only one of several organizational options. Large firms with an integrated managerial hierarchy could in parallel forge external networks, which themselves could be viable alternatives to internalizing production or marketing. Vertical supply and distribution chains, industrial clusters, and cartels necessitated interfirm cooperation and pointed to its advantages. Business groups and holding companies facilitated horizontal and vertical synergies, and served to dilute financial and commercial risks.

European trading firms, for example, were active in developing territories through networks and shared partnerships in Asia, Latin America, and Africa. Several of the largest British houses from the 1890s added a parent holding company to oversee from London their chain of businesses. The Netherlands traders, Internatio and Borsumij, founded headquarters functions to supervise their networks of firms and agents, mostly based in the Dutch East Indies (Jonker and Sluyterman, 2005). Industry–bank cooperation in Germany was extended to the holding-company multinational, Deutsche Überseeische Elektrizitäts-Gesellschaft (DUEG), which financed, built, and managed electrical utilities before the First World War (Jones, 2005a; Fitzgerald, 2017). While the Mitsui and Nissan *zaibatsu* established management teams, they constituted holding companies overseeing multifarious enterprises in China and the Japanese empire during the inter-war decades (Kawabe, 1987; Patrikeff and Shukman, 2007; Yonekawa, 1990; Matsusaka, 2003). By the 1970s, European firms such as Unilever or Ciba-Geigy favoured matrix organizations combining international product, functional, and geographic imperatives, which encouraged national subsidiary decision-making and variation (Franko, 1976; Jones, 2000; Fitzgerald, 2003; Jones, 2005b; Fitzgerald, 2015).

Chandler emphasized how managerial hierarchies were needed to utilize the core capabilities of large firms, and how the headquarters should set the overall company strategy (Chandler, 1962, 1977, 1990). Similarly, mainstream FDI theory has stressed the objectives of the parent multinational and the role of a cross-border managerial hierarchy in utilizing the firm's ownership advantages or core capabilities in foreign markets. Leadership in technology, management

Robert Fitzgerald

know-how, or brands could overcome the problems of being foreign in host markets. FDI was not just the investment of capital but the transfer of resources that had underpinned success in a home economy, and, it followed, a firm had as a result to learn the lessons of international management and cross-border control (Hymer, 1960; Dunning and Lundan, 2008). For historians, Hymer's ground-breaking thesis (1960) does not indicate why and how strategies and organizational structures might evolve after the initial act of FDI. As capital demands rose, large-scale trading firms in Britain incorporated before 1914 to retain the City of London's confidence; moreover, a headquarters could manage the rising transcontinental flow of imported goods and strengthen the hold on final European markets. The evolving organizational requirements of these resource-seeking multinationals differed from the marketing-seeking manufacturers of a later generation. As sales in foreign markets grew to a critical point, US multinationals in Europe from the late 1960s onwards loosened parental control, and bolstered local management teams and product development through the founding of region-wide subsidiaries (Wilkins, 1974; Jones, 2005a; Fitzgerald, 2015). European economic integration supplied a further motive. Originally motivated almost entirely by tariffs and import quotas, Japanese multinationals such as Toyota, Panasonic, or Mitsubishi Corporation from the late 1990s accepted the need for European-wide operations and more product customization, although they found the transformation away from parental and ex-patriate control difficult to implement (Fitzgerald and Lai, 2015; Fitzgerald and Rui, 2016). Firm strategies and histories as well as market context have been relevant. From manufacturing basic autos in developing markets, Suzuki preferred to retain advantages in the close direction of its subsidiaries, even in the case of joint ventures. With its low-cost production and research base in China, Huawei Technologies emerged as the world leader in telecommunications infrastructure, and gained from the global centralization of research and production (Jones, 2000; Fitzgerald, 2015; Fitzgerald and Rui, 2016).

International business writers have built on internationalization theory, which argues that the relative costs and risks of conducting an activity inhouse or externally determine the scope and size of firms (Coase, 1937; Williamson, 1975). Buckley and Casson (1985) utilize this transaction cost analysis to explain why multinationals abandon strategies of exporting and licensing in foreign markets for extensive FDI commitments. To safeguard proprietorial knowledge or reputation, or to minimize negotiating and monitoring costs, multinationals might favour the control and coordination of their activities within cross-border managerial hierarchies. Nonetheless, where host country local firms are entrenched, or potential rivals possess advantages, a multinational or its subsidiary might seek to reduce costs or risks through vertical integration, acquisition, alliances, or joint ventures. Through the development of internalization theory and the use of transaction costs analysis, Hennart (1982) provided new insights into the strategies of mining multinationals. Aluminium smelters before 1914 did not integrate backwards with Malayan mines, whose bauxite contained so few impurities that its processing was not asset-specific. The same was true of smelters buying their tin from South East Asia in the inter-war years, while the particularities of Bolivian lode deposits necessitated cross-border vertical integration and organization. Although transportation and Canadian labour costs induced Alcan to build primary smelters in Australia, Britain, Norway, India, and Japan in the 1960s, the main cause was pressure from foreign governments (Rodrik, 1982). Unlike Ford, General Motors from the 1920s onwards preferred to acquire existing firms such as Opel, Vauxhall, or Holden, furthering quick access to the three foreign markets whose sales potential the company believed justified wholly or majority-owned subsidiaries (Wilkins and Hill, 1964; Wilkins, 1974). Fiat from the 1970s based its entry-mode strategy on joint ventures, because it lacked capital, but could exploit its experience of building low-cost cars in foreign markets (Fitzgerald, 2015).

Both the concepts of cross-border ownership advantage and transaction costs are focused on matters of firms, competitors, or markets, and, arguably, location advantages do not give due prominence the impact of national governments on multinational strategy and organization. In general, government policies were the determining factor on entry-mode and joint venture formation. From Brazil in the 1950s to China in the 1990s, usually in resource-rich developing economies and in industrializing nations, entry to the host market was conditional on the founding of joint ventures through which it was assumed, often incorrectly, technology and know-how would be effectively transferred (Jones, 2005a; Fitzgerald, 2015). Transaction cost theory tended to overlook the gains and difficulties of the organizational learning and adaptation implicit in alliances and joint ventures, and the ways in which the interactions between multinational subsidiaries growing in capabilities and the parent business might develop. "New" internalization theory makes a greater attempt to distinguish between non-location-bound advantages, such as technology, and location-bound advantages, such as business networks and political contexts (Rugman and Verbeke, 2001; Buckley and Strange, 2011).

Dunning's highly influential "eclectic paradigm" or "OLI" framework (2008) incorporates Hymer's ownership or "O" advantages, and outlines the circumstances in which a firm would transfer those advantages from a home to a host economy. Dunning utilizes transaction cost analysis to propose internalization (I) advantages, by which multinationals achieve security and efficiencies through cross-border control and coordination. He adds the notion of locational (L) advantages, which are required to justify FDI, such as access to research and development (R&D) networks, lower costs, human skills, intermediate inputs, infrastructure, cheaper finance, and nearness to customers and consumer markets, plus tariffs, import quotas, subsidies, and other government policies. As with its predecessors, the OLI framework has given precedence to the transfer of capabilities and the creation of subsidiaries that become mini-versions or extensions of the parent company. FDI theory has in general been influenced by the particular history of the post-war international economy: the rapid expansion of manufacturing multinationals with parent concerns seeking to transfer core capabilities, and the dominance of US companies that possessed leading capabilities in technology, management, products, brands, and capital. Japanese manufacturing multinationals followed these approaches to multinational growth and organization (Fitzgerald, 2015). As we have seen, the role of subsidiaries and their managements has been depicted as too passive, and organizational practice was highly varied, due to industry, national market, and political factors. Dunning, in later writings, saw his eclectic paradigm as a highly flexible framework capable of explaining complex international business networks founded on vertically integrated operations and dispersed capabilities. But others disagree that the OLI framework easily accommodates structures beyond the parent–daughter format (Mathews, 2002). Dunning in later adaptions of his theory acknowledged the influence of the political, economic, and social contexts in both home and host nations, but the OLI framework concentrates on firm-level considerations rather than national and global forces (Dunning and Lundan, 2008).

Subsidiaries, networks, and governments

Amongst recent debates in international business theory, the role of multinational subsidiaries, cross-border networks, emerging economy firms, and national institutions have been prominent in attempting to address acknowledged gaps. Using Chandler's strategy-structure perspective, Bartlett and Ghoshal (1989) proposed that the local organization of a multinational varied according to the degree it wanted subsidiaries to adopt parental firm practices, fulfil a specialized role, or evolve some optimal hybrid model. But the schema says nothing about which strategic or organizational factors inhibit the internal transfer of practices (Birkinshaw, 2001). Other critics, wary of parent company strategies, look instead to the duality of the headquarters–subsidiary relationship, subsidiary-level decision-making, and local environment effects on the subsidiary. A subsidiary with its own specific capabilities can in addition contribute positively to the whole multinational and its international competitiveness (Beechler *et al.*, 1998). Admittedly, business historians have instinctively taken the parent business and its strategy as their starting point, and international business history would gain from fuller analysis of subsidiaries and their impact on host economies. The long-term political as well as the economic consequences of multinationals controlling natural resources, key infrastructure, and major industries in developing countries lend themselves to historical investigation. Nonetheless, amongst some of the lessons available from business history are: the effects on political and economic development in Africa and Latin America (e.g. Fieldhouse, 1978; Bucheli, 2005); the adaptation of products, brands, and marketing to different national markets and stages of development (e.g. Fitzgerald, 1995; Cox, 2000; Jones, 2005b; Lopes, 2006); and the politics and managerial challenges of automobile production in developed and industrializing economies (e.g. Wilkins and Hill, 1964; Bonin *et al.*, 2003).

The evolution of vertically integrated cross-border networks since the 1990s has increased the opportunity for subsidiaries to play major roles within a global organization (Dorrenbacher and Geppert, 2003; Forsgren *et al.*, 2007). The spread of manufacturing and deregulation has given impetus to FDI strategies of out-sourcing, off-shoring, export-orientated subsidiaries, and efficiency-seeking on labour, transport, or production costs (Dunning and Lundan, 2008; Fitzgerald, 2015). Many multinationals have adopted an organizational model of cross-border vertical production and marketing chains mixing direct control and contracting-out. The classic definition of a multinational in having ownership control of at least one subsidiary capable of undertaking or replicating that firm's main commercial operations simplifies the diversity of multinational organizational arrangements and requirements. The influence of multinationals goes extensively beyond its directly owned or controlled subsidiaries. Planning and contracting by the parent firm has, to an important extent, replaced ownership as the main means of coordinating over productive resources. As well as being well placed to extricate lessons from comparisons with the pre-1914 international economy, business historians can through case studies assess how far reaching organizational changes have altered from the period before the 1990s. The concept of the global factory envisages a strategic role for subsidiaries within flatter organizational hierarchies and cross-border value chains. But there are Japanese examples of core value-added and strategic activities being centralized and cross-border value chains reducing local management autonomy. Historical continuity is hidden amongst more apparent historical change (Buckley, 2009; Fitzgerald and Lai, 2015).

Emerging economy multinationals have been distinguished by their use of international interfirm networks and alliances as a means of expansion. Where the exploitation of home-grown capabilities does not explain multinationalization, as assumed in mainstream FDI theory, strategic alliances and the acquisition of subsidiaries have acted to enhance the competitiveness of the parent business (Mathews, 2002). The Linkage, Leverage, and Learning or LLL model proposed by Mathews hints at different organizational needs and abilities for developing economy multinationals, and at the formation of business networks different from hierarchical parent–subsidiary relationships. Taiwanese firms such as Acer, Foxconn, or TECO have shown a high capacity for working through cross-border networks in which finance, ownership, production, and marketing are geographically dispersed for reasons of strategic advantage or political necessity (Mathews, 2002; Fitzgerald, 2015). Business historians have employed the late development framework to explain the rapid industrialization of continental Europe and subsequently East Asia. State ownership is another distinguishing feature of many emerging economy multinationals. Institutionalist perspectives have so far focused on inward FDI and the organizational tensions created by pressures for internal cross-border and external local alignment (Morgan *et al.*, 2001). They have also side-lined entrepreneurship, managerial agency, and firms in driving economic change, and downgraded transnational forces and the global economy's long history.

Kojima and Ozawa took national and international factors as their starting-point for exploring the link between outward FDI, economic development, trade, and government policy (Kojima, 1978; Ozawa, 1991). The Japanese state, from the 1950s, supported FDI that secured the raw materials and components needed for industrialization; to promote industrialization at home, other forms of FDI were prohibited. Once Japan had reached an advanced stage of economic development, the government loosened capital controls, and, with rising tariff and quota barriers overseas, manufacturing firms sought to transfer their leading capabilities in production, products, and technology to what were preferably wholly owned subsidiaries (Fitzgerald and Lai, 2015; Fitzgerald and Rui, 2016). Better known for identifying management as a key source of firm growth, and influencing both Chandler and the resource-based view (or RBV) of business strategy, Penrose (1959, 1968) wrote a major study of the international oil industry. She notes its managerial bureaucracies, and she describes the importance of cross-border coordination in extracting natural resources from territories that were not the dominant final markets. Above all, she recognized the formative interactions of multinationals and governments, and the impact of these interactions on ownership, internal structures, and networks. Penrose recorded too the practical difficulties of operating in developing economies. With many newly established, decolonized states being highly dependent on the commodity exports foreign firms controlled, the post-war period was marked by clashes between the international property rights of multinationals and national sovereignty. More generally, government policy has historically been a main motive for joint ventures and local ownership participation, and especially so in developing economies. Federal regulations in the US have limited FDI in certain sectors such as real estate and media, just as anti-trust laws have made US multinationals comparatively wary of international alliances and agreements. The relationship between states and multinationals has fundamentally shaped government policies and company strategies, pointing to the need to be wary of privileging firm-centric calculations. The historical importance of government policy meant that FDI was never entirely footloose, despite periods of low regulation before 1914 and since the 1990s (Jones, 2005; Fitzgerald, 2015).

International business theory has paid too much attention to entry mode and strategies, and spent less time discussing how strategies are developed and implemented; it has focused on home-grown capabilities, but less on how capabilities are reconfigured through entrepreneurial processes, market creation in host economies, and learning processes; and it has emphasized the role of the parent multinational, and overlooked subsidiaries and the impact of multinationals on host economies. Investment in governance and management can be conceived as part of strategic implementation. Organizations are not an outcome or solution in themselves, but as part of a continuous process responding to firm-centric, national, and global factors. Where they can be guided by theory or explicit frameworks, business historians have the case-based methods and the contextual, comparative, and complexity approaches to investigate issues of international business, and to assess trends in continuity versus change.

Trends in multinational business organization

What distinguishes multinational business organization is the particular need to deal with cross-border transactions and the economic and political environments of distinct territories. Numerous inter-related factors affect the internal organizational options and adjustments of firms, and include the required or preferred degree of home nation or headquarters control over subsidiaries; the strategic intent, ability, or need to transfer technologies and other capabilities across borders; the initial role and subsequent evolution of subsidiaries, and host environments; global, regional, or industry determinants of cross-border ownership, supply, distribution, product development, human resource, and production integration, or their decentralization; and the strengths and failings of entrepreneurs, managers, and deal-makers (Fitzgerald and Rui, 2016). Differing levels of economic development, the market, and institutional circumstances of home and host nations, diplomatic and power relations between polities, and industry-specific factors are all external influences on trends and patterns in multinational strategies and structures, meaning that outcomes are never uniform. Multinationals tend to respond to broad trends in international political economy, while being key players in their formation. Drawing on a historical perspective, the following sections review the relationship between FDI patterns, multinational organization, national politics, inter-state relations, and economic development. It considers the period to the First World War, and the links between trade, FDI, developing economies, and colonialism; the disruptions to trade between 1914 and 1948, noting new developments in multinational activity; the increase in manufacturing FDI in developed economies during the decades of post-war recovery, the division of the international economy during the Cold War, and the effects of decolonization on multinationals, from 1948; and the period of deregulation, off-shoring, and contracting-out from the 1980s onwards during which multinationals adopted or adapted new organizational forms.

Trade and empire: 1850 to 1914

International trade in merchandise quadrupled between 1850 and 1880, and tripled between 1880 and 1913, when it was equal to 8.7 per cent of global GDP. Levels of accumulated FDI rose markedly throughout the latter half of the nineteenth century to reach between 9.0 and 11.1 per cent of global gross domestic product (GDP) by 1913 (Maddison, 1999; Dunning and Lundan, 2008; Fitzgerald 2015). With international trade driving global business, European and North American multinationals emerged. They forged flexible networks that could transfer the capital, people, knowledge, and technology needed in the production of commodities; coordinate diverse commercial activities in developing territories; and create the essential infrastructure and international transport systems through which goods passed. Two heavily related and dynamic aspects of nineteenth century history were the growth of the international economy and imperialism. Multinationals were active participants in the process of colonization and economic transformation, as well as eventual beneficiaries of imperialism (Jones, 2000; Fitzgerald, 2015).

Industrialization and rising consumption in advanced economies relied on foreign investment in commodity production in less developed territories. Trade-related FDI and the international division of labour between industrialized or developed nations and commodity producers in developing territories were foundations of the period's international political economy. Trading firms emerged as leaders in multinational enterprise, and they organized the finance, personnel, technology, processing, and transportation of commodities required by manufacturers and consumers in Europe and the United States. They could face in undeveloped locations enormous logistical problems, lack of infrastructure, and institutional gaps, and they responded entrepreneurially and flexibly to regional and local contexts by undertaking banking, finance, shipping, processing, plantation management, mineral and oil extraction, insurance, agency management, and other commercial activities through networks and inter-locking partnerships. Trading firms replaced monopolistic chartered companies, which had administered territories. But colonization in Asia and Africa significantly reduced the commercial risks of

Western investors. European and US trading firms brought investments in plantations, mines, oil wells, ports, shipping lines, railways, and processing, and they transferred key personnel, technology, and management know-how. But they also gained organizationally and commercially from their networks with local Asian and Latin American enterprise. They gained disproportionately from the exploitation of natural resources in foreign and colonized lands (Jones, 2000, 2005a; Jonker and Sluyterman, 2005; Fitzgerald, 2015).

Trading, banking, mining, infrastructure, and utility multinationals during this period registered in Europe, where the capital for ventures was raised, yet the operational activities of these "free standing companies" occurred almost entirely in foreign or colonial markets. These multinationals forged commercial networks with each other and with local traders and businesses, including plantation and mine owners in Latin America, and notable Chinese and Indian investors and merchants in Asia. Connections within the governments and ruling elites of Latin America were as important as commercial networks, as were links with the governments of China, Japan, or Siam, and numerous colonial administrations such as the Dutch East Indies or Nigeria. The largest trader, Mackinnon, MacKenzie, operated in Europe, East Africa, the Middle East, India, Australia, and Japan, and, as we have noted, many of the biggest founded corporate headquarters to coordinate their global businesses. The Japanese trading companies which emerged in the last quarter of the nineteenth century gained responsibility for managing Japan's import and export trade, and they had to supplant established European and US networks in Asia and worldwide. For both reasons, with government support, they established large managerial companies. Their overseas offices, nonetheless, created networks of business partners, shippers and agents, involving Western and Chinese enterprises. Internationalized clusters and economically developed zones – such as London's finance and commodity markets, Singapore, Hong Kong, Shanghai, Suez, Panama, Calcutta, Valparaiso, Sao Paolo, or the Rand – improved returns to scale and scope, networking, and deal-making. Multinationals were key players in financing and building much of the infrastructure in these enclaves, and in creating and expanding the local, regional and global dimensions of these transnational nodes (Jones, 2000, 2005a; Jonker and Sluyterman 2005; Fitzgerald, 2015).

By 1914, perhaps 55 per cent of total FDI stock was invested in natural resources, both renewable and non-renewable; some 20 per cent in railways; 10 per cent in trade, distribution, public utilities, and banking; and about 15 per cent in manufacturing. Approximately 64 per cent of FDI was located in developing economies (Fitzgerald, 2015). The free standing company was prominent for trading, banking, utility, and mining multinationals, but not for manufacturers. Multinational organization for most sectors in this period ran counter to the idea of parent firms transferring, through a managerial hierarchy, capabilities developed in a home economy to foreign subsidiaries. Power and economic relations between territories, calculations of commercial and political risk, and relations with governments and colonial administrations all shaped the internal and external dimensions of firms. Some multinationals did not adopt the free standing company model when expanding in search of supplies. Examples include United Fruit which managed plantation, railway, and shipping interests in Central America, US miners in Mexico, food and soap manufacturer Lever Brothers with its palm oil estates in the Belgian Congo, and Dunlop which owned rubber sources in South East Asia (Fieldhouse, 1965; Wilkins, 1974; Bucheli, 2005; Fitzgerald, 2015).

There existed, too, early pioneers in multinational manufacturing, where companies adopted marketing-seeking strategies in developed economies for their products. The Swiss-based Nestlé needed to sell in larger markets; Courtauld sought to exploit its rayon technology; Singer sewing machine, Ford automobile, and Westinghouse wanted to exploit their distinctive products or technologies; and armaments producer Vickers won government orders by founding joint ventures (Wilkins, 1974; Coleman, 1969; Trebilcock, 1977; Bucheli, 2005; Jones, 2005a; Fitzgerald, 2015, 2017). The creation of these subsidiaries involved the transfer of technologies and know-how from the parent company, but the subsidiaries for practical reasons exercised high levels of autonomy, with management adapting ownership advantages and evolving locally specific capabilities. British Westinghouse – later part of Metropolitan-Vickers and Associated Electrical Industries – provides a clear case of how leading technologies and management systems failed until adapted to host market contexts (Fitzgerald, 2017). Specially formed overseas banks were integral to the international economy, while European and US-based banks maintained corresponding partners in foreign markets and avoided FDI. Marine and fire insurance as well as reinsurance did internationalize. The aim was to spread risks, but regulations and differentiated markets meant that subsidiaries were effectively autonomous. Complex regulations and high capital ratios blocked the internationalization of life insurance (Jones, 1993, 2005a; Fitzgerald, 2015).

War and economic setbacks: 1914–1948

The First World War inevitably disrupted capital and trade flows, and brought about the sequestration of German overseas assets. These losses and those following the Russian Revolution were the first recorded examples of governments permanently seizing FDI. Yet the international business system that re-emerged in the 1920s had notable similarities to the period before the conflict. Imperial control remained, and European colonization was expanded to the Middle East. The decline in commodity prices hurt the activities and profitability of traders, but Western firms extended their investments in natural resources, such as rubber, cocoa, or oil (Dalton, 1965; McCann, 1976; Galey, 1979; Grandin, 2009; Jones, 1981; Ferrier, 1982; Sluyterman *et al.*, 2007; Fitzgerald, 2015). To further local industrialization and economic development, radical and nationalist governments in Latin America sequestrated mineral rights, or placed restrictions on multinational utilities, traders, and insurance businesses, altering their governance and reducing parent company control. The multinational organization and business approaches of multinationals in most sectors remained intact (Fitzgerald, 2015).

In 1938, developing economies were the location for nearly 66 per cent of FDI stock (Fitzgerald, 2015). Nonetheless, we can see the growth in manufacturing FDI during the 1920s and 1930s, in which US firms particularly transferred home-grown technologies, systems, or products to subsidiaries in Canada and Europe. Ford preferred to develop greenfield sites in Ontario, Cologne, or Dagenham, UK, while General Motors converted Opel (Germany), Vauxhall (UK), or Holden (Australia) into subsidiaries (Fitzgerald, 2015). Mining and oil businesses grew rapidly too in the inter-war period, and transferred capital, technology, and personnel. The Great Depression of 1929–1931 was the significant turning point. Tariffs hurt trading firms, but encouraged manufacturing FDI. Multinational activities in public utilities declined in favour of national government and municipal initiatives. Policies of nationalism and autarky in Germany and Japan reduced the control that parent firms could exercise over their subsidiaries. Manufacturing, oil, and mining showed the higher incidence of cross-border management and parent–subsidiary relationships, while networks continued to be more operationally significant in the service sectors. On the whole, international cartels tended to be undermined by external price competition, except where collusion had legislative backing as in the cases of tin, rubber, and tea (Jones, 2000, 2005a; Fitzgerald, 2015).

Cold War and decolonization: 1948–1980

Exports grew markedly during the post-war decades: they amounted to 10.2 per cent and 12.5 per cent of world GDP in 1980 and 1990 respectively, and, by 2006, the figure had reached 29.3 per cent. Multinationals controlled in 2000 approximately two-thirds of merchandise and service exports, much of it through intra-trade within their cross-border organizations. Outward FDI stock in 1993 at 11.3 per cent of global GDP finally overtook the previous high point of 1914 (Maddison, 1999; WTO, 2000, 2007, 2010; UNCTAD 1991, 2000; Fitzgerald, 2015). The impact of FDI and especially US multinationals established, by the 1960s, the idea of the multinational as a business distinct from purely domestic firms. Once the multinational had been defined, theorists looked to explain which strategies or organization obtained success in foreign markets, and how firms might transfer their capabilities in the creation of competitive subsidiaries. The work of theorists reflected growing political and popular awareness of multinationals in the international economy and of their impact upon individual states (Hymer, 1960; Vernon, 1966; Buckley and Casson, 1985; Dunning and Lundan, 2008).

As in the inter-war years, the common strategy of post-war manufacturing multinationals was market-seeking within developed economies, and firms sought overseas customers for goods in which they had a price, product, production, or marketing leadership. After the Second World War, US oil and chemical firms led the surge in FDI, and they were followed by manufacturers generally. Corporations in the US had made breakthroughs in mass manufacturing and marketing, and built teams of managers and technicians to deal with increasingly large and complex operations. They evolved organizational hierarchies with a strategic headquarters at the top, but they devolved in principle major responsibility for products or geographical area to a layer of divisional management, which in turn oversaw departments in charge of business functions such as production or marketing. The emergence of large firms with competitive resources and capabilities increased the likelihood of FDI. Where host market sales justified investment, US manufacturers preferred wholly owned or directly controlled subsidiaries that safeguarded and better utilized technological and managerial know-how transferred from the parent company, although political and economic contexts necessitated variations (Wilkins, 1974; Jones, 2005; Fitzgerald, 2015).

To facilitate international expansion, some large US firms could use their multidivisional model of devolved management, and formed an overseas division to supervise national subsidiaries. Goodyear, for example, created the Goodyear International Company in 1957, and expanded from Latin America and South Africa to France, Italy, and Germany over the course of ten years. Marketing-seeking manufacturers transformed world investment patterns and the homogenization of consumer tastes. The figure for FDI stock located in developing territories had fallen to 32.3 per cent by 1960. Manufacturing was responsible, in 1978, for 52 per cent of world FDI stock, services 26 per cent, and natural resources 22 per cent (Wilkins, 1974; Jones, 2005; Dunning and Lundan, 2008; Fitzgerald, 2015).

With US multinationals possessing 7500 subsidiaries in 1950, and 23,000 in 1966, they faced a huge organizational challenge. An immediate strategic objective from the 1950s was to build a cross-border organization to facilitate the flow of superior resources and capabilities from the parent firm. The second task in practice was to allow subsidiaries enough operational freedom to meet the specific needs of a national market. The clash between headquarters control and decentralization increased where a subsidiary grew in size and importance within a multinational. Headquarters control and monitoring had limitations, and international coordination could depend on the subsidiary having expatriate managers or staff loyal to and familiar with the parent firm. The sharing of senior personnel also assisted the transfer of capabilities or defined best practice, and at the parent business aided understanding of a subsidiary's circumstances. While ownership and management were international, the cross-border integration of production remained minimal. Manufacturing subsidiaries tended to serve national markets, even if they coordinated with the parent in general management or product development. Mining and oil companies similarly transferred personnel, technology, and know-how, but government policies and notably in developing economies, the political and logistical advantages of local support and participation, and risk-sharing meant that joint ventures were more common than in manufacturing, as indeed was nationalization. Geology determined resource-seeking strategies and the locale of production. Mining and oil firms were less likely than manufacturers to produce and sell in the same country, and therefore their international coordination was organizationally important, although levels of extraction, processing, and marketing integration varied between mineral types. Distribution subsidiaries tended to be directly owned by the multinational, unlike over time production facilities. Multinationals operating in developing nations faced different organizational challenges from those carrying out main-line activities in developed economies. Case studies show the effective transfer of technologies and management know-how by multinationals to their foreign subsidiaries in developed countries, although the effects on national economies as a whole are less clear. In developing economies, with FDI biased to mining, oil, and plantations, the benefits to host nations appear limited to political and business elites and geographically to particular enclaves (Wilkins, 1974; Jones, 2005a; Fitzgerald, 2015).

Progressive General Agreement on Tariffs and Trade (GATT) rounds, European Economic Community (EEC) policies, and falling transport costs all encouraged gains from cross-border interaction and undermined the autonomy of subsidiaries. From 1965, trade barriers for automobiles between the United States and Canada ended, and "continentalism" increasingly affected a wide swathe of goods and commodities. The EEC established internal free trade from 1968. The founding of Ford Europe the year before signalled the response of multinationals to cross-border interaction and production (Fitzgerald, 2015). Regional headquarters and structures were a trend of the 1970s and 1980s, although some multinationals preferred worldwide product divisions. They drew control from both the parent firm and individual national subsidiaries, simultaneously centralizing and decentralizing managerial decision-making, and converging and diverging products and systems. Over time, regional and international product divisions might evolve into matrix organizations accommodating the two organizational imperatives of product and geography. Matrix structures that additionally incorporated support services such as accounting, personnel or R&D were rarer, and became associated with slow decision-making and internal conflicts. Traders Cargill-Tradax supplies one illustration (Broehl, 2008). In mining and oil, centralized functional organizations found less value in founding a separate international division, since upstream extraction, processing, downstream sales, technology, capital, personnel had to be coordinated globally (Chalmin, 1990; Jones, 2005a; Fitzgerald, 2015).

British multinationals, like their US rivals, tended towards parent–subsidiary structures and international divisions, but there are suggestions of less monitoring by the parent and greater subsidiary autonomy in practice. Multinationals from continental Europe were more inclined to form holding companies that incorporated nationally based subsidiaries and the main business, and such holding companies exercised minimal direct managerial control or monitoring over formal subsidiaries. Federal antitrust law moved US firms away from holding-company structures, but their lead in technology, management, products, production, or marketing explained the greater concern of US multinationals overall for organizational integration. Many European firms relied on the head of the parent firm exercising control or coordination through personal relationships with the heads of subsidiaries. Anglo-Dutch Unilever and Nestlé viewed national consumer markets as distinct, with their own products and brands, and cross-border coordination brought seemingly few returns to scale or other efficiencies. Unilever's organization continued to be essentially multi-domestic, while Procter and Gamble from the United States had a more international cross-border approach. Unilever's attempts in the 1970s at product standardization in Europe brought mixed results. Swiss pharmaceutical Ciba and Dutch electronics producer Philips record how managers returning from the United States brought the latest ideas on organization back to Europe. Ciba adapted the multi-divisional form by introducing divisional boards, and its merged successor Ciba-Geigy founded a matrix structure in which overseas divisions reported to product and area heads at the main firm. Philips' matrix plotted overlying lines between product divisions and national firms, and between line management and technical support (Franko, 1976; Jones, 2005a, 2005b; Fitzgerald, 2015).

Deregulation and cross-border production: from 1980

The production, human resource management, and technological achievements of manufacturers underpinned the rise of the Japanese economy in the post-war decades. The lifting of Japanese capital controls, the increasing value of the yen, and the imposition of tariffs and import quotas in Europe and the United States explain their move from exports to FDI from the 1980s onwards. As well as staffing newly found subsidiaries with expatriate managers, the parent firm and its production departments maintained a centralized control of international operations, in order to transfer as much as practicable what were perceived as best practice capabilities. The founding of European-wide headquarters by Japanese multinationals from the late 1990s hinted at the need for decentralizing to some extent decision-making and product development, although arguably Japanese multinationals found this organizational shift difficult to achieve (Fitzgerald and Rui, 2016).

If the post-war decades had been characterized by the spread of manufacturing FDI and directly controlled subsidiaries, the period from the 1990s saw across all sectors movement towards joint ventures and business alliances in order to share R&D, production, or marketing costs. The lowering of investment barriers and privatizations encouraged international mergers and acquisitions (M&As), and transformed entry mode strategies and the speed by which firms could internationalize. International M&As reached their peak in 2000 when they accounted for 99.5 per cent of all FDI (UNCTAD, 2001). They stimulated, too, a greater tendency amongst multinationals to engage in asset-seeking approaches by multinationals. Contrary to established theories of FDI, multinationals did not need ownership advantages or competitive capabilities to overcome the disadvantage of operating in foreign markets, but could buy foreign firms that already possessed advantages and capabilities. The fall of the Berlin Wall and the Communist bloc, the reduction of controls over utilities and services by nation states, and the creation of the European Single Market opened up opportunities for both FDI and international M&As from the 1990s onwards. The spread of industrialization to developing economies and especially to Asia established firms with cost advantages which could buy an established technology, product, or brand. For example, Tata from India acquired Jaguar Land Rover, in the UK, just as the private Chinese firm of Geely became the owner of Sweden's Volvo. Organization building proved inevitably more difficult than acquisitions, and it was unclear to what extent technological or managerial know-how was effectively fed back to an acquiring multinational or could upgrade performance in its home economy (Fitzgerald, 2015).

The worldwide spread of industrialization, the lowering of investment barriers, and the evolution of internationally connected and export-orientated clusters furthered strategies of offshoring, cost-cutting, and economy-seeking FDI (UNCTAD, 2001). By 2005, natural resources accounted for nearly 8 per cent of world FDI stock, manufacturing nearly 30 per cent, and services approximately 61, with 1–2 per cent unspecified. Developing economies, the locale for just over 1 per cent of world FDI stock in 1990, could claim nearly 10 per cent by 2005. Levels of FDI assets reached in 2009 the remarkable figure of 35 per cent of global GDP, although trends in growth, trade, and investment turned downwards thereafter in the wake of the global financial crisis for which multinational banks bear the main responsibility (UNCTAD, 2007, 2010; Fitzgerald, 2015). But this impressive measure underestimated the importance of major multinationals since they could not capture trends in the organization of international business since the 1990s: focusing on core operations, companies increasingly coordinated or controlled cross-border networks of contracted suppliers and allied firms, and their importance to the international economy went beyond fully owned subsidiaries or joint ventures. Post-1990 trends had parallels with the organization of the international economy before 1914. Broad transformations in international political economy induced multinationals to reconsider the scope of parent–daughter structures in favour of global value chains and contracting-out. Multinationals increasingly combined full equity, partial equity, strategic partners, and networks of contracted partners, suppliers and distributors. Multinationals became more deeply engaged in the cross-border organization of production chains in addition to international ownership and management (Dunning and Lundan, 2008). Federative structures utilized the vertical control of major products, technologies, key production stages, or brands within an integrated organization alongside the horizontal coordination of contractors and business partners through networks. International production prompted the notion of the global factory, in which subsidiaries could operate as world production hubs and contribute to production chains within a comparatively flat hierarchy. Taiwan's Foxconn and Singapore's Flextronics in electronics, Japan's Denso Corporation in auto-parts, and Hong Kong's Li & Fung in fashion emerged as significant multinationals by undertaking contracted production and coordinating complete product lines on behalf of other companies. Organizational forms of contracting-out and off-shoring have spread manufacturing and support services internationally, but, through deregulation and the extension of low-skill, low value-added production chains, it has become more problematic for host nations to capture the benefits of global business (Jones, 2005a; Fitzgerald, 2015; Fitzgerald and Rui, 2016).

Conclusion

Through their research, business historians have widely acknowledged the role of multinational enterprises in the making of global business. They have the methodological tools to provide empirically grounded cases of multinationals, which shaped as well as responded to complex economic, political, social, international, and comparative contexts. Multinationals must balance external consistency with local environments alongside internal consistency through cross-border organization, and business historians could usefully explore this dilemma and its commercial, political, and cultural consequences more explicitly. There was never a single managerial approach suited to all contexts and industries, and strategic and organizational imperatives evolved over time. The development of global business organization, capabilities, products, and services was a necessarily contingent and negotiated process, and business history's situated approach is well suited to understanding the many factors involved. Business organization deals with the creation, transfer, monitoring, and utilization of key capabilities that underpin economic growth, and multinationals have controlled the resources in finance, technology, management knowledge, personnel, skills, and products required by nation states. Business history has provided insights into the impact of multinationals on the evolution of the global economy, and, when theory has indicated narrower options, into the variety of organizational forms that multinationals have adopted. But much is left to research on the relationship between multinationals with both home and host governments, on the barriers to transferring and utilizing the resources and capabilities owned by multinationals, and on the wide-ranging effects of multinationals on host economies and economic opportunities.

References

Bartlett, C.A. and Ghoshal, S. (1989), *Managing Across Borders* (Cambridge, MA: Harvard Business Press).

Beechler, S., Bird, A., and Taylor, S. (eds) (1998), *Japanese MNCs Abroad: Individual and Organizational Learning* (New York: Oxford University Press).

Birkinshaw, J. (2001), "Strategy and Management in MNE Subsidiaries", in Rugman, A.M. and Brewer, T. (eds), *The Oxford Handbook of International Business* (Oxford: Oxford University Press), 380–401.

Bonin, H., Lung, Y., and Tolliday, S. (eds) (2003), *Ford, 1903–2003: The European History*, 2 vols (Paris: Editions P.L.A.G.E.).

Broehl, W.G. (2008), *Cargill: From Commodities to Customers* (Lebanon, NH: University Press of New England).

Bucheli, M. (2005), *Bananas and Business: The United Fruit Company in Colombia, 1899–2000* (New York: New York University Press).

Buckley, P. (2009), "The Impact of the Global Factory on Economic Development", *Journal of World Business*, 44, 2, 131–143.

Buckley, P.J. and Casson, M. (1985), *The Economic Theory of the Multinational Enterprise* (London: Macmillan).

Buckley, P.J. and Strange, R. (2011), "The Governance of the Multinational Enterprise: Insights from Internalization Theory", *Journal of Management Studies*, 48, 2, 460–470.

Chalmin, P. (1990), *The Making of a Sugar Giant: Tate and Lyle, 1859–1989* (Chur: Harwood Academic Publishers).

Chandler. A.D. (1962), *Strategy and Structure: Chapters in the History of the American Industrial Enterprise* (Cambridge, MA: MIT Press).

Chandler, A.D. (1977), *The Visible Hand: The Managerial Revolution in American Business* (Cambridge, MA: Harvard University Press).

Chandler, A.D. (1990), *Scale and Scope: The Dynamics of Industrial Capitalism* (Cambridge, MA: Harvard University Press).

Chandler, A.D. and Mazlish, B. (eds) (1977), *Leviathans: Multinational Corporations and the New Global History* (Cambridge: Cambridge University Press).

Coase, R.H. (1937), "The Nature of the Firm", *Economica*, 4.

Coleman, D.C. (1969), *Courtaulds: An Economic and Social History*, vols 1–2 (Oxford: Clarendon Press).

Cox, H. (2000), *The Global Cigarette: Origins and Evolution of British American Tobacco, 1880–1945* (Oxford: Oxford University Press).

Dalton, G. (1965), "History, Politics, and Economic Development in Liberia", *Journal of Economic History*, 25.

Dorrenbacher, C. and Geppert, M. (2003), *Politics and Power in the Multinational Corporation: The Role of Institutions, Interests and Identities* (Cambridge: Cambridge University Press).

Dunning, J.H. and Lundan, S. (2008), *Multinational Enterprises and the Global Economy* (Aldershot: Edward Elgar).

Fieldhouse, D. (1965), *Colonial Empires: A Comparative Survey from the 18th Century* (New York: Delacorte Press).

Fieldhouse, D. (1978), *Unilever Overseas* (London: Croom Helm).

Ferrier, R.W. (1982), *The History of the British Petroleum Company*, vol. 1 (Cambridge: Cambridge University Press).

Fitzgerald, R. (1995), *Rowntree and the Marketing Revolution, 1862–1969* (Cambridge: Cambridge University Press).

Fitzgerald, R. (2003), "Corporate Governance, Business Organization and Competitiveness: British and Japanese Business in the Inter-War Period", in Fitzgerald, R. and Abe, E. (eds), *The Development of Corporate Governance in Japan and Britain* (London: Gower Press), 58–96.

Fitzgerald, R. (2015), *The Rise of the Global Economy: Multinational Enterprise and the Making of the Modern World* (Cambridge: Cambridge University Press).

Fitzgerald, R. (2017), "International Business and the Development of British Electrical Manufacturing, 1886–1929", *Business History Review*, 91, 31–70.

Fitzgerald, R. and Lai, J. (2015), "Strategic Capabilities and the Emergence of the Global Factory: Omron in China", *Asia Pacific Business Review*, 21, 3, 333–363.

Fitzgerald, R. and Rui, H. (2016), "Whose Fall and Whose Rise? Lessons of Japanese MNCs for Chinese and Emerging Economy MNCs", *Asia Pacific Business Review*, 22, 4, 534–566.

Forsgren, M., Holm, U., and Johanson, J. (2007), *Managing the Embedded MNC: A Business Network View* (Montpellier: Edward Elgar).

Franko, L. (1976), *The European Multinationals* (Stamford, CT: Greford Publishers).

Galey, J. (1979), "Industrialist in the Wilderness: Henry Ford's Amazon Venture", *Journal of InterAmerican Studies and World Affairs*, 21.

Grandin, G. (2009), *Fordlandia: The Rise and Fall of Henry Ford's Forgotten Jungle City* (New York: Picador).

Hennart, J.-F. (1982), *A Theory of Multinational Enterprise* (Ann Arbor, MI: University of Michigan Press).

Hymer, S. (1960), "The International Operations of National Firms: a Study of Direct Foreign Investment" (MIT: PhD thesis).

Jones, G. (1981), *The State and the Emergence of the British Oil Industry* (Basingstoke: Edward Elgar).

Jones, G. (1993), *British Multinational Banking, 1830–1990* (Oxford: Clarendon Press).

Jones, G. (2000), *Merchants to Multinationals* (Oxford: Oxford University Press).

Jones, G. (2005a), *Multinationals and Global Capitalism: From the Nineteenth to the Twenty-First Century* (Oxford: Oxford University Press).

Jones, G. (2005b), *Renewing Unilever: Transformation and Tradition* (Oxford: Oxford University Press).

Jonker, J. and Sluyterman, K.E. (2005), *At Home on the World Markets: Dutch International Trading Companies from the 16th Century to the Present* (Montreal: McGill Queen's University Press).

Kawabe, N. (1987), "Development of Overseas Competition by General Trading Companies, 1868–1945", in Yonekawa, S. and Yoshihara, H. (eds), *Business History of General Trading Companies* (Tokyo: Tokyo University Press), 71–103.

Kojima, K. (1978), *Direct Foreign Investment: A Japanese Model of Multinational Business Operations* (London: Croom Helm).

Lopes da Silva, T. (2006), *Global Brands: the Evolution of Multinationals in Alcoholic Beverages* (Cambridge: Cambridge University Press).

McCann, T.P. (1976), *An American Company: The Tragedy of United Fruit* (New York: Random House).

Maddison, A. (1999), *Monitoring the World Economy* (Paris: OECD).

Mathews, J.A. (2002), *Dragon Multinationals: A New Model for Global Growth* (Oxford: Oxford University Press).

Matsusaka, Y.T. (2003), *The Making of Japanese Manchuria, 1904–1932* (Cambridge: Cambridge University Press).

Morgan, G., Kristensen, P.H., and Whitley, R. (eds) (2001), *The MNC Firm: Organizing Across Institutional and National Divides* (Oxford: Oxford University Press).

Ozawa, T. (1991), "Japan in a New Phase of MNC-ism and Industrial Upgrading: Functional Integration of Trade, Growth and FDI", *Journal of World Trade*, 25, 1, 43–60.

Patrikeff, F. and Shukman, H. (2007), *Railways and the Russo-Japanese War: Transporting War* (New York: M.E. Sharpe).

Penrose, E. (1959), *The Theory of the Growth of the Firm* (Oxford: Oxford University Press).

Penrose, E. (1968), *The Large International Firm in Developing Countries: The International Petroleum Industry* (New York: Praeger).

Rodrik, D. (1982), "Changing Patterns of Ownership and Integration in the International Bauxite-Aluminium Industry", in Jones, L.P. (ed.), *Public Enterprise in Less Developed Countries* (Cambridge: Cambridge University Press), 182–214.

Rugman, A.M. and Verbeke, A. (2001), "Subsidiary-Specific Advantages in Multinational Enterprises", *Strategic Management Journal*, 22, 3, 237–250.

Sluyterman, K.E., Howarth, S., Jonker, S., and Van Zanden, J.L. (2007), *A History of Royal Dutch Shell*, vols 1–4 (Oxford: Oxford University Press).

Trebilcock, C. (1977), *The Vickers Brothers* (London: Europa).

United Nations Conference on Trade and Development (UNCTAD) (1991, 2000, 2001, 2007, 2010), *World Investment Report* (Geneva: UNCTAD).

Vernon, R. (1966), "International Investment and International Trade in the Product Cycle", *Quarterly Journal of Economics*, 95.

Wilkins, M. (1974), *The Maturing of Multinational Enterprise: American Business Abroad from 1914 to 1970* (Cambridge, MA: Harvard University Press).

Wilkins, M. and Hill, F. (1964), *American Business Abroad: Ford on Six Continents* (Detroit, MI: Wayne State University Press).

Williamson, O.E. (1975), *Markets and Hierarchies: Analysis and Antitrust Implications* (New York: Macmillan).

World Trade Organization (2000, 2007, 2010), *International Trade Statistics* (Geneva: WTO).

Yonekawa, S. (ed.) (1990), *General Trading Companies: A Comparative and Historical Study* (Tokyo: Tokyo University Press).

35

BUSINESS AND SUSTAINABILITY

Ann-Kristin Bergquist

Introduction

This chapter provides a long-term business history perspective on sustainability. The twentieth century is unique in history, not only because of its enormous technological progress and rise in the standard of living, but because no other century in human history can be compared with the twentieth century for its growth in energy use, depletion of natural resources and an overall growth of problems related to global environmental sustainability (McNeill, 2000; UNEP, 2016).[1] It has often been asserted that industrial capitalism, globalization and multinational companies have been central actors in this development (Wright and Nyberg, 2015).

Business historians have shown how business has driven economic growth since the Industrial Revolution. They have also detailed how firms, especially large manufacturing ones, contributed to the commercialization of new products and processes, which embodied innovative technologies that critically impacted the world economy since the nineteenth century (Chandler *et al.*, 1997; Jones and Zeitlin, 2008). It could be provocatively suggested that business historians have, therefore, documented how business made the world unsustainable (Bergquist, 2019). The creation of modern capitalism was essentially the story of manufacturing firms growing large by employing enormous amounts of fossil fuels: the railroad industry, the oil industry, the electric industry, the chemical industry, the car industry and others are examples. Fossil fuels and natural resource depletion have been crucial components of both the past two centuries of economic expansion, and of today's current environmental crisis.

It is often assumed among scholars and business practitioners that business challenges related to sustainability are a recent phenomenon. But as business and environmental historians have increasingly shown, ideas and concerns about pollution and nature conservation date back to at least the nineteenth century. A handful of entrepreneurs even then began thinking that pollution prevention, recycling, renewable energy and providing healthy food were their responsibilities (Rosen, 1995; Jones, 2017a; Bergquist and Lindmark, 2016). Incipient steps towards pollution control and creation of green businesses was taken as a first reaction towards industrialization in the late nineteenth and early twentieth centuries, but a much broader and more forceful social movement only emerged in the 1960s. The environmental awakening in the late 1960s mobilized a mass movement, a development of new institutions, including a complex of laws and organizational bodies to protect the environment (Brenton, 1994; Jones, 2017a). Harsh critique against the business community was coupled with this environmental awakening, initially in the United States (Carroll *et al.*, 2012; Rome, 2017). Environmental regulation emerged as a serious challenge in polluting industries, with operations based in Western countries (Coglianese and Anderson, 2012; Gunningham *et al.*, 2003).

Since the 1960s and 1970s, the issue of business and the environment grew to become broader and much more complex. The Brundtland report in 1987 brought environmental issues into the concept of sustainable development paraphrased as: 'meeting the needs of the present generation without comprising the ability for future generations to meet their own needs' (WCED, 1987). In the 2000s, the 'greening' label started to morph into 'sustainability' and sustainability became translated into business language, such as the 'triple bottom line' and 'eco-efficiency' and became diffused into virtually every major corporation in the world (Ehrenfeld, 2012; Jones, 2017a). The issue of business and the environment also received increasing attention in academic research from the mid-1980s, including the field of business administration. The development is mirrored in *The Oxford Handbook of Business and the Natural Environment* (Bansal and Hoffman, 2012), which included 38 overview chapters of different subfields in business strategy, organizational theory, marketing, accounting, international business, finance and other fields.

Business history was for a long time silent about the topic with only a handful of scholars engaged in it. A first call to integrate the natural environment in business history was made in a special issue in *Business History Review* in 1999 (Rosen and Sellers, 1999). In 2011, the editors of the same journal noticed that business historians had still devoted surprisingly little attention to the environment, and called for an incorporation of sustainability in mainstream business history (Friedman & Jones, 2011). The earliest theme in business historical research, dating to the 1990s, was focused on how business and governments had responded to industrial pollution problems in the nineteenth and the first part of the twentieth century (e.g. Rosen and Sellers, 1999; Rosen, 1995, 2003; Uekötter, 1999, see also Chapter 36 by Stokes and Miller in this volume). Since then, there has been an expansion of research that has covered the period after the 1960s (Bergquist 2019). Existing research does not cover all industries and all different time periods, so the coverage of the literature in this chapter is mainly centred on the Western world. The chapter begins with an overview of the current debate of sustainability and its historical roots, before turning to how business has responded to this challenge over time.

Business and sustainability: defining the challenge

The issue of sustainability is deeply rooted in the Industrial Revolution. Before the Industrial Revolution, however, the pre-modern growth conditions were constrained by ecological factors (Pomeranz, 2000; Clark, 2007). The pre-industrial growth was situated in an organic energy regime, based on human and animal muscle power for mechanical power and on wood and other biomass for heat (Wrigley 2010). With the Industrial Revolution, these growth restrictions were crossed when coal replaced firewood and charcoal. The key technology that brought coal into the energy system was the steam engine, which laid the foundation for intensified industrialization, the growth of large firms and exponential economic growth based on fossil fuels.

Core inventions of the Second Industrial Revolution such as electricity, the combustion engine, advances in the chemical industry spurred an economic growth driven by the expansion of big business (Chandler *et al.*, 1997). But this also urged forward further environmental degradations, which from the 1950s onwards began to accelerate tremendously (McNeill and Engelke, 2014). Many natural scientists have suggested that our planet has entered a new geological age, the so-called Anthropocene, as an effect of accumulated human economic activity

(Steffen *et al.*, 2015). The previous age, the Holocene began 10,000 to 12,000 years ago, when the climate became warmer and much more stable. It is argued that the Anthropocene begins around 1800 with the onset of industrialization, with rapid expansion in the use of fossil fuels being its central feature (Steffen *et al.*, 2007). The 1950s thus mark the beginning of the second stage of the Anthropocene – a stage that has been coined the Great Accelera-tion. The Anthropocene and Great Acceleration debate essentially draws attention to the explosion of population growth and an unsustainable and exponential energy use after 1945 and its negative impact on the Earth system, most critically climate change, loss of biosphere integrity, land-system change and altered biogeochemical cycles (Steffen *et al.*, 2015). Fossil fuel based capitalism, with its deep roots in the nineteenth and twentieth century, are integ-rated with this debate (McNeill and Engelke, 2014; Bergquist, 2019). The historical develop-ment of carbon dioxide (CO_2) emissions is illustrated in Figure 35.1, and demonstrates the acceleration of these emissions since the 1950s.

The concept of sustainable development has been abundantly debated and, unlike climate change, sustainability and sustainable development did not emerge as a scientific concept (Cohen *et al.*, 1998; Robinson, 2004). In research, the concept of corporate sustainability is still developing (Whiteman *et al.*, 2013) and scholars are debating the usefulness of the concept at the business level (Bergquist *et al.*, 2019). The business historian Geoffrey Jones (2017a) has shown that sustainability should be understood as a concept that has been socially and politically constructed, also by business, and has reflected the interests and values of those entrepreneurs and organizations being involved. For instance, when sustainability became widely translated into business strategies in the 1990s, one critical issue emerged about how to 'measure' sustainability, how to evaluate and claim that a business practice or a product is 'green' and what criteria should be used to weigh such claims (Jones, 2017a; Robinson, 2004).

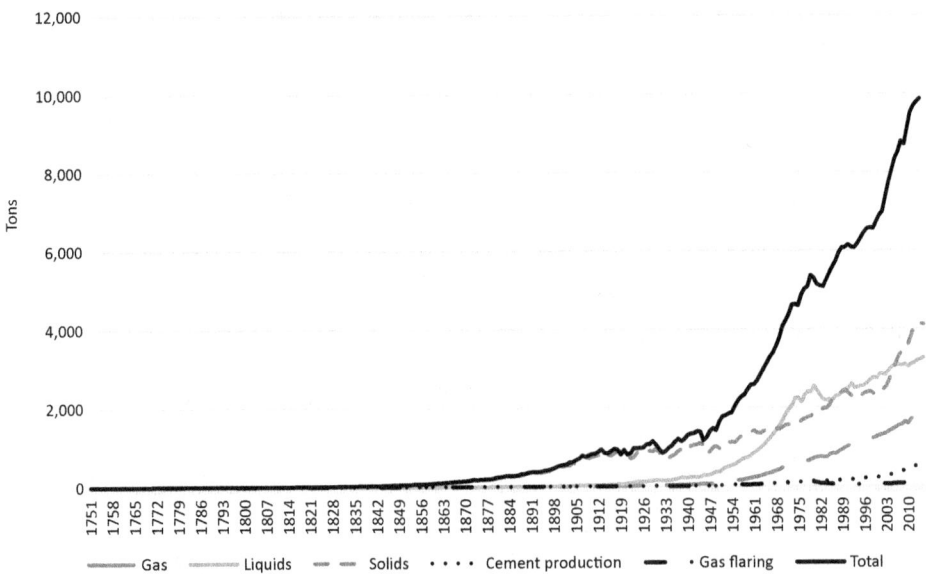

Figure 35.1 Carbon dioxide emissions from fossil fuels, 1751–2007 (tons)

Source: Boden *et al.* (2017).

Corporate practices in responding to the sustainability challenge, again with climate change as its central issue, involve an understanding of how business has captured and constructed the concept.

Business and the first wave of environmentalism

Seen in a long-term perspective, the reaction towards the environmental destruction caused by industrial growth came in two waves (e.g. Guha, 2000; Weber and Soderstrom, 2012; Jones, 2017a). A *first wave* of environmentalism occurred in the nineteenth century, which came to proceed step-by-step with the Industrial Revolution up until the 1930s. It included anti-pollution movements and the first local anti-pollution legislation in the United States and Western Europe, along with a growing nature conservation movement, which, among other things, triggered the establishment of national parks. The initiatives were at first isolated and sporadic, but gained force as the nineteenth century ended and the evils of polluted cities, industries and impoverished communities generated a fledging social movements in the United States (Post, 2012: 542) but also in Europe (Rootes, 2004). A *second wave* of environmentalism emerged in the 1960s but had other characteristics than the first wave. Besides turning into a mass movement, the second wave was based on a dramatic expansion of science and rational models of knowledge about nature as well as the emergence of an anti-establishment and politically left-leaning critique of capitalism after the Second World War. The first wave was primarily a cultural movement with limited mass mobilization and protest capacity to stop the course of industrialization (Weber and Soderstrom, 2012).

Research looking at the forceful impact on the natural environment caused by the industrial capitalism was first driven by environmental historians (Worster, 1979; Cronon, 1991). The seminal work of Worster (1979) delivered a harsh critique of capitalism, which became formative for the subject (Rome, 2017). The one-sided perception of business and capitalism as a dark destructive force turned out to be more complicated and diverse when business historians like Christine Meisner Rosen began to take a closer look into processes 'inside' the business community. She demonstrated how business in the late nineteenth century responded with great variety to controlling smoke in industrializing American cities, where some businessmen voluntary committed themselves to smoke abatement and supported regulation, while some actors were engaged in organized resistance to impose controls (Rosen, 1995). The importance of awareness of the variety of business responses among individual entrepreneurs, managers, industries and countries was stressed by Christine Meisner Rosen and Christopher Sellers (1999) when they argued for an 'ecocultural' history of business.

Manufacturing industries

Technological inventions, such as steam power, and later the electricity and the combustion engine, formed clusters of innovations that not only enabled business corporations to utilize an enormous amount of fossil fuels, metals and wood fibres in production, but also possibilities for firms to grow very large (Chandler, 1990). Along with the rise of modern science, fossil fuel enabled massive increases in productivity through the spread of factory production and economies of scale and scope. This in turn drove global commerce (Jones, 2008), but also environmental degradation to an extent that the world had not experienced before (McNeill, 2000).

The breakthrough of industrial capitalism and the first wave of globalization thus gave rise to very serious negative externalities, and organized local protests, conflicts and even governmental interventions emerged in more seriously damaged areas. One battle was played out in industrial cities, concerning issues around coal smoke (Uekötter, 2009; Rosen, 1995) and another battle emerged in mining and metals smelting districts (Maysilles, 2011; LeCain, 2000, 2009; Newell, 1997). In the early nineteenth century, the magnitude of conflicts and the level of environmental destruction was most serious in the United States, where large copper corporations, such as the Anaconda Company, came under pressure to control emissions of sulphur and arsenic into the air (LeCain, 2009). New technologies were developed to curb the worst problem and was spread to Europe through business networks (Bergquist and Lindmark, 2016). Studies of the US copper industry (LeCain, 2000) and petroleum industry (Gorman, 1999) show that pollution was basically viewed as an 'efficiency' problem. Crude wasted in pipeline leaks was equal to wasted money and sulphur discharged from metal smelter smokestacks was viewed as wasted money as well, as sulphur was a profitable by product. A definition of pollution as an efficiency problem also emerged in the Swedish pulp and paper industry, whose biggest problem at the time was water pollution (Söderholm & Bergquist, 2012). German pulp and paper industry advanced technology to recycle chemicals, triggered both by public complaints over water pollution as well as by cost saving motives (Mutz, 2009).

Although the emissions of pollutants were much lower per produced ton of copper, pulp or crude oil in 1920 than it had been in 1890, the total level of pollution yet continued to increase as the total level of production expanded. However, when the notion of 'eco-efficiency' became widespread more than a century later as a new business concept to implement sustainable development (Ehrenfeld, 2012), it was related to the same ideas of efficiency that had appeared many decades earlier. The rationale behind the eco-efficiency concept was simply to produce more value with less environmental impact. There exists a number of examples of how polluting firms were challenged to curb their avalanche environmental impact as the Second Industrial Revolution took hold, but, indeed, it did not change the course of unsustainable development in manufacturing industries.

Origins of green business

Business history research has recently shown that in parallel to the growth of manufacturing firms, there were also alternative green businesses active in healthy food and in wind and solar energy. Jones (2017a) has shown that from the mid-nineteenth century to the early twentieth century Europe and the United States saw the emergence of what can be likened to 'proto-green' industries created by a cohort of unconventional entrepreneurs. The foundation for future business in healthy and organic food was laid already in the late nineteenth and early twentieth centuries (Jones, 2007a). Also the wind and solar industry originates from entrepreneurial achievements that date back to the late nineteenth century. With further achievements on the technology, wind power for electricity generation came to boom in Denmark during the First World War. The challenge for the wind and solar energy business to grow and scale was, however, overwhelming as long as coal and, later, oil remained cheap, especially during the decades after the Second World War. But, as Jones (2017a) demonstrates, these early ventures laid the basis for technologies, techniques and ideologies which created the foundation for future green large and global firms, such as Whole Foods Market and Vestas.

Household waste in cities has been a well-known nuisance problem since medieval ages, but with industrialization the amount of waste turned into a large-scale challenge. Recycling had already attracted business entrepreneurs in countries, including the United States, Denmark, Germany and Hungary, from the nineteenth century (Jones, 2017a). But by the twentieth century with the rise of mass production and mass consumption, waste became a seriously growing problem, especially in modern cities in the United States and in Europe. Both municipal and private companies developed to meet the emerging challenges related to the accelerating waste generation (Jones, 2017a: 138–151). Both private and public waste companies played a decisive role in Germany and Britain after the Second World War, when the amount of waste exploded. Besides cleaning up the streets and collecting households' waste, private and public companies took early responsibility for recycling (Stokes *et al.*, 2013). But the waste business in Germany, Great Britain and the United States developed without having a foundation of environmental belief or great environmental concerns. As in the case of the wind and solar industry, most of these early ventures in the waste and recycling business struggled to achieve profitability without public funds. It was only in the 1960s when environmental considerations began to impact environmental policies towards waste management that it grew into a big, even global, business (Jones, 2017a).

Environmental concerns on hold

The first wave of environmentalism that had emerged as a direct reaction to the consequences of the Industrial Revolution declined in the 1930s. People and governments became occupied with the hardships of the Great Depression and the Second World War and little attention was paid to the effects of a growing population and rapid industrial growth on the environment. After the Second World War, citizens were absorbed by materialism and a careless optimism on the one hand, and the Cold War and the threat of nuclear annihilation on the other (Shabecoff, 2000). Yet new technologies and explosive economic expansion created escalating environmental pressures. As stressed by environmental historians, the postwar period constituted an acceleration of environmental unsustainability compared to previous periods (McNeill and Engelke, 2014). After 1945, the world economy became driven by enormous quantities of fossil fuels – mostly oil. Since the turn of the twentieth century, oil production increased from 20 million tons in 1900 to three billion tons in 1990 (McNeill, 2000). This was reflected in the growth of the number of cars, which increased from around 40 million after 1945 to nearly 700 million by 1996 (Steffen *et al.*, 2007).

The growth in big business was based on fossil fuels and steel. In 1955, the largest corporations in the United States was General Motors, followed by Exxon Mobil, U.S. Steel and General Electric (Fortune 500 database). In the United States, the petroleum industry did not operate free from environmental regulatory constraints, but was not really challenged by them either. Many efforts to increase the efficiency with which companies extracted, transported and refined petroleum did overlap with efforts to address pollution concerns (Gorman, 2001: 269). Between the end of the Second World War and the 1960s, the German industry was not under much pressure either. The German legal system formally prioritized economic performance over protection of victims of pollution (Jones and Lubinski, 2014). Environmental concerns and pressure on industry was also on hold in the Scandinavian countries. In Sweden, who had had a serious parliamentary debate about enforcing an extensive industrial pollution control system in the early 1900s, shelved the initiative in the 1920s (Bergquist and Lindmark, 2016) and the issue did not return as a serious concern to industry or the government before the 1960s (Söderholm and Bergquist 2012). A first wake-up call that things were getting out of control, at least in Europe, came with the Great Smog in London in 1952. The first European international convention concerning air pollution was held in Milan in 1957 (Bergquist, 2017).

Although the anti-pollution and nature conservation movement became subdued in the 1930s, entrepreneurs in organic food were still active, if marginal, in countries like Britain, Germany and the United States. In 1959 the retail shop Wholefood, was opened in London. But this particular business and equivalent ventures remained niche businesses (Jones, 2017a).

Barber (2016) moreover shows that solar heating experiments in buildings were undertaken in the United States between 1939 and 1949, but as the war restrictions reduced and oil became cheaper, investments in solar heating waned. The corporations and governments around the world were by the 1960s heavily invested in a present and future empowered by oil and there was a rapid loss of sustainability in both the United States and the rest of world (Barber, 2016: 205).

A more radical and popular debate started, however, in the United States, with the publication of Rachel Carson's book *Silent Spring* (1962). Carson was a skilful writer and popularized the existing knowledge of the dangers of indiscriminate use of pesticides in agriculture. It was the beginning of an explosion of popular literature reflecting new scientific knowledge about invisible threats in the environment: radiation, heavy metal waste and other problems. The first mass movement for environmental protection thus started in the United States and focused on domestic issues (Porter and Brown, 1996) but other countries had their own debates in the 1960s. Political and public concern about air, soil and water pollution started overall to occur in non-communist industrial countries. In 1967, the Organisation for Economic Co-operations and Development (OECD) established advisory groups for different environmental problems, among them auto exhaust emissions, and environmental impact from sulphur products and detergents. The list of issues that the OECD found urgent, were extended every year after 1967 (Long, 2000). The second wave of environmentalism was on rise.

Business and the second wave of environmentalism

An extensive academic literature has covered the rise of environmentalism in the 1960s and the early 1970s. A complex of many factors came to lay the foundation of the adoption of the sustainability concept in the 1990s. The publication of *Silent Spring*, the United Nations Conference on the Human Environment held in Stockholm in 1972, the Arab Oil Embargo in 1973 along with publication of the book *Limits of Growth* (Meadows *et al.*, 1972) by the Club of Rome in 1972 have been widely seen as core formative events. Devastating environmental catastrophes caused by corporations in the 1970s and the 1980s, most notably the Bhopal catastrophe in 1984 and Exxon Valdez oil spill in 1989, also raised new levels of pressure on business, especially on multinationals. This interplayed with scientific findings regarding the impact of different pollutants causing acid rain, ozone depletion, eutrophication, mercury intoxication and eventually climate change and a wide range of other issues. There was an outbreak of new non-governmental organizations (NGOs), governmental institutions and national and supranational legislation from the late 1960s and the 1970s, which came to impact business in several ways (Coglianese and Anderson, 2012: Weber and Soderstrom, 2012). The impact of this historical shift has only recently started to be given broader coverage in the business history literature (Jones, 2017a; Berghoff and Rome, 2017; Bergquist, 2019).

Corporate environmentalism

The 1960s was a period when corporations started to grow their environmental awareness. In the United States, public attention and criticism was directed towards the chemical industry, automobile emissions and oil spills. Attention to environmental issues increased in Europe as well (Andersen and Liefferink, 1997). Japan had its own debate in the 1960s centred on the disaster in Minamata, where mercury emissions from Japan's leading petrochemical manufacturer Chisso Corporation caused the deaths of an estimated 1,000 Japanese citizens (Almeida and Brewster Stearns, 1998).

The management scholar Andrew J. Hoffman's work (Hoffman, 1997) on the US history of corporate environmentalism has been frequently cited to describe different modes of business responses to the environmental issue from the 1960s. Hoffman identified a movement along an evolutionary adaptive learning process forming specific attitudes or modes of business responses during certain sub-periods.

According to Hoffman and Bansal's (2012) periodization (Figure 35.2) corporate environmentalism in the 1960s and 1970s embraced the recognition that corporate environmental issues are a problem that necessitated regulatory control, and business responded with a strategy of regulatory compliance. In the 1980s and the early 1990s, business adopted a more pro-active and strategic approach, which was a response to, among other things, a number of devastating catastrophic events, such as the Bhopal catastrophe in 1984. A third wave of corporate environmentalism, then came to embrace the concept of *sustainability*. This shift begun in the latter part of the twenty-first century and came to focus on the merger of environmental and social issues with the global economy. The shift was driven by a series of events and issues that had forced an expansion of the scope of environmentalism to include considerations for a restructuring of global economies (Hoffman and Bansal, 2012: 7–9). The most important issue for business in the third wave was, and still is, climate change.

Hoffman's seminal framework (1997) covering the period from the 1960s to the late 1990s is based on empirical studies of the US chemical and petroleum industry, which responded reactively and defensively to environmental regulations in the 1970s. This view has also been supported by business historical studies such as Archie B. Carroll *et al.* (2012) who have argued that most American companies were resisting environmental regulations in the 1970s along with delaying investments as long as possible. Only a minor number of American executives perceived that they had major responsibility towards the natural environment (Carroll *et al.*, 2012: 254–255). Results from McCarthy's (2007: 190) research on the environment and US car industry also supports this view.

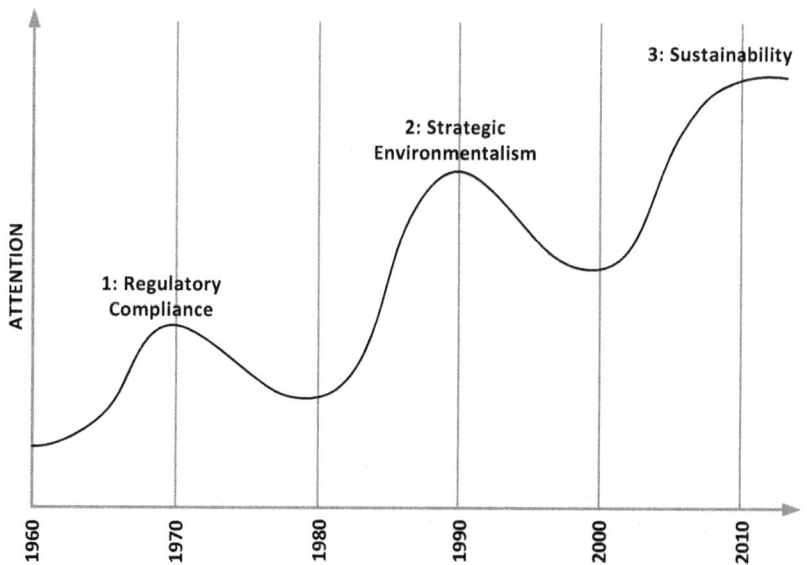

Figure 35.2   Waves of corporate environmentalism, 1960–2010

Source: Hoffman and Bansal (2012: 5).

Business history research gives no clear and coherent picture of how manufacturing companies responded to the new complex of environmental issues emerging since the 1960s. The way national polices shaped business strategies to manage growing environmental concerns is likewise uncertain. Boulett (2006) has explored the development of modes of corporate responses to the environmental issues in the French industry 1950–1990 and identified three stages of business behaviour: inattention, adaptation and integration. Inattention dominated until the end of the 1950s, but, in the 1970s, specific adaptive behaviours were progressively gaining momentum, often as a result of public action. The scope of this initial dynamic was mostly national, but this trend was reinforced after 1979 by external forces, such as European regulation and internationalization. Growing signs of integration into management practices can be found in the second half of the 1980s. Boulett stresses, however, that not all corporations have gone through these stages at the same rate and that the large French corporations adopted various attitudes depending on, among other things, specific geographical contexts.

Jones and Lubinski (2014) have explored the development of environmental strategies in the German chemical industry from the 1950s to the 1980s and found that it diverged from their American counterparts in the 1970s by acting proactively and using public relations strategies not only to contain fallout from criticism, but also as opportunities for changes in corporate culture. This reflected not only the broader emergence of environmental issues in German society and government, but also the fact that the pro-active strategy was driven by geographical circumstances.

In exploring the development of environmental strategies and clean technology development in the Swedish pulp and paper industry, Bergquist and Söderholm (2011, 2015) stressed the importance of factors beyond firm boundaries, and how different styles of national regulations may lead to different corporate responses to environmental challenges. They argued that in the Swedish case, the cooperative and flexible style in Swedish environmental policies helps to explain why and how Swedish pulp and paper took a world leadership in developing cleaner technologies in the 1970s and the 1980s. Challenges in creating effective public policies that incentivize or force companies to undertake efficient measures is discussed in recent business history research by Halvorson (2019), who explored the business and government relations and the new deregulation policies emerging in the United States in the late 1970s. Müller (2019) has also demonstrated how loopholes in US public policies enabled companies to externalize their environmental costs to markets in the global South in the 1970s and the 1980s.

International business scholars have stressed that the interactions between governmental environmental policy and the strategies of multinationals have been much more complex than equivalent business–government interactions at the national level. From the 1960s, environmental policies diverged across countries, and multinationals have had to comply with different national jurisdictions (Rugman and Verbeke, 1998). The impact of such complexities has been clearly demonstrated by Jones' (2005) history of Unilever between 1965 and 1990. Unilever experienced increased environmental pressure already starting in the 1960s, but remained reactive towards the environmental issue in the 1970s and the 1980s. Its highly diversified nature handicapped the development of a strong corporate-wide environmental strategy. Another complicating factor was that the company had to struggle with figuring out what to do in different legal jurisdictions and countries with lower level of incomes (Jones, 2005: 342–347).

Sluyterman's study of Royal Dutch Shell (Sluyterman, 2010, 2007: 303–365) provides an example of the devastating costs to reputation that followed the company's inability to meet the social and environmental expectations from its stakeholders. Shell's presence in South Africa, the planned sinking of the Brent Spar in the North Atlantic Sea in the early 1990s along with the environmental and human rights concern in Nigeria, contributed to a situation in which

Shell's reputation and legitimacy eroded. This resulted in a situation when the company seriously had to rethink the company's ethics, values and coordination to be able to meet the emerging complex challenge related to sustainability .

There is still no comprehensive business history account of how the environmental issue challenged business corporations from the 1960s, although there was a dramatic expansion in the scope, volume and detail of, for instance, environmental law during the past decades. The dominant research stream in international business literature on sustainable development has not focused much on challenges and business responses at the firm level, as the dominant research stream has been of macro-economic and quantitative nature (Van Tulder *et al.*, 2014).

Sustainability as mainstream business

In the 1990s, capitalism was getting redefined as an agent capable of meeting the world's needs. This was a big shift from the discourse of the 1970s. A number of different industries, even oil and gas, which had been resisting environmental regulations in the 1970s, declared that they now had reached the point when the ongoing degradation of the environment had to be dealt with urgently, including climate change. Sustainability suddenly emerged as something that was compatible with profits and something that could enhance value also in large multinational corporations. Carroll *et al.* (2012: 349.) suggest that this happened as global competition increased in the 1990s, and companies' international images and brand reputation became more vulnerable. European oil companies came out in support of the Kyoto Protocol in 1997 and formulated proactive climate strategies (Boon, 2019). In 2000, British Petroleum embarked on a massive $200 million campaign to position itself as a leading environmental and safety company with the slogan 'Beyond Petroleum' (Gendron *et al.*, 2017). Two years later the presidents of DuPont, Anova Holding AG and the Royal Dutch Shell published the book *Walking the Talk: The Business Case for Sustainable Development*, and argued that they were now more convinced than ever that companies can do themselves good through doing the right for society at large and the environment (Holliday *et al.*, 2002: 8).

Jones (2017a) suggests a number of overlapping factors that help to explain why mainstreaming of sustainability in business happened. First of all, the environmental issue became redefined under the category of sustainability by the Brundtland report in 1987. As the concept of sustainability merged both social issues and economic growth, it was compatible with large corporations. Second, the sustainability concepts were made readily adaptable to firms by arguments, definitions, certifications and metrics developed by leaders of green thought such as John Elkington (1997) and Paul Hawken (1993; see also Rome, 2017). A third factor contributing to the mainstreaming of sustainability was the growing market preferences for greener products in the 1990s. Large corporations from food and beauty to energy companies needed to gain value from green reputations. A fourth factor that was some businesses, like the re-insurance industry, faced a serious future threat from global warming, because they were directly exposed to underwriting climate-related risks (Haueter and Jones, 2017). A fifth factor has to do with a shift in government policies, and new regulatory tools that reduced financial barriers of investing in sustainability, such as renewable energy and organic food. Finally, a sixth factor was related to the new and powerful role of NGOs. The growing number of NGOs got increasing opportunities to expose poor environmental practices, but they also provided institutional capacity to enhance big business reputations through partnerships. Corporations could, for instance, use NGOs for product certifications and to form alliances involving matters such as supply chain management (Jones, 2017a, 360–363). One of many examples is the Swedish furniture company IKEA who in 2007 partnered with the World Wildlife Fund (Strand, 2009).

One striking feature in global business from the 1990s was the megatrend of business, voluntary action to protect the environment. This development has been perceived as a reflection of the new role played by various sets of stakeholders who expected global firms to take responsibility for sustainability issues, especially multinational companies due to their enormous power. Costumers, investors, consumers, NGOs and other stakeholders demanded 'facts', not only a green rhetoric. Large corporations in the 1990s began issuing sustainability reports alongside their business reports (Berghoff, 2017). An array of codes, standards, guidelines and frameworks were developed to guide companies in integrating sustainability and corporate social responsibility into their business strategies and management processes. The development was explosive, and more than 300 global corporate standards could be identified in the early 2000s, each with its own history and criteria (Marimon *et al.*, 2012). In 1996, the International Organization for Standardization (ISO), launched the environmental management system, ISO 14001, and already in 2002, the system had been adopted by nearly 50,000 facilities in 118 countries (Prakash and Potoski, 2006: 25).

Another matrix, the Global Reporting Initiative (GRI) was created in 1997 under the initiative of the non-profit organization North American Coalition for Environmentally Sustainable Economies (CERES), with the United Nations Environmental Programme as a joint partner from 1999. The Triple Bottom Line concept, which had been launched by John Eklington (1997) in the early 1990s, laid the foundation for the GRI, a framework for principles for environmental, social and sustainability reporting (Gray and Harremans, 2012: 410; Jones, 2017a). The purpose of the GRI was to enable the diffusion of sustainability records and to provide information guidelines to present a clearer vision of the human and ecological impacts, not the least from large enterprises (Marimon *et al.*, 2012). During the first year (1999) 12 large corporations joined the GRI, among them the US based General Motors, Procter & Gamble and Acea, and the UK based British Airways, the Japanese Panasonic Corporation and the Swedish SCA and Electrolux. The number of firms that had been listed in 1999 (12), had increased to over 6,000 in 2016 (GRI Database, 2017).

The origins and growth of these new 'green institutions', such as green certification which came to lay the foundation of the expansion of green business markets, has been explored by Jones (2017a). The aim with certification was essentially to define what sustainability was in different contexts. Even though certification has been fundamental to the creation and expansion of green markets, the creation of certifications and new accounting principles also provided metrics that enabled big business to demonstrate publicly that it was becoming sustainable. Certification, environmental reporting and green-washing also made the boundaries of the concept of sustainability so wide that any corporation, even oil companies, could be engaged in it (Jones, 2017a: 233–262, 379).

Scholars have raised great concerns whether certifications and new metrics are accurate signals of firms' environmental conduct, and that future research should pay much more attention to firms' actual outcomes. The literature covering the outcomes from multinational corporations' adoption of sustainability policies is still scarce (Christmann and Taylor, 2012; Van Tulder *et al.*, 2014) and it is difficult to conclude to what degree this global trend has delivered meaningful results (Bergquist *et al.*, 2019). It also appears as if the trend has mostly concerned multinational companies based in Western countries. A recent overview covering the business history of emerging markets (Austin *et al.*, 2017) gives no evidence that the same mainstreaming of sustainability happened in large corporations based in Latin America or in Asia.

The scaling of green business

Climate change and other issues of sustainability will require, as it has been stated, a future 'green growth' transition that needs to be large, system-wide and structural, in other words, a new industrial revolution based on renewable energy (Bowen *et al.*, 2016). Business history research has pointed at the historical circumstances that prevented growth in the renewable energy industry, and perhaps, even more importantly, it has pointed at what kind of factors supported its expansion.

Jones' (2017a, 2017b) research on the origin and stepwise scaling of the wind and solar industry contributes with important insights about several important factors that obstructed its growth over the past century. The history of wind and solar power companies shows in its essence the great difficulties that entrepreneurs faced in raising the amount of capital needed to finance innovation and compete with fossil fuels and nuclear energy before the 1980s. The reason why the world has seen a considerable growth in the solar and wind industry, as well as in the waste-to-energy and recycling business, is the crucial policy shift which emerged among some governments in the 1980s. Subsidies and tax incentives came to help companies to compete with fossil fuels, as they could afford innovation and, more importantly, to scale up their businesses. Thus Jones (2017a) argues that clustering of the wind power industry in Denmark can largely be explained by a functioning governmental policy to support its growth. Likewise, the fluctuating public polices in the United States helps to explain why the leadership in wind and solar technologies faltered, giving the opportunity for Europe and then China to take a leadership position.

The business of organic food and drink has expanded from being marginal small businesses in the 1980s into a global industry in the 2000s (Jones, 2017a, 2018). The market growth in consumption of organic food as well as organic agriculture shows, however, wide geographical variations (Jones and Mowatt, 2016). In the United States, organic food production expanded from the 1980s in California, while in Europe it was most evident in Germany, Switzerland and Denmark. However, when the production globalized from the 1980s, there was, as Jones (2017a) shows, an increasing divorce between production and consumption of organic food, which raised new environmental concerns regarding increasing carbon footprint of the industry because of long-distant trade. One example is the American-based Whole Foods Market, founded in 1980, that sourced organic food on an industrial scale from different parts of the world as the company scaled in the US market. The largest regional source of organic food production was, in 2014, located in Australia and the Pacific Islands (Jones, 2017a:176–201), while the major organic tea growing nations were found in South Asia, East Africa and China (Jones, 2018).

One of the more unsustainable global industries with a considerable growth in recent decades is international tourism. From the 1980s it has expanded from 200 million international tourist arrivals to more than one billion arrivals each year since 2010 and exerts an enormous pressure on the environment (Mowforth and Munt, 2015). Business history research has covered how eco-tourism emerged as an important alternative business sector from the 1990s (Jones, 2017a) with one important cluster developed in Costa Rica (see also Chapter 17 by Giacomin in this volume). The growth of the eco-tourism industry represents not only an illustrating case of green business clustering, but also problems related to green-washing. As Jones and Spadafora (2017) demonstrate in their study of Costa Rica, the problem with green-washing emerged when other businesses sought to take advantage to free ride on the national image that had been created there. Overall, once the global eco-tourism market had been proven, conventional firms sought to enter the business segment.

The threat of green-washing represents a general problem in the scaling of green business. When conventional industries entered the green market segment, it involved a complex of problems around green-washing and social constructions of sustainability. In the 1990s, large conventional corporations started to acquire visionary green firms to enhance a greener brand value. This meant that many green firms came to be reduced to only one component inside global corporations, co-existing with environmentally damaging activities (Jones, 2017a).

The world has not seen a decline in global environmental challenges in the past decades, in fact the opposite. One structural aspect raised as a roadblock to sustainability is shareholder capitalism developed from the 1980s, which have provided a constant incentive for firms to take decisions focused on short-term returns (Wright and Nyberg, 2015). Indeed, as recent business history research has proven, quarterly capitalism is not aligned with the long-term investment horizons needed for green business either (Jones, 2017a).

Conclusions

Fossil fuel laid the foundation of Western industrial capitalism and its success. The creation of modern capitalism and big business was essentially the story of manufacturing firms growing large by employing enormous amounts of fossil fuels. Business historians have spent generations exploring that story, and the question why some countries and firms proved more successful in building capitalist enterprise than others. However, today's debates around sustainability are about moving beyond this past focus. There now exists, after a lag, a growing stream of research on the environmental consequences of capitalist growth.

As this chapter has shown, this growing new research has two dimensions. The earliest theme to be explored, in literature dating from the 1990s, is the story of when, how and why some conventional industries sought to become less polluting. This stream of research has dated this phenomenon back to the late nineteenth century, showed that it gained momentum and complexity from the 1960s, and resulted in a mainstreaming of sustainability rhetoric, and sometimes practice, in large corporations from the 1980s, primarily in Western developed countries. Scholars have explored business responses to a wide set of environmental issues, including public pressure, environmental regulations and technological challenges, both in different industries and geographical contexts.

A more recent stream of research is the story of how for-profit entrepreneurs developed entire new product categories such as organic food, and wind and solar energy, which were explicitly focused on sustainability. Again this process has been traced back to the nineteenth century. The process has been explored in different industries and geographies, and it has been shown to have laid the technological and intellectual basis for a range of today's green businesses, even if these early green entrepreneurs were rarely able to build scalable businesses before the 1980s. With the rise in green consumerism and public policy support in some Western countries for sustainability during the 1990s, the two historical trends met, as the concept of sustainable development spread to large conventional corporations and green business firms scaled or were acquired by conventional big businesses.

Business history research has further demonstrated that a major barrier to sustainability emerged in the 1990s as the very concept of sustainability became socially constructed in a sufficiently broad fashion as to permit even firms in the most unstainable industries to be certified and win awards for being sustainable. At the same time, those environmental improvements made in large corporations, not the least heavy polluting industries, should not neglected.

The issue of sustainability has become a mainstream topic in business administration research with a growing number of subfields devoted to the issue. Future business history research needs to be more fully incorporated in these debates by researching what historically shaped factors have facilitated or blocked businesses committing themselves to change their direction towards an environmentally sustainable value creation. One issue to delve into is simply why it has been so difficult for both green entrepreneurs as well as large multinational corporations to live up to their green visions, even when they have had the best intentions. Business historians have to pay attention not only to barriers founded in organizational and technological inertias, but also to the very rules of the market economy and the role of governments. The concept of sustainability, and how it has been translated into business practice, also calls for a specific historical scrutiny, as it appears that the concept has been used to avoid costly, but necessary, actions to protect the environment (Bergquist *et al.*, 2019).

Since the 1960s, corporations have faced increasing criticism from a range of stakeholders over environmental problems caused by economic growth, but yet global environmental challenges are not decreasing: in fact the opposite. Subfields within science have also become increasingly focused on the historical dynamics of capitalism, centred on the Great Acceleration and Anthropocene debates, which have engaged scholarly work by environmental historians. Today no other issue dominates the concerns about sustainability more than climate change, and the issue cuts across not only virtually all industries but also the whole global economy. It is thus a matter of urgency to make issues of sustainability – and "unsustainability" – a mainstream topic in business history, as business historians have unique skills to contribute with important knowledge about the grandest challenge of our time.

Note

1 In 2016 the United Nations presented its most authoritative study ever published – the 'Global Environmental Outlook (GEO-6): Regional Assessments' report – on the state of the planet's health, which concluded that the environment is deteriorating even faster than previously thought.

References

Almeida, Paul and Brewster Stearns, Linda (1998), 'Political Opportunities and Local Grassroots Environmental Movements: The Case of Minamata', *Social Problems*, 45 (1), 37–60.

Andersen, Mikael Skou and Liefferink, Duncan (eds) (1997), *European Environmental Policy: The Pioneers* (Manchester: Manchester University Press).

Austin, Gareth, Dávila, Carlos and Jones, Geoffrey (2017), 'The Alternative Business History; Business in Emerging Markets', *Business History Review*, doi:10.1017/S0007680517001052.

Bansal, Pratima and Hoffman, Andrew J. (eds) (2012), *The Oxford Handbook of Business and the Natural* (Oxford; New York: Oxford University Press).

Barber, Daniel A. (2016), *A House in the Sun: Modern Architecture and Solar Energy in the Cold War* (New York: Oxford University Press).

Berghoff, Hartmut (ed.) (2017), 'Shades of Green: A Business-History Perspective on Eco-Capitalism', in Berghoff, Hartmut and Rome, Adam (eds), *Green Capitalism? Business and the Environment in the Twentieth Century* (Philadelphia, PA: University of Pennsylvania Press), 13–31.

Berghoff, Hartmut and Rome, Adam (eds) (2017), *Green Capitalism? Business and the Environment in the Twentieth Century* (Philadelphia, PA: University of Pennsylvania Press).

Bergquist, Ann-Kristin (2017), 'Dilemmas of Going Green: Environmental Strategies in the Swedish Mining Company Boliden 1960–2000', in Berghoff, Hartmut and Rome, Adam (eds), *Green Capitalism? Business and the Environment in the Twentieth Century* (Philadelphia, PA: University of Pennsylvania Press), 149–171.

Bergquist, Ann-Kristin (2019), 'Renewing Business History in the Era of the Anthropocene', *Business History Review*, 93 (1), 3–24.

Bergquist, Ann-Kristin and Lindmark, Magnus (2016), 'Sustainability and Shared Value in the Interwar Swedish Copper Industry', *Business History Review*, 90 (2), 197–225.

Bergquist, Ann-Kristin and Söderholm, Kristina (2011), 'Green Innovation Systems in Swedish Industry, 1960–1989', *Business History Review*, 54 (4), 677–698.

Bergquist, Ann-Kristin and Söderholm, Kristina (2015), 'Transition to Greener Pulp: Regulation, Industry Responses and Path Dependency', *Business History*, 57 (6), 862–884.

Bergquist, Ann-Kristin, Ehrenfeld, John, Cole, Shawn A., King, Andrew A. and Schendler, Auden (2019), 'Understanding and Overcoming Roadblocks to Environmental Sustainability: Past Roads and Future Prospects', *Business History Review*, 93 (1), 27–148.

Blowfield, Michael (2013), *Business and Sustainability* (Oxford: Oxford University Press).

Boden, T.A., Marland, G. and Andres, R.J. (2017), 'Global, Regional, and National Fossil-Fuel CO2 Emissions', Carbon Dioxide Information Analysis Center, Oak Ridge National Laboratory, U.S. Department of Energy, Oak Ridge, TN, http://cdiac.ornl.gov/ftp/ndp030/global.1751_2014.ems (accessed October 9, 2017).

Boon, Marten (2019), 'A Climate of Change? The Oil Industry and Decarbonization in Historical Perspective', *Business History Review*, 93 (1), 101–125.

Boulett, Daniel (2006), 'La Gestion De L'environnement Dans Les Entreprises Industrielles en Face: Une Mise En Perspective Historique (1950–1990)', *Entreprises et Historie*, 45, 54–73.

Bowen, Alex, Duffy, Chris and Fankhauser, Sam (2016), 'Green Growth and the New Industrial Revolution', *Policy Brief*, London School of Economics and Political Science, London.

Brenton, Tony (1994), *The Greening of Machiavelli: The Evolution of International Environmental Politics* (London: Earthscan Publication Ltd).

Carroll, Archie B., Lipartito, Kenneth J., Post, James E. and Werhane, Patricia H. (2012), *Corporate Responsibility: The American Experience* (Cambridge: Cambridge University Press).

Carson, Rachel (1962), *Silent Spring* (Boston, MA: Houghton Mifflin).

Chandler, Alfred D. (1990), *Scale and Scope: The Dynamics of Industrial Capitalism* (Cambridge, MA: Belknap Press of Harvard University Press).

Chandler, Alfred D., Amatori, Franco and Hikono, Takashi (1997), *Big Business and the Wealth of Nations* (Cambridge; New York: Cambridge University Press).

Christmann, Petra and Taylor Glen (2012), 'International Business and the Environment', in Bansal, Pratima and Hoffman, Andrew J. (eds), *The Oxford Handbook of Business and the Natural* (Oxford; New York: Oxford University Press), 50–69.

Clark, Gregory (2007), *A Farewell to Alms: A Brief Economic History of the World* (Princeton, NJ: Princeton University Press).

Coglianese, Cary and Anderson, Ryan (2012), 'Business and Environmental Law', in Bansal, Pratima and Hoffman, Andrew J. (eds), *The Oxford Handbook of Business and the Natural Environment* (Oxford; New York: Oxford University Press), 140–157.

Cohen, Stewart, Demeritt, David, Robinson, Johan, and Rothman, Dale (1998), 'Climate Change and Sustainable Development: Towards Dialogue', *Global Environmental Change*, 8 (4), 341–371.

Cronon, William (1991), *Nature's Metropolis: Chicago and the Great West* (New York: W.W. Norton).

Ehrenfeld, John R. (2012), 'Beyond the Brave New World: Business and Sustainability', in Bansal, Pratima and Hoffman, Andrew J. (eds), *The Oxford Handbook of Business and the Natural Environment* (Oxford; New York: Oxford University Press), 611–629.

Elkington, John B. (1997), *Cannibals with Forks: The Triple Bottom Line of 21st Century Business* (Oxford: Capstone Publishers).

Fortune 500 Database, http://archive.fortune.com/magazines/fortune/fortune500_archive/full/1955/ (accessed April 15, 2019).

Friedman, Walter and Jones, Geoffrey (2011), 'Business History: Time for Debate', *Business History Review*, 85 (1), 1–8.

Gendron, Corinne, Girard, Bernard., Ivanaj, Silvester., Ivanaj, Vera., and Friser, Alice. (2017), 'Rôle et responsabilités des hauts dirigeants face aux changements climatiques: réflexions à partir du cas e BP', *Entreprises et Historie*, 1 (86): 34–53.

GRI (Global Reporting Initiative) Database, http://database.globalreporting.org (accessed May 23, 2017).

Gorman, Hugh. S. (1999), 'Efficiency, Environmental Quality, and Oil Field Brines: The Success and Failure of Pollution Control Self-Regulation', *Business History Review*, 73 (4), 601–640.

Gorman, Hugh S. (2001), *Redefining Efficiency: Pollution Concerns, Regulatory Mechanisms and Technological Change in the US Petroleum industry* (Akron, OH: University of Akron Press).

Gray, Rob and Herremans, Irene (2012), 'Sustainability and Social Reporting and the Emergence of the External Social Audits: The Struggle of Accountability?' in Bansal, Pratima and Hoffman, Andrew J. (eds),

The Oxford Handbook of Business and the Natural Environment (Oxford; New York: Oxford University Press), 140–157.

Guha, Ramachandra (2000), *Environmentalism: A Global History* (New York: Longman).

Gunningham, Neil, Kagan, Robert A. and Thornton, Dorothy (2003), *Shades of Green: Business, Regulation and Environment* (Stanford, CA: Stanford Law and Politics).

Halvorsen, Charles (2019), 'Deflated Dreams: The EPA's Bubble Policy and the Politics of Uncertainty in Regulatory Reform', *Business History Review*, 93 (1), forthcoming.

Haueter, Neils Viggo and Jones, Geoffrey (2017), *Risk in Reinsurance: Managing Risk in Reinsurance. From City Fires to Global Warming* (Oxford: Oxford University Press).

Hawken, Paul (1993), *The Ecology of Commerce* (New York: HarperCollins).

Hoffman, Andrew J. (1997), *From Heresy to Dogma: An Institutional History of Corporate Environmentalism* (San Francisco, CA: New Lexington Press).

Hoffman, Andrew J. and Bansal, Pratima (2012), 'Retroperspective, Perspective and Prospective: Introduction', in Bansal, Pratima and Hoffman, Andrew J. (eds), *The Oxford Handbook of Business and the Natural Environment* (Oxford; New York: Oxford University Press), 140–157.

Holliday, Charles O. Jr., Schmidheiny, Stephan and Watts, Philip (2002), *Walking the Talk: The Business Case of Sustainable Development* (Sheffield: Greenleaf).

Jones, Geoffrey (2005), *Renewing Unilever: Transformation and Tradition* (Oxford; New York: Oxford University Press).

Jones, Geoffrey (2008), 'Globalization', in Jones, Geoffrey and Zeitlin, Jonathan (eds), *The Oxford Handbook of Business History* (Oxford: Oxford University Press).

Jones, Geoffrey (2017a), *Profits and Sustainability: A Global History of Green Entrepreneurship* (Oxford: Oxford University Press).

Jones, Geoffrey (2017b), 'Entrepreneurship, Policy and Geography of Wind Energy', in Berghoff, Hartmut and Rome, Adam (eds), *Green Capitalism? Business and the Environment in the Twentieth Century* (Philadelphia, PA: University of Pennsylvania Press), 206–231.

Jones, Geoffrey (2018), *Varieties of Green Business: Industries, Nations and Time* (Northampton, MA: Edward Elgar).

Jones, Geoffrey and Lubinski, Christina (2014), 'Making "Green Giants": Environment Sustainability in the German Chemical Industry 1950s–1980s', *Business History*, 56 (4), 623–649.

Jones, Geoffrey and Mowatt, Simon (2016), 'National Image as a Competitive Disadvantage: The Case of the New Zealand Organic Food Industry', *Business History*, 58 (8), 1262–1288.

Jones, Geoffrey and Spadafora, Andrew (2017), 'Creating Ecotourism in Costa Rica, 1970–2000', *Enterprise & Society*, 18 (1), 146–183.

Jones, Geoffrey and Zeitlin, Jonathan (eds) (2008), *The Oxford Handbook of Business History* (Oxford: Oxford University Press).

LeCain, Timothy J. (2000), 'The Limits of "Eco-Efficiency": Arsenic Pollution and the Cottrell Precipitator in the U.S. Copper Smelting Industry', *Environmental History*, 5 (3), 336–351.

LeCain, Timothy. J. (2009), *Mass Destruction: The Men and Giant Mines that Wired America and Scarred the Planet* (New Brunswick, NJ: Rutgers University Press).

Lindmark, Magnus and Bergquist, Ann-Kristin (2009), 'Expansion for Pollution Reduction? Environmental Adaptation of a Swedish and a Canadian Metal Smelter 1960–2005', *Business History*, 50 (4), 530–546.

Long, Bill L. (2000), *International Environmental Issues and the OECD 1950–2000* (Paris: OECD).

McCarthy, Tom (2007), *Auto Mania: Cars, Consumers, and the Environment* (New Haven, CT: Yale University Press).

McNeill, John R. (2000), *Something New Under the Sun: An Environmental History of the Twentieth-Century World* (New York: W. W. Norton).

McNeill, John R. and Engelke, Peter (2014), *The Great Acceleration: An Environment History of the Anthropocene since 1945* (Cambridge, MA: Belknap Press of Harvard University Press).

Marimon, F. Frederic, Alonso-Almeida, Maria Del Mar, Rodriguez, Martha Del Pila, Alejandro, Cortez and Aimer, Klender (2012), 'The World Wide Diffusion of Global Reporting Initiative: What is the Point?' *Journal of Cleaner Production*, 33, 132–144.

Maysilles, Duncan (2011), *Ducktown Smoke: The Fight over One of the South's Greatest Environmental Disasters* (Chapel Hill, NC: University of North California Press).

Meadows, Donella H., Meadows, Dennis, L., Randers, Jergen and Behrens, William, W. (1972), *The Limits to Growth* (New York: Universe Books).

Mowforth, Martin and Munt, Ian (2015), *Tourism and Sustainability: Development, Globalization and New Tourism in the Third World* (Abingdon: Routledge).

Müller, Simone (2019), 'Hidden Externalities: The Globalization of Hazardous Waste', *Business History Review*, 93 (1), 51–74.

Mutz, Mattias (2009), 'Managing Resources: Water and Wood in the German Pulp and Paper Industry 1870s–1930s', *Jahrbuch für Wirtshaftsgeschitcthe/Economic History*, 59 (2), 45–68.

Newell, Edmund (1997), 'Atmospheric Pollution and the British Copper Industry, 1960–1920', *Technology and Culture*, 38 (3), 655–689.

Pomeranz, Kenneth (2000), *The Great Divergence: China, Europe, and the Making of the Modern World Economy* (Princeton, NJ: Princeton University Press).

Porter, Gareth and Brown, Janet Welsh (1996), *Global Environmental Politics*, 2nd edition (Boulder, CO: Westview Press).

Post, James E. (2012), 'Business, Society and the Environment', in Bansal, Pratima and Hoffman, Andrew J. (eds), *The Oxford Handbook of Business and the Natural Environment* (Oxford; New York: Oxford University Press), 537–555.

Prakash, Aseem and Potoski, Matthew (2006), *The Voluntary Environmentalists: Green Clubs, ISO 14001 and Voluntary Environmental Regulations* (Cambridge: Cambridge University Press).

Robinson, John (2004), 'Squaring the Circle? Some Thoughts on the Idea of Sustainable Development', *Ecological Economics* 48, 369–384.

Rome, Adam (2017), 'The Ecology of Commerce: Environmental History and the Challenge of Building a Sustainable Economy', in Berghoff, Hartmut and Rome, Adam (eds), *Green Capitalism? Business and the Environment in the Twentieth Century* (Philadelphia, PA: University of Pennsylvania Press), 13–31.

Rome, Adam (2019), 'Du Pont and the Limits of Corporate Environmentalism', *Business History Review*, 93 (1), 75–99.

Rootes, Christopher (2004), 'Environmental Movements', in Snow, David A., Soule, Sarah A. and Kriesi, Hanspeter (eds), *The Blackwell Champion to Social Movements* (Malden, MA: Blackwell), 608–640.

Rosen, Christine Meisner (1995), 'Businessmen Against Pollution in Late Nineteenth Century Chicago', *Business History Review*, 69 (3), 351–397.

Rosen, Christine Meisner (2003), ' "Knowing" Industrial Pollution: Nuisance Law and the Power of Tradition in a Time of Rapid Economic Change, 1840–1864', *Environmental History*, 8 (4), 656–597.

Rosen, Christine Meisner and Sellers, Christopher C. (1999), 'The Nature of the Firm: Towards an Eco-cultural History of Business', *Business History Review*, 73 (4), 577–600.

Rugman, Alan M. and Verbeke, Alain (1998), 'Corporate Strategies and Environmental Regulations: An Organizing Framework', *Strategic Management Journal*, 19 (4), 363–375.

Shabecoff, Philip (2000), *Earth Rising: American Environmentalism in the 21st Century* (Washington, DC: Island Press).

Sluyterman, Keetie (2007), *Keeping Competitive in Turbulent Markets, 1973–2007: A History of Royal Deutsch Shell*, Vol. 3 (Oxford: Oxford University Press).

Sluyterman, Keetie (2010), 'Royal Dutch Shell: Company Strategies for Dealing with Environmental Issues', *Business History Review*, 84 (2), 203–226.

Söderholm, Kristina and Bergquist, Ann-Kristin (2012), 'Firm Collaboration and Environmental Adaptation: The Case of the Swedish Pulp and Paper Industry 1900–1990', *Scandinavian Economic History Review*, 60 (2), 183–211.

Steffen, Will, Crutzen, Paul J. and McNeill, John R. (2007), 'The Anthropocene: Are Humans Now Overwhelming the Great Forces of Nature?' *Ambio*, 36 (8), 614–621.

Steffen, Will, Richardson, Katherine, Rockström, Johan, Cornell, Sarah E., Fetzer, Ingo, Bennett, Elena M., Biggs, Reinette, Carpenter, Stephen R., de Vries, Wim, de Wit, Cynthia A., Folke, Carl, Gerten, Dieter, Heinke, Jens, Mace, Georgina M., Persson, Linn M., Ramanathan, Veerabhadran, Reyers, Belinda and Sörlin, Sverker (2015), 'Planetary Boundaries: Guiding Human Development on a Changing Planet', *Science*, 347 (6223).

Stokes, Raymond, Köster, Roman and Sambrook, Stephen C. (2013), *The Business of Waste: Great Britain and Germany, 1945 to the Present* (Cambridge: Cambridge University Press).

Strand, Robert (2009), 'Corporate Responsibility in Scandinavian Supply Chains', *Journal of Business Ethics*, 85, 179–185.

Uekötter, Frank (1999), 'Divergent Responses to Identical Problems: Businessmen and the Smoke Nuisance in Germany and the United States', *Business History Review*, 73, 641–676.

Uekötter, Frank (2009), *The Age of Smoke: Environmental Policy in Germany and the United States, 1880–1970* (Pittsburgh, PA: University of Pittsburgh Press).

UNEP (United Nations Environment Program) (2016), "Summary of the Sixth Global Environment Outlook GEO-6 Regional Assessments: Key Findings and Policy Messages", UNEP/EA.2/INF/17.

Van Tulder, Rob, Verbeke, Alain and Strange, Roger (2014), 'Taking Stock of Complexity: In Search of New Pathways to Sustainable Development', in Van Tulder, Rob, Verbeke, Alain and Strange, Roger (eds), *International Business and Sustainable Development* (Bingley: Emerald), 1–20.

Weber, Klaus and Soderstrom, Sara B. (2012), 'Social Movements, Business and the Environment', in Bansal, Pratima and Hoffman, Andrew J. (eds), *The Oxford Handbook of Business and the Natural Environment* (Oxford; New York: Oxford University Press), 248–265.

Whiteman, Gail, Walker, Brian and Perego, Paolo (2013), 'Planetary Boundaries: Ecological Foundations for Corporate Sustainability', *Journal of Management Studies*, 50 (2), 307–336.

World Commission on Environment and Development (WCED) (1987), *Our Common Future* (Oxford: Oxford University Press).

Worster, Donald (1979), *Dust Bowl: The Southern Plains in the 1930s* (New York: Oxford University Press).

Wright, Christopher and Nyberg, Daniel (2015), *Climate Change, Capitalism, and Corporations: Processes of Creative Self-Destruction* (Cambridge: Cambridge University Press).

Wrigley, Anthony (2010), Energy and the English Industrial Revolution (New York: Cambridge University Press).

36

POLLUTION AND CLIMATE CHANGE

Raymond G. Stokes and Christopher W. Miller

Introduction

Manufacturing anything entails waste, regardless of product or of the efficiency of the process by which it is made. Waste, in turn, invariably includes pollution of some sort, in other words contamination of the surrounding physical environment. Thus, from at least the beginning of the industrial revolution, manufacturing operations (as well as other functions undertaken by firms such as moving goods and people from one place to another) have been associated with "negative externalities" involving (usually unspecified) costs associated with environmental degradation that were only very rarely recognized by the companies concerned. It was not until well into the second half of the twentieth century that such pollution could routinely be detected by any other means than the human senses of sight and smell. As a result, the problems associated with pollution by industrial companies were for the most part perceived as profoundly local or regional. Political and regulatory action to address them beyond the regional level therefore began only gradually. In other words, it is only relatively recently that broad consensus has emerged of industrial pollution that: involves dangers that cannot be seen or smelled, but rather must be detected by other – often highly technical – means; affects very wide geographic areas, indeed often with global effects; and, has an impact not only on those alive at present, but also future generations (Chick 2015). Pollution control, we have all come to realize, requires concomitant trans- and international action by actors at various levels operating in the public, private, and third sectors.

This chapter traces the evolution of the incidence, perceptions, and management of industrial pollution from the local to the global level. Focusing on industrial, and mostly multinational, firms – but placing them in political, economic, and regulatory context, in particular in relation to the growth and impact of global environmental consciousness (environmentalism) – it highlights ongoing tensions to the present day between: local and broader-level impact and action; reactive compliance vs. proactive action; and, perceptions of pollution amelioration as a more or less prohibitive cost to be avoided or else as a more or less attractive and lucrative business opportunity to be embraced. It also addresses the roles of multinational firms and of environmental movements in the globalization of the incidence and management of pollution, most recently and centrally in relation to climate change. Along the way, it comments on how far scholarship in business and management studies, business and environmental history, science and technology studies, and other fields has engaged with these tensions, sketching out at the same time some essential areas for additional research.

For reasons of space, we limit our overview in the main part of this chapter to cases where a particular firm, of whatever size, causes or tries to limit pollution directly as part of its supply chain, manufacturing processes, or product design. This will include attention to issues relating to the impact of production on climate change. But we will not examine cases from non-manufacturing industry, including services, agriculture, and extractive industries, although we will touch on some of the main literature that addresses these sectors. Nor will we deal with cases where the relationship between pollution and manufacturing is indirect, e.g., when pollution and/or climate change arise through use or disposal of manufactured products by the consumer, although again we will touch on some literature on this. In addition, we *will* be briefly considering how far manufacturing firms think of minimization of environmental damage when designing such products. In what follows, therefore, we will look at companies active in industries such as oil refining, electronics, chemicals, and automobiles, including their supply chains and product design. We will not, however, deal with issues relating to pollution caused by consumer use or disposal of petroleum products, mobile phones, plastics, or cars.

We begin with a short overview of existing literature on the subject.

Literature review

In his 2001 history of corporate environmentalism, Hoffman (2001) analyzes the incidence of articles on pollution and the environment in chemical and petroleum industry trade journals (among other sources). He demonstrates that issues relating to pollution and its amelioration came to the fore and subsequently grew in importance only in the late 1960s and early 1970s, largely as a response to the environmental movement and increased willingness of governments to engage in environmental regulation. Earlier, Hays (1987) located the rise of "environmentalism" and also of greater public awareness of pollution in the context of broader social and economic change in America in the period after 1955. These developments became even more pronounced in the 1960s and early 1970s, when increasing affluence caused the public as consumers to demand higher standards of quality in their surrounding world.

Not surprisingly, scholarship on the impact of industry on the physical environment lagged somewhat behind this change in societal and industrial consciousness. This trend is documented using bibliometric analysis in a 1998 special issue of *Technology and Culture* on the relationship between technology and the environment (Stine and Tarr 1998: 605). Importantly, although some of the literature that has since appeared deals with the period since the 1960s and the apparent dawning of corporate consciousness in this regard, much of it looks backward to developments that occurred before the 1960s. Desrochers (2007: 356, 358), for example, notes that various American trade journals in the 1920s and 1930s dealt with "waste recovery practices" of Ford and other automobile manufacturers, and that books on industrial waste recovery began to appear already in the late nineteenth and early twentieth centuries. More recently, Jones (2017) traces "green business" (i.e., firms engaging in design and production of goods and provision of services meant to minimize environmental damage or even to avoid it entirely) back to the early twentieth century. Bergquist and Lindmar (2016) similarly find evidence of early "sustainability" as a business practice. It is, though, questionable just how representative these firms are. For instance, Wlasiuk's (2014) study of Standard Oil's refining operations and the manufacturing cluster that grew up alongside it in the Calumet in the late nineteenth and early twentieth century emphasizes the extent to which the pursuit of profit by business was anything but green, at least in the early days of industrialization. More-over, terms such as "green business" and "sustainability" did not come to be used as they are now until very recently and even now are sometimes used imprecisely (e.g., Bansal and DesJardine 2014).

In any event, broadly speaking, scholarship in this area since the 1970s has come from two general fields: environmental studies and science and technology studies (STS) on the one hand; and business and management studies on the other. In spite of some heroic efforts to integrate them, for instance in the historical branches of the fields, they have only very recently begun to speak to one another. Stine and Tarr (1998: 621), for instance, noted that "historians of techno-logy have on the whole neglected ... the environmental consequences of industry and manu-facturing," while Rosen and Sellars (1999: 577) point out that "Business history has never paid much attention to the environment." Both statements would have to be revised somewhat given literature that has appeared since they were written (e.g., LeCain 2009; Elmore 2015; Jones 2017; Berghoff and Rome 2017; Smith and Greer 2017), but they continue to hold true to a surprising extent.

One area of relevant scholarship is located primarily in environmental studies and/or STS. However, to the extent this literature deals with industry and manufacturing, it tends to "black-box" the firm. In other words, this literature is usually more concerned with the general impact of industrial production and technologies on the environment than decision-making, strategy, or management *within* the firms that form the locus for that production and those technologies (e.g., Brüggemeier 1994; Cioc 2009). This is true even for LeCain's (2009) innovative history of the development and deployment of "mass destruction" technologies for producing copper, which mentions firms but does not really engage with their behavior as firms per se. In other words, one can turn Rosen and Sellars' (1999) observation on its head: environmental studies and STS have rarely paid much attention to the firm, although again this has begun to change recently (e.g., Wlasiuk 2014).

Literature on pollution and the environment in business and management studies, on the other hand, deals directly with the firm and its managers. Scholarship here focuses on three main areas. The first involves the impact of business on the environment, the frequent resistance of managers to engage with this impact, and the effects of regulation on business behavior (e.g., Smith 2000). The second relates to the claim by Michael Porter and others that the active embrace of environmentalism by business encourages innovation and leads to profit (Porter and van der Linde 1995; Desrochers 2007). And, third, there are the more general issues of corpo-rate environmentalism on the one hand (e.g., Hoffman 2001) and the idea of "green business" on the other (Jones 2017; Desrochers 2012).

Despite this large and growing scholarly literature on business and pollution, very little of it engages explicitly or deeply with the global dimensions of the subject. The few exceptions, such as LeCain (2009) and Chick (2015), often do not foreground the firm, but rather focus on tech-nology and national-level economic and environmental policy respectively, although Elmore's (2015) innovative history of Citizen Coke illustrates how studies of the development of global firms and their supply chains can be linked effectively to consideration of both local and global environmental issues. In the section which follows, we consider the issues treated by Elmore in his case study more generally, exploring the evolving relationship between business in manufac-turing industries and pollution from the late nineteenth century to the late twentieth century, and thematizing in particular the local and global dimensions of this relationship.

The globalization of industrial pollution

Pre-global? From the industrial revolution to the 1960s

The first industrial revolution that started in the second half of the eighteenth century has long been viewed as a purely British affair which then spread to other areas in continental Europe and North America, and eventually around much of the world (Ashton 1996; Trebilcock 1981). However, one of the most important recent treatments of the industrial revolution and the spread of industrialization, while continuing to emphasize the centrality of Britain in the process, places these developments in a global context (Allen 2017, 2009). Other recent scholarship focuses even more heavily on the interconnections between early industrializers and suppliers of key raw materials (such as cotton and tin) located around the world (Beckert 2014; Ingulstad *et al.* 2015). In addition, European (and eventually American) machinery was sent to all parts of the world for use in processing agricultural products and other applications. Examples include the cases of sugar machinery produced in Glasgow for processing sugar cane on plantations in the Caribbean (Singerman 2014), and of thread manufacturers J & P Coats, which had established manufacturing operations in a wide range of countries by the 1880s (Stopford and Dunning 1982: 238–239).

One of the implications of this emerging consensus on the global interconnections underpinning the development of manufacturing industry from its very beginnings is that industrial pollution, too, has been a global phenomenon from the outset, although this has rarely been pursued in the literature to date. One exception is LeCain (2009), who notes the global implications of the technologies of "mass destruction" initially developed for copper mining. But his primary focus is copper mining and smelting in the United States rather than around the world. Elmore's (2015) study of Coca Cola and its supply chains is more global in orientation, but it remains unusual in the literature. In any event, as we argue below, there are important differences between the early global effects of industrialization and business in relation to pollution and more recent impacts as a result of increased scale and scope of globalized business on the one hand and the potential reach of international regulation on the other.

Whatever the global impacts, the incidence and effects of pollution by manufacturing companies and their suppliers were at the outset primarily local or regional, at least in terms of perception. The increasing use of coal to carry out all sorts of industrial operations, for instance, led to belching smokestacks that polluted the air of the cities that were increasingly the locus of manufacturing. But, initially at least, because of prevailing wind currents, visible air pollution from coal-burning could for the most part be avoided by the wealthier inhabitants of urban areas, who could afford to reside in districts upwind of factories. Those who lived downwind were generally much less fortunate, of course, but the smoke mostly dissipated not far beyond the town limits in any case (Heblich *et al.* 2016). This is true even in relation to particularly toxic smoke pollution in smelting of copper, for instance, although Bergquist and Lindmar (2016) underscore the international dimension of this in terms of flows of knowledge that shaped the development of pollution-abatement technologies.

Water pollution had the potential for reaching a far larger catchment area: large rivers like the Rhine flowed through and/or formed the boundary between several different countries (Blackbourn 2006: 71–111; Cioc 2009). But in practice visible or odorous water pollution resulting from industrial operations also usually dissipated rapidly, thus (apparently) affecting only a limited region. Lakes, of course, were by definition local or regional, while pollution going into the ocean dissipated for the most part owing to wave action. Groundwater contamination by industry sometimes affected drinking water, but again the effect was almost invariably local (Mosley 2013).

Similarly, contamination of the land itself through industrial production from the late eighteenth century onwards also happened routinely, not least through the widespread practice of burying waste that was often toxic. But even when this form of pollution was uncovered – often only years after it occurred – the damage was limited to small geographical areas for the most part (Colten 1991).

Two things are worth highlighting at this point. First, industrial pollution in any of its forms in the nineteenth and first half of the twentieth centuries may well have had effects that went beyond the local or regional. However, because industrial contamination at that time could rarely be detected by anything other than human senses (except through emergent biological and chemical understanding of water pollution from the late nineteenth century), contemporaries were largely unaware of these impacts. Second, it is significant that pollution of air, water, and land was not caused solely by industry. Indeed, arguably the bulk of the problems that arose from pollution came from increasing population, urbanization, and agriculture (all of which were of course affected or even caused in part by industrialization) rather than directly from industry (Hays 1987). Thus, it is not surprising that "from the beginning of the Industrial Revolution through the mid-1900s industry in general did not have protection of the environment or public health as a significant philosophical or operating concern" (Center for Chemical Process Safety 2006: 297). And this observation applies not just to manufacturing, but also to product design through the mid-twentieth century, as the cases of DDT (dichlorodiphenyltrichloroethane) and CFCs (chlorofluorohydrocarbons) outlined below will illustrate.

This did not mean there were no early attempts to mitigate pollution arising from manufacturing or consumption. In many cases, such action arose in response to outcries from those affected by water or air pollution, which eventually resulted in regulation and/or legal action to curb it. Complaints about water and groundwater pollution at chemical firm BASF in Ludwigshafen, Germany, for example, were rife from the start of the firm's existence in the mid-1860s, and sometimes led to changes in the company's behavior. Still, the risks and unpleasantness associated with such pollution were often deemed acceptable in view of the contribution of the company to the economy (von Hippel 2004: 76–79). Public concern elsewhere also led to lawsuits and regulation to minimize pollution, for instance in the case of the meatpacking industry in the United States in the late nineteenth century (Rosen 2007). Outcry by citizens also resulted in smoke abatement regulation in a number of cities in the United States by 1900 and later in Britain (Mosley 2013), and there were similar attempts by local and regional authorities through the first half of the twentieth century to curb the effects of pollution upon the environment. Nevertheless, although moves were made at national levels to tackle air and water pollution (as early as the 1930s in the United States), such efforts were successfully resisted by companies and their trade associations, which limited regulation to the local or, at most, state level rather than the national level. National-level regulation did not start in earnest in the United States (or elsewhere) until the 1960s (Smith 2000: 790–795, 804–809).

But still, even from the earliest days of industrialization, businesses were not just prodded into action to reduce or eliminate pollution; they also acted at times on their own volition. Indeed, the practices of recovery (or salvage) – what we would now call recycling (a term not used in its current sense until at least the late 1960s (Stokes *et al.* 2013: 213–216)) – and reuse of waste products have been around from the very start. Rag and bone men, for instance, collected castoffs for use in various production processes, while scrap dealers facilitated recovery and reuse (Zimring 2005; Thorsheim 2015). What is more, a key new industry – organic chemicals, which initially focused exclusively on production of synthetic dyestuffs – emerged in the last third of the nineteenth century; at the outset its raw materials were based virtually entirely on using toxic wastes produced through coking of coal for the iron and steel industries (Smith

2000: 785–786). Thus, as Desrochers (2012) has pointed out, business people thinking in terms of what we would now call a "circular economy," where what had been waste becomes something of value, existed long before the recent past when that phrase came into general use.

This did not mean, however, that businesses in general were striving for sustainability in the way we now understand it. To the extent that the circular economy has existed for much of the past 200 years, it was largely a function of three things. First, poverty or materials shortages (e.g., in times of war or severe economic disruption) were the major driving forces behind it, not environmental consciousness (Clapp 2014; Stokes *et al.* 2013). Second, regulation and lawsuits were often important factors in the use of alternative materials or chemicals (e.g., Rosen 2007). Third, some – but not many – lucrative industries such as organic chemicals could be built on the back of the use of waste products as valuable raw materials (Smith 2000: 788–789; Desrochers 2009).[1] But in all three cases, "loop closing" or circular economy occurred only when it was profitable, unavoidable, or specifically targeted by regulation or lawsuits, and only very rarely out of concern by business people for the environment or for what we would now call sustainability.[2] Indeed, as Hays (1987) and others have pointed out, "environmentalism" as we now understand it did not exist before the 1960s, while "sustainability" is even more recent (Bansal and DesJardine 2014). In other words, insofar as a circular economy existed through the late twentieth century, it did not apply to the economy as a whole, but rather only to narrow parts of industry and even then often to just selected parts of production processes. Moreover, pollution minimization as a criterion for product or process design seems to have been extraordinarily rare until at least the 1970s or 1980s, as we will come to below.

All of these industries and production processes had important national and even international dimensions in terms of raw materials flows, transport, and markets. Still, manufacturing-related pollution was usually localized, certainly in terms of perception. And, as outlined above, through the 1950s, except for local and regional cases, industry as a whole remained largely immune to being held accountable for the pollution caused, because public outcries usually did not reach beyond the regional level, and also because industrial pollution was often viewed as the price of prosperity.

Emergent globalized awareness of industrial pollution, 1960s–1980s

There is a scholarly consensus that this all changed fundamentally beginning in the 1960s. Despite visionary precursors of "green business" from before that period (Jones 2017), there is little doubt that a sea change in the scale of the perceived link between business and pollution occurred in that decade. One of the key precipitants of that change was the publication of Rachel Carson's (1962) *Silent Spring*. Carson's book (also serialized in the *New Yorker*) was immensely influential and was noteworthy not just because of its emphasis on the invisible threat posed by pesticides, especially DDT, but also because of its direct attack on the organic chemical industry. This was perhaps ironic given the industry's late nineteenth century roots in repurposing toxic waste into useful commodities. Though Carson was concerned about the application of this industrial product in agriculture, which makes this example apparently tangential to industrial pollution as defined at the outset of this chapter, DDT use was still arguably "direct" industrial pollution as defined here because consideration of potential environmental implications played no role whatsoever in the development of the pesticide as a commercial product.

But Carson's book did more than target the chemical industry and its products; it also focused on three dimensions of pollution that had hitherto been largely absent from discussion and debate. First, DDT's most important environmental impacts were not perceptible via the senses alone, but rather only with the aid of sophisticated science-based techniques and analysis. Second, because pesticides were produced, marketed, and distributed by multinational firms, they had effects that reached beyond the local to national and even global levels. And, third, pesticides' effects were not just immediate and/or localized, but also extended over time, with effects being reported many years later in parts of the world where DDT was never used, including the Arctic (Semeena and Lammel 2005).[3]

All three of these new dimensions indicated the start of an accelerating trend toward internationalization and then globalization of perceptions of the relationship between business and pollution and of notions of what could be done about it. The emergence of organized environmental activism by the late 1960s and 1970s – which was inspired in part by the work of Carson and other influential commentators – was therefore another factor in this process (Hays 1987). Friends of the Earth, for example, was founded in 1969 in San Francisco, and developed a network of affiliates in the 1970s in other countries (Stokes *et al.* 2013: 161–164), thereafter growing rapidly in prominence and influence. Such organizations formed an important part of the process whereby growing concerns about the environment pushed environmental issues further up the political agenda especially in industrialized countries, simultaneously internationalizing environmental consciousness and movements. Their cause was furthered by a series of oil spills (Hoffman 2001) and high-profile industrial pollution scandals. The latter included the Seveso disaster in Italy in 1976, when a large cloud of gas containing dioxins was released into the air; the legacy of toxic waste from Hooker Chemical that affected the Love Canal housing estate, first reported in the *New York Times* in 1978; the Three Mile Island nuclear power plant accident in Pennsylvania in 1979; and "the world's worst industrial disaster" involving release of highly toxic methyl isocyanate and other poison gases at a Union Carbide chemical plant in Bhopal, India, in 1984 (UK HSE 2017; Beck 1979; US NRC 2014; Taylor 2014 – quotation from Taylor).

All of this led in turn to extensive regulations on pollution at national rather than just local or regional levels starting in the 1970s. Seven months after the celebration of the first Earth Day on 22 April 1970, for instance, the US Environmental Protection Agency (EPA) began operating, with a remit to develop and enforce anti-pollution legislation and regulations (US EPA 1992). The end of that decade also witnessed one of the first major international agreements, the Convention on Long-range Transboundary Air Pollution. Signed in 1979 by a number of European countries, the convention aimed to limit emissions (primarily from electricity-generation plants, but also from other sources) that led to acid rain. A version of it was later ratified in North America as well (UNECE 2017). Just as with environmental science and activism, then, there has been a growing tendency toward internationalization and eventually globalization of regulations and controls, although effective enforcement at international/global levels has often proved challenging.

All in all, regulation, along with major attacks in the media and by activist groups on chemical and oil firms in particular, put business on the defensive at first, a stance reinforced by continuing pressure to change environmental practices by groups and organizations ranging from consumers to investors and churches. That said, it must be recognized that companies have become increasingly proactive in a number of ways, too, especially since the 1980s and 1990s, with many large corporations in particular embracing environmentalism, previously regarded as "heresy," in the form of the "dogma" of corporate environmentalism (Hoffman 2001). Growing consensus about the effect of burning fossil fuels on global climate change has been a key factor in this process as well. In any event, many of these proactive measures have in turn constituted a significant part of the process of globalization of industry and economy that has since taken place, with both positive and negative consequences.

Firm environmental strategies in the globalized economy

Such proactive measures vary widely by industry, technology, markets, and corporate culture of individual firms, but there are five key (and sometimes overlapping) strategies that companies have developed and deployed. Some have become both more intensive and more extensive since the late 1980s/early 1990s, largely in response to developments in climate change science. It is worth looking at each in turn to illustrate not just the varieties of strategies that have been deployed, but also the complexities of assessing their global impacts.

The first involves companies taking advantage of business opportunities that arise because of environmental regulation or legislation rather than simply reacting defensively. The US government's imposition of legally binding emissions and fuel consumption targets on the American automobile industry in the 1970s is a case in point. Although the extent of innovation fostered by this legislation and regulation, the opportunity costs of it, and the long-term impact on competitiveness are a matter of debate, it is clear that US auto producers devoted extensive R & D (research and development) resources to altering engine design and developing new technologies such as the catalytic converter that may well have enhanced competitiveness in the long run (Stewart 2010). Another example comes from the emerging waste management industry in the 1970s and 1980s. In Germany, increasingly strict recycling and waste reduction targets set by the federal government starting in the 1970s led to opportunities for growth and/or market entry for a range of private-sector recycling firms and eventually to the emergence of the innovative Dual System in the early 1990s. In contrast, much more lax approaches to waste reduction and recycling in Britain during this same period meant a much more modest (and much slower growth in) private-sector presence in the waste management industry, despite the commitment of Conservative governments of the time to privatization in this and other areas (Stokes *et al.* 2013: 298–305).

On the other hand, regulation sometimes only *appears* to foster innovation, as demonstrated in Nil Disco's recent case study of the development of water pollution treatment and abatement technologies starting in the 1970s at BASF. Disco successfully challenges the widely accepted view that legislation and regulation improved water quality in the Rhine River by indicating that improvements began well *before* the legislation was passed. In fact, the improvements came about primarily because BASF was effectively forced to develop environmentally friendly water treatment technologies in response to polluted water coming from upriver that increasingly interfered with the firm's production processes. These technologies, moreover, subsequently became an important source of revenue for the firm (Disco 2017).

A second strategy embraced by some firms since the 1990s entails putting pressure on a firm's supply chain to conform to a certain level of environmentally responsible practice, now widely recognized as "green supply chain management" (Walton *et al.* 1998). Such practices have since been implemented by many companies in a range of industries, sometimes to impressive effect. Apple is perhaps the most prominent example in recent years of this practice. Since 2013, when more than three-quarters of its total carbon output came from its supply chain, the company has been involved in attempts to force its global network of suppliers to reduce their output of carbon, waste, and effluents substantially. In 2016, the company announced that the 96 percent threshold of renewable energy used in its own operations would be extended to companies in its extensive supply chain. The targets will have to be met by 2020. Similar targets on net zero deforestation were also set. Apple's program boasts impressive figures as evidence of its success: 14 billion liters of freshwater were saved, carbon emissions were reduced by 150,000 metric tons, and 200,000 tons of waste were diverted from landfills in 2016 alone (Apple 2017). The extent to which Apple is at all representative is questionable, however. After all, it is one of the few firms in the world that can contemplate buying tens of thousands of acres of forests for conservation, or investing in the construction of massive solar energy plants for its own use. Moreover, the extent to which Apple's sub-contractors depend on it so heavily has arguably created a condition where the firm can force compliance with its objectives across a range of companies that would otherwise be difficult to achieve.

A third strategy embraced by some firms is also related to the emergence of global value chains and asymmetric power relationships between large firms, their subsidiaries, and original equipment manufacturers (OEM): it involves the offshoring (or international outsourcing) of manufacturing. This of course frequently has nothing to do with pollution minimization and can in fact lead to higher levels of pollution than had been the case before the offshoring of production. But, by simply moving the problem elsewhere, very often to developing countries that generally have far less stringent environmental and safety regulations compared to those in place in developed countries, a company can claim to be much more environmentally friendly than it in fact is. As a recent study of data on more than 8,000 US-based companies from 1992–2009 demonstrated, firms based in the United States tended to offshore pollution-intensive industries while shifting domestic production to less pollution-intensive operations (Li and Zhou 2017).

A fourth strategy, however, is far more positive and involves targeting product and process design, development, and deployment in order to minimize or even ameliorate environmental damage. As mentioned above, DDT was developed without any such considerations in mind, as was true for most products of the chemical (and other) industries through the 1960s. Growing public outcry led first to defensiveness, and then to strategies involving environmentally friendly product development, which were motivated in part by the desire to become (and be seen to be) part of the solution rather than part of the problem. Such considerations were part of German chemical firms' "high chem" strategies, especially from the late 1970s and early 1980s (Allen 1989; Jones and Lubinski 2014), and similar strategies were pursued in firms based elsewhere from about the same time.

The race to develop replacements for CFCs illustrates the complexities of such developments well. CFCs were initially developed at a laboratory associated with General Motors, with further development, initially primarily as a refrigerant, by DuPont. By the late 1940s, CFCs were the dominant chemical used in household refrigerators, and chemists soon found a range of other applications for them. Viewed for the next two decades as safe and environmentally benign, CFCs were linked from the early 1970s onwards to ozone depletion, and eventually climate change, which provided a compelling motivation for international agreements to curb their use. Chemical firms caused this problem in the first place, of course, but many of them soon realized that success in finding replacements would not just reshape public perceptions of firms in the industry, but would also be extraordinarily lucrative. Here it is important to note that environmental criteria formed a key part of the product design specification for any replacements, something that has become increasingly widespread in a number of industries. Unfortunately, in this case, the first replacement for CFCs, hydrofluorocarbons (HFCs), was found to add to climate change rather than the reverse (Hoffman 1990). But, eventually, alternatives were found that avoid ozone depletion and do not contribute to climate change.

The fifth of the major strategies involves "green business," although here it is useful to distinguish between two types. The first is the rarer of the two, but has become increasingly important, especially with growing understanding of the dangers of climate change. It involves establishment of firms whose very reason for existence is tied directly to environmental protection and sustainability, for instance in the renewable energy sector. Such companies tend to be characterized by heavy dependence on subsidies, which can make them vulnerable to government policy changes, as happened in the renewable energy sector in the United Kingdom in the 1980s (Wilson 2010). Often, too, the technologies such companies develop and deploy have the effect of offshoring rather than eliminating pollution. So, for instance, wind turbines and batteries for electric automobiles use significant quantities of rare earths, which cause environmental degradation where they are mined as well as when they need to be disposed of (Charalambides *et al.* 2016; Ali 2014), while electricity for charging electric automobiles is usually generated at power plants that use fossil fuels.

The second and much more common type of "green business," though, seeks to *eliminate* negative environmental impacts wherever possible (with the aim of being carbon neutral, or better). Again, this is something that has become much more widespread in the last three decades in the face of growing awareness of climate change and ongoing globalization of business and the economy, particularly since the publication of the "Our Common Future" report by the United Nations in 1987 (WCED 1987). That said, green business also has meant many different things to different organizations and sectors. It has included, for instance, exploring new materials and production methods to avoid exploiting existing finite, and/or polluting resources or processes (which, of course, overlaps with strategy four outlined above), "offsetting" carbon emissions through planting trees, designing logistical systems, and managing supply chains to minimize packaging and fossil fuel use, or recycling and recovering waste to eliminate the use of landfill sites.

However, at its heart, green business, insofar as sustainability is its core value, is based on the idea that the pursuit of longer-term goals instead of merely maximizing short-term profit is worthwhile. But this of course necessarily entails fundamental changes in longstanding business practices. Unilever, for example, recently felt unable to fulfill its fiduciary duty to shareholders (detailed in quarterly earnings reports) while simultaneously pursuing a sustainable business model, and thus shifted to semi-annual reports to better manage conflicts between the two more effectively (Bansal and DesJardine 2014). Another way that companies have implemented sustainability is based on carbon trading schemes devised by governments and international bodies, and involves assigning costs for internal accounting for carbon footprint of the firm's operations. Such assigned costs often exceed those set in public carbon-trading schemes ("Carbon Copy" 2013). In essence, then, this way of implementing strategies for greening business involves adoption of accounting procedures to internalize the negative externalities associated with pollution, particularly in regard to climate change.

These changes in business behavior have also stemmed to some degree from changing perceptions of the respective roles of government and business in causing and dealing with climate change. One influential study published online in 2013, for example, notes that half of all industrial pollution (in the form of carbon dioxide and methane) emitted between 1751 and 2010 has been produced since 1984, and furthermore that nearly two-thirds of these emissions came from just 90 firms, mostly in the extractive and energy industries. The study argues on the basis of this finding that such firms rather than nation-states should be held responsible for dealing with climate change, not least because many of them are investor-owned, headquartered in rich countries, and "possess the financial resources and technical capabilities to develop and contribute to climate change mitigation and adaptation" (Heede 2014: 235–236; quotation 236). In other words, changes in business behavior have occurred, but still more are needed. And this suggests that the "Porter hypothesis" (Porter and van der Linde 1995) is either not viable or that company executives have not yet fully grasped its potential (Bansal and DesJardine 2014).

Conclusion: local to global, heresy to dogma

Pollution has been a by-product of manufacturing from the earliest days of the industrial revolution, and there are some ways in which this "negative externality" has been global in impact from the outset in terms of supply chains, product design, and markets. In these senses at least, there has been a certain continuity in the global impact of pollution from business from the earliest days of industrialization to the present. But there have also been significant changes over time in the scale, perception, and global impact of pollution by business, accompanied (and in part caused) by changes in the ways in which society and institutions have placed pressure on business to alter practices. Awareness of climate change has made change in business practice more urgent and critical. All of this has involved, too, new forms of reactive and proactive/strategic response by business to such pressure.

One of the most significant changes has been the transformation of perception beginning in the early 1960s toward viewing industrial pollution as an issue that transcends the local or regional level. Here, one of the most important factors propelling change has been the increasingly sophisticated role of science in understanding pollution, particularly when combined with increased media attention and growing social and environmental movements. We share the view of other scholars that the publication of *Silent Spring* in 1962 marked a watershed: increased public understanding of the global harm of pollution which *could not be humanly perceived* and could cause damage thousands of miles away altered the spatial and temporal perceptions of industrial pollution dramatically.

In many ways, then, the late 1960s and 1970s marked a period when pollution abatement moved first from a local to a national, and then to an international and global, phenomenon. Certainly, the impact on business practice was most evident from this point. Of course, businesses were still faced with the same – and local – problems they had been faced with for many decades: rivers needed to be cleaned, land treated, and air filtered. And we have noted that there are some scholars who see the beginnings of "green business" and "sustainability" in the early twentieth century. But we have contended that firms engaged in this early on were rare exceptions, and that it is important to recognize that words such as sustainability were not used in their current way until very recently. We have therefore argued that the key transformation lay in the fact that "environmentalism," which emerged in the 1950s and 1960s and at first put business on the defensive, was increasingly embraced by business as "corporate environmentalism," encompassing everything from sourcing of raw materials to management of supply chains, design of products, and packaging and offsetting (or, if particularly challenging, offshoring) of damaging emissions. As Hoffman (2001) points out, what had been heresy in 1960 had become dogma by the close of the twentieth century, a conversion hastened and made more urgent by growing awareness of climate change and its causes starting in the late 1980s. Since then, being (or at least appearing to be, in particular in highly industrialized countries) environmentally responsible has been central to business practice, especially in large, multinational firms. More than that, environmental protection and amelioration have become vital shapers of product and process design for many companies, while becoming the main business of many others, although the process of globalization since the 1980s has also made offshoring of pollution caused by manufacturing to the developing world an important strategy for appearing green in the developed world.

In part for this reason, there is little evidence to support the contention of Michael Porter (Porter and van der Linde 1995) and many others that, essentially, "greed is green" (Desrochers 2013). Or, perhaps better put: there is little evidence to support the idea that business people are acting in ways that suggest they share this view. Even consensus on the centrality of climate change as a global challenge that businesses in particular have a responsibility to address has not generally led to qualitatively different behavior from that typical in the past. Full adherence to the dogma of sustainability would inevitably require firms to choose between short-term commitments to shareholder value and long-term commitments to corporate environmentalism and sustainability. It would also require that commitment to globalization of manufacturing be accompanied by commitment to a globalized vision of the environment that would not simply offshore pollution to the developed world. What has occurred instead may be best described as moderate greening, whereby only some processes, products, and materials have been changed for environmental reasons, but where firms still often make less than optimal choices for the environment, and continue to pollute in some – reduced (although the jury is out on this, too), but still quite significant – ways.

Notes

1 Smith (2000) notes the limits to waste utilization as a complete explanation for the development of the organic chemicals industry.
2 Bergquist and Lindmar (2016), and especially Jones (2017), highlight some important exceptions for the period before the 1980s, but they are not the norm.
3 Chick (2015) emphasizes changing perceptions of the geographical and intergenerational reach of pollution and their effects on environmental policy, while Bansal and DesJardine (2014) stress the intergenerational aspects of sustainability in business.

References

Ali, Saleem H. (2014), "Social and environmental impact of the rare earth industries," *Resources* 3, 123–134, doi: 10.3390/resources3010123.

Allen, Christopher (1989), "Political consequences of change: The chemical industry," in Peter Katzenstein, ed., *Industry and politics in West Germany* (Ithaca, NY: Cornell University Press), 157–184.

Allen, Robert C. (2009), *The British industrial revolution in global perspective* (Cambridge: Cambridge University Press).

Allen, Robert C. (2017), *The industrial revolution: A short introduction* (Oxford: Oxford University Press).

Apple (2017), "Apple supplier responsibility," available at: https://images.apple.com/uk/supplier-responsibility/pdf/GBEN_Apple_Supplier_Responsibility_2017.pdf (viewed 25 May 2017).

Ashton, T.S. (1996), *The industrial revolution, 1760–1830* (Oxford: Oxford University Press; originally published 1948).

Bansal, Pratima and Mark DesJardine (2014), "Business sustainability: It's about time," *Strategic Organization* 12, 70–78.

Beck, Eckardt C. (1979), "The Love Canal tragedy," *EPA Journal* (January), available at: https://archive.epa.gov/epa/aboutepa/love-canal-tragedy.html (viewed 31 March 2017).

Beckert, Sven (2014), *Empire of cotton: A new history of global capitalism* (London: Allen Lane).

Berghoff, Hartmut and Adam Rome, eds. (2017), *Green capitalism? Business and the environment in the twentieth century* (Philadelphia, PA: University of Pennsylvania Press).

Bergquist, Ann-Kristin and Magnus Lindmar (2016), "Sustainability and shared value in the interwar Swedish copper industry," *Business History Review* 90, 197–225.

Blackbourn, David (2006), *The conquest of nature: Water, landscape, and the making of modern Germany* (London: Pimlico).

Brüggemeier, Franz-Josef (1994), "A nature fit for industry: The environmental history of the Ruhr Basin, 1840–1990," *Environmental History Review* 18, 35–54.

"Carbon copy" (2013), *The Economist* (14 December), 62.

Carson, Rachel (1962), *Silent spring* (New York: Houghton Mifflin).

Center for Chemical Process Safety (2006), "Historical perspective on air pollution control," in *Safe design and operation of process vents and emission control systems* (Hoboken, NJ: John Wiley & Sons), 297–307.

Charalambides, G., K. Vatalis, V. Karayannis, and A. Baklavaridis (2016), "Environmental defects and economic impact on global market of rare earth metals," *IOP Conference Series: Materials Science and Engineering* 161.

Chick, Martin (2015), "The changing role of space and time in British environmental policy since 1945," *Revue Francaise d'Histoire Economique* 3, No. 1, 72–89.

Cioc, Mark (2009), "The Rhine as a world river," in Edmund Burke and Kenneth Pomeranz, eds., *The environment and world history* (Berkeley, CA: University of California Press), 165–190.

Clapp, B.W. (2014), *An environmental history of Britain since the Industrial Revolution* (Abingdon: Routledge).

Colten, Craig (1991), "A historical perspective on industrial wastes and groundwater contamination," *Geographical Review* 81, 215–228.

Desrochers, Pierre (2007), "How did the invisible hand handle industrial waste? By-product development before the modern environmental era," *Enterprise & Society* 8, 348–374.

Desrochers, Pierre (2009), "Victorian pioneers of corporate sustainability," *Business History Review* 83, 703–729.

Desrochers, Pierre (2012), "Freedom versus coercion in industrial ecology: A reply to Boons," *EconJournal Watch* 9, 78–99.

Desrochers, Pierre (2013), "Greed is green: How the profit motive helps the environment," 19 April, available at www.aei.org/publication/greed-is-green-how-the-profit-motive-helps-the.../print/ (viewed 13 December 2017).

Disco, Nil (2017), "The power of positive thinking: From the Chemicals Convention to the Rhine Action Plan, 1970–1990," in Ralf Banken and Ben Wubs, eds., *The Rhine: A transnational economic history* (Baden Baden: Nomos), 355–378.

Elmore, Bartow J. (2015), *Citizen Coke: The making of Coca-Cola capitalism* (New York: W.W. Norton).

Hays, Samuel (1987), *Beauty, health, and permanence: Environmental politics in the United States, 1955–1985* (Cambridge: Cambridge University Press).

Heblich, Stephan, Alex Trew, and Zylberberg Yanos (2016), "East side story: Historical pollution and persistent neighborhood sorting," CESifo Working Paper Series No. 6166, available at: https://ssrn.com/abstract=2884598 (viewed 19 February 2018).

Heede, Richard (2014) (published online November 2013), "Tracing anthropogenic carbon dioxide and methane emissions to fossil fuel and cement producers," *Climate Change* 122, 229–241.

Hoffman, A.J. (2001), *From heresy to dogma: An institutional history of corporate environmentalism* (Stanford, CA: Stanford Business Books).

Hoffman, John S. (1990), "Replacing CFCs: The search for alternatives," *Ambio* 19, 329–333.

Ingulstad, Mats, Andrew Perchard, and Espen Storli, eds. (2015), *Tin and global capitalism: A history of the devil's metal, 1850–2000* (Abingdon: Routledge).

Jones, Geoffrey (2017), *Profits and sustainability: A history of green entrepreneurship* (Oxford: Oxford University Press).

Jones, Geoffrey and Christina Lubinski (2014), "Making 'green giants': Environmental sustainability in the German chemical industry, 1950s–1980s," *Business History* 56, 623–649.

LeCain, Timothy J. (2009), *Mass destruction: The men and giant mines that wired America and scarred the planet* (New Brunswick, NJ: Rutgers University Press).

Li, Xiaoyang and Yue M. Zhou (2017), "Offshoring pollution while offshoring production?" *Strategic Management Journal*, on-line version: DOI: 10.1002/smj.2656.

Mosley, Stephen (2013), *The chimney of the world: A history of smoke pollution in Victorian and Edwardian Manchester* (London: Routledge).

Porter, Michael E. and Claas van der Linde (1995), "Green and competitive: Ending the stalemate," *Harvard Business Review* (September–October), 120–134.

Rosen, Christine Meisner (2007), "The role of pollution regulation and litigation in the development of the U.S. meatpacking industry, 1865–1880," *Enterprise & Society* 8, 297–247.

Rosen, Christine Meisner and Christopher C. Sellers (1999), "The nature of the firm: Towards an ecocultural history of business," *Business History Review* 73, 577–600.

Semeena, V.S. and G. Lammel (2005), "The significance of the grasshopper effect on the atmospheric distribution of persistent organic substances," *Geophysical Research Letters* 32: L07804, doi: 10.1029/2004GL022229.

Singerman, David (2014), "Inventing purity in the Atlantic sugar world, 1860–1930," PhD dissertation, MIT.

Smith, Andrew and Kirsten Greer (2017), "Uniting business history and global environmental history," *Business History* 59, 987–1009.

Smith, John K. (2000), "Turning silk purses into sows' ears: Environmental history and the chemical industry," *Enterprise & Society* 1, 785–812.

Stewart, Luke A. (2010), "The impact of regulation on innovation in the United States: A cross-industry literature review," available at: itif.org (viewed 26 May 2017).

Stine, Jeffrey K. and Joel A. Tarr (1998), "At the intersection of histories: Technology and the environment," *Technology and Culture* 39, 601–640.

Stokes, Raymond, Roman Köster, and Stephen Sambrook (2013), *The business of waste: Great Britain and Germany, 1945 to the present* (Cambridge: Cambridge University Press).

Stopford, John and John Dunning (1982), *The world directory of multinational enterprises*, vol. 1 (Detroit, MI: Gale Research).

Taylor, Alan (2014), "Bhopal: The world's worst industrial disaster, 30 years later", *Atlantic* (2 December), available at: www.theatlantic.com/photo/2014/12/bhopal-the-worlds-worst-industrial-disaster-30-years-later/100864/ (viewed 31 March 2017).

Thorsheim, Peter (2015), *Waste into weapons: Recycling in Britain during the Second World War* (Cambridge: Cambridge University Press).

Trebilcock, Clive (1981), *The industrialization of the continental powers, 1780–1914* (London: Longman).

UK HSE (Health and Safety Executive) (2017), "Icmesa Chemical Company, Seveso, Italy, 10 July 1976', available at: www.hse.gov.uk/comah/sragtech/caseseveso76.htm (viewed 31 March 2017).

UNECE (UN Economic Commission for Europe) (2017), available at: www.unece.org/env/lrtap/30anniversary.html (viewed 30 March 2017).

US EPA (Environmental Protection Agency) (1992), "The guardian: Origins of the EPA," *EPA Historical Publication* 1 (Spring), available at: https://archive.epa.gov/epa/aboutepa/guardian-origins-epa.html (viewed 31 March 2017).

US NRC (Nuclear Regulatory Commission) (2014), "Backgrounder on the Three Mile Island Accident," available at: www.nrc.gov/reading-rm/doc-collections/fact-sheets/3mile-isle.html (viewed 31 March 2017).

Von Hippel, Wolfgang (2004), "Becoming a global corporation: BASF from 1865 to 1900," in Werner Abelshauser, Wolfgang von Hippel, Jeffrey Allan Johnson, and Raymond G. Stokes, eds., *German industry and global enterprise. BASF: The history of a company* (Cambridge: Cambridge University Press), 5–114.

Walton, Steve V., Robert B. Handfield, and Steven A. Melnyk (1998), "The green supply chain: Integrating suppliers into environmental management processes," *International Journal of Purchasing and Materials Management* (Spring), 2–11.

WCED (United Nations World Commission on Environment and Development) (1987), "Our Common Future", available at: www.un-documents.net/our-common-future.pdf (viewed 13 March 2018).

Wilson, J. Campbell (2010), "A history of the UK renewable energy programme, 1974–88: Some social, political, and economic aspects," PhD dissertation, University of Glasgow.

Wlasiuk, Jonathan (2014), "A company town on common waters: Standard Oil in the Calumet," *Environmental History* 19, 687–713.

Zimring, Carl (2005), *Cash for your trash: Scrap recycling in America* (New Brunswick, NJ: Rutgers University Press).

37

THE GREAT DIVERGENCE AND THE GREAT CONVERGENCE

Geoffrey G. Jones

Introduction

Over the last decade the Great Divergence, or the timing of when the wealth gap between the Western world and the Rest of the world opened up, has become a prominent issue in the discipline of economic history. The debate has been conducted at a macro-economic level, however, and business historians have made hardly any contribution. They have made a potentially richer contribution to the less explored question of why the Rest failed to catch up after the gap had opened up, though most of this literature has not been structured in terms of the Great Divergence. This chapter begins with these two debates before turning to the Great Convergence of the last three decades. By 2017 China was the world's second largest economy. It accounted for nearly 15 percent of world GDP. Asia as a whole accounted for 34 percent of world GDP; the United States and Canada for 28 percent; and Europe for only 21 percent (World Economic Forum, 2017). While many developing economies, especially in Africa, were still desperately poor compared to the West, the scale and speed of the Great Convergence was nevertheless striking.

The Great Divergence

Although the data is highly contested, most economic historians would agree that the large inequality which became evident in the nineteenth century between regions is relatively "new," at least in historical terms. The timing, however, remains contentious. A consensus that incomes had diverged between Europe and China in the early modern period was disrupted around 2000 when Pomeranz put the term "the Great Divergence" into scholarly usage by suggesting that certain regions of China, India, and Western Europe were at broadly similar levels of agricultural productivity, commercial development, and the ability of some firms to raise capital, in the middle of the eighteenth century. The Great Divergence in wealth between the West and the Rest, then, began with the Industrial Revolution and the advent of modern economic growth in Britain (Pomeranz, 2000).

The Pomeranz hypothesis provoked a surge of quantitative research on comparative income levels. Research has focused on two indices – GDP (gross domestic product) per capita and real wage levels. This research has mostly suggested that income levels between Europe and Asia already diverged widely by the eighteenth century, reflecting trends which had begun at least 300 years earlier and reflecting a variety of factors including the agricultural system, fertility rates, the flexibility of labor supplies, and differences in state capacity. However there were "little divergences" both in Europe, between a more successful England and Low Countries versus Spain and Italy, and in Asia, between Japan versus China and India. By the turn of the nineteenth century the real income gap was between the most advanced countries in Europe – Britain, the Netherlands, and Belgium – and other regions, whether China, India, or central and southern Europe. What happened during the nineteenth century was that much more of the West caught up to the advanced North Sea countries, but the Rest did not (Broadberry and Gupta, 2006; Van Zanden, 2009; Allen *et al.*, 2011; Li and Van Zanden, 2012; Broadberry, 2013; Broadberry *et al.*, 2017).

A critique of this entire literature is that historical Chinese data simply does not support the use being made of it to derive these statistics. Deng and O'Brien have written extensively why available data in China cannot be compared to that available in Western countries such as Britain and the Netherlands. Their own estimates, using an entirely different approach, suggests that China may have been falling behind the West from the early seventeenth century, but their primary achievement has been to cast doubt on what was becoming a consensus in economic history – that the Great Divergence really did start in the early modern period. (Deng and O'Brien, 2016a, 2016b, 2017).

Beyond the shaky data on which it rests, a striking feature of the Great Divergence debate is that it has been "conducted at the macro-level, i.e. macro regions (e.g. the Yangtze Delta and Western Europe), macro sectors (e.g. technology, services, industry, farming, and governance), and macro issues (e.g. growth, development, living standards" (Zan and Deng, 2017, p. 5). There have also been fascinating general theories of the causes of the divergence between the West and China in particular. Controversially, Vries (2015) has pointed to the influence of the strong British state as opposed to the weak one. Mokyr (2017) has seen political fragmentation in early modern Europe promoting a culture of innovation. Rosenthal and Wong (2011) also point to the benefits of fragmentation rather than China's stability. Hoffman (2015) points to the ability of European states to mobilize "gunpowder technology" for both military and economic advantage. Raj (2017) has identified the importance of the emergence of impersonal markets in early modern Europe, driven by trade along the Atlantic coast and the availability of trade related printed books and the European postal system.

These studies (and others) provide the basis for business historians to contribute far more to the Great Divergence debates through work on specific firms, industries, and methods. Accounting historians are already doing such work (Soll, 2014). Zan and Deng point to improved management accounting methods which appeared in early modern Europe, especially sixteenth-century Venice, and the lack of any equivalent in China. They speculate that this may be due not to bad luck that archives were not preserved, but rather a reflection of different attitudes toward finance and money than in the West (Zan and Deng, 2017). Business historians have a real opportunity to engage in the Great Divergence debate by investigating managerial practices and systems in the early modern period.

The failure to catch up

A much less explored question, and one to which business historians can contribute more, is why it took the Rest so long to catch up after the Great Divergence had happened. While many regions of Europe caught up with the home of modern industrialization around the North Sea, it took the Rest of the world much longer. Bénétrix *et al.* (2015) have shown that from the late nineteenth century, the "periphery" began to follow the path of industrialization set in the West. Some Latin American countries began such "convergence" from the 1870s, followed by some Asian countries after 1890, followed again by parts of sub-Saharan Africa and the Middle East during the interwar years. Yet the emergence and growth of modern industrial sectors was not sufficient to close the substantial income gaps which had opened. This was primarily because dynamic and innovative firms were slow to emerge from these regions.

Most of the existing explanations for the slowness of catch-up have been at the macro-level, and have only implicitly explained the lack of emergence of modern firms. These explanations can be crudely summarized as falling into three buckets. The first, and initial, explanatory bucket is the role of culture. The West had the "right" culture, and the Rest had "wrong" cultures for capitalist enterprise. Writers from Weber (2011) to Landes (1998) to Mokyr (1990, ch. 9) have made this argument, as has more recently Ferguson (2011) when he identified the Protestant work ethic as one of the West's "killer apps." However leaving aside the well-known criticisms of such cultural generalizations, these studies have never explained how exactly culture impacts firm formation and quality of business decision-making.

The second big explanation is that, following the work of North, the West had the "right" institutions to promote capitalist economic growth, and the Rest did not (North, 1990, 2005). This has led to debates about the long-term impact of particular colonial regimes, such as North America had the "right" sort of colonialism, while the Rest did not, and about countries with common law having the "right" legal regime for encouraging capitalist development, and the Rest not. A big problem is that this literature has largely used property rights laws as a proxy for institutions (Jones, 2013, pp. 14–18). It is not evident that the West had superior property rights regimes to parts of the Rest. British India has the common law system. The widespread existence of market activities and the importance of private property in nineteenth century (and earlier) China would not suggest an overwhelmingly poor property rights regime (Faure, 2006; Deng, 2000). While the lack of company law in that country might have made capital-raising hard, when China finally introduced a Company Law Act enabling limited liability in 1904, few Chinese companies registered under the act (Kirby, 1995).

Nor is it evident that business enterprises were simply passive recipients of legal regimes. Musacchio has raised serious doubts concerning the adverse impact of civil law regimes on financial and economic development. Brazil was a French civil law country with apparently inadequate creditor protection and contract enforcement, but Musacchio found that Brazilian firms used their own byelaws to offer strong protection for equity investors (Musacchio, 2008).

Finally, education (or lack of it) has been used as an explanatory factor for global wealth and poverty (Easterlin, 1981).While plausible, the link with the development of modern business has never been clearly established. Eighteenth- and nineteenth-century China had widespread literacy, which did not translate into the creation of modern firms (Deng 2000). Probably the greatest negative consequence of low education levels was raising the cost of skilled labor. In the case of colonial India, the high cost of skilled labor has been identified as one possible explanation why the country remained inclined to small-scale traditional manufacture (Roy, 2000, ch. 7).

Context – whether institutional, cultural, or educational – matters for capitalist development, but the existing Great Divergence literature, primarily written by economists, has yet to provide firm evidence of how exactly it shaped entrepreneurship and business. Baumol's work on differences in what he terms the rules of the game between society enables a more explicit connection to be built. Baumol argued that the contribution of entrepreneurship to societies varied because of the allocation between productive activities such as innovation and unproductive activities such as rent seeking or organized crime. This allocation, Baumol suggested, was in turn influenced by the relative pay offs offered by a society to such activities (Baumol, 1990).

Maurer's study of the Mexican financial system from the late nineteenth century shows how this context played out in one country by demonstrating how the existence of an undemocratic political system and selective enforcement of property rights shaped the financial and business system. Limited in its ability to raise taxes to finance infrastructure projects as well as fend off political opponents, the Mexican government of the dictator Porfirio Diaz relied on banks to provide credit, while the banks relied on the government to enforce property rights. A select few bankers were given extensive privileges producing a highly concentrated banking system. Each bank grew fat in its own protected niche. To overcome the problems associated with information asymmetry, banks lent to their own shareholders and other insiders. In the case of the textile industry, banks did not lend to the best firms, but the best-connected firms. Poorly defined property rights prevented those excluded from the insider networks from pledging collateral and finding another financial route (Maurer, 2002).

More broadly, institutional and societal context was a major factor explaining why technological catch-up was a huge entrepreneurial challenge for entrepreneurs in nineteenth-century India, Mexico, and elsewhere in the Rest. The new advanced technologies of the West were embedded in quite different (not better or worse) institutional, economic, and social contexts from in the Rest. Entrepreneurs could not simply import them and they would work. Factor endowments fundamentally shaped the commercial viability of different transferred technologies (Roy, 2009). Relevant technologies needed to be identified, they needed to be adapted, they needed to be financed, and they needed to be used. This was challenging and costly, although not impossible (Beatty, 2003a, 2003b). This explains, in part, why there were such significant regional differences in entrepreneurial performance in many nineteenth century Latin American countries, despite having the same laws, language, and culture at the national level (Cerutti, 1996).

Closer examination of the "institutional arrangements" which promoted growth in many countries raise many questions about the "right" and "wrong" institutions which promoted entrepreneurship and firm growth. For example, the historical evidence does not support the argument that the protection of intellectual property rights and patents was important to promoting entrepreneurship from an institutional perspective. The evidence that patents in Britain played an important role in the Industrial Revolution and later is weak. The cost of obtaining a patent in eighteenth-century Britain was high, and they were difficult to enforce (Mokyr, 2009). Arapostathis and Gooday (2013) showed that British inventors around 1900 emphasized the importance of patents for personal profits. Moser showed that, historically, in countries with patent laws the majority of innovations have occurred outside the patent system, while conversely countries without patent laws produced as many innovations as countries with patent laws during the same time periods, and their innovations were of comparable quality (Moser, 2013). None of this is to deny, however, that institutional frailty of one kind or another was widely found in Africa, Asia, and Latin America, and often provided challenges to the growth of modern business enterprises (Austin et al., 2017).

The role of colonialism poses a particular challenge to institutional explanations of variations in the allocation of entrepreneurial energy. Most economics research on the impact of colonialism on the Great Divergence focuses on the highly exploitative first stages of European colonialism, especially in Latin America. However the policy regime of empires changed over time. While traditional Indian handicraft industries suffered from British free trade policies in the nineteenth century, during the interwar decades British India was protectionist, including against British imports (Morris, 1983). The British brought not only political stability to nineteenth-century India, after decades of turbulence, but also their legal system with protection of property rights and contract enforcement. The British administrators in India simplified and codified British laws in ways which appear to have made them even more enterprise-friendly.

Yet, when investments began in large-scale industry from the mid-nineteenth century, they were clustered geographically and ethnically. Scotsmen developed the modern jute industry of Calcutta from the 1860s, whilst the tiny ethnic minority of Parsees developed the textile industries on the west coast. Modern indigenous entrepreneurship became concentrated ethnically. Subsequently Marwaris, originating from Rajasthan, and the Vanias from Gujarat joined the Parsees as dominant entrepreneurial groups, a situation which lasted until the early twenty-first century (Tripathi, 2004: Markovits, 2008). Roy (2018) has, however, stressed that communal sentiments appear less important than exposure to international merchants, markets, technologies, and engineers in explaining why some merchants were able to transition to modern industry. Location in port cities and in trade routes to them seems to have greatly facilitated the transition to industry of traditional banking and merchant groups.

Market size might be important. The growth and size of the American market provides a key component of the Chandlerian explanation for the emergence of large integrated firms in the United States (Chandler, 1977). It seems plausible that in the case of both Britain, the first industrializer, and Japan, the first non-Western country to create modern business enterprises, the identification of entrepreneurial opportunities, and the building of managerial structures which permitted their exploitation, may have been facilitated by geographically compact domestic markets and unusually large capital cities.

The market opportunities for firms and entrepreneurs in most of Asia, Latin America, and Africa were more constrained. They often faced great difficulties if they wanted to sell beyond their local markets because of poor transport and communications infrastructure. In India, market conditions have been identified as one explanation why India's powerful and rich merchants in the seventeenth and eighteenth centuries left manufacturing in the hands of small artisans, pointing to fragmented markets, inadequate transport infrastructure, and lawlessness (Tripathi, 2004). These constraints were relaxed as the British colonial regime promoted transport infrastructure, but a well-established argument in the literature on nineteenth century India has maintained that the small scale of the domestic market retarded the growth of a modern machinery industry (Morris, 1983).

Yet, it was often foreign firms, or ethnic minorities, which took advantage of expanding opportunities. Variations in entrepreneurial cognition may have been important. Most local entrepreneurs may not have been well-informed about the pace of change in advanced economies, and less knowledgeable about their markets, including the market for skilled expertise. A lack of English-speaking ability might have constrained access to advanced knowledge in Latin America. The former imperial powers, Spain and Portugal, were in the backward south of Europe, and were not as a result a good role model for how to begin modern industrialization

As Casson (1991) has suggested, cultural differences toward information and "trust" levels may have been especially important in explaining variations in the quality of entrepreneurial judgments. It is evident that business enterprises in many non-Western societies were often challenged to grow beyond a certain size because their societies found it hard to "trust" non-family members as either managers or equity holders.

However many of the allegedly cultural explanations of why businesses in the Rest looked different from those in the West turn out to be misconceived. Much of the early literature on Latin American entrepreneurship in the nineteenth century blamed lack of economic growth on an alleged commercial and speculative ethos of the region's entrepreneurs. The diversified business groups, primarily family-owned, which appeared during the nineteenth century in

Latin America (and elsewhere) were regarded as inherently inefficient, and primarily vehicles for rent-seeking. However, such groups are now better understood as rational responses to weaknesses in capital markets, shortage of managerial resources, and high transactions costs. Within such conditions, business groups can, and often are, often the most effective forms of business organization (Jones and Khanna, 2006).

Indeed, as entrepreneurs in the Rest began catching up with their Western counterparts, they were often successful in developing hybrid organizational forms adapted to their local contexts (Lopes *et al.*, 2018). In China, the new modern business enterprises which appeared in early twentieth century typically combined the formal organization of Western-style corporations with traditional, well-established business practices from China's pre-industrial past. A study of the rapid growth of Shanghai's print machinery industry from the late nineteenth century has shown that in this industry, unlike others such as textiles, Chinese entrepreneurs were so successful that they were able to replace foreign machine imports with products from the local machine industry (Reed, 2004).

The pre-eminence of ethnic and religious minorities in entrepreneurial activity points toward a combination of contextual explanations for the slow growth of modern business enterprise. As many countries in the Rest began to industrialize, minorities or immigrants were especially important in new firm creation. These included Chinese in South-East Asia, Indians in East Africa, Lebanese in West Africa, Italians in Argentina, and French in Mexico. Their success has often ascribed to particular ethical or working practices, but their role is more plausibly explained as a demonstration of the challenges faced by entrepreneurs in societies where trust levels were poor, information flows inadequate, institutions weak, and capital scarce. In such situations, small groups with shared values held major advantages as entrepreneurs. If in addition, they established an intermediary role between locals and Western firms, they could secure easier access to knowledge and information from and about Western countries.

The prominent roles of particular ethnic and religious groups in Indian modern industry can be explained in such terms. The role of the tiny Parsee community around Bombay has been variously described as the result of close relations with the colonial authorities, "outsider" minority status, and a "Protestant" style work ethic (Desai, 1968). However the Marwaris were far less close to the British. Indeed, a number of families, like the Bajaj, became active in the Independence struggle. Other explanations for their pre-eminence have been found in unique cost accounting methods and the work ethos (Timburg, 1978).

Wolcott has combined both cultural and institutional factors to explain the pre-eminence of Indian minorities. She relates the situation to India's caste system, and argues that the payoffs to entrepreneurship differed across caste lines. Members of the moneylending and trading castes like the Marwaris could enforce contracts through reputation and membership deterred cheating. As a result, they were efficient at providing financial and other resources to entrepreneurs within their own castes. However, the large number of potential entrepreneurs outside these groups lacked privileged access to these informal financial networks, reducing their incentives to engage in productive entrepreneurship (Wolcott, 2010).

The ethnic clustering in modern entrepreneurship in India, and elsewhere, was striking, but, as Roy has suggested, another way to look at such clustering was geographically. Before 1914 Bombay and Calcutta accounted for half the modern factories in India, and even more of related services such as banking and insurance. Unlike other cities in India, they had grown through the activities of the East India Company, and were outward-oriented and cosmopolitan. In these two port cities, Roy observes, "modern Indian business enterprise and business families congregated and recreated a globalized world with strong Indian characteristics" (2012).

Lewis (2016) has demonstrated the economic and social vibrancy of port cities in South-East Asia in the interwar years.

The emergence of hubs such as Bombay, and modern entrepreneurship in general, also took place within the context of the wider political economy environment. Explanations for why ethnic Chinese business became disproportionately important in South-East Asia typically stress cultural factors, including the role of family, dialect groups, and the Confucian value system. With respect to the latter, it has often been argued that social trust, the social obligations that bind family and lineage, was strengthened by the Confucian belief, and that provided the bedrock of commercial networking. Yet while some or all of these features may be significant, the growth of Chinese entrepreneurship in South-East Asia also has to be placed within a wider political economy context. From the fourteenth century, the region's rulers favored foreign over local merchants because the latter might pose a political threat. Through the seventeenth century, local trading communities, whether Malay or Filipino, continued to flourish, but the Chinese role was strengthened by the arrival of Western merchants, for the Chinese positioned themselves as intermediaries. By the late nineteenth century, the Chinese had secured the position of revenue farmers across the region, both in colonial and non-colonial areas. This made them indispensable for local and colonial governments, while providing a source of funds for their business interests (Brown, 2000).

It was also within the context of Western geo-political power that European and US firms surged abroad to the Rest looking for commodities and markets. By 1914 world FDI (foreign direct investment) was not only substantial compared to world output; it was also primarily located in the non-Western world. Latin America and Asia were especially important as host regions, representing 33 and 21 percent respectively of the total world stock of FDI (Jones, 2005, p. 23). If domestic entrepreneurship in the Rest struggled to get traction, it needs to be explained why foreign entrepreneurship did not exercise a more productive effect on local business systems.

The industrial composition of this FDI provides a partial answer. Possibly one-half of total world FDI was invested in natural resources, and a further one-third in services, especially financing, insuring, transporting commodities, and foodstuffs. Manufacturing FDI primarily went to serve the markets of the West, whilst most FDI in the Rest was either in resources or services.

Yet the establishment and maintenance of mines, oil fields, plantations, shipping depots, and railroad systems involved the transfer of packages of organizational and technological knowledge to host economies. Given the absence of appropriate infrastructure in developing countries, foreign enterprises frequently not only introduced technologies specific to their activities, but also social technologies such as police, postal, and education systems. Between the late nineteenth century and 1914, residents of most of the world's cities were provided with access to electricity, in their homes or at work, or else in the form of street lighting (Hausman *et al.*, 2008).

However spillovers and linkages to local entrepreneurs were limited by the nature of global capitalism at the time. Many natural resource investments were enclavist. Minerals and agricultural commodities were exported with only the minimum of processing. Most value was added to the product in the developed economies. Foreign firms were large employers of labor at that time, but training was only provided to local employees to enable them to fill unskilled or semi-skilled jobs. The nature of the industries and these employment practices meant that the diffusion of organizing and technological skills to developing economies was far less than to developed economies. Technological diffusion worked best when there were already established firms which could be stimulated to become more competitive by foreign firms, or had the capacity to absorb workers who moved on from foreign firms (Jones, 2014).

Nor were foreign companies typically transformers of domestic institutions. While theoretically they may have been channels to transfer aspects of the institutional arrangements in their home countries to their hosts, for the most part they reinforced local institutions. This was most directly seen in the concession system. In order to entice firms to make investments in mines, railroads, and so on, foreign firms were often given large concessions often involving freedom from taxation and other requirements over very long periods (Jones, 2005). Concessions worked to lock-in already sub-optimal institutional arrangements. In Mexico, President Diaz's contracts and concessions to the British engineering contractor Weetman Pearson was effective in securing major infrastructure improvements in railroads, ports, and the drainage of Mexico City, and Pearson also laid the basis for the successful Mexican oil industry. Yet Pearson's very success strengthened the autocratic and crony capitalist regime of Diaz (Garner, 2011).

The nature of the first global economy, then, meant that there was limited diffusion of entrepreneurship and organizing capabilities from Western firms in the Rest. Their primary impact was often to lock-in countries as resource providers, and to reinforce institutional constraints on domestic entrepreneurship rather than removing them. This partly explains why the domestic entrepreneurial response to globalization was weaker than might have been imagined, which at its heart lay in a lagged understanding of the opportunities offered by the new global economy combined with problems building effective business organizations which could absorb foreign technological and organizational skills. Public policy was one way to break constraints on local entrepreneurs, but few governments in developing countries had either the autonomy or the capacity to pursue effective public policies.

Yet by 1914 the evidence, patchy as it might be, suggests that the lag was being addressed in India, China, and some countries in Latin America, especially Argentina, where five large business groups had built diversified businesses spanning manufacturing, finance, and resources (Barbero, 2015, pp. 8–14). During the interwar years, there were significant examples of strong locally owned business enterprises emerging in India, China, Egypt, Turkey, and elsewhere (Koll, 2003: Zelin, 2005: Davis, 1983: Colpan and Jones, 2016). However after World War II, many governments opted for state-led industrialization programs which frequently disrupted local firms, whilst blocking or discouraging foreign firms. Protectionism and restrictions on foreign firms provided a context for new local firms to emerge, but these policies also provided incentives for firms to build skills in political contacts rather than technology (Jones, 2013).

Although there was significant per capita GDP growth in many developing countries between 1960 and 1980, there had been very little closing of the income gap with the developed West (Weisbot and Ray, 2011) The "economic miracle" of the 1950s and 1960s made Japan the only case of a spectacular catch-up, with a number of other smaller East and South-East Asian economies such as Singapore and Taiwan following at a distance. Elsewhere, state interventionist regimes encountered growing problems of macro-economic instability and hyper-inflation by the 1970s which in some cases, such as Brazil, became extremely severe in the following decade (Jones, 2013; Weisbot and Ray, 2011).

The Great Convergence

The fast economic growth seen in China and India, and certain other regions of the Rest, still left a huge income gap between much of the developing world and the West (Weisbot and Ray, 2011). Still the emergence of highly competitive and globally active firms from China and elsewhere was a striking development. However the growth of these businesses provide only limited support for North-style institutional arguments. China's resurgence began under Deng Xiaoping, who had little concern with controls over the executive, human rights, political rights, or intellectual property protection. There is more support for Baumol's argument that shifts in the rules of the game more broadly can stimulate productive entrepreneurship. Policy liberalization and deregulation were important in allowing capitalist enterprise to flourish, even in Communist China.

Interestingly, many of the businesses which flourished with liberalization over the last thirty years had been founded and grew in the earlier era of import substitution. This policy regime provided local firms with opportunities to achieve scale within their protected domestic markets. A pioneer of this strategy was post-1945 Japan, which excluded most inward FDI, enabling automobile firms like Toyota and Nissan, and their electronics equivalents, to scale at home before seeking foreign markets (Mason, 1992). Two decades later it was in the context of a protected local market, and a repressive military regime, that South Korean chaebols such as Samsung got started. Similarly Cemex, now one of the world's largest cement companies, was founded in Mexico in 1906, and was able to grow in a sheltered environment slowly becoming a regional player and then, in the 1970s, a national player. As the Mexican and other economies liberalized, it was well positioned to expand globally. In 1992, Cemex began globalization by purchasing Spain's two largest cement companies.

In India, the era of the so-called "License Raj" between the 1950s and 1980s also enabled firms to grow within their domestic market. Arguably, it laid the basis for the country's subsequently successful IT (information technology) services sector. Postwar India had growing numbers of engineers owing to the many national institutes, engineering universities, and regional colleges established after 1947. However, it had little choice but to be totally dependent on US computer makers. During the 1960s and 1970s a handful of locally owned firms were established to develop and run applications software for Indian companies and research institutions that had brought or leased mainframes from IBM and other US companies. Tata, which had remained India's largest business group, established the first of these firms, Tata Consulting Services in 1968. This and other ventures remained small, however, until 1977, when, after the Indian government tightened the laws on foreign ownership of firms, IBM and other US firms divested.

The departure of IBM opened new opportunities for local firms. TCS developed a relationship with another US computer maker, Burroughs, which provided an important channel of new technology. In 1982 the start-up Infosys was founded by the dynamic entrepreneur Narayana Murthy. The Indian firms built a strong trade association, NASSCOM, which sought to enhance and certify the quality of Indian firms. By the time policy regulation got underway in 1991, which gave Indian IT firms a freer hand in establishing marketing offices abroad and serving foreign clients, it had built strong organizational capabilities. The software industry became focused on Bangalore, where the British had established India's first aircraft factory during World War II, and which was the home of two of India's premier institutes of higher education in pure science. Like Silicon Valley, there was also a pleasant climate, at least before pollution began to increase. The government's establishment of a Software Technology Park, or export zone, in Bangalore in 1990, and an influx of expertise and contracts from the many expatriate Indians employed in Silicon Valley, were other influential factors in the growth of the Bangalore cluster (Parthasarathy and Aoyama, 2006).

The liberalization of policies toward foreign firms was important too in the Great Convergence. China is a showcase for the transforming impact of global capitalism, as foreign firms played a key initial role in China's economic growth, and accounted for a high percentage of China's exports (Vogel, 2011). It is less evident that multinationals had a truly transformational effect on the Rest, even though almost everywhere policy regimes sought to attract them. In countries where export-oriented FDI was concentrated within free trade zones, linkages with local firms were particularly weak (Jones, 2014).

Nevertheless, certain aspects of global capitalism as it evolved from the 1980s delivered more opportunities for firms and entrepreneurs based in the Rest. An important development was the disintegration of the boundaries of M-form firms from the 1980s as many large Western corporations suffered from growing managerial diseconomies and low rates of innovation caused by size and diversification. The result was divestment of "non-core" businesses, outsourcing of many value-added activities, and the formation of alliances with other firms which acted as suppliers and customers, or as partners in innovation. While large Western corporations remained powerhouses of innovation spending and market power, they formed components of a world-wide web of inter-firm connections. As Baldwin (2017) argues, developments in informational technology enabled multinational firms to move both labor-intensive jobs and technological knowledge much easier than in the past.

The disintegration of production systems and their replacement by networks of inter-firm linkages lowered barriers for new entrants from the Rest. Within a network-type global economy, firms from emerging markets were able to piggy back on incumbent Western or Japanese firms as customers through subcontracting, linkages, and leverages (Mathews, 2002). The spectacular growth of Taiwan's personal-computer industry from the 1980s, for example, was based on contract manufacturing for Western firms. However despite their technical capabilities, manufacturing prowess, and scale, most leading Taiwanese firms except Acer did not develop their own capabilities in branding and marketing. The nature of the relationship with established companies in the West, as well as local competition, seems to have constrained capability development among most firms (Yu and Shih, 2014).

The Taiwanese electronics contract manufacturer Foxconn, founded by Terry Gou in 1974 (initially called Hon Hai) grew to be a $140 billion company in 2017 with plants all over the world. A central driver of this growth was its role as the largest components supplier to Apple. Apple began outsourcing to Foxconn in the late 1990s. Gou developed close relations with local government officials in China who provided cheap land and subsidies for plants to manufacture Apple products. When the iPhone was launched in 2007, Foxconn secured agreement with the local government in Zhengzhou to subsidize the building of an industrial park located inside a bonded zone, with customs facilities at the factory gate to facilitate iPhone exports. The located government recruited and trained the manufacturing workforce which by 2016 amounted to 350,000 workers. Billions of dollars of financial incentives were provided by the local government also (Barboza, 2016). By then Foxconn manufactured 90 percent of Apple's iPhones. Foxconn did not develop its own brands, but in 2016 it did acquire the troubled Japanese electronics company Sharp, which had an extensive branded consumer products business. By that year, Foxconn's annual revenues had reached $140 billion.

In some cases, contractors created their own brands in time. The growth of Galanz was one example. Founded in 1978 by Liang Qingde as a company that dealt in the trading of duck feathers, Galanz began producing OEM Toshiba-branded microwave ovens in 1993. Galanz later purchased the appliance division from Toshiba. By the following decade, Galanz had become the world's largest microwave manufacturer (Mathews, 2002).

If a major constraint for firms based in the Rest was not only the existence of entrepreneurial opportunities, but also the building of organizational capabilities to exploit them, then a number of developments during the second global economy alleviated this challenge, and facilitated "accelerated internationalization" (Matthews and Zander, 2007).

First, diaspora assumed a renewed importance as transferors of entrepreneurship and capital, and means by which firms could access management talent. The revitalized use of diaspora reflected changes in policies in China and India especially made them more attractive locations to do business, encouraging diaspora to return. After 1980, ethnic Chinese firms based in Hong

Kong and Taiwan, and later elsewhere, became the leading foreign investors as China liberalized its economy. They enjoyed connections (*guanxi*) in China, which reduced the transactions costs of investment by offering contacts with public authorities and inside information, and were welcomed by the Chinese government. Many engineers settled in Silicon Valley and made up a quarter of the workforce by the 1990s. As the Indian economy grew from the 1990s, there has been a significant reverse flow back to India. This was assisted by the Indian government's new policy in 2003 of granting dual nationality to some overseas Indian residents abroad. These diaspora links provided valuable connections between Silicon Valley and Bangalore, encouraging business connections and capital flows (Pandey *et al.*, 2004; Oonk this volume).

Second, both business schools and management consultants provided much easier access to new management knowledge, and they have played important roles in building organizational capabilities in firms. In postwar Europe both US management consultancies and business schools were influential diffusers of American managerial knowledge to Europe and other developed countries. The impact on emerging markets only became stronger later. McKinsey opened in India in 1992. From the 1980s leading US business schools have internationalized their faculty and student body (Kipping, this volume).

Many of the most successful companies from the Rest used US consulting firms to provide advice on strategy, sent senior managers on executive programs at the top business schools, and recruited MBAs as graduates. None of this meant that such firms evolved as replicas of US firms, but it did mean that they had faster and better access to information about the latest managerial ideas in ways which were impossible fifty years ago. Cemex's global growth, for example, was led by a new generation of the founding Zambrano family. Lorenzo Zambrano, the architect of a new international strategy, had been educated at Stanford Business School, and sought strategy advice from Boston Consulting Group (Lessard and Reavis, 2009).

A final, important, factor in the growth of global firms from some emerging markets was support from their host governments. The important role of governments in promoting catch-up in this era echoed the model of the economic historian Alexander Gershenkron, writing in the early 1960s about the first global economy, who argued that governments would be important forces in countries seeking to catch-up from economic backwardness (Gershenkron, 1962; Colli this volume) The spectacular growth of Gulf-based airlines such as Emirates and Qatar provided a prominent example, but it was in China where some of the striking results were seen. China was among the governments which used state-owned firms as national champions to pursue strategic objectives (Child and Rodriques, 2005). The growth of Chinese firms to dominate the global solar industry provided one such example (Jones, 2017, pp. 342–345). A related category were highly politically connected firms such as HNA, which grew rapidly from the 2000s from its original business of Hainan Airlines into a diversified conglomerate, which included for a time major holdings in Western businesses such as Hilton and Deutsche Bank before coming under pressure from the Chinese government to curb unrelated diversification (Weinland *et al.*, 2017).

However, while official blessing was key to growth for all Chinese corporations, some businesses had less direct support from the government. This smaller category of firms was often founded by victims of the Cultural Revolution in their youths. They included Zong Qinhou (Wahaha), and Ren Zhengfei (Huawei). The fast speed of the globalization of Huawei, the Chinese internet router company, was striking. Ren Zhengfei certainly received credit from the state-owned development bank in the firm's early years. Wireless networking was also a strategic industry for the Chinese government, not least because the equipment was the hardware which enabled the government to monitor activity on the internet. However Huawei's growth was not a simple story of growth based on political contacts and support, despite repeated allegations from the US government. Ren Zhengfei implemented an effective strategy of building businesses in remoter and outlying cities in China before targeting the major cities where the American firm Cisco and others had built an internet router market from the 1990s. He then repeated the strategy globally, first selling to developing and transition countries like Russia, Brazil, and Thailand, before moving to more advanced markets, especially in Europe. Huawei also invested heavily in research, creating research centers in numerous locations around the world including Bangalore and Silicon Valley. Innovation was supported by an aggressive corporate culture which rewarded talent (Jones, 2013).

The growth of powerful globally active corporations from the Rest was a singular feature of contemporary global economy and a driver of the Great Convergence. Huawei and Foxconn had many equivalents in other countries and in different industries, such as Bimbo in Mexico, Concha y Toro in Chile, Natura in Brazil, the Tata group in India, and MTM in South Africa.

Conclusion

This chapter has sought to integrate a business history perspective into debates about the Great Divergence and its consequences, and the more recent Great Convergence. While recognizing that the context of institutions, education, and culture play a role in explanations of wealth and poverty, the chapter calls for a closer engagement with the processes of how these factors translate into generating productive firms and entrepreneurs.

In explaining why the development of modern business enterprise in the Rest lagged, the recasting of existing literature into the framework of the Great Divergence debate permits important insights. The societal and cultural embeddedness of new technologies provide one important explanatory factor. Evidently, the challenges were sufficiently great in the Rest that minorities held significant advantages in capital-raising and trust levels which enabled them to flourish as entrepreneurs. They also benefitted from a greater willingness to engage Western firms and colonial governments. In contrast, multinationals often proved disappointing diffusers of organizational skills and information to the Rest, and had limited importance in relieving the institutional, human capital, or other constraints faced by local entrepreneurs. By the interwar years, there is evidence of emergent modern entrepreneurship and business enterprise in Asia, Latin America, and Africa. However many governmental policies after 1945 designed to facilitate catch-up ended up crippling such emergent business enterprises without putting effective alternatives in place.

The second wave of globalization from the 1980s, which has experienced considerable economic and political turbulence since 2008 and showed evidence of going into reverse, provided more opportunities for catch-up from the Rest. Firms from emerging markets had the opportunity to access the global networks which in part replaced large integrated firms. There were also new ways for firms in the Rest to access knowledge and capital, and governments in a number of countries proved effective supporters of corporate catch-ups. Business historians have an enormous opportunity to contribute to understanding these processes.

References

Allen, Robert C., Bassino, Jean-Pascal, Ma, Debin, Moll-Murata, Christine, and Van Zanden, Jan Luiten (2011), "Wages, Prices, and Living Standards in China, Japan, and Europe, 1738–1925," *Economic History Review*, 64, (1), 8–38.

Arapostathis, Stathis and Gooday, Graeme (2013), *Patently Contestable: Electrical Technologies and Inventor Identities on Trial in Britain* (Cambridge, MA: MIT Press).

Austin, Gareth, Dávila, Carlos, and Jones, Geoffrey (2017), "The Alternative Business History: Business in Emerging Markets," *Business History Review*, 91, (3), 537–569.

Baldwin, Richard (2017), *The Great Convergence: Information Technology and the New Globalization* (Cambridge, MA: Belknap Press).

Barbero, Maria Ines (2015), "Business Groups in Nineteenth and Twentieth Century Argentina," in Geoffrey Jones and Andrea Lluch (eds.), *The Impact of Globalization on Argentina and Chile: Business Enterprises and Entrepreneurship* (Northampton, MA: Edward Elgar).

Barboza, David (2016), "How China Built 'iPhone City' with billions in perks for Apple's Partner," *New York Times*, December 29.

Baumol, William J. (1990), "Entrepreneurship: Productive, Unproductive, and Destructive," *Journal of Political Economy*, 98, (5), 893–921.

Beatty, Edward (2003a), "Approaches to Technology Transfer in History and the Case of Nineteenth Century Mexico," *Comparative Technology Transfer and Society*, 1, (2), 167–200.

Beatty, Edward (2003b), "Bottles for Beer: The Business of Technological Innovation in Mexico, 1890–1920," *Business History Review*, 83, 317–348.

Bénétrix, Agustin, O'Rourke, Kevin, and Williamson, Jeffrey (2015), "The Spread of Manufacturing to the Poor Periphery 1870–2007," *Open Economies Review*, 26, (1), 1–37.

Broadberry, Stephen (2013), "Accounting for the Great Divergence," London School of Economics, *Economic History Working Papers*, 184 (November).

Broadberry, Stephen, Guan, Hanhui, and Li, David Daoki (2017), "China, Europe and the Great Divergence: A Study in Historical Accounting, 980–1850," *University of Oxford, Department of Economics Working Papers*, 155 (April).

Broadberry, Stephen and Gupta, Bishnupriva (2006), "The Early Modern Great Divergence: Wages, Prices and Economic Development in Europe and Asia, 1500–1800", *Economic History Review*, 59, (1), 2–31.

Brown, Rajeswary A. (2000), *Chinese Big Business and the Wealth of Asian Nations* (London: Palgrave).

Casson, Mark (1991), *The Economics of Business Culture* (Oxford: Clarendon Press).

Cerutti, Mario (1996), "Estudios regionals e historia empresarial en Mexico (1840–1920): Una revision de lo producido desde 1975," in Carlos Davilla (ed.) *Empresa e historia en América Latina* (Bogota: Tercer Mundo/Colciendas).

Chandler, Alfred D. (1977), *The Visible Hand* (Cambridge, MA: Harvard University Press).

Child, John and Rodriques, Suzana B. (2005), "The Internationalization of Chinese Firms: A Case for Theoretical Extension?" *Management and Organization Review*, 1, (3), 381–418.

Colpan, Asli and Jones, Geoffrey (2016), "Business Groups, Entrepreneurship and the Growth of the Koç Group in Turkey," *Business History*, 58, (1), 69–88.

Davis, Eric (1983), *Challenging Colonialism: Bank Miṣr and Egyptian Industrialization, 1920–1941* (Princeton, NJ: Princeton University Press).

Deng, Kent (2000), "A Critical Survey of Recent Research in Chinese Economic History," *Economic History Review*, LIII, (1), 1–28.

Deng, Kent and O'Brien, Patrick (2016a), "China's GDP Per Capita from the Han Dynasty to Communist Times," *World Economics Journal*, 17, (2), 79–123.

Deng, Kent and O'Brien, Patrick (2016b), "Establishing Statistical Foundations of a Chronology for the Great Divergence: A Survey and Critique of the Primary Sources for the Construction of Relative Wage Levels for Ming-Qing China," *Economic History Review*, 69, (4), 1057–1082.

Deng, Kent and O'Brien, Patrick (2017), "How Well did Facts Travel to Support Protracted Debate on the History of the Great Divergence between Western Europe and Imperial China," *MPRA Paper* No. 77276, March 5.

Desai, Ashok (1968), "The Origins of Parsi Entrepreneurship," *Indian Economic and Social History Review*, 5, (4) 307–318.

Easterlin, Richard A. (1981), "Why Isn't the Whole World Developed?" *Journal of Economic History*, 41, (1), 1–19.

Faure, David (2006), *China and Capitalism* (Hong Kong: Hong Kong University Press).

Ferguson, Niall (2011), *Civilization: The West and the Rest* (London: Allen Lane).

Garner, Paul (2011), *British Lions and Mexican Eagles: Business, Politics, and Empire in the Career of Weetman Pearson in Mexico, 1889–1919* (Stanford, CA: Stanford University Press).

Gershenkron, Alexandra (1962), *Economic Backwardness in Historical Perspective* (Cambridge, MA: Harvard University Press).

Hausman, William J., Hertner, Peter, and Wilkins, Mira (eds.) (2008), *Global Electrification: Multinational Enterprise and International Finance in the History of Light and Power 1878–2007* (Cambridge: Cambridge University Press).

Hoffman, Philip T. (2015), *Why did Europe Conquer the World?* (Princeton, NJ: Princeton University Press).

Jones, Geoffrey (2005), *Multinationals and Global Capitalism* (Oxford: Oxford University Press).

Jones, Geoffrey (2013), *Entrepreneurship and Multinationals: Global Business and the Making of the Modern World* (Northampton, MA: Edward Elgar).

Jones, Geoffrey (2014), "Business History and the Impact of MNEs on Host Economies," *Research in Global Strategic Management*, 16, 177–198.

Jones, Geoffrey (2017), *Profits and Sustainability: A History of Green Entrepreneurship* (Oxford: Oxford University Press).

Jones, Geoffrey and Khanna, Tarun (2006), "Bringing History (Back) into International Business," *Journal of International Business Studies*, 37, (4), 453–468.

Kirby, William C. (1995), "China Unincorporated: Company Law and Business Enterprise in Twentieth-Century China," *Journal of Asian Studies*, 54, (1), 43–63.

Koll, Elisabeth (2003), *From Cotton Mill to Business Empire* (Cambridge, MA: Harvard University Press).

Landes, David S. (1998), *The Wealth and Poverty of Nations* (New York: W.W. Norton).

Lewis, Su Lin (2016), *Cities in Motion: Urban Life and Cosmopolitanism in Southeast Asia 1920–1940* (Cambridge: Cambridge University Press).

Li, Bozhong and Van Zanden, Jan Luiten (2012), "Before the Great Divergence? Comparing the Yangzi Delta and the Netherlands at the Beginning of the Nineteenth Century," *Journal of Economic History*, 72, (4), 956–989.

Lessard, Donald R. and Reavis, Cate (2009), "CEMEX: Globalization 'The Cemex Way,'" *MITSloan Management Case*, 09–039, March.

Lopes, Teresa, Casson, Mark, and Jones, Geoffrey (2018), "Organizational Innovation in the Multinational Enterprise: Internalization Theory and Business History," *Journal of International Business Studies*. https://doi.org/10.1057/s41267-018-0156-6.

Markovits, Claude (2008), *Merchants, Traders, Entrepreneurs: Indian Business in the Colonial Era* (New York: Palgrave Macmillan).

Mason, Mark (1992), *American Multinationals and Japan* (Cambridge, MA: Harvard University Press).

Mathews, John A. (2002), *Dragon Multinational: A New Model for Global Growth* (Oxford: Oxford University Press).

Matthews, John A. and Zander, Ivo (2007), "The International Entrepreneurial Dynamics of Accelerated Internationalization," *Journal of International Business Studies*, 38, 2007, 387–403.

Maurer, Noel (2002), *The Power and the Money: The Mexican Financial System, 1876–1932* (Stanford, CA: Stanford University Press).

Morris, Morris D. (1983), "The Growth of Large-Scale Industry to 1947," in Dharma Kumar (ed.) *The Cambridge Economic History of India* (Cambridge: Cambridge University Press).

Mokyr, Joel (1990), *The Lever of Riches* (Oxford: Oxford University Press).

Mokyr, Joel (2009), "Intellectual Property Rights, the Industrial Revolution, and the Beginnings of Modern Economic Growth," *American Economic Review Papers and Proceedings*, 99, (2), 349–355.

Mokyr, Joel (2017), *A Culture of Growth: The Origins of the Modern Economy* (Princeton, NJ: Princeton University Press).

Moser, Petra (2013), "Patents and Innovation: Evidence from Economic History," *Journal of Economic Perspectives*, 27, (1), 23–44.

Musacchio, Aldo (2008), "Can Civil Law Countries get Good Credit Institutions? Lessons from the History of Creditor Rights and Bond Markets in Brazil," *Journal of Economic History*, 68, (1), 80–108.

North, Douglas C. (1990), *Institutions, Institutional Change and Economic Performance* (Cambridge: Cambridge University Press).

North, Douglas C. (2005), *Understanding the Process of Economic Change* (Princeton, NJ: Princeton University Press).

Pandey, Abhishek, Aggarwal, Alok, Devane, Richard, and Kuznetsov, Yevgeny (2004), "India's Transformation to Knowledge-Based Economy: Evolving Role of the Indian Diaspora," *Evalueserve*, July. Accessed July 8, 2016, at http://info.worldbank.org/etools/docs/library/152386/abhishek.pdf.

Parthasarathy, Baliji and Aoyama, Yuko Y. (2006), "From Software Services to R&D Services: Local Entrepreneurship in the Software Industry in Bangalore, India," *Environment and Planning A*, 38, 1269–1285.

Pomeranz, Kenneth (2000), *The Great Divergence* (Princeton, NJ: Princeton University Press).

Raj, Prateek (2017), "Origins of Impersonal Markets in Commercial and Communication Revolutions of Europe," Stigler Center for the Study of the Economy and the State, *New Working Paper Series No. 1*, July.

Reed, Christopher A. (2004), *Gutenberg in Shanghai: Chinese Print Capitalism 1876–1937* (Honolulu, HI: University of Hawaii Press).

Rosenthal, Jean-Laurent and Wong, R. Bin (2011), *Before and Beyond Divergence: The Politics of Economic Change in China and Europe* (Cambridge, MA: Harvard University Press).

Roy, Tirthankar (2000), *The Economic History of India 1857–1947* (New Delhi: Oxford University Press).

Roy, Tirthankar (2009), "Did Globalization Aid Industrial Development in Colonial India? A Study of Knowledge Transfer in the Iron Industry," *Indian Economic and Social History Review*, 46, 4, 579–613.

Roy, Tirthankar (2012), "Beyond Divergence: Rethinking the Economic History of India," *Economic History of Developing Regions*, 27, (1), 557–565.

Roy, Tirthankar (2018), *A Business History of India: Enterprise and the Emergence of Capitalism from 1700* (Cambridge: Cambridge University Press).

Soll, Jacob (2014), *The Reckoning: Financial Accountability and the Rise and Fall of Nations* (New York: Basic Books).

Timburg, Thomas A. (1978), *The Marwaris: From Traders to Industrialists* (New Delhi: Vikas).

Tripathi, Dwijendra (2004), *Oxford History of Indian Business* (New Delhi: Oxford University Press).

Van Zanden, Jan Luiten (2009), "The Skill Premium and the 'Great Divergence,'" *European Review of Economic History*, 13, 121–153.

Vogel, F. (2011), *Deng Xiaoping and the Transformation of China* (Cambridge, MA: Belknap Press).

Weber, Max (2011), *The Protestant Ethic and the Spirit of Capitalism* (Oxford: Oxford University Press).

Weinland, Don, Massoudi, Arash, and Fontanella-Khan, James (2017), "HNA's Buying Spree Surpasses $40bn with CWT Deal," *Financial Times*, April 9.

Weisbot, Mark and Ray, Rebecca (2011), "The Scorecard on Development, 1960–2010: Closing the Gap?" *DESA Working Paper*, No 106, June. Accessed June 20, 2016 at www.un.org/esa/desa/papers/2011/wp106_2011.pdf.

Wolcott, Susan (2010), "An Examination of the Supply of Financial Credit to Entrepreneurs in Colonial India," in David S. Landes, Joel Moykr, and William J. Baumol (eds.) *The Invention of Enterprise* (Princeton, NJ: Princeton University Press).

World Economic Forum (2017), Accessed August 8, 2017, at www.weforum.org/agenda/2017/03/worlds-biggest-economies-in-2017.

Yu, Howard H. and Shih, Willy C. (2014), "Taiwan's PC Industry, 1976–2010: The Evolution of Organizational Capabilities," *Business History Review*, 88, (2), 329–357.

Zan, Luca and Deng, Kent (2017), "Micro Foundations in the Great Divergence Debate: Opening up a New Perspective," London School of Economics, *Economic History Working Papers*, No. 256, January.

Zelin, Madeleine (2005), *The Merchants of Zigong* (New York: Columbia University Press).

INDEX

Note: page numbers in **bold** denote tables, those in *italics* denote figures.

Hopkins, Terence 280
horizontal integration 204
host economies 18–19, 21, 98, 203, 268, 534–535, 543, 584
hotels 24, 38, 236, 238, 255, 270, 425
House of Worth 426
Hower, Ralph H. 130
HSBC *see* Hongkong and Shanghai Banking Corporation
Huawei 28–29, 532, 588–589
Hudson, Peter 82
Hudson's Bay Company 203, 254, 425
Hughes, Samuel 193
Hugo Boss 288
Humphrey, John 282
Humphries, Jane 74
Hunt, Edwin S. 181
Hymer, Stephen 5, 96, 532–533
Hyundai 399, 401

IBM 116, 144, 586
IG Farben 491
illegal drug trafficking, global growth of 525
imagined futures, role in entrepreneurship 58, 61
Imagining Britain's Economic Future (Thackeray et al.) 82
IMF (International Monetary Fund) 493
imitation of goods 502–512; complexity of the phenomenon 504; the concept of imitation 502; evolution of the regulatory environment on wine 506–508; imitation strategies in wines 508–510; literature review 503–505; Pears soap example 504–505; strategies for dealing with 510–511; wines 505–506
imperialism: American 519; British 22, 63, 254, 319, 323; the concept 77; gendered perspective 73, 77, 79–80; global business as product of 486–487; multinationals as beneficiaries of 536; translation of imperialism and colonialism to globalization 69, 76–82; *see also* colonialism
Imperial Leather (McClintock) 78
imperial power 46, 518; association with dominance in global business 45–47
India: and the automobile industry 398–399, 402; Bhopal disaster 552, 553, 570; Britain's trade with 203, 208, **209**, 210–212; and business groups 239; clustering 270, 583; and colonial protection of foreign merchants' property rights 486; and colonial protection of property rights 582; and the communications industry 325; consultants' role 140, 145–146, 150–151; and diaspora networks 192–193, 195, 588; executive training 131; Gandhi's campaign against British imperialism 22; and the Great Convergence 585–588; and the Great Divergence 582–583; and the insurance industry 364, 367; and the IT industry 145,

150–151, 588; performance of firms affiliated with business groups 239; ratio of inward FDI ratio 27; and the telegraph network 323; textile and apparel industry 411; Unilever's business interests 26
Indonesia: and the automobile industry 398; clustering 268; FDI status 23; indigenization strategy 494; and the palm oil industry 270–272
industrial concentration 265–268; from districts to clusters 266–267; examples of 265–266; as foundation of cluster scholarship 265–267; literature review 266; new industrial districts, learning regions, and self-containment 265–266; *see also* clusters
Industrial Revolution: and the beginning of the "great divergence" 578; and British trade 46; environmental impact 567–569; and the first globalization wave 18; and the first wave of environmentalism 549; and the Great Divergence 578; and the insurance industry 366–367, 372; and the luxury industry 425; patents laws and 581; role of the Caribbean sugar trade 280; and the roots of sustainability 547; and the shipping industry 444, 446; and the sustainability issue 547; women's role 74
industrial structures 531
industries: automobile industry 392–407; commodities trading 455–464; electric power industry 332–346; film industry 377–389; global communications 315–327; healthcare 349–359; insurance 363–374; luxury consumer goods 424–434; oil industry 467–477; shipping industry 438–450
inequality: connection between violence and 82; as driver of corruption 517; gender inequality 70, 83; the oil industry and 467; racial 70, 80; and the rise of populism 29; *see also* Great Divergence
informal businesses, gendered perspective 79
information technology, and the Great Convergence 586–587
Infosys 586
infrastructure: business and the creation of 211, 250; demands of the shipping industry 449; and entrepreneurship 39–44; examples of 39; infrastructure investment 45; international business enterprises' role in establishing 20; invisible infrastructure and the generation of global knowledge 45–47; in less developed economies 268–269, 584; markets as 41–42; and the oil industry 474; social infrastructure 42–44; typology of physical infrastructure **48–49**; use of joint-stock ownership to enable investment in 203; *see also* physical infrastructure; social infrastructure
inner circles, role of in international business networks 253–255

Price Waterhouse 112
Principles of Economics (Marshall) 265
privatization 294, 296, 298, 300, 303, 305–307,
    325, 357, 475, 496, 522, 541, 571
Procter & Gamble 418, 541, 556
Producing Fashion (Blaszczyk) 81
productivity 26, 128, 181, 287, 355, 405, 449,
    549, 578
professional managers 25, 222
property rights 46, 96, 486, 491, 493, 581–582
protectionism 18, 29, 257, 285, 428, 490, 496,
    504, 509, 581, 585
Proton 402
psychic distance 127–128, 130
public policy 5, 392, 585
Puerto Rico, investment incentives package 286
Putin, Vladimir 324, 475

race and entrepreneurship, literature review 76
racial and gendered perspectives on
    entrepreneurship *see* gendered and racial
    perspectives of entrepreneurship
Raj, Prateek 579
Ralli 460
Ramírez Pérez, Sigfrido 100
Rana Plaza disaster, Bangladesh 289
Rappaport, Erika 81
Rauch, J. E. 259
raw materials 18, 25, 35, 46, 160, 162–164,
    167–168, 174, 181, 259, 271, 280, 282–284,
    340, 429, 445, 456, 458, 461–462, 467, 535,
    567–569; *see also* natural resources
recruitment 126, 220, 254
recycling, early types of 568–569
regulation of trade, contribution of merchant
    guilds to 162
Reliance Industries 236
religious perspectives, on capitalism 179
Renault 394, 401, 403–405
renewable energy sector: environmental and
    sustainability issues 572–573; reduction of
    barriers to investment 555; scaling issues 557
reputation, importance for entrepreneurs 43
research and development (R&D) 61, 241, 243,
    271, 321, 325, 358, 398, 404, 533, 540–541,
    571
resilience 64, 173, 350, 404, 487; as prominent
    feature of global business 26
resources: allocation and reconfiguration in
    entrepreneurial processes 60–62; international
    transfer of 10
retailing 27, 40, 219, 222–223, 228, 240, 510
Retinger, Joseph 257
Reuters 322–323
Rijkens, Paul 257
The Rise of the Global Company (Fitzgerald) 97
Rivoli, Pietra 285

Robertson, H. M. 363
Rochdale Pioneers co-operative 217–218, 222
Roche 490, 492–493
Rockefeller, John D. 472
Rodney, Walter Anthony 78
Rollings, N. 256
Rooth, Tim 99
Rose, Mary 73
Rosen, Christine Meisner 549, 566
Rosenberg, E. S. 259
Rosenthal, Caitlin 82
Rosenthal, Jean-Laurent 579
Rosser, Gervase 163
Rotary International 254
roundabout production 280
The Routledge Companion to Business History
    (Webster) 220
Rouzaud, Claude 429
Roy, Tirthankar 582–583
Royal African Company 425
Royal Dutch Shell 62, 471–473, 491, 554–555
Royal Exchange Assurance (REA) 366, 371
RT 324
rubber 20, 206, 237, 281, 537–538
rubber and palm oil plantation cluster, Southeast
    Asia 270–272
Ruppert, Anton 433
Russia 22, 29
Russian Revolution 20, 22, 98, 490–491, 538

Sabel, Charles 281
Said, Edward 78
Salmon, Lucy Maynard 73
Samsung 236, 586
Samuel, Marcus 471
Sapori, Armando 172
Sarbanes-Oxley Act 525
Saudi Basic Industries Corporation 236
Saunier, P.-Y. 251
Saxenian, A. 266
SCA 556
Scale and Scope (Chandler) 531
Scediwy, R. 220
Schiller, Karl 287
Schmitter, P. C. 255
Schröter, Harm G. 343
Schug, Albert 364
Schumpeter, Joseph 57–58
scientific management 140, 147
Scott, Joan 72, 83
Scott, Peter 99
Scranton, Philip 73, 265
Sealand 449
Sears 26, 418
second global economy: definition 7; ending of
    18; global business and 27–28; origins 24–27;
    political risks and nationalism 495–497

Printed in the United States
by Baker & Taylor Publisher Services